The American Drug Scene

An Anthology

Fifth Edition

James A. Inciardi
University of Delaware

Karen McElrath
Queen's University

New York   Oxford
OXFORD UNIVERSITY PRESS
2008

Oxford University Press, Inc., publishes works that further Oxford University's
objective of excellence in research, scholarship, and education.

Oxford   New York
Auckland   Cape Town   Dar es Salaam   Hong Kong   Karachi
Kuala Lumpur   Madrid   Melbourne   Mexico City   Nairobi
New Delhi   Shanghai   Taipei   Toronto

With offices in
Argentina   Austria   Brazil   Chile   Czech Republic   France   Greece
Guatemala   Hungary   Italy   Japan   Poland   Portugal   Singapore
South Korea   Switzerland   Thailand   Turkey   Ukraine   Vietnam

Copyright © 2008 by Oxford University Press, Inc.

Published by Oxford University Press, Inc.
198 Madison Avenue, New York, New York 10016
http://www.oup.com

Oxford is a registered trademark of Oxford University Press

ISBN 978-0-19-533246-9

Printing number: 9 8 7 6 5 4 3

Printed in the United States of America
on acid-free paper

Contents

Part I. Theoretical Perspectives on Drug Use and Addiction

---

* Indicates chapters that are new to the Fifth Edition.

---

* Indicates chapters that are new to the Fifth Edition.

---

* Indicates chapters that are new to the Fifth Edition.

* Indicates chapters that are new to the Fifth Edition.

---

* Indicates chapters that are new to the Fifth Edition.

---

* Indicates chapters that are new to the Fifth Edition.

Preface

The American Drug Scene, Fifth Edition, is a collection of both classic and contemporary essays and articles on the changing patterns, problems, perspectives, and policies related to both legal and illicit drug use. In these 44 selections, as well as in the commentaries that precede them, the information presented is both contemporary and historical, theoretical and descriptive.

The breadth of coverage includes all the major drugs of abuse (amphetamines and methamphetamine, opiates, marijuana, cocaine and crack, hallucinogens, and "club drugs"), as well as such legal substances as alcohol, tobacco, and prescription drugs.

Other areas covered include such topics as drugs, violence, and street crime; substance abuse prevention and treatment; injection drug use; the social construction of drug problems and moral panics; and the drug legalization debate.

One of the many strengths of The American Drug Scene, Fifth Edition, is the inclusion of the social contexts that frame and influence drug use. Moreover, thought-provoking introductions to each section and each article guide the reader by identifying and explaining central issues, key concepts, and relationships among topics.

The Fifth Edition includes 13 new articles that address recent and emerging patterns of drug use and policy debates, such as methamphetamine, MDMA/Ecstasy, "binge" drinking, OxyContin, and Ritalin.

Of special interest are the original essays, which focus on topics of current concern and controversy. Examples include women and drug treatment and what the media has referred to as an "epidemic" of OxyContin abuse.

Discussion questions and suggested readings and websites also expand the usefulness of this edition.

If anything has been learned about the drug problem in the United States, it is an awareness that the problem is continually shifting and changing. There are fads, fashions, and even rages in the drugs of abuse. Heroin, marijuana, cocaine, LSD, and numerous other drugs have all had their periods of currency. And although one substance may be a drug of choice for just a few months, the popularity of others often endures for years, or even generations. Drug "epidemics" (periods during which there are many new users) seem to come and go as well. The United States experienced an epidemic of cocaine use during the 1880s and 1890s, followed by a decline in popularity early in the twentieth century and a reemergence in the 1970s. Several heroin epidemics occurred during the second half of the twentieth century, and a crack cocaine epidemic began in the mid-1980s. In the 1990s, heroin—previously a popular drug—was in the news once again. And now there is methamphetamine as well as "club drugs" or "dance drugs," such as Ecstasy.

The tenor and direction of drug control policies tend to shift as well. Although major changes in drug policy are infrequent, intermittent fads and fashions have characterized periodic "wars on drugs." Such initiatives as "zero tolerance," asset forfeiture, mandatory minimum sentences for small-time traffickers, compulsory treatment for drug-involved offenders, and numerous others have experienced periods of acceptance and disfavor. And not surprisingly, the public, political, and ideological reactions to the policies of White House incumbents are abundant, ardent, and enduring.

We hope that readers find the material interesting, stimulating, and instructive. ◆

James A. Inciardi
University of Delaware

Karen McElrath
Queen's University

Acknowledgments

The editors would like to thank the following individuals for their valuable assistance in preparing this edition: Krisha Martinez, Jennifer L. Syvertsen, Claude Teweles, Monica Gomez, and Scott Carter. We also acknowledge the very helpful comments and suggestions from several reviewers: Jan Bending (University of Cincinnati), Ida Dupont (Pace University), Matthew Durington (Towson University), Sean P. Griffin (Pennsylvania State University), Jerome L. Himmelstein (Amherst College), Eric L. Jensen (University of Idaho), David Khey (University of Florida), Leah Moore (University of Central Florida), and John Myers (Rowan University). ✦

About the Editors

James A. Inciardi, Ph.D., is Director of the Center for Drug and Alcohol Studies at the University of Delaware; Professor in the Department of Sociology and Criminal Justice at Delaware; Adjunct Professor in the Department of Epidemiology and Public Health at the University of Miami School of Medicine; a guest professor in the Department of Psychiatry at the Federal University of Rio Grande do Sul in Porto Alegre, Brazil; and a member of the Internal Advisory Committee of the White House Office of National Drug Control Policy. Dr. Inciardi is a recipient of a Merit Award from the National Institutes of Health and is the author or editor of more than 450 articles, chapters, and books in the areas of substance abuse, criminology, criminal justice, history, folklore, public policy, HIV/AIDS, medicine, and law.

Karen McElrath, Ph.D., is a reader in the School of Sociology, Social Policy, and Social Work at Queen's University in Belfast, Ireland. Prior to that appointment, she was Associate Professor in the Department of Sociology, University of Miami. She has served as adviser to the Northern Ireland Affairs Committee, House of Commons, and has held advisory membership on several local and regional boards. She has conducted studies with Ecstasy users, and more recently she has engaged in research with people who inject drugs. Her current studies focus on stigma and injecting drug use, blood-borne viruses and injecting drug use, and research rapport as it relates to the validity of findings. ✦

About the Contributors

Frederick L. Altice is a research physician affiliated with the Yale University AIDS program.

Harry J. Anslinger (deceased) was the first U.S. Commissioner of Narcotics and presided over the Federal Bureau of Narcotics from 1930 through 1962.

Mark A. Bellis is Director of the Centre for Public Health at Liverpool John Moores University (England).

Carol J. Boyd is a research scientist at the Substance Abuse Research Center, University of Michigan.

Robert S. Broadhead is a professor of sociology at the University of Connecticut.

Archie Brodsky is a research associate in psychiatry with the Massachusetts Mental Health Center, affiliated with Harvard Medical School.

John J. Casey is president and managing partner at Evans Hagen and Company.

Michael C. Clatts is the Director of the Institute for International Research on Youth at Risk at National Development and Research Institutes. He also is an associate professor in the Department of Sociomedical Sciences at the Mailman School of Public Health at Columbia University.

William Cloud is an associate professor in the Graduate School of Social Work at the University of Denver.

Courtney Ryley Cooper (deceased) was a journalist and author of such "true crime" classics as *Ten Thousand Public Enemies* (1935), *Here's to Crime* (1937), and *Designs in Scarlet* (1939).

Kathleen Daly is a professor in the School of Criminology and Criminal Justice at Griffith University, Brisbane (Australia).

Vincent P. Dole (deceased) was a professor and senior physician emeritus with Rockefeller University in New York City and founder of the methadone maintenance treatment modality for narcotics addiction.

Eloise Dunlap is a sociologist with the National Development and Research Institutes.

Samuel R. Friedman is Director of the Social Theory Core in the Center for Drug Use and HIV Research, National Development and Research Institutes.

Lloyd A. Goldsamt is a deputy director of the Institute for International Research on Youth at Risk at National Development and Research Institutes, Inc.

Paul J. Goldstein is a professor of epidemiology in the School of Public Health and a fellow at the Great Cities Institute in the College of Urban Planning and Public Affairs, University of Illinois, Chicago.

Robert Granfield is a professor in the Department of Sociology, University of Buffalo.

Lester Grinspoon is an emeritus professor of psychiatry at Harvard Medical School and has published widely in the area of drug abuse.

Jean-Paul C. Grund is a drug researcher working for UNAIDS, Vienna, on the Task Force on HIV prevention among IDUs in Central Eastern Europe and the Newly Independent States.

Karen B. Halnon is an associate professor of sociology at Pennsylvania State University.

Thomas E. Hanlon is affiliated with the Friends Research Institute in Baltimore, Maryland.

Michael L. Hirsch is Chair of the Division of Liberal Studies, Huston-Tillotson University.

Karen Hughes is a joint manager of the Sexual Health and Behavioural Epidemiology Team in the Centre for Public Health at Liverpool John Moores University (England).

Dana Hunt is a principal scientist with Abt Associates Inc.

James A. Inciardi See "About the Editors."

Curtis Jackson-Jacobs is a graduate student in the Department of Sociology, UCLA.

Philip Jenkins is a distinguished professor of religious studies and history at Pennsylvania State University.

Bruce D. Johnson is the Director of the Institute for Special Populations Research, National Development and Research Institutes.

Charles D. Kaplan is a professor in the Department of Psychiatry and Neuropsychology, Maastricht University, The Netherlands.

Mara L. Keire is a lecturer of history at Queen Mary, University of London.

Brian C. Kelly is an advanced doctoral student in the medical anthropology track in sociomedical sciences at Mailman School of Public Health, Columbia University.

Thomas H. Kerr is a community health researcher working in Vancouver who specializes in HIV/AIDS and injection drug use research. He is a doctoral student in educational psychology at the University of Victoria (Canada).

Marion C. Kiley is a research administrator at the Center for Drug and Alcohol Studies of the University of Delaware.

Timothy W. Kinlock is a researcher with the Social Research Center, the Friends Research Institute, Baltimore, Maryland.

Herbert D. Kleber is a professor of psychiatry and Director of the Division on Substance Abuse at the College of Physicians and Surgeons of Columbia University and the New York State Psychiatric Institute.

Steven P. Kurtz is a scientist at the Center for Alcohol and Drug Studies of the University of Delaware.

Stephen E. Lankenau is an assistant professor of research in the Department of Pediatrics at the University of Southern California.

Marie Claire Leger is a graduate assistant for internal medicine in the Department of International Programs and Studies, University of Illinois, Urbana-Champaign.

Alfred R. Lindesmith (deceased) was a professor of sociology at Indiana University and one of the first researchers to conduct sociological studies of addiction.

Helen Lowey is a public health specialist with the Health Protection Agency (England).

Lisa Maher is an associate professor in the National Centre in HIV Epidemiology & Clinical Research at the University of New South Wales (Australia).

Sean Esteban McCabe is a research associate professor at the Substance Abuse Research Center, University of Michigan.

Karen McElrath See "About the Editors."

Marissa A. Miller is the Antimicrobial Resistance Program Director at the National Institute of Allergy and Infectious Diseases.

Toby Miller is a professor of cultural studies and cultural policy in the Department of Cinema Studies at New York University.

Michele Morales is a clinical social worker at the University of Michigan.

David F. Musto is a professor of psychiatry and social history at Yale University.

Ethan A. Nadelmann is the founder and executive director of the Drug Policy Alliance.

Mark Nichter is a professor in the Department of Anthropology at the University of Arizona.

David N. Nurco (deceased) was a research professor in the Department of Psychiatry at the University of Maryland School of Medicine.

Marie Nyswander (deceased) was a physician and clinician with Rockefeller University in New York City and co-founder of the methadone maintenance treatment modality for narcotics addiction.

Stanton Peele is a professor, consultant, psychologist, and attorney who has published widely in the area of addiction.

Todd G. Pierce is a medical anthropologist and ethnographer who has published in the areas of drug abuse and HIV risk behaviors.

Edward Preble (deceased) was an anthropologist and ethnographer with Manhattan State Hospital and spent much of his career conducting street studies of the New York City drug scene.

Craig Reinarman is a professor of sociology at the University of California, Santa Cruz.

Peter Reuter is a professor at the School of Public Policy and the Department of Criminology of the University of Maryland.

Marsha Rosenbaum is the Director of the Lindesmith Center–West in San Francisco.

Harvey A. Siegal (deceased) was a sociologist, ethnographer, and professor and director of Substance Abuse Intervention Programs at Wright State University School of Medicine in Dayton, Ohio.

Stephen J. Sifaneck is affiliated with the Institute for Special Populations Research, National Development and Research Institutes.

Hilary L. Surratt is an associate scientist at the Center for Drug and Alcohol Studies of the University of Delaware.

Jennifer L. Syvertsen is a research associate at the Center for Drug and Alcohol Studies of the University of Delaware.

Kenneth D. Tunnell is a professor in the Department of Criminal Justice and Police Studies at Eastern Kentucky University.

Dorinda L. Welle is the Director of Youth and Community Development Research in the Institute for International Research on Youth at Risk, National Development and Research Institutes.

Amy M. Young is an assistant professor in the Department of Psychology at Eastern Michigan University. ✦

Introduction

The American drug scene has a long and enduring history. To begin with, the drinking of alcohol to excess is centuries old. In *The Life and Times of the Late Demon Rum*, the celebrated American social historian and biographer J. C. Furnas suggests that alcohol came to the colonies with the first English and Dutch settlers and that the drinking of "spirits" and "strong waters" was a problem since the first days of the emerging American republic. Tradition had taught that rum, gin, and brandy were nutritious and healthful. Distilled spirits were viewed as foods that supplemented limited and monotonous diets; as medications that could cure colds, fevers, snakebites, and broken legs; and as means of relaxation that would relieve depression, reduce tension, and enable hardworking laborers to enjoy a moment of happy, frivolous camaraderie. By the early 1700s nearly all Americans of every occupation and social class drank alcoholic beverages in quantity, sometimes to the point of intoxication; and by the end of the eighteenth century the daily per capita drinking of Americans was almost a half pint of hard liquor.

The use of other drugs for the enhancement of pleasure and performance or for the alteration of mood also dates back several centuries. Perhaps it all began with Thomas Dover, who developed a form of medicinal opium sold as Dover's Powder. Introduced in England in 1709 and in the colonies several years later, it contained one ounce each of opium, ipecac (the dried roots of a tropical creeping plant), and licorice, combined with saltpeter, tartar, and wine. The attraction of Dover's Powder was in the euphoric and anesthetic properties of opium. For thousands of years opium had been a popular narcotic. A derivative of the oriental poppy (*Papaver somniferum L.*), it was called the "plant of joy" some 4,000 years ago in the "fertile crescent" of Mesopotamia.

The introduction of Dover's Powder in the colonies apparently started a trend. By the latter part of the eighteenth century, medications containing opium were readily available throughout urban and rural America. They were sold over the counter in pharmacies, in grocery and general stores, at traveling medicine shows, and through the mail. They were marketed under such labels as Ayer's Cherry Pectoral, Mrs. Winslow's Soothing Syrup, McMunn's Elixir, Godfrey's Cordial, Scott's Emulsion, and Dover's Powder. Many of these remedies were seductively advertised as "painkillers," "cough mixtures," "soothing syrups," "consumption cures," and "women's friends." Others were promoted for the treatment of such varied ailments as diarrhea, dysentery, colds, fever, teething, cholera, rheumatism, pelvic disorders, athlete's foot, and even baldness and cancer. The drugs were produced not only from imported opium but also from white opium poppies that were being legally grown in the New England states, Florida and Louisiana, the West and Southwest, and the Confederate States of America during the Civil War.

For thousands of years, opium had been the only known product of the oriental poppy. In 1803, however, a young German pharmacist, Frederick Serturner, isolated the chief alkaloid of opium. Serturner had hit upon morphine, which he named after Morpheus, the Greek god of dreams. The discovery had profound effects on both medicine and society, for morphine is the greatest single pain reliever the world has ever known. After the hypodermic syringe was invented in 1853, the use of morphine by injection in military medicine during the Civil War and the Franco-Prussian War granted the procedure legitimacy and familiarity to both physicians and the public. Furthermore, hypodermic medication had its pragmatic aspects—it brought quick local relief, its dosage could be regulated, and it was effective when oral medication was impractical. The regimen, however, was used promiscuously, for many physicians were anxious to illustrate their ability to quell the pain suffered by their patients, who, in turn, expected instant relief from discomfort.

Beyond opium and morphine, the over-the-counter medicine industry expanded even further in the 1880s to include cocaine and heroin. By the close of the nineteenth century, it was estimated that millions of Americans were addicted to over-the-counter medications, and agitation had begun for controls over the manufacture and distribution of products containing cocaine, opium, and their various derivatives.

One result was the passage of the Pure Food and Drug Act in 1906, which prohibited the interstate transportation of adulterated or misbranded food and drugs. The act brought about the decline of over-the-counter medications because the proportions of alcohol, opium, morphine, heroin, cocaine, and a number of other substances in each preparation now had to be indicated. As a result, most of the remedies lost their appeal.

The Pure Food and Drug Act merely imposed standards for quality, packaging, and labeling; it did not actually outlaw the use of cocaine and opiate drugs. Public Law No. 47, 63rd Congress (H.R. 1967), more popularly known as the Harrison Act, sponsored by New York Representative Francis Burton Harrison and passed in 1914, ultimately served that purpose. At the same time, the new legislation went a long way toward altering public and criminal justice responses to drug use in the United States for generations to come. The Harrison Act required all people who imported, manufactured, produced, compounded, sold, dispensed, or otherwise distributed cocaine and opiate drugs to register with the Treasury Department, pay special taxes, and keep records of all transactions. As such, it was a revenue code designed to exercise some measure of public control over drugs rather than to penalize all the users of narcotics in the United States. In effect, however, penalization is specifically what occurred. Although subcultures and criminal cultures of drug users already existed prior to the passage of the Harrison Act, the legislation served to expand their membership. Since then, drug use has generally been viewed not only as a social problem in the United States but as a criminal problem as well.

From the 1920s through the beginning of the twenty-first century, there have been many drugs of abuse—heroin, cocaine, crack, LSD, PCP, Ecstasy, the amphetamines and methamphetamines, and numerous others—all of which are discussed in the following chapters. In addition to describing the drugs, their patterns of use, and their impact on society, chapters examine such other topics as the links between drug use and crime, the AIDS/drug connection, treatment and prevention initiatives, and alternative drug control policies.

Before proceeding with this material, however, it is important that readers have some understanding of the variety of drug-related terms whose meanings are often taken for granted. As such, this introduction closes with a short glossary of the most important definitions.

Basic Drug Groups

Drugs: any natural or artificial substances (aside from food) that by their chemical nature alter the functioning of the body.

Psychoactive drugs: drugs that alter perception and consciousness, including analgesics, depressants, stimulants, and hallucinogens.

Analgesics: drugs used for the relief of varying degrees of pain without rendering the user unconscious. There are both narcotic and nonnarcotic varieties of analgesics.

Depressants: drugs that act on and lessen the activity of the central nervous system (CNS), diminishing or stopping vital functions.

Sedatives: CNS depressant drugs that produce calm and relaxation. Alcohol, barbiturates and related compounds, and minor tranquilizers are sedative drugs.

Hypnotics: CNS depressant drugs that produce sleep. Barbiturates, methaqualone, and chloral hydrate are hypnotic drugs. As such, a number of drugs are both sedatives and hypnotics.

Stimulants: drugs that stimulate the central nervous system and increase the activity of the brain and spinal chord. Amphetamines and cocaine are CNS stimulant drugs.

Hallucinogens: drugs that act on the central nervous system, producing mood and perceptual changes varying from sensory illusions to hallucinations. Sometimes referred to as "psychedelics," hallucinogenic drugs include marijuana, hashish, LSD, PCP, and psilocybin.

Use, Abuse, and Dependency Terms

Drug misuse: the inappropriate use of a prescription or nonprescription drug; that is, using it in greater amounts than, for purposes other than, or for longer than it was intended.

Drug abuse: any use of an illegal drug, or the use of a legal drug in a manner that can cause problems for the user.

Addiction: drug craving accompanied by physical dependence, which motivates continuing usage, resulting in a tolerance to the drug's effects and a syndrome of identifiable symptoms when the drug is abruptly withdrawn. Narcotics, barbiturates, and cocaine are addicting drugs.

Dependence: a concept that indicates the central role that a substance has come to play in an individual's life, with evidence of problems relating to control of intake and the development of physical and psychological difficulties, despite which the individual continues to use the substance.

Neuroadaptation: the chemical and biological changes that occur in the brain in response to the use of psychoactive drugs.

Tolerance: a state of acquired resistance to some or all of the effects of a drug. Tolerance develops after the repeated use of certain drugs, resulting in a need to increase the dosage to obtain the original effects.

Cross-tolerance: among certain pharmacologically related drugs, tolerance of the effects of one carrying over to most or all others. For example, a person who has become tolerant of the euphoric effects of secobarbital is likely to be tolerant of the euphoric effects of all other short-acting barbiturates.

Cross-addiction: also referred to as cross-dependence, a situation in which dependence on drugs of the same pharmacological group is mutual and interchangeable. For example, persons addicted to heroin can use methadone or some other narcotic in place of the heroin without experiencing withdrawal.

Withdrawal: the cluster of reactions and behavior that ensue upon the abrupt cessation of a drug on which the user's body is dependent.

Detoxification: the removal of physical dependency.

Drug Reactions

Potentiation: the ability of one drug to increase the activity of another drug when the two are taken simultaneously. Potentiation can be expressed mathematically as $a + b = A$. For example, aspirin (a) plus caffeine (b) increases the potency of the aspirin (A).

Synergism: similar to potentiation, a situation in which two or more drugs are taken together and the combined action dramatically increases the normal effects of each drug. A synergistic effect can be expressed mathematically as $1 + 1 = 5$; it typically occurs with mixtures of alcohol and barbiturates.

Antagonism: a situation in which two drugs taken together have opposite effects on the body. An antagonistic reaction can be expressed mathematically as $1 + 1 = 0$; it typically occurs with certain mixtures of depressants and stimulants.

Idiosyncrasy: an abnormal or peculiar response to a drug, such as excitation from a depressant or sedation from a stimulant.

Side effect: any effect other than what the drug was intended for, such as stomach upset from aspirin.

Routes of Drug Administration

Intravenous: injected into the vein.

Intramuscular: injected into the muscle.

Cutaneous: absorbed through the skin.

Subcutaneous: inserted under the skin.

Insufflation (inhalation): drawn into the lungs through the nose or mouth.

Oral: swallowed and absorbed through the stomach.

Vaginal: absorbed through vaginal tissues.

Anal: absorbed through rectal tissues.

Sublingual: absorbed through the tissues under the tongue.

Drug Schedules Under the Controlled Substances Act

The Comprehensive Drug Abuse and Control Act of 1970 brought together under one law most of the federal drug control legislation that had been enacted since the early part of the nineteenth century. Title II of the law, known as the Controlled Substances Act, categorized certain substances into five "schedules" and defined the offenses and penalties associated with the illegal manufacture, distribution, dispensation, and possession of any drug in each schedule.

Schedule I includes drugs with a high potential for abuse, with no currently accepted medical use in the United States, and with a lack of accepted safety when used under medical supervision. Schedule I lists a variety of opiates and their derivatives, numerous hallucinogenic substances, and a variety of other substances, including heroin, LSD, marijuana, mescaline, peyote, psilocybin, methaqualone (Quaalude), Ecstasy, and GHB.

Schedule II includes drugs for which there is a high potential for abuse; these are drugs that are currently used for medical treatment in the United States and that if abused could lead to dependence. Examples of Schedule II drugs include opium, morphine, cocaine, methadone, Ritalin, methamphetamine, amphetamine, and Oxy-Contin.

Schedule III includes drugs that have a potential for abuse less than those in Schedules I and II, that are currently accepted for medical use in the United States, and that may lead to moderate or low physical dependence or high psychological dependence. Examples of Schedule III drugs include anabolic steroids; any compound or mixture containing amobarbital, secobarbital, or pentobarbital; and hydrocodone.

Schedule IV includes drugs that have a low potential for abuse and are currently accepted for use in the United States. If abused, these drugs could lead to limited physical or psychological dependence. Examples of Schedule IV drugs include the long-acting barbiturates such as phenobarbital; minor tranquilizers such as Librium, Valium, Xanax, and Miltown; and chloral hydrate.

Schedule V includes drugs that have a potential for abuse and dependence lower that those listed in Schedule IV. Examples of Schedule V drugs are those that contain limited quantities of narcotics, such as codeine cough syrup.

References

Furnas, J. C. (1965). *The Life and Times of the Late Demon Rum*. New York: Putnam.

Inciardi, J. A. (2002). *The War on Drugs III: The Continuing Saga of the Mysteries and Miseries of Intoxication, Addiction, Crime, and Public Policy*. Boston: Allyn and Bacon. ✦

Part I

Theoretical Perspectives on Drug Use and Addiction

Why do people take drugs? For the enhancement of pleasure or performance? To relieve anxiety or boredom? As an escape from reality? To suppress feelings of sorrow, inadequacy, guilt, or other emotional pain? Likely for all of these reasons and many more. In fact, there may be as many reasons for taking drugs as there are people who use them. Moreover, theories of drug use and abuse are legion—so much so that one publication of the National Institute on Drug Abuse devoted its entire 488 pages to outlining the major views.

Although many early explanations of substance abuse considered it to be a moral weakness, a number of modern investigators have described drug users as maladjusted, hostile, immature, dependent, manipulative, and narcissistic individuals, suggesting that drug use is just one more symptom of their disordered personalities. Others suggest that because drug use is an integral part of the general culture that surrounds the user, it is learned behavior. And there are other explanations: the bad-habit theory, disruptive-environment theory, cognitive-control theory, social-deviance theory, biological-rhythm theory, subcultural theory, social-neurobiological theory, and many, many more.

Quite popular for many years was the theory of the "addiction-prone personality," elucidated by Dr. Kenneth Chapman of the U.S. Public Health Service several decades ago:

> . . . the typical addict is emotionally unstable and immature, often seeking pleasure and excitement outside of the conventional realms. Unable to adapt comfortably to the pressures and tensions in today's speedy world, he may become either an extremely dependent individual or turn into a hostile "lone wolf" incapable of attaching deep feelings toward anyone. In his discomfort, he may suffer pain—real or imaginary. The ordinary human being has normal defense machinery with which to meet life's disappointments, frustrations, and conflicts. But the potential addict lacks enough of this inner strength to conquer his emotional problems and the anxiety they create. In a moment of stress, he may be introduced to narcotics as a "sure-fire" answer to his needs. Experiencing relief from his pain, or an unreal flight from his problems, or a puffed-up sense of power and control regarding them, he is well on the road toward making narcotics his way of life.

Stated differently, when "stable" people are introduced to drugs, they will discard them spontaneously before becoming dependent. Those who have "addiction-prone" personalities, because of psychoses, psychopathic or psychoneurotic disorders, or predispositions toward mental dysfunctioning, "become transformed into the typical addict."

1

For a number of contemporary theorists, drug use is related to a more basic need for *pleasure*, plain and simple. For example, there is extensive physiological, neurological, and anthropological evidence to suggest that we are members of a species that has been honed for pleasure. Nearly all people want and enjoy pleasure, and the pursuit of drugs—whether caffeine, nicotine, alcohol, opium, heroin, marijuana, or cocaine— seems to be universal and inescapable. It is found across time and across cultures. The process of evolution has for whatever reasons resulted in a human neurophysiology that responds both vividly and avidly to a variety of common substances. The brain has pleasure centers—receptor sites and cortical cells—that react to "rewarding" dosages of many substances. Or, as University of California pharmacologist Larry Stein explained it in 1989,

> The fact that we respond to a reward shows just how deeply embedded in the design of the brain this reinforcement mechanism is. Dopamine and the opioid peptides are transmitters in very powerful control systems based on a certain chemistry. . . . Along come poppy seeds and coca leaves that have chemicals very similar to these central systems. They go right in, do not pass GO. To say that cocaine or amphetamines, or heroin or morphine, should be highly appealing is an understatement.

Regardless of the theory put forth, it would appear that drug users are of four basic types: *experimenters, social-recreational users, involved users,* and *dysfunctional abusers.*

The *experimenters* are by far the largest group of drug users (not including alcohol users). They most frequently try one or more drugs once or twice in a social setting, but the drug does not play a significant role in their lives. They use their drug of choice experimentally because their social group finds the drug's effects pleasurable. Experimenters do not seek out a drug but may use it when someone presents it to them in an appropriate setting. In this situation, they may smoke marijuana or "snort" cocaine once or twice because the drug does something to them. As a college senior commented about his first cocaine experience,

> I generally don't use drugs, except maybe a little grass now and then. My only experience with coke was a few weeks ago in the dormitory. My roommate came in with a couple of other guys and started getting high on it. They kept trying to get me to do some, and finally I snorted some just for the heck of it. When I did, it was quite a blast at first, from my head all the way down, and then I felt like I was floating. After, I felt a little weird. . . . It was good.

Social-recreational users differ from experimenters primarily in terms of frequency and continuity of consumption. For example, they may use drugs when they are at a party and someone presents the opportunity. Drugs still do not play a significant role in these users' lives. They do not actively seek out drugs but use them only because it does something to them—it makes them feel good. A 28-year-old Miami woman related,

> Partying can be even more fun with a few lines of coke. I never have any of my own, but usually I'll tie in with some guy who does. We'll get a little stoned, and maybe go to bed. It's all in good fun. . . . Another time I was on a double date and this guy had some good toot. We drove up to Orlando and went into Disney World. Do you know what it's like goin' through the haunted mansion stoned like that? It's a whole different trip.

The great majority of alcohol use occurs in a social-recreational context.

For *involved users,* a major transition has taken place since the individual engaged in social-recreational use. As users become "involved" with a particular drug, they also become drug seekers, and their drug of choice becomes significant in their lives. Although they are still quite able to function—in school, on the job, or as a parent or spouse— their proficiency in many areas begins to decline markedly. Personal and social functioning tends to be inversely related to the amount of time involved users spend using drugs. They still have control over their behavior, but their use of the drug occurs with increasing frequency for some adaptive reason; their drug does something *for* them.

Involved users are of many types. Some use drugs to deal with an unbearable work situation, indulging in controlled amounts several times a day. Others use drugs to enhance performance or bolster their self-esteem. And still a third group regularly use drugs to deal with stress, anxiety, or nagging boredom. As one involved cocaine user, a self-employed accountant, put it,

> I seem to be always uptight these days with almost everything I do. Everybody seems to always want something—my clients, my wife, the bank, the world. . . . A few lines [of cocaine] every two [to] three hours gets me through the day—through the tax returns, the tension at home, the bills, sex, whatever. Without the coke I'd probably have to be put away somewhere.

The *dysfunctional abusers* are what have become known as the "cokeheads," "alcoholics," and "addicts." For them, drugs have become the significant part of their lives. They are personally and socially dysfunctional and spend all of their time involved in drug seeking, drug taking, and other related activities. Moreover, they no longer have control over their drug use.

In the six chapters that follow, a variety of perspectives on drug use and addiction are presented, including the sociological work of Alfred R. Lindesmith. The disease concept of addiction is reviewed, the theory and research on how marijuana use is learned behavior is explored, and a historical view of the "femininity of addiction" is presented. Part I also offers a sociopharmacological perspective of drug use that focuses on how social, economic, and health inequalities create conditions conducive to drug use, and how the social order needs to change in order to effectively reduce harmful drug consumption. Part I concludes with a discussion of "drug scares" in the United States.

Reference

Chapman, K. (1951). "A Typical Drug Addict." *New York State Health News*, August 28, 1951.

Additional Readings

Durrant, Russil, and Jo Thakker. (2003). *Substance Use and Abuse: Cultural and Historical Perspectives*. Thousand Oaks, CA: Sage Publications.

Goldstein, Avram. (2001). *Addiction: From Biology to Drug Policy*. New York: Oxford University Press.

Hallstone, Michael. (2002). "Updating Howard Becker's Theory of Using Marijuana for Pleasure." *Contemporary Drug Problems*, 29 (4): 821–844.

McLellan, A. Thomas, David C. Lewis, Charles P. O'Brien, and Herbert D. Kleber. (2000). "Drug Dependence, a Chronic Medical Illness: Implications for Treatment, Insurance, and Outcomes Evaluation." *Journal of the American Medical Association*, 284 (13): 1689–1695.

Schivelbusch, Wolfgang. (1992). *Tastes of Paradise: A Social History of Spices, Stimulants, and Intoxicants*. New York: Pantheon.

Zoha, Luigi. (2000). *Drugs, Addiction, and Initiation: The Modern Search for Ritual*. Santa Rosa, CA: Daimon Publishers. ✦

1

A Sociological Theory of Drug Addiction[1]

Alfred R. Lindesmith

Various theories have been developed to explain drug use and addiction. Current explanations are grounded in the sociological, psychological, or biological sciences. Some theories are interdisciplinary in that they seek to combine two or more of these perspectives. Regardless of where they originate, theories of addiction are important in that they contribute to our understanding of the causal factors that lead to drug dependence. If we are able to identify the causal processes, we are in a better position to develop social policies and treatment initiatives that can serve addicts more effectively.

In this essay, dating back to 1938, the late Alfred R. Lindesmith criticizes the psychiatric explanation of opiate addiction. Psychiatrists, he argues, attach moral labels (e.g., "psychopaths") to addicts and assume that the continued use of opiates results from the addict's need to "escape from life." Although Lindesmith recognizes that users experience euphoria during their early stages of narcotics use, he disagrees with psychiatrists' assertions that the continuous use of opiate drugs is always for the sake of a "high." His sociological theory assumes that opiate addiction results from the conscious awareness that continued drug use is necessary to eliminate or prevent the pain associated with opiate withdrawal. Addicts do not use opiates to escape from life; rather, they do so to avoid withdrawal.

The problem of drug addiction has been an important one in this country for several decades and has proved to be a difficult one to handle from a theoretical, as well as from a therapeutic, standpoint. In spite of more than a half-century of experimentation with "cures," the drug addict has continued to relapse and thereby aroused the wonder and ire of those who have attempted to treat him. It has frequently been said that the drug user cannot be cured "if he doesn't want to be cured"; but this appears to beg the question, for it is the very essence of addiction that the victim desires to use the drug—and also, at the same time, desires to be free of it. An indication of the strength of the addict's attachment to his drug is furnished by the fact that when the Japanese government in 1929 permitted unregistered opium-smokers in Formosa to register and gave them the choice of applying for either a cure or a license, only thirty out of approximately twenty-five thousand asked for the cure.[2]

Current explanations of the drug habit appear to center about a few general conceptions and modes of approach, none of which have led to convincing results. Psychiatrists have often regarded the use of opiates as an escape from life and have viewed addicts as defective persons seeking to compensate for, or avoid, their inferiorities and mental conflicts.[3] As would be expected, addicts have been labeled as "psychopaths," with the assumption that the attachment of this ambiguous label in some mysterious way explained the phenomenon. Various statements, as to the percentage of defective persons among addicts, have not been accompanied by any comparison with the percentage of defective persons in the general, non-addicted population. In fact, the need or desirability of this sort of comparison does not seem to have occurred to the majority of these writers.

This point of view contrasts the "psychopath," who is assumed to be susceptible to addiction, with "normal" persons, who are presumed by implication to be immune, or, if they accidentally become addicted, they are said to quit and remain free. No evidence has been produced, however, which indicates that any but an exceedingly small percentage of addicts ever remain free of the drug for long periods of years,[4] and no "normal" person has ever been shown to be immune to the subtle influence of the drug. It appears from an examination of the literature that all "normal" persons who have been foolhardy enough to imagine themselves immune and have consequently experimented upon themselves and taken the drug steadily for any length of time, have become addicts, or "junkers," as they usually style themselves.[5] The contention that any type of person can be readily cured of the drug habit in a permanent sense is without any support in terms of actual evidence. We have found that narcotic agents and others who are in close contact with the actual problem ordinarily acquire a wholesome fear of the drug and do not delude themselves concerning their own capacity to resist its influence.

A French medical student,[6] in the course of writing a thesis on morphine, decided to experiment upon himself. For five consecutive days, he took an injection each evening at about nine o'clock. He reported that after three or four injections he began to desire the next ones, and that it cost him a decided effort to refrain from using it the sixth night. He managed to carry out his plan, but clearly implied that, if he had continued the experiment for a short time longer, he believed that he would have become addicted. The addict, in his opinion, is *un homme perdu*, who is rarely able ever again to retain his freedom. This account constitutes an interesting document for the individual who believes that he or anyone else is immune to addiction by reason of a superabundance of will-power or because of an absence of psychopathy. In 1894, Mattison advised the physician as follows:

> Let him not be blinded by an underestimate of the poppy's power to ensnare. Let him not be deluded by an over-confidence in his own strength to resist; for along this line, history has repeated itself with sorrowful frequency, and—as my experience will well attest—on these two treacherous rocks hundreds of promising lives have gone awreck.[7]

Sir William Willcox states:

> We know people who say: "I am a man, and one having a strong will. Morphine or heroin will not affect me; I can take it as long as I like without becoming an addict." I have known people—sometimes medical men—who have made that boast, and without exception they have come to grief.[8]

The conception of opiates as affording an escape from life also does not appear to be satisfactory or correct in view of the well-known fact that the addict invariably claims that all the drug does is to cause him to feel "normal." It is generally conceded that the euphoria associated with the use of opiates is highly transitory in character, and, while it is true that during the initial few weeks of use the drug may cause pleasure in some cases and may function as a means of escape, still, when addiction is established, this no longer holds true. The drug addict, who is supposed to derive some mysterious and uncanny pleasure from the drug, not only fails to do so as a rule but is also keenly aware of the curse of addiction and struggles to escape it. Far from being freed from his problems, he is actually one of the most obviously worried and miserable creatures in our society.

Finally, we may call attention to the fact that the current conception of the addict as a "psychopath," escaping from his own defects by the use of the drug, has the serious defect of being admittedly inapplicable to a certain percentage of cases. L. Kolb, for example, finds that 86 percent of the addicts included in a study of his had defects antedating and presumably, explaining the addiction. One may, therefore, inquire how addiction is to be explained in the other 14 percent of the cases. Are these persons addicts, because they are free from defects? The assumption is sometimes made that those in whom defects cannot be found have secret defects which explain the addiction. Such an assumption obviously places the whole matter beyond the realm of actual research. Moreover, one may ask, who among us does not have defects of one kind or another, secret or obvious?

In general, it appears that the conception of the drug addict as a defective psychopath prior to addiction is more in the nature of an attempt to place blame than it is an explanation of the matter. It is easy and cheap to designate as "inferior" or "weak" or "psychopathic" persons whose vices are different from our own and whom we consequently do not understand.[9] Similarly, the "causes" of addiction as they are often advanced—"curiosity," "bad associates," and the "willingness to try anything once"—suffer from the same moralistic taint. Undoubtedly, these same factors "cause" venereal disease; yet, science has ceased to be concerned with them. In the case of drug addiction, we still are more interested in proving that it is the addict's "own fault" that he is an addict than we are in understanding the mechanisms of addiction.

It was noted long ago that not all persons, to whom opiate drugs were administered for sufficiently long periods of time to produce the withdrawal symptoms, became addicts. It frequently occurs in medical practice that severe and chronic pain makes the regular administration of opiates a necessity.[10] Some of the persons who are so treated show no signs of the typical reactions of addicts and may even be totally ignorant of what they are being given. Others to whom the drug is administered in this way return to it when it has been withdrawn, and become confirmed addicts. This fact caused German and French students of the problem to adopt distinct terms for the two conditions—those who received the drug for therapeutic reasons and who showed none of the symptoms of the typical "craving" of addicts were spoken of as cases of "chronic morphine poisoning," or "morphinism"; whereas, addicts in the ordinarily accepted sense of the word were called "morphinomanes" or, in German, *Morphiumsüchtiger*.[11]

Attempts have been made to introduce such a usage in this country, though without success, and it is consequently awkward to try to refer to these two conditions. In this paper, the term "habituated" will be used to refer to the development of the mere physiological tolerance; whereas, the term "addiction" will be reserved for application to cases in which there is added to the physiological or pharmacological tolerance a psychic addiction, which is marked by the appearance of an imperious desire for the drug and leads to the development of the other characteristic modes of behavior of the drug addict, as he is known in our society. For persons who are merely habituated to the drug without being addicted, there is no need for special conceptual treatment any more than persons who have had operations need to be set off as a distinct class. Once the drug has been removed, these persons show no craving for it or any tendency to resume its use, unless, perhaps, the disease for which the opiate was originally given reappears.

Any explanation of the causation of drug addiction must attempt to account for this fact, that not all persons who are given opiates become addicts. What are the factors which cause one man to escape, while the next, under what appear to be the same physiological conditions, becomes an incurable addict? Obviously, the factor of the patient's knowledge of what he is being given is an important one, for clearly, if he is ignorant of the name of the drug, he will be unable to ask for it or consciously to desire it. The recognition of the importance of keeping the patient in ignorance of what drugs he is being given is quite general. Various devices which serve this end, such as giving the drug orally rather than hypodermically, keeping it out of the hands of the patient and permitting no self-administration, mixing the dosage of opiates with other drugs whose effects are not so pleasant and which serve to disguise the effects of the opiate, etc., have been advocated and have become more or less routine practice. But in some cases, individuals who are fully aware that they are receiving morphine (or some other opium alkaloid) may also not become addicted, even after prolonged administration.[12] Other factors, besides ignorance of the drug administered, must therefore operate to prevent the occurrence of addiction in such cases. What seems to account for this variability—and this is the crux of the theory being advanced—is not the knowledge of the drug administered, but the knowledge of the true significance of the withdrawal symptoms when they appear and the use of the drug thereafter for the consciously understood motive of avoiding these symptoms.[13] As far as can be determined, there is no account in the literature of anyone's ever having experienced the full severity of the withdrawal symptoms in complete knowledge of their connection with the absence of the opiate drug, who has not also become an addict. Addiction begins when the person suffering from withdrawal symptoms realizes that a dose of the drug will dissipate all his discomfort and misery. If he then tries it out and actually feels the almost magical relief that is afforded, he is on the way to confirmed addiction. The desire for the drug, and the impression that it is necessary, apparently become fixed with almost incredible rapidity, once this process of using the drug to avoid the abstinence symptoms has begun. Among confirmed addicts, it appears to be the general rule also that those who have the greatest difficulty in obtaining regular supplies of narcotics ("boot and shoe dope fiends") are precisely those who develop the most intense craving for it and use it to excess when the opportunity presents itself. In other words, deprivation is the essential factor both in the origin of the craving and in its growth.

In order to prove the correctness of the theory advanced, it is necessary to consider, first, its applicability to the general run of cases—that is, to determine whether or not addicts become addicted in any other way than through the experience with withdrawal—and whether there are non-addicts, in whom all of the conditions or causes of addiction have occurred without actually producing addiction. We do not have the space here to go into an extended analysis and explanation of any large number of cases. We can only state that, from our analysis of the cases that have come to our attention, both directly and in the literature, it appears to be true without exception that addicts do, in fact, become addicted in this manner and that addiction does invariably follow whenever the drug is used for the conscious purpose of alleviating withdrawal distress. That this is the case is strikingly brought out by the addict's own argot. The term "hooked" is used by drug users to indicate the fact that a person has used the drug long enough so that, if he attempts to quit, withdrawal distress will force him to want to go on using the drug. At the same time, "to be hooked" means to be addicted, and anyone who has ever been "hooked" is forever after classified by himself, as well as by other addicts, as belonging to the in-group, as an addict, a "user" or "junker," regardless of whether he is using the drug at the moment or not.[14] Similarly, a person who has not been "hooked," regardless of whether he is using the drug or not, is not classified as an addict.[15] It is a contradic-

tion in terms of addict argot, therefore, to speak of "a junker who has never been hooked" or of an individual who has been "hooked" without becoming an addict. Addict argot admits no exceptions to this rule. We found that drug users invariably regard any query about a hypothetical addict who has not been compelled to use the drug by the withdrawal distress, or about a hypothetical non-addict who has, as incomprehensible nonsense. To them, it is self-evident that to be "hooked" and to be an addict are synonymous.[16]

As we have indicated, our own experience is in entire accord with this view of the addict, as it is crystallized in his vernacular. In addition, we have found certain types of cases which bear more directly upon the theory and which offer conclusive and, we may say, experimental verification of the theory. It is upon cases of this type which we wish to concentrate our attention.

Crucial instances which strongly corroborate the hypothesis are those cases in which the same person has first become habituated to the use of the drug over a period of time and then had the drug withdrawn without becoming addicted; and then, later in life, under other circumstances, become a confirmed addict. Erwin Strauss[17] records the case of a woman

who received morphine injections twice daily for six months, from February to July of 1907, on account of gall stones. After her operation in July, the drug was removed and the patient did not become an addict[18] but went about her duties as before, until 1916, nine years later, when her only son was killed at the Front. She was prostrated by her grief and, after intense anguish and thoughts of suicide, she thought of the morphine which had been administered to her nine years before. She began to use it, found it helpful, and soon was addicted. *What is particularly noteworthy is that, when asked if she had suffered any withdrawal symptoms when the drug was withdrawn the first time in 1907, she stated that she could not recall any.* [Italics are mine.]

Another case of the same kind was interviewed by the writer:

A man, Dr. H., was given morphine regularly for a considerable period of time when he underwent three operations for appendicitis with complications. He was not expected to live. As he recovered, the dosage of morphine was gradually reduced and completely withdrawn without any difficulty. Although the patient suffered some discomfort during the process and knew that he had been receiving morphine, he attributed this discomfort to the processes of convalescence. Dr. H. had occasion to see drug addicts in his medical practice and had always felt a horror of addiction and had sometimes thought he would rather shoot himself than be one. This attitude of horror remained unaltered during the hospital experience just related. Several years later, Dr. H. contracted gall-stone trouble and was told that an operation would be necessary. Opiates were administered, and Dr. H., who wished to avoid another operation at all costs, administered opiates to himself, hoping that the operation might not be necessary. He began to use the drug for pains of less and less significance, until he found himself using it every day. He became apprehensive during this process, but reasoned with himself that there was nothing to be alarmed about, inasmuch as drug addiction was certainly not the horrible thing it was supposed to be and he was certain that he would have no difficulty in quitting. His horror of addiction disappeared. When he attempted to quit, he found that it was more difficult than he had supposed. He, of course, noticed the regular recurrence of the withdrawal illness and *then realized in retrospect that he had experienced the same symptoms, without recognizing them, several years before.* [Italics are mine.]

A third case of the same kind is briefly mentioned by Dansauer and Rieth,[19] and two others have come to the attention of the writer. Obviously, the number of instances in which a coincidence of this kind is likely to occur is very small, but those that have been found, unequivocally and without exception, indicate that, if morphine is withdrawn carefully, without the patient's recognizing or noticing the symptoms of abstinence, no craving for the drug develops. The typical phenomena which signalize addiction, such as the tendency to increase the dose inordinately, to exhibit and feel a powerful desire to obtain the drug at any cost, and to be unhappy without it—these phenomena do not put in their appearance, until the patient has discovered that there are withdrawal symptoms of a persistent severe character and has used the drug for a time, solely or chiefly to prevent these symptoms from appearing. In the argot of the addict, when this has occurred, the person is "hooked"; he "has a habit." If he quits before it occurs or if he resolutely refrains from using the drug to alleviate the abstinence symptoms the first time he experiences them, he may still escape. If the symptoms occur in their full intensity, however, the impulse to seek relief in the drug, when it is known that only the drug will give relief, is irresistible—especially since the patient is not likely to realize that the danger of addiction is present. He thinks only of the fact that he can obtain relief from those terrible symptoms, which, to the uninitiated, may be genuinely terrifying.

As an illustration of the process of the establishment of addiction which we are attempting to isolate, another case of a man who became addicted in medical practice may be cited:

Mr. G. was severely lacerated and internally injured as the result of an accident. He spent thirteen weeks in a hospital, during which time he received frequent doses of morphine, some hypodermically and some orally. He paid no attention to what it was that was being used on him and felt no effects of any unusual character, except that the medicine to some extent relieved him of pain. He was discharged from the hospital and, after several hours, began to develop considerable discomfort and irritability and the other symptoms of morphine withdrawal. He had no idea what was the matter. In about twelve hours, he was violently nauseated and, during his first night at home, called his family physician in at two o'clock in the morning, fearing that he was about to die. The physician also was not certain what was wrong, but gave him some mild sedatives and attempted to encourage him. The violence of the symptoms increased during the next day, to such an extent that Mr. G. began to wish that he would die. During the course of the second night, the family physician decided that he was perhaps suffering from withdrawal of opiates and gave Mr. G. an injection of morphine to find out. The effect was immediate; in about twenty minutes, Mr. G. fell asleep and slept on in perfect comfort for many hours. He still did not know what he had been given, but when he woke up the next day the doctor told him and said, "Now we are going to have a time getting you off!" The dosage was reduced and in a week or two the drug was entirely removed, but Mr. G., during this short time, had become addicted. After the drug had been removed for a few days, he bought himself a hypodermic syringe and began to use it by himself.[20]

It may seem surprising, at first glance, that many addicts do not know what is wrong with them the first time that the abstinence symptoms occur. This is not difficult to understand when one realizes that many persons seem to think that withdrawal symptoms are purely imaginative or hysterical in character. Even in spite of the occurrence of these symptoms in animals, which have been subjected to the prolonged administration of opiates, and in spite of their occurrence in patients who have no idea what opiates are or that they have been given any, students of drug addiction have sometimes asserted that these symptoms have no physiological basis. In view of this belief among the instructed, it is easy to understand the layman who believes the same thing when he begins to experiment with the drug. Furthermore, there is nothing whatever in the initial effects of the drug to furnish the slightest clue as to what happens later. As the use of the drug is continued, in the same proportion that tolerance appears, and the positive effects diminish, the withdrawal symptoms increase, until they obtrude themselves upon the attention of the individual, and finally become dominant. In most cases of confirmed addiction, the drug appears to serve almost no other function than that of preventing the appearance of these symptoms.

One of the most difficult features of addiction to account for, by means of any explanation of the drug habit in terms of the positive effects, or euphoria, supposed to be produced by it, is the fact that during the initial period of use there takes place a gradual reversal of effect, so that the effects of the drug upon an addict are not only not the same as their effects upon a non-addicted person, but they are actually, in many respects, the precise opposite.[21] This is true both of the physiological and of the psychological effects. The initial dose causes one to feel other than normal; whereas in the case of the addict, the usual dose causes him to feel normal when he would feel below normal without it. The euphoria initially produced by the drug has often been emphasized as a causative factor, but inasmuch as this euphoria, or "kick," disappears in addiction, the continuation of the drug habit cannot be explained in this way.[22] Moreover, when administered therapeutically to allay pain, there is often absolutely no euphoria produced even in the initial period, and the patient may nevertheless become addicted. In fact, it is possible for a person to be unconscious during the entire initial stage when tolerance is established and still become addicted, as a consideration of the implications of the case of Mr. G. shows. It is this reversal of effect which accounts at one and the same time for the seductive aspect of opiates, as well as for their insidiousness. As they cease to produce pleasure, they become a necessity and produce pain if removed. The euphoria produced by the drug at first makes it easy to become addicted, but does not account for the continuance of the habit when the euphoria is gone. A theory which makes the withdrawal distress central in addiction takes account of this reversal of effects.

It follows, if one believes that the drug habit is to be accounted for on the basis of the extraordinary or uncanny state of mind it is sometimes supposed to produce, that addicts should be able to recognize such effects immediately and easily. It is a notorious fact, however, and one that baffles the addicts, as well as those who study them, that under certain conditions the drug user may be completely deceived for varying periods of time into believing that he is receiving opiates, when he actually is not, or that he is not receiving any when, as a matter of fact, he is. We shall not elaborate this point any more than to call attention to the fact that it has been put into practice as a principle in a number of gradual reduction cures, wherein, without the addict's knowledge, the amount of the drug was gradually reduced and finally withdrawn entirely, while injections of water or a saline solution were continued.[23] Then, when the addict had been free of opiates for several days, or a week, or even more, he was told that he had not been getting any of his drug for some time and usually discharged, sometimes in the vain hope that this experience might prove to him that it was only his "imagination" which led him to think he needed his drug! The fact that such a thing is possible is evidence that the direct positive effects per se are not sufficiently extraordinary to make addiction intelligible.

The tendency of the addict to relapse may be readily explained in terms of the viewpoint outlined as arising from the impression that is made upon him when he observes the remarkable and immediate effects the drug has in dissipating unpleasant physical or mental states. What the addict misses when he is off the drug is not so much the hypothetical euphoria as the element of control. On the drug, he could regulate his feeling tone; when he is not using it, it appears to him that he is the passive victim of his environment or of his changing moods. During the initial period of use, the only effects of an injection to which attention is paid are ordinarily the immediate ones lasting but a few minutes or, at most, a half-hour or an hour or so. This episodic significance of injections changes into a continuous twenty-four-hour-a-day sense of dependence upon the drug only after the addict has learned from the recurrence of the beginnings of withdrawal symptoms, as the effects of each shot wore off, that the drug was necessary to the continuance of his well-being. He learns to attribute effects to the "stuff," which are in part imaginary—or rather, projections of the need for it which he feels. When he is off, every vicissitude of life tends to remind him of his drug, and he misses the supporting and sustaining sense of its presence. And so, the ordinary pleasures of life are dulled, something seems to be amiss, and the unhappy addict eventually relapses—either deliberately or otherwise. If he does not relapse, it appears that he nevertheless remains susceptible to it for long periods of years. Cases of relapse after as long as ten or more years of abstinence are recorded.[24]

The thesis of the paper is that addiction to opiate drugs is essentially based upon the abstinence symptoms which occur when the effects of the drug are beginning to wear off rather than upon any positive effects or uncanny or extraordinarily pleasurable state of mind erroneously supposed to be produced by the drug in continued use. Addiction is established in the first instance in a process involving:

> 1. The interpretation of the withdrawal symptoms as being caused by the absence of opiates. . . .[25]
>
> 2. The use of the drug for the consciously understood purpose of alleviating these symptoms or of keeping them suppressed.

As a result of this process there is established in the addict the typical desire for the drug, a constant sense of dependence upon it, and the other attendant features of addiction. The attitudes which arise in this experience persist when the drug has been removed and predispose toward relapse. When the point is reached at which withdrawal symptoms intrude themselves upon the attention of the individual and compel him to go on using the drug, he also has forced upon him the unwelcome definition of himself as a "dope fiend." He realizes then what the craving for drugs means and, applying to his own conduct the symbols which the group applies to it, he is compelled to readjust his conception of himself to the implications of this collective viewpoint. He struggles against the habit and then eventually accepts his fate and becomes "just another junker." Obviously, when the withdrawal distress has entered into the conscious motives of the person, and he realizes that he must anticipate the recurrence of these terrible symptoms, if he does not assure himself of a supply of the drug, and when the definition of self as an addict has occurred, the drug user becomes ripe for assimilation into the culture of drug addiction, as it exists chiefly in our underworld.

The proposed theory has advantages and implications beyond those already mentioned. It is applicable in form to all cases and, as indicated, an extensive exploration of the literature, as well as many interviews with addicts, has so far failed to uncover a single negative case, even of a hearsay type. Moreover, it harmonizes and rationalizes various aspects of the habit which have often been regarded as paradoxical or contradictory in character—as, for example, the fact that addicts claim they do not obtain pleasure from the drug, the initial reversal of effects, and the strange tendency of addicts to relapse when, from a medical standpoint, they appear to be cured.

A number of further implications of the point of view presented seem to have important bearings on certain theories of social psychology and of sociology. Thus, students of the writings of George H. Mead will notice that the hypothesis follows the lines of his theory of the "significant symbols" and its role in human life. According to the view presented, the physiological effects of the drug do not become effective in influencing the psychic and social life of the person, until he has applied to them the "significant symbols" (or perhaps, in Durkheimian language, "collective representations") which are employed by the group to describe the nature of these effects. Addiction, in other words, appears as a process which goes on, on the level of "significant symbols"—it is, in other words, peculiar to man living in organized society in communication with his fellows.[26]

This theory rationalizes and explains the reasons for the ordinary rules-of-thumb employed in the therapeutic administration of morphine to prevent addiction. Some of these rules and practices include (1) keeping the patient in ignorance of the drug being used, (2) mixing other drugs with different and less pleasing effects with the opiate, (3) varying the mode of administration and disguising the drug in various kinds of medicines. The significance of these practices appears to be that they prevent the patient from attributing to morphine the effects which it in fact produces—in other words, they prevent the patient from applying certain collective symbols to his own subjective states, prevent the whole experience from being associated with the patient's preconceptions of drug addiction, and so prevent addiction.

The proposed hypothesis has the further advantage of being essentially experimental in character, in the sense that it is open to disproof, as, for example, by anyone who doubts it and is willing or foolhardy enough to experiment on himself with the drug. As has been indicated, the writer has been unable to find any record in the literature of an experiment of this character which, prolonged enough to be a test—that is, which lasted long enough so that the withdrawal distress upon stoppage of the drug was pronounced—did not result in addiction. This appears to constitute an exception to what is often assumed to be true of knowledge in the field of the social sciences—namely, that it confers, *ipso facto*, the ability to control. It is in accord with the well-known fact that addiction to narcotic drugs is peculiarly prevalent in those legitimate professions in which theoretical knowledge of these drugs is most general—that is, in the medical and allied professions.

A further significant implication of the viewpoint presented is that it offers a means of relating phenomena of a purely physiological variety to cultural or sociological phenomena. The interpretation of withdrawal distress, which we have emphasized as a basic factor in the beginning of addiction, is, it should be emphasized, a cultural pattern, a social interpretation present in a formulated fashion in the social milieu exactly like other knowledge or beliefs. When the organic disturbances produced by the withdrawal of the drug intrude themselves upon the attention of a person, they impede his functioning and assume the nature of a problem, demanding some sort of rationalization and treatment. The culture of the group supplies this rationalization by defining the situation for the individual and, in so doing, introduces into the motives and conceptions which determine his conduct other factors which lead to addiction whenever the drug is continued beyond the point at which this insight occurs.

Finally, we should like to emphasize again the methodological implications of the study. A great deal of argumentation has taken place in sociology on the matter of methodology—whether universal generalizations are possible or not, concerning the role of statistical generalizations and of quantification generally, and concerning the so-called case method. Most of these arguments have tended to take place on an abstract level; whereas, it would seem that in the final analysis, they can be settled only in terms of actual results of research. We, therefore, regard it as significant that the theory advanced in this study is not quantitative in form, nor is it a purely intuitive generalization which is not subject to proof, but that it is experimental in form, in spite of the fact that it is based upon the analysis of data secured largely in personal interviews. It is, moreover, stated in universal form and is, therefore, not dependent upon or relative to a particular culture or a particular time. As such, it provides the possibility of its own continuous reconstruction and refinement, in terms of more extended experience and of more elaborated instances. In other words, it provides a place for the exceptional or crucial case, which George H. Mead has described as the "growing point of science."[27]

Comment

The writer does not state whether his study relates to any one form of drug addiction, but it seems he is concerned chiefly, if not solely, with morphine addiction. At least, he discusses addiction in which withdrawal symptoms are prominent, and so his theory does not seem to apply to types of addiction, such as cocaine, hasheesh, and others, in which withdrawal symptoms are absent or of a minor nature.

It is stated that "addiction begins when the person suffering from withdrawal symptoms realizes that a dose of the drug will dissipate all his discomfort and misery." And, furthermore: "If he fails to realize the connection between the distress and the opiate, he escapes addiction." How often does this occur? Conceivably, in some patients who have received such drugs to alleviate pain or as sedatives. But we presume that the author does not intend to suggest that many drug addicts are established in the course of medical treatment. Apart from such cases, may we not consider that an individual who persists in securing drugs and administering them to himself, until he is likely to suffer withdrawal symptoms of any degree, is in

fact already an addict? And that withdrawal symptoms are then a complication in the course of drug addiction, dependent on the fact that tolerance for the drug has been acquired? But that does not explain why the individual became an addict, although it might be offered as a reason for the difficulty in giving up the addiction, if he so desires or is requested. We would again recall the forms of drug addiction, in which there are few or no withdrawal symptoms.

The cases quoted by the author as crucial for the corroboration of his hypothesis are not convincing. The case quoted from Strauss does not seem to lend any support to the hypothesis. This woman did not become an addict because of withdrawal symptoms, but in an effort to secure relief from a state of acute mental depression. As the case report states: "She began to use it, found it helpful, and soon was addicted." When it is stated that persons may relapse "after as long as ten or more years of abstinence," then surely the renewal of addiction is not due to withdrawal symptoms.

Throughout the paper, there are several statements which call for comment. Thus, it is said that current theories of drug addiction tend to be moralistic, rather than scientific. This does not seem a correct interpretation of the many physiological and psychiatric studies on the subject. Again, references should be given for the statement—in regard to the nature of withdrawal symptoms—that "students of drug addiction have sometimes asserted that these symptoms have no physiological basis." It is stated that "the victim desires to use the drug—and also at the same time desires to be free of it." In what proportion of cases? Too often, one has found the addict seeking a "cure" with the aim of having his tolerance cut down because of financial difficulties, or because the dosage was too high for practical purposes. The author talks of "the drug," but experience with drug addicts shows so often that they have been addicted to several drugs, depending on available supplies and, after a period of abstinence through failure of supplies, would start in afresh on drugs of which they had no previous experience. What were they seeking, if not some form of satisfaction or pleasure or relief from a state of emotional distress or difficulty of life?

One cannot pass over a striking statement: "This appears to constitute an exception to what is often assumed to be true of knowledge in the field of the social sciences—namely, that it confers, *ipso facto,* the ability to control." We are reminded of the musings of one, Burns, who had knowledge but had not always the ability to control—and had knowledge of that also. Thus, in the "Unco Guid, or the Rigidly Righteous":

> One point must still be greatly dark,
> The moving why they do it;
> And just as lamely can ye mark
> How far perhaps they rue it.

Rejoinder

Comment section by:
David Slight
Department of Psychiatry
University of Chicago

A considerable portion of Dr. Slight's comments are based upon an implicit conception of method which is fundamentally different from our own. We assume, and stated in our article, that a scientific explanation must be stated in terms of factors or processes which are present in all the members of the class to which the generalization is supposed to apply. There is no evidence in Dr. Slight's comments that he has taken any account of this principle, and it is for this reason that he has failed to discuss the main issues. When he asserts, concerning the case given by Strauss, "This woman did not become an addict because of withdrawal symptoms, but in an effort to secure relief from a state of acute mental depression," he does not take into account a fact which is known to all—that many addicts begin to use the drug under circumstances which have no connection whatever with "mental distress." Some addicts, for example, first tried the drug in connection with a sex affair with a prostitute, and others first learn about the drug in medical practice. One may also ask if it would not be reasonable to suppose that the woman in this case experienced mental depression at some time during her six-month attack of disease nine years before she became an addict? Why did she not

become addicted then? Dr. Slight does not touch this problem.

In the sentence beginning "Apart from such cases . . ." Dr. Slight appears to imply either that no addicts are created in medical practice or that, if they are, they should be excluded from the argument. Medical practice today does create new addicts—not many, but some. They are addicts in precisely the same sense as others are, and any generalization must include them. Concerning the latter part of this same sentence, we may say for a rather large percentage even of addicts on the street that the withdrawal symptoms are not at first understood. This was true in about 50 percent of our cases. A number of them had to have the symptoms explained to them by addicts or by doctors.

The implication that knowledge of the drug being given and of the withdrawal symptoms is irrelevant, and that the sheer brute fact of having used the drug long enough to produce withdrawal symptoms in itself constitutes addiction is directly contradicted in medical practice itself. The patient who is given morphine in hospitals is kept in ignorance of what is happening to him, and this is done for the explicit purpose of preventing addiction. Medical men quite generally maintain that this practice has, in fact, been very effective. Several decades ago, when such techniques were not as widely employed, medical practice did, in fact, create many new addicts.

The principle that an explanation must be applicable to *all*, rather than to some, of the cases is again ignored when he asks, "What are they [the addicts] seeking if not some form of satisfaction or pleasure or relief from a state of emotional distress or difficulty in life?" This view is simply the current common-sense misconception of the problem, and it explains nothing. It entirely ignores those cases in which addiction is a consequence of the sheer accident of disease. In terms of this view, how is one to account for continued addiction in that group of addicts for whom the major "emotional distress or difficulty in life" is the addiction itself?

The questions of fact which Dr. Slight raises cause us to wonder where he obtained the information upon which he bases his statements. He is correct when he surmises that we were concerned only with opiate addiction, but he repeatedly refers to the use of other drugs and says that addicts shift readily from one drug to another, depending upon available supply. This is incorrect. Opiate addicts shift only from one opiate to another. Chicago addicts use mainly heroin, for which they may pay as much as two hundred dollars an ounce. As a consequence, they cannot afford to use other drugs, and very few do. If an addict is utterly unable to obtain an opiate, he does only one thing—he "kicks his habit"; that is, he breaks the continuity of his addiction. During abstinence, some addicts may try other drugs or drink whiskey, but that does not prove that all forms of drug-taking are alike any more than the fact that some disappointed lovers turn to drink proves that sex activity and alcoholism are alike.

Notes

1. The study on which this paper is based was carried out at the University of Chicago under the direction of Dr. Herbert Blumer.

2. Report to the Council of the League of Nations by the Committee of Enquiry into the Control of Opium Smoking in the Far East, II (1930), p. 420.

3. This general view is not only widespread among psychiatrists, but is popularly held as well. The great majority of writers in medical journals on this subject assume it. It may be found elaborated in a typical form in the following articles by L. Kolb: "Pleasure and Deterioration from Narcotic Addiction," *Jour. Ment. Hyg.*, Vol. IX (October, 1925); "Drug Addiction in Relation to Crime," *ibid*, (January, 1925); "The Struggle for Cure and the Conscious Reasons for Relapse," *Jour. Nerv. and Ment. Dis.*, Vol. LXVI (July, 1927); and "Drug Addiction—A Study of Some Medical Cases," *Arch. Neurol. and Psychiat.*, Vol. XX (1928). It is also developed by Dr. Schultz in "Rep. of the Comm. on Drug Addicts to Hon. R. C. Patterson, etc.," as reported in *Amer. Jour. Psychiat.*, Vol. X (1930–31).

4. Dansauer and Rieth ("Über Morphinismus bei Kriegsbeschädigten," in *Arbeit und Gesundheit Schriftenreihe zum Reichsorbeitsblatt*, Vol. XVI [1931]), found that 96.7 percent of 799 addicts had relapsed within five years after taking a cure. Relapse after more than ten years is sometimes mentioned. We ourselves were acquainted with an addict who stated that he had abstained for fifteen years before resuming the drug. We have never encountered or read an authentic account of any so-called cured addict who did not show by his attitudes toward the drug that the impulse to relapse was actively present.

5. It is characteristic of practically all addicts, prior to their own addiction, that they do not expect or intend to become addicts.

6. L. Faucher, *Contribution de l'étude du rêve morphinique et de la morphinomanie* (Thèse de Montpellier; No. 8 [1910–11]).

7. *JAMA*, Vol. XXIII.

8. *Brit. Jour. Inebriety* XXXI, 132.

9. The aim of this paper is to present a sociological theory of opiate addiction which appears to offer possibilities for a rational and objective understanding of the problem without any element of moralization. This theory is based upon informal and intimate contact over a long period of time with approximately fifty drug addicts. The main points of the theory have been tested in the material available in the literature of the problem, and no conclusions have been drawn from case materials collected, unless these materials were clearly corroborated by case materials in the literature.

10. Dansauer and Rieth (*op. cit.*) cite two hundred and forty such cases. Many of these cases had used the drug for five or more years without becoming addicts.

11. See e.g., Levinstein, *Die Morphiumsucht* (1877); F. McKelvey Bell, "Morphinism and Morphinomania," *N.Y. Med. Jour.*, Vol. XCIII (1911); and Daniel Jouet, *Étude sur la morphinisme chronique* (Thèse de Paris [1883]).

12. The case of Dr. H., cited later in this paper, is such a case.

13. Withdrawal distress begins to appear after a few days of regular administration but does not ordinarily become severe until after two, three, or more weeks, when its severity appears to increase at an accelerated rate. In its severe form, it involves acute distress from persistent nausea, general weakness, aching joints and pains in the legs, diarrhea, and extreme insomnia. In isolated cases, death may result from abrupt withdrawal of the drug.

14. We have checked this point with addicts who had voluntarily abstained for as long as six years. They unhesitatingly declared themselves to be addicts who happened not to be using drugs at the time—i.e., "junkers" or "users" who were "off stuff."

15. A type of individual who uses the drug without being hooked, is the one who uses it, say once a week, and thus avoids the withdrawal distress. Such a person is called a "joy-popper" or "pleasure-user" and is not regarded as an addict, until he has used the drug steadily for a time, experienced withdrawal distress, and become hooked. He then permanently loses his status as a "pleasure-user" and becomes a "junker." An addict who has abstained for a time and then begins to use it a little bit now and then is not a "pleasure-user"—he is just "playing around." See D. W. Maurer's article in the April, 1936, issue of *American Speech*.

16. As the other evidence which indicates how central and how taken for granted the role of withdrawal distress in addiction is, we may mention that the addict's word "yen" refers simultaneously to withdrawal distress *and* to the desire for the drug. Also, "to feel one's habit" means to feel the withdrawal distress. Addicts call cocaine non-habit-forming, because it does not cause withdrawal distress when stopped.

17. "Zuer Pathogenese des chronischen Morphinismus," *Monatschr. fur Psychiat. und Neruol.*, Vol. XLVII (1920).

18. As defined, e.g., in the *Report of the Departmental Committee on Morphine and Heroin Addiction to the British Ministry of Health:* "A person who, not requiring the continued use of a drug for the relief of the symptoms of organic disease, has acquired, as a result of repeated administration, an overwhelming desire for its continuance, and in whom withdrawal of the drug leads to definite symptoms of mental or physical distress or disorder."

19. *Op. cit.*, p. 103.

20. Interviewed by the writer.

21. This had been partially emphasized by Erlenmeyer, as quoted by C. E. Terry and Mildred Pellens, *The Opium Problem* (1928), pp. 600 ff.; and it has been noted, in one way or another, in much of the physiological research that has been done on morphine effects.

22. The English Departmental Committee in 1926 (*op. cit.*) stated that, whatever may have been the original motive, the use of the drug is continued not so much from that original motive as "because of the craving created by the use" (quoted in Terry and Pellens, *ibid.*, pp. 164–65).

23. *Ibid.*, pp. 577 ff., quoting C. C. Wholey; *ibid.*, pp. 572 ff., quoting M. R. Dupony. A number of addicts have somewhat sheepishly admitted to us that they had been deceived in this manner for as long as ten days.

24. Rolb, "Drug Addicts—A Study of Some Medical Cases," *loc. cit.*

25. It is significant to note that this belief that withdrawal distress is caused by the absence of the opiate is not adequate or correct from the standpoint of physiological theory.

26. Very young children, the feeble-minded, and the insane would not be expected to have the necessary sophisticated conception of causality or the ability to manipulate "significant symbols" which, as we have indicated, are necessary preconditions of addiction.

    Dr. Charles Schultz, in a study of 318 cases found only 14 patients, or less than five percent, who were "probably high-grade morons, and even these gave the impression of having their dull wits sharpened by the use of drugs" (*loc. cit.*). Regarding insanity—it has been noted that it confers immunity to addiction, and that insanity appears to occur less frequently among the blood realtions of addicts than among the blood relatives of samples of the general population. O. Wuth, "Zur Erbanlage der Süchtigen," *Z. für die Ges. Neur. und Psychiat.*, CLIII (1935), pp. 495 ff.; Alexander Pilcz, "Zur Konstitution der Süchtigen," *Jahrb. für Psychiat.*, LI (1935), pp. 169 ff.; Jouet, *op. cit.*; Sceleth and Kuh, *JAMA*, LXXXII, p. 679; P. Wolff, *Deutsche medizinische Wochenschrift*, Vol. LVII, in his report on the results of a questionnaire, etc. Note the testimony of Gaupp, Bratz, and Bonhoeffer.

    On the immunity of children, see R. N. Chopra et al., "Administration of Opiates to Infants in India," *Indian Med. Gaz.*, LXIX (1934), pp. 489 ff.; "Opium Habit in India," *Indian Jour. Med. Research*, Vol. XV (1927); "Drug Addiction in India and Its Treatment," *Indian Med. Gaz.*, LXX (1935), pp. 121 ff.

27. In an essay, "Scientific Method and the Individual Thinker," in *Creative Intelligence* (1917).

For Discussion

Can Lindesmith's theory apply to drug users for whom the drug of choice is not accompanied by withdrawal symptoms? Why or why not?

2

Some Considerations on the Disease Concept of Addiction

Jennifer L. Syvertsen

In this essay, the author considers the evidence that drug addiction is a chronic and relapsing disease influenced by a complex array of biological, psychosocial, and environmental factors. Although addiction shares many characteristics with other medical diseases, it has not traditionally been regarded as such. The history of addiction theory is reviewed, and special consideration is given to its fluid nomenclature, including what precisely constitutes an addiction diagnosis. Etiologic agents are defined and detailed, and treatment outcomes are measured. Even though relapse is a common occurrence, studies suggest that treatment can produce beneficial, even if incremental, results. Challenges to conventional conceptualization, treatment, and assessment have been increasingly raised, suggesting that addiction research and clinical practice will continue to evolve into the future.

Drug addiction is a chronic and relapsing disease, characterized by changes in the brain and compulsive drug taking and drug behaviors (National Institute on Drug Abuse [NIDA] 1999). The initiation, development, and progression of drug addiction are synergistically influenced by a wide range of biological, psychosocial, and environmental factors, but its manifestations are the same among its sufferers: a loss of control, craving, distortions in perception and thought, and continued drug use despite myriad adverse consequences. While drug abuse refers to the use of psychoactive drugs that leads to impaired functioning, including potentially risky and hazardous behaviors (Landry 1994), abuse differs from addiction in that an abuser can choose whether or not to use drugs. An individual suffering from addiction, however, increasingly loses that volition (Leshner 1998).

Addiction is also characterized by salience and ambivalence. *Salience* refers to the degree of focus on a particular activity as compared with other activities; that is, for a drug-addicted individual, the use of drugs becomes a compulsively important priority in his or her life, even at the expense of other activities and interests (Loonis, Apter, and Sztulman 2000; Gardner 2001). *Ambivalence* refers to the inability to decide between two equally powerful, opposing choices. For addicted persons, periods of denial tend to alternate with periods of attempted sobriety; the tension between these two opposing forces likely explains why most addicted individuals vacillate between periods of addiction and abstinence throughout their drug-using life (Senay 1998). These phenomena, along with the compulsivity of use even in the face of physical, psychological, and social consequences, are essential elements in understanding the nature of addiction.

Because of its complex etiology and characteristics, drug addiction has a particularly strong association with relapse (Curry, Marlatt, Peterson, and Lutton 1988). Relapse, the resumption of pretreatment patterns of drug use or the development of new patterns of drug use after an unspecified period of abstinence, is also complex and initiated by multiple and interactive risk factors (Donovan 1996). While the designation of drug addiction as a chronic and relapsing disease is a central theme in addiction literature (Landry 1994; O'Brien and McLellan 1996; Hser, Anglin, Grella, Longshore, and Prendergast 1997; McLellan et al. 2000; White, Boyle, and Loveland 2002), the disease concept of drug addiction has evolved considerably over the past two centuries in the context of medicine, public health, and clinical diagnosis (Meyer 1996). This paper traces the linguistic, cultural, and medical development of the disease concept of addiction before detailing the factors effecting its initiation, development, and progression among individuals. Finally, treatment outcomes and relapse potential are discussed.

A Brief History

References to chronic intoxication as a disease of the body and soul can be traced back to ancient civilizations of Egypt and Greece, but in America the disease concept of addiction is relatively new (White 2000a). The view of addiction as a disease rather than a vice first arose in the late eighteenth century, in conjunction with a sudden increase in the consumption of alcohol in America (White et al. 2002). Early disease concept advocates viewed chronic drunkenness as a symptom of a disease, rather than as a disease in its own right. However, expanding knowledge of the physical manifestations of consistent alcohol consumption bolstered a new medical perspective. The Swedish physician Magnus Huss identified the physical manifestations resultant of chronic alcohol exposure, and new terms were coined in 1849: *alcoholism*, to mean a chronic state of alcohol intoxication characterized by physical pathology and impaired social functioning, and its accompanying descriptor, *alcoholic*, or the individual afflicted with this condition (White 1998). Huss promoted the theory of "alcoholism" as a disease and called for health professionals to study and offer treatment for the condition (White 2000a). Other late eighteenth- and nineteenth-century professional literature eventually agreed, and numerous publications began to conceptualize alcoholism as a chronic and progressive disease.

By extension, the disease concept was applied to other drugs as well (White et al. 2002). The issue came to the forefront in the nineteenth century as indiscriminate prescribing of opiates by physicians, widespread availability, and an influx of opium smoking by immigrants from Asia contributed to epidemic levels of narcotic use. Moreover, innovations such as the isolation of morphine and the introduction of the hypodermic syringe led to more severe and compulsive opiate use (White 2000a; Reisine and Pasternak 1996). The cultural perception of opiate use transformed from health misfortune, to vice, to disease in and of itself. Initially, the perception of opiate addiction was tainted by the cultural climate of the time: the predominantly white middle-class users who orally ingested and injected opiates were increasingly thought of as suffering from a "disease," while Chinese immigrants who mostly smoked opium were subjected to persecution and racism and stigmatized as having a "vice" (White 1998, 2000a). However, as the professional literature began to publish mounting evidence of opiate addiction as a chronic and relapsing disease, the media latched onto the idea and perpetuated a medical concept of opiate addiction into mainstream culture as well (White 1998, 2000a).

The rise in narcotic use also generated the first formal attempts to categorize levels of drug abuse (Grant and Dawson 1999). During this time period, a mixture of medical and moral language was common throughout the literature (White 2000a). Professionals began to specialize in the treatment of alcohol, opium, morphine, and cocaine "inebriety," a term that emerged to encompass a wide spectrum of problematic drug use. Other new classifications included *morphinism, narcotism,* and *narcomania*—the "ism" referring to perpetual states of drug use and the "mania" referring to craving and subsequent binging. Around the same time, the slang *dope fiend* became popular, reflecting the general public's enduring negative perception of drug users: "dope" referred to products containing heroin or cocaine, and "fiend" is a derivative of a German word meaning diabolical or hated (White 1998).

The word *addiction*, derived from the Latin word *addicere*, meaning to admire or surrender to a master, first appeared in the literature in the mid-1890s. The term *addict* appeared around 1910 to replace another earlier term, *habitué* (White 1998). With the term *alcoholism* popularized in reference to drinking, the words *addiction* and *addict* came to symbolize the chronic, progressive disease concept of drug use and the individual who suffers from it (White 2000a).

Currents Issues in Addiction

From the mid-twentieth century forward, the disease concept of addiction has been widely accepted. Influential groups, including the National Council on Alcoholism and Drug Dependence as well as the American Society of Addiction Medicine, have adopted the view that addiction is a chronic and relapsing disease. The stance is central to their policy positions (White et al. 2002).

Furthermore, more scientific attempts to quantify and categorize addiction as a disease have emerged. Diagnoses of addiction can be made with the American Psychiatric Association's (APA) *Diagnostic and Statistical Manual of Mental Disorders*, fourth edition (DSM-IV APA 1994) and the World Health Organization's (WHO) *International Classification of Diseases 10* (ICD-10 WHO 1992). Significantly, both of these diagnostic tools use the term *substance dependence* as a synonym for *addiction*, although it was not always that way. In 1968, the term *drug dependence* replaced the term *drug addiction* in both assessment tools. Prior to this, *drug dependence* had not been used in reference to compulsive drug use (Maddux and Desmond 2000). Theoretically, the idea was to produce a term applicable to drug abuse in general.

Both diagnostic systems attempt to define and quantify the multidimensional aspects of the same condition. The *DSM-IV,* most commonly used in the United States, assesses *substance-related disorders,* which are broken down into two categories: *substance use disorders* and *substance-induced disorders.* Substance use disorders are composed of syndromes related to the pathological use of substances, including substance abuse and dependence (addiction); substance-induced disorders are disorders created by substance use, such as intoxication and withdrawal, and psychiatric syndromes, including anxiety, mood disorders, and dementia. *Substance or drug dependence (addiction)* is defined as a pathologic condition manifested by three or more of seven criteria, which fall into three general categories: physiological states (tolerance and withdrawal) behavior with negative consequences (preoccupation with use, substantial time using or recovering from the ef-

fects, continuing use in the face of physical and emotional problems); and a loss of psychological freedom (inability to quit or cut down, using more often or for longer than intended) (APA 1994).

Importantly, pharmacologic definitions of dependence are often confused with addiction and abuse, but clinically, physical dependence, tolerance, and addiction are all separate phenomena (Kowal 1999; Savage et al. 2001). *Physical dependence* is a state of adaptation by the body to a specific drug class, and *withdrawal* is the physical process the body goes through when administration of the drug is abruptly ceased or lowered. *Tolerance* describes the state of adaptation in which the same amount of a drug has progressively less effect on an individual or when increasingly higher doses of a drug are needed to achieve the same effect (Landry 1994). Physical dependence and withdrawal can develop with the repeated administration of several classes of drugs, including antidepressants, antipsychotics, and opiates; these are the body's normal physiological responses to certain classes of drugs (Kirsh et al. 2002). However, physiological adaptation is not in itself sufficient to warrant a diagnosis of addiction or dependence (McLellan et al. 2000). The disease is characterized by an element of compulsion in the individual's drug use that supersedes the physical aspects; the overarching concept of addiction implies persistent substance use despite physical, psychological, and social implications for the user (McLellan et al. 2000; Tims, Leukefeld, and Platt 2001).

The confusion in addiction nomenclature is further complicated by issues in the growing field of pain management. While considerations should be made by physicians treating pain patients with a history of drug abuse, the prevailing concern among many in the medical field is that the prescription of pain medication to patients will unintentionally breed a new generation of "addicts." Consequently, patients who suffer from chronic pain are often undertreated. Further complicating matters is the concept of *pseudoaddiction,* or the apparent abuse of medications brought on by unrelieved pain (Kirsh et al. 2002). On the surface, the patient exhibits the aberrant behaviors consistent with a diagnosis of addiction, but pseudoaddiction is distinguished from the true disease of addiction in that the abusive behaviors cease once the pain has been effectively treated (Savage et al. 2001).

Because of the aforementioned issues, experts from a variety of backgrounds argue that the distinction between physical dependence and drug dependence is unnecessarily muddled. Numerous others suggest that the word *addiction* promotes social stigmatization. Maddux and Desmond (2000) conducted a search of the Medline database and found that of the 272 articles that incorporated *addiction* or *dependence* in the title, 41 percent used *addiction* and 59 percent chose *dependence*, demonstrating a wide use of both terms. The authors of the essay (an editorial in the well-respected journal *Addiction*) advocate the use of the word *addiction*, noting that "terms that are intrinsically useful, clear and appropriate tend to survive. Those that are less useful or clear . . . tend to fade away."

Already, social scientists have expanded upon the current terms in order to provide a better linguistic paradigm in which to frame the multiple layers of the disease. Since addiction tends to vacillate between periods of use and abstinence that occur over an extended period of time, researchers have designated this process an "addiction career" or "dependence career" (Hser et al. 1997). A career perspective advances the theory that perception, action, skills, thought processes, and the like change and develop at different stages throughout an individual's life. During career development, decisions occur when old roles are replaced with new or modified roles. The career concept frames addiction within a longitudinal approach, recognizing that drug use and its effects are a dynamic and permanent feature in the individual's life (Hser et al. 1997). In other words, once an addiction has developed, it is a constant underlying feature of that individual's life and the possibility of relapse is ever present, even if the addiction has been in remission for many years. The idea of recovery is to build upon the stage in an addiction career in which drug use does not play a salient role in the individual's life.

Risk Factors and the Etiology of Addiction

As previously stated, the disease concept of drug addiction has evolved considerably over the past two centuries in the context of medicine, public health, and clinical diagnosis (Meyer 1996). Too, the evolution of the language of addiction is reflective of innovations in its conceptualization as a disease. By situating "addiction" within a historical context, our current understanding of drug addiction at the individual level is elucidated.

Drug addiction develops and intensifies through the synergistic interaction of multiple variables. O'Brien (1996) breaks down these variables into three main categories—agent (drug), host (user), and environment (social and cultural context)—which provide a useful framework to unravel the complex etiology of drug addiction.

Agent

The initial choice of whether or not to try drugs is volitional, but the drug of choice is often influenced by external factors, such as price and availability (O'Brien and McLellan 1996). Drug availability varies by region, as do the effects of the specific drugs chosen for consumption.

Pharmacologic factors, the effects of drugs on the body, increase one's risk for continued use and the development of an addiction. Drugs that produce particularly euphoric results are more reinforcing to the user (O'Brien 1996). Furthermore, the route of administration can potentiate a drug's effect, which has a significant impact on abuse potential (Landry 1994; O'Brien 1996). Inhaled drug vapors reach the brain within 7 seconds; injecting into the veins produces effects in 20 seconds; injecting into the muscle takes 4 minutes; snorting takes 3 to 5 minutes; and liquid or solid ingestion takes 20 to 30 minutes. The faster the drug reaches the brain and the higher concentration of a drug that reaches the brain, the more intense the euphoria and, therefore, the greater the risk of developing an addiction (Landry 1994).

Host

The effects of drugs tend to vary among individuals (O'Brien 1996), and literature suggests that genetic makeup plays a significant role in the risk of developing addiction (McLellan et al. 2000; Meyer 1996). Genetics influence the effects of the initial use of a drug, and any pleasurable effects are in turn likely to reinforce further use of the substance (O'Brien and McLellan 1996). Studies with alcoholics suggest that genetics increase the risk for developing addiction but do not necessarily determine the outcome. For example, genetic influences account for approximately 40 to 60 percent of the risk of developing an alcohol use disorder (Schuckit 2000). Research also indicates that the first-degree relatives of alcoholics have a three- to fourfold higher prevalence of alcoholism compared with those who do not have a history of alcoholism in their family (Schuckit 1999).

An addicted brain is physically and chemically different than a nonaddicted brain. There is a host of neurobiological changes that accompany the progression from voluntary to compulsive drug use, and research suggests that chronic drug use leads to long-term and permanent changes in the brain, even after an individual has ceased using drugs (NIDA 1999; Gardner 2001; Begley 2001; O'Brien and McLellan 1996). The compulsive aspect of drug addiction in and of itself is likely a consequence of drug-induced alterations in brain functioning (NIDA 1999). Significantly, once addiction has taken hold, these brain changes lock an addict into a perpetual risk for relapse (O'Brien and McLellan 1996).

Drug use permanently alters the pleasure and reward circuits in the brain, creates a vulnerability to other drugs that stimulate the reward system even if the individual has no experience using them, and renders an addict vulnerable to internal and external cues associated with drug taking (Gardner 2001). The integration of the reward circuitry with emotional, motivational, and memory centers in the brain enables the individual to experience the pleasure from drugs while simultaneously learning to recognize the signals associated with the rewards. For example, repeatedly associating a friend, a place, or even an emotional state with using drugs can result in a conditioned learning process (McLellan et al. 2000), not unlike Pavlov's famous experiment with salivating dogs. These cues can also trigger relapse, even among persons who have been abstinent for long periods of time (McLellan et al. 2000; Gardner 2001).

Chronic drug use also permanently affects the release and reuptake of dopamine in the reward pathways of the brain. Drugs affect dopamine functioning in different capacities, but all abusable drugs seem to stimulate it in some matter (Gardner 2001). Dopamine is a neurochemical deep within the brain responsible for inducing pleasure; essentially, when people use drugs, they are turning on their brain's pleasure circuit. Eventually, however, chronic drug use starts to have the opposite pleasure-producing effects, and not only do dopamine levels in the brain actually decrease, the brain begins to have trouble producing it at all. The lack of dopamine then begins to evoke feelings of depression and drug craving (Leshner 1998).

Comorbid psychiatric conditions in individuals may play an important role in the development of addiction as well. For example, early antisocial and delinquent behavior may be indicative of problems with addiction later on (Landry 1994). However, the use of drugs can exacerbate or even create new psychiatric symptoms and behavioral problems that may not have developed otherwise (O'Brien 1996). Another theory posits that the more unconventional and risk-taking the individual, the more likely he or she is to experiment with drugs; by extension, the more extreme these personality traits, the more severe involvement with drugs and the more dangerous the drugs of choice (Goode 1999).

The inability to cope with stress, negative self-image, depression, anxiety, and even shyness are also common cofactors that can initiate substance use, which may later progress into an addiction (Landry 1994; O'Brien 1996). Stress in particular has been shown to play a key role in perpetuating patterns of use, especially relapse (NIDA 2002; Sinha 2001). In fact, many of the host factors that initially contribute to the addiction process are also important in the relapse process. Sometimes an individual will "lapse" or "slip": engage in a minor indulgence in his or her former drug-taking activities, without ever fully reverting to former drug use patterns. However, sometimes a lapse (or two) can initiate what is often referred to as "reinstatement"—that is, one or two lapses can essentially reinstate the addiction. In order to cope with the negative feelings the lapse brought on, the individual reverts to his or her old coping behavior (drug use), at which point the relapse process is already under way (Gardner 2001).

Although various drugs and their interaction with an individual's biology and personality can influence the onset and course of addiction, there are also a range of environmental and cultural factors that contribute to the course of the disease and can potentially threaten one's efforts to recover from it (NIDA 1999).

Environmental Factors

Environmental factors encompass the physical, economic, political, and sociocultural aspects of the drug user's life. As such, an individual's potential for addiction is complicated by variables such as cultural traditions, economic conditions, social controls, and the influence of other drug users (Bakalar 2001). Environmental influences, "cues" that become associated with drugs— people, places, and things—can reinforce drug use and can also trigger cravings that sustain an individual's risk for relapse, even after treatment (Gardner 2001; Bakalar 2001).

Since drug use is learned and reinforced through socialization (Goode 1999), peer influences and social pressures are important environmental factors that can influence the course of addiction (O'Brien and McLellan 1996). For example, adolescents are influenced by their peers' use of drugs and attitudes regarding such use. Those whose friends have access to drugs have an increased exposure and, consequently, increased risk of becoming a user. Family influences, including substance abuse by parents or other family members, inconsistent discipline, and lack of warmth and emo-

tional support, are all conducive to the onset of drug use as well (Landry 1994).

Unequal social, economic, and health policies also contribute to conditions in which drug use thrives (Friedman 2002). Studies suggest that inner-city inhabitants, who often live in a culture of violence and economic and educational disadvantage, have an increased likelihood of developing an addiction (Landry 1994; O'Brien 1996). Several developments over the past few decades have exacerbated the drug problem in many of these areas: the deterioration of the economic structure of the lower sector of the working class, a growing economic polarization, and the political and physical decay of many inner-city communities can all translate into feelings of despair, hopelessness, and depression, making drug abuse an attractive escape (Goode 1999). A culture of drug-induced escapism is not limited to urban landscapes, however, as similarly socioeconomically disadvantaged rural areas, for example, have been associated with prescription drug addiction (Clancy 2000; Alcoholism & Drug Abuse Weekly 2002; Department of Justice 2002a, 2002b).

Recovery and Treatment Outcomes

Given the complex nature of addiction, it is not surprising that relapse is a common occurrence. In fact, relapse may even be considered a part of the learning process that ultimately initiates permanent recovery (Tims, Leukefeld, and Platt 2001). Relapse does not mean that addicts must start all over again, especially if they continue with treatment rather than drop out, return to abstinence as soon as possible, and move forward from the point in their recovery process where they previously left off. The relapse itself can provide key information as to what instigated the behavior in the first place, and that information can be used to formulate strategies to prevent it from happening again (Washton 1989).

It is important to recognize that while there are general strategies that have proven successful for many individuals, no single type of treatment is guaranteed successful for everyone. Effective treatment must address issues beyond the drug use itself. Complications in treating drug abusers include polydrug use, comorbid psychiatric conditions, criminal activity, and social issues, such as homelessness and unemployment (Anglin and Hser 1990). Recovery requires a multidimensional approach, and often long-term monitoring and multiple experiences in treatment in order to prevent relapse and achieve lasting results (NIDA 1999).

The American Society of Addiction Medicine (ASAM) promotes a continuum-of-care model, which acknowledges that episodes of addiction manifest with different severity and circumstances among individuals, and that treatment needs to address the multiple and changing needs of the individual at different points in time (ASAM 1996). The basic guiding principles of placement criteria include clinical objectivity and a choice of four general treatment levels: outpatient, intensive outpatient, residential, and intensive inpatient. Within each of these four levels lie continuum-of-care options that address and respond to the variation in patients' needs over time. ASAM discourages using previous treatment failure as a condition for placement and instead relies on clinically determined need to fit the patient into the most optimal treatment. While there are no specific criteria for the length of stay in treatment, patients with more severe problems need to have the option of extended care. Finally, twelve-step and self-help groups are important dimensions in care; ASAM recognizes that the spiritual component can be significant in all levels of the recovery process but does not make any specific recommendations within the various levels of care. The ASAM continuum of care is the ideal way that addicted patients should be treated, but it is not necessarily how they really are treated in practice. As addiction medicine advances, the field will increasingly recognize the need to incorporate these guidelines and ideas into treatment (Senay 1998).

Just as addiction treatment is evolving, so too are the methods to evaluate the success of such episodes of care. Significantly, recent literature has called into question conventional evaluation methods and calculations of "success" among drug treatment outcomes (McLellan et al. 2000; O'Brien and McLellan 1996; McLellan 2002; White et al. 2002; Hser et al. 1997; Miller 1996). If drug addiction is a chronic, relapsing disease that can be controlled but not cured, then why is care provided and outcome measured in predominantly acute terms? Relapse rates depend on the exact definition of "relapse" and at what point in time the follow-up study is conducted; therefore, inconsistencies plague addiction literature. It has been suggested that researchers and clinicians abandon the notion of relapse entirely and instead employ terminology that more accurately describes the normal course of events that takes place in recovering from addiction (Miller 1996).

Since many drug addicts experience multiple episodes of treatment, abstinence, and subsequent reentry into treatment, researchers have built upon the "career" concept to designate this process as a "treatment career." Treatment careers can be lengthy, especially if initiated early, and are often punctuated with periods of sobriety in between phases of drug use. Again, the career framework proves useful in conceptualizing the chronic nature of addiction and the cyclical processes of treatment and relapse (Hser et al. 1997). Further, White and colleagues (2002) have proposed implementing a "recovery management" model in addiction treatment, which requires a shift in thinking from a dichotomous concept of treatment outcome to instead focus on the processes involved in long-term recovery and improvement in the quality of life for the patient. It shifts the focus to the *management* of the disease, instead of the *cure* or *acute* treatment of the disease. This appears to build upon ASAM's continuum-of-care model in practice, and extends Hser and colleagues' (1997) career concepts to include "recovery career" in addition to addiction and treatment careers in linguistic conceptualization.

Although most of the addiction literature deals with predictors of relapse (Brewer, Catalano, Haggerty, Gainey, and Fleming 1998; Dekimpe, Van de Gucht, Hanssens, and Powers 1998), treatment retention (Zhang, Friedmann, and Gerstein 2003; Grella, Hser, Joshi, and Anglin 1999; Greenfield and Fountain 2000), ethnicity and gender issues (Prendergast and Hser 1998; Fiorentine and Hillhouse 1999; Comfort and Kaltenbach 2000; Petry 2003), the relationship of social support (Dobkin, De Civita, Paraherakis, and Gill 2002) and counseling (Joe, Simpson, Dansereau, and Rown-Szal 2001; Etheridge, Craddock, Hubbard, and Rounds-Bryant 1999) to treatment success, and treatment outcomes for specific drugs, like narcotics (Bailey and Hser 1994; Gruber, Chutuape, and Stitzer 2000; Katz, Gruber, Chutuape, and Stitzer 2001; Booth, Crowley, and Zhang 1996; Ghodse et al. 2002) and cocaine (Siegal, Li, and Rapp 2002; Simpson, Joe, Fletcher, Hubbard, and Anglin 1999), there are a few valuable studies that specifically evaluate drug addiction as a chronic and relapsing disease.

Overall, treatment outcomes of drug addiction display success rates similar to those of other chronic diseases. McLellan et al. (2000) undertook a literature review to compare drug dependence with other chronic illnesses, including diabetes, hypertension, and asthma. Each condition is a chronic, medical disease that shares common etiological agents, including genetic influence, personal choice, and environmental factors, which in turn influence the course and outcome of the disease. They found that success rates and incidence of relapse were remarkably similar across all four diseases. For example, one-year follow-up studies showed that 40 to 60 percent of addiction patients remain continuously abstinent. Like diabetics who do not adhere to their diet and medication, drug addicts who do not remain in treatment or who discontinue recommended measures such as self-help groups typically have a poor prognosis. Low socioeconomic status, lack of social support, and comorbid psychiatric conditions were found to be significant contributors among all four diseases in predicting low adherence to treatment and, consequently, poor treatment outcome.

Although treatment utilization and adherence vary among drug users, multiple treatment admissions are very common. A comprehensive study by Anglin, Hser, and Grella (1997) looked at prior treatment episodes among a sample of 10,010 clients enrolled in the Drug Abuse Treatment Outcome Study (DATOS) from 1991 to 1993 in 96 treatment programs across 11 U.S. cities. Approximately half of the patients entered treatment for the first time, while the other half had at least one prior treatment episode; many of these had multiple prior treatments and lengthy periods of time involved in treatment. Clients averaged a history of 2.9 prior drug treatment episodes before enrolling in DATOS, though the number varied by treatment modality; outpatient methadone treatment (OMT) clients had the highest number of previous treatments at 7 1, while outpatient drug-free (ODF) and short-term inpatient (STI) clients had the lowest number of previous treatments, averaging 2.3. Concordantly, the length of clients' "treatment careers," measured by the time between first treatment and current enrollment, varied by modality. The average treatment career was 3.1 years, with OMT clients averaging careers of 7.1 years and ODF and STI clients both averaging careers of 2.1 years. Overall, severe addiction characteristics and engagement in risky behavior were associated with a greater number of previous treatment episodes (Anglin et al. 1997)

Prior treatment influences current treatment adherence and outcome, which impact future treatment utilization and effectiveness (Hser et al. 1997). Research suggests that treatment processes differ among patients with and without previous experience (Hser, Joshi, Anglin, and Fletcher 1999), and although evidence is limited, it is likely that incremental gains are achieved through multiple treatment episodes (Hser et al. 1997). For example, a study of 276 drug abusers seeking treatment referral showed that successful abstinence for at least three months after a previous episode of treatment was among the factors that significantly increased the subject's likelihood of actually reentering treatment. Among a sample of 789 cocaine-abusing DATOS patients, those with prior treatment experience had greater perceived needs in many aspects of their lives besides their drug problems, were less likely to have received one-on-one counseling, and were less likely to have followed program rules and regulations. Accordingly, increasing individual counseling and fostering greater program compliance had a greater impact on those with prior treatment histories, compared with those who had no prior treatment experience (Hser, Joshi et al. 1999). Another study conducted by Hser, Grella and colleagues (1999) among clients in DATOS long-term residential programs found that individuals with prior treatment histories were generally more difficult to treat, but that their likelihood of abstinence was similar to that of individuals with no prior treatment experience, as long as they remained in treatment for a sufficient time period.

In general, strategies that encourage entry into treatment, prolong the time spent in treatment, and facilitate reentry into treatment when warranted are more apt to produce better posttreatment outcomes (Hser et al. 1997).

Final Thoughts

Drug addiction challenges not only those suffering from the disease but also the health care workers, clinicians, and policy makers who aim to ameliorate its effects on individuals and society. Such challenges stem from the myriad of biological, psychological, social, economic, and cultural factors that influence the initiation, progression, and ultimate recovery from addiction in profound ways.

Treatment needs to individually address the multidimensional aspects of drug addiction. Adherence to a prescribed treatment regimen is essential, and individual effort must extend beyond the acute episode of intervention. And even though relapse is a common occurrence, it does not render treatment ineffective. In fact, it may be the way in which we evaluate treatment outcomes that is ineffective. As McLellan et al. (2000) observe, when patients with diabetes, hypertension, and asthma do not maintain their treatment regimen and symptoms reemerge ("fall off the wagon," in addiction slang), it is considered a demonstration of how treatment is a "success" because it held the symptoms at bay. However, when addicted individuals relapse into drug use after not complying with their treatment regimen, it is typically viewed as a "failure" of the

treatment and, by extension, a failure of the individual.

The process of recovery deserves recognition as just that—a process. Future research and clinical practice should continue to highlight the processes that facilitate recovery, rather than fixate on the assignment of an arbitrary treatment outcome. A focus on long-term, holistic development from drug addiction and the lifestyle changes and strategies of patients are important future considerations in the field. The study of the culture of recovery is vital to advancements in the addiction field.

Recent calls for change in how we treat individuals and evaluate outcomes demonstrate that the addiction field is continually evolving in interdisciplinary thought and practice. New additions to the addiction lexicon, including the "career" perspective, for example, have given rise to a more realistic framework in which to understand the complex, multidimensional components of addiction and the processes that underlie sustained recovery. Perhaps a completely new nomenclature will arise to replace the ambiguity and disagreement that carry on over the very words *addiction* and *drug dependence*. In turn, the innovative ideas, research methods, and clinical practice of the future will engender a more complete understanding of the chronic, relapsing nature of the disease and will ultimately give rise to the most effective strategies yet to help individuals overcome addiction once and for all.

References

Alcoholism and Drug Abuse Weekly. (2002). Maine Analysis Demonstrates Far-Reaching Harm From OxyContin. (2002, February 11) *Alcoholism and Drug Abuse Weekly*, 14: 1–3.

American Psychiatric Association. (1994). *Diagnostic and statistical manual of mental disorders* (4th ed.). Washington, DC: Author.

American Society of Addiction Medicine [ASAM]. (1996). *Patient Placement Criteria for the Treatment of Substance Related Disorders*, ed. 2 (ASAM PPC-2). Chevy Chase, MD: Author.

Anglin, M. D., and Hser, Y.-I. (1990). Treatment of Drug Abuse. In: M. Tonry and J.Q. Wilson [Eds.], *Drugs and Crime* (pp. 393–458). Chicago: The University of Chicago Press.

Anglin, M. D., Hser, Y.-I., and Grella, C. E. (1997). Drug Addiction and Treatment Careers Among Clients in the Drug Abuse Treatment Outcome Study (DATOS). *Psychology of Addictive Behavior*, 11 (4): 308–323.

Bailey, R. C., and Hser, Y.-I. (1994). Influences affecting maintenance and cessation of narcotics addiction. *Journal of Drug Issues*, 24 (1/2): 249–273.

Bakalar, J. (2001). The Varieties of Addiction. In: S. Chen and E. Skidelsky [Eds.], *High Time for Reform: Drug Policy for the 21st Century* (pp. 39–50). London: The Social Market Foundation.

Begley, S. (2001). How it all starts in your brain. *Newsweek*, 137 (7): 40–42.

Booth, R. E., Crowley, T. J., and Zhang, Y. (1996). Substance abuse treatment entry, retention and effectiveness: out-of-treatment opiate injection drug users. *Drug and Alcohol Dependence*, 42: 11–20.

Brewer, D. D., Catalano, R. F., Haggerty, K., Gainey, R. R., and Fleming, C. B. (1998). A meta-analysis of predictors of continued drug use during and after treatment for opiate addiction. *Addiction*, 93 (1): 73–92.

Clancy, Mary Anne. (2000, May 13) Down East high: Washington County pill addicts have health officials worried. *Bangor Daily News*. Retrieved January 2003 from Lexis-Nexis on-line subscription.

Comfort, M., and Kaltenbach, K. A. (2000). Predictors of Treatment Outcomes for Substance-Abusing Women: A Retrospective Study. *Substance Abuse*, 21 (1): 33–45.

Curry, S., Marlatt, G. A., Peterson, A. V., and Lutton, J. (1988). Survivial Analysis and Assessment of Relapse Rates. In: D. M. Donovan and G. A. Marlatt [Eds.], *Assessment of Addictive Behaviors* (pp. 454–473). New York: The Guilford Press.

Dekimpe, M. G., Van de Gucht, L. M., Hanssens, D. M., and Powers, K. I. (1998). Long-Run Abstinence After Narcotics Abuse: What Are the Odds? *Management Science*, 44 (11): 1478–1492.

Department of Justice (DOJ). (2002a, July). *Kentucky Drug Threat Assessment*. National Drug Intelligence Center. Product No. 2002-S0382KY-001. Retrieved February 2003. Available: *http://www.usdoj.gov/ndic/pubs/1540/index.htm*.

———. (2002b, April). *Maine Drug Threat Assessment*. National Drug Intelligence Center. Product No. 2002-S0377ME-001. Retrieved February 2003. Available: *http://www.usdoj. gov/ndic/pubs/909/index.htm*.

Dobkin, P. L., De Civita, M., Paraherakis, A., and Gill, K. (2002). The role of functional social support in treatment retention and outcomes among outpatient adult substance abusers. *Addiction*, 97, 347–356.

Donovan, D. M. (1996). Assessment issues and domains in the prediction of relapse. *Addiction*, 91 (Suppl.): S29–S36.

Etheridge, R. M., Craddock, S. G., Hubbard, R. L., and Rounds-Bryant, J. L. (1999). The relationship of counseling and self-help participation to patient outcomes in DATOS. *Drug and Alcohol Dependence*, 57, 99–112.

Fiorentine, R., and Hillhouse, M.P. (1999). Drug Treatment Effectiveness and Client-Counselor Empathy: Exploring the Effects of Gender and Ethnic Congruency. *Journal of Drug Issues*, 29 (1): 59–74.

Friedman, S. R. (2002). Sociopharmacology of drug use: initial thoughts. *International Journal of Drug Policy*, 13, 341–347.

Gardner, D. (2001). Addiction and Free Will. In: S. Chen and E. Skidelsky [Eds.], *High Time for Reform: Drug Policy for the 21st Century* (pp. 29–38). London: The Social Market Foundation.

Ghodse, A. H., Reynolds, M., Baldacchino, A. M., Dunmore, E., Byrne, S., Oyefeso, A., Clancy, C., and Crawford, V. (2002). Treating an opiate-dependent inpatient population: A one-year follow-up study of treatment completers and noncompleters. *Addictive Behaviors*, 27, 765–778.

Goode, E. (1999). *Drugs in American Society*, Fifth Edition. Boston: McGraw-Hill College.

Grant, B. F., and Dawson, D. A. (1999). Alcohol and Drug Use, Abuse, and Dependence: Classification, Prevalence and Comorbidity. In: B. S. McCrady and E. E. Epstein [Eds.], *Addictions: A Comprehensive Guidebook* (pp. 9–29). New York: Oxford University Press.

Greenfield, L., and Fountain, D. (2000). Influence of Time in Treatment and Follow-Up Duration on Methadone Treatment Outcomes. *Journal of Psychopathology and Behavioral Assessment*, 22 (4): 353–364.

Grella, C. E., Hser, Y.-I., Joshi, V., and Anglin, M. D. (1999). Patient histories, retention, and outcome models for younger and older adults in DATOS. *Drug and Alcohol Dependence*, 57, 151–166.

Gruber, K., Chutuape, M. A., and Stitzer, M. L. (2000). Reinforcement-based intensive outpatient treatment for inner city opiate abusers: a short-term evaluation. *Drug and Alcohol Dependence*, 57, 211–223.

Hser, Y.-I., Anglin, M. D., Grella, C., Longshore, D., and Prendergast, M. L. (1997). Drug Treatment Careers: A Conceptual Framework and Existing Research Findings. *Journal of Substance Abuse Treatment*, 14 (6): 543–558.

Hser, Y.-I., Grella, C. E., Hsieh, S., Anglin, M. D., and Brown, B. S. (1999). Prior treatment experience related to process and outcomes in DATOS. *Drug and Alcohol Dependence*, 57, 137–150.

Hser, Y.-I., Joshi, V., Anglin, M. D., and Fletcher, B. (1999). Predicting post-treatment cocaine abstinence: What works for first-time admissions and treatment relapsers? *American Journal of Public Health*, 89 (15): 666–671.

Joe, G. W., Simpson, D. D., Dansereau, D. F., and Rown-Szal, G. A. (2001). Relationships Between Counseling Rapport and Drug Abuse Treatment Outcomes. *Psychiatric Services*, 52 (9): 1223–1229.

Katz, E. C., Gruber, K., Chutuape, M. A., and Stitzer, M. L. (2001). Reinforcement-based outpatient treatment for opiate and cocaine abusers. *Journal of Substance Abuse Treatment*, 20 (1): 93–98.

Kirsh, K. L., Whitcomb, L. A., Donaghy K., and Passik, S. D. (2002). Abuse and addiction issues in medically ill patients with pain: Attempts at clarification of terms and empirical study. *Clinical Journal of Pain*, 18 (Suppl. 4): S52–S60.

Kowal, N. (1999). What is the issue? Pseudoaddiction or undertreatment of pain. *Nursing Economic$*, 17 (6): 348–350.

Landry, M. J. (1994). *Understanding Drugs of Abuse: The Processes of Addiction, Treatment, and Recovery*. Washington, DC: American Psychiatric Press.

Leshner, A. I. (1998). Addiction as a Brain Disease: What the Research Shows. *Brain Work: The Neuroscience Newsletter*, 8 (3): 6–8.

Loonis, E., Apter, M. J., and Sztulman, H. (2000). Addiction as a Function of Action System Properties. *Addictive Behavior*, 25 (3): 477–481.

Maddux, J. F., and Desmond, D. P. (2000). Addiction or dependence? [Editorial]. *Addiction*, 95 (5): 661–665.

Maine Analysis Demonstrates Far-Reaching Harm from OxyContin. (2002, February 11). *Alcoholism and Drug Abuse Weekly*, 14, 1–3.

McLellan, A. T. (2002). Have we evaluated addiction treatment correctly? Implications from a chronic care perspective [Editorial]. *Addiction*, 97, 249–252.

McLellan, A. T., Lewis, D. C., O'Brien, C. P., and Kleber, H. D. (2000). Drug Dependence, a Chronic Medical Illness: Implications for Treatment, Insurance, and Outcome Evaluation. *Journal of the American Medical Association*, (284) 13: 1689–1695.

Meyer, R. E. (1996). The disease called addiction: Emerging evidence in a 200-year debate. *The Lancet*, 347 (8995): 162–167.

Miller, W. R. (1996). What is relapse? Fifty ways to leave the wagon. *Addiction*, 91 (Suppl.): S15–S27.

National Institute on Drug Abuse [NIDA]. (1999). *Principles of Drug Addiction Treatment: A Research-based Guide*. Bethesda, MD: National Institutes of Health Publication No. 99–4180.

NIDA. (2002). NIDA Community Drug Alert Bulletin—Stress & Substance Abuse. Accessed September 2, 2003. Available online: *http://165.112.78.61/StressAlert/StressAlert. html*.

O'Brien, C. P. (1996). Drug Addiction and Drug Abuse. In: J. G. Hardman and L. E. Limbird, Eds-in-Chief; P. B. Molinoff and R. W. Ruddon, Eds.; and A. G. Gilman, Consulting Ed. , *Goodman & Gilman's The Pharmacological Basis of Therapeutics*, Ninth Edition (pp. 557–577). New York: McGraw-Hill, Health Professions Division.

O'Brien, C. P., and McLellan, A. T. (1996). Myths about the treatment of addiction. *The Lancet*, 347 (8996): 237–240.

Petry, N. M. (2003). A comparison of African American and non-Hispanic Caucasian cocaine-abusing outpatients. *Drug and Alcohol Dependence*, 69, 43–49.

Prendergast, M. L., and Hser, Y.-I. (1998). Ethnic differences in longitudinal patterns and consequences of narcotics addiction. *Journal of Drug Issues*, 28 (2): 495–517.

Reisine, T., and Pasternak, G. (1996). Opioid Analgesics and Antagonists. In: J. G. Hardman and L. E. Limbird, Eds-in-Chief; P. B. Molinoff and R. W. Ruddon, Eds.; and A. G. Gilman, Consulting Ed., *Goodman & Gilman's The Pharmacological Basis of Therapeutics*, Ninth Edition (pp. 521–555). New York: McGraw-Hill, Health Professions Division.

Rippere, V. (1978). "Drug addiction" and "drug dependence": A note on word meanings. *British Journal of Addiction*, 73 (4): 353–358.

Savage, S., Covington, E. C., Heit, H. A., Hunt, J., Joranson, D. , and Schnoll, S. H. (2001). *Definitions Related to the Use of Opioids for the Treatment of Pain*. American Academy of Pain Medicine, American Pain Society and American Society of Addiction Medicine. Accessed November 12, 2003. Available: *www.asam.org*.

Schuckit, M. A. (1999). New findings on the genetics of alcoholism. *Journal of the American Medical Association*, 281 (20): 1875–1876.

——. (2000). Genetics of the risk of alcoholism. *American Journal of Addictions*, 9 (2): 103–112.

Senay, E. C. (1998). *Substance Abuse Disorders in Clinical Practice*. New York: W. W. Norton & Company.

Senay, E. C., Adams, E. H., Geller, A., Inciardi, J. A., Muñoz, A. , Schnoll, S. H., Woody, G. E., and Cicero, T. J. (2003). Physical dependence on Ultram (tramadol hydrochloride): both opioid-like and atypical withdrawal symptoms occur. *Drug and Alcohol Dependence*, 69, 233–241.

Siegal, H. A., Li, L., and Rapp, R. C. (2002). Abstinence trajectories among treated crack cocaine users. *Addictive Behaviors*, 27 (3): 437–449.

Simpson, D. D., Joe, G. W., Fletcher, B. W., Hubbard, R. L., and Anglin, M. D. (1999). A National Evaluation of Treatment Outcomes for Cocaine Dependence. *Archives of General Psychiatry*, 56 (6): 507–514.

Sinha, R. (2001). How does stress increase risk of drug abuse and relapse? *Psychopharmacology*, 158, 343–359.

Tims, F. M., Leukefeld, C. G., and Platt, J. J. (2001). Relapse and Recovery. In: F. M. Tims, C. G. Leukefeld, and J. J. Platt [Eds.], *Relapse + Recovery in Addictions* (pp. 3–17). New Haven: Yale University Press.

Washton, A. M. (1989). *Cocaine Addiction: Treatment, Recovery, and Relapse Prevention*. New York: W. W. Norton & Company.

White, W. L. (1998). *Slaying the Dragon: The History of Addiction Treatment and Recovery in America*. Bloomington, IL: Chestnut Health Systems.

——. (2000a). Addiction as a Disease: Birth of a Concept. *Counselor*, 1 (1): 46–51, 73.

——. (2000b). The Rebirth of the Disease Concept of Alcoholism in the 20th Century. *Counselor*, 1 (2): 62–66.

White, W. L., Boyle, M., and Loveland, D. (2002). Alcoholism/Addiction as a Chronic Disease: From Rhetoric to Clinical Reality. *Alcoholism Treatment Quarterly*, 20 (3/4): 107–130.

World Health Organization [WHO]. (1992). *International classification of diseases and related health problems* (10th Rev.). Geneva: Author.

Zhang, Z., Friedmann, P. D., and Gerstein, D. R. (2003). Does retention matter? Treatment duration and improvement in drug use. *Addiction*, 98, 673–684.

For Discussion

1. Should drug addiction be treated, evaluated, and insured just like diabetes, hypertension, and asthma? If addiction is a chronic, medical disease that shares similar etiologic agents with other chronic diseases like diabetes, why is there such a stigma attached to addiction and not to the others?

2. Is applying the term *career* to concepts of drug addiction, treatment, and recovery a useful approach to understanding the nature of the disease? In what ways is an addiction career similar to and dissimilar from other "careers"?

3. Which term is more appropriate to describe the biopsychosocial disease we have evaluated, *addiction* or *dependence*? What are some possible arguments for and against each one? What are some alternative terms to addiction and dependence that would better characterize the disease?

3

The Use of Marijuana for Pleasure

A Replication of Howard S. Becker's Study of Marijuana Use

Michael L. Hirsch
Randall W. Conforti
Carolyn J. Graney

Howard S. Becker was perhaps the first of many researchers to examine the sociological aspects of marijuana use. His major efforts in this regard appear in his classic work *Outsiders: Studies in the Sociology of Deviance* (Free Press, 1963). Based on interviews with 50 marijuana users, Becker proposed that gleaning pleasure from marijuana smoking occurs through a learning process. Further, he noted that marijuana users progress through a series of stages. Beginners learn to master techniques (e.g., inhalation, appropriate dosage) from experienced users. Occasional users smoke marijuana intermittently, that is, when the opportunity arises. More frequent use characterizes regular users who must arrange for a steady supply of marijuana for self-use.

In the following essay, Michael L. Hirsch, Randall W. Conforti, and Carolyn J. Graney report on an attempt to replicate Becker's original study. Their research was based on interviews with 50 marijuana users, half of whom were college undergraduates. Although they found some support for Becker's model, they also noted some discrepancies.

It seems an historic truism that the presence of drugs or drug use within a given cul-

ture engenders controversy or public debate about the relationship of drugs to the larger social order (Braudel 1981). American culture is no exception. Within recent historical memory, our culture has both criminalized and decriminalized the production and use of alcoholic beverages. We currently are involved in a debate about drug use that ranges from those who would declare a war on the traffickers and users of materials deemed illicit, to the suggestion that drug use generally should be decriminalized (Ridding 1989; Keer 1988).

Historically, sociologists (and other social scientists) have contributed to the debate surrounding drug use. This is done not by choosing sides, but rather by providing interested parties with explorations of the relationship between social context and drug use (Conforti, Hirsch, and Graney 1989; Yamaguchi and Kandel 1985; Seeman and Anderson 1983; Radosevich et al. 1979; Alexander 1963). This includes understandings of how drug use is related to cultural belief systems (Room 1976; Mulford and Miller 1959), typologies of drug users (Bloomquist 1971), and conceptualizations of drug addiction (McAuliffe and Gorden 1974; Ray 1964).

In the field of sociology, the work of Howard S. Becker stands out as both the touchstone of sociologically inspired drug research (Becker 1953) and the work responsible for the development of what has come to be known as labelling theory in the study of deviance (Becker 1963, 1964). In part, Becker's work has remained relevant because of the enduring nature of the drug debate itself. Questions of individual predispositions to drug use/criminal behavior, challenged by Becker as early as 1953, have re-emerged as behavioral explanations today (e.g., Walters and White 1989). In addition, Becker's thesis that an understanding of marijuana use could be obtained by approaching the drug as an object from which individuals learn to derive pleasure is itself worthy of re-examination. The utility of such a conception is likely to extend beyond the use of marijuana to drugs such as cocaine and crack.

It is because of the explanatory power of Becker's initial approach and the needs of policy makers/drug counselors today that a re-examination of Becker's work is warranted. In doing such a re-examination, the authors have chosen as their vehicle a replication of Becker's original work. Though the value of replicative work has generally been noted (e.g., Denzin 1989; Schwartz and Jacobs 1979), attempts at replication are particularly important (and rarely attempted) when dealing with contextual models (given the fluidity of contextual reality). In what follows, recent efforts to corroborate Becker's work will be discussed. General points of confirmation will be noted, as well as extensions of his original work, reasons for these extensions, and suggestions for further research.

Method

In Becker's original research (1953), the snowball-sampling method was utilized as the means of obtaining 50 marijuana users willing to be interviewed. Snowball sampling, noted for its strength in penetrating relatively closed populations and its utility in network analysis but not for yielding representative samples (True 1989), yielded a mixed demographic sample in Becker's work. (His sample was somewhat heavily weighted toward musicians who made up approximately ½ of the subjects. In a recent phone interview Becker reported not having kept any more detailed information about his sample than what is reported above.) Site selection, determined by Becker's Chicago residency, was not stated as a methodological issue in the original research.

Becker's interviews were conducted informally, with no set questionnaire format being utilized. Interviewees were asked general questions by Becker regarding their initiation to and use of the drug. They were not directed toward any specifics by Becker, as he took notes of their commentary (Becker's recollection in a recent phone interview). It is from such an informal conversational style that Becker gathered his data, and it is upon this data that Becker bases his stage theory/typology of users.

Like Becker's, our research is based upon data gathered from 50 marijuana users. Also, like Becker's, our respondents were obtained through the use of the snowball-sample method. However, whereas Becker's respondents were all derived within one municipal area (Chicago), our respondents are split between two municipal areas, Milwaukee and the Fox River Valley in Wisconsin (the respective homes of the authors).

Demographically, more information is available regarding our respondents than for Becker's. In comparison to Becker's sample, in which musicians account for 50 percent of the sample, 50 percent of our sample is made up of undergraduate students from both metropolitan areas. The remaining 25 respondents come from a wide range of social positions which include house painters, mechanics, nurses, lawyers, teachers, and middle managers. Respondents in our sample ranged in age from 18 to 44 and included 32 men and 18 women. All of our respondents were of European descent. The greatest methodological difference between Becker's work and our own is in the interview process itself. Whereas Becker's interview process was informal in nature, we took a number of set questions into the interview. Our questions, drawn from the discussions reported by Becker, were designed to yield data similar to that which he obtained (Becker 1953, 1963). Thus, whereas Becker abstracts a "becoming-a-user pattern" from his informal interviews, we specifically questioned respondents about their earliest contacts with the drug and asked them to reconstruct chronologically their relationship to the drug. Such reconstruction was to include both behavioral and attitudinal aspects, and when such information was not forthcoming in a given interview, respondents were specifically asked to fill in omissions, if possible.

Within the format of this more formal interview procedure, several questions were included with the hope of extending Becker's original work. One advantage of replicative research in this instance was the possibility of asking questions designed to extend the research in the direction where deficiencies in the original work were suspected. In this case we questioned Becker's "becoming-a-user" pattern for what we perceived as its neglect of the period of time which preceded the point of an individual's stated willingness to try the drug. Other questions were asked about projections toward future use on the part of reporting individuals, fears they associated with the use of the drug, opinions on legalization, etc. This was information absent from Becker's original work, yet deemed of interest by our research team.

Results

Becker's Path to Pleasurable Usage and Stages of Marijuana Use

Becker's original work (1953) surrounds his belief that the use of marijuana could be constructively approached, if the drug itself was conceived of as an object from which pleasure could be derived. Unless an individual develops "a conception of the drug as an object which could be used for pleasure . . . marijuana use was considered meaningless and did not continue" (Becker 1953). Beginning his life histories of marijuana use with individuals at a "point of willingness to use the drug," Becker outlines a three-stage process through which individuals obtain a conception of the drug as an object from which pleasure may be derived. This process includes: 1) learning a technique which supplies "sufficient dosage for the effects of the drug to appear"; 2) both experiencing and recognizing the effects of the drug; and 3) learning to enjoy the effects (Becker 1953). In addition, Becker notes that, at each juncture on the way toward pleasurable use of the drug, the initiate is aided by and dependent upon the guidance of others.

In subsequent discussions of the same data, Becker (1963) utilizes the concept "career" as a way to understand behavioral patterns related to marijuana use. For Becker, a behavioral career is a ". . . sequence of movements (on the part of the individual) from one position to another" within the social milieu (Becker 1963). Here, focusing on the individual, Becker constructs a three-stage model to describe the changes an individual goes through on the path to becoming a bona fide user of the drug (Figure 3.1). His stages include: 1) the beginner, a person involved in initial encounters with the drug (the stage within which the above three steps are subsumed); 2) the occasional user, one whose drug use is sporadic or determined by chance; and 3) the regular user, one whose

systematic (daily) use has led him or her to procure personal supplies of the drug [it is important to note that Becker views stages 1 and 2 as transitional, stage 3 seemingly the only stable use pattern] (Becker 1963).

Figure 3.1

Our Construction

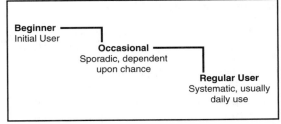

Verification of Becker's Path and Stages of Marijuana Use

Whereas Becker begins his life histories "with the person having arrived at the point of willingness to try marijuana" (Becker 1953), we have included in our life histories the orientations individuals had to the drug before an opportunity to use the drug arose in their life. Our logic for doing so is as follows: as it seems unlikely that those who "arrived at the point of willingness to try marijuana" have reached that point by the same path, it should be of interest to those studying drug-use patterns how different people "arrive" at this same point of willingness.

Preconceptions of the Drug

One half of our respondents held what may be considered negative preconceptions about the drug, the remaining one half being split between those with neutral preconceptions (37 percent) and positive preconceptions (13 percent). Among those holding negative positions were those who recounted anti-drug instruction, knowledge of family members who had varying drug problems, and those who associated the use of marijuana with the socially undesirable. Among those holding neutral positions were those who had no real knowledge of the drug (positive or negative reports), those who held some intellectual curiosity regarding its use, and those who saw it as relatively harmless, equating its use with the use of tobacco and/or alcohol. Among those holding positive views of the drug were those who thought it was "cool" to smoke the drug, had hearsay evidence regarding its "enjoyable" effects, and had early in their lives seen people enjoying themselves with the drug.

Becoming Willing to Use the Drug

How individuals come to be willing to use the drug of course varies with their original preconceptions. For those who were positively oriented to the drug, a willingness to experiment already existed; they lacked only the opportunity. For those with neutral orientations to the drug, "willingness to use the drug" per se often didn't develop. Instead, opportunities to try the drug arose (most often in situations where peers or siblings were using it) and respondents found themselves trying the drug without any forethought regarding its use. Those with negative preconceptions went through the greatest changes on their way toward a willingness to try the drug. Among this group, two avenues were associated with the change in their orientations to the drug. For some, willingness first appeared after encounters with others who commanded their respect and who either used the drug in front of them or discussed its use with them. For others, a willingness to use the drug arose as part of a more general movement away from an unquestioned willingness to uphold the status quo.

First Encounters

All of the respondents in our study reported first-use encounters as having involved other individuals closely associated with and important to their day-to-day life activities. Of those cited as involved in initiations were close friends, boyfriends or girlfriends, family members (siblings and cousins [one person reported smoking with her mother sometime after her initial use]), classmates, and roommates. Initiation gatherings ranged from experimentation with only one other present, to contexts of larger social groupings, here parties being most often cited. It is important to note that none of our respondents spoke of initially using the drug while alone or alone with a stranger or group of strangers.

The Path to the Pleasurable Usage of Marijuana

Our respondents generally corroborate Becker's description of the elements making up the path toward the pleasurable usage of marijuana (as well as the importance others play in learning the proper use of the drug, recognition of its effects, and their enjoyment of the effects). Our research suggests that Becker's three-step presentation is simplistic. There is much to be learned by more closely examining the variance that exists between individual paths to pleasurable usage.

Experiences on the way toward pleasurable use of the drug vary a great deal. There are those who get high, perceive that they are high, and enjoy the high the first time they smoke; and those that smoke 30–40 times over the course of a 2–3-year period before they get high for the first time. Although Becker (1953) states that "[T]he novice does not ordinarily get high the first time he smokes marijuana . . ." we found that 34 percent of our respondents reported getting high the first time they used the drug. The majority of these reported favorable encounters (although two reported the ill effects of nausea and vomiting; there were a few neutral reactions reported as well). An additional 32 percent reported getting high after the first 2–3 attempts, 30 percent after several attempts and the remaining 6 percent after 30–40 uses.

Our respondents' reasons for continued experimentation with the drug after the initial encounter varied in relation to the results of the first experience and the original reasons for their use of the drug. Others did not get high the first time and defined the feeling of "being high" [as] enjoyable. An attempt to re-create that state was motivation enough to try the drug again, for those who did not get high the first time, as well as those who got high but had neutral or negative reactions. When their original willingness to try the drug was associated with a positive motivation toward its use (including those whose original preconception had been negative), this motivation continued even after the failure of the first attempt. Most had anticipated the possibility of "not getting high" their first attempt. Among this group, second and third attempts at using the drug tended to be more deliberately planned and executed than were their initial attempts. One respondent continued his experimentation by stealing small amounts of the drug from his parents' supply.

Such planned attempts by the above group were in sharp contrast to those who had neutral orientations to the drug at the time of its first use. For this group, later attempts at "getting high" proved to be much more passive and haphazard. Whereas the above mentioned group had been more likely to seek out the drug after their initial use, further experimentation by this latter group was often as unexpected as was their initial use. However, regardless of original motivations and results of initial use, once an individual's own experience with the drug proved to be favorable, continued use was predicated on the desire to re-experience pleasurable sensations.

Career Patterns of Use

In our attempt to corroborate this part of Becker's work, our respondents were asked to reconstruct chronologically their relationship to the drug, beginning with their preconceptions and moving to present use. In comparing Becker's model to our information, we find that his model is somewhat descriptive of the behavioral transitions experienced by individuals experimenting with the drug's use. As it now stands, however, his model is both sequentially incomplete and conceptually limited. Conceptual limitations become evident, as we attempt to place our respondents into his classification system.

The first sequential limitation is the most obvious; we have already discussed its absence. This is Becker's exclusion of a stage, wherein individuals develop a willingness to experiment with the drug. Given its importance to an understanding of drug use, the

addition of an orientation stage to Becker's model seems to be reasonable.

Other sequential limitations, blurred with the model's conceptual limitations, become evident when we look beyond the beginner stage and attempt to place respondents into the occasional and regular use categories. Becker's criteria for placement . . . occasional use being chance usage and regular use being systematic usage with self-procuring behaviors . . . makes it difficult to place those whose occasional use is at times systematic (e.g., attending parties hoping the drug will be available), and those whose regular use is at times augmented by chance occurrence (e.g., a weekend user who happens to smoke during the week, if confronted with an unexpected opportunity). We must also ask if it is meaningful to extend the regular use category from those who systematically procure and use the drug 2–4 times per month or year to those whose systematic procurement translates into a daily use frequency of 4–9 times. Would it be at all meaningful to create an abuse/addiction category to deal with those whose use may be self-defined as problematic? If so, how would we place such a category into the current model? Also, though Becker's work suggests that both the beginner and the occasional use categories are transitional stages, the majority of our respondents seem to have maintained a use pattern which falls in between his occasional and regular use categories. How do we account for such non-transition within his framework?

It is at this point in our attempt to replicate Becker's work that we are faced with our greatest challenge. If we stay with Becker's model, we find that we are unable to categorize individuals who consider themselves to be drug abusers, who have quit using the drug, who have never used the drug and are orienting toward its use (or not orienting toward its use, for that matter), or whose patterns fall between his occasional and regular use categories. If we respond to these limitations by constructing a typology of present career use patterns, an approach that would allow for the classification of all respondents, we risk losing the temporal progression of the original model.

Discussion

A comparison of our work with Becker's reveals a general corroboration of his thesis, i.e., the utility of understanding marijuana as an object from which individuals learn to derive pleasure, as well as points of contention regarding the process through which individuals learn to derive enjoyment from the drug, and regarding his typology/stage theory of drug use patterns. We will begin our discussion with points of contention, move to points of confirmation, and conclude with suggestions regarding the direction of future research.

Points of Contention

As noted above, in his analysis of the data, Becker derives a three-step process through which individuals learn to derive pleasure from the use of marijuana. Our research leads us to question the reliability of Becker's description of this process for, as we note above, a large percentage of our respondents reported both getting high and enjoying the high at the time of their first use. As we look to explain the discrepancy between the two studies, several factors come to our attention, all of which relate to the time lapse between the original work and our replicative efforts.

First, we must recognize the existence of both the availability of technologies specifically designed to increase the drug dosage an individual is able to take in a single encounter and the availability of more powerful strains of the plant marijuana. Both the technologies for the smoking of the drug and the nature of the drug being smoked have increased the likelihood that an individual's first encounter will result in the presence of the drug's effects.

In addition to the above changes, cultural attitudes have changed to the extent that first encounters themselves may have taken place in settings that were less clandestine or anxiety-provoking than was true of the time Becker did his research. It is likely that all of these factors taken together have changed first encounters to such an extent that we may no longer rely on Becker's model to understand the reality of initial encounters.

Our next departure from Becker's work is more critical and relates to the utility of his typology/stage theory of use patterns. As noted above, Becker's typology (Figure 3.1) suggests that those who come to enjoy the effects of the drug progress in their use of the drug to the point of regular use. The suggestion that all marijuana smokers are or will become regular (daily) users of the drug is not corroborated by the information provided by our informants, many of whom have used the drug for years but do not fit into his regular use category. It is possible that marijuana users in Becker's time all progressed to regular use of the drug, but we find this to be unlikely. Instead, we believe it is time to abandon Becker's model altogether and consider a more recent alternative offered by Van Dijk (1972).

Van Dijk's model (Figure 3.2) begins with initial contact with the drug and moves through three possible stages, experimentalism, integrated use, and excessive use, toward the possibility of addiction. The advantages of such a model over Becker's relates both to the inclusion of the stated possibility of an addictive use category (the initial three categories here being equated to Becker's three stages in order) but also the possibility of stabilized intermediate use patterns. In addition, Van Dijk's model explicitly allows for the return to earlier patterns of drug use, as well as the discontinuing of drug use at any stage.

Though such a model of use is superior to Becker's in terms of its explanatory power, both models neglect that stage prior to first contact with the drug which has been pointed to in our research of users' preconceptions. If we were to amend Van Dijk's model to include such a stage (Figure 3.3), we would have a model which not only allows us to place all of our respondents within stated categories, but would also allow us to visualize how preconceptions influence the continuation of experimentation after initial contact with the drug.

Points of Convergence

The major point of convergence between Becker's work and our own lies in our belief in the utility of approaching marijuana as an object from which individuals must learn to

Figure 3.2

Van Dijk's Model

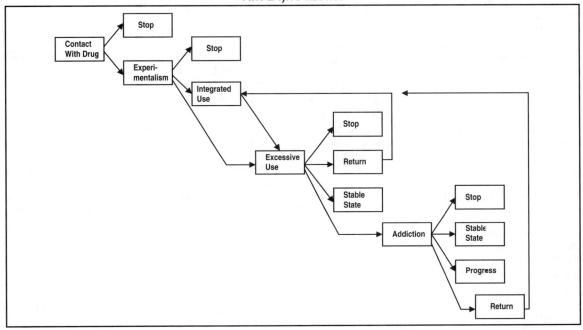

Figure 3.3

Revised Model

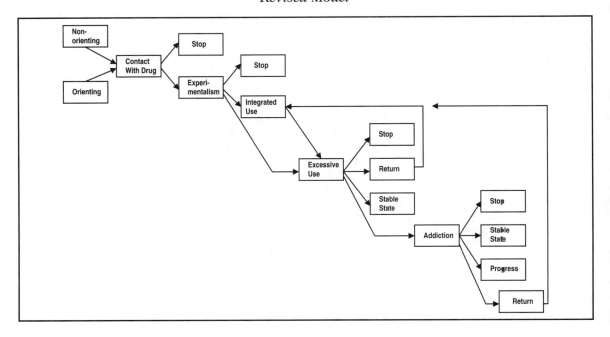

derive pleasure, before drug use behavior will be evidenced. It is in the reconstruction of our respondents' relationships to the drug that we are able to gain an understanding of the motivations which led to both initial experimentation with the drug and subsequent or continued use. The explanatory power of such an approach derives from the focus upon the interactive environment, within which individuals learn to use and enjoy the drug. Such a focus argues against, then and now, theoretical positions which seek to explain drug use by positing predispositions toward drug use/criminal behavior in the individuals themselves.

Directions of Future Research

Though our review of Becker's work is not without criticisms, we believe his work has raised questions that need to be answered. First, his structural/interactive approach to understanding marijuana use does point to the normative components of the learning situation which influence drug use. What Becker does not address (nor do we in this work) is the way in which other individuals, in similar situations to those who become marijuana users, do not become users themselves. If the structural/interactive model is to gain in the power of explanation, we must be willing to explore the life worlds of both the user as well as the non-user, in an attempt to understand the movement of some toward drug use and the continued non-use on the part of others.

Second, we believe that there is great utility in the manner of research Becker began and we have continued. We believe much could be learned, if we expanded our study of drug use by undertaking similar research of other drugs, both legal (e.g., alcohol and tobacco) and illegal (e.g., crack, cocaine, LSD, etc.). Though we may assume similar "becoming-user" patterns will hold for all drugs, differences may exist between them as well. In any event, much may be gained by just such a comparison.

Finally, we believe much could be gained by cross-cultural studies of drug use as well. In particular, it would be of interest to study the differences in drug use experience between cultures which hold the same drug to be licit and illicit. Such comparisons may yield information regarding the role cultural norms play in the regulation of drug use and, perhaps, the control of drug effects.

Conclusion

There is no doubt that Becker's work will continue to serve as a benchmark for those generally interested in drug use. Our attempt to replicate his work was motivated both by a desire to venerate an old master and [by] a desire to continue to improve our stock of knowledge regarding drug use. In the comparative dialogue created by our replicative attempt, we have noted cultural changes that contributed to the variance between our respective results, attempted to correct what we believe to have been inadequacies in the original work, and also raised questions which go beyond the scope of this research.

References

Alexander, C. N., Jr. (1963). Consensus of mutual attraction in natural cliques: A study of adolescent drinkers. *American Journal of Sociology* 69, 395–403.

Becker, H. S. (1953). Becoming a marijuana user. *American Journal of Sociology* 59, 235–242.

——. (1963). *Outsiders: Studies in the sociology of deviance.* New York: The Free Press.

——. (1964). *The other side.* London: The Free Press.

Bloomquist, E. R. (1971). *Marijuana: The second trip.* Beverly Hills: Glencoe Press.

Braudel, F. (1981). *The structures of everyday life* (Vol. 1). New York: Harper and Row.

Conforti, R. W., Hirsch, M. L., and Graney, C. (1989). *The use of marijuana for pleasure.* Conference paper, Spring 1990 Midwest Sociology Convention.

Denzin, N. K. (1989). *The research act.* Englewood Cliffs: Prentice-Hall.

Keer, P. (1988). The unspeakable is debated: Should drugs be legalized? *The New York Times.*

McAuliffe, W. E., and Gorden, R. (1974). A test of Lindesmith's theory of addiction: The frequency of euphoria among long-term addicts. *American Journal of Sociology* 79, 795–801.

Mulford, H., and Miller, D. (1959). Drinking behavior related to definitions of alcohol: A report of research in progress. *American Sociological Review* 24, 385–389.

Radosevich, M., Lanza-Kaduce, L., Akers, R. L., Krohn, M. D., et al. (1979). The sociology of adolescent drug and drinking behavior: A review of the state of the field. *Deviant Behavior* 1, 15–35.

Ray, M. B. (1964). The cycle of abstinence and relapse among heroin addicts. In H. S. Becker (ed.), *The other side* (pp. 163–178). London: The Free Press.

Ridding, A. (1989). Western panel is asking end to all curbs on drug traffic. *The New York Times.*

Room, R. (1976). Ambivalence as a sociological explanation: The case of cultural explanations of alcohol problems. *American Sociological Review* 41, 1047–1062.

Schwartz, H., and Jacobs, J. (1979). *Qualitative sociology: A method to the madness.* New York: The Free Press.

Seeman, M., and Anderson, C. S. (1983). Alienation and alcohol: The role of work, mastery, and community in drinking behavior. *American Sociological Review* 48, 60–77.

True, J. A. (1989). *Finding out: Conducting and evaluating social research.* Belmont: Wadsworth.

Van Dijk, W. K. (1972). *Complexity of the dependence problem: Interaction of biological with psychogenic and sociogenic factors. Biochemical and pharmacological aspects of drug use.* Haarlem: DeErven F. Bohn.

Walters, G. D., and White, T. (1989). The thinking criminal: A cognitive model of lifestyle criminality. *Criminal Justice Research Bulletin* 4, 1–10.

Yamaguchi, K., and Kandel, D. B. (1985). On the resolution of role incompatibility: A life event history analysis of family roles and marijuana use. *American Journal of Sociology* 90, 1284–1293.

For Discussion

Hirsch and his colleagues expand upon Becker's theory of marijuana use. To what extent can their theory apply to other drug use?

Reprinted from: Michael L. Hirsch, Randall W. Conforti, and Carolyn J. Graney, "The Use of Marijuana for Pleasure: A Replication of Howard S. Becker's Study of Marijuana Use." In *Handbook of Replication Research.* Copyright © 1990 by Select Press. Reprinted by permission. ✦

4

Dope Fiends and Degenerates

The Gendering of Addiction in the Early Twentieth Century

Mara L. Keire

In the late nineteenth century, the majority of "addicts" in the United States were women from middle-class backgrounds who used drugs for medicinal purposes. This profile changed significantly in the twentieth century, when most "addicts" were men from lower- or working-class backgrounds. In the next article, Mara Keire discusses these major demographic changes. She introduces the concept of the "femininity of addiction" and argues that our perception of addicts and addiction continued into the twentieth century, despite the demographic changes in the profile of drug users. She also argues that these cultural perceptions served as powerful influences in the area of drug policy.

As historian David Courtwright describes in *Dark Paradise: Opiate Addiction in America Before 1940*, the typical addict of the late nineteenth century was an older middle-class woman who first started taking drugs for medical reasons, while the typical twentieth-century addict was a young man of the urban lower classes who had originally experimented with drugs for pleasure.[1] This demographic shift was dramatic, and Courtwright convincingly argues that the contrast between the ailing matron and the hustling junkie was significant in shaping our national narcotics policy.[2] But in the face of these undeniable demographic differences, important cultural continuities remained. These cultural continuities bridged the demographic shift and connected the medical addicts of the 1880s and 1890s to the dope fiends of the 1910s and 1920s.

The most important cultural continuity was the perceived femininity of addiction. Starting in the 1870s, doctors injected women with morphine to numb the pain of "female troubles," or to turn the willful hysteric into a manageable invalid. Up through the turn of the century, morphine was a literal prescription for bourgeois femininity.[3] Thus, by the 1890s, when the first drug epidemic peaked, approximately two-thirds of the medical addicts were women, making women medical addicts almost half of all addicts in the United States. As a result of this thirty-year association of women with addiction, both users and observers saw drug addiction as something feminine as late as the 1930s, long after men had become the majority of users.[4]

To show how the femininity of addiction connected the older medical addicts to the nascent urban drug culture of the early twentieth century, this article will focus on drug use among the sporting class in the urban red-light district. I have two reasons for analyzing drugs in the vice district. First, the urban tenderloin was the location of cities' disreputable leisure, and as such it was the site of the new addiction.[5] Second, the new addicts either came from the sporting class, which was comprised of prostitutes, pimps, thieves, gamblers, gangsters, entertainers, fairies, and johns; or, they were youths who admired the sporting men and women. In their efforts to join the ranks of the sporting class, the new addicts emulated the sporting class's manners and mores—including their drug use.[6] By focusing on drug use by prostitutes, pimps, and the gay men known as fairies, I will demonstrate how the continued cultural association of addiction with femininity shaped the perception of addiction throughout society, and influenced the decision of men to incorporate drug use into their rejection of conventional male gender roles.[7]

This article is divided into four parts, including a theoretical intermission. The first section is a brief description of drugs in the vice district. In the second section, I focus on opiate use by pimps and prostitutes, paying particular attention to reformers' interpretations of the meaning of underworld addiction. After the section on pimps and prostitutes, I halt the historical narrative in order to discuss subcultures and subcultural style. When I re-engage the narrative, I conclude by analyzing cocaine use among fairies as exemplary of how the nineteenth-century feminization of drugs shaped twentieth-century male drug use.

Drugs in the District

Although never as prevalent as drinking, drug taking was an integral part of life in the urban vice districts. At the turn of the century, the members of the sporting class who took drugs mostly smoked opium. They bought their opium at Chinese restaurants, laundries, and opium dens, but the drug was also readily available in brothels.[8] Indeed, a 1905 study on prostitution found it just as noteworthy when opium was absent as when it was present.[9] By the early teens, both the urban vice districts, and drug use within them, had become more diverse. No longer just saloons, parlor houses, and cribs, the vice districts included dance halls, poolrooms, cabarets, gambling dens, movie theaters, and cigar shops. Concurrent with this diversification of services, there was a diversification in drug use. Anti-vice investigators were as likely to hear about people using morphine, heroin, and cocaine as smoking opium. While brothels and Chinese establishments continued as mainstays to the drug trade, saloons, dance halls, and disreputable pharmacies became increasingly important sites of supply.[10] These circumstances changed dramatically during World War I, when the war fervor enabled reformers to close the red-light districts and Federal officials to strengthen the enforcement of narcotics laws.[11]

As drug use diversified between 1910 and 1920, different cliques within the sporting world distinguished themselves through the types of drugs they used. As the price of opium rose, opium smoking, once so ubiquitous, became associated with the upper echelons of the sporting world—actors and actresses, high-rolling gamblers, and wealthy slummers.[12] Prostitutes and their pimps continued to consume opiates, although it became more likely that they were taking cheaper drugs like morphine than that they were smoking opium.[13] Meanwhile, reformers observed with growing alarm the gangs of boys who were adding cocaine and heroin use to their delinquent activities.[14] It was in the face of these continuities—opium smoking by prostitutes, gamblers and entertainers—and changes—heroin and cocaine use within the growing youth culture—that members of the sporting class and outside observers interpreted the new patterns of drug use. They did so by drawing on, but altering, an older cultural reference: the femininity of drug use.

Prostitutes and Pimps

With prostitutes, the association of addiction with women was literal and direct. Prostitutes were women and prostitutes took drugs.[15] In his 1880 study of Chicago opiate addicts, Charles W. Earle observed that nearly three quarters of the addicts were women, and that fully a third of these women were prostitutes.[16] Thus the cultural continuity in the early twentieth century was twofold. Prostitutes had taken drugs in the earlier period and women had taken drugs for medical reasons. Like nineteenth-century matrons, prostitutes took drugs to treat a whole range of problems euphemistically called "female troubles." These ailments included dysmenorrhea, injuries from childbearing, ovarian cysts, uterine cancer, and venereal diseases.[17] The Chicago Vice Commissioners believed that a high percentage of prostitutes became addicts, either as a result of self-medication or a doctor's prescription, because their work increased their vulnerability to venereal diseases.[18]

In addition to the medical explanation, there was a moral explanation for prostitutes' addiction that also drew on "common sense" assumptions about women's nature. Like most of their contemporaries, anti-vice reformers believed that women were inherently modest and sexually unaggressive.[19] For women to act so contrary to their natures—to submit to sex with countless strangers—something must have undermined their essential purity. Anti-vice reformers found the cause in drugs, alcohol, and the imperatives of addiction—but not always the culprits. Many reformers asserted that prostitutes had no choice in either their addiction or their work: "white slavers" used intoxicants to trick young women into prostitution, and then they forced their prostitutes to continue drinking or taking drugs so that they would not resist their sexual servitude. Anti-vice reformers interpreted prostitutes' dependence on drugs and alcohol as proof that prostitutes found their work distasteful. They believed that prostitutes' addiction was a sign of the extremes to which the agents of vice had to go to overcome women's innate morality.[20]

While the medical and moral explanations had a logical coherence, prostitutes' behavior challenged reformers' image of them as passive victims. The occasional report of a prostitute helpless within a brothel, stupefied by "a deadly drug," and covered with abscesses, reinforced reformers' conception of the world.[21] More often than not, however, the stories from the street called into question the morality tales that reformers sought to tell. For example, in a 1908 report to the United States delegation of the International Opium Convention, a "newspaper detective" described the daily routine of a Baltimore streetwalker. She solicited until two or three in the morning, at which time she took her earnings, bought the night's supply of opium, returned home to her pimp, and together they smoked for the next few hours. She then slept until six or seven in the evening, took a shot of morphine, and went back out on the street to earn more money so that she and her pimp could have more opium.[22] This story was shocking in part because of its role inversion—it was the woman who was leaving the house, earning the money, and providing for the man. Yet, despite the role inversion, this story had a domestic inevitability that the detective did not find as horrifying as what a different investigator witnessed six years later in New York City. In a saloon at the corner of Fourth Avenue and Thirteenth Street, an investigator watched two women crush tablets of heroin and snort them with no self-consciousness about the other patrons. That these women took drugs in a public place, not a private room, was part of what the investigator found so repugnant.[23] The difference between the private opium smoking in 1908 and the public heroin consumption in 1914 challenged reformers' explanations of prostitutes' addiction. The more active and public role that prostitutes displayed in acquiring and taking their drugs in the 1910s called the prostitutes' assumed powerlessness into question.

Evidence that prostitutes introduced young men to drugs was even more damaging to their image as passive victims than the agency they exhibited in acquiring their drugs. One of the most scandalous discoveries made by the Chicago Vice Commissioners was that messenger boys working in the Levee, Chicago's red-light district, were learning drug use from prostitutes.[24] The messenger boys' stories probably resembled the one that an addict told sociologist Bingham Dai in the early 1930s. In his youth, the man had worked as a messenger boy in Butte, Montana's restricted district. There he attracted the attention of several prostitutes who were looking for pimps. At first he was bashful, but eventually the messenger boy raised his courage to talk to one of them. After confirming with a fellow messenger that the prostitute was a good money-maker, he agreed to be her pimp, and started living with her. In the course of their relationship, she slept with him, gave him money, and taught him to smoke opium.[25] It was stories like these that led researchers to sum up the causes of the new addicts' habits with phrases like "bad associates" and "tenderloin life."[26]

While the investigative reports gradually undermined the progressive-era portrayal of prostitutes, urban reformers generally remained sympathetic to prostitutes, even addicted prostitutes, but reviled their pimps. Reports of the pimps' addiction only increased this antipathy. With pimps and prostitutes alike, their drug use was a sign of how far they had fallen, but for prostitutes it reinforced a victimization that was consistent with gender roles in mainstream society. Women were supposed to be helpless, ailing, and even addicted—after all, it is likely that some reformers had older female relatives who were themselves addicts.[27] The pimps' addiction, however, was an affront to American masculinity, for as Surgeon General H. S. Cumming asserted in 1925, "opium makes a man effeminate."[28]

If the dominant nineteenth-century image of a female addict was the ailing middle-class matron, the stereotyped male addict of that period was the pig-tailed Chinese coolie or perhaps an aesthete inspired by Thomas De Quincey or Samuel Taylor Coleridge. Either image implied an orientalized decadence at odds with middle-class masculinity.[29] In the early twentieth century, these images translated into a feminization of male addicts, including pimps. Exhibiting their biases about the nature of men and addicts, contemporary commentators did not believe that boys became addicts because they aspired to be pimps, but rather that they became pimps because drug use made them unfit for any kind of active work. According to public health official Lawrence Kolb, "the ultimate effect [of opiates] is to create a state of idleness and dependency which naturally enhances the desire to live at the expense of others and by anti-social means."[30] In other words, addiction made men less manly.

The pimp's addiction represented just one aspect of his deviation from mainstream male gender roles. Pimps lived off the earnings of "immoral women"—and the more money that their prostitutes earned, the better they could dress, the more drinks they could buy for their fellows, and the higher the stakes at which they could gamble.[31] The flamboyance of the pimp's life had a direct correlation with how much money his prostitutes were earning. As such, the pimp's relationship to prostitutes resembled an inversion of the bourgeois gender relations that Thorstein Veblen described.[32] Women's work supported men's conspicuous consumption. Thus, the pimp did not just deviate from the bourgeois masculine ideal: he lived its inverse.

Nevertheless, as historian Natalie Zemon Davis reminds us in her 1975 essay, "Women on Top," inversions are rarely simple and they "*undermine* as well as reinforce" hierarchies of power.[33] The pimp threatened conventional gender roles because he offered a masculine model that linked male domination to supposedly feminine patterns of consumption and idleness. The pimp inverted

middle-class conventions, but he was not an invert in the emerging medical sense of the term—he was a heterosexual male. The pimp retained his masculinity because he retained his power over women. Although the pimp transgressed bourgeois gender roles, his gender relations were consistent with identity.[34] Thus, even though middle-class reformers portrayed the pimp as a feminized villain, within the sporting class, pimps were the height of suave masculinity.

Middle-class reformers recognized this conundrum and feared that pimps provided a viable, although perverse, alternative for working-class youths. They believed that young men in the ghetto would eschew the bourgeois values of hard work and restraint and embrace the sporting class's leisure and free-spending conviviality.[35] Some observers, including sociologist Frederic M. Thrasher, warned that the increasing drug use among boys in urban gangs was an indication that they were choosing to emulate the sporting class.[36] Like the messenger boy in Butte, Montana, urban youths were trying drugs because they were "part and parcel of the role of a successful pimp."[37] By the early 1920s, the majority of new drug users were urban youths who imitated the lifestyle of the sporting class. These young men took drugs despite their long-standing association with femininity, because ironically that association was an integral part of the pimp's heightened masculinity.[38]

Theoretical Intermission

Up to this point, I have interpreted the femininity of drug use from the perspective of middle-class observers. I will now switch perspectives and address how a particular group within the sporting class—fairies—used cocaine as a way to signal their social and sexual identity. In order to do so, I must discuss at greater length subcultures and the transmission of cultural style.[39]

The sporting class was a distinct urban subculture. Although contemporaries defined the people associated with the urban vice district as a separate class, values and style, not income or family, defined membership. The elements that set the sporting class apart from respectable society were not only how they spent their time, but also their clothing and public presentation. The members of the sporting class, like those of other subcultures, adopted distinctive clothes and body language in order to announce their participation in that subculture. These stylistic elements were their signifiers.[40] Signifiers were not only physical objects—for example, a prostitute's ankle-flashing short skirt—they were also cultural messages: at the turn of the century, a short skirt equaled sexual availability. Thus a pimp's flashy clothing and jewelry were signifiers of his group identity, his wealth, the quality of his prostitutes, and his rejection of the work ethic of respectable men.

The sporting class, however, also had distinct divisions. The most notable distinction was between those who worked in the district and those who played in it. For prostitutes, their revealing dress and cosmetics were literal advertisements of who they were and what they were selling. Thus the adoption of the prostitute's distinctive trademarks of short skirts, cigarettes, a slow saunter, and bold eye contact, were "professional" signifiers. Other members in the sporting class—the consumers—had choices in their identification. The gang members, fairies, and charity girls (sexually-active young women who were not prostitutes) adopted certain types of dress and gestures to signal what were usually leisure-time identities.[41] This distinction is crucial. Although the sporting class consisted of both consumers and producers, these two groups had vastly different reasons for adopting their cultural signifiers. Producers used signifiers to make their living; consumers used them to express their identity.

The people who set the tone and offered the cultural models within the tenderloin were the madams, pimps, and prostitutes—the people who worked in the district. The prostitutes provided, while pimps and madams enabled, the sexual commerce that was the foundation upon which all other activities in the district were built. As a result of their centrality, the successful madams, pimps, and prostitutes had the highest status within the district and established the cultural styles. Charity girls, fairies, and other groups who were socializing in the district by choice rather than financial necessity looked up to the sporting-class elite. In forming their own group identities, gang members, fairies, and charity girls often appropriated elements of the sporting elite's style as signifiers of their own subcultural identity.[42] Fairies, for example, borrowed heavily from the "professional" signifiers of prostitutes to create their leisure-time identities—signifiers they later carried beyond the district into the general culture.

Fairies

The keynote of fairies' subcultural identity was their effeminacy. In *Gay New York*, historian George Chauncey has ably described fairies and their subcultural style. He argues that fairies, who socialized in the urban tenderloin and the most transgressive commercial dance halls, self-consciously rejected masculine gender roles by selectively adopting "feminine" signifiers. As he observes, "In the right context, appropriating even a single feminine—or at least unconventional—style or article of clothing might signify a man's identity as a fairy." These cultural cues could be suede shoes or a red tie, plucked eyebrows or bleached hair, and most stereotypically an exaggerated walk, a limp wrist, or arms akimbo.[43] Cocaine was another signifier that some fairies adopted to distinguish themselves from conventional society. These fairies chose cocaine because, like their contemporaries, they associated drug use with femininity.

Fairies took prostitutes as their model of femininity. Chauncey argues that fairies purposely adopted prostitutes' style and slang. An important element of prostitutes' style was drug use, which fairies copied as well. New York Police Commissioner Theodore A. Bingham described this cultural transmission when he wrote to public health reformer Hamilton Wright that:

> the classes of the community most addicted to the habitual use of cocaine are the parasites [*sic*] who live on the earnings of prostitutes, prostitutes of the lowest order, and young degenerates who acquire the habit at an early age through their connection with prostitutes and parasites [*sic*].[44]

While fairies may have taken prostitutes as their feminine model, these "degenerates" reinterpreted that femininity in the process of making it their own. Like all cultural transfers, there was an alteration in the process. Prostitutes used a range of drugs, but they were best known as opiate addicts. Fairies, on the other hand, were most closely associated with cocaine.

There are two possible explanations for why fairies incorporated cocaine, instead of the opiates, into their subcultural style. The first is functional: cocaine provided an excuse for "trade," conventionally masculine men who were sexually interested in fairies, to approach fairies. As an anti-drug reformer noted, "the practice of sniffing also leads to more social contagion, since the offer of a pinch of cocaine may be as simple a gesture as to offer a cigarette." In saloons and dance halls, cocaine functioned in much the same way as cigarettes did when men were picking up each other.[45] Other drugs, which involved more paraphernalia, could not function in this simple fashion.[46] The second reason for fairies' choice of cocaine was its physical effects. Prostitutes may have taken opiates to anesthetize themselves to their work, but fairies' identities were tied to their leisure, not to their work. One of the keynotes of their leisure identity was a bright flamboyance which suggests why fairies favored cocaine over the opiates. Cocaine could produce a brittle effervescence that made it more attractive to fairies than the effects of opiates, which suggested a laid-back "hipness" inconsistent with fairies' cultural style.[47] These functional and physical explanations of fairies' cocaine use explain why fairies chose cocaine over other drugs, but not why they incorporated drug use into their cultural style. Fairies made cocaine part of their subculture because it was a feminine signifier.

One of the best examples of the association of a fairy with cocaine use was in the story of Daisy, a regular at Martin's Saloon in Brooklyn. At Martin's, Daisy flirted with the patrons, borrowed a powder puff from investigator Natalie Sonnichsen, sang a dirty song, and performed a dance imitating sodomy with Elsie, another fairy. In order to confirm the disreputable goings-on, the gen-

eral secretary of the Committee of Fourteen, an anti-vice association, sent out a male investigator, S. M. Auerbach, to determine whether the fairies were soliciting. When Auerbach approached Daisy, he began the conversation by asking Daisy whether he was a "cocaine fiend," and if he had any "coca" to spare. Although Daisy was all out, he readily admitted that he was a "fiend." While Auerbach did not use this exchange as the first step to setting up a date, Daisy let Natalie know that he "had designs on Mr. A."[48] Daisy's story illustrates the subcultural style that fairies adopted. Daisy signaled that he was a fairy by using feminine gestures such as borrowing Natalie Sonnichsen's powder puff. Daisy's style was not, however, a demure femininity—his outrageous antics were more playful versions of prostitutes' public sexuality. Moreover, Daisy's frenetic sociability suggested to Auerbach that Daisy was a "cocaine fiend" which gave Auerbach, who was quintessentially "trade," an excuse to approach Daisy. In other words, for Daisy, cocaine was one of a range of feminine signifiers that he adopted in order to communicate his identity as a fairy.[49]

Fairies' adoption of cocaine as a signifier meant that cocaine eventually became a general gay signifier, and with that shift the association of drugs and femininity became increasingly tenuous. By the 1920s, the association of drugs with homosexuality had spread beyond the urban vice district. When the Hollywood [s]candals of the early twenties revealed that movie stars were using drugs, the media began speculating about the sexual orientation of leading actors and directors.[50] It was the association of drugs with fairies that informed John Dos Passos' characterization of Tony Garrido in *The Big Money*, the final book of his U.S.A. trilogy. Tony was an attractive Cuban expatriate, but it was his addiction as much as his "mincing walk" that confirmed his homosexuality to his wife Margo Dowling.[51] Whether they were playing off of these associations or informing them, members of wealthy gay artistic circles continued using cocaine into the 1930s.[52]

Although the connection between drug use and homosexuality became increasingly tenuous after World War II, drugs continued to appeal to people disaffected with conventional society, including gay men like William Burroughs and Allen Ginsberg. Even though the hustling junkie now seems more masculine than feminine, William Burroughs was "queer," and it was through his infamous addiction, as well as his sexual preference, that he communicated his rejection of mainstream masculinity.[53] The Beats were a long way from the ailing matrons of the nineteenth century, but the fairy and the pimp—alternative masculine models from the progressive-era vice districts—provide the genealogical link that spans the seemingly unbridgeable demographic difference between nineteenth- and twentieth-century addicts.

Conclusion

Since the 1970s, historians have argued that the demographic differences between the ailing matrons of the late nineteenth century and the dope fiends of the early twentieth century powerfully influenced Federal enactment of anti-drug laws. Historians have not, however, recognized how the femininity of addiction—the cultural continuity that connected the old and new addicts—shaped the early enforcement of narcotics laws. The perception in the 1920s that addicts were unmanly—weak, untrustworthy, and constitutionally flawed—informed how agents enforced, judges interpreted, and the public supported narcotics laws as ad hoc responses hardened into long-term Federal policy.

The "deviant" gendering of drug addicts tipped the balance from uneasy toleration to unquestioned prohibition. David Musto has argued that the passage of narcotics laws and their stringent enforcement required a reviled "other" in order to create an anti-drug consensus.[54] These "others" have included the "cocaine-crazed" Southern black men at the turn of the century, the marijuana-smoking Mexican migrant of the late 1930s, and, most recently, the pregnant crack whore. In each of these cases, however, race and class alone were not enough to create public consensus—it was their alternative, and often threatening, sexual roles that decisively alienated drug users from the

mainstream. This process of "othering" was necessarily multivalenced, and the allegations of deviant sexuality and the transgression of conventional gender roles critically reinforced other, more obvious, racial and class antipathies toward drug users.

Ironically, this process of "othering" often strengthened the cultural appeal of drug use. Media representation made casual drug use within subcultures an emblematic signifier of those cultures. Criminal prosecution turned drug users into romantic outlaws, while labeling simplified complicated subcultural rituals into easily imitated affectations. As a result, people who felt disaffected with conventional society could express their alienation by taking drugs and—however tenuous their connection—signal their affinity for the reviled others. Thus, the association of drugs with transgressive subcultures has meant that although the particular cultural connotations have changed, the overriding reason for drug experimentation in the twentieth century has been rebellion against the restrictions of conventional society. The gendering of addiction at the turn of the century continues to haunt reform efforts, for the recurring tension between othering and embracing the other remains the central conundrum of America's ongoing "war on drugs."

Notes

1. David T. Courtwright, *Dark Paradise: Opiate Addiction in America Before 1940* (Cambridge, Mass., 1982), 1–4.

2. David T. Courtwright, Herman Joseph, and Don Des Jarlais, *Addicts Who Survived: An Oral History of Narcotic Use in America, 1923–1965* (Knoxville, Tenn., 1989), 3–5.

3. For a discussion of bourgeois feminine ideals, hysteria, and the ailments of women's reproductive system, see Carroll Smith-Rosenberg, "Puberty to Menopause: The Cycle of Femininity in Nineteenth-Century America," and "The Hysterical Woman: Sex Roles and Role Conflict in Nineteenth-Century America," in *Disorderly Conduct: Visions of Gender in Victorian America* (New York, 1985), 182–216. Smith-Rosenberg beautifully describes nineteenth-century doctors' understanding of female health and their resulting advice, but she does not examine the therapeutic measures that doctors adopted to treat their patients. On doctors' use of opiates to treat hysteria and "female troubles," see H. H. Kane, *Drugs That Enslave: The Opium, Morphine, Chloral and Hashisch Habits* (Philadelphia, 1881; reprint, New York, 1981), 18, 25; Charles F. Terry and Mildred Pellens, eds., *The Opium Problem* (New York, 1928), 96–100; David T. Courtwright, "The Female Opiate Addict in Nineteenth-Century America," Essay in *Arts and Sciences* 10 (1982): 163–164; H. Wayne Morgan, *Drugs in America: A Social History, 1800–1980* (Syracuse, 1981), 39–40. For the congruence between addiction and gender roles for middle-class women, compare Smith-Rosenberg's descriptions with Kane, *Drugs That Enslave*, 49; T. D. Crothers, *Morphinism and Narcomanias From Other Drugs: Their Etiology, Treatment, and Medicolegal Re-*

lations (Philadelphia, 1902; reprint, New York, 1981), 104; and F. E. Oliver, "The Use and Abuse of Opium," Massachusetts State Board of Health, *Third Annual Report* (Boston, 1872), 162–177 in *Yesterday's Addicts: American Society and Drug Abuse, 1865–1920*, ed. H. Wayne Morgan (Norman, Okla., 1974), 49.

4. David Courtwright argues that during the "first wave" of American drug use, 1870–1940, the peak of opiate addiction was in the mid-1890s. At that point, he estimates that in the United States there could have been no more than 313,000 addicts or 4.59 per thousand. Within the addict population, almost half were women medical addicts from the middle class. After the effective prohibition of narcotics in the late 1910s, and the creation of the Federal Bureau of Narcotics, the available numbers become so politically loaded and statistically unreliable, that Courtwright, even after an exhaustive search, was not able to produce equivalent numbers for the later period. He does posit, however, that in 1920 there could have been no more than 210,000 addicts, or approximately 2 addicts per thousand. Moreover, the number of addicts kept declining through World War II. From contemporary observations, it is clear that from 1900 onwards, there were progressively fewer medical addicts and that there were proportionally more recreational addicts—most of whom were young men from the city. Courtwright, *Dark Paradise*, 28, 36, 34, 113–115.

5. John Phillips, "Prevalence of the Heroin Habit: Especially the Use of the Drug by 'Snuffing,'" *Journal of the American Medical Association* 59 (1912): 2147; Clifford B. Fan, "The Relative Frequency of the Morphine and Heroin Habits: Based Upon Some Observations at the Philadelphia General Hospital," *New York Medical Journal* 101 (1915): 893; Courtwright, *Dark Paradise*, 90, 192 n22; Morgan, *Drugs in America*, 57, 91.

6. Richard Dewey to Hamilton Wright, 5 November 1908, file: "U.S. Data: Rhode Island to Wyoming," box 2, entry 47, Record Group 43, National Archives at College Park, Maryland (hereafter, NARG followed by the record group number); Joseph McIver and George E. Price, "Drug Addiction: Analysis of One Hundred and Forty-Seven Cases at the Philadelphia General Hospital," *Journal of the American Medical Association* 66 (1916): 477; L. L. Stanley, "Morphinism and Crime," *Journal of the American Institute of Criminal Law and Criminology* 8 (1918): 749–756 in *Yesterday's Addicts*, 83.

7. I use the term "fairies" deliberately. Historian George Chauncey has convincingly argued that in the early decades of this century, people did not see sexuality as a binary heterosexual/homosexual split. Instead, he argues, it was not just sexual preference, but also style that determined sexual labels. Fairies—a self-description—were flamboyantly effeminate men who took the "woman's role." There was also a class dimension to this category. Fairies were usually from the working class, while "queers," who were less overt in their sexual display, were from the middle class. See George Chauncey, *Gay New York: Gender, Urban Culture, and the Making of the Gay Male World, 1890–1940* (New York, 1994), 12–23.

8. "Prostitution in Precinct XV," 119011, 2, Committee of Fifteen, Rare Books and Manuscripts Division, New York Public Library; "Several Raids Made on 'Joints' Last Night," *New York News*, 17 March 1901, Newspaper Clippings, Committee of Fifteen; "Quan Yick Nam," 19 February 1901, Committee of Fifteen; "Arthur F. Wilson States," 1 March 1901, Committee of Fifteen.

9. "Parlor Houses," file 6.8, box 91, Lillian Wald Papers, Columbia University.

10. *New Orleans Item*, 9 August 1907, 25 July 1914, 13 November 1915, 23 December 1910, and 22 January 1915.

11. On the closing of the red-light districts as a wartime measure, see Allan M. Brandt, *No Magic Bullet: A Social History of Venereal Disease in the United States Since 1880, With a New Chapter on AIDS* (New York, 1987), 70–77. On how concerns about war preparedness influenced the more stringent interpretation of the Harrison Act, see David F.

Musto, *The American Disease: Origins of Narcotic Control, Expanded Edition* (New York, 1987), 135, 328 n35.

12. Frank A. McGuire and Perry M. Lichtenstein, "The Drug Habit," *Medical Record* 90 (1916): 185; McIver and Price, "Drug Addiction," 478; Courtwright, *Dark Paradise*, 83–84.

13. [Vice Commission of Newark, New Jersey], *Report on the Social Evil Conditions of Newark, New Jersey to the People of Newark* (n.p., ([1914]), 126–130; Courtwright, *Dark Paradise*, 2.

14. Jane Addams, *The Spirit of Youth and the City Streets* (New York, 1909; reprint, Urbana, 1972), 63–67; Pearce Bailey, "The Heroin Habit," *The New Republic* 6 (1916): 314–316 in *Yesterday's Addicts*, 172.

15. Male prostitution was a barely recognized phenomenon during the Progressive era.

16. Charles W. Earle, "The Opium Habit: A Statistical and Clinical Lecture," *Chicago Medical Review* 2 (1880): 442–446 in *Yesterday's Addicts*, 53. In Earle's sample of 235 addicts, 169 were women. Earle wrote that a third of these women were prostitutes, which would mean that approximately 56 women were addicts—making prostitutes approximately a quarter of all drug users in the sample.

17. Courtwright, *Dark Paradise*, 52.

18. Vice Commission of Chicago, *The Social Evil in Chicago: A Study of Existing Conditions, with Recommendations* (Chicago, 1911), 84–87, 289. See also Ruth Rosen, "Introduction" in *The Maimie Papers*, ed. by Ruth Rosen and Sue Davidson (Old Westbury, 1977), xiv, xli n5. Interestingly, at the municipal maintenance clinic in Shreveport, Louisiana, which was open from 1919 to 1923, the most frequently given explanation for opiate addiction was venereal disease. Of the 449 patients, 28.5 percent (121 men, 8 women) said they had started taking opiates because of "venereal disease" or "gonorrhea." When "blood poisoning" and "french fever," both of which were euphemisms for sexually transmitted diseases, are added to the tally the percentage increases to 30.0 percent (127 men, 8 women), History Sheets. Narcotics Division, Louisiana State Board of Health, Willis Butler Papers, Department of Archives and Special Collections, Noel Memorial Library, Louisiana State University in Shreveport.

19. On nineteenth-century feminine ideals, see Nancy F. Cott, "Passionlessness: An Interpretation of Victorian Sexual Ideology," *Signs* 4 (1978): 219–236 in *Women and Health in America*, ed. Judith Walzer Leavitt (Madison, 1984), 57–69; Carroll Smith-Rosenberg and Charles Rosenberg, "The Female Animal: Medical and Biological Views of Woman and Her Role in Nineteenth-Century America," *Journal of American History* 60 (1973): 332–356 in *Women and Health*, 12–27; and Ronald G. Walters, ed., *Primers for Prudery: Sexual Advice to Victorian America* (Englewood Cliffs, 1974), 6.

20. *The Social Evil in Chicago*, 285; Sara Graham-Mulhall, "Experiences in Narcotic Drug Control in the State of New York," *New York Medical Journal* 113 (1921): 106–11 in *Yesterday's Addicts*, 211; The Vice Commission of Philadelphia, *A Report on Existing Conditions with Recommendations to the Honorable Rudolph Blankenburg, Mayor of Philadelphia* (n.p., 1913), 34; George J Kneeland, *Commercialized Prostitution in New York City* (New York, 1917; reprint, Montclair, N.J., 1969), 15–16. This explanation also had a racist version in which authors asserted that opium smoking was the only way that white prostitutes could endure having sex with Chinese men; for a typical example, see I. L. Nascher, *The Wretches of Povertyville: A Sociological Study of the Bowery* (Chicago, 1909), 134.

21. Christina Kuppinger, "Report for May, To the Officers and Directors of the Midnight Mission," May 1911, file 2, box 5, Ernest Bell Papers, Chicago Historical Society.

22. "Baltimore Notes," 17 July 1908, file: "Miscellaneous Correspondence," box 2, entry 48, NARG 43; "Philadelphia Notes," 20–21 July 1908, 2, 5–6, file: "Miscellaneous Correspondence," box 2, entry 48, NARG 43.

23. "135 Fourth Avenue—Saloon Hangout—Drugs," box 28, Committee of Fourteen Papers, Rare Books and Manu-

scripts Division, New York Public Library. See also "317 West 41st Street—Black and Tan Saloon—Drugs," box 28, Committee of Fourteen.

24. *The Social Evil in Chicago*, 242–244. Although he did not state whether they were messenger boys, L. L. Stanley found in a study of 100 prisoners in San Quentin that 15 had learned drug use from prostitutes; Stanley, "Morphinism and Crime," in *Yesterday's Addicts*, 80–83. This pattern continued into the 1940s; see Teddy's interview in Courtwright et al., *Addicts Who Survived*, 51.

25. Bingham Dai, *Opium Addiction in Chicago* (1937; reprint, Montclair, N.J., 1970), 144–148. See also Stanley, "Morphinism and Crime," in *Yesterday's Addicts*, 85.

26. S. Dana Hubbard, "The New York City Narcotic Clinic and Differing Points of View on Narcotic Addiction," New York City Department of Health, *Monthly Bulletin* 10 (1920) in *The Opium Problem*, 123–124; "The First Annual Summary of the Clinical Work on Opium Addiction in Philadelphia General Hospital for the Philadelphia Committee by the Clinical Staff," Part II (1926), 6–7, file 552, box 1, sub-series 1, series IV, Bureau of Social Hygiene Papers, Rockefeller Archive Center, Tarrytown, New York.

27. Ann Douglas Wood, "'The Fashionable Disease': Women's Complaints and Their Treatment in Nineteenth-Century America," *The Journal of Interdisciplinary History* 4 (1973): 25–52 in *Women and Health*, 227; Barbara Ehrenreich and Deirdre English, *For Her Own Good: 150 Years of the Experts' Advice to Women* (Garden City, 1978), 23, 92–96, 103; Brian Dijkstra, *Idols of Perversity: Fantasies of Feminine Evil in Fin-de-Siècle Culture* (New York, 1985), 25–37. Harriet Beecher Stowe's daughter Georgiana is an example of an addict within a reform family; Courtwright, "The Female Opiate Addict," 163–164.

28. H. S. Cumming, "Control of Drug Addiction Mainly a Police Problem," *The American City Magazine* (November 1925), file 126, box 3, sub-series 1, series III, Bureau of Social Hygiene; John S. Haller, Jr. and Robin M. Haller, *The Physician and Sexuality in Victorian America* (Carbondale, Ill., 1974), 302. One of the physical effects of opiate addiction is male impotence. Knowledge of this side effect may be one reason that people associated addiction with effeminacy; see Kane, *Drugs That Enslave*, 45; W. M. Kraus, "An Analysis of the Action of Morphine Upon the Vegetative Nervous System of Man," *Journal of Nervous and Mental Diseases* 48 (1918) in *The Opium Problem*, 461; and W. Hale White, *Materia Medica, Pharmacy, Pharmacology and Therapeutics* (1924) in *The Opium Problem*, 462; Morgan, *Drugs in America*, 189 n56.

29. Morgan, *Drugs in America*, 35–37, 54–55. On turn-of-the-century conceptions of manliness and fears about the "feminized male," see E. Anthony Rotundo, "Roots of Change: The Women Without and the Woman Within," in *American Manhood: Transformations in Masculinity from the Revolution to the Modern Era* (New York, 1993), 247–283.

30. Clifford G. Roe and Clare Teal Wiseman, *The Prosecutor: A Four-Act Drama* (n.p., 1914), 33–34; W. A. Bloedorn, "Studies of Drug Addicts," *U.S. Naval Medical Bulletin* 11 (1917) in *The Opium Problem*, 494; Lawrence Kolb, "Drug Addiction in Its Relation to Crime," *Mental Hygiene* 9 (1925): 75.

31. Ruth Rosen, *The Lost Sisterhood: Prostitution in America, 1900–1918* (Baltimore, 1982), 109.

32. Thorstein Veblen, *Theory of the Leisure Class*, with an introduction by Robert Lekachman (1899; reprint, New York, 1979), 80–82.

33. Natalie Zemon Davis, "Women on Top," in *Society and Culture in Early Modern France* (Stanford, 1975), 131. Emphasis in original.

34. In turn-of-the-century medical literature, "invert" was the term for gay men who transgressed gender boundaries and were more like women than men; see John D'Emilio and Estelle B. Freedman, *Intimate Matters: A History of Sexuality in America* (New York, 1988), 226; Chauncey, *Gay New York*, 48–49.

35. "The White Slavery Films: A Review," *The Outlook* 106 (1914): 345–350; James Bronson Reynolds to Frederick H. Whitin, 24 October 1914, box 3, Committee of Fourteen. Bruce Raeburn of the William Ransom Hogan Jazz Archive at Tulane University has observed that jazz great Jelly Roll Morton's boast that he was a pimp exemplifies the pimp's prestige in the early twentieth century.

36. Frederic M. Thrasher, "Drug Addiction and Adolescent Behavior (Study Completed July 5, 1929)" (typescript), 15, 28, file 128, box 3, sub-series 1, series III, Bureau of Social Hygiene. Although John Devon was not a pimp, the things that Leroy Street admired about him—his leisure, his dress, and his worldliness—were the kinds of things that urban youths admired in pimps. It was as a result of this type of hero worship that Leroy Street and others picked up their idols' drug habits; Leroy Street in collaboration with David Loth, *I Was a Drug Addict* (New York, 1953), 11–13.

37. Dai, *Opium Addiction in Chicago*, 149.

38. McIver and Price, "Drug Addiction," 477; C. Edouard Sandoz, "Report on Morphinism to the Municipal Court of Boston," *Journal of Criminal Law, Criminology, and Police Science* 13 (1922): 24, 36; "The First Annual Summary of the Clinical Work on Opium Addiction in Philadelphia General Hospital for the Philadelphia Committee by the Clinical Staff," Part II (1926), 3, file 552, box 1, sub-series 1, series IV, Bureau of Social Hygiene; Terry and Pellens, eds., *The Opium Problem*, 474. The argument can be made that pimps were the antecedents for hipster jazz musicians; Jill Jonnes, "The Sky Is High and So Am I," in *Hep-Cats, Narcs, and Pipe Dreams: A History of America's Romance With Illegal Drugs* (New York, 1996), 119–140. Howard Becker's description of dance musicians and marijuana smoking also shows the clear continuities between drug use and alternate masculine models; Howard S. Becker, *Outsiders: Studies in the Sociology of Deviance* (New York, 1963).

39. For an excellent discussion of subcultures and group identity, see Dick Hebdige, *Sub-culture: The Meaning of Style* (London, 1979). See also Ken Gelder and Sarah Thornton, eds., *The Subcultures Reader* (London, 1997).

40. For a further explanation of signifiers, see "Myth Today," in Roland Barthes, *Mythologies*, trans. Annette Lavers (Paris, 1957; reprint, New York, 1972), 109–159.

41. Frederic M. Thrasher, *The Gang: A Study of 1,313 Gangs in Chicago*, 2d rev. ed. (Chicago, 1927), 68–69, 79; Chauncey, *Gay New York*, 44, 51–56; Kathy Piess, *Cheap Amusements: Working Women and Leisure in Turn-of-the-Century New York* (Philadelphia, 1986), 57, 62–67.

42. Thrasher, *The Gang*, 252, 255–257, 262; Peiss, *Cheap Amusements*, 66.

43. George Chauncey, *Gay New York*, 51–55, quotation on page 51.

44. Chauncey, *Gay New York*, 60–61, 69, 286; Theo. A. Bingham to Hamilton Wright, 23 June 1909, file: "United States Data, New York," box 1, entry 47, NARG 43. See also the story of a fairy who started taking morphine on the advice of prostitutes in Dai, *Opium Addiction in Chicago*, 163. It is important to note that although "degenerate" had a variety of meanings in the medical literature, in common parlance it generally denoted homosexuality; Charles Johnston, alias Hattie Ross, to Robert S. Bickerd, 29 July 1910, box 1, Committee of Fourteen.

45. The quotation is from page 9 of an unidentified report in file 51, box 7, Bureau of Social Hygiene, Rockefeller Boards, Record Group 2, Rockefeller Family Archives, Rockefeller Archive Center; Chauncey, *Gay New York*, 64, 188. See also, *The Social Evil in Chicago*, 290.

46. Courtwright et al., *Addicts Who Survived*, 97.

47. The term "hip" was originally associated with opium smoking which occurred "on the hip;" see Jonnes, *Hep-Cats, Narcs, and Pipe Dreams*, 125.

48. "Martin's Saloon. Opposite Jackson Avenue Park," 1 August 1912; "Martin's Saloon," 8 August 1912; and "Martin's Saloon. Jackson Avenue," 14 August 1912, box 29; and

"Dance Hall and Martin's Saloon," 15 August 1912, box 28, Committee of Fourteen. Cocaine and fairies were associated with other transgressive places where "anything went," see "Memo," 18 August 1913, box 3, Committee of Fourteen; "Re saloons etc., Queens Boro," 24 July 1913, 5–6, box 29, Committee of Fourteen; George Chauncey, Jr., "Christian Brotherhood or Sexual Perversion? Homosexual Identities and the Construction of Sexual Boundaries in the World War I Era," *Journal of Social History* 19 (1985): 189–212 in *Hidden From History: Reclaiming the Gay and Lesbian Past*, eds. Martin Bauml Duberman, Martha Vicinus, and George Chauncey, Jr. (New York, 1989), 297. I would like to thank George Chauncey for bringing it to my attention that the Newport investigation targeted sexual perversion and cocaine use, see U.S. Senate, 67th Cong., 1st sess., Committee on Naval Affairs, *Alleged Immoral Conditions at Newport (R.I.) Naval Training Station* (Washington, D.C., 1921), 17 reprinted in Jonathan Katz, ed., *Government Versus Homosexuals* (New York, 1975).

49. There are a number of examples of cocaine functioning as a gay signifier in German and Swiss medical literature. For an overview of this literature, see Oriana Josseau Kalant, ed. and trans., *Maier's Cocaine Addiction (Der Kokainzsmus)* (1926; reprint, Toronto, 1987), 43, 50–54, 160–162, 167, 182–185.

50. *Sins of Hollywood: A Group of Actual Happenings Reported and Written by a Hollywood Newspaper Man* (Hollywood, 1922) in *The Movies in Our Midst: Documents in the Cultural History of Film in America*, ed. Gerald Mast (Chicago, 1982), 177, 180; "Slain Film Director Believed Victim of Love Revenge Plot," *New York Herald*, 3 February 1922, William Desmond Taylor Clippings, Library of the Performing Arts at Lincoln Center.

51. John Dos Passos, *The Big Money* (1933; reprint, New York, 1969), 287–90, 402–403.

52. Barry Paris, *Louise Brooks* (New York, 1989), 239, 367–369.

53. Jonnes, *Hep-Cats, Narcs, and Pipe Dreams*, 208–210; William S. Burroughs, *Queer* (New York, 1985).

54. Musto, *The American Disease*, 5–8, 11, 43–44, 219–223.

For Discussion

Discuss whether the "gendering of addiction" applies in contemporary society.

5

Sociopharmacology of Drug Use

Initial Thoughts

Samuel R. Friedman

Samuel Friedman introduces the concept of "sociopharmacology" as it relates to drug use. A sociopharmacological approach to drug use takes into account the particular social, economic, and political context in which drug use occurs. By using several examples, Friedman illustrates the importance of sociopharmacology in terms of its ability to explain drug use. He suggests that social order and social context, rather than the individual, represent the underlying "causes" of drug use.

Introduction

Much research on drug use has focused on individual characteristics of the drug users and the psychopharmacology of drug use. Such research investigates how the psychological traits of drug users and chemical traits of drugs lead to addiction and to its associated problems. At its 'best', this research medicalises addiction and its associated problems. At its worst, it legitimates the demonising of drug users and a war on drugs that, in the United States alone, spends $11 billion annually on law enforcement and interdiction without reducing heroine or cocaine availability or purity or increasing their prices. This drug war approach has, however, helped mask the consequences of social structures based on racial and gender inequality and on economic exploitation by leading millions to see their consequences for local communities and individuals to be the product, instead, of individual criminality and drug use. Millions of drug users have been incarcerated as a result of this scapegoating policy; and it has not prevented the spread of injection drug use, and its related lethal blood-borne infections such as HIV, hepatitis B and C, and endocarditis around the world (Friedman, 1998a; Schiraldi, Holman & Phillip, 2000; Stimson, 1993; Stimson, Ball & Des Jarlais, 1998).

Whether through medicalisation or demonisation, such research defines the user as the problem, and thus ignores socioeconomic and other issues that create vulnerabilities to harmful and/or chronic drug use among individuals, neighbourhoods, and population groups. We offer the concept of 'sociopharmacology of drug use' as a partial contribution to developing an alternative way of thinking and acting on drug-related issues.

Our concept of 'sociopharmacology' attempts to locate drug use in a broader socioeconomic context, as it intersects with the histories and physiologies of individuals, the social, political and economic histories and current realities of different populations, communities and countries, and the pharmacology of drugs. We thus look at the social 'causation' of drug use patterns, where our concept of 'causation' is not one of forces with deterministic impact on individuals, but rather one in which social structures and processes [a]ffect the likelihood that individuals will use various drugs. Human subjectivity and agency are important; but what Durkheim (1982) called 'social facts' nonetheless emerge out of the play of multilevel influences and individual and collective dialectical reactions to these forces. Here, then, our argument parallels those of other students of the social epidemiology of disease, morbidity, and mortality (Armstrong, Barnett, Casper & Wing, 1998; Armstrong & Castorina, 1998; Berkman & Kawachi, 2000; Casper, Wing & Strogatz, 1991; Diez-Roux, Nieto, Muntaner, et al., 1997; Diez-Roux, Nieto, Caulfield, Tyroler, Watson & Szklo, 1999; Elreedy, Krieger, Ryan, Sparrow, Weiss & Hu, 1999; Fife & Mode, 1992; Hu, Frey, Costa, Massey, Ryan, Flemming, D'Errico, Ward & Buehler, 1994; Kaplan, Pamuk, Lynch, Cohen & Balfour, 1996; Kennedy, Kawachi, & Prothrow-Stith, 1996; Lynch, Kaplan, Pamuk, Cohen, Heck, Balfour & Yen, 1998; O'Campo, Xue, Wang & O'Brien Caughy, 1997; Simon, Hu, Diaz & Kerndt,

1995; Wallace & Wallace, 1999; Zierler & Krieger, 1997), as well as of substance use (Bell, Carlson & Richard, 1998; Brugal, Domingo-Salvany, Maguire, Cayla, Villalbi & Hartnoll, 1999; Faris & Dunham, 1939; Chein, Gerard, Lee & Rosenfeld, 1964; Diez-Roux et al., 1997; Kleinschmidt, Hills & Elliott, 1995; Nurco, 1972; Nurco, Shaffer & Cisin, 1984; Redlinger & Michel, 1970).

This concept of sociopharmacology differs from Rhodes' (1996) concept of 'social pharmacology'. Rhodes, like Becker (1977), focuses on how social and cultural forces affect 'knowledge about the perceived and expected "pharmacological" effects of drugs'. Rhodes also discusses the cultural concept of disinhibition due to drug use, and its potential as an excuse for engaging in unsafe sex, in terms of social contexts (or what Mills, 1940, referred to as a 'vocabulary of motives'). We, by contrast, focus on social causation of drug use patterns in populations and subpopulations rather than on perceptions of drug effects.

Similarly, our concept differs from analyses of small group, role, and folk cultural regulatory mechanisms that shape how drug users use their drugs or that help them maintain controlled levels of use or safer injection practices (Friedman et al., 1998b; Friedman, Curtis, Neaigus, Jose & Des Jarlais, 1999; Friedman, Kang, Deren, Robles, Colón, Andia, Oliver-Valdez & Finlinson, 2002; Neaigus, Friedman, Curtis, Des Jarlais, et al., 1994; Southgate & Hopwood, 2001; Zinberg, 1984). It may have more in common with the way in which Southgate and Hopwood (2001) discuss the social roots of their 'folk pharmacology' in the economic and social structures of gay life in Sydney, Australia (see below).

To What Degree Is There Drug Use That Is Not Socially Caused?

As will be discussed below, our theory of drug use is based on the hypothesis that certain parts of the social order are more likely to use drugs; and, beyond that, the drugs which are used in a given social location will be those which seem to them to produce moods or consciousness that help people deal with problems with which society con-

fronts them. Thus, we posit that much harmful drug use is socially caused by ways in which the social order itself causes pain or other reactions in some people that they attempt to medicate with the drugs. To some degree, however, there is probably a residual degree of drug use, including harmful drug use, which would be present in any social order. One way to think about this is that, even in a truly decent society, many people would use some potentially addictive substances during particular social or cultural events. Some of these people might, as a consequence, become addicted and come to use drugs in ways harmful to themselves or others. In addition, some harmful drug use, including the use of potentially-addictive drugs, would be likely to occur because some substances are fun or otherwise pleasing enough so some people will knowingly risk the dangers. Additional drug use might arise as a form of pain medication by people who have undergone traumatic experiences.

What would be done in such a society to help those who develop drug problems? It is difficult to imagine the details of a decent society—but we suspect that human solidarity, values of human respect and equality, the possibility for a desirable future, science, and love would be mobilized to reduce and prevent such harm. (Similar needs might exist in relationship to the dangers of other dangerous pursuits, such as over-devotion to down-hill skiing.)

Social Factors Which May Underlie Harmful Drug Use: Preliminary Thoughts

Unfortunately, the world as it is seems to be far from ideal. Billions of people have real pressures on them that are almost insupportable, whether as a consequence of living in a poor nation; being part of an oppressed people or community; having been sexually or physically abused as a child; having an uncertain, degrading, boring, or highly risky employment situation; or living with a spouse, child, parent, or other person in a relationship that is fraught with tension or violence. We suggest that such pressures are likely to lead some of those exposed to them to use particular drugs in harmful ways. Other factors will also be involved in determining which individuals among those exposed to the pressures actually take up various forms of drug use. The study of this aspect of the problem is important, and has been the major focus of prior research in the field to such an extent that these issues of social causation have been inadequately studied.

For the lucky and wealthy, such social pressures are episodic. For the overwhelming majority of the population, however, they are chronic. Members of the blue, pink, or white collar working class generally face more of these problems than do the corporate rich or those of otherwise wealthy family (Mishel, Schmitt & Bernstein, 1999; UNDP, 1999), although other problems, such as sexual abuse, may be more equally distributed among economic categories. Racial/ethnic stratification, such as the subordination of African Americans, Latino/as, and others in United States and, generally, the Americas, or of non-whites in South Africa, or of Catholics in Ulster, is usually associated with worse health and living conditions for the subordinated groups (Geschwender, 1978; Omi & Winant, 1994). Gender relationships are deeply complicated by issues of class and race/ethnicity, but the greater burdens and stresses that women face even if they do not have an explicit history of sexual abuse and/or violation, domestic violence, and/or survival sex work, have been widely documented (Albeda & Tilly, 1997; Folbre, 1993a, b; Goldberg & Kremen, 1990; Zierler & Krieger, 1997). Elsewhere, Friedman (1991) suggested that 'dignity-denial' is deeply rooted in such social structures of modern capitalism as the workplace, racial and gender subordination, and organisational structures. One possible result of such dignity-denial is the use of drugs or other substances as a source of solace or self-medication against the pain of not being respected as an equal human being.

Although such pressures may be chronic, their intensity varies over time. Recent decades may have been a period in which these pressures have intensified. Economic conditions worsened during the period from ap-

proximately 1970–1999 in a great many countries. Relevant data from a number of countries are presented in Table 5.1 and in Fig. 5.1 and Fig. 5.2. These show that profit rates have been decreasing, unemployment increasing, and inequality increasing over recent decades. As described elsewhere (Friedman, 1998a, b; Friedman, Southwell, Bueno, Paone, Byrne & Crofts, 2001), these economic pressures and their associated politics of scapegoating have contributed to overwork, cutbacks in social and health services, a sense of increasing inequality, widespread imprisonment of scapegoated groups including racial/ethnic minorities and drug users, and the weakening of community social ties all over the world.

We hypothesise that large numbers of people use pharmacologically active substances to help them deal with these pressures and, perhaps, to deal with trauma or with mental illness (which may be derived from these or related pressures). Some use occurs among people who may (also) enjoy using pharmacologically active substances—at least at first. Such substances include marijuana, tobacco, heroin, alcohol, amphetamines, cocaine, and caffeine. Some of these substances, of course, are tolerated, others celebrated, and still others are proscribed. A major focus of a sociopharmacology of drugs should be to study what kinds of socially derived pressures are associated with what kinds of substance use. One potentially important aspect of such research will be to study if and how occupa-

Table 5.1

Differences Between Postwar Boom Period and Since in Selected Economic Characteristics of G-7 Industrialised Countries

Net profit of private business	
1950–1969	18.0%
1970–1990	13.0%
Unemployment rate	
1950–1973	3.1%
1973–1993	6.2%

G-7 countries: Canada, France, Germany, Italy, Japan, United Kingdom, United States.
Source: Brenner, 1998, p. 5.

tional and industrial characteristics of job[s] are associated with particular kinds of drug use in both formal and informal work sectors. There is some literature suggesting that occupation is associated with use of specific psychoactive substances (Ebie & Pela, 1981; Mongkolsirichaikul, Mokkhavesa & Ratanabanangkoon, 1988; Philpot, Harcourt & Edwards, 1989; Roberts & Lee, 1993; Stratford, Ellerbrock, Akins & Hall, 2000; Watts & Short, 1990). Winnick (1964) shows that narcotic addiction among physicians, and perhaps jazz musicians, is associated with the occupational characteristics of their jobs. There has been considerable speculation that caffeine and amphetamines are used to stay alert in some jobs such as truck driving; that other drugs (nicotine, marijuana) are used to deal with boredom in occupations such as routine assembly line work; that opiates are used to cope with painful or otherwise insufferable working conditions such as those associated with sex work; and that steroids and amphetamines are sometimes used to enhance performance in professional sports. Southgate and Hopwood (2001) describe drug use in Sydney as a form of socially regulated pleasure

seeking based on the economic and social structures of the gay community. Left implicit in their discussion is the extent to which social stigmatisation of gays, and struggles against this, also structure these mores and behaviors.

Living in a local area that is socioeconomically deprived may be related to substance use and its related harms. Bell et al. (1998) review a number of studies which show that census tract level analysis of drug use and of its potential socioecological causes provide[s] useful insight into drug use (Faris & Dunham, 1939; Chein et al., 1964), heroin or narcotics addiction (Redlinger & Michel, 1970; Nurco, 1972), and multiple indices of social pathology (Nurco et al., 1984). Bell et al. (1998) themselves show that, in Houston, four identifiable socioecological factors help differentiate census tracts (social disorganisation, economic success, threat of violence, and chronic disease); and that narcotic offenses load heavily (0.50) on a social disorganisation factor. Brugal et al. (1999) report that unemployment rates in small areas within Barcelona are associated with neighborhood population-prevalences of opiod ad-

Figure 5.1

Income Inequality: Deciles D9/D1

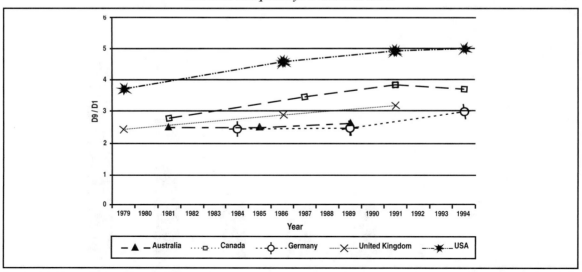

Source: Ruiz-Huerta, Martinez, Ayala. Earnings inequality, unemployment and income distribution in the OECD, Working Paper number 214, LIS. 1999.

diction. Diez-Roux et al. (1997) showed that deprived neighbourhoods have higher levels of smoking, as well as higher cholesterol and body mass index. Kleinschmidt et al. (1995) also showed that smoking is influenced by neighbourhood deprivation.

These data, however, are merely indicative. More research is clearly needed on ways in which social statuses, pressures, and locations are related to drug use and to drug related harm.

There are probably also important cultural and marketing elements in much substance use (in addition to the social and economic ones already discussed). In some areas, psychoactive substances such as coca leaves, mushrooms, or poppy derivatives are part of traditional cultures. In others, these same substances are deeply stigmatised—which may lead them to seem attractive to the rebellious or alienated. Marketing dynamics, as shaped by interactions among producers, distributors, and police forces, affect where which drugs are available at given times. Examples of this are the diffusion of heroin use in Southeast Asia and cocaine use in South America after attempts to disrupt drug trafficking (Friedman et al.,

1998a; Stimson et al., 1998; Stimson, 1993). This may help explain why some substances are used more in some localities than in others.

Implications for Theory, Research, and Action

These thoughts have implications for future research that embrace both macro-social issues and the links between the macro and the micro.

First, research is needed to determine the social distribution of the use of various drugs among different social and socioeconomic categories of the populations of different countries. This should include consideration of routes of administration, frequency and patterns of use, and other variables that may affect the likelihood of drug-related harm. These data will allow testing and exploration of the underlying theory of (partial) social causation of drug use.

Second, if the underlying theory is correct, then data on drug-related harm are likely to point to the ills and contradictions of society. Research should be conducted on

Figure 5.2

Ratio of Chief Executive Officer Pay to Factory Worker Pay, United States of America.

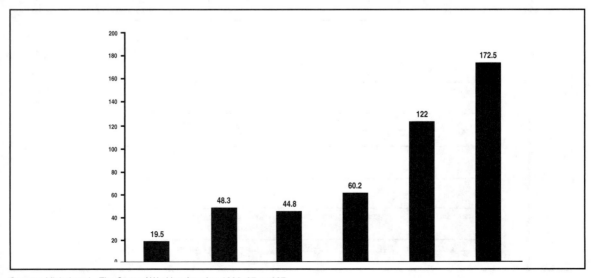

Source: Mishel et al., *The State of Working America*, 1996–97, p. 227.

how such data might identify nations, communities, occupations, and populations whose conditions create vulnerability to drug-related harm. Such data can concomitantly help identify points of social strain or contradiction within populations. The large extent of substance use in the United States probably suggests serious social dysfunction at the macro level. Research is also needed on how social, economic and health policies, or a lack thereof, create conditions that increase demand for harmful drug use and/or make it more likely that large numbers of people will engage in drug production, distribution, and sale.

Individualistic theories of drug use have been used to stigmatise and even demonise individual drug users as being weak or criminal. The sociopharmacological approach, by way of contrast, suggests that if anyone or anything should be demonised, it should be the social order, not the individual user. Whereas individualistic perspectives have justified blaming and incarcerating hundreds of thousands of people in ways that divert attention from and exacerbate serious socioeconomic problems and contradictions, a sociopharmacological view suggests that action should be focused on social change rather than on blaming the victim. This argument, of course, parallels arguments against 'blaming the victim' in other fields of research and action (Chambliss, 1999; Ryan, 1976).

Nonetheless, current drug use patterns do cause misery among drug users, their families, and their neighbors. Although it can be argued that many of these harms are a consequence of legal repression and/or social stigmatisation of drug users, the current pains remain to be addressed. Research and programmes are needed to reduce these harms. Such programmes should help them deal with chemistry-related issues, health-related issues, and issues that concern how they can get along better with family members and neighbours. To the extent that the harmful drug use is the result of social pressures, programs to ameliorate these harms should probably include a mixture of training in ways to more safely deal with these social pressures by personal adjustment and training, and organising for individual and social collective self-defense against these pressures and their causes. Research is needed on how best to provide resources to individuals, communities, and other social groups that they can use to ameliorate both the conditions that lead to harmful drug use and also to reduce harmful drug use among drug users.

To the extent that drug use is the result of social contradictions or occupational necessity, laws that punish users and dealers are at best mistaken efforts based on misdiagnosis of the roots of the problem. However, such laws should not usually be seen as 'mistakes' by well-meaning lawmakers but as serving the function of scapegoating the vulnerable. This serves to remove accountability both from the socioeconomic system and also from those people who benefit from the existing social order by dividing and weakening opposition to the nearly insupportable pressures the system puts on most people (Friedman, 1998a, b; Friedman et al., 2001).

Finally, to the extent that drug-related harm stems from basic social structures and processes, the highest-priority research and action should probably focus on social change and how to get it. This might include research on 'noncompliant elites and ruling classes' and how they can be induced or coerced into needed social changes (or, failing that, replaced). That is, the primary research focus should be on changing society rather than on changing drug users.

References

Albeda, R., & Tilly, C. (1997). (Eds.). *Glass ceilings and bottomless pits: women's work, women's poverty*. Boston: South End Press.

Armstrong, D. L., Barnett, E., Casper, M., & Wing, S. (1998). Community occupational structure medical and economic resources, and coronary mortality among US blacks and whites, 1980–1988. *Annals of Epidemiology 8*, 184–191.

Armstrong, D. L., & Castorina, J. (1998). Community occupational structure, basic services, and coronary mortality in Washington State, 1980–1994. *Annals of Epidemiology 8*, 370–377.

Becker, H. (1977). Knowledge, power and drug effects. In P. E. Rock (Ed.), *Drugs and politics* (pp. 167–190). Somerset, NJ: Transaction Books.

Bell, D. C., Carlson, J. W., & Richard, A. J. (1998). The social ecology of drug use: a factor analysis of an urban environment. *Substance Use and Misuse 33*, 2201–2217.

Berkman, L. F., & Kawachi, J. (2000). *Social epidemiology*. New York: Oxford.

Brenner, R. (1998). The economics of global turbulence. *New Left Review 229*, 1–264.

Brugal, M. T., Domingo-Salvany, A., Maguire, A., Cayla, J. A., Villalbi, J. R., & Hartnoll, R. (1999). A small area analysis estimating the prevalence of addiction to opioids in Barcelona, 1993. *Journal of Epidemiology and Community Health 53*, 488–494.

Casper, M., Wing, S., & Strogatz, D. (1991). Variation in the magnitude of black-white differences in stroke mortality by community occupational structure. *Journal of Epidemiology and Community Health 45*, 302–306.

Chambliss, W. (1999). *Power, politics and crime.* Boulder, CO: Longview Press.

Chein, I., Gerard, D. L., Lee, R. S., & Rosenfeld, E. (1964). *The road to H.* New York: Basic.

Diez-Roux, A. V., Nieto, F. J., Caulfield, L., Tyroler, H. A., Watson, R. L., & Szklo, M. (1999). Neighborhood differences in diet: The Atherosclerosis In Communities (ARIC) Study. *Journal of Epidemiology and Community Health 53*, 55–63.

Diez-Roux, A. V., Nieto, F. J., Muntaner, C., et al. (1997). Neighborhood environments and coronary heart disease: a multilevel analysis. *American Journal of Epidemiology 146*, 48–63.

Durkheim, E. (1982). *The rules of the sociological method.* New York: Free Press (W. D. Halls, Trans.).

Ebie, J. C., & Pela, O. A. (1981). Some sociocultural aspects of the problem of drug abuse in Nigeria. *Drug and Alcohol Dependence 8* (4), 301–306.

Elreedy, S., Krieger, N., Ryan, P. B., Sparrow, D., Weiss, S. T., & Hu, H. (1999). Relations between individual and neighborhood-based measures of socioeconomic position and bone lead concentrations among community-exposed men. *American Journal of Epidemiology 150*, 129–141.

Faris, R. E., & Dunham, H. W. (1939). *Mental disorders in urban areas.* Chicago: University of Chicago Press.

Fife, D., & Mode, C. (1992). AIDS incidence and income. *Journal of Acquired Immune Deficiency Syndrome 5*, 1105–1110.

Folbre, N. (1993a). *Who pays for the kids? Gender and the structures of constraint.* London: Routledge.

Friedman, S. R. (1991). Alienated labor and dignity denial in capitalist society. In B. Berberoglu (Ed.), *Critical perspectives in sociology* (pp. 83–91). Kendall/Hunt.

——. (1998a). The political economy of drug-user scapegoating—and the philosophy and politics of resistance. *Drugs: Education, Prevention and Policy 5* (1), 15–32.

——. (1998b). HIV-related politics in long-term perspective. *AIDS Care 10* (Supplement 2), S93–S103.

——. (1993b). *Women's work in the world economy.* New York: New York University Press.

Friedman, S. R., Curtis, R., Neaigus, A., Jose, B., & Des Jarlais, D. C. (1999). *Social networks, drug injectors' lives, and HIV/AIDS.* New York: Kluwer/Plenum.

Friedman, S. R., Friedmann, P., Telles, P., Bastos, F., Bueno, R., Mesquita, F., & Des Jarlais, D. C. (1998a). New injectors and HIV-1 risk. In G. V. Stimson, D. C. Des Jarlais, & A. L. Ball (Eds.), *Drug injecting and HIV infection: global dimensions and local responses* (pp. 76–90). London: UCL Press.

Friedman, S. R., Furst, R. T., Jose, B., Curtis, R., Neaigus, A., Des Jarlais, D. C., Goldstein, M., & Ildefonso, G. (1998b). Drug scene roles and HIV risk. *Addiction 93* (9), 1403–1416.

Friedman, S. R., Kang, S.-Y., Deren, S., Robles, R., Colón, H. M., Andia, J., Oliver-Velez, D., & Finlinson, A. (2002). Drug-scene roles and HIV risk among Puerto Rican injection drug users in East Harlem, New York City and Bayamón, Puerto Rico. *Journal of Psychoactive Drugs,* in press.

Friedman, S. R., Southwell, M., Bueno, R., Paone, D., Byrne, J., & Crofts, N. (2001). Harm reduction—a historical view from the left. *International Journal of Drug Policy 12*, 3–14.

Geschwender, J. (1978). *Racial stratification in America.* Dubuque, IA: William C. Brown.

Goldberg, G. S., & Kremen, E. (Eds.). (1990). *The feminization of poverty: only in America?* New York: Praeger.

Hu, D. J., Frey, R., Costa, S. J., Massey, J., Ryan, J., Fleming, P. L., D'Errico, S., Ward, J. W., & Buehler, J. (1994). Geographical AIDS rates and sociodemographic variables in the Newark, New Jersey, metropolitan area. *AIDS and Public Policy 9*, 20–25.

Kaplan, G. A., Pamuk, E. R., Lynch, J. W., Cohen, R. D., & Balfour, J. L. (1996). Inequality in income and mortality in the United States. *British Medical Journal 312*, 999–1003.

Kennedy, B. P., Kawachi, I., & Prothrow-Stith, D. (1996). Income distribution and mortality: cross-sectional ecological study of the Robin Hood index in the United States. *British Medical Journal 312*, 1004–1007.

Kleinschmidt, I., Hills, M., & Elliott, P. (1995). Smoking behaviour can be predicted by neighborhood deprivation measures. *Journal of Epidemiology and Community Health 49* (Suppl. 2), S72–S77.

Lynch, J. W., Kaplan, G. A., Pamuk, E., Cohen, R. D., Heck, K., Balfour, J. L., & Yen, I. H. (1998). Income inequality and mortality in metropolitan areas of the United States. *American Journal of Public Health 88*, 1074–1080.

Mills, C. W. (1940). Situated actions and vocabularies of motives. *American Sociological Review 5*, 904–913.

Mishel, L., Schmitt, J., & Bernstein, J. (1999). *The state of working America, 1998–1999.* Ithaca, NY: Cornell University Press.

Mongkolsirichaikul, D., Mokkhavesa, C., & Ratanabanangkoon, K. (1988). The incidence of amphetamine use among truck drivers from various regions of Thailand. *Journal of the Medical Association of Thailand 71* (9), 471–474.

Neaigus, A., Friedman, S. R., Curtis, D. C., Des Jarlais, D. C., et al. (1994). The relevance of drug injectors' social networks and risk networks for understanding and preventing HIV infection. *Social Science and Medicine 38* (1), 67–78.

Nurco, D. N. (1972). An ecological analysis of heroin addicts in Baltimore. *International Journal of the Addictions 7*, 341–353.

Nurco, D. N., Shaffer, J. W., & Cisin, I. H. (1984). An ecological analysis of the interrelationships among drug abuse and other indices of social pathology. *International Journal of the Addictions 19*, 441–451.

O'Campo, P., Xue, X., Wang, M. C., & O'Brien Caughy, M. (1997). Neighborhood risk factors for low birthweight in Baltimore: a multilevel analysis. *American Journal of Public Health 87*, 1113–1118.

Omi, M., & Winant, H. (1994). *Racial formation in the United States.* New York: Routledge.

Philpot, C. R., Harcourt, C. L., & Edwards, J. M. (1989). Drug use by prostitutes in Sydney. *British Journal of Addiction 84* (5), 499–505.

Redlinger, L. J., & Michel, J. B. (1970). Ecological variations in heroin abuse. *Sociological Quarterly 11*, 219–229.

Rhodes, T. (1996). Culture, drugs and unsafe sex: confusion about causation. *Addiction 91*, 753–758.

Roberts, R. E., & Lee, E. S. (1993). Occupation and the prevalence of major depression, alcohol, and drug abuse in the United States. *Environmental Research 61* (2), 266–278.

Ryan, W. (1976). *Blaming the victim.* New York: Random House.

Schiraldi, V., Holman, B., & Phillip, B. (2000). *Poor prescriptions: the cost of imprisoning drug offenders in the United States.* Washington, DC: Justice Policy Institute.

Simon, P. A., Hu, D. J., Diaz, T., & Kerndt, P. R. (1995). Income and AIDS rates in Los Angeles County. *AIDS 9* (3), 281–284.

Southgate, E., & Hopwood, M. (2001). The role of folk pharmacology and lay experts in harm reduction: Sydney gay drug using networks. *International Journal of Drug Policy 12*, 321–335.

Stimson, G. V. (1993). The global diffusion of injecting drug use: implications for human immunodeficiency virus infection. *Bulletin on Narcotics XLV* (1), 3–17.

Stimson, G. V., Ball, A., & Des Jarlais, D. C. (1998). *Drug injecting and HIV infection*. London: UCL Press.

Stratford, D., Ellerbrock, T. V., Akins, J. K., & Hall, H. L. (2000). Highway cowboys, old hands, and Christian truckers: risk behavior for human immunodeficiency virus infection among long-haul truckers in Florida. *Social Science and Medicine 50* (5), 737–749.

United Nations Development Programme. (1999). *Human development report 1999*. New York: Oxford.

Wallace, D., & Wallace, R. (1999). *A plague on your houses: how New York was burned down and national public health crumbled*. New York: Verso.

Watts, W. D., & Short, A. P. (1990). Teacher drug use: a response to occupational stress. *Journal of Drug Education 20* (1), 47–65.

Winnick, C. (1964). Physician narcotic addicts. In H. S. Becker (Ed.), *The other side: perspectives on deviance* (pp. 261–279). New York: The Free Press.

Zierler, S., & Krieger, N. (1997). Reframing women's risk: social inequalities and HIV infection. *Annual Review of Public Health 18*, 401–436.

Zinberg, N. E. (1984). *Drug, set and setting: the basis for controlled intoxicant use*. New Haven, CT: Yale University Press.

For Discussion

1. How is drug use attributable to social disorder? How could more egalitarian social, economic, and health policies help decrease the illegal drug market?

2. Do you think there is a link between occupation and the choice of drug? By extension, what kind of connection exists between being a student and engaging in substance use?

Reprinted from: Samuel Friedman "Sociopharmacology of Drug Use: Initial Thoughts." In *International Journal of Drug Policy*, 13, pp. 341–347. Copyright © 2002 by Elsevier Science B.V. Reprinted with permission. ◆

6

The Social Impact of Drugs and the War on Drugs

The Social Construction of Drug Scares*

Craig Reinarman

In this article, Craig Reinarman describes historical and contemporary drug scares in the United States. These scares, which have targeted opium, alcohol, LSD, and more recently crack cocaine, have much in common. According to the author, drug scares are created or constructed by powerful people who are threatened by the traits of people who use drugs. He links drug scares to racism and class bias. Drug scares, in turn, influence drug policy, so that policies are misguided. Reinarman suggests that drug scares occur far more often in the United States than elsewhere.

The CIA, the government, and the media in general have gotten away with the kind of shenanigans that you've heard about today, in my view, because of a carefully cultivated anti-drug hysteria. I want to tell you a little bit about that cultivation process. It's a good deal older history, but I think a crucial piece of the puzzle you're examining.

And I should just add that while it is my view that a war on drugs is not the most appropriate, effective, or humane form of drug policy, it is certainly the right metaphor. We have the Army, Navy, Air Force, Marines, Coast Guard, CIA, DEA, FBI, every state level and local police agency, and a network of secret informants, some of whom make up to $500,000 a year, fighting that war.

Drug wars, anti-drug crusades, and other periods of marked public concern about drugs are never merely reactions to the various troubles people can have with drugs. These drug scares are recurring cultural and political phenomena in their own right and must, therefore, be understood sociologically on their own terms. It is important to understand why people ingest drugs and why some of them develop problems that have something to do with having ingested them. But the premise of this testimony is that it is equally important to understand patterns of acute societal concern about drug use and drug problems. This seems especially so for U.S. society, which has had recurring anti-drug crusades and a history of repressive anti-drug laws.

Many well-intentioned drug policy reform efforts in the U.S. have come face to face with staid and stubborn sentiments against consciousness-altering substances. The repeated failures of such reform efforts cannot be explained solely in terms of ill-informed or manipulative leaders. Something deeper is involved, something woven into the very fabric of American culture, something which explains why claims that some drug is the cause of much of what is wrong with the world are believed so often by so many. The origins and nature of the appeal of anti-drug claims must be confronted if we are ever to understand how "drug problems" are constructed in the U.S. such that more enlightened and effective drug policies have been so difficult to achieve.

I want to summarize briefly some of the major periods of anti-drug sentiment in the U.S. and draw from them some of the basic ingredients of which drug scares and drug laws are made. I also want to offer a beginning interpretation of these scares and laws based on those broad features of American culture that make self-control continuously problematic.

Drug Scares and Drug Laws

What I have called drug scares have been a recurring feature of U.S. society for 200 years (Reinarman and Levine, 1989a). They are relatively autonomous from whatever drug-related problems exist or are said to exist.[1] I call them "scares" because, like Red Scares, they are a form of moral panic ideologically constructed so as to construe one or another chemical bogeyman, à la "communists," as the core cause of a wide array of pre-existing public problems.

The first and most significant drug scare was over drink. Temperance movement leaders constructed this scare beginning in the late 18th and early 19th century. It reached its formal end with the passage of Prohibition in 1919.[2] As Gusfield showed in his classic book *Symbolic Crusade* (1963), there was far more to the battle against booze than long-standing drinking problems. Temperance crusaders tended to be native born, middle-class, non-urban Protestants who felt threatened by the working-class, Catholic immigrants who were filling up America's cities during industrialization.[3] The latter were what Gusfield called "unrepentant deviants" in that they continued their long-standing drinking practices despite middle-class W.A.S.P. norms against them. The battle over booze was the terrain on which was fought a cornucopia of cultural conflicts, particularly over whose morality would be the dominant morality in America.

In the course of this century-long struggle, the often wild claims of Temperance leaders appealed to millions of middle-class people seeking explanations for the pressing social and economic problems of industrializing America. Many corporate supporters of Prohibition threw their financial and ideological weight behind the Anti-Saloon League and other Temperance and Prohibitionist groups because they felt that traditional working-class drinking practices interfered with the new rhythms of the factory, and thus with productivity and profits (Rumbarger, 1989). To the Temperance crusaders' fear of the barroom as a breeding ground of all sorts of tragic immorality, Prohibitionists added the idea of the saloon as an alien, subversive place where unionists organized and where leftists and anarchists found recruits (Levine, 1984).

This convergence of claims and interests rendered alcohol a scapegoat for most of the nation's poverty, crime, moral degeneracy, "broken" families, illegitimacy, unemployment, and personal and business failure problems whose sources lay in broader economic and political forces. This scare climaxed in the first two decades of the 20th century, a tumultuous period rife with class, racial, cultural, and political conflict brought on by the wrenching changes of industrialization, immigration, and urbanization (Levine, 1984; Levine and Reinarman, 1991).

America's first real drug law was San Francisco's anti-opium den ordinance of 1875. The context of the campaign for this law shared many features with the context of the Temperance movement. Opiates had long been widely and legally available without a prescription in hundreds of medicines (Brecher, 1972; Musto, 1973; Courtwright, 1982; cf. Baumohl, 1992), so neither opiate use nor addiction was really the issue. This campaign focused almost exclusively on what was called the "Mongolian vice" of opium smoking by Chinese immigrants (and white "fellow travelers") in dens (Baumohl, 1992). Chinese immigrants came to California as "coolie" labor to build the railroad and dig the gold mines. A small minority of them brought along the practice of smoking opium—a practice originally brought to China by British and American traders in the 19th century. When the railroad was completed and the gold dried up a decade-long depression ensued. In a tight labor market, Chinese immigrants were a target. The white Workingman's Party fomented racial hatred of the low-wage "coolies" with whom they now had to compete for work. The first law against opium smoking was only one of many laws enacted to harass and control Chinese workers (Morgan, 1978).

By calling attention to this broader political-economic context I don't want to slight the specifics of the local political-economic context. In addition to the Workingman's Party, downtown businessmen formed merchant associations and urban families formed improvement associations, both of which fought for more than two decades to reduce the impact of San Francisco's vice districts on the order and health of the central business district and on family neighborhoods (Baumohl, 1992).

In this sense, the anti-opium den ordinance was not the clear and direct result of a sudden drug scare alone. The law was passed against a specific form of drug use engaged in by a disreputable group that had come to be seen as threatening in lean economic times. But it passed easily because this new threat was understood against the broader historical backdrop of long-standing local concerns about various vices as threats to public health, public morals, and public order. Moreover, the focus of attention [was on] dens where it was suspected that whites came into intimate contact with "filthy, idolatrous" Chinese (see Baumohl, 1992). Some local law enforcement leaders, for example, complained that Chinese men were using this vice to seduce white women into sexual slavery (Morgan, 1978). Whatever the hazards of opium smoking, its initial criminalization in San Francisco had to do with both a general context of recession, class conflict, and racism, and with specific local interests in the control of vice and the prevention of miscegenation.

A nationwide scare focusing on opiates and cocaine began in the early 20th century. These drugs had been widely used for years, but were first criminalized when the addict population began to shift from predominantly white, middle-aged women to young, working-class, males, African Americans in particular. This scare led to the Harrison Narcotics Act of 1914, the first federal anti-drug law (see Duster, 1970).

Many different moral entrepreneurs guided its passage over a six-year campaign: State Department diplomats seeking a drug treaty as a means of expanding trade with China, trade which they felt was crucial for pulling the economy out of recession; the medical and pharmaceutical professions whose interests were threatened by self-medication with unregulated proprietary tonics, many of which contained cocaine or opiates; reformers seeking to control what they saw as the deviance of immigrants and Southern African Americans who were migrating off the farms; and a pliant press which routinely linked drug use with prostitutes, criminals, transient workers (e.g., the Wobblies), and African Americans (Musto, 1973). In order to gain the support of Southern Congressmen for a new federal law that might infringe on "states' rights," State De-

partment officials and other crusaders repeatedly spread unsubstantiated suspicions, repeated in the press, that, e.g., cocaine induced African American men to rape white women (Musto, 1973: 6–10, 67). In short, there was more to this drug scare, too, than mere drug problems.

In the Great Depression, Harry Anslinger of the Federal Narcotics Bureau pushed Congress for a federal law against marijuana. He claimed it was a "killer weed" and he spread stories to the press suggesting that it induced violence especially among Mexican-Americans. Although there was no evidence that marijuana was widely used, much less that it had any untoward effects, his crusade resulted in its criminalization in 1937—and not incidentally, a turnaround in his Bureau's fiscal fortunes (Dickson, 1968). In this case, a new drug law was put in place by a militant moral-bureaucratic entrepreneur who played on racial fears and manipulated a press willing to repeat even his most absurd claims in a context of class conflict during the Depression (Becker, 1963). While there was not a marked scare at the time, Anslinger's claims were never contested in Congress because they played upon racial fears and widely held Victorian values against taking drugs solely for pleasure.

In the drug scare of the 1960s, political and moral leaders somehow reconceptualized this same "killer weed" as the "drop out drug" that was leading America's youth to rebellion and ruin (Himmelstein, 1983). Biomedical scientists also published uncontrolled, retrospective studies of very small numbers of cases suggesting that, in addition to poisoning the minds and morals of youth, LSD produced broken chromosomes and thus genetic damage (Cohen et al., 1967). These studies were soon shown to be seriously misleading if not meaningless (Tijo et al., 1969), but not before the press, politicians, the medical profession, and the National Institute of Mental Health used them to promote a scare (Weil, 1972: 44–46).

I believe that the reason even supposedly hard-headed scientists were drawn into such propaganda was that dominant groups felt the country was at war and not merely with Vietnam. In this scare, there was not so much a "dangerous class" or threatening racial group as multi-faceted political and cultural conflict, particularly between generations, which gave rise to the perception that middle-class youth who rejected conventional values were a dangerous threat.[4] This scare resulted in the Comprehensive Drug Abuse Control Act of 1970, which criminalized more forms of drug use and subjected users to harsher penalties.

Most recently we have seen the crack scare, which began in earnest not when the prevalence of cocaine use quadrupled in the late 1970s, nor even when thousands of users began to smoke it in the more potent and dangerous form of freebase. In fact, when this scare was launched, crack was unknown outside of a few neighborhoods in a handful of major cities (Reinarman and Levine, 1989a) and the prevalence of illicit drug use had been dropping for several years (National Institute on Drug Use, 1990). This most recent scare instead began in 1986 when freebase cocaine was renamed crack (or "rock") and sold in pre-cooked, inexpensive units on ghetto street corners (Reinarman and Levine, 1989b). Once politicians and the media linked this new form of cocaine use to the inner-city, minority poor, a new drug scare was underway and the solution became more prison cells rather than more treatment slots.

The same sorts of wild claims and Draconian policy proposals of Temperance and Prohibition leaders re-surfaced in the crack scare. Politicians have so outdone each other in getting "tough on drugs" that each year since crack came on the scene in 1986 they have passed more repressive laws providing billions more for law enforcement, longer sentences, and more drug offenses punishable by death. One result is that the U.S. now has more people in prison than any industrialized nation in the world—about half of them for drug offenses, the majority of whom are racial minorities. In each of these periods more repressive drug laws were passed on the grounds that they would reduce drug use and drug problems. I have found no evidence that any scare actually accomplished those ends, but they did greatly expand the quantity and quality of social control, particularly over subordinate groups perceived as dangerous or threatening. Reading across these historical episodes one can abstract a recipe for drug scares and repressive drug laws that contains the following seven ingredients:

1. ***A Kernel of Truth:*** Humans have ingested fermented beverages at least since human civilization moved from hunting and gathering to primitive agriculture thousands of years ago (Levine, forthcoming). The pharmacopia has expanded exponentially since then. So, in virtually all cultures and historical epochs, there has been sufficient ingestion of consciousness-altering chemicals to provide some basis for some people to claim that it is a problem.

2. ***Media Magnification:*** In each of the episodes I have summarized and many others, the mass media has engaged in what I call the routinization of caricature—rhetorically re-crafting worst cases into typical cases and the episodic into the epidemic. The media dramatize drug problems, as they do other problems, in the course of their routine news-generating and sales-promoting procedures (see Brecher, 1972: 321–34; Reinarman and Duskin, 1992; and Molotch and Lester, 1974).

3. ***Politico-Moral Entrepreneurs:*** I add the prefix "politico" to Becker's (1963) concept of moral entrepreneur in order to emphasize the fact that the most prominent and powerful moral entrepreneurs in drug scares are often political elites. Otherwise, I use the term just as he intended: to denote the enterprise, the work, of those who create (or enforce) a rule against what they see as a social evil.[5]

In the history of drug problems in the U.S., these entrepreneurs call attention to drug using behavior and define it as a threat about which "something must be done." They also serve as the media's primary source of sound bites on the dangers of this or that drug. In all the scares I have noted, these entrepreneurs had interests of their own (often financial) which had little to do with drugs. Political elites typically find drugs a functional demon in that (like 'outside agitators") drugs allow them to deflect attention from other, more systemic sources of public problems for which they would otherwise have to take some responsibility. Unlike almost every other political issue, however, to be "tough on drugs" in American political culture allows a leader to take a firm stand without risking votes or campaign contributions.

4. ***Professional Interest Groups:*** In each drug scare and during the passage of each drug law, various professional interests contended over what Gusfield (1981: 10–15) calls the "ownership" of drug problems—"the ability to create and influence the public definition of drug problem" (1981: 10), and thus to define what should be done about it. These groups have included industrialists, churches, the American Medical Association, the American Pharmaceutical Association, various law enforcement agencies, scientists, and most recently the treatment industry and groups of those former addicts converted to disease ideology.[6] These groups claim for themselves, by virtue of their specialized forms of knowledge, the legitimacy and authority to name what is wrong and to prescribe the solution, usually garnering resources as a result.

5. ***Historical Context of Conflict:*** This trinity of media, moral entrepreneurs, and professional interests typically interact in such a way as to inflate the extant "kernel of truth" about drug use. But this interaction does not by itself give rise to drug scares or drug laws without underlying conflicts which make drugs into functional villains. Although Temperance crusaders persuaded millions to pledge abstinence, they campaigned for years without achieving alcohol control laws. However, in the tumultuous period leading up to Prohibition, there were revolutions in Russia and Mexico, World War I, massive immigration and impoverishment, and socialist, anarchist, and labor movements, to say nothing of increases in routine problems such as crime. I submit that all this conflict

made for a level of cultural anxiety that provided fertile ideological soil for Prohibition. In each of the other scares, similiar conflicts—economic, political, cultural, class, racial, or a combination—provided a context in which claims makers could viably construe certain classes of drug users as a threat.

6. ***Linking a Form of Drug Use to a "Dangerous Class":*** Drug scares are never about drugs per se, because drugs are inanimate objects without social consequences until they are ingested by humans. Rather, drug scares are about the use of a drug by particular groups of people who are, typically, already perceived by powerful groups as some kind of threat (see Duster, 1970; Himmelstein, 1978). It was not so much alcohol problems per se that most animated the drive for Prohibition but the behavior and morality of what dominant groups saw as the "dangerous class" or urban, immigrant, Catholic, working-class drinkers (Gusfield, 1963; Rumbarger, 1989).[6] It was Chinese opium smoking dens, not the more widespread use of other opiates, that prompted California's first drug law in the 1870s. It was only when smokable cocaine found its way to the African American and Latino underclass that it made headlines and prompted calls for a drug war. In each case, politico-moral entrepreneurs were able to construct a "drug problem" by linking a substance to a group of users perceived by the powerful as disreputable, dangerous, or otherwise threatening.

7. ***Scapegoating a Drug for a Wide Array of Public Problems:*** The final ingredient is scapegoating, i.e., blaming a drug or its alleged effects on a group of its users for a variety of pre-existing social ills that are typically only indirectly associated with it. Scapegoating may be the most crucial element because it gives great explanatory power and thus broader resonance to claims about the horrors of drugs (particularly in the conflictual historical contexts in which drug scares tend to occur).

Scapegoating was abundant in each of the cases noted above. To listen to Temperance crusaders, for example, one might have believed that without alcohol use, America would be a land of infinite economic progress with no poverty, crime, mental illness, or even sex outside marriage. To listen to leaders of organized medicine and the government in the 1960s, one might have surmised that without marijuana and LSD there would have been neither conflict between youth and their parents nor opposition to the Vietnam War. And to believe politicians and the media in the past six years is to believe that without the scourge of crack the inner cities and the so-called underclass would, if not disappear, at least be far less scarred by poverty, violence, and crime. There is no historical evidence supporting any of this.

In short, drugs are richly functional scapegoats. They provide elites with fig leaves to place over unsightly social ills that are endemic to the social system over which they preside. And they provide the public with a restricted aperture of attribution in which only a chemical bogeyman or the lone deviants who ingest it are seen as the cause of a cornucopia of complex problems.

Toward a Culturally-Specific Theory of Drug Scares

Various forms of drug use have been and are widespread in almost all societies comparable to ours. A few of them have experienced limited drug scares, usually around alcohol decades ago. However, drug scares have been far less common in other societies, and never as virulent as they have been in the U.S. (Brecher, 1972; Levine, 1992; MacAndrew and Edgerton, 1969). There has never been a time or place in human history without drunkenness, for example. But in most times and places, drunkenness has not been nearly as problematic as it has been in the U.S. since the late 18th century (Levine, forthcoming). Moreover, in comparable industrial democracies, drug laws are generally less repressive. Why then do claims about the horrors of this consciousness-altering chemical have such unusual power in American culture?

Drug scares and other periods of acute public concern about drug use are not just discrete, unrelated episodes. There is a historical pattern in the U.S. that cannot be understood in terms of the moral values and perceptions of individual anti-drug crusaders alone. I have suggested that these crusaders have benefited in various ways from their crusades. For example, making claims about how a drug is damaging society can help elites increase the social control of groups perceived as threatening (Duster, 1970), establish one class's moral code as dominant (Gusfield, 1963), bolster a bureaucracy's sagging fiscal fortunes (Dickson, 1968), or mobilize voter support (Reinarman and Levine, 1989a,b). However, the recurring character of pharmaco-phobia in U.S. history suggests that there is something about our culture which makes citizens more vulnerable to anti-drug crusaders' attempts to demonize drugs. Thus, an answer to the question of America's unusual vulnerability to drug scares must address why the scapegoating of consciousness-altering substances regularly resonates with or appeals to substantial portions of the population.

There are three basic parts to my answer. The first is that claims about the evils of drugs are especially viable in American culture in part because they provide a welcome vocabulary of attribution (cf. Mills, 1940). Armed with "drugs" as a generic scapegoat, citizens gain the cognitive satisfaction of having a folk devil on which to blame a range of bizarre behaviors or other conditions they find troubling but difficult to explain in other terms. This much may be true of a number of other societies, but I hypothesize that this is particularly so in the U.S. because in our political culture individualistic explanations for problems are so much more common than social explanations.

Second, claims about the evils of drugs provide an especially serviceable vocabulary of attribution in the U.S., in part, because our society developed from a temperance culture (Levine, 1992). American society was forged in the fires of ascetic Protestantism and industrial capitalism, both of which demand self-control. U.S. society has long been characterized as the land of the individual "self-made man." In such a land, self-control has had extraordinary importance. For the middle-class Protestants who settled, defined, and still dominate the U.S., self-control was both central to religious world views and a characterological necessity for economic survival and success in the capitalist market (Weber, 1930 [1985]). With Levine (1992), I hypothesize that in a culture in which self-control is inordinately important, drug-induced altered states of consciousness are especially likely to be experienced as "loss of control," and thus to be inordinately feared.[7]

Drunkenness and other forms of drug use have, of course, been present everywhere in the industrialized world. But Temperance cultures tend to arise only when industrial capitalism unfolds upon a cultural terrain deeply imbued with the Protestant ethic.[8] This means that only the U.S., England, Canada, and parts of Scandinavia have Temperance cultures, the U.S. being the most extreme case.

Some might object that the influence of such a Temperance culture was strongest in the 19th and early 20th century and that its grip on the American zeitgeist has been loosened by the forces of modernity and now, many say, postmodernity. The third part of my answer, however, is that on the foundation of a Temperance culture, advanced capitalism has built a postmodern, mass consumption culture that exacerbates the problem of self-control in new ways.

Early in the 20th century, Henry Ford pioneered the idea that by raising wages he could simultaneously quell worker protests and increase market demand for mass-produced goods. This mass consumption strategy became central to modern American society and one of the reasons for our economic success (Marcuse, 1964; Aronowitz, 1973; Ewen, 1976; Bell, 1978). Our economy is now so fundamentally predicated upon mass consumption that theorists as diverse as Daniel Bell and Herbert Marcuse have observed that we live in a mass consumption culture. Bell (1978), for example, notes that while the Protestant work ethic and deferred gratification may still hold sway in the workplace, Madison Avenue, the media, and malls have inculcated a new indulgence ethic in the leisure sphere in which pleasure-seeking and immediate gratification reign.

Thus, our economy and society have come to depend upon the constant cultivation of new "needs," the production of new desires. Not only the hardware of social life such as food, clothing, and shelter but also the software of the self—excitement, entertainment, even eroticism—have become mass consumption commodities. This means that our society offers an increasing number of incentives for indulgence—more ways to lose self-control—and a decreasing number of countervailing reasons for retaining it.

In short, drug scares continue to occur in American society in part because people must constantly manage the contradiction between a Temperance culture that insists on self-control and a mass consumption culture which renders self-control continuously problematic. In addition to helping explain the recurrence of drug scares, I think this contradiction helps account for why in the last dozen years millions of Americans have joined 12-Step groups, more than 100 of which have nothing whatsoever to do with ingesting a drug (Reinarman, forthcoming). "Addiction," or the generalized loss of self-control, has become the metametaphor for a staggering array of human troubles. And, of course, we also seem to have a staggering array of politicians and other moral entrepreneurs who take advantage of such cultural contradictions to blame new chemical bogeymen for our society's ills.

Notes

1. In this regard, for example, Robin Room wisely observes "that we are living at a historic moment when the rate of (alcohol) dependence as a cognitive and existential experience is rising, although the rate of alcohol consumption and of heavy drinking is falling." He draws from this a more general hypothesis about "long waves" of drinking and societal reactions to them: "[I]n periods of increased questioning of drinking and heavy drinking, the trends in the two forms of dependence, psychological and physical, will tend to run in opposite directions. Conversely, in periods of "wetting" of sentiments, with the curve of alcohol consumption beginning to rise, we may expect the rate of physical dependence . . . to rise while the rate of dependence as a cognitive experience falls" (1991: 154).

2. I say "formal end" because Temperance ideology is not merely alive and well in the War on Drugs but is being applied to all manner of human troubles in the burgeoning 12-Step Movement (Reinarman, forthcoming).

3. From Jim Baumohl I have learned that while the Temperance movement attracted most of its supporters from these groups, it also found supporters among many others (e.g., labor, the Irish, Catholics, former drunkards, women), each of which had its own reading of and folded its own agenda into the movement.

4. This historical sketch of drug scares is obviously not exhaustive. Readers interested in other scares should see, e. g., Brecher's encyclopedic work, *Licit and Illicit Drugs* (1972), especially the chapter on glue sniffing, which illustrates how the media actually created a new drug problem by writing hysterical stories about it. There was also a PCP scare in the 1970s in which law enforcement officials claimed that the growing use of this horse tranquilizer made a severe threat because it made users so violent and gave them such super-human strength that stun guns were necessary. This, too, turned out to be unfounded and the "angel dust" scare was short-lived (see Feldman et al., 1979). The best analysis of how new drugs themselves can lead to panic reactions among users is Becker (1967).

5. Becker wisely warns against the "one-sided view" that sees such crusaders as merely imposing their morality on others. Moral entrepreneurs, he notes, do operate "with an absolute ethic," are "fervent and righteous," and will use "any means" necessary to "do away with" what they see as "totally evil." However, they also "typically believe that their mission is a holy one," that if people do what they want it "will be good for them." Thus, in the case of abolitionists, the crusades of moral entrepreneurs often "have strong humanitarian overtones" (1963: 147–8). This is no less true for those whose moral enterprise promotes drug scares. My analysis, however, concerns the character and consequences of their efforts, not their motives.

6. As Gusfield notes, such ownership sometimes shifts over time, e.g., with alcohol problems, from religion to criminal law to medical science. With other drug problems, the shift in ownership has been away from medical science toward criminal law. The most insightful treatment of the medicalization of alcohol/drug problems is Peele (1989).

7. See Baumohl's (1990) important and erudite analysis of how the human will was valorized in the therapeutic temperance thought of 19th-century inebriate homes.

8. The third central feature of Temperance cultures identified by Levine (1992), which I will not dwell on, is predominance of spirits drinking, i.e., more concentrated alcohol than wine or beer and thus greater likelihood of drunkenness.

Source Note

*This testimony adapted from Reinerman's article in P. and P. Adler, eds., "The Social Construction of Drug Scares," *Constructions of Deviance: Social Power, Context, and Interaction*, (Wadsworth Publishing Co., 1994), pp. 92–103.

Sources

Aronowitz, Stanley, *False Promises: The Shaping of American Working Class Consciousness*, (New York: McGraw-Hill, 1973).

Baumohl, Jim, "Inebriate Institutions in North America, 1840–1920," *British Journal of Addiction* 85: 1187–1204, (1990).

——, "The 'Dope Fiend's Paradise' Revisited: Notes from Research in Progress on Drug Law Enforcement in San Francisco, 1875–1915," *Drinking and Drug Practices Surveyor* 24: 3–12, (1992).

Becker, Howard S., "History, Culture, and Subjective Experiences: An Exploration of the of the Social Bases of Drug-Induced Experiences," *Journal of Health and Social Behavior* 8: 162–176, (1967).

Bell, Daniel, *The Cultural Contradictions of Capitalism*, (New York: Basic Books, 1978).

Brecher, Edward M., *Licit and Illicit Drugs*, (Boston: Little Brown, 1972).

Cohen, M. M., K. Hirshorn, and W. A. Frosch, "In Vivo and in Vitro Chromosomal Damage Induced by LSD-25," *New England Journal of Medicine* 227: 1043, (1967).

Courtwright, David, *Dark Paradise: Opiate Addiction in America Before 1940*, (Cambridge, MA: Harvard University Press, 1982).

Dickson, Donald, "Bureaucracy and Morality," *Social Problems* 16: 142–156, (1968).

Duster, Troy, *The Legislation of Morality: Law, Drugs, and Moral Judgment*, (New York: Free Press, 1970).

Ewen, Stuart, *Captains of Consciousness: Advertising and the Social Roots of Consumer Culture*, (New York: McGraw-Hill, 1976).

Feldman, Harvey W., Michael H. Agar, and George M. Beschner, *Angel Dust*, (Lexington, MA: Lexington Books, 1979).

Gusfield, Joseph R., *Symbolic Crusade: Status Politics and the American Temperance Movement*, (Urbana: University of Illinois Press, 1963).

——, *The Culture of Public Problems: Drinking-Driving and the Symbolic Order*, (Chicago: University of Chicago Press, 1981).

Himmelstein, Jerome, "Drug Politics Theory," *Journal of Drug Issues* 8, (1978).

——, *The Strange Career of Marijuana*, (Westport, CT: Greenwood Press, 1983).

Levine, Harry Gene, "The Alcohol Problem in America: From Temperance to Alcoholism," *British Journal of Addiction* 84: 109–119, (1984).

——, "Temperance Cultures: Concern About Alcohol Problems in Nordic and English-Speaking Cultures," in G. Edwards et al., Eds., *The Nature of Alcohol and Drug Related Problems* (New York: Oxford University Press, 1992).

——, *Drunkenness and Civilization*, (New York: Basic Books, forthcoming).

Levine, Harry Gene and Craig Reinarman, "From Prohibition to Regulation: Lessons from Alcohol Policy for Drug Policy," *Milbank Quarterly* 69: 461–494, (1991).

MacAndrew, Craig and Robert Edgerton, *Drunken Comportment*, (Chicago: Aldine, 1969).

Marcuse, Herbert, *One-Dimensional Man: Studies in the Ideology of Advanced Industrial Society*, (Boston: Beacon Press, 1964).

Mills, C. Wright, "Situated Actions and Vocabularies of Motive," *American Sociological Review*, 39: 101–112, (1974).

Moltoch, Harvey and Marilyn Lester, "News as Purposive Behavior: On the Strategic Uses of Routine Events, Accidents, and Scandals," *American Sociological Review*, 39: 101–112, (1974).

Morgan, Patricia, "The Legislation of Drug Law: Economic Crisis and Social Control," *Journal of Drug Issues*, 8: 53–62, (1978).

Musto, David, *The American Disease: Origins of Narcotic Control*, (New Haven, CT: Yale University Press, 1973).

National Institute on Drug Abuse, *National Household Survey on Drug Abuse: Main Findings 1990*, (Washington, DC: U.S. Department of Health and Human Services, 1990).

Peele, Stanton, *The Diseasing of America: Addiction Treatment Out of Control*, (Lexington, MA: Lexington Books, 1989).

Reinarman, Craig, "The 12-Step Movement and Advanced Capitalist Culture: Notes on the Politics of Self-Control in Postmodernity," in B. Epstein, R. Flacks, and M. Darnovsky, Eds., *Contemporary Social Movements and Cultural Politics*, (New York: Oxford University Press, forthcoming).

Reinarman, Craig and Ceres Duskin, "Dominant Ideology and Drugs in the Media," *International Journal on Drug Policy*, 3: 6–15, (1992).

Reinarman, Craig and Harry Gene Levine, "Crack in Context: Politics and the Media in the Making of a Drug Scare," *Contemporary Drug Problems*, 16: 535–577, (1989a).

——, "The Crack Attack: Politics and Media in America's Latest Drug Scare," in Joel Best, Ed., *Images of Issues: Typifying Contemporary Social Problems*, (New York: Aldine de Gruyter, 1989b), pp. 115–137.

Room, Robin G.W., "Cultural Changes in Drinking and Trends in Alcohol Problems Indicators: Recent U.S. Experience," in Walter B. Clark and Michael E. Hilton, Eds., *Alcohol in America: Drinking Practices and Problems*, (Albany: State University of New York Press, 1989), pp. 149–162.

Rumbarger, John J., *Profits, Power, and Prohibition: Alcohol Reform and the Industrializing of America, 1800–1930,* (Albany: State University of New York Press, 1989).

Tijo, J. H., W. N. Pahnke, and A. A. Kurland, "LSD and Chromosomes: A Controlled Experiment," *Journal of the American Medical Association* 210: 849, (1969).

Weber, Max, *The Protestant Ethic and the Spirit of Capitalism,* (London: Unwin, 1983 [1930]).

Weil, Andrew, *The Natural Mind,* (Boston: Houghton Mifflin, 1972).

For Discussion

1. What types of drug scares have occurred in the area where you reside? What role did the media play? What policies were enacted as a result?

2. Why do some people believe that drug scares are factual? What influences their opinions?

Part II

Alcohol and Tobacco

A major element in the American drug scene is the use and abuse of *legal* drugs—alcohol, tobacco, prescription stimulants and sedatives, anabolic steroids, and other substances as well—as a response to boredom, frustration, stress, and loneliness or, as in the case of steroids, for the enhancement of physical performance. Because these drugs are legal, they are potentially available to everyone, and the use of alcohol and tobacco is particularly widespread.

Alcohol is the most widely used drug in the United States. Estimates of people aged 12 and over who have used alcohol in their lifetime hover in the 80 to 85 percent range. Moreover, every year almost 120 million people from that same category (over 50 percent of the population) have at least one drink every month. Of that number, some 55 million people are what might be called "binge drinkers" (five or more drinks on the same occasion). These high numbers are even more telling when statistics on alcohol-related mortality are considered. More than 100,000 deaths each year are connected to alcohol consumption. Causes of these alcohol-related deaths run the gamut from drunk driving, homicide and suicide, and certain alcohol-related illnesses to 12 ailments solely attributable to alcohol abuse, such as alcoholic cirrhosis of the liver and alcohol dependence syndrome.

Although the majority of those who use alcohol are social recreational drinkers, problem drinking is widespread, and the costs of drinking are staggering—well in excess of $100 billion annually. Despite these costs, alcohol remains something of a social enigma. On the one hand, alcohol is the biggest killer drug in the United States; it causes more havoc, violence, damage, and death than all other drugs combined, legal *and* illegal. On the other hand, when used responsibly and in moderation, it can be a relatively safe and pleasant drug for the majority. In fact, there is evidence suggesting that when used regularly in small amounts, alcohol can even be healthful, reducing blood cholesterol.

The "problem" seems not to lie with alcohol per se but with its misuse. Because alcohol is legal, it is readily available to anyone deemed to be of age. Moreover, alcohol has had numerous roles—social, medical, and religious—in human cultures around the globe for thousands of years. For these reasons, many users fail to understand that it is a dangerous drug, with a high addiction potential and the prospect of severe physical harm through overuse.

While the use of alcohol in moderation may be beneficial to the body, such is not the case with tobacco. Consider the numbers:

- In 2005, almost 29 percent of men aged 12 and over in the United States reported having smoked cigarettes in the past month.

- For the same year, 23 percent of women aged 12 and over reported having smoked cigarettes in the past month. Together the figures represent 26 percent of the U.S. population aged 12 and over.

- Each year in the United States, there are more than 440,000 tobacco-related deaths, the great majority of which are from cardiovascular disease and lung cancer. However, a significant number of these deaths are among nonsmokers, the result of chronic inhalation of secondhand smoke.

- Eighty percent of all smokers began smoking before age 20, and the average age when smoking begins is 15.4 years.

Like alcohol, tobacco is something of a social enigma. Cigarette smoking is considered the most important preventable cause of death in the United States, yet cigarettes are one of the most heavily advertised products. Cigarette advertising themes typically associate smoking with high-style living, healthy activities, and economic, social, and professional success. And interestingly, cigarette advertising campaigns increasingly target women, minorities, and blue-collar workers—groups that account for an increasing proportion of the cigarette-smoking population.

If cigarettes were outlawed in the United States, there would be both costs and benefits. On the positive side, a ban on cigarettes would result in

- **Longer lives.** There is strong evidence supporting links between smoking and heart disease, lung cancer, and a shortened life span. A ban could reduce human suffering, lengthen life, and increase productivity.

- **Health care savings.** Studies suggest that the billions of dollars now spent each year on smoking-related diseases could be saved.

- **Less illness.** It is generally agreed that smokers are ill more often, and remain ill longer, than nonsmokers. A ban would reduce smoking-related absenteeism, saving companies billions of dollars each year.

- **Increased productivity.** Without cigarette breaks, smokers would gain a month's work each year.

- **Fewer fires.** The costs from smoking-related accidental fires are considerable, whether measured in lives, lost productivity, or property damage.

On the other hand, a ban on producing, manufacturing, using, and exporting tobacco products would result in numerous costs for the U.S. economy:

- **Job losses.** Farm sales of tobacco total $1 billion annually in North Carolina, accounting for more than a third of the tobacco grown in the United States. Tobacco product manufacturing is a $14.8 billion industry with a payroll of more than $500 million. A ban could devastate the state's economy.

- **Reduced tax revenues.** Every year, cigarette taxes generate approximately $15 to 20 billion in state and federal taxes. This revenue would vanish.

- **Reduced exports.** Even though its use has declined, tobacco still generates over one billion dollars in trade surplus annually.

- **Farm reductions.** Tobacco farming would disappear, and the potential for replacement crops is uncertain.

- **Reduced pension funds.** Because over 400,000 people die prematurely each year as a result of tobacco-related illnesses, they do not live long enough to collect all or part of their accumulated social security and other pension benefits. As such, reductions in the number of tobacco-related deaths would put considerable pressure on government and private pension funds.

Completely outlawing tobacco products is unlikely. It would be unworkable, and few Americans, smokers and nonsmokers alike, support the idea. In a 2003 Gallup poll, for example, 84 percent of the adult population (smokers and nonsmokers) felt that smoking should remain a legal, personal choice. Interestingly, however, in terms of smoking in the workplace, 97 percent felt that it should be banned, or at least limited to special smoking areas.

In the chapters that follow, the focus is on alcohol and tobacco.

Additional Readings

Brower, Aaron M. (2002). "Are College Students Alcoholics?" *Journal of American College Health*, 50: 253–255.

Furnas, J. C. (1965). *The Life and Times of the Late Demon Rum*. New York: Capricorn Books.

Goodman, Jordan. (1993). *Tobacco in History: The Cultures of Dependence*. London: Routledge.

Landman, Anne, Pamela M. Ling, and Stanton A. Glantz. (2002). "Tobacco Industry Youth Smoking Prevention Programs: Protecting the Industry and Hurting Tobacco Control." *American Journal of Public Health*, 92: 917–930.

Perkins, Wesley H. (2002). "Surveying the Damage: A Review of Research on Consequences of Alcohol Misuse in College Populations." *Journal of Studies on Alcohol*, suppl. 14: 91–100.

Yen, Karl L., Elizabeth Hechavarria, and Susan B. Bostwick. (2000). "Bidi Cigarettes: An Emerging Threat to Adolescent Health." *Archives of Pediatrics & Adolescent Medicine*, 154 (12): 1187–1189. ✦

7

A Brief History of Alcohol

Harvey A. Siegal
James A. Inciardi

Alcohol has had an enduring history. In the following essay, Harvey A. Siegal and James A. Inciardi contemplate the likely origins of alcohol use and its
early evolution. A number of interesting facts about
alcohol are also examined, including the different
kinds of alcohol, the meanings of "proof" and
"blood alcohol content," and how alcohol affects
the body.

The desire to temporarily alter how our
minds process the information brought by
our senses is perhaps one of the oldest and
most pervasive of humanity's wishes. In fact,
some researchers have suggested that the
need to do so is as powerful and permanent
as the in-born drives of self-preservation,
hunger, and security (Weil 1972). In its pursuit, people have, at various times and in various places, subjected their bodies to
beatings and mutilation, starvation and sensory deprivation; they have focused their
minds solely on a single object, or let consciousness expand without direction; and
they have often pursued a more direct route,
changing the brain's chemistry by ingesting
a chemical substance. Of all of these, the
chemical that has probably been used by
more of the earth's people in more places and
times is one of the by-products of a simple
organism's conversion of sugar and water
into energy. It is ethanol, or beverage alcohol. Each year, countless millions of people
experience, both positively and negatively,
the effects of this domesticated drug we call
alcohol.

More is known about alcohol than any
other drug; yet, how much more remains to
be learned staggers the imagination. Our experiences with this most familiar and comfortable of drugs could readily constitute a
social history of civilization. We've lauded
and vilified it. We've brought it into our most
important religious rituals and have included it as part of our significant rites-of-
passage. Conversely, we've discouraged its
use, even prohibited its manufacture and
sale by constitutional amendment. Wars
have been fought over it, and underworld
empires have been built on the proceeds
from its sales. It's been acclaimed as having
the power to comfort and cure and is held responsible for thousands of deaths each year,
billions of dollars in losses, and an incalcula-
ble amount of human suffering. All of us, in
some way, have been touched or influenced
by this drug, so let's take a brief look at its
history.

Early History

Like many significant inventions, the specifics of alcohol's discovery are not known.
We conjecture that it likely occurred during
the neolithic age. Perhaps someone left wild
berries, fruit, or even grapes in a vessel for a
few days. When they returned, airborne
yeasts had already begun fermenting the
mixture. The result—which we call "wine"—
undoubtedly proved to be more interesting
and enjoyable than the original fruit, and,
like other innovations, it did not take people
long to improve their invention.

As people settled into communities and
began cultivating plants and domesticating
animals instead of just simply hunting and
gathering their food, they found that a surplus often ensued. Surplus grains could also
be fermented once the starch in them—
which by itself would not ferment—could be
rendered into sugar. To accomplish this, as is
still done in parts of the world today, these
early agriculturists found that chewing the
grain somehow changes it into a fermentable mixture. We know now that the chemical responsible for this transformation—
ptyalin—is found naturally in saliva. Other
societies discovered that by allowing the
grain to germinate, then roasting the new

shoots, the fermentation process could be initiated. In this way, the beverage we know as "beer" came into being. People discovered that not only fruits, berries, and grains could be used to produce alcohol, but leaves, tubers, flowers, cacti, and even honey could be fermented as well.

These early concoctions (roughly designated as wines or beers), however, were limited in their alcoholic strength. As yeasts metabolize the sugar, carbon dioxide (which is what makes bread rise, wine bubble, or gives beer a head) and alcohol are released as by-products. When the alcoholic content of the mixture exceeded 11 percent or 12 percent the process slowed markedly; as it approached 14 percent, the yeasts were rendered inactive (i.e., killed), and the process of fermentation stopped entirely. In addition to the limitation imposed by the biology of the yeasts, the alcoholic content could be affected by the producers themselves. For example, including more sugar (or fermentable material) would increase the amount of alcohol that would be produced. Whether the producers were willing to allow the yeasts the time necessary to complete the fermentation process or were too eager to consume the brew to wait, this influenced its alcohol content.

It was not until the time of the Crusades that Europeans were able to consume alcoholic beverages more potent than beer or wine. The Crusaders returned from the Holy Lands having learned a process known as "distillation." To distill wine, it first would be heated. Because alcohol has a lower boiling point than water, it would vaporize first. Then, as this vapor cooled, it condensed back into liquid form. This distillate made a considerably more potent beverage. In fact, beverages of quadruple potency now became possible. These were known as "distilled spirits" or "liquors," referring to the essence of the wine.

Aqua Vitae: The Water of Life

What is this drug which has been called by some the "water of life"—*aqua vitae*, in scholastic Latin, or *ambrosia*, the nectar of the gods—and "the corrupter of youth" and the "devil's own brew" by others? Ethyl alcohol or ethanol (whose chemical formula is C_2H_5OH) is a clear, colorless liquid with little odor but a powerful burning taste. Ethanol is just one of many alcohols such as methyl (wood) and isopropyl (rubbing) alcohol. All others are poisonous and cannot be metabolized by the body.

In addition to ethanol and water, alcoholic beverages generally contain minute amounts of substances referred to as "congeners." Many of these chemicals are important to the flavor, appearance, and aroma of the beverage. Brandy, for example, is relatively rich in congeners while vodka contains relatively few. Alcoholic beverages differ in strength. Beer generally has an alcoholic content of 5 percent; malt liquors are slightly higher. Natural wine varies in alcoholic content between 6 percent and 14 percent. Fortified wines—i.e., those that have had additional alcohol added—contain between 17 percent and 20 percent alcohol. Liquor or spirits contain approximately 40 percent ethanol. The common designation of "proof" originated centuries ago in Britain as a test for the potency of a beverage. To accomplish this test, if gun powder saturated with alcohol burned upon ignition, this was taken as "proof" that the liquor was more than half pure alcohol. In the United States, proof is calculated as being roughly twice the proportion of ethanol by unit volume of beverage; for example, an 86-proof Scotch is 43 percent alcohol.

Although the relative strengths of the beverages differ, current standard portions that are consumed actually provide the same amount of ethanol to the drinker. For example, the same quantity of alcohol is consumed if someone drinks either a 12-ounce can or bottle of beer, a three- to four-ounce glass of wine, or a mixed drink made with one and one-half ounces (i.e., one shot) of distilled spirits. Thus, the claim that "I don't drink much alcohol, but I do drink a lot of beer" is simply not true.

Alcohol's Effects

Unlike most other foods, alcohol is absorbed directly into the bloodstream without digestion. A small amount passes directly through the stomach lining itself; most, however, progresses on to the small intestine, where it is almost entirely absorbed. The feeling of warmth that one experiences after taking a drink results from the irritating effect that alcohol has on the tissues of the mouth, esophagus (food-tube), and stomach. Alcohol does not become intoxicating until the blood carrying it reaches the brain. The rapidity with which this occurs is in large measure determined by the condition of the stomach. An empty stomach will facilitate the absorption of the alcohol, while a full stomach retards it. To some degree, the type of beverage consumed has an effect on absorption, as well. Beer, for example, contains food substances which tend to retard this absorption. Drinks which are noticeably carbonated—such as champagne—seem to "quickly go to one's head," since the carbon dioxide facilitates the passage of alcohol from the stomach to the small intestine.

Alcohol is held in the tissues of the body before it is broken down (i.e., metabolized), like any other food or chemical substance. The body metabolizes alcohol at a steady rate, with the individual being able to exercise virtually no control over the process. Therefore, a healthy man who weighs approximately 160 pounds, drinking no more than three-fourths of an ounce of distilled spirits every hour, could consume more than a pint in a day's time without experiencing any marked intoxication. If the same quantity was consumed over an hour or two, however, the person would be very drunk. Today, much research is directed at finding an "antidote" for alcohol: a chemical that would either break down the alcohol itself, or accelerate the body's metabolic process. Although several promising lines of research are under way, it will likely be many years before something is commercially available. Finally, the belief that black coffee (i.e., caffeine) is an "antidote" is without fact. What the caffeine does do, however, is to stimulate the drinker—the intoxicated person is still "drunk," but he or she may, after several cups of black coffee, feel more awake.

Ethanol is broken down (metabolized) by the liver. In experiments, animals have had their livers removed, and then were given ethyl alcohol. The alcohol remained, much like wood (methyl) alcohol, in their bodies without being metabolized and exhibited

the toxic effects—such as nerve damage—brought on by unpotable alcohols. How does this process work? The liver produces and holds the enzymes responsible for alcohol metabolism. Once in the liver, alcohol combines with its enzymes. Alcohol is initially transformed into acetaldehyde, a chemical considerably more toxic than alcohol. Almost instantaneously, other enzymes convert the acetaldehyde into acetic acid (the same compound that constitutes vinegar), an essentially innocuous substance. The acetic acid is then further metabolized into carbon dioxide and water. Interestingly, one of the treatment strategies for managing alcoholism employs this metabolic process itself. In it, disulfiram (Antabuse), a chemical which compromises the body's capacity to convert acetaldehyde to acetic acid, is used as an adversive agent. By itself, disulfiram has little effect on a patient who takes a daily dose of it. If alcohol is consumed while disulfiram remains in the body, the produced acetaldehyde collects quickly, much to the great discomfort of the drinker. The patient is warned of this unpleasant effect, and the consequent fear of it can help increase his or her motivation to abstain from alcohol.

Alcohol does have some nutritional value. The primitive brews and concoctions were probably richer in nutritional value, especially carbohydrates, vitamins, and minerals, than the highly refined beverages we consume today. Alcohol itself is a rich source of calories which are converted into energy and heat. An ounce of whiskey, for example, provides approximately 75 calories, the equivalent of a potato, an ear of corn, a slice of dark bread, or a serving of pasta. The caloric content of mixed drinks is greater, since the sweeteners of the mixer provide additional calories. These extra calories are, of course, fattening, if the drinker does not reduce his or her intake of other foods.

The fact that alcohol provides sufficient calories for subsistence provides an additional health hazard. Many heavy drinkers express a preference to "drink their meals." While alcohol does provide calories, other nutrients, such as proteins, vitamins, and minerals vital to health and well-being, are entirely lacking. These heavy drinkers often suffer from chronic malnutrition and vitamin-deficiency diseases. In fact, adult malnutrition apart from heavy drinking is extremely rare in the United States.

Alcohol exerts its most profound effects on the brain. The observable behavior produced by drinking is as much a result of the social situation in which a person drinks as it is the drinker's mood and expectations about what the drinking will do and the actual quantity of alcohol consumed. For example, after drinking the identical quantity and type of beverage, one might experience euphoria or depression, while another may feel full of energy or simply wish to sleep; or a drink found initially stimulating might encourage sleep. Pharmacologically, alcohol is a central nervous system depressant drug. Currently, neuroscientists are studying the operation of specific biochemical mechanisms, but some research has suggested that alcohol acts most directly on those portions of the brain which control sleep and wakefulness.

The amount of alcohol within a person is conventionally described as Blood Alcohol Content (B.A.C.). This measures the proportion of alcohol that might be found within an individual's bloodstream and can be assessed by analyzing body substances such as blood, breath, or urine. Although, as we mentioned, the effects vary by both drinking situation and the experience that the drinker has had, we can roughly expect to see some of the following occur. After two or three drinks in a short period of time, a person of about 160 lbs. will begin to feel the effects of the drug. These include feelings of euphoria, freeing of inhibitions, and perhaps impaired judgment. Such a person would have an approximate B.A.C. of 0.04 percent.

If our subject has another three drinks in a short period, his or her B.A.C. will elevate to around 0.1 percent. Now, besides affecting the higher centers of thought and judgment located in the cerebral cortex, the alcohol is beginning to act on the lower (more basic) motor areas of the brain. By law, in virtually all the states, this person would now be judged incapable of operating a motor vehicle and, if caught doing so, would be charged with Driving Under the Influence (DUI). The person would have some difficulty walking and appear to lurch somewhat; there would be noticeable decline in activities requiring fine hand-eye coordination; and one's speech would be somewhat slurred.

At higher concentrations of alcohol, from 0.2 percent B.A.C. and up (resulting from the consumption of at least 10 ounces of spirits), more of the central nervous system is affected. The drinker has difficulty coordinating even the simplest of movements and may need assistance to even walk. Emotionally, he or she appears very unstable and readily changes from rage to tears and then back again. At 0.40 percent to 0.50 percent B.A.C., alcohol depresses enough of the central nervous system's functions that the drinker may lapse into a coma. At concentrations of 0.60 percent B.A.C. and above, the most basic centers of the brain—those that govern respiration—are so suppressed that death may occur.

Alcohol and Health

Abusive drinking has a profoundly negative influence on virtually every one of the body's organ systems. This negative impact occurs directly through the irritating and inflaming properties the drug has, and indirectly as an effect of alcohol's metabolism by the liver. Further, like many other drugs, tolerance (both physiologic and psychologic) to alcohol occurs. As such, one needs to drink more to achieve the desired effects. Naturally, the more one drinks, the greater the (potential and actual) damage caused by alcohol.

Alcohol irritates the lining of the stomach, which in turn causes an increase in the amount of gastric juices secreted. These irritate, inflame, and ultimately can chemically abrade the stomach's lining, causing ulcers. Alcohol can damage the small intestine itself, compromising the organ's ability to absorb nutrients, especially vitamins. Other organs that are involved in the digestive process, such as the pancreas are damaged as well; adult-onset diabetes is typically linked to abusive drinking.

Because the liver is responsible for metabolizing the alcohol consumed, it is this organ which is most affected. Not only is the liver abused by the irritating and inflaming properties of alcohol, but, as it metabolizes the drug, proteins broadly described as "free fatty acids" are released. These settle throughout the liver and other internal organs, ultimately compromising their function by blocking blood and other vessels. The livers of alcohol abusers are characterized by fatty deposits, dead and dying tissues, and evidence of scarring. Ultimately, the organ may be so compromised that it fails entirely, and death follows.

Although there is support for the notion that very moderate alcoholic consumption—i.e., never more than two glasses of wine a day—has healthful benefits, heavy drinkers have increased rates of cardiovascular problems. Heart disease is more prevalent among this group—who are more likely to be heavy cigarette smokers as well—than the general population.

Chronic abuse of alcohol can have disastrous effects on the central nervous system. Alcohol is a tolerance-producing and ultimately addicting drug. For the addicted person, withdrawal distress can be life threatening. Longer term, permanent damage can include dementia, profound memory loss, the inability to learn, and impaired balance and coordination. Alcoholic people have higher rates of depression, suicide, and evidence of other mental illnesses.

Alcohol abuse is linked with automobile accidents, especially among adolescents. It is estimated that almost one-half of fatal crashes involve drinking. Other accidents, drownings, burns, and trauma are strongly associated with drinking. Drinking has been associated with violence, especially domestic violence and child abuse. Finally, when consumed by a pregnant woman, alcohol can cause profound damage to the fetus. Babies born suffering from fetal alcohol syndrome are less likely to survive, more likely to fail to thrive, and manifest both physiologic and psychologic developmental problems.

Alcohol, humanity's oldest domesticated drug, is also one of its greatest enemies. In the United States, we estimate that there are almost 10 million alcohol dependent or alcoholic people and perhaps twice that proportion of "problem drinkers." We estimate that each year alcohol abuse costs our nation well in excess of one hundred billion dollars in terms of loss, health care, and decreased productivity. We do pay a large personal and societal price for this chemical comfort.

A Note on the Social History of Alcohol in the United States

Most societies have used alcohol medicinally, ritually, or recreationally. Colonial America was no exception. Beer and wine were made and universally consumed. Distilling grain into "ardent spirits" as a way of promoting the production, storage, and shipment of agricultural products was encouraged. Drunkenness seldom occurred in public and was reportedly not widespread. As the country moved from colonial to revolutionary America, the scene changed; towns grew and social-control mechanisms became more formal. Intoxication was reviled, and drunkenness was defined as a private weakness and a social ill. Thus, America's "drinking problem" began to emerge.

Shortly thereafter, the beginnings of a temperance movement appeared. Initially dominated by a New England aristocracy interested in maintaining the old social order, the movement was concerned about alcohol use at all levels of society. Calvinist temperance preachers expressed fear of the common man who, with drink, spoke profanely, engaged in infidelities, and did not work as he should. By the 1830s, the temperance movement had lost its aristocratic air and become more egalitarian (and middle class) with the inclusion of Methodist, Baptist, and Presbyterian preachers. From the Civil War until the 1890s, the movement attempted to sell the virtues of the well-regulated middle-class life to the working and lower classes. The message was simple: remain sober, work hard, and become a member of the middle class (Gusfield 1962).

At the forefront of the temperance movement in the late 1890s was the Women's Christian Temperance Union (WCTU) and its dynamic leader, Frances Willard. While leading the WCTU in its crusade to abolish drink, she was simultaneously involved in a variety of progressive social reform movements, ranging from women's suffrage to the labor unions' right to strike, to calls for universal childhood education. The WCTU, along with the Anti-Saloon League and the Methodists' Board of Temperance, spearheaded the drive that led to the passage of the Eighteenth Amendment to the U.S. Constitution. When ratified in 1920, the amendment prohibited the manufacture, sale, and transportation of intoxicating liquors (Gusfield 1962).

Prohibition was deemed successful, at first. Hospital admissions related to alcohol consumption—liver disease—declined as many people practiced abstinence. Nevertheless, heavy drinkers continued to drink, and a newly created crime—bootlegging—emerged and took hold. In fact, it is generally conceded that American organized crime was born out of the era of prohibition. By the early 1930s, abstinence was no longer the social norm. A movement to repeal the Eighteenth Amendment grew. Supporters of the repeal argued that the Eighteenth Amendment violated personal liberties, was in fact unenforceable, and created crime (R. W. Howland and T. W. Howland 1978). The noble experiment came to an end on December 5, 1933, when the Twenty-first Amendment repealed the Eighteenth. Although prohibition resulted in fewer alcohol-related illnesses, it was a miserable failure in almost every other aspect. Hoping to restore a moral order to America, its chief contribution was to foster crime and support a profound disrespect for the law.

The lessons learned from alcohol are both valuable and complex. There is, simultaneously, great good and danger in psychoactive drugs. The challenge to us all lies in learning as much about them as we can. If we choose to imbibe, we should do so in a responsible manner that will not endanger the health and well-being of others or ourselves.

References

Gusfield, J. R. (1962). "Status conflicts and the changing ideologies of the American temperance movement." In *Society, Culture, and Drinking Patterns*, D. J. Pittman and C. R. Snyder (eds.), New York: John Wiley and Sons.

Howland, R. W., and T. W. Howland. (1978). "200 years of drinking in the United States." In *Drinking: Alcohol and American Society—Issues and Current Research*, J. A. Ewing and B. A. Rouse (eds.), Chicago: Nelson-Hall.

Weil, A. (1972). *The Natural Mind*. Boston: Houghton Mifflin.

For Discussion

1. Compare the role of bars with the role of shooting galleries discussed in Chapter 18.

2. Review the health consequences of alcohol use. How is it that alcohol use has remained legal for most of the past century at a time when legislation sought to control the use of other drugs?

8

Gateway to Nowhere

How Alcohol Came to Be Scapegoated for Drug Abuse

Stanton Peele
Archie Brodsky

Stanton Peele and Archie Brodsky argue that some United States drug policies are guided by the assumption that alcohol, tobacco, and marijuana serve as "gateways" to "harder" substances, such as cocaine and heroin. Citing data that dispute the theoretical assumptions of the gateway theory, the authors provide critical commentary about the alleged cause-and-effect relationship between "soft" and "hard" substances. Moreover, the authors suggest that drug policies based on the gateway theory may in fact be counterproductive.

The "gateway" theory of drug use holds that exposure to "entry" drugs—notably alcohol, cigarettes, and marijuana—reliably predicts deeper and more severe drug involvements. U.S. drug czar Barry McCaffrey has incorporated the gateway theory as an integral part of the country's drug policy. However, although most heavier drug users undoubtedly were once lighter drug users, this association does not establish a causal connection. Few young people progress from lighter to heavier drug use; in fact, the dominant trend is for young people to reduce illicit drug use and to stabilize drinking with maturity. The gateway theory may actually be counterproductive if we consider that in non-temperance cultures that manage alcohol successfully, alcohol is generally introduced to young people at an early age. Other evidence suggests that moderate-drinking

and drug-using young people, even when such behavior is illegal, are better off psychologically and are more likely to make a successful transition to adulthood than abstainers. Overriding all such profiles of moderate and abusive users of drugs and alcohol are social-epidemiologic models which indicate that the best predictors of abusive substance use are social, family, and psychological depredations that occur independent of supposed gateway linkages.

The National Drug Control Strategy for 1997 unveiled by U.S. drug czar Gen. Barry R. McCaffrey (Office of National Drug Control Policy, 1997) adopts a "zero-tolerance" policy toward youthful alcohol, tobacco, and marijuana use. The strategy regards all of these as "gateway behaviors" leading to serious drug abuse. In support of this contention, the strategy cites a report by the Center on Addiction and Substance Abuse (CASA, 1994) entitled *Cigarettes, Alcohol, Marijuana: Gateways to Illicit Drug Use*. The CASA report has been widely influential, in part because CASA president Joseph A. Califano, Jr., is a former Secretary of the U.S. Department of Health, Education, and Welfare.

Califano and CASA relied on data from a 1991 government survey to show that both adolescents and adults who have used cigarettes, alcohol, and marijuana are hundreds of times more likely to use cocaine than those who have never used any of the three substances. Califano's conclusion: The most critical step in stamping out dangerous drug abuse is to prevent young people from embarking on the road to perdition through the gateway of smoking, drinking, or using marijuana.

According to *The National Drug Control Strategy*, "Drug policy must be based on science, not ideology." This pronouncement is belied by the document's uncritical reliance on the "gateway" concept, whose enthusiastic acceptance by public officials and agencies has not been accompanied by any real scientific scrutiny. For example, the findings of the annual national surveys of high-school student drug use conducted at the University of Michigan over the past two decades offer little support for the gateway theory; instead, they show historical fluctuations in drug use. No one has shown a consistent pattern of youthful alcohol, marijuana, and cigarette use trends that presages cocaine and heroin use trends (Zimmer and Morgan, 1997).

The 1996 survey results (Johnston et al., 1997) continued a recent mild upward trend in use of marijuana, but not other illegal drugs. Along with a slight upturn in marijuana use among high school seniors, tobacco use was also up, while "binge" drinking (five or more drinks at one time within the past two weeks) remained at roughly the same level (30 percent of high school seniors) in 1996. Although the incidence of such drinking is lower than the highs of over 40 percent in the late seventies and early eighties, this does not signify a lessening of overall alcohol excess among young Americans. Researchers at the Harvard School of Public Health have labeled 44 percent of U.S. college students as binge drinkers (50 percent of men had 5+ drinks, 39 percent of women had 4+ drinks) (Wechsler et al., 1994). What lies in store for these young people as they mature?

When young people get away from home by going to college, their binge drinking rises; in time, however, their drinking declines (as does their drug use) as they assume adult roles (Bachman et al., in press). Given that so many young people ultimately do moderate their drinking, why are we failing so badly with the prohibitionist alcohol-education message in which Gen. McCaffrey places such confidence? This failure has more than temporary consequences. Unfortunately, despite the overall drop-off from early problem drinking, a higher than average percentage of those who display unhealthy early drinking will develop adult drinking problems (Schulenberg et al., 1996).

The Reign of Ideology

It is not news that the government and government-related agencies want to prevent everyone from using illegal drugs and young people from sampling legal substances, such as alcohol, as well. As a part of this campaign, the Califano report marked a well-worn tendency to oversimplify complex matters and to tell people what they want and expect to hear. Remember that Robert L. DuPont, an anti-drug activist (he testifies, for example, on behalf of school systems seeking to implement drug tests), former White House drug chief, and the first director of the National Institute on Drug Abuse, was the first to popularize the gateway concept in 1985, with his book, *Getting Tough on Gateway Drugs: A Guide for the Family.*

Warnings against gateway or "stepping-stone" drugs are standard practice by educators, the media, and public-health advocates. These alarmist warnings fuel the War on Drugs in its most indiscriminate form. Hearing of the gateway theory, we may hesitate to teach teenage children to drink responsibly. We begin to fear that exposing them to mild, positive drinking will open the floodgate and sweep them into the crack house.

What makes far more sense is to acknowledge the obvious to children—that there is healthy and unhealthy drinking. Both research and common sense tell us that the young people least likely to drink disruptively are those who were introduced to alcohol by moderate-drinking parents, rather than being initiated into drinking by their peers. Vaillant (1983) found that young Italian-American men tracked from adolescence were only one-seventh as likely to become alcoholics in adulthood as neighboring Irish-Americans in Boston. Yet, it was the Italian-American families who introduced children to alcohol in a family context early in life, while the Irish-Americans urged children to abstain. Likewise, children who learn to drink wine at family social and religious ceremonies are not likely to be found taking crack on our city streets.

But reasonable souls who wouldn't mind having their kids learn in school that alcohol is a normal amenity of life for adults who can use it in moderation are out of luck, at least in the United States. Although Prohibition ended in the United States sixty years ago, only drug-education programs with an uncompromisingly prohibitionist message—even toward alcohol—can be federally funded. On Main Streets across America, billboards and banners proclaim to our young that "Alcohol Is a Liquid Drug." This announcement provides no useful guidance for coming to terms with a substance that is legal, and that most Americans currently use.

The gateway theory also leads to the coercive treatment of many adolescents. In his book *The Great Drug War*, Arnold Trebach (1987) described how 19-year-old Fred Collins was pressured into residential treatment at Straight Inc. in Florida. Confined for four months, Collins was subjected to constant surveillance and indoctrination, accompanied by sleep and food deprivation. Collins escaped, and a jury awarded him $220,000 from Straight. At the trial, Collins was shown to have occasionally indulged in beer and marijuana. But to many in the treatment community, this "proved" he was headed for the disaster of addiction.

Collins embodies the gateway model's credibility gap—the disparity between the image and the reality of mainstream youth who start down the supposed primrose path to chemical enslavement. He illustrates, too, the costs of trying to make the relatively benign reality conform to the malign image. Among these costs are needless grief for parents and children and money wasted on unnecessary or ineffective treatment. At the same time, frightening warnings that young people can plainly see are untrue lead most to dismiss useful and realistic messages about harmful alcohol or drug use. After all, today's college students, nearly half of whom are binge drinkers, have been shaped by years of anti-drug and anti-alcohol education programs.

A Misleading Oversimplification

The cause-and-effect relationships that Califano's report took to be self-evident are in fact the subject of much scholarly debate. As (New York) City University Medical School pharmacologist John Morgan and his colleagues (1993, p. 217) noted, "This gateway concept seems to resemble driving slowly and safely as a gateway to driving recklessly and unlawfully. The reckless driver has always driven carefully at some point. How often does careful driving proceed to recklessness and does the careful driving cause the recklessness?"

It is true that users of narcotics and cocaine typically smoke cigarettes, drink alcohol (often to excess), and use other drugs as well. That is hindsight; looking from the other direction, adolescents and young adults who have had some experience with tobacco, alcohol, and marijuana are somewhat more likely to try "hard" drugs as well. But these generalizations do not mean that "soft" drug use causes, or even predisposes, a young person to use "hard" drugs.

One of the most prominent gateway advocates is epidemiologist Denise Kandel of Columbia University. But Kandel (1989) takes pains to point out that most youths stop at some point on the progression to hard drugs. Even among those who misbehave with drugs and alcohol, most eventually stop using drugs and moderate their alcohol use. Few of the teenagers who drink, even with the problems this causes, will turn into chronic problem drinkers, let alone crackheads. What we really need to figure out is who those few are who progress to extreme drug use, and what distinguishes them from the majority who would never even consider passing through the gateway.

An Enduring Myth

For what is at best a shallow half-truth, the notion of an inexorable progression from tasting forbidden fruit to self-destruction has had a remarkably enduring appeal for Americans. Its roots lie in the nineteenth-century temperance movement's image of "the fatal glass of beer"—that first sip taken by the innocent farm boy in the sinful city. The Currier & Ives print "The Drunkard's Progress" was one of many temperance tales that began with a man tippling and ended in suicide or murder.

Although Prohibition's repeal discredited the idea that alcohol addicts any and every user, this magical potency was then transferred to narcotics. At the same time, marijuana was misclassified as a narcotic. When marijuana became a staple on college campuses in the 1960s and 1970s, however, this myth also had to be discarded. But marijuana continued to be demonized—only now as a stepping stone to heroin addiction. Eventually, alcohol and cigarettes were made additional stepping stones to drug addiction. Thus, we still see the shadow of "the fatal glass of beer" in the title of an article by Kandel and Yamaguchi (1993) in *The American Journal of Public Health*, "From Beer to Crack."

But this model of drug use succeeds little better than the temperance version. In the Harvard alcohol survey, seven in ten students drank in the last month. But according to a 1994 government survey, only 12 percent of 18–25-year-olds and 6 percent of 12–17-year-olds had taken marijuana during the past month, only 1 percent of 18–25-year-olds and 0.3 percent of 12–17-year-olds had taken cocaine, and far fewer had taken crack or heroin (National Household Survey on Drug Abuse, 1996). Based on such information, the stepping-stone theory had to be watered down into the notion of gateway drugs. In this view, alcohol and cigarettes—along with marijuana—don't guarantee, but only make it more likely, that some will use harder drugs.

But even this revision doesn't work. If a substantial segment of Americans have used marijuana for years without getting involved with other illegal drugs, then not only is the old stepping-stone theory a shibboleth, but so too the weaker gateway version. What is true of marijuana is even more true of alcohol, since such a large majority of Americans drink. And a study from the National Development and Research Institutes (Golub and Johnson, 1994) found that the relationship between alcohol use and more serious drug abuse has been *decreasing* during the past three decades.

Alcohol, which can be used in a variety of healthy and unhealthy ways, is just too mainstream to be connected reliably to drug use. This has been truer the more illicit drugs have been marginalized. Cultural myths die hard, but the fatal-glass myth has lingered particularly long. It is time to pull the plug on it. To do something about the destructive consequences of drug abuse, we need to jettison entirely our temperance mentality.

Easy Image, Hard Reality

The Califano report conjures up an "Invasion of the Body Snatchers" image of America, as beer and cigarettes steal the souls of innocent children. This latter-day "Demon Rum" scenario is just another case of looking for our keys under the street light rather than where we actually lost them. For the hard reality to which all research points is that some young people are more vulnerable to destructive habits than others. They are more vulnerable because of psychological maladjustment, family disruption, and economic and social deprivation. For example:

- Kandel (1989) identified depressive symptoms, parental drug use, and the lack of a close parent-child relationship as risk factors for progressing to more serious drug use.
- Sociologist Richard Clayton (1985) found that truancy was a strong prior predictor of cocaine use among high-school students *independent of any other substance use*.
- Grace Barnes (1987) of the New York State Division of Alcoholism and Alcohol Abuse found that children from broken homes were far more likely to use illicit drugs. However, single parents could overcome this risk by providing "appropriate levels of nurturance and control."

The focus should not be on gateway drugs but on the highly dysfunctional lives of adolescent drug abusers. Two UCLA psychologists, Michael Newcomb and Peter Bentler (1989), found that the most destructive teenage drug use occurred among youths whose lives were characterized by limited opportunities (often resulting from inner-city conditions), internal emotional distress, and unhappiness. Among those in the inner city, even when they were able to stop taking drugs, their lives in other respects (e.g., crime, early pregnancy) did not improve. UC Berkeley psychologists Jonathan Shedler and Jack Block (1990) actually found that young people who experimented with drugs were better adjusted than frequent users and abstainers. These researchers were also able to predict drug problems for teens based on psychological profiles constructed when the subjects were small children! More recently, Pape and Hammer (1996) found a similar pattern with respect to alcohol use by male adolescents in Norway: that those who got drunk for the first time at either a very early or a late age had elevated levels of psychological problems; those who first got drunk in mid-adolescence were most likely to develop normally.

The lives of young people at serious risk for drug abuse have been best described by the problem-behavior theory of University of Colorado psychologist Richard Jessor (1987). Jessor has shown that drug abuse is one of a cluster of problem behaviors that also include truancy, delinquency, unhealthy eating habits, excessive TV watching, reckless driving, and premature or reckless sexual behavior. These behaviors do not cause one another; rather, they are common manifestations of traumatized and aimless lives.

Looked at from the opposite direction, Donovan and Jessor (1985) find the risk of problem behavior is reduced by high self-esteem, a sense of personal control, placing a high value on health, and participation in constructive mainstream activities such as school and church. Jessor and his colleagues summed up some of these positive factors as "an orientation toward, commitment to, and involvement with the prevailing values, standards of behavior, and established institutions of American society" (Costa, Jessor, and Donovan, 1989, p. 842).

Direction for Policy

A drug policy based on the mechanistic "gateway" model is a policy badly in need of reconsideration. It should be replaced by one grounded in a real understanding of why people use and abuse drugs. After decades of continuous effort, we still face substantial drug use among young people, including periodic rises like that noted in the Michigan survey. Obviously, the ultimate solution for youthful drug abuse and much else ailing America is to strengthen personal values and family lives and to allow more people to buy into the American dream. But, while we struggle to achieve this elusive goal, we can try to do the following:

- Acknowledge the difference between exposure to drugs and drug abuse, and especially between controlled and destructive drinking.

- With those young people most at risk for becoming involved with drugs, warnings to avoid any use of drugs, alcohol, and cigarettes have thus far been futile. It is more useful to require (and help) them to take responsibility for their actions, to escape destructive situations, and to contribute to society.

No drug makes people use it or other drugs. The causes of drug abuse are life conditions that motivate people to act destructively toward themselves and others. Liberals identify these as social and economic circumstances involving a loss of opportunity and hope. Conservatives identify them as a breakdown of moral standards and public order. Either of these explanations has a lot more going for it than Demon Rum.

References

Bachman, J. G., Wadsworth, K. N., O'Malley, P. M., Johnston, L. D., and Schulenberg, J. E. (in press). *Smoking, Drinking and Drug Use in Young Adulthood: The Impacts of New Freedoms and Responsibilities*. Mahwah, NJ: Erlbaum.

Barnes, G. M., and Windle, M. (1987). "Family factors in adolescent alcohol and drug abuse," *Pediatrician* 14: 13–18.

Center on Addiction and Substance Abuse at Columbia University. (1994). *Cigarettes, Alcohol, Marijuana: Gateways to Illicit Drug Use*. New York: Author.

Clayton, R. R. (1985). "Cocaine use in the United States: In a blizzard or just being snowed?" In N. J. Kozel and E. H. Adams (eds.), *Cocaine Use in America: Epidemiologic and Clinical Perspectives*. Rockville, MD: National Institute on Drug Abuse, 8–34.

Costa, F. M., Jessor, R., and Donovan, J. E. (1989). "Value on health and adolescent conventionality: A construct validation of a new measure in Problem-Behavior Theory," *Journal of Applied Social Psychology* 19: 841–861.

Donovan, J. E., and Jessor, R. (1985). "Structure of problem behavior in adolescence and young adulthood," *Journal of Consulting and Clinical Psychology* 53: 890–904.

DuPont, R. L., Jr. (1985). *Getting Tough on Gateway Drugs: A Guide for the Family*. Washington, DC: American Psychiatric Press.

Golub, A., and Johnson, B. D. (1994). "The shifting importance of alcohol and marijuana as gateway substances among serious drug users," *Journal of Studies on Alcohol* 55: 607–614.

Jessor, R. (1987). "Problem-Behavior Theory, psychosocial development, and adolescent problem drinking," *British Journal of Addiction* 82: 331–342.

Johnston, L. D., O'Malley, P. M., and Bachman, J. G. (1997). *National Survey Results on Drug Use from the Monitoring the Future Study, 1975–1996*. Vol. I.—*Secondary School Students*. Rockville, MD: U.S. Department of Health and Human Services, National Institute on Drug Abuse.

Kandel, D. B. (1989). "Issues of sequencing of adolescent drug use and other problem behaviors." In B. Segal (ed.), *Perspectives on Adolescent Drug Use*. New York: Haworth, 55–76.

Kandel, D. B., and Yamaguchi, K. (1993). "From beer to crack: Developmental patterns of drug involvement," *American Journal of Public Health* 83: 851–855.

Morgan, J. R., Riley, D., and Chesher, G. B. (1993). "Cannabis: Legal reform, medicinal use and harm reduction." In N. Heather, A. Wodak, E. Nadelmann, and P. O'Hare (eds.), *Psychoactive Drugs and Harm Reduction*. London: Whurr, 211–229.

National Household Survey on Drug Abuse: Main Findings 1994. (1996). Rockville, MD: U.S. Department of Health and Human Services, Substance Abuse and Mental Health Services Administration.

Newcomb, M. D., and Bentler, P. M. (1989). "Substance use and abuse among children and teenagers," *American Psychologist* 44: 242–248.

Office of National Drug Control Policy. (1997). *The National Drug Control Strategy: 1997*. Washington, DC: Author.

Pape, H., and Hammer, T. (1996). "Sober adolescence—Predictor of psychological maladjustment in young adulthood?" *Scandinavian Journal of Psychology* 37: 362–377.

Schulenberg, J. E., O'Malley, P. M., Bachman, J. G., Wadsworth, K. N., and Johnston, L. D. (1996). "Getting drunk and growing up: Trajectories of frequent binge drinking during the transition to young adulthood," *Journal of Studies on Alcohol* 57: 289–304.

Shedler, J., and Block, J. (1990). "Adolescent drug use and psychological health," *American Psychologist* 45: 612–629.

Trebach, A. S. (1987). *The Great Drug War*. New York: Macmillan.

Vaillant, G. E. (1983). *The Natural History of Alcoholism: Causes, Patterns, and Paths to Recovery*. Cambridge, MA: Harvard University Press.

Wechsler, H., Davenport, A., Dowdall, G., Moeykens, B., and Castillo, S. (1994). "Health and behavioral consequences of binge drinking in college: A national survey of students at 140 campuses," *Journal of the American Medical Association* 272: 1672–1677.

Zimmer, L., and Morgan, J. P. (1997). *Marijuana Myths, Marijuana Facts*. New York: The Lindesmith Center.

For Discussion

1. What criteria can best differentiate between "soft" and "hard" drugs?

2. Is it possible that the "gateway theory" might serve the interests of public officials involved in the drug war? If so, how?

9

Drinking Like a Guy

Frequent Binge Drinking Among Undergraduate Women

Amy M. Young
Michele Morales
Sean Esteban McCabe
Carol J. Boyd
Hannah D'Arcy

In this article, Amy Young et al. use focus groups to explore perceptions of gender and alcohol use among female undergraduate students. Drinking patterns varied across four groups of respondents, as did "self-presentations" and initial interactions with other focus group members. The authors discuss various themes that emerged from the interviews. For example, some females perceived that drinking heavily made them more attractive to men. The authors conclude that drinking "like a guy" actually reinforces traditional views about gender and heterosexual relations.

Introduction

Binge drinking, defined as four alcoholic beverages in a sitting for women (five beverages for men), represents the most significant health risk behavior among college students today (Hingson et al., 2002; Perkins et al., 2002; Wechsler and Wuethrich, 2002). Binge drinking has serious ramifications for the lives of those who engage in this activity, in terms of academic impairment, blackouts, personal injuries, sexual harassment and assault, and impaired driving; and can have profound consequences for those who reside near binge drinkers in terms of property damage, fights and interpersonal vio-

lence, and noise disturbances (Perkins, 2002). Traditionally, male undergraduate students have been more likely than their female counterparts to engage in binge drinking (O'Malley and Johnston, 2002) and frequent binge drinking, defined as binge drinking three or more times in the last 2 weeks. However, recent assessments of college drinking have noted a pronounced increase in frequent binge drinking among female undergraduate students (Wechsler et al., 2002). The purpose of this investigation was to explore why there has been an increase in frequent binge drinking among college women.

While many background and personality characteristics contribute to alcohol consumption among college students (see Baer, 2002 for a review), it is widely accepted that there is an "alcohol rite of passage" that exists on college campuses (Schulenberg and Maggs, 2002; Wechsler and Wuethrich, 2002). "Heavy alcohol consumption" permeates practically every aspect of the undergraduate collegiate experience; there is a widespread belief among college students that it is acceptable, if not expected, that they will engage in excessive drinking during their college years. For many undergraduates, the term "partying" is synonymous with "alcohol consumption" with the social event being robbed of its purpose without the presence of alcohol (Ahuvia and Steinmetz, 1999). Given such a culture, it is not surprising that college students have had the highest rate of binge drinking since substance use rates have been monitored (Johnston et al., 2000).

Historically, male college students have been most involved in the drinking culture on their campuses; however, research based on large epidemiological studies suggests that with each new cohort of students that enters higher education, gender differences within this age group are diminishing. Whereas only 6% of college women drank more than once a week in the early 1950s (Straus and Bacon, 1953), by 2001, researchers estimated that two out of every five college women engaged in binge drinking (O'Malley and Johnson, 2002; Wechsler and Wuethrich, 2002). In Wechsler and colleagues' (Wechsler et al., 2002) analysis of data from the College Alcohol Study (CAS) spanning from 1993 to 2001, there was a striking increase in college women's drinking. While the rate of binge drinking for women did not change between these periods, the number of women abstainers and frequent binge drinkers increased, indicating a polarization of drinking patterns. Specifically, the rates of female frequent binge drinkers increased from 17.1% in 1993 to 20.9% in 2001. Coinciding with this increase in frequent binge drinking among college women, Wechsler and colleagues also found a rise in the percentage of college women who drank on 10 or more occasions in the past 30 days (12.3% to 16.8%) and the percentage of women who consume alcohol with the intention of getting drunk (35.6% to 42.4%). In conjunction, these findings suggest that the rate of college women's extreme drinking has increased dramatically over the past decade and may soon match the rate of college men's.

Changes in the rate of college women's drinking appear to coincide with changes in the nature of their drinking. Table 9.1 presents a summary of the research on gender differences in the reasons for drinking reported by college students. Since the current study focuses specifically on "heavy drinking" college women, we present research separately for "heavy drinking" students (when available) and for all students who consume alcohol (regardless of amount or frequency consumed). Studies that focused specifically on other subgroups of college drinkers (e.g., studies focusing on problem drinkers) were not included, since such findings are likely skewed and not informative of all "heavy drinking" college students (even though problem drinking students, for example, are commonly heavy drinkers).

Presented chronologically, the studies suggest that gender differences in the reasons for drinking appear to be diminishing. Research based on data collected in either the 1970s or the 1980s typically reveal[s] gender differences. For example, Moos, Moos, and Kulik (1976) found that "heavy drinking" female college students were more likely than their "light drinking" counterparts to report feeling lonely, angry, depressed, and restless; in contrast, no differ-

ence in affective states was reported for the "heavy drinking" men when compared to their "light drinking" counterparts. In a study of college students at 34 colleges and universities across New England, Wechsler and McFadden (1979) found that 20% of the college men reported "drinking to get drunk," in contrast to only 10% of the college women. Focusing on the subgroup from this sample who were heavy drinkers, Wechsler and Rohman (1981) reported that "heavy drinking" college men were more likely than "heavy drinking" college women to report "drinking to get drunk" (32% vs. 25.8%, respectively), but were less likely to report drinking to change emotional states, including "drinking to relax" (26.9% vs. 38.8%), "drinking to forget problems" (9.9% vs. 13.6%), and "drinking to reduce negative affect" (7.9% vs. 19.7%). Likewise, Klein (1992), examining data collected in 1987, found among all levels of drinkers that males were more likely than female drinkers to report various types of drinking motives. Klein associated this finding with the fact that college men are more likely than college women to consume alcohol in general; thus, it is not surprising that they would be more likely to endorse more drinking motives. The one exception to the trend of gender differences in drinking motives from studies based on 1970s and 1980s cohorts of college students is Perkins' (1997) study, which examined data collected on three cohorts of college students (1982, 1987, and 1991). For all three cohorts, no gender differences were found in stress-related drinking motives.

In contrast, though, research examining gender differences in drinking motives among samples collected during the 1990s reveal[s] similarities in the reasons for drinking among male and female college students. For example, Carey and Correia (1997) found no differences between male and female college students in the endorsement of either positive or negative drinking motives. Likewise, McCabe (2002) noted that men and women were just as likely to report "drinking to get drunk" and "drinking to reduce negative affect." Focusing specifically on "heavy drinking" college students, McCabe also reported that the strong association between "drinking to get drunk" and

Table 9.1

Gender Differences in Reasons for Drinking Among All Drinkers and Heavy Drinkers: Parameters and Processes

Author, year published, year of data collection[a]	Study participants	Instruments+	Results and Limitations	
			All drinkers	**Heavy drinkers**
Moos et al. (1976)	753 undergraduate students from a large, state university; 53% female	Single item adjectives regarding feelings		Heavy drinking females were more likely than their light drinking counterparts to report feeling lonely, angry at minor frustrations, depressed, and restless; *lack of standardized measures*
Wechsler and McFadden (1979); data collected in 1977	7,170 undergraduate students from 34 colleges and universities in New England; 55% female	Single item indicators of reasons for drinking	Gender differences present in endorsement of drinking to get drunk (10% of women versus 20% of men); *narrow range of drinking motives included*	
Wechsler and Rohman (1981)	Reports on a subgroup of sample reported in Wechsler and McFadden (1979) that are heavy drinkers (244 males & 68 females)	Single item indicators of reasons for drinking		Gender differences present in endorsement of various drinking motives, including drinking: to get drunk (m = 32.0%, f = 25.8%), to relax (m = 26.9%, f = 38.8%), to forget problems (m = 9.9%, f = 13.6%), to cheer up (m = 7.9%, f = 19.7%)
Ratliff and Burkhart (1984)	A sub-sample of 140 undergraduate students who represented the top and bottom quartile in terms of level of alcohol consumption; participants selected from larger sample of 663 students from a southern university; 50% female	RFDS; BDI; RSE		No gender differences in positive motives for drinking; men more likely than women to report negative or escapist reasons for drinking; no gender differences in affective distress

(continued on next page)

Table 9.1 (continued)

Gender Differences in Reasons for Drinking Among All Drinkers and Heavy Drinkers: Parameters and Processes

Author, year published, year of data collection[a]	Study participants	Instruments+	Results and Limitations		
			All drinkers	Heavy drinkers	
Klein (1992); data collected in 1987	526 undergraduate students from a midsized private Midwestern university; 42% female	23 single item indicators of drinking motivations	Males were more likely to endorse reasons for drinking than females (regardless of type of reason); *low response rate & did not use standardized measure of motives*	
Perkins (1997); data collected in 1982, 1987, 1991	Three cohorts of undergraduate students from a liberal arts college in New York State—1982 (n = 1,514), 1987 (n = 860), 1991 (n = 1,151)	Stress scale included 4 items pertaining to reduction of academic stress, to relieve anxieties, to forget disappointments, and for sense of well-being	No gender differences in the percentage reporting stress-motivated reasons for drinking for all three, cohorts; *narrow range of motivations for drinking examined*	
Carey and Correia (1997)	139 undergraduate students at a larger private university; 61% female	RFDS	No gender differences in the percentage endorsing positive or negative reasons for drinking; *small convenience sample*	
McCabe (2002); data collected in 1999	2,041 undergraduate students at a large Midwestern public university		No gender differences in the percentage endorsing drinking to get drunk or drinking to reduce negative affect; *narrow range of motivations for drinking examined*	The association between "drinking to get drunk" and binge drinking similar for both males and females; *narrow range of motivations for drinking examined*

[a]Year of data collection is absent if it was not included in article; + description of measure provided when a standardized instrument was not used or described in methods section; RFDS = Reasons for Drinking Scale (Farber et al., 1980); BDI = Beck Depression Inventory (Beck, 1967); RSE = Rosenburg Self Esteem Scale (Rosenburg, 1965).

binge drinking was just as prevalent for female "heavy drinking" students as for male "heavy drinking" students.

It is important to note, though, that these aforementioned changes in the rate of and reasons for college women's drinking may be culturally specific to American students. While males consistently have consumed more alcohol than females across all cultures and time periods, there is considerable variation in [the] degree to which males drink more than females, and such variation has been associated with how a particular culture within a given time period constructs appropriate drinking behaviors for males and females (Wilsnack et al., 2000; Wilsnack and Wilsnack, 1997). Thus, these changes in the drinking patterns of American female college students may be a function of historical changes in the symbolic meaning of drinking behaviors for American college students, that when enacted, serve as a gendered expression of "who one is" for both the performer and any observers. One might expect, though, that the drinking habits of male and female college students may be becoming more similar in cultures that have also witnessed a merging of gender roles (as with the United States).

Recent reports published in the popular press offer possible explanations for the rise in undergraduate women's binge drinking. According to these reports, the most recent generation of college women (i.e., enrolled the beginning of the 21st century) fully endorse equality in gender roles and believe that they should have full access to any opportunity offered to men, including the opportunity to engage in the "alcohol rite of passage" on college campuses (Morse and Bower, 2002; Ehrenreich, 2002). These changing beliefs about drinking and gender roles appear to coincide with the alcohol industry's marketing efforts to make alcohol consumption appealing to women by implying that women can obtain gender equality and power by "drinking like a guy" (Wilsnack, see Wechsler and Wuethrich, 2002, pp. 206).

Previous research documenting the association between traditional gender roles and drinking patterns among men and women lends support to the notion that the change in gender roles among the most recent generation of college students might affect their drinking. For men, drinking has been a means of expressing traditionally defined masculine behaviors, such as stamina, a willingness to take risks, and power (Driessen, 1992; McClelland, 1972; McDonald, 1994). Traditional gender roles for women, on the other hand, have been viewed as having a restraining effect on women's drinking. Women's "heavy drinking" has long had a negative stigma, with alcoholic women being viewed as promiscuous and abandoning their responsibilities as wife and mother (Blume, 1997; Sandmaier, 1980). Ethnography (Gefou-Madianou, 1992; McDonald, 1994) and cross-cultural studies (Wilsnack et al., 2000) indicate that the most pronounced gender differences in drinking patterns occur in societies with a strong observance of traditional gender roles. Thus, it may be that the most recent generation of American female college students does not feel confined by traditional gender roles and thus, confined by traditional norms for women's drinking. "Drinking like a guy" may mean that these women do not feel held back by the negative stigma traditionally associated with women's drinking; additionally or alternatively, it may mean that they are striving for the positive social rewards associated with men's drinking, such as having stamina, power, or control. Thus, the purpose of this exploratory study was to examine whether the notion of "drinking like a guy" holds particular resonance for the most recent generation of female college students, and if so, to explore why undergraduate women drink in this fashion.

Method

During March of 2003, focus groups were conducted with alcohol-consuming female undergraduate students. Focus group methods are often used as a follow-up to assist in interpreting survey results (Morgan, 1996). Advantages of focus groups include the unique potential to capture the social interaction between participants in a naturalistic setting, and to encourage participatory analysis of data as they emerge. Interactions between members were used as an additional source of data.

Participants were recruited from a list of respondents from the 2001 Student Life Survey (SLS), a biannual random sample survey of students at a large public university with approximately 24,000 undergraduate students. The 2001 SLS used a web-based data collection method and obtained an overall response rate of 69% for female participants. Additional information about the 2001 SLS data collection procedures and overall sample characteristics are available (McCabe, 2002).

There were 1,231 undergraduate women who participated in the web-based 2001 SLS. The demographic characteristics of this sub-sample are presented in Table 9.2, while Table 9.3 displays their level of alcohol consumption. The majority of the 1,231 undergraduate women were White (73%) and living in a house or apartment (48%) or residence halls (40%). Particularly noteworthy [are] the high rates of alcohol consumption among this sub-sample. For instance, 25% of the sample met the criteria for frequent binge drinking (engaged in binge drinking three or more times in last 2 weeks). Moreover, 26% reported that the average number of drinks per week was seven or more. Thus, this pool of potential participants for the focus groups demonstrated similarly high levels of alcohol consumption as the female participants of the 2001 College Alcohol Study (CAS).

Following approval from the university IRB for the present study, a list was generated of all first- and second-year female participants from the 2001 Student Life Survey who were willing to be recontacted for follow-up studies.[1] All potential participants for the focus groups were sent an e-mail explaining the purpose of the study, what their involvement would entail, and that they would be compensated with a $20 gift certificate for their participation. Those women who were interested in participating in the focus groups were instructed to contact the research team.

A phone screening was conducted with all students who were interested in focus group participation. Students were asked whether they were currently a student, their current

Table 9.2

Selected Demographic and Lifestyle Characteristics of the 1,231 Undergraduate Female Participants of the 2001 Student Life Survey

Ethnicity	
White	73%
Asian	13%
African American	5%
Hispanic	3%
Other/Refused	6%
Class year	
Freshman	25%
Sophomore	25%
Junior	28%
Senior	22%
Age	
18	14%
19	27%
20	29%
21	19%
22 or more	11%
Living arrangements	
Residence hall	40%
Sorority	8%
House or apartment	48%
Other	4%
Sorority affiliation	
None	82%
Member	18%
Sexual orientation	
Heterosexual	97%
Lesbian or bisexual	3%

living situation, current alcohol consumption (number of occasions drank during past year and month, number of times binge drank in past 2 weeks), and sorority affiliation.

Participants

Information from the phone screening was combined with the 2001 Student Life Survey data to generate lists of potential focus group participants based on drinking behaviors during early college years (freshman or sophomore years) and during later college years (junior or senior years). Four lists were created for nonsorority-affiliated women, including a Stable High group of women who were frequent binge drinkers (i.e., drank four or more drinks at least three times in a 2-week period) at both time peri-

Table 9.3

Drinking Behaviors of the 1,231 Undergraduate Female Participants of the 2001 Student Life Survey

Past year alcohol use
None.	11%
1 to 2 times.	10%
3 to 9 times.	17%
10 to 39 times.	36%
40 or more times	26%

Past month alcohol use
None	22%
1 to 2 times.	21%
3 to 9 times.	38%
10 or more times	19%

Past year # times drunk
None	26%
1 to 2 times.	16%
3 to 9 times.	22%
10 to 39 times.	25%
40 or more times	10%

Past month # times drunk
None	43%
1 to 2 times.	25%
3 to 9 times.	24%
10 or more times	8%

Binge drinking in past two weeks
None	47%
1 to 2 times.	29%
3 to 9 times.	18%
10 or more times	7%

Average drinks per week
None	35%
1 to 6	40%
7 to 20	24%
21 or more	2%

How high/buzzed usually get
Not at all.	12%
A little.	36%
Moderately.	45%
Very drunk/wasted	7%

Recent drinking behavior
No recent drinking	22%
Moderate drinking only	25%
Some binge drinking	29%
Frequent binge drinking.	25%

ods, a Stable Low group of women who were nonbinge drinkers (i.e., had not consumed four or more drinks in the past 2 weeks) at both time periods, a Decreasers group of women who were frequent binge drinkers in 2001 but were nonbinge or binge drinkers in 2003, and an Increasers group of women who were nonbinge or binge drinkers in 2001 but were frequent binge drinkers in 2003. While separate focus groups were intended for sorority- and nonsorority-affiliated women for a total of eight groups, unfortunately there were not enough sorority members to conduct multiple focus groups for each drinking pattern. Thus, there were four groups of each drinking pattern for the nonsorority women and one group of sorority-affiliated women with varying drinking patterns (although all sorority women were drinking at least moderate amounts of alcohol at both time points). Ten women were randomly selected from each of the five lists for focus group participation. Since eight women were "no shows," the final sample consisted of 10 women in the Stable Low group and eight women in each of the other four groups for a total of 42 women. The drinking patterns of the actual focus group participants are presented in Table 9.4.

Interestingly, the first and second authors who were conducting the focus groups both noted that the personalities and self-presentation of focus group participants were strikingly similar among women within a given group, yet distinct from the characteristics of the women of the other groups. Women in the Stable High group were notable for being gregarious, stylish, and "happy-go-lucky." For example, women in this group easily and quickly initiated conversations with each other while waiting for the focus group activities to begin. Moreover, group cohesion was easily established and the conversation was lighthearted and free-flowing from the start. Members of this group were also distinct in their self-presentation; they appeared more cosmopolitan than women of the other groups, with their dress and hairstyles reflecting the latest trends of large metropolitan cities of the United States (i.e., they were not necessarily *internationally* cosmopolitan). Also, women in this group were notably thinner than members of the other groups, which is particularly striking given the fact that women in this group consume more calories through alcoholic beverages than other groups (due to the initial group selection process). Not surprisingly, women in this group selected only noncaloric refreshments (e.g., water or diet soda) during the focus group. (By contrast, participants of other groups selected a wide range of the food and beverages that were provided during the focus groups.) In sum, women of the Stable High group gave the impression of the idealized version of young collegial women commonly portrayed by current popular culture in the United States: upbeat, sociable, and friendly; engaging yet not necessarily introspective nor deep; and stylish, trendy, and unrealistically thin.

Participants of the Stable Low group presented themselves in stark contrast to the Stable High group. The Stable Low group participants first appeared shy and slow to warm up to other members in the group. While waiting for the group to start, they did not initiate conversations with each other, but remained seated quietly. Although this group first appeared timid, it became apparent that they were not necessarily bashful. Once the focus group activities had started and a rapport among group members was established, the women did not appear socially ill at ease and were not afraid to express their opinions. When the women had a better sense of the other members of the focus group, the conversation was free-flowing and continuous. In contrast to the researchers' initial impression that these women were bashful or socially ill at ease, it became evident that these women were cautious, in terms of wanting and waiting to read the social context before joining the conversation. In addition to their initially reserved interaction style, women of this group also were distinguishable for their non-self-aggrandizing self-presentation; their dress and style was plain and inconspicuous. The women wore clothes that were comfortable, simple, and unadorned. In contrast to the Stable High group, the self-presentation and social interactions of the Stable Low group suggested that they did not feel compelled to attract attention to themselves nor need to be the focal point of the social group.

The remaining three focus groups, including the two groups whose drinking patterns changed over time as well as the sorority group containing women with varying drinking patterns, were indistinguishable

Table 9.4

Frequency for Number of Times Binge Frank in Past 2 Weeks for Focus Group Participants in 2001 and 2003

Focus group 2003	2001	
Stable high (n = 8)		
No binge drinking	—	—
Once	—	—
Twice	1	1
3–5 Times	4	5
6–9 Times	3	2
Stable low (n = 10)		
No binge drinking	10	10
Once	—	—
Twice	—	—
3–5 Times	—	—
6–9 Times	—	—
Decreasers (n = 8)		
No binge drinking	—	1
Once	—	6
Twice	1	1
3–5 Times	6	—
6–9 Times	1	—
Increasers (n = 8)		
No binge drinking	6	—
Once	2	—
Twice	—	2
3–5 Times	—	6
6–9 Times	—	—
Sorority (n = 8)		
No binge drinking	2	—
Once	—	6
Twice	4	6
3–5 Times	2	1
6–9 Times	—	—

from each other, but distinct from the two aforementioned groups. These characteristics and the self-presentation style of these groups fell between the Stable High and Stable Low groups. These women were generally friendly and socially at ease, but not as overflowing in their sociability nor as magnetic as the Stable High group. Moreover, members of these groups were less hesitant and cautious than the participants in the Stable Low group.

Data Collection and Analysis

The focus groups were led by the first author and assisted by the second author. Focus groups were conducted in the last week of March 2003 in a conference room that was purposefully selected to provide an atmosphere distinct from a classroom. Prior to the focus groups, participants were informed of the purpose of the study, what their participation would entail, and their option to decline participation at any point of the study. All participants signed a consent form prior to their participation.

Focus group discussions were prompted by formal, pre-established questions, in prompt follow-up questions to participants' comments, and three focus group activities designed to elicit information on drinking during college. The discussions lasted approximately 90 to 120 minutes and were audio-recorded and subsequently transcribed. Themes were identified independently by the first author and an additional member of the research team. Discussions among the two individual coders were used to develop uniformity in labeling themes that had been identified. Representative quotes were then extracted from the transcripts for each theme. This method of analysis is commonly used for focus group data (Krueger, 1994).

Findings reported here primarily center around one of these three focus group activities presented to participants. In this activity, participants were asked to read and respond to excerpts from the popular press articles that related the increase in college women's drinking to changes in gender roles and the relevance of "drinking like a guy" to the current generation of female college students (Morse and Bower, 2002). The excerpts from the article are provided in the Appendix section.

Results

The focus groups provide preliminary support to the idea that the increase in drinking among a sub-group of college women is due to changing gender roles and expectations for women. Before reviewing findings pertaining to college women and drinking, however, we discuss themes that emerged in the groups about men, masculinity, and competitive drinking, because these topics provide a critical context for understanding why women's drinking has increased.

College Men, Drinking Abilities, and Sexual Attraction

An unexpected theme to emerge from the focus groups was college men's attentiveness to their own and [others'] drinking capacity. A predominant theme in all discussions was the belief that male college students view the ability to drink large quantities of alcohol as a skill that was to be developed, honed, and used competitively to test one's manhood. College women, on the other hand, were perceived by group participants as being far less attentive to the ability to drink large quantities of alcohol. The following conversation among the Increasers group was a typical discussion of this topic.

Participant #1: . . . I feel like, like if I drink a lot and I don't seem that drunk, guys will notice more than girls will. Girls don't really comment on other girls drinking, like "oh wow you drink so much." Like guys are the ones who are like "Oh you're keeping up with me" or something.

Participant #2: They track it.

Participant #3: They do. Like before I started my ex-boyfriend whatever and we were drinking beers one night and he noticed that I finished my beer before him and I felt like he thought that his ego was shattered (laughter). And he got another one and he's like "OK, GO!" and we were drinking them, and I thought, "What are you doing?" I thought it was ridiculous. But I guess it was like a huge thing, like all of my guy friends always notice when I'm drinking or how much I'm drinking, and my girlfriends . . . like my best girlfriend, we never pay attention, it's not a big deal.

Moderator: And the others agree with that?

Participant #4: I agree with that.

Participant #5: It's an ego thing.

Participant #6: Yeah, I think boys pay attention.

Participant #4: I think they're impressed but it's also kind of intimidating too. Like if a girl drank 12 beers and didn't pass out or didn't get sick, they'd notice and think it was cool but also be a little bit I don't know . . .

Participant #3: Afraid?

Participant #4: Yeah, afraid.

Focus group participants also noted that college men were aware of and uncomfortable when someone was not drinking and would encourage alcohol consumption among nondrinkers. The following discussion among the Stable High group illustrates this point:

Participant #1: The guys are just . . . If you go with your guy friends and you're not drinking like I was at the bar on Saturday night and I was just drinking water, and I mean they're like, "Why aren't you drinking?" Out of everyone's mouth, "Why aren't you drinking? Why aren't you drinking? Why aren't you drinking?" So they are definitely . . . they are . . . it's like some discrepancy you know when your friend that's usually drinking with you isn't drinking like you kind of want to know what's wrong or something's going on. The guys are definitely not . . . I don't think they're that comfortable when that happens. You know, if you're their drinking buddy and you're not drinking they're going to feel weird about it. At first.

Participant #2: Yeah, I think guys push you more . . .

Participant #3: Yeah.

Participant #4: . . . around my guy friends but the girls I think will be more understandable [sic: understanding] when you're not drinking. The guys will just be pushing drinks in your face and it takes you a while to just be like "No, no, no." But girls will just back off and say OK.

While college men's attentiveness to drinking capacities may not be new to this generation of students, what appears to have changed is the fact these standards are now used to judge college women. In all of the groups, women spoke about how male college students were attracted to women who could drink large quantities of alcohol, as illustrated by the following conversation that took place in the Sorority group discussion:

Participant #1: Like when they say, "Guys think it's cool," or whatever, like I know

with my group of guy friends they definitely push all the girls, like "Oh you can drink it, come on," you know?

Moderator: They sort of take notice?

Participant #1: Like, yeah, they definitely they take notice, and it's like, if you're drinking less, it's kind of looked down on more or something, it's like whoever can drink more. So, it's not like a badge of honor [reference to excerpt], I don't know, but it's kind of, I don't know, considered cooler by guys that you're friends with.

As illustrated in the following discussion among the Increasers group, males also took notice of the type of alcohol consumed by women. Types of drinkers were perceived in gendered terms and women who consumed "guy drinks" were considered more attractive and sexually appealing by college men.

Participant #2: . . . when she said that I immediately thought of how one of the drinks that most people think of as a guy drink is like a beer and how so many guys are like, "Oh that girl is drinking beer, that's so hot."

Participant #3: Yeah.

Participant #2: Instead of like the girl that's walking around with the orange juice and the vodka, the girl that's drinking the beast just out of the cup just like every other guy, a lot of guys will be like "Oh that's awesome."

Participant #4: It's like a girl they can have fun with as well as be sexually attracted to, be in love with, like a friend and a girlfriend, you know? That seems to be like a real trend that I've noticed that a lot of guys that are with serious girlfriends can have fun with them.

As evident in the end of the discussion above, women related these changes in what men found attractive in women's drinking habits to general changes in gender roles. These changes were also noted in other groups, as illustrated in the following discussion that occurred among the Stable Low group:

. . . my boyfriend says one of the things he likes about me is that I can play one on one with him and it's a toss up on who is going to win. Guys, more and more, tend to like the fact that women can compete with them in many different aspects. They can have intelligent conversations with them, they can beat them in basketball and you know, one of the things, maybe drinking them under the table. It's one more thing that tries to get women up on the same level as men.

Thus, while our research question was primarily focused on women's gender role beliefs and drinking behaviors, the seemingly inconsequential topic of what college women believe college men find appealing came to the forefront during the focus group discussions. The topic of men's preferences seemed to be prominent in these discussions because it appeared to play a dominant role in shaping women's drinking behaviors. While not all focus group participants felt that "drinking like a guy" described their own behavior, they all felt the pressure to do so because of the impression they could make on their male peers.

Association Between Drinking Levels and 'Drinking Like a Guy'

There appeared to be a strong association with the amount of alcohol consumed by focus group participants and the endorsement of "drinking like a guy" as a descriptor of one's own behavior. When presented with the article excerpts describing "drinking like a guy," all participants of the Stable High group felt it accurately described them. Thus, the discussion about the article excerpts for the Stable High group focused around clarification of what it means to "drink like a guy" (elaborated below) as opposed to questioning its appropriateness. In contrast, many of the women of the other groups felt that the descriptions did not fit their own behavior, despite the fact that they knew of women who drank in this manner. For example, the response below was from a woman in the Decreaser group:

It's not like going to be someone's goal to go out and like, "Hey let's drink guys under the table." You know it's just kind of like, if it happens, it happens. But I feel like a goal would be more like let's just go out and have fun and like relax and forget about our exam or something.

However, the above response was followed by the comment below from another member of the Decreaser group:

I think the first one [first excerpt], just completely describes one of my best friends. She can drink any guy under the table, very very proud of it and she will tell anybody. They just did this thing, I don't know if you guys have heard of it before, it's called like the Century Club where you drink 100 shots of beer in 100 minutes. And she did that a couple weekends ago and she's been bragging about it ever since. So that when I read this I thought "that's her right there" you know? She will drink any guy under the table and she's very proud of it.

Interestingly, a few of the participants of the Decreasers group felt that the excerpt described them in their earlier college years, when they were drinking "heavily." For example:

I was going to say my freshman/sophomore year when I drank a lot I had almost all guy friends and they compete with each other to see who can drink a lot. And so I think to fit in with that, if you really want to be one of the guys, you're probably going to instinctively try to compete with them also.

The fact that "drinking like a guy" was strongly endorsed by the Stable High group, and partially endorsed by the Decreasers group for the period of time in which they were drinking "heavily," suggests that "drinking like a guy" is a phenomenon of particular relevance to undergraduate women who engage in frequent binge drinking.

'Drinking Like a Guy' or 'Drinking to Be Liked by a Guy'?

In this following section, we review the major themes that emerged during the Stable High group's discussion of the article excerpt. Although all of the women in the Stable High group agreed that the descriptions reflected their own drinking behaviors, they did not feel that the descriptions were completely accurate. Thus, the following review clarifies what it meant to the Stable High group to "drink like a guy."

The article excerpts imply that competition underlies "drinking like a guy." While focus group participants perceived that competition was the primary reason why their male peers drank "heavily" (as discussed earlier), only one of the eight focus group members felt that "drinking like a guy" for them had to do with direct competition.

> I know I definitely think like that [the first excerpt] sometimes because I have an older brother and a lot of guy friends. I just grew up around guys a lot and I'm very competitive in sports and that type of thing. So I don't like to have people beat me like at drinking games, regardless of what it is. It's just like a competitive nature type thing. I wouldn't say it's like a feminism thing; it's just kind of like, I like to win. You know like regardless of what it is. I definitely like to have a high tolerance, and like to be able to drink with guys and like to play a Power Hour or do Century Club with them just to show that I can do it. So, I don't know . . . I think that's applicable.

In contrast, most of the Stable High group felt that "drinking like a guy" had more to do with wanting to "hang out" with their male peers and having a special, elite position within a male group.

> Definitely like you know, being known as like the girl who like, you know you always hang out with the guys and they like to hang out with you. And it's like you're one of their own because you can flip the cup over and chug it the fastest. And it really annoys me when you watch girls and they're like, "how do you do it?" (laughter) cause they're trying to do it just to get the boy's attention or something. So he'll help you flip the cup over and be like, "Oh you're OK." I'm not that girl. I like to be able to be like, "Look, I can do it too."

There are two aspects of the above quote that are particularly noteworthy. First, the participant's word choice conveys how she perceives herself belonging among this group of male peers. While it is grammatically correct to say *"you're one of them* because you can flip the cup over after and chug it the fastest," she chose the words "it's like *you're one of their own* because you can flip the cup over after and chug it the fastest." It is likely that she used the grammatically incorrect version because it conveyed a very different meaning than the correct version. "You're one of them" implies that she has an equal position as the males in the group, or she is *just like* them. However, the participant's actual word choice ("you're one of their own") suggests that her belonging to the group is based upon her belonging *to them*. That is, her connection to the group is not based on a "full membership," but instead her connection is to the males who occupy a full membership in the group. In this sense, the word choice of the participant suggests that her relationship to her male peers is of a traditionally heterosexual nature: her femaleness offers her a special position within the group, one in which she belongs to the group only as an appendage to male participants, who occupy "full" membership positions.

Indeed, there was an underlying assumption among participants that "drinking like a guy" did not bring women's heterosexuality into question; in fact, "drinking like a guy" increased women's (hetero)sexuality. Respondents from all of the groups were quick to point out that the term "drink like a guy" is not accurate. Women don't want to "be *like* a guy" because embedded in this statement is a questioning of their sexuality. As illustrated in the statement below from a sorority group participant, women who drink "heavily" do so to be *liked by* a guy, or to confirm their heterosexuality.

> I don't really agree with them. [The first excerpt] says they [women] drink for power, that is if she drinks like a guy she'll be like a guy. I don't agree with that at all. I don't think that women drink to be like a guy. I think that some women drink to become more like desirable to men and think that some women drink to make themselves feel better about their own power, but I don't know that it's to be like a guy.

The second striking aspect of the quote, "you're one of their own," is that the participant makes the distinction between interacting with male peers in a traditional feminine fashion, as exemplified by the girls who don't know how to flip the cup and chug, and how she sees herself interacting with male peers. Whereas the participant views a traditional female approach as appearing weak, helpless, and simply an attempt to get a male's attention, the participant in the quote sees herself as being able to drink as he does, and therefore having a special position within her male peer group; special because it differentiates and *elevates* her position from other females. While the participant implies that she, in contrast to the other woman, is not trying to get the male's attention, her final statement ("Look, I can do it too") suggests that she is seeking approval for her behavior, whether it be approval from herself, the other female, or the male(s) present.

In fact, women in the Stable High Group took great strides to differentiate themselves from what they referred to as the "girly-girl" female drinker. Participants appeared to use the term to describe women who appear weak and childlike and associated it with the inability to tolerate large quantities of alcohol.

> I mentioned earlier that I have a lot of guy friends and they're primarily who I drink with. You know, so as a result, I don't want to be the girl . . . I don't want to be that girly girl who is like tagging along with a bunch of like guys who are like mildly buzzing and I'm wasted.

The term "little girl" was also used in a similar fashion as "girly-girl" to express the social role associated with not being able to drink "heavily." Although the following response was provided by a member of the Decreaser Group regarding her earlier years in college when she drank "heavily," the response clearly demonstrates the statement a female would be making about her social role if she were unable to "hold her liquor":

> Like, when I first came, I literally was only friends with guys because I had a guy friend from California that I knew here and they kind of like took me in as their little sister. And I spent all my time there, day and night. If I wanted to hang out with them and play drinking games, I felt like I had to be one of the guys. So there definitely. . . . They never pressured me to drink. They were never like, "Oh

there's (her name). She can't hold her liquor." But there definitely was this internal pressure to want to be able to be one of the guys and just to hang out and not be seen as a little girl who would throw up and couldn't hold her liquor.

While the term "little sister" implies that there is a nonsexual nature to the participant's relationship to these male friends, the term "little sister" negates her statement about being "one of them" (i.e., being an equal to them). The role of little sister clearly identifies her femaleness and her lower social status, and implies that she feels they are protective of her. While this quote may not imply a heterosexual relationship, it does suggest a patriarchical social structure.

Not surprising given their explicit interest in being considered "one of the guys," almost all members of the Stable High Group expressed a preference for socializing with males over females, as illustrated in the following discussion among this group:

> *Participant #1:* I have probably more fun hanging out with guys and not drinking than hanging out with girls and not drinking.
>
> *Participant #2:* That's very true.
>
> *Participant #3:* Me too.
>
> *Participant #4:* Yeah.
>
> *Moderator:* So what would that be like to be with your girlfriends and not drinking? (laughter)
>
> *Participant #2:* They're not fun.
>
> *Participant #1:* Catty.
>
> *Participant #3:* There's not that many girls . . . I don't know, I just think there are some girls that are like "ha-ha-ha" that you can have fun with but they are few and far between.
>
> *Participant #1:* And some girls always talk about the stuff . . . I mean, boys . . .
>
> *Participant #3:* Yeah they talk about boys . . .
>
> *Participant #1:* And you're like, "Whatever, I don't want to talk about that right now." But guys are like "We don't care." And you can't get in a fight with a guy cause like you know guys just beat each

other up and it's fine but girls it like takes like two weeks and there's feelings hurt and everything (laughter) so I almost prefer to hang out with guys too cause they're really low maintenance.

Participant #4: Exactly.

The fact that the Stable High Group preferred socializing with males instead of females suggests that this group, in contrast to other women, may be particularly vulnerable to college men's opinions about women's drinking habits.

Tolerance Means Control

While these women expressed a clear preference to socializing with male over female peers, they recognized and spoke about their physical difference from males in terms of alcohol tolerance. In fact, there was considerable discussion among the Stable High Group about the physical disadvantage they faced when drinking with their male peers, but that they had overcome this limitation through diligently building up their alcohol tolerance, awareness of their limits, and careful selection of alcoholic beverages with lower alcohol content when drinking with males.

I think it's definitely important to know your level. You do want to be able to drink as much as possible, just so you are comfortable in any situation drinking. And I think it's kind of frustrating as a female that you can drink for [two] hours and the guys can be up for nine drinking. And as a girl, you're or I'm, you know, like if I'm going to, the guys push me to drink more because I'm so like . . . you know by the time that I feel like I'm done drinking they've just begun. So it's definitely trying to push your limit to maintain with them.

Participant #1: You don't want to get drunk too fast cause then you like sober up or you get really sick or you start passing out at the bar because you're so tired. . . . It's like about maintaining it and not, cause you want to like, yeah last all night and not miss anything because sometimes people pre-party too hard and they don't even make it to the bar. (Laughter)

Participant #2: I find that when I drink with my guy friends, I drink beer. Like if I go to the sports bar with my best friend [male name]. There's just no way in hell, I'm getting a Long Island. I find that I drink different things [when drinking with males versus females], not necessarily differently.

Participant #3: I definitely agree with that because with my guy friends it's like the keg-erator and at my house it's like wine and cosmos. It's like totally different. But I'm able to drink beer, a lot of my girlfriends like hate it so, you know.

Moderator: So to be with the guys, you really need to . . .

Participant #4: Well especially with the drinking games, guys always are playing drinking games: beer pong, float cup, something, Beirut and it always has to do with beer because if you played those games with anything else . . .

Participant #2: You'd die. (laughter)

Interestingly, women of the Stable High group associated their ability to build a tolerance for alcohol equal to men with a sense of control.

I would feel kind of embarrassed if I got drunk off of like two or three drinks. I would just like to go out and always have a drink in my hand, always be drinking and not worry that oh, am I going to be sick later, am I not going to be able to control myself. I just like to have that power and know, know that I can be under control.

In contrast, the other focus groups associated drinking with a lack of control. For example, the following discussion occurred among the Stable Low Group:

Participant #1: I said that they (college women who drink a lot) kind of do it (drink heavily) to show they can. To show they can be one of the guys, like they can go drink for drink with a guy to show that they can do it too.

Moderator: Why would they do that?

Participant #1: I don't know it's just . . .

Participant #2: Cause a guy always likes a girl that can keep up with them.

Participant #3: Like drinking, like my friends, one of our girlfriends can chug a beer.

Participant #4: It's something to brag about.

Participant #2: Yeah.

Participant #1: Right.

Moderator: Guys might admire that?

Participant #3: Yeah.

Participant #5: Yeah.

Participant #1: I don't know why.

Participant #2: I don't know why but they do.

Participant #4: They do.

Participant #2: It's not too bright.

Participants: Yeah (laughter).

Participant #2: I think there's an element of carelessness. Girls go out and drink and then they don't think about what they're doing, they don't think about . . . like they tend to lose their sense of . . .

Participant #3: Control?

Participant #2: Yeah. And I think they do it for that reason. They go out and drink just to not have to worry about anything. And then they just become careless. And they don't think about their actions.

While the participants of the above group were fully aware of the positive male attention they would receive for being able to drink "heavily," they were unwilling to do so because of the perceived loss of control associated with being intoxicated. Interestingly, the above group viewed "heavy alcohol consumption" by women as being thoughtless, whereas the women in this study who drank the most (i.e., the Stable High group) described themselves as planful and purposeful in their drinking behaviors (e.g., building a drinking tolerance and knowledge of their tolerance). While this discrepancy could simply be due to the fact that college women who drink "heavily" have a different perception of themselves than how others perceive them, the discrepancy may also be due to the fact that the Stable High group was describing how they manage to "match a guy, drink

for drink," while the conversation among the Stable Low group was in reference to avoiding sexual assault. That is, it may be that the Stable High group was planful in their drinking, allowing them to keep up with their male peers, but careless in considering the ramifications of heavy intoxication in a predominantly male social setting. Unfortunately, data from the focus groups did not address this distinction.

Discussion

Findings from this study suggests that "drinking like a guy" is a concept of particular relevance to the most recent generation of undergraduate women and may explain why there has been a dramatic increase in the rate of frequent binge drinking among this group. All of the women participating in the focus groups could speak to the notion of college women attempting to "drink like a guy," and women who were frequent binge drinkers throughout their college years (i.e., the Stable High group) felt that this description was applicable to their own behaviors. While this study only focused on the most current generation of female students, and therefore cannot speak to transitions from previous cohorts, what appears to be distinct for the most current group of college students is the change in what college men find appealing in college women. Participants of the focus groups noted that the changes in gender roles translated into college men finding it attractive when their female peers were able to "match them, drink for drink." Women who were frequent binge drinkers throughout college (i.e., the Stable High group) appeared the most vulnerable to men's opinions because of their preference to socialize with male peers over female peers.

It has been previously suggested by the popular press and academic researchers (e.g., Ehrenreich, 2002; Morse and Bower, 2002; Wilsnack; see Wechsler and Wuethrich, 2002) that college women try to "drink like a guy" because these women believe that drinking in a traditionally "masculine" manner (e.g., "heavy alcohol consumption," consumption of alcoholic drinks typically consumed by males) would provide them with gender equality and power. Findings from this study suggest that women who engage in frequent binge drinking are copying the drinking behaviors of their male peers (e.g., to flip the cup over and drink as fast and furiously as he does), but are not motivated to obtain what their male peers have (i.e., power or equality) nor to be like their male peers. Focus group participants were steadfast that women who "drank like a guy" did not want to be *like* a guy; that is, they did not want a social position that was exchangeable with their male peers. Instead, copying the drinking behaviors of their male peers provided college women with a special position among male drinking groups because such behaviors were sexually appealing to their male peers and elevated their social position in contrast to other females. Thus, we suggest that drinking in a masculine manner may *appear* to offer women equality and power because it has become socially acceptable for college women to behave as college men do; however, the social dynamics between men and women continue to be traditionally heterosexual and patriarchal when college women "drink like a guy," and thus counteract any appearances of equality. In this sense, "drinking like a guy" may allow women to feel powerful without ever exercising real power in social situations, and therefore, without women ever jeopardizing the status quo of gender relationships.

We caution these interpretations, though, with the recognition that our study was based on qualitative data. While focus groups provide an ideal method to generate new ideas of particular relevance to an understudied population (in this case, college women and excessive drinking), follow-up quantitative studies with random sample surveys are necessary to confirm any generated suppositions. The richness of qualitative data obtained through the focus groups of this study provides an excellent point from which to develop additional larger studies to further evaluate gender roles and excessive alcohol consumption among undergraduate women.

Given the finding from the present study that men's opinions play an important role in college women's decision to drink excessively, additional qualitative research is needed to provide information from the point of view of college males. While women's perceptions about men's opinions are more important than men's actual opinions when considering how women behave, this additional information is critical to have a full understanding of the relationship between gender roles and excessive drinking among college students.

Alcohol consumption has been the most significant health risk behavior on college campuses (Hingson et al., 2002; Perkins et al., 2002; Wechsler et al., 2002). College men have traditionally been at the forefront of excessive drinking; however, findings from our research suggest that a subgroup of college women may quickly be surpassing men in terms of the health risks of college drinking. Twenty-five percent (25%) of the women who participated in the Student Life Survey (of which focus group participants for this study were selected) engaged in frequent binge drinking. While findings from this study offer some possible explanations for why there has been such a dramatic increase in frequent binge drinking among women, we are still left with many questions unanswered. Most prominent is the need to address the health ramifications of excessive drinking for undergraduate women. Since previous research has documented that women cannot drink like men without experiencing higher levels of intoxication and vulnerability to sexual assault (Abbey 1996; Blume 1994; Koss et al., 1987), it is vital that future research explore in greater detail the consequences of frequent binge drinking among undergraduate women.

How might excessive drinking during the college years affect women's lives as they move beyond the college context? While we can only speculate, the exploration of such a question is a worthwhile endeavor. Previous research has documented that excessive drinking during the college years is typically short-lived as students "mature out" of such risky behavior once they leave the college setting (Schulenberg et al., 1996). The decrease in alcohol consumption following college may be due simply to the fact that students are no longer inundated with an alcohol-saturated social climate; however, it also appears that changes in drinking patterns correspond with changes in psychosocial developmental challenges as students transition from the "emerging adulthood" period (ages 18–25) to young adulthood. Research suggests that college students use excessive alcohol consumption to address the normative developmental challenges associated with emerging adulthood, such as self-exploration and differentiation from family of origin (Schulenberg and Maggs, 2002); the resolution of such issues along with the emergence of the new developmental concerns of adulthood, including the undertaking of adult roles (e.g., partner/spouse, worker, and parent) and responsibilities, may serve to temper alcohol consumption once students reach young adulthood (Bachman et al., 1997). This is not to say that college drinking does not have implications for later life stages, though. In fact, "heavy alcohol consumption" during college has been found to be associated with alcohol use related problems 10 years following graduation (O'Neill et al., 2001). Such findings in conjunction with the documented recent increase in college women's alcohol consumption (e.g., Wechsler et al., 2002) suggest that during the next decade we may witness an increase in alcohol use related problems among college-graduated adult women in their late 20s and early 30s, as the current generation of college women transitions into young adulthood. The possibility that excessive-alcohol-consuming college women may develop alcohol dependency during adulthood is only corroborated by the fact that women's alcohol use more commonly and quickly turns to alcohol abuse (Fillmore et al., 1997). For previous generations, women's alcohol misuse may have been restrained by the fact that they were less likely than men to start drinking or to drink consistently. While gender norms about women's drinking may have been inappropriately confining of women's behaviors, such norms consistently have served to moderate women's alcohol use (Wilsnack and Wilsnack, 1997), and likely have had a positive, indirect effect of minimizing women's alcohol use related problems. As beliefs about appropriate behavior for women change from restricting women's alcohol consumption to actually encouraging it, as

we found in this study, the implications for problem drinking for women during adulthood are truly troubling and worthy of future research. Only time (and careful research) will tell what will happen to the current generation of college women who drink excessive amounts of alcohol to demonstrate women's "liberation" and "equality." Will their exhibition of bodily control over excessive consumption of alcohol turn to a realization that alcohol now controls their lives?

Appendix

Excerpts from "Women on a Binge" (Morse and Bower, 2002) presented to focus group participants as one of the group activities.

"(Name of a student), 22, has two goals for her senior year at Syracuse University: 'Learn how to drive a stick shift, and drink a guy under the table.' The pert advertising major has nearly mastered her first objective . . . but the second goal gives her a bit more trouble. . . . 'You don't want to be that dumb girly girl who looks wasted and can't hold her liquor. I know it's juvenile, but I've had boys comment how impressed they are at the amount of alcohol I've consumed,' says (the student). 'To be able to drink like a guy is kind of a badge of honor. For me, it's a feminism thing."'

" '(College women) are no longer confined by the stereotypic notions of femininity,' says Devon Jersild, a journalist who talked with college age women for her book, *Happy Hours: Alcohol in a Women's Life*. They associate drinking with power and they think that if they drink like a guy, they will be like a guy.' "

Note

1. Since the focus group study was to be conducted in the spring of 2003, it was anticipated that participants of the 2001 Student Life Survey who were in their third or higher year of college would have already graduated.

References

Abbey, A., Ross, L. T., McDuffie, D., McAuslan, P. (1996). Alcohol and dating risk factors for sexual assault among college women. *Psych. Women's Quart.* 20: 147–169.

Ahuvia, A., Steinmetz, D. (1999). Campus drinking and alcohol related policies and programs: An exploratory study. (Prepared for Binge Drinking Task Force, Office of the Vice President for Student Affairs, University of Michigan). Ann Arbor, MI.

Baer, J. S. (2002). Student factors: understanding individual variation in college drinking. *J. Stud. Alch.* 14: 40–53.

Blume, S. B. (1994). Women and addictive disorders. In: *Principles of Addiction Medicine*. Miller, N. W., ed. Chevy Chase, MD: American Society of Addiction Medicine, 1–16.

——. (1997). Women and alcohol: Issues in social policy. In: *Gender and Alcohol: Individual and Social Perspectives*. Wilsnack, R. W., Wilsnack, S. C., eds. New Brunswick, NJ: Rutgers Center of Alcohol Studies, 462–489.

Boyd, C. J., McCabe, S. E. (2001). 2001 Student Life Survey Report. Ann Arbor, MI: University of Michigan Substance Abuse Research Center.

Carey, K. B., Correia, J. (1997). Drinking motives predict alcohol-related problems in college students. *J. Stud. Alc.* 58: 100–106.

Driessen, H. (1992). Drinking on masculinity: Alcohol and gender in Andalusia. In: Alcohol, Gender and Culture. Gefou-Madianou, D., ed. London: Routledge, 71–79.

Ehrenreich, B. *Time*, April 1, 2002.

Fillmore, K. M., Golding, J. M., Leino, E. V., Motoyoshi, M., Shoemaker, C., Terry, H., Ager, C. R., Ferrer, H. P. (1997). Patterns and trends in women's and men's drinking. In: *Gender and Alcohol: Individual and Social Perspectives*. Wilsnack, R., Wilsnack, S., eds. New Brunswick, NJ: Rutgers Center of Alcohol Studies, 21–48.

Gefou-Madianou, D. (1992). Introduction: Alcohol commensality, identity transformations and transcendence. In: *Alcohol, Gender, and Culture*. Gefou-Madianou, D., ed. New York.

Hill, S. Y. (1995). Mental and physical health consequences of alcohol use in women. In: *Recent Developments in Alcoholism: Volume 12: Alcoholism and Women*. Galanter, M., ed. New York: Plenum Press, 181–197.

Jersild, D. (2001). *Happy Hours: Alcohol in a Woman's Life*. New York: Cliff Street Books.

Johnson, L. D., O'Malley, P. M., Bachman, J. G. (2000). *Monitoring the Future: National Survey Results on Drug Use. 1975–1999*, Vol. 2, NIH Publication No. 00-4803. Bethesda, MD: Department of Health and Human Services.

Klein, H. (1987). Self reported reasons for why college students drink. *J. Alc. Drug. Educ.* 37: 14–28.

Knight, J. R., Wechsler, H., Meichun, J., Seibring, M., Wetzman, E. R., Schuckit, M. A. (2002). Alcohol abuse and dependence among U.S. college students. *J. Stud. Alch.* 63: 263–270.

Koss, M. P., Gidycz, C. A., Wisniewski, N. (1987). The scope of rape: incidence and prevalence of sexual aggression and victimization in a national sample of higher education students. *J. Consult. Clin. Psych.* 55: 162–170.

Krueger, R. A. (1994). *Focus Groups: A Practical Guide for Applied Research*. Thousand Oaks, CA: Sage.

McCabe, S. E. (2002). Gender differences in collegiate risk factors for heavy episodic drinking. *J. Stud. Alch.* 63: 49–56.

McDonald, M. (1994). Drinking and social identity in the west of France. In: *Gender, Drinking and Drugs*. McDonald, M., ed. Providence, RI: Berg, 99–124.

Moos, R. H., Moos, B. S., Kulik, J. A. (1976). College-student abstainers, moderate drinkers, and heavy drinkers: A comparative analysis. *J. Youth Adol.* 5: 349–360.

Morse, J., Bower, A. Women on a binge. *Time*, 2002, April 1, 56–61.

O'Malley, P. M., Johnston, L. D. (2002). Epidemiology of alcohol and other drug use among American college students. *J. Stud. Alch. Supp.* 14: 23–39.

O'Neill, S. E., Parra, G. R., Sher, K. J. (2001). Clinical relevance of heavy drinking during the college years: Cross-sectional and prospective perspectives. *Psych. Add. Beh.* 15: 350–359.

Perkins, H. W. (1999). Stress-motivated drinking in collegiate and postcollegiate young adulthood: Life course and gender patterns. *J. Stud. Alc.* 60: 219–227.

——. (2002). Surveying the damage: A review of research on consequences of alcohol misuse in college populations. *J. Stud. Alc. Supp.* 14: 91–100.

Ratliff, K. G., Burkhart, B. R. (1984). Sex differences in motivations for and effects of drinking among college students. *J. Stud. Alc.* 45: 26–32.

Sandmaier, M. (1980). *The Invisible Alcoholics: Women and Alcohol Abuse in America*. New York: McGraw-Hill Book Co.

Schulenberg, J. E., Wadsworth, K. N., O'Malley, P. M., Bachman, J. G., Johnston, L. D. (1996). Adolescent risk factors for binge drinking during the transition to young adulthood: Variable and pattern-centered approaches to change. *Dev. Psych.* 32: 659–674.

Schulenberg, J. E., Maggs, J. L. (2002). A developmental perspective on alcohol use and heavy drinking during adolescence and the transition to young adulthood. *J. Stud. Alch. Supp.* 14: 54–70.

Straus, R., Bacon, S. (1953). *Drinking in College*. New Haven: Yale University Press.

Wechsler, H., Davenport, A., Dowdall, G., Moeykens, B., Castillo, S. (1994). Health and behavioral consequences of binge drinking in college: A national survey of students at 140 campuses. *JAMA 272: 1672–1677*.

Wechsler, H., Dowdall, G. W., Davenport, A., Rimm, E. B. (1995). A gender-specific measure of binge drinking among college students. *Amer. J. Public Hlth.* 85: 982–985.

Wechsler, H., Lee, J. E., Kuo, M., Seibring, M., Nelson, T. F., Lee, H. (2002). Trends in college binge drinking during a period of increased prevention efforts. Findings from 4 Harvard School of Public Health College Alcohol Study surveys: 1993–2001. *J. Amer. Coll. Hlth.* 50: 203–17.

Wechsler, H., McFadden, M. (1979). Drinking among college students in New England. *J. Stud. Alc.* 40: 969–996.

Wechsler, H., Rohman, M. (1981). Extensive users of alcohol among college students. *J. Stud. Alc.* 42: 149–155.

Wechsler, H., Wuethrich, B. (2002). *Dying to Drink: Confronting Binge Drinking on College Campuses*. St. Martin's Press.

Wilsnack, R. W., Vogeltanz, N. D., Wilsnack, S. C., Harris, T. R. (2000). Gender differences in alcohol consumption and adverse drinking consequences: Cross-cultural patterns. *Addiction* 95: 251–265.

Wilsnack, R. W., Wilsnack, S. C. (1997). Introduction. In: *Gender and Alcohol: Individual and Social Perspectives*. Wilsnack, R., Wilsnack, S., eds. New Brunswick, NJ: Rutgers Center of Alcohol Studies, 1–18.

For Discussion

1. Think about how the authors defined binge drinking in this study. How would you critique this definition?

2. How do you think male undergraduate students would perceive women who drink heavily, had males been interviewed for this study? Would their perceptions be similar to the perceptions among female respondents?

10
Smoking

What Does Culture Have to Do With It?

Mark Nichter

Ethnicity and culture are two important concepts in sociological study. Mark Nichter deconstructs these concepts and describes their importance in the study of tobacco smoking. He suggests that culture has many significant dimensions and that tobacco smoking is just one dimension of symbolic behavior. Nichter suggests that tobacco smoking is best understood through the interaction of individual and wider social, political, and economic factors. He poses a number of significant questions for future research into tobacco smoking.

A better understanding of tobacco uptake, trajectories of use, expressions of dependence and quitting attempts requires a careful consideration of the interaction between individual and contextual factors, the way in which nested social contexts interface and influence one another and an appreciation of risk and protective factors. The study of nested contexts is challenging. A move from the study of additive to interactive factors influencing tobacco use demands both a new vision of what types of data need to be collected and new methods of data analysis. The papers in [*Addiction* 98] go a long way towards summarizing what we know about family, peer, neighborhood, media, economic and political economic influences on tobacco use. Rather than revisit themes already covered . . . I wish to raise a few additional issues related to ethnicity and 'culture' as a context influencing adolescent smoking. Ways will then be suggested in which ethnographic studies of smoking can add to our understanding of smoking behavior as a phenomenon influenced by both structural

locations which bound subjective experience and cultural play which involves experimentation with self-image and identity (Pavis et al. 1998).

Let me comment first on the role of 'culture,' a factor influencing tobacco use that was raised. . . . When [*Addiction* 98] was first discussed, 'culture' was considered as a context meriting its own review. Given that a Surgeon General's Report (U.S. Department of Health and Human Resources 1998) had recently summarized ethnic differences in rates of smoking, it appeared redundant to restate what is already known and more useful to consider how cultural norms and institutions, gender roles and aesthetics played out in each of the other contexts being addressed. I would urge future researchers investigating 'culture' and tobacco use to continue to look at the interaction between culture and social and economic contexts, and to consider 'culture' on two fronts: (a) culture as it is commonly regarded in relation to ethnic differences, and (b) popular culture as an ongoing project subject to both the identity needs of youth and the influence of an advertising industry that manipulates these needs to sell cigarettes and develop market niches.

Ethnicity and culture are terms that public health researchers need to differentiate and take seriously, especially when studying adolescence (Fergerson 1998).[1] When using the term 'ethnicity' it is important to differentiate between an ethnic identity one assumes in context and an ethnic label that is imposed by others. One's ethnic identity is an identity one chooses to assume on the basis of some sense of social and political affiliation. Far from being fixed or static, which would render ethnicity a reified construct (a 'thing'), ethnic identity may be claimed or distanced in particular contexts, at particular times, and for particular reasons. One's sense of ethnic identity is situational and changes in accord with life-style, residence, etc. At its core, ethnic identity is based on shared meanings that emerge from collective experiences and as such it is produced and reproduced in social interaction. An ethnic label, on the other hand, is a static designation assigned to a person by someone else. It is based on a set of criteria that distinguishes them from others in the eyes of whomever it is that controls the categorization scheme. The history of ethnic categorization in the United States has been politically motivated and has been influenced by a changing agenda (Edmontson & Schultze 1994).

Ethnic labeling, whether by skin color, language or region of origin, lumps people together who may have as many differences as similarities. Lumping has diverse ramifications. It can contribute to misleading and sometimes disempowering stereotypes as well as provide an opportunity for those labeled to gain critical mass and mobilize forces toward particular ends. For example, diverse groups categorized as Hispanic may mobilize as a collective based on the common experience of oppression and assume an ethnic identity as much for political as cultural reasons.

When ethnicity is employed as a category in public health, it is important to be clear about one's assumptions and how ethnic designation is going to be used in data analysis. Is an ethnic label being used to examine the possible role of biological differences? Is ethnicity a proxy for a whole bundle of social and economic factors associated with the position a group of people has been forced to assume as a result of a history of discrimination or oppression (e.g. as a marker of social inequity and structural violence)? Or is ethnicity being examined to determine whether the distinctive characteristics of an ethnic group's 'culture' are protecting or exposing this group to particular types of risk? If the latter is the case, we must bear in mind that 'culture' is one of the most highly debated concepts in cultural anthropology (Sewell 1999).

Culture is commonly thought of as an enduring set of social norms and institutions that organize the life of members of particular ethnic groups, giving them a sense of continuity and community. It is often described rather vaguely as an all-encompassing associational field in which ethnicity is experienced. Numerous anthropologists have discussed the limitations of such conceptualization of 'culture', especially in complex societies subject to the forces of modernity. When 'culture' is thought about in terms of consensus and as a template for ideal behavior, the positions of different stakeholders (defined by gender, generation, class, power relations, etc.) are forgotten and heterogeneity is ignored. A processual rendering of culture is more productive. Such an approach directs attention to cultural dimensions of social transactions and asks what is cultural about particular types of behavior in different contexts. Culture is treated more as an adjective than a noun (Appadurai 1996).

Why is a discussion of ethnicity and culture important for tobacco research? There has been mounting criticism of late about the way in which race/ethnicity has been used in public health research as a set of pigeonholes, if not black boxes. This fosters an analysis of 'difference' that focuses on individual and group traits rather than the contexts in which people live (Lillie-Blanton & LaVeist 1996). Despite warnings against reading too much into aggregate (e.g. state, national) data on smoking and ethnicity, it is easy to overlook ethnic heterogeneity and see ethnicity as a risk factor rather than a risk marker. A question often posed in debates about ethnicity and smoking is the following: are cultural factors responsible for ethnic differences in levels of smoking (at different ages by gender), or is ethnicity merely a marker for multiple social and economic factors predisposing one to smoke or abstain from smoking? Adopting an 'action is in the interaction' perspective, I would argue that there is a much better way of framing this important issue. Two questions appear more relevant to ask:

1. Is smoking behavior in particular social and economic contexts influenced by cultural norms and processes and if so, how?

2. What has smoking come to represent to those sharing an ethnic identity in an environment in which the tobacco industry often targets ethnic pride in marketing campaigns?

I would argue that it is far more productive to look for cultural differences in smoking after first accounting for other factors known to predispose an individual to smoke, including education, social class, economic insecurity, stressors (e.g. discrimination), other drug use, etc. Following an analysis which pays credence to the shortcomings of quantitative research—for example, that it often overlooks important differences between socio-economic indices (King 1997)—ethnic differences should be examined more closely. At a minimum the following three issues should be addressed by ethnographic research. What is the role that cultural institutions, values, and processes play in: (1) protecting against smoking in the general population, as well as particular patterns of smoking among males and females, (2) fostering smoking as a normative behavior within particular gender and age cohorts and (3) affecting the distribution of particular smoking trajectories (e.g. early versus late onset of smoking, smoking characterized by rapid versus slow escalation, etc.). This ethnographic analysis would serve as a complement to assessments by researchers who examine intraethnic group differences by examinations of social class, education, residence, racial segregation and acculturation.

What cultural factors might be productive to examine more closely when researching smoking trajectories? Parenting styles and respect for elders are two variables highlighted in the Surgeon General's Report as important factors influencing smoking behavior. Beyond noting that these factors affect smoking uptake and age of initiation, we need to consider how and in what ways they affect youth once they begin smoking. What verbal and non-verbal messages do youth receive from male and female parental figures in different ethnic communities at different points in their smoking trajectories? Once someone becomes a smoker, are they urged to quit or is their behavior accepted? How does respect for elders influence when and where youth may smoke, and how does this differ by not only age and gender, but by employment status? How do cultural sanctions influence patterns and levels of smoking?

The messages youth receive about smoking must not be looked at in isolation. It is not just the content of the message that makes a difference, but the meaning and social relations it evokes. Several publications have suggested that authoritarian parental

messages protect African American youth against higher rates of smoking (Koepke, Flay & Johnson 1990; Distefan, Gilpin et al. 1998; Clark, Scarisbrick-Hauser et al. 1999). We need to understand youth response to these messages in terms of their relationships with the people delivering them as well as other messages they receive. What protective role do associated messages play such as those which emphasize maintaining a positive self image in the face of adversity and messages which remind youth that one's behavior reflects not only on their person, but family and community? In what contexts do such messages matter and in what contexts do they fall on deaf ears? In contexts where such messages matter, do they contribute to reported ethnic differences in peer group influence (Unger et al. 2001) or are other factors involved? And, are there gender and age differences in the ways youth respond to both peer influence and the messages of elders?[2]

In addition to examining the influence of family and peers it might be useful to focus attention on the influence of role models which include, but are not limited to these two groups of people. For example, among African American families, senior women (mothers, grandmothers, extended and fictive kin) often, but not always, act as effective role models for the young as providers and survivors. Their message about smoking has been fairly consistent and clear—it does not look good for young African American men or women to smoke and it does not reflect well on their family; but what happens, for example, to the many African American men and women who join the armed forces when they turn 18 years of age? What influence do older officers who smoke have on new recruits in their units? Given high rates of smoking uptake and relapse in the military among young recruits (Bray et al. 1988, 1999), studying the influence of officers as role models would seem worthwhile.

Another issue worth considering is how core cultural values affect smoking behavior once uptake has occurred. For example, the importance accorded to social exchange and reciprocity within different ethnic groups may be an important factor to investigate. Being offered and accepting or refusing a cigarette within Filipino-American communities, for example, may carry a locus of meaning far different than within African American or mainstream Anglo communities, and this meaning may differ by gender (Nichter et al. 2002). Similarly, cultural values may influence peer group norms and boundary setting related to tobacco use. For example, I have observed that peers sometimes play a dual role in both encouraging smoking uptake and limiting where, when and how much friends smoke; that is, they are at once a risk and a protective factor that may affect smoking trajectories (Nichter 1999). The role of peers in establishing boundaries for acceptable behavior has also been noted by Tessler (2000), Kobus (2003) and Maggs (1997) in her research on alcohol use. An issue worth exploring is whether peer relations vary within different ethnic groups such that friends are more or less likely to act as boundary setters circumscribing the behaviors of peers. For example, would Native American youth be less likely to limit friends' smoking behavior due to deep-seated cultural norms valuing autonomy than, for example, Mexican Americans?

Another important issue in need of investigation is the meaning that smoking assumes during socially constructed life transitions. The study of smoking transitions in particular ethnic communities would benefit from ethnographies of what else is occurring at times when significant shifts in smoking appear to be taking place. Such research needs to pay special attention to cultural perceptions of age appropriate behavior, normative transgressions and risk taking (Lightfoot 1997; Turbin, Jessor & Costa 2000; Burton et al. 1996), and behaviors associated with assuming greater adult responsibility. In order to understand better the role that smoking plays as a marker of gender and age identity, we need to examine social constructions of adolescence as well as femininity/masculinity. Perceptions of when adolescence begins and ends often differ by gender in accord with roles and expectations, the division of labor within the household and the availability (political economy) of paid work outside the home. While girls in some ethnic group contexts are expected to bear the responsibilities of adult women early (e.g. become child-care providers if not mothers), in other groups young women are encouraged to stay at school for long periods of time; in some contexts, adolescence may be much longer for boys than girls because transitions to employment and marriage take place much later. The point being made is that comparisons of male and female smoking within and across groups need to be contextualized and not merely be based on physical age.

Let me next draw attention to aesthetics and style as important cultural factors influencing smoking, because they are often associated with ethnic identity. At a recent conference I attended, one speaker cited as a reason for lower rates of African American smoking among youth was that smoking was a 'white thing'. An African American woman in the audience corrected the speaker by stating, 'Not acting white isn't what our youth are all about, it is being Black and being proud. Smoking is not a "Black thing."'[3] The woman went on to suggest that the reason black youth did not take to smoking was 'mostly because it wasn't important to their styling'. Her words echo the findings of a multi-site study in the United States, where researchers found that black girls in comparison to white girls were far more likely to think that 'not smoking' enhanced their self-image (Mermelstein 1999). Smoking, put simply, was not equated with style. Ethnographies of African American perceptions of beauty and individual expression have drawn attention to the importance of styling and cool pose to ethnic identity as well as courtship rituals (Majors & Billson 1992; Parker et al. 1995).

Styling can act as both a protective and risk factor for smoking. A better appreciation of cultural aspects of style and the way status is displayed in ethnic communities might provide us with a better understanding of why certain marketing pitches for cigarettes work well in these communities and what kind of tobacco control messages might be best suited for them. It would also be wise to monitor changes in perceptions of 'smoking as stylish' as a barometer of how well the advertising industry is doing in making smoking culturally acceptable in different ethnic groups.[4] In this regard, it is important to bear in mind that the advertising industry is in the business of positioning products to enable people to position themselves as part of an ongoing cultural project.

This brings me to the importance of studying popular culture and the way youth negotiate their identities in consumer society. One of the primary ways we structure time, define who we are and express social relations is through acts of consumption. Consumption events punctuate the flow of everyday life as we move from school or work to leisure time. They help us to rekey our moods and states of mind. Consumption practices also play a role in fantasy and social performance, image experimentation and image management, social affiliation and the expression of group and individual boundaries. In particular, cigarettes serve as symbols as well as props that allow people to imagine as well as act out constantly varying roles on the stage of everyday life (Danesi 1999). Youth create, appropriate and assign meaning to smoking at the same time as they are being primed to interpret smoking in particular ways.

There is nothing new in recognizing all of this. What is called for is a more sophisticated approach to studying the meaning of smoking in popular culture, an approach that accounts for both the expression of agency and the social meaning of smoking performances. Here it is vital to recognize that, although it may be possible to link cigarettes with particular meanings among certain groups and in certain situations, tobacco use is better conceived as a form of imaginative play involving symbols and mutually understandable cues rather than discrete messages sent through a code (Bateson 1972). While it is true that smokers may send messages through their tobacco use, most do not consciously or explicitly set out to send particular messages. The interaction of a smoker's cognitive and emotional situation, their facility in performing smoking routines and the widely distributed cultural imagery that they work off of is glossed over in an analysis of tobacco as a code of meaning (a semiotic). What is required are studies of tobacco use that attend to the stage (context) in which smoking occurs, cultural meanings associated with tobacco, and processes of self-expression which involve performance. Smoking is but one part of image management. For this reason it is important to study smoking as it is combined and contrasted with other expressive acts such as sports, substance use and dress in a constantly evolving fashion system. It is entire ensembles of symbolic behavior that make cultural statements more often than single acts such as smoking a cigarette. When one takes up or gives up smoking, they often make shifts in an array of interrelated behaviors.

In this light we need to deepen our understanding of the importance of smoking in movies and community-based marketing strategies where youth are paid to smoke in particular spaces. Most research on smoking in the movies focuses attention on the number of times smoking occurs, whether main characters smoke cigarettes and if smoking occurs in particularly memorable scenes. The assumption is that youth will want to imitate attractive main characters and that a transfer of positive arousal will occur from scenes to products. Another dimension of tobacco use may be just, if not more important. Background smoking as well as smoking featured in the foreground of movies gives youth ideas about when, where and how to smoke in a manner which enables a range of social performances. At a time when smoking is increasingly being regulated, the tobacco industry will need to provide youth with new images of smoking in spaces and at times when it is feasible. Researchers monitoring smoking in the media need to look beyond the cigarette to the context in which it is smoked and what is signaled by particular smoking gestures. Researchers monitoring community-based tobacco strategies need, similarly, to pay more attention to where 'paid smokers' are positioned and the spaces and times in which cigarettes, small cigars, and other tobacco products are being fashioned to appear normative.

Let me turn briefly to a few other issues related to smoking environments and how they may affect smoking trajectories as well as expressions of tobacco dependence. The study of human geography investigates what behaviors and forms of social interaction and identities are associated with place. This discipline might have much to contribute to studies of what types of smoking occur in different smoking environments. Such studies might provide, for example, valuable insights into smoking topography. At a time when constraints on where and when one may smoke are increasing, more attention needs to be focused on the relaxed and pressured manner in which people smoke in different spaces. Chapman, Haddad & Sindhusake (1997) have called our attention rightly to changes in the depth of smoke inhalation and rates of inhalation by those forced to smoke outside of work sites. Payne (2001) has noted further that women are more likely than men to be employed in work sites where smoking bans lead smokers to smoke both harder and faster. She hypothesizes that gender differences in smoking topography may affect trajectories of lung cancer. Whether or not this is the case, gender-sensitive studies of the way people smoke at different times and in different places are worth doing. Given all the restrictions on youth smoking, it might be valuable to investigate not only how many cigarettes youth smoke a day, but also when youth engage in rushed and relaxed smoking. It is worth considering more closely how smoking trajectories among youth are affected by access to times and spaces where smoking can occur in particular ways. For example, are smoking transitions more likely to take place when youth have access to relaxed smoking environment, such as in a car?

It is very important that we consider the impact of smoking opportunities and constraints on expressions of dependence. Recent research suggests that it may be better to conceptualize tobacco dependence in terms of degrees, not absolutes, and as multi-dimensional phenomena (Shadel et al. 2000). It is likely that youth and adult expressions of dependence differ or that the order in which signs of dependence appear may be different for smokers of different ages (Nichter et al. 2002). It is reasonable to hypothesize that expressions of dependence among youth may be associated with smoking opportunities and constraints over the course of the day and week. In order to test

this hypothesis, measures of dependence sensitive to youth and their life world will need to be developed (Nichter 2000). Such measures will have to be sensitive to patterns of smoking, the plans youth make to smoke, and the salience of particular cigarettes in their day.

A last point I would like to raise is related to the way modernity itself may be a context we need to consider in relation to tobacco use. Today youth live in an age of increasing time compression, greater opportunities for arousal and diminishing tolerance for 'boredom,' and the proliferation of products that promise instant gratification. Cigarettes have been engineered biologically to be a fast and effective nicotine delivery device and engineered socially (advertised) to be an antidote for boredom. There may be biocultural reasons why nicotine, like caffeine, is appealing to youth in today's world. Consider, for example, that a significant percentage of youth are placed in an environment where they are required to multi-task at school when experiencing mild to moderate sleep deprivation (Wahlstrom 1999). Youth today are going to bed later than ever before because they have the opportunity and means to be in constant contact with their friends through cell phones and instant messaging, have access to hundreds of television programs thanks to cable technology, are able to experiment with new identities at will in computer chat rooms and they can spend hours searching the web to complete school assignments. Yet they are subject to early wake up times demanded by school schedules more geared to the political economy of adults than the lives of youth.

Does the pharmacology of nicotine make tobacco attractive to youth given these conditions? Anthropologists who have studied the history of substance use from coca leaves to sugar, coffee and tea have observed that 'food drugs' tend to become popular when they match the biocultural demands of work cycles as well as facilitate the practice of ideologies at the site of the body, through trade, etc. (Mintz 1985 and 1997; Jankowiak & Bradburd 1996 and 2003; Gladwell 2001). If such is the case for tobacco, we need to reflect on both the appeal of tobacco as a symptom of our times and the tobacco industry as the purveyor of a form of ideology. This ideology is clearly a form of capitalism based on the promotion of dependence. Indeed, one could argue that tobacco is the best example of a dependence industry affecting the world on multiple fronts ranging from the micro (cellular) to the macro (society, global relations). Nicotine delivery devices render tobacco as addictive as possible, tobacco agriculture makes farmers more dependent on fertilizers than almost any other crop and politicians and state governments easily become addicted to tobacco generated revenues. The ideology of dependence propagated by the tobacco industry is an important political economic dimension of 'culture' which we must not fail to appreciate.

Notes

1. For a complete discussion of the meaning of 'race,' see Freeman (1998).

2. See for example the study by Simons-Morton et al. (2001), which suggests gender differences in the effect of 'peer pressure' on smoking and drinking among younger adolescents.

3. While it is important to recognize cultural aesthetics as an expression of core values and improvisation, it is also important to recognize that an 'oppositional cultural frame of reference' (Cross 1995; Ogbu 1994) does affect choices in style and self-presentation. This may impact on smoking.

4. Conspicuous consumption among blacks is also an expressive act having collective significance best understood against the backdrop of a history of racism (Lamont & Molnar 2001). This is tapped into and used as a marketing strategy to sell tobacco products.

References

Appadurai, A., ed. (1996) *Modernity at Large: Cultural Dimensions of Globalization*. Minneapolis: University of Minnesota Press.

Bateson, G. (1972) *Steps to an Ecology of the Mind*. New York: Ballantine Books.

Bray, R. M., Sanchaez, R. P., Orenstein, M. L., Lentine, D., Vincus, A., Baird, T. V., Walker, J. A., Wheeless, S. C., Guess, L. L., Kroutil, L. A. & Iannacchione, V. G. (1999) *1998 Department of Defense Survey of Health Related Behaviors Among Military Personnel* (Report RTI/70/7034/006-FR). Research Triangle Park, NC: Research Triangle Institute.

Bray, R. M., Marsden, M. E., Guess, L. L., Wheeless, S. C., Iannacchione, V. G. & Kessling, S. R. (1988) *1988 Worldwide Survey of Substance Abuse and Health Behaviors Among Military Personnel* (Report RTI/4000/06-02FR). Research Triangle Park, NC: Research Triangle Institute.

Burton, L., Obeidallah, D. A. & Allison, K. (1996) Ethnographic insights on social context and adolescent development among inner-city African-American teens. In: Jessor, R., Colby, A. & Shweder, R. A., eds. *Ethnography and Human Development: Context and Meaning in Social Inquiry*, pp. 396–418. Chicago: University of Chicago Press.

Chapman, S., Haddad, S. & Sindhusake, D. (1997) Do workplace bans cause smokers to smoke 'harder'? Results from a naturalistic observational study. *Addiction*, 92, 607–610.

Clark, P., Scarisbrick-Hauser, A., Gautam, S. P. & Wirk, S. (1999) Anti-tobacco socialization in homes of African-American and White parents, and smoking and non-smoking parents. *Journal of Adolescent Health*, 24, 329–339.

Cross, W. E., Jr. (1995) Oppositional identity and African American youth: issues and prospects. In: Hawley, W. D. & Jackson, A. W., eds. *Toward a Common Destiny: Improving Race and Ethnic Relations in America*, pp. 185–204. San Francisco: Jossey-Bass.

Danesi, M. (1999) *Of Cigarettes, High Heels, and Other Interesting Things. An Introduction to Semiotics*. New York: St Martin's Press.

Distefan, J., Gilpin, E., Choi, W. S. & Pierce, J. P. (1998) Parental influences predict adolescent smoking in the United States, 1989–93. *Journal of Adolescent Health*, 22, 466–474.

Edmontson, B. & Schultze, C., eds. (1994) *Modernizing the US Census; Panel on Census Requirements in the Year 2000 and Beyond*. National Research Council. Washington, DC: National Academy Press.

Fergerson, G. (1998) Whither 'culture' in adolescent health research [Commentary]? *Journal of Adolescent Health*, 23, 150–152.

Freeman, H. P. (1998) The meaning of race in science—considerations for cancer research. *Cancer*, 82, 219–229.

Gladwell, M. (2001) The critics. A critic at large. Java man: how caffeine created the modern world. *The New Yorker*, 7, 76–80.

Jankowiak, W. M. & Bradburd, D. (1996) Using drug foods to capture and enhance labor performance: a cross-cultural perspective. *Current Anthropology*, 37, 717–720.

——, eds. (2003) *Stimulating Trade: Drugs, Governments and Western Economic Expansion*. Columbia University Press, in press.

King, G. (1997) The 'race' concept in smoking: a review of the research on African Americans. *Social Science and Medicine*, 45, 1075–1087.

Kobus, K. (2003) Peer contributions to adolescent smoking. *Addiction*, 98 (Supplement 1), 37–55.

Koepke, D., Flay, B. R. & Johnson, C. A. (1990) Health behaviors in minority families: the case of cigarette smoking. *Family Community Health*, 13, 35–43.

Lamont, M. & Molnar, V. (2001) How blacks use consumption to shape their collective identity: evidence from marketing specialists. *Journal of Consumer Culture*, 1, 31–46.

Lightfoot, C. (1997) *The Culture of Adolescent Risk-Taking*. New York: Guilford Press.

Lillie-Blanton, M. & LaVeist, T. (1996) Race/ethnicity, the social environment, and health. *Social Science and Medicine*, 43, 83–91.

Maggs, J. L. (1997) Alcohol use and binge drinking as goal-directed action during the transition to postsecondary education. In: Schulenberg, J., Maggs, J. L. & Hurrelman, K., eds. *Health Risks and Developmental Transitions During Adolescence*, pp. 345–371. Cambridge, UK: Cambridge University Press.

Majors, R. & Billson, J. M. (1992) *Cool Pose: The Dilemmas of Black Manhood in America*. New York: Lexington Books.

Mermelstein, R. (1999) Explanations of ethnic and gender differences in youth smoking: a multi-site, qualitative investigation. *Nicotine and Tobacco Research*, 1, S91–S98.

Mintz, S. (1985) *Sweetness and Power: The Place of Sugar in Modern History*. New York: Penguin.

Nichter, M. (1999) Anthropology's contribution to the study of tobacco consumption: what do we know, what do we need to find out? Paper presented at the Society for Applied Anthropology Annual Meeting, Tucson, AZ.

——. (2000) Assessing nicotine dependence among adolescents: the devil is in the details. Paper Presented at the 11th World Conference on Tobacco or Health, Washington, DC.

Nichter, M., Nichter, M., Thompson, P. J., Shiffman, S. & Moscicki, A.-B. (2002) Using qualitative research to inform survey development on nicotine dependence among adolescents. *Drug and Alcohol Dependence*, 68, S41–S56.

Ogbu, J. U. (1994) From Cultural Differences to Differences in Cultural Frame of Reference. In: Greenfield, P. & Cocking, R., eds. *Cross Cultural Roots of Minority Child Development*, pp. 365–392. Hillsdale, NJ: Erlbaum.

Parker, S., Nichter, M., Nichter, M., Vuckovic, N., Sims, C. & Rittenbaugh, C. (1995) Body image and weight concerns among African American and white adolescent females: differences that make a difference. *Human Organization*, 54, 103–114.

Pavis, S., Cunningham-Burley, S. & Amos, A. (1998) Health related behavioural change in context: young people in transition. *Social Science and Medicine*, 47, 1407–1418.

Payne, S. (2001) 'Smoke like a man, die like a man'?: a review of the relationship between gender, sex and lung cancer. *Social Science and Medicine*, 53, 1067–1080.

Sewell, W. H., Jr. (1999) The concepts of culture. In: Bonnell, V. E. & Hunt, L., eds. *Beyond the Cultural Turn: New Directions in the Study of Society and Culture*, pp. 35–61. Berkeley, CA: University of California Press.

Shadel, W., Shiffman, S., Niaura, R., Nichter, M. & Adams, D. B. (2000) Current models of nicotine dependence: what is known and what is needed to advance understanding of tobacco etiology among youth. *Drug and Alcohol Dependence*, 59, S9–S21.

Simmons-Morton, B., Haynie, D. L., Crump, A. D., Eitel, P. & Saylor, K. E. (2001) Peer and parent influences on smoking and drinking among early adolescents. *Health Education and Behavior*, 28, 95–107.

Tessler, L. (2000) Locations of self in smoking discourses and practices: an ethnography of smoking among adolescents and young adults in the United States. Master's Thesis, Tucson, University of Arizona.

Turbin, M. S., Jessor, R. & Costa, F. M. (2000) Adolescent cigarette smoking: health-related behavior or normative transgression? *Prevention Science*, 1, 115–124.

US Department of Health and Human Resources (1998) *Tobacco Use Among U.S. Racial/Ethnic Minority Groups—African American, American Indians and Alaska Natives, Asian Americans and Pacific Islanders, and Hispanics. A Report of the Surgeon General*. Atlanta, GA: US Department of Health and Human Services, Centers for Disease Control and Prevention: National Center for Chronic Disease Prevention and Health Promotion, Office on Smoking and Health.

Unger, J., Rohrbach, L. A., Cruz, L., Baezconde-Garbanati, K., Ammann, H., Palmer, P. H. & Johnson, C. A. (2001) Ethnic variation in peer influences on adolescent smoking. *Nicotine and Tobacco Research*, 3, 167–176.

Wahlstrom, K. L., ed. (1999) *Adolescent Sleep Needs and School Starting Times*. Bloomington, IN: Phi Delta Kappa Educational Foundation.

For Discussion

1. Does the tobacco industry take advantage of ethnic and cultural stereotypes in its advertising? How effective are these strategies?

2. In what ways does popular culture influence smoking, regardless of ethnic identity?

Part III

Marijuana

Marijuana is a derivative of the Indian hemp plant *Cannabis sativa L.,* an annual shrub that flourishes in most warm and temperate climates and varies in height from three to ten feet or more. The leaves are long, narrow, and serrated and form a fan-shaped pattern; each "fan" has from 3 to 15 leaves, but typically only five or seven. The leaves are shiny and sticky, and their upper surfaces are covered with short hairs. Three psychoactive preparations can be derived from cannabis:

1. *Marijuana,* the crushed and dried twigs, leaves, and flowers

2. *Hashish,* the resinous extract obtained by boiling in a solvent the parts of the plant that are covered with the resin or by scraping the resin from the plant

3. *Hashoil,* a dark, viscous liquid produced by a process of repeated extraction of cannabis material

The active ingredient in cannabis is *delta-9-tetrahydro-cannabinol,* or simply THC. The THC content of most marijuana ranges from 1 to 16 percent, depending on where and how it was grown; in hashish, this figure can be as high as 20 to 30 percent, and it is twice that for hashoil.

Cannabis products vary in both name and form in different parts of the world. In Asia, for example, there is "ganja," "charas," and "bhang." *Ganja* consists of the young leaves and flowering tops of the cultivated female plant and its resin, pressed or rolled into a sticky mass, then formed into flat or round cakes. Its color is dark green or greenish brown, and it has a pleasant smell and characteristic taste. *Charas* is the prepared resin separated from the tops of the female plant. It is pounded and rubbed until it is a gray-white powder and then made into cakes or thin, almost transparent sheets, or it is left in dark brown lumps. *Bhang* consists of the older or more mature leaves of the plant and is often used by boiling it in water and adding butter, to make a syrup. Bhang is less potent than ganja, which in turn is considerably weaker than charas.

In the Middle East the word *hashish* is usually applied to both the leaves and the resin or a mixture of the two. In North Africa, the resin and tops usually reduced to a coarse powder, known as *kif* in Morocco and *takrouri* in Algeria and Tunisia; in Central and Southern Africa, *dagga* refers to the leaves and tops.

Despite these many differences in nomenclature, the subjective effects of marijuana are essentially the same, although varying in intensity depending on THC content. At social-recreational use levels, these effects include alteration of time and space perception; a sense of euphoria, relaxation, well-being, and disinhibition; dulling of attention; fragmentation of thought and impaired immediate memory; an altered sense of identity; and exaggerated laughter and increased suggestibility. At doses higher than the typical recreational levels, more pronounced distortions of thought may occur, including a disrupted sense of one's own body, a sense of personal unreality, visual distortions, and sometimes hallucinations, paranoid thinking, and acute psychotic-like symptoms.

Although marijuana is one of the oldest psychoactive drugs, its use in the United States is relatively recent. At the beginning of the twentieth century, what was referred to in Mexico as "marijuana" (also "marihuana" and "mariguana") began to appear in New Orleans and a number of the Texas border towns. By 1920, the use of marijuana had become visible among members of minority groups—blacks in the South and Mexicans in the Southwest. Given the social and political climate of the period, it is not surprising that the use of the drug became a matter of immediate concern. The agitation for reform that had resulted in the passage of the Pure Food and Drug Act in 1906 and the Harrison Act in 1914 was still active, and the movement for national prohibition of alcohol was at its peak. Moreover, not only was marijuana an "intoxicant of blacks and wetbacks" that might have a corrupting influence on white society, but it was considered particularly dangerous because of its alien (spelled "Mexican") and un-American origins.

Through the early 1930s, state after state enacted anti-marijuana laws, usually instigated by lurid newspaper articles depicting the madness and horror attributed to the drug's use. Even the prestigious *New York Times,* with its claim of "All the News That's Fit to Print," helped reinforce the growing body of beliefs surrounding marijuana use. In an article headlined "Mexican Family Go Insane" and datelined Mexico City, July 6, 1927, the *Times* reported:

> A widow and her four children have been driven insane by eating the marihuana plant, according to doctors, who say that there is no hope of saving the children's lives and that the mother will be insane for the rest of her life. The tragedy occurred while the body of the father, who had been killed, was still in a hospital. The mother was without money to buy other food for the children, whose ages range from 3 to 15, so they gathered some herbs and vegetables growing in the yard for their dinner. Two hours after the mother and children had eaten the plants, they were stricken. Neighbors, hearing outbursts of crazed laughter, rushed to the house to find the entire family insane. Examination revealed that the narcotic marihuana was growing among the garden vegetables.

Popular books of the era were as colorful as the press in describing marijuana and the consequences of its use. A 1928 book, aptly titled *Dope: The Story of the Living Dead,* by Winifred Black, offered the following about "hasheesh":

> And the man under the influence of hasheesh catches up his knife and runs through the streets hacking and killing everyone he meets. No, he has no special grievance against mankind. When he is himself, he is probably a good-humored, harmless, well-meaning creature; but hasheesh is the murder drug, and it is the hasheesh which makes him pick up his knife and start to kill.
>
> Marihuana is American hasheesh. It is made from a little weed that grows in Texas, Arizona, and Southern California. You can grow enough marihuana in a window-box to drive the whole population of the United States stark, staring, raving mad . . . but when you have once chosen marihuana, you have selected murder and torture and hideous cruelty to your bosom friends.

In other reports, the link between the anti-marijuana sentiment and prejudice was apparent. On January 27, 1929, the *Montana Standard* reported on the progress of a bill that amended the state's general narcotic law to include marijuana:

> There was fun in the House Health Committee during the week when the Marihuana bill came up for consideration. Marihuana is Mexican opium a plant used by Mexicans and cultivated for sale by Indians. "When some bean field peon takes a few rares of this stuff," explained Dr. Fred Fulsher of Mineral County, "he thinks he has just been elected president of Mexico so he starts to execute all of his political enemies . . ." Everybody laughed and the bill was recommended for passage.

Although marijuana is neither Mexican opium nor a narcotic of any kind, it was perceived as such by a small group of legislators, newspaper editors, and concerned citizens who were pressuring Washington for federal legislation against the drug. Their demands were almost immediately heard by Harry J. Anslinger, the then recently installed Commissioner of the Treasury Department's Bureau of Narcotics in 1930. Although it would appear that Anslinger was an ultra-right-wing conservative who truly believed marijuana to be a threat to the future of American civilization, his biographer maintained that he was an astute government bureaucrat who viewed the marijuana issue as a mechanism for elevating himself and the Bureau of Narcotics to national prominence. Using the mass media as his forum, Anslinger described marijuana as a Frankenstein drug that was stalking American youth. In an issue of *American Magazine* he wrote, for example,

> The sprawled body of a young girl lay crushed on the sidewalk the other day after a plunge from the fifth story of a Chicago apartment house. Everyone called it suicide, but actually it was murder. The killer was a narcotic known to America as marijuana, and to history as hashish. It is a narcotic used in the form of cigarettes, comparatively new to the United States and as dangerous as a coiled rattlesnake.

Anslinger's crusade resulted in the signing into law of the Marijuana Tax Act on August 2, 1937, classifying "the scraggly tramp of the vegetable world" as a narcotic and placing it under essentially the same controls to which the Harrison Act had subjected opium and coca products.

Currently, marijuana is the most widely used illegal drug in the United States. Government statistics estimate that almost 95 million Americans aged 12 and over (40 percent) have tried it, and of that number, there are over 14 million current users of the drug. In 2004, marijuana was used by 75 percent of illicit drug users.

From 1960 through the end of the decade, the number of Americans who had used marijuana at least once had grown from a few hundred thousand to an estimated 8 million. By the early 1970s, marijuana use had increased geometrically throughout all strata of society, but by the onset of the 1980s evidence indicated that marijuana use was declining. In 1975, for example, surveys showed that some 30 million people were users. By the early 1980s, this figure had dropped to 20 million, with the most significant declines among people ages 25 and under. Perhaps the younger generation had begun to realize that although marijuana was not the "devil drug," "assassin of youth," or "weed of madness" that Harry Anslinger and his counterparts had maintained, it was not a totally innocuous substance either. Perhaps the change occurred because of the greater concern with health and physical fitness that became so much a part of American culture during the 1980s, or as an outgrowth of the antismoking messages that appeared daily in the media. Whatever the reason, it was clear that youthful attitudes had changed. Over the period from 1979 through the beginning of 1990, the proportion of seniors in American high schools who saw "great risk" in using marijuana even once or twice rose from 9.4 percent to 24.5 percent, while the proportion who had ever experimented with marijuana declined from 60.4 percent to 32.6 percent. However, beginning in 1992 national surveys reflected an upswing in marijuana use among youth and a corresponding decrease in perceived harmfulness. Prevalence rates peaked in the late 1990s, and although there has been a modest decline in use among youth since then, the perceived risk associated with using marijuana has continued to decline. The general public's opinion regarding marijuana has also shifted over time: one-third of Americans favor the legalization of marijuana, nearly double the percentage since 1986. Further, according to a 2002 *Time/CNN* poll, 80 percent of Americans believe that adults should be allowed to use marijuana for medicinal purposes.

In the following chapters, a variety of perspectives are presented, ranging from Harry J. Anslinger's "assassin of youth" viewpoint to Lester Grinspoon's thoughts on medical marijuana. There is also a cross-cultural examination of "blunts" and "blowtjes." Concluding Part III is an article that first appeared in the magazine *High Times*, "The Power of Four-Twenty." Karen Bettez Halnon presents a sociological analysis of "420" and its various meanings that those "in the know" of the marijuana subculture share.

Additional Readings

Black, Winifred. (1928). *DOPE: The Story of the Living Dead*. New York: Star Company.

Bock, Alan W. (2000). *Waiting to Inhale: The Politics of Medical Marijuana*. Santa Ana, CA: Seven Locks Press.

Earleywine, Mitch. (2002). *Understanding Marijuana: A New Look at the Scientific Evidence*. New York: Oxford University Press.

Russo, E., M. Dreher, and M. L. Mathre. (Eds.). (2002). *Women and Cannabis: Medicine, Science and Sociology*. Binghamton, NY: Haworth Press.

Sloman, Larry. (1979). *Reefer Madness: The History of Marijuana in America*. Indianapolis: Bobbs-Merrill.

Sussman, Steve, Alan W. Stacy, Clyde W. Dent, Thomas R. Simon, and C. Anderson Johnson. (1996). "Marijuana Use: Current Issues and New Research Directions." *Journal of Drug Issues*, 26: 695–733. ✦

11

Marijuana

Assassin of Youth

Harry J. Anslinger
Courtney Ryley Cooper

In the 1930s, Harry J. Anslinger was appointed Commissioner of the Federal Bureau of Narcotics. The following article is one of many that he wrote describing marijuana as a "Frankenstein" drug that was stalking American youth. As a result of Anslinger's crusade, on August 2, 1937, the Marijuana Tax Act was signed into law, classifying the scraggly tramp of the vegetable world as a narcotic and placing it under essentially the same controls as the Harrison Act had done with opium and coca products.

The sprawled body of a young girl lay crushed on the sidewalk the other day after a plunge from the fifth story of a Chicago apartment house. Everyone called it suicide, but actually it was murder. The killer was a narcotic known to America as marijuana, and to history as hashish. It is a narcotic used in the form of cigarettes, comparatively new to the United States and as dangerous as a coiled rattlesnake.

How many murders, suicides, robberies, criminal assaults, holdups, burglaries, and deeds of maniacal insanity it causes each year, especially among the young, can be only conjectured. The sweeping march of its addiction has been so insidious that, in numerous communities, it thrives almost unmolested largely because of official ignorance of its effects.

Here indeed is the unknown quantity among narcotics. No one can predict its effect. No one knows, when he places a marijuana cigarette to his lips, whether he will become a philosopher, a joyous reveler in a musical heaven, a mad insensate, a calm philosopher, or a murderer.

That youth has been selected by the peddlers of this poison as an especially fertile field makes it a problem of serious concern to every man and woman in America.

There was the young girl, for instance, who leaped to her death. Her story is typical. Some time before, this girl, like others of her age who attend our high schools, had heard the whispering of a secret which has gone the rounds of American youth. It promised a new thrill, the smoking of a type of cigarette which contained a "real kick." According to the whispers, this cigarette could accomplish wonderful reactions and with no harmful aftereffects. So the adventurous girl and a group of her friends gathered in an apartment, thrilled with the idea of doing "something different" in which there was "no harm." Then a friend produced a few cigarettes of the loosely rolled "homemade" type. They were passed from one to another of the young people, each taking a few puffs.

The results were weird. Some of the party went into paroxysms of laughter; every remark, no matter how silly, seemed excruciatingly funny. Others of mediocre musical ability became almost expert; the piano dinned constantly. Still others found themselves discussing weighty problems of youth with remarkable clarity. As one youngster expressed it, he "could see through stone walls." The girl danced without fatigue, and the night of unexplainable exhilaration seemed to stretch out as though it were a year long. Time, conscience, or consequences became too trivial for consideration.

Other parties followed, in which inhibitions vanished, conventional barriers departed, all at the command of this strange cigarette with its ropy, resinous odor. Finally there came a gathering at a time when the girl was behind in her studies and greatly worried. With every puff of the smoke the feeling of despondency lessened. Everything was going to be all right—at last. The girl was "floating" now, a term given to marijuana intoxication. Suddenly, in the midst of laughter and dancing, she thought of her school problems. Instantly they were solved. Without hesitancy she walked to a window and leaped to her death. Thus can marijuana "solve" one's difficulties.

The cigarettes may have been sold by a hot tamale vendor or by a street peddler, or in a dance hall or over a lunch counter, or even from sources much nearer to the customer. The police of a Midwestern city recently accused a school janitor of having conspired with four other men, not only to peddle cigarettes to children, but even to furnish apartments where smoking parties might be held.

A Chicago mother, watching her daughter die as an indirect result of marijuana addiction, told officers that at least fifty of the girl's young friends were slaves to the narcotic. This means fifty unpredictables. They may cease its use; that is not so difficult as with some narcotics. They may continue addiction until they deteriorate mentally and become insane. Or they may turn to violent forms of crime, to suicide or to murder. Marijuana gives few warnings of what it intends to do to the human brain.

The menace of marijuana addiction is comparatively new to America. In 1931, the marijuana file of the United States Narcotic Bureau was less than two inches thick, while today the reports crowd many large cabinets. Marijuana is a weed of the Indian hemp family, known in Asia as *Cannabis Indica* and in America as *Cannabis Sativa*. Almost everyone who has spent much time in rural communities has seen it, for it is cultivated in practically every state. Growing plants by the thousands were destroyed by law-enforcement officers last year in Texas, New York, New Jersey, Mississippi, Michigan, Maryland, Louisiana, Illinois, and the attack on the weed is only beginning.

It was an unprovoked crime some years ago which brought the first realization that the age-old drug had gained a foothold in America. An entire family was murdered by a youthful addict in Florida. When officers arrived at the home they found the youth staggering about in a human slaughterhouse. With an ax he had killed his father, his mother, two brothers, and a sister. He seemed to be in a daze.

"I've had a terrible dream," he said. "People tried to hack off my arms!"

"Who were they?" an officer asked.

"I don't know. Maybe one was my uncle. They slashed me with knives and I saw blood dripping from an ax."

He had no recollection of having committed the multiple crime. The officers knew him ordinarily as a sane, rather quiet young man; now he was pitifully crazed. They sought the reason. The boy said he had been in the habit of smoking something which youthful friends called "muggles," a childish name for marijuana.

Since that tragedy there has been a race between the spread of marijuana and its suppression. Unhappily, so far, marijuana has won by many lengths. The years 1935 and 1936 saw its most rapid growth in traffic. But at least we now know what we are facing. We know its history, its effects, and its potential victims. Perhaps with the spread of this knowledge the public may be aroused sufficiently to conquer the menace. Every parent owes it to his children to tell them of the terrible effects of marijuana to offset the enticing "private information" which these youths may have received. There must be constant enforcement and equally constant education against this enemy, which has a record of murder and terror running through the centuries.

The weed was known to the ancient Greeks and it is mentioned in Homer's *Odyssey*. Homer wrote that it made men forget their homes and turned them into swine. Ancient Egyptians used it. In the year 1090, there was founded in Persia the religious and military order of the Assassins, whose history is one of cruelty, barbarity, and murder, and for good reason. The members were confirmed users of hashish, or marijuana, and it is from the Arabic *"hashshashin"* that we have the English word "assassin." Even the term "running amok" relates to the drug, for the expression has been used to describe natives of the Malay Peninsula who, under the influence of hashish, engage in violent and bloody deeds.

Marijuana was introduced into the United States from Mexico, and swept across America with incredible speed. It began with the whispering of vendors in the Southwest that marijuana would perform miracles for those who smoked it, giving them a feeling of physical strength and mental power, stimulation of the imagination, the ability to be "the life of the party." The peddlers preached also of the weed's capabilities as a "love potion." Youth, always adventurous, began to look into these claims and found some of them true, not knowing that this was only half the story. They were not told that addicts may often develop a delirious rage during which they are temporarily and violently insane; that this insanity may take the form of a desire for self-destruction or a persecution complex to be satisfied only by the commission of some heinous crime.

It would be well for law-enforcement officers everywhere to search for marijuana behind cases of criminal and sex assault. During the last year a young male addict was hanged in Baltimore for criminal assault on a ten-year-old girl. His defense was that he was temporarily insane from smoking marijuana. In Alamosa, Colo., a degenerate brutally attacked a young girl while under the influence of the drug. In Chicago, two marijuana-smoking boys murdered a policeman.

In at least two dozen other comparatively recent cases of murder or degenerate sex attacks, many of them committed by youths, marijuana proved to be a contributing cause. Perhaps you remember the young desperado in Michigan who, a few months ago, caused a reign of terror by his career of burglaries and holdups, finally to be sent to prison for life after kidnapping a Michigan state policeman, killing him, then handcuffing him to the post of a rural mailbox. This young bandit was a marijuana fiend.

A sixteen-year-old boy was arrested in California for burglary. Under the influence of marijuana he had stolen a revolver and was on the way to stage a holdup when apprehended. Then there was the nineteen-year-old addict in Columbus, Ohio, who, when police responded to a disturbance complaint, opened fire upon an officer, wounding him three times, and was himself killed by the returning fire of the police. In Ohio a gang of seven young men, all less than twenty years old, had been caught after a series of 38 holdups. An officer asked them where they got their incentive.

"We only work when we're high on 'tea,' " one explained.

"On what?"

"On tea. Oh, there are lots of names for it. Some people call it 'mu' or 'muggles' or 'Mary Weaver' or 'moocah' or 'weed' or 'reefers'—there's a million names for it."

"All of which mean marijuana?"

"Sure. Us kids got on to it in high school three or four years ago; there must have been twenty-five or thirty of us who started smoking it. The stuff was cheaper then; you could buy a whole tobacco tin of it for fifty cents. Now these peddlers will charge you all they can get, depending on how shaky you are. Usually though, it's two cigarettes for a quarter."

This boy's casual story of procurement of the drug was typical of conditions in many cities in America. He told of buying the cigarettes in dance halls, from the owners of small hamburger joints, from peddlers who appeared near high schools at dismissal time. Then there were the "booth joints" or Bar-B-Q stands, where one might obtain a cigarette and a sandwich for a quarter, and there were the shabby apartments of women who provided not only the cigarettes but rooms in which girls and boys might smoke them.

"But after you get the habit," the boy added, "you don't bother much about finding a place to smoke. I've seen as many as three or four high school kids jam into a telephone booth and take a few drags."

The officer questioned him about the gang's crimes: "Remember that filling-station attendant you robbed—how you threatened to beat his brains out?"

The youth thought hard. "I've got a sort of hazy recollection," he answered. "I'm not trying to say I wasn't there, you understand. The trouble is, with all my gang, we can't remember exactly what we've done or said. When you get to 'floating,' it's hard to keep track of things."

From the other youthful members of the gang the officer could get little information. They confessed the robberies as one would vaguely remember bad dreams. "If I had killed somebody on one of those jobs, I'd never have known it," explained one youth. "Sometimes it was over before I realized that I'd even been out of my room."

Therein lies much of the cruelty of marijuana, especially in its attack upon youth.

The young, immature brain is a thing of impulses, upon which the "unknown quantity" of the drug acts as an almost overpowering stimulant. There are numerous cases on record like that of an Atlanta boy who robbed his father's safe of thousands of dollars in jewelry and cash. Of high school age, this boy apparently had been headed for an honest, successful career. Gradually, however, his father noticed a change in him. Spells of shakiness and nervousness would be succeeded by periods when the boy would assume a grandiose manner and engage in excessive, senseless laughter, extravagant conversation, and wildly impulsive actions. When these actions finally resulted in robbery the father went at his son's problem in earnest—and found the cause of it a marijuana peddler who catered to school children. The peddler was arrested.

It is this useless destruction of youth which is so heartbreaking to all of us who labor in the field of narcotic suppression. No one can predict what may happen after the smoking of the weed. I am reminded of a Los Angeles case in which a boy of seventeen killed a policeman. They had been great friends. Patrolling his beat, the officer often stopped to talk to the young fellow, to advise him. But one day the boy surged toward the patrolman with a gun in his hand; there was a blaze of yellowish flame, and the officer fell dead.

"Why did you kill him?" the youth was asked.

"I don't know," he sobbed. "He was good to me. I was high on reefers. Suddenly I decided to shoot him."

In a small Ohio town, a few months ago, a fifteen-year-old boy was found wandering the streets, mentally deranged by marijuana. Officers learned that he had obtained the dope at a garage. "Are any other school kids getting cigarettes there?" he was asked.

"Sure. I know fifteen or twenty, maybe more. I'm only counting my friends."

The garage was raided. Three men were arrested and 18 pounds of marijuana seized. "We'd been figuring on quitting the racket," one of the dopesters told the arresting officer. "These kids had us scared. After we'd gotten 'em on the weed, it looked like easy money for a while. Then they kept wanting more and more of it, and if we didn't have it for 'em, they'd get tough. Along toward the last, we were scared that one of 'em would get high and kill us all. There wasn't any fun in it."

Not long ago a fifteen-year-old girl ran away from her home in Muskegon, Mich., to be arrested later in company with five young men in a Detroit marijuana den. A man and his wife ran the place. How many children had smoked there will never be known. There were 60 cigarettes on hand, enough fodder for 60 murders.

A newspaper in St. Louis reported after an investigation this year that it had discovered marijuana "dens," all frequented by children of high-school age. The same sort of story came from Missouri, Ohio, Louisiana, Colorado—in fact, from coast to coast.

In Birmingham, Ala., a hot tamale salesman had pushed his cart about town for five years, and for a large part of that time he had been peddling marijuana cigarettes to students of a downtown high school. His stock of the weed, he said, came from Texas and consisted, when he was captured, of enough marijuana to manufacture hundreds of cigarettes.

In New Orleans, of 437 persons of varying ages arrested for a wide range of crimes, 125 were addicts. Of 37 murderers, 17 used marijuana, and of 193 convicted thieves, 34 were "on the weed."

One of the first places in which marijuana found a ready welcome was in a closely congested section of New York. Among those who first introduced it there were musicians, who had brought the habit northward with the surge of "hot" music demanding players of exceptional ability especially in improvisation. Along the Mexican border and in seaport cities it had been known for some time that the musician who desired to get the "hottest" effects from his playing often turned to marijuana for aid.

One reason was that marijuana has a strangely exhilarating effect upon the musical sensibilities (Indian hemp has long been used as a component of "singing seed" for canary birds). Another reason was that strange quality of marijuana which makes a rubber band out of time, stretching it to unbelievable lengths. The musician who uses "reefers" finds that the musical beat seemingly comes to him quite slowly, thus allowing him to interpolate any number of improvised notes with comparative ease. While under the influence of marijuana, he does not realize that he is tapping the keys with a furious speed impossible for one in a normal state of mind; marijuana has stretched out the time of the music until a dozen notes may be crowded into the space normally occupied by one. Or, to quote a young musician arrested by Kansas City officers as a "muggles smoker":

> Of course I use it—I've got to. I can't play any more without it, and I know a hundred other musicians who are in the same fix. You see, when I'm "floating," I own my saxophone. I mean I can do anything with it. The notes seem to dance out of it—no effort at all. I don't have to worry about reading the music—I'm music-crazy. Where do I get the stuff? In almost any low-class dance hall or night spot in the United States.

Soon a song was written about the drug. Perhaps you remember:

> *Have you seen*
> *That funny reefer man?*
> *He says he swam to China;*
> *Any time he takes a notion,*
> *He can walk across the ocean.*

It sounded funny. Dancing girls and boys pondered about "reefers" and learned through the whispers of other boys and girls that these cigarettes could make one accomplish the impossible. Sadly enough, they can—in the imagination. The boy who plans a holdup, the youth who seizes a gun and prepares for a murder, the girl who decides suddenly to elope with a boy she did not even know a few hours ago, does so with the confident belief that this is a thoroughly logical action without the slightest possibility of disastrous consequences. Command a person "high" on "mu" or "muggles" or "Mary Jane" to crawl on the floor and bark like a dog, and he will do it without a thought of the idiocy of the action. Everything, no matter how insane, becomes plausible. The underworld calls marijuana "that stuff that makes you able to jump off the tops of skyscrapers."

Reports from various sections of the country indicate that the control and sale of marijuana has not yet passed into the hands of the big gangster syndicates. The supply is so vast and grows in so many places that gangsters perhaps have found it difficult to dominate the source. A big, hardy weed, with serrated, swordlike leaves topped by bunchy small blooms supported upon a thick, stringy stalk, marijuana has been discovered in almost every state. New York police uprooted hundreds of plants growing in a vacant lot in Brooklyn. In New York State alone last year 200 tons of the growing weed were destroyed. Acres of it have been found in various communities. Patches have been revealed in back yards, behind signboards, in gardens. In many places in the West it grows wild. Wandering dopesters gather the tops from along the right of way of railroads.

An evidence of how large the traffic may be came to light last year near La Fitte, La. Neighbors of an Italian family had become amazed by wild stories told by the children of the family. They, it seemed, had suddenly become millionaires. They talked of owning inconceivable amounts of money, of automobiles they did not possess, of living in a palatial home. At last their absurd lies were reported to the police, who discovered that their parents were allowing them to smoke something that came from the tops of tall plants which their father grew on his farm. There was a raid, in which more than 500,000 marijuana plants were destroyed. This discovery led next day to another raid on a farm at Bourg, La. Here a crop of some 2,000 plants was found to be growing between rows of vegetables. The eight persons arrested confessed that their main source of income from this crop was in sales to boys and girls of high-school age.

With possibilities for such tremendous crops, grown secretly, gangdom has been hampered in its efforts to corner the profits of what has now become an enormous business. It is to be hoped that the menace of marijuana can be wiped out before it falls into the vicious protectorate of powerful members of the underworld.

But to crush this traffic we must first squarely face the facts. Unfortunately, while every state except one has laws to cope with the traffic, the powerful right arm which could support these states has been all but impotent. I refer to the United States government. There has been no national law against the growing, sale, or possession of marijuana.

As this is written a bill to give the federal government control over marijuana has been introduced in Congress by Representative Robert L. Doughton of North Carolina, Chairman of the House Ways and Means Committee. It has the backing of Secretary of the Treasury Morgenthau, who has under his supervision the various agencies of the United States Treasury Department, including the Bureau of Narcotics, through which Uncle Sam fights the dope evil. It is a revenue bill, modeled after other narcotic laws which make use of the taxing power to bring about regulation and control.

The passage of such a law, however, should not be the signal for the public to lean back, fold its hands, and decide that all danger is over. America now faces a condition in which a new, although ancient, narcotic has come to live next door to us, a narcotic that does not have to be smuggled into the country. This means a job of unceasing watchfulness by every police department and by every public-spirited civic organization. It calls for campaigns of education in every school, so that children will not be deceived by the wiles of peddlers, but will know of the insanity, the disgrace, the horror which marijuana can bring to its victim. And, above all, every citizen should keep constantly before him the real picture of the "reefer man"—not some funny fellow who, should he take the notion, could walk across the ocean.

In Los Angeles, Calif., a youth was walking along a downtown street after inhaling a marijuana cigarette. For many addicts, merely a portion of a "reefer" is enough to induce intoxication. Suddenly, for no reason, he decided that someone had threatened to kill him and that his life at that very moment was in danger. Wildly he looked about him. The only person in sight was an aged bootblack. Drug crazed nerve centers conjured the innocent old shoe-shiner into a destroying monster. Mad with fright, the addict hurried to his room and got a gun. He killed the old man, and then, later, babbled his grief over what had been wanton, uncontrolled murder.

"I thought someone was after me," he said. "That's the only reason I did it. I had never seen the old fellow before. Something just told me to kill him!"

That's marijuana!

For Discussion

This article was published a few years after alcohol prohibition was repealed. Is it likely that the United States government will always keep some drugs illegal? How might the government benefit from certain drug prohibitions?

Reprinted from: Harry J. Anslinger and Courtney Ryley Cooper, "Marijuana: Assassin of Youth." In *American Magazine*, July 1937. ◆

12
Medical Marihuana in a Time of Prohibition

Lester Grinspoon

The use of marijuana for medicinal purposes has been debated for several years. In this article, Lester Grinspoon describes the legal debates and legislation regarding marijuana. He discusses various methods and sources for accessing marijuana for medical purposes and describes the problems associated with these sources of access. He argues that marijuana has great potential for treating various illnesses and symptoms but notes that current legislation is restrictive and actually impedes our understanding of the full benefits of medicinal marijuana. He also suggests that laws regarding marijuana should mirror the laws regarding the regulation of alcohol.

> "A new scientific truth does not triumph by convincing its opponents and making them see the light, but rather because its opponents eventually die and a new generation grows up that is familiar with it."
> —Max Planck

The medical value of marihuana has become increasingly clear to many physicians and patients. There are three reasons for this. First, it is remarkably non-toxic. Unlike most of the medicines in the present pharmacopeia, it has never caused an overdose death. Its short-term and long-term side effects are minimal compared with medicines for which it will be substituted. Second, once patients no longer have to pay the prohibi-tion tariff, it will be much less expensive than the medicines it replaces. Third, it is remarkably versatile. Case histories and clinical experience suggest that it is useful in the treatment of more than two dozen symptoms and syndromes, and others will undoubtedly be discovered in the future.

As clinical evidence of marihuana's medical efficacy and safety accumulates and firsthand experience of its value becomes more common, the discussion is turning to how it should be made available. When I first considered this issue in the early 1970s, I thought the main problem was its classification in Schedule I of the Comprehensive Drug Abuse and Control Act of 1970, which describes it as having a high potential for abuse, no accepted medical use in the United States, and lack of accepted safety for use under medical supervision. At that time I naively believed that a change to Schedule II would overcome a major obstacle, because clinical research would be possible and prescriptions would eventually be allowed.

I was the first witness at a joint meeting of the Drug Enforcement Administration and the Food and Drug Administration that was convened to consider a petition for rescheduling introduced by the National Organization for the Reform of Marijuana Laws in 1972. At that time I had already come to believe that the greatest harm in recreational use of marihuana came not from the drug itself but from the effects of prohibition. But I saw that as a separate issue; I thought that, like opiates and cocaine, cannabis could be used medically while remaining outlawed for other purposes. I also thought that once it was transferred to Schedule II, research on marihuana would be pursued eagerly, since it had shown such interesting therapeutic properties. From this research we would eventually be able to determine how it should be used medicinally, how prescriptions could be provided, and who would be responsible for quality control. I have begun to doubt this, 25 years later. It would be highly desirable if marihuana could be approved as a legitimate medicine within the present federal regulatory system, but it now seems to me unlikely.

First, I should note that cannabis has already been a legally accepted medicine in the United States several times. Until 1941, when it was dropped after the passage of the Marihuana Tax Act, it was one of the drugs listed in the U.S. Pharmacopeia. If it had not been removed at that time, it would have been grandfathered into the Comprehensive Drug Abuse and Control Act as a prescription drug, just as cocaine and morphine were. Again, in the late 1970s and early 1980s, cannabis was used medically by hundreds of patients (mainly in the form of synthetic tetrahydrocannabinol) in projects conducted by several of the states for the treatment of nausea and vomiting in cancer chemotherapy. This episode ended because each state program had to comply with an enormous federal paperwork burden that was more than the physicians and administrators involved could bear. The federal government itself approved the use of cannabis as a medicine in 1976 by instituting the Compassionate IND program, under which physicians could obtain an individual Investigational New Drug application (IND) for a patient to receive cannabis. This program too was so bureaucratically burdened that in the course of its history only about three dozen patients ever received marihuana, and only eight are still receiving it. When the program was discontinued permanently in 1992, James O. Mason, the chief of the Public Health Service, gave the following reason: "If it is perceived that the Public Health Service is going around giving marihuana to folks, there would be a perception that this stuff can't be so bad. It gives a bad signal. I don't mind doing that if there is no other way of helping these people . . . But there is not a shred of evidence that smoking marihuana assists a person with AIDS." In effect, this action was analogous to the recall of a prescription drug, without any evidence of toxic effects to support it.

Today, even transferring marihuana to Schedule II would not be enough to make it available as a prescription drug. Such drugs must undergo rigorous, expensive, and time-consuming tests before they are approved by the Food and Drug Administration for marketing as medicines. The purpose is to protect the consumer by establishing safety and efficacy. Because no drug is completely safe or always efficacious, an approved drug has presumably satisfied a risk-benefit analysis. When physicians prescribe for individual patients they conduct an informal analysis of a similar kind, taking into account not just the drug's overall safety and efficacy, but its risk and benefits for a given patient with a given condition. The formal drug approval procedures help to provide physicians with the information they need to make this analysis.

This system is designed to regulate the commercial distribution of drug company products and protect the public against false or misleading claims about their efficacy and safety. The drug is generally a single synthetic chemical the company has developed and patented. It submits an application to the Food and Drug Administration and tests it first for safety in animals and then for clinical efficacy and safety. The company must present evidence from double-blind controlled studies showing that the drug is more effective than a placebo and as effective as available drugs. Case reports, expert opinion, and clinical experience are not considered sufficient. The standards have been tightened since the present system was established in 1962, and few applications that were approved in the early 1960s would be approved today on the basis of the same evidence.

Certainly we need more laboratory and clinical research to improve our understanding of medicinal cannabis. We need to know how many patients and which patients with each symptom or syndrome are likely to find cannabis more effective than existing drugs. We also need to know more about its effects on the immune system in immunologically impaired patients, its interactions with other medicines, and its possible uses for children.

But I have come to doubt whether the FDA rules should apply to cannabis. There is no question about its safety. It is one of humanity's oldest medicines, used for thousands of years by millions of people with very little evidence of significant toxic effects. More is known about its adverse effects than about those of most prescription drugs. The American government has conducted a decades-long multimillion-dollar research program in a futile attempt to demonstrate toxic effects that would justify the prohibition of cannabis as a non-medical drug. Should time and resources be wasted to demonstrate for the FDA what is already so obvious?

As for efficacy, some believe that has been proven too, although most disagree. During the 1970s and 1980s several of the state-sponsored research projects I mentioned suggested that marihuana had advantages over both oral tetrahydrocannabinol and other medicines in the treatment of nausea and vomiting from cancer chemotherapy. But as long as the imprimatur of science can be given only to rigorous double-blind controlled studies, the case for marihuana has not been made. The assertion that it is a useful medicine rests almost entirely on case reports and clinical experience, just as it did in the late 19th and early 20th centuries.

A double-blind controlled study may be the best way to prove the relative value of a new medicine whose advantages over established drugs are not obvious. But it is not the only way to demonstrate efficacy. The focus of controlled trials is usually statistical differences in effects in groups of patients, but medicine has always been concerned mainly with individuals, whose needs can be obscured in such experiments, especially when little effort is made to identify distinctive characteristics that affect their responses. The value of case reports and clinical experience is often underestimated. They are the source of much of our knowledge of synthetic medicines as well as plant derivatives. Controlled experiments were not needed to recognize the therapeutic potential of chloral hydrate, barbiturates, aspirin, curare, or lithium. The therapeutic value of penicillin was widely recognized after it had been given to only six patients. Similar evidence revealed the use of propranolol for hypertension, diazepam for status epilepticus, and imipramine for childhood enuresis. These drugs had originally been approved by regulators for other purposes.

As early as 1976 several small and imperfect studies, not widely known in the medical community, had shown that an aspirin a day could prevent a second heart attack. In 1988 a large-scale experiment demonstrated effects so dramatic that the researchers decided to stop the experiment to publish the life-saving results. On one estimate, as many as 20,000 deaths a year might have been prevented from the mid 1970s to the late 1980s if the medical establishment had been quicker to recognize the value of aspirin. The lesson is suggestive: marihuana, like aspirin, is a substance known to be unusually safe and with enormous potential medical benefits. There is one contrast, however; it was impossible to be sure about the effect of aspirin on heart attacks without a long-term study involving large numbers of patients, but innumerable reports show that cannabis often brings immediate relief of suffering that can be measured in a single person.

Case histories are, in a sense, simply the smallest research studies, and the case reports on marihuana are numerous and persuasive. There is an experimental method known as the N-of-1 clinical trial, or the single-patient randomized trial. In this type of experiment, active and placebo treatments are administered randomly in alternation or succession to a patient. The method is often useful when large-scale controlled studies are impossible or inappropriate because the disorder is rare, the patient is atypical, or the response to the treatment is idiosyncratic.

Some medical marihuana patients I know of carried out similar experiments on themselves by alternating periods of cannabis use with periods of no use. They had such symptoms as nausea and vomiting, muscle spasms, compromised vision, seizures, and debilitating pruritus. It is certain that cannabis won its reputation as a medicine partly because many other patients around the world have carried out the same kind of experiment. Admittedly, in these experiments cannabis could not be administered completely at random and there was no placebo, but in any case its psychoactive effects are usually unmistakable, and few patients or observers could be deceived by a placebo. Case histories and other reports of clinical experience are sometimes disparagingly dismissed as merely "anecdotal" evidence, which is said to be irrelevant because only apparent successes are counted and failures are ignored. It is true that cannabis may be useful for some people with, say, multiple sclerosis, chronic pain, or depression, and not for others. But cannabis is so safe that if even a few patients with a given symptom could get that kind of relief, they should be allowed access to it.

Even if it made sense to put marihuana through the FDA process, there would be other problems in taking the conventional route to medical legitimacy. As I have mentioned, FDA procedures are designed for single chemical compounds, but marihuana is a plant material containing many chemicals. Also, it is taken chiefly by smoking, and no other drug in the present pharmacopeia is delivered by this route. Furthermore, thousands of people are already getting relief from cannabis, and they would not be risking severe penalties if they did not believe that it was more useful than conventional medicines. Can we expect them to put their pain and suffering on hold for years while the established procedures grind away?

Patients, their families, and others are becoming increasingly impatient for a legal means of obtaining medical cannabis. The most dramatic manifestation of this impatience has been the referenda allowing distribution of medicinal cannabis that have been passed in several states. In 1996 California became the first state to approve such a law. Within weeks of the vote, more than a dozen cannabis clubs opened to help sick people in need of relief, and the membership of one quickly grew to 8000. Many Americans believe that this is the best temporary approach to the problem of making medical cannabis available.

Among those who understand the present importance of the cannabis clubs or cooperatives, there are two views on their organization. One model follows the conventional delivery system for medicine: the patient who needs medicinal cannabis (read medicine) goes to the buyers club (read pharmacy) and presents a note from a physician which certifies that the patient has a condition for which the physician recommends cannabis (read prescription) to the staff of the buyers club (read pharmacist). If both the doctor and the buyers club behave responsibly and ethically, only those who have a certified need for the medicine can receive it, and those who are certified now have a reliable source. They are relieved of the anxiety of having to find it on the street or grow their own.

In a buyers club of this kind, the patient is of course not expected to take the medicine on the premises. In contrast, the second distribution model resembles a social club more than a pharmacy. The dispensing area is plastered with menus offering types, grades, and prices. Large rooms are filled with brightly colored posters, lounge chairs and sofas, tables, magazines, and newspapers. While some people remain only long enough to buy their medicine, most stay to smoke and talk. There are animated conversations, laughter, music, and the pervasive pungent odor of cannabis. The atmosphere is informal, welcoming, and warm, providing support for patients who may be socially isolated and have little opportunity to share concerns and feelings about their illnesses. This type of club is a blend of Amsterdam-style coffeehouse, American bar, and medical support group.

Most people who recognize the importance of the buyers clubs believe that the first model, epitomized by the now closed Oakland Club, is preferable to the second model, represented by the now closed San Francisco Cultivators' Club. The San Francisco model, largely because of the on-site cannabis smoking and relaxed atmosphere, seems more casual in its commitment to confirming medical need, and this has made even the supporters of buyers clubs a little nervous. Yet the importance of the social aspect cannot be underestimated. It is becoming increasingly clear that emotional support— contacts with and help from friends, family, co-workers, and others—plays an important role in battling illness. This support improves the quality of life and may even prolong the life of people with various illnesses, including cancer. The San Francisco buyers club was not designed by psychiatrists and social scientists to provide supportive group therapy, but there is reason to believe it did. One of the properties of marihuana may have contributed to its effectiveness: when people use cannabis, they tend to be more sociable and find it easier to share difficult thoughts and feelings. If there is even a kernel of truth to the idea that talking about the stress, setbacks, and triumphs in the battle against an illness can help a patient cope and recover, it is clear that the San Francisco model provides the best kind of environment for the dispensing of marihuana.

Unfortunately, even many supporters of medical cannabis regarded the language of California Proposition 215 as permitting the legal use, cultivation, and distribution of marihuana too broadly. The initiatives passed more recently in several states have more tightly drawn limitations. They will not permit cannabis clubs with the medical and psychiatric advantages of the San Francisco model, and they allow such a short list of medical uses that only a few of the patients who could find marihuana helpful will be allowed to use it. But in any case, buyers clubs have to be regarded as a stopgap measure. The federal government is not going to allow the development of a separate distribution system for one medicine. It has already succeeded in closing most of the California buyers clubs, and if it is as successful elsewhere, they will not long endure.

Other present approaches to making marihuana medically available have even more serious drawbacks. Marihuana is now classified as a Schedule I drug, which means that it is legally defined as too dangerous for use even under medical supervision. But for the sake of argument, let us suppose that the government comes to its senses and marihuana is moved to Schedule II. This would allow investigators to do the studies which lead to FDA approval for medical use. But where will the money to finance these studies come from? New medicines are usually introduced by drug companies, which spend an estimated US$200,000,000 or more on the development of each product. They are willing to undertake these costs only because they hope for large profits during the 20 years they own the patent. Obviously pharmaceutical companies cannot patent marihuana and, in fact, may oppose its acceptance as a medicine because it will compete with their own products. Only the U.S. government has sufficient resources to explore medical marihuana. But its record on the matter is, to put it mildly, not reassuring. The government has opposed any loosening of restrictions on clinical research with cannabis, including the research needed for

FDA approval. I believe the government will ultimately have to provide some support for this research because of public pressure, but it will arrive slowly. A study of marihuana in the treatment of the AIDS wasting syndrome has recently been approved and funded after 4 years of obstruction. But this happened only because the political climate had changed after the California initiative, and even so, the main subject of the study had to be changed from medical efficacy to safety.

But let us suppose that studies are somehow completed showing that marihuana is safe and effective as a treatment for the weight reduction syndrome of AIDS, and physicians are able to prescribe it for that condition. This will present unique problems. When a drug is approved for one medical purpose, physicians are generally free to write off-label prescriptions—that is, prescribe it for other conditions as well. Dronabinol (Marinol), a synthetic form of tetrahydrocannabinol, was approved as a prescription drug in 1986 for the treatment of nausea and vomiting in cancer chemotherapy, and later for the treatment of the weight reduction syndrome of AIDS. However, presumably because it was thought to be susceptible to medically questionable use, it became the first FDA-approved drug for which off-label use was forbidden. The ban has proved too difficult to enforce, and doctors have prescribed it off-label, although somewhat timidly. If marihuana is approved as a medicine, how will this concern about off-label prescriptions be dealt with?

Present state and federal schemes for making cannabis medically available invariably specify that it must be used for the treatment of illnesses defined as "serious," "life-threatening," "terminal," or "debilitating." Which of the many symptoms and syndromes for which cannabis is useful should be considered "serious"? For example, what about premenstrual syndrome? Surely women who suffer from this disorder consider it a serious problem, and many of them find that marihuana is the most useful treatment. What about intractable hiccups or the loss of erectile capacity in paraplegics? The people who suffer from these rare problems know how debilitating they can be.

Generally speaking, the more dangerous a drug is, the more serious or debilitating must be the symptom or illness for which it is approved. Conversely, the more serious the health problem, the more risk is tolerated. If the benefit is very large and the risk very small, the medicine is distributed over the counter (OTC). OTC drugs are considered so useful and safe that patients are allowed to use their own judgment without a doctor's permission or advice. Thus, today anyone can buy and use aspirin for any purpose at all. This is permissible because aspirin is considered so safe; it takes "only" 1000–2000 lives a year in the United States. The remarkably versatile ibuprofen and other NSAIDs can also be purchased over the counter, because they too are considered very safe; "only" 7000 Americans lose their lives to these drugs annually. Acetaminophen, another useful OTC drug, is responsible for about 10% of cases of end-stage renal disease. The public is also allowed to purchase many herbal remedies whose dangers have not been determined and which probably have only placebo effects.

Compare these drugs with marihuana. Today no one can doubt that it is, as DEA Administrative Judge Francis L. Young put it, "among the safest therapeutic substances known to man." If it were now in the official pharmacopeia, it would be a serious contender for the title of least toxic substance in that compendium. In its long history, marihuana has never caused a single overdose death. Yet government schemes for its medical use are always cloaked in language suggesting that it is too dangerous to be used except under the most stringent limitations. In several states, medical marihuana initiatives require patients to register, and in two states they will need identification cards to protect them from arrest.

As a Schedule II drug, marihuana would be classified as having a high potential for abuse and limited medical use. Restrictions on these drugs are becoming tighter. Nine states now require doctors to make out prescriptions for many of them in triplicate so that one copy can be sent to a centralized computer system that tracks every transaction. In 1989 New York State added the benzodiazepines (Valium and related drugs)

to the list of substances monitored in this way. Research has shown that since then many patients in New York who have a legitimate need for benzodiazepines are being denied them, and less safe and effective drugs are being substituted. Increased regulation caused by fear of drug abuse has been to the disadvantage rather than the advantage of patients.

In such situations physicians are often afraid to recommend what they know or suspect to be the best medicine because they might lose their reputations, licenses, and careers. Pharmacies might be reluctant to carry marihuana as a Schedule II drug, and physicians would hesitate to prescribe it. Through computer-based monitoring, the DEA could know who was receiving prescription marihuana and how much. It could hound physicians who by its standards prescribed cannabis too freely or for off-label purposes the government considered unacceptable. The potential for harassment would be extremely discouraging. Unlike other Schedule II drugs such as cocaine and morphine, cannabis has many potential medical uses. Many patients might try to persuade their doctors that they had a legitimate claim to a prescription. Physicians would not want the responsibility of making such decisions if they were constantly under threat of discipline by the state. A physician who prescribed marihuana for chronic pain, for example, might be subjected to the same harassment as those whom the DEA considers to be dispensing opioids too liberally. Since the passage of the medical marihuana initiative in California, I have heard from many patients who say their doctors are afraid to recommend (not prescribe) marihuana because of threats from the federal government—even though those threats have been declared by the courts to be legally baseless.

There is actually no case for the present restrictions—unless third-party reefer-madness anxiety counts as a risk. The Schedule II classification of cannabis would not be accurate. It does not have a high potential for abuse, and above all, it does not have limited medical uses. For example, a physician might sensibly and safely prescribe it for muscle spasms and chronic pain resulting from a variety of conditions, from paraplegia to premenstrual syndrome. If the government and medical licensing boards insist on tight restrictions, challenging physicians as though cannabis were a dangerous drug every time it is used for any new patient or any new purpose, there will be constant conflict with one of two outcomes: patients do not get all the benefits they should from this medicine, or they get the benefits by abandoning the legal system for the black market or their own outdoor or closet gardens.

Then there is the question of who will provide the cannabis. The federal government now provides cannabis from its farm in Mississippi to eight patients who have residual Compassionate INDs. But surely the government could not or would not produce marihuana for many thousands of patients receiving prescriptions, any more than it does for other prescription drugs. But if production is contracted out, will the farmers have to enclose their fields with security fences? How would the marihuana be distributed? If through pharmacies, how would they provide secure facilities capable of keeping fresh supplies? When urine tests are demanded for workers, how would patients who use marihuana legally as a medicine be distinguished from those who use it for other (disapproved) purposes?

If the full potential of cannabis as a medicine were to be achieved in the setting of the present prohibition system, all of these problems and more would have to be addressed. A delivery system that successfully navigated this minefield would be so cumbersome, inefficient, and bureaucratically top-heavy that patients would continue to grow their own or buy it on the illicit market. The authorities could claim that a legal medical distribution apparatus existed, but most patients would find themselves in the same situation they are in today. The Compassionate IND program, the federal government's last scheme to satisfy these needs, lasted from 1976 to 1992 but never supplied more than a few dozen patients with cannabis.

Some believe a solution to the "medical marihuana problem" (restricting the use of cannabis for medical purposes only) will be found in the isolation of individual cannabinoids, the manufacture of synthetic cannabinoids, and the development of analogs (chemical cousins of cannabinoids). Supposedly, these drugs, sometimes in combination, will make the natural product superfluous. Their use in the form of parenterals, nasal sprays, vaporizers, skin patches, pills, and suppositories will allegedly make it unnecessary to expose the lungs to the particulate matter in marihuana smoke. Furthermore, the commercial products may lack psychoactive effects, which is apparently very important to some people. A pain researcher at the Memorial Sloan-Kettering Cancer Institute recently said that he was excited by the new analogs because "the euphoria sparked by cannabinoids . . . is undesirable in chronically ill patients." Not everyone will agree that freedom from the psychoactive effects is an advantage, but some cannabinoids and analogs may be preferable to whole smoked or ingested marihuana for other reasons. For example, cannabidiol may be more effective as an anti-anxiety drug when it is taken without THC, which sometimes generates anxiety. Other cannabinoid analogs may occasionally prove more useful than marihuana because they can be administered intravenously. For example, loss of consciousness occurs in 15–20% of patients who suffer a thrombotic or embolic stroke, an even higher proportion after a hemorrhagic stroke, and some who develop a brain syndrome after a severe blow to the head. The cannabinoid analog dexanabinol (HU 211) has recently been shown to limit brain swelling and protect brain cells from damage in these circumstances. It is apparently not psychoactive and can be given intravenously to an unconscious person.

The modern pharmaceutical laboratory will undoubtedly develop other cannabinoid-related products with properties that whole marihuana and marihuana extracts lack. There are already two known receptors for cannabinoids with different anatomical distributions and only partially overlapping functions. New agonists, antagonists, and inverse agonists will be developed for these receptors (and possibly for others still to be discovered), some of which may have therapeutic potential. For example, tetrahydrocannabinol and possibly other cannabinoids enhance appetite. Perhaps pharmacologists will develop cannabinoid inverse agonists which inhibit appetite and act as non-toxic weight reduction medicines. A better understanding of brain functions will also result from this kind of research.

But these encouraging developments have a worrisome downside. South American Indians have chewed the coca leaf for thousands of years with little apparent abuse and few ill effects, but since the isolation of methylbenzoylecgonine (cocaine) from the leaf's other natural alkaloids, some users have developed serious problems. Similarly, opium in its natural form is less risky than, say, the potent synthetic opioid fentanyl. HU 211 (dexanabinol) is not psychoactive, but its stereoisomer, HU 210, synthesized in the same laboratory, is hundreds of times more psychoactive than THC. Other analogs may be equally potent. The danger is that they will bear the same relationship to marihuana that fentanyl bears to opium.

There are other reasons why isolated cannabinoids and cannabinoid analogs will probably never completely displace marihuana itself as a medicine. It was once widely believed that the availability of dronabinol would make medical marihuana superfluous. Dronabinol is packed in sesame oil, partly for easier absorption, but also because it makes smoking impossible and therefore was thought to make non-medical use unlikely. But patients have generally not found dronabinol to be nearly as useful as whole smoked marihuana. Even among those who judge it equally effective, many find that street marihuana is less expensive. If the advent of prescribable dronabinol did not make marihuana medically obsolete, it is hard to believe that the arrival of new analogs will do so. I believe that many if not most patients who could get benefits from the new analogs will choose instead to smoke the more easily accessible and less expensive marihuana.

In evaluating the prospects for cannabis analogs, we must consider what a pharmaceutical product requires for economic success:

1. It must be as useful as or more useful than competitive medicines for a particular symptom or syndrome, or it must have a wide variety of approved medicinal uses.

2. It must not have more undesirable side effects than competitive medicines.

3. It must have a mode of delivery which is as good as or better than available alternatives.

4. It must be priced competitively.

5. It must have a risk-benefit ratio which is at least as good as that of competitive medicines.

6. It must not be restrictively scheduled under the federal Comprehensive Drug Abuse and Control Act. The more restrictive the schedule, the more serious the impact on marketability and the cost of development.

Now compare the anticipated analogs with whole marihuana:

1. Except in a few situations, such as intravenous injection in an unconscious person, analogs or combinations of analogs are unlikely to be more useful than natural cannabis for most specific symptoms. Nor are they likely to have a much wider spectrum of therapeutic uses than the natural product, which contains the cannabinoids (and synergistic combinations of cannabinoids) from which the analogs are derived. In fact, one result of the development of new analogs may be to identify new medical uses for marihuana in its natural form. Shortly after dexanabinol, which is both a potent antioxidant and an NMDA antagonist, was found to protect brain cells against damage after a stroke or trauma, it was shown that THC and cannabidiol, also potent antioxidants, provide the same kind of protection. In fact, given the urgency of retarding the pathological process set in motion by a stroke or brain trauma, it may be more medically sensible to allow patients with closed head injuries to smoke the more accessible marihuana immediately upon regaining consciousness as they await transportation to a hospital to receive dexanabinol.

2. The analogs may not cause such minor side effects as inflammation of the sclera of the eyes or increased heart rate, but these are not medically significant. Except for infrequent orthostatic hypotension (faintness on standing up), pulmonary exposure to smoke and, in the opinion of some, the psychoactive effect (the high), marihuana has few medically significant side effects.

3. Inhalation devices now being perfected protect the lungs by separating the cannabinoids in whole marihuana from burnt plant products. When these devices are manufactured in large numbers, they will provide an inexpensive, safe, and highly effective means of delivery. Again, except for a few situations such as unconsciousness and pulmonary impairment, it is doubtful that a better means of delivery will be available for analogs.

4. Given the cost of development, the new analogs will be expensive. They will probably cost much more than whole smoked marihuana even at the inflated prices imposed by the prohibition tariff. Suppose, for example, that a new analog is an antinauseant comparable with the prescription drug ondansetron in effectiveness and price. Today a patient suffering from the nausea of cancer chemotherapy might require from one to four 8 mg ondansetron pills at $30–40 apiece. Many patients will probably get equally effective relief from a few puffs of a marihuana cigarette— cost $5 at today's street price, 30 cents if marihuana is produced as a medicine.

5. The potential benefits of whole smoked marihuana are extraordinarily high compared with the risks. For example, the therapeutic ratio of marihuana is not known because it has never caused an overdose death. It has been estimated on the basis of extrapolation from animal data to be 20,000–40,000:1. Even if the therapeutic ratio of a new analog is also high, it is unlikely to be as safe as whole marihuana because it will be physically possible to ingest much more of the analog.

6. Any new cannabinoid analog with psychoactive properties would presumably have to be placed in a restricted schedule by the federal government. The Unimed Corporation, which makes dronabinol, is now attempting to have it transferred from Schedule II to Schedule III. That would allow physicians to write prescriptions which could be refilled up to three times, reducing the inconvenience and cost to the patient. Yet THC in the form of dronabinol is chemically the same as the THC in whole marihuana, which remains in Schedule I. It will become increasingly difficult to justify such inconsistencies, which might be regarded as hypocritical.

Ultimately, I do not believe the full potential of cannabinoids as medicines can be realized through the use of prescription analogs as long as the crushing, costly prohibition on natural marihuana is maintained. Will prescription analogs be approved for all of the present and future medical uses of whole cannabis? If not, will off-label prescriptions of the analogs be allowed? And if prescription drugs are available, will they always be sought? For example, minor stomach upset is almost always quickly relieved with a few puffs of cannabis. Will people suffering from this symptom go to the trouble and expense of seeking a prescription? When it is generally appreciated that marihuana usually relieves not only gastric distress, but many other common symptoms such as headache, insomnia, tension, pain and dysphoria, it may come to be regarded much as aspirin is today.

In fact, the range of beneficial uses of marihuana is so broad that it may ultimately be wrong to single out the strictly medical uses for approval. Many people use it not only to ease everyday discomforts, but also to heighten creativity or help them in their work. It can serve as an intellectual stimulant, promote emotional intimacy, or enhance the appreciation of food, sex, natural beauty, music, and art. Cannabis use simply cannot be made to conform to the boundaries established by present medical institutions. In this case the demand for legal enforcement of a distinction between medical and non-medical use may be incompatible with the realities of human need. I know that to say this is to invite the charge that medical marihuana advocates are only using medicine as a stalking horse for the legalization of non-medical use. This false accusation is actually a mirror image of the view taken by enemies of marihuana. They are unwilling to admit that it can be a safe and effective medicine largely because they are committed to exaggerating its dangers when used for other purposes. Nevertheless, it would be hypocritical to deny that there is a connection. For 28 years I have been urging the legalization of marihuana for general use. At one time I thought medical use could be treated as a distinct issue, because even people who might never see the urgency of legalizing non-medical use would respond to medical need. Now I have changed my mind. On the contrary, I believe that making marihuana fully available as a medicine is one of the reasons for general legalization.

Ideally, cannabis should be available under more or less the same rules now applied to alcohol. At present, I fear, the political and legal system is too ossified to accommodate that change. But I believe enforcement of the laws against marihuana will be increasingly neglected because of the same kind of public pressure that has led to the enactment of the medical marihuana initiatives in five states. If I am correct, anti-marihuana statutes will come to resemble the laws against oral sex which still exist in several states but are ignored so totally that most people do not even know they exist. As the number of people arrested for possession declines, cannabis in its natural form, along with isolated cannabinoids and analogs, will be used more freely as a medicine. As a result, the public will be in a better position to learn about its virtues, and our understanding of those virtues will in turn make the laws more difficult to enforce. I hope and expect that this process will bring the era of prohibition to a de facto end. Only then will it be possible to realize the full potential of this remarkable substance, and its medical potential in particular.

For Discussion

1. Is medical marijuana a distinct issue apart from the wider legalization debate? Can medical marijuana be legal without easing the drug laws in general?

2. What do you consider to be the most important forces prohibiting marijuana from gaining medical legitimacy?

Reprinted from: Lester Grinspoon, "Medical Marihuana in a Time of Prohibition." In *International Journal of Drug Policy*, 10, pp. 145–156. Copyright © 1999 by Elsevier Science B.V. Reprinted with permission. ✦

13

Blunts and Blowtjes

Cannabis Use Practices in Two Cultural Settings and Their Implications for Secondary Prevention

Stephen J. Sifaneck
Charles D. Kaplan
Eloise Dunlap
Bruce D. Johnson

In this article, Stephen Sifaneck and his colleagues use data from two cultures to explore cannabis smoking patterns and the implications for health and prevention. They describe primary prevention and introduce the concept of "secondary prevention." The authors note how cannabis preparations and social context differ across the two cultures. However, other behaviors, e.g., self-regulation, were practiced by users in both cultures. The article demonstrates the importance of acknowledging differences in rituals and subcultural norms that often vary across cultures. The authors argue that prevention efforts must recognize these differences and respond accordingly.

Introduction

Over the last the ten years the use of cannabis in the United States and the Netherlands has remained consistently more prevalent among youth and young adults than it was throughout the 1980s (Johnston, O'Malley & Bachman 1999; Golub & Johnson 2001; Korf & van der Steenhoven 1993; Cohen & Kaal 2001). National and local government agencies have been addressing this trend with traditional methods of preven-

tion supported by new messages which utilize different forms of media and focus specifically on marijuana. The dangers of marijuana are vigorously highlighted in order to discourage new users and to persuade current users to cease using. "Primary prevention" strategies consistent with the values of a drug-free society continue to characterize the American response (Cohen 1993; Botvin 1990). Scaring youths away from drugs by illustrating their dangers and negative outcomes, and the 'responsible' choice of completely avoiding illicit drugs, are the reoccurring themes in the television and newspaper advertisements developed by the Partnership for a Drug-Free America. The Center for Substance Abuse Prevention (CSAP) articulates "The term 'prevention' is reserved for those interventions that occur before the initial onset of the disorder" (Center for Substance Abuse Prevention 1995). In the Netherlands, where the epidemiological trend regarding marijuana is similar, prevention efforts are consistent with its specific policy on cannabis and its general commitment to harm reduction. Prevention is aimed at tightening up the regulations governing the coffeeshop system—where the retail sales of marijuana and hashish are tolerated and health education efforts targeted at the problematic cannabis use of youth. The intention of separating hard (heroin, cocaine, amphetamine) and soft (marijuana, hashish) drug markets, by tolerating the retail sale of cannabis in coffeeshops is to prevent young cannabis users who are experimenting with cannabis from using more dangerous drugs. In the Netherlands, the harm-reduction approach to cannabis can be compared to the work done on controlled drinking and risk reduction among youth in the United States (Marlatt, Baer & Larimer 1995).

This diverse array of prevention efforts, developed in two different cultural and political settings, have been largely uninformed by research of the new and emerging groups of cannabis users which seem to be accounting for the increase in reported prevalence over the last decade. For the most part, cannabis users are typically all lumped into a single youthful category that does not differentiate from the groups that began smoking cannabis more then a generation earlier in the 1960s. American prevention efforts have undervalued the role of changing social meanings of cannabis and related use practices in the groups that are already using it.

This paper analyzes these newly emerged meanings in two contrasting social and policy contexts, the United States (US) and the Netherlands (NL). These analyses are extremely valuable for the development of future prevention strategies. Without a more thorough understanding of these meanings and use practices, it is likely that prevention efforts will be misunderstood, ignored, or even increase use through heightening the anxiety and cognitive dissonance already associated with cannabis. Furthermore, related to these meanings are specific ritualized practices that function to regulate use. Hence, the description and analysis of these rituals can also contribute to "secondary prevention" by identifying naturally occurring customs of social control which create acceptable norms of use and strengthen self-regulation. These practices provide opportunities for prevention work that is not only aimed at abstinence (primary prevention), but, also, secondary prevention, with the intent of reducing the harm associated with the use of cannabis with active users.

Generators of Meaning and Practices: Artistic, Drug, and Sacred Subcultures in the Last 50 Years

One factor for the recent international popularity of cannabis has been the emerging youth subcultures of the 1980s and 1990s which rejected the polarization between "just say no" youth and cocaine using youth. Specifically Hip-Hop and Rastafarianism (re)emerged embracing cannabis as their primary, and often exclusive, drug of choice, but with meanings and rituals that distinguish them from earlier cannabis using subcultures (Sifaneck & Kaplan 1995). Popular culture is also portraying today's cannabis users as trend setters in the social world of illicit drug taking. A number of cover articles about cannabis users of the 1990s have appeared, including the *New York Times Magazine* (1995), the *Village Voice* (1993), *Paper* (1994), and the *Face* (1994). Feature films in-

cluding "Friday" (1995) and "Kids" (1995) have illustratively depicted the lifestyles of these new cannabis users. Even though these new cannabis subcultures borrow rituals and technologies from previous drug subcultures, some of the innovations are unique.

The relationship between cannabis use and subcultures has a long tradition in sociological research. In the 1970s focus shifted from subcultures largely defined by specific artistic scenes (Winick 1960; Becker 1963), to subcultures defined by the use and sales of specific drugs (Johnson 1973). Primary deviance, like drug experimentation, was hypothesized only to lead to secondary deviance (drug dealing, use of hard drugs) if a person became a participant in a drug using subculture through selling drugs. Users who get involved in heavy use subsequently get involved in dealing to support their habits (Johnson 1973; Wood 1988; Sifaneck 1996). After involvement in drug dealing, users may develop connections with hard drugs. Subcultures and the behavior of drug dealing were theorized to be the intervening variables in the progression of deviant behavior (Johnson 1973). Later in the 1970s, investigations into the subculture of Rastafarianism provided an opportunity to explore a context not only where cannabis is used, but where it is truly sacred and endowed with meaning and significance (Hebdige 1979).

Beck and Rosenbaum's (1994) seminal study of MDMA (ecstasy) use recognized the often blurred lines between drugs defined in subcultures and the relationship of these meanings to the larger popular culture. Beck and Rosenbaum articulate:

> Insulated well-defined subcultures gave way to larger more amorphous "social worlds" of illicit drug users. . . . We now had user populations whose identities were substantially shaped and informed by mass communication and the media. (1994)

In a fast paced, information laden, postmodern world, subcultural practices are co-opted, marketed, and quickly adopted by the popular culture. For instance, Hip-Hop and Rastafarian styles of hair and dress are replicated and adopted by persons who are clearly outside the subculture. This happens when subcultural art forms (rap, graffiti, reggae) get marketed through the mass media to a larger audience. To a lesser extent, this is also true for subcultural drug use practices. This will later be exemplified by the practice of blunt smoking.

Methods

Ethnographic research is extremely valuable for understanding both the subcultural features, and the ritualized use practices of cannabis in natural settings. Ethnography is also an important tool for specifying the contexts of illicit drug use. For example, there is a growing tradition of HIV/AIDS-related ethnographic research which has been able to identify practices that both contribute to and impede efforts of a subculture to self-regulate in the interest of harm reduction (Grund, Kaplan & De Vries 1993). By relating cannabis smoking to the broader context of drug use, strategies for secondary prevention and intervention can be identified, developed, and applied. Future research with cannabis smokers should take place in the context of natural settings and most current use practices. This research can only take place after an adequate ethnographic analysis of such subcultural contexts. The following paper utilizes the analysis of both primary and secondary ethnographic data. Sifaneck and Kaplan have undertaken extensive ethnographic research on the cannabis situation in the Netherlands. Sifaneck's dissertation entitled "Regulating Cannabis: An Ethnographic Analysis of the Sale and Use of Cannabis in New York City and Rotterdam" involved extensive participant-observation with users and sellers of cannabis in the United States and the Netherlands. Sifaneck has studied and documented changes in the sale and use of cannabis in New York City over the past ten years. Kaplan has researched the drug scene, taught and lived in the Netherlands since the early 1980s. Both researchers have previous collaborations and are continuously observing developments in the cannabis scenes in both cultural settings.

Secondary ethnographic data was obtained by interviewing practicing ethnographers involved with drug research. These people included Dr. Adrian Jansen, Dr. Ansley Hamid, Dr. Richard Curtis, Errol K. James, Charles Small, and Joseph Richardson. The intention of using such secondary data was to corroborate our own observations, as well as to provide insights on developments not observed during the primary field research. The approach employed is certainly unconventional, but proved to be comprehensive and very fruitful in gathering data. It was a way to overcome generalizations generated through the observations of a single researcher in the field. Through analysis of primary and secondary ethnographic data this paper will explore two more recent modes of cannabis use practices and smoking styles: the American "blunt" and the Dutch "blowtje." A blunt is a hollowed out cheap cigar filled with marijuana, and a blowtje is a modern Dutch style joint which is mixed with tobacco, and is constructed with a large rolling paper and a cardboard filter.

A comprehensive ethnographic approach is an appropriate methodology for this cross-cultural investigation into the subcultural influences which provide contexts for distinct cannabis smoking practices in two different modern Western cultures. Even though the phenomenon of "blunts" has been sporadically mentioned in the drug abuse literature, analysis of the cultural significance, and social and health implications that a relatively novel cannabis use practice presents have been ignored. The Dutch cannabis use practice of the blowtje has been an equally ignored phenomenon. The intention of the following paper is to shed light on these newer drug use phenomena, and discuss their implications for health, prevention, and the reduction of drug related harm.

Blunts and Blowtjes: A Cross-Cultural Ethnographic Analysis of Two Cannabis Use Practices

A Common Antecedent: The Rastafarian Spliff

One striking characteristic of the "blunt," and to a lesser extent the "blowtje," is that they both express, in terms of immenseness and design, the look, and "style" of an important symbol of the Rastafarian subculture, the Jamaican "spliff." Jamaica is the sacred center of the Rastafarian movement which has become a worldwide subculture which embraces a pan-African, anti-imperialist, and working-class revolutionary ideology (Hebdige 1979). Reggae music became a predominant vehicle of the subculture to "spread the word," and obtain supporters from a racially and geographically diverse population. Since "ganja" (marijuana) is plentiful in Jamaica, ganja smokers (often Rastafarians) prefer to roll their joints so that they are relatively large. Large rolling papers and "fronto leaves" (broad tobacco leaves) are the norm when rolling spliffs in Jamaica. The name "fronto" is derived from the opposite phonetics expressed in the word "tobacco." Since tobacco contained the sound "back" Rastafarians interpreted this to mean backwards, or non-progressive. Part of the Rastafarian ideology is the promotion of progress, and the notion never to go backwards, thus the word "fronto" was adopted, containing the sound "front" suggesting a progressive "forwardness" (Small 1996). In Jamaica, locally grown and roughly manicured marijuana is sold by the half (14 grams) or whole (28 grams) ounce to the neophyte tourist consumer. For the American tourist these prices are at least 4–5 times lower than retail market prices in the United States. However, one must keep in mind that tourist prices are super-inflated, although they seem extremely inexpensive to the American or European traveler. For the Jamaican "spliff" smoker, marijuana is plentiful, but generally of a low and unmanicured quality, thus large joints are necessary to obtain a fulfilling high. In a number of Brooklyn neighborhoods during the 1980s fronto leaf was sold in health food stores, owned by and catering to Jamaican and other Caribbean immigrants. Large glass jars of fronto leaf were displayed next to herbal teas and dried fruit. Very often, these stores would also sell marijuana. In the New York setting, spliffs that were rolled with fronto leaf by these new Caribbean immigrants in the late 1970s and early 1980s were the predecessors to the modern blunts. In the Dutch setting, spliff smoking was an influence, spread in part, by immigrants from Suriname and the Dutch Antilles (Curacaos, Aruba, etc.,) and by members of the Rastafarian subculture. These cultural forces would eventually influence the design and style of the modern blowtje.

The Demise of the Trey and the Loose Joint and the Rise of the Blunt: Instabilities of the New York Market

"Blunts" explicitly emerged as a phenomenon in New York City during the mid 1980s, where small groups (3–5) of youth would pool their limited resources to purchase generally a "dime" ($10) or "nickel" ($5) bag of marijuana (James 1994). During the late 1980s, in New York City's inner-city markets, these were relatively small amounts: a nickel consisting of approximately .75 of 1 gram, and a dime averaging slightly more than 1.5 grams. When rolling a traditional marijuana joint, 1 gram may be used to construct 2–3 joints. Joints of this size are meant to be consumed by one or two persons. Blunts are generally shared among larger groups of users. For the original blunt smokers, the blunt smoking phenomenon was born out of the scarce conditions of New York's cannabis market in the mid 1980s. Today single (loose) "joints" and "trey" (3 dollar) bags of marijuana are no longer available in New York's retail market, while cannabis prices throughout the 1990s averaged about four to five times higher than prices in the late 1970s (Small 1996; Sifaneck 1996; Hamid 1995). Throughout the 1980s marijuana prices gradually inflated, and peaked around 1989, while cocaine prices concomitantly plummeted (Rhodes, Hyatt & Scheiman 1994). This unique market condition of abundant and inexpensive cocaine (very often in the form of crack) reinforced the functionality of sharing expensive and often scarce marijuana.

When making a blunt, the user must first purchase an inexpensive, low-quality cigar. "Philly Blunts" from which the blunt label is derived, is a popular "old school" brand, but other cheap cigars ("White Owls," "Dutch Masters," and "Optimos") represent a fair section of this tobacco/paraphernalia market. There exists some urban street mythology concerning the effects of the highs, as well as the burning duration of the different brands. The tobacco inside the cheap cigar is hollowed-out leaving the empty shell. Since the production of these particular cigar brands is low-cost, the shell is not pure broad leaf tobacco, but a tobacco/paper composite. (However, the fronto leaf, used in the traditional spliff making process, is pure broad leaf tobacco.) The cigar is split lengthwise down the center, and the tobacco inside is emptied out. The shell is then reduced or shortened to about two-thirds of the original cigar's length. The cigar-shell is then re-filled with marijuana and rolled-up like a large cigarette. Generally, the whole dime or nickel is used in the construction, and the blunt is shared in a group of three or more users. Since "blunts" have come into fashion, however, personal blunt smoking among wealthier users is not uncommon. The original blunt smokers of the mid 1980s, predominantly African-Caribbean, African-American, and Latino youth residing in the inner-city, saw their new method of preparation as an economical way to consume expensive marijuana, and also a ritual of a group market transaction and preparation process.

The use of blunts is an integral element in the "Hip-Hop" youth subculture which has emerged in most American cities. Other elements of this subculture include rap music, dance styles, a continuously evolving argot (including unique terms for marijuana), graffiti art, and styles of dress which include baggy pants, sport team jackets and caps, oversized jewelry, and a changing array of accessories. Hats and shirts with the "Philly Blunt" logo, and other references to blunts and marijuana smoking are common icons which are displayed prominently on "street gear" or the fashions of Hip-Hop. The argot of the Hip-Hop subculture includes many novel and innovative terms for marijuana (chronic, ism, boom, live, lah, dro), and blunts making previous slang obsolete. The new argot serves the function of keeping conversations about marijuana only recognizable to members of the subculture (Kaplan, Kampe, Antonio & Farfan 1990). In short, the social meanings and rituals of marijuana use have changed from previous

American generations, as a result of different sentiments, attitudes, and ideologies regarding the drug use of youth subcultures. For example, there are rap songs about how to roll blunts and smoking them. Phallic shaped blunts are also an expression of "phatness," an important concept of the Hip-Hop subculture. "Phat" or "fat" is a term analogous with excellent, and the blunt is one expression of many, including "forties" (40-ounce bottles of beer or malt-liquor), and oversized baggy pants and sweatshirts. "Phat" also means healthy, where many overly thin folks in the inner-city are perceived either as crack smokers or victims of the AIDS epidemic.

The use of blunts may be an indication of a "stepping off" or "maturing out" pattern from using hard drugs to only using marijuana, and also a "keeping off" pattern of abstaining from hard drug use altogether (Winick 1963; Sifaneck & Kaplan 1995). While rap music lyrics are embracing marijuana use and blunt smoking, they are also being critical of cocaine and crack-cocaine use. A special type blunt termed a "wulla" or "whoolie" emerged during the height of the crack epidemic in the late 1980s. The "wulla" not only contained marijuana, but also crack and/or cocaine. Regular "wulla" smokers were predominantly former crack smokers who previously consumed their crack from a "pipe" or a "stem," where a whole "hit" would be smoked at one time. Crack or cocaine in the wulla is crushed and spread on top of the marijuana throughout the blunt shell, and then smoked in a gradual manner, thus, titrating the cocaine dose. Peer pressures within Hip-Hop milieus encouraged wulla smokers eventually to abstain from adding crack and cocaine to their blunts (Curtis 1995). Presently, we observe a low prevalence of wulla use, while blunt use is more popular than ever. A more recent development in blunt construction is evidence to the fact that blunts attempt to replicate the look of "spliffs." A few blunt smokers were observed to place rolling paper around the blunt shell, to give it more of the appearance of a spliff (Richardson 1995). The extra paper does not serve a technical function, rather it is simply stylistic.

From the Stickje and Hippie Joint to the Coffeeshop Blowtje: The Gradual Evolution and Normalization of the Dutch Cannabis Market and Culture

In contrast to the developments in New York, the Caribbean influence on cannabis smoking practices in the Netherlands seem more limited despite a relatively large population of immigrants from the Antilles, the former Dutch colonies in the Caribbean. Some Jamaican influence on the Dutch cannabis culture did occur in the 1970s with Bob Marley and the worldwide reggae movement. However, well before that time there [were] already active cannabis and psychedelic subcultures in the Netherlands. In the 1960s an active psychedelic culture sprung up around Jasper Grootveld and the "Magic Center." One of Grootveld's claims to fame was implanting an electrode in his brain to effect "self-stimulation." Young people throughout the Netherlands were experimenting with drugs and other types of "consciousness expansion." Amsterdam was seen as a cosmic center, possessing geodesic conditions, including the ability to contact extra-terrestrials (Bongers, Snelders & Plomp 1995). Grootveld prophesied that "Klaas" was coming, which, in a sense, came true when Princess Beatrix married Prince Klaus ("Klaas" in Dutch) from Germany. This caused much national rumbling, since Dutch-German relationships were still rather uneasy at the time. The Provos, another radical group of the time, threatened to put LSD in the water of the horses of the coronation carriage. Other subcultural groups included the "Pleiners" who hung around the Leidsplein (an urban square) in Amsterdam and were the audience for the new Paradiso and Melkweg youth culture projects. The Paradiso and the Melkweg (translates to Milky Way) were the first environments where the retail sale of cannabis was tolerated by "house dealers" (Jansen 1989).

The considerable Moroccan worker migration in the 1950s provided a bridge for contact with hashish sources, which still provide the most prominent supply in present day coffeeshops (retail establishments which sell cannabis in the Netherlands). Tangier and Marrakesh were popular destinations for international beatnik and hippie travelers in the late 1950s and 1960s, and a stop-over in Amsterdam was often on the itinerary. In the late 1960s, hashish, not marijuana, was the most prominent form of cannabis available in the Netherlands. Only later in the 1970s did the substantial Surinam and Antillian migration occur, which would augment the cannabis scene with marijuana (ganja) and Caribbean influences. The origin of the blowtje was influenced by indigenous tobacco smoking subcultures in the Netherlands. In the late 1960s a trend emerged among youthful tobacco smokers who wished to distinguish themselves from conventional cigarette smokers by rolling their own cigarettes with long-cut "shag" tobacco. This was an old Dutch working class practice, which could also be observed in England, where high tobacco taxes made pre-rolled cigarettes too expensive. Youth subcultures with leftist politics and sympathies perceived the practice of rolling shag tobacco as a symbolic and practical identification with the working class. In the 1970s the practice of rolling shag tobacco was common in the Dutch and German critical intellectual scene. Colorful designer Drum and Samson tobacco cans (shag tobacco brands) were subcultural status symbols.

In the 1960s a hashish-tobacco cigarette made with one paper was called a "stickje" (translates small stick). If two small papers were used in the construction it was called a "joint," also referred to as "American hippie style." This linguistic evidence is illustrative of the American influence on the Dutch cannabis culture transplanted by traveling hippies from the United States. As cannabis smoking became more socialized and more public, larger group smoking became a trend among hippies throughout the world. In the Netherlands, the hippie-style joint made with two papers was replaced by the blowtje, originally made with three cigarette rolling papers. When making a blowtje the user must procure a number of things, all of which are available at the "coffeeshop" where the retail sale of small amounts (5 grams or less) of hashish and marijuana to persons over 18 years of age is tolerated. The collection of essentials to construct a blowtje include: (1) a small amount of high-quality marijuana or hashish (usually about .25 of a gram), (2) a large rolling paper (equivalent to the size of 3 shag tobacco cigarette rolling papers), (3) tobacco (shag or from an American cigarette—approximately two-thirds of one cigarette), [and] (4) a cardboard filter tip ("tipje" in Dutch). The construction process in somewhat elaborate. First, the cardboard tip is placed at the end of the large rolling paper—which is not folded in a perpendicular fashion, but at an angle. Then, the tobacco is spread out carefully inside the paper, creating "a bed" where the cannabis will be placed. The user then adds a small amount of marijuana or hashish, placing slightly more in the end opposite the filter. When the blowtje is rolled, the end which is lit is larger in girth than the end with the filter; creating a joint which is shaped liked a baseball bat, and also resembles the shape of a spliff. The inclusion of tobacco in the Dutch blowtje initially served a technical function. Throughout the 1970s, hashish was the most common form of cannabis available, and tobacco was needed in order for the hashish to burn properly in the form of a joint. Modern blowtje smokers who use marijuana instead of hashish also argue that tobacco is needed in order to insure that the blowtje burns properly. Since the locally grown "Nederweit" (translates to Netherlands' weed) is extremely fresh, and often moist, the addition of the tobacco produces a drier smoking mix which burns more evenly. The addition of tobacco in the blowtje also allows users to use a small amount of cannabis in the construction of their blowtjes, which will be further discussed.

As the blowtje became rooted as the predominant smoking mode, changes in the cannabis subculture were taking place. The practice of smoking cannabis in a group lost popularity. This was reinforced by the emergence of the coffeeshops which provided a social context and a form of consumption that encouraged each patron to order and prepare their own cannabis. Smoking one's own blowtje in the coffeeshop became the norm, and this was supported by the emergence of a new smoking style and related argot. Dutch smokers inhale or "blow" (a term reserved for cocaine in American drug argot) their cannabis in a casual manner like a tobacco cigarette. Unlike American cannabis smokers, who are likely to inhale deeply and hold the smoke in their lungs (sometimes referred to as "holding the hit"), Dutch smokers literally "blow" the smoke in and out of their lungs, avoiding deep inhalation. Thus, the blowtje, and the Dutch cannabis smoking subculture in general, has important roots in tobacco smoking styles as well as international and indigenous subcultural influences. Dutch cannabis smokers distinguish among themselves by the amount and kind of tobacco (shag or American) and cannabis (marijuana or hashish) they prefer. Light processed American tobacco and the darker and heavier less/un-processed Dutch shag tobacco can be widely observed in the blowtje mix. However, there are also a small minority of smokers who do not mix their cannabis with tobacco. Some of these smokers reject the tobacco convention, simply because they do not like the taste and/or the effect of the tobacco. Others may also be concerned about the increased health risks posed by smoking both substances simultaneously. Very often these cannabis users will use a small Moroccan hashish pipe, and avoid the rolling process altogether.

A recently emerged smoking phenomenon in the Dutch cannabis culture is the "blowtje gezond." Its name is derived from the popular Dutch bakery sandwich known as the "broodje gezond," which literally translates to "healthy sandwich." This small bakery bun is filled with cheese, a boiled egg and vegetables—not exactly fat or cholesterol free, but its vegetable laden appearance is its claim of healthfulness. A "blowtje gezond" is simply a Dutch blowtje constructed without the tobacco, and was observed being sold by a few coffeeshops in Rotterdam and Amsterdam. This is an important, although limited development, because it is an indication that the Dutch cannabis culture has come to realize the increased health risks posed by using cannabis and tobacco simultaneously. This may also be an indication of a marketing strategy to encourage smoking without tobacco, which is reinforced by the national campaigns against tobacco use in the Netherlands. Despite these campaigns and new cannabis products, most Dutch cannabis users rarely smoke marijuana and hashish without the tobacco, and when they do, they label the joint as "puur" (pure). "I only smoke pure joints when I am in the sunshine" a young male Rotterdammer commented. "If I see someone smoking a pure joint, I say either he is an American or an old time hippie" responded a young female user in her twenties.

Discussion

Cannabis Market Reinforcements, Self-Regulation and Implications for Secondary Prevention

The ethnographic descriptions in this paper underlie the importance of understanding the specific processes of how these subcultures adapt to market variations. Subcultural drug use practices must adapt themselves to specific market conditions; the subculture and the market reinforce each other in affecting the individual conduct and self-conception of the user. In the field of drug abuse research this process of multiple causality has been described as "causal reinforcement" (Swierstra 1990). Blunts and blowtjes represent two distinct emerging conceptions of cannabis use that serve different self-regulatory functions for the user than their common antecedent the Rastafarian spliff. The blunt is an attempt at economizing an expensive product in a relatively scarce market. The blowtje is the result of the opposite market condition: an abundance of high quality, moderately priced cannabis. In the New York City market, sharing the drug is part of the ritual, in the Dutch market sharing is unnecessary. They are both, however, attempts at self-regulation. In the case of blunts, self regulation takes place collectively inside a group. This also was the case for the prior hippie generation who "could not help but get stoned" through a ritual of sitting in a circle and passing a joint around with each individual taking a turn. However, one essential difference is the self in the group process. The self in "the

blunt era" is characterized by the process of trying to deal with threats and insecurity in the market environment; be it crack or law enforcement. This kind of self is evidenced by the rich repertoire of argot terms. A drug argot has been argued to indicate a form of intense social control that maintains in-group cohesion by hiding the practices which the terms refer to from normal language (Kaplan et al. 1990). The language acts as a means of strengthening the security of the self within the subculture.

In the Dutch context, new cannabis preparations are continually offered in the coffeeshop much like new beers and other alcohol are in an American bar. The individual experiences smoking cannabis from a connoisseur's perspective, not seeking new sensation, but refinements of tried and true products. The lack of drug argot terms is striking when compared to the American context. The old language is maintained with modest addition of innovation. This indicates that the cannabis subculture is being increasingly integrated into normal Dutch society and therefore has no real survival need to hide and promote in-group subcultural cohesion in any form other than a cannabis users association, an interest group protecting the connoisseur consumer self. Part of the preparation ritual in the American context is the "scoring" of the marijuana which is not necessary in the coffeeshop setting. Since generally a five or ten dollar amount is the least one can purchase on the regular retail market, it makes the phenomenon of "going in on" (willing to contribute money towards the purchase of) a function of the ritual. In this sense, the sharing of the cost becomes an integral part of the procurement process. The sharing which ensues when the blunt is smoked is an extension of this functionality. This is a process of group self-regulation, much like the type observed by Grund in his extensive field research with Dutch heroin users, where market scarcity was a determining factor in the sharing process (Grund, Kaplan & De Vries 1993). In the American context, scarcity of injection equipment has demonstrated itself as the most important factor affecting needle sharing among injection drug users (Des Jarlais, Friedman, Sothern & Stoneburner 1988).

The self-regulation practiced by Dutch cannabis users, through the employment of the blowtje, is oriented in individual rather than the collective behavior observed by American blunt smokers. This is a result of the normalized or "pseudo-legal" market which provides the context for cannabis use (Jansen 1989). In such a normalized market, the cannabis offered is high quality, relatively low-priced, and includes a diverse array of types of marijuana and hashish from across the globe. Today's modern Dutch cannabis users do not share joints. Such a practice is perceived by them as anachronistic and subsequently labeled as "hippie-style." "Blowtjes" are truly personal joints, and contain a surprisingly small amount (less than $\frac{1}{3}$ of a gram) of cannabis (marijuana or hashish) mixed with about $\frac{2}{3}$s of the tobacco in an average cigarette. Blowtjes are not passed in circles, but held personally by each user in the coffeeshop.

The potency of cannabis also effects regulation and consumption. The disparities in the potencies of cannabis available to the average consumer are an indirect result of the market conditions surrounding its use. In the Netherlands, where cultivating marijuana is tolerated, although not officially sanctioned, the most popular marijuana presently sold and consumed is "Skunk"—more formally known as a variety of cannabis—indica. This type of cannabis is generally grown hydroponically indoors throughout the Netherlands, under extremely controlled conditions. The "Nederweit" (translates Netherlands' Weed) produced possess[es] a THC content which often approaches 20%. This widely available, high potency cannabis, which most Dutch users choose to consume, allow[s] them to use a very small amount (about .25 of a gram) in their blowtje construction. The self-titrating behavior of using more potent cannabis in lesser amounts, observed during our fieldwork with Dutch users, has also been observed in controlled laboratory settings with American users (Heishman, Stitzer & Yingling 1989).

In the New York City blunt smoking context, the cannabis most widely available is imported from Mexico, and to a lesser extent from Jamaica. These varieties of cannabis, which are grown outdoors, have a considerably lower THC content than the Dutch grown Nederweit. This helps to explain why blunt smokers use a relatively large amount of cannabis (from 1–1.5 grams) in the construction of their blunts. It is also evidence to the fact that differences in the criminality of the market (semi-decriminalized vs. pseudo-legal) seem to effect the potency and quality of cannabis normally available at the retail level (Sifaneck 1996). This, in turn, has an effect on how and why users choose to self-regulate their use.

Secondary prevention strategies can be informed by research that identifies the parameters involved in cannabis self-regulation. For instance, in an important experimental psychological study of cannabis and driving, Robbe (1994) concluded that the harm of cannabis is strongly associated with parameters such as the volume of smoke taken into the lungs and the number of puffs or draws in a smoking session in which this volume is regulated. This was also observed by Azorlosa, Heishman, Stitzer and Mahaffey (1992) in similar controlled laboratory settings. These parameters still need to be documented in their natural settings in order to identify the full range of behaviors and constraints that operate to control the volume of smoke and the frequency of puffs. In the Netherlands, courses are being given to problematic cannabis users in order to adjust their use towards a less harmful direction (Bourghuis 1994). These secondary prevention efforts are largely non-existent in the US. However, there is evidence that similar functions are being initiated by organized American groups that promote cannabis and psychedelic drugs (Jenks 1995). These groups do not promote an indiscriminate use of cannabis, but instead offer users social support and accurate information on how to use cannabis in more responsible ways. Both the Dutch courses and the American organizations rely on the experiences of cannabis users. The future development of preventative cannabis education can benefit from the input of ethnographic studies. For instance, Dutch blowtje smokers do not hold smoke in their lungs as long as their American counterparts. American cannabis users generally "hold the hit" in an attempt to economize the smoke. These parameters are in need of future elaboration in natural setting research. The qualitative results of our research provide a basis for looking in more detail at these behavioral parameters.

Clearly more research is needed in understanding how processes such as cultural diffusion apply to the situation of diverse cannabis smoking behaviors and use practices. In the literature on health behavior, there is ample evidence that healthy lifestyles can diffuse over national, class and ethnic boundaries. The same processes can apply for unhealthy lifestyles. Future ethnographic research should not only be advised to search for "common antecedents" of lifestyles and subcultures, but also to look for how current smoking styles are anchored in the specific development of regional subcultural practices (Becker 1970). A "cross-fertilization" of tobacco and cannabis styles, as we have documented in the Netherlands, may prove to be a useful hypothesis guiding future research in other settings as well.

Evidence has suggested that smokers of both cannabis and tobacco have increased risks of lung and other cancers, than do sole smokers of tobacco (Tashkin, Coulson, Clark, Simmons, Bourque, Duann, Spivey & Gong 1987). If this evidence is correct, it should call for an intervention with cannabis users by dissemination of accurate information regarding the risks posed by the different methods of consuming the drug. Such a secondary preventative effort would be aimed at current users encouraging them to adjust their practices and patterns in less harmful directions. This should include information on the harms of various use practices, as well as information to guard against harmful chronic use patterns. One suggestion might be to encourage current blunt smokers to replace the blunt shell (made of tobacco, paper, and glue) with a large rolling paper, thus eliminating the health risks posed by consumption of the tobacco. Users would still have the convenience and functionality that the blunt provided: a joint large enough to be shared in a small group. Some Dutch coffeeshops have taken the lead in providing such information aimed at sec-

ondary prevention to [their] consumers. Other coffeeshops are offering the use of bongs (water pipes) and water vaporizers to their customers. Water pipes and vaporizers also offer a tobacco free alternative for blowtje smokers. Previous and ongoing research has determined carcinogens and tars are filtered out through the water inside the bong, making it a safer smoking method (Doblin 1995). This is a particularly important issue for persons with AIDS (PWAs) who are using cannabis to combat the wasting syndrome. Patients with such a compromised immune system have to insure that the safest and most effective way is used to ingest marijuana.

Harm reduction measures must include cannabis users in their efforts; and the medicinal use of cannabis might provide the basis for self-regulatory intervention in the future. Just as a generation has observed the devastating effect of crack-cocaine on many users, another generation could learn an experience based lesson in self-regulating and modifying its drug consumption (Furst, Johnson, Dunlap & Curtis 1999). While persons who smoke only cannabis seem to experience lung-related health problems infrequently, there may be an increase of health problems among persons who simultaneously smoke cannabis and tobacco. In the light of the new national and local (especially in Mayor Bloomberg's New York City) campaigns against the use of tobacco by young people, similar efforts should educate youth about the harms posed by the different ways of consuming cannabis. Such efforts, however, should not exclude those youth who have already begun experimenting with the drug.

References

Azorlosa J. L., S. J. Heishman, M. Stitzer & J. M. Mahaffey. 1992. Marijuana smoking: effect of varying tetrahydrocannabinol content and number of puffs *J Pharmacology Experimental Therapeutics* 261 (1): 114–122.

Beck J. & M. Rosenbaum. 1994. *Pursuit of Ecstasy: The MDMA Experience* Albany: SUNY Press.

Becker H. S. 1963. *Outsiders: Studies in the Sociology of Deviance* NY: Free Press.

——. 1970. History, culture and subjective experience: an exploration of the social bases of the drug induced experience. Pp. 307–327 in H. S. Becker ed. *Sociological Work: Method and Substance.*

Bongers H., S. Snelders & H. Plomp. 1995. *De Psychedelische (R)evolution: Geschiedenis en Recente Ontwikkelingen in het Onderzoek Naar Veranderde Bewustzijnsstaten* Amsterdam: Bres.

Botvin G. J. 1990. Substance abuse prevention: theory, practice, and effectiveness. Pp. 461–519 in M. Tonry & J. Q. Wilson eds. *Drugs and Crime* 13 Chicago: U Chicago Press.

Bourghuis M. 1994. Where do youngsters turn? *Jellinek Qrtrty* 1 (2): 4–5.

Center for Substance Abuse Prevention (CSAP). 1995. CSAP's Update on Marijuana. Information folder presented at the First National Conference on Marijuana Use, Prevention, Treatment and Research. Washington D.C., July.

Cohen J. 1993. Achieving a reduction in drug-related harm through education. Pp. 65–76 in N. Heather, A. Wodak, E. Nadelmann & P. O'Hare eds. *Psychoactive Drugs and Harm Reduction: From Faith to Science* London: Whurr Publishers.

Cohen P. D. A. & H. L. Kaal. 2001. *The Irrelevance of Drug Policy: Patterns and Careers of Experienced Cannabis Use in the Populations of Amsterdam, San Francisco and Bremen. Final Report.* Den Haag: Dutch Ministry of Health, Welfare, and Sport.

Curtis R. 1995. Personal communication. Anthropology Department, John Jay College of Criminal Justice, City University of New York.

De Jarlais D. C., S. R. Friedman, J. L. Sothern & R. Stoneburner. 1988. The sharing of drug injection equipment and the AIDS epidemic in New York City. In R. J. Battjes & R. W. Pickens eds. *National Institute on Drug Abuse Research Monograph 80: Needle Sharing Among Intravenous Drug Abusers* Washington DC: USGPO.

Doblin R 1995 Personal Communication. Preliminary results of water pipe/vaporizer research.

Furst R. T., B. D. Johnson, E. Dunlap & R. Curtis. 1999. The stigmatized image of the 'crack-head': a sociocultural exploration of a barrier to cocaine smoking among a cohort of youth in New York City *Deviant Behavior* 20 (2): 153–181.

Golub A. & B. D. Johnson. 2001. The rise of marijuana as the drug of choice among youthful adult arrestees *National Institute of Justice Research in Brief June 2001.* Washington DC: U.S. Department of Justice.

Grund J. P. C., C. D. Kaplan & M. De Vries. 1993. Rituals of regulation: controlled and uncontrolled drug use in natural settings. Pp. 77–92 in N. Heather, A. Wodak, E. Nadelmann & P. O'Hare eds. *Psychoactive Drugs and Harm Reduction: From Faith to Science* London: Whurr Publishers.

Hamid A. 1995. Personal communication. Anthropology Department, John Jay College of Criminal Justice, City University of New York.

Hebdige D. 1979. *Subculture: The Meaning of Style* London and New York: Methuen.

Heishman S. J., M. Stitzer & J. E. Yingling. 1989. Effects of tetrahydrocannabinol content on marijuana smoking behavior, subjective reports, and performance *Pharmacology Biochemistry Behavior* 34: 173–179.

James E. K. 1994. Personal communication. Center for Social Research, Graduate Center for the City University of New York.

Jansen A. C. M. 1989. *Cannabis in Amsterdam: A Geography of Hashish and Marijuana* Muiderberg: Coutinho.

Jenks S. M. Jr. 1995. An analysis of risk reduction among organized groups that promote marijuana and psychedelic drugs *J Drug Issues* 25 (3): 629–647.

Johnson B. D. 1973. *Marijuana Users and Drug Subcultures* NY: Wiley.

Johnston L., P. O'Malley & J. G. Bachman. 1999. *National Survey Results from the Monitoring the Future Study 1975–1998.* Rockville, MD: National Institute on Drug Abuse, U. S. Department of Health and Human Services, National Institutes of Health.

Kaplan CD, H Kampe, J Antonio & F Farfan 1990 Argots as a code-switching process: a case study of the sociolinguistic aspect of drug subcultures. In R Jacobson ed *Code-switching as a Worldwide Phenomenon* NY: Peter Lang.

Korf DJ & P van der Steenhoven 1993 *Antenne 1993: Trends in Alcohol, Tabak, Drugs en Gokken bijjonge Amsterdammers* Jellinek Reeks no. 2. Amsterdam: Jellinek-centrum.

Marlatt G. A., J. S. Baer & M. Larimer. 1995. Preventing alcohol abuse in college students. In G. A. Marlatt, J. S. Baer & M. Larimer eds. *Alcohol Problems Among Adolescents* Northvale, NJ: Lawrence Erlbaum.

Rhodes W, R Hyatt, & P Scheiman 1994 The price of cocaine, heroin and marijuana *J Drug Issues* 24 (3): 383–402.

Richardson J. 1995. Personal communication Predoctoral Research Fellow, Behavioral Scientists Training Program, National Development and Research Institutes, NY.

Robbe HWJ 1994 *Influence of Marijuana on Driving.* Maastricht, NL: Institute for Human Psychopharmacology, Limburg U.

Sifaneck SJ 1996 Regulating Cannabis: An Ethnographic Analysis of the Sale and Use of Cannabis in New York City and Rotterdam. Ph.D. Dissertation, Ph.D. Program in Sociology, The Graduate Center of the City University of New York.

Sifaneck SJ & CD Kaplan 1995 Keeping off, stepping on, and stepping off: the steppingstone theory reevaluated in the context of the Dutch cannabis experience *Contemporary Drug Problems* xxii 3: 513–546.

Small C 1996 Personal communication. Research Associate, Institute for Special Populations Research, National Development and Research Institutes, New York, NY.

Swierstra, KE 1990 *Drugscarrieres; Van Crimineel tot Conventioneel* Groningen: Stichting Drukkerji C. Regenboog.

Tashkin D. P., A. Coulson, V. A. Clark, M. Simmons, L. B. Bourque, S. Duann, G. H. Spivey & H. Gong. 1987. Smokers of marijuana alone, smokers of marijuana and tobacco, smokers of tobacco alone, and non-smokers *American Rev Respiratory Disease* 135: 209–216.

Winick C 1960 The use of drugs by jazz musicians *Social Problems* vol. 7.

——. 1963 Maturing out of narcotic addiction. *UN Bull on Narcotics* 14 (1): 1–7.

Wood E. 1988. Drug selling and dealing among adolescents, in C. Carpenter, B. Glasser, B. D. Johnson & J. Loughlin eds. *Kids, Drugs and Crime*, Lexington, MA: DC Heath and Company.

For Discussion

1. Using alcohol as an example, discuss how cultural influences can aid or impede prevention efforts in certain countries.

2. Think about primary and secondary prevention. Is one more important than the other? Why or why not?

Reprinted from: Stephen J. Sifaneck, Charles D. Kaplan, Eloise Dunlap, and Bruce D. Johnson, "Blunts and Blowtjes: Cannabis Use Practices in Two Cultural Settings and Their Implications for Secondary Prevention." In *Free Inquiry in Creative Society*, 31 (1), pp. 3–13. Copyright © 2003 by Free Inquiry in Creative Society. Reprinted with permission. ✦

14

The Power of 420

Karen B. Halnon

In this article, Karen Halnon describes marijuana users' perceptions of the concept of "420." Although it has various meanings for users, Halnon suggests that the phrase offers a collective identity for users. She traces the folklore associated with 420 and explores users' perceptions of the origins of the phrase. Although she concludes that its origins are unclear, she notes that 420 has important symbolic meaning for users, many of whom incorporate "cherished rituals" in drug use lifestyles.

Marijuana smokers, like other close-knit groups, have a special language. But often people in the straight-and-narrow world just don't understand it. Strange and alien to outsiders are words such as *nugs, dank, permagrin, wake n' bake, blunt, bogarting, Rastafarian, Towlie,* or even *coffee shops.* After 30 years of full-blown marijuana counterculture, outsiders still remain oblivious to the most special marijuana catchphrase of all: "Four hundred and twenty what?"

What outsiders miss, the discerning (and very possibly slightly reddened) eye can find all around. The 420 imprimatur is on bongs, T-shirts, patches, and coffee mugs. Marijuana fans find it frequently in stoner magazines, headshops, and in music lyrics. They feel lucky if they have 420 phone numbers, street addresses, or birthdays. This number is found at smoker Websites, on *Saturday Night Live,* and in news media on or around every April 20. For many smokers, 420 is guiding light and inspiration. Basically, for those with a raised consciousness of it, 420 is part of everyday life.

Curious about this hidden yet vibrant phenomenon, I did some research. The results of my sociological investigation were fascinating. Especially intriguing was the potency of 420, unique in the multiple ways it inspires and cultivates identity, community, and even reality.

It's difficult to even think of another *single numerical expression* that compares. 411 or 911? Lucky 7? Demonic 666? Trinitarian 3? Sexual 69? Tragic 9/11? LSD-25? Or even the infinite 3.1416 . . . ? While these numbers are significant, none by themselves embrace and reflect a community to the extent that 420 does.

In documenting 420, I hope to express the sociological "surprise" of 420. However, sociological surprises do not necessarily provide new information. The surprise of sociology comes when it shines new light on our everyday behaviors and experiences. Everyone on the inside knows that 420 is a most special number. My goal is to explain some of the sociological reasons for its special status as spirit and guide for marijuana smokers. In doing so, I drew upon the insights of nearly a hundred 420 smokers.

Learning the 'Secret Code'

Learning is extremely important in achieving an identity. In fact, it is the basic and necessary way any identity is achieved. And, if learning takes place with friends or family, achieving that identity is even more likely.

Following this pattern, most pot-smokers first learn about 420 from high-school or college friends, or from brothers or sisters. One smoker learned about it from "good friends in the military" who "introduced 4:20 as an alternative to 16:20 military time." Others explained that they "became part of the 'crew' by hitting 420," or learned about it when "sharing marijuana with new friends" at rock concerts—Phish shows in particular.

One of the first lessons smokers learn is that while the meaning of 420 is obvious to insiders as universal or as an international symbol for marijuana, marijuana smoking, and marijuana subculture, it's also a "secret code" or "secret advertiser." Smokers recounted comedic stories, such as where a high school teacher asked a student what time it was, and he replied "Four-twenty," eliciting the laughter of in-group classmates and the bewilderment of his teacher. Another smoker explained that 420's "secret" quality allowed him to get a pro-marijuana symbol past high-school authorities, sneaking a criminal-style number-420 mug shot in the yearbook without the faculty editor noticing. Others explained that it allowed them to wear blatant symbols of marijuana to school (420 written on hats, T-shirts, and the like) without encountering the negative sanctions associated with less obscure symbols, such as marijuana leaves. Still others explained that 420, as secret code, allowed them to safely and accurately identify others who smoke marijuana. For example, one smoker explained, "420 is like a secret advertiser . . . a good way to keep scattered tabs on who puffs."

All of this is fascinating to the sociologist because secrets and humor are very effective means of binding groups closer together. Secrets create a social boundary between outsiders and insiders. Humor, at least for those who share in it, enhances feelings of relaxation and [warmth]. Together, secrets and humor cultivate closeness, commitment, and group solidarity.

420 'Time'

Smokers explained that 420 is "a time that is in-between day and night, a break . . . a good time to relax and chill." Others said, "If my friends and I are ever up at 4:20 A.M., we always celebrate by smoking a bowl or joint. It is simply a justified reason to smoke."

For novices, 420 motivated smoking behavior by organizing time. The newly inducted learn that 420 means "a" or "the" "time to smoke." For example, smokers explained how they learned that 4:20 in the afternoon was "prime time" for smokers, the "pot smoker's happy hour," the "best time to smoke," or the "international smoke time." One smoker expressed the general sentiment of the novice: "You have to smoke at 4:20 if you have herb." Smokers explained how they set their alarm clocks, or how clocks in general served as reminders to smoke at 4:20. Nearly all smokers agreed that for the novice, 420 becomes an excuse or a reason to smoke, and frequently involves excessive smoking.

This pattern is sociologically significant, because a crucial ingredient in the recipe for identity achievement is immersion into identity-shaping activities. In other words, smoking lots of weed in the beginning normalizes getting high and increases the chances of defining oneself as a smoker of weed. The sociologist would also take important note of the fact that the organization of time is one of the most basic frameworks that supports and legitimates a "reality." Stated otherwise, 420 time lends legitimacy or a sense of truthfulness to pot-smoker reality.

Putting such sociological value aside, more seasoned smokers complained and resisted. They complained that such time structuring created a "ritualistic use of 420" or that it turned "marijuana-smoking into a joke." One smoker, who described himself as "patriotic to the weed," claimed that 420 should not be guided by time, but rather a more spontaneous "pledge and a tribute."

Whether a novice or seasoned user, what nearly everyone agreed upon is that 4:20 (P.M. or A.M.) means a source of unity or oneness in the pot-smoker community. It was variously described as a "time to unite with all smokers," a "smoker's club," and a way to "bring users together for smoking, community and solidarity." Smokers repeatedly claimed that 420 created a "common bond" among friends and fellow smokers. They know that when they light up at 4:20, thousands, if not millions, of others are doing the same for the same reason.

420 'Origin' Conversations

Most pot-smokers would probably accept as fact that 420 originated in San Rafael, CA, with the "Waldo Family," and Steve Waldo who used the expression "420 Louie" in high school. Waldo used it as a secret code to remind friends to meet for smoking sessions at the Louis Pasteur statue, 70 minutes after the 3:10 dismissal. However, regardless of whether or not the smokers I talked with actually knew about the veracity of Waldo's claim, they were generally uninterested in determining 420's true origin. One expressed a typical view: "The actual meaning of 420, or where it came from, seems unimportant to me compared to the feeling of 420. That is the true meaning." Another smoker was of a similar opinion: "Most people do not desire to know where 420 came from, but rather enjoy it for its cultural importance." A third, after reviewing a number of possible theories, explained, "While some of these reports are more believable than others, they all represent how important the number is to the marijuana community." Emphasizing the value of learning from talking about 420, a fourth smoker expressed this general point: "I think the most valid meaning of 420 origins is the underlying things you learn."

What fascinated me about origin theories was that while smokers actively discussed and debated them, they didn't care about learning the truth. This apparent contradiction made more sense when I realized that the dozens of theories discussed and debated, though often wrong or unprovable, were equivalent to a 101 course in marijuana cultural literacy. It is, as smokers repeatedly told me, more important to discuss and debate than to discover truth, because of the underlying things that can be learned.

Smokers learn, for example, about taking a defiant attitude toward police enforcement of anti-marijuana laws, and about the meaning and importance of people and things such as Jerry Garcia and the Grateful Dead, Cheech and Chong, Jamaica, Haight-Ashbury, Amsterdam, and THC. While these 101 lessons are an important part of the socialization of new smokers, origin conversations are important for all smokers. They provide a subject for many deep, philosophical and scientific conversations. Smokers said that stoner philosophizing about origins was especially meaningful when sharing a bowl, joint, or bong, and in effect was a learning session. Exploring, but not necessarily proving, origin theories provides many important lessons in marijuana culture. In other words, 420 origins serve as a good, celebratory, and often humorous, teacher.

The most common origin theory proffered by smokers is that 420 is or was a Los Angeles "police code for marijuana-smoking in progress." Researching the validity of this claim, I called the Los Angeles Police Department and asked if 420 was the "real" police code for marijuana smoking in progress. The answering officer explained that 420 in the "penal book" referred to "preventing or ob-

structing entry upon or passage upon public lands." I then asked what the police code would be for marijuana-smoking in progress. He said the California Health and Safety Code for "any narcotic drug," including marijuana, is 11350.

Steve Waldo, writing in *High Times* ("4:20 & the Grateful Dead," May '01 HT), explained further:

> Although it has often been rumored, 420 is not a police code for drug-law enforcement. Drug enforcement in California, and in San Rafael, is part of the state Health and Safety Code, in which all sections have five- and six-digit numbers, sometimes separated by a decimal point. Pot-related activities and violations fall in the middle [11300s].

The police-code origin theory, while false, calls attention to the fact that marijuana is an illegal substance, pointing to a central value difference between what is law and what is valued among marijuana-smokers. To embrace the police code as smoking symbol is to learn to stand in defiance against laws that make smoking illegal. To call attention to California is to learn about a state that is the leader in the fight to legalize the medical use of marijuana.

A second origin theory is that 420 references THC (delta-9 tetrahydrocannabinol) as "the number of chemicals in THC," the "number of molecules in marijuana," or the "number of elements in the marijuana plant." Skeptical about these biochemistry claims, I solicited evaluation from Peter Webster, Review Editor of the *International Journal of Drug Policy*, who responded to my e-mail query as follows:

> THC, or the principal active ingredient of cannabis, is a single chemical entity, i.e., one chemical. There are however many other closely-related but less psychoactive chemicals in cannabis, some which may be more important in medical applications. Each, however, is a different chemical since its molecular structure is unique. Again, THC is ONE chemical. "Marijuana" contains perhaps many thousands of different molecular entities, from the couple of hundred cannabinoids such as THC to chlorophyl, fats, fibers such as lignin, cellulose,

sugars, enzymes, and a wide range of other organic chemicals, to minerals, water, etc. [There are a] number of elements: carbon, hydrogen, oxygen, nitrogen, sulfur, chlorine, sodium, potassium, iron, magnesium, phosphorous, many trace metals, and probably many others in trace amounts . . . in effect, most elements in the first part of the periodic table, and probably even some traces of heavy metals—whatever is in the environment in which it grows.

While also false, the THC origin theory aids in learning about the primary psychoactive ingredient in marijuana, which is standard knowledge for any marijuana smoker.

A third set of related theories revolved around Jerry Garcia and the Grateful Dead. Smokers claimed, for example, that 420 was the "address of the Grateful Dead's home at Haight Ashbury," that "pot smoking is almost synonymous with the Grateful Dead," and that 420 refers to the "exact time of Jerry Garcia's death." In researching these claims I found that according to Rebecca Adams in *Deadhead Social Science,* "By late 1966, the Dead were headquartered at 710 Ashbury, near its intersection with Haight, the symbolic heart of the hippie community." And according to the *San Francisco Bay City Guide* (March 2001), "The Grateful Dead were one-time residents of the Haight (710 Ashbury Street)." Finally, while staying in San Francisco, I took a cab to Haight-Ashbury myself to confirm the 710, not 420, address.

In researching the exact time of Jerry Garcia's death, I found that, according to *People* magazine['s] (Aug. 21, 1995) cover story, he died on Wednesday, August 9, 1995 at 4:23 A.M. exactly. Other newspaper articles similarly reported that Garcia passed away in his bed at Forest Knoll after being found by a nurse who tried to revive him. The time of death again was 4:23 A.M. Thus, a third origin theory, while false again, aids in cultivating marijuana-culture literacy through its focus on classic stoner musician Jerry Garcia, stoner band the Grateful Dead, and the quintessential 1960s drug/hippie community, Haight-Ashbury.

A fourth set of origin theories revolved around times that are, like the theories above, significant to marijuana-smoker culture. One explanation is that 420 means teatime in Amsterdam or Holland. Probably, as in Britain, the time is closer to 4:30. Another explanation was that Tommy Chong (of Cheech and Chong, stars of marijuana cult film *Up in Smoke*) was born on April 20. In fact, he was born May 24, 1938.

Another explanation states that 420 originated from "the date Haille Sallasie visited Jamaica for the first time." The late Ethiopian emperor, venerated by Rastafarians as signifying the rebirth of black rule in Africa, visited Jamaica for three days in April 1966, but he arrived on the 21st.

Thus, a fourth set of origin theories aid smokers in learning about the importance of Amsterdam, a city that tolerates "soft drug" use and where marijuana can be smoked freely in coffeeshops; educates them as to a major marijuana cult film and its figures; and reveals the ritualization of ganja by Rastafarians.

Smokers also claimed that 420 originated from the first recorded use of marijuana. In researching this claim, I found that 2737 B.C. is frequently reported in academic texts as the earliest reference to use of marijuana because of its mention in a Chinese treatise by Emperor Shen Nung. However, Erich Goode (in *Drugs in American Society,* 5th ed.) tells us that "there is no definite date of the earliest recorded use of marijuana, although descriptions of cannabis use can be found in ancient texts from China, India, Persia, Assyria, Egypt, Greece, and Rome. For example, Marijuana is mentioned as a 'healing herb' in *The Divine Husbandman's Materia Medica,* circa first or second century A.D. In 650 B.C. the use of cannabis is mentioned in Persia and Assyria. In 400 B.C. the use of cannabis is mentioned in Rome." This time origin theory, while false or unprovable again, shows that marijuana-smoking has a long and deep historical tradition, and thus naturalizes its use for marijuana smokers.

Drawing more generally upon the illegal drug culture is the theory that 420 originated from the date Albert Hoffman discovered LSD-25. LSD-25 was first synthesized at Sandoz Laboratories in Basel, Switzerland, in 1938. It was re-shelved until April 16, 1943 when Hoffman made a "fresh batch," swallowed 250 micrograms, and experienced the first extremely intense acid trip "for science" (*Acid Dreams*, Martin Lee and Bruce Shalin). This origin theory teaches smokers about Albert Hoffman and LSD, and by doing so asserts the value of using illegal drugs.

Perhaps the most creative but dubious time theory was that 420 originated from the position of a "dangling doobie" in the mouth of a Jamaican getting off work. The position of the joint was said to resemble an analogue clock at 4:20. A final but certainly not exhaustive explanation is that 420 originated from Hitler's birthday. One smoker explained, "Hitler represents in sharp opposite contrast all that the marijuana smoking community stands for." This theory, like the theories above, cannot be proven to have any direct reference to 420. And even though Hitler was in fact born on April 20, 1889, there is no evidence that 420 originated from that date. By learning the dangling doobie and Hitler theories smokers learn about the value of Jamaica and Jamaican weed, and the peaceful, laid-back spirit among smokers.

To summarize, by discussing and debating numerous 420 origin theories marijuana smokers are able to share stories filled with an array of important symbols of marijuana smoker culture: Jamaica, California, Rastafarians, Cheech and Chong, Haight-Ashbury, the Grateful Dead, Jerry Garcia, hippies, THC. Through these conversations, smokers also learn many other lessons about the importance of defying laws and legal authorities that prohibit marijuana-smoking; the value and significance of locales where it is legal or at least tolerated; the deep historical tradition of marijuana-smoking; the spiritual justifications for it; and the easy, relaxed attitude of marijuana smokers.

What is most important is not determining the true origin of 420, but rather engaging in conversations filled with lessons for marijuana-smokers. Because these origin theories are either wrong or unprovable, they provide for an ongoing learning conversation. The sociological significance of ongoing conversations—especially if they are rich in memory, tradition, common beliefs, and values—is that they are a basic and necessary means of maintaining any kind of relationship. The value of 420 origin stories is

similar to that of retelling stories in a close-knit family. Stories—whether true, false, or embellished—strengthen the family's sense of belonging, identity and values, bringing it closer together. Even if we suspect that Aunt Lucy or Uncle John is not telling the truth, that doesn't stop us from reveling in their old stories. The retelling itself becomes a cherished ritual and a means of communicating what is valued and important to the family. This said, the definitiveness of the Waldo theory is, at best, a mixed blessing to the pot-smoker community.

The Pot-Smokers' Holiday

April 20—especially at 4:20 P.M.—is the "pot-smokers' holiday," also variously described as the "hippie New Year," "national smoke time," "national pot smoking day," "the holiday," "pot appreciation day," "the ultimate session," or "a day of tribute to the scene." One enthusiastic smoker reported, "Every group has its holidays and pot-smokers are no exception. April 20th is the day of worship observed by smokers around the world." Another said, "It's comforting to know that hundreds of thousands of other people are lighting up with me on 4/20. It's about the community identity of marijuana-smokers."

For marijuana-smokers, April 20 is especially imbued with emotional and spiritual meaning because it produces an intense collective bonding among them. Smokers emphasized the special quality of the Holiday: "We are talking about the day of celebration, the real time to get high, the grand master of all holidays: April twentieth."

That statement also reveals a sense of family within the pot-smoking culture. "Tokers are brothers and sisters, therefore more closely connected than any other association." Another smoker expressed the anticipation and joy of the Holiday: "At 4:19 P.M., everyone suddenly got quiet and the countdown began. When the time turned to 4:20 it was like New Year's. Everyone was cheering and shouting, jumping, hugging, and of course smoking. It really was incredible. I felt connected not only to the people around me, but to everyone else in the world who was doing the same thing at that exact moment."

While 4/20 celebrations give smokers a sense of worldwide community, they also reinforce old friendships, or create new ones at rallies. Friends travel long distances, even across the country, to party together. As a result, friendships are refreshed or "become stronger than ever." And people who might be strangers in other settings bond through their common allegiance to marijuana. One smoker explained, "It is a time when you can approach people that you do not really know and indulge in pot-smoking with them. You develop friendships with people because of the activities on 4/20 and at 4:20."

The sense of worldwide "we-ness" and the friendships established and renewed at 4/20 celebrations are due in large part to the fact that April 20 is a public forum for the fight for legalization. A smoker explained, "It is an exercise in solidarity, all of the pot-smokers coming together to smoke and the police being utterly powerless to do anything about it. I think this is the most valid expression of 420 as it puts the recreational use of marijuana in full view of the public, which is perhaps the first step towards gaining legitimacy." In a sentiment echoed by others, one smoker explained that "4/20 at 4:20 is a time to come together, to share one's lifestyle with others who feel the same way, to come together and stand strong and proud for marijuana." Said another, "Personally, I feel it (April 20) to be a political statement. It is a good time to gather to show one's support of legalization of marijuana."

As a matter of efficient crowd control, police and university authorities generally tolerate the short—and seldom dangerous—yearly public statements by pot-smokers. One smoker said that not only is 4/20 a time to stand proud for marijuana, but that "it's a day of tolerance and the authorities let us 'hippies' have our fun and smoke pot." Another said in proud defiance, "Pronounced 'four twenty,' it is a day of police non-enforcement of drug laws in certain areas, and a day to celebrate a ritual that has survived thousands of years, only to be condemned by our American government . . . It's one of the most liberating feelings to smoke pot in public and not be afraid of being caught."

The experience of such a holiday provides [a] pot-smokers with hope and inspiration—or with a vision of a future when they will be liberated from repressive antimarijuana laws.

The Sociological Surprise of 420

In this article I have attempted to explain the sociological surprise of 420, or how that special number is imbued with the ability to cultivate especially strong marijuana-smoker identity. As "secret code," it creates a social boundary between outsiders and insiders, and enhances a sense of "we-ness" among insiders. As "time," it legitimates smoker reality and structures and motivates excessive smoking behavior among novices, thus providing a valuable "immersion" experience. As "origin conversation," it facilitates learning about many important fundamental facts and values of the marijuana and illegal drug-user cultures. As "pot-smokers' holiday," it provides special family holiday ritual, a "day of tolerance," and a public opportunity to "stand proud for marijuana." Most important, as pot smokers' holiday, 420 creates an intense sense of group belonging among friends, strangers, crowds, and across geographical boundaries. Sociologists call this "collective consciousness," or a kind of mystical, spiritual, or extraordinary sense of belonging, where the group exists as a reality greater than itself.

In sum, the ultimate sociological surprise or fascination of 420 is that a single expression has the unique and powerful ability to cultivate, support, and reinforce pot-smoker identity, community, solidarity, and reality itself. The modest surprise offered here is a more comprehensive explanation of what smokers already know.

For Discussion

1. Do users of other drugs—cocaine, heroin—share a secret subculture similar to that of marijuana smokers? What makes the subculture of marijuana users unique among drug users?

2. Does the sense of belonging that a subculture provides attract people to try drugs? Once a person is initiated, does being a part of a group reinforce continued drug use?

3. How did the concept of 420 become so important if no one really knows what it means?

Part IV

Heroin and Other Opiates

In pharmacology, a science that focuses on the chemical nature, structure, and action of drugs, *narcotics* include the natural derivatives of *Papaver somniferum L.*—the opium poppy—having both analgesic and sedative properties, and any synthetic derivatives of similar pharmacological structure and action. Thus, the range of substances that can be properly called narcotics is quite limited and encompasses four specific groups:

Natural opiates

- opium, derived directly from *Papaver somniferum L.*
- morphine and codeine, derived from opium

Semisynthetic opiates (or opioids)

- heroin
- hydromorphone (Dilaudid)
- oxycodone (OxyContin, Percocet)
- hydrocodone (Vicodin)
- fentanyl (Duragesic)

Synthetic opiates with high potency

- methadone
- meperidine (Demerol)

Synthetic opiates with low potency

- propoxyphene (Darvon)
- pentazocine (Talwin)

There are many other opiates (also referred to as narcotics), but the examples listed are the best known. The most widely used in the drug culture are methadone and heroin. Methadone was synthesized during World War II by German chemists when supply lines for morphine were interrupted. Although chemically unlike morphine or heroin, it produces many of the same effects. Methadone was introduced in the United States in 1947 and quickly became the drug of choice in the detoxification of heroin addicts.

Since the 1960s, methadone has been in common use for the treatment of heroin addiction. Known as "methadone maintenance," the program takes advantage of methadone's unique properties as a narcotic. Like all narcotics, methadone is cross-dependent with heroin. As such, it is a substitute narcotic that prevents withdrawal. More important, however, methadone is orally effective, making intravenous use unnecessary. In addition, it is a longer-acting drug than heroin, with one oral dose lasting up to 24 hours. These properties have made methadone useful in the management of chronic narcotic addiction. Yet on the other hand, methadone is also a primary drug of abuse among some narcotic addicts, resulting in a small street market for the drug. Most illegal methadone is diverted from legitimate maintenance programs by methadone patients. Hence, illegal supplies of the drug are typically available only where such programs exist.

Heroin has a somewhat longer and more curious history. In 1874, British chemist C. R. A. Wright described a number of experiments he had carried out at London's St. Mary's Hospital to determine the effect of combining various acids with morphine. Wright produced a series of new morphine-like compounds, including what became known in the scientific literature as diacetyl-morphine. His discovery of *diacetylmorphine* had been the outgrowth of an enduring search for more effective substitutes for morphine. This interest stemmed not only from the painkilling qualities of opiate drugs but also from their sedative effects on the respiratory system. Wright's work went for the most part unnoticed, however.

Some 24 years later, in 1898, pharmacologist Heinrich Dreser reported on a series of experiments he had conducted with diacetylmorphine for Friedrich Bayer and Company of Elberfeld, Germany. He noted that the drug was highly effective in the treatment of coughs, chest pains, and the discomforts associated with pneumonia and tuberculosis. Dreser's commentary received immediate notice, for it had come at a time when antibiotics were still unknown and pneumonia and tuberculosis were among the leading causes of death. He claimed that diacetylmorphine had a stronger sedative effect on respiration than either morphine or codeine, that therapeutic relief came quickly, and that the potential for a fatal overdose was almost nil. In response to such favorable reports, Bayer and Company began marketing diacetylmorphine under the trade name of *heroin*—so named from the German *heroisch*, meaning heroic and powerful.

Although Bayer's heroin was promoted as a sedative for coughs and as a chest and lung medicine, it was advocated by some as a treatment for morphine addiction. This situation seems to have arisen from three somewhat related phenomena. First was the belief that heroin was nonaddicting. Second, since the drug had a greater potency than morphine, only small dosages were required for the desired medical effects, thus reducing the potential for the rapid onset of addiction. And third, at the turn of the twentieth century, the medical community did not fully understand the dynamics of cross-dependence. *Cross-dependence* refers to the phenomenon that among certain pharmacologically related drugs, physical dependence on one will carry over to all the others. As such, for the patient suffering from the unpleasant effects of morphine withdrawal, the administration of heroin would have the consequence of one or more doses of morphine. The dependence was maintained and withdrawal disappeared, with the two combining to give the appearance of a "cure."

Given the endorsement of the medical community, with little mention of its potential dangers, heroin quickly found its way into routine medical therapeutics and over-the-counter patent medicines. However, the passage of the Pure Food and Drug Act in 1906 and the Harrison Act in 1914 restricted the availability of heroin, and the number of chronic users declined.

Although opiate use in its various forms has been common throughout United States history, its current and most typical manifestation—the intravenous use of heroin—apparently developed during the 1930s and became widespread after 1945. Between 1950 and the early 1960s, most major cities experienced a low-level spread of heroin use, particularly among the black and other minority populations. Thereafter, use began to grow rapidly, rising to peaks in the late 1960s and then falling sharply. The pattern was so ubiquitous that it came to be regarded as "epidemic" heroin use. More recent "epidemics" occurred in 1973–1974, 1977–1978, and 1982–1983, defined as such on the basis of the number of new admissions to heroin-treatment facilities. Yet interestingly, no one really knew how widespread heroin use was during those years, and even today the estimates are often little more than scientific guesses.

Currently, the most common form of opiate use involves prescription painkillers—such drugs as Vicodin, OxyContin, Percocet, and numerous others. The chapters that follow explore issues related to heroin and prescription painkillers. Patterns of heroin use among both street-based and young white users are explored. The emergence of OxyContin, a potent prescription painkiller, is reported on at length, with special attention given to the media hype surrounding the abuse of the drug.

Additional Readings

Courtwright, David T. (2001). *Dark Paradise: Opiate Addiction in America* (2nd ed.). Cambridge: Harvard University Press.

Davenport-Hines, Richard. (2002). *The Pursuit of Oblivion: A Global History of Narcotics, 1500–2000*. New York: W. W. Norton & Company.

Inciardi, James A., and Lana D. Harrison. (Eds.). (1998). *Heroin in the Age of Crack-Cocaine*. Thousand Oaks, CA: Sage Publications.

Kandall, Stephen R. (1996). *Substance and Shadow: Women and Addiction in the United States*. Cambridge: Harvard University Press.

Meier, Barry. (2003). *Pain Killer: A "Wonder" Drug's Trail of Addiction and Death*. New York: Rodale.

Spunt, Barry. (2003). "The Current New York City Heroin Scene." *Substance Use & Misuse*, 38(10): 1539–1549. ✦

15

'Dope Fiend' Mythology

Alfred R. Lindesmith[1]

Alfred Lindesmith reviews the public images of drug addicts. For example, common perceptions link addicts with crime, including violence and sexual aggression. Lindesmith argues that many of these images are inaccurate, and he attempts to dispel these myths. He suggests, for example, that crimes by drug users tend to be property offenses such as theft. He argues that these crimes are committed largely because drugs are illegal and quite costly. Lindesmith also describes the public image of the drug dealer who entices nonusers into drug initiation. Collectively, these negative images represent what Lindesmith refers to as "dope fiend mythology" and serve to reinforce punitive drug policies.

During the last fifty or so years there has grown up in the United States a body of stereotyped misinformation about drug addicts.[2] Sensational articles and newspaper accounts have harped upon the theme of the "dope-crazed killer" or the "dope fiend rapist" until the public has learned to depend upon this sort of literature as it depends upon the output of fanciful detective mysteries. The fact that the monstrous persons depicted exist mainly as figments of the imagination does not alter the fact that this mythology plays an important role in determining the way in which drug addicts are handled. Among serious students of the problem and among others who have some actual first-hand contact with drug users, as for example prison officials, it has always been recognized that the American public is singularly misinformed on this subject. Nevertheless, the organization of the machinery of justice that deals with this problem is more directly based upon the superstitions of the man on the street than it is upon anything that has been done in the name of impartial and objective analysis. It is the purpose of this paper to indicate and examine some of these popular fallacies, to analyze their function, and to point to the obstacles that stand in the way of a more realistic appraisal of the problem.

Drug addicts are often regarded as the most dangerous and heinous criminals and are linked up with killing and rape. This delusion has been smashed so many times that it is useless to devote serious attention to it.[3] Suffice it to say that students of drug addiction have always been in unanimous agreement that the crimes of rape and murder are rarely committed by drug users. Every publication of crime statistics proves this over and over again for anyone who cares to read.[4] Likewise it has been known in this country for almost a century that the principal drugs of addiction, opium and its derivatives, inhibit rather than stimulate the sex function. The drug addict is ordinarily not interested in sex and is frequently virtually impotent. The overwhelming proportion of law violations committed by drug users is made up of violations of the narcotic laws and petty offenses against property.[5]

The drug user must, of course, violate the narcotic laws. While it is technically true that the use of drugs is not in and of itself a crime, nevertheless, in practice the addict is treated as a criminal and the laws which hedge about him make it virtually impossible for him to avoid violating the narcotic laws daily. His thieving activities are very simply explained in terms of the prices he pays for his drugs. It is frequently estimated that the average cost of a drug habit in this country is somewhere between two and five dollars a day. One must add to this the fact that the drug user must spend a large proportion of his time maintaining his contacts with the peddlers. This means that if he is to maintain a habit he must find some means of making money quickly. The three principal methods utilized by American addicts are theft, prostitution, and drug peddling.

In general, drug users are harmless and not at all dangerous, except that they steal. They rarely carry guns. A gun to most addicts would simply mean another object which could be sold or pawned in order to buy another "bindle of junk." The G men who deal with criminals like Dillinger have dangerous occupations, but the narcotic agent who deals with addicts does not. The vengeance of the drug peddler is directed mainly toward the stool pigeon or informer, not toward the agent. A few years ago a Chicago drug peddler, who was not himself an addict, shot and killed an addict named Max Dent. He did so because the latter had betrayed him to the law. In the terms of the underworld he was a "rat" and according to the code of the underworld no treatment is too harsh for such a person. It is probable that of the relatively few murders attributed to drug law violators, many are of this type. The general public has nothing of this kind to fear. Now and then someone will have his pocket picked or other property stolen by a drug user, and frequently the prostitute is a drug user, but the principal depredations of drug addicts are carried out in stores, and particularly in the large department stores of our cities, where the opportunities for shoplifting are at maximum.

The public stands in virtually no danger of violence at the hands of drug users, except in those relatively rare instances when a user of the drug happens, for example, to be at the same time a professional holdup man. However, addiction is rather infrequent among underworld characters who utilize force or the threat of it. It is more common among such types as pickpockets and shoplifters and other types that do not resort to violence. Even in those cases when an addict is also a gunman, the danger resides not in the use of the narcotics but in the presence of the gun. The use of narcotics probably inhibits more than it encourages the use of violence.

The most substantial effect of the narcotic problem upon the public is the economic one. Aside from direct theft from private citizens, the public pays for the cost of the user's expensive habit and supports the underworld illicit traffic in opiates—one of the big and profitable industries of our country. It does so when it shoulders part of the losses from thefts from merchants when these merchants succeed in passing these losses on to their patrons. The contributions of respectable citizens to prostitutes also frequently serve to give financial support to the illicit traffic. In addition, the public pays for the enforcement of the laws and the penal institutions in which addicts are incarcerated. Instead of being concerned over this invisible and unnecessary form of taxation in the interests of an underworld business, the public has permitted itself to become aroused and indignant over dangers that are often fictitious.

It is often thought that addicts are easily recognizable either by reason of peculiar irresponsible behavior or unusual external appearances or both. This notion is false. Medical men often find it impossible to detect the drug user even after a thorough physical examination. Thus Chopra, a student of addiction in India, who has had experience with thousands of drug users, asserts:

> We know from our extensive experience with opium addicts in India, that it is impossible to detect a person taking opium in small or in moderate quantities, even after a careful physical examination.[6]

E. S. Bishop, a prominent American medical authority, states that if an addict maintains good elimination "he will escape detection."[7] Even when an addict uses large quantities of drugs the matter of determining that fact is often very difficult, the only sure way being to catch him in the act of using it or to find actual traces of the drug in his body. The drug addict driving a car is not a dangerous person—not nearly as dangerous as the respectable citizen who has had a couple of cocktails or a few glasses of beer. Assuming that the addict has his usual dose, there is no evidence to indicate that his skill at driving a car would be any greater if he were not using the drug. Moreover, it is quite well known that many drug users have carried on for many years in occupations requiring skill and intelligence, as for example, the medical profession.

There are certain external indications of drug addiction, but none of these signs is reliable.[8] In fact, it is one of the most remarkable things about drug addiction that the steady use of opiate drugs produces virtually no known significant pathological symptoms. In a recent authoritative study conducted by well-known biochemists, medical men, and physiologists, the results of which were published by the American Medical Association, the following assertions are made:

> The study shows that morphine addiction is not characterized by physical deterioration or impairment of physical fitness aside from the addiction per se. There is no evidence of change in the circulatory, hepatic, renal or endocrine functions. When it is considered that these subjects had been addicted for at least five years, some of them for as long as twenty years, these negative observations are highly significant.[9]

The same authors state:

> In a few recognized cases of opium addiction that have come to autopsy, whether the drug was being taken at the time of death or not, the pathologic changes found have been insignificant.[10]

Concerning the emaciated appearance of some addicts that has sometimes been assumed to be characteristic of drug users, these authorities state:

> We believe that the existence of considerable emaciation in certain cases is caused by the unhygienic and impoverished life of the addict rather than by the direct effects of the drug.[11]

Other students have reached similar conclusions. Thus Terry and Pellens, after an exhaustive and critical examination of an extensive literature, assert:

> Only in cases where large doses of the drug are being consumed can casual observation or even a fairly careful examination determine the existence of the condition. . . . It has been reported that for many years husbands and wives, to say nothing of other members of the family, have lived in complete ignorance of the existence of this condition in one or the other and that quite possibly the average physician, unaccustomed to dealing with the condition, might have difficulty in determining its existence.[12]

In view of the above results of research, the belief that a drug addict automatically becomes a moral degenerate, liar, thief, etc., because of the direct influence of the drug, is simply nonsense quite on a par with a belief in witchcraft. It is true that many American addicts belong to underworld or semi-underworld groups and that their behavior, from the viewpoint of a respectable citizen, is often despicable and reprehensible, but it is also true that there are many drug addicts, even in the United States, whose behavior does not fall in these categories and who maintain their self-respect and social status. There is no necessary or invariable connection between the taking of any kind of drug and moral degeneration. This fact is brought out by the consideration of the way in which wealthy addicts with political influence manage to protect themselves from arrest and detection and from a loss of social status. As Dr. Lichtenstein states:

> To call addiction a disease when applied to the wealthy, and a vice when referring to the underworld addict is nothing short of criminal, and such distinction serves but to becloud the situation and to interfere with the ultimate solution of the problem. At present a poor addict is an underworld addict. . . . We as physicians have no right to refuse treatment to the poor addict. Similarly, hospitals have no right to refuse such people treatment, and we, the general public, are entirely to blame if by forcing the addict to take treatment in a penal institution, we make of him a criminal,—and that is exactly what we are doing.[13]

In other words, it is not the effect of the drug that produces the alleged deterioration of character in the addict, but rather the social situations into which he is forced by the law and by the public's conception of addiction which does the damage. Well-to-do addicts who are in a position to protect themselves against these influences often live useful and productive lives.

It is beyond question that most of the addicts who are arrested and imprisoned in the United States belong to the poor and helpless class known as the "underworld group." Thus W. L. Treadway reports that of a total of 2,407 narcotic law violators studied, a little more than one-third or 925 were regularly employed. Of the same total only about one-seventh, or 352, were reported to have been in "comfortable" economic circumstances before arrest.[14] It is sometimes assumed that this situation is inevitable and natural, but statistical data from other countries reveal that such is not the case. In Formosa, for example, in 1905 more than 90 percent of the addicts are reported as having regular occupations and about 70 percent were reported as married and living with their families.[15] R. N. Chopra, speaking of addicts in India, states:

> Our cases [were] comprised of a fairly large number of good citizens, agriculturists who were working like normal individuals without any appreciable change in their social behavior.[16]

This author also notes a tendency for members of the underworld to seek regular employment and to leave the underworld when they become addicts. It should be remembered that addicts in India are not regarded or treated as criminals. Chopra has the following general comment to make on Indian opium users:

> Opium addicts in this country are not liars or moral wrecks as has been ascribed by some authors elsewhere. Some of our addicts were upright, straightforward and self-respecting individuals. We have observed that moderate consumers of the drug and a majority of those taking even larger doses are generally inoffensive to society. . . . The opium addicts in India are not much objected to by the people at large, but persons taking large doses of the drug, and those who smoke opium, are shunned by respectable citizens lest their children and youths should acquire the habit by force of example. The harm done by an opium addict is mainly confined to himself and not to society.[17]

Chopra found that about two-thirds of Indian addicts showed no appreciable changes in their general behavior as a consequence of the habit, and described the changes in the other one-third of the cases as being mainly of very minor character.[18] If our addicts appear to be moral degenerates and thieves, it is we who have made them that by the methods we have chosen to apply to their problem. By making it impossible for drug users to obtain low cost legitimate drugs, we have created a huge illicit traffic and impoverished the addict. The price of illicit drugs is ordinarily estimated

at anywhere from ten to twenty times the cost of legitimate drugs. It is in the desperate attempt of the drug user to meet these enormous prices that he resorts to theft and prostitution. If we were to set about deliberately to produce thieves and prostitutes we could scarcely improve on this situation.

It may be argued that addicts are thieves and prostitutes before becoming addicts, and no doubt that is sometimes true. A number of investigations indicate, however, that more than half of our addicts have no criminal records of any kind prior to addiction.[19]

An English writer correctly appraised our situation when he wrote:

> In the United States of America a drug habitué is regarded as a malefactor, even though the habit has been acquired through the medicinal use of the drug, as in the case, e.g., of American soldiers who were gassed or otherwise maimed in the Great War. The Harrison Narcotic Law was passed in 1914 by the Federal Government of the United States with general popular approval. It placed severe restrictions upon the sale of narcotics and upon the medical profession, and necessitated the appointment of a whole army of officials. In consequence of this stringent law a vast clandestine commerce in narcotics has grown up in that country. The small bulk of these drugs renders the evasion of the law comparatively easy, and the country is overrun by an army of peddlers who extort exorbitant prices from their hapless victims. It appears that not only has the Harrison Law failed to diminish the number of drug takers—some contend, indeed, that it has increased their numbers—but, far from bettering the lot of the opiate addict, it has actually worsened it; for without curtailing the supply of the drug it has sent up the price tenfold, and this has had the effect of impoverishing the poorer class of addicts and reducing them to a condition of such abject misery as to render them incapable of gaining an honest livelihood.[20]

The whole blame for addiction is sometimes placed upon the shoulders of the well-known "bogey man," the dope peddler, who is blamed for spreading the habit for the alleged purpose of extending his market.[21] In this connection it should be remembered that the peddler depends upon the enormous prices that he is able to obtain. The situation that makes these prices possible is created directly by our present laws. Prospects of profits of more than a thousand percent inevitably attract business talent in a country like ours. Peddlers and smugglers in such a situation are quite inevitable—as inevitable as bootleggers in the prohibition era. The drug peddler does not create this situation, he only takes advantage of the opportunities that are presented.[22]

The peddler of drugs, contrary to a widespread belief, does not ordinarily attempt to induce non-users to try the drug. Isolated instances of this may occur, but the general rule is quite the opposite. The reasons for this are obvious once they are considered, and it is not because the peddler is virtuous and innocent—he is far from that. He does not try to seduce non-users because it does not pay and because it is too dangerous. The ordinary peddler who makes the actual contacts with consumers leads a very precarious existence outside of prison, living in constant fear of the law. He is arrested and evidence against him is obtained through the use of drug-using stool pigeons posing as bona fide customers.[23] Addict informers must be used for this purpose because peddlers have long since learned the elementary fact that if they did no business with non-addicts it would be impossible for the narcotic agent to obtain direct evidence unaided. If peddlers attempted to extend their markets to non-users, they would facilitate their own arrest. The sentences imposed upon them in such circumstances would also certainly be more severe than they otherwise are.

Inducing non-addicts to try the drug is not profitable because the non-user is not initially interested in paying the high prices. Peddlers cannot give away quantities of the drug sufficient to establish addiction and stay in the business. The drug user is in the business for profit and usually to maintain his own habit. The product he handles often brings as much as $200 an ounce—several times its weight in gold. He can no more afford to give it away than a jeweler can afford to give away diamonds. Moreover, most of the peddlers who are arrested and sent to prison are poor. According to W. L.

Treadway, of a group of 2,407, 2,055 were not in comfortable economic circumstances prior to arrest.[24] They were, in other words, what is known as "boots" or "boot and shoe dope fiends." Persons of this type living from hand to mouth and spending a large proportion of their time in penal institutions are in no position to give anything away or to take any unnecessary risks.

The large-scale smuggler and peddler likewise cannot promote the wider use of drugs because he must keep the nature of his business secret. He extends his market by "muscling in" on someone else's business and lets the spread of the habit take care of itself, knowing that with our laws as they are and with human beings what they are, there will always be those who will permit their curiosity to overcome their judgment and keep the market lively.[25]

Another current myth is that all addicts, in accordance with the proverb that "misery loves company," have a positive mania for making new addicts. This is nothing but gratuitous slander of an unfortunate and helpless group. This particular myth is current in the United States, but it is curiously absent in other countries of the world. Drug addicts have been observed and studied for at least three-quarters of a century in this country and in Europe, but the idea that each addict makes it his purpose to obtain new recruits is emphasized in only one country—the United States. In England, France, Germany, Russia, India, etc., it has not been noticed.[26] Throughout the nineteenth century it was not noticed in the United States either.[27] Curiously enough, this myth appears to have only local circulation and a very recent origin.

It is true that people become addicts through association with persons who are already addicted, but that does not mean that the user deliberately makes an addict of the non-user. It is through contacts with the user of the drug that the non-addict has his curiosity aroused to the point where he wants to experiment with the drug. Frequently, probably usually, the beginner is warned solemnly against the dangers involved, but he goes ahead in spite of these warnings, believing in his own powers of resistance. The inconsistency of the attempt to blame the addict for making new addicts is indicated by the fact that, once addicted, no one is inclined to excuse the addict on the grounds that he was innocently lured into the habit by another user. In fact, quite a different position is taken. Not only is the user blamed for spreading the habit, but the new addict is immediately declared to be fully responsible for his own addiction and is punished accordingly.

The assumption that all addicts try to spread the habit is given as a justification for imprisoning them under the erroneous assumption that the habit cannot be spread in prison. However, if this is a reason for incarcerating the drug user, he should be tried in court for that offense. Evidence should be presented to prove that he has in fact attempted to induce a non-addict to become an addict. The victims of venereal disease also sometimes deliberately infect others, but that is not regarded as an excuse for sending all the victims of this disease to prison.

Drug addicts in the United States are punished for being addicts. The establishment of narcotic farms has been a gesture in another direction, but is essentially futile as long as the general social and legal situation of the drug user remains what it is. Regardless of attempts to pretend otherwise, the narcotic farms are regarded as prisons by the addicts. They are places where one "does time." The addict who earnestly wishes to break his habit has virtually no other course open to him except to go to prison—unless, of course, he has money. Sending the addict to prison serves no useful purpose. In fact, the stigma of the prison sentence with its resultant social disgrace and loss of employment and position and the extensive acquaintanceships with drug users and peddlers established in prison, merely aggravates the plight of the addict when he is released and makes it harder for him to break away from his habit.[28]

A. M. Turano, in an excellent article on addicts entitled "Punishment for Disease," summarized the official attitude toward treating addicts as follows:

> Thus it appears, on the whole, that in begrudgingly offering medical care, the law stands at the bedside of the addict as a fumbling nurse with healing balm in one hand and a primitive tomahawk in the other, unable to decide whether to attack the disease or punish its owner for having acquired it.[29]

As August Vollmer says, "Drug addiction . . . is not a police problem; it never has been, and never can be solved by policemen."[30]

Why then does the situation continue as it is? It is at this point that the mythology surrounding drug addiction plays its part. An ideology, based on the distortion and misrepresentation of fact, has been given a veneer of plausibility, which has made it attractive as well as exciting to the man on the street. This ideology serves to justify the severe treatment generally accorded the drug user, and is utilized by vested interests to frighten the public into appropriating more and more funds to combat the great "dope menace." Solemn discussions are carried on about lengthening the addict's already long sentence and as to whether or not he is a good parole risk. The basic question as to why he should be sent to prison at all is scarcely mentioned. Eventually, it is to be hoped that we shall come to see, as most of the civilized countries of the world have seen, that the punishment and imprisonment of addicts is as cruel and pointless as similar treatment for persons infected with syphilis would be.

However, if we are to continue to punish the drug user for his misfortune, turning him over to the tender mercies of policemen for "treatment," the mythology we have described will be useful. We can continue to offer him the haven of a penitentiary instead of a hospital and justify ourselves by pointing out that, after all, he deserves nothing better. Besides being a vicious and degenerate person seeking to infect others, he is naturally inclined toward theft, prostitution, and any crime whatever. If we throw him into prison, he will only be able to spread the habit to other prisoners. The final ironic touch is the argument that the incarceration of addicts deprives peddlers of their market. On this basis all honest persons should be thrown into prison so that pickpockets would have only each other to steal from.

The "dope fiend" mythology serves, in short, as a rationalization of the status quo. It is a body of superstition, half-truths, and misinformation that bolsters an indefensible repressive law, the victims of which are in no position to protest. The treatment of addicts in the United States today is on no higher plane than the persecution of witches of other ages, and like the latter it is to be hoped that it will soon become merely another dark chapter of history.

Notes

1. Review Editor of the [*Journal of Criminal Law and Criminology*]. Professor of Sociology at the State University, Bloomington, Indiana.

2. This article will be concerned only with the users of opiate drugs. Marijuana and cocaine users represent an entirely different problem. One of the reasons for confusion in this field is that the users of totally different types of drugs are not distinguished. The bad reputation of the opiate user is earned for him in part by the cocaine and marijuana users.

3. See, e.g., Dr. Lawrence Kolb, "Drug Addiction in Relation to Crime," *Mental Hygiene* IX (1925), p. 74ff. Also, Terry and Pellens, *The Opium Problem*, 1928.

4. See page 12 of the annual report on the *Traffic in Opium and Other Dangerous Drugs for the Year Ended December 31, 1936*, by the Bureau of Narcotics. Also see Supplement No. 143 to the *Public Health Reports*, "A Statistical Analysis of the Clinical Records of Hospitalized Drug Addicts," by Michael J. Pescor.

5. Thus the annual report of the Bureau of Narcotics for 1936 summarizes approximately 13,000 felonies committed by 4,975 drug users. Of this total, about one-sixth of one per cent, or 23 cases, are classified as "murder or manslaughter" and rape is not even listed. In contrast, 8,427 of the felonies were classified as "narcotic convictions," 1,898 as "miscellaneous," 1,313 "grand larceny," 609 "burglary," 278 "felonious assault," 278 "highway robbery," 100 "concealed weapons," and 87 "forgery."

6. *The Indian Journal of Medical Research* XX, p. 561.

7. *The Narcotic Drug Problem*, Macmillan, 1921, p. 47.

8. I refer to the external appearance of the skin and to the reactions of the eye.

9. *Opium Addiction*, 1929, p. 115.

10. *Ibid.*, p. 19.

11. *Ibid.*, p. 20.

12. *Op. cit.*, p. 2. On page 514 these authors state: "In spite of frequently repeated statements that the use of opium and its derivatives causes mental and ethical degeneration in all cases, we are inclined to believe that this alleged effect has not been established."

13. Appendix 12 of *Documentation of Fifth Annual Conference of Committees of the World Narcotic Defence Association and International Narcotic Education Association*, held in New York in 1932.

14. "Some Epidemiological Features of Drug Addiction," *British Journal of Inebriety* XXVIII (1930), pp. 50–54.

15. A. Hischman, (1912), *Die Opiumfrage*. p. 46.

16. "The Opium Habit in India," *Indian Journal of Medical Research* XV (1927).

17. *Ibid.* See also the other articles by this author in the same journal and also in *The Indian Medical Gazette*.

18. See also A. H. Lindesmith, "A Sociological Theory of Drug Addiction," *American Journal of Sociology* XLIII (1938), pp. 593–609, for material on the "normality" of the drug user.

19. Thus Michael J. Pescor (*op. cit.*) makes this statement on the basis of the results of the study of 1,036 cases, "If the addict is basically a criminal, it is likely that he would have committed anti-social acts prior to his addiction; yet three-fourths of the patients had no delinquency record prior to addiction" (p. 8). Substantially the same result is reported by Bingham Dai, *Opium Addiction in Chicago*, Shanghai, The Commercial Press, 1937.

20. Harry Campbell, "The Pathology and Treatment of Morphia Addiction," *British Journal of Inebriety* XX (1923), pp. 147–148.

21. Even Terry and Pellens are guilty of repeating this sort of thing of peddlers (*op. cit.*, p. 87). They also say that peddlers give away enough of the drug to addict a person and then charge enough to make up for their losses. No evidence has been produced to show that this sort of thing is actually done.

22. The implication is clear. The way to eliminate the peddler is to eliminate his profit.

23. This use of addicted informers is one of the unfortunate and unpublicized aspects of the enforcement of narcotic laws. The informer uses some of the money that he is paid by the government to buy illicit drugs from peddlers whom he has not betrayed to the law. It is stated that in the past local Narcotic Bureaus actually doled out the drug themselves to the informers working for them. The practice of using stool pigeons has the effect of placing some of the responsibility for the way in which the law is enforced upon one of the most despised underworld types.

24. *Locus cited.* This indicates the significant fact that the profits of the drug traffic do not end up in the pockets of the people who are sent to prison for peddling drugs. It may safely be asserted that the persons who profit from the drug traffic are not addicts and that they do not spend much time in prison.

25. It would be positively silly to suppose that the late Rothstein of New York, who is reputed to have made a great deal of his fortune through handling drugs, would have taken the risk of urging the habit upon someone so as to increase his profit by a few dollars.

26. The literature offers instances in which addicts have deliberately imposed the habit upon someone, but they are rare, and as far as I know no competent student of addiction in European countries has ever maintained that all, or most or even many, addicts sought to do this.

27. See Calkins, *Opium and the Opium Appetite*. Philadelphia, 1871. This is one of the most informative books of the nineteenth century on this subject. Literally hundreds of cases are cited and many different shades of opinion are discussed, but the idea under consideration had obviously not occurred to anyone at that time.

28. Thus there is a population of about 1,600 at the Annex of the Fort Leavenworth Penitentiary. Assuming that there are about 100 new cases admitted each month, an inmate has the opportunity of meeting 2,800 drug peddlers and addicts in the course of a year. When released, he may meet former prison comrades in almost any city in the United States and each such meeting represents a temptation to resume the use of the drug. This situation also facilitates the peddling of drugs and entry into other criminal occupations.

29. *The American Mercury* XXXVI, December, 1935.

30. *The Police and Modern Society*, Berkeley. 1936, p. 118. See also Harry Elmer Barnes, *Society in Transition*, 1939, on this problem.

For Discussion

What are the images of the twenty-first-century "dope fiend"? Have these images changed since Lindesmith's article was first published in 1940–1941?

16

OxyContin

Miracle Medicine or Problem Drug?

James A. Inciardi
Jennifer L. Syvertsen

OxyContin, a powerful prescription painkiller, has generated considerable attention since its introduction to the market in 1996. In this next essay, the authors dissect whether an "epidemic" of Oxy-Contin abuse really exists, or if the media have sensationalized recreational use among a certain segment of the population.

They examine the diversion of OxyContin to the black market for nonprescribed reasons and carefully scrutinize government data to try to ascertain the extent of its misuse. Initial reports of abuse can be traced back to Maine, and the trend subsequently spread down the East Coast into parts of Appalachia. The authors consider the popularity of OxyContin in these areas in the context of the region's cultural and socioeconomic features. Abuse has allegedly infiltrated other parts of the country as well, and many have blamed an onslaught of media coverage for contributing to a national "epidemic." The authors examine the media's coverage of the drug in detail, both from national and international outlets, and reveal striking similarities to media coverage of the "crack epidemic" of the 1980s. While the abuse of OxyContin does indeed exist, it appears to be just the latest drug trend that the media have blown out of proportion.

If anything has been learned about the drug problem in the United States, it is that patterns of drug abuse are continually shifting and changing. Fads and fashions in the drugs of abuse seem to come and go; drugs of choice emerge and then disappear from the American drug scene; and still others are reconstituted, repackaged, recycled, and be- come permanent parts of the drug-taking and drug-seeking landscape. And as new drugs become visible, there are the concomitant media and political feeding frenzies, followed by calls for a strengthening of the "war on drugs." It happened with heroin in the 1950s, with marijuana and LSD in the 1960s, with Quaalude® and PCP in the 1970s, and with methamphetamine, "ice," ecstasy, crack and other forms of cocaine in the 1980s and 1990s (Jenkins 1999; Inciardi 2002a). The most recent entry to the drug scene to receive this focused attention is OxyContin®, a narcotic painkiller several times more potent than morphine.

Since OxyContin was first introduced to the market in early 1996, it has been hailed as a breakthrough in pain management. The medication is unique in that its time-release formula allows patients to enjoy continuous, long-term relief from moderate to severe pain. For many patients who had suffered for years from chronic pain, it gave them relief from suffering. But during the past few years OxyContin has received a substantial amount of negative attention—not for its medicinal effects, but for its addiction liability and abuse potential. Within this context, this essay examines the brief but eventful history of OxyContin, as well as available data on its use and misuse, media coverage, and the public health consequences that such attention has generated.

OxyContin and Oxycodone

The active ingredient in OxyContin is "oxycodone," a drug that has been used for the treatment of pain for almost 100 years. Oxycodone is a semi-synthetic narcotic analgesic most often prescribed for moderate to severe pain, chronic pain syndromes, and terminal cancers. When used correctly under a physician's supervision, oxycodone can be highly effective in the management of pain, and there are scores of oxycodone products on the market—in various strengths and forms. Popular brands include Percocet® and Percodan,® Roxicet® and Roxicodone,® and Endocet,® OxyIR,® and Tylox® to name but a few. However, no oxycodone product has generated as much attention as OxyContin.

Produced by the Stamford, Connecticut-based pharmaceutical company, Purdue Pharma L.P., OxyContin is unique because unlike other oxycodone products that typically contain aspirin or acetaminophen to increase or lengthen their potency, Oxy-Contin is a single entity product that can provide up to 12 hours of continuous pain relief. Tablets are available in 10, 20, 40, and 80-milligram doses. The company also introduced a 160-milligram dose in July 2000 for its opioid tolerant patients, only to later withdraw it from the market amidst controversy over its alleged abuse (DEA 2002a).

When the clinical trials for OxyContin were reviewed by the Food and Drug Administration (FDA), the drug was demonstrated to be an effective analgesic in individuals with chronic, moderate to severe pain. Yet it was also judged by the FDA to carry a substantial risk of abuse because of its properties as a narcotic. As a result, OxyContin was approved by the FDA but placed in Schedule II of the Controlled Substances Act (CSA), which is the tightest level of control that can be placed on an approved drug for medical purposes. The placement of OxyContin in Schedule II warned physicians and patients that the drug carried a high potential for abuse and that it needed to be carefully managed, particularly among those at risk for substance abuse. In addition, in the *Physicians Desk Reference* and on the drug's package insert, OxyContin carries a boxed warning (more commonly known as the infamous "black box"), which boldly indicates:

WARNING:
OxyContin is an opioid agonist and a Schedule II controlled substance with an abuse liability similar to morphine.

Oxycodone can be abused in a manner similar to other opioid agonists, legal or illicit. This should be considered when prescribing or dispensing OxyContin in situations where the physician or pharmacist is concerned about an increased risk of misuse, abuse, or diversion.

OxyContin Tablets are a controlled-release oral formulation of oxycodone hydrochloride indicated for the management of moderate to severe pain when a continuous, around-the-clock analgesic is needed for an extended period of time.

OxyContin 80 mg and 160 mg Tablets ARE FOR USE IN OPIOID-TOLERANT PATIENTS ONLY. These tablet strengths may cause fatal respiratory depression when administered to patients not previously exposed to opioids.

OxyContin TABLETS ARE TO BE SWALLOWED WHOLE AND ARE NOT TO BE BROKEN, CHEWED, OR CRUSHED. TAKING BROKEN, CHEWED, OR CRUSHED OxyContin TABLETS LEADS TO RAPID RELEASE AND ABSORPTION OF A POTENTIALLY FATAL DOSE OF OXYCODONE.

Importantly, this "black box," voluntarily inserted in the packaging information by Purdue Pharma in 2001, alerts potential users with the notice that taking broken, chewed, or crushed leads to rapid release and absorption of a potentially fatal dose of the drug. But even before the insertion of the "black box," drug abusers had figured out how to compromise OxyContin's controlled release formula and set off on a powerful high by injecting or snorting dissolved tablets or by crushing and ingesting them.

Despite the numerous controls and warnings required by the FDA, OxyContin has been a major economic success for Purdue Pharma, accounting for some 80% of the company's total business (Greenwald 2003). Prescriptions have risen steadily since the drug's introduction, as the number of prescriptions dispensed increased 20-fold from 1996 through 2000 (Nagel & Good 2001). More than 7.2 million prescriptions were dispensed in 2001 and retail sales totaled more than $1.45 billion, representing a 41% increase in sales between 2000 and 2001 alone. Retail sales increased again in 2002, topping $1.59 billion. In terms of dollar amount, OxyContin now ranks the highest in retail sales of all brand-name controlled substances (DEA 2002a). Federal regulators, however, are put off by these numbers, and focus on the *diversion* of OxyContin to illegal markets, and reports of OxyContin abuse and overdose deaths.

Diversion of OxyContin

Prescription drug diversion involves the unlawful movement of regulated pharmaceuticals from legal sources to the illegal marketplace, and OxyContin's attractiveness to drug abusers has resulted in its diversion in a number of ways. The major mechanisms include the illegal sale of prescriptions by physicians and pharmacists; "doctor shopping" by individuals who visit numerous physicians to obtain multiple prescriptions; the theft, forgery, or alteration of prescriptions by patients; robberies and thefts from pharmacies and pharmaceutical warehouses; and thefts of samples from physicians' offices as well as thefts of institutional drug supplies by health care workers. In all likelihood, OxyContin has been diverted through all of these routes.

Diversion has also occurred by means of fraud, particularly through the abuse of medical insurance programs, a phenomenon observed and investigated most often in a number of rural communities. Medicaid fraud, for example, presents an inexpensive mechanism for abusing drugs and oftentimes an easy route to a lucrative enterprise. For example, a Medicaid patient may pay only $3 for a bottle of a hundred 80-milligram OxyContin tablets. In areas where employment and money are scarce resources, the temptation to sell some of the pills for the going "street price" of $1 per milligram provides an opportunity to earn money. In this example, the $3 bottle from the pharmacy can net the patient up to $8,000 on the illegal market (Moore 2000). If the patient needs more pills before a legitimate refill is possible, he or she may simply "doctor shop" a number of physicians for additional prescriptions and pay cash for the new supplies to avoid having the pharmacist check with the Medicaid people.

Going further, just one corrupt physician, pharmacist, health care worker, or other employee in the healthcare field can have a significant impact on the availability of the product as well. For example, before he was arrested in 2002, a Pennsylvania pharmacist had illegally sold hundreds of thousands of painkillers, including OxyContin, over a three-year period. He made $900,000 on his transactions (only to lose it all in the stock market). Although he operated an independent neighborhood pharmacy, he was reportedly the state's third-largest purchaser of OxyContin (Slobodzian 2002). Similarly, a number of physicians in eastern Kentucky were arrested in 2003 for a variety of diversion schemes. One saw as many as 150 patients each day, writing narcotic prescriptions for them after a visit of less than three minutes. Another physician traded painkillers for sex with female patients who he had addicted to narcotics. A third opened an office in a shopping mall where he generated prescriptions—one after another—almost as quickly as he could write them (Alford 2003).

As to how much diversion of OxyContin actually occurs is impossible to calculate, because there is not a single national reporting system on pharmaceutical diversion. Furthermore, of the more than 23,000 federal, state, and municipal law enforcement agencies in the United States, well under 10% have a specific focus on prescription drug diversion (Inciardi & Cicero 2002). Nevertheless, some data are available which at least suggest the extent of OxyContin diversion, relative to other drugs of abuse, including narcotic painkillers. In a 2001 survey of 34 police agencies with pharmaceutical diversion units, for example, a total of 5,802 cases of diversion (of any drug) were reported during the calendar year (Inciardi 2002b). The reporting agencies were asked to indicate which drugs were most commonly diverted, and in how many cases each was investigated. The most commonly diverted pharmaceutical drug was hydrocodone (Vicodin,® Lortab,® and similar narcotic analgesics), noted in 31% of the total cases. This was followed by oxycodone in 12% of the cases, and alprazolam (Xanax®) in 6% of the cases. Of the 701 cases involving an oxycodone product, 416 were OxyContin. Overall, OxyContin was represented in only 7% of the drug diversions, a rather small proportion given the attention the drug has received. In addition, the data documented that the diversion of OxyContin was part of a much broader pattern of prescription drug diversion. That is, in the great majority of cases in which OxyContin had been diverted, a wide spectrum of other drugs were being diverted at the same time.

OxyContin Abuse: Do the Figures Add Up?

Although there are several sources of national data on drug abuse that have been operating for decades, the collection of specific data on OxyContin abuse is quite recent. In the Monitoring the Future Survey, a government-sponsored study of drug abuse among high school students and young adults that has been conducted annually since 1975, the collection of information on OxyContin began only in 2002—and this was initiated at the request of Purdue Pharma. The 2002 survey found that 4% of 12th graders, 3% of 10th graders, and 1.3% of 8th graders had used OxyContin at least once during the past year. Interestingly, the use of Vicodin (a brand of hydrocodone) in the past year was at least double that of OxyContin—9.6% for 12th graders, 6.9% for 10th graders, and 2.5% for 8th graders (Johnston, O'Malley & Bachman 2003). In the 2001 National Household Survey on Drug Abuse, another government survey conducted annually, only "lifetime use" (at least once in a person's lifetime "to get high") data were collected for OxyContin. For persons ages 12 and over, less than one half of one percent reported ever using OxyContin to get high (SAMHSA 2002).

Because the Monitoring the Future and the National Household surveys are conducted with a high degree of scientific rigor, the estimates they generate for society's more "stable," at-home and/or in-school populations have a high degree of reliability. These should be contrasted with data from the Drug Abuse Warning Network, which tend to be somewhat problematic. More commonly known as DAWN, this large-scale information collection effort was designed to monitor changing patterns of drug abuse in the United States, and to serve as an early warning system for police, prevention, and treatment agencies. Hundreds of hospital emergency rooms and county medical examiners in major metropolitan areas across the United States report regularly to the DAWN system. However, because of the focus on metropolitan areas, the limitation to drug overdoses and other adverse reactions that result in a trip to the emergency room or county morgue, and the lack of information on specific brands of prescription drugs, DAWN data must be examined with considerable caution. Nevertheless, major pronouncements about drug abuse in the United States are often based solely on DAWN.

With regard to OxyContin, DAWN data indicate that the incidence of emergency room visits related to narcotic analgesic abuse has been on the rise since the mid-1990s, more than doubling between 1994 and 2001. The category with the largest increase during this period was oxycodone, at 352%, and most of the increases in narcotic analgesic mentions occurred toward the end of the decade, after OxyContin had been released to the market. Oxycodone mentions surged 186% from 1999 to 2000 and again by 70% from 2000 to 2001 (Crane 2003). But since DAWN does not publish specific brand names of drugs, it is impossible to ascertain the exact number of episodes specifically related to OxyContin at any given time.

Going further, since many OxyContin overdoses likely occur outside the DAWN reporting system—in rural areas such as Maine, West Virginia, and Kentucky—DAWN data are of no use for estimating the extent of the problem. To fill this gap, the Drug Enforcement Administration (DEA) started actively collecting and analyzing data from medical examiners in an attempt to establish the extent of the "OxyContin problem." Medical examiner reports from 2000–2001 from 32 states reported that 949 deaths were associated with oxycodone, of which almost half (49%) were "likely" related to OxyContin (DEA 2002b). However, careful scrutiny of the data paints a more cautious picture: because there are a multitude of oxycodone products on the market, it is impossible to determine the specific brand of drug found in a cadaver. Nevertheless, out of the 949 deaths, DEA reported that 146 were "OxyContin verified," while another 318 were "OxyContin likely." To make things even more complicated, the majority of the toxicological analyses reported "poly" or "multiple-drug use," suggesting that the death may have been the result of an overdose induced by a combination of substances, not just oxycodone by itself (DEA

2002b). When taking all of these factors into consideration, it is very difficult to establish a direct link between OxyContin and cause of death.

A recent study published in the *Journal of Analytical Toxicology* attempted to more scientifically unravel the questions about OxyContin-related deaths. Based on data from over 1,000 deaths reported by medical examiners and coroners' offices from 23 states from August 27, 1999, through January 17, 2002, the study results were an interesting contrast to those fostered by DEA. The conclusion was that OxyContin alone was found in only 1.3% of the cases examined. Of the 1,014 cases, 90.6% of the deaths involved drug abuse; the remainder were due to other causes. Of the drug abuse deaths, 96.7% were found to have multiple drugs present (Goldberger 2003). DEA officials counter that poly-drug use is often part of patients' overall treatment regimen, such as the co-administration of anti-depressants. They emphasize that it should not be surprising to find that many of the deaths were associated with multiple drugs but insist that this should not override the significance of OxyContin's role in the patient's death (DEA 2002b).

The DEA Office of Diversion Control has attempted to bolster its case against OxyContin by stressing that property and other crimes related to the abuse of the drug increased by as much as 75% in some parts of the United States (DEA 2001a), with new OxyContin-related arrests increasing from 67 in 2000 to 277 in 2001 (DEA 2002a). Although no one is questioning the validity of these arrest figures, there is a problem with this kind of data. The 19th century French sociologist Emile Durkheim once commented that a community has as much crime as it has people to count it (Durkheim 1933). In other words, the DEA arrest data, to a very great extent, follows a "Field of Dreams" scenario—"if you look for it, you will find it." If DEA had placed the same focus on the trafficking and illegal distribution of Xanax or some other highly abusable prescription drug as it had on OxyContin, increasing numbers of arrests would have occurred as well.

An Emerging National Epidemic?

OxyContin abuse first surfaced in rural Maine during the late 1990s, soon after spreading down the east coast and Ohio Valley, and then into rural Appalachia. Communities in western Virginia, eastern Kentucky, West Virginia, and southern Ohio were especially hard hit, and a number of factors characteristic of these areas seem to correlate with their apparent high rates of abuse. In northern Maine and rural Appalachia, for example, there are aspects of the culture that are markedly different from those in other parts of the country. Many of the communities are quite small and isolated, often situated in the mountains and "hollers" (small crevice-like mountain dens and valleys) a considerable distance from major towns and highways. As a result, many of the usual street drugs are simply not available. Instead, locals make due with resources already on hand, like prescription drugs. In addition, isolation impacts heavily on options for amenities and entertainment—a major contrast to the distractions of metropolitan areas. Many substance abuse treatment clients in these rural areas have told their counselors that they started using drugs because of boredom. Many start abusing drugs quite young, as well. According to one treatment counselor in Maine, the average age of drug experimentation and abuse in that state is nine. Young people begin with marijuana and alcohol, progressing on to other drugs as they move into their teenage years (Clancy 2000).

Many adults in these rural areas tend to suffer from chronic illnesses and pain syndromes, born out of hard lives of manual labor in perilous professions—coal mining, logging, fishing, and other blue-collar industries which often result in serious and debilitating injuries. As a result, a disproportionately high segment of the population lives on strong painkillers. The use of pain pills evolves into a kind of coping mechanism, and the practice of self-medication becomes a way for life for many. As such, the use of narcotic analgesics has become normalized and integrated into the local culture (DOJ 2002a).

No one understands this cycle better than the people who live in the region and who are most affected by the problem. As the director of Kentucky's Division of Substance Abuse summarized, there is "a cultural history of solving problems through medication" (Gowda 2003). A Kentucky prosecutor who focuses on drug crimes concurred: "A lot of places, you got a headache, you'll tough it out," he says. "Down here," he continues, "it's like, 'Well, my grandfather's got some drugs. I'll take that and it'll go away.' And it just escalates" (Breed 2001).

Data suggest that the abuse of OxyContin may be escalating in certain areas. For example, the number of patients in Kentucky seeking treatment for oxycodone addiction increased 163% from 1998 to 2000 (DOJ 2002a). While OxyContin is not necessarily always the cause, officials there say that it is one of the most widely abused oxycodone products. Crime statistics seem to support the claim, as Kentucky is one of the leading states for OxyContin-related crimes. Between January 2000 and June 2001 alone, 69 of the state's 1,000 pharmacies reported OxyContin-related break-ins (DOJ 2002a).

Drug treatment admissions from several states may also offer evidence to support a growing trend in OxyContin abuse. Programs in Pennsylvania, Kentucky, and Virginia have reported that 50% to 90% of newly admitted patients identified OxyContin as their drug of choice (Nagel & Good 2001). Figures obtained by DEA from the American Methadone Treatment Association also suggest[s] an increase in the number of patients admitted for OxyContin abuse (DEA 2002a). Moreover, according to the Maine Office of Substance Abuse, the number of narcotics-related (excluding heroin) treatment admissions increased from 73 in 1995 to 762 in 2001 (DOJ 2002b). While OxyContin cannot take all of the blame, officials say it is nonetheless a major contributor and also point out that opiate-based prescription drugs in general outpaced the percentage increases for all other types of drugs in the state. Treatment admissions for these drugs increased 78% from 1998 to 1999 (199 to 355) and another 47% from 1999 through September 2000 (355 to 521), which suggest a possible increase in OxyContin use (DOJ 2002b).

A separate study conducted by Maine's Substance Abuse Services Commission and the Maine Office of Substance Abuse found that treatment admissions for narcotic abuse increased 500% since 1995, and that opiate-related arrests comprised more than 40% of the Maine Drug Enforcement Agency's caseload. The study, commissioned because of the publicity the state received for being one of the first to identify OxyContin abuse, analyzed several aspects of prescription opiate abuse. The study linked the use of narcotics with increased rates of crime, emergency medical treatment, and outbreaks of hepatitis C. While OxyContin was not the only opiate abused in the state at the time, it constituted the centerpiece of the study results published in the *Alcoholism & Drug Abuse Weekly* (Maine Analysis 2002).

Based on these and similar reports in a few other states, it has been suggested in numerous media outlets that the abuse of OxyContin is on the rise, and that its popularity is rapidly spreading beyond the rural East Coast to other parts of the United States. At the same time, however, there is also concern that the media has played an integral role in boosting the drug's popularity.

The Media Frenzy

Media outlets in Maine began reporting on OxyContin abuse in early 2000. The *Bangor Daily News*, for example, ran several features which included information not only about the properties of the drug, but also about: (1) how to compromise its time-release mechanism, (2) the tactics of diversion that people were using to obtain the drug (including Medicaid fraud), and (3) the concerns of the medical profession about the potential for abusing the drug. In addition, numerous examples of alleged OxyContin-related crimes were described in detail.

A smattering of news articles followed in other parts of the nation, but in May of 2000 the *Boston Globe* became the first major daily to focus on OxyContin. The lead commanded readers' attention by reporting that even a town sheriff in rural Maine was "scared" of the situation—because of an unusually large number of people being arrested for drug-related crimes, the sheriff noted, the inmate population at the local jail had grown well over capacity (Gold 2000). The following month, the New Orleans *Times-Picayune* quoted a local DEA supervisor who referred to OxyContin as the "new Vicodin" (hydrocodone). In the same article, an anonymous prescription drug abuser added: "You get kind of a Vicodin feeling, but a little heavier [with OxyContin]" (Cannizaro 2000).

Media coverage changed dramatically after Kentucky's sensational "Operation OxyFest 2001," when more than 100 law enforcement officers from numerous jurisdictions worked together to arrest 207 suspected OxyContin users and dealers throughout the state. The arrests made for good headlines, and many local officials were more than happy to vie for their personal 15 minutes of fame. The most colorful of these was Detective Roger Hall of the Harlan County Kentucky Sheriff's Department, who was quoted as saying that abusers "will kick a bag of cocaine aside to get Oxy" (Kaushik 2001). Never mind that comparing cocaine, a stimulant, to OxyContin, a depressant, is like comparing Mountain Dew to Chamomile tea, the national media had their hook and a sexy sound bite and they certainly ran with it.

A blitz of national media coverage followed. The Associated Press, *Time, Newsweek, New York Times*, and other media giants, as well as local newspapers across the nation all ran alarming stories about the potentially lethal and dangerous new drug. Much of the initial coverage of OxyContin seemed to follow a similar formula: it started off with the personal tale of a chronically ill patient for whom OxyContin had suddenly made life worth living, followed by a contrasting tale of a lowly, depraved junkie who had become a slave to the drug, all the while littering the piece with both information and misinformation about the drug. And slang labels like "OC's," "Oxys" and "hillbilly heroin" started to permeate the national vocabulary.

As has historically been the case with drugs, coverage of the issue was generally presented in terms of black and white, good vs. evil. "The media presented the drug prob-

lem as a war of the holy people against the depraved people, and we haven't gone far past that moralizing tone," noted nationally respected media critic Norman Solomon (Kaushik 2001). Headlines screamed about OxyContin-related crimes, including pharmacy break-ins and terrifying accounts of elderly patients' homes being invaded and raided for the drug. Some stories of robberies appeared in local media outlets, only to be followed by a string of copycat attempts (Kaushik 2001). There were numerous stories of physicians who ran "pill mills" to feed the addiction of their clients, and contrasting stories of other doctors who had been scared off from prescribing the drug. There were numerous reports of pharmacies that had stopped stocking the drug for fear of inviting crime.

The major television networks, not to be outdone, recognized the potential to capitalize on the OxyContin media frenzy. For example, ABC's "20/20" prime time news magazine story was called "What the doctor ordered: Young people hooked on a miracle painkiller." But the story was clearly a set-up. In her opening remarks, Barbara Walters gravely warned that every family with children should pay attention to the impending segment. Then correspondent Lynn Sherr talked about her trip to Portsmouth, Ohio, to document one physician's "pill mill" that fed the addiction of locals and others who said they traveled from as far away as Texas to obtain painkiller prescriptions. The camera showed the orthopedic surgeon's dilapidated office, a broken X-ray machine and even beer cans littering the waiting room. At a dramatic high point in the segment the camera zoomed in on the lengthy list of prescriptions that the aberrant physician had written for his patients. Never mind that most of the scripts had been for Lortab® (hydrocodone) and Soma® (a muscle relaxant); the cameras cleverly focused on but a few OxyContin prescriptions—highlighting and enlarging them for the audience to see. And then, after detailing a sad story of a young, married man's overdose death, blamed on the physician's unscrupulous prescribing practices, and the plea bargain he reached with the local prosecutor, Ms. Sherr closed the story by saying she wasn't sure of the exact statistics, but "several dozen" people in Kentucky had already died from OxyContin overdoses. She called the situation "insidious" (Sherr 2001).

Numerous sources have likened the "OxyContin epidemic" to that of the "crack epidemic" of the 1980s, and as far as the media coverage of the issues is concerned, there are indeed striking similarities. Media hype tends to have a profound influence on the public's perception of the issues.

For example, the journalism watchdog group Fairness and Accuracy In Reporting (FAIR) did an interesting analysis of media coverage and public opinion back in the 1980s, during the height of the crack scare. FAIR reported that in 1985, *The New York Times* published an average of 36 articles per month on drug use and trafficking. In November 1985, crack warranted front-page coverage and the *Times* assigned a full-time reporter to the drug beat. Between July and October 1986, the *Times* increased its coverage to a monthly average of 103 articles, with coverage peaking in September at 169 articles. This coincided with Ronald and Nancy Reagan's infamous "Just Say No" speech, to which Congress responded by approving a new $1.7 billion drug package, apparently appeasing the media and the public alike, as coverage and worries over the drug issue subsided (Fink 1992).

A second wave of public drug fear coincided with coverage of George Bush's presidential election in 1988, in which drug abuse was a central campaign issue. In September of that year, in sync with Bush's Oval Office speech on the evils of drugs, the *Times* published 238 articles on drugs, which breaks down to almost seven per day. By the close of September, 64% of the American public agreed that drugs were more grave a threat than nuclear war, environmental destruction, AIDS, and poverty (Fink 1992).

In a similar manner, the media introduced the OxyContin "epidemic" to the general public. A study printed in the *Journal of Toxicology* tracked articles from two large regional newspapers that associated adverse human health effects with drugs, toxins, or other poisonous chemical substances. Within this criterion, articles on chemical and biological warfare (which dramatically

spiked after September 11) were the most prevalent topic, followed by therapeutic drugs. Of the individual non-warfare articles, the two topics with the greatest coverage were medical marijuana (29 stories) and OxyContin abuse (20 stories) (Suchard 2002).

In 2001, the international media began following their American counterparts, as outlets in Europe and more recently Australia began to publish sensational articles about OxyContin. For example, *The Mirror* (England) featured a story that proclaimed, "A dangerous new drug is on the verge of flooding Ireland's inner city," and that "OxyContin is fast replacing other hard drugs as a way for pushers to trap new customers" (Hafford 2001). An *Observer* (England) headline reported in April 2002 that an 18-year-old girl became the UK's first OxyContin overdose victim, a drug that "already killed over 300 in America" (Tough 2002). Interestingly, the story accompanying the headline was actually a feature that had previously appeared in the *New York Times Magazine* in July of 2001. At about the same time, a story called "Epidemic fear as 'hillbilly heroin' hits the streets" accounted the overdose death of the 18-year-old girl, who reportedly drank, smoked and ingested "up to seven oxycodone pills" in a night of partying with her friends. The piece also reported that OxyContin was becoming popular in Manchester and Ireland and reiterated that the drug was responsible for "hundreds of deaths in America . . . prompting fears among police, customs officers and drug workers that it could give rise to a whole new generation of addicts" (Thompson 2002).

Other stories followed, patterning themselves after the media reports seen in the United States. But some readers quickly realized that much of it was media hype. The "Hillbilly Heroin" story in the *Observer* prompted a biting Letter to the Editor from a New Yorker who offered his own perspective on the matter: "The OxyContin scare in the U.S. is as much a product of the media as it is a genuine 'epidemic'; few of the people who become addicted here were taking it for legitimate reasons in the first place. Is it really a surprise that people who already abuse drugs will seek the latest 'stronger than heroin' substance" (Szalavitz 2002)?

While OxyContin stories continue to fill the airwaves and printed page, from the serious to the ridiculous, the frenetic pace began to ease in early 2003. But as Dr. Steven D. Passik wrote in a Letter to the Editor of the *Journal of Pain and Symptom Management* in March 2003: ". . . I have lost even more respect for the media . . . the media's loss of interest in the story shows that they were less concerned about the suffering in places like Eastern Kentucky and Maine, and more concerned about making headlines and capturing the fickle American attention span and demonizing the pharmaceutical industry. The OxyContin story has gone the way of Monica, Mark McGuire's supplements, and countless other pseudo-scandals" (Passik 2003).

Postscript

It would appear that although the abuse of OxyContin is indeed real, it is just one of many drugs that are abused by individuals whose drug taking and drug seeking behaviors focus on prescription painkillers. It also appears that the media stories may have contributed to shifting OxyContin abuse from a regional problem to a national problem. And clearly, OxyContin abuse is anything but an "epidemic." Nevertheless, all of the attention given to OxyContin has prompted U.S. government involvement. In response to the heightened awareness of OxyContin abuse and diversion, the DEA launched its own comprehensive plan to prevent the illegal distribution of the product. Their broad goals include enforcement and intelligence; regulatory and administrative authority; industry cooperation; and awareness, education and outreach initiatives (DEA 2001b). Industry cooperation is an integral part of the plan, including encouraging Purdue Pharma to adopt a balanced marketing plan. As recently as January 2003, the FDA sent Purdue a letter contending that the company improperly disclosed information on OxyContin's risks, including a "particularly disturbing" ad that ran in the November issue of the *Journal of the American Medical Association*. In response, Purdue has

pledged that all future advertisements will balance information about the benefits and risks of their product, as required by the federal Food, Drug and Cosmetic Act (Mishra 2003).

There have also been calls to reformulate the drug, to make it more difficult for abusers to compromise its time-release mechanism. Purdue has pursued alternative formulas, but success has been elusive thus far. Clinical trials found that when naloxone, a narcotic blocker, was added to OxyContin, it sometimes blocked pain relief for patients who ingested the tablets correctly. The company is pursuing an alternate approach by shifting from a tablet to a capsule that contains similar beads of the oxycodone combined with naltrexone, another narcotic blocker. If taken correctly, only the OxyContin beads would dissolve in the system, but if an abuser were to crush the pill, it would crush and activate the naltrexone, therefore masking the drug's effects. The company said complete testing could take as long as five years (Neergaard 2002). Even if this is accomplished, drug abusers are clever people and will likely compromise the new formulation in due course.

In the meantime, Purdue has launched its own public relations offensive. Among the initiatives, they have created educational and outreach materials, including a series of print and television ads and Painfully Obvious,™ a program that provides resources to educate parents, teachers and students about the dangers of prescription drug abuse (Hogen 2002).

Despite the bad press and pressure from the government, the success of OxyContin has not faltered. Only time will tell if the success will be short-lived or if the negative attention will slowly start to chip away at product confidence. In the meantime, those who use it correctly will continue to enjoy consistent pain relief, while those who abuse it will surely continue to inflict pain on the company, law enforcement, the community, and themselves.

References

Alford, Roger. (2003) Doctors Lured to Help in Appalachia Now Sit in Prison, *Miami Herald*, May 11: 13A.

Breed, Allen G. (2001, June 16) In Appalachia and beyond, OxyContin abuse called 'a plague.' *Associated Press State and Local Wire.* Retrieved January 2003 from Lexis-Nexis on-line subscription.

Cannizaro, Steve. (2000, June 27) Potent new painkiller on the street, cops say; Task force investigating street sales of 'new Vicodin.' The *Times-Picayune.* Retrieved January 2003 from Lexis-Nexis on-line subscription.

Clancy, Mary Anne. (2000, May 13) Down East high: Washington County pill addicts have health officials worried. *Bangor Daily News.* Retrieved January 2003 from Lexis-Nexis on-line subscription.

Crane, Elizabeth. (2003, January) *The DAWN Report: Narcotic Analgesics.* Substance Abuse and Mental Health Services Administration: Office of Applied Studies. Retrieved February 2003. Available: *http://www.samhsa.gov/oas/2k3/pain/DAWNpain.pdf*

Department of Justice (DOJ). (2002a, July) *Kentucky Drug Threat Assessment.* National Drug Intelligence Center. Product No. 2002-S0382KY-001. Retrieved February 2003. Available: *http://www.usdoj.gov/ndic/pubs/1540/index.htm*

——. (2002b, April) *Maine Drug Threat Assessment.* National Drug Intelligence Center. Product 2002-S0377ME-001. Retrieved February 2003. Available: *http://www.usdoj.gov/ndic/pubs/909/index.htm*

Drug Enforcement Administration (DEA). (2001a, July) *Alert: Working to Prevent the Diversion and Abuse of OxyContin.* Office of Diversion Control. Retrieved January 2003. Available: *http://www.deadiversion.usdoj.gov/pubs/brochures/alert_oxycontin/oxybrochure.pdf*

——. (2001b, June 22) *Drugs and Chemicals of Concern: Action Plan to Prevent the Diversion and Abuse of OxyContin.* Diversion Control Program. Retrieved March 2003. Available: *http://www.deadiversion.usdoj.gov/drugs_concern/oxycodone/abuse_oxy.htm*

——. (2002a, June 11) *OxyContin Diversion and Abuse.* Office of Diversion Control. Retrieved January 2003. Available: *http://www.deadiversion.usdoj.gov/drugs_concern/oxycodone/oxy_061102.pdf*

——. (2002b, May 16) *Summary of Medical Examiner Reports of Oxycodone-Related Deaths.* Diversion Control Program. Retrieved January 2003. Available: *http://www.deadiversion.usdoj.gov/drugs_concern/oxycodone/oxycontin7.htm*

Durkheim, Emile. (1933) *The Division of Labor in Society* (New York: Macmillan).

Fink, Micah. (1992, September) *Don't forget the hype: Media, drugs, and public opinion* [Published On-line]. Fairness and Accuracy in Reporting. Retrieved January 2003. Available: *http://www.fair.org/extra/best-of-extra/drugs-hype.html*

Gold, Donna. (2000, May 21) A prescription for crime: Abuse of 2 painkillers blamed for rise in violence in Maine's poorest county. *The Boston Globe.* Retrieved January 2003 from Lexis-Nexis on-line subscription.

Goldberger, Bruce. (2003, February 26) Oxycodone rarely the sole cause of drug abuse deaths, new study finds: Landmark analysis sets standard for interpretation of deaths involving drug abuse. *Journal of Analytical Toxicology.* Retrieved February 2003. Available: *http://www.eurekalert.org/pub_releases/2003-02/pn-ort022603.php*

Gowda, Vanita. (2003, January) Not what the doctor ordered. *Congressional Quarterly DBA Governing Magazine.* Retrieved February 2003 from Lexis-Nexis on-line subscription.

Greenwald, Judy. (2003) Drug maker holds off lawsuits claiming painkiller is unsafe. *Business Insurance;* 31: 4.

Hafford, Rory. (2001, October 27) Hillbilly Heroin; new drug catches gardai on the hop. *The Mirror.* Retrieved February 2003 from Lexis-Nexis on-line subscription.

Hogen, Robin. (2002, February 2) *Purdue launches public service advertising campaign to raise awareness of prescription drug abuse* [On-line Press Release]. Retrieved February 2003. Available: *http://www.pharma.com/pressroom/news/20020402.htm*

Inciardi, James A. (2002a) *The War on Drugs III: The Continuing Saga of the Mysteries and Miseries of Intoxication, Ad-*

diction, Crime, and Public Policy (Boston: Allyn and Bacon).

——. (2002b) "Prescription Drug Diversion," *College on Problems of Drug Dependence,* June 8–12, Quebec City.

Inciardi, James A. and Theodore J. Cicero (2002) "Research on the Diversion of Prescription Drugs" *First Annual West Coast Training Conference of the National Association of Drug Diversion Investigators,* Marina del Rey, CA, May 21–24.

Jenkins, Philip. (1999) *Synthetic Panics: The Symbolic Politics of Designer Drugs* (New York: New York University Press).

Johnston, L. D., O'Malley, P. M., and Bachman, J. G. (2003) *Monitoring the Future national survey results on drug use: Overview of key findings, 2002.* NIH Publication No. 03-5374. Bethesda, MD: National Institute on Drug Abuse.

Kaushik, Sandeep. (2001, June 4) *OxyCon game: Anatomy of a media-made drug scare* [Published On-line]. Alternet.org: Drug Reporter. Retrieved January 2003. Available: *http://www.alternet.org/story.html?StoryID=10955*

Maine Analysis Demonstrates Far-Reaching Harm from OxyContin. (2002, February 11) *Alcoholism and Drug Abuse Weekly;* 14: 1–3.

Mishra, Raja. (2003, January 24) OxyContin ads to carry prominent warning of risks. *The Boston Globe.* Retrieved February 2003 from Lexis-Nexis on-line subscription.

Moore, Michael O'D. (2000, May 13) Drug abuse spurs pain management debate. *Bangor Daily News.* Retrieved February 2003 from Lexis-Nexis on-line subscription.

Nagel, Laura M. and Good, Patricia M. (2001) *DEA Industry Communicator: Special OxyContin Issue. Vol. 1.* United States Department of Justice Drug Enforcement Administration Office of Diversion Control. Retrieved February 2003. Available: *http://www.deadiversion.usdoj.gov/pubs/nwslttr/spec2001/index.html*

Neergaard, Lauren. (2002, June 18) Abuse-resistant OxyContin hits snag. *The Associated Press.* Retrieved March 2003 from Lexis-Nexis on-line subscription.

Passik, Steven D. (2003) Same as it ever was? Life after the OxyContin media frenzy [Letter to the Editor]. *Journal of Pain and Symptom Management;* 25: 199–201.

Sherr, Lynn. (2001, February 9) What the doctor ordered; Young people hooked on a miracle painkiller. ABC News 20/20 broadcast. Transcript available: *http://www.transcripts.tv/2020.cfm*

Slobodzian, Joseph A. (2002, December 3) Delco pharmacist pleads guilty in illegal drug sales. *The Philadelphia Inquirer.* Retrieved March 2003. Available: *http://www.philly.com/mld/philly/archives/*

Substance Abuse and Mental Health Services Administration (SAMHSA) (2002). *Results from the 2001 National Household Survey on Drug Abuse: Volume III.* Rockville, MD: SAMHSA, Office of Applied Studies. Available: *http://www.samhsa.gov/oas/nhsda.htm*

Suchard, J. (2002) Newspaper Coverage of Clinical Toxicology. *Journal of Toxicology: Clinical Toxicology;* 40: 629.

Szalavitz, Maia. (2002, March 31) Drug Abuse [Letter to the Editor]. *The Observer.* Retrieved March 2003. Available: *http://www.observer.co.uk/letters/story/0,6903,576767,00.html*

Thompson, Tony. (2002, March 24) Epidemic fear as 'hillbilly heroin' hits the streets. *The Observer.* Retrieved March 2003. Available: *http://www.observer.co.uk/uk_news/story/0,6903,672984,00.html*

Tough, Paul. (2002, April 7) Hillbilly Hell: Last month, 18-year-old Samantha Jenkinson from Hull became the first person in the UK to die from an overdose of OxyContin. But the prescription painkiller has already killed 300 in America. Paul Tough traces the spread of 'hillbilly heroin' from the Appalachian backwoods to the teen party scene in Britain. *The Observer.* Retrieved January 2003 from Lexis-Nexis on-line subscription.

For Discussion

1. Are reports of OxyContin abuse overblown by the media? Why has OxyContin been singled out as a problem drug when other prescription drugs are abused in substantial numbers as well?

2. Does media attention pique individuals' curiosity to try drugs, or does it create a certain amount of fear that prohibits experimentation with particular drugs? Does media influence even matter?

Adapted from: James A. Inciardi and Jennifer L. Syvertsen, "OxyContin and Prescription Drug Abuse." In *Consumers' Research* 86 (7): 17–21. Copyright © 2003 by *Consumers' Research*. Reprinted with permission. ✦

17

The OxyContin Epidemic and Crime Panic in Rural Kentucky

Kenneth D. Tunnell

In this article, Kenneth Tunnell critically examines conflicting reports about OxyContin abuse and the alleged links to criminal activity. Using the state of Kentucky as a case study, he describes how the relationship between OxyContin use and crime was socially constructed, influenced in part by class bias, the media, and the police. Additionally, he provides several explanations that might account for the high rates of OxyContin use in Kentucky.

OxyContin (trade name), an oxycodone drug, was approved by the Food and Drug Administration (FDA) in 1995 and first marketed in 1996 by Purdue Pharma of Stamford, Connecticut (U.S.A.). Among the most powerful analgesics currently manufactured, OxyContin is a synthetic opioid. Opioid drugs (which include opium, heroin, morphine, codeine, hydrocodone, and oxycodone) are produced from the opium poppy. Opiate agonists, such as OxyContin, provide pain relief by acting on opioid receptors in the brain and the spinal cord and directly on tissue (OxyContin Diversion and Abuse 2002). OxyContin is a single-entity product unlike most oxycodone drugs (e.g., Percodan and Percocet), which typically contain aspirin or acetaminophen. A marked improvement, OxyContin reportedly is 16 times more powerful than similar narcotics (Sappenfield 2001). Designed as an orally administered, time release analge-sic, OxyContin provides significant and sustained pain relief and, due to its addictive propensity, is listed as a Schedule II narcotic (i.e., drugs approved for medical use that have a high potential for abuse) under the Controlled Substances Act.

OxyContin Abuse

OxyContin abuse was first noted in Maryland, the eastern part of rural Maine, eastern Ohio, the rust-belt areas of Pennsylvania, and the southern Appalachian region of West Virginia, Virginia, and Kentucky. During the year 2000, the 10 states with the highest OxyContin prescription rates (per 100,000 population) and those with problems of abuse were, in descending order: West Virginia, Alaska, Delaware, New Hampshire, Florida, Kentucky, Pennsylvania, Maine, Rhode Island and Connecticut (Hutchinson 2001). West Virginia, particularly its southern region, and southeastern Kentucky have long histories of pharmaceutical abuse (DEA Briefs and Background 2002).

As prescriptions dramatically increased, concerns were raised about this new drug that was sweeping across some communities. The apprehensions, galvanized by citizens' complaints, increases in drug-related arrests, politicians' dire warnings, and newspapers' headlines, soon took an all too familiar shape—a new drug-abuse epidemic fueling myriad social problems. As is shown in the remainder of this paper, OxyContin use increased markedly after its introduction. OxyContin related problems likewise increased. In some locales, OxyContin likely was connected to some increases in index crimes. But, similar to marijuana, opium, LSD, crack, and MDMA, OxyContin also has been the subject of drug panics. The politics of drug panics, often involving people with good intentions, politicians, newsmakers, and moral entrepreneurs, produce their own unintended dysfunctions and uninformed public policies (see, e.g., Duster 1970; Reinarman and Levine 1989; Humphries 1993; Jenkins 1999; Presdee 2000). These drugs' use, their pharmacological effects, and their relationships to crime have been socially constructed and, in public dialogues, often bear little resemblance to empirical reality. As is shown in this paper detailing the growth of OxyContin use, crime-related increases either have not occurred or have been greatly mischaracterized or exaggerated by both public and private sector officials.

OxyContin *abuse* has been made possible largely by its diversion. OxyContin is illegally acquired with fraudulent prescriptions; through illegal sales; by pharmacy theft and doctor shopping; from loosely organized rings of individuals diverting and then selling it; and by way of foreign diversion and smuggling into the U.S. (often via the Internet). When OxyContin abuse dramatically increased, authorities in Pennsylvania, Florida, Ohio, Kentucky, and Georgia reported swelling numbers of pharmacy robberies, burglaries, and theft to get Oxy-Contin (OxyContin: Pharmaceutical Diversion 2002). Some individuals have been known to acquire OxyContin from parents and grandparents or to buy it from elderly patients who hold valid prescriptions (Sappenfield 2001). OxyContin's black market price is about one dollar per milligram (Dangers of OxyContin 2001; Addressing OxyContin Abuse 2001).

During the late 1990s, OxyContin became the stuff of frequent front-page news stories. News articles consistently increased in number from no stories from its introduction in 1996 through 1999 to 17 in 2000, to 404 in 2001, and declining to 247 in 2003 (Lexis-Nexis search by keyword "OxyContin"). News coverage and the campaigns of public and private sector officials fueled a moral panic about a new drug of abuse (Goode and Ben-Yehuda 1994). Their panic may have resulted from the sheer number of new OxyContin prescriptions, which in and of itself may have been negatively and sensationally interpreted and reported.

There are various methods of abusing OxyContin. In some cases tablets are crushed and snorted. In others, the powder is diluted and intravenously injected. A less often used delivery style is to peel off the outer coating and chew the tablets (Sullivan 2001). These abuse techniques result in the sudden absorption of the analgesic rather than as designed—slowly and continuously

over several hours. Not surprisingly, overdoses and deaths have occurred, although the exact number is unknown. OxyContin-related overdose deaths are difficult to disaggregate, and the actual number likely will never be known with any degree of certainty. This is due in part to poly-drug use, in some cases OxyContin mixed with alcohol and in others OxyContin with depressants. Furthermore, data do not distinguish accidental deaths from suicides.

Conflicting estimates, however, have been published by the media and various office holders. For example, in September 2003, the *New York Times* reported that OxyContin was blamed for 500 to 1,000 deaths per year. Yet an article from March in *The Journal of Analytical Toxicology* examined records of 919 oxycodone-related deaths in 23 states across three years. In only 12 cases Oxy-Contin alone was found. The remaining deaths were due to an overdose of oxycodone or poly-drug use. Almost all the victims had at least three other drugs in their systems, with alcohol, Valium and cocaine comprising the bulk. The conclusion, in the *Journal*, was that these deaths occurred in drug-abusing individuals. OxyContin, it was discovered, was rarely the sole cause of death (Satel 2003).

National data consistently indicate, however, increases in the number of new pharmaceutical abusers (but not solely oxycodone) and narcotic-related emergency incidents. During the 1980s, the National Household Survey on Drug Abuse reported generally fewer than 500,000 people yearly who first used prescription drugs for non-medical purposes. By 1998, the number of first-time users was at 1.6 million persons. Since then, persons reporting at least one non-medical use of OxyContin have increased from 221,000 in 1999 to 1,900,000 in 2002 (National Survey on Drug Use and Health 2003). Federal data indicate that emergency room visits involving oxycodone increased with the introduction of OxyContin. Between 1990 and 1996, emergency room treatment of oxycodone remained stable. After 1996, when OxyContin was first marketed, the number of oxycodone-related emergency room visits skyrocketed from 100 in 1996 to nearly 15,000 in 2002 (Clines and Meier 2001; Emergency Department Trends 2003). Nonetheless, emergency rooms that treat drug-related emergencies report that oxycodone (there is no separate category for OxyContin) is mentioned by patients in less than one percent of all cases (viz., 0.95%). Oxycodone ranks 18th, with alcohol first, acetaminophen sixth, and ibuprofen 13th in frequency of mentions (see Table 17.1). Although OxyContin use and its connection to drug-related emergencies have increased, oxycodone products evidently remain far less widely used than rhetoric often suggests.

OxyContin Diversion and Containment

Illegal acts by doctors and pharmacists are the primary means of diverting narcotics, some of which are illicitly sold. Some narcotics users "doctor shop" to find physicians who write prescriptions; in some cases they find multiple doctors to write multiple prescriptions. In some regions of the United States (and particularly in southern Appala-

Table 17.1

Drugs mentioned in emergency department drug abuse episodes, 2001, by rank, number of mentions, and percentage of mentions

Rank	Drug Name	Mentions by Number	Mentions by Percent
1	alcohol in combination	218,005	18.71
2	cocaine	193,034	16.56
3	cannabis	110,508	9.48
4	heroin	93,064	7.99
5	narcotic analgesics	32,196	2.76
6	acetaminophen	30,888	2.65
7	benzodiazepines	30,302	2.60
8	alprazolam	25,644	2.20
9	drug unknown	21,657	1.86
10	clonazepam	19,117	1.64
11	acetaminophen-hydrocodone	19,058	1.64
12	amphetamine	17,285	1.48
13	ibuprofen	17,123	1.47
14	methamphetamine	14,923	1.28
15	lorazepam	11,902	1.02
16	diazepam	11,447	0.98
17	carisoprodol	11,239	0.96
18	oxycodone	11,100	0.95

Source: *Drug Abuse Warning Network.*

chia), "pain clinics" are the primary source of OxyContin prescriptions (many of which result in illegal diversion). But over-prescribing remains the single most common source for OxyContin (and for other oxycodone and hydrocodone narcotics) (Johnson 2003a; OxyContin: Pharmaceutical Diversion 2002).

Because of this, medical providers have been prosecuted. For example, a Florida physician who overprescribed OxyContin, and whom prosecutors likened to a drug dealer, was convicted on four counts of manslaughter, five counts of unlawful delivery of a controlled substance, and racketeering. The Drug Enforcement Administration (DEA) spokesperson in the case claimed the conviction should "send a very strong message to the medical community that they treat these very potent drugs . . . with respect." Similar charges against other medical doctors have been filed in California and Kentucky. In Virginia, a retired physician was held under house arrest allegedly for overprescribing OxyContin. In Canada, doctors' licenses have been suspended for trafficking in oxycodone. Some concerns have been raised within the medical community that authorities have become overly aggressive at containing even legitimate OxyContin use ("Panhandle doctor's OxyContin conviction to send message").

Other control measures have been initiated. For example, the Vermont welfare system no longer pays for prescribed OxyContin ("State won't cover painkiller"). In some cases, OxyContin has been removed from pharmacy shelves because of its adverse effects, pharmacists' fear of robbery, and the stigma now associated with even its legitimate use. Some pharmacies, in efforts to deter burglars and robbers, now post signs reading "No OxyContin." In one Virginia town, police supplied the six local pharmacies with fingerprinting equipment, and OxyContin patients are required to provide fingerprints ("Pulaski hopes fingerprint system will stamp out OxyContin abuse").

Once OxyContin abuse became publicly recognized, Purdue Pharma was implicated as partly culpable. Purdue for a time manufactured a single OxyContin tablet of 160 milligrams.[1] By comparison, Percocet and

Tylox contain 5 milligrams of oxycodone, and Percodan contains 2.25 milligrams. Allegations were raised that Purdue did not provide adequate instructions for physicians, who prescribed OxyContin for minor rather than for intense, cancer-related pain. Furthermore, there is some intimation that Purdue offered incentives to doctors for prescribing the drug (OxyContin Diversion and Abuse 2002).

In Virginia, seven plaintiffs filed federal suit against Purdue Pharma, claiming it had encouraged doctors to prescribe OxyContin for treating all sorts of pain (A.F. McCaulley vs. Purdue Pharma et al.). Furthermore, the attorney general for McDowell County, West Virginia, filed suit against Purdue for marketing OxyContin irresponsibly (State of West Virginia vs. Purdue Pharma et al.; Sappenfield 2001). Filed in 2001, these cases remain pending; one is scheduled for trial in late 2004. In U.S. District Court in Kentucky, plaintiffs' attempts to restrict access to OxyContin were denied when the court ruled that "plaintiffs have failed to produce any evidence showing that Purdue Pharma's marketing, promotional, or distribution practices have ever caused even one tablet of OxyContin to be inappropriately prescribed or diverted" (Federal judge in Kentucky rejects injunction on OxyContin 2002; Foister et al. vs. Purdue Pharma). The FDA, however, recently reprimanded Purdue for an advertisement in a medical journal that overstated the drug's use while understating its risks (Camp 2003c).

With news of increasing abuse and overdose deaths, Purdue limited the abuse of the drug by discontinuing its 160 milligram tablet, trained physicians to recognize fraudulent claims for the drug, and financially participated in a federal plan to monitor prescriptions in certain states (Sappenfield 2001). Purdue Pharma sent letters to 800,000 doctors in July 2001 recommending that OxyContin be prescribed only to patients in serious and continuous pain rather than to those recovering from surgery or those experiencing mild or temporary pain (Sullivan 2001). Purdue has distributed tamper-proof prescription pads to physicians and has sent pharmacists information for spotting abuse and fraudulent prescriptions

(Ukens 2001). Purdue initiated research and development to produce an abuse-resistant tablet or capsule, although its efforts, like those of other pharmaceutical manufacturers, have proved unsuccessful. During the summer of 2003, Purdue Pharma announced that it would spend $130 million annually to help curb addiction and to remedy the distorted image associated with OxyContin use. Although allegations that the company indirectly contributed to OxyContin abuse are common, Purdue apparently is making great strides toward preventing future problems, including developing an alternative drug that is more tamperproof and less addictive (Rosenberg 2001).

At the height of the OxyContin scare, the FDA issued warnings about oxycodone abuse within depressed regions of the United States (most notably in Appalachia) and mandated that OxyContin packaging display a "black box" warning, the strongest warning recommended by the FDA. A black box warning means that an admonitory statement is placed within a shaded box to caution both physicians and patients about the drug's dysfunctions (Sullivan 2001).

Kentucky as Case Study

For decades pharmaceutical drug abuse has been a significant social problem in southern Appalachia. More recently, prescription drug abuse in southern Appalachia has changed from well known and widely used narcotics (e.g., Valium and Xanax) to newer and more powerful analgesics such as OxyContin, Lorcet, Lortab, and Vicodin[2] (Kaushik 2001).

In Kentucky, news headlines have documented especially the OxyContin problem, detailing addictions, drug rehabilitation clinics and their scarce resources, OxyContin-fueled property crimes, pharmacy robberies, and drug overdoses and deaths. In southeastern Kentucky, news stories highlighted the emergence of a satellite industry selling fake Magnetic Resonance Imaging reports on an official hospital letterhead with phony patient identification numbers and the name of a doctor. With the report, patients get prescriptions (Mueller 2003), some of which are sold on the black market.

The former police chief of Hazard, Kentucky (Perry County) reported that in a one-year period (1999–2000), the number of complaints about OxyContin called in to his office increased from one every three months to three to four daily. The Perry County Park became known as "Pillville," an indication of its open-air drug-market atmosphere. The OxyContin problem in eastern Kentucky, and specifically in Hazard, was a featured *Newsweek* cover story that, like many popular press articles detailing Appalachian problems, sensationalized and distorted the people and their ways of life (Rosenberg 2001; cf. Blee and Billings 1999; Giardina 1999; Tunnell 2004a).[3]

In Kentucky, prescription-drug abuse historically has been limited mainly to the respectable classes, while the less privileged used alcohol and illicit drugs. But OxyContin, unlike other pharmaceuticals, first took hold among working and lower classes and drifted upward into the respectable classes. Beattyville, Kentucky, a town of about 1,200 residents, has been particularly hard hit. With a 25% poverty rate and 42% of its residents earning less than $15,000 yearly, social classes are polarized (Lasseter and Estep 2003a & b). This polarization, to some extent, is at the root of both the drug problem and the public response to it. For example, some claim that local elites became concerned about drug use only after it "crawled up from the streets into polite society." Before then, drug abuse had been ignored by the privileged, since their drug use had remained concealed and mainly unaffected by cultural controls (Lasseter and Estep 2003b: 1). Similarly, opium drug use in the early 20th century became a publicly recognized problem when lower-class use became defined as immoral despite the long-term opiate use and the legal buying and selling of morphine and heroin among the upper classes (Duster 1970: Chapter 1) With increased law-enforcement attention given to Kentucky's OxyContin problem, the local elite eventually witnessed the arrest of some of its own, including a former high school homecoming queen and the daughters of a circuit court judge, a local school board member, a reputable businessman, and a prosecutor.

Other affluent locals charged include medical doctors who overprescribed the analgesic (Sappenfield 2001; Sullivan 2001). One Harlan County urologist who was arrested for improperly dispensing the drug "was seeing 120 patients daily [and] was charging each person a $65 fee that resulted in an OxyContin prescription" (Dangers of OxyContin 2001). Records confirm that in one day he saw 133 patients. He currently is serving a 20-year federal prison sentence (Camp 2003b).

Five medical doctors practicing in a small pain clinic in South Shore (Greenup County), Kentucky, were indicted on several counts of illegally overprescribing drugs (Mueller and Camp 2003). Three of the five were granted Kentucky medical licenses notwithstanding histories of criminal, civil and professional charges in other states (including possession of illegal machine guns and drug addictions). The state's medical licensure board is not accustomed to finding criminal misdeeds among fellow doctors. Recognizing the current reality, one board member said, "Until a very few years ago, you just didn't think about physicians having felony convictions" (Camp and Mueller 2003). As a result of criminal conduct among local privileged classes, social control measures that until now were applied almost solely to the disreputable, the unlicensed and the uncredentialed have been applied to them. For example, doctors in Kentucky (and other states) now must submit to criminal background checks and fingerprinting to obtain and to annually renew their medical licenses.

In the midst of these events, a task force headed by the Kentucky State Police Commissions proposed new policies to further contain OxyContin abuse (Kentucky: House bill restricts use of OxyContin 2001). The committee's recommendations included: requiring a patient's identification when filling an OxyContin prescription; a public education campaign on OxyContin abuse and related hazards; tougher law enforcement measures for containing drug abuse; and the electronic tracking of prescription drug sales for specific pharmaceuticals, most notably addictive analgesics (Kentucky: OxyContin traffic sparks new controls 2001). The tracking program, Kentucky All-Schedule Prescription Electronic Reporting System (KASPER), enacted in 1998, is designed for doctors and pharmacists to monitor patients' prescriptions, the prescriptions' sources, and frequency of refill. Law enforcement personnel use it to investigate patients, physicians, and pharmacists who they suspect misuse or overprescribe pharmaceuticals. The Supreme Court affirmed the legality of drug tracking in a 1997 case despite the challenges from Civil Libertarians (State monitoring programs seen as key to tackling OxyContin abuse 2002). Seventeen states have some tracking database, although systems are not linked. Of those 17, only one—Kentucky's—was implemented after the introduction of OxyContin.

Constructing Kentucky's Problem

The OxyContin abuse problem became widely recognized through the efforts of the media and various office holders. As has been the case with drugs from marijuana and opium to crack and MDMA, the problem was described using particular imagery and rhetoric and relied on particular sources with little verification of their claims (cf. Tunnell 2004b: Chapter 1). For example, much of the public discourse about OxyContin was its relationship to Kentucky's (and the region's) significantly worsening crime problem. Claims of increases in crime and increases related to only one variable, OxyContin, were reported as fact, when in reality the crime problem undoubtedly is more complex than this simple relationship suggests.

In Greenup County, Kentucky, the commonwealth's attorney claimed that the circuit court's docket increased almost 25% during the year 2005 because of cases of prescription drug abuse (Gil 2002). Greenup County indeed witnessed dramatic increases in arrests for prescription drugs, including OxyContin. The county's arrest increases, however, were mainly for prescription drugs other than OxyContin, such as barbiturates and Benzedrine, and for Kentucky's locally produced drug—marijuana. Marijuana-re-

lated arrests, though, have decreased in recent years, more than likely a result of law enforcement's concerted efforts on drugs such as OxyContin. Furthermore, the county experienced decreases in index crimes after the introduction of OxyContin. Tables 17.2 and 17.3 illustrate Greenup County's drug arrest trends and index crimes, respectively. Two points of clarification about these data are warranted. First, drug arrest raw numbers may or may not indicate changes in patterns of drug use. They may reflect changes in enforcement priorities or styles. Second, arrests for opium-based drugs (which include OxyContin) increased over time. Synthetic-drug arrests (including methamphetamine) remained at zero for several years before increasing dramatically in 2001, while marijuana-related arrests decreased. These changes indicate changes in use and enforcement imperatives. OxyContin use, in this region of the country, increased during the late 1990s, as did methamphetamine use and the operation of clandestine manufacturing laboratories. Marijuana use likely remained stable, as law enforcement gave synthetic and opium-related drugs greater attention and resources.

The Hazard, Kentucky, police chief reported that 90% of thefts and burglaries in

Table 17.2

Greenup County, Kentucky, drug arrests, 1995–2001

Drug Type	1995	1996	1997	1998	1999	2000	2001
Opium or cocaine and their derivatives[1]							
	1	10	5	11	6	17	134
Marijuana							
	43	101	112	164	95	112	58
Synthetic narcotics that can cause drug addiction[2]							
	0	0	0	0	0	0	198
Other dangerous non-narcotic drugs[3]							
	9	14	23	34	137	197	0

[1] This category includes morphine, heroin, codeine and OxyContin.
[2] This category includes Demerol, methamphetamine and methadone.
[3] This category includes barbiturates and Xanax.
Source: *Crime in Kentucky.*

his area were to get money to buy OxyContin (Alford 2001). He offered no explanations for thefts and burglaries prior to 1996 (when OxyContin was first marketed) or for fluctuating crime rates since then. For example, as Table 17.4 illustrates, the year before Oxy-Contin was manufactured, Perry County (which includes Hazard) had 303 crimes per 10,000 population. In 1996 it had 260; in 1997, 251; in 1998, 272; in 1999, 264; in 2000, an increase to 382; and in 2001 a decrease to 308.6 per 10,000 population. A less sensationalistic interpretation is that crime rates in Perry County, as nearly everywhere, fluctuate, with some years experiencing increases and others experiencing decreases. Yet this universal feature of crime goes unreported. Statewide crime rates in Kentucky, as Table 17.5 illustrates, also have fluctuated, but with lower rates in 2001 than in 1996. Although there was a slight increase in robbery and burglary, larceny rates declined. As is shown in each table, larceny, the least serious and most frequently occurring index crime in the United States, accounts for the bulk of all reported crimes. Linking any crime increases directly to the introduction of OxyContin has not been established.

A Kentucky State Police captain reportedly claimed that "with drugs such as cocaine and marijuana, police could occasionally work their way to Mr Big." But, regarding OxyContin and other narcotics, the captain stated that "each day brings a new kingpin," depending on who "got their prescription filled" (Johnson 2003a: A8). This is a poor analogy, especially given that a prescription translates to about 30 pills—hardly a "kingpin's" normal inventory. Yet such rhetoric, and from an official on whom the public is likely dependent for information, is often compelling evidence when few alternative sources of information are available.

In February 2001, "Oxyfest," the biggest drug raid in Kentucky history, netted 201 alleged OxyContin dealers in a two day federal and state law enforcement crackdown ("Police arrest 201 in OxyContin crackdown" 2001). U.S. Attorney General Joseph Famularo, justifying the arrests, claimed that during the previous year, OxyContin had caused 59 deaths in Kentucky alone (Alford 2001; "Raids in Kentucky aim at deadly new drug" 2001). Purdue Pharma dismissed his estimates as "inflammatory." Although published widely, his claims are not supported by data.

Next door, in mountainous Pulaski, Virginia, the police chief reported (in October 2000) that about 90% of all thefts, burglaries and shoplifting incidents in the area were linked to the OxyContin trade. In Tazewell, Virginia, similar claims were made "that OxyContin addiction is behind 80 to 95 percent of all crimes committed there" (Drugs and Chemicals of Concern 2001). Yet according to state data, narcotics offense rates, while varying wildly from year to year, were about the same in 2000 as in 1995. The *Washington Times* quoted an ATF agent assigned to southwest Virginia as having said that "every year from 1996 to 1999, the crime rate doubled directly because of the influx of

Table 17.3

Greenup County, Kentucky, index crimes per 10,000 population, 1995–2001

Year	Index Crime Rate (excluding arson)
1995	147.0
1996	144.3
1997	153.0
1998	144.5
1999	147.0
2000	139.0
2001	130.9

Source: Crime in Kentucky.

Table 17.4

Perry County, Kentucky, index crimes* per 10,000 population, 1995–2001

Year	Crime Rate	Rate (controlling for larceny)
1995	303.7	119.4
1996	260.8	115.8
1997	251.1	116.1
1998	272.9	117.7
1999	264.8	110.6
2000	382.1	151.0
2001	308.6	133.1

*Total index crimes excluding arson.

Source: Crime in Kentucky.

Table 17.5

Kentucky crime index rates per 100,000 inhabitants, 1996–2001

Year	Violent Crime	Property Crime	Murder	Rape	Robbery	Assault	Burglary	Larceny	Vehicle Theft
1996	320.5	2845.8	5.9	31.7	93.8	189.2	688.4	1896.3	261.1
1997	316.9	2810.1	5.8	33.4	90.7	187.0	681.6	1880.4	248.1
1998	284.0	2605.3	4.6	29.3	75.4	174.7	637.4	1750.1	217.8
1999	308.3	2645.1	5.1	29.0	78.4	195.8	635.7	1785.5	223.9
2000	294.5	2665.2	4.8	27.0	80.6	182.2	262.2	1809.6	229.5
2001	250.4	2669.4	4.6	25.8	82.1	137.9	639.3	1795.9	234.1

Source: Crime in Kentucky.

Table 17.6

Average incidents per 10,000 population for Lee, Scott, Tazewell, and Wise counties, Virginia, 1994–2002

Year	1994	1995	1996	1997	1998	1999	2000	2001	2002
Index crimes	126.3	132.5	162.9	176.5	199.1	252.1	247.3	260.7	270.7
Index minus larceny	51.2	57.3	68.7	73.4	87.3	145.4	104.4	99.2	93.8
Narcotic offenses	NA	20.0	15.3	16.4	37.1	11.04	29.0	32.1	23.7

Index Crimes excludes arson.
Index Crimes minus Larceny excludes arson and controls for larceny.
Source: Crime in Virginia: Virginia Uniform Crime Reports.

OxyContin" (Taylor 2003). The crime rate did not double during that time, as any interested party could determine from data that are public record. The three largest counties in southwest Virginia did indeed witness some increases in crime (and also some decreases) between 1996 and 2002. In fact, the crime rate did indeed double between 1994 and 2002, but increases were due almost solely to hikes in larceny rates (the most frequently occurring and least serious index crime). Table 17.6 illustrates that region's dynamic crime patterns.

Beyond the region, in October 2003 the *Boston Herald* reported that "[OxyContin] is seen as fueling a crime wave around the country, particularly in poor areas" (Lasalandra 2003). According to this story, a national crime wave is associated with the use of this one drug. No such crime wave exists, as crime rates in the United States for years have steadily decreased. Property crime (the type most commonly associated with drug abuse) decreased from a high of 5,140 per 100,000 population in 1991 to 3,624 per 100,000 in 2002. Violent-crime rates declined 33.8% between 1993 and

2002; property-crime rates declined 23.5% during the same period. For the first half of 2003 (the most recent data), property crimes decreased 0.8%, indicating that the downward trend of the past 12 years is continuing. The percentage of households experiencing any type of criminal victimization has steadily decreased from 25% in 1994 to 16% in 2000. The raw number of households experiencing crime likewise shows steadily decreasing trends (Uniform Crime Reports 2003; Sourcebook of Criminal Justice Statistics 2002). Furthermore, as Figure 17.1 shows, the 10 states with the highest per capita OxyContin use have lower property crime rates than the 10 states with the lowest per capita OxyContin use. Not only is claiming a national crime wave an exaggeration, those very states with the highest OxyContin use per capita have experienced declining crime rates since OxyContin was first marketed, although differences between these two groups of states are narrowing and are not significant. Similar trends exist for violent crime. Although drastic increases in OxyContin-related crimes are not occurring at the aggregate, some communities undoubtedly have experienced increasing drug-abuse and predatory-crime problems. Likewise, the decreasing trends in national crime rates might have been even greater had it not been for the increasing abuse of drugs such as OxyContin.

Kentucky's newly elected governor (and the first Republican in 32 years, whose campaign emphasized declining morals in the state and in government) issued a white paper on crime and justice issues that claimed: "The prescription drug abuse problem has steadily increased during the past three decades. Drug use continues to be the number one concern in Kentucky law enforcement" (Fletcher and Pence 2003: 32). This manifesto, like contemporary public discourse on drug use, does not distinguish between abuse and use or the process by which prescription-drug abuse came to be defined as the "number one concern."

The governor's report states: "Drug abuse continues to be recognized by practitioners as the nucleus of the majority of the criminal activity in the state" (Fletcher and Pence 2003: 32). Alcohol (its manufacture is a major Kentucky industry), the drug most commonly associated with criminal behavior, is exempt from the governor's indictment. The report continues: "We are confronting an epidemic . . . OxyContin problems [are] overwhelm[ing] the law enforce-ment communities. . . . Substance abuse is increasingly linked to violent crimes. . . . Over the past eight years, crime has increased in Kentucky" (Fletcher and Pence 2003: 33 & 37). Yet rather than discussing Kentucky's dynamic crime rates (based on population), the fact that crime in Kentucky did not increase during that period, or that violent crime rates were lower in 2001 (the most recent data) than in 1996, the authors sensationalize crime and victimization by publishing the number of crimes that occur each minute (see Table 17.5).

Explanations

OxyContin abuse is a highly localized problem requiring specific interpretations. Probable explanations for OxyContin abuse within rural eastern Kentucky include: prescription drug use is a culturally entrenched phenomenon; Kentucky leads the nation in prescription drug use, in part because the state has the fourth highest cancer rate in the nation; Kentucky has an above-average older population that uses prescription drugs; Kentucky's highest levels of chronic illnesses and debilitating diseases contribute to increasing numbers of pharmaceutical prescriptions and addictions; prescription fraud largely has been ignored by medical, academic, and legal communities; OxyContin is a very powerful drug whose

Figure 17.1

Property crimes by states with highest and lowest OxyContin prescriptions per capita: 1988–2000

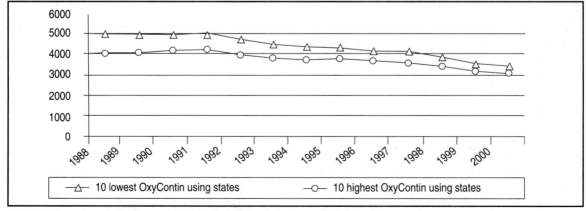

SOURCE: U.S. Census Bureau. Statistical Abstract of the United States: 2002 (122 edition). Washington, DC: U.S. Government Printing Office.

design makes it easy to abuse; and Purdue Pharma aggressively promoted OxyContin. This last explanation is particularly telling.

Over the first five years of manufacture, OxyContin sales totaled $2 billion, considerably higher than the company's projected $350 million. According to the *Wall Street Journal*, sales and marketing projections for OxyContin took shape during 1995, when Purdue planned on committing 70% of its sales force's time to OxyContin immediately after its introduction into the market ("Painkiller's sales far exceeded levels anticipated by maker"). After five years, the sales force was expected to devote 40% of its time to OxyContin. But by spring 2002, Purdue Pharma's sales force was spending 80% of its time promoting it. Marketing strategies specifically targeted those medical doctors known for prescribing large numbers of painkillers. Sales representatives personally called on hospital committees responsible for deciding which drugs to use. The company's plan also included using a "Speakers' Bureau"—a group of about 1,000 doctors to lecture during hospital programs on OxyContin's benefits. All told, Purdue's sales force and strategies cost the company about $500 million (Camp 2003c). In all fairness, promotional measures evidently are the norm within the pharmaceutical industry (Silverman, Lee, and Lydecker 1981: Chapter 1; 1982: Chapter 4; 1992: Chapter 3; Angell 2004). Purdue's efforts, however, paid off in a big way. During 2000, Purdue Pharma's revenue from OxyContin sales was eight times the projected volume. Given the drug's popularity and the demand for it, Purdue Pharma expanded production, marketing, and sales. According to the DEA, OxyContin retail sales are now greater than any other brand-name controlled pharmaceutical (Ambien, a sleeping pill, ranks second, and Xanax eighth) and totaled $1,485,974,000 in 2001—a 41% increase over 2000 sales (OxyContin Diversion and Abuse 2002).

Another explanation for high levels of OxyContin in southeastern Kentucky is the dual role of the DEA. Other than enforcing federal drug laws, the DEA is responsible for determining manufacturing quotas for legal, prescription drugs, including powerful analgesics. The Controlled Substances Act mandates that the DEA prevent, detect, and investigate the diversion of legally manufactured controlled substances, all while ensuring that there are adequate supplies to meet legitimate medical needs. The agency recently authorized a sharp increase in production of specific addictive analgesics. In 1998 over 56 million new prescriptions were written for hydrocodone products. Since 1990, hydrocodone national consumption has increased by 300% (Drug Enforcement Administration, Office of Diversion Control). The 2003 quota for hydrocodone, for example, was 14% higher than in 2002 and 75% higher than a decade ago (Camp 2003a). Oxycodone (which includes OxyContin) production, authorized by the DEA, also has increased significantly across the past 10 years. Table 17.7 shows that the production quotas steadily increased with the exception of one year (2002). The DEA's role is more than simply a dual one; it is a conflicting role. It is authorized to ensure ample supplies of addictive pharmaceuticals. This charge, however, means that the DEA's policies contribute to oversupplies of drugs that in turn impact the risk of drug abuse and its associated dysfunctions.

Both corporate and government policies and practices, particularly the DEA's charge, have contributed to the growth of OxyContin use and abuse in a number of states, most

Table 17.7

Oxycodone aggregate production quota history in kilograms of anhydrous acid or base, 1993–2003

Year	Production Quota
1993	3520
1994	3853
1995	4794
1996	5571
1997	8323
1998	12118
1999	18517
2000	35850
2001	46680
2002	34482
2003	41182

Source: *Diversion Control Program, Drug Enforcement Administration, U.S. Department of Justice.*

notably in southern Appalachia and specifically in southeastern Kentucky. Data show that parts of eastern Kentucky ranked highest nationally in per capita narcotics distribution during the period 1998–2001. Although distributed legally, some drugs are diverted into illegal black markets. An axiom about narcotic dispersal is that the more drugs legally bought and sold in a particular area, the more that will be illegally diverted (Johnson 2003a; 2003b). Thus, we can anticipate that those areas with the greatest legal distribution of OxyContin will witness greater levels of diversion through informal social networks (e.g., family or friends) or more formal drug black markets (e.g., buyers of OxyContin who in turn resell the drug to street-level dealers or directly to users). This universal feature of dispersal, however, pertains to certain classes of drugs. For example, Ambien, a mild sleeping pill, is unlikely to be a significant black market product. Analgesics, on the other hand, are demanded by a steady population of consumers whose wants and needs are met by ready suppliers, who rather than create the product, devise processes by which to acquire and sell it.

Although eastern Kentucky's counties led the nation in per capita narcotics distribution from 1998 through 2001, narcotics - distribution increased nationally during the late 1990s as chronic pain was treated more aggressively than previously (Johnson 2003a). This positive development for patients and medical providers likely has contributed to some diversion and abuse. The American Pain Society, for example, representing 3,500 pain specialists (viz., doctors, nurses and pharmacists), during its 2002 annual convention endorsed the use of OxyContin for severe cases of osteoarthritis (Tanner 2002). A year before, medical doctors adopted a new, aggressive approach to treating pain by recognizing it as a vital sign. This means that doctors began measuring and managing pain as they would any other vital sign—blood pressure, for example. Congress, during the 2000 session, declared the first years of the 21st century as the "Decade of Pain Control and Research" (Kalb 2001: 45). It seems that even these progressive measures by Congress and the medical

community may have contributed inadvertently to drug-abuse problems.

During the year 2000, 190 million prescriptions for opioids (Darvon, Vicodin, Dilaudid, Demerol and OxyContin) were filled. About 5.8 million (3%) were for OxyContin (Drug Intelligence Brief 2002). The seven areas of the United States that received the greatest distribution of narcotics per capita between 1998 and 2001 were (in descending order) (1) Johnson, Martin, and Lawrence Counties, Kentucky; (2) Perry, Knott, and Leslie Counties, Kentucky; (3) Pike County, Kentucky; (4) Cabell and Wayne Counties, Kentucky; (5) Hillsborough County, Florida; (6) Del Norte, Humboldt and Trinity Counties, California; and (7) Mingo and Logan Counties, West Virginia (Johnson and Ware 2003). Nine of these 15 counties (60%) are in southeastern Kentucky, and 11 of the 15 (73.3%) are located in the southern Appalachian region. Again, the sheer volume of prescriptions in this corner of the country translates into the potential, at least, for abuse, addictions, and diversion.

Drug abuse is a culturally entrenched problem within rural southeastern Kentucky, and one that impacts crime and justice. For example, in drug cases that actually are tried in court, juries, despite evidence, often acquit—according to some, because of the region's long-term trade in moonshine and marijuana. The "moonshine mentality," as it is called, refers to the acceptance of manufacturing illegal drugs for outside communities if that provides revenue for Kentuckians. A few counties in southeastern Kentucky are nearly wholly dependent on the marijuana industry, for example. Marijuana is the primary income-producing product for the counties' residents. Even those not directly involved often have family members or friends who are, and as a result they at least tacitly support the growing and selling. Legitimate businesses profit, since community members are able to participate in consumption at levels greater than they would if illicit production were not a part of the community (Potter et al. 1990). Cloward and Ohlin (1960) likely would consider the marijuana situation indicative of an organized criminal subculture, as it is neatly integrated into legitimate businesses and life-styles within the community. Some speculate that this acceptance of moonshine and marijuana is a component of illegal transactions involving other, harder drugs, including narcotics and methamphetamine labs (although labs are more prevalent in non-Appalachian western Kentucky). According to some, this mentality, along with a historical distrust of government, makes it difficult to win criminal convictions. One prosecutor claims that "Eastern Kentuckians fear the government more than they fear drugs" (Estep and Lasseter 2003). Fear, suspicion, and conspiracy theories abound, as some suggest a "cycle of community suspicion" among eastern Kentuckians who distrust centralized systems. People willingly believe conspiracy theories about the drug trade, which in turn increases levels of distrust in government to address the issue. The suspicion is hardly misplaced, given that several law enforcement agents and circuit court judges have been arrested for participating in drug trafficking. During 2002, two candidates for sheriff's office in two separate counties were assassinated. Each murder was connected, in part, to drug trafficking (Lasseter and Estep 2003c). Said one community spokesman: "Most people feel deep down that the system is set up to allow drug crime to go on. It's so ethereal." Another local therapist noted "an umbrella of fear" and that the entire community structure seemingly supports the drug trade.

Another sign of cultural entrenchment is the U.S. Department of Justice's reporting that pharmaceutical addiction has its roots in southeastern Kentucky's local industries, and most notably in coal mining. Painkillers, allegedly dispensed to miners by mining camp doctors, were the means by which work could continue. Self-medication followed, as did abuse and addiction, ironically, among people who were unlikely to use traditionally available illicit drugs (Lasseter and Stephenson 2003: 5).

From 1998 through 2000, treatment for the abuse of pharmaceutical drugs accounted for 20% of all treatment admissions in the state of Kentucky (Other Dangerous Drugs 2002). According to one published report, Kentucky ranks 44th nationally in spending on mental health and substance abuse treatment, although research shows that it would actually save money—nearly $18,000 yearly to incarcerate compared with about $2,800 for residential treatment (Johnson 2003b).

Rural areas are facing some of the same problems as urban areas except with far fewer resources, social capital, and collective efficacy for significantly addressing them (Duncan 2001). In Kentucky, with the collapse of infrastructural enterprises such as mining and family farming, rural areas have become especially financially distressed. In the southeastern part of the state, for example, poverty and unemployment are consistently higher than elsewhere. Poverty is a persistent feature of many of those Kentucky counties (Duncan 1999). Rural areas have always been disproportionately poor, but global economic changes of the 1980s further devastated already poor rural areas (Tickamyer 1992). Furthermore, social services, including drug abuse treatment, are less readily available in rural than in urban areas, often leaving rural drug abusers with fewer resources than their urban counterparts (Warner and Leukefeld 2001).

Conclusion

Like all social problems, the origins of OxyContin abuse are located in social events that require social explanations. Kentucky's problem with OxyContin abuse has particular social antecedents. They include: Purdue's sales and marketing strategies, Congress's declaration of the "decade of pain control and research," the medical community treating pain differently (as a vital sign), the DEA granting increases in manufacturing, and a history of pharmaceutical use and abuse in rural Kentucky. Each of these contributes to OxyContin abuse in Kentucky. On the other hand, the OxyContin epidemic's relationship to crime in Kentucky evidently is a socially constructed one with little empirical support. Granted, crime in some Kentucky counties is increasing while overall state rates are not. OxyContin abuse likely is connected, to some measure, to those increases. Furthermore, in those counties the raw number of crimes is increasing while populations (as is the case in many rural areas) are decreasing (see, e.g., Duncan 2001). In those counties, the result is marked *rate* increases at a pace that likely would not occur with positive population gains. This further skews the impression of a nearly bivariate OxyContin–crime relationship. This association complicates the panic about this drug, for there is both alarm about abuse and addiction and fear about drug-fueled crimes.

Whenever drug scares emerge, such as this most recent one with OxyContin, the role of the mass media and its focus on a drug at a particular point and time must be examined. Questions must be raised about how the public comes to accept their stories. There was a dramatic increase in news stories given to OxyContin from zero news or health articles in 1998 (and 1999) to a high of 404 stories in 2001. Such news saturation about one particular phenomenon contributes to a particular interpretation about dynamic social events. The *Lexington Herald-Leader*, the major newspaper serving the bluegrass and the eastern Kentucky regions, ran a 12-part series titled "Prescription for Pain" between January 19 and February 16, 2003 (and a Sunday, December 7, insert of 20 pages) that detailed the OxyContin problem and its alleged connection to a worsening crime problem. Although some might argue that this is in-depth reporting of a new drug of abuse, others might argue that the coverage presents a skewed and misleading impression of the drug's pervasiveness and its connections to changes in local and national crime rates. The coverage detailed Kentucky's problem of narcotics abuse, yet it inaccurately presented a causal relationship with crime increases.

At times, media coverage, indirectly at least, romanticized the drug and its effects. However unwittingly, the media likely participated in promoting this new drug. It gained a popularity it might never have acquired had it simply been ignored or been given far less sensational treatment. "Instead, the substance is described in the most exaggerated terms, stressing its extremely powerful, pleasurable, and enduring effects in a way that in other contexts would be seen as unabashed advertising" (Jenkins 1999:

18). A cynical question has arisen: "Given the damage that drugs can do, what's the harm in a little hysteria?" (Reinarman and Levine 1989: 567 & 568). Over time and across several panics involving drugs and other bogeymen, it is obvious that drug scares are not very effective at reducing abuse; they also tend to assign blame to individuals when explaining complex social problems. Rather than reducing the dysfunctional consequences of drug use, for example, scares may actually "promote the behavior that they claim to be preventing" (Reinarman and Levine 1989: 567 & 568). They also, as history and this OxyContin case show, are not particularly good forums for disseminating accurate information.

The media and public officials likely were greatly alarmed because OxyContin prescriptions and its use dramatically increased. This major change in the amount of prescribed oxycodone and the new drug's sheer analgesic power in and of themselves may have been interpreted as a negative development, and one that, in the eyes of law enforcement and the media, was bound to be related to crime. OxyContin prescription increases alone have panicked otherwise well-intentioned people. As the evidence shows in this paper, the prescription increases were dramatic. They may have led officials in the private and public sectors to assume the worst—that since OxyContin's use and its diversion had markedly increased, crime must also be on the rise and directly related to it.

Yet the OxyContin-crime panic, like others, is a socially constructed occurrence. Drug scares usually result in an extreme reaction to a perceived drug problem that may not necessarily correspond to its actual social or individual harm. A panic may arise regardless of a drug's pervasiveness or increases and decreases in its use. Drug scares, it has been noted, "are independent phenomena, not necessarily related to actual trends or patterns in drug use or trafficking" (Brownstein 1995: 55). On the other hand, panics do not simply materialize. Rather, they emerge "out of very real conditions of social life" (Goode and Ben-Yehuda 1994: 49). The myths about drugs, for example, that take shape through panics and publicized reporting about them, affect perceptions and definitions of situations. These myths may represent explanations and realities to those who define them as such. They may represent the best explanations conceivable to those who hold them. Contra-realities are likely unthinkable.

Drug scares as moral panics are symbolic crusades that involve particular interest groups or agencies that lead the way in labeling the drug as dangerous (Gusfield 1963). In some cases they benefit. This historically has been the case as public officials, often aided by media outlets, make less than honest claims for greater crime-fighting resources and social control initiatives. The OxyContin–crime propagated relationship evidently is only the latest in this long history.

Notes

1. The 160 milligram tablet was sold only in the United States. OxyContin sales in Canada included tablets of 80 milligrams and in Mexico up to 40 milligrams (Drug Enforcement Administration, Office of Diversion Control). As demand for OxyContin began to outpace local supplies, dealers began making journeys into Mexican border towns and acquiring and transporting the drug from there. Purdue Pharma discontinued its production of OxyContin in Mexico in 2001 (Lasseter and Stephenson 2003: 7).

2. Lorcet and Lortab are brand names for the drug Vicodin, a non-single entity hydrocodone. An analgesic for moderately severe pain, Vicodin is an addictive drug.

3. Two sentences from the *Newsweek* article are illustrative: "Hazard has a long tradition of self-medication. Moonshine and marijuana, grown in its fertile soil, have long helped blot out depression, boredom, even physical pain . . . OxyContin seemed like the most potent antidote yet to the local despair" (Rosenberg 2001: 49). What Rosenberg fails to acknowledge is that moonshine is made and marijuana grown largely as revenue-producing export products. Granted, these drugs are used locally, but Hazard, Kentucky, is "wet" and spirits are legally bought and sold.

References

Alford, Roger. 2001. "Across the east, abuse of painkiller meant for cancer patients is rising." *Inquirer*. February 10: A5.

Addressing OxyContin abuse. 2001. *FDA Consumer* 35 (4): 3.

Angell, Marcia. 2004. *The Truth About the Drug Companies.* New York: Random House

Blee, Kathleen M. and Dwight B. Billings. 1999. "Where bloodshed is a pastime: Mountain feuds and Appalachian stereotyping." Pp. 119–137 in Dwight Billings, Gurney Norman, and Katherine Ledford (eds.), *Confronting Appalachian Stereotypes.* Lexington: University of Kentucky Press.

Brownstein, Henry H. 1995. "The media and the conjunction of random drug violence." Pp. 45–65 in Jeff Ferrell and Clinton R. Sanders (eds.), *Cultural Criminology.* Boston: Northeastern University Press.

Camp, Charles B. 2003a. "Agency OKs more pills to chase." *Lexington Herald Leader.* January 19: A9.

——. 2003b. "Denied in Virginia, licensed in Kentucky." *Lexington Herald-Leader.* January 31: A8.

——. 2003c. "Strategy tainted busy doctors, hit Kentucky." *Lexington Herald-Leader.* August 17: A1.

Camp, Charles B. and Lee Mueller. 2003. "Questionable practices." *Lexington Herald-Leader.* January 31: A1.

Clines, Francis X. and Barry Meier. 2001. "Cancel painkillers pose new abuse threat." *New York Times.* February 9: A1 & 21.

Cloward, Richard A. and Lloyd Ohlin. 1960. *Delinquency and Opportunity.* New York: The Free Press.

Dangers of OxyContin. 2001. *Federal Document Clearing House Congressional Testimony.* December 11.

DEA Briefs and Background. 2002. *Drugs and Drug Abuse, State Factsheets.* Washington, DC: U.S. Department of Justice.

Drug Intelligence Brief: OxyContin, Pharmaceutical Diversion. 2002. Drug Enforcement Administration. *www.dea.gov* (March).

Drugs and Chemicals of Concern. 2001. Diversion Control Program. Drug Enforcement Administration. Washington, DC: U.S. Department of Justice.

Duncan, Cynthia M. 1999. *Worlds Apart: Why Poverty Persists in Rural America.* New Haven: Yale University Press.

——. 2001. "Social capital in America's poor rural communities." Pp. 60–86 in Susan Saegert, J. P. Thompson, and M. R. Warren (eds.), *Social Capital and Poor Communities.* New York: Russell Sage.

Duster, Troy. 1970. *The Legislation of Morality.* New York: The Free Press.

Emergency Department Trends. 2003. *Drug Abuse Warning Network, Final Estimates 1995–2002.* September.

Estep, Bill and Tom Lasseter. 2003. "Moonshine mentality." *Lexington Herald-Leader.* February 3: A1.

Federal judge in Kentucky rejects injunction on OxyContin. 2002. *Pain and Central Nervous System Week.* January 21: 14.

Fletcher, Ernie and Stephen B. Pence. 2003. "Hitting the ground running." Pp. 12–39 in *Restoring Hope.* Lexington, KY: Friends of Ernie Fletcher.

Giardina, Denise. 1999. "Appalachian images: A personal history." Pp. 161–173 in Dwight Billings, Gurney Norman, and Katherine Ledford (eds.), *Confronting Appalachian Stereotypes.* Lexington: University of Kentucky Press.

Gil, Gideon. 2002. "Prescription for abuse." *Louisville Courier-Journal.* October 20: A1.

Goode, Erich and Nachman Ben-Yehuda. 1994. *Moral Panics: The Social Construction of Deviance.* Cambridge: Blackwell.

Gusfield, Joseph R. 1963. *Symbolic Crusade,* Urbana, IL: University of Illinois Press.

Humphries, Drew. 1993. "Crack mothers, drug wars, and the politics of resentment." Pp. 31–48 in Kenneth D. Tunnell (ed.), *Political Crime in Contemporary America.* New York: Garland.

Hutchinson, Asa. 2001. Statement of Asa Hutchinson, Administrator, Drug Enforcement Administration. Before the House Committee on Appropriations Subcommittee on Commerce, Justice and State: December 11, DEA Congressional Testimony. Washington, DC: U.S. Department of Justice.

Jenkins, Philip. 1999. *Synthetic Panics.* New York: New York University Press.

Johnson, Linda J. 2003a. "Many pills diverted to illegal sales." *Lexington Herald-Leader.* January 19: A1 & 8.

——. 2003b. "Antidote for addiction sits on shelf." *Lexington Herald-Leader.* February 9: A1 & 14.

Johnson, Linda J. and C. Ware. 2003. "Eastern Kentucky: Painkiller capital investigation reveals narcotics flood mountain counties at highest in nation." *Lexington Herald-Leader.* January 19: A1.

Kalb, Claudia. 2001. "Playing with pain." *Newsweek* 137 (15): 45–47.

Kaushik, Sandeep. 2001. "An Oxy Con Job?" *Cleveland Free Times.* May 2: 1.

Kentucky: House bill restricts use of OxyContin. 2001. *Crime Control Digest* 35 (10): 6.

Kentucky: OxyContin traffic sparks new controls. 2001. *Crime Control Digest* 35 (39): 6.

Lasalandra, Michael. 2003. "Harvard, drug maker skirt pain-center controversy." *www.bostonherald.com*. October 13.

Lasseter, Tom and Bill Estep. 2003a. "Addicted and corrupted." *Lexington Herald-Leader*. January 26: A1 & 8.

——. 2003b. "Pushing for justice." *Lexington Herald-Leader*. January 27: A1 & 8.

——. 2003c. "A climate of fear, mistrust." *Lexington Herald-Leader*. February 3: A1.

Lasseter, Tom and David Stephenson. 2003. "Home grown drug lords." *Lexington Herald-Leader*. December 7: Insert.

Mueller, Lee. 2003. "Fake MRI reports get drugs for many." *Lexington Herald-Leader*. February 16: A1 & 15.

Mueller, Lee and Charles Camp. 2003. "Suspect clinic fueled a lavish lifestyle." *Lexington Herald-Leader*. January 31: A8.

National Survey on Drug Use and Health. 2002. 2003. Substance Abuse and Mental Health Administration. Washington, DC: U.S. Department of Health and Human Services: September 5.

Other Dangerous Drugs. 2002. *Kentucky Drug Threat Assessment*. National Drug Intelligence Center, Washington, DC: U.S. Department of Justice: July.

OxyContin Diversion and Abuse. 2002. *Information Bulletin*. National Drug Intelligence Center. Johnstown, PA: U.S. Department of Justice: January.

OxyContin: Pharmaceutical Diversion. 2002. *Drug Intelligence Brief*. Drug Enforcement Administration. Washington, DC: U.S. Department of Justice: March.

Painkiller's sales far exceeded levels anticipated by maker. 2002. *Wall Street Journal*. May 16: 4.

Panhandle doctor's OxyContin conviction to send message. 2002. *Rocky Mountain News*. February 20: A1.

Police arrest 201 in OxyContin crackdown. 2001. *Organized Crime Digest* 22 (3): 4.

Potter, Gary W., Larry Gaines, and Beth Holbrook. 1990. "Blowing smoke: An evaluation of Kentucky's Marijuana Eradication Program." *American Journal of Police* 9 (1): 97–116.

Presdee, Mike. 2000. *Cultural Criminology and the Carnival of Crime*. London: Routledge.

Pulaski hopes fingerprint system will stamp out OxyContin abuse. 2001. *Roanoke Times*. June 11: A1.

Raids in Kentucky aim at deadly new drug. 2001. *New York Times*. February 8: A4.

Reinarman, Craig and Harry G. Levine. 1989. "Crack in context: Politics and the media in the making of a drug scare." *Contemporary Drug Problems* 16: 535–578.

Rosenberg, Debra. 2001. "How one town got hooked." *Newsweek* 137 (15): 48–52.

Sappenfield, Mark. 2001. "Rise of 'hillbilly heroin' creates alarm in East." *Christian Science Monitor* 93 (159): 1.

Satel, Sally. 2003. "OxyContin half-truths can cause suffering." *USA Today*. October 26: A1.

Silverman, Milton, Philip R. Lee, and Mia Lydecker. 1981. *Pills and the Public Purse*. Berkeley, CA: University of California Press.

——. 1982. *Prescriptions for Death*. Berkeley, CA: University of California Press.

——. 1992. *Bad Medicine*. Stanford, CA: Stanford University Press.

Sourcebook of Criminal Justice Statistics. 2002. "Estimated percent distribution of households experiencing crime." P. 206. Washington, DC: Bureau of Justice Statistics.

State monitoring programs seen as key to tackling OxyContin abuse. 2002. *Drug Week*. February 22: 15–16.

State won't cover painkiller. 2001. *New York Times*. July 21: A3.

Sullivan, Patrick. 2001. "OxyContin-abuse problem appears limited to U.S." *Canadian Medical Association Journal* 165 (5): 624–625.

Tanner, Lindsey. 2002. "OxyContin recommended for arthritis." *www.nlm.nih.gov/medline*. March 14.

Taylor, Guy. 2003 "OxyContin a scourge for users in rural areas." *The Washington Times*. September 2: 1.

Tickamyer, Ann R. 1992. "The working poor in rural labor markets: The example of the southeastern United States." Pp. 41–61 in Cynthia M. Duncan (ed.), *Rural Poverty in America*. New York: Auburn House.

Tunnell, Kenneth D. 2004a. "Cultural constructions of the hillbilly heroin and crime problem." Pp. 133–142 in Keith Hayward, Jeff Ferrell, Mike Presdee, and Wayne Morris (eds.), *Cultural Criminology Unleashed*. London: Cavendish.

——. 2004b. *Pissing on Demand: Workplace Drug Testing and the Rise of the Detox Industry*. New York: New York University Press.

Ukens, Carol. 2001. "Propelling pain." *Drug Topics* 145 (5): 24.

Uniform Crime Reports. 2003. Crime in America. Washington, DC: United States Department of Justice.

Warner, Barbara D. and Carl G. Leukefeld. 2001. "Rural–urban differences in substance use and treatment utilization among prisoners." *American Journal of Drug and Alcohol Abuse* 27 (2): 265–280.

For Discussion

1. If pharmaceutical companies intentionally fail to provide accurate information about their manufactured drugs, should they be held criminally liable? Why or why not?

2. The author of this article discusses the sociological concept "moral panic." What types of moral panics have emerged at your college, university, or area of residence?

18

Taking Care of Business

The Heroin Addict's Life on the Street

Edward Preble
John J. Casey

"Taking Care of Business," one of the classic papers in the drug field, begins with a brief history of heroin use and distribution in New York City from World War I through the late 1960s. The authors note trends in price, availability, and legitimate opportunities for heroin users. The primary focus of the article, however, is the various levels of heroin distribution. Importantly, Preble and Casey dispel the widely held belief that individuals use heroin as an escape. Rather, they argue, heroin allows individuals to experience purposeful lives. The daily activities in which heroin users are involved are highly rewarding to them, particularly when legitimate opportunities are not generally available.

Introduction

This report is a description of the life and activities of lower-class heroin users in New York City in the context of their street environment. It is concerned exclusively with the heroin users living in slum areas, who comprise at least 80 percent of the city's heroin-using population. They are predominantly Negro and Puerto Rican, with some Irish, Italian, and Jewish.

It is often said that the use of heroin provides an escape for the user from his psychological problems and from the responsibilities of social and personal relationships—in short, an escape from life. Clinical descriptions of heroin addicts emphasize the passive, dependent, withdrawn, generally inadequate features of their personality structure and social adjustment. Most sociological studies of heroin users make the same point. Thus, Chein et al. (1964) reported that street-gang members are not likely to become heroin users, because they are resourceful, aggressive, well-integrated boys who are "reality-oriented" in their street environment. They held that it is the passive, anxious, inadequate boy, who cannot adapt to street life, who is likely to use heroin. Similarly, Cloward and Ohlin (1960) referred to heroin users as "retreatists" and "double failures" who cannot qualify for either legitimate or illegitimate careers. Unaggressive "mamma's boys" is the usual stereotype these days for the heroin addict, both for the students of narcotic use and the public at large. Experienced researchers and workers in the narcotics field know that there is no such thing as "the heroin addict" or "the addict personality." However, most attempts to generalize—the goal of all scientific investigation—result in some version of the escape theory.

The description which follows of the activities of lower-class heroin users in their adaptation to the social and economic institutions and practices connected with the use of heroin contradicts this widely held belief. Their behavior is anything but an escape from life. They are actively engaged in meaningful activities and relationships seven days a week. The brief moments of euphoria after each administration of a small amount of heroin constitute a small fraction of their daily lives. The rest of the time they are aggressively pursuing a career that is exacting, challenging, adventurous, and rewarding. They are always on the move and must be alert, flexible, and resourceful. The surest way to identify heroin users in a slum neighborhood is to observe the way people walk. The heroin user walks with a fast, purposeful stride, as if he is late for an important appointment—indeed, he is. He is hustling (robbing or stealing), trying to sell stolen goods, avoiding the police, looking for a heroin dealer with a good bag (the street retail unit of heroin), coming back from copping (buying heroin), looking for a safe place to take the drug, or looking for someone who beat (cheated) him—among other things. He is, in short, *taking care of business*, a phrase which is so common with heroin users that they use it in response to words of greeting, such as "how you doing?" and "what's happening?" *Taking care of biz* is the common abbreviation. *Ripping and running* is an older phrase which also refers to their busy lives. For them, if not for their middle- and upper-class counterparts (a small minority of opiate addicts), the quest for heroin is the quest for a meaningful life, not an escape from life. And the meaning does not lie, primarily, in the effects of the drug on their minds and bodies; it lies in the gratification of accomplishing a series of challenging, exciting tasks, every day of the week.

Much of the life of the heroin user on the street centers around the economic institutions of heroin distribution. Therefore, this report features a description of the marketing processes for heroin, from importation to street sales. The cost of heroin today is so high and the quality so poor that the street user must become totally involved in an economic career. A description of typical economic careers of heroin users will be presented. Preceding these two sections is a brief historical account of heroin use in New York City from World War I to the present, in which it will be seen that patterns of heroin use have changed at a pace and in a direction in correspondence with the social changes of the past fifty years. Theories and explanations about heroin use, based upon observations of fifty, twenty-five, or even five years ago, are inadequate to account for the phenomenon today. It is hoped that this contemporary account of the social setting for heroin use will provide useful data for the modifications of theory and practice which should accompany any dynamic social process.

Methodology

The data on which this report is based have come from interviews with patients at the Manhattan State Hospital Drug Addiction Unit and from participant observation and interviews with individuals and groups in four lower-class communities in New York City—East Harlem, Lower East Side, Yorkville, Claremont (Bronx). The communities represent the neighborhoods of approximately 85 percent of the addict patients

at Manhattan State Hospital. The anthropologist's role and approach to the heroin-using study of informants was in the tradition of Bronislaw Malinowski (1922) and William F. Whyte (1955), which, in Whyte's words, consists of "the observation of interpersonal events." Another dimension was added with the modified use of research techniques, introduced by Abraham Kardiner and his collaborators (1939) in their psychosocial studies of primitive and modern cultures. The main feature of this methodology is the life-history interview with individual subjects. Initial and subsequent contacts with the research informants occurred, in all cases, with their voluntary consent and cooperation. The anthropologist had the advantage of twelve years experience of street work and research in the study neighborhoods, and was able to enlist the assistance of long-time acquaintances for this special project. Four major ethnic groups were represented among the approximately 150 informants: Irish, Italian, Negro, and Puerto Rican.

History of Heroin Use in New York City

The recent history of heroin use in the city can be broken down into six time periods: (1) between World War I and World War II, (2) during World War II, (3) 1947 to 1951, (4) 1951 to 1957, (5) 1957 to 1961, and (6) 1961 to the present.

1. Between World War I and World War II

Prior to World War II the use of heroin was limited, for the most part, to people in the *life*—show people, entertainers, and musicians; racketeers and gangsters; thieves and pickpockets; prostitutes and pimps. The major ethnic groups represented among these users were Italian, Irish, Jewish, and Negro (mostly those associated with the entertainment life). There were also heroin users among the Chinese, who had a history of opium use. The distribution of heroin by those who controlled the market was limited mostly to these people, and there was little knowledge or publicity about it.

2. During World War II

World War II interrupted the trade routes and distributorships for illicit heroin supplies, which resulted in a five-year hiatus in heroin use.

3. 1947 to 1951

When World War II ended, there was a greatly expanded market for heroin in the increased population among Negroes from the South and among migrating Puerto Ricans who came to New York during the war in response to a manpower shortage. In 1940, the Negro population in New York City was 450,000; in 1960, it was over 1 million. In 1940, the Puerto Rican population was 70,000; in 1960, it was over 600,000. As with all new immigrants in New York, they worked at the lowest economic levels, settled in slum neighborhoods, and were the victims of unemployment, poverty, and discrimination. From 1947 to 1951, the use of heroin spread among lower-class Negro and Puerto Rican people and among other lower-class, slum-dwelling people, mainly the Irish and Italians. The increased rate of use was gradual, but steady, and did not attract much attention. Most of the users were young adults in their twenties and thirties. They were more or less circumspect in their drug consumption, which they were able to be because of the relatively low cost and high quality of the heroin.

During this period, heroin was sold in number-five capsules (the smallest capsules used for pharmaceutical products). These *caps* could be bought for about one dollar apiece, and two to six persons could get high on the contents of one capsule. Commonly, four persons would contribute one quarter each and *get down on a cap*. There was social cohesion, identification, and ritual among the users of this period. Sometimes as many as twenty people would get together and, in a party atmosphere, share the powder contents of several capsules which were emptied upon a mirror and divided into columns by means of a razor blade, one column for each participant. The mirror was passed from person to person and each one would inhale his share through the nose by means of a tapered, rolled-up dollar bill which served as a

straw, and was called a *quill*. A twenty, fifty, or hundred dollar bill was used on special occasions when someone wanted to make a show of his affluence. Since heroin was so inexpensive during this time, no addict had to worry about getting his fix; someone was always willing to loan him a dollar or share a part of his drug. The social relationships among these addicts were similar to those found in a neighborhood bar, where there is a friendly mutual concern for the welfare of the regular patrons. The most important economic factor in these early post-war days of heroin use was that heroin users were able to work even at a low-paying job and still support a habit, and many of them did. Relatively little crime was committed in the interest of getting money to buy heroin. A habit could be maintained for a few dollars a day, at little social or economic cost to the community.

4. 1951 to 1957

Around 1951, heroin use started to become popular among younger people on the streets, especially among street-gang members who were tired of gang fighting and were looking for a new high. As heroin use had become more common in the latter days of the previous period, the more street-wise teenagers learned about it and prevailed upon the experienced users to introduce them to it. Contrary to popular reports, experimentation with heroin by youths usually began at their initiative and not through proselytism. The stereotype of the dope *pusher* giving out free samples of narcotics to teenagers in school yards and candy stores, in order to addict them, is one of the most misleading myths about drug use. Also, contrary to professional reports about this development, it was not the weak, withdrawn, unadaptive street boy who first started using heroin, but rather the tough, sophisticated, and respected boy, typically a street-gang leader. Later, others followed his example, either through indoctrination or emulation. By 1955, heroin use among teenagers on the street had become widespread, resulting, among other things, in the dissolution of fighting gangs. Now the hip boy on the street was not the swaggering, leather-jacketed gang member, but the boy nodding on the corner, enjoying his heroin high. He was the new hero model.

As heroin use spread among the young from 1951, the price of heroin began to rise in response to the greater demand, and the greater risks involved in selling to youths. Those who started using heroin as teenagers seldom had work experience or skills and resorted to crime in order to support their heroin use. They were less circumspect in their drug-using and criminal activity, and soon became a problem to the community, especially to those who were engaged in non-narcotic illegal activities, such as bookmaking, loan-sharking, and policy (the gambling game popular among working-class people, in which a correct selection of three numbers pays off at 50 to 1). The activities and behavior of young drug users brought attention and notoriety to the neighborhood, which jeopardized racketeer operations. It was not uncommon for a local racketeer to inform the parents of a young heroin user about his activities, hoping that they would take action.

5. 1957 to 1961

In 1957, the criminal organization, or *syndicate*, which had been mainly responsible for heroin distribution (according to law-enforcement agencies and government investigation committees), officially withdrew from the market. This resulted from two conditions: the passage of stricter federal laws that included provision for conspiracy convictions, and the related fact that illegal drug use was receiving increased attention from the public and officials, especially as a result of the increased involvement of youth with heroin. The risks had become too great, and the syndicate did not want to endanger the larger and more important sources of revenue, such as gambling and loan-sharking. However, the instruction to get out of narcotics was more honored in the breach than in the observance by certain syndicate members. Those who stayed involved in narcotics operated independently. Some made it their primary operation, while others would make only one or two big transactions a year when they needed to recoup quickly from an unexpected financial loss in some other operation. Dealing irregularly in nar-

cotics for this purpose became known as a *fall-back*—a quick and sure way to make money. The syndicate also stayed involved indirectly through loan-shark agreements. In these transactions, large sums of money were lent to narcotic dealers for a period of one month at a fixed rate of return. No questions were asked regarding its use. By this means, the syndicate avoided some of the undesirable aspects of narcotic distribution and still participated in the profits. The official withdrawal of the syndicate from narcotics created opportunities for independent operators, which resulted in a relatively free market.

6. 1961 to the Present

The next major development in the history of heroin use in the city occurred in November 1961, when there was a critical shortage of heroin. Known as a *panic*, this development, whatever its cause, had a profound effect on the course of heroin use in the city. The panic lasted only for a few weeks. During this time, the demand for the meager supplies of heroin was so great that those who had supplies were able to double and triple their prices and further adulterate the quality, thus realizing sometimes as much as ten times their usual profit. By the time heroin became available again in good supply, the dealers had learned that inferior heroin at inflated prices could find a ready market. Since that time, the cost of heroin on the street has continued to climb, through increased prices, further adulteration, and *short counts* (misrepresentation of aggregate weight in a given unit). A few minor panics—about two a year—help bolster the market. Today, an average heroin habit costs the user about $20 a day, as compared to $2 twenty years ago. This fact is responsible for a major social disorder in the city today. It has also had important effects on the personal, social, and family relationships of the heroin users themselves. There is no longer social cohesion among addicts. The competition and struggle necessary to support a habit has turned each one into an independent operator who looks out only for himself. Usually, addicts today will associate in pairs (partners), but only for practical purposes: in a criminal effort which requires two people (as when one acts as lookout, while the other commits a burglary), to share in the price of a bag of heroin, to assist in case of an overdose of drugs, to share the use of one set of works (the paraphernalia used to inject heroin). There is no longer a subculture of addicts, based on social cohesion and emotional identification, but rather a loose association of individuals and parallel couples. Heroin users commonly say, "I have no friends, only associates."

The economic pressures on heroin users today are so great that they prey on each other, as well as on their families and on society at large. An addict with money or drugs in his possession runs a good risk of being *taken off* (robbed) by other addicts. An addict who has been robbed or cheated by another addict usually takes his loss philosophically, summed up by the expression, "That's the name of the game." Referring to a fellow addict who had cheated him, one victim said, "He beat me today, I'll beat him tomorrow." Another addict who specializes in robbing other addicts said, "I beat them every chance I get, which is all the time." Sociability, even among partners, extends no farther than that suggested by the following excerpt: "You might be hanging out with a fellow for a long time, copping together and working as crime partners. You might beat him for a purpose. You might beat him, because maybe you bought a bag together and you know it's not going to do both any good, so you beat him for it. But then you try to go and get some money and straighten him out; make it up to him." Another informant summed up the attitude between partners this way: "I'm looking out for myself—I might be sick tomorrow; anyway, he's got something working for him that I don't know about." Sometimes, a distinction is made between a hustling partner and a crime partner (*crimey*), where it is suggested that the latter is more dependable; however, as one informant put it, "There are larceny-minded crimeys." The causes of these changes in the relationships of heroin users to each other, to family members, and to other members of the community are to be found in the economic practices of heroin distribution.

The Distribution of Heroin in New York City

Heroin contracted for in Europe at $5000 per kilo (2.2 pounds) will be sold in $5 bags on the street for about one million dollars, after having passed through at least six levels of distribution. The following description of the distribution and marketing of heroin, from the time it arrives in New York until it reaches the hands of the heroin user in the street, is a consensus derived from informants in the hospital and in the street representing different ethnic and racial groups from different parts of the city. There are many variations to the account given here at all levels of the marketing process. For example, as in the marketing of any product, a quantity purchase can be made at a lower price; and a dealer who makes a rapid turnover of the product for a wholesaler will receive higher benefits for his work. All the way down the line, the *good customer* is the key to a successful operation. He is one who buys regularly, does a good volume of business, does not ask for credit or try to buy short (offer less than the established price), and can be trusted. The following account does not include all the many variations, but can be taken as a paradigm.

Opium produced in Turkey, India, and Iran is processed into heroin in Lebanon, France, and Italy, and prepared for shipment to the East Coast of the United States. A United States importer, through a courier, can buy a kilogram of 80-percent heroin in Europe for $5000. The quality is represented to him in terms of how many cuts it will hold (that is, how many times it can be adulterated). In earlier days, when the marketing of heroin was a more controlled operation, the word of the European seller was accepted. Now, it is customary for the importer to test it, either by means of scientific instruments, or through a reliable tester—an addict who makes experimental cuts, uses the drug, and reports on its quality. The importer, who usually never sees the heroin, sells down the line to a highly trusted customer through intermediaries. If it is a syndicate operation, he would only sell to high level, coded men, known as *captains*. These men are major distributors, referred to as *kilo connections* and, generally, as *the people*.

Major Distribution

The *kilo connection* pays $20,000 for the original kilogram (kilo, kee), and gives it a one and one cut (known as *hitting it*); that is, he makes two kilos out of one by adding the common adulterants of milk sugar, mannite (a product from the ash tree, used as a mild laxative), and quinine. The proportions of ingredients used for the cutting vary with the preferences of the cutter. One may use 5 parts milk sugar, 2 parts quinine, and 1 part mannite; while another may use 2 parts milk sugar, 3 parts quinine, and 1 part mannite. All three of these products are quickly soluble with heroin. A match lit under the cooker (bottle cap) will heat and dissolve the mixture into a clear liquid in a few seconds. The milk sugar contributes the bulk, the mannite inflates the volume—described as *fluffing* it up—and the quinine heightens the sensation of the *rush* when, upon injection into the vein, the mixture first registers on the nervous system. In the cutting procedure, the substance to be cut is placed under a fine sieve, often made from a woman's nylon stocking stretched over a coat hanger. The adulterants are sifted on top of it, then the new mixture is sifted through several more times. After the cut, the kilo connection sells down the line in kilos, half kilos, and quarter kilos, depending upon the resources of his customers. He will get approximately $10,000 per half kilo for the now adulterated heroin.

The customer of the kilo connection is known as *the connection* in its original sense, meaning that he knows *the people*, even though he is not one of them. He may also be called an *ounce man*. He is a highly trusted customer. (One common variation here is that the kilo connection may sell to a third line man, known, if a syndicate operation, as a *soldier* or *button man*. He, in turn, will make a one and one cut and sell to the connection.) Assuming that the connection buys directly from a kilo connection, he will probably give the heroin a one and one cut (make two units of each one), divide the total aggregate into ounces, and sell down the line at $700 per ounce. In addition to the adultera-

tion, the aggregate weight of the product is reduced. Known as a *short count*, this procedure occurs at every succeeding level of distribution. At this stage, however, it is called a *good ounce*, despite the adulteration and reduced weight.

The next man is known as a *dealer in weight*, and is probably the most important figure in the line of distribution. He stands midway between the top and the bottom, and is the first one coming down the line who takes substantial risk of being apprehended by law-enforcement officers. He is also the first one who may be a heroin user himself, but usually he is not. He is commonly referred to as one who is *into something* and is respected as a big dealer who has put himself in jeopardy by, as the sayings go, *carrying a felony with him* and *doing the time*; that is, if he gets caught, he can expect a long jail sentence. It is said of him that "he let his name go," or "his name gets kicked around," meaning that his identity is known to people in the street. This man usually specializes in cut ounces. He may give a two and one cut (make three units of each one) to the good ounce from the connection and sell the resulting quantity for $500 per ounce. The aggregate weight is again reduced, and now the unit is called a *piece*, instead of an ounce. Sometimes, it is called a *street ounce* or a *vig ounce* (*vig* is an abbreviation for *vigorish*, which is the term used to designate the high interest on loans charged by loan sharks). In previous years, twenty-five to thirty level teaspoons were supposed to constitute an ounce; today, it is sixteen to twenty.

The next customer is known as a *street dealer*. He buys the *piece* for $500, gives it a one and one cut and makes *bundles*, which consist of twenty-five $5 bags each. He can usually get seven bundles from each piece, and he sells each bundle for $80. He may also package the heroin in *half-bundles* (ten $5 bags each), which sell for $40, or he may package in *half-loads* (fifteen $3 bags), which sell for $30 each. This man may or may not be a heroin user.

The next distributor is known as a *juggler*, who is the seller from whom the average street addict buys. He is always a user. He buys bundles for $80 each and sells the twenty-five bags at about $5 each, making just enough profit to support his own habit, day by day. He may or may not make a small cut, known as *tapping the bags*. He is referred to as someone who is "always high and always short"; that is, he always has enough heroin for his own use and is always looking for a few dollars to get enough capital to cop again. The following actual account is typical of a juggler's transactions: he has $25 and needs $5 more to buy a half-load. He meets a user he knows who has $5 and would like to buy two $3 bags; he is short $1. The juggler tells him he needs only $5 to cop, and that, if he can have his $5, he will buy a half-load and give him his two $3 bags—$1, in effect, for the use of the money. When the juggler returns, he gives the person his two bags. In the example here, the person had to wait about two hours for the juggler's return, and it was raining. For taking the risk of getting beat for his money by the juggler, for the long wait and the discomfort of the weather, the juggler was expected to go to the *cooker* with him (share the use of some of the heroin), with the juggler putting in two bags to the other person's one bag and sharing equally in the total. The juggler had his fix and now has eleven bags left. He sells three bags for $9. From the eight bags he has left he uses two himself to get straight—not to get high, but enough to keep from getting sick so that he can finish his business. Now, he sells four bags for $12 and has three left. He needs only $7 more to cop again, so he is willing to sell the last three bags for the reduced price, and he can begin a similar cycle all over again. He may do this three or four times a day. The juggler leads a precarious life, both financially and in the risks he takes of getting robbed by fellow addicts or arrested. Most arrests for heroin sales are of the juggler. Financially, he is always struggling to stay in the black. If business is a little slow, he may start to get sick or impatient and use some of the heroin he needs to sell, in order to recoup. If he does this, he is in the red and temporarily out of business. A juggler is considered to be doing well if he has enough money left over after a transaction for cab fare to where he buys the heroin. One informant defined a juggler as a "non-hustling dope fiend who is always messing the money up."

Other Specialists

There are ancillary services provided by other specialists in the heroin-marketing process. They are known as: (1) lieutenants, (2) testers, (3) drop-men, (4) salesmen, (5) steerers, (6) taste faces, and (7) accommodators.

1. *Lieutenant:* Very often, a connection or weight dealer will have in his employ a trusted associate who handles the details of transactions with the street-level dealers. He arranges for deliveries, collects the money, and acts as an enforcer, if things go wrong. He may work for a salary or a commission, or both. Sometimes, he will be given some *weight* (part of a kilo) to sell on his own as a bonus.

2. *Tester:* Heroin dealers down the line are likely to keep a trusted addict around to test the quality of the drug for them. In return for this service, he gets all the heroin he needs and pocket money.

3. *Drop-man:* This person, often a young, dependable non-user, is used by sellers to make deliveries. He works for cash and may make as much as $500 for a drop [on] behalf of a top-level seller. He may also handle the transfer of money in a transaction. He is usually a tough, intelligent, trusted street youth who is ambitious to work his way up in the criminal hierarchy.

4. *Salesman:* Sometimes, the type of person used as a drop-man will be used as a street salesman of heroin for a fairly big dealer. The use of this kind of salesman is growing, because of the unreliability of addict jugglers and the desirability of having a tough person who can be trusted and not be easily robbed and cheated by addicts. Sometimes, these boys are about 16 to 18 years old and may be going to school. Being young, they usually do not have a police record, and they attract less attention from the police. One informant summed up their attributes this way: "The police won't pay much attention to a kid, but if they do get busted (arrested) they don't talk; they want to be men . . . they (the dealers) trust a guy that don't use it, because they know the guy ain't going to beat

him. They got a little gang, and nobody is going to get their stuff, because they're going to gang up on the guy. In that case, they can use a gun in a hurry. The kids that sell the stuff, they don't use it. They buy clothes or whatever they want with the money." They often sell on consignment, starting with a small advance (usually a bundle) and working up to more if they are successful.

5. *Steerer:* The steerer is one who in race-track parlance would be known as a *tout*, or in a sidewalk sales operation as a *shill*. He is one who tries to persuade users to buy a certain dealer's bag. He may work off and on by appointment with a particular dealer (always a small street dealer or juggler) in return for his daily supply of drugs. Or he may hear that a certain dealer has a good bag and, on a speculative basis, steer customers to him and then go to him later and ask to be taken care of for the service. This is known as *cracking* on a dealer. One of his more subtle selling techniques is to affect an exaggerated-looking high, and, when asked by a user where he got such a good bag, refer him to the dealer. Usually, he is a person who stays in the block all day and is supposed to know what is going on; he is, as they say, *always on the set*.

6. *Taste face:* This is a derogatory term given to one who supports his habit by renting out works—loaning the paraphernalia for injecting heroin—in return for a little money or a share of the heroin. Possession of works (hypodermic needle, eyedropper fitted with a baby's pacifier nipple, and bottle cap) is a criminal offense, and users do not want to run the extra risk of carrying them; thus, they are willing to pay something for the service. Although they perform a useful service, these people are held in contempt by other users. Taste refers to the small amount of heroin he is given (known as a *G shot*) and face is a term applied to anyone on the street who is known as a *creep, flunky,* or *nobody*.

7. *Accommodator:* The accommodator is a user who buys at a low level—usually from a juggler—for someone new to the neighborhood who has no connections. These purchases are for small amounts bought by users from other parts of the city or the suburbs. The accommodator receives a little part of the heroin or money for his services. Sometimes, he will also cheat the buyer by misrepresenting the price or the amount, or just by not coming back. However, he has to be somewhat reliable, in order to support his habit regularly in this way. Many selling arrests by undercover narcotics police are of these low-level accommodators.

The Street Bag of Heroin

The amount of heroin in the street bag is very small. A generous estimate of the aggregate weight of a $5 bag is ninety milligrams, including the adulterants. Assuming, as in the above account, that the original kilo of 80-percent heroin is adulterated twenty-four times by the time it reaches the street, the amount of heroin would be about three milligrams. There is considerable fluctuation in the amount of heroin in the retail unit, running the range from one to fifteen milligrams, which depends mainly upon the supply available in the market. The important point is that, no matter how small the amount, heroin users are never discouraged in their efforts to get it. The consensus figure of three milligrams is a good approximation for an average over a one-year period. This is the average analgesic dosage that is used in those countries, such as England, where heroin can be prescribed in medical practice. It is a minimal amount, being considered safe for someone who does not use opiates. It is equivalent to about ten milligrams of either morphine or methadone.

In controlled experiments with opiate addicts, as much as sixty milligrams of morphine have been administered four times a day (Martin, personal communication 1967). Each dosage is equivalent to about twenty milligrams of heroin, which is seven times the amount in the average street bag. In another experiment, it was found that the average heroin addict "recognized" heroin at a minimum level of about fifteen milligrams—five times the amount in the street bag (Sharoff, personal communication 1967). The average dosage of methadone used in opiate-maintenance treatment is one hundred milligrams—about ten times the amount in the street bag. One informant said of the effects of a street bag today: "All it does is turn your stomach over so that you can go out and hustle, and you had better do it fast." Heroin users who are sent to jail report that they are surprised when they do not experience serious withdrawal symptoms after the abrupt cessation of heroin use. Physicians working in the withdrawal wards of narcotic treatment centers refer to the abstinence syndrome among most of their patients today as "subclinical."

The amount of heroin in the street unit has resulted in an institution known as *chasing the bag*. In a community with a high incidence of heroin use, there will be two, three, or four competing bags on the street; that is, bags which have come down through different distributorship lines. Because of the low quality of the heroin, users want to get the best one available on a given day. The number of times it has been cut and the ingredients that were used to cut it are the main considerations. The dealer who has the best bag on the street at a given time will sell his merchandise fast and do a big volume of business. A dealer with a good bag who works hard can sell forty to fifty bundles a day. A good bag dealer can sell seventy-five to one hundred bags a day. By keeping the quality relatively high—for example by giving a one and a half cut to a quantity represented as being able to hold two cuts—he makes less profit on each unit. However, this loss can be offset by the greater volume and the reduced price he gets from his wholesaler, as a result of buying more often and in large quantities. Those with inferior bags on the street do not have a rapid turnover, but they know that sooner or later they can sell their stock, since the demand tends to exceed the supply. There are also other factors operating in their favor. Some users are not known to the dealer of the best bag and cannot buy from him except through the mediation of someone else. This service costs the prospective buyer something and he has to weigh that consideration against the better bag. Usually, however, if he is sure that one bag is much better than another one, he will find the price to pay for the service to get it; the quality of the bag, not the money, is always the primary consideration.

Another condition favorable to the dealers of inferior bags is that a user who hustles for his drugs is too busy to be around all the time waiting for a particular bag to come on the street. He is usually pressed for time and has to take what is available. If the dealer of the good bag is out recopping, the user cannot afford to wait for what may be a long time. The dealer of an inferior bag, whose heroin moves more slowly, is reliable; that is, he is always around and can be depended upon. Even in extreme cases, where a bag is so bad that the dealer builds up a surplus because of slow business, he knows that sooner or later a temporary shortage of heroin— even for a few days—will insure his selling out. Heroin does not spoil and can be easily stored for an indefinite period.

Sometimes, the dealer of an exceptionally good bag will be approached by his competitors, and they will make a deal, whereby he agrees to leave the street on the condition that they buy their bundles from him. In such a deal, those buying the good bundles will *tap the bags* (adulterate them a little more) and put them on the street at the same price. This is one of the many variations in marketing heroin.

It is common practice for a new dealer to come on the street with a good bag and keep it that way, until he has most of the customers. Then, he will start to adulterate the heroin, knowing that his reputation will carry him for a few days; by that time, he has made a good extra profit. When he starts losing customers in large number, he can build the bag up again. Users are constantly experimenting with the products of different dealers, comparing notes with other users, and attempting to buy the best bag that is around. As one informant put it: "You keep searching. If the guy is weak and you buy from him and it's nothing, then you go to Joe or Tom. Like you get a bag over here now, you run over there about in an hour and get another bag from the other guy, and get another from this other guy after a while. You just go in a circle to see. You run in different directions." One informant said, "There are no longer dope addicts on the street, only hope addicts." A report on the street that a heroin user died of an overdose of heroin results in a customer rush on his dealer for the same bag.

Economic Careers of Heroin Users

The nature of the economic careers of heroin users on the street is epitomized in the following quote from a research informant: "I believe in work to a certain extent, if it benefits my profit; but I do believe there is more money made otherwise." Another informant, in referring to a fellow user, said: "He just got no heart to be pulling no scores. He can't steal, he don't know how to steal. You can't be an addict that way. I don't know how he's going to make it."

Virtually all heroin users in slum neighborhoods regularly commit crime, in order to support their heroin use. In addition to the crimes involving violation of the narcotic laws, which are described above, heroin users engage in almost all types of crime for gain, both against property and the person. Because of the greatly inflated price of heroin and because of its poor quality, it is impossible for a heroin user to support even a modest habit for less than $20 a day. Since the typical street user is uneducated, unskilled, and often from a minority racial group, he cannot earn enough money in the legitimate labor market to finance his drug use; he must engage in criminal activity. It is a conservative estimate that heroin users in New York City steal $1 million a day in money, goods, and property. About 70 percent of the inmates in New York City Department of Correction institutions are heroin users whose crimes were directly or indirectly connected with their heroin use.

As with non-addict criminals, addict criminals tend to specialize in certain activities, depending upon their personalities, skills, and experience. One of the myths derived from the passivity stereotype of the heroin user is that the heroin user avoids crimes of violence, such as robbery, which involve personal confrontation. This no longer seems to be the case. A 1966 New York City Police Department study of the arrests of admitted narcotic (primarily heroin) addicts for selected felonies, other than violations of narcotic laws, showed that 15.1 percent of the arrests were for robbery ([City of] New York Police Department 1966). This compared with 12.9 percent robbery arrests of all arrests (addict and non-addict) during the same year. Murder arrests among the addicts amounted to 1 percent of the selected felonies, as compared to 1.4 percent of all arrests in the same categories. The biggest differences between addict arrests and all arrests in the seventeen felony categories selected for study were in the categories of burglary and felonious assault. Among the addicts, 40.9 percent were burglary arrests, compared to 19.7 percent of all arrests; felonious assault constituted 5.6 percent among the addicts, compared to 27.9 percent of all arrests. What these figures reveal is not that heroin users avoid crimes of violence, as compared to non-addicts, but that they avoid crimes not involving financial gain, such as felonious assault. Where financial gain is involved, as in robbery, the risk of violence is taken by heroin users in a higher percentage of cases than with non-addicts. These statistics confirm the observations and opinions of street informants, both addict and non-addict. The high percentage of burglaries committed by heroin users is often cited as evidence that, in comparison with non-addict criminals, they prefer nonviolent crime. What is overlooked here is that burglary, especially of residences, always involves the risk of personal confrontation and violence. Of the 1745 burglary arrests of admitted addicts in 1966, 975 (51 percent) were residence burglaries.

Analysis of the data from the informants for this study showed the following, with regard to principal criminal occupations, not including those connected with narcotic-laws offenses: burglar—22.7 percent, *flatfooted hustler*—12.2 percent, shoplifter—12.1 percent, robber—9.0 percent. *Flatfooted hustler* is a term used on the street for one who will commit almost any kind of crime for money, depending upon the opportunities. As one self-described flatfooted hustler put it: "I'm capable of doing most things—jostling (picking pockets), boosting (shoplifting), con games, burglary, mugging, or stick-ups; wherever I see the opportunity, that's where I'm at." The main advantage of crimes against the person is that the yield is usually money, which does not have to be sold at a discount, as does stolen property. It is easily concealed and can be exchanged directly for heroin. In the case of stolen goods and property, the person has to carry the proceeds of, say, a burglary around with him, as he looks for a direct buyer or a fence. . . . This exposes him to extra risk of apprehension. When he does find a buyer, he can only expect to get from 10 percent to 50 percent of the value, the average being about 30 percent, depending upon the item—the more expensive the item, the higher the discount.

The distribution and sales of goods and property stolen by heroin users has become a major economic institution in low-income neighborhoods. Most of the consumers are otherwise ordinary, legitimate members of the community. Housewives will wait on the stoop for specialists in stealing meat (known as *cattle rustlers*) to come by, so that they can get a ham or roast at a 60-percent discount. Owners of small grocery stores buy cartons of cigarettes stolen from the neighborhood supermarket. The owner of an automobile places an order with a heroin user for tires, and the next day he has the tires—with the wheels. During the Easter holidays, there is a great demand for clothes, with slum streets looking like the streets of the Garment District.

It has often been noted that retail stores in a slum neighborhood have higher prices than those in more affluent neighborhoods, and this has been attributed to discrimination and profiteering at the expense of poor people with little consumer education and knowledge. Although such charges have some foundation, another major cause of higher prices is the high rate of pilferage by heroin users and others from such stores, the cost of which is passed on to the consumer. One chain store operation which locates exclusively in low-income neighborhoods in New York City is reportedly in bankruptcy due to a 10 percent pilferage rate. This rate compares to about 2 percent citywide.

One economic institution that has resulted directly from the increased criminal activity among heroin users is the *grocery fence*. He is a small, local businessman, such as a candy store owner, bar owner, or beauty parlor owner, who has enough cash to buy stolen goods and property on a small scale and has a place to store them. He then sells the items to his regular customers, both for good will and a profit. He provides a service for the user in providing him with a fast outlet for his goods.

The heroin user is an important figure in the economic life of the slums. In order to support a $20-a-day habit, he has to steal goods and property worth from $50 to $100. Usually, he steals outside his neighborhood, not out of community loyalty, but because the opportunities are better in the wealthier neighborhoods; and he brings his merchandise back to the neighborhood for sale at high discounts. This results, to some extent, in a redistribution of real income from the richer to the poorer neighborhoods. Although non-addict residents in the slums may deplore the presence of heroin users, they appreciate and compete for their services as discount salesmen. The user, in turn, experiences satisfaction in being able to make this contribution to the neighborhood.

The type of criminal activity he engages in, and his success at it, determine, to a large extent, the addict's status among fellow addicts and in the community at large. The appellation of *real hustling dope fiend* (a successful burglar, robber, con man, etc.) is a mark of respect and status. Conversely, *non-hustling dope fiend* is a term of denigration applied to users who stay in the neighborhood begging for money or small tastes of heroin, renting out works, or doing small-time juggling. There are also middle-status occupations, such as *stealing copper*, where the person specializes in salvaging metal and fixtures from vacant tenement buildings and selling to the local junkman. About the only kinds of illegal activity not open to the heroin user are those connected with organized crime, such as gambling and loan sharking. Users are not considered reliable enough for work in these fields. They may be used as a lookout for a dice game or policy operation, but that is about as close as they can get to organized criminal operations.

Respite from the arduous life they lead comes to heroin users when they go to jail, to a hospital, or, for some, when they take short-time employment at resort hotels in the mountains. In the present study, it was found that 43 percent of the subjects were in some type of incarceration at any given period of time. In jail they rest, get on a healthy diet, have their medical and dental needs cared for, and engage in relaxed socialization which centers around the facts and folklore of the heroin user's life on the street.

If a user has been making good money on the street, he eventually builds up a tolerance to heroin which gets to the point where he can no longer finance the habit. He may then enter a hospital for detoxification. If he stays the medically recommended period of time—usually three weeks—he can qualify for Department of Welfare assistance, which eases the economic pressures on him when he resumes his heroin-using life on the street. More often than not, however, he will leave the hospital when his tolerance has been significantly lowered, which occurs in about a week.

Some users solve the problems of too much physical and economic pressure which build up periodically by getting temporary employment out of the city, usually in the mountain resort hotels. There are employment agencies in the Bowery and similar districts which specialize in hiring drifters, alcoholics, and drug addicts for temporary work. In the summer, there is a demand for menial laborers in the kitchens and on the grounds of resort hotels. The agencies are so eager to get help during the vacation season that they go to the street to solicit workers. Some of them provide a cheap suitcase and clothes for those who need them. One informant reported about a particular agency man this way: "He'll grab you out of the street. He'll say, 'Do you want a job, son? I'll get you a good job. You want to work up in the country and get fat? You'll eat good food and everything.'" The agency charges the worker a substantial fee, which is taken out of his first check, and makes extra money by providing private transportation at a price higher than the bus fare. The heroin user usually works through one pay period and returns to the city somewhat

more healthy, with a low heroin tolerance, and with a few dollars in his pocket.

It can be seen from the account in this section that the street heroin user is an active, busy person, preoccupied primarily with the economic necessities of maintaining his real income—heroin. A research subject expressed the more mundane gratifications of his life this way:

> When I'm on the way home with the bag safely in my pocket, and I haven't been caught stealing all day, and I didn't get beat, and the cops didn't get me—I feel like a working man coming home; he's worked hard, but he knows he done something, even though I know it's not true.

Conclusions

Heroin use today by lower-class, primarily minority-group, persons does not provide for them a euphoric escape from the psychological and social problems which derive from ghetto life. On the contrary, it provides a motivation and rationale for the pursuit of a meaningful life, albeit a socially deviant one. The activities these individuals engage in, and the relationships they have in the course of their quest for heroin, are far more important than the minimal analgesic and euphoric effects of the small amount of heroin available to them. If they can be said to be addicted, it is not so much to heroin as to the entire career of a heroin user. The heroin user is, in a way, like the compulsively hardworking business executive, whose ostensible goal is the acquisition of money, but whose real satisfaction is in meeting the inordinate challenge he creates for himself. He, too, is driven by a need to find meaning in life which, because of certain deficits and impairments, he cannot find in the normal course of living. A big difference, of course, is that with the street user, the genesis of the deficits and impairments is, to a disproportional degree, in the social conditions of his life.

In the four communities where this research was conducted, the average median family income is $3500, somewhat less than that of family Welfare Department recipients. Other average population characteristics for the four communities include: public welfare recipients—four times the city rate; unemployment—two times the city rate; substandard housing—two times the city rate; no schooling—two times the city rate; median school years completed—eight years. Neither these few statistics nor an exhaustive list could portray the desperation and hopelessness of life in the slums of New York. In one short block where one of the authors worked, there was an average of one violent death a month over a period of three years—by fire, accident, homicide, and suicide. In Puerto Rican neighborhoods, sidewalk *recordatorios* (temporary shrines at the scenes of tragic deaths) are a regular feature.

Given the social conditions of the slums and their effects on family and individual development, the odds are strongly against the development of a legitimate, non-deviant career that is challenging and rewarding. The most common legitimate career is a menial job, with no future except in the periodic, statutory raises in the minimum-wage level. If anyone can be called passive in the slums, it is not the heroin user, but the one who submits to and accepts these conditions.

The career of a heroin user serves a dual purpose for the slum inhabitant; it enables him to escape, not from purposeful activity, but from the monotony of an existence severely limited by social constraints, and, at the same time, it provides a way for him to gain revenge on society for the injustices and deprivation he has experienced. His exploitation of society is carried out with emotional impunity on the grounds, for the most part illusory, that he is *sick* (needs heroin to relieve physical distress), and any action is justified in the interest of keeping himself well. He is free to act out directly his hostility and, at the same time, find gratification, both in the use of the drug and in the sense of accomplishment he gets from performing the many acts necessary to support his heroin use. Commenting on the value of narcotic-maintenance programs, where addicts are maintained legally and at no cost on a high level of opiate administration, one informant said:

> The guy feels that all the fun is out of it. You don't have to outslick the cop and other people. This is a sort of vengeance. This gives you a thrill. It's hiding from

them. Where you can go in the drugstore and get a shot, you get high, but it's the same sort of monotony. You are not getting away with anything. The thing is to hide and outslick someone. Drugs is a hell of a game; it gives you a million things to talk about.

This informant was not a newcomer to the use of heroin, but a 30-year-old veteran of fifteen years of heroin use on the street. *Soldiers of fortune* is the way another informant summed up the lives of heroin users.

Not all, but certainly a large majority of, heroin users are in the category, which is the subject of this paper. It is their activities which constitute the social problem which New York City and other urban centers face today. The ultimate solution to the problem, as with all the problems which result from social injustice, lies in the creation of legitimate opportunities for a meaningful life for those who want it. While waiting for the ultimate solution, reparative measures must be taken. There are four major approaches to the treatment and rehabilitation of heroin users: (1) drug treatment (opiate substitutes or antagonists), (2) psychotherapy, (3) existentialist-oriented group self-help (Synanon prototype), (4) educational and vocational training and placement.

To the extent that the observations and conclusions reported in this paper are valid, a treatment and rehabilitation program emphasizing educational and vocational training is indicated for the large majority of heroin users. At the Manhattan State Hospital Drug Addiction Unit, an intensive educational and vocational program, supported by psychological and social treatment methods, has been created in an effort to prepare the patient for a legitimate career which has a future and is rewarding and satisfying. The three-year program is divided into three parts: (1) eight months of education, vocational training, and therapy in the hospital; (2) one month in the night hospital, while working or taking further training in the community during the day; (3) twenty-seven months of aftercare, which includes, where needed, further education and training, vocational placement, and psychological and social counseling. With this opportunity for a comprehensive social reparation, those who have not been too severely damaged by society have a second chance for a legitimate, meaningful life.

References

Chein, Isidor, et al. *The Road to H: Narcotics, Delinquency, and Social Policy*. New York: Basic Books, Inc., 1964.

City of New York, Police Department. Statistical Report: *Narcotics*, 1966.

Cloward, Richard A., and Ohlin, Lloyd E. *Delinquency and Opportunity*. Glencoe, IL: The Free Press, 1960.

Kardiner, Abraham, et al. *The Individual and His Society*. New York: Columbia University Press, 1939.

Malinowski, Bronislaw. *Argonauts of the Western Pacific*. London: Routledge and Kegan Paul Ltd., 1922.

Martin, W. R., Personal Communication, 1967.

Sharoff, Robert, Personal Communication, 1967.

Whyte, W. F. *Street Corner Society*. Chicago: The University of Chicago Press, 1955.

For Discussion

The authors argue that the daily activities in which heroin users are involved create purposeful lives among users, particularly when legitimate educational and work opportunities are limited. However, some heroin users, e.g., physicians, are employed in prestigious careers in which a sense of purpose is derived from their work. How would Preble and Casey explain heroin use among these individuals?

19

Gen-X Junkie

Ethnographic Research With Young White Heroin Users in Washington, D.C.

Todd G. Pierce

In this next article, Todd Pierce uses ethnographic research to study drug users' social networks. He traces the evolution of networks from their formation to their dissolution. By comparing data on young white heroin users with older African American users, Pierce finds important age/ethnic differences in the areas of networks and risk behaviors. He also documents users' perceptions about their own addictions. Pierce's work and his emphasis on social networks demonstrate the importance of understanding subcultural differences when developing effective harm reduction interventions.

Introduction: Research Objectives, Design, and Population

Historically, both ethnographic and epidemiologic research conducted with IDUs [intravenous drug users] focuses on people from poor socioeconomic situations. They are easier to access on the streets, monetary incentives for interview participation is very attractive, the ethnographer can be fit within the IDUs world view (often as an HIV counselor, outreach worker, or case manager), and they are at the most risk for HIV because intravenous drug use or sex-for-crack exchanges are overrepresented in poorer populations.

Beyond the possible political implications, maintaining this exclusive and extended focus (fifteen some-odd years of HIV research with these populations) also limits our theoretical understanding of the nature of networks of IDUs and the gambit of risk behaviors. This project focuses on economi-cally well-off white IDUs or those who grew up in that socioeconomic condition. "Studying up" or "sideways," meaning the study of people with either the same or greater levels of mainstream power (than that of the researcher's), allows us to better understand the range of behaviors we are investigating while also allowing us to create a better cultural comparative model. As Murphy (1987) points out, IDUs can be found in every part of our society, not just the inner city.

Ethnographic data for this study were based on a network analysis of the IDUs. These networks of IDUs were extracted from larger complex units of social analysis: metropolitan areas, suburban communities, inner city or downtown club scenes, drug market and use areas, etc. (see Hannerz, 1980: 170–201). The networks were made up of an "extremely complex interlinkage" (Hannerz, 1992: 69) of networks with their own "perspectives" (*ibid.*) or world views on how they structure meaning within their perceived realities. For the purposes of this study, selected network variables (i.e., IDUs, young, white) were sampled for analysis. Network analysis can be a very powerful tool for social sciences (Aldrich, 1982: 293), but to fully understand these networks we must also consider the interlinking networks that make up the sampled networks (i.e., the wider communities from which the network members come, their histories, economies, and so on) and must analyze both the group and individual levels within their social and cultural contexts (Curtis et al., 1995; see also Bolt, 1957; Mitchell, 1969; Barnes, 1972).

The core sample for this study was drawn from a snowball sampling design and consisted of 12 white intravenous drug users (six male/six female) ranging in ages from 19 to 31. The snowball sample was achieved through the ethnographer's networking through the social networks of the IDUs first, and then introduced to the IDUs from their friends and other IDUs. The typical scenario would occur over a game of eight ball (pool) where the ethnographer's opponent would ask what the ethnographer did for a living, and then when told that he studied heroin users, the opponent would say "Oh, I have a friend that you should meet. He's a junkie." Then the ethnographer would give the opponent his business card and tell him to give it to the friend to arrange for a meeting.

In total, 12 egocentric networks were studied. The sample of networks contained two or three core or main members as well as periphery and outer periphery members. Primary analysis for each network was based on dyadic and triadic core relationships within each network (Neaigus et al., 1995). Each network had members that connected one network to the next (a "bridger"). Bridged networks contained white, black, and Hispanic members. Most of the 12 IDUs in the main sample came from a white, suburban, middle- or upper-middle-class background. Several were from very "well-off" families. All had at least a high school education, while some had either a four-year college degree or some college. Other individuals in the study included eight who were either heroin or cocaine snorters, cocaine injectors, or rehabilitated heroin injectors. In addition to these eight, about 25 peripheral network members were included in the study. These members were part of the social environment of the 12 core IDUs and were either cocaine snorters or sexual conjugates (sex partners) of the core. The individuals and the networks studied were part of extremely complex micro- and macro-cultural formations, which in turn influenced their drug-use behaviors (see Grund et al., 1991; Singer et al., 1992; Watters, 1988, 1989).

Through intensive participant observation, the ethnographer accessed drug users within the music and club "scene" of Washington, DC, and created relationships with several heroin IDUs, which led to the meeting of other IDUs (the snowball). Ultimately, he was exposed to a multitude of aspects of the users' lives. These aspects included the activities and rituals of club life, after-hours bars, pool halls, family life and relations, sexual relationships, friendships, and involvement with the drug economy and other users.

All subjects for this project were informed of the ethnographer's research objectives and were guaranteed confidentiality. Almost all of the subjects for the study admitted to wanting to participate because of the money offered for the interviews, but later came to rather enjoy working with the ethnographer.

After a time the ethnographer and the subjects became close friends and colleagues, working together in this ethnograph[ic] endeavor.

Research Methodology

A variety of ethnographic research methods were employed at different levels throughout the research. All methods were embedded within the context of intensive participant observation. The ethnographer participated in all life activities with most of the research subjects, save for drug use, though he did drink alcohol. An average of 50 hours of participant observation were conducted every week for approximately 104 weeks. The ethnographer often ate, slept, and socialized at the informants' houses, as did the informants at the ethnographer's house. Toward the end of the research project, several subjects divulged their addictions to their families. Because the ethnographer knew the families, the subjects also told them what the ethnographer was up to. This compromised the ethnographer's research status, since the proverbial cat had been let out of the bag. But, in fact, this actually aided the family because they were able to talk to the ethnographer about addiction and were happy their family member was working with him. It aided in creating an open and respectful relationship for all parties concerned.

Life histories (Langness, 1965; see also Langness and Frank, 1981; Kroeber, 1961) were obtained from all of the core sample members. These interviews typically lasted two to three hours and were conducted either at the ethnographer's office, home, or a coffee shop. The respondents were paid $30 to $40 for the interview, depending on how long it took to do. The interviews investigated the respondent's life from birth to the present, covering all aspects of life, and focusing on drug use as it occurred.

Even recall interviews (Agar, 1980) were utilized to elicit data on past injection events to establish a self-report record of injection behaviors, their contexts, and network dynamics. The event recalls attempted to reconstruct specific events or instances within the respondent's recent life history. These interviews were conducted in coordination with the life histories and took place at the same time/place. Directed observations (developed for the Needle Hygiene Project but modified to include network-focused data collection for this project) (see Note 1) of injection events (see Note 2) were conducted with individual and multiperson injection events to record personal and network-based injection rituals. These observations were performed within the natural contexts of the individual's and network's injection locations. The observations aimed at data on network dynamics, needle hygiene practices, and other injection behaviors as they occurred within different times and spaces so as to capture variations on the injection theme in relation to contexts. All observational data were recorded in tables designed specifically for this task (previously utilized for the Needle Hygiene Project) and within field notes for future analysis.

Network plots, or diagrams that illustrate network connections and relations, were created with each informant. These plots depicted network membership, relationships, positions within other cultural and behavioral realms, and relations within socioeconomic structures (including relations within the drug economy and supply of drugs and needles). These plots were updated periodically and when changes occurred within the networks. Informants regularly aided the ethnographer in keeping track of the plots and verified field note data for him during sporadic and periodic follow-up sessions as a means of ensuring data reliability and to check the validity of data. Also, a comparative model was used within the analysis so as to help establish differences and ranges in behaviors and meanings within and between different types of networks. Different young white networks were compared for variations in structure, formation, changes over time, and possible dissolution. Also, the young white networks were compared to older black IDU networks on which data had also been collected during the same years (see Note 3). These black networks offered completely different structural dynamics than the white, which aided in creating a range of possibilities for comparisons. The exact same research methods were used with all networks. These comparisons will be utilized throughout the network descriptions to illustrate distinct differences between certain network characteristics and behaviors.

Network Attributes: Formation, Change, and Dissolution

Network Formation

When studying the creation of an IDU network, you must first ask whether networks formed before or after drug use were put into the mix. In most cases the networks studied in DC turned to injecting drugs after network formation. This point is central for our understanding of risk networks because it helps us better understand the foundations of the network itself (thus a better understanding of the risk relations). In most cases the network members knew each other and had a relationship prior to drug use. Those who did not know their network before "using" acquired them after accessing key roles within their drug environment (i.e., drug running).

What was discovered in DC was that there were two general ways young white IDU networks formed. The first was a network relationship that stemmed from long-term friendships. The second was centered around IDUs that had an ability to cop dope successfully.

Cindy's network is a good example of a long-term friendship network. Her network had three main members who were IDUs, one of which was her boyfriend (her main sex partner). She also had a number of other sexual partners who were part of her network, but they were not IDUs. The main members of the network, Cindy (age 20), her boyfriend Jimmy (age 31), and her best friend Sandy (age 19), had had a relationship before shooting up together. Cindy and Sandy had known each other since the age of 13 or 14. They had literally grown up together and had been hanging out in the rock and roll "scene" since their early teenage years. Cindy had started injecting with one of her boyfriends when she was in her late teens. Sandy had acquired a snorting habit by using with several of her friends, but then asked Cindy to help her in administering her first injection. The ethnographer witnessed her first injection (Pierce, forthcoming: 1), and interviewed Sandy the next day to discuss the event, and why she did it with Cindy:

> She's (Cindy) been an intravenous drug user for years, and she never wanted me to, she wouldn't, we hadn't done heroin together. We never have done heroin together until this [past] weekend, because she doesn't want me to get like her, she doesn't want me to shoot up heroin. She doesn't like this, but she saw that I was going to do it anyway. And she's lonely, really. She's very lonely. She's got her boyfriend, and he's not very nice to her, and she kind of didn't want me to do it, but she really like, I mean that's what she told me afterwards. She said "I really enjoy doing this with you, even though it's very bad." Then she's like "Okay, fine. Let's get the heroin, let's get the needles. We'll do this." She taught me how to do it. I've seen it done before, I just never went that step until this weekend. (Pierce Interview: WX: 14)

This scenario was common for most of the users in the study. In fact, all of the users [were] "turned on" to injection through a friend who was using. In such cases the formation of both young white and black injection networks came from much deeper sociocultural roots, i.e., neighborhood communities or schoolmates, than simply the need to inject. People are generally social beings, and form networks within their lives to satisfy different social needs they have (i.e., feeling accepted, belonging, loved). Different networks fulfill different needs. Some networks, like the family, may fulfill a need for stability or safety, others may be for advancement of knowledge, or adventure. Like many social activities, the first time one does something, it is usually done with somebody else who can experience it with you or show you how to do it.

In order to bring a network analysis to a deeper level here, we ask why and how people associate with each other in different cultural surroundings. Though anthropologists and sociologists alike have tackled this issue in some depth (indeed, historically this has been the mission of both disciplines), the topic cannot be given the proper attention in this discussion. But the bottom line is that most people do not experiment with heroin or start injecting it on their own. They are brought into a risk network of current users or they create a network of experimental users who eventually develop substantial habits (see Note 4). In order to fully understand the creation and the dynamics of a network, one must first understand the nature of its formation.

With experimentation come new experiences and the feelings and knowledge that come with them. The evolution of a person's drug addiction is a learning process that is often learned with their network, but also on their own through trial and error. Sandy explains for us the feelings she had about injecting heroin as opposed to just snorting it:

> I'm used to needles because I have a bad history with asthma, and I'm just used to needles from getting blood drawn, and whatever, and I find it kind of . . . it's hard to explain, it's a lot more sexy, almost. It's a lot more, you're really getting into the whole feel of the high. It's part of . . . the preparation's almost like, it's an anticipation . . . you're not just spreading a few lines out and snorting it this time. You're now cooking it and you're putting a needle in your vein. It's, if you have time to kind of sit there and do it, like have the whole symbolism thing, it's, it makes it a lot more impressive in your mind. It's uh, I don't, it's hard to explain. It's almost a fun thing, but it's not fun. I mean the pain of the needle, or whatever, that's not fun, but it's, you've got these little toys to play with, and you've got all this stuff that you have, that's illegal. And if you get caught, you feel like shit with it, but when you have it, it's almost like it's, it's more . . . almost like a toy . . . drugs. To play with, I don't know, it's not a happy thing, if you really think about it, but it gets you really excited about the whole thing and it's fun. . . . It's almost like a permanent thing in your mind. You're really going to get high. It's really happening, you're really getting prepared for this whole thing, things like that, it's just the whole anticipation of getting high. You've got to do all [these things], it's part of the whole process. (Pierce Interview: WX: 14)

How these new experiences are discussed and learned within a network and certain socioeconomic contexts are important for understanding the injection processes, the personal nature and the social nature of the drug-using rituals (see Note 5). Also, the behavior that is learned through trial and error as an individual IDU builds a habit is important because it illustrates how some behaviors are not taught or discussed. Many aspects of drug misuse were not discussed by network members, such as morning sickness from withdrawal symptoms. In one discussion with the ethnographer, early on in her addiction, Sandy had described having a headache all day long. The ethnographer asked her how much dope she was using. She replied "three or four bags a night." Essentially, she was binging on heroin, but only at night instead of a constant stream of use throughout the day. And she was unaware of the detox effects occurring in the morning. Nobody from her network had told her! Even though her network members were very experienced users. In fact, it was the ethnographer who had to educate her on her biophysical reactions to the drugs. "Man, you just don't know why you have these headaches all day do you? You're dope sick!" She was horrified upon learning this. It was as if the reality of her level of use had just set in. That's when her long uphill struggle to recovery started, after the fact. A few days after learning this she told the ethnographer her headaches were all better, now she "got off E" (see Note 6) in the morning with that coveted first shot of dope for the day.

This transference of cultural information (or lack of it) is important for understanding risk reduction in injection behaviors because it tells us how people learn (or do not learn) certain behavioral procedures for injecting drugs. And, to make matters more complicated, this transference of information happens differently for all subpopulations or microcultures.

The second type of network formation is centered around copping dope. Young, new, white IDUs generally have a lot of difficulty trying to cop dope off the street. They fall prey to more experienced IDUs who will "take" them for all they are worth. They are literally sitting ducks for a "hard-core" street junkie who knows the ropes. Also, dealers do not trust people whom they do not know well, and so will be reluctant to sell to them. Therefore, the young white user must earn

his stripes on the streets by going through a series of rip-offs and takes, gaining access to a runner, and then establishing a steady relationship. Not all young white IDUs can or want to do this. It is a risky endeavor, and the stakes are high when playing the street game. Only a few users from this study were any good at copping their own dope; even fewer held the highly respected runner position.

What this meant was that users who were not very adept at copping for themselves sought out users who could do that for them (for a small fee, usually in the form of money or drugs). In the first type of network formation discussed earlier, the network members were forced to go through trial and error routines in order to cop. In most cases only one of the members would do the copping for the entire network. Some of these successful buyers would find routes to copping other than the streets, like a dealer at a night club or an acquaintance from another network who had access to the drug. If a trusting relationship could be established with that acquaintance, then maybe the buyer and his or her network would join up with the runner's network, thus expanding the network based on the need for drugs (on the seeker's side), the need for money (on the runner's side), and trust. The runner then becomes the bridger of the two networks (the runner's own network and that of the seeker).

A good example of such network formation was Ken's, a 25-year-old white male, with long brown hair and tattoos. He's a musician, works at different clubs as a doorman, and plays a good game of pool. He is the center of his network because he is a drug runner. He was taught how to deal drugs by an older black man (Q) who had been running drugs for about 20 years, and who is also part of Ken's network. Ken has six network members, both male and female; all are white except for Q. His network members are not only customers for drugs, but they are also friends. He has known many of them for several years and socializes with them outside the context of injecting or scoring drugs. Although they pay him either in drugs or money for helping them score, the relationship doesn't stop there.

They will often eat meals together, stay at each other's apartments, go out on the town together, etc.

Ken is a bridger to Q's network, which consists of about 30 people from different ethnic and socioeconomic backgrounds. Although Ken has injected with Q at Ken's apartment (which doubles as an exclusive shooting gallery), there is no risk of HIV infection between the two men or the two networks. This is because there is no direct or indirect sharing occurring during injection episodes. In networks that do directly or indirectly share drug-use equipment, bridgers can be a very high-risk agent for the network members because they can spread the virus from one network to the next. But because Ken's network is very safe in their drug-use behaviors, there is no (or extremely low) risk of infection.

There are other ways that networks form as well, most of which happen by the pure chance of being at the same place at the same time. A good example of this might be if one user sees another trying to cop some dope on the street and decides to approach the person to either aid in copping or to maybe ask if the person knows where they can get a good deal. They might even go as far as to pool their money in an attempt to cop a higher quantity of dope. This is rare, but it does happen.

IDUs from the study also reported making contacts at methadone clinics and NA meetings. In these environs it might be more risky to approach somebody because they are all supposed to be cleaning up. But they usually can tell if somebody is high, and so they approach them anyway. DC does not have a needle exchange program, and needles cannot be legally purchased without a prescription (a topic that will be covered later). But IDUs that I have worked with in Hartford, Connecticut, have reported making network connections at needle exchange points (see Note 7). These connections are usually for the purpose of locating "good dope" rather than network expansion per se.

A nice example of how networks are created can be drawn from the ethnographer's own experiences when meeting the respondents for this project. The ethnographer was not familiar with DC nor its drug scene. He did not know anybody when he moved into town, but found in-roads to one or two IDUs located within the alternative punk scene (see Note 8) (from which the ethnographer himself hails). These in-roads occurred within the social networks of the IDUs and through participating in social activities (like pool, as described earlier). The ethnographer then had those IDUs introduce him to other IDUs in their network, or members of other networks. The chain of people made up the sample for the study: it is not much different for an IDU who moves into town and doesn't know anybody, let alone other IDUs. This sort of network begins with a superficial "weak link" or peripheral connection within a network (as opposed to long-term "core" connections like Cindy and Sandy's), but that changes over time as relationships are developed.

The differences found between the way younger white risk networks formed in comparison to older African American networks is revealing. Most of the black IDUs studied had grown up in neighborhoods with a long history of drug economies. Many had relatives working within that economy as drug dealers, hustlers of some sort, and users. Their neighborhoods were inundated with drugs, and they quickly learned what it was all about at a young age. Many of the black IDUs had histories of incarceration because of their dealings with the drug market. Many of the users (almost all of them) had grown up knowing each other, but had entered the drug scene at different points in their lives. Their networks were much larger than the whites, yet they tended to have a small core network in which they created relationships based on either sexual relations or hustling schemes. The number of people they might inject with is much higher and changes more rapidly, but those people appear to be drawn from a limited number of people within their neighborhood.

The young white IDUs, in contrast, tend to come from suburban communities that do not have a visible active drug economy of nearly the scale that is found in poorer urban neighborhoods. They learn about drugs in their teenage years, and in many cases pass through a series of drugs before ending up on heroin (see Note 9). Their networks are small, with only a few people at the core (close sexual relations and best friends), and those networks are usually formed around trying to cop dope. They do not cop in their home neighborhoods (dealers are hard to find in Bethesda, MD), they do not use them frequently, and they have very few run-ins with the law.

In sum, one critical difference between the black low-income (or informal economy incomes only) networks and white middle-class networks was that the black networks were focused on getting money to buy the dope (they knew exactly how to go about getting it, but couldn't afford it), while the whites were focused on purchasing it (they had sufficient economic means to afford it, but were not good at getting it). Exact opposites in that respect, but both working for the same goal: Dope.

Network Changes

Networks were tracked over time to examine changes in size, relationships, risk behavior, and drug-use activities such as copping and connections within the street economy. The core of the networks changed very little. When it did, it was often spurred on by one of the members cleaning up off drugs (rehabilitating) or through changes within relationships, e.g., two or more of the network members might get into a dispute over some topic, maybe over drugs or some other social issue. Over the one year of the study, the IDUs became better at copping for themselves as well as better at finding sources of new needles.

When rehabilitation of a person occurs, it can cause the network to splinter into two or more separate groups, depending on that person's role within the network. Ken's group is a good example of this sort of splintering. Ken cleaned up about halfway through the study. This caused his network members to form three different networks with other IDUs or primary dyadic relations. As soon as Ken is taken out of the picture, a drastic change occurs as the remaining members scramble for resources. Because Ken was the main drug supply for many of the network members, they now had to find their own way to cop drugs. To lessen this burden, Ken gave several of the network

members the information and phone numbers they would need to cop the drugs.

Each of the members still consider Ken a friend, but he "had to do what he had to do," which meant clean up. But they were then stuck for another way to get drugs. Also, the members reverted to their main partners as a core network for support. The network did not actually dissolve completely; it just changed on a drug-use level.

As discussed earlier, networks also change as the members meet other people who can cop for them or offer something the network can use, i.e., money. This brings us back full circle to network formation. Networks also change when members move to other cities. In most cases the original network is kept while members from the new location are added on, thus making the IDU who moved a bridger of two networks. This happened with Cindy's network. She moved with her boyfriend to a beach in Virginia where they created a large network for whom they ran drugs from DC. They would drive back and forth in her sports car every couple of days on drug runs. Cindy hid the 10 packs of dope in a condom that she inserted into her vagina, just in case the police pulled them over. This new "beach" network was abandoned as soon as the summer was over and Cindy moved back to DC.

Network Dissolution

The most drastic change that any network can go through is total dissolution. This can happen through extreme splintering or when all or most of the network members quit using drugs (kick, clean up, rehabilitate, etc.). This happened with Cindy's network. By the end of the study Cindy and Sandy had cleaned up, Cindy had broken up with her boyfriend, and all other members had been dropped, save for a few sex partners (who changed every couple of months). Her boyfriend continued to use, but with a new network. In Cindy's network case, two of the three main or core members had cleaned up, and this caused the network to dissolve completely. Although the network may have been created before any of the members were IDUs (meaning long-term friendship-based nets), upon dissolution those ties were in most cases severed as well. Many of the IDUs had to change their social environments in order to stay clean, which meant getting rid of old friends and the places they socialized at. Cindy's boyfriend was cut out of the picture completely, but Sandy was kept as a friend because they were trying to clean up together. Even though they remained friends, they did not socialize together as much as they used to. They both began to rebuild their lives separately by creating new networks of friends and relationships.

Another network that dissolved was centered around a 25-year-old woman named Carol and her 22-year-old boyfriend Jim. They had three main members to their network and several not so important members. In this network's case the main core people were very different in terms of social status. Carol had a B.A. in philosophy and was very driven toward an upwardly mobile lifestyle, while her boyfriend was an untrained artist who also played the drums and was using drugs at a higher rate than Carol. Jim lived at an apartment that was paid for by his mother's husband (stepfather), but was thrown out after he had attempted suicide. The stepfather thought it was bad for his image to have the stepson around, so he evicted him.

When Jim moved to a homeless shelter, he and Carol (who was living with her parents) decided they should kick their habits. In short, Carol was able to kick and he was not, even though they were both taking methadone. This caused a tremendous strain on their love relationship, and ultimately ended in dissolution of the relationship. During their attempt at kicking they had severed ties with the other network members, at least that is what Carol thought. Jim continued contact with several of them after they had supposedly broken up. She discovered this and eventually left town so that she could be away from the environment completely. In this case the core members of the network changed, the dynamics of the network changed, and a different network was maintained by one of the original core members. This is not a case of splintering, but rather a reorganization.

Drug Use Behaviors: Needle Procurement, Needle Hygiene, and HIV Risk

Unlike most IDU subpopulations, the young white IDUs in this study were extremely safe users. As noted by many researchers, seropositivity levels will vary from population to population based on several factors (Price et al., 1995; see also Allen et al., 1992; Berkelman et al., 1989; Des Jarlais et al., 1988; Quinn et al., 1989; Siegal et al., 1991). Actual seropositivity data for the sample networks were not gathered. Self-report data indicated that only one member of the study was HIV-positive, but he did not directly or indirectly share any of his drug-use paraphernalia. In fact, there was almost no direct or indirect sharing of syringes or drug-use equipment observed within any of the direct observations of injection events of the networks. Most of the IDUs studied have the resources to buy their own bags of dope, which decreases the chance of indirect sharing occurring. And because most come from a well-educated and well-off economic background, they have had access to a wealth of information about HIV, safe sex, safe drug use, and safe cleaning practices. Basic concepts of viral transmission were well known by all of the IDUs studied, which made them very conscious of their behaviors.

The young white subpopulation worked with might be considered sexually liberal due to the high rate of sexual partners they had. Several of the participants had an average of one new partner a month, in many cases they had co-occurring sexual relationships (affairs or multiple partners), and in some cases there were group sexual encounters (two men and one woman, or two women and one man). These cases usually occurred when the participants were intoxicated (drunk), but were reportedly consensual events. New partners or new sexual adventures were always reported to the ethnographer as if they were telling stories of a great hunting expedition. One informant, Cindy, would even run up to the ethnographer with a smile and say, "I have a new one for my network plot!" And 9 times out of 10 she meant a new sexual partner. Although most are aware of and practice safe sex, there were many reports of unsafe sex, usually during sex when drunk.

Syringe procurement was usually done by buying the needles off the street or from a pharmacy. Although the latter is not legal in DC (you must have a prescription), it was easily done by a well-dressed young white person. The typical scenario was that the IDU cleaned themselves up, dressed up in their finest clothes, and came up with a line for why they needed the needles. One informant (Carol) said she needed them to inject vitamin B. In most cases the pharmacist took the line and made them sign a waver, releasing the pharmacy of any legal responsibilities they might have for selling the works to someone without a prescription.

When purchasing on the street, young white IDUs have to trek into some pretty rough areas to find sellers. A large network of black sellers (the network discussed above in the discussion on network formation) sold works as their hustle. Most of the works they sell are new and in sealed packages. But in some cases they will use the needles and then try to sell them as new, without cleaning them first. This is looked down upon by most sellers, and they will often yell at those who do. It is considered a very bad thing to do, even among other needle sellers. But it does happen, which puts the young white user at risk when purchasing a needle from the street.

Awareness of needle hygiene and hygienic drug use is well known among this population. It is enforced by many of them in conversation and in practice. One of the networks worked with had an HIV-positive member who had contracted HIV from sharing needles in the 1980s. He was an older IDU, but was very aware of his HIV status and so made sure he did not share liquids or syringes with anybody else. He did not disclose his status to anybody besides the ethnographer, but promoted safe use within his network ". . . because it's the right thing to do." As discussed earlier, direct sharing was extremely rare within the white networks that were observed. In fact, the only direct sharing observed was between two core members of a network that had two outer periph-

ery members within it as well. This core is made up of a 31-year-old man named Tim and his 22-year-old girlfriend Lucy. They keep their own sets of works, but they get them mixed up on occasion.

Because they divide their bags of dope in liquid (they are a live-in couple and pool all resources), they do partake in indirect sharing. They also have unprotected sex. This does not create any real risks for them or their network because it is a contained sharing of fluids. They do not indirectly or directly share with anybody else, nor do they routinely have sex with other people (Lucy does have sex with other women on occasion). This would place her at some small risk of HIV transmission, in which case, if infected, she could then infect Tim. This is a possible risk, but slim in comparison to other risky behaviors (such as unprotected vaginal or anal sex and sharing needles). In sum, young white IDUs were found to be at little risk for HIV in comparison to older black IDU networks. This had a lot to do with socioeconomic and educational levels as well as the level of drug use. While indirect sharing (through the sharing of cookers, cottons, or rinse water) is almost nonexistent in this population, it is the norm within the older black population. While direct sharing of syringes/needles is close to nil within the younger white population, it does happen on occasions within the older black networks.

Level of drug use and economic resources are key to understanding the differences between different types of IDU risk networks. The young white users who began to build up substantial heroin habits began to use up more than their economic resources could support. This eventually made them have to rely on street hustles to get by. By that time, when they had used their other resources, they had potentially gained access to dealers for whom they could run drugs. This helped them carry their habits for a while longer. That, too, would only last so long before they exceeded that resource. Then they were left to the streets with virtually no knowledge of the cultures of the street economy, and so they became prey to those who are accustomed to it, i.e., those who are from a poorer socioeconomic condition and who are very familiar with the streets. When this happens to young white middle-class heroin users, it is usually time for them to kick.

Kicking the Dope: Economic Loss, Cultural Stresses, and Transitions

Heroin addiction has taken on many cultural symbols within the larger part of American society, both in the way it is imagined and in the ways we have treated it. These symbols are utilized by the user and the non-user alike when discussing drug use and addiction. A young white heroin user's addiction is commonly couched within a context of personal trauma or depression. It is the saddened "rock star" or the depressed inner turmoil of the teenager. Their pain is imagined as being inner pain, with psychological issues that must be addressed. A poor black user's addiction is often discussed in relation to larger exterior circumstances. He or she is often discussed in terms of systemic poverty and institutionalized racism. The "system" has gone wrong, not the addict. This is a terribly interesting and important fact, and must be kept in mind when studying these sorts of microcultures. The users at both ends of the economic spectrum will often use this discourse. The white users often referred to personal problems in their lives that led them to drug use. The black users often referred to a lack of jobs and opportunities and to poverty as being causes of their drug addictions.

Also, the way in which heroin addiction is discussed and illustrated by the popular media and academia reflects the same discourse used by the addicts themselves (see Note 9). It is common to see writings on heroin addiction (or drug addiction in general) among minorities being represented with statistics and graphical charts. This is a depersonalized way of representing real people. On the other hand, young white addicts are often represented, especially in the media, through documentaries in a journalistic style—very personal, very tragic. Interestingly enough, the users do read these types of reports or are at least familiar with the discourse, and mimic its rhetoric. This is the mimetic process that Taussig describes (1993) that often leads to mimetic excess: copies of copies of copies, for which there is

no original. We are left only with creations of perceived realities controlled through specific discourses (e.g., journalism, social or medical sciences, anthropology, etc.).

Understanding how an addict perceives his or her addiction, how and why they became an addict, is important for trying to understand why they want to clean up, and how they do it.

Cleaning up off a heroin habit is an interesting topic because it relates to all the topics discussed above: The reasons why networks form, their changes, their dissolution, their risk behaviors, etc. What was discovered through watching several of the younger white IDUs enlarge their habit size was that they went through the phases of use and economic support discussed above, but they had also undergone stresses as they underwent transitions from the white suburban life they grew up with and knew so well to the urban ghetto and the street-based economies of the drug world. The users were quickly losing parts of their "selves" as the different cultural roles that created them, i.e., the student, the daughter or son, the champion horse rider, the hard worker, the brother or sister, etc., began to slip away as the drugs took over their lives (chemically, socially). They slowly but surely moved closer to the street environment, to the home of "the real junkies," the hardened street addict that researchers of today are so familiar with. They didn't realize that these street junkies were no different than themselves, just better at surviving within their own environment.

Beyond being traumatic to the young white user emotionally, heading to the street life can often be deadly as they do the wrong things in the street because they don't know the proper roles in that environment. Also, they must learn the street way of using, where you do NOT divide bags of dope in powder form because you might end up ripping someone else off of their 0.02 cc of dope or end up with less cut than them. Thus the users now find themselves in a world of higher risk for HIV and no way to get out, except to kick.

In most cases kicking came well before that point, not because they couldn't afford the drugs. Rather, it was also personal stresses that caused the kick. The fear of losing friends, family, and social status was enough stress to force the IDUs to clean up. These cultural and social forces can be a powerful influence in a person's life, more powerful than dope. When these things are slowly being torn away, and the user sees himself or herself changing both physically and culturally, it scares the living daylights out of them. And when the next stop is some street corner or a shooting gallery, it's often enough to help them try to kick. Although many of the white IDUs had visited such locations, it was only because they were trying to cop. But they were not part of that scene, and they didn't know how to act or play the role when there.

Kicking dope happened a lot with the young white IDUs in the study. Many of them had attempted it numerous times with some success. They might stay clean for a few months, half a year, maybe a few years. But then they'd end up using again, building a habit, losing cultural identities, running short of money, and then kicking completely or ending up on the streets. In most cases kicking was done informally, without knowledge of their habit or cleanup being divulged to anyone outside their drug use and close social networks. This was either done through "chipping" one's way down to detox (meaning they used less and less each day), the straight kick (no drugs to help the pain of withdrawal), or they used drugs purchased on the street to ease the pain of the kick (drugs that help you sleep it off were preferable). The ethnographer aided several IDUs who asked him to help them kick. One stayed at his apartment during the initial kick.

Compared to the older black IDUs, the younger white IDUs attempted kicking much more. The process of using, stresses, and kicking discussed above occurred rapidly and multiple times for most, while the older black IDUs were able to maintain a consistent habit for up to 20 years. This is because they have a limited economic resource that is determined, by and large, by their particular hustle. For instance, a needle seller knows he can sell only so many needles in a day, and so he pretty much knows how much dope he will be able to shoot in a day. This amount may vary on "good" days, but it is pretty constant. The white user, on the other hand, will build a large habit quickly, and thus he or she will "crash and burn" quickly, which leads to the repeated kicks. Many of the older black IDUs talk about wanting to kick, but because they are from the streets they do not feel the cultural stresses that might influence a kick attempt at the same level by the younger whites. Many of the older black IDUs kicked only when forced to do so by the law (either when locked up or forced into a rehab clinic for a 21-day detoxification).

Recommendations: Understanding Variation in Networks and HIV Risk

This research with young white IDUs offers the drug research and HIV intervention fields several insights. For one, through an ethnographic approach to network analysis, one that not only includes risk relations but also socioeconomic and cultural variables, we can better understand the possible range of HIV risk-related behaviors among injection drug users. Also, through an understanding of the different processes IDUs from different socioeconomic backgrounds go through within their histories of drug use, we can better understand the root causes of drug addiction and rehabilitation.

Future ethnographic research with IDUs should attempt to create more culturally comparative research models that analyze networks across different ethnic, gender, and socioeconomic ranges. This will help assist harm reduction and HIV prevention more effectively because it will allow us to better understand the finer points and differences in drug addiction, drug-use behaviors, and HIV risk.

Notes

1. The Needle Hygiene Project (NHP) was a seven-city ethnographic study that was conducted in 1993. The methodology for this project demanded that the ethnographers be able to collect comparative data across all sites. To do this, the ethnographers utilized a method they developed called "directed observation" of injection drug use behaviors. Todd Pierce, M.A., Michael Clatts, Ph.D., Steve Koester, Ph.D., and Laurie Price, Ph.D., developed this method and the NIDA Field Manual for this seven-city project.

2. An injection event is defined as the observed time of injection behaviors. The parameters of the event are determined by the ethnographer's presence at the location of the behaviors (i.e., shooting galleries). The event can be brief or several hours long, and may include several actual injection "episodes." Data collected for "events" include the

macro- and microlevel environmental situation of the event (i.e., location, time of day, police presence), how the money for drugs and syringe were obtained (the "hustle"), how drugs and injection equipment were actually obtained, how they were used, and by whom, throughout the event, and disposal of equipment, as well as all microcultural dynamics of the users in the event (power relations, etc.).

3. Twenty egocentric black networks (10 male/10 female) were studied for this project, forming four separate clusters of networks. The exact same ethnographic methods used for data collection on the whites were also used for the blacks and Latinos that were part of the study. The Latinos from the study are not discussed in this article. In DC, Latino IDUs are uncommon, and were often bridgers or peripheral members of either black or white networks.

4. I am making a generalization across all types of heroin users and injection networks here—white, black, and Latino. Although there may be cases of individuals using on their own, it is very rare that they started using alone at the start of their injection use. It is also rare that they continue to use alone. Many "older" or seasoned IDUs will report being "loners," but with only a little ethnographic investigating it is found that they indeed have an extensive network of people they use with on occasion.

5. I am not supporting the "gateway" theoretical discussions here. On the contrary, there is an incredible difference between smoking marijuana and injecting heroin. Unfortunately, there is neither the time nor space to debate this topic within this text. One suggestion I can propose for this debate would be to consider gateway networks as a key factor in drug misuse. Social networks, including drug use networks, do not form due to a predetermined or acquired biophysical condition, i.e., drug misuse and the biochemical changes the brain goes through with this "disease." This can be illustrated by my argument that most first-time experiences an individual has usually occur with someone else (smoking, drinking, sex, dancing, eating, and so on). The jury is still out on the genetically predetermined drug addict, which is also used in the gateway discourse. To that end of the debate I would have to pose the question: Is it because one or both parents were addicts, or was it growing up in an environment of addicts where the youth is constantly surrounded with their behavioral routines?

6. "Get off E" is to satisfy the "craving" for heroin. The term is allegorical to a car that has an empty gasoline tank.

7. Research in Hartford, Connecticut, was conducted during 1990–1994 under the direction of Merrill Singer, Ph.D., at The Hispanic Health Council of Hartford, Connecticut, funded by HIN for the NIDA Cooperative Agreement and Needle Hygiene Project.

8. The "alternative" punk scene refers to the punk rock microcultures that had developed during the early 1970s and had developed and changed throughout the 80s and 90s. Although these microcultures (Hannerz, 1992) differ in many ways, there are some common links in ideologies and cultural material (i.e., music, clothing style).

9. For popular representations of heroin addiction, see the texts *Junky* by W. S. Burroughs (1977) (which was first published as *Junkie* under the pen name William Lee). Also, see the writings of Jim Carroll [*The Basketball Diaries*, (1987) and *Forced Entries* (1987)]. For recent articles in popular magazines, refer to *Details*, April 1996, pp. 68–70, "Love in Vein"; or *Newsweek*, August 1996 lifestyle report, "Rockers, Models, and the *New* Allure of Heroin" (emphasis added). From 1988 to 1997 a slew of major motion pictures were produced that either directly or indirectly illustrated the junky lifestyle. Also, on any given day in America you can see portrayals of junked-out models on the nod in blue jeans and perfume commercials. Heroin chic!

References

Agar, M. (1980) *The Professional Stranger: An Informal Introduction to Ethnography*. New York: Academic Press.

Aldrich, H. (1982) "The origins and persistence of social networks." In Marsden and Man (eds.), *Social Structure and Network Analysis*. Beverly Hills, CA: Sage.

Allen, D. M., Onorato, I. M., Green, T. A.; and the Field Service Branch of the CDC (1992) "HIV infection in intravenous drug users entering drug treatment, United States 1988 to 1989," *Am. J. Public Health* 82: 541–546.

Barnes, J. (1972) *Social Networks*. Reading, MA: Addison-Wesley.

Berkelman, R. L., Heyward, W. L., Stehr-Green, J. K., and Curran, J. W. (1989) "Epidemiology of human immunodeficiency virus infection and acquired immunodeficiency syndrome," *Am. J. Med.* 86: 761–770.

Bolt, E. (1957) *Family and Social Network. Roles, Norms, and External Relationships in Ordinary Urban Families*. London: Tavistock.

Burroughs, W. S. (1953) *Junky*. New York: Penguin Books, Ace Books, 1977.

Carroll, J. (1987a). *The Basketball Diaries. The Classic About Growing Up Hip on New York's Mean Streets*. New York: Penguin Books.

——. (1987) *Forced Entries: The Downtown Diaries: 1971–1973*. New York: Penguin Books.

Curtis, R., Freedman, S., Neaigus, A., Jose, B., Goldstein, M., and Ildefonso, G. (1995) "Street-level drug markets: Network structure and HIV risk," *Soc. Networks* 17: 229–249.

Des Jarlais, D. C., Friedman, S. R., and Stroneburner, R. L. (1988) "HIV infection and intravenous drug use: Critical issues in transmission dynamics, infection outcomes, and prevention," *Rev. Infect. Dis.* 10: 151–158.

Grund, J., Kaplan, C., and Adriaans, N. (1991) "Needle sharing in the Netherlands: An ethnographic analysis," *Am. J. Public Health* 81: 1602–1607.

Hannerz, U. (1980) *Exploring the City: Inquiries Toward an Urban Anthropology*. New York: Columbia University Press.

Hannerz, U. (1992) *Cultural Complexity: Studies in the Social Organization of Meaning*. New York: Columbia University Press.

Katel, P., and Hager, M. (1996) "Rockers, models and the new allure of heroin." *Newsweek*, pp. 50–56. August 26.

Kroeber, A. E. (1961) *Ishi in Two Worlds: A Biography of the Last Wild Indian in North America*. Berkeley, CA: Sage Press.

Langness, L. L. (1965) *The Life History Method in Anthropology*. New York: Holt, Rinehart and Winston.

Langness, L. L., and Frank, G. (1981) *Lives: An Anthropological Approach to Biography*. Novato, CA: Chandler and Sharp.

Mitchell, J. C. (1969) "The concept and use of social networks." In J. C. Mitchell (ed.), *Social Networks in Urban Situations*. Manchester, UK: Manchester University Press.

Murphy, S. (1987) "Intravenous drug use and AIDS: Notes on the social economy of needle sharing," *Contemp. Drug Problem*, pp. 373–395.

Neaigus, A., Friedman, S., Goldstein, M., Ildefonso, G., Curtis, R., and Jose, B. (1995) "Using dyadic data for a network analysis of HIV infection and risk behaviors among injection drug users." In Needle, Coyle, Genser, and Trotter (eds.), *Social Networks, Drug Abuse, and HIV Transmission* (NIDA Research Monograph 151). Rockville, MD: NIDA.

Pierce, T. G. (forthcoming) *Use Twice and Destroy: An Ethnography of Young White Heroin Users*.

Price, R., Cottler, L., Mager, D., and Murray, K. (1995) "Injection drug use, characteristics of significant others, and HIV-risk behaviors." In Needle, Coyle, Genser, and Trotter (eds.), *Social Networks, Drug Abuse, and HIV Transmission* (NIDA Research Monograph 151). Rockville, MD: NIDA.

Quinn, T. C., Zacarias, F. R. K., and St. John, R. K. (1989) "HIV and HTLV-1 infections in Americans: A regional perspective," *Medicine* 68: 189–209.

Scott, H., and Drake, S. (1996) "Love in vein." *Details Magazine* (New York, NY), pp. 68–70.

Siegal, H. A., Carlson, R. G., Falck, R., Li, L., Forney, M. A., Rapp, R. C., Baumgartner, K., Myers, W., and Nelson, M. (1991) "HIV infection and risk behaviors among intravenous drug users in low seroprevalence areas in the Midwest," *Am. J. Public Health* 81: 1642–1644.

Singer, M., Zhongke, J., Schensul, J., Weeks, M., and Page, J. (1992) "AIDS and the IV drug user: The local context in prevention efforts," *Med. Anthropol.* 14: 285–306.

Taussig, M. (1993) *Mimesis and Alternity: A Particular History of the Senses*. New York: Routledge, Chapman and Hall.

Watters, J. (1988) "Meaning and context: The social facts of intravenous drug use and HIV transmission in the inner city," *J. Psychoactive Drugs* 20: 173–177.

Watters, J. (1989) "Observations on the importance of social context in HIV transmission among intravenous drug users," *J. Drug Issues* 19: 9–26.

For Discussion

Given the importance of social networks in the lives of drug users, how might these networks be used to generate more positive outcome for drug users?

Part V

Cocaine and Crack

Although chewing coca leaves for their mild stimulant effects had been a part of South America's Andean culture for perhaps a thousand years, for some reason the practice never became popular in either Europe or the United States. During the latter part of the nineteenth century, however, Angelo Mariani of Corsica brought the unobtrusive Peruvian coca shrub to the notice of the rest of the world. After importing tons of coca leaves to his native land, he produced an extract that he mixed with wine and called Vin Coca Mariani. The wine was an immediate success, publicized as a magical beverage that would free the body from fatigue, lift the spirits, and create a lasting sense of well-being. Vin Coca brought Mariani immediate wealth and fame, a situation that did not go unnoticed by John Styth Pemberton of Atlanta, Georgia. In 1885, Pemberton developed a product that he registered as French Wine Coca—Ideal Nerve and Tonic Stimulant. It was originally a medicinal preparation, but the following year he added an additional ingredient, changed it into a soft drink, and renamed it Coca-Cola. Although the extracts of coca may have indeed made Pemberton's cola "the real thing," the actual cocaine content of the leaves was (and remains) quite low—1 percent or less by weight.

The full potency of the coca leaf had remained unknown until 1859, when cocaine was first isolated in its pure form. Yet little use was made of the new alkaloid until 1883, when Dr. Theodor Aschenbrandt secured a supply of the drug and issued it to Bavarian soldiers during maneuvers. Aschenbrandt, a German military physician, noted the beneficial effects of cocaine, particularly its ability to suppress fatigue. Among those who read Aschenbrandt's account with fascination was a struggling young Viennese neurologist, Sigmund Freud. Suffering from chronic fatigue, depression, and various neurotic symptoms, Freud obtained a measure of cocaine and tried it himself. Finding the initial results to be quite favorable, Freud decided that cocaine was a "magical drug."

In July 1884, less than three months after Freud's initial experiences with cocaine, his first essay on the drug was published. Freud then pressed the drug onto his friends and colleagues, urging that they use it both for themselves and their patients; he gave it to his sisters and his fiancée and continued to use it himself. By the close of the 1880s, however, Freud and the others who had praised cocaine as an all-purpose wonder drug began to withdraw their support for it in light of an increasing number of reports of compulsive use and undesirable side effects. Yet by 1890 the patent-medicine industry in the United States had also discovered the benefits of the unregulated use of cocaine. The industry quickly added the drug to its reservoir of home remedies, touting it as not only helpful for everything from alcoholism to venereal disease but also as a cure for addiction to other patent medicines. Because the new tonics contained substantial amounts of cocaine, they did indeed make users feel better, at least initially, thus spiriting the patent-medicine industry into its golden age of popularity.

By the early years of the twentieth century, however, the steady progress of medical science had provided physicians with an even better understanding of the abuse liability of cocaine. In 1906 the Pure Food and Drug Act was passed, bringing about a significant decline in the use of cocaine. The use of the drug did not entirely disappear, however. The drug moved underground, to the netherworlds of crime, the bizarre, and the avant-garde, where it remained for some 40 years. Its major devotees included prostitutes and poets, artists and writers, jazz musicians, fortune-tellers, and criminals. By the 1950s, cocaine use had spread to such other exotic groups as the "beatniks" of New York's Greenwich Village and San Francisco's North Beach, and the movie colony of Hollywood. It was used to such an extent among the urban "smart set" that coke became known as "the rich man's drug."

During the late 1960s and early 1970s, cocaine use began to move from the underground to mainstream society. At that time, most users viewed cocaine as a relatively "safe" drug. They inhaled it in relatively small quantities, and use typically occurred within a social-recreational context. But as the availability of cocaine increased during the late sixties, so too did the number of users and the mechanisms for ingesting it. Some users began to sprinkle street cocaine on tobacco or marijuana and smoke it as a cigarette or in a pipe, but this method did not produce effects distinctly different from inhalation, or "snorting."

A new alternative—freebasing, or the smoking of "freebase" cocaine—soon became available. Freebase cocaine is actually a different chemical product from cocaine itself. In the process of freebasing, street cocaine—which is usually in the form of a hydrochloride salt—is treated with a liquid base (such as ammonia) or baking soda to remove the hydrochloric acid. The free cocaine, or cocaine base (and hence the name "freebase"), is then dissolved in a solvent such as ether, from which the purified cocaine is crystallized. These crystals are then crushed and used in a special glass pipe.

Smoking freebase cocaine provides a more potent rush and a more powerful high than inhaling regular cocaine. By 1977, it was estimated that there were some four million users of cocaine, with as many as 10 percent of these freebasing the drug exclusively. Yet few outside of the drug-using and drug research and treatment communities were even aware of the existence of the freebase culture. Fewer still had an understanding of the new complications that freebasing had introduced to the cocaine scene.

The complications are several. First, cocaine in any of its forms is highly seductive. With freebasing, the euphoria is more intense than that achieved when the drug is inhaled. Moreover, this intense euphoria subsides into irritable craving after only a few minutes, thus influencing many users to continue freebasing for days at a time until either they or their drug supplies are fully exhausted. Second, the practice of freebasing is expensive. When a user snorts cocaine, a single gram can last the social user an entire weekend or longer. With street cocaine ranging in price anywhere from $50 to $200 a gram depending on availability and purity, even this method of ingestion can be a costly recreational pursuit. With freebasing, the cost factor can undergo a geometric increase. Habitual users have been known to freebase continuously for three or four days without sleep, using up to 150 grams of cocaine in a 72-hour period. Third, one special danger of freebasing is the proximity of highly flammable ether (or rum when it is used instead of water as a coolant in the pipe) to an open flame. This problem is enhanced by the fact that the user is generally suffering from a loss of coordination produced by the cocaine or a combination of cocaine and alcohol. As such, in many freebasing situations the volatile concoction has exploded in the face of the user.

Freebasing is but one variety of cocaine smoking. Common in the drug-using communities of Colombia, Bolivia, Venezuela, Ecuador, Peru, and Brazil is the use of coca paste, known to most South Americans as "basuco," "susuko," and "pasta basica de cocaina." Coca paste is an intermediate product in the processing of the coca leaf into cocaine. In the initial stages of coca processing, the leaves are pulverized, soaked in alcohol mixed with benzene (a petroleum derivative used in the manufacture of motor fuels, detergents, and insecticides), and shaken. The alcohol/benzol mixture is then drained, sulfuric acid is added, and the solution is shaken again. Next, a precipitate is formed when sodium carbonate is added to the solution. When the result is washed with kerosene and chilled, crystals of crude cocaine, or coca paste, are left behind. While the cocaine content of leaves is relatively low—0.5 to 1 percent by weight—paste has a cocaine concentration ranging up to 90 percent, but more commonly about 40 percent. Coca paste is typically smoked straight or in cigarettes mixed with either tobacco or marijuana.

Beyond coca, cocaine, freebase, and basuco, there is also *crack* cocaine. Contrary to popular belief, crack is not a product of the 1980s. Rather, it was first reported in the literature during the early 1970s. At that time, however, knowledge of crack, known then as "garbage freebase," seemed to be restricted to segments of cocaine's freebasing subculture. Crack is processed from cocaine hydrochloride by using ammonia or baking soda and water and heating it to remove the hydrochloride. The result is a pebble-sized crystalline form of cocaine base.

Contrary to another popular belief, crack is neither "freebase cocaine" nor "purified cocaine." Part of the confusion about what crack actually is comes from the various ways the word "freebase" is used in the drug community. "Freebase" (the noun) is a drug, a cocaine product converted to the base state from cocaine hydrochloride after adulterants have been chemically removed. Crack is converted to the base state without removing the adulterants. "Freebasing" (the act) means to inhale vapors of cocaine base, of which crack is but one form. Finally, crack is not purified cocaine; the baking soda remains as a salt after it is processed, which reduces the overall purity of the product. And interestingly, crack gets its name from the fact that the residue of baking soda often causes a crackling sound when heated.

The rediscovery of crack during the early 1980s seemed to occur simultaneously on the East and West coasts. As a result of the Colombian government's attempts to reduce the amount of illicit cocaine production within its borders, it apparently, at least for a time, had successfully restricted the amount of ether available for transforming coca paste into cocaine hydrochloride. The result was the diversion of coca paste from Colombia, through Central America and the Caribbean, into South Florida for conversion into cocaine. Spillage from shipments through the Caribbean corridor acquainted local island populations with coca paste smoking, which developed into the forerunner of crack cocaine in 1980. Known as "baking-soda base," "base-rock," "gravel," and "roxanne," the prototype was a smokable product composed of coca paste, baking soda, water, and rum. Immigrants from Jamaica, Trinidad, and locations along the Leeward and Windward Islands chain introduced the crack prototype to Caribbean inner-city populations in Miami and New York, where it was ultimately produced from cocaine hydrochloride rather than coca paste.

Apparently at about the same time, a Los Angeles basement chemist rediscovered the rock variety of baking-soda cocaine, and it was initially referred to as "cocaine rock." It was an immediate success, as was the East Coast type, for a variety of reasons. First, it could be smoked rather than snorted. When cocaine is smoked, it is more rapidly absorbed and reportedly crosses the blood-brain barrier within a few seconds. Hence, it creates an almost instantaneous high. Second, it was cheap. While a gram of cocaine for snorting may cost $50 or more, depending on its purity, the same gram can be transformed into any number of "rocks," depending on their size. For the user, this meant that individual "rocks" could be purchased for as little as $2, $5, $10, or $20. For the seller, $50 worth of cocaine hydrochloride (purchased wholesale for $30) could generate as much as $150 when sold as rocks. Third, it was easily hidden and transportable, and when hawked in small glass vials, it could be readily scrutinized by potential buyers.

By the close of 1985, crack had come to the attention of the media and was predicted to be the "wave of the future" among substance abusers, and by mid-1986 national headlines were calling crack a glorified version of cocaine and the major street drug of abuse in the United States. Also, there was the belief that crack was responsible for rising rates of street crime.

As the media blitzed the American people with lurid stories depicting the hazards of crack, Congress and the White House began drawing plans for a more concerted war on crack and other drugs. At the same time, crack use was reported in Canada, England, Finland, Hong Kong, Spain, South Africa, Egypt, India, Mexico, Belize, and Brazil. By the middle of the 1990s, however, the use of crack had begun to decline in many of America's inner-city communities. In other locales, more hard-core users continued to ingest the drug.

Within the context we have outlined, the following chapters examine the history of cocaine, patterns of cocaine use, and the current controversies related to the sentencing of crack users in the federal courts.

Additional Readings

Belenko, Steven R. (1993). *Crack and the Evolution of Antidrug Policy.* Westport, CT: Greenwood Press.

Bourgois, Philippe. (2003). "Crack and the Political Economy of Social Suffering." *Addiction Research & Theory, Special Issue: Crack Chronicles,* 11 (1): 31–37.

Inciardi, James A., and Hilary L. Surratt. (2001). "Drug Use, Street Crime, and Sex-Trading Among Cocaine-Dependent Women: Implications for Public Health and Criminal Justice Policy." *Journal of Psychoactive Drugs* 33 (4): 379–389.

Sabet, Kevin A. (2005). "Making It Happen: The Case for Compromise in the Federal Cocaine Law Debate." *Social Policy and Administration* 39 (2): 181–191.

Sterk, Claire E. (1999). *Fast Lives: Women Who Use Crack Cocaine.* Philadelphia: Temple University Press.

Streatfeild, Dominic. (2001). *Cocaine: An Unauthorized Biography.* New York: Thomas Dunne Books. ✦

20
America's First Cocaine Epidemic

David F. Musto

Widespread public perception would suggest that cocaine emerged initially as a drug of choice in the 1980s. In this essay, this myth is dispelled with a description of the drug's popularity beginning in the late 1800s. Using several illustrations, the author discusses the three phases of this first cocaine epidemic. He describes the four-decade process in which cocaine initially was readily available and endorsed by the medical community but then was prohibited.

Only a decade ago, many prominent Americans tolerated and even touted the use of cocaine. From Capitol Hill to Wall Street, the young and moneyed set made the drug its favorite "leisure pharmaceutical." Some talked of decriminalizing the "harmless" white powder. But that changed after cocaine overdoses killed several celebrities—including Hollywood's John Belushi in 1982 and college basketball star Len Bias in 1986. Last year, the drug claimed 1,582 lives in the United States and was a factor in countless crimes. Crack, a cheap form of cocaine, is now considered a scourge of the nation's ghettos; teenage dealers wage murderous turf battles within blocks of the Capitol dome. Lawmakers clamor for a war on drugs but despair of finding a way to win it. All this has a familiar ring to it, says Yale's David Musto. Here he recalls what happened a century ago, when America entered its first cocaine craze.

"I have tested [the] effect of coca," wrote a youthful Sigmund Freud in his famed essay *On Coca* (1884), "which wards off hunger, sleep, and fatigue and steels one to intellectual effort, some dozen times on myself." Like other doctors who had tested the drug, he found that the euphoria it induced was not followed by depression or any other unpleasant aftereffects. "Furthermore," wrote Freud, "a first dose or even repeated doses of coca produce no compulsive desire to use the stimulant further."

With obvious wonder, Freud described the remarkable experiments of 78-year-old Sir Robert Christison, a world-famous toxicologist at the University of Edinburgh: "During the third experiment he chewed two drams of coca leaves and was able to complete [a 15-mile] walk without the exhaustion experienced on the earlier occasions; when he arrived home, despite the fact that he had been nine hours without food or drink, he experienced no hunger or thirst, and woke the next morning without feeling at all tired."

Freud's "song of praise to this magical substance," as he described it, was only one of many that were sung by various medical authorities before the turn of the century. Indeed, Freud had become interested in coca because American physicians, the drug's earliest and heartiest enthusiasts, had "discovered" that it could reduce the cravings of opiate addicts and alcoholics. Freud's interest was not academic. He was seeking a cure for the addiction of his colleague, Ernst von Fleischl-Marxow. "At present," Freud observed in 1884, "there seems to be some promise of widespread recognition and use of coca preparations in North America, while in Europe doctors scarcely know them by name."

In America, where the cocaine fad would reach greater heights than in Europe, the ability to cure opiate addictions was regarded as only one of cocaine's marvelous powers. While morphine and other torpor-inducing opiates were beginning to seem positively un-American, cocaine seemed to increase alertness and efficiency, much-prized qualities in the industrializing nation. In 1880, Dr. W. H. Bentley, writing in Detroit's *Therapeutic Gazette*, hailed coca as "the desideratum . . . in health and disease." The gazette's editors, quoting another medical journal, cheerily endorsed this view: "One feels like trying coca, with or without the opium-habit. A harmless remedy for the blues is imperial. And so say we."

Encouraged by the nation's leading medical authorities, and with no laws restricting the sale, consumption, or advertising of cocaine (or any other drugs), entrepreneurs quickly made cocaine an elixir for the masses. Lasting from around 1885 to the 1920s, America's first great cocaine epidemic went through three phases: the introduction during the 1880s, as cocaine rapidly gained acceptance; a middle period, when its use spread and its ill effects came to light; and a final, repressive stage after the turn of the century, when cocaine became the most feared of all illicit drugs.

North Americans, to be sure, were not the first inhabitants of this hemisphere to discover or extol the powers of the "magical leaf." For centuries before (and after) the arrival of the Europeans, the Indians of the Andes had chewed coca leaves to gain relief from hunger and fatigue. The drug spread beyond South America only after 1860, when an Austrian chemist named Albert Niemann learned how to isolate the active ingredient, cocaine. When Freud published his first praise of the elixir, pure cocaine, along with the milder coca, was already available to Americans in drug and grocery stores, saloons, and from mail-order patent-medicine vendors. By 1885, the major U.S. manufacturer, Parke, Davis & Co., of Detroit and New York, was selling cocaine and coca in 15 forms, including coca-leaf cigarettes and cheroots, cocaine inhalant, a Coca Cordial, cocaine crystals, and cocaine in solution for hypodermic injection.

Parke, Davis reported that it had repeatedly stepped up production during 1885 in order to satisfy the public's growing appetite. A Parke, Davis advertisement informed doctors of the drug's uses:

> An enumeration of the diseases in which coca and cocaine have been found of service would include a category of almost all the maladies that flesh is heir to. . . . Allowing for the exaggeration of enthusiasm, it remains the fact that already cocaine claims a place in medicine and surgery equal to that of opium and quinine, and coca has been held to be better adapted for use as a popular restorative and stimulant than either tea or coffee.

The American craving for cocaine was not satisfied by domestic producers alone. From Paris came a variety of popular cocaine concoctions manufactured by Angelo Mariani. "Vin Mariani," a mixture of wine and coca, arrived on the drugstore shelf with a raft of celebrity endorsements, including those of Pope Leo XIII, Thomas Edison, Sarah Bernhardt, Emile Zola, Henrik Ibsen, and the Prince of Wales. "Since a single bottle of Mariani's extraordinary coca wine guarantees a lifetime of a hundred years," exclaimed novelist Jules Verne, "I shall be obliged to live until the year 2700." Mariani boasted that Ulysses S. Grant took another of his products, "Thé Mariani," once a day during his last illness in 1885, allowing the ex-president to complete his famous *Memoirs*.

For consumers on a budget, the new wonder drug was available in less exalted forms. Coca-Cola, for example, contained a minute amount[1] of cocaine—enough to provide a noticeable lift, if not a "high." The "real thing" began life as a coca wine in 1885. In deference, ironically, to the widespread temperance sentiment of the day, the company replaced the alcohol content of the drink with soda water and flavorings, which allowed it to market Coke as a healthful "soft drink"—a "brain tonic" to relieve headaches and cure "all nervous affections." With the successful marketing of Coca-Cola and similar refreshers, the neighborhood drugstore soda fountain of late-19th-century America came to serve as the poor man's Saratoga Springs. There, the weary citizen could choose from among dozens of soda pop pick-me-ups, including Cola Coke, Rocco Cola, Koca Nola, Nerv Ola, Wise Ola, and one with the simple and direct name, Dope.

Cocaine also was offered as an asthma remedy and an antidote for toothache pain. (Other patent medicines contained opiates, such as morphine and heroin.) Dr. Nathan Tucker's Asthma Specific, a popular catarrh powder, or snuff, considered to be an excellent cure for hay fever and asthma, contained as much as half a gram of pure cocaine per package. Thanks to its remarkable ability to shrink the nasal mucous membranes and drain the sinuses, cocaine became the official remedy of the American Hay Fever Association.

In the six states and innumerable counties that were "dry" during the mid 1890s, workingmen found snuffs, soft drinks, and other cocaine products a cheap substitute for hard liquor. In states where teetotalers had not prevailed, bartenders often put a pinch of cocaine in a shot of whiskey to add punch to the drink. Peddlers sold it door to door. And some employers in the construction and mining industries found practical uses for the drug, reportedly distributing it to their workers to keep them going at a high pitch.

How much cocaine did Americans consume? Judging from its wide legal availability, and given its seductive appeal, it is safe to assume that they were using substantial amounts by the turn of the century. The limited import statistics for the leaf and manufactured cocaine suggest that use peaked shortly after 1900, just as cocaine was being transformed in the public mind from a tonic into a terror.[2] Legal imports of coca leaves during that period averaged about 1.5 million pounds annually and the amount of cocaine averaged 200,000 ounces. (Today, the United States has roughly three times the population it did in 1900 but consumes more than 10 times as much cocaine—perhaps 2.5 million ounces annually.)

At first, there were few reports of chronic cocaine abuse. Confronted with one example in 1887, Dr. William A. Hammond, former Surgeon General of the Army, and one of the most prominent cocaine advocates of the era, dismissed it as a "case of preference, and not a case of irresistible habit." However, by 1890 the *Medical Record* cited some 400 cases of habit mostly among people being treated, as Freud and others had recommended, for addiction to morphine and other opiates.

In fact, Freud himself watched his friend Ernst von Fleischl-Marxow disintegrate into a state of "cocainist" delirium before he died in 1891. Freud claimed that he had not intended for von Fleischl-Marxow to inject the drug, and he withdrew his support for its use as a treatment for morphine addiction. But he never publicly renounced other uses of the drug.

By the turn of the century, cocaine was becoming more and more suspect. A thorough investigation by a committee of the Connecticut State Medical Society in 1896 concluded that cocaine cures for hay fever and other ailments had been a major cause of drug dependency, and "the danger of addiction outweighs the little efficacy attributed to the remedy." It recommended that cocaine be made available only to physicians, for use as a local anesthetic. Scattered newspaper reports—"Another Physician a Victim To The Baneful Drug"—books such as Annie Meyers' *Eight Years in Cocaine Hell* (1902), word of mouth, and articles in *Ladies' Home Journal*, *Collier's*, and other popular magazines brought more bad news. The debilitating effects of Sherlock Holmes's cocaine habit were familiar enough to earn a place in an 1899 Broadway play bearing the name of the brilliant British detective.

Once the miracle drug of upper-class professionals, cocaine came to be considered a curse of both the American demimonde and pathetic middle-class victims of patent medicines. The "Report of Committee on the Acquirement of Drug Habits" in the *American Journal of Pharmacy* (1903) declared that most users were "bohemians, gamblers, high- and low-class prostitutes, night porters, bell boys, burglars, racketeers, pimps, and casual laborers." That year, reflecting the public's growing suspicion of cocaine, the Coca-Cola company replaced the stimulant with a milder, more acceptable one, caffeine—the first, one might say, of the "new formula" Cokes.

A 1909 *New York Times* report on "The Growing Menace of the Use of Cocaine"— published even as use was declining—noted that the drug was used at lower-class "sniff parties," destroying "its victims more swiftly and surely than opium." In the *Century Magazine*, Charles B. Towns, a national anti-drug activist, issued a grave warning: "The most harmful of all habit forming drugs is cocaine. Nothing so quickly deteriorates [sic] its victim or provides so short a cut to the insane asylum."

As early as 1887, the states had begun enacting their own (largely ineffective) laws against cocaine and other drugs. In 1913, New York passed the toughest statute to date, completely outlawing cocaine, except for certain medical uses. By the beginning of World War I, all 48 states had anti-cocaine laws on the books. Fourteen states also inaugurated "drug education" programs in the public schools.

And what role did the federal government play? A small one, at first. According to the Constitutional doctrines of the day, Washington had virtually no power to police the drug trade directly. The federal Pure Food and Drug Act of 1906 merely required labelling of any cocaine content in over-the-counter remedies. But official Washington was jolted by the effects of the cocaine "epidemic" in its own backyard, much as it has become alarmed today by hundreds of crack cocaine-related killings in the Federal District. For years, the District of Columbia's chief of police, Major Sylvester, had been warning Congress (which then governed the city directly) of cocaine's horrifying effects. "The cocaine habit is by far the greatest menace to society, because the victims are generally vicious. The use of this drug superinduces jealousy and predisposes [sic] to commit criminal acts," he declared. In 1909, President Theodore Roosevelt's Homes Commission presented the testimony of Sylvester and other officials to an alarmed Congress, which promptly restricted legal drug sales in the nation's capital.

At the same time, the drug problem took on an international dimension. Roosevelt's State Department, under Elihu Root, had assumed the lead in attempting to regulate the free-wheeling international opium trade. Root's motives were mixed. By siding with the Chinese against Britain and other European powers that were reaping large profits in the Chinese opium market, Root hoped to gain trade concessions from the Chinese. Moreover, Root hoped, like some officials in Washington today, that he could solve America's drug problem by stamping out the cultivation of opium poppies and coca bushes abroad. But a nation that led such an international moral crusade, Root realized, would have to have exemplary anti-drug laws of its own.

In 1910, President William Howard Taft presented a State Department report on drugs to Congress. Cocaine officially became Public Enemy No. 1:

> The illicit sale of [cocaine] . . . and the habitual use of it temporarily raises the power of a criminal to a point where in

resisting arrest there is no hesitation to murder. It is more appalling in its effects than any other habit-forming drug used in the United States.

The report also stirred racist fears, adding that "it has been authoritatively stated that cocaine is often the direct incentive to the crime of rape by negroes of the South, and other sections of the country." (Likewise, opium was considered to be a special vice of the nation's Chinatowns.) Terrifying rumors told of criminals who gained superhuman strength, cunning, and efficiency under the influence of cocaine. Convinced that black "cocaine fiends" could withstand normal .32 caliber bullets, some police departments in the South reportedly switched to .38 caliber revolvers.

By December 1914, when Congress passed the Harrison Act, tightly regulating the distribution and sale of drugs, the use of cocaine and other drugs was considered so completely beyond the pale that the law itself seemed routine. The *New York Times* did not even note the passage of the Harrison Act until two weeks after the fact. The vote was overshadowed by a popular crusade against a more controversial target, Demon Rum, a crusade which brought thousands of temperance demonstrators to Washington that December. From the gallery of the House of Representatives, temperance advocates hung a Prohibition petition bearing six million signatures.

But the public's adamant anti-cocaine sentiment, which had reduced the drug's appeal after the turn of the century and resulted in legal restrictions, now facilitated operation of the laws. Unlike Prohibition, which was not backed by a public consensus, the Harrison Act—which Congress made more restrictive over the years—was largely successful.

What happened to cocaine? Of course, some Americans continued to acquire and use it, but their numbers eventually shrank. Peer pressure and the threat of punishment combined to drive cocaine underground. Only occasional—and often negative—references to it appeared in movies and popular songs during the 1920s and 1930s. Cole Porter announced, "I get no kick from cocaine" in his 1934 musical, *Anything Goes*, and an impish Charlie Chaplin, in the movie *Modern Times* (1936), gained such superhuman strength from sniffing "nose powder" that he was able to break out of jail.

By the time I was in medical school, during the late 1950s, cocaine was described to medical students as a drug that used to be a problem in the United States. It was news to us.

The people who had lived through the nation's first cocaine epidemic and knew that the euphoria induced by the drug was a dangerous delusion had grown old and passed from the scene. Cocaine's notorious reputation died with them. By the 1960s, America was ready for another fling with this most seductive and dangerous drug.

Notes

1. Coca-Cola's cocaine content was .0025 percent in 1900, and may have been greater during the 1880s.

2. It is also difficult to determine how many Americans were addicted to cocaine. Because they can live with their addictions for 20 or 30 years, opium addicts (of whom there were perhaps 250,000 around the turn of the century) are a relatively stable population, and thus easier to count. Cocaine addicts, on the other hand, do not live long if they do not quit, so their ranks are constantly changing.

For Discussion

It is believed that use of cocaine was minimal between 1930 and 1960. Discuss alternative explanations for the drug's alleged lack of popularity during these decades.

Reprinted from: David F. Musto, "America's First Cocaine Epidemic." In *The Wilson Quarterly*, Summer 1989, pp. 59–64. Copyright © 1989 by The Woodrow Wilson International Center for Scholars. Reprinted by permission. ✦

21

African Americans, Crack, and the Federal Sentencing Guidelines

James A. Inciardi
Hilary L. Surratt
Steven P. Kurtz

Historically, various antidrug policies have targeted ethnic minorities. Current federal law allows for more severe penalties for possession of crack-cocaine than for cocaine powder, and this sentencing policy has been criticized on the grounds that it discriminates against African Americans.

Media portrayal has contributed to the perception that crack-cocaine is used disproportionately among African Americans, and these media portrayals are described briefly in this essay. The authors then report findings from their study of an ethnically diverse sample of cocaine users in Miami. The results show that crack use does not differ substantively across ethnic groups. Moreover, although crack users engage in various criminal activities, the authors observed only a few ethnic differences in relation to the crack-crime connection.

> This one provision, the crack statute, has been directly responsible for incarcerating nearly an entire generation of young black American men for very long periods. It has created a situation that reeks with inhumanity and injustice. The scales of justice have been turned topsy-turvy so that those masterminds, the kingpins of drug trafficking, escape detection while those whose role is minimal, even trivial, are hoisted on the spears of an enraged electorate and at the pinnacle of their youth are imprisoned for years while those responsible for the evil of the day remain free.

— (United States District Court Judge Clyde S. Cahill, 1994)

Although Judge Cahill's remarks are both melodramatic and somewhat overstated, his point is well taken. Under the current federal sentencing scheme for cocaine offenses, crimes involving *crack*-cocaine are punished far more severely than those involving *powder*-cocaine (U.S. Sentencing Commission 1993). In fact, the Federal Sentencing Guidelines treat a given amount of crack as equivalent to 100 times the amount of powder-cocaine. Thus, this 100-to-1 ratio results in sentences for crack defendants that are considerably more severe than sentences for those whose offenses involve other forms of cocaine (see Figure 21.1). In addition to the disparities in the crack and powder cocaine Sentencing Guidelines, the 100-to-1 ratio is also used in the determination of statutory *mandatory minimum sentences* that are intended to heavily penalize drug traffickers. Thus, the mandatory minimum sentence of 5 years for the sale of 500 grams of powder cocaine (10 years for 5,000 grams) is applied to the sale or possession of just 5 grams of crack (and 10 years for 50 grams of crack).

This oddity in the federal sentencing scheme is best illustrated with the story of Derrick Curry, a 20-year-old African American college student who was also a small-time crack dealer (see Leiby 1994). In 1990,

Figure 21.1

Minimum Sentences (in Years) for First Offenders Under Federal Sentencing Guidelines

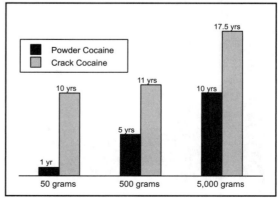

Curry was one of several Washington, D.C.-area men involved in the distribution of crack who were under surveillance in a joint F.B.I./D.E.A. sting operation. At one point in the investigation, undercover agents had supplied Curry—who was no more than a low-level drug courier—with a cellular phone in exchange for crack. All of his telephone conversations about his crack deliveries were recorded, and eventually were used as evidence against him. On the day of Curry's arrest, agents found just over a pound of crack in his car, along with a criminal justice textbook (mine as a matter of fact) and a spiral notebook with his name on it. He was eventually convicted by a federal jury of conspiracy and distribution of crack, and sentenced to prison for 19 years and 7 months, with no possibility of parole.

Derrick Curry's sentence, by almost any available standard, is incomprehensibly severe. It is nearly three times the prison sentence served by most murderers in the United States; it is four times the prison sentence served by most kidnappers; it is five times the prison sentence served by most rapists; and it is ten times the prison sentence served by those who illegally possess guns.

2006 Law Update. In *United States v. Booker,* decided by the U.S. Supreme Court in 2005, the Sentencing Guidelines were rendered advisory to the sentencing judge rather than mandatory. Sentencing judges were thereby authorized discretion to consider the individual circumstances and characteristics of the case at hand, in addition to the Guidelines. Because the ruling in *Booker* affected only the Sentencing Guidelines and not statutory minimum sentences, however, this judicial sentencing discretion is available only in those crack-cocaine cases where mandatory minimum sentences do not apply (i.e., where the amounts of the drug are less than 5 grams, about 25% of all cases), or in those cases in which the judge is determining additional penalties beyond the applicable statutory minimum (King and Mauer 2006).

Although many who opposed the crack-powder discrepancies embedded in the Sentencing Guidelines initially hoped that the *Booker* case would lead to a reduction in dis-

crepant sentencing in at least those cases where judges were authorized the exercise of discretion, such hopes appear to be unfounded. A study of 24 written federal court decisions in 2005 involving crack-cocaine offenses—and which cited *Booker* in support of the decision—*did* find that some judges justified lower-than-Guideline sentences for crack offenders because they perceived the 100-to-1 ratio to be unfair. Several judges described the ratio as "excessive" or as "too severe." A number of them determined that a 20-to-1 ratio was more appropriate, because that was the most recent ratio recommended (unsuccessfully) to the Congress by the U.S. Sentencing Commission (USSC).

At this writing, however, at least two circuit courts have struck down sentencing judges' authority to justify below-Guideline sentences on the basis of the unfairness of the Guideline-determined sentence or of Congressional policy (USSC 2006), holding that only Congress has the power to change the law. Further, national sentencing data post-*Booker* generally show that sentences for crack offenses have been maintained within the Sentencing Guidelines (USSC 2006).

Many African American defendants have argued in the federal courts, unsuccessfully for the most part, that this sentencing scheme discriminates against them on the basis of race. They point to the fact that, at least in the public's perception, crack-cocaine is primarily associated with black sellers and users, whereas powder cocaine is primarily associated with white users and sellers (Cauchon 1993).

To a large extent, this perception of crack as a "black" or "African American" drug can be traced to the mass media. In their many analyses of the crack epidemic, journalists have portrayed crack use and crack-related crime as essentially problems of blacks in inner-city neighborhoods. Magazine photographs show young African American men and women smoking crack in abandoned buildings, minority youths with guns in their jeans holding handfuls of crack, and even the former (and once again current) Washington, D.C., mayor Marion Barry smoking crack. Headlines proclaim "A Tide of Drug Killings: The Crack Plague Spurs More Inner

City Murders" and "Prisoners of Crack: Eight Years of Reagan Politics Corrupted a Generation of Urban Black Americans and Devastated Their Communities." Feature articles highlight "Drugs and the Black Community" and "The New Criminal Recruits of the Inner City, the Children Who Deal Crack." Altogether, journalists have presented a crack/crime/African American interconnection that would appear to be a simple, well-established fact of American life.

The problem with these representations is that only part of it all has been clearly and accurately documented in media reports—that crack has had a destructive impact on black inner-city communities. The evidence presented for more specific crack/crime/African American connections is far more tenuous, leaving a series of unanswered questions. Is the crack/crime association mere sensationalism, or are crack users commonly involved in criminal behavior? Is any crack/crime relationship really a more general cocaine/crime association, or are crack users more crime-involved than other cocaine users? Is it really so that most crack users are African Americans, as typically portrayed in media reports? Are users of any and all forms of cocaine predominantly African Americans, or are African American cocaine users more likely than white or Latino/a users to use cocaine in the specific form of crack? Hasn't crack spread well beyond inner-city neighborhoods into working-class suburbs, and if so, isn't there a white crack/crime problem? Are any such ethnic differences anything more than socioeconomic differences?

These questions, even without answers, suggest a considerably more complex relationship between crack use, crime by crack users, and race/ethnicity than that implied by mass media reports. Much of the complexity is due to the fact that multiple considerations other than race/ethnicity are at issue. These factors cannot be disentangled with urban war zone reporting techniques, but instead require scientific methods of sample selection and data analysis.

The Crack/Crime Connection

The relationship between crack use and crime has received considerable attention since the late 1980s, but the available studies have rarely examined race/ethnic differences. Nevertheless, at least the crack/crime linkages appear to be rather clear cut, particularly with regard to crack selling and violence (Goldstein et al. 1991; Hamid 1990; Inciardi, Lockwood, and Pottieger 1993, pp. 116–31; Inciardi and Pottieger 1991; Klein and Maxson 1985; McBride and Swartz 1990). The media reports appear to be correct in implying that crack users are commonly involved in criminal behavior.

Prior research is also fairly consistent in its answer to another question about the crack/crime/race connection. Many studies suggest crack users are more often African Americans. For example, a disproportionate amount of crack use among African Americans is indicated in official statistics from the Substance Abuse and Mental Health Services Administration (SAMHSA) *National Survey on Drug Use and Health* (formerly the *National Household Survey*). In 1991, 4.3 percent of blacks surveyed had used crack, compared with only 1.5 percent of whites and 2.1 percent of Latinos/as. (By 2003, these statistics were similar except that the proportion of whites who had used crack had doubled to 3.3 percent, reducing, but not eliminating, the observed ethnic differences). Race/ethnic differences in lifetime crack use were especially large among people aged 26 to 34 years old: the 9.2 percent of blacks reporting use is some three times that of the 2.8 percent for whites or 3.7 percent for Latinos/as (National Institute on Drug Abuse 1991). However, because whites represent the majority of the U.S. population, these percentage estimates imply that in terms of absolute numbers, most crack users are *not* African Americans, but whites. NIDA's estimates of current crack use—defined as use in the past month—are 0.7 percent for blacks, 0.4 percent for Latinos/as, and 0.2 percent for whites. This translates to population estimates of 172,000 black crack users, 68,000 Latino/a crack users, and 238,000 white crack users. That is, of the 479,000 crack users estimated for the 1991 U.S. household population, 49.9 percent were white, 14.2 percent were Latino/a, and only 35.9 percent were African Americans.

While SAMHSA's *National Survey on Drug Use and Health* provides the *best available evidence* on race/ethnic distributions of crack users, it should also be noted that this does not mean it is necessarily a *good* estimate. Very low percentage estimates in this type of study—such as those given for current crack use—mean less reliable estimates. Further, as a survey of the general household population, the NIDA study does not include populations critical to examining race/ethnic differences in crack use, such as runaways and other homeless people, addicts in residential treatment, incarcerated populations, and those living on the street and in drug subcultures that are generally inaccessible through standard survey methods. Some other official statistics do include some of these populations—notably SAMHSA's Drug Abuse Warning Network (DAWN)—but they cannot separate crack use from other cocaine use and they do not report statistics in a way that permits extrapolation to population estimates.

Beyond these two points—a strong crack/crime relationship and no more than a weak crack/black association—very little published research exists on ethnic differences specifically among *crack users,* let alone ethnic differences in crimes among crack users. In fact, there is surprisingly little research on ethnic differences concerning any type of illegal drug use or its correlates. Moreover, the work that has been done is suspect for purposes of understanding race-ethnicity/drug-use relationships because it is almost all based on samples of either students or drug treatment patients, and ethnic minorities have both higher rates of school dropout and lower rates of treatment seeking than whites (Collins 1992; Rebach 1992).

The most research attention in this regard has focused on adolescents, primarily students. The findings generally show that ethnic differences in drug use are explained by background variables, particularly income and availability (Adlaf, Smart, and Tan 1989; Kandel, Single, and Kessler 1976; Maddehian, Newcomb, and Bentler 1986; Wallace and Bachman 1991). More important, studies indicate that most drug use rates including those of alcohol, cocaine, pills of all types, cigarettes, hallucinogens, and inhalants—are *lowest* among black adolescents (Bachman et al. 1991; Kandel, Single, and Kessler 1976; National Institute on Drug Abuse 1991; Rebach 1992; Segal 1989). Latino/a males, however, are generally found more likely to have used cocaine than either whites or blacks (Bachman et al. 1991; Marin 1990; SAMHSA 2003; Wallace and Bachman 1991).

Among adult drug users, most research on ethnic differences comes from studies of heroin addicts in treatment in which, usually, only two ethnic categories are compared: black and white, or Latino/a and white Anglo. These studies suggest that minorities, including African Americans, Puerto Ricans, and Mexican Americans, are overrepresented among heroin users (Anglin et al. 1988; Ball and Chambers 1970; Kleinman and Lukoff 1978). Studies of cocaine and crack users also indicate disproportionate use among minorities (Carroll and Rounsaville 1992; Johnson, Elmoghazy, and Dunlap 1990). As in the studies of students, however, ethnicity generally is found to interact with other variables. In particular, an interaction effect between gender and ethnicity has been documented in several studies (Austin and Gilbert 1989; Prendergast et al. 1989), and other researchers have presented their results separately for males and females to clarify the ethnic differences within gender categories and to avoid the complexity of this interaction (Anglin et al. 1988; Wallace and Bachman 1991).

More recently, treatment status also has been recognized as an important confounding factor in the study of ethnic differences in drug use. One recent study, for example, found that 55 percent of 298 cocaine users in treatment were white, whereas among 101 cocaine users *not* in treatment, only 14 percent were white (Carroll and Rounsaville 1992). Treatment status of cocaine users also appears to be entangled with gender and other differences (Boyd and Mieczkowski 1990; Brunswick, Messeri, and Aidala 1990; Chitwood and Morningstar 1985; Griffin et al. 1989; Rounsaville and Kleber 1985).

Altogether, social science research pertinent to the alleged crack/crime/black linkage can be summarized as follows. First, it is limited, particularly on the specific topic of crack. Second, it has documented a *crack/crime* association. Third, it suggests that any *black/crack* association is a limited one—higher rates of crack use for blacks than for whites and Latinos/as, but fewer black crack users than non-black crack users. Fourth and most important, it repeatedly documents the complexity of drug use/race-ethnicity relationships and the consequent requirement for a large, demographically diverse sample in order to study this subject adequately. Drug users who differ in ethnicity invariably also differ in ways that have nothing to do with ethnicity, such as gender, and in additional ways that are correlated with ethnicity, such as income levels and residence patterns, and in still other ways, such as treatment status, for which relationships to ethnicity are still not well understood. These other differences tend either to explain the drug/ethnicity differences or to make the sample size too small for the kind of analysis that would even permit study of this possibility. For the specific problem of the crack/crime/black association alleged in media reports, many of these methodological difficulties are overcome in a recent study of a large, demographically diverse sample of cocaine users.

Studying Crack/Crime Connections

Drug use patterns and criminal behavior were the focus of a study conducted in the Miami, Florida, metropolitan area (Inciardi and Pottieger 1994). A total of 699 cocaine users were interviewed, 349 of them in residential treatment at the time and 350 on the street. Eligible participants were those who reported any cocaine use during the "last 90 days on the street." For the street sample, this was the 90 days prior to interview. For the treatment sample, it was the most recent continuous 90 days on the street prior to treatment entry. This 90-day period was required to be within the two years prior to interview. Questions about drug use and criminal behavior were asked during an interview lasting 30 to 60 minutes, and respondents were paid $10 for their time. Legal protection for subjects was assured by anonymity and a Certificate of Confidentiality from the

National Institute on Drug Abuse. This guaranteed that project employees could not be compelled by any court or law enforcement agency to reveal information sources or questionnaire data. Treatment program clients were assured that neither participation nor nonparticipation would affect their program status and that their answers would not be seen by counselors or other program personnel.

Selection of both street and treatment respondents was guided by subsample targets for gender, age, and ethnicity in order to ensure a demographically diverse sample. In the treatment programs, this generally meant returning repeatedly to interview every new client in the hard-to-fill subsamples (younger and white or Latino/a). On the street, subsample targets meant pushing the interview process into a variety of neighborhoods to get the required race-ethnic diversity. Street respondents were located through standard multiple starting-point "snowball sampling" techniques in neighborhoods with high rates of cocaine use by a street interviewer familiar with and well known in the target areas. The details of how this kind of street data collection is done are described elsewhere (Inciardi, Horowitz, and Pottieger 1993, pp. 64–67; Inciardi, Lockwood, and Pottieger 1993, pp. 147–51).

The final sample was 66 percent male and 34 percent female. The 285 black respondents comprised 34 percent of the males and 54 percent of the females; the 273 white respondents were 36 percent of the males and 46 percent of the females; and the 141 Latino/a respondents (108 of them Cuban) made up the remaining 30 percent of the male respondents. Forty-six percent of the respondents were ages 20 to 29, while 28 percent were ages 13 to 19, and 26 percent were 30 to 49 years old.

Questions about cocaine use in the last 90 days on the street were asked separately for six types of cocaine use: snorting, intravenous (IV) use, crack smoking, other (pure, ether-based) freebasing, coca paste smoking, and any other (new) form of cocaine. For each cocaine type, respondents were asked how many days cocaine was used and the usual number of doses per day. "Amount of cocaine use" was then calculated by multiplying "number of usual doses per day" by "number of days that dosage was used," to arrive at an estimated total quantity for each cocaine type used in the respondent's last 90 days on the street. These figures permitted calculation of each cocaine user's "primary cocaine type"—the one cocaine form, if any, which accounted for 75 percent or more of all cocaine used by each respondent. The resulting estimated totals for each cocaine type were recoded into variables ranging from zero (none) to six (1,350+ doses).

Measures for illegal activities were constructed in a similar fashion. For each of 23 crime types, respondents were asked on how many days the offense was committed and the usual number of offenses per day. Total crimes for the 90 days were then computed for each specific offense type. These numbers were combined into totals for six general crime types—violence-related, major property crime, petty property crime, prostitution and procuring, drug trafficking or manufacture, and street-level drug sales.

The Nature of the Connection

This analysis focuses on two issues: (1) the primary type of cocaine used; and (2) the crack/crime connection, in general and by race-ethnicity, and specifically among African Americans.

The first question addressed is that of whether black cocaine users were more likely than their white and Latino/a counterparts to have crack as their "primary cocaine type." A breakdown by ethnicity alone suggests no black/crack association: the only apparent differences in primary cocaine type by ethnicity are (1) a preference for snorting among Latinos/as (31.9 percent, compared with 12.3–13.2 percent of blacks and whites) and thus *less* preference for crack (58.2 percent, compared with 74.5 percent for both blacks and whites), and (2) more injection use among blacks (8.4 percent, compared with 1.4 percent–1.8 percent of Latinos/as and whites).

Because prior research suggests that gender, age, and treatment status might all be related to race-ethnic differences in cocaine-type preference, these three factors were

held constant so that a clearer picture of the relationship between race-ethnicity and primary cocaine type could be examined. The results indicate that among users ages 13 to 29 years who were interviewed on the street, there were very few differences in cocaine use by either ethnicity or gender. Crack was the primary cocaine type for every single street respondent under age 20, and for over 90 percent of street respondents ages 20 to 29, with the sole exception of Latino males. For the older cocaine users interviewed on the street, in contrast, both ethnic and gender differences appear. Among whites ages 30 to 49 years, all of the women and most of the men had crack as their primary cocaine type; Latino/a men ages 30 to 49 were split exactly 50-50 between crack and snorting; and black cocaine users ages 30 to 49 were clearly *least* likely to have crack as their primary cocaine type. In fact, among cocaine users ages 30 to 49 interviewed on the street, it was not crack but injection cocaine that was the primary cocaine type much more likely among blacks than among whites and Latinos/as.

The treatment groups present an even more complicated picture. Over 40 percent of the adolescent respondents used cocaine primarily by snorting, as did more than 20 percent of all women and all Latinos/as. Further, a significant minority of respondents in an apparently random selection of gender, age, and ethnicity subgroups used such a variety of cocaine forms that no one type accounted for 75 percent of their total use. This pattern of "No Primary Cocaine Type" was not seen for even one street respondent. Thus, crack use was clearly less common among the cocaine users in treatment than among their counterparts interviewed on the street, with a particularly strong contrast between users under age 30.

In a follow-up analysis, correlates of having crack as a primary cocaine type were computed. The results indicate that in this sample of 699 cocaine users, the only significant crack/ethnicity correlation indicates that Latino/a males are less likely to prefer crack. That is, being black (or white, for that matter) was unrelated to having crack as a primary cocaine type. Being younger or female, in contrast, was related to a preference for crack use. Street respondents were also much more likely than treatment respondents to have crack as a primary cocaine type.

For still another way of looking at the crack/black connection, correlates were computed for amount of crack used in the last 90 days by only the 499 respondents who were primary crack users. The prior analyses suggest *among cocaine users,* being black is *not* associated with being a crack user. This analysis asked whether *among crack users,* blacks use *more* crack than whites and Latinos/as. The results showed no relationship between amount of crack used and ethnicity or gender. Amount of crack used by primary crack users was significantly, although weakly, correlated with being in treatment, and was clearly related to being older.

The second question of interest is that of whether the crack/crime relationship documented in prior studies is indicative of a more general cocaine/crime association, or whether crack users are actually more crime-involved than other cocaine users. Analysis of only the 298 primary crack users interviewed on the street indicated that the crack/crime correlation among this subgroup is stronger than the general cocaine/crime correlation for all 699 cocaine users. These results suggest that the crack/crime association reported by other researchers is more than just a part of some general correlation between cocaine use and crime.

Given a definite crack/crime connection but only a very weak crack/black connection, the question for analysis necessarily shifts to that of whether there are differences in the crack/crime relationship for crack users of different ethnicities. Far too many crack users are *not* black for the crack/crime association to be a black phenomenon. Thus, is the white or Latino/a crack/crime connection different in degree or type from that for blacks?

This more detailed analysis of the crack/crime relationship was done for only the 298 primary crack users ages 13 to 49 years who were interviewed on the street. As seen in Table 21.1, respondents on the street—regardless of gender or ethnicity—were much more consistent than any other subgroup of cocaine users in preferring crack as their primary cocaine type. Confining further analysis to this subsample thus permits the clearest view of the crack/crime/race-ethnicity relationship because complications of treatment status can be ignored. Further, youth and adult crack users who are not in treatment are also the crack users who present the most obvious problem to policy makers and the criminal justice system, as well as to their families and neighborhoods. Thus, the "street crack user" subsample is arguably also the most appropriate and important one in which to more closely examine the crack/crime relationship.

The criminal involvement of this subsample is extensive, as shown in Table 21.1. Over 96 percent of each gender/race-ethnic category is involved in dealing drugs, most respondents committed petty property crimes, and some also committed major property crimes (burglary or motor vehicle theft) or violent offenses (robbery, assault, or weapons use). However, gender and race-ethnic differences also appear—more prostitution and procuring for women, and especially black women; more major property crimes for men, and especially Latino/a men; more petty property crimes among women; and more violent offenses among black women.

The extent to which these gender and ethnic variations in level of criminal involvement are related to amount of crack used varies greatly by crime type. In fact, strong correlations were found between amount of crack used and involvement with drug sales in most gender and ethnic subgroups. Prostitution was also correlated with amount of crack used for both black and white women. Violence-related offenses, in contrast, were related to the amount of crack used only among white females. Major property crimes, petty property crimes, and drug trafficking were not significantly related to amount of crack used for any of the subgroups.

A final question is why this apparent pattern of ethnic differences in the crack/crime relationship exists. While no differences are apparent among male respondents, the contrast between white and black female respondents seen in Table 21.1 is what would be expected in a sample if the difference

Table 21.1

Type of Crime Committed in the Last 90 Days by 298 Primary Crack Users Interviewed

Crime Type Committed	Male			Female	
	Black (n = 59)	White (n = 65)	Hispanic (n = 50)	Black (n = 56)	White (n = 68)
Violence-Related	19	16	12	22**	12
Major Property	8	13	16	2	0
Petty Property	39	43	41	50	56
Prostitution/Procuring	1	0	0	39**	29
Drug Trafficking	0	0	0	1	0
Drug Dealing	59	65	50	54	65

**Chi-square significant at p = .05.

were primarily one of differing socioeconomic status. In Miami, as in many other cities across the country, general socioeconomic indicators, such as income, education, and residential patterns, show markedly greater poverty among blacks than among whites.

One aspect of ethnic socioeconomic differences is the availability of economic resources. When respondents in this study were asked about sources of legal income or support, results indicated that job income was highly unusual. In the female street crack user subsample, current job income was reported by only one of the women ages 13 to 49. Welfare, disability, or other assistance were also rare; such income was reported by four of the 124 women ages 13 to 49 (3.2 percent of this subgroup). Unexpectedly, some kind of investment income was actually more common—15 of the respondents in this subsample reported this type of income. Unlike job income or government assistance, furthermore, reports of investment income were significantly more likely among white than black women. Thus, total numbers of female respondents with employment, assistance, and investment income indicate that whites were more likely to have such conventional economic resources than were blacks.

Most respondents, however, did have some legal source of support—most commonly, parents, spouse, or other people. Thus, only one in four of the female street crack user subsample reported obtaining over half of her living expenses from crime. However, economic support from parents, spouse, or other people may have a very different kind of crack/crime relevance—some persons who help pay for a crack user's living expenses may also help support a crack/crime lifestyle. Respondents were asked three questions about living circumstances: (1) Persons lived with last week, including (a) parents (with or without siblings), (b) spouse/opposite-sex partner, and (c) other people; (2) Do any of these people use crack or other cocaine?; and (3) Do any deal it? All co-residents reported as dealers were also reported as users. Results in the female street crack user subsample indicated that *every* respondent living with a spouse or person other than a parent reported living with another cocaine user. In contrast, only 47.8 percent of those living with their parents reported living with other cocaine users.

For the total 124 female street crack users, co-residence with a cocaine user was significantly related to race-ethnicity: 92.9 percent of black respondents reported co-resident cocaine involvement while only 45.6 percent of white respondents did so. In fact, black women were over 15 times more likely than white women to reside with a cocaine user. The relevance of greater cocaine involvement of co-residents is demonstrated by its marked correlations with other crack/crime indicators. Female respondents who reported greater cocaine involvement of co-residents were also significantly more likely to report obtaining more living expenses from crime and more overall crime.

Although no causal inferences can be made from this analysis, it does suggest that crime and crack use are part of a more general lifestyle that includes such everyday elements as persons with whom one lives and ways of meeting living expenses. The results also indicate that ethnic differences—particularly black/white differences—exist in both elements of that lifestyle and influences upon it. White respondents had less apparent need to commit crimes in order to pay for living expenses and were also less likely to reside with other cocaine-involved persons. Black respondents tended to show the opposite pattern—more living expenses paid for by crime, and more cocaine involvement among co-residents. These results suggest that differences that appear to be ethnic are in fact socioeconomic in nature. That is, it is socioeconomic factors such as (1) the degree of access to income sources other than crime and (2) the likelihood of living in a high drug/crime-rate environment that are important for understanding the crack/crime connection.

Discussion

In the 1991 case of *State v. Russell* (477 N.W.2d 886 [Minn. 1991]), the Minnesota Supreme Court invalidated a state law that punished the possession of crack-cocaine more harshly than that of powder-cocaine. The court invalidated the differential punishment largely on the grounds that it constituted an "illicit racial discrimination"—most people convicted of possessing powder-cocaine were white, while most of those convicted of possessing crack were black.

More specifically, under Minnesota Statute 152.023(2), a person is guilty of a "third-degree" offense if he or she possesses three or more grams of cocaine base ("crack-cocaine"). Under the same statute, a person must possess ten or more grams of cocaine powder to be guilty of the same offense. A person who possesses less than ten grams of powder is guilty of a fifth-degree offense (Section 152.025). Pursuant to these statutes, possession of three grams of crack carries a penalty of up to 20 years in prison,

while possession of an equal amount of powder-cocaine carries a penalty of up to five years in prison.

In *State v. Russell*, five African American men who were charged with violating Section 152.023(2) jointly moved the trial court to dismiss the charges on the grounds that the statute had a discriminatory effect on black persons and violated the equal protection guarantees of both the Minnesota and U.S. constitutions. The trial court noted that crack was indeed used primarily by African Americans, and powder-cocaine primarily by whites. Among the many statistics provided to the trial court were those showing that of all people charged with possession of cocaine base in 1988, 97 percent were black; of those charged with possession of powder-cocaine, 80 percent were white. The trial court agreed with the defendants and invalidated the sentencing scheme.

On an appeal brought by the state, it was contended that the state legislature had a permissible and legitimate interest in regulating the possession and sale of both crack- and powder-cocaine, and that it was reasonable for lawmakers to believe that the three grams of crack/ten grams of powder classification would regulate the possession of those drugs by the "street level" dealers at whom the statute was primarily aimed. The Minnesota Supreme Court was not persuaded, however, and affirmed that the sentencing scheme was in violation of the state constitution on equal protection grounds.

On the basis of the analysis in this chapter, is it possible that the Minnesota Supreme Court's holding in *Russell* was wrongly decided? Harvard law professor Randall Kennedy has argued that the Minnesota case was erroneously decided, and on several grounds (Kennedy 1994). Primarily:

> The portrayal of Minnesota's sentencing statute as a "burden" to blacks as a class is simplistic. Assuming that one believes in criminalizing the distribution of crack cocaine, punishing the conduct is a public good. It is a "burden" on those who are convicted of engaging in this conduct. But it is presumably a benefit for the great mass of law-abiding people. (pp. 1266–1267)

And Professor Kennedy added:

The Minnesota Supreme Court condemned the statute as imposing a racially discriminatory burden. But what is "racial" about punishment? Justice Wahl [writing the opinion for the court] writes as though the punishment falls upon blacks as a class. But to the extent that the heavier punishment for possession of crack falls upon blacks, it falls not upon blacks as a class but rather upon a subset of the black population—those in violation of the law who are apprehended (p. 1269).

Whether or not one agrees with Professor Kennedy's contentions, the analysis in this chapter suggests that crack may not be an "African American drug" and powder-cocaine a white American drug. The difference is not a race-ethnic matter, but one of socioeconomic status. However, one could argue that the research data presented here are from but one study and from one community, collected in a manner that may not be representative of the crack and cocaine using populations. Indeed, this would be a legitimate criticism, for drug users in Miami are certainly not representative of the nation as a whole. But nevertheless, other data are accumulating which tend to corroborate the Miami findings. In fact, a reanalysis of data from SAMHSA's 1988 *National Survey* compared race-ethnic group differences in crack smoking (Lillie-Blanton, Anthony, and Schuster 1993). The findings provided evidence that given similar social and environmental conditions (neighborhood, education, income, age, and gender), crack use does not depend on race-specific factors. This would clearly suggest that race-specific explanations of crack use likely obscure the role that social and environmental factors play in the overall epidemiology of crack use.

Most recently, the striking down of the Sentencing Guidelines by the U.S. Supreme Court as mandatory in *Booker* gave many critics of the 100-to-1 policy hope that the penalties for crack and powder cocaine would become more equal and more fair. Blog networks that cover legal issues, like *Sentencing Law and Policy* and *stopthedrugwar.org*, track almost every new crack case in which a judge attempts to sentence defendants outside of the policy. In fact, however, *Booker* has had a minimal effect in reducing sentences for crack offenses, as appellate courts have held that the power to change the Sentencing Guidelines and mandatory minimum sentences for drug offenses rests with Congress and not the courts. In this regard, the best hope for change may be the introduction of a bill in July 2006—*The Drug Sentencing Reform Act of 2006*—by a bipartisan group of U.S. senators that would reduce the disparity in federal sentencing guidelines from 100-to-1 to 20-to-1. No action has been taken by the Congress so far, however, and it is quite possible that the new bill will suffer the same fate as a similar effort that failed in 2002.

References

Adlaf, Edward M., Reginald G. Smart, and S. H. Tan (1989) "Ethnicity and Drug Use: A Critical Look," *International Journal of the Addictions* 24: 1–18.

Anglin, M. Douglas, Mary W. Booth, Timothy M. Ryan, and Yih-Ing Hser (1988) "Ethnic Differences in Narcotics Addiction. II. Chicano and Anglo Addiction Career Patterns," *International Journal of the Addictions* 23: 1011–27.

Austin, Gregory A., and M. Jean Gilbert (1989) "Substance Abuse Among Latino Youth," *Prevention Update* 3: 1–26.

Bachman, Jerald G., John M. Wallace, Patrick M. O'Malley, Lloyd D. Johnston, Candace L. Kurth, and Harold W. Neighbors (1991) "Racial/Ethnic Differences in Smoking, Drinking, and Illicit Drug Use Among American High School Seniors, 1976–89," *American Journal of Public Health* 81: 372–77.

Ball, John C., and Carl D. Chambers (1970) "Overview of the Problem," pp. 5–21 in John C. Ball and Carl D. Chambers (eds.), *The Epidemiology of Opiate Addiction in the United States* (Springfield, IL: Charles C. Thomas).

Boyd, Carol J., and Thomas Mieczkowski (1990) "Drug Use, Health, Family and Social Support in 'Crack' Cocaine Users," *Addictive Behaviors* 15:481–85.

Brunswick, Ann, Peter A. Messeri, and Angela A. Aidala (1990) "Changing Drug Use Patterns and Treatment Behavior: A Longitudinal Study of Urban Black Youth," pp. 263–311 in R. R. Watson (ed.), *Drug and Alcohol Abuse Prevention* (Clifton, NJ: Humana Press).

Carroll, Kathleen, and Bruce J. Rounsaville (1992) "Contrast of Treatment-Seeking and Untreated Cocaine Abusers," *Archives of General Psychiatry* 49: 646–71.

Cauchon, Dennis (1993) "Crack Sentencing Disparities Weighed," *USA Today*, November 10, p. 10A.

Chitwood, Dale D., and Patricia C. Morningstar (1985) "Factors Which Differentiate Cocaine Users in Treatment From Nontreatment Users," *International Journal of the Addictions* 20: 449–59.

Collins, R. Lorraine (1992) "Methodological Issues in Conducting Substance Abuse Research in Ethnic Minority Populations," *Drugs and Society* 6: 59–77.

Goldstein, Paul J., Patricia A. Belluci, Barry J. Spunt, and Thomas Miller (1991) "Volume of Cocaine Use and Violence: A Comparison Between Men and Women," *Journal of Drug Issues* 21: 345–67.

Griffin, Margaret L., Roger D. Weiss, Steven M. Mirin, and Ulrike Lange (1989) "A Comparison of Male and Female Cocaine Abusers," *Archives of General Psychiatry* 46: 122–26.

Hamid, Ansley (1990) "The Political Economy of Crack Related Violence," *Contemporary Drug Problems* 17: 31–78.

Inciardi, James A., Ruth Horowitz, and Anne E. Pottieger (1993) *Street Kids, Street Drugs, Street Crime* (Belmont, CA: Wadsworth).

Inciardi, James A., Dorothy Lockwood, and Anne E. Pottieger (1993) *Women and Crack-Cocaine* (New York: Macmillan).

Inciardi, James A., and Anne E. Pottieger (1991) "Kids, Crack and Crime," *Journal of Drug Issues* 21: 257–70.

——. (1994). "Crack Cocaine Use and Street Crime," *Journal of Drug Issues*, 24: 273–292.

Johnson, Bruce D., Elsayed Elmoghazy, and Eloise Dunlap (1990) "Crack Abusers and Noncrack Drug Abusers: A Comparison of Drug Use, Drug Sales, and Nondrug Criminality," paper presented at the Annual Meeting of the American Society of Criminology, Baltimore, MD, November 8.

Kandel, Denise B., Eric Single, and Ronald Kessler (1976) "The Epidemiology of Drug Use Among New York State High School Students: Distribution, Trends and Changes in Use," *American Journal of Public Health* 66: 43–53.

Kennedy, Randall (1994) "The State, Criminal Law, and Racial Discrimination: A Comment," *Harvard Law Review* 107: 1255–78.

King, Ryan S., and Marc Mauer (2006) *Sentencing with Discretion: Crack Cocaine Sentencing After Booker* (Washington, DC: The Sentencing Project).

Klein, Malcolm W., and Cheryl Maxson (1985) " 'Rock' Sales in South Los Angeles," *Sociology and Social Research* 69: 561–65.

Kleinman, Paula Holzman, and Irving Faber Lukoff (1978) "Ethnic Differences in Factors Related to Drug Use," *Journal of Health and Social Behavior* 19: 190–99.

Leiby, Richard (1994) "A Crack in the System," *Washington Post*, February 20, pp. F1, F4–F5.

Lillie-Blanton, Marsha, James C. Anthony, and Charles R. Schuster (1993) "Probing the Meaning of Racial/Ethnic Group Comparisons in Crack Cocaine Smoking," *Journal of the American Medical Association* 269: 993–97.

Maddehian, Ebrahim, Michael D. Newcomb, and Peter M. Bentler (1986) "Adolescents' Substance Use: Impact of Ethnicity, Income and Availability," *Advances in Alcohol and Substance Abuse* 5: 63–78.

Marin, Barbara V. (1990) "Latino/a Drug Abuse: Culturally Appropriate Prevention and Treatment," pp. 151–65 in R. R. Watson (ed.), *Drug and Alcohol Abuse Prevention* (Clifton, NJ: Humana Press).

McBride, Duane C., and James A. Swartz (1990) "Drugs and Violence in the Age of Crack Cocaine," pp. 141–69 in Ralph Weisheit (ed.), *Drugs, Crime and the Criminal Justice System* (Cincinnati: Anderson).

National Institute on Drug Abuse (1991) *National Household Survey on Drug Abuse: Population Estimates* (Rockville, MD: National Institute on Drug Abuse).

Prendergast, Michael L., Gregory A. Austin, Kenneth I. Maton, and Ralph Baker (1989) "Substance Abuse Among Black Youth," *Prevention Research Update* 4: 1–27.

Rebach, Howard (1992) "Alcohol and Drug Use Among American Minorities," *Drugs and Society* 6: 23–57.

Rounsaville, Bruce J., and Herbert D. Kleber (1985) "Untreated Opiate Addicts: How Do They Differ from Those Seeking Treatment?" *Archives of General Psychiatry* 42: 1072–77.

Segal, Bernard (1989) "Drug-Taking Behavior Among School-Aged Youth: The Alaska Experience and Comparisons with Lower 48 States," *Drugs and Society* 4: 1–17.

Substance Abuse and Mental Health Services Administration (SAMHSA) (2003) *National Survey on Drug Use and Health* (Rockville, MD: Substance Abuse and Mental Health Services Administration).

U.S. Sentencing Commission (1993) *Hearing on Crack Cocaine* (Washington, DC: November 9).

——. (2006) *Final Report on the Impact of* United States v. Booker *on Federal Sentencing* (Washington, DC: March).

Wallace, John M., and Jerald G. Bachman (1991) "Explaining Racial/Ethnic Differences in Adolescent Drug Use: The Impact of Background and Lifestyle," *Social Problems* 38: 333–57.

For Discussion

1. Would we expect to find similar results from studies conducted in other communities? Why or why not?

2. The Federal Sentencing Guidelines were introduced in part to minimize disparities by reducing judicial discretion. Are the guidelines fair and just with regard to the sentencing statutes for cocaine and crack cocaine? Why or why not?

22

An Ethno-epidemiological Model for the Study of Trends in Illicit Drug Use

Reflections on the 'Emergence' of Crack Injection

Michael C. Clatts
Dorinda L. Welle
Lloyd A. Goldsamt
Stephen E. Lankenau

In this chapter, Clatts et al. note the limitations of drug monitoring systems for uncovering particular patterns of drug use. Moreover, these systems offer little explanation as to *why* patterns occur. The authors describe how efforts to monitor the use of crack cocaine have ignored the possibility of injecting the drug. Their studies have demonstrated the importance of ethnography for assisting epidemiology as a monitoring tool.

Introduction

Sentinel drug forecasting systems often fail to adequately identify and assess emerging trends in the use of illegal drugs, with the result that public health systems are rarely able to adequately mobilise local, regional, and national prevention and treatment systems in a timely manner. The spread of crack cocaine in the USA in the 1980s is a prime ex-ample. Drug forecasting systems were slow to identify and track the rapid diffusion of crack smoking and both research and prevention lagged well behind the epidemic. When the epidemic did become apparent, much of the early information came from popular media that provided potent images of unbridled violence and luric sex, and subsequently, of public health and law enforcement's alleged control and triumph over the epidemic. In a tragic twist of "art imitating life," much of the research on crack use has reflected similarly erroneous assumptions about the nature of crack use, often playing upon and reinforcing stereotypical images of one type of user and one type of mode of administration, in an epidemiological trend that had a singular "start" and "end."

Despite the propositions made in the USA from sentinel data that the use of crack cocaine is waning, there is potent evidence that it remains prevalent among many groups of drug users, and indeed that both its use and its mode of administration have become more elaborate in the US. As far back as the late 1980s, there has been ample evidence of the emergence of the use of injection as a mode of administration in the use of crack cocaine. Despite its implications for the heightened risk for transmission of viral pathogens prevalent among IDU populations, including HIV, HBV, and HCV, the use of injection as a mode of administration in the use of crack remains virtually unrecognised in any of the "early warning systems" upon which public health programmes are reliant. Similarly, few service providers in the US are aware of crack injection, with the result that clients who report the use of crack are assumed to be crack smokers and are therefore not adequately screened or educated about injection risk

Researchers and service providers alike in the US have often tended to assume a uniformity across drug types and drug forms in the technical practices employed in preparing drug solutions for injection. At an epidemiological level, a failure to recognise variability in the behavioural practices themselves, has served to confound our understanding of how and why the prevalence of certain types of blood-borne pathogens, such as HIV-1 infection, for example, vary so widely at the regional and national level. In fact, however, recent research has shown these practices to be far more variable than has heretofore been appreciated in the epidemiological literature. For example, in an earlier study of heroin injection in the mid 1990s, we used ethnographic observation to document as yet unrecognised variability in the injection paraphernalia and technical practices that IDU's in the United States employ in preparing heroin for injection, and further showing that differences in paraphernalia selection processes and drug preparation practices, rather than [being] random or haphazard, were in fact direct responses to differences in the form of heroin that was available in a given time and place (Clatts, Heimer, Abdala, Goldsamt, Sotheran, Anderson, Gallo, Hoffer, Luciano & Kyriakides, 1999a). In subsequent laboratory studies in which these same observational data were used to model the potential effects of this variability on survival (and transmissibility) of HIV-1 in cookers, we showed that this unrecognised variability had significance for understanding regional differences in the prevalence of HIV infection among US IDU populations, a longstanding epidemiological puzzle (Clatts et al., 1999a). This study also showed the malleability of these practices, and the rapid shifts in drug preparation practices that attended shifts in situational fluctuations in the availability of particular forms of heroin, thereby challenging received notions of the nature of the drug injection processes which have represented them, variously, as chaotic and irrational, or alternatively as ritualised and static. In contrast, we demonstrated the importance of the macro and micro environment in injection processes, as well as the importance of understanding the "agency" of the injector in understanding injection decision-making.

Following our work in modeling variability in heroin injection practices, we initiated a similar study of crack injection. In this paper, we present some of [our] preliminary work on crack injection, and based on our experience in this study, we offer some reflections on ways that ethnography might contribute to monitoring trends in the use of illegal drugs, and identifying emerging behavioural practices that need to be antici-pated in mounting public health responses to the spread of blood-borne pathogens and other kinds of poor health outcomes among populations involved in drug abuse. We describe the current epidemiology of crack use in the US, including both its known and perhaps as yet unrecognised role in the injection-mediated spread of viral pathogens prevalent among drug users. With the overall goal of demonstrating the potential uses of ethnography in identifying emerging trends in the epidemiology of drug use, we highlight our methodological approach to the study of macro and micro level antecedents to the use of injection as a mode of administration in the use of crack, and we show how understanding variability in the behavioural practices used [in] preparing crack-based drug solutions may inform both research and prevention. We also highlight the unique contributions that ethnography can make in capturing the "voice" of drug injectors, showing the relevance of eliciting this kind of data in understanding emerging patterns in drug abuse.

The Epidemiology of Cocaine Injection and HIV

Cocaine injection has long been associated with increased risk for infection with HIV and other blood-borne pathogens (Anthony, Vlahov & Nelson, 1991; Battjes, Pickens & Haverkos, 1994; Bux, Lamb & Iguchi, 1995; Chaisson, Bacchetti & Osmond, 1989; Doherty, Garfein & Monterroso, 1996; Joe & Simpson, 1995; Meandzija, O'Connor & Fitzgerald, 1994; Nemoto, 1994). Associations between cocaine injection and HIV infection remain even after controlling for frequency and duration of injection (Rezza, Sagliocca & Zaccarelli, 1996; Thomas, Vlahov & Solmon, 1995), a fact attributed to higher-risk injection practices (notably "booting"; Greenfield, Bigelow & Bronner, 1992), higher levels of sexual risk (Bux et al., 1995; Hudgins, McCusker & Stoddard, 1995), and "binge injection" (Strathdee et al., 1997). Moreover, many studies have reported an elevated risk of seroconversion associated with cocaine injection (Anthony et al., 1991; Chaisson et al., 1989), including abrupt outbreaks of new HIV infections (Strathdee et al., 1997).

The emergence of crack—a cheap and potent form of cocaine that historically has been associated with the use of "smoking" as a mode of administration—only served to expand the size and composition of populations using cocaine-based substances. Before the late 1970s, many practical problems associated with the distribution and marketing of powder cocaine served to functionally limit the types of populations involved in chronic use as well as the ways in which it could be used in many of these groups. For example, the cost of a single dosage unit of powder cocaine was generally much more expensive than other illegal drugs such as heroin. In addition, the supply of powder cocaine was generally less dependable, and often involved a different distribution system than other street drugs such as heroin. Moreover, powder cocaine is especially susceptible to degradation from exposure to moisture, functionally limiting its shelf life and therefore its resale value in street drug markets.

Cocaine in the form of crack overcame several of these obstacles. Crack begins as cocaine HCl, and ammonia or baking soda is added to remove the hydrochloride and to create the pebble-sized crystalline freebase form. The pebble-sized "rocks" may be sold in the US in units for as little as $3.00, significantly less than the cost for a minimum amount of powder cocaine. Thus, transforming cocaine into crack form also facilitates expansion of distribution, particularly in street drug markets, since (relative to powder cocaine) the rock form can be divided into smaller, cheaper units that will accommodate the resources available to a larger population of potential users. With this marketing innovation, crack cocaine became accessible to poor populations at high risk for drug abuse (Golub & Johnson, 1997), including many populations of drug users that could not otherwise afford to purchase a minimum dose of powder cocaine (Clatts, 1998; Bourgois, 1995). In addition, many users believe that "rocking-up" powder cocaine serves to preserve powder cocaine, helping to protect it from moisture and extending its shelf life and marketability. Fi-

nally, and at least relative to "snorting," smoking delivers a fairly powerful and immediate dose to the brain, resulting in a "rush" whose intensity is not as easily or economically achieved in snorting powder cocaine.

Crack use began to appear in US cities as early as 1981 (Inciardi, 1987). By 1988, crack distribution had become so widespread in inner-city neighbourhoods that, in locales such as New York City, the income from crack distribution surpassed that of all other illegal drugs (Johnson, Golub & Fagan, 1995). The introduction of crack cocaine led to rapid adoption of crack smoking by injection drug users and other populations of drug users, so that by the early 1990s, many injection drug users reported smoking crack and also injecting other drugs (Carlson, Siegal, Falck & Wang, 1998). For example, in NIDA's NADR national database of 26,229 drug injectors recruited in research studies from 47 US cities, nearly half (49.4%) reported that they had used crack at least occasionally, most often with their more established heroin use (Chitwood, 1993).

Crack use has also been associated with HIV risk factors, including higher numbers of sexual partners, higher rates of STDs, and higher rates of HIV infection (Inciardi, 1987; Chaisson, Stoneburner, Hilderbrandt, Ewing, Telzak & Jafee, 1991; Jones et al., 1998). In studies of out-of-treatment, adult drug users, for example, Booth, Watters and Chitwood (1993) showed an increased risk for HIV associated with crack use (presumed to be smokers), particularly among those who also injected drugs (presumed to be heroin). Crack users were more likely to report sex with an injector, to have exchanged sex for money and/or drugs, to use drugs before or during sex, and to have had unprotected sexual intercourse. Crack users also injected (heroin) more frequently than non-crack smoking injectors, and reported higher overall frequencies of drug use (Booth et al., 1993).

While the injection of cocaine hydrochloride has been described since the time of Arthur Conan Doyle, crack injection has remained largely outside the purview of mainstream public health surveillance and forecasting systems. Moreover, as noted above, research in out-of-treatment populations of crack users (including virtually all of the studies cited above) have presumed smoking as the exclusive mode of administration in the use of this substance. As early as the late 1980s, a number of anecdotal reports appeared, principally from ethnographers, describing the emergence of injection as a mode of administration in the use of crack cocaine (cf. Clatts, 1989). The first published report of crack injection in the United States came from Johnson and Ouellet (1996), followed by a report from Carlson (2000) working in Ohio. Subsequently, injection of crack cocaine has been reported in diverse US populations (Clatts & Davis, 1999; Hunter, Donoghoe & Stimpson, 1995), across several US cities (including Atlanta, Boston, Denver, and Austin, Texas; Community Epidemiology Working Group, 1998), as well as in drug using populations outside the US (Hunter et al., 1995; Millson et al., 1998). Particularly noteworthy are studies in London that showed that once crack injection is introduced to a community, rapid adoption of the practice follows, as injection drug users adopt the practice and people who have previously only smoked cocaine initiate injection. A London study, for example, showed that the prevalence of crack injection increased from 1 to 27% in an injection drug using population over a 4-year period (1990–1993; Hunter et al., 1995).

Like any drug that is marketed in dry form, however, crack cocaine must somehow be transformed into soluble form [if] it is to be injected. Common types of acids used in the preparation of crack-based solutions include fresh lemon juice, reconstituted lemon concentrate, citric acid, and vinegar. Choice of acid may be contingent on variations in "taste" of drugs, or on choices made relative to injectors' perceptions of which acid is best to inject (Carlson et al., 1998).

Curiously, however, there remains a dearth of epidemiological research on crack injection, despite the fact that there is ample evidence of the use of injection as a mode of administration in the use of this substance. Crack injection may contribute to our understanding of the prevalence and distribu-

tion of blood-borne pathogens among crack users, and were this practice to become widespread and common, it may significantly exacerbate syringe-mediated transmission risk in a number of already vulnerable populations. The dearth of information about the types of users in which crack injection is prevalent, and the types of behavioural practices with which crack injection is associated, thwarts our epidemiological understanding of the spread of HIV and other pathogens prevalent among IDUs, as well as our ability to target effective prevention messages and strategies where they are most needed.

If we are to begin to understand the potential epidemiological significance of crack injection, at least two key questions emerge. First, what are the specific behavioural practices employed in preparing crack cocaine for injection and how might variability in the distribution of these practices contribute to our understanding of risk for transmission of blood-borne pathogens? Second, how are the various practices used to prepare crack for injection distributed amongst IDU populations and at the level of the individual injector, how are they acquired? Third, to the extent that some form of trend may be discernable in the adoption of crack injection, how have particular social, economic, and political factors contributed to the use of injection as a mode of administration in the use of crack cocaine?

The Use of Ethnography in the Study of Crack Injection

Ethnography, following Malinowski's earlier vision, is still often presented as an "organic" process in which research questions continue to "emerge" over the course of extended study. Unfortunately, this impression of ethnographic research, while in some contexts valid, may serve to undermine how the method is understood outside the various disciplines in which it has historically been practiced. Ironically, while this impression may have served to reinforce an understanding of ethnography's utility in identifying changes in patterns of consumption and administration in the use of drugs [emerging] at the local level, the impression of ethnography as an amorphous mode of inquiry perhaps undermined an understanding of the capacity of the method to be used as an effective tool in developing comparative data bases as well as in monitoring changes in drug abuse over both time and place.

Our ongoing research on crack injection employs a targeted ethnographic approach to several key epidemiological questions. We have detailed the theoretical and methodological underpinnings of ethno-epidemiology in several publications (Clatts, Sotheran, Heimer & Goldsamt, 1999b; Clatts & Sotheran, 2000; Clatts, Welle & Goldsamt, 2001), and continue to build this model through our ongoing study of crack injection. Ethnography informs the epidemiology through its focus on drug injectors, the physical and social contexts in which they inject drugs, and the contextual factors that exacerbate or attenuate the various behavioural practices used to inject drugs and associated with HIV risk. In addition, an ethnographic epidemiology seeks to detail the material and behavioural sources of HIV risk, as well as unintended consequences of the social and political environments which serve to constrain how illegal drugs are acquired and used. As we detail the study and some preliminary findings (below), additional dimensions of this synthetic approach will become apparent.

We employ a "controlled comparison design," conducting parallel ethnographic inquiry in six cities in North America, where pilot work has evidenced the prevalence of crack injection: New York City; Bridgeport, CT; Chicago, IL; Atlanta, GA; Los Angeles, CA; and Toronto, Canada. The study design includes a preliminary "community assessment" phase, in which ethnographers identify local knowledge of crack injection at the systems level (e.g. public health departments), service delivery level (hospitals, drug treatment programs, social service agencies, street outreach programs, precincts, needle exchanges), and street level (e.g. individual users and members of their social groups/networks). Injectors are invited to participate in a semi-structured ethnographic interview focused on drug use history, initiation into crack injection, settings/venues for crack injection, and unin-

tended consequences of crack injection. The ethnographic interview additionally elicits participants' rationale for injecting crack. Ethnographic interviews serve as a means to develop adequate rapport and facilitate access to settings and groups in which crack injection is occurring, thereby facilitating access to settings and groups in which firsthand observation of drug acquisition strategies and injection practices can be accomplished. In the following section, we detail our current work on crack injection to demonstrate the relevance of ethnography in identifying drug injection practices as these practices are embedded in micro and macro contexts. It is in studying the relationship of micro and macro level contexts that we seek to build "up" an understanding of local and regional trends in the use of drugs.

Ethnographers often refer to their research activities—that is, to the process of talking, listening, and observing—as if they were inalienable processes. On some levels this is true, both in relation to how use of the methods might appear to a casual observer of the ethnographer, as well as in the way in which the ethnographer might use different types of data and sources of information in representing a particular finding. However, the components of the method can be disentangled at an operational level and the kind of information acquired from each part of the process can be distilled from the whole, thereby providing the basis for comparisons between behavioural practices, injection groups, and injection settings, and thus providing the basis for conducting parallel lines of inquiry across dimensions of both time and place.

Physical Settings, Drug Administration, and Drug Markets

Users' decisions whether to use and how to administer powder or crack cocaine are often situationally determined. In the case of crack injection, our investigation of physical settings has identified fluctuations in local cocaine markets that have informed individuals' decisions to use and inject crack cocaine. Thus, one of the unintended consequences of interdiction and pressure on "supply" of cocaine may be that it results in at least short-term gaps in local supply, as well as associated shifts in cost, purity, and availability of powder cocaine. At the level of local drug markets, changes in the quality, availability, and cost of powder cocaine may have unintended consequences for how the drug is used, and may situate the emergence [of] injection as a mode of administration.

It is interesting to note that relative to the general literature on drug injection, our preliminary findings suggest a lesser role for injection groups in the case of crack injection: in most of the cities studied, crack injectors report injecting alone rather than in groups. Thus we find variability not only within macro- and micro-level settings, but also in the relative significance of macro-level versus micro-level settings in informing the environmental dimensions of crack injection. The ways in which these situational factors are related to episodic shifts in modes of administration are not anticipated in drug forecasting systems.

The Use of Targeted Observation in Identifying Sources of HIV Transmission

The prominence of macro-level environmental dimensions in the emergence of crack injection does not preclude the use of targeted participant-observation at the micro-level. Accurate accounts of the full range of behavioural practices associated with drug preparation and injection are particularly difficult to obtain from self-reports, and are best gleaned from systematic observations of drug injection events. Prior to our current research on crack injection, the full range of behavioural practices used to prepare and inject crack cocaine, including potential sources of variability within these practices that may exacerbate or attenuate risk for transmission of blood-borne pathogens, had not been described. We are investigating variability across both material and behavioural dimensions. For example, crack injection observations are capturing the types of acids used to dissolve crack, the duration of exposure to acidic environments, the use and duration of heating of drug solu-

tions, the entry of blood into syringes, the volume of blood "booted" into the syringe, and the practices associated with "binge" injection.

Observations of crack injection events are informed by targeted epidemiological questions about the viability of HIV and other blood-borne pathogens when exposed to specific conditions (such as heat) or liquids (such as acids) in the course of transforming drugs into soluble form for injection. In some respects, our observational protocol more closely resembles the highly detailed cataloguing of materials and observation of practices common to a more traditional anthropology (for example, Firth, 1966), and it provides the basis for understanding the role of "material culture" in drug use practices. Over the course of our prior work, we have developed a targeted observational methodology to facilitate the laboratory modeling of the effects of specific drug preparation and injection practices on the transmission of viral pathogens among drug users (Clatts et al., 1999a). Following this model used in our prior work on heroin, we have conducted targeted observations of events involving the injection of crack, coded these observations, and are now utilising the observational data to model the practices involved in the preparation and injection of the drug solution. In particular, our research group, including the team of laboratory virologists with whom we collaborate, are investigating the viability of HIV-1 when exposed to the conditions and materials established in the preparation and injection of crack cocaine, particularly the effects of acids on the viability of HIV-1.

Documenting Variability: The Use of Targeted Participant-Observation

Our approach challenges the notion of "drug injection" as a uniform epidemiological category, and prioritises the elicitation of variability in the behavioural practices used to prepare drugs for injection, including the influence of situational factors derived from either the physical or social environment in producing this variability. This was a purposeful choice on our part, and was intended as a corrective response to the fact that an understanding of variability—historically, one of the most salient functions of ethnographic methods—especially in US-based research, had been largely overshadowed in drug research by an interest in central tendencies. Much of the drug research prior to the emergence of HIV, for example, focused largely on "the heroin addict" chasing a fairly static drug habit located within a monolithic and a historical "culture of sharing." Early epidemiological studies placed much less emphasis on the drug user, examining the ways that the drug itself "structured" the seemingly invariable characteristics of drug use. In large measure, drug research (including much of the early work conducted in the context of HIV prevention among drug using populations) had become content with descriptions of a unified drug user "subculture" and facile "predictions" of the type of "behavioural animal" that the use of a particular type of drug could be expected to produce.

Despite efforts by some ethnographers (cf. Preble & Casey, 1969; Agar, 1973) to detail the everyday strategies with which heroin users actively and purposely organised their drug use, economic activities, and social relationships, much of the US-based ethnographic research on drug abuse that emerged in the 1990s, particularly that which was conducted in the context of HIV research, aimed at populating the notion of a drug "subculture" and an assumption about the presence of a system of shared values, norms, and practices among drug users. In this context, qualitative and quantitative drug research produced surprisingly complementary portraits of a population of drug users with a unified set of drug use practices. This effort, while perhaps springing from an interest in depathologising drug injectors, nevertheless had the unfortunate consequence of over-stating the degree to which interactions among drug users can be seen as deriving from some kind of social order. An attention to social order came at the expense of attention to the economic imperatives that are critical to understanding interactions among drug users, particularly the high level of contingency that governs everyday exchanges. As one drug user commented in response to a question about his social networks, "I have no friends out here, only associates," an apt description of his view of the social world of drug users on the streets that highlights the brittleness and contingency that characterises the nature of these social relations. In our experience, the building blocks of social relations among drug users are not those of [a] unique local drug subculture, but rather are grounded in emerging micro-level and macro-level markets.

As noted in the Section 1 of this essay, similarly problematic assumptions have attended the use of crack cocaine, with the result that our understanding of them has often lacked sufficient attention to complexity. Early on, researchers noted an association between smoking crack and high risk sexual behaviour. In both epidemiological reports, the popular press, and indeed among many drug users themselves, crack, sex, and violence became inseparable images in which the substance was used to define both the type of person the user was and the types of behavioural practices in which they were likely engaged. Epidemiologists were quick to report the central tendency associations between crack use and sexual risk, with limited reflection on the interaction of both behavioural complexes and background socioeconomic factors. These perceptions were also reproduced at the street level. Longtime heroin users who had begun to switch from powder cocaine to the use of crack, often in the context of concomitant use of heroin, contributed these stereotypical images of the crack user through their own efforts to distinguish themselves from "crack heads" who they represented as having descended to the lowest form of drug use. None of these constituencies sought to reconcile the inherent conflict between the image of the user and the multiple realities of the use of crack cocaine.

Quite apart from the social and political implications of these images, however, the ethnographic goal of documenting variability in drug use practices and users' perspectives on the logic of the use of one type of practice versus another has the potential to enhance our understanding of the distribution of HIV risk and other unintended consequences associated with injection drug use. By documenting sources of variability in injection drug use, the traditional "drug-driven" methodology and its mono-causal explanatory framework can be overcome. Through the targeted use of participant-observation, variability can be documented along numerous dimensions populated and shaped by drug users themselves, including setting, social group, the discrete type and form of drug solutions, and injection practices. Thus, the research focus shifts from documenting characteristics and effects of either the drug itself, or the drug "subculture," to identifying the variable and ever-shifting practices and materials with which users orchestrate the use of illegal drugs.

In the course of our current work on crack injection, it has become apparent that the ethnographic study of variability of drug injection practices yields valuable information about emerging drug use trends, their causes and consequences. Whereas sentinel systems work from the institutional level "down" to document drug use trends, ethnographic approaches can work from the "ground up," first documenting variability in practices, and then establishing the relevance of the agency of the user and the contexts of use for the understanding of wider drug use trends. A perfect illustration of this is found in how powder cocaine users, faced with decreased availability of affordable powder cocaine, innovate ways to break crack—a far cheaper form of cocaine—into soluble form for injection. The most important question in understanding the appearance of crack injection may not be whether it is a "trend" or not. Rather it lies in understanding how this practice may be related to periodic changes in the availability of powder cocaine, and thereby contribute to our understanding of how episodic uses of alternative drug forms and alternative modes of administration are operant in increases in injection-mediated risks. Sentinel systems can say little about why drug use trends occur; however, ethnographic approaches can elucidate, through a dual attention to variability and voice, the situated changes in drug use practices that institutionally-based information systems cannot capture.

At the macro or community level, our prior research on heroin injection demonstrated the significance of physical settings and injection groups as they variously inform the stratification of HIV risk among IDUs. Similarly, our study of crack injection has aimed to describe both the physical and social settings in which crack is injected, with a specific interest in describing the social hierarchies of injection groups. By identifying social status and resource differences across dimensions such as race, ethnicity, gender, age, injection experience, access to the drug, knowledge of needle safety, and the use of needle exchange, the distribution of risk within injection groups can be described in [a] social context.

Documenting Voice: The Use of Semi-structured Ethnographic Interviews

Although systematic observations of crack injection provide unprecedented detail about material and behavioural sources of risk, it is also imperative to obtain injectors' own accounts and interpretations of the use of these materials and methods. Whereas observations provide a window onto variability, ethnographic interviews give voice to injectors' drug use history and the ways they organise and understand crack injection in the "real world." Without this dimension of voice, observations of injection behaviour lack an interpretive context. Ethnographic research has distinguished itself for its willingness to consider even the most stigmatised persons to evidence agency and adaptability and to ascribe meaning to their experiences or practices. Through the analysis of open-ended accounts of subjects' drug use, antecedents to decisions about modes of [administration] (including transition to injection) can be identified, with direct relevance for the development of prevention and outreach. Since a structured interview or survey cannot adequately anticipate the content of new practices or emergent trends, semi-structured ethnographic interviews are imperative in giving the subject ample means to describe practices and trends that researchers cannot adequately anticipate.

In our current work, ethnographic interviews focus on five areas: (1) initiation into injection drug use; (2) initiation into crack injection; (3) injection "training," i.e. sources of knowledge about the technical aspects of the preparation of crack based solutions for injection; (4) patterns of crack injection; and (5) unintended consequences of crack injection, particularly consequences for vein health. We have also sought to describe crack users' rationales for employing injection as a mode of administration in the use of crack-cocaine, in order to identify antecedents to transition to injection. Although we anticipated initiation into crack injection to be a significant area of investigation, we were surprised to discover its potential for variability and hence complexity. Preliminary analysis of our data indicate that transitions into crack injection are not strictly linear but evidence significant complexity, in some cases spanning multiple "drug use careers." Many users have reported several years time in between their first injection event (which often involved heroin) and their first injection of crack cocaine. Other typically younger injectors have described their first crack injection event as their initiation into injection drug use.

Injecting Alone: Crack Injection on the Margins

Given our prior work with heroin injectors who have developed an elaborate language for the various dimensions of heroin use and "the life" that supports it (Clatts et al., 1999), we were initially surprised to find that crack users who acknowledged the use of injection had not elaborated a unique terminology to describe the practices and materials used in crack injection. When crack injection is recognised as a relatively new or emerging practice, the apparent lack of "slang" terminology would not be unusual. In fact, however, many users report having employed injection as a mode of administration in the use of crack, at least episodically, for many years. In some respects, this makes the absence of an elaboration of language to describe the practice all the more remarkable.

Moreover, the demonstrable lack of "voice" among crack injectors is evidenced along other dimensions as well. Crack injec-

tors provided limited rationale for injecting crack; many described a rather unpleasant "high" which rated poorly compared to crack smoking and other drug use. Supporting this picture of a "social poverty" of crack injection, most crack injectors reported injecting alone rather than in injection groups and in private rather than public settings. In fact, some crack injectors noted that they were not "initiated" into crack injection by any particular person, but gathered the information "on their own" and began injecting crack "solo": a relatively unique picture for injection drug use that challenges received notions about the import of social pressure and socialisation in the initiation of drug use.

Although many of these preliminary findings suggest that crack injectors may be avoiding some of the very factors—needle sharing, injection groups, public settings—that can contribute to HIV risk, the emergent picture of the "lone" crack injector adverse to revealing their involvement in crack injection points to the degree of stigma that surrounds crack use in general. Many of the participants in our study had begun to inject crack in neighbourhood milieus where crack had come to be associated with any number of social ills, and where crack smokers were shunned as "crack heads." Injection crack use brings into play additional dimensions of stigma: not only is injection drug use stigmatised and the possession of syringes criminalised, but the phenomenon of crack injection is typically treated as an all-out impossibility by outreach workers, drug treatment providers, emergency room personnel, and not a few drug researchers. Many crack injectors described their own revulsion at first ever hearing about crack injection: "That's sick!" "That's crazy!" "I've tried everything but I would never try THAT!" After subsequently having "tried" crack injection, crack injectors are especially reluctant to discuss their ongoing use. Thus, crack injectors might be understood to be located on the margins or borders of micro social contexts (e.g. local drug user networks) and macro social contexts (e.g. community and service systems).

Accounts of initiation into crack injection, for example, lack the kind of elaborate narrative that is often found among users of other drugs, notably heroin. As a kind of "non-event," then, the use of injection in the use of crack may represent a situational "development," rather than the sudden adoption of an entirely new practice. Indeed the fact that crack users, including many who have used crack for several years, report the use of injection as an episodic event serves to challenge assumptions about the role that injection has often been thought to play in signaling the escalation of addiction and routinisation of a "drug habit." Preliminary data suggest that initiation into crack injection may in fact be a more "gradual" process, characterised by accumulated shifts in drug form, mode of administration, and in some cases, drug type: shifts that may move to and from different modes of administration on a situational basis.

While admittedly preliminary, these data challenge the addiction model, which would posit sustained individual factors in explaining initiation and onset of injection, and argue instead for an occupational hazards model in which initiation may more properly be seen as a consequence of sustained exposure to a set of operant conditions which favor the routinisation of one mode of administration over another. For example, the local emergence of crack injection seems to be constituted by shifts in drug form (as users switch from the use of powder cocaine to the use of "rock" crack cocaine) as well as shifts in mode of administration (as users switch from smoking crack to injecting it, or from sniffing powder cocaine to injecting crack cocaine). Some users have also reported alternating drug form (powder vs. crack cocaine) and mode of administration (sniffing cocaine or injecting heroin/cocaine "speedballs" vs. injecting crack) in response to cocaine market trends.

It should be noted as well, that some subjects have reported years of heroin injection, followed by a switch to crack injection, suggesting that a third dimension in the emergence of crack injection—shift in drug type—is also evidenced. Again, these are exactly the type of situationally-based trends that sentinel systems fail to register in a timely way. Moreover, even when these systems identify a trend, it is precisely these types of processes that trend data are ill-suited to describe or explain in relation to the development of practical interventions. It will be interesting to see how innovations in trend theory . . . will contribute to the further development of an ethno-epidemiological approach to studying episodic patterns of drug injection as well as longer term drug use trends.

Conclusion

There are a number of lessons to be drawn from our ongoing work in developing an ethnographic approach that can capture variability while also informing our understanding of emerging drug trends. Certainly ethnography has a significant role to play in identifying drug use trends as well as episodic patterns in drug use. Our current work on crack injection has underscored the value of the study of types and sources of variability on two fronts. First, documenting variability in the use, preparation, and administration of illegal drugs facilitates the identification of sources of HIV risk. This is best illustrated through our prior work in New York and Denver, where we identified regional differences in the availability and use of "powder" versus "tar" heroin, and documented differences (variability) in the material culture and associated behavioural practices that IDUs employ in preparing these different forms for injection (Clatts et al., 1999a). In Denver, where tar heroin was predominantly available, injectors typically used spoons and heavier types of metal vessels to prepare heroin solutions, and were observed heating heroin solutions for extended intervals. In New York City, where powder heroin was widely marketed, most injectors used thinner types of heating vessels and prepared their drug solutions without heating the drug solution prior to injection. Those NY injectors who did apply heat did so for significantly shorter intervals than injectors using tar heroin in Denver. A minority of injectors in each city who were observed using the form of heroin more common in the other city (i.e. powder in Denver and tar in NY) were observed to immediately adapt their preparation practices.

Ongoing laboratory studies of HIV transmissibility used these observation-based models of heroin injection practices in order to examine the effects of exposure [to] HIV-1 in heating cookers[;] laboratory studies showed that different heating practices have different effects on the viability of HIV-1 (ibid.). Depending on the virus liter, the type of "cooker," the heat source, and volume of solution being examined, we extrapolated that the virus would be inactivated following 7–15 s of heating. Applying the observational data to the laboratory simulations revealed that inactivation would occur in only 6% of the injections observed in NYC. In contrast, the heating practices observed in Denver would be sufficient to inactivate the virus in 57% of the injections. These data suggest that dramatic regional differences in seroprevalence may, at least in part, be attributable to the effect of regional differences in the way in which drug solutions are prepared and their differential impact in inactivating HIV-1.

Importantly, however, these regional differences in the preparation of drug solutions are themselves constructed through the forms of heroin available in local drug markets. In other words, regional variations in the marketing of heroin directly informed more general "drug use trends" as well as the consequent patterns of HIV seroprevalence in New York and Denver. The significant differences in seroprevalence between East coast and West coast IDU populations is a longstanding epidemiological puzzle, and one that has confounded attempts at explanation even when controlling for differences in historicity, syringe sharing, and injection networks among local IDU populations. Our findings suggest that the heating practices employed by heroin injectors using tar heroin appear to contribute some measure of protection against the viability of HIV-1, and hence to attenuate its transmission (at least in the context of multi-person use of injection paraphernalia such as "cookers" which are typically used to prepare drugs for injection and to divide them for the purposes of drug sharing). Thus, it may be that some types of heroin injection (as informed by local availability of powder vs. tar heroin)

are less likely to result in transmission (as a function of heating).

This brings home the second lesson of our ongoing work thus far: For the purposes of developing an ethnographic approach that can inform our understanding of emerging drug use trends, it becomes imperative to consider variability of injection practices in relation to macro contexts such as local and regional drug markets. Beyond the "thick description" of exoticised behavioural practices among local groups, ethnography has the potential to demonstrate unrecognised variability within assumed epidemiological categories (such as injection drug use) and thereby contribute to unraveling complexities in the spread of blood-borne pathogens that are not easily illuminated by other types of data.

By examining a practice—namely, crack injection—which many have assumed to be logically "impossible," we continue to identify sources of injection risk that have gone unexamined for nearly 20 years. In the case of crack injection, it became paramount to foreground "voice"—that is, to undertake direct observation and to elicit descriptions of users' own experience, rather than relying simply on the available epidemiological literature to inform our understanding of how and why users might employ injection as a mode of administration in the use of crack cocaine. At the same time, the effort to elucidate "voice" of crack injectors underscored the multiple sources of stigma that crack injectors confront. Thus, by attending to the complementary dimensions of variability and voice, ethnography can expose and critically examine assumptions of uniformity across drug users, drug types, drug forms, and drug preparation and injection practices. Community assessments in particular can enable ethnographers to identify and connect macro-level processes (such as changes in drug form, drug availability, and price) with micro-level sources of risk practices and protective factors. Rather than search for a universal theory of "drug use" or aim to describe discrete subcultures of "drug users," an ethnographic epidemiology can employ a unique approach in its regional grounding, eye for material culture, ear for "indigenous" description of disregarded practices, and willingness of ethnographers to immerse themselves in challenging local milieus where practices obtain their everyday "logic."

Ethnography, in contrast to approaches developed by sentinel systems, is inherently about implementing systematic methods in an ongoing, open investigation, utilising methods that enable the identification of new sources of variability, assign an interpretive role to drug users themselves, and provide direction in understanding how and why certain drug use trends are sustained over time and how and why others appear episodically. As a field-based research approach, ethnography can enhance the ways that sentinel systems identify and track drug use trends and sources of HIV risk. Through the application of community assessments, targeted observations, and ethnographic interviewing, it becomes possible to elucidate particularly localised domains of variability as they are embedded in micro and macro contexts. By locating ethnographic sentinel systems "on the ground" where emergent practices and trends develop and inform each other, it may be possible to eventually include and track a wider range of hidden drug user populations and obscured sources of injection-mediated HIV risk—such as those implicated in crack injection. Such an integration of epidemiological goals and ethnographic methods may well carry drug research towards a field-based ethno-epidemiology that can discern the relationship between variability of injection practices and emerging drug use trends.

References

Agar, M. (1973). *Ripping and running*. New York: Academic Press.

Anthony, J. C., Vlahov, D. & Nelson, K. E. (1991). New evidence on intravenous cocaine use and the risk of infection with human immunodeficiency virus type 1. *American Journal of Epidemiology* 134, 1175–1189.

Battjes, R. J., Pickens, R. W. & Haverkos, H. W. (1994). HIV risk factors among injecting drug users in five US cities. *AIDS* 8, 681–687.

Booth, R. E., Watters, J. K. & Chitwood, D. D. (1993). HIV risk related sex behaviors among injection drug users, crack smokers, and injection drug users who smoke crack. *American Journal of Public Health* 83, 1144–1148.

Bourgois, P. (1995). *Search of respect: selling crack in El Bario*. New York: Cambridge University Press.

Bux, D. A., Lamb, R. J. & Iguchi, M. Y. (1995). Cocaine use and HIV risk behavior in methadone maintenance patients. *Drug and Alcohol* 37, 29–35.

Carlson, R. G. (2000). Shooting galleries, dope houses, and injection doctors: examining the social ecology of HIV risk behaviors among drug injectors in Dayton, OH. *Human Organization* 59 (3), 325–333.

Carlson, R. G., Siegal, H. A., Falck, R. S. & Wang, J. (1998). Crack cocaine injection in the heartland: an ethnographic perspective. Presented at the annual meetings of the society for applied anthropology, San Juan, Puerto Rico.

Chaisson, R. E., Bacchetti, P. & Osmond, D. (1989). Cocaine use and HIV infection in intravenous drug users in San Francisco. *Journal of the American Medical Association* 261, 561–565.

Chaisson, M. A., Stoneburner, R. L., Hilderbrandt, D. S., Ewing, W. E., Telzak, E. E. & Jafee, H. A. (1991). Heterosexual transmission of HIV-1 associated with use of smokable freebase cocaine (crack). *AIDS* 5, 1121–1126.

Chitwood, D. D. (1993). Epidemiology of crack use among injecting drug users and sex partners of injecting drug users. In B. S. Brown, et al. (Ed.), *Handbook on AIDS, IV drug users, and sexual behaviors in the US—trends, issues, and intervention strategies*. New York, NY: Greenwood Press.

Clatts, M. C. (1989). Substance abuse and AIDS prevention strategies for homeless youth: an ethnographic perspective. Paper presented at the third international gay and lesbian health conference, San Francisco, CA.

——. (1998). Ethnographic observations of men who have sex with men in public: notes and queries toward an ecology of sexual action. In W. Leap (Ed.), *Gay sex, public space* (pp. 141–156). Columbia University Press.

Clatts, M. C. & Davis, W. R. (1999). A demographic and behavioral profile of homeless youth in New York City: implications for AIDS outreach and prevention. *Medical Anthropology Quarterly* 13 (3), 365–374.

Clatts, M. C., Heimer, R., Abdala, N., Goldsamt, L. A., Sotheran, J. L., Anderson, K. T., Gallo, T. M., Hoffer, L. D., Luciano, P. A. & Kyriakides, T. (1999a). HIV-1 transmission in injection paraphernalia: heating drug solutions may inactivate HIV-1. *JAIDS* 22 (2), 194–199.

Clatts, M. C., Sotheran, J. L., Heimer, R. & Goldsamt, L. A. (1999b). Interdisciplinary research on transmission of blood-borne pathogens among drug injectors: applications of ethnography in epidemiology and public health. In P. A. Marshall, M. Singer, M. C. Clatts, R. Needle & E. Lambert (Eds.), *Integrating cultural, observational, and epidemiology approaches in the prevention of drug abuse and HIV/AIDS: current status and future prospects* (pp. 74–93). Rockville, MD: National Institutes on Drug Abuse.

Clatts, M. C. & Sotheran, J. L. (2000). Challenges in research on drug and sexual risk practices of men who have sex with men: applications of ethnography in HIV epidemiology and prevention. *AIDS and Behavior* 4 (2), 169–179.

Clatts, M. C., Welle, D. L. & Goldsamt, L. A. (2001). Reconceptualizing the interaction of drug and sexual risk among MSM speed users: notes toward an ethno-epidemiology. *AIDS and Behavior* 5 (2), 115–130.

Community Epidemiology Working Group (1998). *Epidemiologic trends in drug abuse, vol. 1: highlights and executive summary*. Bethesda, MD: National Institutes of Health, Division of Epidemiology and Prevention Research, National Institute of Drug Abuse.

Doherty, M. C., Garfein, R. S. & Monterroso, E. (1996). Younger age of initiating injecting drug use is associated with risky behavior and HIV infection in short-term injectors. Presented at the XI international conference on AIDS, Vancouver, Canada.

Firth, R. (1966). *Malay fisherman*. New York: Norton.

Golub, A. & Johnson, B. D. (1997). *Crack's decline: some surprises across US cities. Research in brief. Washington, DC: US Department of Justice, National Institute of Justice*.

Greenfield, L., Bigelow, G. E. & Brooner, R. K. (1992). HIV risk behavior in drug users: increased blood "booting" during cocaine injection. *AIDS Education Prevention* 4, 95–107.

Hudgins, R., McCusker, J. & Stoddard, A. (1995). Cocaine use and risky injection and sexual behaviors. *Drug and Alcohol Dependence* 37, 7–14.

Hunter, G. M., Donoghoe, M. C. & Stimpson, G. V. (1995). Crack use and injection on the increase among injecting drug users in London. *Addiction* 90, 1397–1400.

Inciardi, J. A. (1987). Beyond cocaine: basuco, crack, and other coca products. *Contemporary Drug Problems* 14, 461–492.

Joe, G. W. & Simpson, D. D. (1995). HIV risks, genders, and cocaine use among opiate users. *Drug and Alcohol Dependence* 37, 23–28.

Johnson, W. A. & Ouellet, L. J. (1996). The injection of crack cocaine among Chicago drug users. *American Journal of Public Health* 86 (2), 266.

Johnson, B. D., Golub, A. & Fagan, J. (1995). Careers in crack, drug use, drug distribution and non-drug criminality. *Crime and Delinquency* 41, 275–295.

Jones, D. L., Irwin, K. L., Inciardi, J., Bowser, B., Schilling, R., Word, C., Evans, P., Faruque, S., McCoy, H. V. & Edlin, B. R. (1998). The high-risk sexual practices of crack-smoking sex workers recruited from the streets of three American cities. The multicenter crack cocaine and HIV infection study team. *Sexually Transmitted Diseases* 25, 187–193.

Meandzija, B., O'Connor, P. G. & Fitzgerald, B. (1994). HIV infection and cocaine use in methadone maintained and untreated intravenous drug users. *Drug and Alcohol Dependence* 36, 109–113.

Millson, P., Myers, T., Calzavara, L., Rea, E., Wallace, E., Major, C. & Fearon, M. (1998). Prevalence of HIV and other blood-borne viruses and associated risk behaviors in Ontario injection drug users. Unpublished manuscript.

Nemoto, T. (1994). Patterns of cocaine use and HIV infection among injection drugs in a methadone clinic. *Journal of Substance Abuse* 6, 169–178.

Preble, E. & Casey, J., Jr. (1969). Taking care of business: the heroin user's life in the street. *International Journal of the Addictions* 4, 1–24.

Rezza, G., Sagliocca, L. & Zaccarelli, M. (1996). Incidence rate and risk factors for HCV seroconversion among injecting drug users in an area with low HIV seroprevalence. *Scandinavian Journal of Infectious Disease* 28, 27–29.

Strathdee, S. A., Patrick, D. M., Currie, S. L., Conelisse, P., Rekart, M. L., Montaner, J. S., Schechter, M. T. & Oshaughnessy, M. C. (1997). Needle exchange is not enough: lessons from the Vancouver injecting drug use study. *AIDS* 11, F59–F65.

Thomas, D. L., Vlahov, D. & Solmon, L. (1995). Correlates of hepatitis C virus infections among injection drugs users. *Medicine* 74, 212–220.

For Discussion

1. The authors provide evidence that systems designed to track and monitor drug use, at times fail to uncover important patterns of use including patterns that pose a risk for blood-borne viruses. Think about some of the regional or local monitoring systems in your area that are designed to track drug use. What types of drug use or drug users might they overlook? What are the consequences?

2. The authors suggest that people who inject crack cocaine might be more stigmatized than people who smoke the drug. Think about other drugs in relation to stigma. For example, is Ecstasy more or less stigmatizing than cocaine? Why?

23

Refining Rock

Practical and Social Features of Self-Control Among a Group of College-Student Crack Users

Curtis Jackson-Jacobs

Most sociological studies of crack cocaine have focused on samples of African Americans or Hispanics. In this article, Curtis Jackson-Jacobs uses observational data collected at several points in time to examine the use of crack among white, middle-class college students. Because of their limited access to crack markets, respondents in this study purchased cocaine powder and transformed it into crack. Rather than smoking the drug simultaneously, respondents "passed the pipe" as a means of controlling or regulating use.

During the 20th century in the United States there were numerous "moral panics" (Ben-Yehuda 1990; Goode & Ben-Yehuda 1994) in which specific drugs were sensationalized and deeply stigmatized. National panics focused on cocaine, opiates, marijuana, alcohol, psychedelics (Musto 1973), and "crack" cocaine (Reinarman & Levine 1997). Just as these "drug scares" (Reinarman & Levine 1997) have developed repeatedly in popular culture, a long history of social research has countered many of these fears. Most notably for marijuana (Becker 1953, 1955) and heroin (Lindesmith 1947; Zinberg 1984), there have been powerful arguments to question the view that drugs are inherently dangerous for individuals and society.

The most recent drug scare in the United States has been "crack" cocaine (Reinarman and Levine 1997). Crack, since it first inspired passionate rhetoric in the mid-1980s, has been widely labeled the most addictive and destructive drug in existence. It has been inextricably associated with poor, addicted black users from urban ghettos. However, social scientists have yet to make as powerful a challenge to the conventional wisdom about crack as they have about other drugs.

In this paper I present results of a study of how one group of college students used crack cocaine. The users described here differ markedly in several social characteristics from users described in other studies of crack users. The four primary participants were all college students from middle-class families, three of them white. When they began smoking they were students with strong conventional ties. The ways of using drugs they employed that afforded them some control were tied to their social world as college students.

I detail the microlevel of drug use: the social practices that regulate the way the drug is introduced into the body. A critical gap in our understanding of how crack use works is highlighted by the experiences of this group. The ways in which crack is consumed, whether in a controlled or a highly compulsive manner, can be understood in terms of the practices surrounding consumption, especially in group context.

The Historical Basis of Social Explanations of Drug Use

Social scientists have traditionally argued that the effects of drug use are inextricably linked with the social contexts of use. First, how people use a drug is not just a function of its chemical properties, but also of local practices developed by groups. Second, the meanings and understandings of drugs people come to accept follow from their social environments.

An important landmark in this line of thinking was the publication of Howard Becker's first article, "Becoming a marihuana user," in 1953. He showed that even the most internal, bodily, or psychological experiences of marijuana use—feeling and enjoying the high—require social learning from other users.

The idea that how and with whom a person uses affect the outcomes of drug use, while not so shocking now, is in stark contrast to the exaggerated images found, for example, in the famous film *Reefer Madness* (1936). When marijuana first became a social concern in America, popular images indicated that the use of marijuana would automatically lead to immediate irrational behavior. Current conceptions of marijuana—that it is relatively harmless as far as drugs go and that it is widely used by many types of people—were certainly not common sense 60 years ago, when marijuana was associated with Mexican immigrants and violent, irrational urban crime (Musto 1973).

Popular ideas about heroin addiction have been refined over time as well. Lindesmith (1947), in his landmark study of opiate users, injected the role of social experience into the picture. He showed that becoming addicted to opiates required learning from others that heroin can be used to relieve withdrawal.

By the 1970s sociologists had shown that the social consequences of heroin use depended largely on the user's social experiences. Yet they were reluctant to go so far as to conclude that some people might use heroin without suffering any serious negative effects, much less show how they would go about it. Lindesmith (1947), for example, discovered some non-addicted "pleasure" users but was unable to say confidently that they would stay that way. Blumer (1967) felt the same way about moderate heroin users. Wouldn't these people, sooner or later, become physically addicted?

The question remained generally unanswered until Zinberg, a psychiatrist, began to study what he called "controlled users" of opiates. His research subjects had used prescription opiates or heroin for years without becoming addicted (Zinberg et al. 1977; Zinberg 1984). Continuing to use heroin without becoming addicted depended on the observance of social norms and practices that limited consumption. The most important and influential feature of this work was the primacy it placed on the analysis of group practices of drug use.

The question now stands for crack also. Researchers have yet to attempt to provide an explanation for how some users, through some practices and in some contexts, are able to control their drug use. In this paper I discuss ways in which control over one's drug intake is not due merely to acts of will; it is based on various practices of consuming the drug, developed through collective efforts to exert self-control.

Popular Understandings of Crack

Crack presents a theoretically important and socially relevant test-case for the sociological study of drug use. Since the 1980s there has been strong public rhetoric supporting the belief that crack is the most dangerous drug in existence and is potent enough to cause addiction automatically upon use (e.g., Reagan 1986).

Popular and scientific understandings of drug use, including crack, have often focused on the role of self-control. The concept of addiction itself engenders a sense of inability to control one's own drug consumption. Two criteria in the *DSM-IV* for diagnosing "substance dependence" are that "the substance is often taken in larger amounts or over a longer period than was intended" and that "there is a persistent desire or unsuccessful efforts to cut down or control substance use" (*DSM-IV-TR* 2000: 197). "Craving," the experience of uncontrollable urges to continue using drugs, has been historically considered central to compulsive drug use (Drummond 2001). Journalists and researchers have provided numerous vivid images of what "out of control" crack use looks like. But we have few images of what it is like to use crack *without* losing control.

I argue here that we can advance our understanding of how crack, self-control and social control interact—as has been done for other drugs—by studying a variety of practices and contexts of use. Some users do have some success at controlling their consumption of crack. The informants described here understood crack as a drug that leads to compulsive behavior and a loss of self-control. How they went about achieving control as a group, in the context of a university campus, is the central issue of this paper.

Sociological Understandings of Crack Cocaine

Early in the 1990s ethnographic studies delved into the hidden worlds of crack houses, street prostitutes, and violent street addicts (for example, Williams 1992; Inciardi et al. 1993a; Ratner 1993). Although ethnography has historically debunked myths of drug use, the ethnographic study of crack users has in many cases confirmed our worst fears (Katz 1997). These researchers, it seems, went to the heart of the social problem: crack use among the desperately poor and addicted individuals who shock and concern us the most. What we see are the desperate worlds of individuals whose use strikes us as "out of control." We find out a lot about what it is to use crack in uncontrolled ways, but we have yet to see images of those who do not slip into the worlds of crime and addiction.

The uniformity of the samples and sites of crack ethnographies may be obscuring the diversity of contexts in which crack is used. The predominant images of "street" users in academic research have exaggerated and oversimplified the dangers of crack cocaine. By focusing only on poor users, the literature has uniformly confused the effects of smoking crack with those of social marginality, and in turn the practices that develop for using crack under such conditions.

A striking theme emerges in the current sociological research on crack users. Users in the various studies get high in the same way. They buy small units of cocaine in rock form and smoke them quickly, giving us a sense of the uncontrolled nature of compulsive use. Crack is then used either individually or in pairs. Users rarely share the drug in groups, as was done here.

Findings related to this theme are discussed in the following sections. The results from my sample provide detailed contrasts to these previous findings, adding a new wrinkle to our understanding of crack use. We have numerous images of users who suffer from addiction and its negative social consequences. The group here adds a sense of how some users manage not to suffer the same troubles.

Physical Interaction With Crack Cocaine

There are two related reasons why it is important to know both how and how fast people actually consume crack cocaine. First, crack's intense highs are followed by intense lows that may drive users to desperately seek another hit (Morgan and Zimmer 1997). Tolerance to crack builds and declines rapidly, meaning that the faster a smoker takes consecutive hits, the higher his tolerance becomes during a binge. Smoking larger hits rapidly increases the psychological impact of smoking crack during each binge. Slowing the rate of ingestion, then, may mitigate compulsion and addiction.

Second, crack is destructive because its users go on long binges costing hundreds of dollars. If the rate of ingestion is cut in half, then so might be the economic cost to the user. This point is especially important, since some researchers claim that the high cost of crack addiction drives users to crime. Street addicts may turn to robbery, drug dealing, and prostitution (Inciardi et al. 1993a, 1993b), while middle-class addicts may sell their Rolexes and Mercedes-Benzes to pay for a continued supply of the drug (Waldorf et al. 1991).

Waldorf et al. (1991) presented a picture of crack addiction that suggests the importance of understanding the temporal patterns of smoking rock cocaine. Although their respondents often felt addicted during a binge, they went for long periods of abstinence between these binges. The users, to some extent, could control at what times they went on binges, but they felt out of control during the binges (see also Reinarman et al. 1997). Likewise, in his study of drug users who injected amphetamines, Moore showed that users sometimes created conditions for "structured irresponsibility and freedom from constraint" (1992: 475). Users committed themselves to relaxed control over drug use during certain time periods, such as vacations.

To understand how other types of drug users control their intoxication, looking at group practices has been productive. Zinberg (1984) found that passing a joint around a room allows marijuana smokers time to pace their use and gauge their high, and that incorporating heroin into a night of dining and talking served to moderate use. Bourgois et al. (1997) found that even among hopelessly addicted street addicts, heroin consumption could be controlled to some extent by concerted efforts to share doses and to inject the drug into the muscle rather than the vein.

Crack users in most ethnographic studies buy small, prepackaged quantities, often on public streets or in busy crack-houses (for example, Bourgois 1995; Ratner 1993; Inciardi et al. 1993a).[1] The widespread success of crack as a consumer good is often attributed to the fact that rock cocaine is a marketing innovation. Packaged in small, cheap, easily concealed and divided units, it is sold in public places much more easily than powder cocaine. When crack is bought in this form, users can quickly put individual hits into a pipe and smoke them.

Cocaine can either be bought in rock form and then smoked or converted from powder into rock and then smoked. The form the drug is in when purchased affects how it is used. One of Ouellet et al.'s (1993) respondents pointed out the ease with which precooked rock is smoked:

The ready rock is already cooked up, and the only thing you have to do, you can be riding down the street and—if you got your pipe in your hand—put you a little grain and throw it right on the pipe and just go on and throw down, go on and smoke. Now if you got the powder, you got to go through all the shit of having your tools and cooking it up, getting you some soda. (75)

French (1993) also noted how buying rock makes use simpler and quicker than buying and then cooking powder. Because the rock can be smoked almost immediately, French called it "the fast food of the drug market" (p. 214).

The characterization of crack as the "fast food of the drug market" is consistent with reports about the rate at which it is used. Although research suggests that users consume the drug rapidly in repeated doses, the attempts to quantify how much and how fast have been limited. Commonly researchers have reported that smokers cannot estimate how much they smoke, simply saying they smoke constantly, as quickly as they can (Bourgois & Dunlap 1993; Ratner 1993; Williams 1992). Inciardi and his associates also had difficulty with this, but they estimated that many participants in one sample smoked up to 50 times a day, while half got high 20 to 30 times (Inciardi et al. 1993a).

Early reports on freebase use suggested that repetition of doses may occur at five to thirty minutes, sometimes for days at a time (Siegel 1982; Murray 1986; Sterk-Elifson and Elifson 1993).[2] Duneier (1999) suggested, in his study of street vendors, that the ones who smoked crack, if they weren't careful, could smoke five-dollar rocks every two or three minutes during a binge. These estimates were echoed by one of Boyle and Anglin's (1993) participants: "Even when that's happening [the rush from the hit], I start this craving, put my hand in my pocket to get more."

The practices and temporal organization of using crack in the contexts described above are fairly uniform in that users smoked individually or in groups of two or three (though many others may have been present, smoking separately), they smoked precooked rock, and they smoked very rapidly. The authors showed that these practices grow from the worlds of street users. The availability of "ready-rock" for sale in repeated small doses, the lack of stable relationships and trust between drug users, and the understanding of crack as simply a means to achieving a high, rather than as a social object, contributed to ways of using crack that seem especially compulsive.

Hidden Samples and Drug Research

For the study of both marijuana and heroin use there was a specific research finding that marked a forward step in these areas. In both cases it was the finding that there are people who "get away with it," which by itself calls into question the potency of a drug to change lives. More importantly, when these people are found, it becomes possible to explore the interaction between pharmacology and sociality. What emerges is a more textured understanding of how different people use drugs and how use varies by social context.

There have been no studies to show that some people, in some places, get away with smoking crack. Is this because we have finally found a drug so powerful that social controls and practices cannot prevent addiction?

Just as Lindesmith and Blumer wondered about the few heroin users who weren't addicted, Waldorf et al. (1991) were ambivalent about whether their "controlled" users would eventually become compulsive users (see also Reinarman et al. 1997). Because of the limited time frame of their interview study, they were unsure whether the users they studied would remain "controlled" or whether they would lose control eventually.

For both heroin and crack research there are several reasons why users who "get away with it" are hard to find. They are not in detention or medical facilities, so they cannot be located by institutional means, a common method of finding drug-using samples (e.g., Boyd & Mieczkowski 1990; Fullilove et al. 1992). Statistical data generally cannot help us figure out if a case represented addicted or controlled use based on standard measurement tools.

An additional obstacle to ferreting out controlled crack users has been the orientation of researchers studying this problem. Researchers like Inciardi and his associates have sought out serious users by entering dangerous crack-houses (Inciardi et al. 1993a), or they have gone to the ghetto for the explicit purpose of finding the most desperate users (Bourgois 1995). Such people are, after all, the ones who are involved in social problems like homelessness, prostitution, and violence. Researchers may not feel any practical incentive to look for moderate crack users, and they are probably even less likely to get funding for such research.

Sample Considerations

This paper presents results of a case study of a small group of crack users. Most of the observations are of four men who were college students.

Given the often much larger samples reported on in other research, the power of

these observations to comment on the literature about crack deserves some attention. This study, despite the limitation of small sample size, has the two distinct advantages of detailed observation over time and a rare sample.

When heroin researchers began to study controlled users, they found respondents through advertisements in university and underground newspapers (Zinberg et al. 1977; Zinberg 1984). While this method produced large samples of about 100 respondents, it did not allow for the type of detailed observation reported here. Interview studies are problematic in that first, the time frame is usually brief, and second, they cannot capture the minute practices and daily interactions that are essential to understanding how drugs are used.

Although the sample is small, this study draws much of its value from its novelty among studies of crack users. There are few reports of non-black, non-Hispanic crack users, and no qualitative studies of college students who use crack.

Site, Sample, and Methods

My informants lived in a town of about 200,000, where they attended a state university. When I first met them, they all lived on the same floor of a dormitory building. When they moved out of the dorm, they lived, like many students, in a small neighborhood called Midtown (like all proper names used here, a pseudonym).

As far as I could tell, there was not a major crack problem in the city, much less in the small student neighborhood where I conducted my fieldwork. In fact it has been consistently described by magazines like *Money* and *Parenting* as one of the country's best and most crime-free cities in which to live and raise a family. There was no visible impoverished ghetto near the neighborhood. The most serious police effort to intervene in substance abuse in Midtown was a task force that infiltrated keg parties with undercover officers.

I met Jon, Martin, Casey and Mark in 1996. I first met Jon, who quickly became a close friend. He was an intellectually engaged student. Before he told me that he used crack, we had attended several lectures on campus (including one on the topic of the CIA and its role in delivering cocaine into the country) as well as small concerts at the student union. We drank beer and talked about sociology or politics. He showed me his artwork and his music. One day I stopped by his dorm room and found him "cooking" crack with an out-of-town friend. I was immediately intrigued and began to watch often and ask questions about the drug.

That year Jon introduced several other residents of the dorm, all new friends of his, to the drug. Martin and Casey, upon Jon's invitation, began to smoke crack with him on a regular basis. Mark became friends with the group but did not use crack until about a year later. During my observation the core group sometimes smoked with other student and non-student friends, about two dozen over the course of the time I knew them. My data do not focus on these people, because they rarely smoked for long. Most of them used the drug only once or twice, curious about and allured by crack's dangerous aura, but never tried it again.

Only one of the primary participants was not white—Casey, who is Korean-American. All the men came from middle-class families. Their parents included a doctor, an engineer, a librarian, and a federal law-enforcement agent.

All the people I observed using crack cocaine also used other drugs as well. They all used marijuana, powder cocaine, and alcohol in varying amounts at various times. Casey, Paul and Martin used LSD and mushrooms on rare occasions. Casey and Paul had begun to use Ecstasy (MDMA) before the study was completed. Jon used heroin on rare occasions and was sometimes joined by the others.

All of them worked jobs and went to school at least part-time. They all had relatively active social lives. They maintained non-using friendship circles, went to parties, and dated with variable frequency. Often they lived in houses where their roommates did not use crack or any drugs. Their dress and appearance did not especially distinguish them from other college students. Their use of crack and other drugs was, for the most part, a relatively minor feature of their lives.

While I lived in Midtown I was hanging out with at least one of them—but usually with all of them—on a daily basis. They were among the few people whom I came to know well in the community. Nearly a year after they began smoking crack together as a group, I asked if I could observe them and take notes for a sociological study. They agreed, and during the fall of 1997 I started to take notes and conduct observations in a structured way. Sometimes only once a month, sometimes four times in a week, one or more of these men would sit in a single room and smoke crack for up to 12 hours. I observed them in several different members' apartments.

I kept taking notes throughout the duration of a one-semester fieldwork seminar. My unstructured observations began in November 1996 and ended in 1998, when I moved out of the state. Soon thereafter, I learned, the group dissolved. Martin continued to go to school in Midtown, Jon transferred to an art college in a large metropolitan city and then returned to Midtown a year later, and Casey transferred to a college in another state.

Mark, I was told, had "lost control" of his drug use. He dropped out of school, ran up large debts, and began hanging out with the few poor adult users from the neighborhood. The last I heard of Mark was that his mother had come to Midtown and taken him back to his hometown about 100 miles away.

After leaving town, I attempted to maintain relationships with the participants. Until recently I spoke with Casey every few months. Casey's use tapered off when he moved to a new town. Martin, according to Jon, graduated in May 2001 and began attending graduate school that fall. He stopped using crack when Jon moved out of town.

My closest relationship has continued with Jon, who recently moved to California with Angie, his girlfriend, both of them using crack "on special occasions." Angie seems to be a bright graduate student in a prestigious department at a well-respected research university. Jon has earned a bachelor's degree and is now bartending while looking for work in the criminal justice system, preferably law enforcement. I continue to visit them and sometimes observe them as they use crack cocaine in a relatively controlled manner.

Physical Interaction With the Drug

The results I present deal with how the group physically interacted with the drug. That is, I describe how they came into bodily contact with the drug at each step, from buying it, to preparing it, to consuming it. What is taken to be "control" over drug use is often related to physical interactions with drugs. Loss of control is often attributed to those who use drugs as quickly as possible and with no effort to limit quantity. Control over duration and quantity of drugs are generally exerted through practices developed in groups (Zinberg 1984).

Specifically, this group practiced three rituals relevant to the current analysis: (1) cooking the drug from powder, (2) cooking several small batches rather than one large batch, and (3) passing the pipe and each hit of crack around the room in turn. The intense rituals these men developed around crack use substantially slowed their rate of consumption. Self-control was not achieved by an act of will alone, but under the conditions developed through these habitual social practices.

Bingeing and Pharmacology

Although my own participants did not smoke continuously, it seemed that they wanted to. Soon after each hit they would stare intently at the drug or at the supplies being used to make it, apparently ready to smoke again as soon as they had finished the last hit.

Like most other crack researchers, I cannot provide precisely quantified estimates of how quickly these men used crack. Fortunately, though, they had a fairly regular routine. From this routine I can extrapolate some rough estimates about the pace of smoking. These estimates were virtually identical to those given by one of the principal informants.

During most binges the group of users I observed smoked altogether either a "teen" (1.75 grams) or a "ball" (3.5 grams) of powder cocaine. Most commonly the binges lasted between four and eight hours, roughly corresponding to whether the group bought a teen or a ball. The number of hits produced from these quantities would be about 16 per gram. Estimating the time between hits in this way, then, I concluded that if four to six users were present, each of them took a hit approximately once every 30 minutes to an hour.

In an interview, Jon reported that the group most commonly smoked a teen in a night. Each gram of cocaine, he said, could be turned into 15–20 hits. At most, he thought, the group smoked one hit per half hour.

Procuring Crack

My participants tried to purchase rock cocaine on a few occasions but were duped each time. They ended up with $20 worth of soap or chopped-up peanuts when they did try to buy the drug on the street (this is common enough that Maher (1997) found it to be an occupational category). Although they suspected that there was a "spot" (a place to buy crack on a street corner) in the neighborhood, they shied away from it. Having been tricked, and lacking a visible public crack market, they chose a steady private, reliable source of powder cocaine.

In the Midtown neighborhood these men knew numerous powder-cocaine users, one or more of whom could usually set up a deal on short notice. At one time Mark lived with a cocaine dealer, Paul, who supplied many other young people in the neighborhood. When Mark lived in this house, there were four women living on the same block who used cocaine on and off. If Paul was unavailable, the group could often get a quantity from these women. They almost always bought from a friend or a friendly acquaintance, or at least from a friend of a friend. It was always done in a private residence. They relied on the same distribution network that supplied cocaine to powder-using college students in the neighborhood.

Smoking Ready-Rock

One of the most important outcomes of buying cocaine from this network was that they bought only powder. As far as I could tell, rock cocaine was not especially popular on campus. Furthermore, they knew of no source for cocaine of any kind in the town besides other college students. So in order to smoke rock, they had to first buy the powder and then convert it into the product that could be smoked.

Isolated in the social world of a university campus, these men had to procure crack in a way that street users do not. As Ouellet et al.'s informant suggested, my sample had to "go through all the shit" of making crack themselves. That is, they had to get supplies and spend time "cooking."

Jon had smoked in houses where rock was sold. I asked if things were different there. Completely, he told me. He had, for a time, frequented what he described as a typical crack-house. There, he said, the smokers all took a corner in the room and smoked with their own pipes. He went there only a few times, mainly because he smoked so much more in this environment. Most often, he said, he bought a "teen" of rock for himself, at a price of $100 or $120. He would then sit in a corner and smoke it by himself within two or three hours. Based on these estimates, he was smoking a hit every three-and-a-half to seven minutes; about eight times as fast as in the group. At times he got himself into one or two hundred dollars debt at this house.

He hated it there; the money just went up in smoke too quickly. A hundred dollars could have lasted him all night if he were smoking crack in a group with Martin, Casey, Mark, and any other friend who was around. Jon's experience suggests the role of social practices, as opposed to simply psychological or chemical properties, in explaining how he used crack. A detailed look at the practices of this group illuminates how they maintained moderate use.

The Cook and the Technique

Most of the individuals I observed were unable or unwilling to risk trying to cook.

Only Jon and Martin would do the deed of turning cocaine into crack. They and Casey and Mark saw it as a very delicate technical process. All the first-time users who tried the drug with the group made no attempts whatsoever to try to cook, instead watching the process closely. The technical knowledge and the mystique surrounding the process meant that the participants would use crack only when they could get hold of Jon or Martin.

Of the various activities performed on a regular basis by the circle of crack smokers, cooking the drug received the most attention. Cooking went on almost non-stop throughout the sessions. The group thought that cooking made an important contribution to the "quality" of the final product, second only to the quality of the cocaine itself.

So heavy on the minds of the group was this skill that some had developed elaborate techniques. Martin spent about 15 minutes describing to me in each detail his own "two-stage cooking" method: "Cook it till it's all brown. . . . Keep cooking it till crust forms. Then cool it. Little rocks'll form and you see some goo. . . . Then cook it again. Two-stage cook."

Often the most minute details of the activity—such as how much baking soda to mix in, how far from the flame to hold the spoon, when to stir the solution, when to extract some substance—were scrutinized. Within a given session, a single batch of powder cocaine was almost always used in cooking rock. Despite the constant quality of the powder cocaine, the quality of rock was subject to frequent appraisals.

They commented continuously on the quality of the final product. There was a constant back-and-forth of comments like the following: "You think I should put more coke in the spoon?" Jon asked Martin on one occasion. "Yeah, and more water." Jon declined, saying, "No, I think I'm just gonna cook it." With hushed voices, long pauses in their speech, and tedious care for the physical materials, they fussed over the process for extended periods.

All this attention to cooking took quite a bit of time. Not only did the group have to wait for a qualified cook to be present, they sat and agonized over every detail of the process. The solution was heated and cooled repeatedly. The product was discussed and played around with. Rather than cook as efficiently and rapidly as possible, they paused and took breaks to evaluate the cook's progress and to discuss technique. Each time someone undertook to turn powder into rock, many minutes went by. Even as these men craved another hit, they waited up to half an hour for the delicate task to be completed.

Small Batches

When a proper cook was present, he cooked only in small batches. That is, rather than cook the entire quantity at once into a large rock, he would repeatedly cook small batches that amounted to a fraction of the cocaine on hand. There were a number of reasons for this.

First, the group felt that cooking small batches afforded them the opportunity to stop smoking at some point. Often Jon would end a session by saying he was going to put the rest away for later. Sometimes this worked, sometimes not. On a successful occasion, Jon put the powder away and suggested that everyone go for a walk. He brought two joints along to alleviate craving for the drug.

Another time he went so far as to ask Martin to lock the drug in a safe in their room: "Set a new combination and don't tell me what it is." At one session Jon announced, "Okay, that's my last one." He proceeded, however, to cook another single-hit quantity.

These men knew that during a binge they would have the urge to smoke all of their cocaine. By cooking small batches they attempted, with variable success, to make it easier to stop. This particular practice was developed in order to exercise control over what was felt to be a drug that might spark a loss of control.

Second, and most importantly, cooking crack took on a special meaning for this group. Embodying the sensuality of crack use, much of the pleasure found in the experience was derived from the ritualized and aesthetic appeal of the activity. As one of Adler's (1985) respondents pointed out, "Half of the Jones [the high] is watching that

stuff form, scraping it up, putting it into the waterbase pipe . . ." (p. 88).

The men I studied were able to distinguish fine differences in the texture and color of their product. They continuously commented on the quality of the final product. Each batch was made a subject of discussion. "Whoa," one of them once exclaimed to Jon, "look at that brown shit!" Jon replied, "It's the best."

One time, when a particularly good batch came out, Martin said to Jon, "That tastes good. How much [powder cocaine] did you put in there?" Jon responded, "Probably half a gram." Commenting on the efficacy of that mixture, Martin said, "It tastes perfect."

Each of them developed his own preference for how the drug should look. As Jon told me, when he cooks he keeps all "the goo and brown resin" for himself. These substances, he explained, give the best high.

When I asked Martin about his most memorable experience smoking crack, he described the best rock he ever smoked. "[Jon] cooked it up, and let the rock dry off. It was really dense gray rock. 'CHINK!' " he mimicked the sound of the rock bouncing on a hard surface. "So I'd rather smoke rock than goo."

Martin went on to tell me about the intensity of his appreciation for crack. He had even found a spiritual leader and developed a spiritual perspective on the drug. His "guru" was an older man who Martin thought had taught him a lot about the drug. Several times he said to me, "Ray was a guru to me." When I asked him why, he responded: "Ray taught me to treat crack like a person. He told me to think of it as a person that was so powerful, spiritually, that when he died he decided to turn himself into something that would last forever."

The cooking ritual, besides transforming powder into rock, also transformed crack from simply a drug into an artistic and spiritual accomplishment. Cooking was not just a practical task. It was an art. Once they had completed the delicate process, they were left with not only a quantity of the drug, but an object in which they had invested their hard-earned skill and their own sense of aesthetic style.

At times, controlling their binge was relevant to how they cooked. In some cases they explicitly tried to "stop early" by cooking just a bit. Most important, though, was the deep aesthetic appeal of cooking. Unlike users who buy precooked rock, during each binge this group was able to repeatedly live the beauty and fascination of watching the substance materialize.

Rather than cook the entire amount at once, they went through an elaborate process of cooking small quantities. Repeating the cooking ritual after each member had taken a hit slowed the process of smoking considerably. Over and over, throughout a binge, the group took time-outs to cook more. These time-outs could have been used to smoke several hits. Were it not for these half-hour cooking breaks, these smokers could have consumed several hits for each hit they actually took.

Passing the Pipe

Once the rock had been produced, the cook would spend several minutes chopping it up. Unlike the pattern described in virtually all other ethnographic accounts of crack circles, these men shared one pipe and took turns smoking. The cook would take the first hit and then pass a rock and the pipe to the next smoker. This continued around the circle. The reverie each smoker fell into after his hit also slowed the process. For up to a minute he might breathe heavily while staring into nothing. The next in line would often request his turn with an impatient gesture.

In this practice we can see the clear competition between compulsion and ritualization. If they had wanted to, they could have all smoked simultaneously; most of the time there were glass stems, antennas with filters, and metal sockets about that served as pipes. This practice was developed with a particular norm in mind—sharing the drug together—but had the effect of limiting use.

Even as they waited I could see they were ready for another hit. They constantly stared at whoever was taking a hit. They fidgeted in anticipation. If they became too impatient, they would nudge a smoker and tell him to pass the pipe.

It would have been just as easy for the men to all smoke at once. Instead, they used a practice common among marijuana smokers: taking turns. This group smoked marijuana together more often than they smoked crack. When they smoked marijuana, they always passed a pipe or a joint around the room. Doing otherwise was considered rude.

Unlike the anonymous and compulsive groups who smoke in the crack-houses described by Inciardi et al. (1993a), Ratner (1993), and others, this group treated crack-cocaine as a ritual and social object. It was not just something to use to get high; it was something to be enjoyed collectively. Like middle-class heroin users who add middle-class rituals like drinking wine to the practice of shooting up (Zinberg 1984), this group imported the practice of passing the pipe, thus imposing control on the rate at which they could smoke.

Just as they waited for the drug to be cooked, these men repeatedly waited for it to be divided and passed. As they waited, the time between hits might have increased as much as twofold. The compulsion to smoke as quickly as possible was moderated by the practice of smoking in turns. Where self-control may not be enough for those who smoke in busy crack-houses or alone in alleys, group regulation served here to slow the rate of crack ingestion.

Conclusion

The role of self-control in crack use was a central concern for this group, as it has been for researchers and the public. Concerted efforts to exercise control were in fact realized through the development of social controls, particularly norms and practices of using crack. The ability to control use was not simply a matter of individual capacity. It depended heavily on the local conditions and habitual practices surrounding these men's crack use.

Of the four main participants, at least three used crack for years without getting into any real trouble. Numerous other students tried the drug with them only once or a few times without continuing. Mark, however, is reported to have "lost control," dropped out of school, and stopped hanging out with his college-student friends.

Before I left town, Mark had befriended some older crack users whom he had met at a restaurant where he worked and through Martin and Casey's roommate Ray. He no longer used the drug under the conditions he had shared with Martin, Jon and Casey. Escalation of his drug use coincided with new, more compulsive ways of using and the disappearance of many of the social controls described above. I lost track of him, except for hearing occasional rumors that he left school, squandered loans, and eventually went back home to live with his mother.

Part of what makes crack so frightening is that some users consume it in ways that appear uncontrolled. Yet few studies have attempted to explain the boundaries of control and loss of control during binges. Politicians, news reporters, researchers, and treatment specialists often claim that it is either the properties of the drug itself or the psychology of the user that structures crack binges (for a review, see Reinarman and Levine 1997).

From the data here, we see the intimate connection between social contexts, group practices, and control over crack use. The conditions of a university campus were such that the users developed long-standing, personalized practices in using crack. Unlike those who use in anonymous, fearful, dangerous environments (Inciardi et al. 1993a), these young men established patterns of use that mitigated the threat of "losing control."

From this group of college students we can see that specific practices and rituals, developed in the context of a friendship group, had a direct effect on how crack was consumed. That crack use on campus takes a completely different shape than it does in the ghetto indicates that the blame for addiction and destructive behaviors lies not so much in the drug but in characteristics of the ghetto. Furthermore, this finding supports the continued value of researching social aspects, not simply chemical and psychological aspects, of drug use.

Notes

1. French (1993) mentioned that users in his Newark sample did their own cooking. He did not discuss how this might have structured their activity.

2. I do not distinguish between "freebase" and crack. The terms are used inconsistently. If there is any real difference between the two substances, it is only that they are cooked using slightly different solutions and that people usually refer to cooking freebase from powder themselves rather than purchasing it in rock form.

References

Adler, Patricia. 1985. *Wheeling and Dealing.* New York: Columbia University Press.

Becker, Howard. 1953. "Becoming a Marihuana User." *American Journal of Sociology* 59: 235–242.

——. 1955. "Marihuana Use and Social Control." *Social Problems* 3: 35–44.

Ben-Yehuda, Nachman. 1990. *The Politics and Morality of Deviance: Moral Panics, Drug Abuse, Deviant Science, and Reversed Stigmatization.* Albany, NY: State University of New York Press.

Blumer, Herbert. 1967. *The World of Youthful Drug Use.* Berkeley, CA: University of California School of Criminology.

Bourgois, Philippe. 1995. *In Search of Respect: Selling Crack in el Barrio.* Cambridge, UK: Cambridge University Press.

Bourgois, Philippe and Eloise Dunlap. 1993. "Exorcising Sex-for-Crack: An Ethnographic Perspective from Harlem." In *Crack Pipe as Pimp: An Ethnographic Investigation of Sex-for-Crack Exchanges,* edited by M. Ratner. Lexington, MA: Lexington Books.

Bourgois, Philippe, Mark Lettiere, and James Quesada. 1997. "Social Misery and the Sanctions of Substance Abuse: Confronting HIV Risk Among Homeless Heroin Addicts in San Francisco." *Social Problems* 44: 155–173.

Boyd, Carol and Thomas Mieczkowski. 1990. "Drug Use, Health, Family and Social Support in 100 Drug Program In-Patients." *Addictive Behaviors* 15: 481–485.

Boyle, Kathleen and M. Douglas Anglin. 1993 " 'To the Curb': Sex Bartering and Drug Use Among Homeless Crack Users in Los Angeles." In *Crack Pipe as Pimp: An Ethnographic Investigation of Sex-far-Crack Exchanges,* edited by M. Ratner. Lexington, MA: Lexington Books.

Diagnostic and Statistical Manual of Mental Disorders DSM-IV-TR. 4th ed., text revision. 2000. Washington, DC: American Psychiatric Association.

Drummond, Colin. 2001. "Theories of Drug Craving, Ancient and Modern." *Addiction* 96: 33–46.

Duneier, Mitchell. 1999. *Sidewalk.* New York: Farrar, Strauss, and Giroux.

French, John. 1993. "Pipe Dreams: Crack and the Life in Philadelphia and Newark." In *Crack Pipe as Pimp: An Ethnographic Investigation of Sex-for-Crack Exchanges,* edited by M. Ratner. Lexington, MA: Lexington Books.

Fullilove, Mindy, E. Anne Lown, and Robert Fullilove. 1992. "Crack 'hos and Skeezers: Traumatic Experiences of Women Crack Users." *Journal of Sex Research* 29: 275–287.

Goode, Erich and Nachman Ben-Yehuda. 1994. *Moral Panics: The Social Construction of Deviance.* Cambridge, MA: Blackwell.

Inciardi, James, Dorothy Lockwood, and Anne E. Pottieger. 1993a. *Women and Crack-Cocaine.* New York: Macmillan Publishing Company.

Inciardi, James, Ruth Horowitz, and Anne Pottieger. 1993b. *Street Kids, Street Drugs, Street Crime: An Examination of Drug Use and Serious Delinquency in Miami.* Belmont, CA: Wadsworth Publishing Company.

Katz, Jack. 1997. "Ethnography's Warrants." *Sociological Methods and Research* 25: 391–423.

Lindesmith, Alfred. 1947. *Opiate Addiction.* Bloomington, IN: Principia Press.

Maher, Lisa. 1997. *Sexed Work: Gender, Race and Resistance in a Brooklyn Drug Market.* Cambridge, UK: Oxford University Press.

Moore, David. 1992. "Deconstruction 'Dependence': An Ethnographic Critique of an Influential Concept." *Contemporary Drug Problems* 19: 459–490.

Morgan, John and Lynn Zimmer. 1997. "The Social Pharmacology of Smokeable Cocaine: It's Not All It's Cracked Up to Be." In *Crack in America*, edited by C. Reinarman and H. Levine. Berkeley: University of California Press.

Murray, John. 1986. "An Overview of Cocaine Use and Abuse." *Psychological Reports* 59: 243–264.

Musto, David. 1973. *The American Disease: Origins of Narcotic Control*. New Haven, CT: Yale University Press.

Ouellet, Lawrence, W. Wayne Wiebel, Antonio Jimenez, and Wendell Johnson. 1993. "Crack Cocaine and the Transformation of Prostitution in Three Chicago Neighborhoods." In *Crack Pipe as Pimp; An Ethnographic Investigation of Sex-for-Crack Exchanges*, edited by M. Ratner. Lexington, MA: Lexington Books.

Ratner, Mitchell, ed. 1993. *Crack Pipe as Pimp: An Ethnographic Investigation of Sex-for-Crack Exchanges*. Lexington, MA: Lexington Books.

Reagan, Nancy. 1986. "The Battle Against Drugs: What Can You Do?" *Vital Speeches of the Day* 53: 645.

Reefer Madness. 1936. Film directed by Louis Gasnier.

Reinarman, Craig and Harry Levine. 1997. "Crack in Context: America's Latest Demon Drug." In *Crack in America*, edited by C. Reinarman and H. Levine. Berkeley: University of California Press.

Reinarman, Craig, Dan Waldorf, Sheigla B. Murphy, and Harry G. Levine. 1997. "The Contingent Call of the Pipe: Bingeing and Addiction Among Heavy Cocaine Smokers." In *Crack in America*, edited by C. Reinarman and H. Levine. Berkeley: University of California Press.

Siegel, Ronald. 1982. "Cocaine Smoking." *Journal of Psychoactive Drugs* 14: 271–359.

Sterk-Elifson, Claire and Kirk Elifson. 1993. "The Social Organization of Crack Cocaine Use: The Cycle in One Type of Base House." *Journal of Drug Issues* 23: 429–441.

Waldorf, Dan, Craig Reinarman, and Sheigla B. Murphy. 1991. *Cocaine Changes: The Experience of Using and Quitting*. Philadelphia: Temple University Press.

Williams, Terry. 1992. *Crackhouse: Notes from the End of the Line*. New York: Addison-Wesley.

Zinberg, Norman, Wayne Harding, and Miriam Winkeller. 1977. "A Study of Social Regulatory Mechanisms in Controlled Illicit Drug Users." *Journal of Drug Issues* 7: 117–133.

Zinberg, Norman. 1984. *Drug, Set, and Setting*. New Haven, CT: Yale University Press.

For Discussion

1. Why has research uncovered so little about the use of crack cocaine among white, middle-class college students?

2. Can friendships between researchers and respondents help or hinder a study? Why?

Part VI

Methamphetamine and Other Stimulants

A drug that has received considerable attention in recent years is methamphetamine, also referred to as "crystal meth" and "crank." A central nervous system stimulant chemically related to the amphetamines, methamphetamine was developed in Japan in 1919 and first used widely during World War II by German soldiers to counter the fatigue of prolonged troop movements. Like the amphetamines, methamphetamine is a potent stimulant with an action on the body similar to the effects of adrenalin. It has been used in the clinical management of psychiatric depression, obesity and weight control, chronic fatigue and narcolepsy, hyperkinetic activity disorders in children, as an analeptic in sedative overdose, and as a vasoconstrictor for inflamed mucosal membranes.

Since the early 1970s, the therapeutic applications of methamphetamine have been notably curtailed. Its use in weight control is highly problematic since its appetite-suppressing effects endure for only a short time and its potential for dependence is considerable. Moreover, other drugs have been found to be more effective in the management of psychiatric depression, and for fatigue it is prescribed only in extraordinary circumstances. Significant, as well, in the restricted clinical use of methamphetamine has been its notable abuse potential. It is typically abused for its energizing and euphoric properties. Although it can be taken orally for such purposes, the effects tend to be far more profound when taken intravenously.

Chronic intravenous use typically leads to psychotic reactions and paranoid delusions.

Although methamphetamine abuse has been a notable part of the American drug scene since the 1960s, it seems to have become more prominent since the latter part of the 1980s, particularly west of the Mississippi. Referred to in the media as the "white man's crack," methamphetamine is produced in illegal laboratories throughout the United States.

Methamphetamine releases high levels of the neurotransmitter *dopamine*, which stimulates brain cells, enhancing mood and body movement. It also appears to have a neurotoxic effect, damaging brain cells that contain dopamine as well as serotonin, another neurotransmitter. Over time, methamphetamine appears to cause reduced levels of dopamine, which can result in symptoms like those of Parkinson's disease, a severe movement disorder.

Methamphetamine is taken orally or intranasally (snorting the powder), by intravenous injection, and by smoking. Immediately after smoking or intravenous injection, the methamphetamine user experiences an intense sensation, called a "rush" or "flash," that lasts only a few minutes and is described as extremely pleasurable. Oral or intranasal use produces euphoria—a high, but not a rush. Users may become addicted quickly, and use it with increasing frequency and in increasing doses.

Animal research going back more than 20 years shows that high doses of methamphetamine damage neuron cell endings. Dopamine- and serotonin-containing neurons do not die after methamphetamine use, but their nerve endings ("terminals") are cut back, and regrowth appears to be limited.

The central nervous system (CNS) actions that result from taking even small amounts of methamphetamine include increased wakefulness, increased physical activity, decreased appetite, increased respiration, hyperthermia, and euphoria. Other CNS effects include irritability, insomnia, confusion, tremors, convulsions, anxiety, paranoia, and aggressiveness. Hyperthermia and convulsions can result in death.

Methamphetamine causes increased heart rate and blood pressure and can cause irreversible damage to blood vessels in the brain, producing strokes. Other effects of methamphetamine include respiratory problems, irregular heartbeat, and extreme anorexia. Its use can result in cardiovascular collapse and death.

In the chapters that follow, methamphetamine is discussed extensively. Also addressed are two other stimulants in widespread use—the amphetamines and Ritalin.

Additional Readings

Braswell, Sterling R. (2006). *American Meth: A History of the Methamphetamine Epidemic in America*. New York: iUniverse Inc.

DeGrandpre, Richard. (1999). *Ritalin Nation*. New York: Norton.

Rodriguez, Nancy, Charles Katz, Vincent J. Webb, and David R. Schaefer. (2005). "Examining the Impact of Individual, Community, and Market Factors on Methamphetamine Use: A Tale of Two Cities." *Journal of Drug Issues* 35 (4): 665–693.

Stoops, William W., Michele Staton Tindal, Allison Mateyoke-Scrivner, and Carl Leukefeld. (2005). "Methamphetamine Use in Nonurban and Urban Drug Court Clients." *International Journal of Offender Therapy and Comparative Criminology* 49 (3): 260–276. ✦

24

History and Epidemiology of Amphetamine Abuse in the United States

Marissa A. Miller

In this chapter, Marissa Miller traces the history of amphetamine use in the United States. Amphetamines were once perceived as safe drugs for treating various medical problems, but, the author notes, more stringent controls on their production were introduced in 1971. Subsequently, the illegal manufacture of methamphetamine, in particular, began to develop. Miller uses data from various sources to describe recent patterns of use. She notes that regional variations in use have emerged and suggests that amphetamine and methamphetamine are likely to represent major drugs of abuse in the future.

Trends in drug abuse are influenced by many factors, including properties of the drug, characteristics of the abusing population, and the environment within which the abuse occurs, as well as broader issues related to drug manufacturing, marketing, and distribution. Many complex and interrelated elements have converged in promulgating past and present epidemics of amphetamine abuse. This chapter will chronicle the unique history of the development of amphetamine and methamphetamine, the medical and nonmedical use of these drugs, and subsequent epidemics of abuse in the United States; describe current patterns and trends of abuse and factors in-

fluencing these trends; explain how legal control of the manufacture and distribution has influenced the availability and propelled the patterns of abuse; and consider the potential for future abuse of methamphetamine and related substances.

Background

Amphetamines are a class of synthetic stimulants that include several specific chemical agents the most common of which are amphetamine (Benzedrine), methamphetamine (Desoxyn), dextroamphetamine (Dexadrine), and benzphetamine (Didrex), plus the combination amphetamine and dextroamphetamine (Biphetamine) (King and Coleman, 1987). Amphetamines were first manufactured in 1887 (Caldwell, 1980). Methamphetamine was first synthesized in 1919 and closely resembles amphetamine in chemical structure and pharmacologic action. Today the term amphetamine refers generally to popular pharmaceutical pills and capsules used licitly and illicitly. Methamphetamine is a related compound that generally is more sought after due to its long-lasting high. Methamphetamine is the only compound in this class of stimulants that is manufactured to any significant extent in clandestine laboratories in the United States and currently is a more prevalent drug of abuse than amphetamine.

Speed is a term used to describe all the synthetic stimulants including amphetamine and methamphetamine. Illicit methamphetamine is known by names such as 'meth,' 'crystal,' and 'crank.' Amphetamine pills and capsules that have found their way onto the streets are commonly referred to as 'denies,' 'dexies,' 'bennies,' and 'uppers.' Street drug terminology is very location specific and not standardized, so wherever possible any new term will be defined in the text.

History of Early Use

Historically, use of the synthetically manufactured amphetamines and methamphetamine can be traced back to the early 1930s, when medicinally useful attributes of these compounds were discovered. Amphetamine and the closely related methamphetamine exhibited bronchodilator and hypertensive properties: They reversed barbiturate anesthesia and treated lung congestion. Between 1932 and 1946, the pharmaceutical industry developed a list of 39 generally accepted clinical uses for these drugs, including the treatment of schizophrenia, morphine and codeine addiction, tobacco smoking, heart block, head injuries, radiation sickness, low blood pressure, and persistent hiccups (Lukas, 1985). They were promoted as being safe without risks (Grinspoon and Hedblom, 1975). From the time of early use the existence of psychoactive properties was also identified in association with these substances. Extensive use, combined with the inherent properties of the drugs, set the stage for later widespread abuse.

Amphetamines rapidly became popular in the United States. Amphetamine tablets could be obtained without prescription until 1951, and amphetamine inhalers were available until 1959. Amphetamines and methamphetamine were widely marketed during the 1950s and 1960s for obesity, narcolepsy, hyperkinesis, and depression. Housewives were prescribed amphetamines for weight loss; others, including students, businessmen, and truck drivers, used them for their anti-fatigue effects (Ellinwood, 1974). Their popularity was bolstered by low cost and long duration of effect (Fischman, 1990). During World War II amphetamines were used extensively by the American, British, German, and Japanese military as stimulants and insomniacs. An estimated 200 million tablets and pills were supplied to American troops during World War II (Grinspoon and Hedblom, 1975). Some of the American soldiers returned home following the war and continued to use stimulants.

The popularity of amphetamines drove production, and production levels served ultimately to drive popularity. Legal production soared from approximately 3.5 billion tablets in 1958 to 10 billion tablets by 1970 (Grinspoon and Hedblom, 1975). During the 1960s, 20 million prescriptions were written each year, predominantly for weight reduction purposes (Ellinwood, 1979; Spotts and Spotts, 1980). Prescribing practices escalated until 1967, when 31 million scripts were written. The prevalence of use was much higher among younger adults and in certain areas of the country such as San Francisco (Mellinger et al., 1971).

In the late 1950s some physicians began prescribing intravenously administered methamphetamine as a treatment for heroin addiction. Other doctors and pharmacists became involved in writing illegal prescriptions for liquid amphetamine ampoules (Lake and Quirk, 1984). These practices contributed to the origination of new abuse patterns involving intravenous injection of methamphetamine. The most popular of the injectable ampoules were made by Abbott (Desoxyn) and Burroughs Wellcome (Methedrine). During the first half of 1962 over 500,000 ampoules were prescribed (Brecher, 1972; Smith, 1969).

During the 1960s speed use spread to a variety of groups throughout the San Francisco Bay area. Haight-Ashbury, a neighborhood of the Bay area, epitomized the 1960s drug subculture. In Haight-Ashbury speed began to replace hallucinogenic drugs such as LSD in popularity (Pittel and Hofer, 1970). Speed use escalated, and a shift from oral preparations to intravenous abuse occurred. By the early 1960s the San Francisco Bay area was home to a large and increasing number of intravenous methamphetamine users. Intravenous use, combined with the development of tolerance, led to escalating use. Serial intravenous speed users became known as 'speed freaks.' A public campaign in response to this trend warned that 'speed kills' (Lukas, 1985). As a result of law enforcement targeting activities, the public health campaign, user demographic changes, and other factors, the prevalence of methamphetamine and amphetamine use dropped after 1972 (Newmeyer, 1988).

Manufacture, Distribution, and Diversion

During the 1960s pharmaceutical amphetamine production soared with the demand from widespread use. However, production levels grew at a rate that far exceeded medical use. One consequence of excessive production combined with widespread popularity was diversion of pharmaceutical grade drugs to illegal traffic and use. The black market in amphetamines involved diversions from pharmaceutical companies, wholesalers, pharmacists, and physicians. It is estimated that up until 1971 between one-half to two-thirds of the 100,000 pounds of pharmaceutical amphetamine produced each year was diverted to black market channels (Grinspoon and Hedblom, 1975). In 1971 the Justice Department began imposing quotas on legal amphetamine production.

The Department of Justice (DOJ) became aware of the magnitude of dispensation of intravenous methamphetamine through illegal prescription writing. The DOJ intervened, and pharmaceutical manufacturers voluntarily removed methamphetamine ampoules from the outpatient prescription marketplace (Spotts and Spotts, 1980). Abbott withdrew Desoxyn in 1962 and Burroughs Wellcome withdrew Methedrine in 1963. This action left intravenous methamphetamine users without a product that could be readily injected. Demand was created for an inexpensive water-soluble powder product.

What resulted was the emergence of the first illicit 'bathtub' methamphetamine laboratories in late 1962 in San Francisco to satisfy the demand for a user-friendly product (Morgan et al., 1994). The early illicit methamphetamine was synthesized from phenyl-2-propanone (P-2-P) and methylamine by a process referred to as the amalgam method, resulting in a racemic mixture of *d-* (the more pharmacologically active form) and *l-*isomer methamphetamine. A few legitimate chemists are believed to have helped several groups develop this manufacturing process (Morgan et al., 1994). The illicit product was less potent and less pure than the pharmaceutical product which is all *d-*isomer methamphetamine. The newly manufactured product became known by a number of street names such as: 'crank,' 'bathtub crank,' 'biker crank,' 'peanut butter,' 'prope-dope,' and 'wire.'

Whereas prior to 1962 the quality and purity of methamphetamine was defined by pharmaceutical supplies, after 1962 the availability and quality of the illicit product was unpredictable. Up until 1974 only 30% of street samples purported to be metham-

phetamine truly were methamphetamine. 'Look-alike' speed, a combination of phenylpropanolamine, ephedrine, and caffeine, sometimes with other constituents, flooded the street market (Lake and Quirk, 1984). From 1975 to 1983 the meth content of street samples increased from 60% to over 90%. Over time, clandestinely manufactured methamphetamine came to dominate the street speed market (Puder et al., 1988).

With the escalation of use during the 1960s came an increase in violence and a diffusion of clandestine manufacturing and distribution of speed outward from Haight-Ashbury to other areas along the West Coast (Smith, 1970). By 1965, outlaw motorcycle gangs, notorious for their depraved and unlawful activities and realizing there was profit to be made, began manufacturing and distributing speed (National Narcotics Intelligence Consumers Committee, 1993). Crank became regarded as the best speed for the biker lifestyle, which emphasized fast high-risk motorcycling, fighting, heavy drinking, partying, and barbiturate use (Thompson, 1967). The combination of the affinity of bikers and their lifestyle for the drug, and the sizeable profits to be made from its manufacture and distribution, led to increasing involvement and dominance over distribution by mid-1960. Biker distribution of crank diffused north to Oregon and Washington State and into Southern California. The laboratories were located primarily in rural areas.

The Department of Justice recognized the involvement of outlaw biker groups, in particular the Hell's Angels, in methamphetamine manufacture and distribution and began targeting these groups. During the 1980s, the law enforcement pressure combined with the dissemination of a new method of synthesis led to significant changes in methamphetamine distribution networks. The shift was to smaller producers and groups of friends or family who cooperated to produce small amounts of methamphetamine in low-tech labs (NNICC, 1993). Beginning around 1980, methamphetamine laboratories began to proliferate around San Diego and use in that area escalated.

The illicit manufacture of methamphetamine is relatively simple and can be carried out by individuals without special knowledge or expertise provided a detailed recipe is available (Irvine and Chin, 1991; Bureau of Justice Statistics, 1992). Laboratory operators include high school dropouts and highly educated chemists. Clandestine laboratories are commonly operated on an irregular basis. Frequently a batch of product is produced and the laboratory is disassembled, stored, or moved to a new location. Sites for laboratories vary from sophisticated underground hideaways to motel rooms, kitchens, or garages (NNICC, 1993). Laboratories tend to be located in more secluded rural sites, initially to avoid discovery due to fumes and odors vented during the production process (Irvine and Chin, 1991). The precursors and methods used in methamphetamine synthesis can vary from laboratory to laboratory. In many cases the producers possess insufficient knowledge and skill to carry out the synthesis appropriately and completely. In these cases the purity and quality of the end product suffer, with the output containing large levels of contaminants and unreacted precursors.

The Drug Enforcement Administration reports that methamphetamine is the most prevalent clandestinely manufactured controlled substance in the United States (DEA, 1993). The number of clandestine methamphetamine laboratories seized rose dramatically during the 1980s, from 88 in 1981 to 652 in 1989. This dramatic increase reflects both increased law enforcement pursuit of clandestine laboratories and the expansion of clandestine production. Since 1989, there has been a decrease in laboratory seizures to 429 in 1990, 315 in 1991, and 288 in 1992. Consistent with previous years, the clandestine manufacture of methamphetamine was located primarily in the West and Southwest United States. During 1992, 78% of the laboratories seized were located in the Denver, Los Angeles, Phoenix, San Diego, San Francisco, and Seattle DEA field areas (NNICC, 1993). Methamphetamine laboratories accounted for more than 87% of all clandestine laboratory seizures during 1992. The decrease in the number of methamphetamine laboratories seized in the United States during the 1990s as compared to the large number of laboratory seizures during 1989, is be-

lieved to be largely a result of the enactment and enforcement of the Chemical Diversion and Trafficking Act of 1988, which placed the distribution of 12 precursor and eight essential chemicals used in the production of illicit drugs under federal control (DEA, 1993).

Currently the ephedrine reduction method is the principal means employed in the manufacture of methamphetamine. This relatively simple process originated in Southern California and now is widespread throughout the United States (NNICC, 1993). The resulting product is the *d*-isomer of methamphetamine. Reportedly, new and altered chemical processes for clandestine manufacturing of methamphetamine are emerging on the West Coast, including the tetrahydrofuran (THF) synthesis (Wrede and Murphy, 1994) and a relatively simple synthesis procedure that is a variation of the ephedrine reduction method that is called 'cold cook' because no external heat source is required for the synthesis to proceed (Dode and Dye, 1994; DEA, 1993).

During 1992 the individuals and groups involved in [the] manufacture and distribution of methamphetamine were diverse and numerous and included independent entrepreneurs, outlaw motorcycle gangs, and Hispanic polydrug trafficking organizations (NNICC, 1993). Independent entrepreneur involvement was broad and distributed nationally. Motorcycle gangs influenced production in select areas, and Mexican traffickers dominated the large-scale production and distribution in [the] San Diego, Riverside, San Bernardino, and Fresno areas of California (NNICC, 1993; DEA, 1993). The Mexican traffickers typically manufacture large quantities of methamphetamine in Mexico and smuggle the finished product into California through heroin and marijuana trafficking routes, with the potential for distribution throughout the United States. Mexican smuggling of precursor chemicals such as ephedrine into California also provides evidence of their domination of methamphetamine production in the West (DEA, 1993). The emergence of this new trafficking and distribution scheme involving large quantities of methamphetamine may serve to drive a new widespread epidemic of use in endemic regions and new areas. Increases in methamphetamine use in Phoenix are attributed to a newly forged trafficking relationship between Mexican nationals and local Hispanics (Dode and Dye, 1994).

This brief but significant history of use and abuse of amphetamine and methamphetamine (decades rather than centuries) has laid the foundation for continued abuse of methamphetamine, the arrival of new dosage forms, and the emergence of new chemically related analogues.

Current Trends of Methamphetamine Abuse

Due to its illicit and illegal nature, the direct, reliable, and consistent measurement of substance abuse is difficult, if not impossible. As a result, the description of patterns and trends of drug abuse are derived from a variety of data sources, some more scientifically rigorous than others. These sources of information are interpreted as available and patterns and trends inferred from them. Data sources include national probability surveys such as the Monitoring the Future study (MTF), nationally representative surveillance systems akin to the Drug Abuse Warning Network (DAWN) and the Drug Use Forecasting system (DUF), state-based treatment data, small-scale field studies, and ethnographic observational research.

DAWN Data

The first measured surge in methamphetamine use following what has been described historically in Haight-Ashbury during the 1960s and early 1970s, occurred during the mid-1980s among metropolitan areas primarily along the West Coast. These increases were first picked up through ethnographic research and field studies (NIDA, 1986; NIDA, 1989), and later recognized through the Drug Abuse Warning Network (DAWN) system and reported through the Community Epidemiology Work Group, a network of researchers from major metropolitan areas of the United States who provide ongoing community level surveillance of drug abuse.

The DAWN is a national surveillance system that monitors hospital emergencies and deaths associated with drug abuse. The DAWN system was begun in the early 1970s as a random sample of hospital emergency departments; over time the number and type of participating hospitals changed, and the representativeness of the sample was compromised. The current system was revitalized, and a new sample drawn in 1986 to represent all hospital emergency departments in the coterminous United States. Nonfederal, short-stay, general hospitals with a 24-hour emergency department are eligible for inclusion in DAWN. Twenty-one Metropolitan Statistical Areas (MSAs) are designated for oversampling. Hospitals outside of these 21 areas are assigned to a national panel and sampled. A total of 685 hospitals were selected for the sample and 508 hospitals (74%) participated in the survey in 1993 (Office of Applied Studies, 1994a). Participation in DAWN is voluntary and involves a designated reporter within each facility reviewing hospital emergency department (ED) admission records.

An episode report is submitted each time a patient visits a DAWN hospital with problems relating to their own drug use. The case definition involves four criteria, all of which must be met: the patient must be treated in the hospital's ED, the presenting complaint must have been induced by or related to drug use at any time preceding the episode, the case must involve the nonmedical use of a legal drug or any use of an illegal drug, and the patient's reason for taking the drug/drugs must include dependence, suicide attempt, or psychic effect. If all the above criteria are met, then the ED visit is deemed a drug episode. For each drug episode, in addition to alcohol in combination, up to four substances may be recorded as drug mentions. Drug episodes are not synonymous with the number of individuals involved in the reported episodes. One person may make repeated visits to one or several EDs with each episode recorded independently.

The limitations of this system are that the data are only as good as the information recorded by the hospital ED staff and reflect only self-reported drug use by the patient without laboratory confirmation. DAWN does not provide a complete image of problems associated with drug use but only reflects the impact of drug use on hospital EDs in the United States and the sort of drug-related problems that bring patients into emergency departments.

The DAWN emergency department data showed statistically significant increases in mentions of methamphetamine/speed in Atlanta, Dallas, Los Angeles, Phoenix, San Diego, and Seattle between 1986 and 1988 (NIDA, 1989). During 1988 and 1989 the national level of methamphetamine/speed emergency room mentions held steady, [and] a drop was experienced in 1990 with a steady increase from 1990 through 1993 (Figure 24.1). In 1993 10,052 episodes (preliminary estimates) involving the use of methamphetamine/speed were reported in the coterminous United States, up from a low of 4,887 reported in 1991, a 106% increase (OAS, 1994b). A total of 466,897 drug-related emergency room episodes were recorded for 1993, cocaine accounted for 123,317 (26.4%) and heroin accounted for

62,965 (13.5%), with meth/speed involved in just over 2% of the episodes, ranking 12th among all drug-related episodes. From 1990 through 1993 national estimates of total drug-related ED episodes increased 26% from 371,208 to 466,897 respectively, and increased 8% between 1992 and 1993. Approximately 10% of the 1992 to 1993 increase is attributable to increases in meth/speed mentions (OAS, 1994b).

West Coast U.S. cities including San Diego, San Francisco, Seattle, and Los Angeles–Long Beach accounted for over 30% of the total 1993 methamphetamine/speed ED mentions (1993 preliminary estimates). Over the six-year period from 1988 through 1993, San Diego exhibited consistently high numbers of methamphetamine/speed ED mentions, leading all other cities during three years of this time period (Figure 24.2). Los Angeles led all MSAs in number of methamphetamine/speed mentions in 1993 with 1,140 accounting for 11% of total U.S. methamphetamine/speed mentions, followed by

Figure 24.1

Estimated Number of Methamphetamine/Speed Emergency Room Mentions in the Coterminous United States by Year: 1988–1993

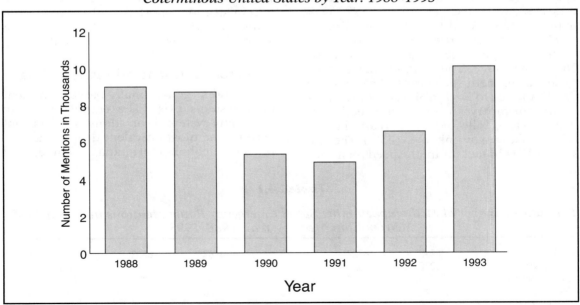

Source: SAMHSA, Drug Abuse Warning Network (April 1994 data file).
Note: The 1993 estimates are preliminary.

Figure 24.2

*Estimated Number of Methamphetamine/Speed Emergency Room Mentions in
Selected U.S. Metropolitan Areas by Year: 1988–1993*

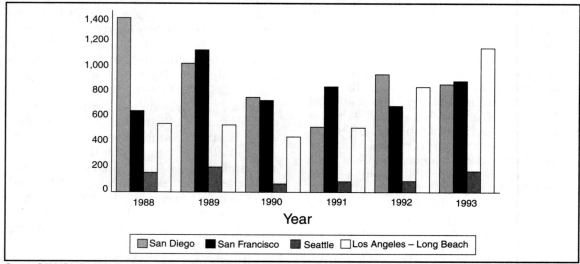

Source: SAMHSA, Drug Abuse Warning Network (April 1994 data file).
Note: The 1993 estimates are preliminary.

San Francisco, San Diego and Seattle with 879, 850, and 161 respectively (Table 24.1).

The profile of a typical methamphetamine user in 1993 is someone in the middle-age range, male, and white (Source: SAMHSA, weighted preliminary 1993 estimates from the April 1994 data file). During 1993, 35% of meth/speed mentions occurred in the 18–25 year age range and 37% in the 26–34 age range. The ratio of males to females using meth/speed ranged from 5:1 in San Francisco to 1.7:1 in San Diego. The predominant motivation for use was dependence (34%), followed by recreational use (27%), followed by unknown (25%). The reason for ED contact for meth/speed mentions was unexpected reaction (37%), overdose (29%), and chronic effects (13%), with withdrawal, seeking detoxification, accident/injury, other, and unknown together comprising the remaining percentage. The route of administration reported for the DAWN mentions was 31% unknown, 27% sniffed or snorted, 22% injected, and 11% oral.

State Treatment Admission Data

Several large nationally based treatment data systems exist. The emphasis within these data systems is on admission data concerning the most prevalent drugs of abuse, namely alcohol, marijuana, cocaine, and

Table 24.1

*Estimated Number of Methamphetamine/Speed Emergency Room Mentions in Selected U.S.
Metropolitan Areas by Year: 1988–1993*

U.S.	8992	8722	5236	4887	6563	10052
San Diego	1372	1021	758	515	931	850
San Francisco	639	1125	740	839	688	879
Seattle	142	201	59	90	99	161
Los Angeles–Long Beach	536	536	442	506	828	1140
Year	1988	1989	1990	1991	1992	1993

heroin. Data singular to methamphetamine were not readily available from these sources. State and city level admissions trends are reported for areas that have a significant methamphetamine problem.

In San Diego during 1993 amphetamine and methamphetamine primary admissions to publicly funded treatment programs totaled 2,376, a 37% increase from 1992 (Haight, 1994). Methamphetamine was the most frequently reported nonalcohol primary drug of abuse among those entering drug treatment programs during 1993, accounting for 41% of all nonalcohol treatment admissions. Numbers of methamphetamine admissions are rivaling alcohol admissions, which historically have been most prevalent. The median age of methamphetamine users entering treatment was 28 in 1993, tending to be younger than cocaine or heroin users. The racial distribution of methamphetamine users entering treatment was 71% white, 5% African American, and 17% Hispanic. An increase was seen in the number of methamphetamine treatment admissions reporting smoking as the preferred route of administration. In 1989, 4% reported smoking as compared to 23% in 1993.

In San Francisco primary admissions for amphetamine abuse totaled 1,357, increasing 17% from 1992 levels (Newmeyer, 1994). Amphetamine admissions accounted for just over 5% of the total non-alcohol admissions, behind heroin (67%) and cocaine (23%). The number and percent[age] of amphetamine admissions has increased steadily each year since 1988 with 534 admissions (3.3%) reported in 1988, and 1,357 (5.2%) reported in 1993.

Statewide methamphetamine treatment admissions in Hawaii have increased from 152 in 1991, to 268 in 1992, to an all-time high of 495 in 1993 (Wood, 1995). These data represent about 90% of the state-supported treatment facilities and do not include two large private facilities. In 1993, methamphetamine admissions accounted for 28% of the total admissions, second only to marijuana admissions (excluding alcohol). The trend of treatment admissions continued to increase into the first half of 1994.

Several drug use indicators including treatment admissions point to escalations of methamphetamine use in Phoenix, Arizona (Dode and Dye, 1994). The number of detoxification admissions for methamphetamine increased by 114% between 1992 and 1993 and ranked second behind heroin among non-alcohol admissions. Admissions of methamphetamine users to treatment through criminal justice programs rose from zero prior to 1992 to 30% in one program and 15% in another program during 1993.

Amphetamine and methamphetamine admissions account for a small proportion of overall admissions in most other cities and States (NIDA, 1994). In Colorado amphetamine admissions comprised 5.6% of the total, a slight increase over 1992. In Texas, Seattle, and Los Angeles amphetamine and methamphetamine admissions account for 3%, and in Minneapolis 2%, of non-alcohol admissions.

DUF Data

The Drug Use Forecasting (DUF) system is a monitoring system collaboratively administered by the National Institute of Justice and 24 booking facility sites across the nation. Interviews and urine drug tests for 10 illicit compounds are conducted at the time of booking of adult male, adult female, and juvenile arrestees, and represent drug use among those involved with the criminal justice system. For approximately 14 consecutive evenings each quarter, local staff interview and obtain voluntary urine specimens from a sample of newly booked arrestees. At each site approximately 225 males are sampled, and in some sites female arrestees and juvenile arrestees/detainees are also sampled. Response rates are 90% for the interview portion and 80% for the urine specimen portion of the system (NIJ, 1994a).

The DUF sample attempts to represent a sufficient distribution of arrest charges by limiting the number of male booked arrestees who are charged with the sale or possession of drugs (otherwise a majority of the sample would be made up of drug charge arrestees). Persons charged with drug charges are more likely to be using drugs at the time of arrest, so this limitation tends to underestimate drug use in the male arrestee population. The DUF sample also generally excludes driving offenses, emphasizing more serious crimes. In contrast, in order to obtain sufficient numbers of arrestees, all adult female and juvenile arrestees brought to the booking center or detention facility during the data collection period are included in the DUF sample, regardless of the charge.

Urine specimens are tested for cocaine, opiates, marijuana, PCP, methadone, benzodiazepines, methaqualone, propoxyphene, barbiturates, and amphetamines. All amphetamine positive results are further tested to eliminate exposure to over-the-counter products. The testing detects drug use that occurred in the previous two to three days for most compounds. PCP and marijuana use may be detected as long as several weeks prior to the testing date.

In 1993 the DUF system collected data from 20,550 adult male booked arrestees in 23 sites (NIJ, 1994a). Data from 8,070 adult female booked arrestees were collected at 20 of these sites. Twelve DUF sites collected male juvenile arrestee/detainee data (NIJ, 1994b). At most sites during 1993 cocaine was the most prevalent drug among male arrestees, followed by marijuana (seven sites reported a rate of marijuana use higher than cocaine). Cocaine use among male adult arrestees ranged from a low of 19% in Omaha, Nebraska, to a high of 66% in Manhattan, New York, with a median percentage of 43. Marijuana use ranged from 21% in Manhattan to 42% in Omaha, with a median value of 28%. Opiate use ranged from a low of 1% in Fort Lauderdale, Florida, to a high of 28% in Chicago, Illinois. Data from 20 sites revealed female arrestees to have marijuana in their urine a median of 16.5% of the time (range of 9% to 25%); and a range of opiate use from 3% to 23%. Results for juvenile arrestees/detainees nearly exclusively showed marijuana and cocaine use.

Overall, during 1993 in the majority of sites amphetamine use was very low or nonexistent. The predominant portion of amphetamine use was clustered in Western cities, including San Diego, California; San Jose, California; Los Angeles, California; Phoenix, Arizona; and Portland, Oregon. The level of amphetamine abuse among adult male arrestees within these sites ranged from 36% in San Diego to 8% in Los Angeles, and 53% in San Diego to 10% in Los Angeles among female arrestees (NIJ, 1994a [Source: DUF 1993 data file]). San Diego had the largest prevalence of amphetamine use for all three user groups during 1993; males (36%), females (53%), and juvenile males (14%) were positive for amphetamine abuse. In San Diego, among male arrestees, amphetamine abuse followed marijuana and cocaine abuse at 36% compared to 40% and 37% respectively. Amphetamine abuse led all other drugs for females in San Diego. Phoenix had the second highest prevalence of amphetamine abuse, with 16% of males and 26% of females testing positive. In all five Western cities the percentage of female arrestees testing positive for amphetamines was higher than the male arrestee counterpart at the same site.

Emergence of Ice

During the mid and late 1980s, ice, a high-potency, high-purity, and smokable methamphetamine hydrochloride was identified as a problem initially by Hawaiian law enforcement sources and later, through Hawaiian drug treatment programs. At the time of the emergence of ice the resident Hawaiian population had limited experience with mainland forms of methamphetamine. Hawaiian users widely believed ice to be a 'new drug,' and not related to other forms of speed. On the street this product, which resembles rock candy in appearance, was most commonly referred to as 'ice,' 'crystal,' 'shabu' (Japanese), or 'batu' (Filipino). In Hawaii the drug is almost exclusively smoked in a glass pipe. The inhalation of vapors leads to rapid absorption into the bloodstream and dissemination to the brain, resulting in the immediate onset of effects, similar to what is experienced by intravenous administration (Chiang and Hawks, 1989).

The unique combination of characteristics of ice—namely, high potency, high purity, and rapid onset of effects by smoking—resulted in an escalation of use among many abusers on the Island of Oahu (Miller and Tomas, 1989). The use pattern that emerged was one of bingeing and crashing, or continuous smoking in runs of three to eight days followed by complete exhaustion, usually characterized by deep prolonged sleep. Many adverse social, psychological, and medical consequences, including rapid addiction were experienced by binge users (Miller, 1991).

The presence of ice in Hawaii dates back to the late 1970s. During the early to mid-1980s ice use was limited to small ethnic gangs, but the outbreak beginning in [the] mid-1980s and peaking in the late 1980s found use spreading to numerous ethnic minorities, the Pacific-Asian majority, Caucasians, both genders, people of all ages, and all socioeconomic classes (Miller, 1991).

Prior to 1990, all the ice entering Hawaii originated from Asian sources, namely Korea, Taiwan, and the Philippines (DEA, 1989). Ice distribution in Hawaii was an economic enterprise developed by organized crime networks in Japan and Korea with large corporate investors (Adamski, 1992; Schoenberger, 1992). Availability of ice in Hawaii was widespread through 1990. By 1991 the availability had decreased, price had skyrocketed, and use indicators were declining (Wood, 1995). Large seizures of ice made by Chinese authorities in 1991 and 1992 confirm that illicit methamphetamine manufacture was also occurring in China. It is believed the Chinese contraband was smuggled into Japan, the Philippines, Hawaii, and the mainland United States during the early 1990s (NNICC, 1993). Current data are not available on the location and extent of ice manufacture within the United States.

Chemical Analogues

Synthesis of designer drugs or chemically related analogues to methamphetamine and amphetamine are emerging as new public health problems. Reports from ethnographers of a sharp increase of use of methylene deoxymethamphetamine (MDMA, XTC, Ecstasy) in association with the 'rave' scene have been received from San Francisco, Dallas, Houston, Miami, and Denver (NIDA, 1994; Kotarba, 1993; and Harrison, 1994). The rave scene is an increasingly popular form of dance and recreation predominantly frequented by young whites, but open to people of all ages, at clandestine locations (frequently abandoned warehouses), where high volume music and high tech entertain-

ment is available. The use of hallucinogens, methamphetamine, or MDMA is often incorporated into the overall experience of the rave (Office of National Drug Control Policy, 1995). MDMA is most commonly swallowed or snorted but can be smoked or injected. In addition to methamphetamine-like effects, MDMA may cause sensory enhancements and distortions and mild visual hallucinations.

To date, MDMA use has not been detected to any large degree on a national level through drug use indicator systems based on drug associated emergency room mentions, medical examiner reports, or within treatment data. Case reports and ethnographic information provide a glimpse of the problem but cannot be relied upon to represent the full scope and extent of this drug problem.

N-methylcathinone hydrochloride (methcathinone, 'cat,' 'goob,' 'sniff,' 'star,' 'wonder star'), a structural and pharmacological analogue of methamphetamine, is a potent and easily manufactured stimulant gaining popularity in the Midwest (Goldstone, 1993; DEA, 1994; Pinkert and Harwood, 1993). Cathinones occur naturally in the leaves of the khat shrub (*catha edulis*), which are chewed in East Africa and southern Arabia for the mild stimulant effects. Methcathinone is typically snorted but can be smoked and injected. Symptoms and adverse effects similar to methamphetamine are reported for methcathinone.

Michigan treatment programs report increasing numbers of methcathinone admissions; as many as 60 treatment admissions were reported statewide between October 1993 and March 1994 (Calkins and Hussain, 1994). Laboratories producing methcathinone were first identified in 1991, when five laboratory sites were seized in the Michigan Upper Peninsula. Methcathinone manufacturing is relatively simple from easily obtained materials; the technology is spreading to other nearby states throughout the Midwest and West (DEA, 1994).

Patterns of Youth Drug Abuse

The Monitoring the Future Study, also known widely as the National High School Senior Survey, has been conducted each year since 1975 under a National Institute on Drug Abuse grant to the University of Michigan Institute for Social Research (Johnston et al., 1991). The 1994 survey represents the 20th annual survey of high school seniors; data on 8th and 10th grade students have been collected since 1991. In 1994 a national probability sample of 15,929 high school seniors in 139 public and private schools nationwide was selected to be representative of all seniors in the continental United States. The students completed self-administered questionnaires during the spring of the year. Questions from the MTF Study solicit responses on use of amphetamines referred to as 'uppers,' 'ups,' 'speed,' 'bennies,' 'decries,' 'pep pills,' and 'diet Pills' (HHS, 1994).

From 1982 to 1992, lifetime, past year, and past month use of stimulants (amphetamines) by high school seniors declined (Figure 24.3). This decline was consistent with an increase in anti-drug attitudes and beliefs in the harmfulness of drug use. Since 1992 there have been significant increases in lifetime, past year, and past month use of stimulants by high school seniors during both 1993 and 1994 (Figure 24.3). During 1991 through 1994 the study also showed a

dramatic upturn in past year use of stimulants among 8th and 10th graders, paralleling the increase seen among seniors (Figure 24.4). Among senior students, lifetime use increased for amphetamines from 13.9% to 15.7%, and increased for crystal methamphetamine (ice) from 2.9% to 3.4% over the 1992 to 1994 period (HHS, 1994). These estimates of drug use prevalence by the MTF study may be underestimates due to the fact that the survey is conducted in secondary school classrooms and does not represent drug use by dropouts. Dropouts have been shown to have much higher drug use than seniors in the MTF study (Gfroerer, 1993).

Since 1991 there has been a steady and accelerating decline in perceived risk of drug use, with only 65% in 1994 reporting a great risk associated with regular marijuana use as compared to 79% of seniors in 1991. Perceived risk of use of other drugs such as cocaine and LSD also declined. This decline in perceived risk of drug use is consistent with the increases in drug use demonstrated during the same time period. Perceived dangers and attitudes of peers toward drug use have been shown to predict future drug use.

Figure 24.3
Estimated Prevalence of Lifetime, Past Year, and Past Month Use of Stimulants Among High School Seniors: 1982–1994

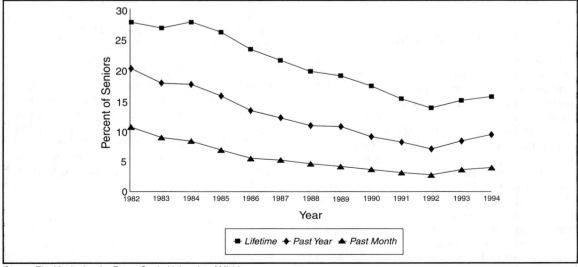

Source: The Monitoring the Future Study. University of Michigan.

Figure 24.4

Estimated Prevalence of Lifetime, Past Year, and Past Month Use of Stimulants Among High School Seniors (1982–1994) and Eighth and Tenth Graders (1991–1994)

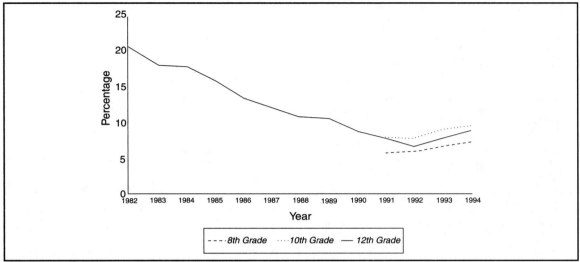

Source: The Monitoring the Future Study. University of Michigan.

Conclusion

In conclusion, methamphetamine abuse is endemic in West Coast U.S. cities and Hawaii. From early use by housewives, students, businessmen, and truck drivers, methamphetamine continues to be a significant drug of abuse in the U.S. Morgan et al. (1994) in their study described current methamphetamine use to be firmly entrenched in disenfranchised communities, among troubled individuals and dysfunctional families, and spreading to new user groups. The favorable side-effects such as euphoria, increased energy levels, sexual enhancement, and weight loss [make] methamphetamine appealing to diverse population subgroups. With the potential for widespread dissemination, factors such as easy availability, low cost, long duration of effect, and multiple methods of administration may also serve to increase its acceptance in new groups and areas.

The potential for expanded methamphetamine use is particularly significant in light of increasing youth use of drugs (including amphetamines), changing attitudes toward drug use in general, the availability of new dosage forms, and new venues for use. Rave scenes, where both methamphetamine and its analogue MDMA are sold and experimented with, serve as sites for spread into younger age cohorts and higher socioeconomic groups than have historically abused methamphetamine. Ice, a smokable form of methamphetamine, continues to wreak havoc and devastation within low socioeconomic status and working-class Hawaiian neighborhoods. Cat, an analogue, is gaining acceptance and use in the Midwest, and the potential for new analogues presenting new threats to the public health is significant.

Methamphetamine poses current challenges to our public health and future legacies for our youth and promises to remain problematic in American society for years to come.

References

Adamski, M. (1992) "Yakuza Investors Sink Roots in Isles," *Honolulu Star Bulletin*, October 16.

Brecher, E. M. (1972) *Licit and Illicit Drugs*. Boston: Little Brown.

Bureau of Justice Statistics (BJS). (1992) *Drugs, Crime and the Justice System—A National Report*. Washington, D.C.: U.S. Department of Justice, U.S. Government Printing Office (NJS-133652).

Caldwell, J. (1980) *Amphetamines and Related Stimulants: Chemical, Biological, Clinical, and Sociological Aspects*. Boca Raton, Florida: CRC Press, Inc.

Calkins, R. F., and Hussain K. L. (1994) "Drug Abuse Trends in Detroit/Wayne County, Michigan." In: *Epidemiologic Trends in Drug Abuse. Volume II: Proceedings of the Com-*

munity Epidemiology Work Group June 1994. Rockville, Maryland: National Institute on Drug Abuse (NIH Pub. No. 94-3854).

Chiang, N., and Hawks, R. (1989) *Pyrolysis Studies: Cocaine, Phencyclidine, Heroin and Methamphetamine.* Technical Review Brief. Rockville, Maryland: National Institute on Drug Abuse.

Dode, I. L., and Dye, C. (1994) "Drug Abuse Trends in Phoenix and Arizona." In *Epidemiologic Trends in Drug Abuse. Volume II: Proceedings of the Community Epidemiology Work Group June 1994.* Rockville, Maryland: National Institute on Drug Abuse (NIH Pub. No. 94-3854).

Drug Enforcement Administration. (1993) *Methcathinone (CAT) Drug Fact Sheet.* Washington, D.C.: U.S. Department of Justice, Intelligence Division (DEA-94007).

———. (1994) *U.S. Drug Threat Assessment: 1993. Drug Intelligence Report.* Washington, D.C.: U.S. Department of Justice (DEA-93042).

———. (1989) "A Special Report on 'Ice'." In *Epidemiologic Trends in Drug Abuse.* (Proceedings of the Community Epidemiology Work Group December 1989.) Supt. of Docs., U.S. Govt. Print. Off., Washington, DC (DHHS Pub. No. 721-757:20058).

Ellinwood, E. H. (1974) "Epidemiology of Stimulant Abuse." In E. Josephson and E. Carroll (eds.), *Drug Use.* Washington, D.C.: Hemisphere Publishing Corporation.

———. (1979) "Amphetamines/Anorectics." In R. DuPont, A. Goldstein, and J. O'Donnell (eds.), *Handbook on Drug Abuse.* Washington, D.C.: National Institute on Drug Abuse.

Fischman, M. W. (1990) "History and Current Use of Methamphetamine in the United States." In: *Cocaine and Methamphetamine: Behavioral Toxicology, Clinical Psychiatry and Epidemiology.* Proceedings from Japan-U.S. Scientific Symposium '90' on Drug Dependence and Abuse. Tokyo, Japan.

Gfroerer, J. (1993) "An Overview of the National Household Survey on Drug Abuse and Related Methodological Research." Proceedings of the Survey Research Section of the American Statistical Association, Joint Statistical Meetings, August 1992. Boston, Massachusetts.

Grinspoon, L., and Hedblom, P. (1975) *The Speed Culture, Amphetamine Use and Abuse in America.* Cambridge, Mass.: Harvard University Press.

Goldstone, M. S. (1993) "Cat: Methcathinone—a New Drug of Abuse." *JAMA* 269, p. 2508.

Haight, M. A. (1994) "Drug Abuse Trends in San Diego County." In *Epidemiologic Trends in Drug Abuse. Volume II: Proceedings of the Community Epidemiology Work Group June 1994.* Rockville, Maryland: National Institute on Drug Abuse (NIH Pub. No. 94-3854).

Harrison, L. (1994) "Raving in Colorado: An Amateur's Field Notes." In *Epidemiologic Trends in Drug Abuse. Volume II: Proceedings of the Community Epidemiology Work Group June 1994.* Rockville, Maryland: National Institute on Drug Abuse (NIH Pub. No. 94-3854).

Health and Human Services. (1994) *HHS Releases High School Drug Abuse and "DAWN" Surveys.* U.S. Department of Health and Human Services Press Release, Monday, December 12.

Irvine, G., and Chin, L. (1991) "The Environmental Impact and Adverse Health Effects of the Clandestine Manufacture of Methamphetamine." In M. A. Miller and N. J. Kozel (eds.), *Methamphetamine Abuse: Epidemiologic Issues and Implications.* NIDA Research Monograph 115. Rockville, Maryland: U.S. Dept. of Health and Human Services.

Johnston, L. D., O'Malley, P. M., and Bachman, J. G. (1991) *Drug Use Among American High School Seniors, College Students and Young Adults, 1975–1990, Volume I—High School Seniors.* Rockville, Maryland: National Institute on Drug Abuse (DHHS Pub. No. [ADM] 91-1813).

King, P. K., and Coleman, J. H. (1987) "Stimulants and Narcotic Drugs." *Pediatric Clinics of North America*, 34 (2): 349–362.

Kotarba, J. A. (1993) *The Rave Scene in Houston, Texas: An Ethnographic Analysis.* Austin, Texas: Texas Commission on Alcohol and Drug Abuse.

Lake, C., and Quirk, R. (1984) "Stimulants and Look-Alike Drugs." *Psychiatric Clinics North America* 7: 689–701.

Lukas, S. E. (1985) *The Encyclopaedia of Psychoactive Drugs. Amphetamines. Danger in the Fast Lane.* New York: Chelsea House.

Mellinger, G. D., Balter, M. B., and Manheimer, D. I. (1971) "Patterns of Psychotherapeutic Drug Use Among Adults in San Francisco." *Archives of General Psychiatry,* November, pp. 385–395.

Miller, M. A. (1991) "Trends and Patterns of Methamphetamine Smoking in Hawaii." In M. A. Miller and N. J. Kozel (eds.), *National Institute on Drug Abuse Research Monograph Series No. 115: Methamphetamine Abuse: Epidemiologic Issues and Implications.* Washington, D.C.: Supt. of Docs., U.S. Govt. Print. Off. (DHHS Pub. No. [ADM]91-1836).

Miller, M. A., and Tomas, J. M. (1989) "Past and Current Methamphetamine Epidemics." In *Epidemiologic Trends in Drug Abuse: Proceedings of the Community Epidemiology Work Group December 1989.* Washington, D.C.: Supt. of Docs., U.S. Govt. Print. Off. No. 721-757:20058).

Morgan, P., Beck, J., Joe, K., McDonnell, D., and Gutierrez, R. (1994) *Ice and Other Methamphetamine Use.* Final Report to the National Institute on Drug Abuse. National Institute of Health. U.S. Government Printing Office.

Morgan, J. P., and Kagan, D. X. (1978) "The Impact on Street Amphetamine Quality of the 1970 Controlled Substances Act." *Journal of Psychedelic Drugs* 10: 303–317.

National Institute of Justice (NIJ). (1994a) *Drug Use Forecasting 1993 Annual Report on Adult Arrestees: Drugs and Crime in America's Cities.* Washington, D.C.: U.S. Department of Justice, National Institute of Justice.

———. (1994b) *Drug Use Forecasting 1993 Annual Report Juvenile Arrestee/Detainees: Drugs and Crime in America's Cities.* Washington, D.C.: U.S. Department of Justice, National Institute of Justice.

National Institute on Drug Abuse. (1986) *Drug Abuse Trends and Research Issues.* Proceedings of the Community Epidemiology Work Group December 1986. Washington, D.C.: U. S. Govt. Print. Off. (DHHS Pub. No. 181-332:60315).

———. (1989) *Methamphetamine Abuse in the United States.* Washington, D.C.: Supt. of Docs., U.S. Govt. Print. Off. (DHHS Pub. No. [ADM]89-1608).

———. (1994) *Epidemiologic Trends in Drug Abuse. Volume 1: Highlights and Executive Summary. Community Epidemiology Work Group (June 1994).* Rockville, Maryland: National Institute on Drug Abuse (NIH Pub. No. 94-3853).

National Narcotics Intelligence Consumers Committee. (1993) *The NNICC Report 1992.* Washington, D.C.: Department of Justice, Drug Enforcement Administration.

Newmeyer, J. A. (1978) "The Epidemiology of the Use of Amphetamine and Related Substances." *Journal of Psychedelic Drugs* 10 (4): 293–302.

———. (1988) "The Prevalence of Drug Use in San Francisco in 1987." *Journal of Psychoactive Drugs* 20 (2): 185–189.

———. (1994) "Drug Use in the San Francisco Bay Area." In *Epidemiologic Trends in Drug Abuse. Volume II: Proceedings of the Community Epidemiology Work Group June 1994.* Rockville, Maryland: National Institute on Drug Abuse (NIH Pub. No. 94-3854).

Office of Applied Studies. (1994a) *Statistical Series: Annual Emergency Room Data 1992 Data from the Drug Abuse Warning Network (DAWN).* Series 1, No. 12 A. Rockville, Maryland: Substance Abuse and Mental Health Services Administration (DHHS Pub. No. [SMA]94-2080).

———. (1994b) *Preliminary Estimates from the Drug Abuse Warning Network 1993, Preliminary Estimates of Drug-Related Emergency Department Episodes. Advance Report Number 8, December 1994.* Rockville, Maryland: Substance Abuse and Mental Health Services Administration.

Office of National Drug Control Policy. (1995) *Pulse Check—National Trends in Drug Abuse*. Washington, D.C.: Executive Office of the President.

Pinkert, D., and Harwood, H. J. (1993) *"Khat* (Cathaedulis): Background and Policy Questions." Prepared for National Institute on Drug Abuse (in draft). Rockville, Maryland: Drug Abuse Policy Center.

Pittel, S. M., and Hofer, R. (1970) "The Transition to Amphetamine Abuse." In E. H. Ellinwood and S. Cohen (eds.), *Current Concepts on Amphetamine Abuse*. National Institute of Mental Health, Washington, D.C.: Supt. of Docs., U. S. Govt. Print. Off. (DHEW Pub. No. [HSM]72-9085).

Puder, K. S., Kagan, D. V., and Morgan, J. P. (1988) "Illicit Methamphetamine: Analysis, Synthesis, and Availability." *American Journal Drug Alcohol Abuse* 14: 463–473.

Schoenberger, K. (1992) "Yakuza Expand on Mainland." *Honolulu Advertiser*, January 5.

Smith, R. C. (1969) "The World of the Haight-Ashbury Speed Freak." *Journal of Psychoactive Drugs* 2 (2): 77–83.

——. (1970) "Compulsive Methamphetamine Abuse and Violence in the Haight-Ashbury District." In E. H. Ellinwood and S. Cohen (eds.), *Current Concepts on Amphetamine Abuse*. National Institute of Mental Health. Washington, D.C.: Supt. of Docs., U.S. Govt. Print. Off. (DHEW Pub. No. [HSM]72-908).

Spotts, J. V., and Spotts, C. A. (1980) *Use and Abuse of Amphetamine and Its Substitutes*. NIDA Research Issues 25. Washington, D.C.: National Institute on Drug Abuse.

Thompson, H. S. (1967) *The Hell's Angels*. New York: Ballantine.

Wood, D. W. (1995) "Illicit Drug Use in Honolulu and the State of Hawaii." In *Epidemiologic Trends in Drug Abuse. Volume II: Proceedings of the Community Epidemiology Work Group*.

Wrede, A. F., and Murphy, L. D. (1994) "Recent Drug Abuse Trends in the Seattle King County Area." In *Epidemiologic Trends in Drug Abuse. Volume II: Community Epidemiology Work Group June 1994*. Rockville, Maryland: National Institute on Drug Abuse (NIH Pub. No. 94-3854).

For Discussion

1. Compare Miller's perspective on methamphetamine with that described by Jenkins in this section.

2. Discuss whether recent patterns of amphetamine and methamphetamine use might have been different if production controls had not been developed in 1971.

25

A Very Childish Moral Panic

Ritalin

Toby Miller
Marie Claire Leger

Ritalin is a medicine that can be prescribed for At-
tention-Deficit/Hyperactivity Disorder (ADHD) in
children. In this chapter, Toby Miller and Marie
Claire Leger trace the history of psychiatry and
children and note the increasing role of the state in
this regard. The authors outline the criticisms surrounding the diagnosis of ADHD and prescriptions
of Ritalin. They also discuss illegal use by school and
college students as well as professionals, explore
the relationship between gender and ADHD, and
link the prevalence of ADHD to culture and
modernity.

Introduction

For years it has been a nostrum of the cultural left to attack the psy-complexes—psychoanalysis, psychology, psychotherapy,
psychiatry, and psychopharmacology. These
complexes are easy marks for accusations
that they generate and sustain false consciousness, bourgeois individualism, racism, and sexism, as well as implicating folks
in the policing apparatus of medicine, therapy, and thought control. The taste for the
psy-complexes is seen as a luxury unavailable to those preoccupied with subsistence,
a manifestation of middle-class guilt at the
ravages of capitalism. It is also a reminder of
the "Red Scare" of 1919, when the United
States government was assured that psychotherapy could defuse the appeal of Marxism
to the urban poor, and the later rise of behav-

iorism, a model of person-as-machine that
promised to manage individual conduct in
the interests of capital. Critics on the left further argue that the pathologization of young
people distracts attention from structural inequalities by psychologizing issues of social
order and disorder. For the right, the psy-
complexes are suspect because they suggest
personal weakness, threaten a lack of productivity, and may imply the use of public resources for personal "development." Each
side revels in denouncing the solipsistic absorption and selfish individualism of those
derided by Bill Clinton as "the worried well."
For their part, corporations promote fast, efficient solutions to life's problems—stop
talking and start swallowing. Reactions
against the psy-complexes have taken a variety of forms: the anti-psychiatry movement
of R. D. Laing and others; critiques of
Freudianism; denial of public funds for therapy; critical press about both counseling and
psycho-pharmacology; and battles within
the psy-complexes between therapeutic and
drug treatments. The practical philosophy
movement in the United States stands in
opposition to pharmacology under the
slogan "More Plato, Less Prozac" (Marinoff,
2000).

Each of the psy-complexes has been subject at one time or another to "moral panics."
This term was coined within critical British
criminology in the early 1970s to describe
media messages announcing an increase in
the crime rate, and the subsequent establishment of specialist police units to deal with
this alleged problem (Thompson, 1998, p. 7;
Erich Goode, 2000). Moral panics were initially theorized as short-lived spasms with a
standard trajectory: exaggeration, prediction, symbolization, and then conclusion.
Next, they were thought of as a series of
waves that spoke of wider ideological contradictions about economic inequality
(Barker, 1999). So we might say that a moral
panic is a sudden, brief, but seemingly thor-
oughgoing anxiety or condemnation concerning particular human subjects or practices. Often generated by the state or the
media and picked up by interest groups and
social movements, its verve is generally disproportionate to the extent of the "problem"
it brings into being, such that the panic's life

266

is determined by the practices of its intellectual progenitors rather than its material outcomes (Jenkins, 1999, pp. 4–5). The literature on moral panics suggests that they function synecdochally: part of society is used to represent (or perhaps distort) a wider problem—youth violence is a suitable case for panic, whereas systemic class inequality is not; adolescent behavior is addressed, but capitalist degeneracy is not (P. Cohen, 1999, pp. 192–193; S. Cohen, 1973, pp. 9–13). Moral panics often take the form of crusades, sustained over a certain period by activists ("moral entrepreneurs") seeking to protect a majority they see as feckless and vulnerable. A "turncoat," a rejected or dissident former insider, is a crucial component of a prominent panic, but the perfect deconstructionist is the professional "expert" (Thompson, 1998, pp. 3, 12, 91).

The dual role of experts and media critics in the constitution of moral panics sees the former testifying to their existence, and the latter sensationalizing and diurnalizing them—making the risk attributed to the particular panic seem like a new, terrifying part of everyday life. The cumulative impact of this alliance between specialist and popular knowledge is a heightened yet curiously normalized sense of risk (Wagner, 1997, p. 46). Particular kinds of individuals are labeled as dangerous for social well-being because of their "deviance" from agreed-upon norms of the general good. Once identified in this way, their life-practices are interpreted from membership of this group. Critics of the moral-panic process propose that we should ask not "Why do people behave like this?," but "Why is this conduct deemed 'deviant,' and whose interest does that serve?" (S. Cohen, 1973, pp. 12–13).

Moral panics are part of today's "risk society," a world characterized by "institutions of monitoring and protection" that seek to protect people from "social, political, economic and individual risks" in the service of the time-discipline required by capitalism. Rather than risk being occasional, it is now a constitutive component of being and social organization (Beck, Giddens, & Lash, 1994, p. 5). Advanced industrial/postindustrial societies induce massively increased feelings of risk in their populations by admitting and even promoting the irrationality of the economy. Simultaneously, environmental despoliation, cycles of recession, the decline of life-long employment, massive international migration, changed gender relations, developments in communication technology, and the rolling back of the welfare state, alongside income redistribution towards the wealthy, have left people in postindustrial societies factoring cost and benefit into the everyday as never before, even as their sense of being able to determine their future through choice is diminished. Put another way, whereas early modernization was primarily concerned with the establishment of national power and the accumulation and distribution of wealth, developed modernity produces new risks for its members beyond those of the nation and affluence. Moral panics become means of dealing with these risks via appeals to "values," a displacement from acknowledging the systemic nature of socioeconomic crises and fissures (Thompson, 1998, pp. 22–23, 62, 88, 140). They both contribute to and are symptomatic of the risk society.

Youth occupy a privileged position in moral panics. Positioned between birth and adulthood, holding both the promise of the future and the key to its potential corruption, youth are both "at risk" and "a source of risk." They must be protected from harm by the family, society, and educational institutions because they embody a threat to order and stability, as provided by those same institutions. From characterizations of youth's hedonistic consumption, to their association with subcultures and resistance—in the form of anti-war movements, global popular culture, and alternatives to traditional lifestyles—panics about youth and youth safety are also panics about moral and social order (Thompson, 1998, p. 1).

The idea of the moral panic is unusual as a sociological concept in that it is freely used and accepted in the mainstream UK media (Barker, 1999)—although the *British Medical Journal* has attacked applying the idea to science (Daniels, 1998). In this paper, we examine the moral panic surrounding Ritalin, an amphetamine-related pill that has been medically prescribed for use by children diagnosed with attention deficit hyperactivity disorder (ADHD) in the United States for over three decades and is now the object of great controversy both here and in other countries.

Our intent here is not to debunk Ritalin, but to follow the agnosticism of Michel Foucault. He was careful to avoid arguing that madness did not exist, or was a product of medicine: "That people are suffering, that people make trouble in society or in their families, that is a reality." He sought to uncover how mental conditions were identified and rendered as problems in need of treatment, with the aim of explaining how these forms of problematization function as techniques, economies, social relations, and knowledges (1994, p. 123). Similarly, we are not arguing here that ADHD is "made-up," nor do we negate the value of decisions made within particular social formations that decree certain forms of conduct (and suffering) to be unacceptable or deny the efficacy and legitimacy of democratically-derived and policed norms. But to regard definitions (for example, as to what is mad or sane) as timeless, spaceless, absolute accounts is to miss the temporal and spatial contingency of the knowledges that are applied to generate social norms. Rather than promoting or condemning Ritalin itself, we suggest that the moral panic associated with it is a routine, generic event that emanates from today's risk society and its political economy and political technology of personhood. Using theoretical insights derived from social constructionism, the history of thought, and the sociology of risk, we examine the human sciences' discourse of personhood, the history of American psy-complexes and the policing of children, and these complexes at work on ADHD and Ritalin. We find new ways to explain the panic, if not to adjudicate on it, and conclude that Ritalin is, as per the wider designer-drug phenomenon, the latest path to the United States upward-mobility fantasy of transcendence, a combination of the pleasure and self-development sides of United States popular culture.

The Psy-complexes

The human subject is generally known via three modes of subjectification: the speaking subject (defined by linguistics); the working subject (from economics); and the living subject (as per the natural sciences, especially biology). These modes define subjects as internally split or separated from others, nominating the sane versus the mad, the well-behaved versus the criminal, and the healthy versus the sick. Such categories are produced through the decisions and apparatuses of institutions that are driven by forms of scientific knowledge. Of course, self-directed techniques also turn a person into a subject: gay versus straight, private versus public, and learn*ed* versus learning. Struggles for power take place over:

> the status of the individual: on the one hand, they assert the right to be different, and they underline everything that makes individuals truly individual. On the other hand, they attack everything which separates the individual, breaks his links with others, splits up community life, forces the individual back on himself and ties him to his own identity in a constraining way. (Foucault, 1982, pp. 781, 777–778)

The raw stuff of human beings, then, is *not* individuals: people *become* individuals through the discourses and institutions of modernity. Over time, rites of passage from traditional societies are increasingly displaced, supplemented, or made purely symbolic by scientific accounts of personhood: status and ancestry join measurement and confession, as ritualistic shame meets inner guilt and state authority. Epistemology shifts, with facts and interpretations deriving from experimentation rather than individual authority. But even as this looser model of power appears, so too do hospitals and psychologists (Foucault calls them "professionals of discipline, normality and subjection"). They utilize the new forms of knowledge to multiply and intensify the expression of power over bodies. For example, adults who lack the ability to narrate their feelings and struggles to the satisfaction of psychologists are incarcerated for failing the duty of disclosure that is the corollary of Enlightenment freedoms (Foucault, 1979, pp. 193, 224, 296; Foucault, 1987, p. 23; Albee, 1977, p. 152).

Crucially, at the beginning of the nineteenth century, psychiatry intervened in the legal field, establishing its right to define individuals as sane or insane through the concept of the dangerous individual and the homicidal maniac, thus claiming a role in the allocation of justice and punishment. By the end of the nineteenth century, however, psychiatry was no longer only interested in the criminal, but had established that there was no qualitative difference between heinous crimes and minor delinquencies—that these were varying degrees of the same thing! Since that time, the concept of the dangerous individual has emerged, an extension of the boy who runs around looking up little girls' skirts, stealing stop signs, or in our case, acting up in class. The model poses several scientific puzzles: Are there individuals who are intrinsically dangerous? By what signs can they be recognized? How should one react to their presence? These quandaries relate to forms of punishment. In the course of the past century, penal law has enlarged, organized, and codified the suspicion and the identification of dangerous individuals, from the rare and monstrous figure of the monomaniac to the common everyday figure of the degenerate, the pervert, the constitutionally unbalanced, and the immature (Foucault, 2000).

Enlightenment knowledges invented collectives as well as individuals. The populace became the province of statistics, bounded not by the direct exertion of juridical influence or domestic authority, but by forms of knowledge that granted "the people" a life that could not be divined from the model of the family (Foucault, 1991a, pp. 98–99). Even as Revolutionary France was embarking on a regime of slaughter, public-health campaigns were underway—an ongoing Janus-faced "game between death and life" (Foucault, 1991b, p. 4). Out of that came the following prospect: "Maybe what is really important for our modernity—that is, for our present—is not so much the étatisation of society, as the governmentalization of the state" (Foucault, 1991a, p. 103). Cholera, sanitation, and prostitution were figured as problems for government to address in the modern era, through "the emergence of the health and physical well-being of the popula-

tion in general as one of the essential objectives of political power." The entire "social body" was assayed and treated for its insufficiencies. Since that time, governing people has meant, most centrally and critically, obeying the "imperative of health: at once the duty of each and the objective of all" (Foucault, 1991b, p. 277). Science and government combined in new environmental-legal relations, under the signs of civic management and economic productivity. In 1855, Achille Guillard invented "demography," merging "political arithmetic" and "political and natural observations," which had been on the rise since the first population inquiries in seventeenth-century Britain. The new knowledge codified five projects: reproduction, aging, migration, public health, and ecology (Fogel, 1993, pp. 312–313). It has been determinate in articulating productivity to fitness since then. These forces coalesce in the psy-complexes, which have attained their most developed form in the United States.

United States psychiatry has twice announced breakthroughs that appeared to guarantee its stature, during the nineteenth century and again in the 1960s. First, moral treatment and the "talking cure" (named by Bertha von Pappenheim), then pharmacology and community care (JFK's promise of two thousand Community Mental Health Centers and the American Psychiatric Association's in-house 1963 declaration that the profession was ready to "inherit the earth") were thought to offer deliverance. There has been a shift—winding, incomplete, and frequently circular—from religious judgment and confessional technique to medicalized chemical intervention and deinstitutionalized help, from carceral buildings and elongated couches to pill-dispensing hospitals and returns to the social (Musto, 1995; Shattuc, 1997, p. 114). Today, more money is spent promoting the new "wonder drugs" in the United States than on all medical school and residency training put together—in 1998, Eli Lilly spent in the United States $95 million to promote Prozac (Maslin, 2000; Bloom, 2000). How did these "breakthroughs" happen?

The key enabling moment for the psy-complexes in the United States is the period after the Second World War. During this period, the Federal Government invented new laws, agencies, and programs that encouraged the development of mental health as an industry. The popularity of Freudian psychoanalysis peaked during this time (between 1940 and 1965), after demonstrating efficacy with soldiers during World War II, although many "cures" may have been more attributable to the war ending than to psychoanalysis (Hale, 1995, p. 382).

Additionally, in 1954, the first psychoactive drug came onto the market. Chlorpromazine (sold as Thorazine) combined with new governmental employment of therapists to reverse the institutional removal of the mentally ill from public life. Two years later, the number of mental-hospital patients declined for the first time since the previous century. Patients were not the only ones to come out. Whereas almost all psychiatrists worked in hospitals in 1940, by 1957 over 80 percent did not. With the advent of Medicare and Medicaid as part of the "Great Society" reforms of the next decade, public hospitals lost more patients. State governments utilized new forms of funding to shift them into non-traditional institutions like private nursing homes, halfway houses, and outpatient care, which were simultaneously ideologized as democratic by the emergent community-care movement (Herman, 1996, pp. 257–259).

The importance of diagnosis became eminently clear with the introduction of psychoactive therapeutic drugs in the 1950s. The availability of effective medicine made diagnosis particularly important, although in psychiatry the effect of a medicine itself often created the diagnostic category of the disease it was "designed" to alleviate. The American Psychiatric Association's *Diagnostic and Statistical Manual of Mental Disorders I (DSM)*, which catalogues mental disorders for the field, was created in 1952 and encompassed an expansionist project, in which broad labels were used for diagnosis with the aim of encompassing the whole of society. *DSM II* was published in 1968, and embodied a psychoanalytic approach to psychiatry.

The status of psychoanalysis began to decline after 1965, however, because of doubts about its scientific validity, its links to the establishment rather than with progressive reform, a renewed interest in genetic/biological causes of mental illness (particularly after the advent of psychotherapeutic drugs in the mid-'50s) and the rising popularity of alternative models. The *DSM III*, published in 1980, was a response to biopsychiatry, and focused on symptoms and description rather than etiology or theory. The purported reason for not focusing on etiology was to avoid controversy about causes amongst different camps of psychiatry, but in actuality, this model was directly opposed to the psychoanalytic perspective and also to the social psychiatry models that had been emerging in the 1960s. The shift from *DSM II* to *DSM III* marked an important moment in the history of psychiatry, as the biopsychiatric model of diagnosis came to dominate over the psychoanalytic model (Cooksey & Brown, 1998, pp. 529–530).

Although the supposed aim of the new diagnostics was to avoid the expansionist tendencies in the 1950s and '60s when there was a greater social and economic attention to mental illness, this counter-tendency is itself expansionist, in the name of biopsychiatry. Nosology as applied to conduct now depends on entirely distinct practices being collocated by clinicians in order to define them as amounting to psychopathology. The result fixes these forms of life as immovable diagnostic things via reification, reductionism, and synecdoche (part of one's "behavior" stands for the totality of one's personality). This has been identified as a danger associated with attention deficit disorder and its relatives (Santostefano, 1999, pp. 322–323).

In 1990, President George Bush the Elder declared the commencement of the "Decade of the Brain." This represented the triumph of the "New Psychiatry," which had mobilized psychosurgery and drug treatments from the 1960s to the point where they were dominant. Identifying the brain as the etiological site of educational, social, personal, and even political problems, psychiatrists have comprehensively medicalized misery, to the point where ideas of early-childhood trauma are deemed outmoded and there are moves to erase psychotherapy from psychiatric education. Pharmaceutical corporations and their prescribing delegates have become the new hospital administrators and therapists, under the slogan "You can't talk to disease" (Breggin, 1994, pp. 11–13, 17, 23, 122). Prior to addressing this topic with reference to ADHD, we need to historicize one more item—the child and its psyche.

Policing the Child

Based on his studies of France, Jacques Donzelot (1979) states that child psychiatry was not originally concerned with psychiatric particularities common to children, *per se*. The early physicians who directed mental asylums, and the alienists and the neurologists who restricted their expertise to a small group composed of the severely insane, were interested in childhood insanity as it was linked to the future health of the adult.

For example, the vagabond became the focus of psychiatric attention in the last decade of the nineteenth century, and problematic children were seen as potential future vagabonds. This attention to children was intended to "preselect and to pretreat," separating troubled children from the normal population (Donzelot, 1979, p. 131). The school became a site for observing the signs of disorders for which children were to be treated, and the family was seen as the originary site of mental illness. Juvenile law at this time was shifting its focus from punishment and repression to education and prevention, and psychiatry played a major role. By the middle of the twentieth century, the damning diagnosis "pervert" became less common, and the shift away from permanent diagnosis and towards "educability" continued.

But child psychiatry became more and more concerned with the proclivities of everyday children. By the early decades of the twentieth century, there was a shift in focus—the "predelinquent" child emerged as a subject of child guidance, and psychiatry grew increasingly interested in the everyday "normal" child, which included all ages and classes (Jones, 1999, p. 9). The asylums of the nineteenth century were replaced by or converted into hospitals, psychiatrists developed an interest in everyday problems and patients—not just the criminally insane—

and psychiatry increasingly focused on the normal (Lunbeck, 1994, pp. 22–24).

An early twentieth-century concentration on deviant children emerged in the United States via the juvenile courts, which were founded in 1899. These courts, which mostly dealt with the poor, were based on the premise that adult courts were too harsh, doling out sentences that were too final and not therapeutic-minded enough for children. The Juvenile Courts linked up to psychiatry early on; in 1909, the Juvenile Psychopathic Institute (JPI) was founded in Chicago. It aimed to improve the juvenile court, while the courts were to seek psychiatric evaluation of perplexing cases. With this union of child law and child psychiatry, progressives hoped to rely on scientific research into the causes of juvenile crimes to eradicate juvenile delinquency. And the turn of the century was an auspicious time to garner public support for this movement, as the mass media were filled with reports of rising crime, justifying immediate social action. The JPI suggested that delinquents were "normal" children, not feebleminded or psychopathic, and its findings were praised by welfare and prison reformers. This inspired a national child-guidance movement, which created more court-affiliated clinics (Jones, 1999, pp. 15, 37–38, 43, 56–57). In 1910, the National Committee for Mental Hygiene (NCMH) was founded in the United States, supported with grants from the Rockefeller Foundation and the Commonwealth Fund. The prevention of mental illness and delinquency was its aim, to be achieved through children. In 1922, the NCMH provided seed money to establish child-guidance clinics, and by 1936 there were 235 such clinics nation-wide (Hale, 1995, p. 87; Jones, 1999, pp. 58–60).

Many current attitudes about children took root in the child-guidance movement during the first half of the twentieth century in the United States (Jones, 1999, p. 4). There was a shift at that time from a focus on heredity as a cause of deviance to the impact of environment on character, the influence of the home, family, and parents on children's development, mother-blaming, the continuum drawn between normal and abnormal children, the negative effects of severe repression on children, and childhood sexuality (Hale, 1995, p. 85). The child-guidance clinic's first patients were young delinquents and their parents, mostly from immigrant families and low socioeconomic groups, but throughout the next few decades, this clientele grew to encompass middle-class children brought by mothers concerned with educational performance and sexual behavior (Hale, 1995, pp. 7, 87). By the 1920s and '30s, child guidance had begun to take an interest in the "problem child," who was "normal" in comparison with nineteenth-century psychiatric subjects, but deviant with respect to authority—for example the family or the school. This problem child could come from any social class (Jones, 1999, p. 7).

After World War II, child psychiatrists associated more with the medical community than with social workers and liberal reformers. In 1952, the American Academy of Child Psychiatry was founded. It restricted membership to medically trained persons who were part of the American Psychiatric Association, and in 1959 child psychiatry became a formal medical sub-specialty. Social-structural factors were not completely eschewed; in 1970, the Joint Commission on Mental Health of Children denounced the nation for ignoring socioeconomic factors that related to the well-being of children (Jones, 1999, pp. 217–218).

Coterminous with this history, we have seen the intense differentiation of United States children from adults. In the hundred years to 1950, the school displaced the factory as the site for disciplining children, parents in the evolving nuclear family were held responsible for their children's welfare and punishable by the state for failing to be responsible adults, and child psychologists emerged to theorize and treat children in terms of "natural" forms and stages of development into adulthood. Protection in the form of policing was an established norm by the 1950s (Steinberg & Kincheloe, 1997, pp. 1–2). In 1958, the National Defense Education Act invented the school-guidance counselor, funding 60,000 jobs.

Almost overnight, children were subject to external testing and self-monitoring against norms of scholastic and occupational achieve-

ment derived from the psyprofessions (Herman, 1996, pp. 257–259).

By this time, the "privatized nuclear household with its male breadwinner, female homemaker, and dependent children" had shifted from an "insurgent ideal" of the white middle class during the nineteenth century to a tentatively achieved but ideologically naturalized norm (Reeves & Campbell, 1994, p. 186). In the 1950s, 80 percent of children lived with their married, biological parents. But that was true of just 12 percent of children by the end of the 1980s. Seven percent of children lived with an employed father and "home-duties" mother (Reeves & Campbell, 1994, pp. 186–189). This is but one of the statistical changes that have generated concerns about youth and their well-being: as suicide rates fell across the population, they rose among young people—the suicide rate among 15–19-year-olds quadrupled between 1950 and 1995, notably among males. Key social measures of unhappiness correlate with youth today in a way that they did not even up to the mid-1970s, and young people report greater distress than before, beyond what old people experience (Putnam, 2000, pp. 261–263). These indices contribute to heightened concern about the welfare of youth; this is coterminous with increased contact with the psy-complexes, which simultaneously functions to protect youth and generate statistics that add to the concern: in the year 2000, 37 percent of US residents aged 15 to 24 were diagnosed as mentally ill (Berman, Strauss, & Verhage, 2000). In 1999, almost 2.98 million prescriptions were written for United States adolescents—over 11,000 new scripts each weekday (Waters, 2000).

The media have also come to take a critical role in the creation of childhood. The proliferation of new media technologies has seen a vast increase in the amount, degree, and speed of textual content experienced by children and young people, with much more of the latter's diurnal experience produced by entertainment corporations and much less by parents. The brief moment of parental dominance in the 1950s was itself clouded by the media—congressional hearings into juvenile delinquency heard again and again from social scientists, police, parents, and others that the emergent mass media were standing between parents and their children, diverting offspring from their parents' values (Gilbert, 1986, p. 3). This trend has continued. Ideologies, institutions, and policies predicated and structured on "tradition" are inadequate in the face of such major social change. On the one hand, children experience the extended working hours and diminished spending power of harried, often single parents. On the other, children are interpellated by the corporate advertising and entertainment as competent, knowledgeable consumers who should not be cowed into submission by authoritarian parental and educational will (Steinberg & Kincheloe, 1997, pp. 2–3, 16–17).

Attention Deficit-Hyperativity Disorder

ADHD and hyperkinetic disorder provide the psy-complexes with their reason for prescribing Ritalin, since stimulants like it are "the cornerstone of therapy" for the disorder (Steinberg, 1999, p. 223). This use of treatment only works, of course, as part of medicalization—there must be a physiological underpinning to these disorders, lest they be dismissed as malingering by sufferers, quick remedies for parents, teachers, or doctors, or self-interest on the part of the psychiatric and pharmaceutical establishments. Five distinct attempts have been mounted to provide a biological basis to the disorders. The first takes the efficacy of treatment as proof of the existence of disease—Ritalin works like a neurotransmitter, repairing concentration and disruptive conduct, so there must have been a problem with neurotransmission in the first place. This neglects the fact that use of Ritalin on "healthy" children also leads to greater obedience and focus. The second removes the blame from neurotransmitters and places it on pregnancy and birth, where prenatal and perinatal traumas are held responsible for early behavioral difficulties. The research only validates such claims up to the age of three years, so it is rarely used to justify Ritalin prescription. The third turns to retarded maturation, "soft signs" of neurologi-

cal function; but again, these signs are encountered in normal children as well. The fourth looks in the direction of physical abnormalities, but there are weak correlations between these difficulties and hyperactivity. Lastly, the inevitable appeal to genetics has produced no absolute proof. Concordance of ADHD among monozygotic twins is only 51 percent, compared to 100 percent concordance with eye color, which suggests only a partial genetic link (Rubinstein, Scrimshaw, & Morrissey, 2000, pp. 42–43; Livingstone, 1997).

Taken together, these five forms of thought offer less than compelling evidence that ADHD "exists" independently of its diagnosis and treatment. They have been described as "highly subjective" even though they are presented as quite the opposite (Messinger, 1978, p. 67). Endless studies that find children are hyperactive at home but not at school or *vice versa*, or hyperactive at both but not at summer camp or in clinicians' rooms, do serious disservice to biological claims (Sandberg & Garralda, 1996, pp. 281–282). The United States National Institutes of Health Consensus Conference has not established any basis for ADHD in brain functioning. So when patients or their significant others present professionals with such queries as "do you test for ADD?," they are reifying a cluster of symptoms and signs into a biological-neurological issue (Diller, 1998, p. 3). Where did such queries, with this earnest backdrop, derive from?

Hyperactivity was first declared in the late 1950s by Europeans, despite its contemporary status as an American disorder. But clinical discussion of unruly conduct amongst children has a much longer history. In its earliest manifestations, such disorders were attributed to moral defects in dealing with authority and self-discipline, evidenced in unruly bodily motions and inattentiveness. This analysis derived from a Social Darwinism employed to explain class difference (Sandberg & Barton, 1996, pp. 1, 5–6). Moral and medical discourses blurred on their way past one another, with each affected by the transaction, as "behavior" came to displace "morality." But the latter heavily coded the former, if in a scientific manner that treated norms as necessary for social cohesion and individual advancement on a secular rather than a God-given basis.

Even before identification of hyperactivity in Europe, George Still identified ADHD-like symptoms in 1902, attributing them to an inherited neurological disorder (Breggin, 1998, p. 179). However, it took the 1917–18 encephalitis epidemic to stimulate this discourse more thoroughly. Clinicians were presented with numerous young patients who behaved oddly, and this served to confirm the diagnosis of unusually lively but unfocused conduct on brain damage or disease. The 1960s witnessed a grand Atlantic bifurcation over the disorder(s). European clinicians began, and have largely continued, to define the problem narrowly and specifically, in terms of "excessive motor activity" probably caused by damage to the brain. In the United States, by contrast, hyperactivity was viewed as part of the problem and brain damage part of the cause, as attention deficits were categorized and counted (Sandberg & Barton, 1996, pp. 2–3, 8).

As per these key differences of opinion over defining ADHD, its diagnosis has remained controversial and at times even appeared ludicrous to the non-initiate. Successive *DSM*s have radically differed in their definitions of ADHD. *DSM-II* offers hyperactivity, impulsiveness, and inattention as three cores; *DSM-III* divides the three into their own groups, with minimal disorders required within each one; and *DSM-IV* clusters them into one multifaceted problem whilst criticizing previous rules of inclusion and exclusion. This version requires a minimum of six forms of inattention/hyperactivity in order for children to qualify (McBurnett, Pfiffner, & Ottolini, 2000, pp. 229–231).

The casual reader of the *DSM* list may be inclined to diagnose him or herself, identifying with such "symptoms" as being easily distractible, clumsy, impatient, explosive, always on the go, fidgety, talking loudly, moving a lot during sleep, immature, and a loner (Accardo & Blondis, 2000b, pp. 4–5). Some of this becomes rather sinister when forms of diagnosis extend to identifying a "double posterior hair whorl," "anterior cow lick," or "electric hair" with a proclivity towards ADHD (Accardo & Blondis, 2000a, p. 153).

There is a long history of attributing deviance to physiology. Take, for example, the sex-variant study carried out in New York City between 1935 and 1941, in which Robert Dickinson traced the genitals of New York women on a plate of glass placed over their vulvas to differentiate lesbians from non-lesbians, or the studies of the criminal anthropologist, Cesare Lombroso, undertaken in Italy in the late nineteenth century, in which prostitutes were examined for signs of physical "degeneracy" (Terry, 199[5]; Horn, 1995). Today, such signs are also visible from within the body. In 1990, a National Institute of Mental Health (NIMH) study included colorful pictures of PET scans, suggesting that a number of adults with a history of ADHD in childhood had decreased brain metabolism. These images were produced and circulated widely in the media. The study was used to assert a biological basis for ADHD (Breggin, 1998): "It is not that your mother got divorced, or that your father didn't wipe you the right way . . . It really is DNA roulette" (Harold Koplewicz quoted in Waters, 2000).

Still, this "roulette" requires interpretation. There is a strong preference in the medical literature on ADHD for knowing and attending to what is described, almost in base-superstructure terms, as "underlying physiology." Yet even these true believers lament the weak correlation of "brain damage with attentional dysfunction" (Lock & Bender, 2000, pp. 30–31), and many admit that "definitions of learning disabilities are astoundingly plastic" and depend on "one's choice of boundaries" (Hinshaw, 2000, p. xv). This dilemma is positively spun as "the heterogeneity of ADHD," a function of its collecting together "a cluster of several behavioral deficits, each with a specific physiologic substrate" (Sieg, 2000, p. 111).

The "true" prevalence of ADHD across gender, geographic, and class lines is a topic that has generated many conflicting opinions, yet certain groups of people are more likely to be diagnosed than others. Boys are four times more likely than girls to receive a diagnosis of ADHD and be prescribed stimulant medication (Woodworth, 2000). Based on census data and other studies, it has been proposed that of children aged between 5 and 17, 5.8 percent of boys and 1.5 percent of girls had ADHD in 1994. However, the ratio was 3.5:1 two years later, while in 1995, 25 percent of Ritalin use was by adults. Clinical numbers suggest males outnumber females 9:1, while the epidemiological ratio is 4:1. In the UK, the figures are 3:1. The gender differences have been explained away as an outcome of the less-violent ways of girls, which lead to fewer referrals than the attention-getting conduct of bratty boys. Recent scholarship regards the association of males with ADHD as largely mythic, proposing that the clinical imbalance derives from under-diagnosis amongst girls and a similar failure to identify ADHD in older women (Quinn & Nadeau, 2000, pp. 216–217). Geographically, ADHD is mostly found in the South and West of the United States amongst upper-middle-class whites living in the suburbs. Outside the United States as well as within, Ritalin is more prevalent in poor urban rather than rural areas (Diller, 1998, pp. 35–36; Hepstintall & Taylor, 1996, p. 330; Luk, 1996, p. 358; Cantwell, 1999, p. 4). African-American families deploy the drug at half to a quarter the rate of their white socioeconomic equals, while use is virtually zero amongst Asian Americans (Diller, 2000). There is conflicting evidence on the impact of class and family background on ADHD diagnoses. Some studies propose a link between disadvantaged families, and others do not. There is a much stronger correlation with attention deficit diagnoses (Sandberg & Garralda, 1996, pp. 283–284).

Responding to the threat to its legitimacy posed by this sociological variety, the American Academy of Pediatrics issued its first detailed guidelines for ADHD diagnosis in 2000. The group is also writing treatment guidelines for children aged 6–12 to emphasize that symptoms may not be apparent in a doctor's office, so doctors should ask parents, caregivers, and teachers about conduct at home and school. The symptoms must be present for six months in at least two of the child's social settings (i.e., home and school) and other conditions should be ruled out (or diagnosed as co-existing conditions) (Hall, 2000). And so, although controversial, diagnosis continues, and once the diagnosis is at-tained, it generally leads to one outcome—the prescription of Ritalin.

Ritalin

Ritalin is related to amphetamines, a class of chemicals that replicates the function of neurotransmitters in arousing the nervous system. Amphetamines were first synthesized in the 1880s, and since the 1920s, their capacities to stimulate activity have been widely appreciated. By 1970, fifteen different pharmaceutical corporations manufactured over thirty kinds, amounting to 12 billion pills annually. Ritalin, with the chemical name methylphenidate, is within this group (Jenkins, 1999, pp. 30–31; Steinberg, 1999, p. 225). Methylphenidate was first synthesized in 1944 as part of a search for a non-addictive stimulant, and used in the United States ten years later, when it was endorsed by the FDA to treat narcolepsy, depression, and lethargy. Researchers recommended the drug for controlling children's behavior in 1963 (Breggin, 1998, p. 180). It was reborn as Ritalin by the pharmaceutical company Ciba-Geigy in the early 1960s as a memory aid for seniors, before being redisposed yet again for use on children (Diller, 1998, pp. 21–22, 25).

Ritalin has been enormously popular since its introduction. By the mid-1960s, it was the drug of choice for treating performance and behavioral issues in United States children, perhaps an early sign that psychoanalysis was on the wane (Sandberg & Barton, 1996, pp. 11–12). In 1970, 150,000 children were on the drug, increasing to 900,000 in 1990. Across the 1990s, the number of United States children and adults diagnosed with ADD/ADHD rose, to 2 million in 1993 and 3.5 million by 1997, with most patients taking Ritalin and some using Dexedrine. During that period, the amount of Ritalin produced increased by 700 percent, an astonishing figure for a controlled substance. Eleven million prescriptions are written in the United States each year and sales went from United States $109 million in 1992 to United States $336 million in four years (Marshall, 2000; Russell, 1997).

Early studies suggested Ritalin increased adherence to norms of polite, restrained conduct, but subsequent research proposes strong correlations with improved academic performance (Trapani, 2000, p. 201; Powers, 2000, p. 486). The drug has latterly been positively linked to more manageable conduct in class, better scholastic results, diminished violence, greater intersubjective pleasure and calm, and higher rates of participation in organized sport (Cantwell, 1999, p. 16). Here lies the point of suspicion for critics on the left. We might translate these correlations a few degrees such that they are viewed as social conformity, preparedness for a conservative role in the work force, suppression of disgruntlement that is a rational response to oppressive institutions and norms, or diversion of energy into reactionary pastimes. A healthier, fitter, more polite population reduces the cost of public health, guarantees a functioning and pliable workforce, and even helps tourism. This long-standing criminological obsession deems familially-based and institutional activities to be worthy, integrative norms, whilst informal leisure is demonized as a danger that should be pacified and redirected into an appropriate sphere—literally, national fitness.

Pediatricians and family practitioners write most prescriptions for Ritalin in the United States—this removes it from the clutches of the traditional gatekeepers of psychiatric drugs, the psychiatrists (Schachar, Tannock, & Cunningham, 1996, pp. 435–436). Of adolescents treated for depression in Oregon in 1998, 60 percent were prescribed drugs not by psychiatrists, but [by] pediatricians. In North Carolina in 1999, the figure was 72 percent (Waters, 2000; Hyman, 2000; Woodworth, 2000). Health Maintenance Organizations (HMOs) have added to this trend of undermining power-brok[er]ing professionals through the discourse of bureaucratic-managerial commodification: "deprofessionalization is one of the outcomes of the new managerialism" (Scheid, 2000). There has been a rapid decline of insurance-company support for family therapy since the advent of wholesale managed care versus fee-for-service, in the mid-1990s. HMOs will only fund four to six visits before the use of drugs (Waters, 2000).

But apart from questions of prevalence and in whose hands prescription lies, some important issues surround the ethics and physiological impact of the drug. True believers argue that Ritalin is safe and effective, that the moral panics surrounding it are driven by illegitimate anxieties about the number and rate of diagnoses. It has a very high rating on the therapeutic safety index, a figure derived from dividing a toxic by a therapeutic dose (Powers, 2000, pp. 477, 483). However, Ritalin can produce anorexia, which is said to end once use is discontinued, while "intermittent drug holidays" are also recommended to ensure normal growth. There is also dispute over its role in the etiology of tics and Tourette's Syndrome (Powers, 2000, pp. 489–490). Long-term use (beyond 14 months) has not been studied, as the pharmaceutical industry is mostly interested in measuring short-term effects of medication, and is ill-disposed to perform long-term studies of the type desired by parents (Hyman, 2000).

Additionally, the "abuse" of Ritalin, characterized as its recreational use, has proved troubling. The Drug Enforcement Administration (DEA) designates it as a Schedule II substance, a categorization that stigmatizes drugs as liable to lead to abuse.[1] In 1995, the supposedly independent patient-rights' group Children & Adults with Attention Deficit Disorders (CHADD) and the American Academy of Neurology submitted an unsuccessful petition to the DEA to lower regulatory controls. The Administration declined, for safety reasons (Diller, 1998, p. 348 n. 86). There have been many reports of Ritalin abuse, starting [in the] 1960s in Sweden. A statement issued by the DEA in 1996 noted that Ritalin abuse had increased significantly since 1990; in 1994, a national high-school survey found that 1 percent of all seniors had taken Ritalin the year before without a prescription. In 1999, the survey found that 3 percent had. In 1990, there were about 271 emergency room reports of Ritalin and 1727 in 1998. From January 1990 to May 1995, methylphenidate ranked in the top ten most frequently reported controlled drugs stolen from Registrants; about 700,000 dosage units of stolen methylphenidate were reported to the DEA's drug-theft database between January 1996 and December 1997. School nurses, "teachers of the year," and principals have been among those found stealing Ritalin from school coffers. In May 2000, the House Education and Workforce Committee held hearings on the recreational use of Ritalin, in which testimony was given stating that one in five college students use Ritalin illegally (Sax, 2000). Responding to concerns about the illicit use of Ritalin by both students and adults in public schools, the United States government launched a study of "Ritalin abuse" in November 2000 (Woodworth, 2000; Thomas, 2000).

Conflict of interest concerns have also caused controversy; in the 1990s, the manufacturer gave CHADD 9 percent of its annual revenue (Russell, 1997).

Media Concern

All of this has, of course, attracted major media attention—Ritalin receives both good and bad press. Recognizing the media's power, Ciba-Geigy (now called Novartis following a merger with Sandoz), the manufacturer of Ritalin, spread the gospel of brain disorders as the key to depression and other abnormalities by financing public television's series *The Brain* (Breggin, 1994, p. 122). But from the 1970s, several horror stories about Ritalin appeared in the *bourgeois* United States press. Congressional hearings were prompted by a story in the *Washington Post* entitled "Omaha Pupils Given 'Behavior' Drugs," which raised the specter of mind control and merged with popular concerns about diet to suggest a more "natural" form of treatment (Diller, 1998, pp. 30–31; Sandberg & Barton, 1996, pp. 3, 18–19). These concerns coalesced with the anti-psychiatry movement of the time, represented by the tragic heroics of Jack Nicholson's character in the film version of Ken Kesey's novel, *One Flew Over the Cuckoo's Nest*. The decade also produced the first pop-psy-complex denunciations of Ritalin, with the publication of *The Myth of the Hyperactive Child, and Other Means of Child Control*, by Peter Schrag and Diane Divoky, and Gerald Coles' *The Learning Mystique* (1987), while Scientology founder and science-fiction writer L. Ron Hubbard also denounced Ritalin (Diller,

1998, p. 31). In the late 1980s there was another round of media attention, with articles appearing in the *New York Times*, the *Wall Street Journal*, the *Washington Post*, and the *Los Angeles Times*, and a segment on Ted Koppel's *Nightline* (Breggin, 1998, pp. 180, 183). Popular literature also appeared favoring the phenomenon around this time, notably Barbara Ingersoll's *Your Hyperactive Child* (1988) and Edward M. Hallowell and John J. Ratey's *Driven to Distraction: Recognizing and Coping with Attention Deficit Disorder from Childhood to Adulthood* (1994) (Eberstadt, 1999). This genre of popular critique drew new strength in the 1990s, in the wake of Prozac's popularization and associated debates about it and other mind-altering antidepressants, via Peter Breggin's *Toxic Psychiatry* (first published in 1991) and *Ritalin Nation* (1998) plus Lawrence Diller's *Running on Ritalin* (1998), Thomas Armstrong's *The Myth of the ADD Child* (1995), and Richard DeGrandpre's *Ritalin Nation* (1999). The debate has trickled into popular literature as well, via Robin Cook's 1994 novel *Acceptable Risk* (Stookey, 1996, pp. 163, 172–173, 175, 180 n. 1).

In the first Bush's decade of the brain, ADHD came to be referred to as the "diagnosis of the decade." Media attention has been "unprecedented" since in terms of "national magazine covers, sciene [*sic*] features in daily newspapers, broadcast television highlights, talk radio topics, and local-news spots" (Hinshaw, 2000, p. xiii). In 1997, *Good Housekeeping* magazine queried "the rush to Ritalin," dubbing it "kiddie cocaine" and suggesting that "at the slightest sign of trouble—a child keeps running back and forth to the water fountain, has an unruly week pushing other kids on the playground, plays drums on his desk with pencils—parents are circled by the school's teachers, psychologists, and even principals, all pushing Ritalin" (Russell, 1997).

Breggin, one of the most visible contemporary critics of pharmacological psychiatry, stigmatizes Ritalin as 'an iatrogenic drug epidemic." He charges it with generating a mindless obedience that suppresses emotions and ideas, diminishes self-esteem, and takes away from a sense of self while questioning the very existence of ADHD

(1994, pp. 303–305, 309). Other medical professionals/populist authors who dissent from the mainstream pose questions about the drug's long-term safety, its role in facilitating or obstructing long-term cures for ADHD, and its capacity to treat-without-understanding, changing behavior by masking a hidden problem, whether biological, familial, or institutional (Diller, 1998, p. 13). DeGrandpre (1999) does not question the existence of the disorder. He takes reports of its increasing incidence literally, but claims that ADHD is prompted by a speedy society rather than abnormal biology. Rapid-fire culture is culpable for producing sensory addicts, addicted to newness and change. DeGrandpre uses the amount of money poured into fleeting pop-culture moments—such as *The Titanic*—to advance this hypothesis. His prescription for the problems is not medication—providing stimulants to sensory addicts just compounds the problem, he says—but to slow society down, to return to a "natural speed and rhythm," to "challenge the dominant paradigm of work work work," and to "overcome cynicism through hope and action" (DeGrandpre, 1999).

A very recent flurry of media attention devoted to children and Ritalin was set off by a study published in the *Journal of the American Medical Association (JAMA)* by Julie Zito and her colleagues. They state that in the last decade, the prescription of stimulants in the treatment of ADHD in United States children aged 5–14 has dramatically increased, and use by those aged 2–4 grew threefold between 1991 and 1995 (Zito, Safer, dos Reis, Gardner, Boles, & Lynch, 2000). The NIMH reacted strongly to these findings, rejecting prescriptions to large numbers of preschoolers, and funding a large research project to evaluate that group (Scandal!, 2000). This round of moral panic continues previous decades' skepticism of psychiatry. It highlights the increasing frequency of prescription of Ritalin, its abuse by "normal" children, and the potential nature of ADHD as a sociocultural phenomenon, which should not be treated with drugs. Major media attention was also paid to the bizarre summer 2000 instances of state intervention against parents who took their children off Ritalin. In one New York case, the local school district informed the Child Protective Services Unit, which accused the parents of child abuse, a charge upheld in court (Leibowitz, 2000). More and more public schools threaten parents with removal of their children from conventional classes absent medication (Diller, 2000).

Conclusion

Some suggest that the psychologization and therapization of teaching have produced the Ritalin trend. They have turned educators towards diagnostics, such that schools are viewed as mental-health institutions. The right derides egalitarianism in progressive educational philosophy for making teachers responsible for students' performance against a presumed *tabula rasa* of equal innate ability. Such conservatives contend that this philosophy, along with a pharamacological replacement of old-style physical sanctions as means of disciplining children, have encouraged educators to put their charges on Ritalin (Livingstone, 1997). Alternatively, it has been suggested that with the introduction of "high stakes" testing into many states—in which funds are allocated to school districts based upon improvements in students' test scores—counselors, teachers, and principals may be more inclined to recommend Ritalin to parents, in a desperate attempt to improve performance; indeed, local property values, jobs, and salaries can depend upon these scores (Sax, 2000).

In the light of these concerns, attempts have been made to study, understand, and reverse the Ritalin trend. In 1999, the Colorado Board of Education resolved to discourage teachers from recommending Ritalin. The following spring, the Federal Government funded a five-year United States $6 million study of the drug's effects (Leibowitz, 2000). Novartis, CHADD, and the American Psychiatric Association now face class-action lawsuits in New Jersey, California, and Texas that they conspired to drive up demand for Ritalin and did not publicize warnings about the nervous and cardiovascular systems. Breggin is a star witness (Diller, 2000; Layton & Washburn, 2000).

Although the United States produces and consumes about 85 percent of all

Ritalin, panics surrounding its increased use are not restricted to American children (Woodworth, 2000). While containing many of the same concerns exhibited in the United States, these panics are also about modernity and power in a global economy. The *Independent* of London warns of increased Ritalin consumption in England, noting that as the latter is customarily 10–30 years behind the United States, it could look forward to an ADHD epidemic, treated with Ritalin; a warning is already in place, as prescriptions in Britain tripled across the 1990s (Lacey, 1996). Just as in the United States, these concerns are not always met with uniform policy responses. In the fall of 2000, Ritalin was banned for preschoolers in the United Kingdom, just weeks before the National Institute for Clinical Excellence advocated *more* prescriptions for children, setting off a flurry of debate (Hinsliff, 2000; Orr, 2000). Within this framework, the under-prescription of Ritalin—whether characterized as the absence of sick children or the absence of pill-happy doctors and parents—can sometimes be as problematic as its over-prescription, signifying non-modernity. For example, one Israeli woman's dissertation, while granting that Ritalin may be over-prescribed in the United States, states that Israel is "behind the United States in knowledge and awareness," that many ADHD children in Israel go undiagnosed (Mason, 1999).

The increasing number of children diagnosed with ADHD is deemed objectionable because the public is worried about real harm done to children in a hyper-speedy age of hyper-competitive parents and because the diagnosis pathologizes children who were previously viewed as normal or mischievous. Critiques of Ritalin evoke nostalgia for a less technological era, one in which "boys would be boys" and that was all there was to say about the topic. Today's fuzzy boundaries that differentiate the normal feisty child from the ill are viewed as problematic. This helps account for the fervent searches conducted for signs of ADHD displayed physically on the body, in the hope that this will clearly distinguish those who need treatment from those who do not. Hair patterns, odd toes, and brain scans are evaluated and categorized with the expectation that they will lead to a concrete and unitary diagnosis, waiting to be read by experts and accepted by parents, teachers, and the public.

"The most important epidemiological question in psychiatry is the following: When is a person malingering? It is the difficulty of answering this question that shakes the very foundation of psychiatry" (Reznek, 1998, p. 214). The absence of objectifiable signs via an underlying cause is matched by a set of symptoms that are always liable to redefinition. Drugs answer the question by sidestepping it—they can make people comport themselves differently, and in the process, lift psychiatry out of its ascientific mire (Reznek, 1998, pp. 214, 220). The pill is a commodity form *par excellence*—truly "consumed," genuinely material and measurable, utterly standard, and infinitely repeatable. It also adheres to bureaucratic norms of reliability and efficiency and infinite substitutability. This amounts to the actuarialization and financialization of the sick mind. For therapists, this threat has encouraged collective action to preserve analysis (Lerner, 2000). For pharmaceutical corporations, it has encouraged competition. Shire, the extraordinary new company that is simply a developer and marketer rather than a researcher and manufacturer of drugs, expanded at unprecedented pace in 2000 on the back of Adderall, a dynamic new alternative to Ritalin that offers three kinds of amphetamine instead of just one and lasts longer. It attained 36 percent of the United States market virtually overnight and led to the acquittal of a man who killed his daughter because it was determined the drug made him psychotic. It is banned in Europe (Clark, 2000a and 2000b; Phalen, 2000). That again forwards the question of United States avant-gardisme.

Americans are world-renowned (and much laughed-at) for (i) putting certain things *in* their mouths (cigarettes, sugar drinks, and fast food); (ii) making words come *out* of their mouths to condemn these very activities; and (iii) exporting this combination of customs to other peoples. Now, Americans' capacities to seek more and more artificial substances to put in their mouths include the promise to make themselves into completely different people. The promise and the risk are, quite literally, to take this American oral fetish and transform it into the ultimate American dream: self-invention. The sense of ethical incompleteness inscribed in Americanness, courtesy of being the underclass of Europe, then inventing personal self-criticism as an invitation to consumerism and a means of surviving and thriving in a risk society, is today producing what Erik Davis diagnoses as "the posthuman self." No wonder the UN finds Europeans prefer downers and United States citizens opt for uppers (Capella & Boseley, 1999)!

The nineteenth century's dangerous individual has become younger, whiter, and middle class in the United States, where people are increasingly "on drugs—SSRIs, hormones, brain boosters, neurotransmitters." Instead of old-style recreational objects that Americans liked to put in their mouths (alcohol, tobacco, coffee, and illegal substances) which had instantaneous joy and release as promises, tied in some cases to the threat of death, disability, or pain, the new, legal, but controlled substances offer a permanent overhaul (Davis, 2000). No huddling outside the office building, no stains on the paperwork or keyboard, no obvious need to be like others. No quick pleasure, no hangover, no snoring or morning cough driving those around you to distraction, no staggering to the bathroom to be ill, no breathlessness walking up two flights of stairs, no emanations from the mouth, hair, or clothes to mark one out. Instead, the personal side to risk is made manageable via a quiet daily insurance that backs up the gains made the day before within one's not-so-hard drive of a body. In this sense, the new drugs are designed for upwardly mobile people who have decided to abandon former existences. For they make us anew, via a form of secular, even scientific transcendence that markets in pill form the grand promise of the United States: that what you were born as will not define you ever more. And once the decision has been made to take these reformatting technologies, they "melt invisibly into the texture of the everyday" (Davis, 2000). Rather than forming relationships with others through the shared experience of inges-

tion, the new drugs forge a new relationship with the self that is nearly invisible to others and oneself after a time. As such, they fulfill the peripatetic individual's *ur*-dream—to learn the code, to crack the means of making oneself anew, to be other than what one came with—and to do so in a seamless way that does not draw attention to itself. No wonder that thirty-eight million people in the United States have tried Prozac and 10.3 million new prescriptions were written for it in 1999 (Erica Goode, 2000).

In the process, the grand project of bringing the mentally ill out into the bright lights of narcissistic day has been accomplished, their new way of seeing the world modeled upon and in turn modeling the behavior of a new citizen, one whose change is invisible, thanks to pharmacology. Perhaps the moral panics about Ritalin will die off once it is recognized as one more cosmopolitan investment in human capital, in a risk society that wagers its future on the very people about whom it most panics. As pharmaceutical companies market their wares more and more effectively to parents, doctors, and teachers, and forces mount in opposition to this new era of swallowing, both sides must make peace with the tension between promises of new applications and fears of doping the future.

Note

1. The DEA designation guarantees good data on levels of prescription, as the state sets an annual quota on the production of Schedule II substances in response to pharmaceutical industry requests and the amount of sales by pharmacies (Diller, 1998, p. 27).

References

Accardo, P. J., & T. A. Blondis. (2000a). The neurodevelopmental assessment of the child with ADHD. In P. J. Accardo, T. A. Blondis, B. Y. Whitman, & M. A. Stein (Eds.), *Attention deficits and hyperactivity in children and adults: Diagnosis, treatment, management*, 2nd ed. (pp. 141–161). New York: Marcel Dekker.

——. (2000b). The Strauss syndrome, minimal brain dysfunction, and the hyperactive child: A historical introduction to attention deficit hyperactivity disorder. In P. J. Accardo, T. A. Blondis, B. Y. Whitman, & M. A. Stein (Eds.), *Attention deficits and hyperactivity in children and adults: Diagnosis, treatment, management*, 2nd ed. (pp. 1–11). New York: Marcel Dekker.

Albee, G. W. (1977). The protestant ethic, sex, and psychotherapy. *American Psychologist*, 32 (2), 150–161.

Barker, M. (1999). [Review of the book *Moral Panics*]. *Sociology*, 33 (2), 224–227.

Beck, U., Giddens, A., & Lash, S. (1994). *Reflexive modernization: Politics, tradition and aesthetics in the modern social order*. Stanford, CA: Stanford University Press.

Berman, S. M., Strauss, S., & Verhage, N. (2000). Treating mental illness in students: A new strategy. *Chronicle of Higher Education*, B9.

Bloom, S. G. (2000, May 23). Sex-free bliss? *Salon*. Retrieved from *http://cobrand.salon.com/health/sex/urge/2000/05/17/sexdrugs/*.

Breggin, P. R. (1994). *Toxic psychiatry: Why therapy, empathy, and love must replace the drugs, electroshock, and biochemical theories of the "new psychiatry."* New York: St Martin's Press.

———. (1998). *Talking back to Ritalin: What doctors aren't telling you about stimulants for children*. Monroe, ME: Common Courage Press.

Cantwell, D. P. (1999). Attention deficit disorder: A review of the past ten years. In J. A. Incorvaia, B. S. Mark-Goldstein, & D. Tessmer (Eds.), *Understanding, diagnosing, and treating AD/HD in children and adolescents: An integrative approach Reiss-Davis Child Study Center*, Vol. 3 (pp. 3–23). Northvale, NJ: Jason Aronson.

Capella, P., & Boseley, S. (1999, February 24). UN agency on the offensive against the abuse of "lifestyle" drugs. *Guardian*, 14.

Clark, A. (2000a, November 18). The man who sold America calmer kids. *Guardian*, 32.

———. (2000b, December 12). Shire in 5.9bn merger. *Guardian*, 27.

Cohen, P. (1999). *Rethinking the youth question: Education, labor, and cultural studies*. Durham, NC: Duke University Press.

Cohen, S. (1973). *Folk devils & moral panics: The creation of the mods and rockers*. St Albans: Paladin.

Cooksey, E., & Brown, P. (1998). Spinning on its axes: DSM and the social construction of psychiatric diagnosis. *International Journal of Health Services*, 28 (3), 525–554.

Daniels, A. M. (1998). [Review of the book *Moral Panics*]. *British Medical Journal*, 7, 1327.

Davis, E. (2000, September 1). Take the red pill. *AlterNet*. Retrieved from *http://www.alternet.org/story.html?StoryID=9722*.

DeGrandpre, R. (1999). *Ritalin nation: Rapid-fire culture and the transformation of human consciousness*. New York: W. W. Norton.

Diller, L. H. (1998). *Running on ritalin: A physician reflects on children, society, and performance in a pill*. New York: Bantam.

———. (2000, September 25). Just say yes to Ritalin. *Salon*. Retrieved from *http://www.alternet.org/story/html?StoryID=9838*.

Donzelot, J. (1979). *The policing of families*. New York: Pantheon.

Eberstadt, M. (1999). Why Ritalin rules. *Policy Review*, 4. Retrieved from *http://www.policyreview.org/apr99/eberstadt.html*.

Fogel, A. (1993). The prose of populations and the magic of demography. *Western Humanities Review*, 47 (4), 312–337.

Foucault, M. (1979). *Discipline and punish: The birth of the prison* (A. Sheridan, Trans). New York: Vintage Books.

———. (1982). The subject and power (L. Sawyer, Trans.). *Critical Inquiry*, 8 (4), 777–795.

———. (1984). *The history of sexuality: An introduction* (R. Hurley, Trans.). Harmondsworth: Penguin.

———. (1987). *Mental illness and psychology* (A. Sheridan, Trans). Berkeley, CA: University of California Press.

———. (1991a). Governmentality (P. Pasquino, Trans). In G. Burchell, C. Gordon, & P. Miller (Eds.). *The Foucault effect: Studies in governmentality* (pp. 87–104). London: Harvester Wheatsheaf.

———. (1991b). *Remarks on Marx: Conversations with Duccio Trombadori* (J. R. Goldstein & J. Cascaito, Trans.). New York: Semiotext(e).

———. (1994). Problematics: Excerpts from conversations. In R. Reynolds & T. Zummer (Eds.), *Crash: Nostalgia for the absence of cyberspace* (pp. 121–127). New York: Thread Waxing Space.

———. (2000). About the concept of the "dangerous individual" in nineteenth-century legal psychiatry. In J. D. Faubion (Ed.), *Power: Essential works of Foucault 1954–1984*, Vol. 3 (pp. 176–200). New York: New Press.

Gilbert, J. (1986). *America's reaction to the juvenile delinquent in the 1950s*. New York: Oxford University Press.

Goode, Erica. (2000, July 18). Once again, Prozac takes center stage, in furor. *New York Times*, pp. F1–F2.

———. (2000). No need to panic? A bumper crop of books on moral panics. *Sociological Forum*, 15 (3), 543–552.

Hale, N. (1995). *The rise and crisis of psychoanalysis in the United States: Freud and the Americans, 1917–1985*. New York: Oxford University Press.

Hall, C. (2000, May 8). Pediatricians' group issues guide for ADD diagnosis. *San Francisco Chronicle*, p. A1.

Hepstintall, E., & Taylor, E. (1996). Sex differences and their significance. In S. Sandberg (Ed.), *Hyperactivity disorders of childhood* (pp. 329–349). Cambridge: Cambridge University Press.

Herman, E. (1996). *The romance of American psychology: Political culture in the age of experts*. Berkeley, CA: University of California Press.

Hinshaw, S. P. (2000). Introduction. In P. J. Accardo, T. A. Blondis, B. Y. Whitman, & M. A. Stein (Eds.), *Attention deficits and hyperactivity in children and adults: Diagnosis, treatment, management*, 2nd ed. (pp. xiii–xvii). New York: Marcel Dekker.

Hinsliff, G. (2000, September 3). Sedative drug ban for under-5s. *The Observer*, 1.

Horn, D. (1995). This norm which is not one: Reading the female body in Lombroso's anthropology. In J. Terry & J. Urla (Eds.), *Deviant bodies* (pp. 109–128). Bloomington, IN: Indiana University Press.

Hyman, S. (2000, May 16). Statement for the record on methylphenidate (Ritalin) for children with ADHD. Retrieved from *http://waisgate.hhs.gov/cgibin/waisgate?WAISdocID+7418017227+3+0+0&WAISaction=retreive*.

Jenkins, P. (1999). *Synthetic panics: The symbolic politics of designer drugs*. New York: New York University Press.

Jones, K. (1999). *Taming the troublesome child: American families, child guidance, and the limits of psychiatric authority*. Cambridge, MA: Harvard University Press.

Lacey, H. (1996, October 27). Drug him when he teases. *Independent*, 12.

Layton, M. J., & Washburn, L. (2000, October 1). "Hyperactive" kids: Victims of a plot?—Lawsuit alleges scheme to sell Ritalin. *Record*, 1.

Leibowitz, D. (2000, August 8). Parents prosecuted for taking son off Ritalin. *Arizona Republic*, 1.

Lerner, S. (2000, April 11). The shrink brigade. *Village Voice*, 32.

Livingstone, K. (1997). Ritalin: Miracle drug or cop-out? *Public Interest*, 127.

Lock, T. M., & Bender, D. B. (2000). In P. J. Accardo, T. A. Blondis, B. Y. Whitman, & M. A. Stein (Eds.), *Attention deficits and hyperactivity in children and adults: Diagnosis, treatment, management*, 2nd ed. (29–56). New York: Marcel Dekker.

Luk, S. L. (1996). Cross-cultural aspects. In S. Sandberg (Ed.), *Hyperactivity disorders of childhood* (pp. 350–381). Cambridge: Cambridge University Press.

Lunbeck, E. (1994). *The psychiatric persuasion: Knowledge, gender, and power in modern America*. Princeton, NJ: Princeton University Press.

Marinoff, L. (2000, July 16). Más platón y menos Prozac. *El Pais*, 14–15.

Marshall, E. (2000, August 4). Epidemiology: Duke study faults overuse of stimulants for children. *Science*, 721.

Maslin, J. (2000, June 29). Exploring a dark side of depression remedies. *New York Times*, p. E11.

Mason, R. (1999, May 19). The gift of clarification. *Jerusalem Post*, 11.

McBurnett, K., Pfiffner, L. J., & Ottolini, Y. L. (2000). Types of ADHD in DSM-IV. In P. J. Accardo, T. A. Blondis, B. Y. Whitman, & M. A. Stein (Eds.), *Attention deficits and hy-*

peractivity in children and adults: Diagnosis, treatment, management, 2nd ed. (pp. 229–240). New York: Marcel Dekker.

Messinger, E. C. (1978). Violence to the brain. *Semiotexte*, (2), 66–71.

Musto, D. (1995, March 31). No cure but care. *Times Literary Supplement*, 4800, 6.

Orr, D. (2000, November 1). Do we need to drug our children? *Independent*, 5.

Phalen, K. F. (2000, September 12). Treatment of Choice. *Washington Post*, p. Z34.

Powers, C. A. (2000). The pharmacology of drugs used for the treatment of Attention Deficit Hyperactivity Disorder. In P. J. Accardo, T. A. Blondis, B. Y. Whitman, & M. A. Stein (Eds.), *Attention deficits and hyperactivity in children and adults: Diagnosis, treatment, management*, 2nd ed. (pp. 477–511). New York: Marcel Dekker.

Putnam, R. D. (2000). *Bowling alone: The collapse and revival of American community*. New York: Simon & Schuster.

Quinn, P. O., & Nadeau, K. G. (2000). Gender issues and Attention Deficit Disorder. In P. J. Accardo, T. A. Blondis, B. Y. Whitman, & M. A. Stein (Eds.), *Attention deficits and hyperactivity in children and adults: Diagnosis, treatment, management*, 2nd ed. (pp. 215–227). New York: Marcel Dekker.

Reeves, J. L., & Campbell, R. (1994). *Cracked coverage: Television news, the anti-cocaine crusade, and the Reagan legacy*. Durham, NC: Duke University Press.

Reznek, L. (1998). On the epistemology of mental illness. *History and Philosophy of the Life Sciences*, 20 (2), 215–232.

Rubinstein, R. A., Scrimshaw, S. C., & Morrissey, S.E. (2000). Classification and process in sociomedical understanding: Towards a multilevel view of sociomedical methodology. In G. L. Albrecht, R. Fitzpatrick, & S.C. Scrimshaw (Eds.), *The handbook of social studies in health & medicine* (pp. 36–49). London: Sage.

Rundle, G. (1999). Ten years of vitamin P. *Arena Journal*, 13, 25–30.

Russell, J. (1997, December 1). The pill that teachers push. *Good Housekeeping*, 110–117.

Sandberg, S., & Garralda, M. E. (1996). Psychosocial contributions. In S. Sandberg (Ed.), *Hyperactivity disorders of childhood* (pp. 280–328). Cambridge: Cambridge University Press.

Sandberg, S., & Barton, J. (1996). Historical development. In S. Sandberg (Ed.), *Hyperactivity disorders of childhood* (pp. 1–25). Cambridge: Cambridge University Press.

Santostefano, S. (1999). A psychodynamic approach to treating Attention Deficit/Hyperactivity Disorder: Recent developments in theory and technique. In J. A. Incorvaia, B. S. Mark-Goldstein, & D. Tessmer (Eds.), *Understanding, diagnosing, and treating AD/HD in children and adolescents: An integrative approach Reiss-Davis Child Study Center*, Vol. 3. (pp. 319–367). Northvale, NJ: Jason Aronson.

Sax, L. (2000). Ritalin: Better living through chemistry? *The World and I*, 15. Retrived from http://www.worldandi.com/public/2000/November/sax.html.

Scandal! They haven't tested Ritalin on the children it's not prescribed for! Scandal! They're going to test Ritalin on the children it's prescribed for. (2001, January 2). *Washington Post*, p. T6.

Schachar, R., Tannock, R., & Cunningham, C. (1996). Treatment. In S. Sandberg (Ed.), *Hyperactivity disorders of childhood* (pp. 433–476). Cambridge: Cambridge University Press.

Scheid, T. L. (2000, August). Commodification and contradiction: The rationalization of mental health care. Paper presented to the American Sociological Association, Washington, D.C.

Schizophrenia may be expanded. (2000, July 26). *Wall Street Journal*, pp. B1, B4.

Shattuc, J. M. (1997). *The talking cure: TV talk shows and women*. New York: Routledge.

Sieg, K. G. (2000). Neuroimaging and attention deficit hyperactivity disorder. In P. J. Accardo, T. A. Blondis, B. Y. Whitman, & M. A. Stein (Eds.), *Attention deficits and hyperactivity in children and adults: Diagnosis, treatment, management*, 2nd ed. (pp. 73–118). New York: Marcel Dekker.

Steinberg, L. (1999). ADD or AD/HD medication treatment. In J. A. Incorvaia, B. S. Mark-Glodstein, & D. Tessmer (Eds.), *Understanding, diagnosing, and treating AD/HD in children and adolescents: An integrative approach Reiss-Davis Child Study Center*, Vol. 3 (pp. 223–234). Northvale, NJ: Jason Aronson.

Steinberg, S. R., & Kincheloe, J. L. (1997). Introduction: No more secrets—Kinderculture, information saturation, and the postmodern childhood. In S. R. Steinberg & J. L. Kincheloe (Eds.), *Kinderculture: The corporate construction of childhood* (pp. 1–30). Boulder, CO: Westview Press.

Stookey, L. L. (1996). *Robin Cook: A critical companion*. Westport, CT: Greenwood Press.

Terry, J. (1995). Anxious slippages between us and them. In J. Terry & J. Urla (Eds.), *Deviant bodies* (pp. 129–169). Bloomington, IN: Indiana University Press.

Thomas, K. (2000, November 27). Stealing, dealing, and Ritalin: Adults and students are involved in abuse of drug. *USA Today*, p. 1D.

Thompson, K. (1998). *Moral panics*. London: Routledge.

Trapani, C. (2000). Psychoeducational assessment of children and adolescents with Attention Deficit Hyperactivity Disorder. In P. J. Accardo, T. A. Blondis, B. Y. Whitman, & M. A. Stein (Eds.), *Attention deficits and hyperactivity in children and adults: Diagnosis, treatment, management*, 2nd ed. (pp. 197–214). New York: Marcel Dekker.

Wagner, D. (1997). *The new temperance: The American obsession with sin and vice*. New York: Westview Press.

Waters, R. (2000, May 2). Generation Rx. *Alternet*. Retrieved from http://www.alternet.org/story.html?StoryID=9722.

Woodworth, T. (2000, May 16). DEA congressional testimony before the Committee on Education and the Workforce: Subcommittee on early childhood, youth, and families. United States Drug Enforcement Administration. Retrieved from http://www.usdoj.gov/dea/pubs/cngrtest/ct051600.htm.

Zametkin, A. J., Nordahl, T. E., Gross, M., King, A. C., Semple, W. E., Rumsey, J., et al. (1990). Cerebral glucose metabolism in adults with hyperactivity of childhood onset. *New England Journal of Medicine*, 323, 1361–1366.

Zito, J., Safer, D. J., dos Reis, S., Gardner, J., Boles, M., & Lynch, F. (2000). Trends in the prescribing of psychotropic medications to preschoolers. *Journal of the American Medical Association*, 283 (8), 1025–1030.

For Discussion

1. The authors note that research has yet to examine the effects of Ritalin over long time periods. Why would this research be important?

2. How might society have responded to children who exhibited traits of alleged ADHD several decades ago, when ADHD had not been recognized as a diagnosis?

26

'The Ice Age'

The Social Construction of a Drug Panic

Philip Jenkins

This chapter focuses on methamphetamine ("ice"). Philip Jenkins traces the brief history, the manufacture, and contemporary usage of the drug. The chapter's major focus, however, is on the media (and government) response to methamphetamine. Jenkins discusses the powerful labels (e.g., epidemic) and media symbolism that emerged during the moral panic over methamphetamine. He also provides an important comparison between the media response to methamphetamine and to cocaine. The author notes that the panic over methamphetamine was not substantiated by drug use indicators, and he provides possible explanations for the moral panic.

In 1989 and 1990 there was much media and political concern about use of the drug "ice," or smokable crystal methamphetamine, which was believed to pose a social threat potentially as great as that of crack cocaine. This concern was not sustained, however, and references to the topic diminished sharply within a few months. The incident thus offers a valuable opportunity to trace the history of a drug panic from its origins to its eclipse. Particular emphasis is placed on the role of domestic political divisions, especially in Hawaii, in citing the panic. It is suggested that this incident illustrates both the manner in which local problems come to be projected on the national political arena and the limitations inherent in such a process. The paper explores the rhetorical devices used to create a sense of impending menace around the supposed danger, and the reasons why such an apparently plausible danger failed to gain more public attention or credence.

Research in illicit drugs has often emphasized the disparity between the perceived threat of a substance and the actual social harm involved. A distinguished literature deals with successive drug "panics," which have focused on marijuana in the 1930s, amphetamines in the 1950s, glue sniffing in the 1960s, and crack cocaine in the last decade (Brecher, 1972; Musto, 1973; Reinarman and Levine, 1989; Goode, 1984:310–34). This is not to argue that any of these substances is harmless or (necessarily) socially acceptable, but in each case, the extravagant claims permit us to employ the term *panic*.

Drug scares generally follow broadly similar patterns in which it is suggested, for example, that the drug in question is currently enjoying an explosive growth in popularity; that it is extremely addictive, and that even occasional use can cause severe physical addiction; and that it is destructive to the user or to others, threatening health or encouraging bizarre and violent behavior. Such claims are buttressed in a number of ways, including the use of exemplary cases and the parading of what appear to be objective statistics and scientific studies; the latter often turn out to be rather questionable on further examination. In addition, claims makers usually demonstrate a certain historical amnesia, often rediscovering problems that in fact are well-established while failing to note how thoroughly earlier panics were discredited.

Social scientists have explained such periodic waves of concern in various ways. Many emphasize the role of political or bureaucratic interest groups seeking to enhance their claims on resources and status. Others stress the role of factors in the broader society, such as ethnic or generational tension and hostility, which come to be symbolized by the drug in question. In this sense it is almost irrelevant whether the claims presented by the rhetoric of a "panic" are well-founded or wholly spurious: The panic itself is valuable in itself for what it suggests about the perceptions of a society as a whole, and specifically of policymakers and legislators. The incident thus has great significance for understanding the social construction of crime and deviance.

Some claims are widely accepted and have the effect of remolding law and public policy: the crack issue has done so in the last decade (Reinarman and Levine, 1989). Other issues, however, are more ephemeral, and the claims appear to enjoy far less success. In recent years we have witnessed a dramatic example of such a short-lived panic in the public reaction to the alleged boom in the use of the drug "ice," or smokable methamphetamine. During 1989 and early 1990, it was widely claimed that this substance was becoming enormously popular in certain regions, and that it had the potential to "sweep the nation" in a few months or years. Dramatic statistics were offered to support these claims; it was suggested that ice was uniquely dangerous in combining extremely addictive qualities with the advantages of cheapness, easy access, and domestic manufacture. The media panic about ice found its focus in Congressional hearings during October 1989 and January 1990. The stage seemed to be set for a repetition of the crack "explosion" of 1986.

This concern about ice was not sustained, however, and media references to the topic diminished sharply within a few months. Outside a few cities and regions, the issue either has ceased to exist or is dormant. The incident thus offers an unusual opportunity to trace the creation of a drug panic from its inception to its eclipse. In understanding the phenomenon, we must emphasize that "ice" originated as a very localized event, confined largely to Hawaii, and that the words *epidemic* and *explosion* arose from partisan and bureaucratic rivalries within that state. The projection of this local concern onto the national stage was made possible by a number of factors, including the existence of specialized agencies and investigative bodies focusing on drug issues, and the intensification of public expectations and fears following the crack scare. I suggest that all these elements still exist and are likely to lead in future to other ephemeral drug panics. The "ice" incident is likely to be repeated in various forms.

The Methamphetamine Industry

Methamphetamine is a stimulant of the central nervous system which, as a street drug, is often known as "speed" or "crank" (Graham, 1976; Grinspoon, 1975; *Methamphetamine Abuse*, 1989; Miller and Kozel, 1991). The illegal manufacture of methamphetamines began in the early 1960s, and networks of clandestine laboratories emerged to produce several synthetic drugs. During the 1970s, such laboratories tended increasingly to shift their production towards methamphetamine and away from other synthetics such as PCP (Jenkins, 1992b). Between 1981 and 1984, methamphetamine producers represented half of all laboratory seizures; by 1988 they exceeded 80 percent (*U.S. Congress: Laboratories*, 1980; *U.S. Congress: Re-emergence*, 1990:25, 90–91).

The attractions of the industry were obvious. The manufacturing process required little expertise; several cheap "hands-on" manuals were available to provide detailed instruction. A laboratory could make as much as five to 10 pounds of methamphetamine in a week, and the pure substance usually was "cut" repeatedly for street sale. The annual production of a laboratory thus might be worth several million dollars (Jenkins, 1992b). In 1989 a Dallas police officer remarked, "We think the profit is much greater when we look at methamphetamine production, as compared to heroin or cocaine. We know that an investment of $3000 to $4000 in chemicals, in glassware, can turn a profit of $25,000 to $30,000." (*U.S. Congress: Re-emergence*, 1990:39).

One appeal of methamphetamine was that the substance was manufactured in the United States and did not need the sophisticated importation and distribution networks required for heroin or cocaine. Laboratories needed no elaborate facilities or natural resources beyond an ample supply of electricity, and distribution demanded little more than convenient access to the interstate highway network (Skeers, 1992; Weingarten, 1989; Witkin, 1989).

During the 1980s, methamphetamine manufacture tended to become strongly regionalized. In the late 1970s and early 1980s, the Philadelphia area was said to be "the speed capital of the world," with networks of hundreds of laboratories in the southern and eastern parts of the state (Jenkins, 1992b; *U.S. Congress: Profile*, 1983). By the mid-1980s, the city of Eugene, Oregon, was believed to enjoy a similar role in manufacturing; other law enforcement sources emphasized the importance of San Diego and the San Francisco Bay area (*Organized Crime in California*, 1989:55; Wiedrich, 1987). In 1987 and 1988 more than 300 methamphetamine laboratories were seized in the San Diego area alone. Centers of methamphetamine use included Denver, Portland (Oregon), Dallas, and Phoenix; some problems also were observed in Los Angeles, San Francisco, and Seattle (*Arrestee Drug Use*, 1990:6; *U.S. Congress: Re-emergence*, 1990:37, 46). Though it is hard to assess the extent of methamphetamine use, there appears to be substantial demand in many parts of the nation (Isikoff, 1989; Miller and Kozel, 1991; Morgan, 1992; *Methamphetamine Abuse in the United States*, 1989).

The Emergence of Ice

Like other drugs, methamphetamine can be taken in various ways: either injected, smoked, or ingested orally. The dominant mode of use tends to reflect the tastes and traditions of local subcultures. In view of the highly regional nature of manufacture and distribution, suppliers do not find it difficult to accommodate these local tastes, and it is natural to find wide disparities in patterns of use. Fashions that emerge in one city or region can become dominant in that area without making much impact elsewhere. In short, there is no such thing as a national market in methamphetamines.

During the 1980s, a vogue for smokable crystal methamphetamine developed in Hawaii and some Western states under the common nickname *ice* (Cho, 1990; Pennell, 1990). A similar, though somewhat less pure, product called glass also made its appearance in California. The manufacturing process has been described as follows:

Two basic methods are used to produce crystal meth. The first and most common method is the reaction of phenyl-2-propanone (P2P or phenylacetone) and methylamine. The second method uses ephedrine as a precursor. The second method uses a simple formula and does not require the use of controlled precursors. It is known as the ephedrine/red phosphorus method and requires the use of a hydrogenator. It takes two to four days to make a batch of ice. . . .

In Honolulu, crystal meth is most commonly smoked with a glass pipe, the bowl of which becomes coated with a milky white, brownish or black residue, depending on the form of crystal meth used. A gram of ice sells for $250 to $400 in Honolulu right now, with a $1/10$ gram paper going for $50 to $75. It is inexpensive to produce, so the profit margin is tremendous (*U.S. Congress: Re-emergence*, 1990:74–75).

The drug itself had long been known and used in this crystal form, but apparently the specific process used to make the extremely pure ice was not yet in use in the United States itself. Instead the substance, like the fashion for its use, had been imported from the Pacific Rim. Amphetamines, specifically methamphetamines, had long been popular in Japan and other East Asian countries. In that region, illicit markets were supplied by sizable narcotic networks with roots in organized crime among both Chinese triads and Japanese *yakuzas* (Delfs, 1991). During the 1970s and 1980s, such networks had collaborated in a variety of activities, including product counterfeiting and trafficking in guns and prostitutes in addition to narcotics; we have much evidence of cooperative endeavors, based (for example) in Taiwan or South Korea (Buruma and McBeth, 1984–85; Posner, 1988). For methamphetamines the *yakuza* had developed manufacturing facilities in South Korea; these supplied much of East Asia, though the triads also were active in Hong Kong (Kaplan and Dubro, 1986:198–200; *U.S. Congress: Re-emergence*, 1990:11, 99). Entrepreneurs and distributors might be nationals of any of a dozen Asian countries.

Though illegal, the amphetamine drug "family" was stigmatized far less severely than opiates, cocaine, or even marijuana. Most estimates place the number of regular amphetamine (*shabu*) users in Japan at more than half a million. In the 1980s, smokable methamphetamine became the drug of choice among upwardly mobile urban dwellers in several Pacific Rim nations, especially Taiwan, South Korea, and the Philippines (Delfs, 1991; McBeth, 1989; Savadove, 1991).

Therefore, it is not surprising to find a similar habit developing in Hawaii, which has so many cultural and economic affinities with the Pacific Rim, and in which Japanese organized crime had developed a strong foothold. In fact, Kaplan and Dubro's (1986) study of the *yakuza* calls Hawaii the "forty-eighth Prefecture," an annex to the 47 administrative units of the Japanese home islands. *Yakuza*-supplied amphetamines were identified in the state during the 1970s, and Korean-manufactured methamphetamines appeared in the following decade (Shoenberger, 1989). Beginning in 1987, island authorities had described an "ice problem," linked in part to Filipino youth gangs and Korean groups (*U.S. Congress: Re-emergence*, 1990:5).

Discovering a Problem

By 1989, law enforcement agencies were finding evidence of localized use of smokable methamphetamine originally in Hawaii and subsequently in and around San Diego. The perceived "wave" of new activity was epitomized by a series of federal drug raids on 20 laboratories in southern California during March, and by a series of smaller raids over the next year (Ford, 1990; Reza, 1989). Concern about the drug in Hawaii was given a new focus in March 1989 by the arrest of a substantial ice-importation ring headed by one Paciano Guerrero (*U.S. Congress: Drug Crisis*, 1990:74–75; *U.S. Congress: Re-emergence*, 1990:70–72).

It might be thought that the perceived boom in the smokable drug reflected strictly local conditions, unlikely to be replicated in other areas. Even in Hawaii, the problem was confined largely to Oahu (*U.S. Congress: Drug Crisis*, 1990:56, 205, 215). Now, however, there began a media campaign to emphasize the perils of the "new" drug, and the danger that this would soon be reflected across the nation. A headline in the *Los Angeles Times*, for example, read "Potent Form of Speed Could Be Drug of 90s" (Corwin, 1989). *The Economist* noted that ice could make crack seem almost benign ("Drugs: Ice Overdose," 1989). Rep. Charles Rangel coined the alliterative description "the narcotics nemesis of the nineties" (*U.S. Congress: Re-emergence*, 1990:59).

The theme was taken up by all the major regional newspapers and national newsmagazines, as well as more specialized publications serving the medical and pharmaceutical communities (Cho, 1990; "Illicit Methamphetamine," 1991; Zurer, 1989). Between September and December 1989, major stories appeared in the *New York Times* (Bishop, 1989), *The Washington Post* (Thompson, 1989), *The Atlanta Constitution* (Curriden, 1989), *The Economist* ("Drugs; Ice Overdose," 1989), *The Boston Globe* (Howe, 1989; Tabor, 1989), *The Chicago Tribune* (Weingarten, 1989), *The Christian Science Monitor* (Larmer, 1989), and *Newsweek* (Lerner, 1989). The tone of the coverage was epitomized by the *New York Times* headline "Fear Grows Over Effects of a New Smokable Drug" (Bishop, 1989). This story was printed on the front page; equal prominence was given to ice-related stories on the front pages of the *Los Angeles Times* (Corwin, 1989) and *The Chicago Tribune* (Weingarten, 1989). In October the *Los Angeles Times* presented a series of four stories on ice within a nine-day period (Corwin, 1989; Essoyan, 1989; Shoenberger, 1989; Zamichow, 1989). Clearly, pronouncements about the new drug were finding a ready and enthusiastic market in the mass media.

The jeremiads about ice were heard most frequently in the last quarter of 1989, though a few stories appeared in early 1990, and television news shows such as *60 Minutes* sustained the focus on methamphetamines in general for a few months more ("Meth," 1990). The height of the panic, however, can be identified clearly between about September 1989 and February 1990. (See Table 26.1 for a chronology of media accounts.)

The peak of public concern can be associated with Congressional hearings on this topic; Rep. Rangel's Subcommittee on Narcotics Abuse and Control held a session titled "The Re-emergence of Methamphetamine" in October. A follow-up session, the

"Drug Crisis in Hawaii," was held in Honolulu the following January (*U.S. Congress: Re-emergence*, 1990; *U.S. Congress: Drug Crisis*, 1990). For criticisms of the latter session as a Congressional junket, see Anderson and Van Atta, 1990). Taken together with the media accounts, the hearings became the chief vehicle for the burgeoning panic about ice. Here it will be useful to analyze the language and rhetoric employed to present the new phenomenon as a major problem.

The Rhetoric of Ice

Certain themes and expressions recur with striking regularity. Ice was new, potent, and dangerous, and had acquired high prestige as the new "in" drug. Taken together, these features meant that the use of ice apparently was about to expand rapidly and to create a national menace at least comparable to crack cocaine.

The experience of Hawaii was recounted often, as in a *Boston Globe* story titled "Ice in an Island Paradise" (Tabor, 1989). The use of ice, in the words of a Congressional report, "has escalated in such leaps and bounds that we have not been able to keep pace" (*U.S. Congress: Re-emergence*, 1990:2). Generally such accounts suggested that what such areas were experiencing today would be the fate of the whole country in a few months or years. Honolulu police chief Douglas Gibb told the story of a New York City Korean gang that had flown some members to Honolulu to attack some local Samoans. "The whole purpose . . . was to come into town to establish a connection for ice, a line for ice to take back to New York" (*U.S. Congress: Re-emergence*, 1990:8). "It is probably only a matter of time until other parts of the country start to see crystal meth and its attendant problems . . . we fully expect the Ice Age to spread east from Hawaii" (p. 77).

The idea that ice was gradually penetrating areas of the mainland gave a local angle to media reporting of the drug in cities such as Atlanta (Curriden, 1989), Boston (Howe, 1989), and Philadelphia (Durso, 1992). In the Congressional hearings, this was a frequent theme. One subcommittee member noted, "We have got ice in Virginia . . . it is for sure coming our way and we had better get ready for it" (U.S. Congress: emergence, 1990:19). Another member stated, "Reports are already filtering in of ice use in New York and Washington DC" (*U.S. Congress: Drug Crisis*, 1990:3). A lengthy investigative account in *Rolling Stone* quoted law enforcement officials, who believed that the Hawaii "epidemic" soon would sweep the mainland and that the drug would surpass both heroin and cocaine, marking a new and still more deadly era in drug abuse (Sager, 1990).

One paradox was that ice, by its nature, negated some of the obvious advantages of methamphetamine: as an imported drug, for example, it encountered the obstacles and expense involved in crossing national borders. The witnesses at the hearings, however, emphasized repeatedly that it would only be a matter of time before domestic manufacturers learned to reproduce Asian techniques; at that point, ice would begin to conquer the American "speed" market. In the words of a Dallas police official, "We have cooks, we have numerous cooks scattered throughout the country, literally thousands of persons who are qualified to make methamphetamine. So, we have the processes in place to make ice. I think we also have a ready consumer market out there, individuals who want the drug. I have no doubt that ice will come to the United States" (*U.S. Congress: Re-emergence*, 1990:39–40).

Particularly evocative was the word *epidemic*, which was employed in most of the accounts, with its implications of plague, disease, and uncontrollable spread (compare Reinarman and Levine, 1989). During the Congressional hearings, U.S. Attorney Daniel Bent described Hawaii ice use as already an "epidemic" (*U.S. Congress: Re-emergence*, 1990:5). When a DEA spokesman was quoted as having denied the validity of the "epidemic," he was taken to task by members of the committee, especially Florida Rep. Tom Lewis, who described the opinion as "irresponsible" and "lackadaisical" (p. 17). "Epidemic" was a politically valuable concept that would not be abandoned easily.

Other significant terms included *deluge*, *plague*, and *crisis*. Congressman Rangel remarked that Honolulu police were "deluged"

Table 26.1

Chronology of Media Accounts, 1989–1991

	1989	
September		
First ice-related stories in mainland newspapers		
Sept. 16	*New York Times*	(Bishop 1989)
October		
Oct. 1	*Boston Globe*	(Howe 1989)
Oct. 8	*Los Angeles Times*	(Shoenberger 1989)
Oct.14	*Los Angeles Times*	(Essoyan 1989)
Oct. 16	*Los Angeles Times*	(Essoyan 1989)
Oct. 16	*Los Angeles Times*	(Zamichow 1989)
Oct. 24	Congressional hearings, *The Re-emergence of Methamphetamine*	
November		
Nov. 6	*Chemical and Engineering News*	(Zurer 1989)
Nov. 21	*Washington Post*	(Thompson 1989)
Nov. 27	*Newsweek*	(Lerner 1989)
Nov. 30	*Atlanta Constitution*	(Curriden 1989)
December		
Dec. 2	*The Economist*	("Drugs: Ice Overdose" 1989)
Dec. 8	*Boston Globe*	(Tabor 1989)
Dec. 8	*Christian Science Monitor*	(Larmer 1989)
Dec. 18	*Jet*	(Carthane 1989)
	1990	
January		
Jan. 13	Congressional hearings on *The Drug Crisis in Hawaii*	
February		
Feb. 8	*Rolling Stone*	(Sager 1990)
February	*Good Housekeeping*	(Holland 1990)
April		
April 22	CBS news program *60 Minutes* broadcasts story on methamphetamine trafficking ("Meth" 1990)	
May		
May 23	*Journal of the American Medical Association*	(Cotton 1989)
August		
Aug. 10	*Science*	(Cho 1990)
	1991	
March		
March 6	*Journal of the American Medical Association*	(Hong, Matsuyama, and Nur 1991)
May		
May 9	*Washington Post*	(Holley, Vernant, and Essoyan 1991)
June		
June 30	*Emergency Medicine*	("Illicit Methamphetamine" 1991)

by ice (U.S. Congress: Re-emergence, 1990:1). Sociologist Elliott Currie spoke of "this hidden methamphetamine plague" (p. 44). The word *crisis* was much used, generally in the context of an "emerging" crisis, to suggest that what had gone before was trivial compared to what would come in future (p. 61). As has been noted, the January hearings of the Narcotics Subcommittee were devoted explicitly to the drug crisis in Hawaii.

The term ice offered great potential for writers, suggesting as it did the phrase *ice age* and thus implying that the drug somehow could dominate American society so strongly that it could give its name to an era. The phrase *The Ice Age* was employed both by Douglas Gibb and Hawaii Rep. Daniel Akaka in the Congressional hearings (*U.S. Congress: Re-emergence*, 1990:3, 77). It was used subsequently for major investigative accounts in *Rolling Stone* in 1990 and in the *Washington Post* in 1991 (Holley, Vernant, and Essoyan, 1991; Sager, 1990; compare LaBianca, 1992). "Ice" also suggested "chilling" in the metaphorical sense of "extremely frightening"; it was used in this sense by several journalists. In late 1989, for example, the *Atlanta Constitution* carried the headline "Police Chilled by New In-Drug: Ice" (Curriden, 1989). Within two weeks, the *Christian Science Monitor* warned similarly, "Ice Chills U.S. Anti-Drug Officials" (Larmer, 1989).

In addition, these arguments were stated by individuals and agencies with great expertise in the field. Every news story was buttressed by the opinions of prominent and credible law enforcement officials, police, and prosecutors from California and Hawaii, together with academics and other experts. In the Congressional hearings, major witnesses included Daniel Bent, the U.S. attorney for Hawaii; Douglas Gibb, the police chief of Honolulu; and David Westrate of the DEA; all were prestigious and experienced officials. Other presentations were made by reputable doctors and academics. The potential "ice epidemic" thus appeared both plausible and threatening.

Ice and Cocaine

One potent element of the attack on ice involved the analogy with cocaine. In seeking to portray a new problem as serious or dangerous, one well-known rhetorical device is to stigmatize that problem by associating it with another, already familiar issue, thus placing it into an existing context. Problem construction is a cumulative or incremental process in which each issue is built, to some extent, on its predecessors. As Best remarks,

As an acknowledged subject for concern, a well established social problem becomes a resource, a foundation upon which other claims may be built. Rather than struggling to bring recognition to a new problem, claimants may find it easier to expand an existing problem's domain. These new claims take the form (new problem) X is really a type of (established problem) Y (1990:65–66).

Issue (X) therefore demands the array of responses and reactions that already have been judged appropriate for Problem (Y). This is the process described by Hall et al. (1978:223) as "convergence."

[C]onvergence occurs when two or more activities are linked in the process of signification so as to implicitly or explicitly draw parallels between them. Thus the image of "student hooliganism" links student protest to the separate problem of hooliganism—whose stereotypical characteristics are already part of socially available knowledge. . . . In both cases, the net effect is amplification, not in the real events being described but in their threat potential for society (1978:223).

By 1989 cocaine, especially crack cocaine, had been invested with an enormous amount of "threat potential," suggested, for example, by the "drug war" rhetoric, which was then at its height. President George Bush had made the "drug war" a major part of his domestic policy; his commitment to drug eradication was symbolized by the appointment of William Bennett as "drug czar." During 1989, American activism against international drug traffickers contributed to the near-civil war in Colombia, beginning in August, and to the invasion of Panama in December. Media coverage in the latter part of the year featured almost daily news of violence and conflict associated with these incidents. In September, President Bush made a nationally televised address on drug control strategy, in which he stated, "All of us agree that the gravest domestic threat facing our nation today is drugs . . . our most serious problem today is cocaine and in particular crack." Producing a sample of crack, which he said had been purchased close to the White House, the president continued, "It's as innocent looking as candy, but it is turning our cities into battle zones, and it is murdering our children. Let there be no mistake, this stuff is poison" ("Text," 1989). President Bush argued that the drug control budget for the coming year should be raised by more than one-third from the 1989 figure, to $8 billion.

If crack was indeed "the gravest domestic threat," then it was a highly effective strategy to suggest that ice was associated somehow with the better-known drug. Superficial parallels also existed. It could be suggested, for example, that crack was an especially virulent and addictive form of powder cocaine, while ice bore a similar relationship to "regular" methamphetamine. Also, the two substances were similar in general appearance and means of ingestion. The ice threat was amplified by its association with crack, an association pursued most vigorously on the Narcotics Subcommittee by Rep. Akaka. From the viewpoint of the media, the analogy with crack made ice an attractive subject because its dangers and thus its social significance could be comprehended easily; thus the drug would be likely to excite public concern and fear.

Ice was said to cause as much social damage as cocaine, in terms of overdoses and emergency room admissions (Gross, 1988; "Illicit Methamphetamine," 1991). Rep. Akaka stated that in Hawaii, ice contributed to the problems that elsewhere were linked to crack: "ice-addicted babies, gang activities, turf battles and hospital emergency cases of overdoses . . . this drug has the capacity to drag our country even deeper into the dark abyss created by crack" (*U.S. Congress: Re-emergence*, 1990:3). "It doesn't make any difference whether it is ice, crack, crank, cocaine. We are losing kids. We are corrupting our police departments. We are corrupting our political arena. We are breaking up families" (p. 17).

U.S. Attorney Daniel Bent stated that ice was "presenting the same problems to Hawaii as crack cocaine has in areas of the Continental United States in terms of its popularity, availability, addiction potential and destructiveness" (*U.S. Congress: Re-emergence*, 1990:64). It was alleged to stimulate violent behavior even more sharply than did crack; Hawaii, it was said, was seeing the birth of a generation of "crystal meth babies" (*U.S. Congress: Drug Crisis*, 1990:2, 226–33; *U.S. Congress: Re-emergence*, 1990:66, 76; for the idea of the "crack baby," however, see Jacobs, 1991). Such remarks made the two drugs appear all but indistinguishable; in fact, Rep. Akaka even asked a witness, "Can you explain to me the differences between crack, crank, ice and croak . . . ?" (*U.S. Congress: Re-emergence*, 1990:54).

In some ways, ice could be made to appear even more dangerous than crack. First, it was superior to crack because of its lower cost and its longer-lasting high. The effects were reported to last from four to 14 hours, as opposed to a few minutes for crack (Carthane, 1989; Holley et al., 1991). Also, ice did not necessarily have to be imported from overseas (though it was imported currently); therefore it did not encounter the stringent restrictions imposed by Customs and the Coast Guard as part of the current "war on drugs." In addition, ice lacked the features that might safeguard individuals from experimenting with other sustances. It did not require injection, as did heroin, and did not yet have the destructive associations of crack cocaine. By 1989, crack had acquired undesirable connotations that deterred many people from using it: It was associated with cultures of violence and extreme urban poverty, and was linked especially with racial minorities.

In contrast, methamphetamine generally was linked to hard work. Insofar as it had any racial overtones, it tended to be favored by white users (*Methamphetamine Abuse in the United States*, 1989; Miller and Kozel, 1991). Nationally, said the congressional account, "the typical methamphetamine user is a white male 22 to 26 years of age, who is employed in a blue-collar job. The most frequently cited occupations are in construction trades and the trucking industry" (*U.S. Congress: Re-emergence*, 1990:87). In the San Diego region, "abusing populations are predominantly white, lower middle income, high school educated, young adults ranging in age from 18–35 years" (p. 111). A Texas police officer stated, "The persons who we most often encounter in Dallas, the users we most often encounter are primarily Caucasian, primarily lower income" (p. 39).

Ice users tend to fit a similar profile. In Hawaii, ice was "popular in the workplace, particularly among blue collar workers, people who do mechanical tasks, and it has also spread into office workplaces as well . . . (it is) the drug of choice for on the job use in Honolulu. . . . It is generally in the blue collar community and the service community" (*U.S. Congress: Re-emergence*, 1990:6–9). In short, ice could appeal to white or Asian middle-class people; teenagers especially were at risk. The title of a *Good Housekeeping* article described ice as "A New Drug Nice Kids Can Get Hooked On" (Holland, 1990). Women also were believed to be particularly vulnerable: "In Honolulu, most ice users range in age from the late teens to the early thirties. The drug is popular with young women, perhaps because users tend to lose weight" (*U.S. Congress: Re-emergence*, 1990:75).

It was suggested that ice might be able to wreak havoc in all sections of society, not merely in the inner cities. Rep. Rangel thus was tapping into potent fears when he wrote, "[W]e shudder to think of what would happen in this country if the devastation of the crack crisis were doubled or even tripled by adding on a whole new layer of illicit drug abuse" (*U.S. Congress: Re-emergence*, 1990:59). This rhetoric was even more powerful in the context of current developments in the "drug war" at home and overseas.

Whatever Became of Ice?

"Ice" thus was attracting quite fervent interest. One might suggest that it had the potential to attract the same kind of fear as crack. The recent precedent of crack cocaine provided a set of stereotyped images and rhetoric on which ice could build readily, with the added "bonus" that ice threatened to reproduce these disturbing images outside the African-American urban community. Ice (it appeared) could cause the same kind of havoc as crack in geographical, social, and ethnic settings still untouched by ice or any other "hard" drug. It would not be difficult to imagine that the new problem could thrive through the use of ethnic and xenophobic stereotypes: the substance was imported from Asia, and had Japanese connotations. *Yakuza* drug dealers might easily acquire the stigma that had adhered earlier to gangsters from immigrant ethnic groups such as Jews and Italians.

In addition, it has been argued that intense media attention to a particular drug might tend to incite interest in the substance, and to lead to experimentation. Prophecies of an "epidemic" thus might be self-fulfilling in that they could unwittingly generate the problem that activists were seeking to avoid (MacDonald and Estep, 1985; compare Young, 1971). In the 1960s this kind of imitation caused glue sniffing to spread at "incredible speed . . . the enemies of glue-sniffing popularized the custom all by themselves" (Brecher, 1972:326, 332). In the 1980s it was suggested that media portrayals of the effects of crack cocaine might have excited interest among users of powdered cocaine. With these precedents in mind, observers of ice warned that ice was being "beautifully advertised by the media" to cocaine users (Cotton, 1990). *The Journal of the American Medical Association* warned, "News articles describing (ice) as like 'ten orgasms pronto' are working like paid ads. . . . If the media says it's an epidemic, drug adventurers say everybody's using it so I've got to try it" (Cotton, 1990).

The ice danger, however, did not materialize as a national crisis, and the prospective "plague" faded rapidly in early 1990. Media accounts became far less frequent from February onwards, and virtually none appeared between August 1990 and spring 1991 (see Table 24.1). In part this silence reflected the new concern of the media with political affairs in Iraq and the Persian Gulf, but the ice panic had been declining sharply for several months before the August invasion of Kuwait. The rather sudden eclipse of the ice problem requires explanation.

Some observers had been skeptical even during the height of the panic, and witnesses at the October hearings faced criticism for their use of the term *epidemic*. The evidence presented also contained clear contradictions—for example, in the damage caused by ice. Early reports of the testimony quoted Chief Gibb's statements that "since 1985, there have been 32 deaths in Honolulu attributed to ice," including eight homicides and seven suicides (*U.S. Congress: Re-emergence*, 1990:76). Gibb, however, also stated that "32 people were confirmed to have crystal methamphetamine in their system at the time of deaths," which does not necessarily establish a causal link between the drug and the fatality (pp. 7–8). Hawaii's Governor Waihee placed the number of deaths at 36, of whom "three died as a direct result, and 32 had traces of the drug in their systems" (p. 80). It was embarrassing when Gibb was publicly challenged on his statistics; as a result, the early claims about the impact of the drug, even in Hawaii, were reduced substantially. Thus it was even more difficult to claim that ice presented a potential national menace.

During the October hearings, one DEA spokesman commented, "I can confirm there is a drug out there called ice, which is certainly bad news. But D.E.A. agents are not looking for it yet. . . . It will take a while for ice to proliferate. When we get reports from police departments that ice has gotten to be at the epidemic state, such as crack did in 1985, then we will move in" (*U.S. Congress: Re-emergence*, 1990:17). Such a drug "explosion" seemed remote, however. In early 1990, testing of arrestees confirmed considerable amphetamine use in San Diego, Portland, Phoenix, and San Jose, but the figures did not appear to be growing.

Moreover, ice as such had made few inroads among the arrestees, though a substantial majority knew the substance by reputation: the media were cited overwhelmingly as the main source. Even in San Diego, almost 70 percent of those who knew about ice based their knowledge on media accounts rather than on information provided by friends or dealers. Nationwide the proportion who admitted ever having used ice nowhere exceeded 3 percent (though no community in Hawaii was included in the survey) (*Arrestee Drug Use*, 1990:6; Pennell, 1990). This picture was confirmed by other survey data. Among male hustlers and sex workers in San Francisco, for example, ice had made very limited inroads, even among heavy users of methamphetamine. Moreover, the number of habitual ice users in such groups remained negligible (Lauderback and Waldorf, 1992).

Largely on the basis of such data and of the reexamination of the drug's impact in Hawaii itself, law enforcement and DEA officials soon were saying that the danger of ice had been substantially overstated. Media rhetoric subsided within a few months of the Congressional hearings. Ice continues to be popular in some regions, but the language of epidemic no longer seems realistic—if it ever did.

The Construction of the Ice Danger

In retrospect it seems certain that the menace of ice was considerably overstated, and we might well ask how such a misperception could emerge. A considerable literature exists on the origins of such scares and perceived social problems; some of the explanations suggested by that literature seem relevant here. Many researchers, for example, follow some form of what is generally known as the "moral entrepreneur" theory. The classic discussion of this term comes from Becker, who emphasized the role of a particular individual in the formulation of American narcotics policy in the 1930s:

> Wherever rules are created and applied we should be alive to the possible presence of an enterprising individual or group. Their activities can properly be called "moral enterprise" for what they are enterprising about is the creation of a new fragment of the moral constitution of society, its code of right and wrong (1963:145).

Such entrepreneurs might have diverse motives. In the case of a drug panic, for example, we might find activism by an interest group or a bureaucratic agency that was seeking to portray a serious social danger in order to focus public attention on issues falling within its scope of activity. This effort would permit the agency to expand its influence and resources, and might allow local authorities and law enforcement agencies to justify and request for federal funding and other support. In such circumstances, we often find a cyclical pattern in which greater concern causes more resources to be devoted to a problem; the result is more detection and more vigorous prosecution of the activity in question. This process in turn generates statistical evidence that can be used to intensify public concern, and thus to argue for still more resources. "Epidemics" thus can be self-sustaining.

Such bureaucratic concerns may have played some role in the case of ice. One recurrent theme of the hearings was the need to strengthen still further the numbers and resources of the DEA (*U.S. Congress: Re-emergence*, 1990:8–9). This agency had grown in numbers from 1,900 in 1980 to 2,900 in 1989. Currently it was requesting 160 new agents, chiefly for international enforcement in Latin America and the Pacific Rim (34–35). An ice panic therefore served the interests of the DEA, but it certainly cannot serve as a full explanation. As we have seen, the DEA was strongly critical of the exaggerated claims made for ice, and during 1990 was instrumental in damping down the nascent panic. In January, for example, the head of the Honolulu office wrote that ice was still confined largely to Hawaii and "very limited West Coast areas"; otherwise, he reported, "we know of no ice samples (having) been analyzed elsewhere in the United States" (*U.S. Congress: Drug Crisis*, 1990:76).

Instead of examining national groups and controversies, it would be more profitable to consider the needs of the political and bureaucratic interests in Hawaii that sponsored most of the extravagant claims about ice and first identified an "epidemic." For example, the major claims makers heard by the Congressional committees included two of the leading figures in the state's law enforcement bureaucracy, police chief Douglas Gibb and U.S. attorney Daniel Bent. The evidence offered by these two witnesses accounted for more than one-third of the total testimony presented during the October hearings, and both men emphasized the "epidemic" quality of the ice threat. As in the case of the DEA, an ice panic would enhance the reputation of local police agencies as well as increasing their access to resources. In addition, the powerful office of U.S. attorney often provides any incumbent with the opportunity to win prestige and visibility that can be translated subsequently into a wider political career. This is not to suggest that either individual was insincere in his claims about the ice problem, but both had

clear bureaucratic interests in formulating the issue in a particular way.

Electoral politics also played a role in shaping official claims and statements. At the opening of the 1989 hearings, which did so much to put ice on the map of American social problems, Congressman Rangel emphasized that the impetus for concern came chiefly from the Hawaii Congressional delegation of Representatives Daniel Akaka and Patricia Saiki. Both in fact had a strong vested interest in appearing to be active and interested in drug issues, and in adopting hard-line antidrug stances. Therefore they stood to benefit from making ice seem as perilous and as threatening as possible; both can be viewed as classical moral entrepreneurs.

This political context can be observed if we describe recent developments in Hawaii, traditionally one of the most loyally Democratic states in the nation (Smith and Pratt, 1992). In the 1980s, for example, both of the Democratic U.S. senators could count regularly on receiving 70 to 80 percent of the votes cast, and the powerful governor's office remained firmly in Democratic hands throughout these years (Benenson, 1991). Republicans were placed extremely poorly; they won offices chiefly when Democratic factions were split, as when Republican Patricia Saiki won the First Congressional District. By 1989 she had retained this position in two elections, but with progressively slimmer majorities. Democrat Daniel Akaka had remained firmly in control of the Second District in every contest since 1976.

Saiki's presence as a Republican representative therefore might appear anomalous, but the Republicans had one major point of potential strength, namely in the general area of law and order. Throughout the decade, Democratic authorities had been involved in a series of scandals; these had exposed alleged links between organized crime and the labor unions, which play so crucial a role in Hawaii Democratic politics. These incidents reached a climax in 1984 with the investigation by Charles F. Marsland, the Republican Honolulu city/county prosecutor, into a series of gangland murders that included the killing of Marsland's own son. Marsland targeted a prominent political ally of Democratic Governor George Ariyoshi as the alleged "godfather" of organized crime in the state (Turner, 1984a, 1984b). The ensuing scandals and lawsuits did not destroy Democratic power. In fact, the next governor, elected in 1986, was a close associate of Ariyoshi, but the incident suggested one area in which Democrats were politically vulnerable: Daniel Akaka himself had been an Ariyoshi protégé. In addition, he is of native Hawaiian descent, and thus could potentially be associated with Larry Mehau, the ethnically Hawaiian "godfather."

In the following years, Saiki and Akaka emerged as powerful figures in Hawaii politics, and they clashed on crime-related issues. In the U.S. Congress, Saiki voted for a measure to extend the death penalty to major drug dealers, which Akaka opposed. The rivalry between the two was especially significant in 1989, when it became increasingly likely that soon they would be vying for a U.S. Senate seat in Hawaii. The junior senator's position currently was held by Spark Matsunaga, a very popular figure first elected in 1972, but a series of health crises beginning in 1984 made it unlikely that Matsunaga would run again in 1990, even if he completed his current term.

Therefore it was likely that within a year, Saiki would challenge Akaka for the hitherto solidly Democratic Senate seat, but the balance in this apparently unequal match could be tipped in a number of ways. One would be the ethnic factor. As noted above, Akaka is a native Hawaiian. The strongest faction in his Democratic party, however, is Japanese-American, a group to which Saiki could be expected to appeal. In addition, it would be natural to portray the relatively liberal Akaka as soft on crime and drugs, and possibly not sufficiently vigorous in the war on local organized crime. As a result, it was important for Akaka to rebut such charges; his membership on the House Subcommittee on Narcotic Abuse provided an ideal opportunity.

Both representatives therefore needed to appear strong on drug issues, and ideally both needed national media credentials as antidrug crusaders. Local ethnic and partisan alignments, however, circumscribed the kinds of rhetoric that would be appropriate in such a campaign. Although organized crime in general could be denounced, it is significant that none of the ice rhetoric focused on the specifically Japanese component of drug manufacture and distribution or on the role of the *yakuza* described so frequently by other law enforcement agencies and investigators. One might suggest that the nature of the forthcoming Hawaii elections made such accusations too sensitive to be presented at that time, for fear of perpetrating ethnic slurs against one of the most influential communities in the islands.

In fact, both Akaka and Saiki succeeded in gaining significant political capital from the ice issue. Saiki earned credit for having brought the problem to national attention and for requesting increased resources, but Akaka also shared the credit, and was not portrayed as soft on the crime issue in any sense. Akaka first used the term *ice age* in the hearings, and drew some of the starkest analogies between ice and crack. Both confirmed their role as standard-bearers of their respective parties. When Senator Matsunaga died a few months later, in April 1990, Akaka was the natural choice to fill the unexpired portion of his term. Both he and Saiki easily won their parties' nominations for the November election ("Hawaiian Politics," 1990). That contest normally would have been a Democratic walkover, but Saiki had established her prestige so firmly that she made it a close race, and lost only narrowly to Akaka. He thereby became the first native Hawaiian to [serve] in the U.S. Senate (Saiki went on to head the federal Small Business Administration) (Reinhold, 1990; Richburg, 1990).

Domestic politics in Hawaii thus made it likely that the state representatives would seek to focus on a crime or drug problem of local significance. It was by no means apparent, however, that these issues would come to wider attention, especially when conditions and controversies in Hawaii so rarely attract the attention of the national media. The opportunity was provided by Akaka's service on the House Narcotics Subcommittee, where he was aided by another representative with a strong record in drug issues and a long career as a "moral entrepreneur." This was a Pennsylvania representative named

Lawrence Coughlin, from the thirteenth district in suburban Montgomery County, outside Philadelphia. Coughlin, the ranking Republican on the Narcotics Subcommittee, was instrumental in bringing Akaka's views to Rangel's attention. His advocacy was significant in showing that ice was causing concern far outside Hawaii, and legitimately could be presented as a national issue.

Other agendas, however, may have been at work here as well. Coughlin's interest in methamphetamine issues dated back at least to the late 1970s, when he had been one of the most active supporters of the theory that Philadelphia was the "speed capital of the world" (Jenkins, 1992a, b). To illustrate this questionable assertion, Coughlin had publicized stories from local Montgomery County newspapers as if they represented conditions throughout the state or the nation, and in effect had generated a mythology about the prevalence of speed in southeastern Pennsylvania. In 1980, largely at Coughlin's behest, the Narcotics Select Committee had been persuaded to hold special hearings in Philadelphia, where local issues and investigations received national attention (*U.S. Congress: Laboratories*, 1980). The campaign to link Philadelphia with speed was so successful that it became the focus of the popular 1985 film *Witness*, whose plot concerns a huge shipment of the precursor chemical P2P. Coughlin thus emerges as a long-standing protagonist of a "speed menace." As a result, it is scarcely surprising to see the limited experience of Hawaii extrapolated to the entire nation in the 1989–1990 hearings, just as had happened with conditions in Philadelphia in 1980.

Transforming Local Issues Into National Problems

In studying social problems, one critical theme is the relationship between local and national perceptions, and the way in which some (but by no means all) local phenomena come to be regarded as issues of far wider significance. The panic about ice serves to remind us that drug problems are extremely localized, and that in crime, as in so much else, it is difficult to generalize about the American experience. Drug problems rarely strike the nation in a regular or homogeneous way. Much has been written about the "crack epidemic" that swept the United States in the mid-1980s, but we must always remember that this phenomenon was highly localized. The "epidemic" initially was centered in the major cities of the east and west coasts, but scarcely penetrated large sections of the midwest until the early 1990s. This situation has many possible explanations—the strength of local traditions and subcultures, patterns of law enforcement, vagaries of manufacture and supply, the interests of criminal groups—but the point is that a "panic" might be well under way in one area years before it is felt elsewhere, and it is by no means inevitable that it ever will move beyond the original region (for the localized nature of drug cultures, see, for example, Weisheit, 1992).

On the other hand, certain extraneous factors demand that a local problem should be viewed in a national context, and that policy responses should be developed accordingly. One important element in this regard is the mass media, which had come, during the 1980s, to treat drug-related stories as events of major significance. Newspapers assigned journalists to cover such stories as their sole or major responsibility; thus the papers had a vested interest in the constant generation of newsworthy items in this area.[1] One way to achieve this goal was to focus on local concerns or incidents, but to project them as if they were of wider, even national significance. A notorious example appeared in 1986 in the CBS television documentary *48 Hours on Crack Street*. This program presented the (then) essentially New York City problem of crack cocaine as if it were already a national epidemic, with vials littering the streets and parks of virtually every community across the country (Reinarman and Levine, 1989). Though largely spurious, this account had enormous influence in generating fears of a national crack epidemic.

In the early 1980s, before the advent of crack, the media often presented the localized PCP problem in Washington, D.C., in such a way as to suggest that it soon would become a national crisis. (Such "extrapolations" are not confined to drug issues: Witness the suggestions, at about that time, that

Los Angeles's distinctive gang problems were spreading to cities throughout the nation.) Once the media present a problem in this way, Congressional hearings permit the issue to be discussed in another national forum, with the certainty that national news coverage will reinforce perceptions of a widespread crisis.

This process of "nationalization" gives rich opportunities to local activists, moral entrepreneurs, or claims makers who wish to draw attention to a particular issue, and who do so by presenting it as more dangerous or more important than it may be in fact. One natural way to do this is to suggest that a local issue either is national in scope or has a strong potential to become so in the very near future: in short, that it is about to "sweep the nation." This process enhances the importance of local campaigns; it also offers the local moral entrepreneurs the opportunity to acquire the status of national leaders and experts, should their analysis be accepted. This enhancement, in turn, can reinforce the position of local figures in their home areas.

The panic about ice is a model example of this process. The use of the drug was a local phenomenon; the national concern about the drug in 1989 derived chiefly from Hawaii's elected officials and law enforcement agencies with a definite political agenda. For two specific reasons, they were relatively successful in projecting their concerns. First, the recent experience of crack made it easy for them to represent ice, in effect, as part of the same problem; this process is known by the rhetorical term *convergence*. The ice phenomenon occurred at precisely the right time, when the rhetoric about crack was still fresh in the public mind and when the "drug war" was reaching a crescendo. It is difficult to imagine that the ice issue would have arisen at all if public expectations had not been conditioned by these recent precedents.

Second, the intense public focus on drug issues during the 1980s had created bureaucracies and political frameworks able to publicize information and opinion about drugs. These groups, such as the DEA, the NIDA, and the Narcotics Subcommittee itself, had excellent media ties and could be relied on to provide newsworthy stories about crime and drug abuse. In the case of the Congressional committee, it is inevitable that members of any political organization charged with investigating drug problems will attempt to attract as much publicity as possible by presenting themselves as concerned, active, well-informed guardians of the public good. There are few better opportunities to do so than by recognizing a problem at an early stage to prevent it reaching crisis proportions. The case of Hawaii offered the committee members the chance to investigate and combat a drug problem in a proactive, farsighted way.

No significant risk was involved in this strategy. If an "ice epidemic" occurred, the committee earned credit for having predicted it and for urging preemptive action; if it faded away, the committee could claim that its forethought had prevented a drug crisis. Conversely, there was much to be lost by cautious or skeptical reactions to an incipient crisis. If the predicted menace actually materialized, an agency or an administration stood to attract most of the blame for the ensuing problems.

None of the factors that produced the ice panic has changed significantly since 1989, or is likely to change significantly in the near future. Therefore it is probable that local drug fads will be presented once again as potential crises, likely to spread rapidly across the entire country. Social scientists must recognize and publicize the social and political factors that generate such misleading expectations.

Note

1. I am indebted to one of the anonymous reviewers for raising this point when I originally submitted this article to *Justice Quarterly*.

References

Anderson, J., and D. Van Atta (1990) "Big Plane Junket for Hill Spouses." *Washington Post*, January 10, p. 3.

Arrestee Drug Use (1990) National Institute of Justice, Research in Action. Washington, DC: U.S. Government Printing Office.

Becker, H. (1963) *Outsiders*. New York: Free Press.

Benenson, B. (1991) "Democrats Reassert Primacy in Hawaii Politics." *Congressional Quarterly*, October 12.

Best, J. (1990) *Threatened Children*. Chicago: University of Chicago Press.

Bishop, K. (1989) "Fear Grows Over Effects of a New Smokable Drug." *New York Times*, September 16, p. 4A.

Brecher, E.M. (1972) *Licit and Illicit Drugs*. Boston: Little, Brown.

Buruma, I., and J. McBeth (1984–85) "An East Side Story . . . ." *Far Eastern Economic Review*, 27 December/3 January, p. 15.

Carthane, A. (1989) "Will New Drug 'Ice' Freeze Hope in Black Communities?" *Jet*, December 18.

Cho, A.K. (1990) "Ice: A New Dosage Form of an Old Drug." *Science* (249):831–34.

Corwin, M. (1989) "Potent Form of Speed Could Be Drug of 90s." *Los Angeles Times*, October 8, p. 1A.

Cotton, P. (1990) "Medium Isn't Accurate Ice Age Message." *Journal of the American Medical Association* (263):2717.

Curriden, M. (1989) "Police Chilled by New In-Drug: Ice." *Atlanta Constitution*, November 30, p. 1.

Delfs, R. (1991) "Cocaine Surge." *Far Eastern Economic Review*, November 21, p. 7.

"Drugs: Ice Overdose" (1989) *Economist*, December 2, pp. 29–30.

Durso, C. (1992) "Powerful Drug 'Ice' Is Found at Lab." *Philadelphia Inquirer*, August 14, p. 1B.

Essoyan, S. (1989) "Use of Highly Addictive 'Ice' Growing in Hawaii." *Los Angeles Times*, October 16, p. 3A.

Ford, A. (1990) "Federal, Local Police Raid House in San Diego." *Los Angeles Times*, July 26, p. 7A.

Goode, E. (1984) *Drugs in American Society*. 2nd ed. New York: Knopf.

Graham, J.M. (1976) "Amphetamine Politics on Capital Hill." In W.J. Chambliss and M. Mankoff (eds.), *Whose Law? What Order?*, pp. 107–22. New York: Wiley.

Grinspoon, L. (1975) *The Speed Culture: Amphetamine Use and Abuse in America*. Cambridge, MA: Harvard University Press.

Gross, J. (1988) "Speed's Gain in Use Could Rival Crack." *New York Times*, November 27, p. A9.

Hall, S., Critcher, C., Jefferson, T., Clarke, J., and Roberta, B. (1978) *Policing the Crisis*. London: Macmillan.

"Hawaiian Politics: Ethnic Pineapple Salad" (1990) *Economist*, October 20, p. 32.

Holland, L. (1990) "All about Ice: New Drug Nice Kids Can Get Hooked On." *Good Housekeeping*, February, pp. 215–16.

Holley, D., E. Vernant, and S. Essoyan (1991) "The Ice Age." *Washington Post*, May 9, p. 1A.

Hong, R., E. Matsuyama, and K. Nur (1991) "Cardiomyopathy Associated with the Smoking of Crystal Methamphetamine." *Journal of the American Medical Association* (265):1152–54.

Howe, P.J. (1989) "Ice Worse Than Crack, Officials Warn." *Boston Globe*, October 1, p. 2.

"Illicit Methamphetamine: Street Drug on the Rise." (1991) *Emergency Medicine*, June 30, pp. 13–17.

Isikoff, M. (1989) "Rural Drug Users Spur Comeback of Crank." *Washington Post*, February 20, p. 3A.

Jacobs, J. (1991) "Debunking the Crack Baby Myths." *Centre Daily Times*, State College, PA, August 11, p. 6k.

Jenkins, Philip (1992a) "Narcotics Trafficking and the American Mafia: The Myth of Internal Prohibition." *Crime, Law, and Social Change* 18:303–18.

Jenkins, Philip (1992b) "The Speed Capital of the World: Organizing the Methamphetamine Industry in Philadelphia 1970–1990." *Criminal Justice Policy Review* 6(1):17–39.

Kaplan, D.E., and A. Dubro (1986) *Yakuza*. Reading, MA: Addison-Wesley.

LaBianca, D.A. (1992) "The Drug Scene's New Ice Age." *USA Today*, January, pp. 54–56.

Larmer, B. (1989) "Ice Chills U.S. Anti-drug Officials." *Christian Science Monitor*, December 8, p. 7.

Lauderback, D., and D. Waldorf (1992) "Whatever Happened to Ice?" Paper presented at meetings of the American Society of Criminology, New Orleans.

Lerner, M. L. (1989) "The Fire of Ice." *Newsweek*, November 27, p. 26.

MacDonald, P.T., and R. Estep (1985) "Prime Time Drug Depictions." *Contemporary Drug Problems* 12(3):419–38.

McBeth, J. (1989) "The Junkie Culture: Supercharged Speed Is Scourge of Manila's Smart Set." *Far Eastern Economic Review*, November 23, pp. 23–25.

"Meth" (1990) Report broadcast on "*60 Minutes*," April 22.

Methamphetamine Abuse in the United States (1989) Rockville, MD: U.S. Department of Health and Human Services.

Miller, M.A., and N.J. Kozel (1991) *Methamphetamine Abuse: Epidemiological Issues and Implications*. Rockville, MD: U.S. Department of Health and Human Services.

Morgan, J.P. (1992) "Amphetamine and Methamphetamine During the 1990s." *Pediatrics in Review* 13(9):330–36.

Musto, D. (1973) *The American Disease: Origins of Narcotic Control*. New Haven: Yale University Press.

Organized Crime in California: Annual Report to the California Legislature (1989) State of California: Department of Justice.

Pennell, S. (1990) "Ice: DUF Interview Results from San Diego." *NIJ Reports* 221:12–13.

Posner, G.L. (1988) *Warlords of Crime*. New York: McGraw-Hill.

Reinarman, C., and H.G. Levine (1989) "The Crack Attack: Politics and Media in America's Latest Drug Scare." In Joel Best (ed.), *Images of Issues*, pp. 115–37. Hawthorne, NY: Aldine.

Reinhold, R. (1990) "Hawaii Race Tests Democratic Hold." *New York Times*, November 1, p. 9B.

Reza, H.G. (1989) "Raids Shut 23 Drug Labs." *Los Angeles Times*, March 20.

Richburg, K.B. (1990) "For Hawaii Democrats, Anxiety Over Safe Seats." *Washington Post*, November 1, p. 7A.

Sager, M. (1990) "The Ice Age." *Rolling Stone*, February 8, pp. 53–57.

Savadove, B. (1991) "High Society: Growing Drug Abuse Reflects Economic Changes." *Far Eastern Economic Review*, September 12, pp. 45–46.

Shoenberger, K. (1989) "South Korea Seen as Major Source of Ice Narcotic." *Los Angeles Times*, October 14, p. 9A.

Skeers, V.M. (1992) "Illegal Methamphetamine Drug Laboratories." *Journal of Environmental Health* 55(3):6–9.

Smith, Z.A., and R.C. Pratt, eds. (1992) *Politics and Public Policy in Hawaii*. Albany: SUNY Press.

Tabor, M. (1989) "Ice in an Island Paradise." *Boston Globe*, December 8, p. 7.

"Text of President's Speech on Drug Control Strategy" (1989) *New York Times*, September 6, p. 4A.

Thompson, L. (1989) "Ice: New Smokable Form of Speed." *Washington Post*, November 21, p. 2.

Turner, W. (1984a) "Hawaii Criminal's Pledge to Talk Seen as Door to Underworld." *New York Times*, July 24, p. 11A.

——. (1984b) "Inquiry on Murders in Hawaii Brings Governor and Prosecutor into Conflict." *New York Times*, August 28, p. 7A.

U.S. Congress: Drug Crisis (1990) *Drug Crisis in Hawaii: Hearing before the Select Committee on Narcotics Abuse and Control House of Representatives 101st Congress, Second Session. January 13. 1990*. Washington, DC: U.S. Government Printing Office.

U.S. Congress: Laboratories (1980) *Illicit Methamphetamine Laboratories in the Pennsylvania/New Jersey/Delaware Area: Hearing before the Select Committee on Narcotics Abuse and Control, U.S. House of Representatives, 96th Congress, Second Session, July 7, 1980*. Washington, DC: U.S. Government Printing Office.

U.S. Congress: Profile (1983) *Profile of Organized Crime: Mid-Atlantic Region: Hearings before the Permanent Subcommittee on Investigations of the Committee on Governmental Affairs, United States Senate, 98th Congress. First Session. February 15, 23, and 24, 1983*. Washington, DC: U.S. Government Printing Office.

U.S. Congress: Re-emergence (1990) *The Re-emergence of Methamphetamine: Hearings before the Subcommittee on Narcotics Abuse and Control. U.S. House of Representatives,*

101st Congress, First Session. October 24, 1989. Washington, DC: U.S. Government Printing Office.

U.S. *Congress: Small Business* (1988) *Impact of Clandestine Drug Laboratories on Small Business: Hearings before the Subcommittee on Regulation and Business Opportunities of the Committee on Small Business, U.S. House of Representatives, 100th Congress, Second Session. Eugene, Oregon. May 13, 1988.* Washington, DC: U.S. Government Printing Office.

Weingarten, P. (1989) "Profits, Perils, Higher for Today's Bootleggers." *Chicago Tribune*, September 14, p. 16.

Weisheit, R.A. (1992) *Domestic Marijuana: A Neglected Industry.* Westport, CT: Greenwood.

Wiedrich, B. (1987) "San Diego Has Become National Center for Manufacture of Methamphetamine." *Chicago Tribune*, April 20, p. 11.

Witkin, G. (1989) "The New Midnight Dumpers." *U.S. News and World Report*, January 9, p. 23.

Young, J. (1971) "Drugs and the Media." *Drugs and Society* 2(1):14–18.

Zamichow, N. (1989) "Navy Hopes Drug Test Will Detect, Deter Meth Users." *Los Angeles Times*, October 16, p. 6A.

Zurer, P.S. (1989) "Federal Officials Plot Strategy to Stop Methamphetamine Spread." *Chemical and Engineering News*, November 6, pp. 13–16.

For Discussion

1. Discuss the possibility of whether drug panics can be productive for society.

2. Who, if anyone, benefits from drug panics?

27

Post-circuit Blues

Motivations and Consequences of Crystal Meth Use Among Gay Men in Miami

Steven P. Kurtz

For this study, Steven Kurtz uses focus group interviews to collect data from gay men in Miami who had used crystal methamphetamine at least six times in the previous year. The author describes methamphetamine use in relation to respondents' relationships, sexual encounters, risk behaviors, and employment. The results suggest that stigmata associated with being gay contributes to initiation into methamphetamin use as well as subsequent use of the drug. The findings also reveal the debilitating effects of the drug on respondents' lives.

I told him before he moved to Miami Beach what was going to happen. Because I've seen this Beach spit so many, you know, chew them up and spit them out. And that's how they end up. He thought living in Miami Beach—every weekend was going to be a circuit party. Every single weekend was going to be a circuit party. "I'll get cracked out [high on crystal meth] on Friday night. I'm gonna crack till Monday morning, I'll go straight to work and I'll sleep on Monday night." And that was exactly what he made it when he came here. Then I remember talking to him one morning—he was cracked out of his skull—and he didn't have enough money to put gas in his car to drive to work, so he had to call in sick. And then he gets sick, he has some kind of gall bladder or something, goes into the hospital, and they find out he's HIV positive. And it's all in a matter of like eight months. And everything was, "Oh, poor me, poor me, poor me." And I have a real hard time mustering up any sympathy. I'm not going to be an asshole to him, but it's like, "You know what? I told you, I told you that! What makes you

think that you are any better any different, any smarter than anybody else that's fallen before you?"

Introduction

In contrast to the 1980s when urban gay communities suffered the initial ravages of AIDS, the 1990s witnessed a gradual return to the sexual freedom, pervasive drug use and all-night dance parties that were hallmarks of the 1970s. MDMA, or ecstasy, gained early popularity and was closely associated with the rise of "techno" dance music and "circuit party" culture. Other "designer" or "club" drugs followed, primarily ketamine (Special K), gammahydroxybutyrate (GHB), and crystal methamphetamine (crystal or "tina") (Kurtz, 1999b; Lewis and Ross, 1995; Li et al., 1998; Mattison et al., 2001; Signorile, 1997; Silcott, 1999). Although methamphetamine has a long history of abuse among a number of populations (Brecht et al., 2004; Kalant, 1966; Kirsch, 1986), in this recent context crystal use spread rapidly among gay men on the West coast and gradually moved east toward the end of the 1990s (Brown, 2002; Halkitis et al., 2003; Heredia, 2003; Reback, 1997). Crystal has now become embedded in many urban gay communities and is strongly associated with sexual behaviors that put men at risk for HIV infection (Frosch et al., 1996; Molitor et al., 1998; Reback, 1997; Semple et al., 2002).

Researchers have found associations between gay men's sexual risk behaviors and the use of other substances as well, including alcohol (Halkitis and Parsons, 2002; Perry et al., 1994); ecstasy (Klitzman et al., 2000); nitrite inhalants (Halkitis and Parsons, 2002; Darrow et al., 1998; Ekstrand et al., 1999; Paul et al., 1994); and cocaine (Chesney et al., 1998; McNall and Remafedi, 1999). The specific mechanisms linking substance use and sexual risk behaviors are not well understood (Clatts et al., 2001; Chesney et al., 1998; Gold et al., 1994; Leigh and Stall, 1993; Stall and Purcell, 2000). One problem is the paucity of studies which have employed event-level measures (Stall and Purcell,

2000) which could help determine, for instance, whether intoxication was designed to achieve unprotected sex (McKirnan et al., 2001), whether unprotected sex was the result of clouded judgment, or whether sexual risk and substance use are related through a third variable, such as sensation-seeking (Dolezal et al., 1997; Kalichman et al., 1996; Ostrow, 2000).

Nevertheless, there is abundant evidence that crystal has an especially synergistic relationship with sex among sizeable numbers of gay men (Frosch et al., 1996; Ireland et al., 1999; Molitor et al., 1998; Reback, 1997; Semple et al., 2002; Signorile, 1997). Unlike ecstasy, for instance, which is often described as a "love drug" but not a "hard sex drug" (Beck and Rosenbaum, 1994; Cohen, 1998; Ireland et al., 1999; Reback, 1997), crystal has been described, more than other drugs, to be especially sexually arousing and disinhibitory (Ireland et al., 1999; Kirsch, 1986; Paul et al., 1993; Reback, 1997; Semple et al., 2002; Zule and Desmond, 1999).

A few studies—all from Sydney, Australia or the West coast of the United States—have employed qualitative research methods to explore more deeply the motivations and meanings that gay men ascribe to crystal. In one such study, Semple et al. (2002) found that HIV-positive men used crystal to both enhance sex (through increased confidence, heightened sensations and loss of inhibitions) and self-medicate negative emotional states related to having HIV. Similarly, Ireland et al. (1999) found that a community sample of men used crystal for its sexual confidence, performance, endurance and disinhibitory qualities. Lewis and Ross (1995) interviewed crystal users as a part of their ethnographic study of Sydney's dance party culture with similar findings; in addition, their respondents indicated that the drug was associated with risky sexual behaviors and a high potential for dependence. In one of the most extensive qualitative studies to date, crystal-using men in Los Angeles described sex-on-crystal as an element of gay cultural identity and inclusion (Reback, 1997). That study also found that some men reported using crystal to escape feelings of boredom, isolation, hopelessness and grief.

There has been little research published on crystal use among gay men on the East coast (Halkitis et al., 2003) and none on gay men in Miami, a city that was at the vanguard of the rise of circuit parties and attendant club drug use—especially ecstasy, GHB, and ketamine—in the 1990s (Albin, 1995; Kurtz, 1999b; Kurtz and Inciardi, 2003; Signorile, 1997). The South Beach Health Survey (Webster et al., 1998), a 1996 population-based study of the drug use and sexual behaviors of gay men living in Miami's "gay ghetto" (Levine, 1979: 384), found that 13% of respondents used drugs other than marijuana and inhalants at least weekly, more than double the rate found in San Francisco in the late 1980s (Stall and Wiley, 1988). Overall, 63% of South Beach Health Survey respondents used illicit drugs other than marijuana in the prior year; 24% reported having been high on drugs or alcohol during anal sex at least half of the time (Webster et al., 1998).

Despite these high background levels of drug use, the incursion of crystal meth in Miami has been recent and rapid, and occurred as the city's reputation as an international mecca of gay nightlife was beginning to wane. The spread of crystal meth also coincided with an alarming rise in already high rates of HIV and syphilis infections among gay men in the area (CDC, 2002; MDCHD, 2003; Stepick et al., 2003). Although the literature on gay men's use of crystal provided some guidance about the likely meanings, motivations and consequences of the spread of the drug, there were important reasons to suspect that conditions in Miami may be different from the Sydney and West coast experiences. First, the lack of history of methamphetamine abuse in Miami made it unlikely that the drug could already have become a key element of gay cultural identity here. Second, the seminal Lewis and Ross (1995) study framed crystal meth as one of several drugs embedded in the ritualistic gay dance party scene, an aspect of gay culture which had almost disappeared from Miami by the time the drug became popular. Within this context, the present study was designed as a qualitative exploration of the motivations for and consequences of crystal use in this new setting.

Methods

Between February and April, 2003, four focus groups of three to four participants each—including a total of 15 men ages 33–50—were conducted by the author. Men were recruited through print media advertisements and screened by telephone to determine if they met eligibility requirements: at least 18 years of age, had sex with another man in the past 30 days, and used crystal meth more than five times during the past year. Eight participants were Hispanic and seven "Anglo" (non-hispanic white). The groups included seven current users as well as eight men recovering from some level of self-described addiction to crystal. Six of the current users said they were HIV-negative, while six of the ex-users reported being HIV-positive.

Subsequent to informed consent using a protocol approved by the University's Institutional Review Board, participants completed a brief demographic and behavioral questionnaire using an identifying pseudonym. This questionnaire was also used to confirm eligibility. In the audio-taped focus group discussions that followed, the participants identified themselves on the tape using the same pseudonym so that the two sources of data could be linked at the individual respondent level. The sessions lasted 60–90 min and were guided by a relatively unstructured interview schedule that included open-ended questions about the initiation, motivations, and health and social consequences of crystal use. Participants were compensated $30 for their participation.

Following Morgan (1997), the small size of the groups was deemed important for two reasons: (1) the study targeted personal meanings attached to private behaviors, and (2) it was anticipated that respondents would be quite deeply involved in the questions of interest. Similarly, the number of groups was considered sufficient when the group discussions reached consensus, or converged, i.e., when additional data collection was not expected to generate new knowledge or themes (Morgan, 1997). One group included only current crystal users, one group only ex-users, and two were mixed. All groups were diverse in terms of HIV status and ethnicity. The study was also informed by a focus group of health professionals held in May 2002 that included a primary care physician specializing in HIV/AIDS, a hospital pharmacologist, a drug treatment program administrator, and an expert on local drug use trends.

Analyses and Interpretation

Focus group sessions were transcribed using pseudonyms to identify individual speakers. The transcribed texts were segmented and coded while retaining their links to the original speakers and contexts (Leap, 1996; Miles and Huberman, 1994) using QSR N6 text analysis software. As this was an exploratory study, the coding themes emerged from the data following a constructivist-oriented grounded theory approach (Charmaz, 2000; Glaser and Strauss, 1967). This inductive method entails synergistic iterations of data collection and analysis in an effort to build theoretical frameworks that explain situations and events as respondents experience them. Therefore, although the interview schedule targeted specific aspects of crystal use, including the motivations for use and any health or social consequences, the coding categories used in the analyses were not predetermined. The results of the author's analyses were reviewed by two of the study participants from different groups as a test of validity.

Results

The Lures of Crystal

As discussed earlier, the rise in the popularity of crystal in Miami has been both recent and rapid, by all accounts having been introduced to the gay scene around the millennium. To better understand how this drug became prevalent so quickly among gay men here, focus group participants were asked to discuss the circumstances surrounding men's initiation to the drug and the benefits they perceived from using it. There were three main patterns to respondents' motivations to use crystal: escaping loneliness, dealing with feelings of sexual unattractiveness, and lowering sexual inhibitions. In a more general sense, these problems appeared to stem from deep-seated feelings of being unloved and unlovable.

Avoiding loneliness and alienation. Focus group participants were unanimous in attributing pervasive drug use among gay men to the social difficulties they face in a homophobic culture. Those problems usually started within men's neighborhoods and families while they were growing up. But men said that the same cultural norms that make growing up gay a difficult, often secretive process contribute to long-term difficulties with intimate relationships. Difficulty with self-disclosure to a partner is exacerbated by the lack of social and institutional support in either gay or mainstream cultures for long-term gay couple relationships. The participants in one focus group shared the following exchange:

> Participant A: What's missing in most of our relationships [is] the commitment . . . that dirty word, *love.* Having somebody there for you. And so I think a lot of people turn to drugs because what we're looking for is just acceptance.

> Participant B: We don't have things like marriage, domestic partner benefits, *any* legal protections as gay couples. So, we're vacillating from having been oppressed to where we're busting out of the closet and we're taking it to the other extreme. I mean, take it on an individual basis: if you're in high school and college, if you're gay, you keep that very much under wraps. And if anything, you go out of your way to keep people from thinking that you might be gay. Then, say you move to a big city where you can be openly gay, you go all out and you go overboard.

In this context, drug use serves as an escape from an unshakable sense of being alone, unacceptable, and unloved; crystal emerged on the Miami scene as the newest way to avoid those realities. As one 38-year-old Anglo put it,

> Despite all the progress in gay rights and everything related to being gay, the reality of it is that, for a lot of gay men, reality still is fairly unpleasant. Crystal fixes that. Or at least it makes it seem that way.

In addition to being an escape, drugs often provide the "courage" necessary to overcome fears of rejection that surface when trying to meet sexual partners. A 50-year-old white man described his need for human connection and the usefulness of crystal in facilitating that:

> I do not have a family. I have no mother, no father, no sister, no brother, no aunts, no uncles, no cousins. So I don't worry what anybody thinks of me because I know I am alone and nobody really cares, you know? I get overwhelmed sometimes by the sense of being so alone in the world that it just becomes so overwhelming to me, and drugs and any kind of mind-altering substance can kind of take that sense away of just being so alone. I can say that when I am on the drug it's easier for me to reach out and just pull somebody into my home, and they'll spend the night and I take them back to where I met them in the morning. I have no illusions that they are probably a crackhead prostitute, you know, from [neighborhood], but it kind of fills the void for me for that evening. And I don't really care what anybody says, it fills the need for human interaction.

This environment is even further complicated by men's isolation *within* a subculture in which drugs are such a common form of escape. A 33-year-old Anglo said:

> I have been at the beach since 1990, and I really had done well not to get so wrapped up in the scene, or the group. I went out and drank every now and then, and every now and again I would do coke or take a roll of ecstasy, whatever. And then right around the millennium, I don't know what happened, but I felt almost defeated by it. Like if you can't beat them, join them. I mean, literally, it was stay home and do absolutely nothing or be in that crowd. I was doing ecstasy and K[etamine] all the time and then that high wasn't enough for me, so next crystal came into the picture.

Dealing with aging and illness. If mainstream American culture debases sex between men, gay ghetto cultures tend to value sexual attractiveness and prowess to a degree that is unreachable for many men (Kurtz, 1999a; Levine, 1998; Signorile,

1997). Aging and illness exacerbate those worries, and represented a second broad set of concerns that led men to experiment with crystal. The doctor with a primarily gay HIV/AIDS medical practice noted that:

> I see guys, when they get into their late thirties and early forties, that's when they get into real trouble. It's this change-of-life gay thing. "I'm in my late thirties, early forties; I've got to get everything I can get now before my hair falls out. Yeah, I've got to do it now before I'm no longer a commodity." And they just get annihilated. See, guys in their twenties, they call it partying. They take ecstasy before they go to [dance club]. These guys in their late thirties are the ones that are doing the, "I need a little bit of this, a little bit of that," and they think they're chemists. They do one little thing, too much of something that doesn't balance out something else, and they're in trouble.

As an example of this "mid-life-crisis" problem, an Anglo in recovery from crystal described the circumstances under which he first tried the drug:

> I'm 49, so at my age, when you get an 18- or 19-year-old who's like, "Hey, I'm yours, just try this," you try it. And we were in the right places where the owners of the bars would come over and meet and greet, and we met stars, and we met people with money, and all of those people do drugs here. And they all offered us drugs. I used to have a penthouse on [street name]. I'd have people show up that I didn't even know, and they'd show up with this bag, and say, "Oh, come on try it, I know you'll like it." It gives you the mentality that you're someone you're not.

Concerns about physical attractiveness brought on by illness also provided the impetus for some men's experimentation with crystal. A 38-year-old white man described his experience:

> I was diagnosed with HIV in 1991, and then in '93 was diagnosed with an HIV-related cancer and I wound up having major surgery and chemotherapy. It was a pretty brutal, long-term kind of thing. I took a good two years to sort of recover, physically at least. I did not want to deal with the mental part, even though I knew

I really needed to. At that point, when I got sort of physically recovered, but not mentally, the drug use started. It was a way to sort of numb the pain, to deal with the body issues that come with it. They sometimes say that people that were fat all their lives and lose weight look in the mirror and they still see a fat person. Well, I still saw somebody who was emaciated, with tubes hanging out of him and all of that stuff. It took a long time to get to the point to where I felt viable and sexually attractive again. Crystal did wonders towards making that happen.

Unbridled sex. As described earlier, crystal has been described by many gay men as increasing sexual arousal and lowering inhibitions. Opposing cultural value systems—the mainstream cultural debasement of sex between men as dirty versus the high valuation within gay ghetto subcultures of sexual variety and freedom—produce conditions under which lowering one's sexual inhibitions is often a goal in itself. All respondents in this study had engaged in sex while using crystal, and all but four of them had done so in group settings. A 33-year-old Latino explained why so much of gay men's sex on crystal is in groups:

> The more the merrier, I mean it's just more, it's sexual. You have a voracious appetite. Maybe you see other people having an orgy . . . that appeals to you. If you're watching porno, it's great to see 15 guys fucking in [a] room, or whatever. And, you wanted to do that, but you just couldn't. I mean, I could personally never go to a bathhouse if I wasn't cracked out of my skull, you know? And so the drug allows me to do things I would never be able to do without it.

A 38-year-old ex-user added that there are practical reasons related to the psychological effects of the drug that sex on crystal works better with more men rather than fewer:

> Being high on crystal in sexual situations, you need excessive amounts of input, of stimulation, just to keep that end of the buzz going. And the chances of getting that to the degree you need with one person over an extended period of time are not too good. You go through phases where you're really into doing

this, then you're into phases when you're really into playing with the VCR and seeing what you can do with that. The most important thing for you is that you are doing it with other people who are of the same mindset, but also at the same level of buzz. It does not matter who you are having sex with, near, or whatever, as long as they are just as high as you and on the same thing. That becomes your overriding concern.

The Tragedies of Meth

Men in recovery described using crystal for various lengths of time before they experienced serious problems. Some had been users for as long as 8–10 years before things got out of control, while others managed only for a few months. Those still using generally confined their use to weekend binges and reported being able to manage their daily lives pretty well, although most of them also experienced some problems. Like the original motivations for using crystal, the events that led men to try to stop using the drug revolved around personal relationships and sex. In contrast to respondents' initial perceptions, crystal was ultimately destructive of both kinds of experience.

Isolation and lost personal relationships. If making "connections" was the common thread in men's stories of their initiation to crystal, regular use of the drug became a barrier rather than an aid to social involvements. Friendships with non-users were early casualties of the drug for many men. A 33-year-old Hispanic man said:

When I came from work on Friday, crystal took me away from friends and took me away from normal things you do in life. I said, "I got my crystal, I'll go into my AOL and that's my company."

Another Latino described how using the drug became a substitute for dating:

It gets to the point where you feel like people are against you. Well, let me say that I've messed up my relationships because I've chosen to be on crystal meth, and then I start thinking to myself, "You know what, I really don't need a relationship." Where before the initial high I was thinking, "Oh yeah, I'm going to have a relationship with this guy, so let me [go meet him]." I've lost many relationships because of my stupid high. Because my mind gets so high up there that I start thinking to myself like, "I don't need someone to make me happy, I can make myself happy." Then afterwards I fucking regret it and I start crying and I feel like shit, you know?

The sexual adventurism and insatiability that served initially to gratify users created insurmountable problems for several men's long-term relationships as well. As one 42-year-old Latino related:

I started to use crystal when I was in a relationship, which I was in for twelve and a half years. Crystal wasn't so much related to sex in the beginning, and then sex became a lot of it. We had sex for a long time, long hours. We already had intimacy because we were lovers for so long, so it was a lot of fun. Then, when we started having problems in the relationship, that's when the crystal use would be a problem. We'd go and start having sex with other guys and having three-ways and four-ways and having guys come to the house. With the internet, that's when we really started going out there and having more partners. That's when we started breaking loose from our relationship, because I'd be working and he would still be on the crystal high, and he would come home looking for sex. And I wanted to do the same thing he did. So we started going to the bathhouse. We started going together, me and him, holding hands and finding partners that we liked. Then that didn't work after a while so it was like, "Okay, you get a room and I'll get a room." And then after that, the crystal just made it worse, because you were never satisfied, but at the same time it was hot sex.

In addition to romantic relationships, several men reported losing their jobs or businesses because crystal use interfered with reporting to work on time, their judgment on the job, and their trustworthiness in the eyes of others. Paranoia was another frequently cited complaint, which led to increasing isolation even from the sex scenes that respondents initially found so "enlightening" and "liberating." As one 36-year-old Hispanic man explained:

And now, it's like fucking sit in front of my computer. You can literally sit there and it's like, "Shit, it's two days later." I've sat there and drank two 2 liter bottles of Diet Coke and I haven't even got up to pee in twenty-four hours. And whacked off, literally whacked off sitting watching the same porno tape that you rented four days ago, twenty times, over and over again, let it rewind, you know, like you've got this parade of men coming in and out of your house. Thank God for auto rewind, it goes right back to the beginning, you don't even have to get up.

Finally, if crystal initially made men feel better about their physical appearance, the direct physical effects of using it eventually kept many long-term users out of the public eye. A 41-year-old Latino said:

One thing with crystal use is that people tend not to see it too much. People who get sucked into crystal use very, very quickly drop out of sight. You don't see what happens to them. You don't see that they've plucked all the hair out of their eyebrows. You don't see the sores on their skin. You don't see the sunken-in cheeks. You don't see their pupils bigger than their whole head. You don't see that really ugly thing, the ugly, physically ugly side of it, because people who get like that have long since disappeared.

Sexual risks and HIV/sexually transmitted infections (STI). If crystal made for uninhibited sex, it also led many to take sexual risks that they would not have if they had not been high on the drug. Many focus group respondents cited health problems, including HIV/STIs, as the critical signal that crystal was taking their lives out of control. The consensus among all of the groups was that men having sex while high on crystal are very unlikely to use condoms or to inquire as to the HIV status of their partners. One HIV-positive 44-year-old Anglo, who began experimenting with crystal after moving from New York following the breakup with his long-time partner, recalled the first sex-on-crystal party he attended:

My [internet] profile always says I had [HIV]. I'm pretty up front about it. And then, you know, it ends up that 5 or 6 people are there that evening and there was a lot of unprotected sex. It freaked me out

because I had really not been around that. Even though I'm not, you know, naive. And I know that had been going on for a while, but not to the level of not really caring of how or who you're having sex with. They didn't even talk about it. That's why I think this drug, it, you know, you don't even care.

Another echoed:

There can be a bowl of condoms sitting right in the middle of the bed and they're not going to get used. Most people on crystal, it's been my experience, it's like saying, "Here, have a 22-pound turkey."

One man in his mid-30s who expressed constant panic over becoming infected, as well as a high level of personal commitment to safe sex, talked about the way he felt after a weekend on crystal:

If you're HIV negative, at the end of it all you're, "God, I can't believe I just had sex with ten guys in two days or whatever." You come with that guilt. I'm not so worried about how much money I spend on the meth, I'm worried, "Did I . . . , I wonder if I was safe to do that?" That's my thing. It's like those two have to be definitely intertwined to show that one does lead to the other. And Miami Beach is a hotbed case in point.

A fourth participant recounted the frightening story of a friend who thought he could place the exact moment of his HIV infection at a sex-on-crystal party:

On crystal, certain things that aren't normally high risk become high risk. When you are having sex for three days straight, and have been masturbating three days straight, and you maybe ran out of lube two days into that, and now you've got a big raw spot on the side of your dick because you just can't manage to leave it alone. And then, somebody manages to get you hard enough to get off . . . I have a friend who's a top, has never put himself on the receiving end of anal sex. He seroconverted once at a party when people were doing crystal. He had sort of rubbed a raw spot on the side of his dick. Somebody came, and he said he remembers reaching down and grabbing a handful of it, because it was the closest thing to use as lube, put it on his dick, and felt a burn, because he had just put something on a raw spot on his skin, and he said it burned a memory in his brain, that that's how he got infected. So even normally, some of the low risk behaviors can—on crystal, because of the type of activity and situations you're in—it can make low risk activity suddenly become high risk. And, to be quite honest, you are with a lot of high-risk people. You know, these are people who . . . people who have lots of sex on crystal eventually are going to be positive, given enough time. It is the rare person who will not at some point succumb, or forget, or be too tweaked to have any decent judgment to exercise. You know you're in a very concentrated viral pool.

Return to reality. In addition to leading to increased risks for HIV and STIs, the experience of sex on crystal became less fulfilling with time. A 34-year-old Latino described the transition he made from his first perceptions of sex on crystal to his now-sober assessment:

For me, once I got into the bathhouse it was amazing. Just walking there and having all these people just walking around. It was like a connection. It was just a spiritual . . . I mean, we were attracting each other and you felt good. It just felt like a connection. You knew that if you'd find it, that that would be the connection to get you to what you needed. In my case I needed what I thought was intimacy. For those twelve hours I thought I was in love. That's why I know the lie. I have no desire to go back to the lie, because I've tasted the truth.

A 46-year-old white man who still participates in the sex-on-crystal scene acknowledged that it didn't take long for him to understand the true nature of the "connection" he is making with other men:

When I first signed up on one of the "party and play" websites, I posted a picture of my face on my profile. I wasn't getting so many hits. When I posted a picture of my dick instead, then I became really popular right away.

Another participant, a 36-year-old Latino, explained that his moment of realization that he needed to quit the drug occurred during a sex-on-crystal party:

At first it was a really [good] drug high, which made for really good sex. Then after a while you realize you just not getting high any more. You have lost your ability to respond to the drug. And you also wake up one day and realize that I am not really having sex with people, I am just having sex near people. I did not like what I was seeing, I did not like what I was becoming. I realized there was just no good end to this. Taken to its logical conclusion, it was just going from bad to worse. I was then looking for a reason to stop.

Trying to Quit Crystal

Even when men reached the low point of understanding the damage that crystal was doing to their lives, quitting the drug was a very difficult passage. The first hurdle was the physical and emotional reaction to coming down from the drug, as explained by a 33-year-old Anglo:

For a while, deep down underneath it all, you still know you got that dread that this high is going to wear off. You're so high that you're like, "Shoot, this is going to be a rough one." In that few minutes in that particular day, that's when you lock the doors and turn on the answering machine. You lay down—that's the worst time, until you fall asleep. "Please let me pass out." That's why you don't stop doing it. Because as soon as you stop doing it, you'll have to deal with that horrible despair and depression. The way to avoid that is, you just don't come down.

But using crystal over even a short period of time also had profound effects on men's ability to distinguish reality from fantasy. A 38-year-old Anglo respondent related how the internalization of the crystal high as "normal" made quitting a tremendous challenge:

A lot of people don't realize exactly how quickly crystal becomes addictive. The thing that makes crystal so insidious is that, even if you were basically a mentally healthy, well adjusted, happy person - beforehand, the first couple of times after you do crystal it manages to convince you that the state you are in when you are high on crystal is the normal, desirable, natural state, and that what happens to you when you are off crystal is the abnormal condition that needs to [be] rectified. *That* becomes the abnormal state. What do you do when you're in an abnormal state? You fix it with something. It becomes this chase, you know, "If I could just do enough crystal, if I can manage to get enough of it into me, that will fix whatever is wrong." I don't think a lot of people are prepared for how fundamentally it changes the way you think on and off the drug.

Discussion

Limitations

The findings of this study may not be generalizable to gay men's experience in other cities. In fact, the difference in the timing and social context of the introduction of crystal to the Miami gay scene was a major impetus for the study. Also, Miami is known as an international center of tourism and entertainment—as well as a high drug trafficking area—and drug use may consequently be more highly normalized in this city than many others. This entertainment focus has been blamed for the dearth of gay community social support systems (Albin, 1995; Levin, 1996; Halden, 1996); gay men may well have a greater sense of isolation than in other locales. As well, the findings of this study may not be representative of the larger population of gay men in Miami who use crystal. Focus group participants were not randomly selected and may have been particularly motivated by the cash incentive or because their experiences with crystal meth were especially debilitating. Although not due to the study design, the men who did participate fell into a rather narrow age range. Further, the results of focus group research are dependent to varying degrees on the makeup of the individual groups, the engagement of the moderator, and the content of the interview schedule (Krueger, 1993). All of that said, the study included Anglo and Hispanic participants (the largest ethnic groups in Miami) as well as HIV-positive and negative men, and there was broad group-to-group validation (Morgan, 1997) of recorded patterns in the motivations and consequences of men's use of crystal.

Conclusions

The associations of crystal with the perceived enhancement of sexual experience and sexual risk-taking found here are confirmatory of other research among gay men. The present study also contributes new findings to the literature in several respects, however. First, the nature of the connection between crystal and sexual behavior as described by the participants appears to be complex, and to some extent quite specific to the individual. Some men said that they used crystal *in order to* be able to have sex or to engage in more diverse sexual activities. Sensation-seeking behavior (Kalichman et al., 1996) is implied in some of the cases, but other men explained that they were unable to ever have sex without being under the influence of some psychoactive substance. At the same time, Reback's (1997) finding that sexual response does not directly follow from the pharmacological effects of the drug was not contradicted here. Rather, men's intentions and expectations, their perceived HIV status, their emotional state, the extent of their experience with using crystal, and situational factors all appear to intertwine with the effects of the drug in ways that result in many men—including those with usually strong commitments to safe sex—engaging in risky behaviors. A multifactoral model of drug use and sexual risk such as that outlined by Ostrow (2000) is indicated.

Other motivations for using crystal described here fit well with Signorile's (1997) "cult of masculinity" thesis about the circuit party subculture (and for that matter, Levine's (1998) thesis about the "homosexual clones" of the 1970s)—that the strong focus on physical appearance and sexual performance is destructive of men's self-esteem, intimate relationships, and the enjoyment of a wide range of life activities. Many participants in the present study emphasized that, initially, crystal helped them to feel more attractive, sexually desirable, and socially connected.

The findings regarding the devastating consequences of crystal use described by the participants in this study break new ground. Paranoia and employment difficulties, both also noted by Semple et al. (2003), were cited here as common problems resulting from continued use of the drug. The extent of the isolation and loss of social relationships attributed by these men to crystal use have not been previously described in the literature, however. Earlier qualitative studies (Lewis and Ross, 1995; Reback, 1997) emphasized men's perceptions that the drug contributed to social bonding within the subculture. Here, even men who continued to use the drug were aware that their relationships to others during a crystal high were quite superficial. Those in recovery often attributed their efforts to quit to a realization that they no longer had any meaningful social support system.

At least in Miami, where the rise in the popularity of crystal coincided with the rapid decline of the dance scene, it might be argued that the sex-on-crystal subculture reveals more fully what the circuit party subculture was better able to hide—that many gay men feel isolated, often use drugs in an attempt to bond with others, and find that connectedness and intimacy remain elusive. This suggests that interventions to reduce drug use and sexual risks among this population may be more successful to the extent they address men's needs for—and skills at attaining—social connectedness to other individuals and to the broader community. As well, community level interventions that target subcultural norms of both drug use and safe sex, and expectations regarding both physical attractiveness and sexual performance, appear to be equally necessary.

References

Albin, G. (1995). To live and die in South Beach. *Out*, 73–77, 125–128.

Beck, J., and Rosenbaum, M. (1994). *Pursuit of Ecstasy: The MDMA Experience*. Albany, NY: State University of New York Press.

Brecht, M., O'Brien, A., von Mayrhauser, C., and Anglin, M. D. (2004). Methamphetamine use behaviors and gender differences. *Addictive Behaviors*, 29, 89–106.

Brown, E. (2002, April 29). Crystal ball. *New York Magazine*. Retrieved on March 12, 2003, from *http://www. newyorkmetro.com/nymetro/urban/gay/features/5948/index.html*.

Centers for Disease Control and Prevention, National Center for HIV, STD and TB Prevention and Divisions of HIV/AIDS Prevention (2002). *HIV/AIDS surveillance report: Year-end edition*, 13, 2–44.

Charmaz, K. (2000). Grounded theory: Objectivist and constructivist methods. In N. K. Denzin and Y. S. Lincoln (Eds.), *Handbook of Qualitative Research* (2nd ed., pp. 509–535. Thousand Oaks, CA: Sage Publications.

Chesney, M. A., Barrett, D. C., and Stall, R. (1998). Histories of substance use and risk behavior: Precursors to HIV seroconversion in homosexual men. *American Journal of Public Health*, 88, 113–116.

Clatts, M. C., Welle, D. L., and Goldsamt, L. A. (2001). Reconceptualizing the interaction of drug and sexual risk among MSM speed users: Notes toward an ethno-epidemiology. *AIDS and Behavior*, 5, 115–130.

Cohen, R. S. (1998). *The Love Drug: Marching to the Beat of Ecstasy*. Binghamton, NY: The Haworth Medical Press.

Darrow, W. W., Webster, R. D., Kurtz, S. P., Buckley, A. K., Patel, K. I., and Stempel, R. R. (1998). Impact of HIV counseling and testing on HIV-infected men who have sex with men: The South Beach health survey. *AIDS and Behavior*, 2, 115–126.

Dolezal, C., Meyer-Bahlburg, H. F. L., Remien, R. H., and Petkova, E. (1997). Substance use during sex and sensation seeking as predictors of sexual risk behavior among HIV+ and HIV-gay men. *AIDS and Behavior*, 1, 19–28.

Ekstrand, M. L., Stall, R. D., Paul, J. P., Osmond, D. H., and Coates, T. J. (1999). Gay men report high rates of unprotected anal sex with partners of unknown or serodiscordant status. *AIDS and Behavior*, 13, 1525–1533.

Frosch, D., Shoptaw, S., Huber, A., Rawson, R. A., and Ling, W. (1996). HIV risk among gay and bisexual male methamphetamine abusers. *Journal of Substance Abuse Treatment*, 13, 483–486.

Glaser, B. G., and Strauss, A. L. (1967). *Discovery of Grounded Theory: Strategies for Qualitative Research*. Hawthorne, NY: Walter de Guyter.

Gold, R., Skinner, M., and Ross, M. (1994). Unprotected anal intercourse in HIV-infected and non-HIV-infected gay men. *Journal of Sex Research*, 31, 59–77.

Halden, L. (1996, October 9). Community missing from Sobe center. *TWN*, 10.

Halkitis, P. N., and Parsons, J. T. (2002). Recreational drug use and HIV-risk sexual behavior among men frequenting gay social venues. *Journal of Gay & Lesbian Social Services*, 14, 19–38.

Halkitis, P. N., Parsons, J. T., and Wilton, L. (2003). An exploratory study of contextual and situational factors related to methamphetamine use among gay and bisexual men in New York City. *Journal of Drug Issues*, 33, 413–432.

Heredia, C. (2003, May 4). Dance of death: First of three parts: Crystal meth fuels HIV. *San Francisco Chronicle*, p. A1.

Ireland, K., Southgate, E., Knox, S., Van de Ven, P., Howard, J., and Kippax, S. (1999). *Using and 'The Scene': Patterns and Contexts of Drug Use Among Sydney Gay Men* [Research Monograph] (Vol. 7). Sydney, Australia: National Centre in HIV Social Research.

Kalant, O. J. (1966). *The Amphetamines: Toxicity and Addiction*. Toronto, Ontario, Canada: University of Toronto.

Kalichman, S. C., Heckman, T., and Kelly, J. A. (1996). Sensation seeking as an explanation for the association between substance use and HIV-related risky sexual behavior. *Archives of Sexual Behavior*, 25, 141–154.

Kirsch, M. M. (1986). *Designer Drugs*. Minneapolis, MN: CompCare Publications.

Klitzman, R. L., Pope, Jr., H. G., and Hudson, J. I. (2000). MDMA ("ecstasy") abuse and high-risk sexual behaviors among 169 gay and bisexual men. *American Journal of Psychiatry*, 157, 1162–1164.

Krueger, R. A. (1993). Quality control in focus group research. In D. L. Morgan (Ed.), *Successful Focus Groups: Advancing the State of the Art* (pp. 65–85). Newbury Park, CA: Sage Publications.

Kurtz, S. P. (1999a). *Without Women: Masculinities, Gay Male Sexual Culture and Sexual Behaviors in Miami, Florida*. Ann Arbor, MI: UMI Dissertation Services.

——. (1999b). Butterflies under cover: Cuban and Puerto Rican gay masculinities in Miami. *The Journal of Men's Studies*, 7, 371–390.

Kurtz, S. P., and Inciardi, J. A. (2003). Crystal meth, gay men, and circuit parties. *Law Enforcement Executive Forum*, 3, 97–114.

Leap, W. L. (1996). *Word's Out: Gay Men's English*. Minneapolis, MN: University of Minnesota Press.

Leigh, B. C., and Stall, R. (1993). Substance use and risky sexual behavior for exposure to HIV: Issues in methodology, interpretation, and prevention. *American Psychologist, 1993*, 1035–1045.

Levin, J. (1996, November 3). Gay identity, defined with defiance. *Miami Herald*, pp. I1–I5.

Levine, M. P. (1979). Gay ghetto. *Journal of Homosexuality*, 4, 363–377.

——. (1998). *Gay Macho: The Life and Death of the Homosexual Clone*. New York: New York University Press.

Lewis, L. A., and Ross, M. W. (1995). *A Select Body: The Gay Dance Party Subculture and the HIV/AIDS Pandemic*. London: Cassell.

Li, J., Stokes, S. A., and Woeckener, A. (1998). A tale of novel intoxication: Seven cases of gamma-hydroxybutyric acid overdose. *Annals of Emergency Medicine*, 31, 723–728.

Mattison, A. M., Ross, M. W., Wolfson, T., and Franklin, D. (2001). Circuit party attendance, club drug use, and unsafe sex in gay men. *Journal of Substance Abuse*, 13, 119–126.

McKirnan, D. J., Vanable, P. A., Ostrow, D. G., and Hope, B. (2001). Expectancies of sexual 'escape' and sexual risk among drug and alcohol-involved gay and bisexual men. *Journal of Substance Abuse*, 13, 137–154.

McNall, M., and Remafedi, G. (1999). Relationship of amphetamine and other substance use to unprotected intercourse among young men who have sex with men. *Archives of Pediatric and Adolescent Medicine*, 153, 1130–1135.

Miami-Dade County Health Department. (2003). *Surveillance Profile June 2002/HIV*. Miami, FL.

Miles, M. B., and Huberman, M. (1994). *Qualitative Data Analysis*. Thousand Oaks, CA: Sage Publications.

Molitor, F., Truax, S., Ruiz, J. D., and Sun, R. K. (1998). Association of methamphetamine use during sex with sexual behaviors and HIV infection among non-injection drug users. *Western Journal of Medicine*, 168, 93–97.

Morgan, D. L. (1997). *Focus Groups as Qualitative Research* (2nd ed.). Thousand Oaks, CA: Sage Publications.

Ostrow, D. G. (2000). The role of drugs in the sexual lives of men who have sex with men: Continuing barriers to researching this question. *AIDS and Behavior*, 4, 205–219.

Paul, J. P., Stall, R., and Davis, F. (1993). Sexual risk for HIV transmission among gay/bisexual men in substance-abuse treatment. *AIDS Education and Prevention*, 5, 11–24.

Paul, J. P., Stall, R., Crosby, G. M., Barrett, D. C., and Midanik, L. T. (1994). Correlates of sexual risk-taking among gay male substance abusers. *Addiction*, 89, 971–983.

Perry, M. J., Soloman, L., Winett, R., Kelly, J., Roffman, R., Desiderato, L., Kalichman, S., Sikkema, K., Norman, A., Short, B., and Stevenson, Y. (1994). High risk sexual behavior and alcohol consumption among bar-going gay men. *AIDS*, 8, 1321–1324.

Reback, C. J. (1997). *The social construction of a gay drug: Methamphetamine use among gay and bisexual males in Los Angeles, Executive Summary, City of Los Angeles, AIDS Coordinator*.

Semple, S. J., Patterson, T. L., and Grant, I. (2002). Motivations associated with methamphetamine use among HIV+ men who have sex with men. *Journal of Substance Abuse Treatment*, 22, 149–156.

——. (2003). Binge use of methamphetamine among HIV-positive men who have sex with men: Pilot data and HIV prevention implications. *AIDS Education and Prevention*, 15, 133–147.

Signorile, M. (1997). *The Signorile Report on Gay Men: Sex, Drugs, and the Passages of life*. New York: Harper Collins Publishers.

Silcott, M. (1999). *Rave America: New School Dancescapes*. Toronto, Ontario, Canada: ECW Press.

Stall, R., and Wiley, J. (1988). A comparison of alcohol and drug use patterns of homosexual and heterosexual men: The San Francisco men's health study. *Drug and Alcohol Dependence*, 22, 63–73.

Stall, R. D., and Purcell, D. W. (2000). Intertwining epidemics: A review of research on substance use among men who have sex with men and its connection to the AIDS epidemic. *AIDS and Behavior*, 4, 181–192.

Stepick, A., Kurtz, S. P., Stepick, C. D., and Stepick, IV, A. (2003). *Syphilis and men who have sex with men: Miami-Dade county* [Research Monograph]. The Immigration & Ethnicity Institute, Florida International University.

Webster, R. D., Darrow, W. W., Buckley, A., and Kurtz, S. P. (1998). *The South Beach Health Survey: HIV Infection and Risky Sexual Behaviors Among Men Who Have Sex with Men*. Miami, FL: Florida International University, Department of Public Health.

Zule, W. A., and Desmond, D. P. (1999). An ethnographic comparison of HIV risk behaviors among heroin and methamphetamine injectors. *American Journal of Drug and Alcohol Abuse*, 25, 1–23.

For Discussion

1. Compare Steven Kurtz's research into methamphetamine use with Philip Jenkins' findings (this section).

2. Would anonymous surveys produce similar findings to those described in this article? Why or why not?

Part VII

Drugs and the Club Culture

During the 1960s, the use of drugs seemed to have leaped from the more marginal zones of society to the very mainstream of community life. No longer were drugs limited to the inner cities and the half-worlds of the jazz scene and the underground bohemian subcultures. Rather, their use had become suddenly and dramatically apparent among members of the adolescent and young adult populations of rural and urban middle-class America. By the close of the decade, commentators were maintaining that ours was "the addicted society," that through drugs millions had become "seekers" of "instant enlightenment," that drug taking and drug seeking would persist as continuing facts of American social life, and that there was a "drug revolution" in which the United States had entered a "new chemical age."

Whatever the ultimate causes of the drug revolution of the sixties, America's younger generations—or at least noticeable segments of them—had embraced drugs. The drug scene had become the arena of "happening" America; "turning on" to drugs to relax and to share friendship and love seemed to have become commonplace. And the prophet—the high priest, as he called himself—of the new chemical age was a psychology instructor at Harvard University's Center for Research in Human Personality, the late Dr. Timothy Leary.

Leary had been an advocate of the use of LSD, and his messages on the idea had been numerous and shocking both to the political establishment and to hundreds of thousands of mothers and fathers across the nation. In *The Realist*, a radical periodical of the 1960s, Leary hypothesized,

> I predict that psychedelic drugs will be used in all schools in the near future as educational devices—not only marijuana and LSD, to teach kids how to use their sense organs and other cellular equipment effectively—but new and more powerful psychochemicals. . . .

Perhaps most frightening of all to the older generation were Leary's comments to some 15,000 cheering San Francisco youths on the afternoon of March 26, 1967. As a modern-day Pied Piper, Leary addressed his audience:

> *Turn on* to the scene, *tune in* to what's happening; and *drop out* of high school, college, grad school . . . follow me, the hard way.

The hysteria over Leary, LSD, and other psychedelic substances had been threefold. First, the drug scene was especially frightening to mainstream society because it reflected a willful rejection of rationality, order, and predictability. Second, there was the stigmatized association of drug use with antiwar protests and anti-establishment, long-haired, unwashed, radical "hippie" LSD users. And third, there were the drug's negative effects, the reported "bad trips" that seemed to border on mental illness. Particularly in the case of LSD, the rumors of how it could "blow one's mind" became legion. One story told of a youth, high on the drug, who took a swan dive in front of a truck moving at 70 mph. Another spoke of two "tripping" teenagers who stared directly into the sun until they were permanently blinded. A third described how LSD's effects on the chromosomes resulted in fetal abnormalities. The stories were never documented and were probably untrue. What were true, however, were the reports of LSD "flashbacks." Occurring with only a small percentage of the users, individuals would re-experience the LSD-induced state, days, weeks, and sometimes months after the original "trip," without having taken the drug again.

Despite the lurid reports, as it turned out LSD was not in fact widely used on a regular basis beyond a few social groups that were fully dedicated to drug experiences. In fact, the psychedelic substances had quickly earned reputations as being dangerous and unpredictable, and most people avoided them. By the close of the 1960s, all hallucinogenic drugs had been placed under strict legal control, and the number of users was minimal.

In the years since, interest in LSD and other hallucinogens periodically re-emerges for short periods of time, and every few years a new "psychedelic" is introduced to the American drug scene.

During the 1990s and on into the twenty-first century, the "fad drugs" have been the "club drugs" or "dance drugs"—all of which have become associated with clubs, electronic music festivals, "circuit parties," and "raves." Raves are all-night dance parties, many of which occur without the appropriate licenses or permits required for holding public events. They are typically held in abandoned warehouses, airplane hangers, open fields, and other venues where large numbers of participants (up to 20,000) can be accommodated. Circuit parties, which have roots in both the rave subculture and AIDS fundraising efforts by the gay community, are annual events (with corporate sponsors) that can attract several thousand men (upwards of 15,000 to 25,000) with the allure of music, laser shows, and dancing. Although many circuit parties are one-night AIDS charity events, they often bloom into weeklong "unofficial" parties at local clubs and venues as well.

At many raves, clubs, and parties, some form of drug use is the norm. The most notable of the "club drugs" are MDMA (Ecstasy), Ritalin, amphetamines and methamphetamine, ketamine, GHB, LSD, cocaine, and a number of prescription drugs. The attraction of these drugs is the seemingly increased stamina that they engender, enabling partygoers to dance all night, as well as the intoxicating highs that are said to deepen the overall experience. Many users tend to experiment with a variety of club drugs in combination, often with alcohol, which can lead to unexpected adverse reactions.

MDMA (Ecstasy). The most popular of the club drugs, and a drug of choice among many youths and adults well beyond the dance subcultures, is MDMA (3,4-methylenedioxymethamphetamine). Better known as "Ecstasy," and sometimes referred to as "X," "N," "XTC," "E," "Adam," "Clarity," and "Lover's Speed," it is a synthetic compound related to both mescaline and the amphetamines and is commonly (however incorrectly) labeled as a hallucinogen.

Ritalin. The trade name for methylphenidate, Ritalin is a medication prescribed for children with attention-deficit/hyperactivity disorder (ADHD), an abnormally high level of activity. It is also occasionally prescribed for treating narcolepsy, a condition characterized by sudden attacks of deep sleep. Because of its stimulant properties, the abuse of the drug has become widespread. Adolescents and young adults reportedly use Ritalin for appetite suppression, wakefulness, increased attentiveness, and euphoria—effects that make it ideal for long nights of dancing (or in the case of some students, studying).

Ketamine. Ketamine, also known as "K," "Special K," "Vitamin K," and "Cat," is an injectable anesthetic that has been approved for both human and animal use in medical settings since 1970. Some 90 percent of the ketamine legally sold today, however, is intended for veterinary use. The drug gained popularity for abuse in the 1980s, when it was realized that large doses caused reactions similar to those of phencyclidine (PCP), such as dreamlike states and hallucinations.

Gamma hydroxybutyrate (GHB). Known on the street as "G," "Grievous Bodily Harm," "Liquid Ecstasy," and "Georgia Home Boy," GHB can be produced as a clear liquid, white powder, tablet, or in capsule form, and it is often used in combination with alcohol, making it extremely dangerous. GHB is often manufactured in homes with recipes and ingredients found and purchased on the Internet. The drug is typically abused either for its intoxicating/sedative/euphoriant properties or for its growth hormone-releasing effects for muscle development.

In the four articles in this section, LSD is discussed at length, as are the various "club drugs." High-risk behavior linked to club drug use is also explored: The nexus of circuit parties, drug use, and unsafe sex among gay men is detailed, as is the practice of Ketamine injection among youth in New York City. This part concludes with a "healthy settings" approach to nightclubs. Given that clubbing and drug use are popular activities among young people around the world, harm minimization initiatives are perhaps the best way to protect the health and lives of these individuals.

Additional Readings

Camacho, Alvaro, Scott C. Matthews, Brian Murray, and Joel E. Dimsdale. (2005) "Use of GHB Compounds Among College Students." *American Journal of Drug and Alcohol Abuse* 31 (4): 601–607.

Cohen, Richard S. (1998). *The Love Drug: Marching to the Beat of Ecstasy.* Binghamton, NY: The Hawthorn Press.

Henderson, Leigh A., and William J. Glass. (1998). *LSD: Still With Us After All These Years.* San Francisco: Jossey-Bass.

Holland, J. (Ed.). (2001). *Ecstasy: The Complete Guide. A Comprehensive Look at the Risks and Benefits of MDMA.* Rochester, VT: Park Street Press.

Leary, Timothy W. (1964). "Introduction." In David Soloman (Ed.), *LSD: The Consciousness-Expanding Drug* (pp. 1–21). New York: G. P. Putnam.

Owen, Frank. (2003). *Clubland: The Fabulous Rise and Murderous Fall of Club Culture.* New York: St. Martin's Press.

Schensul, Jean J., Sarah Daimond, William Disch, Rey Bermudez, and Julie Eiserman. (2005). "The Diffusion of Ecstasy Through Urban Youth Networks," *Journal of Ethnicity in Substance Abuse* 4 (2): 39–71. ✦

28
Rise of Hallucinogen Use

Dana Hunt

Dana Hunt traces the history and "re-emergence" of hallucinogens (e.g., LSD) in the United States. Drawing from basic survey data, Hunt notes that users of LSD tend to be white and from higher income groups. These data also show interesting trends. For example, Hunt notes that the percentage of persons who continue to use LSD (as opposed to using one time only for experimental purposes) is higher than in years past. The author also reviews other data and describes how patterns of LSD consumption differ across geographic regions in the United States and across various university and college settings.

In the public imagination, few periods in history have been so linked to a type of drug as the 1960s were to psychedelics, or hallucinogens. Widespread experimentation with drugs such as LSD, peyote, and psilocybin ("magic mushrooms") influenced many aspects of American pop culture—clothing, music, art, and language. Many people discussed but few followed Timothy Leary's advice to "tune in and turn on." Americans nevertheless tried psychedelic drugs at an unprecedented rate. According to the first National Household Survey on Drug Abuse (NHSDA) in 1972, 5 percent of Americans, almost all of them under the age of 18, had used psychedelics at least once; by 1979 lifetime prevalence was reported as 25 percent among young adults ages 18–25.

In the mid-1980s the use of psychedelics dramatically declined as cocaine became the drug of choice. Law enforcement seizures of LSD and other hallucinogens dropped precipitously, as did emergency room reports of adverse effects of hallucinogen use. How-

Issues and Findings

Discussed in this Brief: The history of hallucinogen use in the United States, a comparison of past and present user groups, and the impact of today's use and distribution patterns on law enforcement and public health and safety.

Key issues: Psychedelic drugs figured prominently in the hippie culture of the 1960s and 1970s, but their popularity declined during the 1980s. Recent studies reveal that hallucinogen use is on the rise in the 1990s, particularly among young adults of the same socioeconomic class as those who embraced these substances in previous decades. While current hallucinogen users seem to have little involvement in criminal activities, their drug-taking behavior places them at risk of harming themselves or others.

Key findings: Five sources were used to study the resurgence of hallucinogen use in this country. Data from these sources indicate that:

- Hallucinogens are relatively inexpensive, domestically produced, and not part of a network of distributors battling over markets or territory.

- Between 1991 and 1996, the percentage of Americans who had used psychedelics at least once in their lives grew from 6 to 14 percent.

- The percentage of high school seniors who believe that trying LSD or using it regularly is a "great risk" has declined significantly. Between 1991 and 1996, the percentage of seniors who said they disapproved of LSD use even once or twice fell from 90 to 80 percent.

- Thirty-four percent of college and university officials reported that hallucinogen use, particularly of LSD and psilocybin, is increasing on their campuses. Campus sources identified hallucinogen users today as mainstream students, not the more marginal or "hippie" students of the 1960s. Private and public campuses are equally likely to report hallucinogen use; religious schools are most likely to report little or no use. Larger campuses and institutions in urban areas report the widest range of drug use.

- The rise in hallucinogen use coincided with the growth of "raves," underground dance parties that cater to those under age 21.

- Systemic violence associated with the trafficking of heroin and cocaine has not been found with hallucinogen trafficking. The Drug Enforcement Administration reports that a relatively small number of producers and distributors located in Northern California have controlled the LSD market for a number of years.

- Repeated doses of hallucinogens or ingestion of multiple substances can produce highly adverse effects, including death. In addition, the auditory and visual distortion resulting from hallucinogen ingestion can last for 10 to 12 hours, thus endangering a user who drives, his or her passengers, pedestrians, and the occupants of other cars in proximity.

Target audience: Drug enforcement and drug treatment practitioners, college and university officials, high school administrators, public health officials, drug policy coordinators, and researchers. ✦

ever, by the early 1990s, interest in hallucinogens seemed to resurface among users whose demographic profile was similar to that of users in the 1960s—young men and women, often middle class, who typically declined to use heroin or cocaine. Reports of LSD use and distribution at places as surprising as the U.S. Naval Academy[1] highlight the return of these drugs among student populations. In addition to familiar hallucinogens, newer compounds have surfaced (see "Drugs Classified as Hallucinogens or Psychedelics").

This research in brief traces the historical use of hallucinogens in the United States and discusses the implications—in terms of law enforcement and public safety—of their current popularity among youths and young adults. To conduct the analysis for the study summarized here, researchers from Abt Associates Inc. relied on national survey data and two telephone surveys conducted specifically for this report (see "Data Sources").

Recent History of Hallucinogen Use

Hallucinogens are not new. Many naturally occurring substances such as peyote, psilocybin, or mescaline have long been used in cultural and religious contexts, and LSD was synthesized in Europe in the late 1930s. However, until the 1950s, when psychiatric researchers investigated the possible therapeutic value of LSD, recognition that certain drugs had hallucinogenic properties was very limited.

LSD did not receive popular attention until the early 1960s, when the late Timothy Leary and Richard Alpert, his colleague at Harvard University, began experimenting with the drug on themselves, other academics, local artists, and students. Leary was dismissed from Harvard for promoting LSD, but he continued to advocate its use as a positive mind-altering experience and identified psychedelics as part of a counter cultural or lifestyle choice. Although non-medical use of LSD continued to rise throughout the 1960s, scientific interest declined. In 1974 the National Institute of Mental Health concluded that LSD had no therapeutic use.[2]

The interest in LSD during the 1960s also prompted users to seek out naturally occurring substances that produced the same experiential effects. In fact, a variety of substances in nature produce transitory visual or auditory distortion, e.g., cannabis, thornapple, peyote, and jimsonweed. One of the oldest hallucinogens known to Western scientists is mescaline, a derivative of the peyote cactus, used for centuries in natural medicines and religious ceremonies. Substances such as peyote, mescaline, and a variety of exotic fungi (e.g., psilocybin mushrooms) can be smoked, brewed in tea, chewed, and incorporated into food. In the 1960s users exchanged and published recipes for preparation of hallucinogens through popular publications of the era.

How many people actually used hallucinogens during the 1960s and 1970s? In 1974, 17 percent of all Americans reported they had used a hallucinogen in their lifetime. Ac-

Figure 28.1

Use of Hallucinogens by High School Seniors

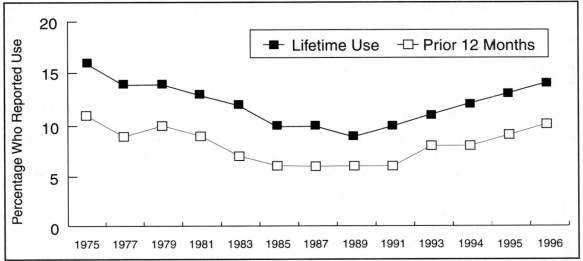

Source: Monitoring the Future Study, University of Michigan.

cording to NHSDA, lifetime prevalence among the young adult population rose to 20 percent in 1977 and 25 percent by 1979.

During the same period, other surveys made similar findings. In 1975 the Monitoring the Future (MTF) Study reported that 16 percent of high school seniors across the country had used hallucinogens at some point. A 1980 survey of New York State high school students showed that, by age 18, 25 percent had used hallucinogens.[3] These figures represented a remarkable rise in the use of drugs that less than 15 years earlier had been virtually unknown.

Who Is Using Hallucinogens Now?

Until the late 1980s and early 1990s, hallucinogens appeared to be out of vogue as the generation of original users aged. By 1982, 6 percent of adults over 26 years old reported that they had used hallucinogens at least once, but fewer than 1 percent reported use in the prior year.[4] In 1992, however, drug ethnographers reporting to *Pulse Check* began noticing increased availability of hallucinogens in many areas of the country. At the same time, researchers studying the emerging music and dance phenomena known as "raves" found LSD, MDMA, ketamine, and 2C-B playing a significant part in these activities.[5]

National survey data supported this observation. Figure 28.1 shows high school seniors' self-reported hallucinogen use for selected years of the MTF study. As these data indicate, the first year (1975) of the survey produced the highest lifetime use (16 percent), followed by a gradual decline that continued until the end of the 1980s. In 1991 the percentage reporting lifetime use again began to rise, reaching 11 percent in 1993, 13 percent in 1995, and 14 percent in 1996. Use in the prior 12-month period also declined throughout the 1980s, reached a low of 6 percent in 1985, then rose to 8 percent in 1993 and 1994, 9 percent in 1995, and 10 percent in 1996. Figure 28.2 indicates that LSD has typically been the most commonly used hallucinogen, although a similar but smaller rise in the use of any hallucinogens is also apparent.

Data from a 1992 Dade County, Florida, survey showed an even higher level of use among high school and college students. The Dade County student survey indicated that 17 percent of high school seniors reported using LSD at least once, a figure almost five times the 1991 level and considerably higher than the level reported in the national MTF study.[6]

In recent years, increased hallucinogen use has been concentrated primarily among white students, a group that has the highest rates of use (both lifetime and annual) for hallucinogens, inhalants, and tranquilizers. According to the 1994 national survey of high school students, 8 percent of white seniors reported using LSD in the prior 12 months compared with less than 1 percent of African-American and 5 percent of Hispanic seniors. Use also appears to be related to so-

cioeconomic status (SES). Data indicate that as the overall use level of LSD began to increase in the late 1980s and early 1990s, a positive relationship between socioeconomic status and use emerged. Students from the highest income groups are now twice as likely as those from the lowest SES group to have used LSD in the previous 12 months. This relationship, however, has nothing to do with price; the cost of hallucinogens is lower than that of both cocaine and heroin.[13]

Although interest in hallucinogens is resurgent, it is difficult to quantify use that

Drugs Classified as Hallucinogens or Psychedelics

The terms "hallucinogen" and "psychedelic" refer to both synthetic and organic substances that can produce visual, auditory, and tactile distortions in users. The group of drugs so designated generally includes:[7]

- LSD (d-lysergic acid diethylamide) and Nexus (4-bromo-2, 5 dimethoxyphenethylamine)— synthetic or laboratory-derived substances that at varying dosages produce degrees of perceptual distortion. LSD is most often soaked into patterned paper, though it may also be distributed in tablet, crystalline, or liquid forms. Nexus is structurally related to mescaline and produces sensory distortion lasting 4 to 8 hours.

- Mescaline, peyote, bufotenine, belladonna, and various fungi—substances derived from plants or other sources in nature that, when smoked, eaten, or otherwise ingested, quickly produce altered perceptual states.

- PCP (phencyclidine) and ketamine hydrochloride (Special K)—central nervous system agents that produce anesthetic, analgesic, and hallucinogenic effects.[8] These substances were originally tested in humans for their anesthetic use during minor surgery, but use was eventually restricted to the tranquilization of large animals in veterinary medicine. PCP and ketamine appear most often in powder form ("dust"), but they can also be found as liquids.

- MDMA (methylene dioxymethamphetamine), or Ecstasy—a synthetic methamphetamine compound that produces both psychedelic and

stimulant effects. MDMA was used clinically until 1988, when the Food and Drug Administration reclassified it as a Schedule I controlled substance (i.e., one with no approved use) because of its abuse potential. MDMA is most often found in the form of tablets or capsules.

Hallucinogens are defined more by the effects they produce than by any common chemical structure. In part the term "hallucinogen" refers to a drug's ability to distort reality. Although persons with psychotic disturbances may hallucinate without an external stimulus, normal individuals can induce the same (but temporary) effect using hallucinogenic drugs.[9] Hallucinogens as a group produce varying levels of visual, auditory, and tactile distortions and/or "out of body" sensations. As with all drugs, the intensity of effect depends not only on ingestion of a specific drug and dose but also on the user's perception or expectation of the experience.[10]

Hallucinogens differ in several ways from other commonly abused drugs such as heroin or cocaine. Although their reality-distorting effects may make them attractive and reinforce repeated usage, most hallucinogens are not physiologically addictive in the same way that opiates or even sedatives are, that is, if tolerance is established, hallucinogens do not produce long-term physiological craving after their effects have worn off.[11] They also differ in the duration of drug action. Unlike the effects of cocaine, which last for only minutes, and those of heroin, which last for a couple [of] hours, the active effects of hallucinogens can continue for several hours. Only methamphetamine can produce a similar long-lasting effect from a single ingestion. ✦

Figure 28.2

Prior-Year Use of Hallucinogens by High School Seniors

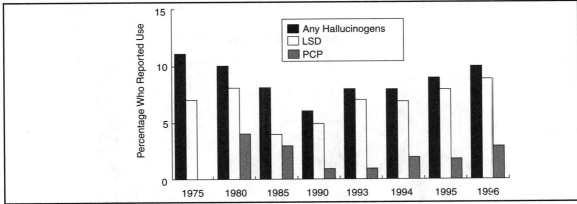

Source: Monitoring the Future Study, University of Michigan.

Data Sources

Data for this report came from the following five sources:

- **National Household Survey on Drug Abuse**. First conducted in 1971, NHSDA is supported by the Substance Abuse and Mental Health Services Administration and is a national probability sample of household members 12 years and older. Respondents are interviewed about their current and past use of a wide range of illegal and legal drugs, including alcohol.

- **Monitoring the Future Study**. Supported by the National Institute on Drug Abuse (NIDA) and conducted annually since 1975, this survey administers questionnaires to a national probability sample of high school seniors in the United States. Questionnaires are also mailed to a sample from each of the previous senior class samples for up to 10 years after high school. Since 1991 the survey has also included samples of 8th- and 10th-grade students.

- *Pulse Check*. Conducted quarterly since 1992 and semiannually since spring 1996 by the Office of National Drug Control Policy (ONDCP), *Pulse Check* gathers information from telephone interviews with 15–20 ethnographic sources, 10–15 police agencies, and 50–60 drug treatment providers from across the country. While not a probability sample, it is nevertheless a timely report from persons working "on the front lines" of law enforcement and drug abuse research and treatment.

- **Survey of colleges and universities**. A random sample of 4-year colleges and universities was developed for this analysis. The sampling was distributed evenly between public and private institutions in all geographic areas. Sources knowledgeable about student drug use (on-campus drug program officers or counselors, student health directors, student affairs officers) were interviewed by telephone in October 1995. Questions were asked about which drugs were used most often on campus and what types of students were using them; if applicable, more detailed information was sought on hallucinogen use. Of the 100 institutions sampled, approximately 50 were determined to be eligible for inclusion in this report.[12]

- **Survey of drug treatment programs for adolescents**. The 1992 NIDA National Drug Abuse Treatment Unit Survey was also used as a framework to develop a random sample of adolescent drug treatment programs from across the United States. Twenty-five program or clinical directors were interviewed by telephone using the same guidelines described above for college sources. ✦

Figure 28.3

Prior-Year Use of Hallucinogens, Cocaine, and Marijuana by High School Seniors

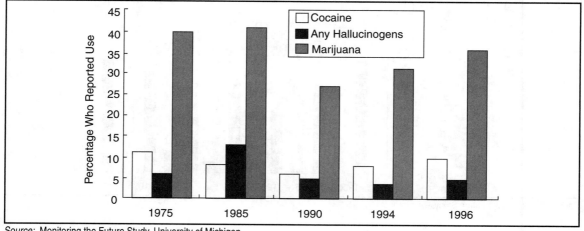

Source: Monitoring the Future Study, University of Michigan.

continues beyond initial experimentation or to determine whether the rise in hallucinogen use is part of a general upswing in the use of all illegal drugs. Figure 28.3 shows trends in hallucinogen, cocaine, and marijuana use among high school seniors in the year prior to the survey.

The overall increase in illicit drug use by teens and young adults is driven by significant growth in the use by high school students of marijuana, hallucinogens, and, to a lesser degree, crack cocaine. From 1993 to 1996, the percentage of 8th, 10th, and 12th graders who reported using marijuana in the previous year rose steadily, reaching 18 percent, 34 percent, and 36 percent respectively. Daily use of marijuana also rose in all high school grades surveyed. As is true for marijuana, the figure in 1996 for prior-year use of hallucinogens continued to rise to levels statistically and significantly higher than 1995 levels among all grades.

The high school senior survey provides data on noncontinuation rates of drug use.[14] Unfortunately, data show that many of these teens persist as users beyond experimentation. Since 1992 noncontinuation rates for LSD have been the lowest reported in 10 years;[15] that is, more students are starting to use hallucinogens and fewer are stopping.

Not surprisingly, data on juveniles involved with the criminal justice system show even higher rates of illicit drug consumption. Figure 28.4, which reports data from 12th graders who have been arrested and tested for drugs as part of the juvenile Drug Use Forecasting (DUF) program and from the MTF study, shows that use of all illicit drugs has increased in the 1990s, but use of LSD and stimulants has doubled. Renewed interest in hallucinogens coincides with a perception of reduced risk and greater peer support for use. The high school survey data indicate a significant decline in the percentage of seniors who feel that trying LSD or using it regularly is a "great risk." In 1991, 90 percent of high school seniors reported that they disapproved of LSD use even once or twice. That number had dropped to 83 percent in 1994 and to 80 percent in 1996. The percentage of high school seniors who said none of their friends used MDMA decreased significantly from 88 percent in 1990 to 76 percent in 1996.

The report also indicates that hallucinogens are increasingly accessible to high school students. In 1992, 45 percent of high school seniors described LSD as "easy or fairly easy to get"; in 1996 that percentage had risen to 51 percent. The survey authors speculate that although attention has been focused on co-

Figure 28.4

Thirty-Day Prevalence for Twelfth Graders, by Drug and Year

Percentage Reporting Past 30-Day Use	1991	1992	1993	1994	1995
Any illicit drug?					
DUF	37.0	44.3	53.7	58.2	62.7
MTF	16.4	14.4	18.3	21.9	23.8
Any illicit drug other than marijuana?					
DUF	12.1	14.5	16.9	19.1	22.3
MTF	7.1	6.3	7.9	8.8	10.0
Marijuana					
DUF	34.9	41.4	51.0	55.2	59.5
MTF	13.8	11.9	15.5	19.0	21.2
LSD					
DUF	3.3	4.3	5.1	5.0	7.2
MTF	1.9	2.0	2.4	2.6	4.0
PCP					
DUF	2.0	1.8	1.9	1.8	3.7
MTF	0.5	0.6	1.0	0.7	0.6
Cocaine					
DUF	4.5	5.3	5.9	5.7	4.9
MTF	1.4	1.3	1.3	1.5	1.8
Crack					
DUF	3.5	2.6	2.5	4.0	5.5
MTF	0.7	0.6	0.7	0.8	1.0
Heroin					
DUF	0.2	0.3	0.4	0.5	1.1
MTF	0.2	0.3	0.2	0.3	0.6
Amphetamine/Stimulants					
DUF	2.9	4.0	6.2	10.2	7.9
MTF	3.2	2.8	3.7	4.0	4.0
Methamphetamine/Ice					
DUF	2.3	3.0	4.6	8.1	7.8
MTF	0.6	0.5	0.6	0.7	1.1

Sources: Drug Use Forecasting Program and Monitoring the Future Study.

caine and crack for many years, little media coverage has been devoted to hallucinogens and fewer opportunities have existed to observe their adverse effects. This situation may have added to "generational forgetting"[16]— today's teens knowing less than teens from the previous generation—to the point that hallucinogens surpass cocaine in popularity for all groups except Hispanics.

NHSDA data (see Figure 28.5) depict a similar, although less dramatic, time trend than that reported in the MTF studies. In the first year of this survey (1972), 5 percent of youths under 18 said they had used a halluci-

nogen one or more times. That figure peaked by 1979 (7 percent of respondents under age 17 and 25 percent between the ages of 18 [and] 25), began to decline, and dropped dramatically for those under 25 in 1985. In the late 1980s and early 1990s, however, the trend began to change somewhat. Among young adults (ages 18–25), lifetime prevalence began to rise from 12 percent in 1985 to 15 percent in 1994. In the most recently published survey, 14 percent of respondents between the ages of 18 and 25 and 5 percent between the ages of 12 and 17 reported using a hallucinogen at least once. As is true for the

Figure 28.5

Lifetime Prevalence of Hallucinogen Use by Age

Age	1972	1977	1979	1982	1985	1991	1992	1993	1994	1995
12–17 Any Use (Hallucinogens)	4.8%	4.6%	7.1%	5.2%	3.2%	3.3%	2.6%	2.9%	4.0%	5.4%
18–25 Any Use (Hallucinogens)	–	19.8%	25.1%	21.1%	11.6%	13.2%	13.4%	12.5%	14.5%	14.1%
26–34 Any Use (Hallucinogens)	–	2.6%	4.5%	6.4%*	16.7%	15.5%	15.6%	15.9%	15.5%	15.2%
35+ Any Use (Hallucinogens)	–	–	–	–	2.2%	5.2%	5.2%	6.6%	6.2%	7.6%

* Includes all users over 26 years old.
Source: National Household Survey on Drug Abuse (1972–1995).

high school survey data, NHSDA data indicate that much of this increase has been among whites and Hispanics (see Figure 28.6). The greatest concentration of reported lifetime use is found among two groups: white youths ages 18–25 (19 percent) and Hispanics ages 18–25 (9 percent).

Although the NHSDA and MTF surveys show increases in hallucinogen use, particularly among the young, data from emergency rooms (ERs) across the country do not. The percentages of ER mentions for LSD or PCP in the Drug Abuse Warning Network (DAWN) are low (fewer than 0.01 percent); this has been the case throughout the past two decades. However, notable increases in ER mentions have been seen in four cities: Atlanta, Washington, D.C., Chicago, and Seattle. Although hallucinogens have long been known to produce some adverse reactions in users, particularly over time, the lower potency of today's hallucinogens may not produce acute incidents requiring emergency medical attention. There is increasing anecdotal evidence, however, that the lower dosage drug is simply being consumed more frequently than in the past.[17]

Variations Across the United States

National probability samples have limited ability to reflect recent changes in drug use because of the time needed to conduct the survey, analyze the results, and report the findings. Therefore, the following sources were used to examine hallucinogen use across the United States in 1996: the ONDCP *Pulse Check* series, Community Epidemiology Work Group (CEWG) at NIDA, and two telephone surveys conducted for this report. Although these sources reveal that a renewed interest in hallucinogens is national in scope, they also show regional variation. Epidemiologists reporting to CEWG from New York, Atlanta, San Francisco, Seattle, Miami, and cities in Texas noted increased hallucinogen use.[18] Other areas, such as New Orleans and Denver, report that LSD is widely available for purchase, but indicator data do not reflect any changes in use.

LSD is produced in domestic labs concentrated in Northern California and shipped by mail or couriers through what law enforcement officials describe as a well-established network of distributors.[19] *Pulse Check* and Drug Enforcement Administration (DEA) sources report that LSD is sold primarily in paper or blotter form, with each sheet divided into squares of single dose units containing approximately 25–60 micrograms of the substance. It may also be sold as "microdots" (small tablets) or in gelatin squares ("window panes"). A dose (approximately 55 micrograms) sells for $1–$10.

The unit dosages consumed by users in the 1990s are less concentrated than those taken in the 1960s—the heyday of LSD consumption—when dosages were typically 100–200 micrograms. In the San Francisco area, *Pulse Check* ethnographers report that users experience shorter "trips," lasting only a few hours, and milder hallucinogenic effects than was true of LSD trips 20 years ago. Interviews with rave-goers also indicate a milder and shorter effect from today's LSD.[20] However, Miami CEWG data show that users may increase the number of doses to make up for reduced potency, thus producing new patterns of use. LSD may also be combined or sequenced with other drugs to enhance or extend its effect. For example, one study describes young users who practice "candy-flipping," or combining in sequence MDMA or methamphetamine with LSD.[21]

Both *Pulse Check* and CEWG sources report user interest in naturally occurring hallucinogens such as peyote or mescaline. In the October 1994 *Pulse Check*, three sources reported that youths had come into emergency rooms exhibiting symptoms brought on by ingesting jimsonweed, a plant in the deadly nightshade family whose active ingredient, belladonna, has hallucinogenic properties. Even in relatively small quantities, however, it is generally toxic. Other drugs that have been mentioned in both sources include peyote, mescaline, psilocybin, and bufotenine, all of which have been relatively absent from the drug culture for many years.

New synthetic drugs have generated renewed interest in hallucinogen use. MDMA is one of the most popular of these newer drugs; other drugs that have surfaced in recent years include Nexus and ketamine. Ketamine use has been reported in New York for more than 2 years, and it is increasingly being used as a "club drug" in New Jersey, Delaware, Washington, D.C., Florida, and Georgia. Ketamine is packaged in baggies or capsules and sells for approximately $10–$20 per dose.

Hallucinogen Use on College Campuses

In October 1995 telephone surveys conducted with 59 college and university officials knowledgeable about student drug use indicated that hallucinogens, particularly

Figure 28.6

Lifetime Prevalence of Hallucinogen Use by Ethnicity

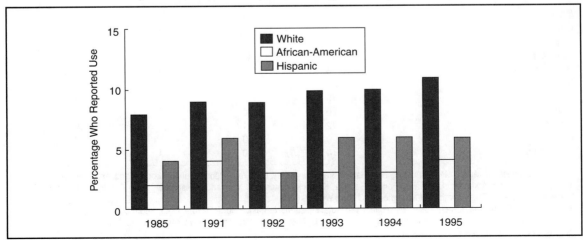

Source: National Household Survey on Drug Abuse.

LSD and psilocybin, are popular in many areas of the country. Of the campuses surveyed, 34 percent reported increasing hallucinogen use, 7 percent reported decreasing use, and 39 percent reported no change. Figure 28.7 shows the drugs used most frequently on campuses across the country. Alcohol and marijuana are the most commonly cited (83 and 78 percent, respectively). However, 44 percent of campuses reported student use of hallucinogens; all cited LSD and 57 percent cited psilocybin and MDMA as the specific hallucinogens students use. Officials at one large Midwestern university claimed that their own campus survey revealed that 10 percent of students had tried hallucinogens at some time, but only 2 percent had used one of these drugs in the prior 30 days. Similar figures from other campus surveys were reported, ranging from 3 percent to 19 percent lifetime prevalence. Many officials stressed that although hallucinogen use was appearing on campus, it was still confined to a small segment of students and dwarfed by marijuana and alcohol consumption. In several instances campus officials also believe that, although hallucinogen use has only recently resurfaced, it may already have peaked.

Campus sources reported that individuals of both genders and all ethnic groups in the student body are hallucinogen users, although the greatest interest seems to be concentrated among younger students. Unlike the 1960s, when hallucinogens were identified with the more marginal or "hippie" culture, today hallucinogens are used among mainstream students.

Private campuses were as likely as public ones to report hallucinogen use, and religious schools were least likely to do so. Because of student accessibility to the off-campus urban club scene, larger campuses and institutions in urban areas reported the widest range of drug use.

Young Users and Treatment

Drug treatment programs across the United States that specialize in treating substance abusers under 18 years old were surveyed about their current population of patients. These sources said their clients use a variety of drugs, although alcohol, marijuana, and hallucinogens (particularly LSD) are the most frequently abused substances. For most youths in treatment, hallucinogen consumption is part of an extensive drug use

Figure 28.7

"What Types of Drugs Are Used Most Often by Students on Your Campus?"

Drug	Region I[a] N = 15	Region II[b] N = 17	Region III[c] N = 11	Region IV[d] N = 16	Total N = 59
Opiates	0	0	1	1	2
Cocaine	1	4	7	4	16
Crack	1	5	1	1	8
Marijuana	12	12	11	11	46
Hallucinogens	2	8	6	10	26
Inhalants	2	0	2	1	5
Tranquilizers	2	0	0	1	3
Methamphetamine	3	0	3	6	12
Alcohol	15	12	11	11	49
Other	1	0	0	1	2
No drug use	1	4	0	4	9

[a]Region I: Connecticut, Maine, Massachusetts, New Hampshire, New Jersey, New York, Pennsylvania, Rhode Island, and Vermont
[b]Region II: Alabama, Arkansas, Delaware, Florida, Georgia, Kentucky, Louisiana, Maryland, Mississippi, North Carolina, Oklahoma, South Carolina, Tennessee, Texas, Virginia, Washington, D.C., and West Virginia
[c]Region III: Illinois, Indiana, Iowa, Kansas, Michigan, Minnesota, Missouri, Nebraska, North Dakota, Ohio, South Dakota, and Wisconsin
[d]Region IV: Arizona, California, Colorado, Idaho, Montana, Nevada, New Mexico, Oregon, Utah, Washington, and Wyoming
Source: Survey of Colleges and Universities.

history; rarely do counselors see adolescents who abuse only hallucinogens. Anecdotal reports from some counselors indicate as many as 80 percent of clients have used hallucinogens; others report diagnosing as many as three or four cases per week of adolescents with hallucinogen-related perceptual disorders. The anecdotal reports attribute the visual system damage to the number of "trips" (including consecutive multiple doses of LSD) that teens often take. The media have reported similar patterns of abuse among young party-goers who ingest large amounts of Ecstasy (seven or eight doses) that may result in long-term, harmful effects on mood, sleep, appetite, and impulse control.[22]

What Are 'Club Drugs'?

Hallucinogens are often reported as part of the "club drug scene"—a term that refers to the use of particular drugs by teens and young adults who frequent music or dance clubs geared to their age group. In general, these are the same youths found in the campus survey: young, often fairly affluent men and women who have limited histories of using drugs such as heroin or cocaine. Urban-area ethnographic sources for *Pulse Check* report hallucinogen use among patrons of the many nightclubs that cater to persons under 21 years of age. Many such clubs serve no alcohol and can attract clientele as young as 13 or 14 years old. In New York City, heroin or cocaine may also be part of the club drug scene, although this seems to be the exception. The most frequently reported club drugs are LSD, MDMA, Nexus, and ketamine. In fact, young club participants in Miami actively scorn "harder" drugs but embrace LSD, MDMA, and other hallucinogens as "safe."

A study conducted by Abt Associates Inc. in 1994 examined "raves," phenomena closely tied to the club culture, and the drugs that may be used there.[23] A rave is a large party where participants often dance all night to "house music," technically synthesized rhythms of 120–180 beats per minute played at earsplitting decibel levels. Raves were fashionable in Europe during the late 1980s and have become popular in the United States in recent years. They attract a predominantly middle-income audience, often high school and college students. Whereas they were once "underground"[24]—the whereabouts of the events passed by word of mouth—raves are now openly advertised and discussed on electronic mail services.

Although the music and frenetic activity of raves have little in common with the almost dreamy pace of the hallucinogen culture of the 1960s, other aspects of the phenomena indicate an active nostalgia for that era: its fashions, emphasis on the "spirituality" of attending raves, promotion of nonviolence, and the use of marijuana and a variety of hallucinogens.

Abt Associates Inc. researchers examined rave activity in New York and San Francisco, informally interviewing participants as well as organizers about various aspects of rave activity, including drug use.[25] They found that the drugs most commonly associated with raves are marijuana and hallucinogens, although methamphetamines and alcohol were evident. Among the hallucinogens, MDMA and LSD were the most popular drugs—the ones some participants associated with the spiritual ethos attached to the events. As was true in the earlier era of hallucinogen use, some rave participants associated a range of benefits, including personal enlightenment, with the use of these drugs. The researchers also found that participants were unaware of the possible harm that repeated or uncontrolled use could produce.

Implications for Law Enforcement and Public Safety

The nature of different drugs (e.g., physical effects produced, costs) is often directly linked to the problems they present for law enforcement. Stimulants (e.g., methamphetamines) and depressants (e.g., alcohol) produce unique psychopharmacological effects (such as agitation, paranoia, or irritability) in users that may make them more difficult for law enforcement officers to restrain. The expense of a drug may also predict users' involvement with income-generating crimes. One researcher characterizes three types of violence or crime associated with drugs:[26]

- Pharmacologic: crime related to a drug's pharmacological effects on the user
- Economic: crime associated with a drug's costs to the user
- Systemic: crime associated with trafficking of a drug

Hallucinogens have not been linked to pharmacologic crime primarily because of their sedative effects. They cost relatively little ($1–$5 per unit dose) for the long-lasting results they produce, and their use is concentrated among middle- to upper-income youths with greater access to funds, a fact that reduces the likelihood that economically driven crime would be associated with their use.

The systemic violence connected to heroin and cocaine trafficking has not been found with hallucinogen trafficking. DEA reports that a relatively small number of producers and distributors located in Northern California have controlled the LSD market for a number of years.[27] A handful of chemists, some of whom have been working since the 1960s and 1970s, synthesize the bulk of the drugs produced and distribute them throughout the country. Quantities are shipped from suppliers to known contacts (often on a prepaid basis) and distributed through established user networks. Although some local production of hallucinogens exists, the chemists or producers involved in such enterprises generally confine their products to local markets and therefore pose little threat to established traffickers. LSD may also be distributed at concerts, although ethnographic research indicates that much of the hallucinogen use associated with raves occurs prior to attendance.

Threats to the safety of users and those with whom they come in contact are major problems associated with hallucinogen use. Health risks for drugs such as MDMA include dehydration, appetite suppression, and heartbeat disruption. Adverse psychological reactions, which some users experience with high and/or repeated doses of hallucinogens, are well documented; they include psychotic episodes, panic disorder, and long-term sensory distortion.

In addition to health risks, concerns for public safety are related to hallucinogen use.

The use of multiple substances is troubling. Any of the club drugs taken alone can impair motor skills; in combination they can produce deadly synergistic effects. The enduring effects of drugs such as LSD or MDMA can pose special problems. For example, ingestion of a drug with the potential to cause visual and auditory distortion lasting 10–12 hours may mean that the user will drive home from a party while still under its influence. The opinion of one experienced [s]tate police source quoted in the October 1994 *Pulse Check* reflects a concern shared by several respondents: "Kids think they're fine to drive, but their reaction time is all off, and they get into trouble."

Summary

As crack has been the drug of the inner city for a decade, hallucinogens appear to be a popular drug among today's young, more affluent users. All sources reported their popularity among nonminority high school and college users who often reside outside the inner cities. The drugs are relatively inexpensive, domestically produced, and part of a stable, noncompetitive distribution network. Despite law enforcement efforts to disrupt the production and distribution of hallucinogens, a small number of manufacturers have provided a relatively steady supply, distributed through local user networks, for more than 20 years. Although rising use may not pose severe threats to law enforcement, it does present problems for public health officials in terms of the health and safety of young users who are rediscovering this family of drugs.

Author's Note

This study was conducted under cooperative agreement 94-IJ-CX-C007, awarded to Abt Associates Inc. by the National Institute of Justice.

Findings and conclusions of the research reported here are those of the author and do not necessarily reflect the official position or policies of the U.S. Department of Justice.

Notes

1. Bradsher, K. (1995) "All midshipmen drug tested after two caught with LSD." *New York Times*, October 18, A18.
2. Henderson, L., and W. Glass (eds.) (1994) *LSD: Still With Us After All These Years*. Lexington, MA: Lexington Books.

3. Kandel, D. (1982) "Epidemiology and psychological perspectives in adolescent drug use," *Journal of the American Academy of Child Psychology* 21(4):328–347.

4. Miller, J., et al. (1982) *National Survey on Drug Abuse: Main Findings*. Washington, D.C.: National Institute on Drug Abuse.

5. Harlow, D. (1994) "Raves and drug use: An exploratory study." A Research Application Review working paper for internal distribution prepared by Abt Associates Inc.

6. Community Epidemiology Work Group (1995) *Epidemiologic Trends in Drug Abuse*. Rockville, MD: National Institute on Drug Abuse.

7. There has long been debate whether marijuana and hashish should be included in the hallucinogen category because the active ingredient in both (tetrahydrocannabinol, or THC) produces some hallucinogenic effects. They were not included in this report.

8. Because PCP is often included in data sets with hallucinogens, it is included in this analysis even though PCP users are demographically different from other hallucinogen users. Its use is more geographically limited, and PCP use constitutes a small portion of reports in the hallucinogen category.

9. Szara, S. (1994) "Are hallucinogens psychoheuristic?" In G. Lin and R. Glennon (eds.), *Hallucinogens: An Update*. NIDA Research Monograph Series 146, Rockville, MD: National Institute on Drug Abuse, pp. 33–52.

   Some users report experiencing "flashbacks" of distorted perception long after the drug is taken, and these often long-delayed reactions are not well understood.

   Strassman, R. (1984) "Adverse reactions to psychedelic drugs: A review of the literature," *Journal of Nervous and Mental Disorder* 172:577–595.

10. Zinberg, N. (1984) *Drug, Set and Setting*. New Haven, CT: Yale University Press. Zinberg called this the impact of "set and setting" on drug use. The set is the expectation the user brings to the experience, e.g., the user is expecting to get high. The setting is the context in which the drug is taken—at a party, while alone, in the hospital. Both have a direct influence on the perception of its effect.

11. Glennon, R. (1994) "Classical hallucinogens: An introductory overview." In C. Lin and R. Glennon (eds.), *Hallucinogens: An Update*. NIDA Research Monograph Series 146, Rockville, MD: National Institute on Drug Abuse, pp. 4–33.

12. Institutions that offered almost exclusively graduate or continuing education programs were eliminated from the analysis in this report because they served a different, older student population than were found in 4-year institutions.

13. Johnston, L., P. O'Malley, and J. Bachman (1995) *National Survey Results on Drug Abuse from the Monitoring the Future Study (1975–1993)*. Rockville, MD: National Institute on Drug Abuse.

14. *Ibid.*, 54. Noncontinuation rates are calculated as the percentage of those who report that they have used a drug at least once in their lives but not in the 12 months prior to the survey.

15. *Ibid.*, 54.

16. *Ibid.*, 12.

17. Community Epidemiology Work Group, *Epidemiologic Trends in Drug Abuse*.

18. *Ibid.*

19. Drug Enforcement Administration (1995) "LSD in the Unites States." Drug Intelligence Report, Washington, D.C.: U.S. Department of Justice.

20. Harlow, "Raves and drug use: An exploratory study."

21. *Ibid.*

22. Blakeslee, S. (1995) "Popular drug may damage brain," *New York Times*, August 15, C5.

23. Harlow, "Raves and drug use: An exploratory study."

24. The underground nature of the initial raves had less to do with drug use and more to do with the fact that initial promoters, often not professional promoters or club owners, did not have permits to hold large gatherings.

25. Harlow, "Raves and drug use: An exploratory study."

26. Goldstein, P. (1985) "The drugs/violence nexus: A tripartite conceptualized framework," *Journal of Drug Issues* 15:493–506.

27. Drug Enforcement Administration, "LSD in the United States."

For Discussion

Legally, should hallucinogenic drugs be treated the same as cocaine and heroin? Why or why not?

Reprinted from: Dana Hunt, "Rise of Hallucinogen Use." In *National Institute of Justice Research Brief*, October 1997. ✦

29

Conceptions of Risk in the Lives of Club Drug-Using Youth

Brian C. Kelly

Considerable discussion has focused on the risks associated with using Ecstasy (MDMA) (e.g., depression, hyperthermia). In this chapter, Brian Kelly describes and compares folk (i.e., people who use the drug) and professional models of risks in relation to Ecstasy use. His study draws on data collected from a sample of young adults who reside in suburban areas of New York City and party in Manhattan. The author found that although folk and professional models of Ecstasy-related risk were similar, respondents tended to gauge risk in terms of their own personal experiences or the experiences of people within their social networks.

Conceptions of Risk in the Lives of Club Drug-Using Youth

As the lighting scheme shifted from staccato bursts of colors to the steady glow of blacklight, I spied Tony dancing rhythmically in the middle of the floor to the pulsing sound of house beats. I waded through the crowd of gesticulating bodies to catch up with him and see how the night had treated him to this point. Having noticed me snaking through the crowd, Tony grinned and pointed at me as I made my way over while he continued to dance. After greeting each other and exchanging the normal pleasantries, I asked him how the night was going for him. He told me that his *"roll"* was wearing off and he needed to take another half pill of ecstasy. *"Why a half pill?"* I asked, somewhat

confused. He replied, *"Moderation brother, moderation. I got to take care of my brain."* I asked him what he meant, still somewhat confused since generally my own idea of taking care of my brain would preclude ecstasy consumption. After he paused with a stylish dance move, he explained that he wanted to achieve his *"roll"*—the high derived from ecstasy use—with as little ecstasy as possible because he asserted that the degree of brain damage is dependent upon quantity consumed.

Club drugs consist of a wide range of substances, from stimulants to depressants to hallucinogens. The unifying classificatory principle is that these substances proliferated with a perceived association with club subcultures. Most notably subsumed under this classification are MDMA (ecstasy), ketamine, methamphetamine, and gamma-hydroxybutyrate (GHB). These drugs produce a wide range of effects and experiences for users. For example, MDMA produces a euphoric, emotional high said to enhance one's feelings of connectivity with those around the user, whereas in contrast, ketamine can produce dissociative effects resulting in a "k-hole," in which the user is withdrawn from others into a state centered upon the self.

The meanings associated with these drugs vary as much as their effects. As noted by Agar, *"a variety of interpretations of the same object are possible, depending on the actors who encounter it and the traditions in which they participate"* (Agar, 1985). People impart different meanings upon club drugs, depending upon how they understand and make sense of the drugs in their lives. For instance, ecstasy has been labeled as both a *"hug drug"* and a dangerous poison. The way in which youth impart meaning on these drugs shapes their understandings of risk. Thus, to better understand the role of these drugs in the lives of youth, we need to ascertain how they understand club drugs and risk in the context of their own lives.

Much of the literature on youth, drug use, and conceptions of risk revolve around HIV risk rather than general conceptions of risk. General risk data suggest that risk perception can significantly influence youth to use or not use drugs (Derzon and Lipsey, 1999).

However, it is also important to explore how youth who do use drugs conceive of the risks. The narrative above provides a brief illustration of how conceptions of risk shape the patterns and practices of club drug use among youth. This paper describes local conceptions of risk that inform current patterns and practices of club drug use among youth. Here, I review the professional literature on club drug risks, then provide a descriptive profile of how club drug-using youth themselves conceive of risk. I examine how these folk models of risk compare with professional models and finally explore how the recognition of the relationship between folk models and professional models might enable health promotion efforts targeting youth.

The Social Nature of Risk

Risk is comprised of two key elements: objective determinants, the probability of a negative outcome given a certain action within a given context, and subjective determinants, the perceived or felt threat of danger given a certain action (Luhmann, 1993). Both are dependent upon the confluence of certain social processes and dialectically influence one another. Objective determinants of risk vary across individuals depending upon biological factors, such as metabolic rate, as well as social factors such as one's position in the class structure or the historical vagaries of one's cultural framework. Subjective determinants of risk pertain more specifically to the ways in which human beings experience risk. Individuals ground subjective assessments of risk within a cultural framework accrued as a byproduct of experience within a given social milieu (Douglas, 1992). Thus, risk assessment is not simply a rational calculus of danger occurring in a psychological vacuum, but is dependent upon systems of belief and systems of value that shape how dangers are perceived. Thus, the perception of risk is always generated through social processes influenced by cultural frameworks. Broader social, political, economic, and cultural forces play themselves out at the local level, thus forming a context that shapes not only

which objective dangers are faced, but subjective conceptions of danger as well.

Within a given society, different sectors of the population have different models of understanding the same phenomena. Even subtle differences may profoundly shape the way in which the world is experienced. Such differences stem not only from the local inflections of culture, but from the different perspectives individuals cultivate through experiencing society from specific positions. These models can be loosely divided into two types, professional and folk models. "Professional models" are those that enjoy privileged status in a society; they are endowed with authority and offer official interpretations of a given practice (Agar, 1985). In this instance, professionals are scientists, public health experts, and politicians.

Alternatively, "folk models" arise popularly through the everyday practices of people in society. Public health professional models of risk often differ from those engaging in them.

Professional Models of Club Drugs and Risk

The following review is a synopsis of a series of dangers that concern scientists and public health experts with regard to ecstasy use.

Neurotoxicity. Neurotoxicity, both acute and long-term, remains a primary concern of scientists and public health experts. There is no universal definition of what comprises neurotoxicity; it may comprise anything related to toxic effects on the brain from serotonin depletion briefly following ecstasy consumption to long-term cognitive impairment (Baggott and Mendelson, 2001). Neurotoxicity could arise in several ways from reductions in cerebral blood flow (Chang et al., 2000), the alteration of axons in the brain due to oxidative stress (Jayanthi et al., 1999; Shankaran, Yamamoto, and Gudelsky, 1999) or other serotonergic changes in the brain. Acute neurotoxic effects include acute memory loss and short-term cognitive impairment in the days following the use of MDMA (Parrott and Lasky, 1998). Long-term neurotoxic effects of MDMA potentially include impaired memory, impulsivity, alteration of mood, and other cognitive impairments (Morgan, 1998). Some animal studies suggest that neurotoxicity is dose-related, with neurotoxic effects correlating with consumption, thus suggesting that binges of ecstasy use pose greater risk of neurotoxicity (O'Shea et al., 1998). Carlson et al. reported that consumption level appears to have an effect on the report of adverse consequences; those who consumed greater amounts of ecstasy reported long-term adverse consequences [at] higher rates (2004). It is unclear whether some long-term effects of MDMA use surface only with aging. Given that for ethical reasons prospective clinical studies on MDMA-naïve humans have not been conducted, much remains unclear about the neurotoxicity of MDMA. Thus, the neurotoxicity ramifications are not yet fully understood.

Depressive disorders. The potential for depressive disorders is related to neurotoxicity via the possibility of permanent alteration of the serotonin system, located in the brain and associated with the regulation of mood and psychological well-being. An acute period of depression in the days following ecstasy consumption has been well documented and is thought to relate to the process of restoration of the serotonin system after its disruption by the induced flooding of serotonin during the ecstasy experience (Curran and Travill, 1997). However, we cannot yet determine the potential inducement of long-term depression, given our inability to distinguish between premorbid or latent depression and ecstasy-induced depression through retrospective assessments. Further research on links between ecstasy use and depressive disorders is necessary.

Hyperthermia. MDMA may contribute to hyperthermia, when core body temperatures rise above the optimal temperature of 98.6°F, to anywhere from 102° to 109°F. The human body cannot sustain metabolic and cardiovascular activity under hyperthermic conditions (Henry and Rella, 2001). At these high temperatures, a number of negative medical outcomes—muscle breakdown, kidney and liver failure, or cerebral edema—and even death may occur. Yet, much of the cause for concern stems from the use of ecstasy under specific conditions rather than simply use of the drug (Henry, 1992). The fear is that youth may use ecstasy and concurrently engage in extended periods of physical exertion through dancing in locations with high ambient temperatures.

Thoracic organ damage. [As with use of] other amphetamine-based substances, ecstasy use raises blood pressure and heart rate and may enable complications related to tachycardia, cardiac arrhythmias, and other heart-related problems (Mas et al., 1999). Though it remains unclear whether MDMA use can trigger adverse cardiac-related outcomes in otherwise healthy adults, the symptoms of high blood pressure and increased heart rate may enable negative health outcomes for those with preexisting cardiac conditions. The effects of ecstasy on hepatic functioning also warrant further investigation. Clinical cases of liver toxicity have been found (Henry, Jeffreys, and Dawling, 1992). Some doctors have expressed concern over the potential for ecstasy-induced hepatitis (Hwang, Daniels, and Holtzmuller, 2002).

Serotonin Syndrome. Serotonin Syndrome is a rare complication resulting from the use of a serotonergic agent such as ecstasy (Sternbach, 1991). The use of ecstasy with MAO inhibitors may contribute to this syndrome, manifesting in tremors, shivers, confusion, muscle spasms, and poorly regulated heart rate and blood pressure. These symptoms may lead to death (Mueller and Korey, 1998).

Dependence. A common concern with all drugs is the potential for dependence; MDMA could be no different. Though physiological dependence and physical withdrawal symptoms do not appear to occur with ecstasy use, the habitual daily use of ecstasy has been reported in some case studies of ecstasy dependence (Jansen, 1998). Thus, individuals may potentially develop psychological dependence upon ecstasy. Indeed, some ecstasy users have self-reported feelings of dependence on the drug, though the prevalence appears to be low (Solowij, Hall, and Lee, 1992).

Sexual risk taking. Youth may potentially engage in risky sexual behavior under the influence of club drugs. Studies have shown the effects of many intoxicating substances on sexual risk taking (Temple, Leigh, and Schafer, 1993; Frosch et al., 1996). MDMA has been reported as a sensual rather than a sexual drug (Buffum and Moser, 1986; Beck and Rosenbaum, 1994). The use of MDMA has been noted to increase empathy with others, contributing to a heightened sense of intimacy, as well as a reported reduction in ability to achieve orgasm. Yet, Topp et al. reported that although roughly half of their cohort of ecstasy-using youth claimed that the use of ecstasy inhibits orgasm, 70% claimed that it improved sex (1999). Among the same population, condom use with casual partners occurred less frequently while individuals were under the influence of ecstasy (Topp et al., 1999). Clinical evaluations of MDMA use and its effect on sexuality also suggest that users report increases in sexual desire and increases with sexual satisfaction (Zemishlany, Aizenberg, and Weizman, 2001). Data also suggest increased impulsivity associated with the use of MDMA, which may enable riskier behaviors to occur *"in the heat of the moment"*(Morgan, 1998).

Public health professionals have little certainty about the dangers associated with ecstasy consumption. We have far more hypotheses than proof established through the scientific method. Adequate funding needs to be directed at researchers engaging in clinical studies that examine the outcomes of ecstasy use as well as social researchers who conduct grounded examinations of the patterns and practices of ecstasy use and its associated harms. The scientific foundations of our knowledge, no doubt, are crucial aspects of the manner in which we proceed in a variety of areas from prevention to intervention to public policy. However, also key to the appropriate development of interventions are the folk models of risk associated with club drugs. It is equally imperative to investigate the question *"How do club drug-using youth conceive of the risks and what do these risks mean to them?"*

Methods

This study is an ethnographic study of club drug use among "Bridge and Tunnel" youth in the New York City metropolitan area. Bridge and Tunnel is local vernacular for youth who hang out or "party" in Manhattan but who reside in suburban neighborhoods surrounding New York City. These youth are thus a population engaged in urban social scenes as well as their everyday suburban existences. Thus, involved in multiple social worlds, these youth provide a window from which to examine the patterns of club drug use in both urban and suburban locales.

The prospect of data collection from a population without roots in the region of study poses numerous challenges. Manhattan has an enormous club scene and a key challenge consisted of creating a social map to identify the key venues in which Bridge and Tunnel youth regularly "hang out." On various nights of the week over a 6-week period, I conducted exploratory fieldwork and "intercept" interviews with suburban youth at the major points of entry in Midtown Manhattan, such as Penn Station and Grand Central Station. I administered a brief, structured interview, which consisted of determining their county of residence, preferred music genre, and the locations in which they prefer to socialize in Manhattan. Based upon direction from this social mapping phase, I conducted informal interviews about the presence of club drugs through participant-observation in environments in which Bridge and Tunnel youth socialize. The first 2 months of participant-observation, which overlapped with the intercept interview period, focused upon defining five key venues for extended participant-observation research and recruitment for an in-depth interview cohort. The duration of the full 18-month fieldwork period extended from March of 2003 through the fall of 2004.

The key feature of the participant-observation method is that the researcher immerses [himself or herself] within the social milieus of local venues. During the cultivation of this extended presence, the fieldworker not only observes social behavior in a given locale, but participates in a variety of activities with the "natives." Such a presence not only subsequently enables the recruitment of interview participants through the development of rapport, but enables the ethnographer to thickly describe emerging trends in club drug use and facilitates the ethnographer's ability to assess patterns of observed behavior and link these observations to interview data to cultivate fuller interpretations of subcultural social norms. Furthermore, it eliminates a need to rely on the self-report of respondents, thus further increasing the validity of the data. All fieldwork resulted in descriptive documentation in fieldnotes, which were written as soon as possible after the event.

Respondents were recruited from the five designated venues through a theoretical sampling scheme, constructed in a targeted fashion, for inclusion into an in-depth interview cohort (Bluthenthal and Watters, 1995; Strauss and Corbin, 1998). The in-depth interview cohort consisted of youth recruited at the designated venues and did not include youth from the social mapping sample. Inclusion criteria for men and women recruited for in-depth interviews was as follows: (a) individuals between the ages of 18 and 25, (b) who have reported the use of one of four club drugs—MDMA, ketamine, methamphetamine, or GHB—within the previous year, (c) who reside in a suburban county outside New York accessible by public transport, and (d) who are willing and able to consent to participation. Respondents participated in one to four anonymous audio-taped interviews, which lasted between 1 and 2.5 hours and were transcribed verbatim.[a]

The interviews consisted of open-ended questions designed to gain an insider's perspective on a range of salient issues pertinent to club drug use (Geertz, 1983). Among others, a series of topical modules included (a) initiation into club drug use, (b) current practices and patterns of use, and (c) conceptions of risk. Ethnographic interview techniques such as critical incident measures as well as analytic contrasts were employed in order to gather detail-rich data with reduced recall bias (Leonard and Ross, 1997). Initial interviews occurred after the occasion of recruitment at a time and location agreed upon with the respondent, often in the suburbs. Follow-up interviews occurred a minimum of 2 weeks from the previous interview so as to allow the respondent time to contemplate issues raised and to allow the investigator time to digest and initially interpret the data so as to more pointedly direct the follow-up interview. A thematic analysis

of data was employed to ascertain the coinciding conceptions of risk among these youth. The quotations employed in the paper provide descriptive evidence of thematic patterns across the interviews. They represent general sentiments expressed by many youth, not simply unique perspectives. All quotations are derived from taped in-depth interviews, except where noted.

The data for this paper was drawn primarily from interviews with 25 Bridge and Tunnel youth hailing from New Jersey, Long Island, and the Mid-Hudson suburbs of New York City. They ranged in age from 18 to 25 with a mean age of 20.5 years. They had an average monthly income of $1,700, with a range of $600 to $4,000 from a variety of jobs, such as part-time florist, selling drugs, and marketing analyst for a multinational corporation. They were well educated; most either [were] currently enrolled in college or [had] completed college. The cohort consisted of 17 White youth, five Latino youth, two Asian youth, and one youth of "mixed" race.[b] Ecstasy appears to be the primary club drug utilized by these youth, which supports existing prevalence data. These youth have all used ecstasy during the course of their lives. Thus, ecstasy resonates most in the lives of these Bridge and Tunnel youth, and for this reason, is the focus of the following examination of risk among club drug-using youth. The average number of ecstasy pills consumed within the last year is roughly 13, with a range of one to 60. In other words, these youth are not heavy consumers of ecstasy. Ketamine has been used to a lesser degree among this group, though it is still prevalent. Methamphetamine and GHB have been used by very few participants.

Pleasure and Danger in the Lives of Club Drug-Using Youth

Youth awareness of danger. The risks of club drugs resonated with most youth in that they perceived they [were] doing something with potential harm. One key aspect about youth awareness of danger associated with the use of club drugs can be seen in the efforts made to cultivate knowledge about these drugs. Youth were often acutely aware of the dangers associated with ecstasy use because of their attempts to accumulate knowledge on the subject. When I asked Jane if there was anything bad about taking ecstasy, she belly laughed as if I had just posed an absurd question and said, "Uhhh, drugs are not good for you! It hurts you. It's terribly stupid . . . most drugs are not good for you." Aside from the knowledge accumulated from drug use prevention education sessions in high school and health classes in college, many youth engage in proactive efforts to cultivate knowledge about the drugs they are using. They turned to a variety of sources to locate such information, but particularly the Internet. They used websites from health education organizations, self-developed websites, and on-line public health journals. These youth also discussed the subject of club drug use and the associated dangers within their social networks. Message boards and chat rooms provide forums to extend social networks as well as arenas for discussing the harms associated with club drugs.

During another interview with Jane I obtained a further understanding of her perspective on the dangers of club drugs. Jane put it this way:

> "OK, whenever I think of it (ecstasy), I know I'm ruining my body. I'm killing my brain. I think about it, like, eventually I'm going to die anyway, so enjoy life. This is one way to enjoy it. So, take all the good stuff and keep in mind the bad stuff. Don't forget about them. Never ignore them, but know what you're doing. Always be prepared. I guess by the age of 30 there will be some retards, maybe, you know, have some side effects. I read they did research on monkeys with ecstasy and it made the monkeys have some sort of imbalance in their brains. So, OK, nothing's perfect. You have to accept that fact to enjoy something. I eat candy, you know. When you overeat, you become fat. If you eat them in normal portions, OK, so you get pimples. But nothing is good with too much, you know."

Jane spoke of keeping in mind the potential harms associated with club drug use. The expectation is that one should remember the dangers of club drugs, "never ignore them," such that this knowledge enables preparation for the use of these drugs. This knowledge of dangers, thus, informs the practices of club drug-using youth. Though the level of knowledge varies within this population, nonetheless, to "know what you're doing" is important among these youth and is impressed upon others within social networks, not for the purposes of popularity but of health concern. Some youth likened it to "doing your homework" before taking drugs. Despite their awareness of the dangers associated with club drug use, some youth valued the other side of the proposition enough to engage in risk taking. Andrew, a 21-year-old Asian male, said,

> "It's the feelings of expression, the connections, and general well-being. When you take the pill, it's not the drug. E makes you open up. You're connected to everyone. I guess in a way, it's like a little bit of heaven."

This type of payoff is part of the reason why youth take risks with club drugs despite being aware of potential dangers.

Networks and the social nature of risk. Social networks are a primary vehicle by which youth gauge the likelihood of danger. Again, it is not due to a lack of awareness that youth continue to use ecstasy but due, at least partly, to their assessments of the probability of danger, which may or may not be accurate. Vicky, a 19-year-old white female, described this process in response to my query about why she uses ecstasy even though she knows that she is risking potentially hazardous outcomes.

> "I always think about, you know, wow this person did it this many times and he's still fine and he's still walking. That's how I look at it. I know it's bad but I know a lot of people who have done a lot and like major amounts and they're still walking today. Nothing ever happened to them, you know."

Though such assessments may not accurately reflect the objective probability of dangers, they nonetheless demonstrate the manner in which youth assess the risks through their social networks. Youth try to assess how much these harms are pertinent to their lives, although they may not have specific probabilities in mind. As noted by Mike, a 25-year-old white male,

"You can get in serious trouble or die I guess theoretically with every drug. I don't really know with ecstasy really. Long-term heavy usage eats away at your brain. It takes away from your memory and stuff like that but that's something I really don't know the odds of."

Though the youth with whom I conducted in-depth interviews had nearly all "heard stories," they generally did not have individuals within their social networks who had experienced ecstasy-related negative health outcomes aside from acute episodes of short-term depression after ecstasy use, which some describe as "terrible Tuesdays." Only one youth knew someone in his network with a negative health outcome related to club drugs. In this instance, the youth's friend died from a suspected overdose of GHB, a dose-sensitive depressant that can adversely affect the central nervous system. These youth may hear little of traumatic outcomes because such outcomes related to ecstasy may be exceedingly rare. Of 19,366 autopsies conducted in NYC from 1997–2000 on decedents with "unexpected" or "suspicious" deaths, "only two were caused exclusively by MDMA" (Gill et al., 2002).

Folk Models of Risk

In contrast to the clinical basis of professional models of risk, folk models of risk are experientially based, framed in ways that youth can and do experience them. Though many areas of consistency between professional and folk models exist, the youth discussed these risks as phenomenological realities rather than clinical incidents. The following are accounts of how Bridge and Tunnel youth conceived of ecstasy risks and accounted for these risks in their lives.

Dehydration/overheating. The potential harms of dehydration and overheating [form] perhaps one of the most common concerns among ecstasy-using youth. Many youth spoke of these potential dangers as significantly serious, potentially mortal, and not simply akin to dehydration associated with binge drinking. They spoke specifically of the potential to pass out, often attributed to a combination of ecstasy consumption, overexertion, hot atmosphere, and not rehydrating oneself, concerns that echo the con-

cerns of professionals. While conducting fieldwork at a rave during the summer of 2003, I witnessed the level of concern for these risks among youth. Midway through the evening, the venue shut off the cold water in the men's bathroom so as to prevent patrons from refilling their bottles with cool water. Later on in the evening, I was talking with some young women and we broached the subject in conversation. I mentioned that I wished I could fill my bottle at the tap in the bathroom. Immediately, one of the girls said to me, "Oh my God, did you know that they shut the cold water off on us. That's so fucked up isn't it? People could die." She then went on a profanity-laden tirade against the venue management. During the next several months, I met several other youth who attended the same rave. Often, when that rave came up in conversation, they mentioned the lack of accessible water and the potential for overheating. They similarly expressed concern that "someone could have gotten hurt."

Memory loss, "burned brains," and feeling "cracked out." Youth spoke of "neurotoxicity" in a variety of different ways, without using the clinical language of neurotoxicity. Instead, they spoke of memory loss and other impairment using expressions such as *"burning your brain"* or feeling *"cracked out."* They addressed the possibility of both acute and long-term effects, suggesting that they concern themselves not only with present dangers but with the potential that their use of ecstasy may *"catch up"* with them in the future.

Many youth spoke of acute effects in the days after taking ecstasy. A widely held perception of the adverse consequences is briefly impaired cognitive capacities. Many youth felt their ability to think is atypical the day following ecstasy consumption. "I just feel really 'cracked out.' I just feel like I'm just useless the next day," said Vicky. Feeling "cracked out" is a reference to another drug, crack, and the supposed detrimental effects on brain function the drug is perceived to have; perhaps a significant connection given that these youth consider crack to be one of the "hardest" drugs. The impairment of feeling "cracked out," however, is generally of short duration, lasting for a day or two following the consumption of ecstasy. The duration of the "cracked out" feeling is short but the qualitative nature of the impairment is significant. The impairment is experienced as something more than simply a hangover, but rather as a cognitive fog as noted by Luis, a 20-year-old Latino male. "It's just messing your brain up completely. Sometimes if I go to work the next day, I can't function. You're like a zombie." Thus, youth are often able to go through their daily routines but cannot function at their usual level.

Youth were also concerned about the potential long-term neurotoxic ramifications of ecstasy use. Jane talked about the possibility of "burning" her brain through the use of ecstasy but didn't perceive it to be a problem in her own life, and she did not see a "burned brain" to be the inevitable result of ecstasy use. Other youth felt similarly. As noted earlier, Mike also talked about the possibility of memory loss because of the consumption of ecstasy. However, as is common among these youth, he framed his comments in a discourse of excessive consumption. Though he mentioned brief cognitive problems in the days after taking ecstasy during the 6 years he has used the drug, as far as his own experiences are concerned, Mike notes, "Long-term, no, I really don't think it affected me in that way." The concern over a burned brain is often tempered by the perception that only excessive ecstasy use triggers damage. The dangers associated with infrequent use, thus, pose few concerns for these youth.

Depression. Depression is another risk widely perceived by youth who use ecstasy. Like the concern about neurotoxic effects leading to "burned brains" and feeling "cracked out," youth expressed concern both for the acute depressive episodes that follow in the wake of ecstasy consumption as well as the potential long-term depression that could ensue following regular consumption of ecstasy. Some youth experienced a period of acute depression in the hours and days that follow the ecstasy high—"post-E depression" as characterized by some. George, a 21-year-old male of mixed descent, said that for him it can last "anywhere from a couple of hours to a couple of days." Later in the interview, George discussed his experiences with post-E depression, which highlight the unpredictable nature of this phenomenon. He notes,

> "Sometimes you feel like shit the next day. Like, you get like depressed for no reason. Usually, if I take it at a party and I dance a lot, I find that afterwards, the next day, I'm just completely fine, like I can just get over it. Sometimes it has a really bad comedown though. Like, if I'm coming down after a party, if I'm going home, everything's quiet, you know, I just start thinking. And I don't even know why, I'm just depressed for no good reason and that's definitely bad."

In using ecstasy, George chances that he may experience a bout of acute depression *"for no good reason."* The post-E depression seems to be somewhat unpredictable; though many ecstasy-using youth have experienced it, not all have. It also varies in intensity and duration. Some youth experienced post-E depression more frequently than George, others far less, and some not at all. Though usually not a problem for George, it remains a risk he is willing to take.

Youth also concerned themselves with the risk of long-term depression. Though some recognized this risk, they also saw it as minimal if they were generally happy individuals. Mary, a 19-year-old Hispanic female, spoke of potential long-term ramifications related to depression by couching her understandings through a discussion of the serotonin system.

> "Your serotonin level is definitely altered afterwards. They say it takes two weeks to get it back to its original status and even then your serotonin level will never be at the original status. You'll never get back to where you were originally. I feel that especially if you have a lot of insecurities and you get down a lot, you know, really pessimistic, then it's not something you should be doing."

Mary expressed particular concern for those with a predisposition towards depression, a sentiment echoed by others. Some ecstasy users conceived of this risk as primarily for those predisposed to depression; thus, that it exacerbates rather than generates long-term depression.

Addiction and loss of control. Some youth saw the potential for addiction with ecstasy, though they generally did not view ecstasy as physically addictive. Will, a 22-year-old white male from New Jersey, characterized a set of actions involving the drug as addictive but not the drug itself.

"I think maybe that whole lifestyle, it's kind of addicting. Some people, that's the only thing they can think about all day is just going to the clubs and doing drugs. It seems like a lot of people are really addicted to it. I guess maybe they're both kind of like a couple (drugs and clubs), almost like they're one thing. One really doesn't go without the other. It's kind of like you need both of them."

Will asserted that people don't get addicted to ecstasy per se, but rather a lifestyle. The drug is not the focal point, but, rather, simply part of a whole experience that is addicting. Interestingly enough, Will also noted that clubs are not a necessary part of the equation of addicting experiences, as he and many of his friends [were] initiated into ecstasy use at house parties during high school and that was still a common pattern of use among his friends.

Other youth framed the risk of losing control in terms of shedding inhibitions and making impulsive decisions. Eddie, a 22-year-old white male, notes,

"What I would take as risky might not be dangerously obvious, for instance, persons that don't really have control. You know, a lot of people take drugs to sort of lose their inhibitions, but if they lose it totally, they could get hurt."

For these youth, the fears of getting hurt through loss of control included driving while under the influence and sexual risk taking.

Adulterated pills. Many youth felt a common risk they take when consuming ecstasy is the danger of using adulterated pills, which contain more substances than simply MDMA or even no MDMA at all. As Tony remarked during our second interview, "It could be not what you're buying at all. Like, it's filth and you have no idea." Many youth echoed these concerns that they're being given something other than MDMA. They seemed to find this particularly disconcert-

ing because it thwarts their efforts to cultivate knowledge about MDMA risk.

Jane related a story of a friend who thought he bought a couple of hits of ecstasy only to find out they were "speed, some sort of amphetamines" upon receiving news of his toxicology report at the hospital after an adverse event related to the drugs. Though among this group this was the only narrative of an acquaintance experiencing an adverse outcome because of adulterated pills, most youth had "heard stories" about adulterated pills. Perhaps justifying these stories, or perhaps the source of them, a testing program supported by the harm reduction organization Dance Safe has regularly revealed the presence of adulterants in pills sold as ecstasy.[c] An analysis of 123 pills from New York tested since September 1, 1999, reveals that 54 (44%) contained only MDMA while slightly more, 56 (45%), contained no MDMA at all. The others (11%) contained a combination of MDMA and other substances. Other substances found in 56% of the pills included methamphetamine, dextromethorphan, amitriptyline, fluoxetine, codeine, diazepam, lidocaine, and acetaminophen, among others.

Discussion

"Although users may think these substances are harmless, research has shown that club drugs can produce a range of unwanted effects, including hallucinations, paranoia, amnesia, and, in some cases, death."
—Alan Leshner, former Director of NIDA[d]

Public health professionals often assume that young people take risks because they do not know any better or they "just don't get it." The pervasive assumption that youth engage in dangerous behaviors because of a lack of knowledge permeates areas of the health literature on topics from drinking to sexual behavior to drug use. This may stem in part from an underestimation of the capabilities of youth, but also from professional treatment of risk. Public health professionals often privilege danger when assessing risk. Discussions of risk focus specifically on danger, which obscures the potential for rational decision making in the face of danger.

In practice, risk assessment proceeds with attentiveness to danger, though how seasoned that attentiveness is varies. What is clear is that youth do not see ecstasy use as a danger-free enterprise and public health messages that assume otherwise will not engage these youth. They view risk as a two-sided proposition: danger on one side but some sort of potential payoff, such as pleasure or connectivity, on the other. These dangers are possible—not certain or perhaps not even probable—and these youth recognize them as such when they make risk assessments. Their conceptions of risk readily account for the known dangers associated with club drugs and they weigh risks based upon a knowledge base cultivated about the dangers of these drugs alongside the potential payoffs. They practice club drug use accordingly.

In a number of areas, youth express the same concerns as public health professionals regarding the risks of ecstasy use, though youth models are filtered down into an experiential understanding. Both professionals and these youth are concerned with depression, neurotoxicity ("burned brains"), addiction, and hyperthermia (overheating and dehydration). Areas of dissonance also exist. Other harms mentioned by professionals, such as Serotonin Syndrome or heart problems, do not enter youth discourse of risk, perhaps because they are exceedingly rare and youth are unlikely to encounter others having experienced such problems. Since I conducted these interviews with general open-ended questions about the risks of ecstasy use rather than listing specific risks for them to identify with, it remains uncertain to what extent these youth are aware of these possible dangers or simply do not find them plausible dangers in their own lives.

Far from being oblivious to the potential harms in their lives, these youth are aware of the dangers they risk when using club drugs. This recognition of harm stems from a general sentiment of the importance of cultivating knowledge about drug-related harms. Furthermore, youth appear to cultivate this knowledge base not for social currency, but as a necessary component for the preservation of their health. They weigh risks based upon knowledge cultivated about these substances alongside that of the potential payoffs, and practice club drug use accordingly. Knowledge acquisition plays a key role in the development of these conceptions of risk. In a certain sense, it is the foundational practice of risk management. As Tony noted in our final interview, "You're not supposed to be on drugs but the smartest thing you can do while you're on drugs is research about it. Know what you should be doing. Know what you shouldn't be doing." Research on the substances while the user is proverbially "on drugs"—not while literally high—ultimately provides the basis for putting risk management strategies into practice. This is about *"know(ing) what you should be doing."* In other words, this is about translating knowledge and conceptions of risk into practice. Knowledge provides youth with the opportunity to strategize drug taking so as to manage the potential dangers.

The fundamental purpose of understanding the conceptions of risk among club drug-using youth is to understand the informal logic that guides their drug-using practices. Youth collectively translate their concerns about risks into strategic practices aimed at minimizing these risks. They depend on a model of risk that is context dependent and they assess the likelihood of adverse outcomes in different ways and primarily relate potential dangers to specific features of context. Risks do not occur in a strict *"if . . . then"* fashion for these youth but as variable. Youth engage in a variety of risk management strategies that stem from the context-specific manner in which they conceive of risks associated with club drug use. The initial case of Tony taking ecstasy in half-pill increments is a vivid example of moderation put into practice. A burned brain from ecstasy is dose-dependent. Tony thus minimizes his intake and subsequent risk while achieving his high. Other risk management practices include other forms of moderation, "preloading" or "postloading," and taking "breaks," periodic interruptions in the regular pattern of ecstasy use so as to replenish one's body, or more specifically to rejuvenate the serotonin system. Thus, these conceptions of risk translate into specific patterns and practices of club drug use.

Limitations. The study is a small one based upon regionally specific youth, and the generalizability remains unclear. It is important to reiterate that this group is a rather well-educated group; most are either currently enrolled in or have graduated from college. The pursuit of club drug-related knowledge, as well as the ability and tendency to pursue such knowledge, may not be universal. These youth are uniquely primed to seek club drug-related knowledge. College education provides unique resources to these youth. For example, some of these youth access on-line public health journals through university subscriptions, opportunities unavailable to those not enrolled in college. Another limitation is that the sample is primarily white, with some Latino and Asian youth. Though the sample represents that suburban counties surrounding NYC are predominantly white, even exclusively white in some neighborhoods, it does not account for black youth.

Implications. An understanding based solely on professional models is incomplete at best. The incorporation of folk models into our understandings of a given phenomenon enables fuller and richer explanations of why the "folk" act as they do. Folk models demonstrate how specific phenomena resonate on the ground. Only through ascertaining fuller understandings of folk models can we adequately inform health promotion efforts and public policy by eliminating the assumptions inherent in professional models.

The analysis of professional and folk models of risk has a number of implications for promoting health among club drug-using youth. One such area is that it allows us to attempt to understand the harmony and discontinuities between how scientists and public health professionals view club drug-related risks and how youth view them. We can thus explore areas for potential mediating health education interventions. Many of the club drug-using youth I have interviewed maintain an interest in harm reduction approaches to club drug use, even if they are unaware of harm reduction as a specific movement. Efforts should be made to enhance existing harm reduction organiza-

tions targeting club drug-using youth and also allow for the development of new organizations through private and public funding streams. Public health professionals have a responsibility not only to prevent club drug use through primary prevention efforts but to offer healthier alternatives through secondary and tertiary prevention so as to minimize the harms associated with club drug use among current users.

One final note: It remains clear that we as professionals still have much to learn about the long-term harms associated with ecstasy use and the use of other club drugs. Efforts to fund such clinical research should be a priority for both public and private funding sources of drug-related research. Furthermore, several public policy recommendations and enactments related to club drugs have occurred in the last several years in the United States, despite a dearth of clinical and behavioral research on these drugs. Only further clinical and social research on club drugs will provide fuller understandings for well-informed drug policy.

Notes

a. Informed consent was obtained from all respondents for the in-depth interviews as per the approved IRB protocol. The study operated under a Federal Certificate of Confidentiality to ensure protection of sensitive data elicited from respondents. All names within this paper are pseudonyms.

b. These youth self-identified with a variety of racial and ethnic identifiers. For the sake of brevity, they have been subsumed under specific identifiers. For example, "Latino" included youth who identified as Latino, Hispanic, and Latin American. "White" includes youth who identified as European, white, and Caucasian.

c. For more information on Dance Safe's pill testing program, visit *www.dancesafe.org* or *www.ecstasydata.org*.

d. This quote comes from Dr. Leshner's article "Club Drugs are Not 'Fun Drugs,' " accessible via *www.clubdrugs.org*, a NIDA-supported informational website about club drugs. Aside from a series of brief articles issued from NIDA, the website also contains basic information about club drugs, trends and statistics, and news updates.

Glossary

Burned brain. Refers to the mental exhaustion, acute or long-term, that may stem from drug use. Similar to the term "burned out."

Cracked out. A short-term feeling of a cognitive fog following a period of drug use. The reference is to the drug "crack" and its association with difficulties of cognitive functioning among users. For example, after a weekend of using ecstasy, the user may feel "cracked out."

K-hole. A state induced through the use of ketamine. The "k-hole" is a state in which the user is dissociated from the body. This feeling of disconnection may result in the user feeling like he or she is trapped in a psychological hole produced by K use.

Post-E depression. A depressive state induced by lowered serotonin levels in the brain after ecstasy consumption.

Roll. The ecstasy high and experience. A youth would "roll" on ecstasy.

Terrible Tuesday. Refers to the arrival of the depressive state on a Tuesday morning following a weekend of ecstasy use. The bottom of the ecstasy crash may arrive about 36 hours after the high. Thus, ecstasy use on a Saturday night and into Sunday morning may result in a "Terrible Tuesday."

References

Agar, M. (1985). Folks and professionals: Different models for the interpretation of drug use. *The International Journal of the Addictions* 20 (1): 173–182.

Baggott, M., Mendelson, J. (2001). Does MDMA cause brain damage? In: Holland, J., ed. *Ecstasy: The Complete Guide.* Rochester, Vermont: Park Street Press.

Beck, J., Rosenbaum, M. (1994). *Pursuit of Ecstasy: The MDMA Experience.* Albany, New York: SUNY Press.

Bluthenthal, R. N., Watters, J. K. (1995). Multimethod research from targeted sampling to HIV risk environments. *NIDA Research Monograph* 157: 212–230.

Buffum, J., Moser, C. (1986). MDMA and human sexual function. *Journal of Psychoactive Drugs* 18 (4): 355–360.

Carlson, R., McCaughan, J. A., Falck, R. S., Wang, J., Siegal, H. A., Daniulaityte, R. (2004). Perceived adverse consequences associated with MDMA/ecstasy use among young adults in Ohio: Implications for intervention. *International Journal of Drug Policy* (in press).

Chang, L., Grob, C. S., Ernst, T., Itti, L., Mishkin, F. S., Jose-Melchor, R., Poland, R. E. (2000). Effect of ecstasy (3,4-methylenedioxymethamphetamine [MDMA]) on cerebral blood flow: A co-registered SPECT and MRI study. *Psychiatry Research* 98: 16–28.

Curran, H. V., Travill, R. A. (1997). Mood and cognitive effects of 3,4-methylenedioxymethamphetamine (MDMA, ecstasy): Weekend "high" followed by mid-week low. *Addiction* 92: 821–831.

Derzon, J. H., Lipsey, M. W. (1999). What good predictors of marijuana use are good for: A synthesis of research. *School Psychology International* 20 (1): 69–85.

Douglas, M. (1992). *Risk and Blame: Essays in Cultural Theory.* New York: Routledge.

Frosch, D., Shoptaw, S., Huber, A., Rawson, R. A., Ling, W. (1996). Sexual risk among gay and bisexual male methamphetamine abusers. *Journal of Substance Abuse Treatment* 13 (6): 483–486.

Geertz, C. (1983). *Local Knowledge: Further Essays in Interpretive Anthropology.* New York: Basic Books.

Gill, J. R., Hayes, J. A., deSouza, I. S., Marker, E., Stajic, M. (2002). Ecstasy (MDMA) deaths in New York City: A case series and review of the literature. *Journal of Forensic Sciences* 47 (1): 121–126.

Henry, J. A. (1992). Ecstasy and the dance of death. *British Medical Journal* 305: 5–6.

Henry, J. A., Jeffreys, K. J., Dawling, S. (1992). Toxicity and deaths from 3,4-methylenedioxymethamphetamine ("ecstasy"). *Lancet* 340: 384–387.

Henry, J. A., Rella, J. (2001). Medical risks associated with MDMA use. In: Holland, J., ed. *Ecstasy: The Complete Guide.* Rochester, Vermont: Park Street Press.

Hwang, I., Daniels, A. M., Holtzmuller, K. C. (2002). "Ecstasy"-induced hepatitis in an active duty soldier. *Military Medicine* 167 (2): 155–156.

Jansen, K. L. R. (1998). Ecstasy (MDMA) dependence. *Drug and Alcohol Dependence* 53 (2): 121–124.

Jayanthi, S., Ladenheim, B., Andrews, A. M., Cadet, J. L. (1999). Overexpression of human copper/zinc superoxide dismutase in transgenic mice attenuates oxidative stress caused by methelyenedioxymethamphetamine (ecstasy). *Neuroscience* 91: 1379–1387.

Leonard, L., Ross, M. (1997). The last sexual encounter: The contextualization of sexual risk behaviour. *International Journal of STD & AIDS* 8: 643–645.

Luhmann, N. (1993). *Risk: A Sociological Theory.* New York: De Gruyter Press.

Mas, M., Farre, M., de la Torre, R., Roset, P., Ortuno, J., Segura, J., Cami, J. (1999). Cardiovascular and neuroendocrine effects and pharmacokinetics of 3,4-methylenedioxymethamphetamine in humans. *Journal of Pharmacology and Experimental Therapeutics* 290: 136–145.

Morgan, M. J. (1998). Recreational Use of "ecstasy" (MDMA) is associated with elevated impulsivity. *Neuropsychopharmacology* 19: 252–264.

Mueller, P. D., Korey, W. S. (1998). Death by "ecstasy": The serotonin syndrome? *Annals of Emergency Medicine* 32: 377–380.

O'Shea, E., Granados, R., Esteban, B., Colado, M. I., Green, A. R. (1998). The relationship between the degree of neurodigestion of rat brain 5-HT nerve terminals and the dose and frequency of administration of MDMA (ecstasy). *Neuropharmacology* 37: 919–926.

Parrott, A. C., Lasky, J. (1998). Ecstasy (MDMA) effects upon mood and cognition: Before, during, and after a Saturday night dance. *Psychopharmacology* 139 (3): 261–268.

Shankaran, M., Yamamoto, B. K., Gudelsky, G. A. (1999). Involvement of the serotonin transporter in the formation of hydroxyl radicals induced by 3,4-methylenedioxymethamphetamine. *European Journal of Pharmacology* 385: 103–110.

Solowij, N., Hall, W., Lee, N. (1992). Recreational MDMA use in Sydney: A profile of "ecstasy" users and their experiences with the drug. *British Journal of Addiction* 87: 1161–1172.

Strauss, A., Corbin, J. (1998). *Basics of Qualitative Research: Grounded Theory Procedures and Techniques.* 2nd Ed. Newbury Park, CA: Sage Publications.

Sternbach, H. (1991). The serotonin syndrome. *American Journal of Psychiatry* 148: 705–713.

Temple, M. T., Leigh, B. C., Schafer, J. (1993). Unsafe sexual behavior and alcohol use at the event level: Results of a national survey. *Journal of Acquired Immune Deficiency Syndromes* 6: 393–401.

Topp, L., Hando, J., Dillon, P., Roche, A., Solowij, N. (1999). Ecstasy use in Australia: Patterns of use and associated harm. *Drug & Alcohol Dependence* 55 (1–2): 105–115.

Zemishlany, Z., Aizenberg, D., Weizman, A. (2001). Subjective effects of MDMA ("ecstasy") on human sexual function. *European Psychiatry* 16 (2): 127–130.

For Discussion

1. The respondents reported that cold water was not available in the restrooms of some club venues. Is this practice acceptable? Why or why not?

2. The author suggests that respondents' knowledge of Ecstasy-related risk may have been enhanced due to their access to resources. Is it important to distribute related knowledge to other users who may not have access to this kind of information? Why or why not?

30

Ketamine Injection Among High-Risk Youth

Preliminary Findings From New York City

Stephen E. Lankenau
Michael C. Clatts

Most studies of injecting drug users (IDUs), are based primarily on heroin users. However, as this article shows, IDUs do not represent a homogeneous group. Stephen E. Lankenau and Michael C. Clatts conduct research into ketamine injectors and find that members of this group differ from what is known about heroin injectors. For example, ketamine users often inject several times during the same episode, and the social setting in which ketamine users inject often includes several other injectors. The authors also observe that a number of ketamine injectors frequently lend or borrow drug paraphernalia from other IDUs. All of these behaviors can increase the possibility of the transmission of infectious disease, including HIV.

Introduction

Ketamine, also known as Special K, or K, is among the several illicit substances recently classified as "club drugs." Ketamine and other so-called club drugs, such as MDMA and GHB, are synthetic substances that are consumed to alter a user's experience within a recreational setting (Curran & Morgan, 2000; Reynolds, 1997). Among these drugs, ketamine is particularly noteworthy because it is commonly administered in multiple ways. Ketamine is sold illicitly in pill, powder, and liquid form, and it may be swallowed, drunk, smoked, sniffed, and injected

(Jansen, 2001). In this article, we describe a small sample of young ketamine injectors living in New York City to highlight the current social and behavioral practices associated with ketamine injection—practices that may place ketamine injectors at risk for infectious diseases.

Ethnographic research that specifically examines injection drug using practices can lead to important discoveries about viral transmission and harm reduction strategies. While the sharing of syringes has been long identified as a primary means of transmitting HIV (Des Jarlais, Friedman, & Stoneburner, 1988), more recently, ancillary injection paraphernalia, such as "cookers," water, heat sources, and filters, have been found to be additional sources of risk for bloodborne pathogens. For instance, based upon ethnographic interviews and observations of heroin injectors preparing both tar and powder heroin in cookers, Clatts et al. (1999) found that tar heroin required longer exposure to a heat source before dissolving in water. Subsequent laboratory studies modeling these findings revealed that heating heroin solutions in a cooker for 15 seconds or more reduced HIV-1 viability below detectable levels.

Similarly, this article uses qualitative interviews to understand infectious disease risk associated with ketamine injection by focusing on specific injection events among a sample of young drug injectors. As this study demonstrates, ketamine injectors utilize a different series of injection practices and different types of paraphernalia compared to other types of injection drug use, such as heroin. Consequently, ketamine injection practices may pose new or different kinds of injection risks.

Ketamine: A Brief History

Ketamine was developed in the United States in 1962 and later patented by Parke-Davis in 1966. Marketed under trade names such as Ketaset and Ketaject, ketamine was promoted as a fast-acting general anesthetic. Ketamine became the most widely used battlefield anesthetic during the Vietnam War (Siegel, 1978) and was approved by the Food and Drug Administration (FDA) for use among children and [the] elderly in

1970. Gradually, ketamine became used less in medical settings after clinical administrations revealed certain complications in some patients, such as vivid dreaming, hallucinations, and confused states (Fine, Weissman, & Finestone, 1974; Perel & Davidson, 1976). Currently, ketamine is dispensed primarily by veterinarians as an animal sedative (Curran & Morgan, 2000). It is also administered to humans by physicians under certain medical circumstances, such as treating postoperative (Nikolajsen, Hansen, & Jensen, 1997) and chronic pain (Fine, 1999) and sedating pediatric patients (Green et al., 1999). In both veterinary and hospital settings, ketamine is administered via injection and is purchased from pharmaceutical companies where it is manufactured as a liquid.

While recreational ketamine use became increasingly popular in the United States and Europe in the last decade, the non-medical use of ketamine extends back to the mid-1960s. Ketamine was dispensed by underground "medicinal chemists" from Michigan as early as 1967 (Jansen, 2001), while solutions of ketamine were sold on the streets in Los Angeles and San Francisco in 1971 (Siegel, 1978). By the late 1970s, the FDA released a report on ketamine abuse, and the National Institutes on Drug Abuse (NIDA) published a monograph on phencyclidine that included an article on ketamine intoxication (Jansen, 2001). Recreational ketamine use—sniffing in particular—became more widespread during the late 1980s and early 1990s in combination with new types of dance music played at house parties and raves (Dotson, Ackerman, & West, 1995). In 1997, New York State passed a law criminalizing the sale or possession of ketamine. Following reports of the sale, theft, and abuse of ketamine, the Drug Enforcement Administration (DEA) placed ketamine into Schedule III of the Controlled Substance Act (CSA) in August 1999. Upon being listed as a Schedule III drug, it became illegal in the United States to possess ketamine for recreational or nonmedical purposes. In New York State, for instance, the possession of ketamine is a misdemeanor offense, which can carry penalties of six months in jail and a $1,000 fine.

There has been some confusion in classifying ketamine in relation to more common illicit drugs, such as MDMA and LSD, since ketamine can produce a range of experiences depending upon dosage. Ketamine can be a stimulant in low doses and can also cause potent psychedelic experiences in moderate and high doses. It has been described as a "dissociative anesthetic," meaning the drug causes users to feel both sedated and separated from their bodies (Jansen, 2001), yet the drug is not a depressant. Rather, ketamine is a derivative of phencyclidine, or PCP, and both are chemical compounds known as arylcyclohexylamines. Like PCP, ketamine stimulates the vital functions of heartbeat and respiration, though ketamine is less toxic and shorter acting than PCP (Weil & Rosen, 1983).

While no epidemiological studies currently exist detailing the extent of the nonmedical use of ketamine or the modes of administering it, a 1999 report on drug use in 21 U.S. cities and metropolitan areas reported ketamine use in eight cities while intramuscular injections of ketamine were reported in three of those cities—Boston, New Orleans, and Minneapolis/St. Paul (CEWG, 1999). In an updated 2000 report, eight additional cities or metropolitan areas reported ketamine use, including two cities—New York and Seattle—that reported ketamine injection, though intramuscular versus intravenous injections were not specified (CEWG, 2000). Additionally intravenous injections of ketamine have been reported among small samples of users (Jansen, 2001; Siegal, 1978) and single individuals (Lilly, 1978). Collectively, these recent reports and older accounts suggest that ketamine use—injection in particular—is occurring in cities across the United States. In particular, as we report in this article, injecting ketamine is an emerging practice among youth that carries certain risks for viral transmission. However, these risks have not been described or examined in previous studies.

Methods and Sample

We first learned that youths were injecting ketamine in New York City while conducting ethnographic research on two other at-risk populations—young men who have sex with men (YMSM) and injection drug users who shoot crack cocaine. In the course of interviewing injection drug users from these two populations, and during conversations with outreach workers who served these populations, we learned that ketamine injection was occurring among street-involved youth. Upon realizing the potential risks associated with ketamine injection practices, we initiated an exploratory study focused on high risk youth who injected ketamine.

Our data was gathered by the lead author who recruited 25 ketamine injectors (n = 25) from street and park settings in Manhattan's East and West Villages. To qualify for an interview, a youth had to meet two criteria: aged between 18 and 25 years old and had ever injected ketamine. Upon meeting the criteria, each youth agreed to a 30-minute, semi-structured interview focusing on the details of their most recent ketamine injection, the effects of injecting ketamine, and their history of ketamine and other injection drug use. Hence, our sample constitutes an active drug using, out-of-treatment, youth population.

Table 30.1 presents the sample demographics of the 25 ketamine injectors recruited into the study. The youths were typically in their early 20s, white, and male. We use the term "street involvement" to describe a particular relationship between youths and informal economic generating activities, such as drug dealing, sex work, and panhandling, or structural housing circumstances, such as homelessness. However, these categories are not mutually exclusive. Nearly all of the youth interviewed were connected to the street economy in some manner, which ultimately had implications for their ketamine use.

Findings

Polydrug Use

The majority of the youth in the sample were injection drug users, or had experimented with injection drug use, prior to injecting ketamine for the first time. The median age at injection initiation of any drug was 17 years old. Over half of the sample (56%) initiated injection drug use with a substance other than ketamine, such as heroin, cocaine, or methamphetamine. However, a relatively large proportion (44%) of the youth began their drug injection career with ketamine. The median age at ketamine injection initiation was 18 years old. Hence, youths were slightly older when they began injecting ketamine compared to other injection drugs.

As the sample's history of injection drug use suggests, these ketamine injectors were polydrug users. Heroin, cocaine, crack, PCP, MDMA, LSD, methamphetamine, and marijuana were drugs commonly used by these young injectors in the months prior to being interviewed. In fact, 56% of the sample used one or more of these drugs before, during, or after their most recent injection of ketamine. However, equally significant is that 44% of the sample did not use any other drugs in addition to ketamine during their most recent injection. In other words, ketamine was the drug of choice for a number of users during a specific drug injection event.

In addition to injecting ketamine, 80% of the youth had sniffed ketamine during their

Table 30.1

Sample Demographics

Age	Median	N
Range 18–25	21	25
Race/Ethnicity	**%**	**N**
African-American/Black	8	2
Caucasian/White	64	16
Latino/Hispanic	24	6
Native American	4	1
Gender	**%**	**N**
Male	92	23
Female	8	2
Street Involvement	**%**	**N**
Homeless	44	11
Sex Work	36	9
Drug Dealing	32	8
Panhandling	20	5

drug-using careers. Youths reported several advantages of injecting ketamine over sniffing the drug: some found that sniffing aggravated their nasal passages and that injecting produced a "cleaner" high; others who developed a tolerance to ketamine from sniffing found that injecting was a more potent and reliable mode of administering the drug. It is noteworthy that 20% (or five youth) had never sniffed ketamine—a more common mode of administering the drug—and had only injected ketamine. In fact, these five youth had all initiated their injection drug use career with either heroin or cocaine prior to their first time injecting ketamine. Additionally, all five injected ketamine intravenously during their last ketamine injection event. This finding indicates that a user's preferred mode of administering certain drugs, like heroin or cocaine, is often transferred to administering a new drug, such as ketamine.

K-Hole

Many injectors reported that a primary reason for injecting ketamine was to "fall into" or achieve a "k-hole." A k-hole is a general term that injectors applied to the intense psychological and somatic state experienced while under the influence of ketamine. K-holes were more reliably achieved—and more intensely experienced—by injecting the drug. After injecting ketamine, users reported feeling a momentary rush of energy followed by physical immobilization and social detachment for the duration of the experience, which could last from 10 to 60 minutes, depending upon the dosage. A k-hole is characterized by a distorted sense of space, such as a small room appearing the size of a football field, and an indistinct awareness of time, such as a few minutes seeming like an hour. As a user's body slowed and disengaged from everyday conceptions of time and space, his or her mind tuned into often pleasant—though sometimes bizarre—experiential realms, such as spiritual journeys, interactions with famous or fictitious persons, and hallucinatory visions. Once the drug was processed by the body, however, users reported that the k-hole ended rather abruptly but could be quickly reentered following another injection of ketamine.

Injection Risk Factors

Figure 30.1 displays several factors present during the youths' last ketamine injection episode that placed them at risk for viral transmission. First, ketamine was almost always injected in a group setting among other injectors. Youths reported that these injection groups were as large as 10 people. Large injection groups pose risks (particularly when paraphernalia is shared) since greater numbers of injectors increase the odds that someone in the group is infected with HIV or hepatitis. Second, multiple injections of ketamine were typical, such as 8 to 10 injections over a period of several hours. Multiple injections increase the likelihood that injection paraphernalia will be shared—particularly when the drug injected is one that produces feelings of disorientation. Third, over half of the injectors reported some form of paraphernalia sharing, such as syringes or bottles of ketamine, but most commonly a bottle of ketamine. Liquid ketamine is typically packaged in a sealed 10 cc bottle with a flat rubber lid that is designed to be pierced by a needle point. Youths reported that two or more injectors would pull shots of ketamine from the same common bottle over the course of administering multiple injections of ketamine. Fourth, a relatively large proportion (though less than half) of injectors obtained their syringe from an indirect source, such as a friend who received needles from a needle exchange, a person on the street selling syringes, or an unfamiliar member of the injection group. Injectors who obtain syringes from such indirect sources increase the possibility of obtaining a used or tainted syringe. Fifth, ketamine was frequently obtained for free—a fact suggesting that ketamine is a social or "party drug." Youths who reported receiving ketamine for free indicated that the injection that followed was often spontaneous. During these unplanned drug injection events, youths reported forgoing certain precautions, such as bringing their own injection paraphernalia to the injection setting.

At the time of the youths' most recent injection, the drug was injected both intramuscularly (68%) and intravenously (32%). As noted earlier, intravenous injectors typically

Figure 30.1

Risk Factors During Last Ketamine Injection Episode (N = 25)

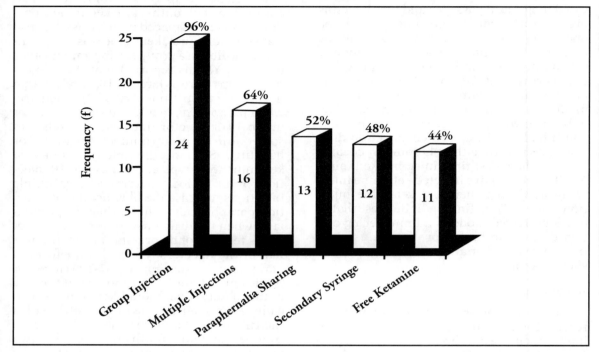

had injected other drugs previous to ketamine, such as heroin or cocaine, and were accustomed to intravenous drug injections. The intramuscular ketamine injectors were either new injection drug users who did not want to inject the drug intravenously or were intravenous drug users who were initiated into ketamine injection by an injection group who administered the drug intramuscularly. Shooting ketamine intramuscularly produced a slower-acting, longer high, whereas administering ketamine intravenously led to a quicker, shorter high. Intravenous injections pose a greater risk for viral transmission than intramuscular injections since intramuscular injections typically do not pull blood into the needle or syringe.

Patterns of Ketamine Use

The frequency of injecting ketamine within the past year varied widely among the youth. For instance, 20% had injected ketamine only one time within the past year, while another 12% had injected ketamine

100 times or more (n = 4 cases or 16% were missing), although 10 was the median number of injections within the past year, or less than once per month. This variability in the number of ketamine injections within the past year reveals two primary facts about ketamine injection and ketamine use.

First, the dynamics surrounding injecting ketamine along with the pharmacological effects of the drug produced a range of experiences that some users found disturbing and impacted upon levels of use. Among youth who injected ketamine only one time in the past year were those who were reluctant to become regular users of drug injection paraphernalia, while others found the effects of ketamine unpleasant, which included vomiting. However, the great majority injected the drug multiple times in the past year—suggesting that most found the experience pleasurable and intriguing. Second, the number of ketamine injections in the past year was also impacted by the availability of the drug. Most reported that the supply of ketamine—particularly liquid ketamine—was variable so that a month or two might pass when the drug was very difficult to obtain. During these dry periods, youths reported injecting ketamine less frequently. In contrast, youths who had a steady supply of ketamine as a result of dealing the drug injected ketamine more frequently in the past year than those youth that did not deal the drug.

During the youths' most recent injection, ketamine was obtained via three primary ways: received from friends for free, obtained as a result of dealing ketamine themselves, or bought from a drug dealer. Dealers obtained ketamine from two main sources: veterinarian offices, where it was stolen or diverted, or Mexico, where it was manufactured and packaged into 10 cc bottles, and could be purchased without a prescription. After obtaining bottles or cases of bottles, dealers sold bottles of liquid ketamine, known as a "lick," or converted it into powder by heating the liquid until it became crystallized. In New York City, bottles of ketamine sold for between $60 and $80, while one bottle could be converted into powder valued at $200 or more.

The majority of youths (72%) reported that their most recent injection of ketamine occurred in New York City (80% when including suburban New Jersey). Other cities where the most recent injection occurred included Portland, Oregon; San Francisco; and rural locations in West Virginia and Montana during outdoor raves. However, this sample population is more mobile than these findings suggest. Including these five sites outside of New York City, youths reported injecting ketamine on other occasions in more than 35 cities and locations across the United State—large cities like Los Angeles and Seattle, but also smaller cities, such as Asheville, North Carolina and Grand Rapids, Michigan. These reports indicate that ketamine is injected across a much broader area than indicated by the current epidemiological data (CEWG, 1999; CEWG, 2000). Additionally, these findings point to the mobility of the youth population under study. Many youth traveled from city to city as a result of homelessness, while others traveled to visit friends or attend raves in other cities.

Ketamine: A Club Drug?

The convention of labeling ketamine as "club drug," while capturing the fact that ketamine is commonly consumed in a social environment, does not accurately locate the settings where ketamine was most often injected among these youth. In fact, only 16% of the injections occurred at raves (more typically outdoor raves), and another 8% happened at indoor house parties. Instead, the most common setting was a street or park (36%), and another 8% injected ketamine inside a public bathroom. The remaining 32% injected inside an apartment or house among groups of injectors numbering between two and six persons. Additionally, after injecting ketamine in these typical settings, none of the youths reported attending a club or rave. (It should be noted that all of the youths had attended raves or clubs on other occasions.) Rather, the youths reported that injecting ketamine often created an experience in its own right that did not require a specialized setting, such as a rave. Interestingly, relatively mundane activities typically followed the injection or injections of ketamine, such as listening to music, watching television, walking the streets, talking about the high, consuming other drugs, or sleeping. Hence, these findings suggest that ketamine is injected recreationally in a variety of settings and is typically injected and experienced apart from the club or rave environs.

Discussion

Our findings indicate that ketamine injectors are an important population of young injection drug users worthy of further study. For as we report, the injection practices, injection groups, and use norms surrounding ketamine differ from heroin, cocaine, crack, and methamphetamine injection drug use: intramuscular injections were more common than intravenous injections; injection groups were often large; multiple injections within a single episode were common; bottles rather than cookers were shared; and the drug was often obtained for free. These findings suggest that the drug injection practices among ketamine injectors place [them] at risk for bloodborne pathogens, such as HIV, HBV, and HCV.

Additional research is necessary to follow young ketamine injectors longitudinally to learn whether, and under what circumstances, they transition to injecting other drugs. The majority of the youths in this sample had injected other drugs prior to ketamine injection initiation, but a large proportion began their injection drug use career with ketamine. The availability and supply of ketamine, which varies over the course of a year, may be an important factor in explaining the transition from ketamine injection to other injection drug use. Additionally, the type of ketamine available to users, such as powder versus liquid, may affect the transition from sniffing to injecting ketamine.

More research is needed to examine how the injection practices and injection groups among young ketamine injectors compare in different cities and locations. For as we indicated, New York City is only one of many cities where youth reported injecting ketamine. We anticipate variability in risk practices across settings since ketamine injection is a relatively new phenomenon and information about how to inject ketamine is diffuse among users.

We also indicated that involvement in the street economy—homelessness, drug dealing, and sex work—was common among this sample of young ketamine injectors. Future studies need to examine how the contingencies surrounding marginalized street existences, such as relationships with sex work partners and within drug dealing networks, affect trajectories into ketamine injection. Additionally, focusing on street-involved youth populations, such as ketamine injectors, is likely to yield information on emerging drug trends since youth are frequently enmeshed in varied drug-using and drug-selling networks.

We reported that a large proportion of users did not combine ketamine with other drugs. Rather, they injected only ketamine during their most recent ketamine injection event. This finding should temper certain assumptions about club drug use—that drugs, such as ketamine, are always or frequently used in combination with other drugs, such as MDMA and GHB, to create a synergistic drug experience. In particular, ketamine injection should not be viewed as synonymous with other club drug use, nor viewed as presenting the same health risks as other club drugs.

Likewise, calling ketamine a "club drug" may be a misnomer. The youths in this study largely reported injecting ketamine in settings other than clubs or raves. Whether due to the disorienting effects of injecting ketamine, the stigma often attached to injection drug use, or the pressure from law enforcement to police and sometimes close clubs, ketamine is most often injected in private dwellings. In other words, ketamine use—at least ketamine injection—has moved outside of the club environs and has become a recreational practice similar to (though not nearly as widespread [as]) smoking marijuana or ingesting LSD.

One limitation to this data, in addition to the small sample size, is the relatively homogeneous demographic profile of the ketamine injectors interviewed: young, male, and white. While this profile may reflect the larger population of ketamine injectors, future research should continue to target street-involved youth but with a greater emphasis on obtaining a sample that includes more women and more members of racial and sexual minorities. Collecting a more diverse sample could reveal different injection practices and injection groups that may have further implications for infectious disease risk.

Lastly, ketamine injectors represent an emerging, though often hidden, population of injection drug users. As these findings indicate, ketamine injectors frequently obtained syringes from sources other than needle exchanges. This lack of direct contact with needle exchanges, while problematic in that ketamine injectors are not using a verifiable distributor of clean syringes, means that ketamine injection practices and related problems are less likely to be reported in syringe exchange data. Similarly, ketamine injectors, particularly those who only inject ketamine, are likely to be missed by studies focusing on heroin, cocaine, or methamphetamine injection. Hence, more studies focusing on ketamine injection are needed to gain additional understanding into the risks and experiences connected to injecting ketamine.

References

Clatts, M. C., Heimer R., Abdala, N., Goldsamt, L., Sotheran, J. L., Anderson, K. T., Gallo, T. M., Hoffer, L. D., Luciano, P. A., & Kyriakides, T. 1999. HIV-1 transmission in injection paraphernalia: Heating drug solutions may inactivate HIV-1. *JAIDS, 22,* 194–199.

Community Epidemiological Working Group (CEWG). 1999. *Epidemiological trends in drug abuse. Volume 1: Proceedings of the Community Epidemiological Work Group.* Bethesda, MD: National Institutes of Health, Division of Epidemiology and Prevention Research, National Institute of Drug Abuse.

——. 2000. *Epidemiological trends in drug abuse. Volume 1: Proceedings of the Community Epidemiological Work Group.* Bethesda, MD: National Institutes of Health, Division of Epidemiology and Prevention Research, National Institute of Drug Abuse.

Curran, V. & Morgan, C. 2000. Cognitive, dissociative and psychotogenic effects of ketamine in recreational users on the night of drug use and 3 days later. *Addiction, 95,* 575–590.

Des Jarlais, D. C., Friedman, S. R., & Stoneburner, R. 1988. HIV infection and intravenous drug use: Critical issues in transmission dynamics, infection outcomes, and prevention. *Review of Infectious Disease, 10,* 151–158.

Dotson, J. W., Ackerman, D. L., & West, L. J. 1995. Ketamine abuse. *Journal of Drug Issues, 25,* 751–757.

Fine, J., Weissman, J., & Finestone, E. C. 1974. Side effects after ketamine anesthesia: Transient blindness. *Anesthesia and Analgesia, 53,* 72–74.

Fine, P. G. 1999. Low-dose ketamine in the management of opioid nonresponsive terminal cancer pain. *Journal of Pain Symptom Management, 17,* 296–300.

Green, S. M., Hummel, C. B., Wittlake, W. A., Rothrock, S. G., Hopkins, G. A., & Garrett, W. 1999. What is the optimal dose of intramuscular Ketamine for pediatric sedation? *Academy of Emergency Medicine,* January 6, 21–26.

Jansen, K. 2001. *Ketamine: Dreams and realities.* Sarasota, FL: Multidisciplinary Association for Psychedelic Studies.

Lilly, J. 1978. *The scientist: A novel autobiography.* Philadelphia: Lippincott.

Nikolajsen, L., Hansen, P. O., & Jensen T. S. 1997. Oral ketamine therapy in the treatment of postamputation stump pain. *Acta Anaesthesiol Scandinavia, 41,* 427–429.

Perel, A. & Davidson, J. T. 1976. Recurrent hallucinations following ketamine. *Anaesthesia, 31,* 1081–1083.

Reynolds, S. 1997. Rave culture: Living dream or living death? In Redhead, S. (Ed.), *The clubcultures reader* (pp. 84–93). Malden, MA: Blackwell Publishers.

Siegel, R. K. 1978. Phenylcyclidine and ketamine intoxication: A study of four populations of recreational users. In Peterson, R. C. & Stillman, R. C. (Eds.), *Phencyclidine abuse: An appraisal* (pp. 119–147). NIDA research monograph 21. Rockville, MD: National Institutes on Drug Abuse (NIDA).

Weil, A. & Rosen, W. 1983. *Chocolate to morphine: Understanding mind-active drugs.* Boston: Houghton Mifflin Company.

For Discussion

How accurate is it to describe ketamine as a "club drug"? Does the setting in which the drug is used have an effect on the intended experience? How, if at all, does the user's route of administration influence the perception of ketamine as a "club drug"?

Reprinted from: Stephen E. Lankenau and Michael C. Clatts, "Ketamine Injection Among High Risk Youth: Preliminary Findings from New York City." In *Journal of Drug Issues* 32 (3), pp. 893–905. Copyright © 2002 by *Journal of Drug Issues.* Reprinted with permission. ✦

31

Healthy Nightclubs and Recreational Substance Use

From a Harm Minimisation to a Healthy Settings Approach

Mark A. Bellis[a]
Karen Hughes[b]
Helen Lowey[b]

Mark Bellis and his colleagues suggest that reducing the harm associated with drug use is best understood from a "healthy settings" approach. Characteristics of the venues in which some drugs are consumed often contribute to injury, ill health, and risk taking among drug users. A "healthy settings" approach offers solutions for minimizing these negative implications of drug taking.

Introduction

In the UK alone, approximately 3.5 million individuals go to nightclubs each week (Mintel International Group, 2000). Most of these are younger people and a large proportion of them consume illegal drugs often in combination with alcohol (Measham, Aldridge, & Parker, 2001). The relationship between recreational drug use and dance music events is now well established (Release, [1997] and Winstock, [Griffiths, & Stewart, 2001]). In the UK, for instance, estimates of ecstasy, amphetamine, and cocaine use in regular clubbers (i.e. attendees at nightclubs) or those travelling abroad to visit international nightclub resorts (e.g. Ibiza) far exceed average levels of consumption by individuals in the general population (Bellis, Hale, Bennett, Chaudry, & Kilfoyle, 2000) (Table 31.1).

The acute and long-term problems relating to *recreational* (i.e. ecstasy, amphetamine, and cocaine) drug use are the subject of a wide range of studies (Parrott [et al., 2001,] and Reneman [et al., 2001]) and form the rationale for a variety of health interventions (Niesnk [et al., 2000] and Page, [2000]). Thus, ecstasy use has been linked to short-term health effects such as hyperthermia (Henry, Jeffreys, & Dawling, 1992) as well as long-term effects such as memory problems (Reneman et al., 2001). Interventions addressing recreational drug use have often been outreach based (Crew 2000, 2001) and focused on disseminating information on adverse effects of drugs and how to avoid them, problems around combining substances (often drugs and alcohol), and courses of action necessary when acute adverse effects are experienced. However, there is now a growing recognition that the adverse effects of club drugs are strongly related to the environment in which they are used rather than resulting solely from the toxic properties of substances themselves (Calafat et al., 2001). Often, reports of ecstasy-related deaths refer to the temperature of the environment—The most likely cause of death is heatstroke. The temperature inside the club had reached 40°C (Burke, 2001) or in other instances the lack of basic facilities to redress the effects of dancing and substance use—A number of people complained about lack of water (Bowcott, 2001).

In this paper, we argue that the relationship between the health effects of substance use and the environment in which [substances] are used is much wider than temperature control and access to water and extends across the entire nightlife setting. We explore the wide range of factors that contribute to risk in nighttime environments and describe initiatives that effectively address these issues without curtailing fun. Consequently, we argue that by adopting a broad settings approach (World Health Organisation, 1997) to nightclubs, inclusive solutions to reducing harm in clubs (including that caused by drugs) can be better devel-

Table 31.1

Levels of Drug Use in Three UK Surveys

	British Crime Survey[a] (%)	Ibiza Uncovered Survey[b] (%)	Dancing on Drugs Survey[c] (%)
Cannabis	22	51	69.5
Ecstasy	5	39	51.4
Amphetamine	5	27	53.5
Cocaine	5	26	27.1

[a] 16–29-year-olds in the general population; drugs used in last 12 months (Ramsay, Baker, Goulden, Sharp, & Sondhi, 2001).

[b] 16–29-year-olds who visited Ibiza during Summer 2000; drugs used in last 6 months (Bellis et al., 2000).

[c] 15–57-year-olds attending dance events; drugs used in last 3 months (Measham et al., 2001).

oped and disseminated. Furthermore, the same approach can also facilitate multidisciplinary involvement in nightlife health, taking health issues solely from health departments and placing the responsibility also in the hands of organisations such as local authorities, police, voluntary organisations, club owners and managers, door staff, and clubbers themselves. Finally, we suggest that with worldwide growth in dance music tourism, this multidisciplinary approach needs to be extended to include travel and tourism organisations and requires collaboration on an international level.

Healthy Settings and Nightclubs

A healthy settings approach (World Health Organisation, 1997) recognises that the effects of any particular setting on an individual's health are related to the general conditions within that setting, perhaps more than they are to provision of health or other care facilities. The nightclub setting at its most basic is a building that provides loud music, often with a repetitive beat, a dance area that usually has low background light and intermittent bright lighting effects and a licensed bar. Developing this environment as a healthy setting must recognise that large numbers of clubbers regularly consume substances such as alcohol, drugs, and tobacco (often in combination) and consequently experience a variety of psychological and physiological effects. Furthermore, the criminal nature of some drug use and environmental factors such as poor ventilation mean substance consumption can directly affect staff,

for example, pressure on door staff to allow drugs into clubs (Morris, 1998) and passive smoking affecting bar staff, respectively (Jones, Love, Thomson, Green, & Howden-Chapman, 2001).

Some settings approaches to club health are well established. Harm minimisation messages advising sipping water, avoiding mixing alcohol with ecstasy, and taking periods of rest provide the essential information for individuals to protect their health (London Drug Policy Forum, 1996). However, without cool areas within the club, often referred to as chill out areas (London Drug Policy Forum, 1996) and access to free cold water, such advice cannot be implemented. Equally, when adverse reactions to drugs are experienced, a separate appropriately stocked first-aid room, trained staff, and access for emergency services are all required to allow the best chance of recovery. However, other often more deleterious effects on health are also related to nightlife and substance use. In the UK in 1999, 19% of all violent acts (n = 3,246,000) occurred outside a pub or club. Overall, 40% of violent incidents were related to alcohol use and 18% to drugs (Kershaw et al., 2000). The paraphernalia of alcohol use also contributes to harm, with 5000 people being attacked with pint glasses every year of whom many are scarred for life (Deehan, 1999). Thus, both the promotion of aggression by, for instance, alcohol (Institute of Alcohol Studies, 2001) and the paraphernalia of substance use play parts in the harm caused by violence.

Less frequently addressed issues, which are important to a settings approach to club health, include the risk of smoking and in particular fire. Large amounts of electrical equipment, the use of old converted premises, low lighting, and a high proportion of smokers (Measham et al., 2001) all contribute to making nightclubs high-risk environments. Additionally, substance use can mean that patrons can be disorientated, leading to further implications particularly if an emergency evacuation of the building is required. A healthy setting should promote well-marked fire exits (some have been known to be camouflaged to fit in with club décor), crowd control training (Newcombe, 1994), and strict compliance with fire limits on the building's capacity (Ministry of Health, 1999). The effects of fires in clubs can be horrific, as graphically illustrated by the loss of life associated with recent incidents (BBC News, 2000; CNN, 2000; and The Guardian, 2001). However, the effects of smoking alone may also be significant. Dancing while holding a cigarette can result in damage to eyes of those nearby (Luke, 1999), whilst non-smoking bar staff are subject to heavy exposure to environmental tobacco smoke while at work (Jarvis, Foulds, & Feyerabend, 1992).

Noise levels in clubs can also pose a substantial risk to health. UK guidance on protection at work suggests earplugs are used when levels regularly exceed 90 dB (Health and Safety Executive, 1999). However, noise levels in many nightclubs reach 120 dB (Royal National Institute for Deaf People, 1999) and at some points noise can approach the pain threshold (140 dB) (Walsh, 2000). However, those utilising the nighttime environment are unlikely to recognise the effects on their hearing. The clubbing experience, especially in conjunction with substance use, distracts from concerns about health effects and in the case of some drugs (e.g. ketamine or cocaine) may even anaesthetise the user against pain (European Monitoring Centre for Drugs and Drug Addiction, 2000). As increasing numbers of young people are exposed to loud music in dance clubs, it would be expected that more young people would develop hearing problems. In fact, a survey by the Medical Research Council Institute of Hearing Research found that 66% of club goers reported temporary hearing problems after attending a nightclub (Smith & Davis, 1999). Policies about maximum noise levels in clubs can address some of these issues. However, noise is not just a concern within the club but may also affect the surrounding environment, either through loud music contaminating nearby residential areas or through the noise of inebriated clubbers appearing on the street when clubs finally close (BBC Devon News, 2001). Such noise may also be associated with violence (often related to alcohol and drug use), lack of appropriate access to public transport (leaving long waits or drink/drug driving as the only alternatives), and difficulties in coordinating an adequate police presence when clubs close (Calafat et al., 2001).

Furthermore, any comprehensive approach to a healthy club setting should recognise the close relationship between substance use and sexual health. A variety of studies identify the relaxation of safe sex measures (particularly condom use) associated with alcohol and drug-taking (e.g. Poulin & Graham, 2001). One study has identified individuals using drugs, particularly GHB, specifically in order to temporarily forget safe sex messages they have previously heard (Clark, Cook, Syed, Ashton, & Bellis, 2001). Addressing such issues means providing safe sex information within the club setting and combining this with easy access to condoms. Fire, noise, sex, and other areas for health promotion and protection in the nighttime environment as well as their relationship with substance use are summarised in Table 31.2.

Disseminating Knowledge and Developing Solutions

The use of substances often contributes to the dangers presented within the nighttime environment. Previously, harm minimisation has tended to focus on direct effects of drug use. However, basic measures to alter the environment can substantially reduce substance-related harm. Measures to reduce violence in and around clubs include training and registration of door staff, good lighting around the main entrance, and public

Table 31.2

Some Wider Club Health Issues, Their Relationship With Substance Use, and Developing a Setting Response

Health risk	Relationship to substance use	Setting response	Groups involved
Dehydration and hyperthermia	Ecstasy alters thermoregulation (McCann, Slate, & Ricaurte, 1996) Increased energetic dancing Alcohol consumption causes dehydration	Prevent overcrowding Well ventilated and temperature control Cool and quieter chill out areas or ability to leave and reenter Access to cool, free water Information on effects of taking drugs Pill testing First-aid room and staff training	Club owners/staff Drug outreach workers Health promotion groups Licensing authority Club goers Local A&E
Fire	High levels of smoking among club goers Intoxication leads to disorientation when exiting clubs Flammable clubbing clothes (e.g. PVC)	Prevent overcrowding High visibility and accessible emergency exits Availability and maintenance of all fire equipment Ensure electrical equipment is safe Encourage use of noncombustible material	Club owners/staff Fire authorities Building inspectors Licensing authority Club goers
Damage to hearing	Alcohol and drugs reduce awareness of potential hearing damage Greater exposure to noise due to prolonged dancing	Set maximum levels on systems Restricted areas around speakers Make earplugs available Information on the effects of excessive noise Information on signs of hearing damage	Club owners/staff Club goers Environmental inspectors Licensing authority Health promotion Club goers
STIs and unwanted pregnancies	Alcohol and drugs reduce inhibitions (Calafat, 2000) Substances help forget safe sex message (Clark et al., 2001)	Easy availability of condoms Information on safer sex	Health promotion Public health department Contraception services Club owners Club goers
Accident Glass Burns Falls General	Disorentation Anaesthetising effect of substances (European Monitoring Centre for Drugs and Drug Addiction, 2000) Lack of fear and increased confidence Increased risk-taking	Toughened glass or plastic bottles No drinking/smoking on dance floor Provide places to dispose of cigarettes Well-lit and clear stairwells Restricted access to potentially dangerous areas Secure fixtures and fittings are secure On-site first-aid	Club owners/staff Public health departments Health promotion groups Licensing authority Club goers
Violence	Alcohol and drugs increase aggression Drug dealing (Morris, 1998) Steroid and cocaine use by door staff (Lenehan & McVeigh, 1998) Increased risk-taking, lower inhibitions	Stagger closing times Increase public transport availability throughout night Plastic/toughened glass Registration and training of door staff Complaints procedures and policing	Club owners/staff Police Licensing authority Club goers Transport authority

Table 31.2 (Continued)

Some Wider Club Health Issues, Their Relationship With Substance Use, and Developing a Setting Response

Health risk	Relationship to substance use	Setting response	Groups involved
Drink/drug driving	Increased confidence Lack of coordination Increased risk-taking, lower inhibitions (Crowley & Courney, 2000)	Provide cheap soft drinks Public transport: taxis, buses, and trains available Information of safety issues Special club buses provided by clubs	Club owners/staff Health promotion group Club goers PoliceTransport authority
Passive smoking	Increased smoking when out Many "occasional" smokers Link between smoking and other substance use (Lewinsohn, Rohde, & Brown, 1999)	Adequate ventilation (especially behind the bar) Adequate "break areas" for staff No smoking areas Information on dangers of smoking	Club owners Outreach workers Smoking prevention groups Health promotion groups Licensing authority Club goers

transport integrated into the nighttime environment so that individuals can quickly and easily leave city centres (London, [1996] and Calafat). Specific measures to reduce spillage of bottles from bars and clubs onto streets can also reduce the risk of glass-related injuries (The Kirklees Partnership, 1999). Inside, club design should anticipate and acknowledge the exuberant behaviour and intoxicated state of patrons by restricting access to any areas where falls are likely and ensuring exits are well lit and distinctive (London Drug Policy Forum, 1996).

Importantly, the process of tackling harm reduction across the entire nightlife setting legitimises the inclusion of a wide variety of organisations and individuals who may have felt that they could not engage in dialogue solely on a drug use agenda. These groups may include club and bar owners, club goers and club staff, event promoters, local authorities and politicians, environmental health officials, and travel and tour operators as well as youth services, health services, police, and other emergency services. Furthermore, sometimes, this mix of individuals produces novel solutions. For example, to reduce night crime and increase public safety, the owners of a number of neighbouring venues have supported the employment [of] a uniformed police officer dedicated to patrolling outside their premises (Greater Manchester Police, 2001). Also, in North Devon, a police initiative involved handing out free lollipops as clubbers left nightclubs in order to reduce noise in the surrounding areas (BBC Devon News, 2001).

International Considerations

The recent clubbing phenomenon probably has its routes in Ibiza where the mix of music (known as the Balearic Beat) and concurrent use of ecstasy rose to popularity (Calafat et al., 1998). Today, travelling in the form of dance music tourism (individuals specifically travelling abroad to attend dance events or choosing to holiday in destinations renowned for their nightlife) is more popular than ever. Major international clubbing resorts include Ibiza in Spain, Rimini in Italy, and Ayia Napa in Cyprus. Clubbing has additional elements of risk when undertaken in an unfamiliar country. Thus, geography abroad is often unfamiliar, and combined with a different language, this can mean health services or other forms of help are difficult to locate and access. Furthermore, accessing items such as condoms or emergency contraception may also prove more difficult. Legislation can be different and poorly understood, leading to unexpected confrontations with judicial services. If drugs are purchased, the supplier will often be untested, raising the possibility of counterfeits. Equally, alcohol measures may vary in size and purity from standard measures within individuals' home countries.

When alcohol and drugs are consumed, a combination of hotter climates, longer periods of dancing, and possible gastrointestinal infections increase the risk of severe dehydration. Importantly, however, along with environmental change, individuals abroad are often free from the social constraints of work and family that restrict their substance use and sexual behaviour (Ryan and Kinder, 1996). Thus, an individual may go clubbing one night per week while at home, whereas during a 2-week trip abroad the same individual may visit a club every night. This in turn can significantly alter an individual's exposure to substances. For instance, around a third of all young people from the UK who visited Ibiza in 1999 used ecstasy while on the island. The vast majority of these also used ecstasy in the UK (Bellis et al., 2000). However, the way in which people used ecstasy while abroad was significantly different. Of ecstasy users, only 3% used the drug 5 or more days a week in the UK while 45% of the same group used the drug 5 or more days a week while in Ibiza. Similar trends in increased frequency of use were also seen for alcohol, amphetamine, and cocaine.

Little is currently known about the health effects of such periods of intense substance use. Clearly, the opportunities for adverse reactions are substantially increased where multiple drugs are being regularly consumed along with alcohol on a nightly basis. Furthermore, intense periods of consumption provide at least the possibility that more frequent drug use could continue when individuals return home, potentially moving individuals' habits further towards problematic use.

In order to address the health needs of the increasingly large numbers of young people who regularly travel to experience international nightlife, new approaches to health promotion and protection are required. New literature and campaigns are needed that provide international information on substance use and nightlife health for those travelling abroad. They should tackle the broad range of risks to health, including environmental considerations, but should also address the changes in substance use that occur while abroad (Bellis et al., 2000). Access to such information can utilise new technologies affiliated with club culture (e.g. the Internet) and popular with the major clubbing age groups (Hughes & Bellis, in press). Good examples of such sites are already available (*www.dancesafe.org* and *www.ravesafe.org*).

Conclusions

Around the world, clubbing is now well established as a major feature of the nighttime environment. It provides a social outlet for millions of individuals every week and developing a popular club scene has reinvigorated many cities bringing money and employment. Substance use in clubs is strongly affiliated with relaxation, exercise (Gaule, Dugdill, Peiser, & Guppy, 2001), and meeting new sexual partners. Whether these pastimes lead to increased well-being or ill health depends on the environment and the specific behaviour of individuals. Developing clubs as a healthy setting requires interventions that protect and promote health while retaining fun as a central feature. Where interventions or regulations substantially reduce fun young people may look elsewhere for their entertainment (e.g. illegal parties). Consequently, organisations need to recognise the importance of involving young people in the development of nighttime health interventions.

Substance use is one of the major risks to health in the nighttime environment both through its direct effects on individuals' health and through the alterations in behaviour and perception that it causes. However, many organisations and individuals do not feel either comfortable or equipped to engage in drug-specific interventions or even discussions. By developing a healthy settings approach to clubs, the emphasis of health interventions can be diverted away from solely drug use to include a wider range of issues. This means key individuals and organisations (including club owners, staff, promoters, and major industries) can be engaged in a harm minimisation agenda that includes drug use along with alcohol, tobacco, transport, security, and other environmental issues. Furthermore, tackling a broad range of issues in the nighttime environment reaches groups that are difficult to reach through education or occupational settings, such as those who play truant or are unemployed.

Some countries have already engaged in this more holistic approach to nighttime health by generating broader guidelines on safer clubs and clubbing (e.g. London, [1996]; Ministry, [1999] and Newcombe, [1994]). However, with cheaper air travel and young people having greater expendable income (Calafat et al., 2001) combined with the international nature of the clubbing phenomenon, a significant proportion of an individual's annual clubbing nights can be spent in nightclubs abroad where risks to health may be even greater. As a result, guidelines are required to provide basic standards for nightclubs on an international basis and different interventions need to be developed to address local and international needs. Efforts to develop international guidelines on club health are already underway (*www.clubhealth.org.uk*). However, empirical evidence on changes in individuals' behaviour when abroad (Bellis et al., 2001) and the resultant effects on health are both rare and urgently needed. Without such intelligence, the appropriate structure of health interventions to minimise harm for millions of dance music tourists remains unclear and the burden of ill health carried especially by younger people may unnecessarily be increasing.

Notes

a. Birkenhead and Wallasey Primary Care Trust, St. Catherine's Hospital, Church Road, Birkenhead, CH42 0LQ, UK.

b. Centre for Public Health, Liverpool John Moores University, 70 Great Crosshall Street, Liverpool, L3 2AB, UK.

References

BBC Devon News (2001). Lollipops gag late-night revellers. *BBC News* (online).

BBC News (2000). Mexico club blaze kills 19. *BBC News*, Friday, 20 October 2000.

Bellis, M. A., Hale, G., Bennett, A., Chaudry, M., & Kilfoyle, M. (2000). Ibiza uncovered: changes in substance use and sexual behaviour amongst young people visiting an international night-life resort. *International Journal on Drug Policy* 11, pp. 235–244.

Bellis, M. A., Hughes, K., Bennett, A., & Chaudri, M. (2001). *Three years of research on risk behaviour in Ibiza* (in preparation).

Bowcott, O. (2001). Ecstasy deaths may have been caused by heat, not a bad batch. *The Guardian*, Saturday, 30 June 2001.

Burke, J. (2001). Ecstasy's death toll "set to go on rising." *The Guardian*, Sunday, 1 July 2001.

Calafat, A., Fernandez, C., Juan, M., Bellis, M. A., Bohrn, K., Hakkarainen, P., Kilfoyle-Carrington, M., Kokkevi, A., Maalste, N., Mendes, F., Siamou, I., Simojn, J., Stocco, P., & Zavatti, P. (2001). *Risk and control in the recreational drug culture: SONAR project*. Spain: IREFREA.

Calafat, A., Stocco, P., Mendes, F., Simon, J., van de Wijngaart, G., Sureda, M., Palmer, A., Maalste, N., & Zapatti, P. (1998). *Characteristics and social representation of ecstasy in Europe*. Valencia: IREFREA and European Commission.

Clark, P., Cook, P. A., Syed, Q., Ashton, J. R., & Bellis, M. A. (2001). *Re-emerging syphilis in the North West: lessons from the Manchester outbreak*. Liverpool: Public Health Sector, Liverpool John Moores University.

CNN (2000). Christmas fire kills at least 309 at China shopping centre. *CNN*, 27 December 2000.

Crew 2000 (2001). Development of strategies for secondary prevention in drug use. Patterns of drug use amongst young people at clubs and pre-club bars in Edinburgh. *Project Report*. Edinburgh: Crew 2000.

Crowley, J., & Courney, R. (2000). The relation between drug use, impaired driving and traffic accidents. *The results of an investigation carried out for the European Monitoring Centre on Drugs and Drug Addictions (EMCDDA), Lisbon*. Proceedings of Road Traffic and Drugs, Strasbourg, 19–21 April 1999. Council of Europe Publishing.

Deehan, A. (1999). *Alcohol and crime: taking stock*. Policing and Reducing Crime Unit, Crime Reduction Research Series Paper 3. London: Home Office.

European Monitoring Centre for Drugs and Drug Addiction (2000). *Report on the risk assessment of ketamine in the framework of the joint action on new synthetic drugs*. Portugal: EMCDDA.

Gaule, S., Dugdill, L., Peiser, B., & Guppy, A. (2001). *Moving beyond the drugs and deviance issues: rave dancing as a health promoting alternative to conventional physical activity*. In: Proceedings of club health 2002. Liverpool John Moores University and Trimbos Institute. Available at: *www.clubhealth.org.uk*.

Greater Manchester Police (2001). *Manchester City Centre venues team up with police to reduce night crime*. Press release.

The Guardian (2001). Dutch fire toll climbs to 10 with 17 fighting for life. *The Guardian*, Wednesday, 3 January 2001.

Health and Safety Executive (1999). *Introducing the noise at work guidelines: a brief guide to the guidelines controlling noise at work*. INDG75 (rev) C150 11/99. Suffolk: HSE Books.

Henry, J. A., Jeffreys, K. J., & Dawling, S. (1992). Toxicity and deaths from 3,4-methylenedioxymethamphetamine ("Ecstasy"). *Lancet* 340, 384–387.

Hughes, K., & Bellis, M. A. (1992). *Disseminating public health information and the public health evidence base: assessing the current and future potential for the Internet and e-mail*. Health Development Agency and North West Public Health Observatory (in press).

Institute of Alcohol Studies (2001). *Alcohol and crime. IAS factsheet*. Cambridgeshire: Institute of Alcohol Studies.

Jarvis, M. J., Foulds, J., & Feyerabend, C. (1992). Exposure to passive smoking among bar staff. *British Journal of Addiction* 87, 111–113.

Jones, S., Love, C., Thomson, G., Green, R., & Howden-Chapman, P. (2001). Second-hand smoke at work: the exposure, perceptions and attitudes of bar and restaurant workers to environmental tobacco smoke. *Australian and New Zealand Journal of Public Health* 25, 90–93.

Kershaw, C., Budd, T., Kinshott, G., Mattinson, J., Mayhew, P., & Myhill, A. (2000). *The 2000 British crime survey*. Home Office Statistical Bulletin 18/00. London: Home Office.

Lenehan, P., & McVeigh, J. (1998). *Anabolic steroids: a guide for professionals*. The Drugs and Sport Information Service, University of Liverpool.

Lewinsohn, P. M., Rohde, P., & Brown, R. A. (1999). Level of current and past adolescent cigarette smoking as predictors of future substance use disorders in young adulthood. *Addiction* 94, 913–921.

London Drug Policy Forum (1996). *Dance till dawn safely: a code of practice on health and safety at dance venues.* London: Drug Policy Forum.

Luke, C. (1999). A little nightclub medicine. In M. Kilfoyle & M. A. Bellis (Eds.), 1999. *Club health: the health of the clubbing nation.* Liverpool: Department of Public Health, Liverpool John Moores University.

McCann, U. D., Slate, S. O., & Ricaurte, G. A. (1996). Adverse reactions with 3,4-methylenedioxymethamphetamine (MDMA: "ecstasy"). *Drug Safety* 15, 107.

Measham, F., Aldridge, J., & Parker, H. (2001). *Dancing on drugs: risk, health and hedonism in the British club scene.* London: Free Association Books.

Ministry of Health (1999). *Guidelines for SAFE dance parties: the big book.* New Zealand: Ministry of Health.

Mintel International Group (2000). *Nightclubs and discotechques: market size and trends.* Report Code 11/2000, London.

Morris, S. (1998). *Clubs, drugs and doormen.* Crime Detection and Prevention Series Paper 86, Police Research Group, London: Home Office.

Newcombe, R. (1994). *Safer dancing: guidelines for good practice at dance parties and nightclubs.* Liverpool: 3D Pub.

Niesnk, R., Nikken, G., Jansen, F., & Spruit, I. (2000). *The drug information and monitoring service (DIMS) in the Netherlands: a unique tool for monitoring party drugs.* Proceedings of club health 2002. Liverpool John Moores University and Trimbos Institute. Available at: *www.clubhealth.org.uk.*

Page, S. (2000). *Death on the dancefloor.* Proceedings of club health 2002. Liverpool John Moores University and Trimbos Institute. Available at: *www.clubhealth.org.uk.*

Parrott, A. C., Milani, R. M., Parmar, R., & Turner, J. D. (2001). Recreational ecstasy/MDMA and other drug users from the UK and Italy: psychiatric problems and psychobiological problems. *Psychopharmacology* 159, 77–82.

Poulin, C., & Graham, L. (2001). The association between substance use, unplanned sexual intercourse and other sexual behaviours among adolescent students. *Addiction* 96, 607–621.

Ramsay, M., Baker, P., Goulden, C., Sharp, C., & Sondhi, A. (2001). *Drug misuse declared in 2000: results from the British crime survey.* Home Office Research Study 224. London: Home Office.

Release (1997). *Drugs and dance survey: an insight into the culture.* London: Release.

Reneman, L., Lavalaye, J., Schmand, B., de Wolff, F. A., van den Brink, W., den Heeten, G. J., & Booij, J. (2001). Cortical serotonin transporter density and verbal memory in individuals who stopped using methylenedioxymethamphetamine (MDMA or "ecstasy"): preliminary findings.

Royal National Institute for Deaf People (1999). *Safer sound: an analysis of musical noise and hearing damage.* London: RNID.

Ryan, C., & Kinder, R. (1996). Sex, tourism and sex tourism: fulfilling similar needs? *Tourist Management,* 17, 507–518.

Smith, P., & Davis, A. (1999). Social noise and hearing loss. *Lancet* 353, 1185.

The Kirklees Partnership (1999). *Boiling point preventer: a code of practice for dealing with drugs and violence in pubs and clubs.* Yorkshire: The Kirklees Partnership.

Walsh, E. (2000). *Dangerous decibels: dancing until deaf.* San Francisco: The Bay Area Reporter, Hearing Education and Awareness for Rockers.

Winstock, A. R., Griffiths, P., & Stewart, D (2001). Drugs and the dance music scene: a survey of current drug use patterns among a sample of dance music enthusiasts in the UK. *Drug and Alcohol Dependence* 64, 9–17.

World Health Organisation (1997). *The Jakarta declaration on leading health promotion into the 21st century.* Fourth international conference on health promotion, Jakarta, 21–25 July 1997.

For Discussion

How beneficial would it be to establish international guidelines for healthy nightclubs? What are the most important issues to address, and how would specific recommendations be enforced?

Part VIII

Drugs and Crime

For generations, while commentators on the American drug scene have been sensationalizing the crimes committed by users of heroin, cocaine, and other drugs, researchers and clinicians have argued a related series of questions. Is criminal behavior antecedent to addiction, or does criminality emerge subsequent to addiction? More specifically, is crime the result of or a response to a special set of life circumstances brought about by the addiction to narcotic drugs? Or conversely, is addiction per se a deviant tendency characteristic of individuals already prone to offensive behavior? Moreover, and assuming that criminality may indeed be a pre-addiction phenomenon, does the onset of the chronic use of narcotics bring about a change in the nature, intensity, and frequency of deviant and criminal acts? Does criminal involvement tend to increase or decrease subsequent to addiction? Furthermore, there are related questions: What kinds of criminal offenses do addicts engage in? Do they tend toward violent acts of aggression? Or are their crimes strictly profit oriented and geared toward the violation of the sanctity of private property? Or is it both?

As early as the 1920s, researchers conducted studies seeking to unravel these very questions. Particularly, Edouard Sandoz at the Municipal Court of Boston and Lawrence Kolb at the U.S. Public Health Service examined the backgrounds of hundreds of heroin users, focusing on the drugs-crime relationship. What they found within crimi-nal justice and treatment populations were several different types of cases. Some drug users were habitual criminals and likely always had been; others were simply violators of the Harrison Act, having been arrested for no more than the illegal possession of narcotics. Moreover, among both types a record of violent crimes was absent.

The analyses provided by Sandoz, Kolb, and others established the parameters of several points of view:

- Addicts ought to be the object of vigorous law-enforcement activity, since the majority are members of a criminal element and drug addiction is simply one of the later phases of their deviant careers.

- Addicts prey upon legitimate society, and the effects of their drug use do indeed predispose them to serious criminal transgressions.

- Addicts are essentially law-abiding citizens who are forced to steal to adequately support their drug habits.

- Addicts are not necessarily criminals but are forced to associate with an underworld element that tends to maintain control over the distribution of illicit drugs.

The notion that addicts ought to be the objects of vigorous police activity, a posture that might be called the *criminal model of drug abuse*, was actively and relentlessly pursued by the Federal Bureau of Narcotics and other law enforcement groups. Their argument was fixed on the notion of criminality, for, on the basis of their own observations, the vast majority of heroin users were members of criminal groups. To support this view, the Bureau of Narcotics pointed to several studies that demonstrated that most addicts were already criminals before they began using heroin. Addicts, the bureau emphasized, represent a destructive force confronting the people of America. Whatever the sources of their addiction, they are members of a highly subversive and antisocial group. For the bureau, this position did indeed have some basis in reality. Having been charged with the enforcement of a law that prohibited the possession, sale, and distribution of narcotics, bureau agents were confronted with *criminal* addicts, often under the most dangerous of circumstances. It was not uncommon for agents to be wounded or even killed in arrest situations, and analyses of the careers of many addicts demonstrated that their criminal records were lengthy. But the bureau was incorrect in its belief that all drug users were from the same mold. Studies of drug-using populations have noted the existence of numerous and alternative patterns of narcotic addiction.

During the years between 1900 and 1960, for example, there was a pattern of addiction characteristic of a core of middle-aged, white Southerners. Identified through patient records at federal drug-treatment facilities, these users were usually addicted to morphine or paregoric, and their drugs had been obtained from physicians through legal or quasi-legal means. As "patients" under treatment for some illness, these addicts were not members of any deviant subculture and did not have contacts with other addicts.

There were also groups of *hidden addicts* who, because of sufficient income or access to a legitimate source of drugs, had no need to make contacts with visibly criminal cultures to obtain drugs. Among these were musicians, physicians, and members of other segments of the health professions.

Finally, there was the stereotyped heroin street addict—the narcotics user of the American inner cities depicted in the mass media. Heroin street addicts were typically from the socially and economically deprived segments of the urban population. They began their careers with drug experimentation as adolescents for the sake of excitement or thrills, to conform with peer-group activities and expectations, or to strike back at the authority structures that they opposed. The use of alcohol, marijuana, codeine, or pills generally initiated them into substance abuse, and later drug intake focused primarily on heroin. Their status of addiction was often said to have emerged as a result of an addiction-prone personality, and they supported their habits through illegal means. Also among this group were polydrug users—those who concurrently abused a variety of drugs.

By mid-century, most law enforcement agencies focused their attention and commentary on those who manifested the pattern of heroin street addiction. Their judgments and assertions were often a response to the clinicians and social scientists of the time who had put forth the notion of what might be called a medical model of drug abuse, as opposed to the *criminal* view held by law enforcement. The medical model, which physicians first proposed in the late nineteenth century, held that addiction is a chronic and relapsing disease. The addict, it was argued, should be dealt with as any patient suffering from some physiological or medical disorder. At the same time, numerous proponents of the view sought to mitigate addict criminality by putting forth the "enslavement theory of addiction." The idea here was that the monopolistic controls over the heroin black market forced "sick" and otherwise "law-abiding" drug users into lives of crime to support their habits.

In retrospect, from the 1920s through the close of the 1960s, hundreds of studies of the relationship between crime and addiction were conducted. Invariably, when one analysis supported the medical model of addiction, the next would affirm the criminal model. Given these repeated contradictions, something had to be wrong—and indeed something was. The theories, hypotheses, conclusions, and other findings generated by almost the entire spectrum of research were actually of little value, for major biases and deficiencies were built into the very nature of their designs. Data-gathering enterprises on criminal activity had usually restricted themselves to drug-users' arrest histories, and there can be little argument about the inadequacy of official criminal statistics as measures of the incidence and prevalence of offense behavior. Those studies that did manage to go beyond arrest figures to probe self-reported criminal activity were invariably limited to either incarcerated heroin users or addicts in treatment settings. The few efforts that did manage to locate active heroin users in the street community typically examined the samples' drug-taking behaviors to the exclusion of their drug-seeking behaviors. Given the many methodological difficulties, it was impossible to draw many reliable conclusions about the nature of drug-related crime—about its magnitude, shape, scope, or direction. Moreover, and perhaps most important, the conclusions being drawn from the generations of studies were not taking a number of important features of the drug scene into account: that there were many different kinds of drugs and drug users; that the nature and patterns of drug use were con-

stantly shifting and changing; that the purity, potency, and availability of drugs were dynamic, rather than static; and that both drug-related crime and drug-using criminals were undergoing continuous metamorphosis. It was not until the 1970s that research began to reliably address these issues in order to generate a better understanding of the drugs-crime connection in the American drug scene. In the following chapters, aspects of this research are presented.

Additional Readings

Bean, Philip. (2001). *Drugs and Crime*. Portland, OR: Willan Publishing.

Mohamed, A. Rafnik, and Erik Fritsvold. (2006). "Damn, It Feels Good to Be a Gansta: The Social Organization of the Illicit Drug Trade Servicing a Private College Campus." *Deviant Behavior* 27: 97–125.

Menard, Scott, Sharon Mihalic, and David Huizinga. (2001). "Drugs and Crime Revisited." *Justice Quarterly* 18 (2): 269–299.

Newcomb, Michael D., Elisha R. Galaif, and Jennifer Vargas Carmona. (2001). "The Drug-Crime Nexus in a Community Sample of Adults." *Psychology of Addictive Behaviors* 15 (3): 185–193.

Seddon, Toby. (2006). "Drugs, Crime, and Social Exclusion: Social Context and Social Theory in British Drugs-Crime Research." *British Journal of Criminology* 46: 680–703.

Walters, Glenn D. (1994). *Drugs and Crime in Lifestyle Perspective*. Thousand Oaks, CA: Sage Publications. ✦

32

The Drugs-Crime Connection

David N. Nurco
Timothy W. Kinlock
Thomas E. Hanlon

The nature of the drug-crime relationship is not altogether clear. Is addiction another expression of a criminal lifestyle? Or do addicts commit crime to support their addictions? In the opening essay of this section, David N. Nurco and his colleagues address these important questions, while discussing a number of problems associated with previous studies. Addicts, they argue, should not be classified as a homogeneous group. Some drug users do not commit crime except for drug possession and sale. For others, criminal activity occurs before the onset of addiction, while some commit crimes to support their addictions. The authors conclude with suggestions for improving our knowledge of the drug-crime connection.

The first recorded speculation regarding a link between narcotic drugs and crime appeared more than a hundred years ago.[1]

Since that time, there has been a long and continuing controversy in the United States about the relationship between narcotic addiction and crime. On one side were those advocating the "criminal model of addiction,"[2] who regarded addicts as confirmed criminals who endanger society by their anti-social behavior. This viewpoint was epitomized by the late Harry J. Anslinger, the first head of the Federal Bureau of Narcotics, who served in this capacity from 1930 to 1962. Similar viewpoints were publicly expressed as early as 1924.

As David Musto noted in his comprehensive historical account, *The American Dis-ease*, it was stated in testimony before Congress that heroin was a stimulus to the commission of crime.[3] In this testimony, Dr. Alexander Lambert, the head of the Mayor's Committee on Drug Addiction for New York City, expressed the view that heroin tended to destroy the sense of responsibility to the herd. The commissioner of health of Chicago, Dr. Herman Bundesen, went even further, stating that "the root of the social evil is essentially in our dope, our habit-forming drugs [the] main cause of prostitution and crime."[4] Although there were differences in emphasis and interpretation among those who held that heroin use promoted crime, it was generally agreed that heroin was destructive and criminogenic.

The other side in this historical controversy took the position that narcotic addicts were not criminals, but deprived or mentally ill individuals who were "forced" into the commission of petty theft in order to support their habit. This viewpoint was emphatically presented by Harry Barnes and Negley Teeters of Temple University in their 1945 textbook, *New Horizons in Criminology*:

> It is now definitely demonstrated that most serious cases of drug addiction are the result of neurotic conditions, namely, mental and nervous disorders growing out of deep-seated mental conflicts in the individual . . . It is not likely, however, that normal person will become an addict. . . . Alarmist literature and the propaganda of the crusaders against drug addiction have created a grotesquely exaggerated impression of the danger to society from the drug addict.[5]

This notion has been frequently referred to as the "enslavement theory of addiction."[6] It was based on a medical model, and the proponents of this view advocated the treatment of narcotic addiction by psychiatrists or other physicians. Those who supported this idea included many clinicians and social scientists of the 1950s and 1960s.

Regardless of which side one took in this controversy, it was often assumed that all narcotic addicts were alike. This concept of uniformity was tacitly assumed by most researchers of the drugs-crime connection before the 1970s.

As researchers from the National Institute of Justice summarized in a comprehensive literature review published in 1980, the majority of studies concentrated on how certain factors affect most addicts, largely ignoring the fact that "these factors all affect addicts differently" and that addicts "should not be viewed as a homogeneous group that follow the same career paths."[7] This appears to be one of the major flaws inherent in earlier research.

Research on the Drugs-Crime Connection

Literature reviews have documented that hundreds of studies of the relationship between addiction and crime were performed from the 1920s to the late 1970s.[8] Several reviewers have commented that these studies contained numerous flaws. As James A. Inciardi has summarized elsewhere,[9] the theories, hypotheses, conclusions, and other findings generated by these studies were of little value, since there were considerable biases and deficiencies in their designs. Given the many methodological difficulties, it was impossible to draw reliable conclusions about the magnitude, shape, scope, or direction of drug-related crime.

In their 1987 review article, "Characterizing Criminal Careers," Alfred Blumstein and Jacqueline Cohen maintained that "even though the subjects of crime and crime control have been major issues of public debate, and despite their regular appearance as one of the nation's most serious problems, significant advances in empirical research related to these issues are relatively recent. . . ." They also emphasized that "more effectively disentangling the apparent drug-crime nexus is of particular concern."[10]

Not until the 1970s and 1980s were more sophisticated studies of the relationship between drug use and crime finally undertaken. In their book, *Taking Care of Business*,[11] published in 1985, Bruce D. Johnson and his associates at the New York State Division of Substance Abuse Services noted that earlier literature reviews had concluded that little was known about the crime rates of heroin abusers and emphasized the need for improved information about the crimi-

nal behavior of drug users. They cited the 1967 report of the President's Commission on Law Enforcement and the Administration of Justice: "Only minimal comprehensive data are available relative to the issue of the drugs/crime relationship";[12] and the 1976 Panel on Drug Use and Criminal Behavior: "Convincing empirical data on drug abuse and crime . . . are generally unavailable—the principal reason being the lack of a long-term, research program in the area."[13]

While there were some notable exceptions, the results of studies revealing differential characteristics among narcotic addicts were usually ignored by policy makers. Examples of these exceptions were the works of Edward Sandoz at the Municipal Court of Boston and Lawrence Holt from the U.S. Public Health Service.[14] Both series of studies suggested that there were different types of addicts. Some were habitual criminals and were so before becoming addicted. On the other hand, others were simply violators of the Harrison Act, having been arrested for illegal possession of narcotics. Unfortunately, the notion of heterogeneity of addicts did not become evident until much later.

Methodological Deficiencies of Early Studies

Evidence of criminal activity among narcotic users is longstanding and abundant; however, it is apparent that relationships among the important variables involved are much more complex than were initially believed. As mentioned, literature reviews of studies conducted on the relationship between narcotic addiction and crime found that these investigations contained several important methodological deficiencies. Among the most commonly mentioned problems were the following:

1. The employment of seriously deficient measures of criminality.

2. The preoccupation with the single-cause issue or the "chicken-egg" question of which came first, crime or drugs.

3. The use of "captive" samples of narcotic addicts.

4. The failure to apply measures of criminal activity over time.

5. The failure to correctly identify the empirical precursors, correlates, possible determinants, and patterns of criminality, and the ignoring of the co-variation of such factors within an addict population.

Measurement of Crime Among Narcotic Addicts

Probably the most serious methodological problem contained in early studies of the relationship between drug use and crime has been the use of official arrest records, or "rap sheets," as indicators of criminal activity. In a review of sixty-five studies to determine the methods of measuring individual criminal behavior, James J. Collins and his co-workers concluded that "arrest data are a seriously deficient indicator of criminal involvement—in fact, it is more accurate to view arrest data as an indicator of criminal justice *system* involvement."[15] In other words, arrest data more properly measure how often one *gets caught* for committing crime, and there is far from a one-to-one relationship between how often someone is caught and how much crime he or she commits.[16]

Several studies employing confidential self-report interview methods have shown that the use of arrest data as an indicator of the amounts and types of crimes actually committed results in gross underestimates.[17] These investigations have found that less than 1 percent of all offenses reported by addicts resulted in arrest. Typical of findings emphasizing the inadequacy of official statistics as measures of the incidence and prevalence of criminal behavior are those of Inciardi.[18] In one of his studies, Inciardi noted that his sample of 573 Miami narcotic abusers had engaged in criminal activity for an average of two years before their first arrest. Also, he indicated that subsequent arrest rates were extremely low. Of 215,105 offenses reported by the respondents over a one-year period, only 609, or one arrest for every 353 crimes committed (0.3 percent), resulted in arrest.[19]

A common finding of the research of Jan M. Chaiken and Marcia R. Chaiken has been that number of arrests is a poor predictor of who the most dangerous criminals are. Analyzing arrest data and self-reported crime in a Rand Corporation study of over two thousand offenders in three states, these investigators concluded that it was impossible to identify serious and frequent offenders from official records, since "the vast majority of those who do commit all of these crimes (robbery, assault, and drug sales) have not been convicted of them."[20] Although all respondents had been arrested, it was found that arrests were so infrequent and the official records so inadequate that it was impossible to distinguish the serious and persistent offenders from the less serious ones. Chaiken and Chaiken found that only about 10 percent of self-reported violent predators could be so identified by arrest records.[21]

In our studies of narcotic addicts in Baltimore, we have obtained similar results.[22] In one of these studies, we analyzed the self-reports and arrest data of a sample of 243 addicts. While these addicts had a total of 2,869 arrests over an eleven-year period, they also had accumulated 473,738 days of crime, resulting in a ratio of arrests to crime days of .006. Not only were arrests an extreme underestimate of how much crime was committed, but also the arrests were biased with regard to both the type of offense committed and the frequency of offenses. Violent crimes were more likely than other crimes to result in arrest, and the probability of arrest decreased for addicts with high crime rates.[23]

The Validity of Self-Reported Crime

Any study relying primarily on informant self-disclosure must eventually come to grips with the issue of the accuracy, or veridicality, of such information.[24] In this context, the self-reports of drug addicts are particularly suspect because of the deviant and illegal nature of their lifestyles. In addition to possible distortions introduced in order to conceal unsavory aspects of their lives, genuine errors in recalling information about events that occurred years earlier can further affect the accuracy of the information obtained. However, evidence in the literature indicates that addicts, as a group, tend to be surprisingly truthful and accurate in their replies to a wide range of questions when interviewed under non-threatening conditions.[25] Validation studies that have been conducted have used the following methods: comparing self-reports of arrests with official records, comparing information on drug use with urinalysis results, and using repeat-interview procedures.

It is, of course, clear that the social context and the conditions under which interviews are conducted may affect the addicts' motivation to be candid, equivocal, or deceitful. Thus, even though interview information is obtained in the context of research, it would be just as unwarranted to maintain that addicts' responses are invariably valid as it would be to assume that they are invalid. Research procedures that appear to be particularly important to the securing of valid interview data include the following: the addict's recognition of the availability of an official record (that allows corroboration of self-report information); the interviewer's thorough knowledge of the addict subculture, as well as his or her competence, experience, and training in interviewing procedures; the absence of an authoritarian or retribution function in the interview; the assurance of confidentiality; and the use of a structured instrument that enables internal consistency checks and the offering of meaningful time-reference points to assist in the recall of information. (The "addict career" interview, which will be discussed in more detail later, is especially useful in this respect.)

The Crime-Days per Year-at-Risk Concept

Several investigators of the drugs-crime connection have been striving to develop a meaningful application of what has been termed "lambda"—the rate of offending per unit of time (usually a year) for a given population at risk. Our own calculations involving a variation of this index have used self-reported information from narcotic addicts, covering varying periods, while addicted and not addicted to narcotics over a lifetime of narcotic drug use. Because narcotic addicts may engage in hundreds of offenses per year, it has proved useful to express the magnitude of their criminal behavior in terms of the number of crime-days per year-at-risk (while at large in the community), rather

than in terms of the total number of offenses committed per year. A *crime-day* is conceptually defined as a twenty-four-hour period, during which one or more crimes are committed by a given individual. Thus, crime-days per year-at-risk is a rate of occurrence that varies from 0 to 365.

Our use of the crime-days per year-at-risk measure has served to document the continuity of high crime rates among narcotic addicts over extended periods. Although there are differences in the types of crimes that individual addicts engage in, their overall high rates of criminality characteristically persist throughout their periods of addiction. The continuity of these high crime rates is remarkable. An analysis of crime-days per year-at-risk for 354 addicts interviewed between 1973 and 1978 revealed that the crime-day means for the first seven addiction periods were 255, 244, 259, 257, 254, 336, and 236, respectively. Thus, the high rate of criminality reported not only was persistent on a day-to-day basis, but also tended to continue over an extended number of years and periods of addiction.[26]

Use of the crime-days per year-at-risk approach has also enabled us to document a reduction in crime when individuals are not actively addicted. Inasmuch as the life course of narcotic addiction or "addict career," while in the community, is characterized by numerous periods of addiction and nonaddiction, it is feasible to compare the amounts of crime committed by individuals when they are addicted and when they are not.[27] When crime rates were compared in this manner, it was found that the number of crime-days per year-at-risk averaged 255 during periods of active addiction and only 65 during periods of nonaddiction.[28] There was, then, a 75-percent decrease in criminality from addiction to nonaddiction. Further analysis showed that there was a decline in annualized crime rates during successive nonaddiction periods as well. Conversely, crime rates during successive addiction periods remained high.

A subsequent study of 250 addicts in Baltimore and New York whom our staff interviewed between 1983 and 1984 provided similar results. It was found that the number of overall crime-days per year-at-risk during periods of addiction averaged 259, while the rate for periods of nonaddiction was 108.[29]

Narcotic Addict Types

There has long been a nagging concern about the order of first occurrence of drug abuse and crime, and about the directional nature of the relationship between the two. Many early studies of the drugs-crime connection were preoccupied with this question. The inquiry was typically stated as an either-or, mutually exclusive one. Addicts either committed crimes to support their habits or were criminals to begin with, addiction merely being one more manifestation of a deviant lifestyle. As mentioned, regardless of whatever side one took, there was general consensus that addicts basically comprised a homogeneous group. Only recently (since the 1970s) have researchers begun to systematically evaluate the differential characteristics of narcotic addicts. A major outgrowth of research, based on an assumption of heterogeneity, has been the derivation of narcotic addict types. Such information is just beginning to be available for consideration by policy makers.

Our own work in this area of research has determined that addicts vary along a host of dimensions, including the degree to which they engage in crime.[30] Some individuals are extremely criminal before they become addicted, while others turn to criminal behavior only as a result of their addiction. There are addicts who do not commit any crime, except for possession of illegal drugs, while others commit several crimes per day and carry weapons while doing so. Certain addicts may maintain rather stable levels of crime, while the criminal behavior of others may trend upward or downward, as addiction careers extend over time. Also, many addicts undergo treatment for their addictions, while others remain addicted for long periods of time, with no intention of being treated for their drug problems. Only by carefully examining the various kinds of narcotic addicts will more effective use be made of treatment facilities and correctional resources.

In one of our studies of addicts, we classified a sample of 460 individuals, according to criminality, employment, and adequacy of income to meet needs.[31] Two of the types generated by this classification were so different from one another that they suggested two distinct ways of dealing with drug activities. The first type, the "successful criminal," is accustomed to having more than enough money from illicit sources to meet his needs. The second type, the "working addict," is employed at least eight hours a day and is only involved minimally in criminal activities. The successful criminal would appear to be a poor candidate for treatment that counsels him to seek a legitimate job, paying far less than his illegal income. For such a strategy to succeed, this type of addict would have to be monitored closely to ascertain whether or not he was returning to drug abuse and crime. Should reinvolvement occur, he should be promptly referred back to the court for disposition. In contrast, the working addict attempts to live in two worlds, the "straight world" and the drug subculture; his struggle to maintain this precarious balance makes him a prime candidate for receiving help in planning for a more legitimate lifestyle. It is believed that such meaningful, pragmatic typologies will ultimately serve to increase the effectiveness of prevention, rehabilitation, and correctional efforts with respect to the individual at risk.

Use of 'Captive' Samples

Several literature reviews have reported that most investigations of the criminal behavior of narcotic addicts have ignored the problem of population representativeness.[32] Many researchers have studied only "captive" addicts (those in jail or in treatment) who may possess characteristics quite different from those of addicts at large in the community. This fact obviously compromises the generalizability of results.

While a truly random sample of narcotic addicts is apparently impossible to achieve, since the activity is illegal and therefore often unseen, making the population incapable of complete enumeration, in the 1970s, attempts were begun to minimize these difficulties. One example was our own study, which employed a "community-wide" population, consisting of all individuals identified as narcotic addicts by the Baltimore City Police over a twenty-year period.[33] Another approach to the representativeness problem has been the use of samples of narcotic abusers "on the street." In this type of research, ethnographic methods have been used. Often researchers employ ex-addicts or become familiar themselves with the addict subculture in various ways. An example of the latter, the setting up of "storefronts," is exemplified by the work in New York City of Edward A. Preble and John J. Casey[34] in the 1960s and of Bruce Johnson, Paul Goldstein, and others in the 1970s and 1980s.[35]

Ethnographic research may provide a means of obtaining valuable insights into the procurement of information regarding the drugs-crime connection that has not been possible through traditional research. As Goldstein summarized in 1981:

> Careful and probing research is needed to explicate the dynamics underlying both drugs and crime, and the multi-faceted relationship between the two phenomena. Ethnographic techniques may well hold the most promise in this regard. Interviewing subjects in institutional settings, or perusing official statistics, is a poor substitute for being with subjects on a daily basis.[36]

Measures of Criminal Activity Over Time

Career patterns of criminal behavior and drug use were typically ignored in earlier research,[37] most studies having dealt with single-event, pre- and post-intervention comparisons of criminal behavior.[38] Systematically measuring criminal activity over time is a relatively new development. As William H. McGlothlin[39] and other reviewers have noted, however, unless suitable adjustments are made, the age of the addict may become a confounding variable. Since research has shown that many individuals tend to "mature out" of both crime and addiction over time, the decreased prevalence of illicit behavior among older (more experienced) addicts may be a phenomenon associated with age. One way of dealing with this methodologically, as Blumstein and Cohen have suggested, is by "tracking carefully the patterns of offending by individual criminals in order to collect reliable data," which "involves the characterization of the longitudi-nal pattern of crime events for offenders and assessment of factors that affect that pattern."[40]

A way of applying this method to the joint study of crime and addiction over time has centered around the notion of "addict careers." As mentioned earlier, the addict career, or the time from the first regular narcotic use to the present, is divided into periods of addiction and nonaddiction. Using this longitudinal method, crime rates can be compared between different addiction status periods, as well as over successive periods of addiction and nonaddiction.[41] This form of interview schedule has also been successfully used by McGlothlin, and later by Douglas Anglin, at UCLA in their follow-up studies of addicts.[42]

Types and Extent of Drug-Related Crime

Many researchers have concluded that the prevalence and diversity of criminal involvement by narcotic addicts are high, and that this involvement is primarily for the purpose of supporting the use of drugs. Further, it has been a consistent finding that initiation into both substance abuse and criminal activity occurs at an early age. In particular, several investigators have found that, among samples of drug-using offenders, those who reported the most crime as adults, including the most violent crime, were characteristically precocious in their drug use and illegal activity.[43]

It has also been a uniform finding that frequency of narcotic use is generally associated with higher crime rates. Johnson and his associates[44] found that the heaviest heroin users were more likely to be classified as serious offenders. In their research, such individuals were found to be disproportionately represented in the highest categories of criminal involvement and had the highest incomes from major crime. Examining a broader range of drug abusers, the Research Triangle Institute group[45] reported that "expensive" drug use was at least a partial explanation for income-generating crime. These investigators found that more-than-once-a-day heroin and cocaine use predicted comparatively high levels of illegal income. Further examination of the drug-use-frequency/income-from-crime relationship suggested that, whereas low-use levels are supportable without resort to illegal activity, frequent daily use rarely is. And Chaiken and Chaiken,[46] classifying prison and jail inmates as addicted heroin users, nonaddicted heroin users, nonheroin drug users, and nondrug users, found that addicted heroin users had markedly higher levels of criminal activity than did nonheroin drug users.

In explanation of the above results, one might argue that those individuals prone to be heavy drug users are also innately prone to become involved in criminal activity. Evidence of a more direct relationship between narcotic drug-use frequency and crime requires longitudinal, intra-subject information on narcotic-abusing individuals over periods varying with respect to frequency of narcotic drug use. In our own studies of addict careers, the consistently high rates of criminality associated with addiction periods and the markedly lower rates found in the nonaddiction periods provide substantial support for a causal component in the relationship of drug use to crime. The most parsimonious explanation of these within-group changes in crime rates with varying amounts of narcotic use is that narcotic addiction contributes to an increase in crime. Without engaging in a discussion of causal analysis, it seems evident from the totality of the data that heroin addiction is criminogenic in the same sense that cigarette smoking or air pollutants are carcinogenic—they can, and often do, lead to increased incidence, although they are not the only causal agents.

Although individual addicts vary with respect to the crime they engage in, narcotic addicts as a group engage in many different types of criminal activity. Examining a sample of male and female narcotic users in Miami between 1978 and 1981, Inciardi found that over a preceding twelve-month period, the 573 individuals in this sample were responsible for over 82,000 drug sales, nearly 6,000 robberies and assaults, 6,700 burglaries, and 900 car thefts, as well as for more than 25,000 instances of shoplifting and 46,000 other types of larceny and fraud. Overall, they were responsible for a total of 215,105 criminal offenses of all types during the twelve-month reporting period, or an average of 375 offenses per narcotic user.[47]

Drug-Distribution Crimes

Drug-distribution crimes (e.g., dealing, copping, tasting) appear to account for a sizable proportion of all crimes performed by narcotic abusers. For Inciardi's sample, drug sales was by far the most frequent crime, accounting for 38 percent of all offenses. The respondents averaged 144 drug sales per year.[48] A sample of 201 heroin abusers studied by Johnson reported committing, on the average, 828 crimes per year per user. The most frequent crime was drug sales, or dealing, which accounted for 34 percent of all crimes. The second most frequent crime was copping (buying for others), which constituted 28 percent of all crimes. Taken together, these and other drug-distribution offenses accounted for 65 percent of all crimes reported.[49]

Our recent studies of addicts interviewed in Baltimore and New York, during 1983 and 1984, also documented the dominance of drug-distribution crimes. This sample of 250 male addicts reported performing drug-distribution crimes on nearly 48,000 days while addicted, the average time spent addicted being nearly eight years. On average, the addicts were involved in drug-distribution crimes 191 days per year. For the entire sample, drug-distribution crimes accounted for 48.3 percent of all crime-days. Comparisons of crime-days frequencies with those reported by an earlier sample of addicts, interviewed during 1973–1978, revealed a higher proportion of drug-distribution crimes and a lower proportion of theft crimes in the more recent sample. In the earlier sample, drug-distribution crimes accounted for only 27 percent of the crime-days, while theft crimes made up 38 percent of the crime-days.[50]

The 100 subjects interviewed in Baltimore were also examined in a separate series of analyses, comparing crime-days results with those for an earlier sample of Baltimore addicts.[51] It was found that, for both black and white addicts, crime increased overall, with the greatest area of increase in drug-distribution crimes. This was true of crimes committed during both addiction periods and nonaddiction periods. Minor differences in study procedures, however, render these findings tentative rather than conclusive.

Violent Crimes

Obviously, because of their severe consequences to victims, policy makers and the media have emphasized violent drug-related crimes. While investigations by us and others have reported that violent crimes make up a small proportion of all crimes committed by addicts, the actual number of such offenses is still large, since addicts commit so many crimes. For example, in Inciardi's sample of 573 narcotic users, the proportion of violent crimes committed in the year before the interview constituted only 2.8 percent of all offenses, but this amounted to nearly six thousand offenses, since a total of 215,105 crimes were committed.[52]

Paul Goldstein[53] has recorded many ethnographic accounts of violent drug-related acts from both perpetrators and victims in New York City. Resulting from this research is his theory that violent crime and drugs can be related in three different ways. The psychopharmacological model of violence implies that individuals act violently because of the short- or long-term effects of the ingestion of certain substances. Crimes resulting from withdrawal effects of heroin or directly related to barbiturate or PCP use are examples of this. The economically compulsive model suggests that violent crime is committed to obtain money to purchase drugs. This applies primarily to expensive drugs, such as heroin and cocaine. The systemic model purports that violence results from the traditionally aggressive patterns of interaction within the drug-distribution system. Killing or assaulting someone for distributing "bad" drugs is an example of this.

A study of 578 homicides in Manhattan in 1981 found that 38 percent of the male victims and 14 percent of the female victims were murdered as result of drug-related activity.[54] This report, published in 1986, stated that the observed proportion of homicides related to drug and other criminal activities was higher than had been reported previously in the United States. The authors concluded that rather than being related to pharmacological actions producing aggressive and homicidal behavior, the effects of drugs were probably indirect and related to drug-seeking activities. They concluded that "the fact that over one-third of male homicide victims in Manhattan in 1981 died in drug-related homicides attests to the magnitude and the impact of the drug problem, particularly with narcotics."[55]

Non-narcotic Drug Use and Crime

While it has been acknowledged that a substantial relationship exists between narcotic addiction and crime, the situation has been somewhat less clear with regard to non-narcotic drugs. In a comprehensive review of the literature published in 1980, Robert P. Gandossy and his associates found the evidence connecting the use of various non-narcotic drugs to crime to be inconclusive.[56] A further problem concerning this issue is that narcotic and non-narcotic drugs are often used in combination. Thus, disentangling their joint relationship to criminal behavior, let alone resolving the issue of cause and effect, is problematical. Research endeavors in the past decade, however, have made several advances in addressing these difficulties.

One method of approaching the issue has been to study the crime rates of individuals, during a particular period in which they were strictly non-narcotic users and had never become addicted to narcotics. Inciardi interviewed a sample of 429 such individuals in the years 1978–1981.[57] Reporting both a high prevalence and a diversity of crimes, these individuals admitted to committing a total of 137,076 offenses, for an average of 320 crimes per user, over a one-year period. This rate was slightly lower and the diversity of crimes somewhat less than those found for a sample of narcotic users interviewed during the same period. Of the crimes committed by the non-narcotic users, drug sales accounted for 28 percent, prostitution for 18 percent, and shoplifting for 16 percent.[58]

Another way of studying the non-narcotic, drug-crime relationship has been to correlate rates of various types of crime with the use of non-narcotic drugs during periods of addiction and nonaddiction to narcotics. Our own findings from this type of approach have consistently indicated that the use of certain non-narcotic drugs by narcotic addicts is associated with the commission of certain types of crime, although this varied somewhat by ethnic group and narcotic addiction status.[59] Cocaine use was found to have a particularly high association with several different types of crime, including theft, violent crimes, drug dealing, and confidence games. This association appeared to be stronger in black and Hispanic addicts than in white addicts.[60]

Treatment and Rehabilitation

Most of the addicts we have studied in over twenty years of research have been arrested a number of times and have spent considerable time in prison. Many addicts have also had at least one treatment experience for narcotic drug abuse. However, these arrests, periods of incarceration, and treatment experiences appear to have had little deterrent effect on subsequent criminal behavior in the community for a good many addicts. As we have indicated elsewhere,[61] the finding of continuity and persistence of criminal behavior among narcotic addicts stands out as a major conclusion of our research.

Some encouraging findings concerning rehabilitation efforts have involved the use of legal pressures accompanied by a monitoring or surveillance component. Studies of the California Civil Addict Program by McGlothlin and Anglin[62] found that court-ordered, drug-free outpatient treatment accompanied by supervision, including urine testing and weekly visits to a parole officer, was associated with reduced criminal activity. Other studies, conducted by investigators at the Research Triangle Institute (RTI) in North Carolina, found that legal pressure was positively related to retention in treatment programs, and that time in treatment was a significant factor in the reduction of criminal behavior following treatment.[63] And, encouraged by their findings in a recently reported study of legal pressure and methadone-maintenance outcome, Anglin and his colleagues[64] argue for greater utilization of community drug treatment by pretrial, probation, and parole agencies.

By far the most ambitious series of studies of the influence of treatment on the behavior of the narcotic addict has been that conducted by the Institute of Behavioral Research at Texas Christian University in Ft. Worth.[65] Based on a client reporting system for community-based drug abuse programs, titled Drug Abuse Reporting Program (DARP), this treatment-outcome evaluation research involved a comparison of the effectiveness of methadone-maintenance programs (therapeutic communities, outpatient drug-free treatments, outpatient detoxification clinics, and no treatment). Major criteria of effectiveness included illicit drug use and criminality, along with alcohol use, employment, and need for further treatment. Post-treatment results over a three-year follow-up period were available for four to five thousand clients, with many individuals being followed for as long as six years after treatment admission.

Findings of the DARP revealed a clear-cut superiority of methadone maintenance, therapeutic community, and outpatient drug-free treatment over outpatient detoxification and no treatment. No further differentiation was made among the three effective treatment approaches, all of which produced a marked reduction in self-reported narcotic drug use and criminal behavior. Regardless of treatment type, outcomes associated with treatments of less than ninety days tended to be poor. Persons with less criminal involvement before treatment and persons employed before treatment were more likely to demonstrate favorable outcomes. As apparent in our own research, criminal activity during follow-up was related to daily drug use. And, consistent with the results of other studies, there was no obvious interaction between client and treatment types in terms of outcome.[66]

For DARP clients, during-treatment performance, including longer program involvement and completion of the program, was also positively related to outcome. As in the RTI studies, the marked improvement that tended to occur after the first few months of treatment, particularly with methadone maintenance, suggested a compliance factor associated with coercive entry and program surveillance. After this marked change, there was continued improvement over time in treatment, which suggested a therapeutic effect, due to the development of motivation that was also instrumental in the clients' remaining in treatment.[67]

Policy Implications

Although narcotic addicts as a group extensively engage in crime, the amounts and types of crimes committed vary considerably across individuals. The criminal activity of most addicts is strongly influenced by current addiction status. Narcotic addicts commit millions of crimes per year in the United States, and many of these offenses are of a serious nature. In a very real sense, it can be said that illicit narcotic drugs "drive" crime. Therefore, there is a pressing need to address the problem by continuing to inform the public and its leaders concerning the magnitude and perseverance of criminal behavior among heroin addicts.

As several recent writers have suggested,[68] one approach to a solution involves the early identification of those individuals prone to commit large numbers of serious crimes. Our studies, as well as those by Chaiken and Chaiken, have indicated that, among offenders, those who are precocious in crime and poly-drug use will most likely become the most dangerous, long-term criminals.[69] In addition, we are currently studying the etiology of drug abuse, with the goal of determining the distinguishing characteristics of those individuals who later become addicts, as opposed to their peers who do not. Such information will eventually be useful in planning prevention and intervention strategies.

Another policy with regard to drug abuse and crime centers on the targeted reduction of the amounts of illicit drugs, especially heroin and cocaine, consumed by daily users. Implementation of this policy would involve identifying criminally active, daily heroin and cocaine users and ensuring that they are treated and closely monitored in order to alter their drug-abuse patterns. Our studies suggest that this particular strategy may work best with addicts minimally involved in crime before becoming addicted and during periods of nonaddiction (i.e., those whose criminal activity is more exclusively related to supporting a habit).[70]

In determining an appropriate disposition of a narcotic drug abuser after arrest, it should again be emphasized that there is not a one-to-one relationship between official arrest records and extent of criminal activity. For a more accurate estimate of the latter, it is important that frequency of narcotic abuse also be determined. From our experiences and those of Johnson and his associates, it appears that the more criminally prone, heaviest narcotic abusers are "slipping through the cracks of the criminal justice system."[71] These individuals are committing more crimes per arrest and are managing to avoid involvement in drug-abuse treatment efforts.

Identifying the "heavy" drug abuser is, however, problematic. While individuals tend to be truthful in reporting drug use in research situations, where confidentiality and immunity from prosecution are ordinarily guaranteed, there is evidence that, on arrest, they are likely to conceal their recent drug use.[72] As a result of this finding, urine testing of arrestees has been recommended as an additional means of identifying those who are habitual drug users. Urine testing has, therefore, been utilized in many jurisdictions as an additional means of identifying arrestees who are drug users. It has recently been estimated that approximately 70 percent of those arrested for serious crimes in major U.S. cities test positive for at least one illicit drug.[73] However, while a single positive urinalysis result is a valid indicator of recent drug use, it is not sufficient to identify an individual as a frequent and persistent drug user. As several researchers have indicated, a series of positive results over a long period of time tends to be a more accurate indicator.[74]

At the very least, it would be advisable for criminal justice authorities to give more concerted attention to evidence concerning the drug activity of individuals who are arrested. One useful approach to this task would be to develop a triage/liaison service within the criminal justice system that would deal exclusively with the disposition of drug-abusing offenders. This service would provide a much-needed link between the criminal justice system and a variety of drug-abuse treatment programs available for rehabilitation. Major functions of the service would include participation in decisions regarding sentencing, parole, and probation, as well as in implementation of procedures for the appropriate placement, monitoring, and evaluation of outcome for all narcotic addict arrestees. Thus, this service would be an important resource to clinicians who treat drug abusers, as well as to judges and other criminal justice system officials who are involved in the disposition of individual cases.

It is important to reiterate that all narcotic addicts are not alike. What works with one type of addict may not work with another. Some addicts commit a considerable amount of crime, regardless of whether they are addicted, and they may engage in crime several years before becoming addicted to narcotics. On the other hand, other addicts may not commit much crime and may only commit crimes directly related to their use of drugs; during periods of nonaddiction, their criminal activities may drop to trivial levels. As we have emphasized, there are clearly different types of addicts and different pathways to addiction. Effective strategies for dealing with the drugs-crime problem will depend, to a significant extent, on recognizing this diversity among addicts and on tailoring counter-measures, both therapeutic and judicial, to individual requirements.

Legalizing Drug Use

Some policy makers have proposed that drug-related crime be curtailed by legalizing the use of illicit drugs, making them openly available at little or no cost. This is offered as an admittedly simplistic solution that requires the development of strategies aimed at preserving the smooth functioning of society and mitigating damage to addiction-prone individuals. Outlandish as it may seem, this is an intriguing notion, the ramifications of which bear consideration, in view of the lack of effectiveness of current methods of controlling drug use that largely involve attempts at cutting off the sources of drug supply.

A look at history is particularly helpful in conceptualizing the polarity of this issue. During the era of prohibition of alcohol use in this country, emphasis was placed on eliminating sources of supply. As a consequence, alcoholism became less of a national problem, but organized crime flourished in its nearly exclusive role as distributor of alcoholic products. The subsequent repeal of the prohibition, while dealing a significant blow to the underworld, undeniably increased the number of alcoholics and problematic drinkers in our society.[75]

We are now faced with an analogous situation. Unless innovative strategies are developed, the alternative to the high level of drug-related crime associated with strict drug control appears to be an inevitable rise in the number of drug-dependent individuals in society. Ignoring ethical and moral issues for the moment, from a purely pragmatic standpoint, there is the question of how many drug-dependent individuals society can tolerate.

Basic unresolved questions make any position taken, with regard to the impact of the legalization of drugs, a matter of educated opinion, at best. No one knows for certain the extent to which legalization of drugs in this country would increase the number of addicts, nor whether such a strategy would eventually undermine the integrity of our society. Few would deny, however, that the greater availability of, and easier access to, drugs would increase drug use (and addiction) beyond current levels. Whether this nation can be adequately prepared to deal with the consequences of this increase is, again, a matter of conjecture that is beyond the scope of this chapter. More pertinent is this question: What would be the impact of open drug availability on drug-related crime?

To a large extent, the amount of drug-related crime committed is proportional to the costs of drugs, and the latter depend[s] to a large extent on supply and demand. On the supply side, there are two important considerations with regard to legalization, both of which have to do with the effects of a vigorously enforced policy of interdiction. When it is most effective, a policy of interdiction reduces the supply of drugs and, as a consequence, raises the prices people have to pay for them. It also increases the risks associated with drug production and distribution and thus increases the compensation demanded by drug suppliers for their services. Again, the end result is higher drug prices. Assuming that interdiction will never entirely eliminate the supply of drugs, the ironic conclusion is that vigorously enforced interdiction may very well be instrumental in increasing drug-related crime.

In view of the above, some would argue that legalizing drugs would lead to substantial reductions in drug costs and a corresponding reduction in drug-related crime. Such an argument, however, assumes exclusive, trouble-free governmental regulation of the drug supply. Such an assumption would appear to be untenable. The possibility of providing a more desirable drug price and/or purity, unrestricted quantity, personal anonymity, lack of restrictions with regard to age, and other similar inducements could readily lead to black-market competition in drug sales and thus continue the involvement of illegitimate sources of drug supply. Also, the argument ignores the impulsivity and lack of control associated with the use of certain drugs and the crime-linked effects of such drugs as PCP (which produces both self-destructive and assaultive behavior) and cocaine (the excessive use of which has been associated with violence stemming from affective disturbance and paranoid ideation).

This leads us to a consideration of the demand side of the equation, relating supply and demand to drug cost and attendant crime. In view of the above, and the fact that greater demand is associated with increased cost, adoption of intervention strategies aimed at diminishing demand for illicit drugs appears to be the most suitable approach to dealing with the issue of drugs and crime. Consequently, an appropriate policy recommendation would be that concerted attempts be made to dissuade individuals from becoming involved with drugs, along with persistent efforts to wean them off drugs when and if they do become involved. Drug-prevention and treatment programs employing both novel and already proven approaches should, therefore, be targeted for increased support on a national level by both governmental agencies and private funding sources. To the extent that it is drug-related, criminal activity in this country

should show discernible signs of abatement with any subsequent decrease in drug demand that can thus be effected.

Notes

1. James A. Inciardi, ed., *The Drugs-Crime Connection* (Beverly Hills, CA: Sage, 1981), 7.
2. James A. Inciardi, *The War on Drugs: Heroin, Cocaine, and Public Policy* (Palo Alto, CA: Mayfield, 1986), 106.
3. David F. Musto, *The American Disease: Origins of Narcotic Control* (New Haven, CT: Yale University Press, 1973).
4. *Ibid.*, 326.
5. Harry E. Barnes and Negley K. Teeters, *New Horizons in Criminology* (New York: Prentice-Hall, 1945), 877.
6. Inciardi, *The War on Drugs*, 148.
7. Robert P. Gandossy, Jay R. Williams, Jo Cohen, and Henrick J. Harwood, *Drugs and Crime: A Survey and Analysis of the Literature* (Washington, DC: U.S. Department of Justice, National Institute of Justice, 1980), 67.
8. See Harold Finestone, "Narcotics and Criminality," *Law and Contemporary Problems* 22 (Winter 1957):72–85; Gregory A. Austin and Dan J. Lettieri, *Drugs and Crime: The Relationship of Drug Use and Concomitant Criminal Behavior* (Rockville, MD: National Institute on Drug Abuse, 1976); Inciardi, *The Drugs-Crime Connection*; David N. Nurco, John C. Ball, John W. Shaffer, and Thomas E. Hanlon, "The Criminality of Narcotic Addicts," *Journal of Nervous and Mental Disease* 173 (1985):94–102; Inciardi, *The War on Drugs*.
9. Inciardi, *The War on Drugs*.
10. Alfred Blumstein and Jacqueline Cohen, "Characterizing Criminal Careers," *Science* 237 (1987):985–91.
11. Bruce D. Johnson, Paul J. Goldstein, Edward Preble, James Schmeidler, Douglas S. Lipton, Barry Spunt, and Thomas Miller, *Taking Care of Business: The Economics of Crime by Heroin Abusers* (Lexington, MA: Lexington, 1985).
12. President's Commission on Law Enforcement and the Administration of Justice, *The Challenge of Crime in a Free Society* (Washington, DC: U.S. Government Printing Office, 1967), 229.
13. Robert Shellow, ed., *Drug Use and Crime: Report of the Panel on Drug Use and Criminal Behavior* (Washington, DC: National Technical Information Service, 1976), 5.
14. Inciardi, *The War on Drugs*.
15. James J. Collins, J. Valley Rachal, Robert L. Hubbard, Elizabeth R. Cavanaugh, S. Gail Craddock, and Patricia L. Kristiansen, *Criminality in a Drug Treatment Sample: Measurement Issues and Initial Findings* (Research Triangle Park, NC: Research Triangle Institute, 1982), 27.
16. Jan M. Chaiken and Marcia R. Chaiken, *Who Gets Caught Doing Crime?* (Los Angeles: Hamilton, Rabinovitz, Szanton, and Alschuler, Inc., 1985).
17. See James A. Inciardi and Carl D. Chambers, "Unreported Criminal Involvement of Narcotic Addicts," *Journal of Drug Issues* 2 (1972):57–64; William H. McGlothlin, M. Douglas Anglin, and Bruce D. Wilson, "Narcotic Addiction and Crime," *Criminology* 16 (1978):293–316; John C. Ball, Lawrence Rosen, John A. Flueck, and David N. Nurco, "Lifetime Criminality of Heroin Addicts in the United States," *Journal of Drug Issues* 12 (1982):225–39.
18. Inciardi, *The War on Drugs*.
19. *Ibid.*, 127.
20. Jan M. Chaiken and Marcia R. Chaiken, *Varieties of Criminal Behavior: Summary and Policy Implications* (Santa Monica, CA: Rand, 1982), 18.
21. Chaiken and Chaiken, *Who Gets Caught Doing Crime?*
22. Ball, Rosen, Flueck, and Nurco, "Lifetime Criminality of Heroin Addicts."
23. *Ibid.*

24. Richard C. Stephens, "The Truthfulness of Addict Respondents in Research Projects," *International Journal of the Addictions* 7 (1972):549–58.

25. See John C. Ball, "The Reliability and Validity of Interview Data Obtained from Narcotic Drug Addicts," *American Journal of Sociology* 72 (1972):549–58; Stephens, "The Truthfulness"; Arthur J. Bonito, David N. Nurco, and John W. Shaffer, "The Veridicality of Addicts' Self-Reports in Social Research," *International Journal of the Addictions* 11 (1976):719–24.

26. John C. Ball, John W. Shaffer, and David N. Nurco, "The Day-to-Day Criminality of Heroin Addicts in Baltimore—A Study in the Continuity of Offense Rates," *Drug and Alcohol Dependence* 12 (1983):119–42.

27. See Ball, Rosen, Flueck, and Nurco, "Lifetime Criminality of Heroin Addicts"; Hall, Shaffer, and Nurco, "The Day-to-Day Criminality"; John W. Shaffer, David N. Nurco, and Timothy W. Kinlock, "A New Classification of Narcotic Addicts," *Comprehensive Psychiatry* 25 (1984):315–28; David N. Nurco, John W. Shaffer, John C. Ball, Timothy W. Kinlock, and John Langrod, "A Comparison by Ethnic Group and City of the Criminal Activities of Narcotic Addicts," *Journal of Nervous and Mental Disease* 174 (1986):112–116.

28. Ball, Shaffer, and Nurco, "The Day-to-Day Criminality," 123.

29. *Ibid.*

30. See David N. Nurco, Ira H. Cisin, and Mitchell B. Balter, "Addict Careers I: A New Typology," *International Journal of the Addictions* 8 (1981):1305–25; "Addict Careers II: The First Ten Years," *International Journal of the Addictions* 8 (1981):1327–56; "Addict Careers III: Trends Across Time," *International Journal of the Addictions* 8 (1981):1357–72; David N. Nurco and John W. Shaffer, "Types and Characteristics of Addicts in the Community," *Drug and Alcohol Dependence* 9 (1982):43–78; Shaffer, Nurco, and Kinlock, "A New Classification"; David N. Nurco, Thomas E. Hanlon, Mitchell B. Balter, Timothy W. Kinlock, and Evelyn Slaght, "A Classification of Narcotic Addicts Based on Type, Amount, and Severity of Crime," *Journal of Drug Issues* (in press).

31. Nurco and Shaffer, "Types and Characteristics."

32. See Gandossy, Williams, Cohen, and Harwood, *Drugs and Crime*; Anne E. Pottieger, "Sample Bias in Drugs/Crime Research: An Empirical Study," in *The Drugs-Crime Connection*, ed. James A. Inciardi (Beverly Hills, CA: Sage, 1981), 207–38; George Speckart and M. Douglas Anglin, "Narcotics and Crime: An Analysis of Existing Evidence for a Causal Relationship," *Behavioral Sciences and the Law* 3 (1985):259–82.

33. David N. Nurco and Robert L. DuPont, "A Preliminary Report on Crime and Addiction Within a Community-Wide Population of Narcotic Addicts," *Drug and Alcohol Dependence* 2 (1977):109–21.

34. Edward A. Preble and John J. Casey, Jr., "Taking Care of Business: The Heroin User's Life on the Street," *International Journal of the Addictions* 4 (1969):1–24.

35. See Paul J. Goldstein, "Getting Over: Economic Alternatives to Predating Crime Among Street Drug Users," in *The Drugs-Crime Connection*, ed. James A. Inciardi (Beverly Hills, CA: Sage, 1981), 67–84; Johnson et al., *Taking Care of Business*.

36. Goldstein, "Getting Over," 82–83.

37. Gandossy, Williams, Cohen, and Harwood, *Drugs and Crime*, 67.

38. See William H. McGlothlin, "Drugs and Crime," in *Handbook on Drug Abuse*, ed. Robert L. DuPont, Avram Goldstein, and John O'Donnell (Washington, DC: National Institute on Drug Abuse and Office of Drug Policy, 1979), 357–64; Gandossy, Williams, Cohen, and Harwood, *Drugs and Crime*, 110.

39. McGlothlin, "Drugs and Crime."

40. Blumstein and Cohen, "Characterizing Criminal Careers," 985.

41. See David N. Nurco, "A Discussion of Validity," in *Self-Reporting Methods in Estimating Drug Abuse*, ed. Beatrice A. Rouse, Nicholas J. Kozel, and Louise G. Richards (Rockville, MD: National Institute on Drug Abuse, 1985), 4–11.

42. See McGlothlin, Anglin, and Wilson, "Narcotic Addiction and Crime"; M. Douglas Anglin and George Speckart, "Narcotics Use, Property Crime, and Dealing: Structural Dynamics Across the Addiction Career," *Journal of Quantitative Criminology* 2 (1986):355–75.

43. See Chaiken and Chaiken, *Varieties of Criminal Behavior*; Shaffer, Nurco, and Kinlock, "A New Classification."

44. Johnson et al., *Taking Care of Business*.

45. James J. Collins, Robert L. Hubbard, and J. Valley Rachal, *Heroin and Cocaine Use and Illegal Income* (Research Triangle Park, NC: Research Triangle Institute, 1984).

46. Chaiken and Chaiken, *Varieties of Criminal Behavior*.

47. *Ibid.*

48. *Ibid.*

49. Johnson et al., *Taking Care of Business*, 77.

50. Nurco, Shaffer, Ball, Kinlock, and Langrod, "A Comparison by Ethnic Group and City."

51. *Ibid.*

52. Chaiken and Chaiken, *Varieties of Criminal Behavior*.

53. Paul J. Goldstein, "Drugs and Violent Behavior" (Paper presented at the annual meeting of the Academy of Criminal Justice Sciences, Louisville, KY, 28 April 1982).

54. Kenneth Tardiff, Elliot M. Gross, and Steven F. Messner, "A Study of Homicide in Manhattan, 1981," *American Journal of Public Health* 76 (1986):139–43.

55. *Ibid.*, 143.

56. Gandossy, Williams, Cohen, and Harwood, *Drugs and Crime*.

57. Inciardi, *The War on Drugs*, 128–30.

58. *Ibid.*

59. See John W. Shaffer, David N. Nurco, John C. Ball, and Timothy W. Kinlock, "The Frequency of Nonnarcotic Drug Use and Its Relationship to Criminal Activity Among Narcotic Addicts," *Comprehensive Psychiatry* 26 (1985):558–66; David N. Nurco, Timothy W. Kinlock, Thomas E. Hanlon, and John C. Ball, "Nonnarcotic Drug Use Over an Addiction Career—A Study of Heroin Addicts in Baltimore and New York City," *Comprehensive Psychiatry* 29 (1988):450–59.

60. *Ibid.*

61. Nurco, Ball, Shaffer, and Hanlon, "The Criminality of Narcotic Addicts."

62. See William H. McGlothlin, M. Douglas Anglin, and Bruce D. Wilson, *An Evaluation of the California Civil Addict Program* (Washington, DC: U.S. Government Printing Office, 1977); M. Douglas Anglin and William H. McGlothlin, "Outcome of Narcotic Addict Treatment in California," in *Drug Abuse Treatment Evaluation: Strategies, Progress, and Prospects*, ed. Frank Tims and Jacqueline P. Ludford (Washington, DC: U.S. Government Printing Office, 1984), 106–28.

63. See James J. Collins and Margaret Allison, "Legal Coercion and Retention in Drug Abuse Treatment," *Hospital and Community Psychiatry* 34 (1983):1145–49; Robert L. Hubbard, J. Valley Rachal, S. Gail Craddock, and Elizabeth R. Cavanaugh, "Treatment Outcome Prospective Study (TOPS): Client Characteristics and Behaviors Before, During, and After Treatment," in *Drug Abuse Treatment Evaluation: Strategies, Progress, and Prospects*, ed. Frank Tims and Jacqueline P. Ludford (Washington, DC: U.S. Government Printing Office, 1984), 42–68.

64. M. Douglas Anglin, Mary-Lynn Brecht, and Ebrahim Maddahian, "Pretreatment Characteristics and Treatment Performance of Legally Coerced Versus Voluntary Methadone-Maintenance Admissions," *Criminology* 27 (1989):537–57.

65. D. Dwayne Simpson and Saul B. Sells, *Highlights of the DARP Follow-Up Research on the Evaluation of Drug Abuse*

Treatment Effectiveness (Ft. Worth: Institute of Behavioral Research, Texas Christian University, 1981).

66. Shaffer, Nurco, Ball, and Kinlock, "The Frequency of Nonnarcotic Drug Use and Its Relationship to Criminal Activity Among Narcotics Addicts."

67. Simpson and Sells, *Highlights of the DARP.*

68. See Chaiken and Chaiken, *Varieties of Criminal Behavior;* Peter W. Greenwood, *Selective Incapacitation* (Santa Monica, CA: Rand, 1982); Nurco, Ball, Shaffer, and Hanlon, "The Criminality of Narcotic Addicts."

69. *Ibid.*

70. See David N. Nurco, Thomas E. Hanlon, Timothy W. Kinlock, and Karen R. Duszynski, "Differential Patterns of Criminal Activity Over an Addiction Career," *Criminology* (in press).

71. Bruce D. Johnson, Paul Goldstein, Edward Preble, James Schneidler, Douglas S. Lipton, Barry Spunt, Nina Duchaine, Reuben Norman, Thomas Miller, Nancy Meggett, Andrea Kale, and Deborah Hand, *Economic Behavior of Street Opiate Users: Final Report* (New York: Narcotic and Drug Research, Inc., 1983), 232.

72. Eric Wish, "Drug-Use Forecasting: New York 1984 to 1986," *National Institute of Justice Research in Action*, February 1987.

73. James R. Stewart (director, National Institute of Justice), *NIJ Reports*, no. 213 (Washington: U.S. Department of Justice, March–April 1989), 1–3.

74. See Chaiken and Chaiken, *Varieties of Criminal Behavior;* Eric D. Wish, Mary A. Toborg, and John P. Bellasai, *Identifying Drug Users and Monitoring Them During Conditional Release* (Washington, DC: U.S. Department of Justice, 1987); Marcia R. Chaiken and Bruce D. Johnson, *Characteristics of Different Types of Drug-Involved Offenders* (Washington: U.S. Department of Justice, 1988).

75. Mark Moore and Dean Gerston, eds., *Alcohol and Public Policy: Beyond the Shadow of Prohibition* (Washington, DC: National Academy Press, 1981).

For Discussion

How might the drugs-crime relationship differ by gender, and what are the implications for drug treatment and policy?

33

Sex Work and Drug Use in a Subculture of Violence

Hilary L. Surratt
James A. Inciardi
Steven P. Kurtz
Marion C. Kiley

In this chapter, Hilary Surratt and her colleagues use the "subculture of violence" perspective to examine childhood trauma and adult victimization among female sex workers who consume drugs. They draw on data collected from 325 women in Miami and highlight findings with qualitative narratives collected through focus groups. Approximately three-quarters of the respondents had consumed crack cocaine in the 30 days prior to the interview, and approximately 14 percent had injected during this time period. The authors found that the women had high rates of victimization during childhood and adulthood and that violence was perceived as normative.

The concept of a *culture of violence,* with origins in the fields of both sociology and anthropology, has been used to explain high rates of homicide and other violent behaviors in certain cultures and segments of society. The concept expresses the notion that cultural values and social conditions rather than simply individual biological or psychological factors are significant causes of violent behavior. For example, the culture of violence thesis has been used to explain the higher rates of violent crime in urban inner-city areas (Gottesman & Brown, 1999) as well as the propensity among males in the American South to use violence to settle disputes (Lundsgaarde, 1977; Montell, 1986; Nisbett & Cohen, 1996). In anthropological writings, the culture of violence concept has been considered when comparing the values, attitudes, and behaviors characteristic of generally peaceful cultures, such as the Limbu of Nepal, with those of violent societies like the Yanomamo of Brazil or the Bena Bena of New Guinea (Largness, 1974; Northrup, 1985).

In the criminology and delinquency literature, a *subculture of violence thesis* has been introduced for the purpose of explaining social-structural causes of violence in urban areas. The general model of such a subculture is one characterized by "dense concentrations of socioeconomically disadvantaged persons with few legitimate avenues of social mobility, lucrative illegal markets for forbidden goods and services, a value system that rewards only survival and material success, and private enforcement of the informal rules of the game" (Gottesman & Brown, 1999, p. 297). In this context, the subculture of violence thesis emphasizes Durkheim's (1893) idea of *anomie* rather than normative socialization. According to Merton (1968), furthermore, inner-city minority nihilism is sourced in the disparity between the cultural ideal of equal opportunity and real structural inequalities. Cloward and Ohlin (1960) emphasized that the form that deviant or criminal behavior takes in response to these anomic conditions—criminal, violent, or retreatist (drug addiction)—depends on the opportunity structures for illegitimate activity. Also, socialization remains an aspect of concern here because the exposure of generations of children to violent life experiences refashions inner-city norms to favor violence over nonviolence (Clark, 1992; Shaw & McKay, 1931). This rendering of the subculture of violence concept has been used to analyze juvenile gang violence (Clark, 1992; Kennedy & Baron, 1993; Thompson & Lozes, 1976; Walker, Schmidt, & Lunghofer, 1993), adolescent delinquency (Bernburg & Thorlindsson, 1999), violence committed by black women against black men (Ray & Smith, 1991), as well as generalized violence in urban inner-city neighborhoods (Baron & Hartnagel, 1998; Clarke, 1998).

Perhaps the best known elucidation of the subculture of violence thesis appeared in the work of Wolfgang and Ferracuti (1967), which concluded that young, lower socio-economic class African Americans possessed a value system in which violence was an acceptable and "normal" part of everyday life in the inner city. In recent years, however, Wolfgang and Ferracuti's point of view has been widely criticized because of its stereotyping of young African American males and its failure to address the social-structural sources of the values in question, including the differential treatment of blacks and whites by criminal justice agencies and the media (Madriz, 1999). Despite these limitations, the subculture of violence thesis can be a useful approach for understanding the extent to which certain types of violence are socially situated rather than for focusing exclusively on individual factors.

Within this context, it has been well documented that women sex workers who walk the boulevards and back streets of urban centers are typically at high risk for assault, rape, and other forms of physical violence—including murder—from a variety of individuals, including muggers, serial predators, drug dealers, pimps, police, "dates" ("johns" or customers), and even passersby (Carmen & Moody, 1985; Dalla, 2002; Inciardi, 1993; Inciardi & Surratt, 2001; Maher, 1997; Miller, 1986; Teets, 1997). Furthermore, street sex workers are embedded in the same violent social spaces where street violence and other subcultures of violence exist. As such, it would appear that to a considerable extent, street sex workers ply their trade in a subculture of violence.

The violence experienced by sex workers has been attributed to a number of enduring social problems, including gender inequality and discrimination against women as well as the attempts by many men to exercise sexual control over women (Weitzer, 2000). Class and racial discrimination are also issues, because a great majority of street sex workers are indigent minority women, many of whom lack the social and work skills that offer alternative options. In addition, many street-based sex workers are also embedded

in a complex of social situations that are independently associated with violent victimization, including homelessness (Davis, 2000; Wenzel, Leake, & Gelberg, 2001) and drug abuse (Baseman, Ross, & Williams, 1999; Davis, 2000; Falck, Wang, Carlson, & Siegal, 2001; Gilbert, El-Bassel, Rajah, Foleno, & Frye, 2001). As such, the sex worker milieu can be an extremely violent one. Furthermore, numerous studies have documented that although sex workers are victimized by a variety of different types of perpetrators, most of the violence they experience comes from their own customers, or dates (Church, Henderson, Barnard, & Hart, 2001; Coston & Ross, 1998; Davis, 2000; Farley & Barkan, 1998; Hoigard & Finstad, 1986; Inciardi, Lockwood, & Pottieger, 1993; Maher, 1997; Silbert & Pines, 1983; Sterk & Elifson, 1990).

The impetus for this analysis of sex work and violent encounters was initially an outgrowth of field work in Miami, Florida, undertaken for the purpose of developing a culturally appropriate HIV and hepatitis prevention-intervention strategy that met the specific needs of street-based, drug-involved, women sex workers. In 1999 and 2000, a number of pilot interviews were conducted with police and public health officials, HIV/AIDS prevention groups, and commercial sex workers in an effort to obtain preliminary data and materials that would inform both logistical and substantive issues related to the implementation of such an intervention program. In addition, focus groups were conducted during the same period with 53 active and former sex workers. These women ranged in age from 21 to 46 years; 60% were African American, 30% were White, and 10% were Latina; and they had a mean of 6 years of sex work and 11-year careers in illicit drug use.

Importantly, most of the women consistently reported in the focus groups that they began their dates in the evening when they were "straight" (i.e., not "high"), and after they were paid for sex, they would immediately buy drugs and get high. As this initial high wore off, they would go back to the streets to find more dates and more drugs. As they did so, they became more intoxicated, their thinking became more impaired, and they "quit thinking and caring," which put them at additional risk not only for HIV and hepatitis infections but also for sexual and physical violence. In fact, the overwhelming majority of the women recalled occasions when they had been assaulted and/or raped by their dates. Only one woman mentioned ever seeking help or counseling, primarily because most were unaware that rape crisis counseling services were available. Others feared that they would be "blamed because of what we do."

Because the sex worker focus group participants regularly encountered physical and sexual violence and considered it to be a "hazard of doing business on the street," the prevention-intervention program that was developed as a result of the field research included strategies for assessing a potential "bad date" and ways of averting potentially dangerous situations. As such, it is not only an HIV/hepatitis prevention program but also a violence prevention initiative for women on the street. The research grant to test the efficacy and effectiveness of the model was funded by the National Institute on Drug Abuse (NIDA) at the close of 2000. The target population includes active, drug-using, female sex workers who are randomly assigned to either a standard public health intervention or the sex worker focused intervention noted above (see Inciardi & Surratt, 2002). This article uses interview and focus group data drawn from a sample of the first 325 women recruited in Miami, Florida, during 2001 and 2002 to examine women's experiences of violent victimization, and it discusses sex work as constituting a subculture of violence.

Methods

The target population of *active, drug-using, female sex workers* is defined in this article as women ages 16 to 49 who have (a) traded sex for money or drugs at least 3 times a week in the past 30 days, and (b) used heroin and/or cocaine 3 or more times a week in the past 30 days. Although it has been argued in the literature that "sex work" and "sex exchange" are behaviorally different phenomena (Cohen & Alexander, 1995), prior research in Miami combined with information

from key informants suggests that these distinctions are less clear in the neighborhoods and "strolls" (locations where sex workers walk the streets soliciting customers) where study participants are recruited. It would appear that among drug-involved sex workers in Miami, virtually all drift back and forth between commercial solicitation on the streets and sex-for-drugs exchanges in automobiles, empty lots and backyards, crack houses, shooting galleries, and stroll motels, as well as behind fences, along the sidewalks of darkened streets, and in the many back alleys that are a characteristic part of the downtown Miami geography. Although most sex workers prefer commercial solicitation along the stroll, they also resort to sex-for-drugs exchanges when they have an immediate need for drugs, money is scarce, and paying dates are few in number.

Participants in the study were located and recruited through traditional targeted sampling strategies (Watters & Biernacki, 1989), which are especially useful for studying drug-involved women in the sex industry. Because it is impossible to achieve a random sample of active sex workers, a purposive, targeted sampling plan was constructed that would best reflect what is typical of the larger population. Such a strategy has been used successfully in recent years in studies of injection and other out-of-treatment drug users (Braunstein, 1993; Carlson, Wang, Siegal, Falck, & Guo, 1994; Coyle, Boruch, & Turner, 1991). Targeted sampling has been referred to as a purposeful, systematic method by which specified populations within geographical districts are identified, and detailed plans are designed to recruit adequate numbers of cases within each of the target areas (Watters & Biernacki, 1989). Several elements are necessary for this approach, including the systematic mapping of the geographical areas in which the target population is clustered, the examination of official *indicator data* (such as police arrest reports), information from professional and indigenous informants, and direct observations of various neighborhoods for signs of sexual solicitation. Periodic updates of these are necessary should the locations of the strolls temporarily shift as the result of urban renewal or police activity.

Because the authors of this article have been conducting street studies in Miami for a number of years, numerous contacts have been built up with drug users and dealers, sex workers, police officers, HIV prevention specialists, and treatment professionals. A number of these informants were contacted prior to the onset of the research to elicit information about where the highest concentrations of active sex workers might be found. In addition, through focus groups with current and former sex workers, the downtown Miami strolls most heavily traveled in the sex industry were specifically described, identified, and subsequently located.

The field office for this study is located just east of Miami's well-known Biscayne Boulevard, a more than 15-mile-long major thoroughfare extending from the Broward County line into downtown Miami. An 80-block stretch at the lower end of "the Boulevard" is a major sex worker stroll. To the east are several gated, barricaded, and somewhat gentrified neighborhoods fronting Miami's Biscayne Bay, and to the west are mainly African American and Haitian residential areas long steeped in poverty. Numerous services for the homeless are found along the southern end of the Boulevard strip as it enters downtown Miami. Despite more than a decade of gradual revitalization, the Boulevard stroll continues its long-held reputation for prostitution, sex trading, drug dealing, fencing operations, and the widespread availability of cheap motels that cater not only to locals but also to those who participate in Miami's sexual tourism industry. Some 90% of the women in the sample who specified a particular neighborhood for their sex work indicated areas within the boundaries of eight zip codes hugging the main stroll. Almost half concentrated their work within three zip codes centered directly along Biscayne Boulevard.

A distinctive feature of this project is the use of active sex workers as client recruiters for sampling purposes. The effectiveness of indigenous client recruiters in drug abuse and HIV prevention research has been well documented (Inciardi, Surratt, & McCoy, 1997; Latkin, 1998; Levy & Fox, 1998; Wiebel, 1990, 1993). Because active sex workers do the recruiting of study participants, and because of their membership in the target population, they know of many locations on and off the Boulevard stroll— such as motels, bars, convenience stores, crack houses and shooting galleries, laundromats, and secluded empty lots—where potential participants can be found. In addition, sex worker recruiters have familiarity with drug user networks, "copping areas," and drug markets; they typically approach potential clients with culturally appropriate language, dress, and methods; and their "insider status" helps to build the trust and confidence necessary for successful outreach and recruitment.

All contacts in the street represent prescreening interviews. Those meeting project eligibility requirements are scheduled for appointments at the project intervention center, where they are rescreened by project staff members. After eligibility is confirmed, informed consent is obtained and urine testing is conducted for cocaine and opiates. Interviews are conducted using a standardized data collection instrument based primarily on the NIDA Risk Behavior Assessment, the Childhood Trauma Questionnaire (short form), and the Georgia State University Prostitution Inventory (Bernstein et al., 1994; Dowling-Guyer et al., 1994; Elifson, 1990; Needle et al., 1995; Weatherby et al., 1994). This interview process takes approximately one hour to complete. After the baseline interview is completed, the client is randomly assigned to one of two alternative HIV and hepatitis prevention interventions, either the sex-worker-focused intervention noted earlier or the NIDA Standard Intervention (Wechsberg et al., 1997). The NIDA Standard Intervention is delivered in two sessions and includes individual pretest counseling covering such topics as HIV disease, transmission routes, risky behaviors, risks associated with crack or cocaine use, unsafe sexual practices, rehearsal of condom use, disinfection of injection equipment, and rehearsal of needle/syringe cleaning. Testing for HIV and hepatitis A, B, and C is provided on a voluntary basis in both interventions, and the clients receive relevant risk reduction literature and service referrals as well as a hygiene kit containing a variety of risk reduction materials. Participants receive their HIV and hepatitis test results three weeks hence, and follow-up assessments and HIV prevention booster sessions are conducted at 3, 6, and 12 months post-Baseline.

Focus group participants were drawn from the larger sample of women enrolled in the study and therefore met all of the eligibility requirements for participation in the project, including active drug use and sex work in the month prior to interview. Six focus groups were conducted in total with an average of four participants per group. All groups were facilitated by a senior researcher experienced in the conduct of qualitative fieldwork. To protect confidentiality, participants were not personally acquainted with one another and names were not used during the groups. Focus groups lasted between 60 and 90 minutes and were audio recorded with the participants' permission for the purposes of transcription.

Results

Recruitment began in March 2001, and through mid-2002, 325 eligible clients had been enrolled into the study. Table 33.1 presents information on the demographic characteristics of the study participants. Their mean age is 38.1 years (*SD* 8.1), and some 24.6% are age 45 or older. In terms of race/ethnicity, the majority (60.3%) is African American, followed by White (23.4%) and Latina (12.9%). The living situation of the clients is typically unstable, with 44.7% reporting that they consider themselves to be homeless. Although most women reporting homelessness were staying in shelters or on the streets, some staying in the homes of other individuals on a nightly or weekly basis also considered themselves to be homeless because of the often precarious nature of the arrangement. Not surprisingly, less than half of the sample completed their high school education, and few had legal employment or income. The majority received less than $1,000 per month, primarily from sex work, a spouse or family members, and public assistance programs.

The drug-use histories of the clients (see Table 33.2) are substantial, with most begin-

Table 33.1

Demographic Characteristics of 325 Drug-Involved, Female Sex Workers in Miami, Florida

Age	
18–24	7.4%
25–34	23.7%
35–44	44.3%
45+	24.6%
Mean age *(SD)*	38.1 (8.1)
Race/ethnicity	
African American	60.3%
White/Anglo	23.4%
Latina	12.9%
Other	23.4%
Level of education	
Less than high school	51.7%
High school graduate	30.1%
At least some college	18.1%
Percent homeless	44.7%
Sources of income	
Prostitution	100.0%
Spouse, family, friends	22.8%
Public assistance	16.9%
Other illegal activity	8.6%
Paid job	4.3%

ning alcohol and marijuana use at a mean age of 15.0 (*SD* 4.7) and 15.5 (*SD* 4.3), respectively, followed by powder cocaine at 20.3 (*SD* 6.1), heroin at 23.4 (*SD* 7.5), and crack cocaine at 25.7 (*SD* 8.0) years of age. On average, the clients' illegal drug-using careers span some 22.3 (*SD* 8.6) years. Reports of past-month drug use indicate that alcohol and crack cocaine are the most widely used substances (75.4% and 74.4%, respectively) by this sample, followed by marijuana (57.8%), powder cocaine (38.4%), and heroin (19.4%). The current use of drugs by injection was reported by 13.8% of the women. The sex work careers of the clients are similarly lengthy, spanning an average of 15.8 years (*SD* 9.2) and a mean of 792.2 (*SD* 1,997.3) sexual partners. Past-month sexual activity included a mean of 35.9 (*SD* 62.1) vaginal sexual contacts and 24.4 (*SD* 56.1) oral sexual contacts. A substantial proportion (26.8%) also engaged in less traditional forms of sex trading in the past month, including anal sex, bondage, sadism, "threesomes," and "golden showers" (sexual acts involving urination).

The substantial level of drug use and sex work engaged in by these women is often associated with violent encounters in their daily lives. In fact, the subculture of violence thesis might suggest that interpersonal conflict and violence have permeated the lives and experiences of these women from an early age. Interesting in this regard are the historical self-reports of trauma experienced by the women as children and adolescents. As indicated by Table 33.3, the prevalence of childhood abuse and neglect in this sample is extremely elevated. 44.9% reported a history of childhood physical abuse, 50.5% reported sexual abuse, and 61.8% reported emotional abuse. Neglect was also common, with 58.5% and 45.2%, respectively, indicating some level of emotional or physical neglect in childhood. Because the data on childhood trauma experiences were collected on a 5-point Likert-type scale ranging from *never* to *very often*, this allowed the women's experiences to be rated and classified by severity. The severity scores on each of the items within the individual subscales *(physical abuse, sexual abuse, emotional abuse, emotional neglect, and physical neglect)* were then summed and recoded into four severity ratings based on criteria from the authors of the childhood trauma scale. Table 33.3 presents the prevalence of each of these categories, ranging from no history to severe history. Among those reporting some history of abuse, *severe* trauma is the most frequent classification, regardless of the type of abuse considered.

Of interest in regard to the subculture of violence thesis, reports of childhood abuse are consistently related to current violent encounters. Tables 33.4 and 33.5 present data on the clients' recent violent victimizations and the associations among childhood and adult victimizations. Of the clients, 41.5% had some violent encounter while engaging in sex work in the past year. Most frequently, clients reported that these incidents involved being "ripped off" (forcibly taking back money paid for sex) by a customer or date (28.9%), being beaten by a date (24.9%), being threatened with a weapon by a date (13.8%), and being raped by a date (12.9%). The women themselves often took extreme measures to escape from violent dates, with 15.4% indicating that they had jumped from cars and 23.7% running away from dates.

Importantly for the subculture of violence thesis, current violent victimization is modestly but consistently correlated with childhood victimization. Table 33.5 presents these relationships in detail. Spearman correlation coefficients were computed because they are most appropriate for the analysis of the ordinal-level abuse history data in this study. Interestingly, the severity of abuse history, be it sexual, physical, or emotional, is consistently associated with more incidents of violence of all types in the past year, with a single exception. On the other hand, the severity of neglect history demonstrates a less consistent pattern of association with current violence (data not shown). These data lend support to the thesis that violence and victimization may be considered as normative occurrences by developing individuals situated in subcultures of violence.

To contextualize the findings from the interview data, a series of six focus groups was conducted with 24 female sex workers during mid- and late 2002. One of the many areas addressed in these sessions concerned sex workers' expectations of violence. A

Table 33.2

Drug-Use Characteristics of 325 Female Sex Workers in Miami, Florida

% Ever Used	
Alcohol	95.7%
Marijuana	92.9%
Cocaine	77.5%
Crack cocaine	81.5%
Heroin	34.5%
Mean Age at First Use (SD)	
Alcohol	15.0 (4.7)
Marijuana	15.5 (4.3)
Cocaine	20.3 (6.1)
Crack cocaine	25.7 (8.0)
Heroin	23.4 (7.5)
% Currently Using (Last 30 Days)	
Alcohol	75.4%
Marijuana	57.8%
Cocaine	38.4%
Crack cocaine	74.4%
Heroin	19.4%
% Currently injecting drugs	13.8%

major theme expressed by the women participating in these groups was that the violent victimizations they experience are inevitable. One woman indicated:

> Prostitution, drugs, and violence go hand in hand; it's all in one palm, OK? And because the prostitute is out there to get drugs and because she has an addiction and—whether it be violence from the date or violence from the dope boy, either way we're looking at it, there's still violence involved.

Or, as another woman reported:

> I think people who have been abused, like from childhood, sexual, or physical . . . I think they become codependent [on it]. Like my first boyfriend . . . I was like codependent on him, even though he was violent, a drug dealer, a drug addict, and you know, I was used to that kind of life-

style anyway cause that's what I had in my parents home. Violence and drugs.

And still another stated:

> It's like there are two worlds, there's a good world and then there's a violent world and it's like alls we know is violence, alls we know is violent men.

These comments, along with many others, suggest that violence is a routine occurrence permeating many aspects of these women's lives and is normative to such a degree that many consider it to be an unavoidable cost of doing business on the street.

Discussion

The interview data collected on this cohort of drug-involved, female sex workers have documented that these women's historical and current life experiences are replete with episodes of victimization and violence. The prevalence of both physical and sexual victimization in childhood and adulthood is extremely elevated in comparison with national estimates. In fact, a recent National Violence Against Women survey sponsored by the National Institute of Justice and the Centers for Disease Control and Prevention placed the percentage of women experiencing rape or physical assault in the past 12 months at 0.3% and 1.9%, respectively (Tjaden & Thoennes, 1998). In this analysis of drug-involved sex workers, the rates of date violence alone are some 43 and 13 times higher, supporting the contention that female sex workers are enmeshed in a social milieu wherein violence is commonplace and victimization is expected.

Table 33.3

Childhood Trauma Histories of
325 Drug-Involved, Female Sex Workers
in Miami, Florida

% Physically Abused	
None	55.1%
Low	13.8%
Moderate	7.1%
Severe	24.0%
% Sexually Abused	
None	49.5%
Low	4.3%
Moderate	12.6%
Severe	33.5%
% Emotionally Abused	
None	38.2%
Low	18.2%
Moderate	13.5%
Severe	30.2%
% Physically Neglected	
None	54.8%
Low	18.5%
Moderate	11.4%
Severe	15.4%
% Emotionally Neglected	
None	41.5%
Low	27.1%
Moderate	10.8%
Severe	20.6%

Table 33.4

Recent Violent Victimizations of
325 Drug-Involved, Female Sex Workers
in Miami, Florida

	Past Month	Past Year
Encountered violent date	20.9%	41.5%
Ripped off	16.6%	28.9%
Beaten	10.8%	24.9%
Threatened with weapon	5.5%	13.8%
Raped	4.0%	12.9%

Table 33.5

Childhood Trauma and Past Year Violent Victimizations Among 325 Drug-Involved, Female Sex Workers in Miami, Florida

	Level of Childhood		
	Physical Abuse	Sexual Abuse	Emotional Abuse
Times encountered violent date	.118*	.124*	.128*
Times ripped off	.152**	.112*	.155**
Times beaten	.138*	.078	.126*
Times threatened with weapon	.121*	.122*	.132*
Times raped	.122*	.176**	.146*
*Spearman correlation coefficients significant at $p < .05$. **Spearman correlation coefficients significant at $p < .01$.			

Numerous remarks and insights from focus group participants also lend plausibility to the idea put forth in this article that street-level sex work operates as a subculture of violence. Although the analysis is limited by the absence of systematic measures of subcultural attitudes about violence (Messner, 1983), behavioral data demonstrate that violent victimization is concentrated among drug-using female sex workers, is perpetrated primarily by men who solicit their sexual services, and is both expected and inevitable. These encounters also serve to extend and deepen the patterns of violence and abuse that were experienced by many women in childhood.

The marginalization of the women sex workers is further extended by the fact that nearly 45% of those in the sample are homeless, the majority have limited education, and very few possess any sort of social or professional ties with the larger community. As such, negotiating the system and network of existing community resources in search of help can be extremely difficult. This fact is evidenced by the women's scant reports of accessing any type of community health or counseling service in the past three months. In spite of the elevated incidence of rape reported by this sample of women, only one (0.3%) indicated that she contacted a rape crisis center for assistance.

The policy and research implications of these findings are several. First, because drug-involved, women sex workers are so marginalized, some type of advocacy is warranted—advocacy in terms of promoting a safer work environment, providing access to mental and physical health care, and extending unbiased treatment by the police and other criminal justice organizations. Organizations such as COYOTE, PONY, and the National Task Force on Prostitution have been established for these very purposes, but their resources are minimal and their presence is limited to but a few places in the United States.

Second, mechanisms need to be established that serve to provide sex workers with alternatives to the street. Virtually all of the women encountered in this project indicated that prostitution is not a chosen career. Rather, for most it is *survival sex,* and for almost all it is the result of a drug habit combined with the lack of other skills or resources. Or as one sex worker indicated:

> When you need *the cracks* [crack cocaine] and you need money for other things 'cause your rent money *went on the boards* [was used to buy crack], you got to survive, and you know, to do that, the pussy works!

The creation of alternatives to the street for this population, however, is not an easy task. Long-term substance abuse treatment that includes strategies for empowerment and the development of positive self-images is only the beginning.

In addition, there is the need for vocational education and the introduction to networks that will enable women to use their newly developed skills rather than their sexuality to support themselves.

Third, because these data clearly document that the risk for violent victimization may exacerbate the potential for acquisition of HIV or some other sexually transmitted infection, existing HIV/AIDS prevention programs for sex workers need to immediately incorporate strategies for violence prevention as well. In addition, studies designed to better understand the precursors and determinants of the violence aimed at women sex workers are needed at multiple sites to better identify mechanisms of violence avoidance.

Fourth, and finally, one of the more daunting and perhaps most difficult of tasks is outreach to the dates of female sex workers. This is a population also in need of empowerment to provide them with alternatives to battering and other violence in their interactions with women. Working with male dates may serve to reduce not only street violence but also other violence against women. Yet members of this population are unwilling to be identified. As such, perhaps the most immediate need is the development of effective strategies for outreach, earning trust, and designing and implementing appropriate interventions for this hard-to-reach population.

References

Baron, S. W., & Hartnagel, T. F. (1998). Street youth and criminal violence. Journal of Research in *Crime and Delinquency*, 35 (2), 166–192.

Baseman, J., Ross, M., & Williams, M. (1999). Sale of sex for drugs and drugs for sex: An economic context of sexual risk behaviors for STDs. *Sexually Transmitted Diseases*, 26 (8), 444–449.

Bernburg, J. G., & Thorlindsson, T. (1999). Adolescent violence, social control, and the subculture of delinquency: Factors related to violent behavior and nonviolent delinquency. *Youth and Society*, 30 (4), 445–460.

Bernstein, D. P., Fink, L., Handelsman, L., Foote, J., Lovejoy, M., Wenzel, K., et al. (1994). Initial reliability and validity of a new retrospective measure of child abuse and neglect. *American Journal of Psychiatry*, 151 (8), 1132–1136.

Braunstein, M. S. (1993). Sampling a hidden population: Noninstitutionalized drug users. *AIDS Education and Prevention*, 5 (2), 131–139.

Carlson, R. G., Wang, J., Siegal, H. A., Falck, R. S., & Guo, J. (1994). An ethnographic approach to targeted sampling: Problems and solutions in AIDS prevention research among injection drug and crack-cocaine users. *Human Organization*, 53, 279–386.

Carmen, A., & Moody, H. (1985). *Working women: The subterranean world of street prostitution*. New York: Harper & Row.

Church, S., Henderson, M., Barnard, M., & Hart, G. (2001). Violence by clients towards female prostitutes in different work settings: Questionnaire survey. *British Medical Journal*, 322, 524–525.

Clark, C. M. (1992). Deviant adolescent subcultures: Assessment strategies and clinical interventions. *Adolescence*, 27 (106), 283–293.

Clarke, J. W. (1998). *The lineaments of wrath: Race, violent crime, and American culture*. Tucson: University of Arizona Press.

Cloward, R., & Ohlin, L. (1960). *Delinquency and opportunity: A theory of delinquent gangs*. Glencoe, IL: Free Press.

Cohen, J. B., & Alexander, P. (1995). Female sex workers: Scapegoats in the AIDS epidemic. In A. O'Leary & L. S. Jemmott (Eds.), *Women at risk, issues in the primary prevention of AIDS*. New York: Plenum.

Coston, C. T. M., & Ross, L. E. (1998). Criminal victimization of prostitutes: Empirical support for the lifestyle/exposure model. *Journal of Crime and Justice*, 21 (1), 53–70.

Coyle, S. L., Boruch, R. F., & Turner, C. F. (Eds.). (1991). *Evaluating AIDS prevention programs* (Exp. ed.). Washington, DC: National Academy Press.

Dalla, R. (2002). Night moves: A qualitative investigation of street-level sex work. *Psychology of Women Quarterly*, 26, 63–73.

Davis, N. J. (2000). From victims to survivors: Working with recovering street prostitutes. In R. Weitzer (Ed.), *Sex for sale: Prostitution, pornography, and the sex industry* (pp. 139–158). New York: Routledge.

Dowling-Guyer, S., Johnson, M., Fisher, D., Needle, R., Watters, J., Andersen, M., et al. (1994). Reliability of drug-users' self-reported HIV risk behavior and validity of self-reported recent drug use. *Assessment*, 1, 383–392.

Durkheim, E. (1893). *The division of labour in society*. Paris: P. U.F.

Elifson, K. (1990). *The Georgia State Prostitution Inventory*. Unpublished questionnaire.

Falck, R. S., Wang, J., Carlson, R. G., & Siegal, H. A. (2001). The epidemiology of physical attack and rape among crack-using women. *Violence and Victims*, 16 (1), 79–89.

Farley, M., & Barkan, H. (1998). Prostitution, violence and posttraumatic stress disorder. *Women and Health*, 27 (3), 37–49.

Gilbert, L., El-Bassel, N., Rajah, V., Foleno, A., & Frye, V. (2001). Linking drug-related activities with experiences of partner violence: A focus group study of women in methadone treatment. *Violence and Victims*, 16 (5), 517–536.

Gottesman, R., & Brown, R. M. (Eds.). (1999). *Violence in America: An encyclopedia* (Vol. 3). New York: Scribner.

Hoigard, C., & Finstad, L. (1986). *Backstreets: Prostitution, money and love*. University Park: The Pennsylvania State University Press.

Inciardi, J. A. (1993). Kingrats, chicken heads, slow necks, freaks, and blood suckers: A glimpse at the Miami sex-for-crack market. In M. Ratner (Ed.), *Crack pipe as pimp: An ethnographic investigation of sex-for-crack exchanges* (pp. 37–68). New York: Lexington Books.

Inciardi, J. A., Lockwood, D., & Pottieger, A. E. (1993). *Women and crack cocaine*. New York: Macmillan.

Inciardi, J. A., & Surratt, H. L. (2001). Drug use, street crime, and sex-trading among cocaine-dependent women: Implications for public health and criminal justice policy. *Journal of Psychoactive Drugs*, 33 (4), 379–389.

———. (2002, July 7–12). *Developing targeted HIV and Hepatitis interventions for drug-using female sex workers in Miami*. Paper presented at the Fourteenth International AIDS Conference, Barcelona, Spain.

Inciardi, J. A., Surratt, H. L., & McCoy, H. V. (1997, Winter). Establishing an HIV/AIDS intervention program for street drug users in a developing nation. *Journal of Drug Users*, 27, 173–193.

Kennedy, L. W., & Baron, S. W. (1993). Routine activities and a subculture of violence: A study of violence on the street. *Journal of Research in Crime & Delinquency*, 30 (1), 88–112.

Langness, L. L. (1974). Ritual, power and male dominance. *Ethos*, 2 (3), 189–212.

Latkin, C. A. (1998). Outreach in natural setting: The use of peer leaders for HIV prevention among drug users' networks. *Public Health Reports*, 113 (Suppl. 1), 151–159.

Levy, J. A., & Fox, S. E. (1998). The outreach-assisted model of partner notification with IDUs. *Public Health Reports, 113* (Suppl. 1), 160–169.

Lundsgaarde, H. P. (1977). *Murder in space city.* New York: Oxford University Press.

Madriz, E. (1999). Overview II. In R. Gottesman & R. M. Brown (Eds.), *Violence in America: An encyclopedia* (Vol. 1, pp. 298–302). New York: Scribner.

Maher, L. (1997). *Sexed work: Gender, race and resistance in a Brooklyn drug market.* Oxford: Clarendon Press.

Merton, R. K. (1968). *Social theory and social structure.* New York: Free Press.

Messner, S. F. (1983). Regional and racial effects on the urban homicide rate: The subculture of violence revisited. *American Journal of Sociology, 88* (5), 997–1007.

Miller, E. M. (1986). *Street woman.* Philadelphia: Temple University Press.

Montell, W. L. (1986). *Killings: Folk justice in the upper South.* Lexington: University Press of Kentucky.

Needle, R., Weatherby, N., Brown, B., Booth, R., Williams, M., Watters, J., et al. (1995). The reliability of self-reported HIV risk behaviors of injection and non-injection drug users. *Psychology of Addictive Behavior, 9,* 242–250.

Nisbett, R. E., & Cohen, D. (1996). *Culture of honor: The psychology of violence in the South.* Boulder, CO: Westview Press.

Northrup, G. (1985). The residential treatment of violent youth viewed as a process of acculturation. *Milieu Therapy, 4* (1), 51–59.

Ray, M. C., & Smith, E. (1991). Black women and homicide: An analysis of the subculture of violence thesis. *The Western Journal of Black Studies, 15* (3), 144–153.

Shaw, C., & McKay, H. D. (1931). *Social factors in juvenile delinquency.* Washington, DC: Government Printing Office.

Silbert, M. H., & Pines, A. M. (1983). Early sexual exploitation as an influence in prostitution. *Social Work, 28,* 285–289.

Sterk, C. E., & Elifson, K. W. (1990). Drug-related violence and street prostitution. In M. De La Rosa, E. Y. Lambert, & B. Gropper (Eds.), *Drugs and violence: Causes, correlates, and consequences* (NIDA Research Monograph Series #103; pp. 208–221). Rockville, MD: National Institutes on Drug Abuse.

Teets, J. M. (1997). The incidence and experience of rape among chemically dependent women. *Journal of Psychoactive Drugs, 29* (4), 331–336.

Thompson, R. J., & Lozes, J. (1976). Female gang delinquency. *Corrective & Social Psychiatry & Journal of Behavior Technology, Methods & Therapy, 22* (3), 1–5.

Tjaden, P., & Thoennes, N. (1998). *Prevalence, incidence, and consequences of violence against women: Findings from the National Violence Against Women Survey.* Washington, DC: National Institute of Justice.

Walker, M. L., Schmidt, L. M., & Lunghofer, L. (1993). Youth gangs. In M. I. Singer, L. T. Singer, & T. M. Anglin (Eds.), *Handbook for screening adolescents at psychological risk* (pp. 400–422). New York: Lexington Books/Macmillan.

Watters, J. K., & Biernacki, P. (1989). Targeted sampling: Options for the study of hidden populations. *Social Problems, 36,* 416–430.

Weatherby, N., Needle, R., Cesari, H., Booth, R., McCoy, C., Watters, J., et al. (1994). Validity of self-reported drug use among injection drug users and crack cocaine users recruited through street outreach. *Evaluation and Program Planning, 17,* 347–355.

Wechsberg, W., MacDonald, B., Inciardi, J., Surratt, H., Leukefeld, C., Farabee, D., et al. (1997). *The NIDA cooperative agreement standard intervention: Protocol changes suggested by the continuing HIV/AIDS epidemic.* Bloomington, IL: Lighthouse Institute.

Weitzer, R. (Ed.). (2000). *Sex for sale: Prostitution, pornography, and the sex industry.* New York: Routledge.

Wenzel, S. L., Leake, B. D., & Gelberg, L. (2001). Risk factors for major violence among homeless women. *Journal of Interpersonal Violence, 16* (8), 739–752.

Wiebel, W. W. (1990). Identifying and gaining access to hidden populations. In E.Y. Lambert (Ed.), *The collection and interpretation of data from hidden populations* (NIDA Research Monograph Series #98, pp. 4–11). Rockville, MD: National Institutes on Drug Abuse.

———. (1993). *The indigenous leader outreach model* (NIH Publication No. 93–3581). Rockville, MD: U.S. Department of Health and Human Services.

Wolfgang, M. E., & Ferracuti, F. (1967). *The subculture of violence: Towards an integrated theory in criminology.* London: Tavistock.

For Discussion

1. Why is "sex work" illegal in most regions of the United States? Would regulating the sex work industry reduce the level of violence?

2. The authors describe the benefits of using "indigenous" workers, in this instance "active sex workers," to recruit respondents for the study. What other types of research might benefit from using indigenous study recruiters? Are there any limitations to this approach?

34

The Drugs/Violence Nexus

A Tripartite Conceptual Framework

Paul J. Goldstein

Most of the research that addresses linkages between drug use and crime focuses on property crime. Less understood is the relationship between drugs and violence. In this regard, Paul J. Goldstein draws from existing research to propose a framework for considering the drugs/violence nexus. One linkage is psychopharmacological—drugs alter behavior by reducing inhibitions or instigating aggression. By contrast, economically compulsive violence occurs when individuals commit violent crimes in their efforts to secure funds to purchase drugs for self-use. Systemic violence is associated with the turf battles and struggles for control in the drug-dealing and drug-trafficking industries.

Drug use, as well as the social context in which that use occurs, are etiological factors in a wide range of other social phenomena. Drug use is known to be causally related to a variety of physical and mental health problems, crime, poor school performance, family disruption, and the like. Previous research has also consistently found strong connections between drugs and violence.

For example, Zahn and Bencivengo (1974) reported that in Philadelphia, in 1972, homicide was the leading cause of death among drug users, higher even than deaths due to adverse effects of drugs; and drugs accounted for approximately 31 percent of the homicides in Philadelphia. Monforte and Spitz (1975), after studying autopsy and police reports in Michigan, suggested that drug use and distribution may be more strongly related to homicide than to property crime. Preble (1980) conducted an ethnographic study of heroin addicts in East Harlem between 1965 and 1967. About fifteen years later, in 1979 and 1980, he followed up the 78 participants and obtained detailed information about what had happened to them. He found that 28 had died. Eleven, 40 percent of the deaths, were the victims of homicide. The New York City Police Department (1983) classified about 24 percent of known homicides in 1981 as drug-related.

The drugs/violence nexus also appears consistently in newspaper headlines. For example, a seventeen-year-old boy who committed suicide by hanging himself in his jail cell had earlier confessed to committing a ritual stabbing and mutilation killing of another youth, because he believed the boy had stolen ten bags of PCP from him (*New York Times*, July 12, 1984). A New York City transit policeman was beaten with his own nightstick and his chin was nearly bitten off by a fare-beater who was high on angel dust (*New York Post*, September 19, 1984). A thirty-nine-year-old mother of three was killed by a stray bullet fired during a fight between drug dealers on the lower east side of Manhattan (*New York Post*, October 10, 1984). A front-page headline in the *New York Times* (October 29, 1984) claimed that "Increase in Gang Killings on Coast Is Traced to Narcotics Trafficking." Less than a month later, another *New York Times* front-page headline announced that "Cocaine Traffickers Kill 17 in Peru Raid on Anti-Drug Team" (November 19, 1984). A Miami police official was quoted on television as saying that one-third of the homicides in Miami in 1984 were cocaine-related.

Even though the relationship between drugs and violence has been consistently documented in both the popular press and in social scientific research, it is only recently that attempts have been made to assess this problem on a national level. One such effort estimated that 10 percent of the homicides and assaults nationwide are the result of drug use (Harwood et al. 1984). Another recent report estimated that, in the United States in 1980, over 2,000 homicides were drug-related and, assuming an average life span of 65 years, resulted in the loss of about 70,000 years of life. This report further estimated that, in 1980, over 460,000 assaults were drug-related, and that, in about 140,000 of these assaults, the victims sustained physical injury, leading to about 50,000 days of hospitalization (Goldstein and Hunt 1984).

While the association between drugs and violence appears strong, and drug use and trafficking appear to be important etiological factors in the incidence of violence, there has been little effort to place this relationship into a conceptual framework to guide further empirical research. The purpose of this paper is to introduce such a framework.

Information for this report was gathered during the course of three separate empirical investigations. Sixty women were interviewed in 1976 and 1977 for a study of the relationship between prostitution and drugs (Goldstein 1979). Between 1978 and 1982, an ethnographic study was undertaken of the economic behavior of 201 street opiate users in Harlem.[1] Finally, in 1984, I began a study of the relationship between drugs and violence on the lower east side of Manhattan.[2] That study is guided by the conceptual framework presented below.

Drugs and violence are seen as being related in three possible ways: the psychopharmacological, the economically compulsive, and the systemic. Each of these models must be viewed, in a theoretical sense, as "ideal types," i.e., as hypothetically concrete ". . . devices intended to institute comparisons as precise as the stage of one's theory and the precision of one's instruments allow" (Martindale 1959:58–59). In fact, it will be shown below that there can be overlap between the three models. However, this overlap does not detract from the heuristic value of the tripartite conceptual framework.

Psychopharmacological Violence

The psychopharmacological model suggests that some individuals, as a result of short- or long-term ingestion of specific substances, may become excitable, irrational, and may exhibit violent behavior. The most relevant substances in this regard are probably alcohol, stimulants, barbiturates, and

PCP. A lengthy literature exists, examining the relationship between these substances and violence (Tinklenberg 1973; Virkunnen 1974; Glaser 1974; Gerson [and Preston] 1979; Ellinswood 1971; Smith 1972; Asnis and Smith 1978; d'Orban 1976; Feldman et al. 1979). Early reports which sought to employ a psychopharmacological model to attribute violent behavior to the use of opiates and marijuana have now been largely discredited (Finestone 1967; Inciardi and Chambers 1972; Kozel et al. 1972; Greenberg and Adler 1974; Schatzman 1975; Kramer 1976). In a classic statement of this point, Kolb argued the following.

> There is probably no more absurd fallacy prevalent than the notion that murders are committed and daylight robberies and holdups are carried out by men stimulated by large doses of cocaine or heroin which have temporarily distorted them into self-imagined heroes incapable of fear. . . . [V]iolent crime would be much less prevalent if all habitual criminals were addicts who could obtain sufficient morphine or heroin to keep themselves fully charged with one of these drugs at all times. (Kolb 1925:78)

Kolb's point must be modified in one very important way. He is correct in claiming that ingestion of opiates is unlikely to lead to violence. However, the irritability associated with the withdrawal syndrome from opiates may indeed lead to violence. For example, in previous research on the relationship between drugs and prostitution, I found that heroin-using prostitutes often linked robbing and/or assaulting clients with the withdrawal experience (Goldstein 1979). These women reported that they preferred to talk a "trick" out of his money, but if they were feeling "sick," i.e., experiencing withdrawal symptoms, that they would be too irritable to engage in gentle conning. In such cases, they might attack the client, take his money, purchase sufficient heroin to "get straight," and then go back on the street. In a more relaxed physical and mental state, these women claimed that they could then behave like prostitutes rather than robbers.

Drug use may also have a reverse psychopharmacological effect and ameliorate violent tendencies. In such cases, persons who are prone to acting violently may engage in self-medication, in order to control their violent impulses. Several subjects have reported doing this. The drugs chosen for this function are typically heroin or tranquilizers.

Psychopharmacological violence may involve drug use by either offender or victim. In other words, drug use may contribute to a person behaving violently, or it may alter a person's behavior, in such a manner as to bring about that person's violent victimization. Previous research indicates relatively high frequencies of alcohol consumption in rape (Amir 1971; Rada 1975) and homicide victims (Shupe 1954; Wolfgang 1958). Public intoxication may invite a robbery or mugging. One study found that, in rapes where only the victim was intoxicated, she was significantly more likely to be physically injured (Johnson et al. 1978).

It is difficult to estimate the true rate of victim-precipitated psychopharmacological violence, because many such instances go unreported and, hence, unrecorded in official records. My own research in New York over the last decade indicated that many intoxicated victims do not report their victimization. Such victims say that they do not wish to talk to the police while drunk or "stoned." Further, since they are frequently confused about details of the event and, perhaps, unable to remember what their assailant looked like, they argue that reporting the event would be futile.

Assuming that the psychopharmacological violence is not precipitated by the victim, the victim can then be just about anybody. Psychopharmacological violence can erupt in the home and lead to spouse or child abuse. Psychopharmacological violence can occur in the workplace, on the streets, in bars, and so on. The incidence of psychopharmacological violence is impossible to assess at the present time, both because many instances go unreported and because when cases are reported, the psychopharmacological state of the offender is seldom recorded in official records.

Economic-Compulsive Violence

The economically compulsive model suggests that some drug users engage in eco-nomically-oriented violent crime, e.g., robbery, in order to support costly drug use. Heroin and cocaine, because they are expensive drugs typified by compulsive patterns of use, are the most relevant substances in this category. Economically compulsive actors are not primarily motivated by impulses to act out violently. Rather, their primary motivation is to obtain money to purchase drugs. Violence generally results from some factor in the social context in which the economic crime is perpetrated. Such factors include the perpetrator's own nervousness, the victim's reaction, weaponry (or the lack of it) carried by either offender or victim, the intercession of bystanders, and so on.

Research indicates that most heroin users avoid violent acquisitive crime, if viable non-violent alternatives exist (Preble and Casey 1969; Swezey 1973; Cushman 1974; Gould 1974; Goldstein and Duchaine 1980; Goldstein 1979; Johnson et al. 1985). This is because violent crime is more dangerous, embodies a greater threat of prison if one is apprehended, and because perpetrators may lack a basic orientation toward violent behavior. Bingham Dai reported similar findings nearly fifty years ago. His study of the criminal records of over one thousand opiate addicts in Chicago revealed that the most common offenses for which they were arrested were violations of the narcotics laws, followed by offenses against property.

> . . . it is interesting to note that comparatively few of them resorted to violence in their criminal activities. The small percentage of addicts, committing such crimes as robbery, assault and battery, homicide, and others that involve the use of force, seems to discredit the view shared by many that the use of drugs has the effect of causing an individual to be a heartless criminal. On the contrary, our figures suggest that most of the crimes committed by addicts were of a peaceful nature that involve more the use of wit than that of force. (Dai 1937:69)

Victims of economic-compulsive violence, like those of psychopharmacological violence, can be anybody. Previous research (Goldstein and Johnson 1983; Johnson et al. 1985) indicates that the most common victims of this form of drug-related violence are people residing in the same neighborhoods as the offender. Frequently, the victims are engaged in illicit activities themselves. Other drug users, strangers coming into the neighborhood to buy drugs, numbers runners, and prostitutes are all common targets of economic-compulsive violence.

While research does indicate that most of the crimes committed by most of the drug users are of the non-violent variety, e.g., shoplifting, prostitution, drug selling, there are little data that indicate what proportion of violent economic crimes are committed for drug-related reasons. No national criminal justice data bases contain information on the motivations or drug-use pattern of offenders as they relate to specific crimes.

Systemic Violence

In the systemic model, violence is intrinsic to involvement with any illicit substance. Systemic violence refers to the traditionally aggressive patterns of interaction within the system of drug distribution and use. Some examples of systemic violence follow below:

1. disputes over territory between rival drug dealers.

2. assaults and homicides committed within dealing hierarchies as a means of enforcing normative codes.

3. robberies of drug dealers and the usually violent retaliation by the dealer or his/her bosses.

4. elimination of informers.

5. punishment for selling adulterated or phony drugs.

6. punishment for failing to pay one's debts.

7. disputes over drugs or drug paraphernalia.

8. robbery violence related to the social ecology of copping areas.

Substantial numbers of users of any drug become involved in drug distribution as their drug-using careers progress and, hence, increase their risk of becoming a victim or perpetrator of systemic violence. Examples of each type of systemic violence mentioned above are readily available.

We recently reported that much of the heroin in New York City is being distinctively packaged and sold under "brand names" (Goldstein et al. 1984). These labeling practices are frequently abused, and this abuse has led to violence. Among the more common abuses are the following: dealers mark an inferior-quality heroin with a currently popular brand name; users purchase the good heroin, use it, then repackage the bag with milk sugar for resale; the popular brand is purchased, the bag is "tapped," and further diluted for resale.

These practices get the real dealers of the popular brand very upset. Their heroin starts to get a bad reputation on the streets, and they lose sales. Purchasers of the phony bags may accost the real dealers, complaining about the poor quality and demanding their money back. The real dealers then seek out the purveyors of the phony bags. Threats, assaults, and/or homicides may ensue.

A common form of norm violation in the drug trade is known as "messing up the money." Basically, this involves a subordinate returning less money to his superior than is expected. For example, a street dealer is given a consignment of drugs to sell and is expected to return to his supplier or lieutenant with a specific amount of money. However, for any of a variety of reasons, he returns with too little money or fails to return at all. Some of the reasons why he might be short on his money are that he used some or all of the drugs himself; he sold all of the drugs, but then spent some or all of the money; he gave out too many "shorts," i.e., he sold the drugs for less than he should have; he was robbed, either of his drugs or of the money that he obtained from selling them.

When a street dealer fails to return sufficient money, his superior has several options. If only a small amount of money is involved, and the street dealer has few prior transgressions and a convincing justification for the current shortage, his superior is likely to give him another consignment and allow him to make up the shortage from his share of the new consignment. Other options include firing the street dealer, having him beaten up, or having him killed.

In a recent study, a lieutenant in a heroin dealing operation had been rather lax in supervising the six street dealers working under him. Just about everybody was "messing up the money," including himself. One day, the supplier and two "soldiers" picked up the lieutenant and took him for a ride in their car. The lieutenant was afraid that he was going to be killed. However, after cruising for a while, they spotted one of the street dealers who had been "messing up the money." The two soldiers jumped from the car and beat him with iron pipes. They positioned him in the street and drove the car over his legs, crippling him for life. The supplier then suggested to the lieutenant that he would be well-advised to run the operation more tightly in the future.

An interesting addendum to this discussion is that the "code of the streets" dictates that "blood cancels all debts." In other words, if a street dealer has "messed up the money" and is subsequently beaten up or wounded, then he no longer owes the money. The shedding of blood has canceled the debt.

The above account illustrates a direct punishment for a norm violation. Violence may also arise in the course of a dispute that stems from a norm violation. I was recently told of such an incident. A drug dealer operated out of an apartment in New York City. Prospective purchasers would line up in the hallway of the apartment house and give their money to a young Hispanic woman who worked for the dealer. The woman would then get the drugs from the dealer and give them to the buyers. Dealers seldom allow customers into the space where the drugs are actually kept.

One day, the line was long and three black men waited patiently to make their purchase. Finally, it was their turn. However, the woman bypassed them in favor of two Hispanic men who were at the back of the line. The Hispanic men made a large purchase, and the woman announced that the dealer had sold out for the day. The blacks were furious. An argument ensued, shots were fired, and one of the Hispanic men was killed. The norm violator in this case, the woman, was fired by the dealer.

A common precipitator of violence in the drug scene is the robbery of a dealer. No dealer who wishes to stay in business can allow himself or his associates to be robbed. Most dealers maintain an arsenal of weapons and a staff that knows how to use them. A subject in a recent study reported going with two friends to "take off" a neighborhood social club that was a narcotics distribution center. In the course of the hold-up, they shot one of the employees and beat up several other men and women. In retrospect, the subject admitted that they had probably used excessive force, but that at the time it had seemed justified because they were outnumbered about fifteen to three. One of the victims recognized one of the robbers. This robber was later shot to death in the street.

The Pulitzer Prize-winning study of narcotics trafficking, *The Heroin Trail*, documents many instances of systemic violence. One concerns Joseph Fucillo, a Brooklyn drug dealer who became a police informant in 1972.

> One day, as his wife watched from the window of their home in the Bensonhurst section of Brooklyn, Fucillo backed his car out of the driveway, and two men in ski masks walked up to it. Two guns fired rapidly and seven bullets went into Fucillo's head. He died. (*Newsday* Staff and Editors, 1974:226)

A pimp stated that he would never allow a "junkie broad" to work for him. One of his reasons was that an addicted woman might be easily turned into an informant by the police. When asked what he would do if one of his women did start to use narcotics, he replied that, if she didn't know too much about his activities, he would just fire her. However, if she did know too much, he would kill her (Goldstein 1979:107).

New York Magazine reported an event that was tragic both in its consequence and in the fact that it is so typical of the current drug scene.

> Sylvester, a sixteen-year-old boy, is stabbed in the chest . . . in the Crown Heights section of Brooklyn. He is taken to St. Mary's Hospital and dies a short time later. According to a witness, Sylvester sold marijuana to a group of adolescents a few days before the incident. His customers were apparently dissatisfied with its quality. Tonight, the teenag-

ers, a group of about eight or ten, find Sylvester on the street and complain about the bad grass. The leader of the group, John Green, demands their money back. Sylvester then picks up a couple of bottles and throws them at the group, running away down the block. The teenagers chase Sylvester down Lincoln Place, where he picks up a stick and starts swinging. Knocking the stick out of his hand, John Green plunges a four-inch knife into Sylvester's chest. Green and the others escape from the scene. At one p.m. Sunday afternoon, in apparent retaliation for the Sylvester murder, John Green is shot once in the left rear side of the body. He too is taken to St. Mary's, where he too dies. (Goro 1977:31)

Violence associated with disputes over drugs has long been endemic in the drug world. Friends come to blows, because one refuses to give the other a "taste." A husband beats his wife, because she raided his "stash."

The current AIDS scare has led to an increasing amount of violence because of intravenous drug users' fear of contracting this fatal disease from contaminated "works." Some sellers of needles and syringes claim that the used works that they are trying to sell are actually new and unused. If discovered by would-be purchasers, violence may ensue. I was recently told of one incident that allegedly led to the death of two men. A heroin user kept a set of works in a "shooting gallery" that were for his exclusive use. One day, another man used these works. The owner of the works discovered what had happened and stabbed this man to death. He later stabbed a friend to death who was present when the stranger had used the works, had done nothing to stop him, and had failed to inform the owner of what had happened.

The social ecology of copping areas is generally well-suited for the perpetration of robbery violence. Most major copping areas in New York City are located in poor ghetto neighborhoods, such as Harlem. In these neighborhoods, drug users and dealers are frequent targets for robberies because they are known to be carrying something of value, and because they are unlikely to report their victimization. Dealers are sometimes forced to police their own blocks, so that customers may come and go in safety.

A subject in a current study earns money by copping drugs for other people. He stated that he was recently forced to protect one of his clients by fighting off two would-be robbers with a garbage-can lid. Interestingly, he knew the two attackers from the street, but he claimed to harbor no ill will towards them. He stated that they did what they had to do, and he did what he had to do.

Victims of systemic violence are usually those involved in drug use or trafficking. Occasionally, non-involved individuals become innocent victims. The case of a woman being killed by a stray bullet fired in a dispute between rival drug dealers was cited earlier. Several cases have been reported where whole families of drug dealers, including wives and young children, have perished in narcotics gang wars. However, the vast majority of victims of systemic violence are those who use drugs, who sell drugs, or are otherwise engaged in some aspect of the drug business.

Various sources have stressed the importance of what I have termed the systemic model in explaining drugs/violence relationships. Blumm (1970) points out that, with the exception of alcohol, most drug users are not violent, but that this point does not apply to the typical dealer for whom there is strong evidence linking drugs and violence. Smith (1972), in his discussion of amphetamines and violence in San Francisco's Haight-Ashbury district, stated that the primary cause of violence on the streets was "burning," i.e., selling phony or adulterated drugs. Several sources suggest that studying the area of systemic violence may be more important than the study of the relationship of drug use to crime on the level of the individual user.

> Racket-associated violence, a result of the intense competition for enormous profits involved in drugs, is flourishing. This is not the "crime in the streets" which is often associated with drugs, but an underworld in which ordinarily those people suffer from violence who in one way or another have become related to the traffic. (Fitzpatrick 1974:360)

Because these criminal entrepreneurs operate outside the law in their drug transactions, they are not bound by business etiquette in their competition with each other, in their collection of debts, or in their non-drug investments. Terror, violence, extortion, bribery, or any other expedient strategy is relied upon by these criminals. . . . (Glaser 1974:53)

Where a commodity is scarce and highly in demand (as may be the case with drugs), extreme measures of control, i.e., homicide, may be involved. Further, in areas of high scarcity and inelastic demand, bitter arguments centering on the commodity are likely to ensue. When such arguments take place in a subculture where violence is the modus operandi, and where implements of violence, e.g., guns, are readily available, homicide is likely to be the result. (Zahn 1975:409)

Zahn pointed out the importance of systemic violence in her recent study of homicide in [the] twentieth-century United States. She showed that homicide rates peaked in the 1920s and early 1930s, declined and leveled off thereafter, began to rise in 1965, and peaked again in 1974. This analysis led to the following conclusion:

In terms of research directions, this historical review would suggest that closer attention be paid to the connection between markets for illegal goods and the overall rate of homicide violence. It seems possible, if not likely, that establishing and maintaining a market for illegal goods (booze in the 1920s and early 1930s; heroin and cocaine in the late 1960s and early 1970s) may involve controlling and/or reducing the competition, solving disputes between alternate suppliers or eliminating dissatisfied customers. . . . The use of guns in illegal markets may also be triggered by the constant fear of being caught either by a rival or by the police. Such fear may increase the perceived need for protection, i.e., a gun, thus may increase the arming of these populations and a resulting increased likelihood of use. For the overall society, this may mean a higher homicide rate. (Zahn 1980:128)

It was stated above that the three models of the drugs/violence nexus contained in the tripartite conceptual framework should be viewed as ideal types, and that overlap could occur between them. For example, a heroin user preparing to commit an act of eco-nomic-compulsive violence, e.g., a robbery, might ingest some alcohol or stimulants to give himself the courage to do the crime. This event now contains elements of both economic-compulsive and psychopharmacological violence. If the target of his robbery attempt was a drug dealer, the event would contain elements of all three types of drug-related violence.

The conceptual framework allows the event to be effectively analyzed and broken down into constituent parts and processes. The roles played in the event by different sorts of drugs can be explicated. In the above example, the need for money to purchase heroin was the primary motivation for the act. Alcohol and stimulants were ingested after the act was decided upon because of the robber's need for courage, and, presumably, because prior experience with these substances led the perpetrator to believe that they would serve that psychopharmacological function.

The choice of target, a drug dealer, is open for empirical investigation. It may turn out that the reason the heroin user needed to commit the robbery was because that dealer had cheated him earlier in the day on a drug purchase, perhaps selling him "dummy" bags. Our robber, needing to "get straight" and not having any more money, decides that robbing this unscrupulous dealer would be an appropriate revenge.

Several subjects in our studies reported committing economic-compulsive acts out of fear of becoming a victim of systemic violence. These were street dealers who had "messed up the money" and who were terrified of what their superiors might do to them. Some had already been threatened. This motivated them to do robberies as a quick way to obtain the money that they owed.

Thus, as the concepts are employed, a fuller understanding of the event emerges. The roles played by specific drugs become clearer. The actor's motivations and the process by which he undertakes to commit a robbery are elaborated upon.

If the above events were to be examined in official crime records, assuming they were reported, they would be listed as robberies. Victim-perpetrator relationships would probably be unknown, though they might be listed as "acquaintance" or "stranger." No mention of drugs would be made.

Victims of systemic violence frequently lie to the police about the circumstances of their victimization. Not a single research subject whom I have interviewed who was the victim of systemic violence and who was forced to give an account of his or her victimization to the police admitted that he or she had been assaulted because of owing a drug supplier money or selling somebody phony or adulterated drugs. All such victims simply claimed to have been robbed.

It would make little difference if the robbery were to develop into a homicide. The classification of the event would change from robbery to homicide, but victim-perpetrator relationship and nature of the homicide would remain unknown or be coded in such a broad fashion that the information would not be very useful. No mention of drugs would be made. Attention will now be focused on the quality of data available on the national level to elaborate on the drugs/violence nexus.

Quality of Data Available on Drugs/Violence Nexus

The drugs/violence nexus is one of the most important criminological and health issues, for which rigorously collected data [are] currently unavailable. While a variety of ethnographic studies focus on violent behavior of drug users, most of this material is not quantitative and does not allow national projections to be made. Official statistics collected in the criminal justice and health care systems do not link acts of criminal violence and resultant injuries or death to antecedent drug activity of victims or perpetrators. Broad recording categories make it virtually impossible to determine whether the offender or victim was a drug user or distributor, or whether the pharmacological status of either victim or offender was related to the specific event.

Uniform Crime Reports (UCR), collected by the Federal Bureau of Investigation, is the most visible source of crime data in the country. However, it is not very useful for an elaboration of the relationship between drugs and violence. UCR is a measure of crimes known to the police. Many crimes are not reported. The 1980 National Crime Survey found that the following proportions of violent victimizations were not reported to the police: 57 percent of the rapes; 41 percent of the robberies; 52 percent of the assaults (BJS 1982:71). UCR data on homicide, due to the presence of a body, is the most reliable crime-incidence category.

Reporting schedules, to which local law-enforcement agencies must adhere, frequently result in data being submitted to UCR before investigative work has been completed; and, hence, large numbers of unknowns usually appear in relevant categories. The New York City Police Department has addressed this issue by holding an annual debriefing of detective-squad commanders about all homicides that occurred in their precincts during the preceding year. It was in the context of these debriefings that the significance of drug-related homicides first emerged and became an important analytic category for the NYPD Crime Analysis Unit. The new data gathered during these debriefings have never been included in UCR, because no structure exists for their transmission. This has led to such curious statistical phenomena as New York City reporting more drug-related homicides for a given year than UCR reports for the nation as a whole, including New York City.

The major difficulty in using UCR to estimate drug-related violent crime is the lack of a descriptive component to supplement the quantitative presentation. The drug-relatedness of violent events is simply not coded. Therefore, it is not possible to link specific violent acts to antecedent drug activities of either victim or perpetrator.

An alternative data source is the National Crime Survey (NCS). This annual report issued by the Bureau of Justice Statistics (BJS) is based on data obtained from a stratified, multi-stage cluster sample. The basic sampling unit is the household. Respondents within households are asked for all instances of victimization in the past year. Projections are then made to the nation as a whole.

As was the case with UCR, the NCS is not very useful for elaborating on the drugs/violence nexus. Street drug users frequently are not part of a household, i.e., they may sleep in abandoned buildings, in subways, on park benches. Thus, a population that is posited to be at especially high risk for drug-related violence is likely to be underrepresented in [these] data. Also, victims may have difficulty recalling specific events or be reluctant to describe them to an interviewer.

Research on the capacity of victims to recall specific kinds of crime . . . indicates that assault is the least well-recalled of the crimes measured by the NCS. This may stem in part from the observed tendency of victims not to report crimes committed by offenders known to them, especially if they are relatives. In addition, it is suspected that, among certain groups, crimes that contain the elements of assault are a part of everyday life and, thus, are simply forgotten or are not considered worth mentioning to a survey interviewer. Taken together, these recall problems may result in a substantial understatement of the "true" rate of victimization from assault. (Bureau of Justice Statistics 1982:94)

A major problem with the NCS is that victims seldom know the motivation of offenders for committing acts of violence. Of course, this is less the case with systemic violence than it is with either psychopharmacological or economic-compulsive violence. With regard to psychopharmacological violence, victims may not be able to discern that assailants are "high" and, even if they could, it would be difficult to ascertain what substances are involved. Similarly, victims of economic-compulsive violence may not know that they are being robbed in order to finance a drug habit.

Summary and Conclusions

Drugs and violence were shown to be related in three possible ways: psychopharmacologically, economic-compulsively, and systemically. These different forms of drug-related violence were shown to be related to different types of substance use, different motivations of violent perpetrators, different types of victims, and differential influence by social context. Current methods of collecting national crime data were shown to be insensitive to the etiological role played by drug use and trafficking in creating violent crime.

No evidence currently exists as to the proportions of violence engaged in by drug users and traffickers that may be attributed to each of the three posited models. We need such data. My own impression, arising from research in New York, is that the area of systemic violence accounts for most of the violence perpetrated by, and directed at, drug users.

Systemic violence is normatively embedded in the social and economic networks of drug users and sellers. Drug use, the drug business, and the violence connected to both of these phenomena, are all aspects of the same general lifestyle. Individuals caught in this lifestyle value the experience of substance use, recognize the risks involved, and struggle for survival on a daily basis. That struggle is clearly a major contributor to the total volume of crime and violence in American society.

Notes

1. This research was supported by the New York State Division of Substance Abuse Services; by a Public Health Service Award from the National Institute on Drug Abuse (RO1-DA 01926); and by an interagency agreement between NIDA (RO1-DA 02355) and the Law Enforcement Assistance Administration (LEAA-J-IAA-005-8).

2. This research is being supported by the New York State Division of Substance Abuse Services and by a Public Health Service Award from the National Institute on Drug Abuse (RO1-DA 03182).

References

Amir, M. 1971. *Patterns in Forcible Rape*. Chicago: University of Chicago Press.

Asnis, S., and R. Smith. 1978. Amphetamine Abuse and Violence, *Journal of Psychedelic Drugs*, 10:317–377.

Biernacki, P. 1979. Junkie Work, Hustles, and Social Status Among Heroin Addicts, *Journal of Drug Issues*, 9:535–550.

Blumm, Richard and Associates. 1970. *Students and Drugs*. San Francisco, CA: Jossey-Bass.

Bureau of Justice Statistics. 1982. *Criminal Victimization in the United States*, 1980. Washington, DC: United States Department of Justice.

Cushman, P. 1974. Relationship between Narcotic Addiction and Crime, *Federal Probation*, 38:38–43.

Dai, B. 1937. *Opium Addiction in Chicago*. Montclair: Patterson Smith.

d'Orban, P. T. 1976. Barbiturate Abuse, *Journal of Medical Ethics*, 2:63–67.

Eckerman, W., J. Bates, J. Rachall, and W. Poole. 1971. *Drug Usage and Arrest Charges: A Study of Drug Usage and Arrest Charges among Arrestees in Six Metropolitan Areas of the United States*. Washington, DC: United States Department of Justice.

Ellinswood, E. 1971. Assault and Homicide Associated with Amphetamine Abuse, *American Journal of Psychiatry*, 127:1170–1175.

Feldman, H., M. H. Agar, and G. M. Beschner (eds.). 1979. *Angel Dust: An Ethnographic Study of PCP Users*. Lexington: Lexington Books.

Finestone, H. 1967. Narcotics and Criminality, *Law and Contemporary Problems*, 22:60–85.

Fink, L., and M. Hyatt. 1978. Drug Use and Violent Behavior, *Journal of Drug Education*, 8:139–149.

Fitzpatrick, J. P. 1974. Drugs, Alcohol, and Violent Crime, *Addictive Diseases*, 1:353–367.

Gerson, L. W., and D. A. Preston. 1979. Alcohol Consumption and the Incidence of Violent Crime, *Journal of Studies on Alcohol*, 40:307–312.

Glaser, D. 1974. Interlocking Dualities in Drug Use, Drug Control, and Crime, in Inciardi, J. A., and C. Chambers (eds.), *Drugs and the Criminal Justice System*. Beverly Hills: Sage Publications.

Goldstein, P. J. 1979. *Prostitution and Drugs*. Lexington: Lexington Books.

——. 1981. Getting Over: Economic Alternatives to Predatory Crime Among Street Drug Users, in Inciardi, J. A. (ed.), *The Drugs/Crime Connection*. Beverly Hills: Sage Publications.

Goldstein, P. J., and N. Duchaine. 1980. Daily Criminal Activities of Street Drug Users, paper presented at annual meetings of the American Society of Criminology.

Goldstein, P. J., and B. D. Johnson. 1983. Robbery Among Heroin Users, presented at annual meetings of the Society for the Study of Social Problems.

Goldstein, P. J., and D. Hunt. 1984. Health Consequences of Drug Use, report to the Carter Center of Emory University and The Centers for Disease Control.

Goldstein, P. J., D. S. Lipton, E. Preble, I. Sobel, T. Miller, W. Abbott, W. Paige, and F. Soto. 1984. The Marketing of Street Heroin in New York City, *Journal of Drug Issues*, 14:553–566.

Goro, H. 1977. Saturday Night Dead, *New York Magazine*, 10:31.

Gould, L. 1974. Crime and the Addict: Beyond Common Sense, in Inciardi, J. A., and C. Chambers (eds.), *Drugs and the Criminal Justice System*. Beverly Hills: Sage Publications.

Greenberg, S., and F. Adler. 1974. Crime and Addiction: An Empirical Analysis of the Literature, 1920–1973, *Contemporary Drug Problems*, 3:221–270.

Harwood, H., D. Napolitano, P. Kristiansen, and J. Collins. 1984. *Economic Costs to Society of Alcohol and Drug Abuse and Mental Illness*. Final Report to the Alcohol, Drug Abuse and Mental Health Administration.

Inciardi, J. A., and C. Chambers. 1972. Unreported Criminal Involvement of Narcotic Addicts, *Journal of Drug Issues*, 2:57–64.

Johnson, B. D., P. J. Goldstein, E. Preble, J. Schmeidler, D. S. Lipton, B. Spunt, and T. Mille. 1985. *Taking Care of Business: The Economics of Crime by Heroin Abusers*. Lexington: Lexington Books.

Johnson, S., L. Gibson, and R. Linden. 1978. Alcohol and Rape in Winnepeg: 1966–1975, *Journal of Studies on Alcohol*, 39:1887–1894.

Klepfisz, A., and J. Racy. 1973. Homicide and LSD, *JAMA* 223:429–430.

Kolb, L. 1925. Drug Addiction and Its Relation to Crime, *Mental Hygiene*, 9:74–89.

Kozel, N., R. Dupont, and B. Brown. 1972. A Study of Narcotic Involvement in an Offender Population, *International Journal of the Addictions*, 7:443–450.

Kramer, J. C. 1976. From Demon to Ally—How Mythology Has and May Yet Alter National Drug Policy, *Journal of Drug Issues*, 6:390–406.

McBride, D. 1981. Drugs and Violence, in Inciardi, J. A. (ed.), *The Drugs/Crime Connection*. Beverly Hills: Sage Publications.

Martindale, D. 1959. Sociological Theory and the Ideal Type, in Gross, L. (ed.), *Symposium on Sociological Theory*. New York: Harper and Row.

Monforte, J. R., and W. U. Spitz. 1975. Narcotic Abuse Among Homicides in Detroit, *Journal of Forensic Sciences*, 20:186–190.

Newsday Staff and Editors. 1974. *The Heroin Trail*. New York: Holt, Rinehart, and Winston.

New York City Police Department. 1983. *Homicide Analysis: 1981*.

Petersen, R., and R. Stillman (eds.). 1978. *Phencyclidine Abuse: An Appraisal*. Rockville, MD: National Institute on Drug Abuse.

Preble, E. 1980. El Barrio Revisited, paper presented at annual meetings of the Society for Applied Anthropology.

Preble, E., and J. Casey. 1969. Taking Care of Business: The Heroin User's Life on the Street, *International Journal of the Addictions*, 4:1–24.

Rada, R. 1975. Alcoholism and Forcible Rape, *American Journal of Psychiatry*, 132:444–446.

Schatzman, M. 1975. Cocaine and the Drug Problem, *Journal of Psychedelic Drugs*, 77–81.

Shupe, L. M. 1954. Alcohol and Crime: A Study of the Urine Alcohol Concentration Found in 882 Persons Arrested During or Immediately After the Commission of a Felony, *Journal of Criminal Law, Criminology, and Police Science*, 44:661–664.

Smith, R. 1972. Speed and Violence: Compulsive Methamphetamine Abuse and Criminality in the Haight-Ashbury District, in C. Zarsfonetis (ed.), *Drug Abuse: Proceedings of the International Conference*. Philadelphia: Lea and Febiger.

Swezey, R. 1973. Estimating Drug-Crime Relationships, *International Journal of the Addictions*, 8:701–721.

Tinklenberg, J. 1973. Drugs and Crime, in National Commission on Marijuana and Drug Abuse, *Drug Use in America: Problems in Perspective*. Appendix, Volume 1, Patterns and Consequences of Drug Use. Washington, DC: United States Government Printing Office.

Virkunnen, M. 1974. Alcohol as a Factor Precipitating Aggression and Conflict Behavior Leading to Homicide, *British Journal of the Addictions*, 69:149–154.

Wolfgang, M. E. 1958. *Patterns in Criminal Homicide*. Philadelphia: University of Philadelphia Press.

Zahn, M. A. 1975. The Female Homicide Victim, *Criminology*, 13:409.

——. 1980. Homicide in the Twentieth Century United States, in Inciardi, J. A., and C. E. Faupel (eds.), *History and Crime*. Beverly Hills: Sage Publications.

Zahn, M. A., and M. Bencivengo. 1974. Violent Death: A Comparison between Drug Users and Non-Drug Users, *Addictive Diseases*, 1:283–296.

For Discussion

The psychopharmacological linkage between drug use and violence assumes that some drug users have little control over their actions. Is it fair to punish these offenders in the same manner that we punish those users who engage in systemic violence?

35

Women in the Street-Level Drug Economy

Continuity or Change?

Lisa Maher
Kathleen Daly

In this article, Lisa Maher and Kathleen Daly use ethnographic research to examine women's roles in the informal drug economy. The authors find that the drug labor market is stratified by gender within which women are more likely than men to occupy lower-level positions. Women are viewed as untrustworthy and unable to engage in and respond appropriately to drug-related violence. Moreover, the authors find that opportunities for sex-for-drug exchanges have declined, and potential earnings from these exchanges are limited.

Images of women in the contemporary drug economy are highly mixed. Most scholars emphasize *change* in women's roles in U.S. drug markets of 1960–1985, organized primarily around heroin, compared to women's roles in more recent drug markets with the advent of crack cocaine (e.g., Baskin et al., 1993; Bourgois, 1989; Dunlap and Johnson, 1992; Inciardi et al., 1993; Mieczkowski, 1994; C. Taylor, 1993). Some emphasize *continuity* from previous decades (Adler, 1985; Koester and Schwartz, 1993; Maher and Curtis, 1992). Others suggest that both change and continuity are evident, with women inhabiting "two social worlds" (Fagan, 1994:212): one of increased participation in, and the other of continued restriction by, male-dominated street and drug networks.

One should expect, on the one hand, to see variation in women's positions in the drug economy. Research on drug markets in New York City (Bourgois, 1995; Curtis and Sviridoff, 1994; Hamid, 1990, 1992; Johnson et al., 1985, 1992; Williams, 1989), Miami (Inciardi et al., 1993), Washington, D.C. (Reuter et al., 1990), Detroit (Mieczkowski, 1986, 1990; C. Taylor, 1990), Chicago (Padilla, 1992), Milwaukee (Hagedorn, 1994), Los Angeles and the West Coast (Adler, 1985; Morgan and Joe, 1994; Skolnick, 1989; Waldorf et al., 1991) reveals differences in the racial and ethnic composition of participants and who controls markets, the kinds of drugs sold, how markets are organized, and participants' responses to law enforcement. Such differences are likely to affect women's positions and specific roles.

At the same time, the varied characterizations of women's roles reflect differences in the theoretical assumptions and methodological approaches taken by scholars. For example, women's increasing presence in the drug economies of the late 1980s and early 1990s is said to reflect (1) emancipation from their traditional household responsibilities (Bourgois, 1989; Bourgois and Dunlap, 1993), (2) an extension of their traditional household responsibilities (Wilson, 1993), and (3) the existence of "new opportunities" in street-level drug markets (Mieczkowski, 1994), especially with increased rates of incarceration of minority group men (Baskin et al., 1993). These explanations reveal different assumptions about changes (or not) in the gendered structure of drug markets and about the links (or not) between women's participation in crime and their domestic responsibilities.

Data sources and methods also affect the quality and content of the inferences drawn. Some have analyzed Uniform Crime Report (UCR) arrest data (e.g., Wilson, 1993), others have interviewed women arrested on drug charges or through snowball samples (e.g., Baskin et al., 1993; Fagan, 1994; Inciardi et al., 1993; C. Taylor, 1993), and a handful have conducted ethnographies of particular neighborhoods (e.g., Bourgois, 1989; Maher and Curtis, 1992). While interview-based studies may offer an empirical advantage over the inferences that can be drawn from

UCR arrest data, the one-time interview may not elicit complete or reliable information about the changing contexts of women's income generation in the informal economy.

This article presents the results of an ethnographic study of women drug users conducted during 1989–1992 in a New York City neighborhood. We assess whether women's involvement in U.S. drug markets of the mid-1980s onward reflects change, continuity, or a combination of change and continuity from patterns in previous decades. We find that contrary to the conclusions of Baskin et al. (1993), Fagan (1994), Inciardi et al. (1993), Mieczkowski (1994), and C. Taylor (1993), crack cocaine markets have not necessarily provided "new opportunities" for women, nor should such markets be viewed as "equal opportunity employers" (Bourgois, 1989; Wilson, 1993). Our study suggests that recent drug markets continue to be monopolized by men and to offer few opportunities for stable income generation for women. While women's *presence* on the street and in low-level auxiliary roles may have increased, we find that their *participation* as substantive labor in the drug-selling marketplace has not.

Women in the Drug Economy

Drug Markets of the 1960s to the Mid-1980s

Prior to the advent of crack cocaine in the mid-1980s, research on women in the drug economy used one or more of four elements to explain women's restricted roles in selling and distributing drugs:[1] intimate relationships with men, the availability of alternative options for income generation, restrictions on discretionary time, and institutionalized sexism in the underworld.

Female heroin users were often characterized as needing a man to support their consumption (e.g., File, 1976; File et al., 1974; Hser et al., 1987; Smithberg and Westermeyer, 1985; Sutter, 1966). They were also described as being "led" into crime by individual men (Covington, 1985; Pettiway, 1987), although this may apply more to white than minority group women (Anglin and Hser, 1987; Pettiway, 1987). The typical pattern was of low-status roles in which participation was short-lived, sporadic, and mediated by intimate relationships with men (Adler, 1985; Rosenbaum, 1981). Alternative sources of income generation, such as prostitution and shoplifting, may have been preferable to female drug users, especially heroin users (File, 1976; Goldstein, 1979; Hunt, 1990; Inciardi and Pottieger, 1986; James, 1976; Rosenbaum, 1981). Some suggest, in addition, that women's household and childcare responsibilities may have limited their full participation in the drug economy (e.g., Rosenbaum, 1981; A. Taylor, 1993; see also Wilson, 1993).

Women's peripheral roles in male-dominated drug selling networks (Auld et al., 1986; Goldstein, 1979; Rosenbaum, 1981) can also be explained by "institutionalized sexism" in the "underworld" (Steffensmeier, 1983; Steffensmeier and Terry, 1986; see also Box, 1983). Steffensmeier (1983:1013–1015) argues that male lawbreakers prefer to "work, associate, and do business with other men" (homosocial reproduction); they view women as lacking the physical and mental attributes considered essential to working in an uncertain and violent context (sex-typing and task environment of crime). In the drug economy, in particular, women are thought to be unsuitable for higher-level distribution roles because of an inability to manage male workers through threatened violence (Waterston, 1993:114).

Crack Cocaine Markets of the Mid-1980s Onward

Women have been depicted as more active participants in selling and distributing drugs in the crack cocaine economy of the late 1980s compared to previous drug eras. While some find that women's roles continue to be mediated by relationships with men (Koester and Schwartz, 1993; Murphy et al., 1991) and that women remain at the bottom of the drug market hierarchy (Maher and Curtis, 1992), others suggest that there has been decisive change. Specifically, it is argued that "drug business" crimes (that is, street-level drug sales) generate a higher share of women's income than in the past, with a concomitant decrease in prostitution-generated income (Inciardi et al., 1993). More generally, it is argued that the crack-propelled expansion of drug markets has provided "new opportunities" for women.

The "new opportunities" argument is made by the majority of those in the field (see, e.g., Baskin et al., 1993; Bourgois, 1989; Bourgois and Dunlap, 1993; Fagan, 1994; Inciardi et al., 1993; Mieczkowski, 1994). It takes two forms: a general claim that women's emancipation in the wider society is evident in "all aspects of inner-city street life" (Bourgois, 1989:643–644) and a more restricted claim that the weakening of male-dominated street networks and market processes has made it possible for women to enter the drug economy. For example, in his study of New York City women, Fagan (1994:210) concludes that

> while women were consigned secondary, gender-specific roles in . . . [drug] businesses in the past, the size and seemingly frantic activity of the current drug markets has made possible for women new ways to participate in street networks. Their involvement in drug selling at high income levels defies the gendered norms and roles of the past, where drug dealing was an incidental income source often mediated by domestic partnerships. . . . [T]he expansion of drug markets in the cocaine economy has provided new ways for women to escape their limited roles, statuses and incomes in previous eras.

While two-thirds of the women in Fagan's (1994) sample did not sell drugs and while most who sold drugs acted alone (p. 197), Fagan was struck by "the emergence of women sellers earning high incomes and avoiding prostitution" (p. 211). He concluded that "two social worlds" of continuity and change characterized women's participation in drug markets. One difficulty in assessing this claim is that no estimate is given of the proportion of women who were earning high incomes from drug business, avoiding prostitution, and "def[ying] the gendered norms and roles of the past."

Fagan's research offers a good comparison to our study. He draws from interviews with 311 women, the majority of whom were drug users or sellers, in two New York City neighborhoods (Washington Heights and

Central Harlem in northern Manhattan). The interviews were conducted during the late 1980s; the sample included women with police arrest records, in residential treatment programs, and those who had not been arrested. The women in our sample lived just a few miles away in Bushwick, a Brooklyn neighborhood. Very few of the Bushwick women were active dealers, and virtually all supported themselves by prostitution. Whereas Fagan sees two worlds of continuity and change, we see just one of continuity. Before describing that social world, we sketch the study site and the methods used in gathering the data.

Research Site and Methods

Research Site

Bushwick, the principal study site, has been described as hosting "the most notorious drug bazaar in Brooklyn and one of the toughest in New York City" (*New York Times*, October 1, 1992:A1). Historically home to large numbers of European Jews, by the 1960s Bushwick was dominated by working-class Italians. Since the late 1960s, the area has become the home of low-income Latino populations, predominantly Puerto Ricans, although Dominicans and Colombians have begun to move in. In 1960 the population was 89% white, 6% black, and 5% Hispanic. By 1990 it was 5% white, 25% black, and 65% Hispanic (Bureau of the Census, 1990). In 1990 Bushwick was Brooklyn's poorest neighborhood with a median household income of $16,287; unemployment was twice the citywide rate; and more than half of all families and two-thirds of all children lived under the official poverty line (Bureau of the Census, 1990).

Between 1988 and 1992 drug distribution in Bushwick was intensely competitive; there were constant confrontations over "turf" as organizations strove to establish control over markets. Like many drug markets in New York City (see, e.g., Curtis and Sviridoff, 1994; Waterston, 1993), Bushwick was highly structured and ethnically segmented. The market, largely closed to outsiders, was dominated by Dominicans with networks organized by kin and pseudo-kin relations.[2]

Fieldwork Methods

Preliminary fieldwork began in the fall of 1989, when the senior author established a field presence in several Brooklyn neighborhoods (Williamsburg, East Flatbush, and Bushwick). By fall 1990 observations and interviews were intensified in Bushwick because it hosted the busiest street-level drug market in Brooklyn and had an active prostitution stroll. As fieldwork progressed, it became apparent that the initial plan of conducting interviews with a large number of women crack users was not, by itself, going to yield a complete picture. For example, few women initially admitted that they performed oral sex for less than $20, and none admitted to participating in sex-for-crack trades.

By the end of December 1991, interviews had been conducted with 211 active women crack users in Williamsburg, East Flatbush, and Bushwick. These were tape recorded and ranged from 20 minutes to 3 hours; they took place in a variety of settings, including private or semiprivate locations (e.g., apartments, shooting galleries, abandoned buildings, cars) and public locales (e.g., restaurants, parks, subways, and public toilets).[3] From January to March 1992, a preliminary data sort was made of the interview and observational material. From that process, 45 women were identified for whom there were repeated observations and interview material. Contact with these women was intimate and extensive; the number of tape-recorded interviews for each woman ranged from 3 to 15. Unless otherwise noted, the research findings reported here are based on this smaller group of 45 Bushwick women.

Profile of the Bushwick Women

The Bushwick women consisted of 20 Latinas (18 Puerto Ricans and 2 Dominicans), 16 African-Americans, and 9 European-Americans; their ages ranged from 19 to 41 years, with a mean of 28 years. At the time of the first interview, all the women used smokable cocaine (or crack), although only 31% used it exclusively; most (69%) had used heroin or powder cocaine prior to using crack. The women's average drug use history was 10.5 years (using the mean as the mea-

sure); heroin and powder cocaine initiates had a mean of about 12 years and the smokable cocaine initiates, about 6 years.

Most women (84%) were born in the New York City area, and more than half were born in Brooklyn. About one-quarter were raised in households with both parents present, and over one-third (38%) grew up in a household in which they were subjected to physical abuse. Most (84%) had not completed high school, and 55% had no experience of formal-sector work. A high proportion were homeless (91%), alternating between the street and short-term accommodations in shelters, apartments of friends, and homes of elderly men (see also Maher et al., 1996). Most women were mothers (80%); the 36 mothers had given birth to 96 children, whose ages ranged from newborns to 26 years. Few of the mothers (9%) had their children living with them during the study period. Fourteen women (31%) had tested positive for HIV, and an additional five women believed that they were HIV positive; but most women said they did not know their serostatus. By the end of the study period, two women had stopped using illicit drugs, and five had died: two from HIV-related illnesses and three from homicide.

These 45 women represent the range of ages, racial-ethnic backgrounds, life experiences, and histories of crack-using women among the larger group of Brooklyn women interviewed. We are cognizant, however, of the limits of using ethnographic research in one area to generalize to other areas. For example, there is a somewhat higher proportion of Latinas (44%) in our sample than in Fagan's (1994:225) sample in Central Harlem (23%) and Washington Heights (33%). A higher share of the Bushwick women had not completed high school, had no experience in the formal labor force, and were homeless.

Structure of New York City Crack Markets

Street-level crack markets have frequently been characterized as unregulated markets of freelancers engaged in individual entrepreneurial activity (Hunt, 1990; Reuter et al., 1990). Some evidence suggests, however, that once demand has been established, the freelance model may be superseded by a more structured system of distribution. When the crack epidemic was at its peak in New York City during the late 1980s, Bushwick (like other neighborhoods) hosted highly structured street-level drug markets with pooled interdependence, vertical differentiation, and a formal, multitiered system of organization and control with defined employer-employee relationships (Curtis and Maher, in press; Johnson et al., 1990, 1992). This model is similar to the "runner system" used in heroin distribution (see Mieczkowski, 1986).

In selling crack cocaine, drug business "owners" employ several "crew bosses," "lieutenants," or "managers," who work shifts to ensure an efficient organization of street-level distribution. Managers (as they were known in Brooklyn) act as conduits between owners and lower-level employees. They are responsible for organizing and delivering supplies and collecting revenues. Managers exercise considerable autonomy in the hiring, firing, and payment of workers; they are responsible for labor force discipline and the resolution of workplace grievances and disputes. Next down the hierarchy are the street-level sellers, who perform retailing tasks having little discretion. Sellers are located in a fixed space or "spot" and are assisted by those below them in the hierarchy: lower-level operatives acting as "runners," "look-outs," "steerers," "touts," "holders," and "enforcers." Runners "continuously supply the sellers," look-outs "warn of impending dangers," steerers and touts "advertise and solicit customers," holders "handle drugs or money but not both," and enforcers "maintain order and intervene in case of trouble" (Johnson et al., 1992:61–64).

In New York City in the early 1990s, it was estimated that 150,000 people were involved in selling or helping to sell crack cocaine on any given day (Williams, 1992:10). Crack sales and distribution became a major source of income for the city's drug users (Hamid, 1990, 1991; Johnson et al., 1994). How, then, did the Bushwick women fit into this drug market structure? We examine women's involvement in a range of drug business activities.

Selling and Distributing Drugs

During the entire three years of fieldwork, including the interviews with the larger group of over 200 women, we did not discover any woman who was a business owner, and just one worked as a manager. The highly structured nature of the market in Bushwick, coupled with its kin-based organization, militated against personal or intimate sexual relationships between female drug users and higher-level male operatives. To the limited extent that they participated in drug selling, women were overwhelmingly concentrated at the lowest levels. They were almost always used as temporary workers when men were arrested or refused to work, or when it was "hot" because of police presence. Table 35.1 shows how the 45 women were involved in Bushwick's drug economy.

Of the 19 women (42%) who had some involvement, the most common role was that of informal steerer or tout. This meant that they recommended a particular brand of heroin to newcomers to the neighborhood in return for "change," usually a dollar or so. These newcomers were usually white men, who may have felt more comfortable approaching women with requests for such information. In turn, the women's perceptions of "white boyz" enabled them to use the situation to their advantage. Although they used only crack, Yolanda, a 38-year-old Latina, and Boy, a 26-year-old African-American woman, engaged in this practice of "tipping" heroin consumers.

> They come up to me. Before they come and buy dope and anything, they ask me what dope is good. I ain't done no dope, but I'm a professional player. . . . They would come to me, they would pay me, they would come "What's good out here?" I would tell them, "Where's a dollar," and that's how I use to make my money. Everyday somebody would come, "Here's a dollar, here's two dollars." (Yolanda) [What other kinds of things?] Bumming up change. [There ain't many people down here with change.] Just the white guys. They give you more faster than your own kind. [You go cop for them?] No, just for change. You tell them what's good on [the] dope side. Tell

Table 35.1

Bushwick Women's Roles in the Drug Economy, 1989–92

	N	%
No Role	26	58
Had Some Role	19	42
	45	100

Of the 19 women with roles in the drug economy during the three-year study period, the following shows what they did. Because most women (*N* = 13) had more than one role, the total sums to greater than 19.

Selling and Distributing Roles	
Owner	0
Manager	0
Regular Seller	0
Irregular Seller	7
Runner	0
Look-out	0
Steerer or Tout	9
Holder	0
Enforcer	0
Selling/Renting Paraphernalia	
Works Sellers	4
Stem Renters	6
Running a Gallery	3
Copping Drugs for Others	14
Other Drug Business Hustles	
Street Doc	1

NOTE: While we have tried to be precise, we should note that it can be difficult to characterize women's roles—not only because drug markets are fluid and shifting but also because some women had varied mixes of roles over time.

them anything, I don't do dope, but I'll tell them anything. Yeah, it's kicking live man. They buy it. Boom! I got my dollar, bye. (Boy)

Within the local drug economy, the availability of labor strongly determines women's participation in street-level distribution roles. Labor supply fluctuates with extra-market forces, such as product availability and police intervention. One consequence of police activity in Bushwick during the study period was a recurring, if temporary, shortage of male workers. Such labor market gaps promoted instability: The replacement of "trusted" sellers (i.e., Latinos) with "untrustworthy" drug users (i.e., women and non-Latinos) eroded the social and kinship ties that

had previously served to reduce violence in drug-related disputes (see also Curtis and Sviridoff, 1994).

Early in the fieldwork period (during 1989 and early 1990), both men and women perceived that more women were being offered opportunities to work as street-level sellers than in the past. Such opportunities, it turned out, were often part of a calculated risk-minimization strategy on the part of owners and managers. As Princess, a 32-year-old African-American woman observed, some owners thought that women were less likely to be noticed, searched, or arrested by police:

> Nine times out of ten when the po-leece roll up it's gonna [be] men. And they're not allowed to search a woman, but they have some that will. But if they don' do it, they'll call for a female officer. By the time she gets there, (laughs) if you know how to move around, you better get it off you, unless you jus' want to go to jail. [So you think it works out better for the owners to have women working for them?] Yeah, to use women all the time.

As the fieldwork progressed and the neighborhood became more intensively policed, this view became less tenable. Latisha, a 32-year-old African-American woman, reported that the police became more aggressive in searching women:

> [You see some women dealing a little bit you know.] Yeah, but they starting to go. Now these cop around here starting to unzip girls' pants and go in their panties. It was, it's not like it was before. You could stick the drugs in your panties 'cause you're a female. Now that's garbage.

Thus, when initially faced with a shortage of regular male labor and large numbers of women seeking low-level selling positions, some managers appear to have adopted the opportunistic use of women to avoid detection and disruption of their businesses. How frequent this practice was is uncertain; we do know that it was short-lived (see also Curtis and Sviridoff, 1994:164).

In previous years (the late 1970s and early 1980s), several Bushwick women had sold drugs in their roles as wives or girlfriends of distributors, but this was no longer the case. During the three-year study period only 12 women (27%) were involved in selling and distributing roles. Of this group of 12, only 7 were able to secure low-level selling positions on an irregular basis. Connie, a 25-year-old Latina, was typical of this small group, and in the following quotation she describes her unstable position within the organization she worked for:

I'm currently working for White Top [crack]. They have a five bundle limit. It might take me an hour or two to sell that, or sometimes as quick as half an hour. I got to ask if I can work. They say yes or no.

Typically the managers said no to women's requests to work. Unlike many male street-level sellers who worked on a regular basis for this organization and were given "shifts" (generally lasting eight hours), Connie had to work off-hours (during daylight hours), which were often riskier and less financially rewarding. Temporary workers were usually given a "bundle limit" (one bundle contains 24 vials), which ensured that they could work only for short periods of time. As Cherrie, a 22-year-old Latina, said,

The last time I sold it was Blue Tops [crack]. That was a week ago. [What, they asked you or you asked them to work?] Oh, they ask me, I say I want to work. [How come they asked you?] I don't know. They didn't have nobody to work because it was too hot out there. They was too full of cops.

Similarly, although Princess was well-known to the owners and managers of White Top crack, had worked for them many times in the past year, and had "proved" herself by having never once "stepped off" with either drugs or money, she was only given sporadic employment. She reported,

Sometime you can't [sell]. Sometime you can. That's why it's good to save money also. So when you don't get work. [How come they wouldn't give you work on some days?] Because of some favor that someone might've done or y'know, jus'... [It's not like they're trying to punish you?] No, but they will do that y'know. Somebody go and tell them something, "Oh,

this one's doin' this to the bags or this one's doin' this to the bottles." OK, well they check the bags and they don' see nothin' wrong, but they came to look at it so they're pissed off so they'll take it away from you, y'know.

Violence and Relationships

In addition to being vulnerable to arrest and street robbery, street-level sellers who use drugs constantly grapple with the urge to consume the product and to abscond with the drugs and/or the money. Retaliation by employers toward users who "mess up the money" (Johnson et al., 1985:174) was widely perceived to be swift and certain. Rachel, a 35-year-old European-American woman, said,

Those Dominicans, if you step off with one piece of it, you're gonna get hurt. They don't play. They are sick people.

The prospect of violent retaliation may deter women from selling drugs. Boy, a 26-year-old African-American woman, put it this way:

I don' like their [the managers'] attitude, like if you come up short, dey take it out on you. . . . I don' sell no crack or dope for dese niggers. Because dey is crazy. Say for instance you short ten dollars, niggers come across you wit bats and shit. It's not worth it, you could lose your life. If dey say you are short, you could lose your life. Even if you were not short and dey say you is short, whatever dey say is gonna go, so you are flicked all the way around.

However, considerable uncertainty surrounds the likelihood that physical punishment will be meted out. This uncertainty can be seen in the comments by Princess, who had a long but sporadic history of street-level sales before and after the advent of crack:

It's not worth it. Number one, it's not enough. Come on, run away, and then *maybe* then these people want to heavily beat the shit out of you. And then they *may* hit you in the wrong place with the bat and *maybe* kill you (emphasis added).

Such disciplinary practices resemble a complex interplay between "patronage" and "mercy," which features in relations of dependence (Hay, 1975). The unpredictability of punishment may work as a more effective form of control than actual punishment itself. In Bushwick, the actuality of violent retaliation for sellers who "messed up" was further mediated by gender and ethnicity. In this Latino- (mainly Dominican) controlled market, the common perception was that men, and black men especially, were more likely than Latinas to be punished for "stepping off." Rachel described what happened after an African-American man had been badly beaten:

> [What happened to him. I mean he stepped off with a package, right?] Yeah, but everybody has at one time or another. But it's also because he's a black and not a Puerto Rican, and he can't, you know, smooze his way back in like, you know, Mildred steps off with every other package, and so does, you know, Yolanda, they all do. But they're Spanish. And they're girls. So, you know, they can smooze their way back in. You know, a guy who's black and ugly, you know, so they don't want to hear about it.

Relationships in the drug economy are fueled by contradictory expectations. On the one hand, attributes such as trust and reliability are frequently espoused as important to drug-selling organizations. On the other hand, ethnographic informants often refer to the lack of trust and solidarity among organization members. This lack of trust is evident in the constant "scams" sellers and managers pull on each other and the ever-present threat of violence in owner-manager-seller relations.

Strategies of Protection and 'Being Bad'

Women who work the streets to sell or buy drugs are subject to constant harassment and are regularly victimized. The Bushwick women employed several strategies to protect themselves. One of the most important was the adoption of a "badass" (Katz, 1988), "crazy," or "gangsta bitch" stance or attitude, of which having a "bad mouth" was an integral part. As Latisha was fond of saying, "My heart pumps no Kool Aid. I don't even drink the shit." Or as Boy put it,

> Ac' petite, dey treat you petite. I mean you ac' soft, like when you dress dainty and shit ta come over here an' sit onna fuckin' corner. Onna corner an' smoke an you dressed to da teeth, you know, you soft. Right then and there you the center of the crowd, y'know what I'm sayin'? Now put a dainty one and put me, she looks soft. Dey look at me like "don't fuck wid dat bitch, she looks hard." Don' mess wit me caus I look hard y'know. . . . Dey don't fuck wit me out here. Dey think I'm crazy.

Acting bad and "being bad" are not the same. Although many Bushwick women presented themselves as "bad" or "crazy," this projection was a street persona and a necessary survival strategy (see also Spalter-Roth, 1988). Despite the external manifestation of aggression, a posture and rhetoric of toughness, and the preemptive use of aggression (Campbell, 1993), women were widely perceived (by men and women alike) as less likely to have the attributes associated with successful managers and street-level sellers. These included the requisite "street cred" and a "rep" for having "heart" or "juice"—masculine qualities associated with toughness and the capacity for violence (Bourgois, 1989; Steffensmeier, 1983; Waterston, 1993). Women's abilities to "talk tough" or "act bad" were apparently not enough to inspire employer confidence. Prospective drug business employers wanted those capable of actually "being bad" (Bourgois, 1989:632). Because female drug users were perceived as unreliable, untrustworthy, and unable to deploy violence and terror effectively, would-be female sellers were at a disadvantage.

Selling Drug Paraphernalia

In Bushwick the sale of drug paraphernalia such as crack stems and pipes was controlled by the bodegas, or corner stores, whereas syringes or "works" were the province of the street. Men dominated both markets, although women were sometimes employed as part-time "works" sellers. Men who regularly sold "sealed" (i.e., new) works had suppliers (typically men who worked in local hospitals) from whom they purchased units called "ten packs" (10 syringes). The benefits of selling syringes were twofold: The penalties were less severe than those for selling drugs, and the rate of return was higher compared to the street-level sale of heroin or crack.[4]

The women who sold works were less likely than their male counterparts to have procured them "commercially." More often they "happened across" a supply of works through a family member or social contact who was a diabetic. Women were also more likely to sell works for others or to sell "used works." Rosa, a 31-year-old Latina, described in detail the dangerous practice of collecting used works strewn around the neighborhood. While she often stored them and later exchanged them for new works from the volunteer needle exchange (which was illegal at the time), Rosa would sometimes select the works she deemed in good condition, "clean" them with bleach and water, and resell them.

Although crack stems and pipes were available from neighborhood bodegas at minimal cost, some smokers chose not to carry stems. These users, almost exclusively men, were from outside the neighborhood. Their reluctance to carry drug paraphernalia provided the women with an additional source of income, usually in the form of a "hit," in exchange for the use of their stem. Sometimes these men were "dates," but more often they were "men on a mission" in the neighborhood or the "working men" who came to the area on Friday and Saturday nights to get high. As Boy put it,

> I be there on the block an' I got my stem and my lighter. I see them cop and I be askin' "yo, you need a stem, you need a light?" People say "yeah man," so they give me a piece.

An additional benefit for those women who rented their stems was the buildup of crack residues in the stems. Many users savored this resin, which they allowed to accumulate before periodically digging it out with "scrapers" fashioned from the metal ribs of discarded umbrellas.

Some women also sold condoms, another form of drug-related paraphernalia in Bushwick. Although condoms were sold at bodegas, usually for $1 each, many of the women obtained free condoms from outreach health workers. Sometimes they sold them at a reduced price (usually 25 cents) to other sex workers, "white boyz," and young men from the neighborhood. Ironically, these same women would then have to purchase condoms at the bodegas when they had "smoked up" all their condoms.

Running Shooting Galleries

A wide range of physical locations were used for drug consumption in Bushwick. Although these sites were referred to generically as "galleries" by drug users and others in the neighborhood, they differed from the traditional heroin shooting gallery in several respects.[5] Bushwick's "galleries" were dominated by men because they had the economic resources or physical prowess to maintain control. Control was also achieved by exploiting women drug users with housing leases. Such women were particularly vulnerable, as the following quotation from Carol, a 40-year-old African-American woman, shows:

> I had my own apartment, myself and my daughter. I started selling crack. From my house. [For who?] Some Jamaican. [How did you get hooked up with that?] Through my boyfriend. They wanted to sell from my apartment. They were supposed to pay me something like $150 a week rent, and then something off the profits. They used to, you know, flick up the money, like not give me the money. Eventually I went through a whole lot of different dealers. Eventually I stopped payin' my rent because I wanted to get a transfer out of there to get away from everything 'cause soon as one group of crack dealers would get out, another group would come along. [So how long did that go on for?] About four years. Then I lost my apartment, and I sat out in the street.

The few women who were able to maintain successful galleries operated with or under the control of a man or group of men. Cherrie's short-lived effort to set up a gallery in an abandoned burned-out building on "Crack Row" is illustrative. Within two weeks of establishing the gallery (the principal patrons of which were women), Cherrie was forced out of business by the police. The two weeks were marked by constant harassment, confiscation of drugs and property, damage to an already fragile physical plant, physical assaults, and the repeated forced dispersal of gallery occupants. Within a month, two men had established a new gallery on the same site, which, more than a year later, was thriving.

Such differential policing toward male- and female-operated galleries is explicable in light of the larger picture of law enforcement in low-income urban communities, where the primary function is not so much to enforce the law but rather to regulate illegal activities (Whyte, 1943:138). Field observations suggest that the reason the police did not interfere as much with activities in the men's gallery was that they assumed that men were better able than women to control the gallery and to minimize problems of violence and disorder.

Other factors contributed to women's disadvantage in operating galleries, crack houses, and other consumption sites. Male drug users were better placed economically than the women in the sample, most of whom were homeless and without a means of legitimate economic support. When women did have an apartment or physical site, this made them a vulnerable target either for exploitation by male users or dealers (as in Carol's case) or for harassment by the police (as in Cherrie's). Even when a woman claimed to be in control of a physical location, field observations confirmed that she was not. Thus, in Bushwick, the presence of a man was a prerequisite to the successful operation of drug-consumption sites. The only choice for those women in a position to operate galleries or crack houses was between the "devils they knew" and those they did not.

Copping Drugs

Many Bushwick women supplemented their income by "copping" drugs for others. They almost always copped for men, typically white men. At times these men were dates, but often they were users who feared being caught and wanted someone else to take that risk. As Rachel explained,

I charge them, just what they want to buy they have to pay me. If they want twenty dollars they have to give me twenty dollars worth on the top because I'm risking my free time. I could get busted copping. They have to pay me the same way, if not, they can go cop. Most of them can't because they don't know the people.

Those who cop drugs for others perform an important service for the drug market because as Biernacki (1979:539) suggests in connection with heroin, "they help to minimize the possibility of infiltration by undercover agents and decrease the chance of a dealer's arrest." In Bushwick the copping role attracted few men; it was regarded by both men and women as a low-status peripheral hustle. Most women saw the female-dominated nature of the job to be part of the parallel sex market in the neighborhood. Outsiders could readily approach women to buy drugs under the guise of buying sex. As Rosa recounted,

You would [be] surprise. They'd be ahm, be people very important, white people like lawyer, doctors that comes and get off, you'd be surprised. Iss like I got two lawyer, they give me money to go, to go and cop. And they stay down over there parking. . . . [How do you meet them?] Well down the stroll one time they stop and say you know, "You look like a nice girl though, you know, you wanna make some money fast?" I say, how? So they say you know, "Look out for me." First time they give me like you know, twenty dollars, you know. They see I came back, next time they give me thirty. Like that you know. I have been copping for them like over six months already.

Sometimes this function was performed in conjunction with sex work, as Latisha's comment illustrates:

He's a cop. He's takin' a chance. He is petrified. Will not get out his car. . . . But he never gets less than nine bags [of powder cocaine]. [And he sends you to get it?] And he wants a blow job, right, okay. You know what he's givin' you, a half a bag of blue (blue bag cocaine). That's for you goin' to cop, and for the blow job. That's [worth] two dollars and fifty. . . . I can go to jail [for him]. I'm a piece of shit.

Women also felt that, given the reputation of the neighborhood as very "thirsty" (that is, as having a "thirst" or craving for crack), male outsiders were more likely to trust women, especially white women, to purchase drugs on their behalf. Often this trust was misplaced. The combination of naive, inexperienced "white boyz" and experienced "street smart" women produced opportunities for additional income by, for example, simply taking the "cop" money. This was a calculated risk and sometimes things went wrong. A safer practice was to inflate the purchase price of the drugs and to pocket the difference. Rosa explained this particular scam,

> He think it a ten dollar bag, but issa five dollar. But at least I don't be rippin' him off there completely. [But you're taking the risk for him.] Exactly. Sometime he give me a hunert dollars, so I making fifty, right? But sometime he don't get paid, he got no second money, eh. I cop then when I come back the car, he say, "Dear I cannot give you nothin' today," you know. But I still like I say, I gettin' something from him because he think it a ten dollar bag.

Similar scams involved the woman's returning to the client with neither drugs nor money, claiming that she had been ripped off or, less often, shortchanging the client by tapping the vials (removing some crack) or adulterating the drugs (cutting powder cocaine or heroin with other substances). These scams reveal the diversity of women's roles as copping agents and their ingenuity in making the most of limited opportunities.[6]

Other Drug Business Hustles

The practice of injecting intravenous drug users (IDUs) who are unable to inject themselves, because they are inexperienced or have deep or collapsed veins, has been documented by others (e.g., Johnson et al., 1985; Murphy and Waldorf, 1991). Those performing this role are sometimes referred to as "street docs" (Murphy and Waldorf, 1991:16–17). In Bushwick, men typically specialized in this practice. For example, Sam, a Latino injector in his late thirties, lived in one of the makeshift huts or "condos" on a busy street near the main heroin copping area. Those who were in a hurry to consume or who had nowhere else to go would use Sam's place to "get off." Sam had a reputation as a good "hitter" and injected several women in the sample on a regular basis. He provided this service for a few dollars or, more often, a "taste" of whatever substance was being injected.

Only one woman in the sample, Latisha, capitalized on her reputation as a good "hitter" by playing the street doc role. Latisha had a regular arrangement with a young street thug named Crime, notorious for victimizing the women, who had only recently commenced intravenous heroin use and was unable to "hit" himself. While women IDUs were likely to have the requisite level of skill, they were less likely than men to be able to capitalize on it because they did not control an established consumption setting.

Discussion

A major dimension of drug economies, both past and present, is the "human qualities" believed necessary for the performance of various roles. Opportunities for income generation are defined, in part, by who has the necessary qualities or traits and who does not. These traits, whether grounded in cultural perceptions of biology and physiology (e.g., strength and capacity for violence), mental states (e.g., courage and aggressiveness), or kinship (e.g., loyalty and trustworthiness), are primarily differentiated along the lines of gender and race-ethnicity. In this study, we found that women were thought to be not as "strong" as men and that men, particularly black men and Latinos, were thought to be more "bad" and capable of "being bad." The gendered displays of violence that men incorporate into their work routines not only cement their solidarity as men, but also reinscribe these traits as masculine (Messerschmidt, 1993). As a consequence, men are able to justify the exclusion of women from more lucrative "men's work" in the informal economy. All the elements of underworld sexism identified by Steffensmeier (1983)—homosocial reproduction, sex-typing, and the qualities required in a violent task environment—featured prominently in Bushwick's street-level drug economy.

The significance of gender-based capacities and the symbolism used to convey them was evident in the women's use of instrumental aggression. Boy's discussion of how to "dress for success" on the streets reveals that power dressing is "dressing like a man" or "dressing down." It is anything but "dressing dainty." Both on the street and in the boardroom, it appears that a combination of clothing and attitude makes the woman (Kanter, 1981, citing Hennig, 1970). In the drug business, conveying the message "don't mess with me" is integral to maintaining a reputation for "craziness," which the women perceived as affording them some measure of protection.

The Bushwick women's experiences within a highly gender-stratified labor market provide a counter to the romantic notion of the informal drug economy as an "equal opportunity employer" (Bourgois, 1989:630). Their experiences contradict the conventional wisdom, shaped by studies of the labor market. [E]xperiences of minority group men (e.g., Anderson, 1990; Bourgois, 1989, 1995; Hagedorn, 1994; Padilla, 1992; C. Taylor, 1990; Williams, 1989), [for whom] the drug economy acts as a compensatory mechanism, offering paid employment that is not available in the formal labor force. While in theory the built-in supervision and task differentiation of the business model, which characterized drug distribution in Bushwick, should have provided opportunities to both men and women (Johnson et al., 1992), our findings suggest that sellers were overwhelmingly men. Thus, the "new opportunities" said to have emerged with the crack-propelled expansion of drug markets from the mid-1980s onward were not "empty slots" waiting to be filled by those with the requisite skill. Rather, they were slots requiring certain masculine qualities and capacities.

Continuity or Change?

Those scholars who emphasize change in women's roles in the drug economy with the advent of crack cocaine are correct to point out the *possibilities* that an expanded drug economy might have offered women. Where they err, we think, is in claiming that such "new opportunities" were in fact made available to a significant proportion of women. Granted, there were temporary opportunities for women to participate in street-level drug distribution, but they were irregular and short-lived and did not alter male employers' perceptions of women as unreliable, untrustworthy, and incapable of demonstrating an effective capacity for violence.

The only consistently available option for women's income generation was sex work. However, the conditions of street-level sex work have been adversely affected by shifts in social and economic relations produced by widespread crack consumption in low-income neighborhoods like Bushwick. The market became flooded with novice sex workers, the going rates for sexual transactions decreased, and "deviant" sexual expectations by dates increased, as did the levels of violence and victimization (Maher and Curtis, 1992). Ironically, the sting in the tail of the recent crack-fueled expansion of street-level drug markets has been a substantial reduction in the earning capacities of street-level sex workers.

Of the four elements that have been used to explain women's restricted involvement in drug economies of the past, we see evidence of change in two: a diminishing of women's access to drug-selling roles through boyfriends or husbands, especially when drug markets are highly structured and kin based, and decreased economic returns for street-level sex work. Because few Bushwick women had stable households or cared for children, we cannot comment on changes (if any) in discretionary time. Underworld institutionalized sexism was the most powerful element shaping the Bushwick women's experiences in the drug economy; it inhibited their access to drug business work roles and effectively foreclosed their ability to participate as higher-level distributors. For that most crucial element, we find no change from previous decades.

How can we reconcile our findings with those of researchers who say that the crack cocaine economy has facilitated "new opportunities" for women or "new ways for women to escape their limited roles, statuses, and incomes [compared to] previous eras" (Fagan, 1994:210)? One answer is that study samples differ: Compared to Fagan's sample, for example, our sample of Bushwick women contained a somewhat higher share of Latinas, whose economic circumstances were more marginal than those of the women in Central Harlem and Washington Heights. It is also possible that Latino-controlled drug markets are more restrictive of women's participation than, say, those controlled by African-Americans. Those who have studied drug use and dealing in Puerto Rican (Glick, 1990) and Chicano (Moore, 1990) communities suggest that "deviant women" may be less tolerated and more ostracized than their male counterparts. For Bushwick, it would be difficult to disentangle the joint influences of a male-dominated and Dominican-controlled drug market on women's participation. While seven women (16%) engaged in street-level sales during the study period, all women—whether Latina, African-American, or European-American—were denied access to higher levels of the drug business.

We lack research on how racial-ethnic relations structure women's participation in drug markets. Fagan's (1994:200–202) comparison of Central Harlem and Washington Heights indicates that a lower proportion of women in Central Harlem (28%) than in Washington Heights (44%) reported being involved in drug selling; similar proportions (about 16%) were involved in group selling, however. While Fagan noted that drug markets in Washington Heights were Latino-controlled, he did not discuss the organization or ethnic composition of drug markets in Central Harlem. His study would appear to challenge any clear links between "Latino culture"—or the Latina share of women studied—and greater restrictions on women's roles compared to other racial-ethnic groups.

While disparate images of women in the drug economy may result from differences in study samples (including racial-ethnic variation in drug market organization, neighborhood-level variation, and when the study was conducted), a researcher's methods and theories are also crucial. For methods, virtually all U.S. studies of women drug users have employed one-time interviews. The ethnographic approach used in this study reveals that in the absence of a temporal frame and observational data, interviews may provide an incomplete and inaccurate picture. For example, in initial interviews with the larger group of Brooklyn women, we found that when women were asked about sources of income, it was more socially desirable for them to say that it came from drug selling or other kinds of crime than from crack-related prostitution (Maher, in press). The one-time interview also misses the changing and fluid nature of relations in the informal economy. For example, for a short period there was a perception in Bushwick that "new opportunities" existed for women to sell crack. That perception faded as it became clear that managers and owners were "using" women to evade the constraints imposed on them by law enforcement and police search practices. Ethnographic approaches can offer a more dynamic contexualized picture of women's lawbreaking. While such approaches are relatively numerous in the study of adolescent and adult men in the United States (e.g., Anderson, 1990; Bourgois, 1989; Sullivan, 1989), they are rarely utilized in the study of women and girls.

For theory, women lawbreakers are rarely studied as members of social networks or as participants in collective or group-based activity (see also Steffensmeier and Terry, 1986). Nor have women been viewed as economic actors in illegal markets governed by occupational norms and workplace cultures (Maher, 1996). Those making a general claim about "women's emancipation" in the current drug economy ignore the obdurateness of a gender-stratified labor market and associated beliefs and practices that maintain it. Those making the more restricted claim that male-dominated street networks and market processes have weakened, thus allowing entry points for women, need to offer proof for that claim. We would expect to see variation in women's roles, and we would not say that Bushwick represents the general case. However, assertions of women's changing and improved position in the drug economy have not been well proved. Nor are they grounded in theories of how work, including illegal work, is conditioned by relations of gender, race-ethnicity, and sexuality (see, e.g., Daly, 1993; Game and Pringle, 1983; Kanter, 1977; Messerschmidt, 1993; Simpson and Elis, 1995).

Our findings suggest that the advent of crack cocaine and the concomitant expansion of the drug economy cannot be viewed as emancipatory for women drug users. To the extent that "new opportunities" in drug distribution and sales were realized in Bushwick and the wider Brooklyn sample, they were realized by men. Women were confined to an increasingly harsh economic periphery. Not only did the promised opportunities fail to materialize, but the expanding crack market served to deteriorate the conditions of street-level sex work, a labor market that has historically provided a relatively stable source of income for women drug users.

Notes

1. *Selling* refers to the direct exchange of drugs for cash; *distributing* refers to low-level distribution roles that do not involve direct sales but provide assistance to sellers.

2. At one level, language served as a marker of identity; "outsiders" were those who were not "Spanish," with country of origin often less salient than an ability to speak Spanish or "Spanglish." However, the distribution of opportunities for income generation also involved finely calibrated notions of ethnicity.

3. Each woman was given $10 or the equivalent (e.g., cash, food, clothing, cigarettes, makeup, subway tokens, or a combination) for the initial tape-recorded interview. However, field observations and many of the repeat interviews were conducted on the basis of relations of reciprocity that did not involve direct or immediate benefit to those interviewed. While this research focused on women's lives, interviews and observations were also undertaken with the women's female kin, male partners, and children.

4. Street-level drug sellers typically made $1 on a $10 bag of heroin and 50 cents on a $5 vial of crack. Syringe sellers made at least $1.50 per unit, depending on the purchase price and the sale price.

5. While consumption settings in Bushwick more closely resembled heroin shooting galleries (see, e.g., Des Jarlais et al., 1986; Murphy and Waldorf, 1991) than crack houses (see, e.g., Inciardi et al., 1993; Williams, 1992), many sites combined elements of both and most provided for polydrug (heroin and crack) consumption (for further details see Maher, in press).

6. By their own accounts, women took greater risks in order to generate income than they had in the past. More generally, the incidence of risky behavior increased as conditions in the neighborhood and the adjacent street-level sex market deteriorated (Maher and Curtis, 1992; see also Curtis et al., 1995).

References

Adler, Patricia A., 1985. *Wheeling and Dealing: An Ethnography of an Upper-Level Drug Dealing and Smuggling Community.* New York: Columbia University Press.

Anderson, Elijah, 1990. *Streetwise: Race, Class and Change in an Urban Community.* Chicago: University of Chicago Press.

Anglin, M. Douglas and Yih-Ing Hser, 1987. Addicted women and crime. *Criminology* 25:359–397.

Auld, John, Nicholas Dorn, and Nigel South, 1986. Irregular work, irregular pleasures: Heroin in the 1980s. In Roger Matthews and Jock Young (eds.), *Confronting Crime.* London: Sage.

Baskin, Deborah, Ira Sommers, and Jeffrey Pagan, 1993. The political economy of violent female street crime. *Fordham Urban Law Journal* 20:401–407.

Biernacki, Patrick, 1979. Junkie work, hustles, and social status among heroin addicts. *Journal of Drug Issues* 9:535–549.

Bourgois, Philippe, 1989. In search of Horatio Alger: Culture and ideology in the crack economy. *Contemporary Drug Problems* 16:619–649.

——, 1995. *In Search of Respect: Selling Crack in El Barrio.* New York: Cambridge University Press.

Bourgois, Philippe and Eloise Dunlap, 1993. Exorcising sex-for-crack: An ethnographic perspective from Harlem. In Mitchell S. Rawer (ed.), *Crack Pipe as Pimp: An Ethnographic Investigation of Sex-for-Crack Exchanges.* New York: Lexington Books.

Box, Steven, 1983. *Power, Crime and Mystification.* London: Tavistock.

Bureau of the Census, 1990. *Brooklyn in Touch.* Washington, D.C.: U.S. Government Printing Office.

Campbell, Anne, 1993. *Out of Control: Men, Women, and Aggression.* London: Pandora.

Covington, Jeanette, 1985. Gender differences in criminality among heroin users. *Journal of Research in Crime and Delinquency* 22:329–354.

Curtis, Richard and Lisa Maher, [in press] Highly structured crack markets in the southside of Williamsburg, Brooklyn. In Jeffrey Fagan (ed.), *The Ecology of Crime and Drug Use in Inner Cities.* New York: Social Science Research Council.

Curtis, Richard and Michelle Sviridoff, 1994. The social organization of street-level drug markets and its impact on the displacement effect. In Robert P. McNamara (ed.), *Crime Displacement: The Other Side of Prevention.* East Rockaway, N.Y.: Cummings and Hathaway.

Curtis, Richard, Samuel R. Friedman, Alan Neaigus, Benny Jose, Marjorie Goldstein, and Gilbert Ildefonso, 1995. Street-level drug markets: Network structure and HIV risk. *Social Networks* 17:229–249.

Daly, Kathleen, 1993. Class-race-gender: Sloganeering in search of meaning. *Social Justice* 20:56–71.

Des Jarlais, Don C., Samuel R. Friedman, and David Strug, 1986. AIDS and needle sharing within the IV drug use subculture. In Douglas A. Feldman and Thomas M. Johnson (eds.), *The Social Dimensions of AIDS: Methods and Theory.* New York: Praeger.

Dunlap, Eloise and Bruce D. Johnson, 1992. Who they are and what they do: Female crack dealers in New York City. Paper presented at the Annual Meeting of the American Society of Criminology, New Orleans, November.

Fagan, Jeffrey, 1994. Women and drugs revisited: Female participation in the cocaine economy. *Journal of Drug Issues* 24:179–225.

File, Karen N., 1976. Sex roles and street roles. *International Journal of the Addictions* 11:263–268.

File, Karen N., Thomas W. McCahill, and Leonard D. Savitz, 1974. Narcotics involvement and female criminality. *Addictive Diseases: An International Journal* 1:177–188.

Game, Ann and Rosemary Pringle, 1983. *Gender at Work.* Sydney: George Allen and Unwin.

Goldstein, Paul J, 1979. *Prostitution and Drugs.* Lexington, Mass.: Lexington Books.

Glick, Ronald, 1990. Survival, income, and status: Drug dealing in the Chicago Puerto Rican community. In Ronald Glick and Joan Moore (eds.), *Drugs in Hispanic Communities.* New Brunswick, N.J.: Rutgers University Press.

Hagedorn, John M., 1994. Homeboys, dope fiends, legits, and new jacks. *Criminology* 32:197–219.

Hamid, Ansley, 1990. The political economy of crack-related violence. *Contemporary Drug Problems* 17:31–78.

———, 1991. From ganja to crack: Caribbean participation in the underground economy in Brooklyn, 1976–1986. Part 2, Establishment of the cocaine (and crack) economy. *International Journal of the Addictions* 26:729–738.

———, 1992. The developmental cycle of a drug epidemic: The cocaine smoking epidemic of 1981–1991. *Journal of Psychoactive Drugs* 24:337–348.

Hay, Douglas, 1975. Property, authority, and the criminal law. In Douglas Hay, Peter Linebaugh, John G. Rule, Edward Palmer Thompson, and Cal Winslow (eds.), *Albion's Fatal Flee*. London: Allen Lane.

Hennig, Margaret, 1970. Career Development for Women Executives. Ph.D. dissertation, Harvard University, Cambridge, Mass.

Hser, Yih-Ing, M. Douglas Anglin, and Mary W. Booth, 1987. Sex differences in addict careers, Part 3, Addiction. *American Journal of Drug and Alcohol Abuse* 13:231–251.

Hunt, Dana, 1990. Drugs and consensual crimes: Drug dealing and prostitution. In Michael Tonry and James Q. Wilson (eds.), *Drugs and Crime. Crime and Justice*, Vol. 13. Chicago: University of Chicago Press.

Inciardi, James A. and Anne E. Pottieger, 1986. Drug use and crime among two cohorts of women narcotics users: An empirical assessment. *Journal of Drug Issues* 16:91–106.

Inciardi, James A., Dorothy Lockwood, and Anne E. Pottieger, 1993. *Women and Crack Cocaine*. New York: Macmillan.

James, Jennifer, 1976. Prostitution and addiction: An interdisciplinary approach. *Addictive Diseases: An International Journal* 2:601–618.

Johnson, Bruce D., Paul J. Goldstein, Edward Preble, James Schmeidler, Douglas S. Lipton, Barry Spunt, and Thomas Miller, 1985. *Taking Care of Business: The Economics of Crime by Heroin Abusers*. Lexington, Mass.: Lexington Books.

Johnson, Bruce D., Terry Williams, Kojo Dei, and Harry Sanabria, 1990. Drug abuse and the inner city: Impact on hard drug users and the community. In Michael Tonry and James Q. Wilson (eds.), *Drugs and Crime. Crime and Justice*, Vol. 13. Chicago: University of Chicago Press.

Johnson, Bruce D., Ansley Hamid, and Harry Sanabria, 1992. Emerging models of crack distribution. In Thomas M. Mieczkowski (ed.), *Drugs and Crime: A Reader*. Boston: Allyn & Bacon.

Johnson, Bruce D., Mangai Natarajan, Eloise Dunlap, and Elsayed Elmoghazy, 1994. Crack abusers and noncrack abusers: Profiles of drug use, drug sales, and nondrug criminality. *Journal of Drug Issues* 24:117–141.

Kanter, Rosabeth Moss, 1977. *Men and Women of the Corporation*. New York: Basic Books.

———, 1981. Women and the structure of organizations: Explorations in theory and behavior. In Oscar Grusky and George A. Miller (eds.), *The Sociology of Organizations: Basic Studies*. 2d ed. New York: The Free Press.

Katz, Jack, 1988. *Seductions of Crime: Moral and Sensual Attractions of Doing Evil*. New York: Basic Books.

Koester, Stephen and Judith Schwartz, 1993. Crack, gangs, sex, and powerlessness: A view from Denver. In Mitchell S. Ratner (ed.), *Crack Pipe as Pimp: An Ethnographic Investigation of Sex-for-Crack Exchanges*. New York: Lexington Books.

Maher, Lisa, (N.D.) *Making It at the Margins: Gender, Race and Work in a Street-Level Drug Economy*. Oxford: Oxford University Press.

———, 1996. Hidden in the light: Discrimination and occupational norms among crack using street-level sexworkers. *Journal of Drug Issues* 26(1):145–175.

Maher, Lisa and Richard Curtis, 1992. Women on the edge of crime: Crack cocaine and the changing contexts of street-level sex work in New York City. *Crime, Law, and Social Change* 18:221–258.

Maher, Lisa, Eloise Dunlap, Bruce D. Johnson, and Ansley Hamid, 1996. Gender, power and alternative living arrangements in the inner-city crack culture. *Journal of Research in Crime and Delinquency* 33:181–205.

Messerschmidt, James D., 1993. *Masculinities and Crime*. Lanham, Md.: Rowman and Littlefield

Mieczkowski, Thomas, 1986. Geeking up and throwing down: Heroin street life in Detroit. *Criminology* 24:645–666.

———, 1990. Crack dealing on the street: An exploration of the FBI hypothesis and the Detroit crack trade. Paper presented at the Annual Meeting of the American Society of Criminology, Baltimore, November.

———, 1994. The experiences of women who sell crack: Some descriptive data from the Detroit crack ethnography project. *Journal of Drug Issues* 24:227–248.

Moore, Joan W., 1990. Mexican American women addicts: The influence of family background. In Ronald Glick and Joan Moore (eds.), *Drugs in Hispanic Communities*. New Brunswick, N.J.: Rutgers University Press.

Morgan, Patricia and Karen Joe, 1994. Uncharted terrains: Contexts of experience among women in the illicit drug economy. Paper presented at the Women and Drugs National Conference, Sydney, November.

Murphy, Sheigla and Dan Waldorf, 1991. Kickin' down to the street doc: Shooting galleries in the San Francisco Bay area. *Contemporary Drug Problems* 18:9–29.

Murphy, Sheigla, Dan Waldorf, and Craig Reinarman, 1991. Drifting into dealing: Becoming a cocaine seller. *Qualitative Sociology* 13:321–343.

Padilla, Felix M., 1992. *The Gang as an American Enterprise*. New Brunswick, N.J.: Rutgers University Press.

Pettiway, Leon E., 1987. Participation in crime partnerships by female drug users: The effects of domestic arrangements, drug use, and criminal involvement. *Criminology* 25:741–766.

Reuter, Peter, Robert MacCoun, and Patrick Murphy, 1990. *Money from Crime: A Study of the Economics of Drug Dealing in Washington, D.C.* Santa Monica, Calif.: Rand Corporation.

Rosenbaum, Marsha, 1981. *Women on Heroin*. New Brunswick, N.J.: Rutgers University Press.

Simpson, Sally S. and Lori Elis, 1995. Doing gender: Sorting out the caste and crime conundrum. *Criminology* 33:47–81.

Skolnick, Jerome H., 1989. *The Social Structure of Street Drug Dealing*. Report to the State of California Bureau of Criminal Statistics and Special Services. Sacramento: State of California Executive Office.

Smithberg, Nathan and Joseph Westermeyer, 1985. White dragon pearl syndrome: A female pattern of drug dependence. *American Journal of Drug and Alcohol Abuse* 11:199–207.

Spalter-Roth, Roberta M., 1988. The sexual political economy of street vending in Washington, D.C. In Gracia Clark (ed.), *Traders Versus the State: Anthropological Approaches to Unofficial Economies*. Boulder, Colo.: Westview Press.

Steffensmeier, Darrell, 1983. Organization properties and sex-segregation in the underworld: Building a sociological theory of sex differences in crime. *Social Forces* 61:1010–1032.

Steffensmeier, Darrell J. and Robert M. Terry, 1986. Institutional sexism in the underworld: A view from the inside. *Sociological Inquiry* 56:304–323.

Sullivan, Mercer L., 1989. *Getting Paid: Youth Crime and Work in the Inner City*. Ithaca, N.Y.: Cornell University Press.

Sutter, A. G., 1966. The world of the righteous dope fiend. *Issues in Criminology* 2:177–222.

Taylor. Avril, 1993. *Women Drug Users: An Ethnography of a Female Injecting Community*. Oxford: Clarendon Press.

Taylor, Carl S., 1990. *Dangerous Society*. East Lansing: Michigan State University Press.

———, 1993. *Girls, Gangs, Women and Drugs*. East Lansing: Michigan State University Press.

Waldorf, Dan, Craig Reinarman, and Sheigla Murphy, 1991. *Cocaine Changes: The Experience of Using and Quitting*. Philadelphia, Pa.: Temple University Press.

Waterston, Alisse, 1993. *Street Addicts in the Political Economy*. Philadelphia, Pa.: Temple University Press.

Whyte, William Foote, 1943. *Street Corner Society*. Chicago: University of Chicago Press.

Williams, Terry, 1989. *The Cocaine Kids*. Reading, Mass.: Addison-Wesley.

——, 1992. *Crackhouse: Notes from the End of the Line*. New York: Addison-Wesley.

For Discussion

1. Discuss the ways in which gender roles within the illegal drug economy reflect gender roles in the greater society.

2. Relate the findings reported by Maher and Daly to Keire's perspective about the gendering of addiction in Part I of this reader.

Part IX

Drug Treatment

Historically, a major approach to eliminating the drug problem in the United States has been "treatment," and a considerable body of literature describes and documents the effectiveness of five major modalities of substance abuse/addiction treatment: chemical detoxification, methadone maintenance, drug-free outpatient treatment, self-help groups, and residential therapeutic communities. Each has its own particular view of substance abuse/addiction, and each affects the client in different ways.

Chemical Detoxification. Designed for persons dependent on narcotic drugs, chemical detoxification programs are typically situated in inpatient settings and endure for 7 to 21 days. The rationale for detoxification as a treatment approach is grounded in two basic principles. The first is a conception of "addiction" as drug craving, accompanied by physical dependence that motivates continued usage, resulting in a tolerance to the drug's effects and a syndrome of identifiable physical and psychological symptoms when the drug is abruptly withdrawn. The second is that the negative aspects of the abstinence syndrome discourage many addicts from attempting withdrawal and hence influence them to continue using drugs. Given this situation, the aim of chemical detoxification is elimination of physiological dependence through a medically supervised procedure.

Methadone, a synthetic narcotic, is the drug of choice for detoxification. Generally, a starting dose of the drug is gradually reduced in small increments until the body adjusts to the drug-free state. While many detoxification programs address only the addict's physical dependence, some provide individual or group counseling in an attempt to address the problems associated with drug abuse, while a few refer clients to other, longer-term treatments.

Almost all narcotics addicts have been in a chemical detoxification program at least once. Studies document, however, that virtually all relapse. Nevertheless, detoxification is temporary treatment that provides addicts with the opportunity for reducing their drug intake; for many, this means that the criminal activity associated with their drug taking and drug seeking is interrupted. Finally, given the association between injection drug use and HIV/AIDS, detoxification programs also provide counseling to reduce AIDS-related risk behaviors.

Methadone Maintenance. Methadone was synthesized during World War II by German chemists when supply lines for morphine were interrupted. Although chemically unlike morphine or heroin, it produces many of the same effects. Methadone was introduced in the United States in 1947, and since the 1960s the drug has been in common use for the treatment of heroin addiction. Known as "methadone maintenance," the treatment program takes advantage of methadone's unique properties as a narcotic. Like all narcotics, methadone is cross-dependent with heroin. As such, it is a substitute narcotic that prevents withdrawal. More important, however, methadone is orally effective, making intravenous use unnecessary. In addition, it is longer acting than heroin, with one oral dose lasting up to 24 hours. These properties have made methadone useful in the management of chronic narcotic addiction.

During the first phase of methadone treatment, the patient is detoxified from heroin on dosages of methadone sufficient to prevent withdrawal without either euphoria or sedation. During the maintenance phase, the patient is stabilized on a dose of methadone high enough to eliminate the craving for heroin. Although this process would appear to substitute one narcotic for another, the rationale behind methadone maintenance is to stabilize the patient on a less debilitating drug and make counseling and other treatment services available.

Studies have demonstrated that while few methadone maintenance patients have remained drug free after treatment, those who remain on methadone have highly favorable outcomes in terms of employment and no arrests. As such, methadone maintenance is effective for blocking heroin dependency.

Drug-Free Outpatient Treatment. Drug-free outpatient treatment encompasses a variety of nonresidential programs that do not use methadone or other pharmacotherapeutic agents. Most are based on a mental health perspective, and the primary services include individual and group therapy, while some offer family therapy and relapse-prevention support. An increasing number of drug-free outpatient programs are including case management services as adjuncts to counseling. The basic case management approach is to assist clients in obtaining needed services in a timely and coordinated manner. The key components of the approach are assessing, planning, linking, monitoring, and advocating for clients within the existing nexus of treatment and social services.

Evaluating the effectiveness of drug-free outpatient treatment is difficult, since programs vary widely—from drop-in "rap" centers to highly structured arrangements that offer counseling or psychotherapy as the treatment mainstay. A number of studies have found that outpatient treatment has been moderately successful in reducing daily drug use and criminal activity. However, the approach appears to be inappropriate for the most troubled and antisocial users.

Self-Help Groups. Self-help groups, also known as 12-step programs, are composed of individuals who meet regularly to stabilize and facilitate their recovery from substance abuse. The best known is Alcoholics Anonymous (AA), in which sobriety is based on fellowship and adhering to the "12 Steps" of recovery. The 12 steps stress faith, confession of wrongdoing, and passivity in the hands of a "higher power," and move group members from a statement of powerlessness over drugs and alcohol to a resolution that they will carry the message of help to others and will practice the principles learned in all affairs.

In addition to AA, other popular self-help groups are Narcotics Anonymous (NA), Cocaine Anonymous (CA), and Drugs Anonymous (DA), all of which follow the 12-step model. All of these organizations operate as stand-alone fellowship programs but are also used as adjuncts to other modalities. Although few evaluation studies of self-help groups have been carried out, the weight of clinical and observational data suggest that they are crucial to facilitating recovery.

Residential Therapeutic Communities. The therapeutic community, or TC, is a total treatment environment in which the primary clinical staff are typically former substance abusers—"recovering addicts"—who themselves were rehabilitated in therapeutic communities. The treatment perspective of the TC is that drug abuse is a disorder of the whole person—that the problem is the *person* and not the drug, that addiction is a *symptom* and not the essence of the disorder. In the TC's view of recovery, the primary goal is to change the negative patterns of behavior, thinking, and feeling that predispose drug use. As such, the overall goal is a responsible, drug-free lifestyle. Recovery through the TC process depends on positive and negative pressures to change, and this change is brought about through a self-help process in which relationships of mutual responsibility to every resident in the program are built.

In addition to individual and group counseling, the TC process has a system of explicit rewards that reinforce the value of achievement. As such, privileges are *earned*. In addition, TCs have their own specific rules and regulations that guide the behavior of residents and the management of their facilities. Their purposes are to maintain the safety and health of the community and to train and teach residents through the use of discipline. TC rules and regulations are numerous, with the most conspicuous being total prohibitions against violence, theft, and drug use. Violation of these cardinal rules typically results in immediate expulsion from a TC. Therapeutic communities have been in existence for decades, and their successes have been well documented.

In the chapters that follow, some approaches to treatment are addressed, with an emphasis on two common treatment modalities—the therapeutic community and methadone maintenance.

Additional Readings

Leukefeld, Carl G., Frank Tims, and David Farabee (Eds.). (2002). *Treatment of Drug Offenders: Policies and Issues.* New York: Springer Publishing Company.

Rawlings, Barbara, and Rowdy Yates. (2001). *Therapeutic Communities for the Treatment of Drug Users.* Philadelphia: Jessica Kingsley Publishers.

Rosenberg, Harold, and Kristina T. Phillips. (2003). "Acceptability and Availability of Harm-Reduction Interventions for Drug Abuse in American Substance Abuse Treatment Agencies." *Psychology of Addictive Behaviors* 17 (3): 203–210.

White, William L. (1998). *Slaying the Dragon: The History of Addiction Treatment and Recovery in America.* Bloomington, IL: Chestnut Health Systems. ✦

36

Gender-Specific Issues in the Treatment of Drug-Involved Women

Hilary L. Surratt

In this chapter, Hilary Surratt notes the increasing numbers of females who are incarcerated for drug offenses, with little opportunity for engaging with drug treatment while in prison. Moreover, treatment needs often differ for women and men, and Surratt describes how women can benefit from treatment programs that acknowledge these needs. The author presents data collected from women enrolled in a residential drug treatment program that allows participants' children to be present. The respondents emphasized that their children's presence encouraged them to engage more fully in the recovery process and assisted with motivation to address their addictions. Several narratives focused primarily on the role of motherhood. The author also describes the limitations of the program.

Substance abuse and dependence are significant problems in the United States, affecting some twenty million individuals (SAMHSA 2005; Uziel-Miller and Lyons 2000; Uziel-Miller et al. 1998; Wright 2004), almost one-third of whom are women (Wright 2004). Compared with men, substance-dependent women tend to differ in terms of precursors and pathways to addiction, the addictive process itself, and patterns of related comorbid conditions (CASA 2006; McMahon et al. 2002). Overall, re-

search has documented consistent gender differences in biological responses to drugs of abuse, with women typically showing greater increases in brain and metabolic activity after exposure, as well as greater and longer-lasting feelings of physical and mental well-being associated with substance use (Fallon et al. 2005; McCance-Katz et al. 2005). As a result, women tend to progress to addiction more quickly than men, have higher severities of negative consequences related to substance abuse, and often have more difficulties achieving abstinence from drugs than their male counterparts (CASA 2006; Zilberman and Blume 2005).

Substance abuse and its associated harms are increasingly affecting the lives of greater numbers of women (CASA 2006). These harms include not only a range of physical and mental health problems, but also social marginalization, separations from children and other family members, homelessness, and arrest and incarceration, to name but a few. The growing number of women involved with the criminal justice system is in many ways a reflection of increasing rates of substance abuse among women, as well as the enactment of tougher drug laws and mandatory sentencing policies as part of the nation's continuing "war on drugs" (Inciardi 2002). At mid-year 2005, for example, 106,174 women were incarcerated in state or federal prisons nationwide, and over 950,000 female offenders were on probation across the country (Glaze and Palla 2005; Harrison and Beck 2006), and many of these were serving sentences for drug-related offenses.

Possession and sale of illicit drugs and other drug-related offenses have contributed significantly to the continuing increases in the female correctional population (Inciardi 2002; Wilsnack et al. 1997). Across the nation, moreover, women are more likely than men to be serving sentences for drug-related offenses and to have committed their crimes under the influence of drugs, but less likely to be incarcerated for violent crimes (Conly 1998). In fact, a nationwide survey of women inmates found that nearly 45 percent were serving time for drug or drug-related charges, up from 15 percent in 1979 (Greenfeld and Snell 1999). Nearly half reported committing their crimes under the influence of drugs or alcohol and approximately 6 in 10 had used illegal drugs in the month before the offense (Mumola and Beck 1997). More recently, studies have indicated even higher levels of drug-involvement among female offenders than male offenders. In a national survey Peugh and Belenko (1999) documented that 79 percent of male and female prisoners in state correctional institutions had histories of substance abuse problems, but females were more likely to have used drugs in the month before their crimes and more likely to have committed their offenses under the influence of drugs. Going further, Staton-Tindall and colleagues (2003) found that 85 percent of female inmates interviewed in Kentucky prisons had used multiple substances in the 30 days prior to their incarceration, a prevalence well beyond that observed for male inmates.

Despite the overwhelming need for treatment among women in criminal justice populations, researchers have estimated that only about 13 percent receive treatment while incarcerated (Blanchard, 1999; Sheridan, 1996). Among the chief reasons for the paucity of institutionally based treatment programs is a lack of funding for treatment space and severe shortages of treatment personnel. One approach to providing substance abuse treatment for offenders has been the creation of "drug courts"—special courts that are given the responsibility for handling criminal cases among drug-involved offenders. Drug courts leverage the coercive power of the criminal justice system to impose judicial supervision, substance abuse treatment, drug testing, and case management of drug-involved offenders (Inciardi, McBride, and Rivers 1996). The primary procedure has been to require the offender, by legislative mandate or court order, to attend substance abuse programs as a form of legal leverage to ensure participation (Shearer, Myers, and Ogan 2001). Drug courts currently operate in all 50 states, and the successful completion of the treatment regimen assigned by the court can result in dismissal of criminal charges, reduced sentences, or lesser penalties for the offender. And with the proliferation of drug courts throughout the United States, treatment populations in many communities are becoming more and more dominated by drug court referrals.

Treatment Needs of Drug-Involved Women

Historically, treatment programs for drug abuse have been developed for male clients, because men represented the majority of drug abusers and because policymakers have been concerned with reducing violent crimes more commonly associated with men's involvement with drugs. As such, many treatment programs fail to address women's most common needs (Ashley, Marsden, and Brady 2003). Numerous studies have documented a variety of gender-specific issues and barriers to treatment that confront women drug abusers, including pregnancy and childcare responsibilities, partner violence and abuse histories of other trauma, resistance from family and friends, stigma associated with women's alcohol and drug use, poverty and financial need, conflict between traditional and changing gender roles, and low social support (Grella 1996; Klee, Jackson, and Lewis 2002; Pottieger and Tressell 2000; Uziel-Miller and Lyons 2000; Wechsberg, Craddock, and Hubbard 1998; Whiteside-Mansell, Crone, and Conners 1999; Wobie et al. 1997). In fact, an analysis of the national Drug Abuse Treatment Outcome Study data found that women entering substance abuse treatment tend to be younger, less educated, and more often unemployed than their male counterparts, with significantly higher levels of emotional and psychological distress, more depression and anxiety, poorer physical health, more physical and sexual abuse histories, and burdened by more child-related responsibilities (Uziel-Miller and Lyons 2000; Wechsberg, Craddock, and Hubbard 1998; Wobie et al. 1997). In addition, because substance abuse among pregnant or parenting women is often viewed as more deviant and stigmatizing than drug or alcohol abuse by men, women's sense of shame and guilt related to their drug use may also be heightened (Klee, Jackson, and Lewis 2002; Whiteside-Mansell, Crone, and Conners 1999). As such, drug abuse is rarely a woman's sole problem, and is likely just one of a myriad of adverse circumstances that profoundly affect the lives of women.

In response to the findings that the antecedents and consequences of substance abuse differ markedly for women and men, the number of specialized treatment programs for drug-abusing women has begun to increase. In this regard, an analysis of national treatment program data by Grella (1999) found that approximately 19 percent of the programs surveyed could be classified as "women only" programs. More recent analyses indicate that 19 percent of community treatment programs offer special therapeutic regimens for pregnant women, and 28 percent include gender-specific programming for other groups of women (Ashley, Marsden, and Brady 2003). And within the criminal justice system, 49 state departments of correction indicate that they have initiatives designed specifically for women, primarily in the areas of parenting, drug abuse treatment, victimization, and life skills (National Institute of Corrections 1998).

Typically, treatment adaptations for gender-appropriate programs include establishing programs staffed by women, changing the nature of staff-client interactions to a more supportive, less confrontational tone, including gender-specific issues in the programming content, and creating safe treatment environments (Kaplan and Sasser 1996). Although the recognition of differences in treatment needs and the implementation of specialized programs have expanded, until recently detailed descriptions of the services provided under the auspices of such programs and data on the effectiveness of these treatment approaches for women were generally absent from the literature. A recent comprehensive review of nearly 40 published studies reported consistent positive associations between specialized treatment programming for women and length of stay in treatment, treatment completion, decreased substance use, and reduced mental health symptoms (Ashley, Marsden, and Brady 2003). These data suggest that the provision of gender-specific treatment is more successful at reducing traditional barriers to treatment entry and

retention for women, and a key component of this success may be the increased availability of ancillary services and tangible support in other areas of importance to women.

One of the most consistent and well-documented findings in the scientific literature on drug abuse relates to gender differences in parenting and childcare concerns. Drug-dependent women are far more likely to be parents and to be living with their children than are their male counterparts (CASA 2006; McMahon et al. 2002), and concern about the effects of drug use on their children is one of the primary motivations for women to seek treatment (Klee, Jackson, and Lewis 2002). Though often situated within a context of extreme poverty and disadvantage, women drug users nevertheless express high levels of commitment to their children and value motherhood as a personally meaningful role (Kearney, Murphy, and Rosenbaum 1994; Sterk 1999; Surratt 2003). For many women, children function as a powerful motivating force toward abstinence from drugs, and pregnancy and motherhood are often looked upon as opportunities for a "new beginning," a chance to become a "good mother," and to promote positive, healthy lifestyle change (Kissin et al. 2004; Klee, Jackson, and Lewis 2002; Lesser, Koniak-Griffin, and Anderson 1999; Murphy and Rosenbaum 1999).

Within this context, a particularly important recent development in substance abuse treatment has been the creation and implementation of programs designed to serve parenting women and their children. Historically, there was a strong belief within traditional residential substance abuse treatment programs for women that having children present would be a deterrent to recovery (Dudley-Grant, Williams, and Hunt 2000). It was believed that women needed time away from maternal responsibilities to focus solely on recovery-related issues, and children were alleged to act as barriers to drug-involved women in admitting and confronting their addiction. The problem was that many women could not enter or complete substance abuse treatment because of childcare responsibilities, and as a result concerns about childcare and children's well-being have acted in some cases as deterrents to women's help-seeking behavior (McMahon et al. 2002; Wilke, Kamata, and Cash 2005).

Ultimately recognizing this dilemma, providers have recently established a larger number of residential treatment programs that accommodate women and their young children. Although there is a growing body of literature describing such model substance abuse treatment programs for parenting women, there is little published research on the treatment processes and outcomes related to participation in these programs (Conners et al. 2001). The most consistent findings from this research have been that women will remain in residential treatment longer and are more likely to complete treatment goals if they are permitted to have their children with them (Greenfield et al. 2004; Uziel-Miller et al. 1998; Wobie et al. 1997). A recent analysis of national data on women entering drug abuse treatment between 1995 and 2001 confirmed these findings, noting that women who brought children into treatment remained in the facility almost twice as long as those who did not (Chen et al. 2004). As such, it appears that enabling parenting women to remain together with their children during residential treatment is an important key to achieving the extended period of stay needed to accomplish treatment objectives (Chen et al. 2004). As retention is a major challenge in many treatment programs, these findings are particularly important indicators of women's potential for success in treatment. Treatment research has consistently found strong associations between length of stay in treatment and post-treatment outcomes including decreased drug use, decreased criminal activity, and increased employment (Anglin and Hser 1991; De Leon 1994; Inciardi, Martin, and Butzin 2004; NIDA 2006).

Although these findings indicate that specialized programs for parenting women are generally effective in reducing drug use and promoting at least short-term abstinence, the processes of engagement and participation through which this occurs are not well understood. This has led some to refer to treatment as a "black box" (Simpson 2001), with little understanding of how and why treatment does and does not work. In this regard, Reisinger and colleagues (2003) have suggested that traditional approaches to substance abuse treatment research, which often focus on discrete outcome measures such as treatment completion, do not fully capture the experiences and engagement of individuals in these programs.

New Approaches to Studying Women in Substance Abuse Treatment

Within the context of these remarks, the balance of this chapter reports the findings of a qualitative study that examined the motivations and experiences of women as they participated in a residential drug abuse treatment program together with their children. The data were collected in 2003 as part of a larger research initiative focusing on identity development among drug-involved women. The sample of women in the specialized treatment program was drawn from "The Village," one of the oldest and largest residential drug abuse treatment facilities in the State of Florida. The Village operates several substance abuse treatment programs in South Florida for adults and adolescents, including the Families in Transition (FIT) program—a 24-hour residential substance abuse treatment program for women and their children under twelve years of age. At any given time, there are nearly 50 women in various phases of the Families in Transition program with their children, and the typical length of stay in primary treatment is approximately six months.

Semi-structured, in-depth interviews were conducted with twelve women in the women and children's substance abuse treatment program. These were organized by an interview guide, containing broad questions about key topic areas: the women's experiences of residency in substance abuse treatment, histories of drug use, previous treatment experiences, experiences of mothering, views of addiction, and views of self in the past, present, and future. Interviews lasted between 60 and 90 minutes, and were audio-recorded for the purposes of transcription. Attempts were made to interview each woman on two occasions, with initial interviews occurring early in each woman's treatment experience, typically within four weeks after admission into the program. The second interview occurred two to three months later, after substantial exposure to primary treatment in the women and children's program. The second interview focused on significant events occurring since the first contact, and the women's experiences in treatment.

Four primary steps were taken to analyze the textual data elicited in the in-depth interviews. These included: (1) initial verbatim transcription and verification of interview audiotapes; (2) a series of four focused readings of these transcripts; (3) the construction and application of a detailed coding scheme based on analyses of the transcripts; and (4) the construction of an interpretive summary for each participant based on specific patterns of coding and a final reading of the full narrative. The word-processing files generated by transcription were converted into files compatible with the qualitative software package N6, which is designed to aid in the storage, coding, retrieval, and analysis of text (Weitzman and Miles 1995).

Analyses of the qualitative interviews revealed that the women universally attributed their motivation for and engagement with the treatment program to the presence of their children, as well as their desire to be responsible caregivers. As a group, the women displayed high levels of acceptance of treatment practices and participated actively in the components of the treatment program. Over time, women in the parental treatment program began to see the tangible benefits of participation in recovery-related activities as they progressed to increased visitations with their children, and ultimately co-residence. As this occurred, women began to interweave recovery and motherhood in their personal narratives, and a sense of personal accomplishment emerged. In this sense, engagement with their children afforded a sense of greater commitment to recovery, and many attributed personal change and development to their participation in this specialized program. In this regard, recovery was empowering for women in this specialized treatment context, supporting their emerging abilities to make positive change and to pursue valued commitments.

Themes surrounding the importance of motherhood were apparent in the narratives of virtually all of the women participating in family-centered treatment. Vanessa, a 37-year-old African American woman, had been a cocaine user for some 16 years when she entered the women and children's residential treatment program. Although Vanessa's initiation into crack cocaine use took place only a year prior to our interview, she recalled a rapid deterioration in her life at that point that she connected to her chronic and compulsive drug use. Although she had participated in treatment for cocaine use on several occasions, this was her first experience in a specialized women and children's facility. Through her interactions with this unique treatment community, she had developed a sense of herself as a recovering addict, but at the same time built a stronger sense of herself as a mother:

> I'm definitely an addict. But I'm workin' on that. I have to learn how to get some. . . . I'm learnin' how to get some control over myself. I did things in my addiction that, I mean, I ignored my kids. I never would do anything to just actually just hurt them, you know, physically or anything like that. But mentally I know I hurt them. I know they're, they're hurt. They do know that somethin' was wrong with mommy. They know mommy wasn't mommy anymore. Um, but they, they really sweet kids. They, they very intelligent kids. All I can do is move on with them, just hold on to them. Ask the Lord to guide me in how to raise them. And they, they precious. They very smart, like I say. They um, they love mommy. They uh, they support mommy. They know that I'm sick. That I'm gettin' well.

Clearly Vanessa viewed recovery as supporting her ability to mother, and in fact she attributed her successful participation in treatment to the structure of the program and the opportunity to maintain and strengthen ties with her children. Growing up for the most part without guardianship due to her mother's heavy drug use and long periods of absence from the family, Vanessa appeared to view recovery as important in its own right, but also as a mechanism for achieving meaningful reconciliation with her children. She vividly described the deprivation of her own childhood, culminating in her first pregnancy at age 13. Her youth and lack of parental role models afforded her a limited understanding of the possibilities for mothering at that time, yet she expressed a strong commitment to altering her own path as a mother:

My mom was a addict. I remember always wantin' my momma. I remember lovin' my mom. And I'd go lookin' for her. I used to walk around lookin' for her 'cause I knew where she'd be hangin' out. I stopped lookin' for her 'cause I started findin' her. And then when I found her I couldn't stand how I'd find her so I stopped looking for her. And my brother, my oldest brother, he took care of all of us. We stayed in the house, we stayed there by ourself. You know, my brother always told us not to let nobody know what was goin' on or else, you know, HRS [Health and Rehabilitative Services] would take us. We never said anything but eventually it came out. We lived for, I maybe was five and I was eight goin' on nine when they found out. My oldest brother, he'd been going to jail since he was ten. Tryin' to take care of us. He been gettin' shot at. He was almost killed and he wasn't but, maybe but eleven years old. Tryin' to break into somebody's house to get money to feed us. Now it's strange that I'm not angry at my mom anymore about me. I've learned that in order for me to recover I have to accept the responsibilities for all my actions. But I, I still sometime think about my brother and I get angry at her. 'Cause he never had a life. It's like, she took his life away from him. I definitely don't ever want to be to a point where I make my kid do somethin' that can get his life taken away from him so I can use. I never meant to, to be the way I am. That's the same way my mom was. She got high. Just didn't care. I want to be, I see myself working. Holding down a job. And I plan to live somewhere along this, somewhere along by this water with my kids. As long as I, I'm able to provide for us, I'm happy. As long as we be together. Long as I can teach them things and they can teach me things. When I was usin', I, I didn't have time for any of it. But now I'm gonna make sure I be there to their schools. To do the things that I need to do to help my kids grow into responsible adults. 'Cause I want them to be able to take of them, and not have to be like me.

For many women, it was precisely the felt connection with their children that initiated and maintained their very participation in treatment, and their commitment to motherhood and "good" mothering that supported their recovery from addiction. This consistently emerged as a central feature of the narratives of women most committed to recovery. Kristen, a 22-year-old mother, placed considerable emphasis on this point:

The first two weeks I was here, I didn't want to be here. I didn't think I had a problem. Once I found out I did, I was like shit! Now what am I gonna do? Well I started, you know, really listening intensely, and I was like ok, I'm gonna do this for K, my daughter. I came in because of my daughter. And I knew that I had to stay because of her. And I didn't want it for me, I wanted it for her and figured I'll do it for her. But you learn in here, you have to want it for yourself. I mean, whatever keeps you in here, wonderful. Like she's the reason I stayed in here and that worked. That's what I needed to get by to this point where I can have it for myself and I want it. And it was just gradually throughout, you know. The classes back-to-back every day, and the counselors and everything that I've heard. And I started wanting a better life for me. That way I could give her a better life. So it's been really a big factor because part of me recovering is getting better so I can be with her.

Here, Kristen assesses her future in recovery in terms of its impact on her goal of raising her child. In this way, her focus was not on recovery as an end in itself, but on what sobriety allowed her to achieve in other areas of her life—in this case the opportunity to re-claim her daughter and to contribute positively to her development.

The centrality and importance of motherhood remained a highly salient goal, even among women who were grappling with extreme poverty, health issues, and prior incidents of abuse and victimization in their childhood and adult lives. Theresa's story was a particularly poignant illustration of the violence endemic to many women's lives.

A 19-year-old African American woman, she came to the women and children's program with a substantial history of cocaine use in spite of her young age, and continued to struggle with the extensive trauma she had undergone in her adolescence:

> I have a really bad anger problem. Maybe 'cause of the things that happened when I was a child. I felt not wanted. I felt left out. It's somethin' that grew inside of me, like anger just grew inside of me. My father passed when I was twelve. My mother wasn't there. You know, and after my father passed like my grandmother didn't really care no more. And I had these anger tantrums. I would act out and stuff. So I guess they couldn't take it anymore. Um, and they kicked me out the house but it was okay. So I got introduced to the street. At the age of twelve I got kicked out the house. I was strippin' in the strip club at fourteen. That's how I made my money. The reason that I used drugs was to hide up, all those hurtin' feelings that's inside me. But when I came down off the drug, it ain't do nothin' but make it worse. And that's why I wanted the drug more and more and more. And I have to relive that, that incident that happened and it's, it's kinda hard but it has helped me a lot. Because at the age of sixteen I was raped by five boys. And when I got raped, I had to take care of myself. It made me feel like I was nothin'. That I, I didn't matter to nobody.

In spite of this traumatic personal history, Theresa displayed remarkable resilience as she organized much of her narrative around the topic of mothering, and her goal of being a "normal mother." Eight months pregnant when she entered treatment, her newborn had been removed from her care immediately after birth, as was her 15-month-old daughter. She had little opportunity to develop an attachment to her youngest daughter, and had had little meaningful contact with her 15-month-old due to her drug using activities over the prior year. Yet the very fact of their young ages afforded Theresa the hope that she could raise her own children and become the mother she would like to be. Since entering the treatment program she had been granted supervised visitation by the court, which positioned her children as highly salient, visible symbols of her recovery:

> The most important thing to me today is gaining custody of my kids back. That's, that's, that's my number one goal that I have to achieve. And I can't stand the fact that somebody else will raise them. Because my, my biological mother is an addict herself. And I'm not. . . . She chose drugs over me. And I'm not gonna choose drugs over my kids. But by me bein' in the program now, this is my first treatment center. It has really taught me how to deal with life on life's terms without the use of drugs. And in order for me to be right for my kids I have to get right for myself first, you know. It's, it's the first thing is stayin' clean. Because if I'm not clean, I'm not gonna be able to take care of my kids the way a normal mother would.

Through her continued participation in the specialized treatment regimen, Theresa began to speak of structuring her life around meaningful participation in recovery-related activities, and emphasized the role of sobriety in achieving her family-related goals. Her words regarding motherhood suggested that the valued goal of becoming a "good mother" was achievable through a process of learning and engagement afforded by the family-centered program activities:

> My momma was never there for me. And I don't, I don't want to use drugs no more because I don't want my children to look at me how I look at my mom. Because the way I used to look at my mom was like ugh, you ain't you momma, you just had me, you know. And I'm learnin' a lot. I wanna, I'm only nineteen years old. I wanna learn how to be a parent to my, to my child. I wanna learn how to raise my children. You know, that's why I go to parenting classes. For me to get off drugs, to get my life back in order, and to become a mother again, those are my goals. To raise my children I have a chance, you know. Because addicts, drug use, it only leads to jail, or institution, or death. You know? And either way it goes, you don't have a mother. And I'm not dead. I'm in a institution but I still have a chance to be with my child, another chance at life for me and my children. I'm gonna try to be the best mother that I can be. And if I'm in

active addiction, I'm not gonna be able to do that.

As suggested in the presentation of individual women's narratives, virtually all of the participants in the women and children's treatment program developed strong commitments to recovery that were uniquely connected to their goals of providing stable and responsible care for their children. The tremendous value of this connection was evident over time, as none of the participants in the women and children's treatment program declined in their commitment to recovery. The findings of this research suggest that women's connections to their children in the specialized treatment program reinforced recovery as meaningful in tangible, concrete ways. In particular, recovery became personally meaningful as it supported a desired path to motherhood.

Discussion

Taken together, these findings clearly demonstrate that substance-abusing women are a highly marginalized and vulnerable population. Frequently situated in a complex of adverse and chaotic social environments, their lives are marked by both intimate partner and community-level violence, poverty, homelessness, disease, and mental illness (Baseman, Ross, and Williams 1999; Davis 2000; Falck et al. 2001; Gilbert et al. 2001; Kettinger, Nair, and Schuler 2000). Chronic drug-using women often inhabit a world of economic deprivation and indigence, where the shifting and precarious nature of their financial resources, health, safety, and fragile social ties often engenders criminal involvement and perpetuates drug-using careers (Boyd 1999; Inciardi 1995). Many of these concerns are magnified even further for women from socioeconomically disadvantaged backgrounds or minority communities. These factors had a substantial impact on the participants in the present study, as many experienced periods of homelessness and very few had histories of stable employment. As such, drug abuse is rarely a woman's sole life problem, but is likely one of a myriad of adverse life events that profoundly affect the lives of women—and for those who are mothers, their children as well.

Nevertheless, research on women drug users has traditionally focused on their lack of parenting abilities and failure to be responsible or responsive caregivers (Blume 1991; Hans 1995; Kumpfer and Bayes 1995; Tarter et al. 1993). In spite of these portrayals, women drug users express high levels of commitment to their children and value motherhood as a personally meaningful role (Kearney, Murphy, and Rosenbaum 1994; Sterk 1999). For many women, becoming a "good mother" is a motivator for abstinence and recovery, and this was the case in this study as well. The women were overwhelmingly concerned not only with avoiding the removal of their children from their care, but also with making positive contributions to their development.

Cultural expectations for mothering emphasize unconditional love, nurturing, and self-sacrifice for one's children (Boyd 1999). While these idealized notions of motherhood may obscure the realities of daily life for many mothers, drug-using mothers are stigmatized by visible shortfalls in these expectations, and they often express guilt for failure to meet personal expectations as well (Baker and Carson 1999; Carter 2002; Lewis, Klee, and Jackson 1995; Murphy and Rosenbaum 1999; Sharpe 2005). Specialized treatment programs for pregnant and parenting women are designed in part to build women's parenting skills and to support women's confidence in their ability to mother, and thus have demonstrated increased retention in treatment and improved outcomes (Clark 2001; Conners et al. 2001; Grella 1999; Kissin et al. 2004; Surratt 2005). The qualitative research described above extends our understanding of family-centered approaches to substance abuse treatment for women by documenting the beneficial synergy between commitments to children and commitments to recovery that support women's meaningful engagement with treatment.

Implications for Future Research

As drug abuse continues to touch the lives of increasing numbers of women, expanded research in formal treatment settings and self-help venues is needed in order to understand women's experiences in these programs and the ways that their participation supports or impedes positive treatment outcomes. Process-oriented research has the potential to unpack the "black box" of treatment, and ultimately to improve the delivery of treatment services to women and their families by refining or redesigning the structure of programs and the meanings of participation in these regimens. One such fundamental redesign in drug abuse treatment has been the creation and expansion of women and children's residential programs. Clearly the structure and design of the parental treatment program described above impacted individual women's experiences of treatment. Participants in this program very clearly understood the paths to recovery and motherhood as intertwined, and each goal was seen to support the other. In fact, most attributed their active engagement in treatment to their children, and this fundamental engagement allowed them to remain in treatment long enough to achieve their treatment goals.

As a final point, it is important to note that while the family-centered treatment program was designed to incorporate children into the facility, this modification did not entail a transformation in the underlying structure of treatment practices or the philosophy of treatment promoted by the program. Rather, the treatment program continued to regard successful recovery as accomplished only for oneself, and the treatment regimen failed to optimize time for interaction between women and their children. It is often the case with women's treatment programs that, in spite of gender-specific modifications to a program's content and design, the fundamental philosophical orientation of the program remains unchanged (Grella 1996, 1999). In other words, the basic assumptions about the nature and process of treatment persist, unaltered by new patterns of staffing or the expanded purview of treatment to address gender-specific topics related to substance abuse. The inherent contradictions in the women and children's treatment program described above were difficult for many women to understand.

Clearly, women's sense of connection to their children was a powerful part of the recovery process in treatment, yet the institutional emphasis on recovery as an individual process often failed to consider or build upon the value of this social connectedness. As such, future research in women and children's programs should examine whether and how children are meaningfully integrated into the treatment community as potentially important participants, and the impact of these factors on women's treatment outcomes. From a social policy perspective, in-depth explorations of such programs could lead to improved programming and structured services for drug-involved women and their children.

References

Anglin, M. D., and Y. I. Hser. (1991). Criminal Justice and the Drug Abusing Offender: Policy Issues of Coerced Treatment. *Behavioral Sciences and Law* 9 (3): 243–267.

Ashley, O. S., M. E. Marsden, and T. M. Brady. (2003). Effectiveness of Substance Abuse Treatment Programming for Women: A Review. *The American Journal of Drug and Alcohol Abuse* 29 (1): 19–53.

Baker, P. L., and A. Carson. (1999). I Take Care of My Kids: Mothering Practices of Substance-Abusing Women. *Gender and Society* 13 (3): 347–363.

Baseman, J., M. Ross, and M. Williams. (1999). Sale of Sex for Drugs and Drugs for Sex: An Economic Context of Sexual Risk Behaviors for STDs. *Sexually Transmitted Diseases* 26 (8): 444–449.

Blanchard, C. (1999). Drugs, Crime, Prison and Treatment. *Spectrum: The Journal of State Government* 72 (1): 26–28.

Blume, S. B. (1991). Children of Alcoholic and Drug Dependent Parents. In *Alcohol and Drugs Are Women's Issues*, ed. P. Roth, 166–172. Metuchen, NJ: Women's Action Alliance.

Boyd, S. C. (1999). *Mothers and Illicit Drugs: Transcending the Myths*. Ontario, Canada: University of Toronto Press.

Carter, C. S. (2002). Perinatal Care for Women Who Are Addicted: Implications for Empowerment. *Health and Social Work* 27 (3): 166–174.

CASA (The National Center on Addiction and Substance Abuse at Columbia University). (2006). *Women under the Influence*. Baltimore, MD: Johns Hopkins University Press.

Chen, X., K. Burgdorf, K. Dowell, T. Roberts, A. Porowski, and J. M. Herrell. (2004). Factors Associated with Retention of Drug Abusing Women in Long-Term Residential Treatment. *Evaluation and Program Planning* 27 (2): 205–212.

Clark, H. W. (2001). Residential Substance Abuse Treatment for Pregnant and Postpartum Women and Their Children: Treatment Policy Implications. *Child Welfare* 80 (2): 179–198.

Conly, C. (1998). *The Women's Prison Association: Supporting Women Offenders and Their Families*. Washington, DC: National Institute of Justice.

Conners, N. A., R. H. Bradley, L. Whiteside-Mansell, and C. C. Crone. (2001). A Comprehensive Substance Abuse Treatment Program for Women and Their Children: An Initial Evaluation. *Journal of Substance Abuse Treatment* 21 (2): 67–75.

Davis, N. J. (2000). From Victims to Survivors: Working with Recovering Street Prostitutes. In *Sex for Sale: Prostitution, Pornography, and the Sex Industry*, ed. R. Weitzer, 139–158. New York: Routledge.

De Leon, G. (1994). Therapeutic Communities. In *Textbook of Substance Abuse Treatment*, eds. M. Galanter and H. D. Kleber, 391–414. Washington, DC: Psychiatric Press.

Dudley-Grant, G. R., I. Williams, and K. Hunt. (2000). Substance Abusing Women with Children in Treatment: A Virgin Islands Residential Model. *Interamerican Journal of Psychology* 34 (1): 17–28.

Falck, R. S., J. Wang, R. G. Carlson, and H. A. Siegal. (2001). The Epidemiology of Physical Attack and Rape among Crack-Using Women. *Violence and Victims 16 (1): 79–89.*

Fallon, J. H., D. B. Keator, J. Mbogori, D. Taylor, and S. G. Potkin. (2005). Gender: A Major Determinant of Brain Response to Nicotine. *International Journal of Neuropsychopharmacology* 8 (1): 17–26.

Gilbert, L., N. El-Bassel, V. Rajah, A. Foleno, and V. Frye. (2001). Linking Drug-Related Activities with Experiences of Partner Violence: A Focus Group Study of Women in Methadone Treatment. *Violence and Victims* 16 (5): 517–536.

Glaze, L. E., and S. Palla. (2005, November). *Probation and Parole in the United States, 2004.* Bureau of Justice Statistics Bulletin. NCJ 210676. US Department of Justice, Office of Justice Programs.

Greenfeld, L. A., and T. L. Snell. (1999, December). *Women Offenders.* Bureau of Justice Statistics Bulletin. NCJ 175688. US Department of Justice, Office of Justice Programs.

Greenfield, L., K. Burgdorf, X. Chen, A. Porowski, T. Roberts, and J. Herrell. (2004). Effectiveness of Long-Term Residential Substance Abuse Treatment for Women: Findings from Three National Studies. *The American Journal of Drug and Alcohol Abuse* 30 (3): 537–550.

Grella, C. E. (1996). Background and Overview of Mental Health and Substance Abuse Treatment Systems: Meeting the Needs of Women Who Are Pregnant or Parenting. *Journal of Psychoactive Drugs* 28 (4): 319–343.

——. (1999). Women in Residential Drug Treatment: Differences by Program Type and Pregnancy. *Journal of Health Care for the Poor and Underserved* 10 (2): 216–229.

Hans, S. (1995). Diagnosis in Etiologic and Epidemiologic Studies. In C. Jones and M. De La Rosa (eds.), *NIDA Technical Review: Methodological Issues: Etiology and Consequences of Drug Abuse among Women.* Rockville, MD: National Institute on Drug Abuse.

Harrison, P. M., and A. J. Beck. (2006, May). *Prison and Jail Inmates at Midyear 2005.* Bureau of Justice Statistics Bulletin. NCJ 213133. US Department of Justice, Office of Justice Programs.

Inciardi, J. A. (1995). Crack, Crack House Sex, and HIV Risk. *Archives of Sexual Behavior* 24 (3): 249–269.

——. (2002). *The War on Drugs III: The Continuing Saga of the Mysteries and Miseries of Intoxication, Addiction, Crime, and Public Policy.* Boston, MA: Allyn and Bacon.

Inciardi, J. A., S. S. Martin, and C. A. Butzin. (2004). Five-Year Outcomes of Therapeutic Community Treatment of Drug-Involved Offenders after Release from Prison. *Crime and Delinquency* 50 (1): 88–107.

Inciardi, J. A., D. C. McBride, and J. E. Rivers. (1996). *Drug Control and the Courts.* Thousand Oaks, CA: Sage Publications.

Kaplan, M. S., and J. E. Sasser. (1996). Women Behind Bars: Trends and Policy Issues. *Journal of Sociology and Social Welfare* 23 (4): 43–56.

Kearney, M., S. Murphy, and M. Rosenbaum. (1994). Mothering on Crack: A Grounded Theory Analysis. *Social Science and Medicine* 38 (2): 351–361.

Kettinger, L. A., P. Nair, and M. E. Schuler. (2000). Exposure to Environmental Risk Factors and Parenting Attitudes among Substance Abusing Women. *American Journal of Drug and Alcohol Abuse* 26 (1): 1–11.

Kissin, W. B., D. S. Svikis, P. Moylan, N. A. Haug, and M. L. Stitzer. (2004). Identifying Pregnant Women at Risk for Early Attrition from Substance Abuse Treatment. *Journal of Substance Abuse Treatment* 27 (1): 31–38.

Klee, H., M. Jackson, and S. Lewis. (2002). *Drug Misuse and Motherhood.* London: Routledge.

Kumpfer, K. L., and J. Bayes. (1995). Child Abuse and Drugs. In *The Encyclopedia of Drugs and Alcohol* (Vol. 1, pp. 217–222). New York: Simon and Schuster.

Lesser, J., D., Koniak-Griffin, and N. L. R. Anderson. (1999). Depressed Adolescent Mothers' Perceptions of Their Own Maternal Role. *Issues in Mental Health Nursing* 20 (2): 131–149.

Lewis, S., H. Klee, and M. Jackson. (1995). Illicit Drug Users' Experiences of Pregnancy: An Exploratory Study. *Journal of Reproductive and Infant Psychology* 13: 219–227.

McCance-Katz, E. F., C. L. Hart, B. Boyarsky, T. Kosten, and P. Jatlow. (2005). Gender Effects Following Repeated Administration of Cocaine and Alcohol in Humans. *Substance Use and Misuse* 40 (4): 511–528.

McMahon, T. J., J. D. Winkel, N. E. Suchman, and S. S. Luthar. (2002). Drug Dependence, Parenting Responsibilities, and Treatment History: Why Doesn't Mom Go for Help. *Drug and Alcohol Dependence* 65 (2): 105–114.

Mumola, C. J., and A. J. Beck. (1997, June). *Prisoners in 1996.* Bureau of Justice Statistics Bulletin. NCJ 164619. US Department of Justice, Office of Justice Programs.

Murphy, S., and M. Rosenbaum. (1999). *Pregnant Women on Drugs: Combating Stereotypes and Stigma.* New Brunswick, NJ: Rutgers University Press.

National Institute of Corrections. (1998). *Current Issues in the Operation of Women's Prisons.* Longmont, CO: U.S. Department of Justice.

National Institute on Drug Abuse. (2006) *Principles of Drug Abuse Treatment for Criminal Justice Populations: A Research Based Guide.* NIH Publication No. 06-5316, Rockville, MD.

Peugh, J., and S. Belenko. (1999). Substance-Involved Women Inmates: Challenges to Providing Effective Treatment. *The Prison Journal* 79 (1): 23–44.

Pottieger, A. E., and P. A. Tressell. (2000). Social Relationships of Crime-Involved Women Cocaine Users. *Journal of Psychoactive Drugs* 32 (4): 445–460.

Reisinger, H. S., T. Bush, M. A. Colom, M. Agar, and R. Battjes. (2003). Navigation and Engagement: How Does One Measure Success? *Journal of Drug Issues* 33 (4): 778–800.

Sharpe, T. T. (2005). *Behind the Eight Ball: Sex for Crack Cocaine Exchange and Poor Black Women.* Binghamton, NY: Haworth Press.

Shearer, R. A., L. B. Myers, and G. D. Ogan. (2001). Treatment Resistance and Ethnicity among Female Offenders in Substance Abuse Treatment Programs. *The Prison Journal* 81 (1): 55–72.

Sheridan, M. J. (1996). Comparison of Life Experiences and Personal Functioning of Men and Women in Prison. *Families in Society: The Journal of Contemporary Human Services* 77 (7): 423–434.

Simpson, D. D. (2001). Modeling Treatment Process and Outcomes. *Addiction* 96 (2): 207–211.

Staton-Tindall, M., C. Leukefeld, and J. M. Webster. (2003). Substance Use, Health, and Mental Health: Problems and Service Utilization among Incarcerated Women. *International Journal of Offender Therapy and Comparative Criminology* 47 (2): 224–239.

Sterk, C. E. (1999). *Fast Lives: Women Who Use Crack Cocaine.* Philadelphia: Temple University Press

Substance Abuse and Mental Health Services Administration, and Office of Applied Studies (SAMHSA). (2005). *Substance Use During Pregnancy: 2002 and 2003 Update.* The NSDUH Report. Available at *http://www.oas.samhsa.gov/2k5/pregnancy/pregnancy.pdf.*

Surratt, H. L. (2003). Parenting Attitudes of Drug-Involved Women Inmates. *The Prison Journal* 83 (2): 206.

——. (2005). *Constructing the Self as Addict: Narratives of Recovery and Resistance among Women in Drug Abuse Treatment.* Doctoral Dissertation, City University of New York.

Tarter, R., T. Blackson, C. Martin, R. Loeber, and H. Moss. (1993). Characteristics and Correlates of Child Discipline Practices in Substance Abuse and Normal Families. *American Journal on Addictions* 21 (1): 18–25.

Uziel-Miller, N. D., and J. S. Lyons. (2000). Specialized Substance Abuse Treatment for Women and Their Children: An Analysis of Program Design. *Journal of Substance Abuse Treatment* 19 (4): 355–367.

Uziel-Miller, N. D., J. S. Lyons, C. Kissiel, and S. Love. (1998). Treatment Needs and Initial Outcomes of a Residential Recovery Program for African-American Women and Their Children. *American Journal on Addictions* 7 (1): 43–50.

Wechsberg, W. M., S. G. Craddock, and R. L. Hubbard. (1998). How Are Women Who Enter Substance Abuse Treatment Different Than Men? A Gender Comparison from the Drug Abuse Treatment Outcome Study (DATOS). *Drugs and Society* 13 (1/2): 97–115.

Weitzman, E. A., and M. B. Miles. (1995). *Computer Programs for Qualitative Data Analysis: A Software Sourcebook.* Thousand Oaks, CA: Sage Publications.

Whiteside-Mansell, L., C. C. Crone, and N. A. Conners. (1999). The Development and Evaluation of an Alcohol and Drug Prevention and Treatment Program for Women and Children: The AR-CARES Program. *Journal of Substance Abuse Treatment* 16 (3): 265–275.

Wilke, D. J., A. Kamata, and S. J. Cash. (2005). Modeling Treatment Motivation in Substance-Abusing Women with Children. *Child Abuse and Neglect* 29 (11): 1313–1323.

Wilsnack, S. C., N. D. Vogeltanz, A. D. Klassen, and T. R. Harris. (1997). Childhood Sexual Abuse and Women's Substance Abuse: National Survey Findings. *Journal of Studies on Alcohol* 58 (3): 264–271.

Wobie, K., F. D. Eyler, M. Conlon, L. Clarke, and M. Behnke. (1997). Women and Children in Residential Treatment: Outcomes for Mothers and Their Infants. *Journal of Drug Issues* 27 (3): 585–606.

Wright, D. (2004). *State Estimates of Substance Use from the 2002 National Survey of Drug Use and Health: Findings.* DHHS Publication No. SMA 04-3907, NSDUH Series H-23. Rockville, MD: Substance Abuse and Mental Health Services Administration, Office of Applied Studies.

Zilberman, M. L., and S. B. Blume. (2005). Drugs and Women. In *Substance Abuse: A Comprehensive Textbook* fourth edition, ed. J. H. Lowinson, P. Ruiz, R. B. Millman, and J. G. Langrod, 1064–1075. Philadelphia: Lippincott, Williams and Wilkins.

For Discussion

1. Are mothers who use drugs treated differently by society than fathers who use drugs? If so, why?

2. Should state and federal prisons be required to offer treatment programs similar to the one described in this article? Why or why not?

37

Advances in Therapeutic Communities

National Institute on Drug Abuse

The therapeutic community (TC) is a drug treatment modality that uses a holistic design for creating lifestyle changes. It is characterized by a democratic philosophy with foundations in social learning theory. In the next article, the historical background regarding TCs is described as well as their organizational and ideological characteristics. TCs have changed in recent years in response to the needs of various subgroups, such as women drug users with children. This article also includes a summary of findings drawn from evaluation studies of TCs.

What Is a Therapeutic Community?

"Therapeutic community," or just "TC" as it is usually referred to by researchers and clinicians in the drug field, is a generic term used to describe a wide spectrum of residential drug abuse treatment approaches. However, fundamental to the TC concept is the necessity for a total treatment environment isolated from the drugs, violence, and other aspects of street life that militate against rehabilitation. The primary clinical staff in TCs are typically former substance abusers who themselves were rehabilitated in therapeutic communities. The treatment perspective in the TC is that drug abuse is a disorder of the whole person; that the problem is the *person* and not the drug; that addiction is a *symptom* and not the essence of the disorder; and that the primary goal is to change the negative patterns of behavior, thinking, and feeling that predispose drug use (De Leon, 1994).

History of Therapeutic Communities

1. Early Roots

The roots of therapeutic communities date back to the "no restraints" therapy for mental patients developed in early nineteenth century France. Treatment was based on work therapy and the provision of recreational facilities, within a "no violence" atmosphere (Kooyman, 1993). Similar programs appeared in other parts of Europe later in the century, but none evidenced any meaningful success. They were usually replaced with more traditional forms of treatment, given that most institutions were understaffed and overpopulated with difficult to treat patients.

During World War II, psychiatrists assigned to England's Army Selection Unit found themselves confronted with growing numbers of soldiers returning from battle suffering from mental breakdowns. Maxwell Jones, a psychiatrist dealing with soldiers at the army's Northfield Hospital, stressed the importance of patients' participation in their own successful recovery (Kooyman, 1993). He described his approach as "democratic therapy," and eventually turned his unit at Henderson into a therapeutic community. Jones made five basic assumptions for patient-staff interactions in his therapeutic community (Jones, 1953):

1. two-way communication at all levels
2. decision-making at all levels
3. shared leadership
4. consensus in decision-making
5. social learning by social interaction, here and now

2. Synanon

Contemporary therapeutic communities in the United States can be traced to Synanon. Synanon seemed to just "happen" by chance in 1958, when its founder, Charles Dederich, an unemployed recovering alcoholic, used his Ocean Park, California, apartment for holding informal therapy "bull sessions" with alcoholic and drug-using friends. Dederich found that people were drawn to him and listened to him. In time, he began to structure his gatherings with different types of group therapy that he had become familiar with at Alcoholics Anonymous and other treatment. Before long, he began to exercise rigid control over the groups, introducing methods of cross examination and ridicule that gave birth to the "encounter group"—a highly confrontational and intense form of verbal communication in a group setting.

Dederich observed that many of the substance abusers in his groups stopped using drugs while they were connected with his groups. Motivated by the idea that he might have found an answer to addiction, he established Synanon House, America's first TC for drug abusers. As the program grew, with houses in several parts of the United States, its methods and procedures evolved into a dynamic that focused on the rehabilitation of drug-involved offenders (Casriel, 1963).

Since the very beginning of its founding, Synanon faced numerous problems, including community resistance to the program. It was argued that Dederich's facility was not only in violation of zoning regulations, but was operating as a hospital without a license. The zoning wars that followed gave Synanon national publicity, both positive and negative, and by 1962 it was claimed by one of Synanon's supporters that the program had attracted more than 19,000 visitors, most of whom were professionals who wished to see Dederich's "anti-criminal society" first hand (Yablonsky, 1967). But despite the adverse publicity, Synanon grew to 500 residents by 1964, 800 by 1967, and 1,400 by 1969 (White, 1998).

3. Synanon II and Synanon III

By 1968, Dederich had shifted his vision of Synanon from rehabilitation to the creation of an alternative community. The process of restructuring one's character became more important than returning an individual back to society (White, 1998). Program graduation was abolished, and addiction was cast as a "terminal disease" that could be arrested only by sustained participation within Synanon. Loyalty oaths were introduced, and only the most committed to the concept remained.

During the early 1970s Synanon underwent yet another transition. In 1974 the Synanon Foundation was chartered as a religion. At the same time, increased paranoia regarding outsiders led to the emergence of paramilitary defense measures that included major weapons purchases and martial arts training. Quickly, Synanon's role in the rehabilitation of addicts disappeared. Its legacy, however, was a new approach to addiction treatment. By introducing the use of recovering addicts as counselors, the treatment approach stepped away from the traditional doctor-patient relationship and created an environment where former users could treat current users through role modeling. In addition, Synanon was successful in stripping the culture of addiction from the addict and replacing it with a culture of recovery.

4. Daytop Village

First known as Daytop Lodge, the Daytop experience began when Herbert A. Bloch, a criminology professor at Brooklyn College; Joseph Shelly, Chief Probation Officer for the New York State Supreme Court; and Alexander Bassin, Director of Research for the State Supreme Court, submitted a proposal to the National Institute of Mental Health for a project to establish a halfway house for drug-involved offenders (Shelly and Bassin, 1965). The project was to be modeled after Synanon, and on April 15, 1963, an initial grant of $390,000 enabled Daytop to open its doors several months later. The initial population was 25 men between the ages of 16 and 45 who had been sentenced to probation with the stipulation that they remain in the program until graduation (Shelly and Bassin, 1965).

By 1965, Daytop Lodge had evolved from its halfway house roots into Daytop Village, a well-organized and tightly structured program for both women and men with an intricate network of treatment approaches. The treatment philosophy during the early years of Daytop was straightforward: *You are an addict because you are stupid, immature, and irresponsible, and cannot bear the realities of life as an adult!* This was the only cause of drug addiction recognized by Daytop, and the program leadership would not permit residents to blame their behavior on parents, peers, neighborhood, or community (Inciardi, 1967). Or stated differently:

> In other words, the concept of the drug addict as [an] ill person and therefore automatically entitled to the recognized prerogatives of the role of the ill in our society in terms of sympathetic understanding, special concern, leniency, and forgiveness is vehemently fought as an ideology. (Shelly and Bassin, 1965)

The new resident at Daytop was considered to be a "child," and as such was given little responsibility. As he or she developed in the program, duties of greater importance were assigned. Treatment was intended to force the "child" to act as an adult, with the resolve that he or she would eventually think as an adult and feel like an adult. When that was accomplished, the resident was ready for graduation—a process that generally endured from 12 to 18 months. Regardless of one's position, however, all had to follow the three cardinal rules: no drugs, no violence, and no shirking of responsibility. Sanctions for breaking the cardinal rules ranged from public ridicule and reduction in status to shaved heads, the wearing of diapers, or expulsion from the program.

As time passed and Daytop grew, the rigidity and severity of sanctions for rule breaking lessened, and other programs adopted the Daytop model—Phoenix House and Delaney Street in New York City, Amity in Tucson, Gaudenzia House in Philadelphia, Gateway House in Chicago, Integrity House in Newark, and Marathon in Coventry, Rhode Island. All of these new programs were started during the 1960s, many by graduates of either Synanon or Daytop.

Criticisms

During their first two decades, TCs received both praise and support. Daytop and Phoenix House, furthermore, expanded into worldwide programs. But TCs also drew numerous criticisms. For example (see White, 1998):

1. The great majority of residents were mandatory rather than voluntary placements.

2. Programs boasted of great successes, but few permitted independent evaluations or provided statistics on the number of dropouts or successful graduates.

3. The TC was an artificial environment that inhibited rather than promoted a graduate's functioning in the outside community.

4. The use of nonprofessional staff ran the risk of serious mistakes in diagnoses and treatment.

5. TCs had few links to other community-based support structures.

6. Programs placed too much emphasis on the charismatic leadership of its director. This dependence, it was claimed, made TCs unstable.

7. The fact that there were only a few key positions in a TC hierarchy made programs vulnerable to abuses of power by those in charge.

8. The costs of treatment were far too high.

All of these criticisms had some validity, and by the latter 1970s and early 1980s a number of TCs had closed, while others had fallen on hard times. Part of this, however, was the result of factors unrelated to the therapeutic community process—it was the era of the "nothing works" philosophy in correctional treatment.

The 'Nothing Works' Era

During the late 1960s and early 1970s, programs to abolish poverty and racial injustice had not lived up to their expectations. There were riots, many were angered over American involvement in Vietnam, and rates of drug abuse and crime were increasing at a rapid pace. Furthermore, there was growing opposition to the many Supreme Court decisions that some claimed, and others denied, were "handcuffing police" and "coddling criminals." During much of this period, researchers in New York had been undertaking a massive evaluation of prior efforts at correctional intervention.

The idea for the research went back to early 1966, when the New York State Governor's Special Committee on Criminal Offenders decided to commission a study to determine what methods, if any, held the greatest promise for the rehabilitation of convicted criminals, including drug-involved offenders. The findings of the study were to be used to guide program development in the state's criminal justice system. The project was carried out by researchers at the New York State Office of Crime Control Planning, and for years they analyzed the literature on hundreds of correctional efforts published between 1945 and 1967.

The findings of the project were put together in a massive volume that was published in 1975 (Lipton, Martinson, and Wilks, 1975). Prior to the appearance of the in-depth report, the article, "What Works?— Questions and Answers About Prison Reform" [appeared] (Martinson, 1974). Written by one of the researchers, Robert Martinson, the article was published in *The Public Interest*. In it he reviewed the purpose and scope of the New York study and implied that with few and isolated exceptions, *nothing works!*

There was little that was really new in Martinson's article. In 1966, Professor Walter C. Bailey of the City University of New York had published the findings of a survey of 100 evaluations of correctional treatment programs with the final judgment that "evidence supporting the efficacy of correctional treatment is slight, inconsistent, and of questionable reliability" (Bailey, 1966). The following year, Roger Hood in England completed a similar review, concluding that the different ways of treating offenders lead to results that are not very encouraging (Hood, 1967). And in 1971, James Robison and Gerald Smith's analysis of correctional treatment in California asked "Will the clients act differently if we lock them up, or keep them locked up longer, or do something with them inside, or watch them more closely afterward, or cut them loose officially?" Their conclusion was a resounding "Probably not!" (Robison, 1971).

But the Martinson essay created a sensation, for it appeared in a visible publication and attracted popular media attention at a time when politicians and opinion makers were desperately searching for some response to the widespread public fear of drug abuse and street crime. Furthermore, as Harvard University's James Q. Wilson explained:

> Martinson did not discover that rehabilitation was of little value in dealing with crime so much as he administered a highly visible *coup de grace*. By bringing out into the open the long-standing scholarly skepticism about most rehabilitation programs, he prepared the way for a revival of an interest in the deterrent, incapacitative, and retributive purposes of the criminal justice system. (Wilson, 1980)

Martinson also created a sensation within the research and treatment communities— mostly negative. He was criticized for bias, major distortions of fact, and gross misrepresentation (Klockars, 1975; Palmer, 1975). And for the most part, his critics were correct. Martinson had failed to include all types of treatment programs; he tended to ignore the effects of some programs on some individuals; he generally concentrated on whether the particular treatment method was effective in *all* the studies in which it was tested; and he neglected to study the new federally funded treatment programs that had begun after 1967. But none of that seemed to matter. The end result was the loss of funding for many treatment programs, both in and out of correctional settings, including many therapeutic communities.

Essential Elements of Modern Therapeutic Communities

The essential elements of modern therapeutic communities consist of a series of concepts, beliefs, assumptions, program components, and clinical and educational practices that are apparent to a greater or lesser degree in every TC. A cataloguing and description of these elements was accomplished by TC researcher George De Leon with the help of a national panel of TC experts (Melnick and De Leon, 1993; De Leon, 1997).

As De Leon has explained, the quintessential element of the TC approach may be termed *community as method* (De Leon, 1997). The essential concepts that characterize community as method include:

Use of Participant Roles: Individuals contribute directly to all activities of daily life in the TC, which provides learning opportunities through engaging in a variety of roles.

Use of Membership Feedback: The primary source of instruction and support for individual change is the peer membership.

Use of Membership as Role Models: Each participant strives to be a role model of the change process. Along with their responsibility to provide feedback to others as to what they must change, members must also provide examples of how they can change.

Use of Collective Formats for Guiding Individual Change: The individual engages in the process of change primarily with peers. Education, training, and therapeutic activities occur in groups, meetings, seminars, job functions, and recreation.

Use of Shared Norms and Values: Rules, regulations, and social norms protect the physical and psychological safety of the community. However, there are beliefs and values that serve as explicit guidelines for self-help recovery and teaching right living.

Use of Structure and Systems: The organization of work (e.g., the varied job functions, chores, and management roles) needed to maintain the daily operations of the facility, is a main vehicle for teaching self-development.

Use of Open Communication: The public nature of shared experiences in the community is used for therapeutic purposes.

Use of Relationships: Friendships with particular individuals, peers, and staff are essential to encourage the individual to engage and remain in the change process.

Use of Language: TC argot is the special vocabulary used by residents to reflect elements of its subculture, particularly its recovery and right living teachings. As with any special language, TC argot represents individual integration into the peer community. However, it also mirrors the individuals' clinical progress.

The basic components of the generic TC program model include the following (De Leon, 1997):

Community Separateness: TC-oriented programs have their own names, often innovated by the clients, and are housed in a space or locale that is separated from other agency or institutional programs and units or generally from the drug-related environment.

A Community Environment: The inner environment contains communal space to promote a sense of commonality and collective activities (e.g., groups, meetings). The walls display signs that state in simple terms the philosophy of the program, the messages of right living and recovery.

Community Activities: To be effectively utilized, treatment or educational services must be provided within a context of the peer community. Thus, with the exception of individual counseling, all activities are programmed in collective formats.

Peers as Community Members: Members who demonstrate the expected behaviors and reflect the values and teachings of the community are viewed as role models.

Staff as Community Members: The staff are a mix of recovered professionals and other traditional professionals (e.g., medical, legal, mental health, and educational) who must be integrated through cross-training that is grounded in the basic concepts of the TC perspective and community approach.

A Structured Day: Regardless of its length, the day has a formal schedule of varied therapeutic educational activities with prescribed formats, fixed times and routine procedures. The structure of the program relates to the TC perspective, particularly the view of the client and recovery.

Phase Format: The treatment protocol, or plan of therapeutic and educational activities, is organized into phases that reflect a developmental view of the change process. Emphasis is on incremental learning at each phase, which moves the individual to the next stage of recovery.

Work as Therapy and Education: Consistent with the TC's self-help approach, all clients are responsible for the daily management of the facility (e.g., cleaning activities, meal preparation and service, maintenance, purchasing, security, coordinating schedules, preparatory chores of groups, meetings, seminar activities).

TC Concepts: There is an organized curriculum focused on teaching the TC perspective, particularly its self-help recovery concepts and view of right living.

Peer Encounter Groups: The peer encounter is the main community or therapeutic group, although other forms of therapeutic, educational, and support groups are utilized as needed. The minimal objective of the peer encounter is to heighten individual awareness of specific attitudes or behavioral patterns that should be modified.

Awareness Training: All therapeutic and educational interventions involve raising the individuals' consciousness of the impact of their conduct and attitudes on themselves and the social environment, and conversely the impact of the behaviors and attitudes of others on themselves and the social environment.

Emotional Growth Training: Achieving the goals of personal growth and socialization involves teaching individuals how to identify feelings, express feelings appropriately, and manage feelings constructively through the interpersonal and social demands of communal life.

Planned Duration of Treatment: How long individuals must be program-involved depends on their stage of recovery, although a minimum period of intensive involvement is required to ensure internalization of the TC teachings.

Continuance of Recovery: Completion of primary treatment is a stage in the recovery process. Thus, whether implemented within the boundaries of the main program or separately as in special halfway houses, the perspective and approach guiding aftercare programming must be continuous with that of primary treatment in the TC.

Clinical Foundations

Little has been written on the specific clinical underpinnings of the treatment techniques applied in therapeutic communities. They tend to vary depending on the client needs, and as such, those described here are what have been found to be most appropriate for those with long histories of both drug abuse and criminality. The great majority of drug-involved offenders found in prison-based therapeutic communities tend to have little or no self-confidence and trust of others, and seem to be out of touch with their feelings. Typically, they cover their feelings of hopelessness, guilt, and worthlessness with facades of strength, invincibility, and control over their immediate situations. Frequently, attempts at control are accomplished through manipulation. In turn, they tend to be both indirect and unable to seek help or to recognize areas where help is essential. Their lives, furthermore, have been marked by chaos and the inability to assume responsibility for themselves or their actions (Kooyman, 1986).

For drug-involved offenders, interactions with police, the courts and the prison system solidify feelings of mistrust. In an attempt to gain control or even survive, drug-involved offenders become increasingly manipulative. The revolving cycle of imprisonment heightens feelings of hopelessness and worthlessness. As well, it diminishes their opportunities to take responsibility for their lives and their actions (Chaiken and Johnson, 1988). In addition, few drug-involved offenders have adequate formal education. Many are from dysfunctional homes, with parents or other family members having histories of drug abuse, criminality, and incarceration. And finally, knowledge and experiences are based on street life. As such, effective treatment techniques must consider clients' educational levels and life experiences. In other words, the representations used in therapy must be relevant to the experiences of the clients. The techniques described here have been tailored for the needs, aptitudes, and experiences of drug-involved offenders.

The fundamental goal of the TC is to create behavior change by having the clients understand their feelings and thoughts and to take responsibility for their decisions and actions. In doing this, many other treatment objectives are accomplished at the same time, including the creating of trust, the instilling of hope, and increasing self-esteem (Hinshelwood, 1986). In many TCs, the theoretical framework in which the treatment is grounded is a simple paradigm in which feelings and thoughts result in behaviors. With this paradigm it is assumed that people choose how they will behave. Thus, they have free choice and are responsible for their own actions. In traditional psychotherapy, the initial focus is on feelings and thoughts. Yet the time and energy spent on feelings and thoughts can be endless, with no noticeable changes in behavior, whereas, in a TC the initial focus is on behavior. This shift in focus is effective, since behaviors are most evident to the clients. By focusing first on behaviors, clients are more likely to become engaged in treatment because they can readily understand and assimilate the treatment plan to change behaviors. In addition, criminal and drug-using behaviors are the crucial elements to be changed in order to reduce risk to self and others.

The initial behavior change occurs through modelling and redirection. During the orientation phase of TC treatment, clients' behaviors are continually addressed by experienced clients and staff. Through daily confrontations, clients' behaviors are redirected. This process teaches clients that old behaviors are unacceptable. As a result, clients begin to adopt new, prosocial behaviors. However, in order for these newly incorporated behaviors to have lasting effects and to avoid regression, inappropriate behaviors, feelings, and thoughts—both current and past—must be addressed.

Clinical Treatment Approaches

Within the framework outlined above, specific clinical techniques tend to vary from one therapeutic community to another. In the state of Delaware, for example, seven TCs are currently operating within the correctional system, and all follow an holistic approach. Different types of therapy—behavioral, cognitive, and emotional—are used to address individual treatment needs (Hooper, Lockwood, and Inciardi, 1993). Briefly:

1. Behavioral Therapy fosters positive demeanor and conduct by not accepting antisocial actions. To implement this, behavioral expectations are clearly defined as soon as a new resident is admitted to the program. At that time, the staff's primary focus is on how the resident is to behave. The client works with an orientation manual which he is expected to learn thoroughly. Once again, the focus is on his or her behavior as opposed to thoughts and feelings. As the client learns and adjusts to the routines of the therapeutic community, more salient issues are dealt with in the treatment process.

2. Cognitive Therapy helps individuals recognize errors and fallacies in their thinking. The object is to help the client understand how and why certain cognitive patterns have been developed across time. With this knowledge the client can develop alternative thinking patterns resulting in more realistic decisions about life. Cognitive Therapy is accomplished in both group and individual sessions.

3. Emotional Therapy deals with unresolved conflicts associated with interactions with others and the resulting feelings and behaviors. To facilitate this treatment strategy, a non-threatening but nurturing manner is required so that clients can gain a better understanding of how they think and feel about themselves as well as others.

Special Population TCs

The recognition that TCs may be most appropriate for "Special Populations" is the most important modification, indeed innovation, in the use of TCs in the last decade. As De Leon has noted, "the quintessential element of the TC approach [is] *community as method.... The purposive use of the peer community [is] to facilitate social and psychological change in individuals*" (De Leon, 1997:5). And when the clients in the community share an identity apart from substance abuse, they have more in common. Their identity as community is actually strengthened by the existence of other shared problems and the potential to assist each other in dealing with these issues. Consequently, the rationale for being part of the community and remaining in it is greater, and when the length [of] time in treatment increases, so does the potential for prosocial changes in other important arenas. It is not surprising that, in general, retention in special population TCs is longer than in standard community-based TCs.

In most cases, special population TCs have demographic or behavioral circumstances that identify their clients apart from their substance use. It may be adolescence, gender, family circumstances, mental health, or criminal justice involvement. Often the factor that makes them "special" is correlated or co-morbid with their substance abuse. The types of special population therapeutic communities are varied and growing—in fact, targeted TCs are the growth area in the TC movement. Here we review some of the most prevalent currently established targeted TCs.

TCs for Adolescents

There have been a significant number of adolescents in TCs since the beginning of the movement. The Drug Abuse Reporting Program (DARP) summarizing treatment modality results up to the mid-1970s found almost one-third of those in TCs were 19 or younger (Sells and Simpson, 1979). In almost all cases youth were treated right along with adults in the same community-based TCs. Such co-mingling often failed to recognize any unique circumstances of adolescence—puberty, identity formation, school problems, vulnerable psychological status but often seemingly invulnerable physical risk—to say nothing of the definitional fact that addiction histories were generally much shorter. At the same time that addiction careers may be shorter for adolescents in TCs, they usually began drug use earlier than adult TC clients (Jainchill et al., 1995) and are less likely to perceive they have a substance abuse problem (De Leon, 1988).

Recently, there have been a number of TCs established exclusively for adolescents, the premise being that an age-segregated community will lead to better peer relations. Others in the TC movement have argued against this, saying that an age-integrated community is better for dealing with family issues. Outcome findings on age-integrated versus age-segregated communities for youth are not yet available (Marshall and Marshall, 1993; Jainchill, 1997), but, other than in juvenile corrections settings, most TCs with adolescents also include adults.

In a recent review of 10 adolescent TC programs, it is apparent that most adolescents do not enter TCs voluntarily. Over two-thirds were referred by the criminal justice system, and another 14% by doctors, counselors or teachers. About 10% were referred by family, and only 8% were self-referred (Jainchill, 1997). Not surprisingly, since age is a known predictor of length of time in treatment, adolescents are less likely to remain in treatment than are adults. As compared to adults, it is not known if compulsory treatment works. In fact, to the extent an adolescent TC resembles a boot camp, it probably does not work very well. Moreover, for adolescents who complete residential treatment, it is not clear what the outcome expectations should be. Even when limited outcome data has shown some reduction in substance use, this has not been true of the "recreational" drugs alcohol and marijuana (Pompi, 1994). It is unreasonable to expect adolescent TC graduates to have the outcome expected of adults—self-reliance—when job, education, and family living circumstances are unlikely to have been resolved. One exception [is] educationally focused TCs like the John Dewey Academy in Massachusetts. This TC is a "college preparatory, therapeutic, residential high school that provides intensive services for gifted, self-destructive adolescents" (Bratter et al., 1997). A combination of a professional and self-help model TC, the John Dewey Academy has had remarkable success in graduating its clients and placing them in college. On the whole, however, adolescent TCs, while having intrinsic appeal as an intervention with youth in crisis and in need of habilitation or rehabilitation, must still be considered an open question.

TCs for Women With Children

Traditionally women have been underserved in terms of substance abuse treatment. A 1979 survey sponsored by NIDA identified only 44 programs in the nation that provided specialized substance abuse treatment services to women (Beschner and Thompson, 1981). Although some early TCs admitted women clients, they as well did not provide specialized programs directed at women, particularly women with children. Stevens and Glider (1994) suggest that two things changed this focus beginning in the 1980s: first, a marked increase in the number of women seeking treatment, particularly for cocaine addiction. These women were often single parents, primary caregivers and increasingly pregnant at the time they presented for treatment. Second, the passage of the 1986 Omnibus Drug Bill led to a marked increase in interest and funding for drug treatment in special populations and drug prevention among high-risk youth. This legislation had implications for other special populations, but the effect was more pronounced for women in need of treatment. The federal agencies now known as the Center for Substance Abuse Treatment and the Center for Substance Abuse Prevention greatly increased the funding for programs for women with children.

As with many special population TCs, there is little outcome data on the effectiveness of TCs designed especially for women with children. However, some preliminary studies do suggest a real benefit for women in terms of retention in treatment and positive changes (Stevens et al., 1997; Winick and Evans, 1997).

TCs for MICA Clients

The mentally ill chemically abusing (MICA) client is a significant and growing problem. For many years the two conditions were rarely treated together. Until the 1960s institutions effectively hid or controlled the substance abusing element among the mentally ill. However, the movement toward deinstitutionalization of the mentally ill has had the effect of increasing the homeless population and of encouraging substance use as a means of self-treating mental illness.

One important variable to ascertain in treating MICA clients is whether substance use precedes or antedates the psychiatric problems (Jainchill, 1994).

TCs for MICA clients retain the peer orientation and, even more than in other TCs, rely on a routinized daily regimen to structure clients' daily lives. They do make modifications in the intensity of group sessions, and allow for more attention to case management needs. Psychotropic medications are allowed when medically indicated. Such TCs have been successfully introduced in both hospital (Silberstein et al., 1997) and community (Sacks et al., 1997) settings. MICA programs are also characterized by the need for a long-term aftercare and support program for clients who do return to the outside community.

TCs in Corrections

The TC has had its greatest impact and widest application in corrections. Correctional systems have long recognized the utility of implementing treatment programs for their "captive" populations, over two-thirds of whom have substance abuse problems (Petersen, 1974). Prison TCs, like other therapeutic communities, are designed to provide a total treatment environment in which a drug user's transformations in behavior, attitudes, emotions, and values are introduced and inculcated. Throughout the 1960s and into the 1970s, TCs were the most visible type of treatment in correctional settings, but by the early 1980s, almost all of these TCs had closed, the result of prison crowding, state budget deficits, staff burnout or blowup, and changes in prison leadership (Camp and Camp, 1990).

Despite these early failures, the correctional TC reemerged in the late 1980s and demonstrated great promise in the treatment of substance abuse (De Leon, 1985; Yablonsky, 1989). TCs modified their approaches from the earlier Synanon models. Staff had more professional training and credentials, inmates were given appropriate power and rewards without too much program control, and TC programs worked with institutional staff rather than in opposition (Wexler, 1995). At the same time, correctional approaches were again becoming more favorable to the concept of rehabilitation, no doubt spurred by the massive prison crowding accompanying the increased use of determinate and mandatory minimum sentences for drug-involved offenders (Inciardi and Martin, 1993; Wexler, 1995). Moreover, correctional administrators and clinicians found TCs useful in improving client attitudes and inmate comportment (Wexler, Falkin, Lipton, Rosenblum, and Goodlue, 1988; Field, 1989; Inciardi and Scarpitti, 1992).

TCs in corrections have moved from the early prison-only applications to a variety of programs combining in-prison, transitional and aftercare elements at the long extreme to short-term (one-to-five month programs) in prisons and jails at the short extreme. The desire to have shorter programs to treat more clients and to treat them cheaper per client is understandable, but as some of the evidence reviewed below reveals, the effects of short-term treatment, while significant, are also relatively short-lived.

Outcome Studies

Apsler (1991) listed factors that singly or jointly would improve treatment outcome research: measures on the variability among treatment programs, long project periods, objective validation of self-report measures, the cooperation of the treatment programs, large samples, multiple measures of treatment experience, and multiple measures of outcomes. Recently, Knight and colleagues (1999) have reiterated this list and added to it the need for common, or at least comparable, indicators across studies.

Because of interest in the past 10 years, particularly by the National Institute on Drug Abuse, TCs have been the subject of a number of studies of effectiveness. Many of the shortcomings noted by Apsler have been addressed through NIDA-funded research during the past decade; a number of studies began reporting encouraging initial results from the use of therapeutic community treatment programs for drug-abusers. Yet even with increased support for research and recognition of the need for outcome data, the systematic assessment of specific, promising, effective, and replicable TC programs

did not advance concomitantly with the increases in the number of new programs. The dilemmas of conducting field studies that can be rigorously evaluated proved difficult to solve. Consequently, most assessments of program effectiveness were *process* rather than *outcome* oriented and did not incorporate multiple outcome criteria. Outcome research, when attempted, involved short follow-up time frames and included only limited use of comparison groups, standardized measurement instruments, multivariate models, and appropriate control variables (Forcier, 1991; Rouse, 1991; Wexler, 1995; De Leon, Inciardi, and Martin, 1995).

The great majority of these outcome studies of TC programs have been in correctional systems (Lipton, 1995; Graham and Wexler, 1997; Inciardi and Lockwood, 1994; Nielsen and Scarpitti, 1997; Knight, Simpson, and Hiller, 1996; Mello et al., 1997; Hiller et al., in press; Wexler et al., 1999). Many of the studies reporting the effectiveness of prison therapeutic communities in reducing relapse and recidivism have documented significant effects, but usually over relatively short terms—6 to 12 months after release from prison (Lipton, 1995; Glider et al., 1997; Inciardi et al., 1997). Very recently, several studies showing TC effectiveness have appeared documenting significant results three years after release from prison (Knight et al., 1999; Wexler et al., 1999; Martin et al., 1999). All of these studies show a pronounced effect of TC treatment when accompanied by transitional treatment and/or aftercare in reducing recidivism three years after release from prison. Recidivism averaged under 30% for the TC/aftercare treated versus about 70% for those not so treated.

Emerging Trends and Research

1. *Modified Therapeutic Communities. Since the 1980s, many therapeutic communities have been modified from the traditional model in a number of ways in an effort to adapt specifically to patient needs and funding limitations. TCs have been modified by using shorter lengths of stay (3, 6 and 12 months) and through establishing day treatment and outpatient programs. Obviously, many of these*

modifications are for cost savings. In addition, as we noted earlier, numerous correctional settings and homeless shelters, as well as medical and mental institutions, have initiated a variety of different types of therapeutic communities. Modified therapeutic communities are also targeting adolescents. Programs have been designed exclusively for juveniles because of their emotional and treatment needs. Other TCs have adapted their programming to address the special needs of addicted mothers and their children, and prison and work release populations.

One of the more notable developments in modified TCs has been the involvement of the client's family. Although having a strong support system has always been important, in recent years families have had extensive involvement in both short-term and long-term TC programs. Important, as well, has been the provision of specialized health care education. Because of the growing number of clients with HIV/AIDS, virtually almost all TCs have instituted risk reduction programs and HIV testing.

Since the majority of modified TCs have a shorter length of stay, aftercare services have been instituted. These serve to extend the period of treatment, with the purpose of providing community support, relapse prevention, and access to community service agencies that can assist in the recovery process.

2. *Multi-modality Approaches. In recent years, multi-modality approaches have emerged that include a combination of therapeutic community concepts and other types of treatment, such as methadone maintenance, family therapy, drug education, AA/NA, relapse prevention, and other treatment approaches. The programs, which often exist in a single community, are ancillary [to], rather than competitive with, one another.*

De Leon has examined the impact of combining TC and methadone maintenance modules in his Passages program. Many of the main components of TCs remained the same; however, certain aspects were changed to accommodate methadone clients. Although TCs are typically "drug free" programs, Passages permitted the use of methadone as an opiate substitute, provided greater emphasis on outreach, increased the flexibility of the format, and reduced the intensity of the personal and interpersonal interactions (De Leon et al., 1995). Detoxification from methadone was not seen as essential to the recovery process, but some clients voluntarily chose detoxification at some point of the program. And although the program was transformed into a day treatment rather than a twenty-four hour residential approach, like typical TCs Passages promoted a culture where clients learned through a self-help process in order to produce change. Although a twist on the usual TC treatment program, outcome data suggested that the Passages program yielded a clinically observable decrease in drug use and improvement in the level of functioning during the first six months.

An alternative form of multi-modality program was instituted at Walden House in San Francisco. Walden House established a TC day treatment program by transferring TC concepts and philosophy to a nonresidential setting (Bucardo et al., 1997). The original purpose of this type of treatment was to assist those individuals who were awaiting acceptance into a therapeutic community. As this treatment method developed, it became its own unique form of intervention. The day treatment program contains the same rules and norms of the original TC by addressing clients as members of a community. In Walden House, the central belief is that each client has the potential for growth and change.

3. *Compulsory Treatment. An important corollary to the extensive and impressive data on treatment outcome being a function of length of time in treatment are the data supportive of compulsory and coerced treatment for drug offenders (Leukefeld and Tims, 1988; Hubbard et al., 1989; De Leon, 1988; Platt et al., 1988). In this regard, evaluation studies have demonstrated that the key variable most related to success in treatment is length of stay, and that those coerced into*

treatment do as well as voluntary commitments and in fact do better because they tend to remain longer in treatment than voluntary commitments.

4. *The TC Treatment Continuum. Recently, Inciardi and colleagues have argued that an integrated continuum of corrections-based TC treatment works best for seriously drug-involved offenders. This continuum involves three stages of therapeutic community treatment, tied to an inmate's changing correctional status: prison "work release" parole or other form of community supervision (Inciardi, Lockwood, and Martin, 1991, 1994).*

The *primary* treatment occurs in a prison-based TC designed to facilitate personal growth through the modification of deviant lifestyles and behavior patterns. Segregated from the rest of the penitentiary, recovery from drug abuse and the development of pro-social values in the prison TC would involve essentially the same mechanisms seen in community-based TCs. Ideally, it should last for 9 to 12 months (Wexler et al., 1988), and client recruits should be within 12 to 15 months of work release eligibility.

Since the 1970s, work release has become a widespread correctional practice for felony offenders being released from prison: Inmates work for pay in the free community but spend their nonworking hours in an institution or a community-based work release facility or "halfway house" (Inciardi, 1999). This initial freedom exposes inmates to old groups and behaviors that can easily lead them back to substance abuse, criminal activities, and reincarceration. Even those receiving intensive TC treatment while in the institution face the prospect of their recovery breaking down. Thus, *secondary* TC treatment is warranted. This *secondary* stage is a "transitional TC"—the therapeutic community work release center—with a program composition similar to that of the traditional TC.

In the *tertiary* or "aftercare" stage, clients have completed work release and are living in the free community under parole or some other form of supervision. Treatment intervention in this stage should involve continued monitoring by TC counselors, including regular outpatient counseling, group therapy, and family sessions.

This model is for correctional clients, but the argument is appropriate to other TC settings, particularly some "special populations." For some long-term TC clients in community or MICA TCs, issues of community reintegration are not paramount because there are no short-term prospects for the client leaving the TC. For most TC clients, however, reintegration into the larger community is a real goal. The rationale for the development of special population TCs and multi-modality approaches are efforts to adapt the traditional TC approach to deal with issues other than substance use. The continuum approach is another important extension of the TC model to provide support in the process of transitions—be it back to the family, gainful employment, self-support—and to tailor that support to the particular demands and risks of the transition.

References

Apsler, R. (1991). "Evaluating the cost-effectiveness of drug abuse treatment services," pp. 57–66 in W. S. Cartwright and J. M. Kaple (eds.), *Economic Costs, Cost-effectiveness, Financing, and Community-based Drug Treatment*, NIDA research monograph 113. Rockville, MD: U.S. Department of Health and Human Services.

Bailey, Walter C. (1966). "Correctional outcome: An evaluation of 100 reports," *Journal of Criminal Law, Criminology, and Police Science* 57(June):153–160.

Beschner, G., and Thompson, P. (1981). *Women and Drug Abuse Treatment: Needs and Services*. DHHS, No. (ADM) 81-1057. Rockville, MD: NIDA.

Bratter, B. I., Bratter, T. E., Bratter, C. J., Maxym, C., and Steiner, K. M. (1997). "The John Dewey Academy: A moral caring community (an amalgamation of the professional model and self-help concept of the therapeutic community)," pp. 179–195 in George De Leon (ed.), *Community as Method: Therapeutic Communities for Special Populations and Special Settings*. Westport, CT: Praeger.

Bucardo, J., Guydish, J., Acampora, A., and Werdegar, D. (1997). "The therapeutic community model applied to day treatment of substance abuse," pp. 213–224 in George De Leon (ed.), *Community as Method: Therapeutic Communities for Special Populations and Special Settings*. Westport, CT: Greenwood Press.

Camp, G. M., and Camp, C. G. (1990). *Preventing and Solving Problems Involved in Operating Therapeutic Communities in a Prison Setting*. South Salem, NY: Criminal Justice Institute.

Casriel, D. (1963). *So Fair a House: The Story of Synanon*. Englewood Cliffs, NJ: Prentice Hall.

Chaiken, M. R., and Johnson, B. D. (1988). *Characteristics of Different Types of Drug-Involved Offenders*. Washington, D. C.: National Institute of Justice.

De Leon, G. (1997). *Community as Method: Therapeutic Communities for Special Populations and Special Settings*. Westport, CT: Greenwood Publishing Group, Inc.

——. (1985). "The therapeutic community: Status and evolution," *International Journal of the Addictions* 20:823–844.

——. (1986). "The therapeutic community for substance abuse: Perspective and approach," pp. 14–18 in George De Leon and James Ziegenfuss (eds.), *Therapeutic Communities for Addictions*. Springfield, IL: Charles C. Thomas.

——. (1988). "The therapeutic community perspective and approach to adolescent substance abusers," *Annals of Adolescent Psychiatry* 15:535–556.

——. (1994). "Therapeutic communities," pp. 391–393 in Marc Galanter and Herbert Kleber (eds.), *Textbook of Substance Abuse Treatment*. Washington, D.C.: American Psychiatric Press.

De Leon, G., Inciardi, J. A., and Martin, S. S. (1995). "Residential drug treatment research: Are conventional control designs appropriate for assessing treatment effectiveness?" *Journal of Psychoactive Drugs* 27(1):85–91.

Field, G. (1989). "The effects of intensive treatment on reducing the criminal recidivism of addicted offenders," *Federal Probation* (December):51–56.

Forcier, M. W. (1991). "Substance abuse, crime and prison-based treatment: Problems and prospects," *Sociological Practice Review* 2(2):123–131.

Glider, P., Mullen, R., Herbst, D., Davis, C., and Fleishman, B. (1997). "Substance abuse treatment in a jail setting: A therapeutic community model," pp. 97–112 in George De Leon (ed.), *Community as Method: Therapeutic Communities for Special Populations and Special Settings*. Westport, CT: Praeger.

Graham, W. F., and Wexler, H. K. (1997). "The amity therapeutic community program at Donovan Prison: Program description and approach," in George De Leon (ed.), *Community as Method*. Westport, CT: Praeger.

Hiller, M. L., Knight, K., and Simpson, D. D. (in press). "Prison-based substance abuse treatment, residential aftercare, and recidivism," *Addiction*.

Hinshelwood, R. D. (1986). "Britain and the psychoanalytic tradition in therapeutic communities," pp. 43–54 in George De Leon and James T. Ziegenfuss (eds.), *Therapeutic Communities for Addictions: Readings in Theory, Research and Practice*. Springfield, IL: Charles C. Thomas.

Hood, R. (1967). "Research on the effectiveness of punishments and treatments," in European Committee on Crime Problems, *Collected Studies in Criminological Research*. Strasbourg: Council of Europe.

Hooper, R. M., Lockwood, D., and Inciardi, J. A. (1993). "Treatment techniques in corrections-based therapeutic communities," *The Prison Journal* 73(September–December):290–306.

Hubbard, R. L., Marsden, M. E., Rachal, J. C., Harwood, H. J., Cavanaugh, E. R., and Ginzburg, H. M. (1989). *Drug Abuse Treatment: A National Study of Effectiveness*. Chapel Hill, NC: University of North Carolina Press.

Inciardi, J. A. (1967). *The Daytop Village Therapeutic Community*. Albany: New York State Division of Parole.

——. (1999). *Criminal Justice*, 6th edition. Ft. Worth, TX: Harcourt Brace.

Inciardi, J. A., and Lockwood, D. (1994). "When worlds collide: Establishing CREST Outreach Center," pp. 63–78 in B. W. Fletcher, J. A. Inciardi, and A. M. Horton (eds.), *Drug Abuse Treatment: The Implementation of Innovative Approaches*. Westport, CT: Greenwood Press.

Inciardi, J. A., Lockwood, D., and Martin, S. S. (1991). *Therapeutic Communities in Corrections and Work Release: Some Clinical and Policy Considerations*. Paper presented at National Institute on Drug Abuse Technical Review Meeting on Therapeutic Community Treatment Research, May 16–17, Bethesda, Maryland.

——. (1994). "Therapeutic communities in corrections and work release: Some clinical and policy implications," pp. 259–267 in F. M. Tims, G. De Leon, and N. Jainchill (eds.), *Therapeutic community: Advances in research and application*, NIDA research monograph 144. Rockville, MD: U.S. Department of Health and Human Services.

Inciardi, J. A., and Martin, S. S. (1993). "Drug abuse treatment in criminal justice settings," *Journal of Drug Issues* 23(1):1–6.

Inciardi, J. A., Martin, S. S., Butzin, C. A., Hooper, R. M., and Harrison, L. D. (1997). "An effective model of prison-based treatment for drug-involved offenders,' *Journal of Drug Issues* 27(2):261–278.

Inciardi, J. A., and Scarpitti, F. R. (1992). *Therapeutic Communities in Corrections: An Overview*. Paper presented at the annual meeting of the Academy of Criminal Justice Sciences, Pittsburgh, Pennsylvania.

Jainchill, N. (1994). "Co-morbidity and therapeutic community treatment," pp. 209–231 in F. M. Tims, G. De Leon, and N. Jainchill (eds.), *Therapeutic Community: Advances in Research and Application*, NIDA Research Monograph 144. Washington, DC: Supt of Docs., U.S. Govt. Print. Off.

——. (1997). "Therapeutic communities for adolescents: The same and not the same," pp. 161–177 in George De Leon (ed.), *Community as Method: Therapeutic Communities for Special Populations and Special Settings*. Westport, CT: Praeger.

Jainchill, N., Bhattacharya, G., and Yagelka, J. (1995). "Therapeutic communities for adolescents," pp. 190–217 in E. Rahdert and D. Czechowitz (eds.), *Adolescent Drug Abuse: Clinical Assessment and Therapeutic interventions*, NIDA Research Monograph 153. Washington, D.C.: Supt of Docs., U.S. Govt. Print. Off.

Jones, M. (1953). *The therapeutic community: A new treatment method in psychiatry*. New York: Basic Books.

Klockars, C. B. (1975). "The true limits of the effectiveness of correctional treatment," *The Prison Journal* 55(Spring–Summer):53–64.

Knight, K., Simpson, D. D., and Hiller, M. L. (1996). *Evaluation of Prison-based Treatment and Aftercare*. Paper presented at the annual meeting of the American Psychological Association, Toronto, Canada.

Knight, K., Hiller, M. L., and Simpson, D. D. (1999). "Evaluating corrections-based treatment for the drug-abusing criminal offender," *Journal of Psychoactive Drugs* 31(3):299–304.

Knight, K., Simpson, D. D., and Hiller, M. (1999). "3-year reincarceration outcomes for in-prison therapeutic community treatment in Texas," *The Prison Journal* 79.

Kooyman, M. (1986). "The psychodynamics of therapeutic communities for the treatment of heroin addiction," pp. 29–42 in George De Leon and James T. Ziegenfuss (eds.), *Therapeutic Communities for Addictions: Readings in Theory Research and Practice*. Springfield, IL: Charles C. Thomas.

——. (1993). *The Therapeutic Community for Addicts*. Amsterdam: Swets and Zeitlinger.

Leukefeld, C. G., and Tims, F. M. (1988). "Compulsory treatment: A review of the findings," pp 236–254 in C. G. Leukefeld and F. M. Tims (eds.), *Compulsory Treatment of Drug Abuse: Research and Clinical Practice*. NIDA Research Monograph 86. Rockville, MD: U.S. Department of Health and Human Services.

Lipton, D., Martinson, R., and Wilks, J. (1975). *The Effectiveness of Correctional Treatment: A Survey of Treatment Evaluation Studies*. New York: Praeger.

Lipton, D. S. (1995). *The Effectiveness of Treatment for Drug Abusers under Criminal Justice Supervision*. Washington, D.C.: National Institute of Justice.

Marshall, M. J., and Marshall, S. (1993). "Homogeneous versus heterogeneous age group treatment of adolescent substance abusers," *American Journal of Drug and Alcohol Abuse* 19:199–207.

Martin, S. S., Butzin, C. A., Saum, C. A., and Inciardi, J. A. (1999). "3-year outcomes of therapeutic community treatment for drug-involved offenders in Delaware: From prison to work release to aftercare," *The Prison Journal* 79:294–320.

Martinson, R. (1974). "What works?—Questions and answers about prison reform," *The Public Interest* 35(Spring):22–54.

Mello, C. O., Pechansky, F., Inciardi, J. A., and Surratt, H. L. (1997). "Participant observation of a therapeutic community model for offenders in drug treatment," *Journal of Drug Issues* 27:299–314.

Nielsen, A. L., and Scarpitti, F. R. (1997). "Changing the behavior of substance abusers: Factors influencing the effectiveness of therapeutic communities," *Journal of Drug Issues* 27(2):279–298.

Palmer, T. (1975). "Martinson revisited," *Journal of Research in Crime and Delinquency* 12 (July):133–152.

Petersen, D. M. (1974). "Some reflections on compulsory treatment of addiction," pp. 143–169 in J. A. Inciardi and C. D. Chambers (eds.), *Drugs and the Criminal Justice System*. Beverly Hills, CA: Sage.

Pompi, K. F. (1994). "Adolescents in therapeutic communities: Retention and posttreatment outcome," pp. 128–161 in F. M. Tims, G. De Leon, and N. Jainchill (eds.), *Therapeutic Community: Advances in Research and Application*. NIDA Research Monograph 144. Washington, DC: Supt of Docs., U.S. Govt. Print. Off.

Robison, J. (1971). "The irrelevance of correctional programs," *Crime and Delinquency* 17 (January):67–80.

Rouse, J. J. (1991). "Evaluation research on prison based drug treatment programs and some policy implications," *The International Journal of the Addictions* 26:29–44.

Sacks, S., De Leon, G., Bernhardt, A. J., and Sacks, J. Y. (1997). "A modified therapeutic community for homeless mentally ill chemical abusers," pp. 19–37 in George De Leon (ed.), *Community as Method: Therapeutic Communities for Special Populations and Special Settings*. Westport, CT: Praeger.

Shelly, J. A., and Bassin, A. (1965). "Daytop Lodge: A new treatment approach for drug addicts," *Corrective Psychiatry* 2(July):180–193.

Silberstein, C. H., Metzger, E. J., and Galanter, M. (1997). "The Greenhouse: A modified therapeutic community for mentally ill homeless addicts at New York University–Bellevue Medical Center," pp. 53–65 in George De Leon (ed.), *Community as Method: Therapeutic Communities for Special Populations and Special Settings*. Westport, CT: Praeger.

Stevens, S. J., Arbiter, N., and McGrath, R. (1997). "Women and children: Therapeutic community substance abuse treatment," pp. 129–141 in George De Leon (ed.), *Community as Method: Therapeutic Communities for Special Populations and Special Settings*. Westport, CT: Praeger.

Stevens, S. J., and Glider, P. J. (1994). "Therapeutic communities: Substance abuse treatment for women," pp. 162–180 in F. M. Tims, G. De Leon, and N. Jainchill (eds.), *Thera-*

peutic Community: Advances in Research and Application, NIDA Research Monograph 144. Washington, DC: Supt of Docs., U.S. Govt. Print. Off.

Wexler, H. K. (1995). "The success of therapeutic communities for substance abusers in American prisons," *Journal of Psychoactive Drugs* 27:57–66.

Wexler, H. K., De Leon, G., Thomas, G., Kressel, D., and Peters, J. (1999). "The Amity prison TC evaluation: Reincarceration outcomes," *Criminal Justice and Behavior* 26(2):147–167.

Wexler, H. K., Falkin, G. P., Lipton, D. S., Rosenblum, A. B., and Goodlue, H. P. (1988). *A Model Prison Rehabilitation Program: An Evaluation of the "Stay'n Out" Therapeutic Community*. New York: Narcotic and Drug Research, Inc.

Wexler, H. K., Melnick, G., Lowe, L., and Peters, J. (1999). "3-year reincarceration outcomes for Amity in-prison therapeutic community and aftercare in California," *The Prison Journal* 79:321.

White, W. (1998). *Slaying the Dragon*. Bloomington, IL: Chestnut Health Systems.

Wilson, J. Q. (1980). " 'What works?' revisited: New findings on criminal rehabilitation," *The Public Interest* 61(Fall):3–17.

Winick, C., and Evans, J. T. (1997). "A therapeutic community program for mothers and their children," pp. 143–159 in George De Leon (ed.), *Community as Method: Therapeutic Communities for Special Populations and Special Settings*. Westport, CT: Praeger.

Yablonsky, L. (1967). *Synanon: The Tunnel Back*. New York: Macmillan.

Yablonsky, L. (1989). *The Therapeutic Community: A Successful Approach for Treating Substance Abusers*. New York: Gardner.

For Discussion

Should therapeutic communities be expected to work for persons regardless of their drug of choice? What groups, if any, might not be suitable for therapeutic communities?

38

Methadone Maintenance

A Theoretical Perspective

Vincent P. Dole
Marie Nyswander

Whereas therapeutic communities view drug addiction as an underlying symptom of other life problems, methadone maintenance treatment sees addiction as a disease rather than an expression of a character or psychological disorder.

When administered orally, methadone serves to "block" the euphoric effects of heroin. That is, when an individual is given sufficient doses of methadone, he or she will be unable to "get high" from heroin. Vincent P. Dole and Marie Nyswander were the first in the United States to introduce methadone as a treatment for heroin addiction. In this article, these investigators discuss issues related to methadone treatment. Their study of methadone clients found that criminal activity decreased greatly when addicts were enrolled in maintenance programs. This finding, they argue, suggests that antisocial behavior, such as criminal activity, occurs as a result rather than a cause of drug addiction.

The Methadone Maintenance Research Program (Dole and Nyswander 1965, 1966; Dole et al. 1966) began in 1963 with pharmacological studies conducted on the metabolic ward of the Rockefeller University Hospital. Only six addict patients were treated during the first year, but the results of this work were sufficiently impressive to justify a trial of maintenance treatment of heroin addicts admitted to open medical wards of general hospitals in the city.

The dramatic improvements in social status of patients on this program exceeded expectations. The study started with the hope that heroin-seeking behavior would be stopped by a narcotic blockade, but it certainly was not expected that we would be able to retain more than 90 percent of the patients and that almost three-fourths would be socially productive and living as normal citizens in the community after only six months of treatment. Prior to admission, almost all of the patients had supported their heroin habits by theft or other anti-social activities. Further handicapped by the ostracism of the community, slum backgrounds, minority group status, school dropout status, prison records, and anti-social companions, they had seemed poor prospects for social rehabilitation.

The unexpected response of these patients to a simple medical program forced us to reexamine some of the assumptions that we brought to the study. Either the patients that we admitted to treatment were quite exceptional, or we had been misled by the traditional theories of addiction (Terry and Pellens 1928). If, as is generally assumed, our patients' long-standing addiction to heroin had been based on weaknesses of character—either a self-indulgent quest for euphoria or a need to escape reality—it was difficult to understand why they so consistently accepted a program that blocked the euphoric action of heroin and other narcotic drugs, or how they could overcome the frustrations and anxieties of competitive society to hold responsible jobs.

Implicit in the maintenance programs is an assumption that heroin addiction is a metabolic disease, rather than a psychological problem. Although the reasons for taking the initial doses of heroin may be considered psychological—adolescent curiosity or neurotic anxiety—the drug, for whatever reason it is first taken, leaves its imprint on the nervous system. This phenomenon is clearly seen in animal studies: a rat, if addicted to morphine by repeated injections at one to two months of age and then detoxified, will show a residual tolerance and abnormalities in brain waves in response to challenge doses of morphine for months, perhaps for the rest of its life. Simply stopping the drug does not restore the nervous system of this animal to its normal, pre-addiction condition. Since all studies to date have shown a close association between tolerance and physical dependence, and since the discomfort of physical dependence leads to drug-seeking activity, a persistence of physical dependence would explain why both animals and humans tend to relapse to use of narcotics after detoxification. This metabolic theory of relapse obviously has different implications for treatment than the traditional theory that relapse is due to moral weakness.

Whatever the theory, all treatment should be measured by results. The main issue, in our opinion, is whether the treatment can enable addicts to become normal, responsible members of society; and, if medication contributes to this result, it should be regarded as useful chemotherapy. Methadone, like sulfanilamide of the early antibiotic days, undoubtedly will be supplanted by better medications, but the success of methadone maintenance programs has at least established the principle of treating addicts medically.

The efficacy of methadone as a medication must be judged by its ability or failure to achieve the pharmacological effect that is intended—namely, elimination of heroin hunger and heroin-seeking behavior, and blockade against the euphoriant actions of heroin. The goal of social rehabilitation of criminal addicts by a treatment program is a much broader objective: it includes the stopping of heroin abuse, but is not limited to this pharmacological effect. Failures in rehabilitation programs, therefore, must be analyzed to determine whether they are due to failures of the medicine, or to inability of the therapists to rehabilitate patients who have stopped heroin use. Individuals who have stopped heroin use with methadone treatment but who continue to steal, drink excessively, or abuse non-narcotic drugs, or are otherwise anti-social, are failures of the rehabilitation program but not of the medication.

When the Food and Drug Administration asks for proof of efficacy of a new drug, it is the pharmacological efficacy that is in question. For example, diphenylhydantoin is accepted as an efficacious drug for prevention of epileptic seizures. Whether or not the treated epileptics obtain employment, or otherwise lead socially useful lives, is not relevant to the evaluation of this drug as an efficacious drug for prevention of epileptic seizures or as an anti-convulsant; similarly with methadone.

With thousands of patients now living socially acceptable lives with methadone blockade, and with many more street addicts waiting for admission, the question as to whether these patients are exceptional is no longer a practical issue. The theoretical question, however, remains: is addiction caused by an antecedent character defect, and does the maintenance treatment merely mask the symptoms of an addictive personality? The psychogenic theory of addiction would say so. This theory has a long history—at least 100 years (Terry and Pellens 1928)—and is accepted as axiomatic by many people. What, then, is the evidence for it?

Review of the literature discloses two arguments to support the psychogenic, or character defect, theory: the sociopathic behavior and attitude of addicts and the inability of addicts to control their drug-using impulse. Of these arguments, the first is the most telling. Even a sympathetic observer must concede that addicts are self-centered and indifferent to the needs of others. To the family and the community, the addict is irresponsible, a thief, and a liar. These traits, which are quite consistently associated with addiction, have been interpreted as showing a specific psychopathology. What is lacking in this argument is proof that the sociopathic traits preceded addiction.

It is important to distinguish the causes from the consequences of addiction. The decisive proof of a psychogenic theory would be a demonstration that potential addicts could be identified by psychiatric examination before drug usage had distorted behavior and metabolic functions. However, a careful search of the literature has failed to disclose any study in which a characteristic psychopathology or "addictive personality" has been recognized in a number of individuals prior to addiction. Retrospective studies, in which a record of delinquency before addiction is taken as evidence of sociopathic tendencies, fail to provide the comparative data needed for diagnosis of deviant personality. Most of the street addicts in large cities come from the slums, where family structure is broken and drugs are available. Both juvenile delinquency and drug use are common. Some delinquents become addicted to narcotic drugs under these conditions, whereas others do not. There is no known way to identify the future addicts among the delinquents. No study has shown a consistent difference in behavior or pattern of delinquency of adolescents who later become addicts and those who do not.

Theft is the means by which most street addicts obtain money to buy heroin and, therefore, is nearly an inevitable consequence of addiction. For the majority, this is the only way that they can support an expensive heroin habit. The crime statistics show both the force of drug hunger and its specificity; almost all of the crimes committed by addicts relate to the procurement of drugs. The rapid disappearance of theft and antisocial behavior in patients on the methadone maintenance program strongly supports the hypothesis that the crimes that they had previously committed as addicts were a consequence of drug hunger, not the expression of some more basic psychopathology. The so-called sociopathic personality was no longer evident in our patients.

The second argument, that of deficient self-control, is more complicated, because it involves the personal experience of the critic as well as that of the patient. Moralists generally assume that opiates are dangerously pleasant drugs that can be resisted only by strength of character. The pharmacology is somewhat more complicated than this. For most normal persons morphine and heroin are not enjoyable drugs—at least not in the initial exposures. Given to a post-operative patient, these analgesics provide a welcome relief of pain, but addiction from such medical use is uncommon. When given to an average pain-free subject, morphine produces nausea and sedation, but rarely euphoria. What, then, is the temptation to become an addict? So far as can be judged from the histories of addicts, many of them found the first trials of a narcotic in some sense pleasurable or tranquilizing, even though the drug also caused nausea and vomiting. Perhaps their reaction to the drug was abnormal, even on the first exposure. However this may be, with repeated use and development

of tolerance to side effects, the euphoric action evolved and the subjects became established addicts.

Drug-seeking behavior, like theft, is observed after addiction is established and the narcotic drug has become euphorigenic. The question as to whether this abnormality in reaction stems from a basic weakness of character or is a consequence of drug usage is best studied when drug hunger is relieved. Patients on the methadone maintenance program, blockaded against the euphorigenic action of heroin, turn their energies to schoolwork and jobs. It would be easy for them to become passive, to live indefinitely on public support, and claim that they had done enough in winning the fight against heroin. Why they do not yield to this temptation is unclear, but in general they do not. Their struggles to become self-supporting members of the community should impress the critics who had considered them self-indulgent when drug-hungry addicts. When drug hunger is blocked without production of narcotic effects, the drug-seeking behavior ends.

So far as can be judged from retrospective data, narcotic drugs have been quite freely available in some areas of New York City, and experimentation by adolescents is common. The psychological and metabolic theories diverge somewhat in interpreting this fact; the first postulates preexisting emotional problems and a need to seek drugs for escape from reality, whereas the alternative is that trial of drugs, like smoking the first cigarette, may be a result of a normal adolescent curiosity and not of psychopathology (Wikler and Rasor 1953). As to the most important point—the reasons for continuation of drug use in some cases and not in others—there is no definitive information, either psychological or metabolic. This is obviously a crucial gap in knowledge. Systematic study of young adolescents in areas with high addiction rates is needed to define the process of becoming addicted and to open the way for prevention.

The other extreme—the cured addict—involves a controversy as to the goal of therapy. Those of us who are primarily concerned with the social productivity of our patients define success in terms of behavior—the ability of the patients to live as normal citizens in the community—whereas, other groups seek total abstinence, even if it means confinement of the subjects to an institution. This confusion of goals has barred effective comparison of treatment results.

Actually, the questions to be answered are straightforward and of great practical importance. Do the abstinent patients in the psychological programs have a residual metabolic defect that requires continued group pressure and institutionalization to enforce the abstinence? Conversely, do the patients who are blockaded with methadone exhibit any residual psychopathology? No evidence is available to answer the first question. As to the latter point, we can state that the evidence, so far, is negative. The attitudes, moods, and intellectual and social performance of patients are under continuous observation by a team of psychiatrists, internists, nurses, counselors, social workers, and psychologists. No consistent psychopathology has been noted by these observers or by the social agencies, to which we have referred patients for vocational placement. The good records of employment and school work further document the patients' capacity to win acceptance as normal citizens in the community.

The real revolution of the methadone era was its emphasis on rehabilitation, rather than on detoxification. This reversed the traditional approach to addiction, which had been based on the assumption that abstinence must come first. According to the old theory, rehabilitation is impossible while a person is taking drugs of any kind, including methadone. The success of methadone programs in rehabilitating addicts who had already failed in abstinence programs decisively refuted this old theory. Indeed, nowhere in the history of treatment has a program with the abstinence approach achieved even a fraction of the retention rate and social rehabilitation now seen in the average methadone clinic. This statement includes all of the abstinence-oriented programs of governmental institutions, therapeutic communities, and religious groups for which any data are available (Brecher 1972; Glasscote [et al.] 1972).

We believe that it is a serious mistake for programs to put a higher value on abstinence than on the patient's ability to function as a normal member of society. After the patient has arrived at a stable way of life with a job, a home, a position of respect in his community, and a sense of worth, it may or may not be best to discontinue methadone, but at least he can consider this option without pressure. The pharmacologic symptoms of withdrawal will be the same, whether or not the addict is socially rehabilitated; but with a job and family there is much more to lose if relapse occurs, and, therefore, the motivation to resist a return to heroin will be strong. The time spent in maintenance treatment does not make detoxification more difficult. It has proved very easy to withdraw methadone from patients who have been maintained for one to eight years when the reduction in dose has been gradual and the patient free from anxiety.

As with heroin, the real problems begin after withdrawal. The secondary abstinence syndrome, first described by Himmelsbach, Martin, Wikler, and colleagues at the United States Public Health Hospital, Lexington, Kentucky, in patients detoxified from morphine and heroin, reflects the persistence of metabolic and autonomic disturbances in the post-narcotic withdrawal period (Himmelsbach 1942; Martin et al. 1963; Martin and Jasinski 1969): these persistent abnormalities in metabolism are clearly pharmacologic, since they occur also in experimental animals addicted to narcotics and then detoxified. Follow-up studies of abstinent ex-addicts have emphasized the frequency of alcoholism and functional deterioration (Brecher 1972). An unfortunate consequence of the early enthusiasm for methadone treatment is today's general disenchantment with chemotherapy for addicts. What was not anticipated at the onset was the nearly universal reaction against the concept of substituting one drug for another, even when the second drug enabled the addict to function normally. Statistics, showing improved health and social rehabilitation of the patients receiving methadone, failed to meet this fundamental objection. The analogous long-term use of other medications, such as insulin and digitalis, in medical practice has not been considered relevant.

Perhaps the limitations of medical treatment for complex medical-social problems were not sufficiently stressed. No medicine can rehabilitate persons. Methadone maintenance makes possible a first step toward social rehabilitation by stabilizing the pharmacological condition of addicts who have been living as criminals on the fringe of society. But to succeed in bringing disadvantaged addicts to a productive way of life, a treatment program must enable its patients to feel pride and hope and to accept responsibility. This is often not achieved in present-day treatment programs. Without mutual respect, an adversary relationship develops between patients and staff, reinforced by arbitrary rules and the indifference of persons in authority. Patients held in contempt by the staff continue to act like addicts, and the overcrowded facility becomes a public nuisance. Understandably, methadone maintenance programs today have little appeal to the communities or to the majority of heroin addicts on the street.

Methadone maintenance, as part of a supportive program, facilitates social rehabilitation; but methadone treatment clearly does not prevent opiate abuse after it is discontinued, nor does social rehabilitation guarantee freedom from relapse. For the previously intractable heroin addict with a pretreatment history of several years of addiction and social problems, the most conservative course, in our opinion, is to emphasize social rehabilitation and encourage continued maintenance. On the other hand, for patients with shorter histories of heroin use, especially the young ones, a trial of withdrawal with a systematic follow-up is indicated when physician and patient feel ready for the test, and when they understand the potential problems after detoxification. The first step of withdrawing methadone is relatively easy and can be achieved with a variety of schedules, none of which have been shown to have any specific effect on the long-range outcome. The real issue is how well the

patient does in the years after termination of maintenance.

References

Brecher, E. M. *Licit and Illicit Drugs.* Mt. Vernon, N.Y.: Consumers Union, 1972.

Dole, V. P., and Nyswander, M. E. A medical treatment for diacetylmorphine (heroin) addiction. *Journal of the American Medical Association,* 193:646–650, 1965.

Dole, V. P., and Nyswander, M. E. Rehabilitation of heroin addicts after blockade with methadone. *New York State Journal of Medicine,* 55:2011–2017, 1966.

Dole, V. P., Nyswander, M. E., and Kreek, M. J. Narcotic blockade. *Archives of Internal Medicine,* 118:304–309, 1966.

Glasscote, R. M. et al. *The Treatment of Drug Abuse: Programs, Problems, Prospects.* Washington, D.C.: The Joint Information Service of the American Psychiatric Association and the National Association for Mental Health, 1972.

Himmelsbach, C. K. Clinical studies of drug addiction, physical dependence, withdrawal and recovery. *Archives of Internal Medicine,* 69:766, 1942.

Martin, W. R., and Jasinski, D. R. Physiological parameters of morphine dependence in intolerance, early abstinence, protracted abstinence. *Journal of Psychiatric Research,* 7:9–17, 1969.

Martin, W. R., Wikler, A., Eades, C. G., and Pescor, F. T. Tolerance to and physical dependence on morphine in rats. *Psychopharmacologia,* 4:247, 1963.

Nyswander, M. E., and Dole, V. P. Methadone maintenance and its implications for theories of narcotic addiction. *Research Publications of the Association for Research in Nervous and Mental Disease,* 49:359–366, 1971.

Terry, C. E., and Pellens, M. *The Opium Problem.* Montclair, N. J.: Patterson Smith, 1928.

Wikler, A., and Rasor, R. W. Psychiatric aspects of drug addiction. *American Journal of Medicine,* 14:566–570, 1953.

For Discussion

1. Experts on methadone maintenance often believe that some heroin users should be treated with methadone periodically throughout their lives. Who should fund life treatment? Is it cost-effective?

2. In the first section of this book, Lindesmith argues that individuals continue to use opiates to eliminate the pain associated with withdrawal. Is the philosophy of methadone treatment consistent with Lindesmith's theory of addiction? If so, how?

Reprinted from: Vincent P. Dole and Marie Nyswander, "Methadone Maintenance: A Theoretical Perspective." In *Theories on Drug Abuse,* Dan J. Lettieri, Mollie Sayers, and Helen Wallenstein Pearson (eds.). National Institute on Drug Abuse, 1980. ✦

39

The Elephant That No One Sees

Natural Recovery Among Middle-Class Addicts[1]

Robert Granfield
William Cloud

Stereotypical perceptions about drug and alcohol dependence often assume that addiction is associated with persons from low-income backgrounds and that persons dependent on drugs need treatment if they are to recover. This article dispels those myths by examining persons from middle-income backgrounds who overcame problems associated with drugs and alcohol without the benefit of formal treatment. Robert Granfield and William Cloud explore the concept of "addict identity" among these respondents and identify reasons that these persons avoided treatment. The authors also note various lifestyle aspects that appear to contribute to natural recovery. Their research findings appear to contradict the assumptions of predominant treatment ideologies.

Introduction

Social deviance literature typically portrays drug and alcohol addicted individuals as possessing distinct subcultural characteristics that marginalize them from the nonaddicted world. Whether this marginalization occurs because of a personality profile which predisposes an individual to addiction or whether it follows from being labeled and stigmatized as "an addict," the outcome is thought to be the same. Such individuals are considered to be distinctly different from the majority of the population. Indeed, the social deviance literature has played a role in classifying addicts as "other," thereby contributing to the production of an outsider status. However, as Waterston (1993:14) has recently argued, such portrayals have contributed to the "ghettoization" of drug users and to the "construction of a false separation between 'them and us.'"

While the social deviance paradigm of addiction has produced insightful material documenting the lifestyle, experiences, and world views of drug and alcohol addicted persons, this literature has excluded groups not conforming to the image of social disparagement. For instance, the social deviance perspective has been instructive in expanding our knowledge of "bottle gangs" and other alcoholic subcultures (Rubington 1967, 1968; Wiseman 1970), "crack whores" or crack-distributing gangs (Ratner 1993; Williams 1989), and the slum-dwelling heroin addict who injects in order to either enhance his/her social status or simply to escape the hopelessness of his/her own economic poverty (Stephens 1991; Hanson et al. 1985). Although such groups can be classified as "hidden populations" due to their powerlessness and poverty as well as the fact that these groups are largely omitted from national surveys (Lambert and Wiebel 1990), their actions are frequently visible. Inner-city heroin addicts, coke whores, and skid row alcoholics often come in direct contact with social control agents such as the police, the courts, treatment programs, hospitals, and researchers. Precisely because these groups are classified as deviant and are "othered," they are subject to social inspection and identification.

Often absent from the research on hidden populations are those drug addicts and alcoholics who fail to fit into the previously constructed categories that are consistent with current models of deviance. One such group that falls into such a category is the population of middle-class addicts. For instance, some heroin-addicted women from middle-class backgrounds are often able to avoid immersion into a heroin-using subculture, and also have better chances of recovery (Rosenbaum and Murphy 1990). According to these authors (1990:125), "it is possible for them to readjust more readily, because they often possess the resources necessary to start a new life." Such limited subcultural involvement may also result in an increased ability to circumvent detection. Similarly, many high-level drug dealers may remain hidden due to the secretive nature of their activity (Adler 1986). Thus, many drug users and drug dealers avoid detection because they occupy otherwise legitimate social roles and lead basically straight, middle-class lives (Biernacki 1986). In fact, recent scholarship has removed drug use from the world of deviance and has advanced alternative perspectives including the arguments that addiction is an act of cultural resistance (Waterston 1993), or one that locates addiction in the larger social, political, and economic contexts (Waldorf et al. 1991). Such views remove the unique characteristics associated with addiction and place it within the context of conventional social life (Becker 1963).

One population that remains hidden due to the fact that they deviate from socially constructed categories regarding addiction are middle-class drug addicts and alcoholics who terminate their addictive use of substances without treatment. Research exploring the phenomena of natural recovery has found that significant numbers of people discontinue their excessive intake of addictive substances without formal or lay treatment. While it is difficult to estimate the actual size of this hidden population because they are largely invisible (Lee 1993), researchers agree that their numbers are large (Goodwin et al. 1971) and some even contend that they are substantially larger than those choosing to enter treatment facilities or self-help groups (Sobell et al. 1993; Peele 1989; Biernacki 1986). Some have estimated that as many as 90% of problem drinkers never enter treatment and many suspend problematic use without it (Hingson et al. 1980; Roizen et al. 1978; Stall and Biernacki 1986). Research in Canada has shown that 82% of alcoholics who terminated their addiction reported using natural recovery (Sobell et al. 1993).

Research on natural recovery has focused on a variety of substances including heroin and other opiates (Valliant 1966; Waldorf and Biernacki 1977, 1981; Biernacki 1986), cocaine (Waldorf et al. 1991; Shaffer and Jones 1989), and alcohol (Valliant and Milofsky 1982; Valliant 1983; Stall and

Biernacki 1986). Much of this literature challenges the dominant view that addiction relates primarily to the substance being consumed. The dominant addiction paradigm maintains that individuals possess an illness that requires intensive therapeutic intervention. Failure to acquire treatment is considered a sign of denial that will eventually lead to more advanced stages of addiction and possibly death. Given the firm convictions of addictionists as well as their vested interests in marketing this concept (Weisner and Room 1978; Abbott 1988), their rejection of the natural recovery research is of little surprise.

Research on natural recovery has offered great insight into how people successfully transform their lives without turning to professionals or self-help groups. The fact that people accomplish such transformations naturally is by no means a revelation. Most ex-smokers discontinue their tobacco use without treatment (Peele 1989) while many "mature out" of a variety of behaviors including heavy drinking and narcotics use (Snow 1973; Winick 1962). Some researchers examining such transformations frequently point to factors within the individual's social context that promote change. Not only are patterns of alcohol and drug use influenced by social contexts as Zinberg (1986) illustrated, but the experience of quitting as well can be understood from this perspective (Waldorf et al. 1991). Others have attributed natural recovery to a cognitive appraisal process in which the costs and benefits of continued drinking are assessed by alcoholics (Sobell et al. 1993).

Perhaps one of the most detailed investigations of natural recovery is Biernacki's (1986) detailed description of former heroin addicts. Emphasizing the importance of social contexts, Biernacki demonstrates how heroin addicts terminated their addictions and successfully transformed their lives. Most of the addicts in that study as well as others initiated self-recovery after experiencing an assortment of problems that led to a resolve to change. Additionally, Biernacki found that addicts who arrest addictions naturally utilize a variety of strategies. Such strategies involve breaking off relationships with drug users (Shaffer and Jones 1989), removing oneself from a drug-using environment (Stall and Biernacki 1986), building new structures in one's life (Peele 1989), and using social networks of friends and family that help provide support for this newly emerging status (Biernacki 1986). Although it is unclear whether the social contexts of those who terminate naturally is uniquely different from those who undergo treatment, it is certain that environmental factors significantly influence the strategies employed in the decision to stop.

While this literature has been highly instructive, much of this research has focused on respondents' circumvention of formal treatment such as therapeutic communities, methadone maintenance, psychotherapy, or regular counseling in outpatient clinics (Biernacki 1986). Many of those not seeking professional intervention may nevertheless participate in self-help groups. Self-help groups have been one of the most popular avenues for people experiencing alcohol and drug problems. This may be due in large part to the fact that groups such as Alcoholics Anonymous (AA), Narcotics Anonymous (NA), or Cocaine Anonymous (CA) medicalize substance abuse in such a way as to alleviate personal responsibility and related guilt (Trice and Roman 1970). Moreover, these groups contribute to the cultivation of a support community which helps facilitate behavioral change.

Despite these attractions and the popularity of these groups, many in the field remain skeptical about their effectiveness. Research has demonstrated that addicts who affiliate with self-help groups relapse at a significantly greater rate than do those who undergo hospitalization only (Walsh et al. 1992). Some have raised concerns about the appropriateness of self-help groups in all instances of addiction (Lewis et al. 1994). In one of the most turgid critiques of self-help groups, Peele (1989) estimates that nearly half of all those who affiliate with such groups relapse within the first year. Peele contends that these groups are not very effective in stopping addictive behaviors since such groups subscribe to the ideology of lifelong addiction. Adopting the addict-for-life ideology, as many members do, has numerous implications for a person's identity as

well as ways of relating to the world around them (Brown 1991).

Somewhere between the two positions of skepticism and optimism are the findings of Emrick et al. (1993). In one of the most comprehensive analyses of AA participation to date, their meta-analysis of 107 various studies on AA effectiveness report[s] only a modest correlation between exposure to self-help groups and improved drinking behavior. They additionally point out the compelling need for further research on the personal characteristics of individuals for whom these programs are beneficial and those for whom they are not.

Given the emerging challenges to the dominant views of recovery, research on recovery will be advanced through an examination of those who terminated their addictive use of alcohol and drugs without the benefit of either formal or informal treatment modalities. While research has provided insight into those who reject formal treatment modalities, we know little about the population who additionally reject self-help groups, particularly those from middle-class backgrounds. This paper examines the process of natural recovery among middle-class drug addicts and alcoholics and first explores the identity of previously addicted middle-class respondents in relation to their past addictions. Next, respondents' reasons for rejecting self-help group involvement or formal treatment are examined. Strategies used by our respondents to terminate their addictions and transform their lives are then examined and the implications of our findings in relation to current addiction treatment are presented.

Method

Data for the present study were collected from a two-stage research design involving 46 former drug addicts and alcoholics. The initial stage of this study involving 25 interviews explored 3 primary areas. These areas included elements of respondents' successful cessation strategies, perceptions of self relative to former use, and attitudes toward treatment. The second stage of the study sharpened the focus of the exploration within these three areas. This was accomplished by constructing a new interview schedule designed to capture the most salient themes that emerged from the first stage of the study. In each phase of this study, lengthy, semistructured interviews with respondents were conducted to elicit thickly descriptive responses. All interviews were tape-recorded and later transcribed.

Strict criteria were established for respondent selection. First, respondents had to have been drug or alcohol dependent for a period of at least 1 year. On average, our respondents were dependent for a period of 9.14 years. Determination of dependency was made only after careful consideration; each respondent had to have experienced frequent cravings, extended periods of daily use, and associated personal problems due to their use. Second, to be eligible, individuals had to have terminated their addictive consumption for a period of at least 1 year prior to the interview. The mean length of time of termination from addiction for the entire sample was 5.5 years. Finally, the sample includes only individuals who had no, or only minimal, exposure to formal treatment. Individuals with short-term detoxification (up to 2 weeks) were included provided they had had no additional follow-up outpatient treatment. Also, individuals who had less than 1 month exposure to self-help groups such as AA, NA, or CA were included. Some of our respondents reported attending one or two of these self-help group meetings. However, the majority of our respondents had virtually no contact with formal treatment programs or self-help groups.

Respondents in this study were selected through "snowball sampling" techniques (Biernacki 1986). This sampling strategy uses referral chains of personal contacts in which people with appropriate characteristics are referred as volunteers. Snowball sampling has been used in a variety of studies involving hidden populations. In particular, snowball samples have been employed in previous studies of heroin users (Cloud 1987; Biernacki 1986) and cocaine users (Waldorf et al. 1991). In the present study, snowball sampling methods were necessary for two reasons. Since we were searching for a middle-class population that circumvented treatment, these individuals were widely distributed. Unlike those in treatment or in self-help groups, this population tends to be more dispersed. Also, these individuals did not wish to expose their pasts as former addicts. Very few people were aware of a respondent's drug- and alcohol-using history, making the respondent reluctant to participate. Consequently, personal contact with potential respondents prior to the interview was necessary to explain the interview process as well as the procedures to ensure confidentiality. While there are limitations to this sampling strategy, probability sampling techniques would be impossible since the characteristics of the population are unknown.

All of our respondents in the present study report having stable middle-class backgrounds. Each of the respondents had completed high school, the majority possessed college degrees, and several respondents held graduate degrees. Most were employed in professional occupations, including law, engineering, and health-related fields, held managerial positions, or operated their own businesses during their addiction. Of the respondents participating in this study, 30 were males and 16 were females. The age range in the sample was 25 to 60 with a mean age of 38.4 years.

Forming a Postaddict Identity

Research within the tradition of symbolic interaction has frequently explored the social basis of personal identity. Central to the symbolic interactionist perspective is the notion that personal identity is constituted through interaction with others who define social reality. From this perspective, the self emerges through a process of interaction with others and through the roles individuals occupy. Symbolic interactionists maintain that the self is never immutable, but rather change is an ongoing process in which new definitions of the self emerge as group affiliation and roles change. Consequently, identities arise from one's participation within social groups and organizations.

The perspective of symbolic interaction has frequently been used when analyzing the adoption of deviant identities. For instance, the societal reaction model of deviance views the formation of a spoiled identity as a consequence of labeling (Lemert 1951, 1974; Goffman 1963). Reactions against untoward behavior in the form of degradation ceremonies often give rise to deviant identities (Garfinkel 1967). In addition, organizations that seek to reform deviant behavior, encourage the adoption of a "sick role" for the purposes of reintegration (Parsons 1951). AA, for instance, teaches its members that they possess a disease and a lifelong addiction to alcohol (Trice and Roman 1970). Such organizations provide a new symbolic framework through which members undergo dramatic personal transformation.

Consequently, members adopt an addict role and identity, an identity that for many becomes salient (Brown 1991; Cloud 1987).[2] One respondent in Brown's study, for instance, indicated the degree of engulfment in the addict identity:

> Sobriety is my life's priority. I can't have my life, my health, my family, my job, or anything else unless I'm sober. My program [participation in AA] has to come first . . . Now I've come to realize that this is the nature of the disease. I need to remind myself daily that I'm an alcoholic. As long as I work my program, I am granted a daily reprieve from returning to drinking.

Brown's (1991:169) analysis of self-help programs and the identity transformation process that is fostered in those settings demonstrates that members learn "that they must constantly practice the principles of recovery in all their daily affairs." Thus, it is within such programs that the addict identity and role is acquired and reinforced (Peele 1989).

If the addict identity is acquired within such organizational contexts, it is logical to hypothesize that former addicts with minimal contact with such organizations will possess different self-concepts. In the interviews conducted with our first set of respondents, a striking pattern emerged in relation to their present self-concept and their past drug and alcohol involvement. They were asked, "How do you see yourself now in relation to your past?" and, "Do you see yourself as a former addict, recovering addict, recovered addict, or in some other way?" A large majority, nearly two-thirds, refused to identify themselves as presently addicted or as recovering or even recovered. Most reported that they saw themselves in "some other way." While all identified themselves as being addicted earlier in their lives, most did not continue to define themselves as addicts. In several cases, these respondents reacted strongly against the addiction-as-disease ideology, believing that such a permanent identity would impede their continued social development. As one respondent explained:

> I'm a father, a husband and a worker. This is how I see myself today. Being a drug addict was someone I was in the past. I'm over that and I don't think about it anymore.

These respondents saw themselves neither as addicts nor ex-addicts; rather, most references to their past addictions were not central to their immediate self-concepts.

Unlike the alcoholics and drug addicts described by Brown (1991) and others, they did not adopt this identity as a "master status" nor did this identity become salient in the role identity hierarchy (Stryker and Serpe 1982; Becker 1963). Instead, the "addict" identity was marginalized by our respondents. Alcoholics and addicts who have participated extensively in self-help groups often engage in a long-term, self-labeling process which involves continuous reference to their addiction. While many have succeeded in terminating addiction through participation in such programs and by adopting the master status of an addict, researchers have raised concern over the deleterious nature of such self-labeling. Peele (1989), for instance, believes that continuous reference to addiction and reliance on the sick role may be at variance with successful and enduring termination of addictive behaviors. Respondents in the first stage of the present study, by contrast, did not reference their previous addictions as being presently central in their lives. Their comments suggest that they had transcended their addict identity and had adopted self-concepts congruent with contemporary roles.

During the second phase of the study, the question around identity was reconstructed.

Since most respondents in the first sample often made extensive and unsolicited comments about how they currently view themselves in relation to their past experiences (former addict, recovering addict, recovered addict, or other), a decision was made to reshape this question for use with the second sample. The question then read, "How do you see yourself today in relation to your own past experiences with drugs and alcohol (e.g., addict, recovering addict, person who had a serious drug and/or alcohol problem or, do you see yourself in some other way)? Please discuss as it relates to your current identity." The solicited responses from this second sample did not differ dramatically from the unsolicited responses from the first sample. Essentially, their former identities as addicts were not currently central in their lives but rather had been marginalized, as had been the case with the first sample of respondents.

Also, during the second stage of the study, an additional question about "addict identity" was constructed and asked. The question read, "To what extent do you freely discuss your previous drug and alcohol experiences with others? Please elaborate." The majority of these respondents were quite selective about with whom they discussed these previous drug experiences. Some stated that they shared these experiences with very close friends. Others stated that they discussed these matters only with people who had known them as addicts. Still others reported that they discussed these experiences with no one. Again one could conclude, as was the case with the first sample, that this second group minimized these experiences in terms of how they presently view themselves.

The fact that our respondents did not adopt addict identities is of great importance since it contradicts the common assumptions of treatment programs. The belief that alcoholics and drug addicts can overcome their addictions and not see themselves in an indefinite state of recovery is incongruous with treatment predicated on the disease concept which pervades most treatment programs. Such programs subscribe to the view that addiction is incurable; programmatic principles may then commit addicts to a life of ongoing recovery, often with minimal success. Some have suggested that the decision to circumvent formal treatment and self-help involvement has empirical and theoretical importance since it offers insight about this population that may be useful in designing more effective treatment (Sobell et al. 1992). While research has examined the characteristics of individuals who affiliate with such groups, few studies have included individuals outside programs. Therefore, there is a paucity of data that examines the avoidance of treatment. We now turn to an examination of respondents' attitudes toward addiction treatment programs.

Circumventing Treatment

Given the pervasiveness of treatment programs and self-help groups such as AA and NA, the decision to embark upon a method of natural recovery is curious. Some of our respondents in the first stage of the study reported having had direct exposure to such groups by having attended one or two AA, NA, or CA meetings. Others in this sample, although never having attended, reported being indirectly familiar with such groups. Only two of them claimed to have no knowledge of these groups or the principles they advocate. Consequently, the respondents, as a group, expressed the decision not to enter treatment, which represented a conscious effort to circumvent treatment rather than a lack of familiarity with such programs.

In order to explore their decisions to bypass treatment, we asked what they thought about these programs and why they avoided direct involvement in them. When asked about their attitudes toward such programs, most of them commented that they believed such programs were beneficial for some people. They credited treatment programs and self-help groups with helping friends or family members overcome alcohol or drug addictions. Overall, however, our respondents in the first sample disagreed with the ideological basis of such programs and felt that they were inappropriate for them.

Responses included a wide range of criticisms of these programs. In most cases, rejection of treatment programs and self-help groups reflected a perceived contradiction between these respondents' world views and the core principles of such programs. Overcoming resistance to core principles which include the views that addiction is a disease (once an addict always an addict), or that individuals are powerless over their addiction, is imperative by those who affiliate with such programs. Indeed, individuals who subscribe to alternative views of addiction are identified as "in denial" (Brissett 1988). Not unlike other institutions such as the military, law school, or mental health hospitals, self-help groups socialize recruits away from their previously held world views (Granfield 1992; Goffman 1961). It is the task of such programs to shape [their] members' views to make them compatible with organizational ideology (Brown 1991; Peele 1989). Socialization within treatment programs and self-help groups enables a person to reconstruct a biography that corresponds to a new reference point.

Respondents in this sample, however, typically rejected specific characteristics of the treatment ideology. First, many expressed strong opposition to the suggestion that they were powerless over their addictions. Such an ideology, they explained, not only was counterproductive but was also extremely demeaning. These respondents saw themselves as efficacious people who often prided themselves on their past accomplishments. They viewed themselves as being individualists and strong-willed. One respondent, for instance, explained that "such programs encourage powerlessness" and that she would rather "trust her own instincts than the instincts of others." Another respondent commented that:

> I read a lot of their literature and the very first thing they say is that you're powerless. I think that's bullshit. I believe that people have power inside themselves to make what they want happen. I think I have choices and can do anything I set my mind to.

Consequently, these respondents found the suggestion that they were powerless incompatible with their own self-image. While treatment programs and self-help groups would define such attitudes as a manifestation of denial that would only result in

perpetuating addiction, they saw overcoming their addictions as a challenge they could effectively surmount. Interestingly, and in contrast to conventional wisdom in the treatment field, the overwhelming majority of our respondents in the first sample reported successful termination of their addictions after only one attempt.

They also reported that they disliked the culture associated with such self-help programs. In addition to finding the ideological components of such programs offensive, most rejected the lifestyle encouraged by such programs. For instance, several of them felt that these programs bred dependency and subsequently rejected the notion that going to meetings with other addicts was essential for successful termination. In fact, some actually thought it to be dangerous to spend so much time with addicts who continue to focus on their addictions. Most of our respondents in this first sample sought to avoid all contact with drug addicts once they decided to terminate their own drug use. Consequently, they believed that contact with addicts, even those who are not actively using, would possibly undermine their termination efforts. Finally, some of these respondents reported that they found self-help groups "cliquish" and "unhealthy." One respondent explained that, "all they do is stand around smoking cigarettes and drinking coffee while they talk about their addiction. I never felt comfortable with these people." This sense of discomfort with the cultural aspects of these programs was often keenly felt by the women in our sample. Most women in this group believed that self-help groups were male-oriented and did not include the needs of women. One woman, for instance, who identified herself as a lesbian commented that self-help groups were nothing but "a bunch of old men running around telling stories and doing things together." This woman found greater inspiration among feminist support groups and literature that emphasized taking control of one's own life.

During the second stage of the study we decided to separate and sharpen our focus on what appeared to be three prominent overlapping themes around attitudes toward treatment. We asked these respondents why they chose not to undergo formal treatment or participate in self-help groups. We also asked about their general impressions of formal treatment, separate from their impressions of self-help groups. We then asked them specifically about their impressions of AA, NA, and other 12-step programs.

The principal reason reported for not undergoing formal treatment was that nearly all of the 21 respondents in the second sample stated directly or in some variation that they felt that they could terminate their addiction without such interventions. Some stated that treatment was not a viable option since it was either too expensive or essentially unavailable. While some of these respondents registered positive attitudes regarding varying treatment modalities, these respondents, nonetheless, reported that such treatment was not necessary in their individual case. In the case of respondent evaluation of 12-step programs, the second sample of addicts was not as critical as the previous sample. However, even among the second group, most believed that the principles espoused by these programs were at variance with their own beliefs about the recovery process.

The Elements of Cessation

The fact that our respondents were able to terminate their addictions without the benefit of treatment raises an important question about recovery. Research that has examined this process has found that individuals who have a "stake in conventional life" are better able to alter their drug-taking practices than those who experience a sense of hopelessness (Waldorf et al. 1991). In their longitudinal research of cocaine users, these authors found that many people with structural supports in their lives such as a job, family, and other involvements were simply able to "walk away" from their heavy use of cocaine. According to these authors, this fact suggests that the social context of a drug user's life may significantly influence the ability to overcome drug problems.

The social contexts of our respondents served to protect many of them from total involvement with an addict subculture. Literature on the sociocultural correlates of heavy drinking has found that some groups possess cultural protection against developing alcoholism (Snyder 1964). In addition, Peele (1989) has argued that individuals with greater resources in their lives are well equipped to overcome drug problems. Such resources include education and other credentials, job skills, meaningful family attachments, and support mechanisms. In the case of our first 25 respondents, most provided evidence of such resources available to them even while they were actively using. Most reported coming from stable home environments that valued education, family, and economic security, and for the most part held conventional beliefs. All of our respondents in the first group had completed high school, nine were college graduates, and one held a master's degree in engineering. Most were employed in professional occupations or operated their own businesses. Additionally, most continued to be employed throughout their period of heavy drug and alcohol use and none of our respondents came from disadvantaged backgrounds.

It might be concluded that the social contexts of these respondents' lives protected them from further decline into alcohol and drug addiction. They frequently reported that there were people in their lives to whom they were able to turn when they decided to quit. Some explained that their families provided support; others described how their nondrug-using friends assisted them in their efforts to stop using. One respondent explained how an old college friend helped him get over his addiction to crack cocaine:

> My best friend from college made a surprise visit. I hadn't seen him in years. He walked in and I was all cracked out. It's like he walked into the twilight zone or something. He couldn't believe it. He smoked dope in college but he had never seen anything like this. When I saw him, I knew that my life was really screwed up and I needed to do something about it. He stayed with me for the next two weeks and helped me through it.

Typically, respondents in our first sample had not yet "burned their social bridges" and were able to rely upon communities of friends, family, and other associates in their lives. The existence of such communities made it less of a necessity for these individuals to search out alternative communities such as those found within self-help groups. Such groups may be of considerable importance when a person's natural communities break down. Indeed, the fragmentation of communities within postmodern society may account for the popularity of self-help groups (Reinarman n.d.). In the absence of resources and communities, such programs allow individuals to construct a sense of purpose and meaning in their lives. Respondents in our first sample all explained that the resources, communities, and individuals in their lives were instrumental in supporting their efforts to change.

In some cases, these respondents abandoned their using communities entirely to search for nonusing groups. This decision to do so was often triggered by the realization that their immediate social networks consisted mostly of heavy drug and alcohol users. Any attempt to discontinue use, they reasoned, would require complete separation. Several from this group moved to different parts of the country in order to distance themselves from their using networks. This finding is consistent with Biernacki's (1986) study of heroin addicts who relocated in order to remove any temptations to use in the future. For some women, the decision to abandon using communities, particularly cocaine, was often preceded by becoming pregnant. These women left boyfriends and husbands because they felt a greater sense of responsibility and greater meaning in their new maternal status. In all these cases, respondents fled using communities in search of more conventional networks.

In addition to relying on their natural communities and abandoning using communities, these respondents also built new support structures to assist them in their termination efforts. They frequently reported becoming involved in various social groups such as choirs, health clubs, religious organizations, reading clubs, and dance companies. Others from this group reported that they returned to school, became active in civic organizations, or simply developed new hobbies that brought them in touch with nonusers. Thus, respondents built new lives for themselves by cultivating social ties with meaningful and emotionally satisfying alternative communities. In each of these cases where respondents formed attachments to new communities, they typically hid their addictive past, fearing that exposure would jeopardize their newly acquired status.

During the second stage of the study we further examined two of the above themes. The first theme that was revisited dealt with "specific strategies used to remain abstinent." Overwhelmingly for this group, severing all ties with using friends emerged as the most important strategy one could undertake in successfully terminating addiction.

The next theme around elements of cessation that was further examined among this second sample included "resources that were perceived as valuable in the process of recovery." After giving examples of resources discovered in the first stage of the study (e.g., family), these respondents also reported that identical or similar resources had been very useful in their own struggles to overcome addictions. They reported being able to draw upon their families, job skills, formal education, economic security, and other conditions that had been identified as instrumental resources by the first sample. Interestingly, will power and determination emerged as important internal resources during the second stage of the study. However, these should be viewed cautiously since "determination" was given as an example of a possible internal resource during the interviews with the second sample.

Given the apparent roles that severing ties with using networks and having resources play in the natural recovery process, one might draw the compelling conclusion that those individuals from the most disadvantaged segments of our society are also least likely to be in a position to overcome severe addiction problems naturally. Unfortunately, these individuals are also at greatest risk for severe drug and alcohol problems, least likely to be able to afford private treatment, and least likely to voluntarily seek public treatment.

Discussions and Implications

While the sample within the present study is small, there is considerable evidence from additional research to suggest that the population of self-healers is quite substantial (Sobell et al. 1992; Waldorf et al. 1991). Despite empirical evidence, many in the treatment field continue to deny the existence of such a population. The therapeutic "field" possesses considerable power to construct reality in ways that exclude alternative and perhaps challenging paradigms. As Bourdieu (1991) has recently pointed out, such fields reproduce themselves through their ability to normalize arbitrary world views. The power of the therapeutic field lies in its ability to not only medicalize behavior, but also in the ability to exclude the experiences and world views of those who do not fit into conventional models of addiction and treatment (Skoll 1992).

Finding empirical support for natural recovery does not imply that we devalue the importance of treatment programs or even self-help groups. Such programs have proven beneficial to addicts, particularly those in advanced stages. However, the experiences of our respondents have important implications for the way in which addiction and recovery are typically conceptualized. First, denying the existence of this population, as many do, discounts the version of reality held by those who terminate their addictions naturally. Natural recovery is simply not recognized as a viable option. This is increasingly the case as media has reified dominant notions of addiction and recovery. Similarly, there is an industry of self-help literature that unquestionably accepts and reproduces these views. Denying the experience of natural recovery allows treatment agencies and self-help groups to continue to impose their particular view of reality on society.

Related to this is the possibility that many of those experiencing addictions may be extremely reluctant to enter treatment or attend self-help meetings. Their resistance may stem from a variety of factors such as the stigma associated with these programs, discomfort with the therapeutic process, or lack of support from significant others.

Whatever the reason, such programs do not appeal to everyone. For such people, natural recovery may be a viable option. Since natural recovery demystifies the addiction and recovery experience, it may offer a way for people to take control of their own lives without needing to rely exclusively on experts. Such an alternative approach offers a low-cost supplement to an already costly system of formal addiction treatment.

A third implication concerns the consequences of adopting an addict identity. While the disease metaphor is thought to be a humanistic one in that it allows for the successful social reintegration of deviant drinkers or drug users, it nevertheless constitutes a deviant identity. Basing one's identity on past addiction experiences may actually limit social reintegration. The respondents in our sample placed a great deal of emphasis on their immediate social roles as opposed to constantly referring to their drug-addict pasts. Although there is no way of knowing, such present-centeredness may, in the long run, prove more beneficial than a continual focusing on the past.

Fourth, for drug and alcohol treatment professionals, as well as those who are likely to refer individuals to drug and alcohol treatment programs, this research raises several important considerations. It reaffirms the necessity for individual treatment matching (Lewis et al. 1994). It also suggests that individuals whose profiles are similar to these middle-class respondents are likely to be receptive to and benefit from less intrusive, short-term types of interventions. Given the extent of the various concerns expressed by these respondents around some of the possible long-term negative consequences of undergoing traditional treatment and related participation in self-help programs, the decision to specifically recommend drug and alcohol treatment is a profoundly serious one. It should not be made capriciously or simply because it is expected and available. A careful assessment of the person's entire life is warranted, including whether or not the condition is so severe and the absence of supportive resources so great that the possible lifelong identity of addict or related internalized beliefs are reasonable risks to take in pursuing recovery. Overall, the findings of this study as well as previous research on natural recovery could be instructive in designing more effective treatment programs (Sobell et al. 1992; Fillmore 1988; Stall and Biernacki 1986).

Finally, the experiences of our respondents may have important social policy implications. If our respondents are any guide, the following hypothesis might be considered: those with the greatest number of resources and who consequently have a great deal to lose by their addiction are the ones most likely to terminate their addictions naturally. While addiction is not reducible to social class alone, it is certainly related to it (Waldorf et al. 1991). The respondents in our sample had relatively stable lives: they had jobs, supportive families, high school and college credentials, and other social supports that gave them reasons to alter their drug-taking behavior. Having much to lose gave our respondents incentives to transform their lives. However, when there is little to lose from heavy alcohol or drug use, there may be little to gain by quitting. Social policies that attempt to increase a person's stake in conventional life could not only act to prevent future alcohol and drug addiction, they could also provide an anchor for those who become dependent on these substances.

Further research on the subject of natural recovery among hidden populations such as the middle class needs to be conducted in order to substantiate the findings we report and related conclusions. One important direction the researchers are presently pursuing is to differentiate the natural recovery experience of individuals who have been addicted to different substances. Such research could increase understanding of how different hidden populations overcome the addictions they experience.

Notes

1. An earlier version of this paper was presented at the American Sociological Association meetings, Los Angeles, Calif., August 1994.

2. In his study of identity transformation of alcoholics, Brown (1991) found that the conversion experience to a "recovering alcoholic" was so powerful that many individuals abandoned their previous careers to become counselors.

References

Abbott, A. 1988. *The system of profession.* Chicago: University of Chicago Press.

Adler, P. 1986. *Wheeling and dealing.* New York: Columbia University Press.

Becker, H. 1963. *The outsiders: Studies in the sociology of deviance.* New York: The Free Press.

Biernacki, P. 1986. *Pathways from heroin addiction: Recovery without treatment.* Philadelphia: Temple University Press.

Bourdieu, P. 1991. The peculiar history of scientific reason. *Sociological Forum* 5(2):3–26.

Brissett, D. 1988. Denial in alcoholism: A sociological interpretation. *Journal of Drug Issues* 18(3):385–402.

Brown, J. D. 1991. Preprofessional socialization and identity transformation: The case of the professional ex. *Journal of Contemporary Ethnography* 20(2):157–178.

Cloud, W. 1987. From down under: A qualitative study on heroin addiction recovery. Ann Arbor: Dissertation Abstracts.

Emrick, C., J. Tonigan, H. Montgomery, and L. Little. 1993. Alcoholics Anonymous: What is currently known? In *Research on Alcoholics Anonymous: Opportunities and alternatives,* eds. B. McCrady and W. Miller. New Brunswick, N.J.: Rutgers Center of Alcohol Studies.

Fillmore, K. M. 1988. Spontaneous remission of alcohol problems. Paper presented at the National Conference on Evaluating Recovery Outcomes, San Diego, Calif.

Garfinkel, H. 1967. *Studies in ethnomethodology.* New Jersey: Prentice-Hall.

Goffman, E. 1961. *Asylums.* Garden City, N.Y.: Anchor Books.

———. 1963. *Stigma.* Englewood Cliffs, N.J.: Prentice Hall.

Goodwin, D., J. B. Crane, and S. B. Guze. 1971. Felons who drink: An eight-year follow-up. *Quarterly Journal of Studies on Alcohol* 32:136–147.

Granfield, R. 1992. *Making elite lawyers: Visions of law at Harvard and beyond.* New York: Routledge, Chapman and Hall.

Hanson, B., G. Beschner, J. M. Walters, and E. Boville. 1985. *Life with heroin.* Lexington, Mass.: Lexington Books.

Hingson, R., N. Scotch, N. Day, and A. Culbert. 1980. Recognizing and seeking help for drinking problems. *Journal of Studies on Alcohol* 41:1102–1117.

Lambert, E., and W. Wiebel. 1990. Introduction. In *The collection and interpretation of data from hidden populations,* ed. E. Lambert. Rockville, Md.: National Institute on Drug Abuse.

Lee, R. 1993. *Doing research on sensitive topics.* Newbury Park, Calif.: Sage.

Lemert, E. 1951. *Social pathology.* New York: McGraw-Hill.

Lemert, E. 1974. Beyond Mead: The societal reaction to deviance. *Social Problems* 21(4):457–468.

Lewis, J., R. Dana, and G. Blevins. 1994. *Substance abuse counseling: An individualized approach.* Pacific Grove, Calif.: Brooks/Cole.

Parsons, T. 1951. *The social system.* New York: The Free Press.

Peele, S. 1989. *The diseasing of America: Addiction treatment out of control.* Lexington, Mass.: Lexington Books.

Ratner, M. 1993. *Crack pipe as pimp: An ethnographic investigation of sex-for-crack exchanges.* New York: Lexington Books.

Reinarman, C. n.d. The twelve-step movement and advanced capitalist culture: Notes on the politics of self-control in postmodernity. In *Contemporary social movements and cultural politics,* eds. M. Darofsky, B. Epstein, and R. Flacks. Philadelphia: Temple University Press. In press.

Roizen, R., D. Cahalan, and P. Shanks. 1978. Spontaneous remission among untreated problem drinkers. In *Longitudinal research on drug use,* ed. D. Kandel. Washington, D.C.: Hemisphere Publishing.

Rosenbaum, M., and S. Murphy. 1990. Women and addiction: Process, treatment, and outcome. In *The collection and interpretation of data from hidden populations,* ed. E. Lambert. Rockville, Md.: National Institute on Drug Abuse.

Rubington, E. 1967. Drug addiction as a deviant career. *International Journal of the Addictions* 2:3–20.

Rubington, E. 1978. Variations in bottle-gang controls. In *Deviance: The interactionist perspective*, eds. E. Rubington and M. Weinberg. New York: Macmillan.

Shaffer, H., and S. Jones. 1989. *Quitting cocaine: The struggle against impulse*. Lexington, Mass.: Lexington Books.

Skoll, G. 1992. *Walk the walk and talk the talk: An ethnography of a drug abuse treatment facility*. Philadelphia: Temple University Press.

Snow, M. 1973. Maturing out of narcotic addiction in New York City. *International Journal of the Addictions* 8(6):921–938.

Snyder, C. 1964. Inebriety, alcoholism and anomie. In *Anomie and deviant behavior*, ed. M. Clinard. New York: The Free Press.

Sobell, L., M. Sobell, and T. Toneatto. 1992. Recovery from alcohol problems without treatment. In *Self control and the addictive behaviors*, eds. N. Heather, W. R. Miller, and J. Greeley, 199–242. New York: Maxwell Macmillan.

Sobell, L., M. Sobell, T. Toneatto, and G. Leo. 1993. What triggers the resolution of alcohol problems without treatment? *Alcoholism: Clinical and Experimental Research* 17(2):217–224.

Stall, R., and P. Biernacki. 1986. Spontaneous remission from the problematic use of substances. *International Journal of the Addictions* 21:1–23.

Stephens, R. 1991. *The street addict role: A theory of heroin addiction*. Albany, N.Y.: State University Press of New York.

Stryker, S., and R. Serpe. 1982. Commitment, identity salience and role behavior: Theory and research example. In *Personality, roles and social behavior*, eds. W. Ickes and E. Knowles. New York: Springer-Verlag.

Trice, H., and P. Roman. 1970. Delabeling, relabeling, and Alcoholics Anonymous. *Social Problems* 17:538–546.

Valliant, G. 1966. A twelve-year follow-up of New York narcotic addicts: Some characteristics and determinants of abstinence. In *Classic contributions in the addictions*, eds. H. Shaffer and M. Burglass. New York: Brunner/Mazel.

——. 1983. *The natural history of alcoholism*. Cambridge: Harvard University Press.

Valliant, G., and E. S. Milofsky. 1982. Natural history of male alcoholism: IV. Paths to recovery. *Archives of General Psychiatry* 39:127–133.

Waldorf, D., and P. Biernacki. 1977. Natural recovery from opiate addiction: A review of the incidence literature. *Journal of Drug Issues* 9:281–290.

——. 1981. Natural recovery from opiate addiction: Some preliminary findings. *Journal of Drug Issues* 11:61–74.

Waldorf, D., C. Reinarman, and S. Murphy. 1991. *Cocaine changes: The experience of using and quitting*. Philadelphia: Temple University Press.

Walsh, D. C., R. Hingson, and D. Merrigan. 1992. The impact of a physician's warning on recovery after alcoholism treatment. *Journal of the American Medical Association* 267:663.

Waterston, A. 1993. *Street addicts in the political economy*. Philadelphia: Temple University Press

Weisner, C., and R. Room. 1978. Financing and ideology in alcohol treatment. *Social Problems* 32:157–184.

Williams, T. 1989. *The cocaine kids*. Reading, Mass.: Addison-Wesley.

Winick, C. 1962. Maturing out of narcotic addiction. *Bulletin on Narcotics* 6:1.

Wiseman, J. 1970. *Stations of the lost: The treatment of skid row alcoholics*. Englewood Cliffs, N.J.: Prentice-Hall.

Zinberg, N. 1986. *Drug, set and setting: The basis for controlled intoxicant use*. New Haven: Yale University Press.

For Discussion

1. Why might some individuals be able to recover on their own, while others struggle through a lifetime of addiction? What does this say about the nature of addiction?

2. What kinds of social policies might "increase a person's stake in conventional life" and help prevent substance dependence?

Part X

Policy Considerations

The federal approach to drug abuse and drug control has included a variety of avenues for reducing both the supply of and the demand for illicit drugs. Historically, the supply-and-demand reduction strategies were grounded in the classic deterrence model: Through legislation and criminal penalties, individuals would be discouraged from using drugs; by making an example of traffickers, the government would force potential dealers to seek out other economic pursuits.

In time, other components were added: treatment for the user, education and prevention for the would-be user, and research to determine how to best develop and implement plans for treatment, education, and prevention.

By the early 1970s, when it appeared that the war on drugs had won few if any battles, new avenues for supply-and-demand reduction were added. Federal interdiction initiatives involved charging Coast Guard, Customs, and Drug Enforcement Administration operatives with intercepting drug shipments coming to the United States from foreign ports, and in the international sector there were attempts to eradicate drug-yielding crops at their source. On the surface, none of these strategies seemed to have any effect, and illicit drug use continued to spread.

The problems were many. Legislation and enforcement alone were not enough, and early education programs of the "scare" variety quickly lost their credibility. Moreover, for most social scientists and clinicians,

treating drug abuse as a medical problem seemed to be the logical answer. But treatment programs did not seem to be working very effectively, probably because the course of treatment was of insufficient length to have any significant impact.

Given the perceived inadequacy of the traditional approaches to drug-abuse control, during the late 1970s federal authorities began drawing plans for a more concerted assault on drugs, both legislative and technological. It began with the RICO (Racketeer-Influenced and Corrupt Organizations) and CCE (Continuing Criminal Enterprise) statutes. What RICO and CCE accomplish is the forfeiture of the fruits of criminal activities by eliminating the rights of traffickers to their personal assets, whether these be cash, bank accounts, real estate, automobiles, jewelry and art, equity in businesses, directorships in companies, or any kind of goods or entitlements obtained in or used for a criminal enterprise.

The new, evolving federal drug strategy considered it crucial to include the U.S. military in its war on drugs. In 1982 the Department of Defense Authorization Act was signed into law, making the entire war chest of U.S. military power available to law enforcement—for training, intelligence gathering, and detection. Beginning in 1982, the "war on drugs" had a new look. Put into force was the Bell 209 assault helicopter, more popularly known as the Cobra. None in the military arsenal were faster, and in its gunship mode it could destroy a tank. In addition, there was the awesome Sikorsky Black Hawk assault helicopter, assigned for operation by U.S. Customs Service pilots. Customs also had the Cessna Citation, a jet aircraft equipped with radar originally designed for F-16 fighters. There was the Navy's EC-2, an aircraft equipped with a radar disk capable of detecting other aircraft from as far as 300 miles away. There were "Fat Albert" and his pals—aerostat surveillance balloons 175 feet in length equipped with sophisticated radar and listening devices. Fat Albert not only could pick up communications from Cuba but also could detect traffic in "Smugglers' Alley," a wide band of Caribbean sky that is virtually invisible to land-based radar systems. There were NASA satellites to spy on drug operations as far apart as California and Colombia, airborne infrared sensing and imaging equipment that could detect human body heat in the thickest underbrush of Florida's Everglades, plus a host of other high-tech devices. In all, drug enforcement appeared well equipped for battle.

The final component added to the drug war armamentarium was "zero tolerance," a 1988 White House antidrug policy based on a number of premises: (1) that if there were no drug abusers there would be no drug problem; (2) that the market for drugs is created not only by availability but also by demand; (3) that drug abuse starts with a willful act; (4) that the perception that drug users are powerless to act against the influences of drug availability and peer pressure is an erroneous one; (5) that most illegal drug users can choose to stop their drug-taking behaviors and must be held accountable if they do not; (6) that individual freedom does not include the right to self- and societal destruction; and (7) that public tolerance for drug abuse must be reduced to *zero*. As such, the zero-tolerance policy expanded the war on drugs from suppliers and dealers to users as well—especially casual users— and meant that planes, vessels, and vehicles could be confiscated for carrying even the smallest amount of a controlled substance.

By the late 1980s, well after the newest "war on drugs" had been declared and put into operation, it had already been decided by numerous longtime observers that the more than 70 years of federal prohibition since the passage of the Harrison Act of 1914 were not only a costly and abject failure but represented a totally doomed effort as well. It was argued that drug laws and drug enforcement had served mainly to create enormous profits for drug dealers and traffickers, overcrowded jails, police and other government corruption, a distorted foreign policy, predatory street crime carried on by users in search of the funds necessary to purchase black-market drugs, and urban areas harassed by street-level drug dealers and terrorized by violent drug gangs. Many of these observations were indeed true.

Within the context of these concerns, the late 1980s also marked the onset of renewed calls for the *decriminalization*, if not the outright *legalization*, of most or all illicit drugs. The arguments posed by the supporters of legalization seem all too logical. First, they argued, the drug laws have created evils far worse than the drugs themselves—corruption, violence, street crime, and disrespect for the law. Second, legislation passed to control drugs failed to reduce demand. Third, an activity that a significant segment of the population of any society is committed to doing should not be made illegal. A social system simply cannot arrest, prosecute, and punish such large numbers of people, particularly in a democracy. And specifically in this regard, in a liberal democracy the government must not interfere with personal behavior if liberty is to be maintained. Fourth, they added, if marijuana, cocaine, crack, heroin, and other drugs were legalized, a number of positive things would happen:

1. Drug prices would fall and subsequently so would crime committed for the purpose of obtaining funds with which to support expensive drug habits.

2. Users could obtain their drugs at low, government-regulated prices and would no longer be forced to engage in prostitution and street crime to support their habits.

3. The fact that the levels of drug-related crime would significantly decline would result in less crowded courts, jails, and prisons and would free law en-

forcement personnel to focus their energies on the "real criminals" in society.

4. Drug production, distribution, and sale would be removed from the criminal arena; such criminal syndicates as the Medellin Cartel and the Jamaican posses would be decapitalized, and the violence associated with drug distribution rivalries would be eliminated.

5. Government corruption and intimidation by traffickers, as well as drug-based foreign policies, would be effectively reduced, if not eliminated entirely.

6. The often draconian measures undertaken by police to enforce the drug laws would be curtailed, thus restoring to the American public many of its hard-won civil liberties.

Those opposed to legalizing drugs argued a counterposition, suggesting that making heroin, cocaine, and other illicit drugs more available would create a public health problem of massive proportions. Several moderating positions were visible as well, including what is known as the "harm reduction" approach. Although an explicit definition of "harm reduction" would be difficult, harm reduction includes a wide variety of programs and policies, including the following:

1. *Advocacy for changes in drug policies*— legalization, decriminalization, ending the drug prohibition, changes in drug paraphernalia laws, reduction of penalties for drug-related crimes, and treatment alternatives to incarceration.

2. *HIV/AIDS-related interventions*—needle/ syringe exchange programs, HIV prevention/intervention programs, bleach distribution, referrals for HIV testing and HIV medical care, referrals for HIV/AIDS-related psychosocial care, and case management.

3. *Broader drug treatment options*—methadone maintenance by primary care physicians, changes in methadone regulations, heroin substitution programs, and new experimental treatments.

4. *Drug abuse management for those who wish to continue using drugs*—counseling and clinical case management programs that promote safer and more responsible drug use.

5. *Ancillary interventions*—housing and other entitlements, healing centers, and support and advocacy groups.

In the five chapters that follow, the arguments for and against legalizing drugs are thoroughly examined, as are alternative drug policy choices.

Additional Readings

Cooper, Hannah, Lisa Moore, Sofia Gruskin, and Nancy Krieger. (2005). "The Impact of a Police Drug Crackdown on Drug Injectors' Ability to Practice Harm Reduction: A Qualitative Study." *Social Science and Medicine* 61 (3): 673–684.

Courtwright, David T. (1991). "Drug Legalization, the Drug War, and Drug Treatment in Historical Perspective." *Journal of Policy History* 3: 393–414.

Gray, James P. (2001). *Why Our Drug Laws Have Failed and What We Can Do About It.* Philadelphia: Temple University Press.

Inciardi, James A. (1999). *The Drug Legalization Debate.* Thousand Oaks, CA: Sage Publications.

——. (2003). "The Irrational Politics of American Drug Policy: Implications for Criminal Law and the Management of Drug-Involved Offenders." *Ohio State Journal of Criminal Law* 1 (Fall): 273–288.

Inciardi, James A., and Lana D. Harrison. (2000). *Harm Reduction: National and International Perspectives.* Thousand Oaks, CA: Sage.

MacCoun, Robert J., and Peter Reuter. (2001). *Drug War Heresies: An Agnostic Look at the Legalization Debate* (RAND Studies in Policy and Analysis). Port Chester, NY: Cambridge University Press.

Trevino, Robert A., and Alan J. Richard. (2002). "Attitudes Towards Drug Legalization Among Drug Users." *American Journal of Drug & Alcohol Abuse* 28 (1): 91–108. ✦

40

Safety First

A Reality-Based Approach to Teens, Drugs, and Drug Education

Marsha Rosenbaum

Marsha Rosenbaum begins this chapter by describing the historical and contemporary nature of drug education, most of which has been based solely on the philosophy of abstinence. She reviews the findings from evaluation studies of drug prevention programs such as Drug Abuse Resistance Education (D.A.R.E.) and discusses the problems associated with these programs. Rosenbaum proposes an alternative strategy that focuses on a "safety first" approach to drug education.

Although often championed as a new form of weaponry in the War on Drugs, drug education in the United States was first conceived over a century ago by the Women's Christian Temperance Union (WCTU), a leading organization of the anti-alcohol crusade.[1] Early programs claimed to be based on scientific research. Standard textbooks, however, were filled with misinformation: Alcohol would cause permanent damage to the liver, lungs, kidneys, heart and brain; and marijuana could drive users insane and cause homicidal rages. All drugs were portrayed as equally dangerous and addicting. Only total abstinence could save an individual from inevitable destruction.

Post–World War II drug education portrayed *alcohol* in a way more consistent with the beliefs and practices of most Americans, making distinctions between use and *abuse,* and characterizing the majority of users as moderate.[2] *Marijuana,* however, continued to be described as causing crime and insanity, leaving its users exceedingly vulnerable to heroin addiction.[3] The purpose of these programs was to frighten young people out of using *illegal* drugs, utilizing scare tactics reminiscent of the movie *Reefer Madness,* a 1936 propaganda film now universally regarded as factually incorrect.[4]

By the late 1960s and early 1970s, it was clear that exaggerations of danger had failed to prevent a generation of young people (the Baby Boomers) from experimenting with marijuana and other drugs. In response, there was an effort by some educators to take a different tack. Whereas abstinence continued to be promoted as the wisest choice, the idea was to give students all available information about drugs so they might use their education to make responsible decisions.[5]

In the early 1980s, America's new First Lady instituted "Just Say No" as official policy, with the simple goal of prevention of drug use.[6] Anti-drug budgets climbed and "abstinence-only" school-based programs proliferated, with federal funding requiring a firm "zero-tolerance" stance.[7] Materials construed as neutral were prohibited.[8] These new programs were considered sophisticated because they utilized psycho-social innovations. Students were given information about the dangers of drugs as well as techniques for countering "peer pressure." Mrs. Reagan instructed inner city children on how to say "no" to drugs, while "feel good" drug education programs gave them a heavy dose of self-esteem and self-control exercises to fill the alleged void that rendered them "at risk" to the lure of mind-altering drugs.[9]

Today's drug education is *extremely* variable in content as well as quality and price. Classes are sometimes offered as early as kindergarten, and in later grades drug education is often taught in courses such as "family life," or "health education." First, a particular program is adopted by a school and then the school's own teachers or outside "experts" teach the program's curriculum. Some offer video presentations, others stickers, posters, and activity books. Some are designed to stand alone, others to be integrated into health or science curricula. Some hand out T-shirts and certificates when students complete the program; others have graduation ceremonies at which students are encouraged to take a pledge to remain drug-free. All programs provide information about the negative consequences of drug use and teach resistance/refusal skills. The majority teach students that *most* people do not use drugs, that *abstinence* is the societal norm, and that it is acceptable not to use drugs.[10]

Does Drug Education 'Work'?

Increased governmental funding for "prevention" in the 1980s resulted in a plethora of "approved" drug-education programs, but it is very difficult to know which, if any, drug education programs really "work." We do know that despite prevention education a majority of students experiment with drugs by the time they reach their senior year of high school. Somewhere there is a "disconnect."

Of 49 programs reviewed in *Making the Grade: A Guide to School Drug Prevention Programs,*[11] only 10 had been subjected to rigorous evaluations. Of these, a handful of programs developed in university settings have shown favorable results in delaying or reducing some drug use. Yet they tend to be rather expensive, hence less available than those programs that are cheaper to administer, aggressively marketed, and of questionable value.[12]

Some researchers question our ability to determine the effectiveness of drug education programs because the evaluations themselves are too simplistic. They tend to measure student *attitudes* about drugs rather than drug use itself. Unfortunately, attitudes formed about drugs during childhood or early adolescence seem to have little bearing on later decisions, and high school students may rhetorically state reasons for avoiding drugs, yet use them anyway.[13] Furthermore, such evaluations tend to report positive findings, while ignoring or even covering up those that show no effectiveness. In a comprehensive evaluation of several of the most popular programs, D. M. Gorman of Rutgers University's Center of Alcohol Studies argues:

> The evidence presented . . . from both national surveys and program evaluations, shows that we have yet to develop successful techniques of school-based drug prevention. The claims made on behalf of this aspect of the nation's drug control policy are largely unsupported by empirical data. Evidence is cited selectively to support the use of certain programs, and there is virtually no systematic testing of interventions developed in line with competing theoretical models of adolescent drug use.[14]

Education researcher Joel Brown and his colleagues conclude that flaws in the way programs are evaluated lead us to believe that drug education is effective, although in reality it is an enormous taxpayer drain with precious few positive effects.[15]

Perhaps no program has been evaluated more than D.A.R.E., which has been tested for its impact on drug use, both immediately after the program's completion and several years later. A study tracking D.A.R.E. students over five years found that the program had "no long-term effects . . . in preventing or reducing adolescent drug use."[16] Another study, funded by the National Institute of Justice, found that "expectations concerning the effectiveness of any school-based curriculum, including D.A.R.E., in changing adolescent drug use behavior should not be overstated."[17] Based on a ten-year follow-up study conducted when D.A.R.E. graduates were twenty years old, a team of researchers led by Donald Lynam at the University of Kentucky concluded that D.A.R.E. created no lasting changes in the outcomes evaluated, including not only legal and illegal drug use, but self-esteem and peer pressure resistance.[18] Other long-term studies have found little or no difference in drug use between D.A.R.E. graduates and non-graduates.[19]

What do students themselves say? A common complaint about the D.A.R.E. program, according to researchers Wysong, Aniskiewicz, and Wright, was from students who did not believe their opinions were taken into account:

> It's like nobody cares what we think . . . The D.A.R.E. cops just wanted us to do what they told us and our teachers never talked about D.A.R.E. . . . . It seems like a lot of adults and teachers can't bring

themselves down to talk to students . . . so you don't care what they think either.[20]

As part of a large evaluation study of drug education in California conducted by Dr. Brown and his colleagues, students were asked to tell "in their own voices" how much their drug use had been influenced by the drug education they had received. Only 15% felt drug education had a "large effect" on their choice of whether to use drugs, and 45% said they were "not affected at all."[21] In conversations with students, Brown also obtained their views on the entire drug education experience. Many felt it was insulting to teach so-called "decision-making skills" when it seemed obvious that the only acceptable decision was to decline to use drugs. Brown believes this basic hypocrisy undermines drug education: "When young people recognize that they are being taught to follow directions, rather than to make decisions, they feel betrayed and resentful. As long as federal mandates force this charade, drug education programs and policies will continue to fail."[22]

> **Long-term studies have found little or no difference in drug use between D.A.R.E. graduates and non-graduates.**

Fundamental Problems With Drug Education

The foundations of conventional school-based drug education are fundamentally flawed. Many programs are based on the conviction that any use of illegal drugs is inherently pathological, dangerous behavior, an indication that something is wrong. Some psychologists define drug use as deviant, aberrant behavior caused by a personality problem. Other explanations suggest a "proneness" on the part of some teenagers to problem behavior such as unconventionality (e.g., sagging pants and exposed bra straps) and willingness to take risks (e.g., driving too fast). Sociological explanations link youthful drug use to weak ties to family religion and school, to "peer pressure," and to membership in drug-using groups. Alternative explanations, not based on the idea that experimentation with drugs is pathological, acknowledge the importance of *culture*. The American people and their children are perpetually bombarded with messages that encourage them to imbibe and medicate [themselves with] a variety of substances. We routinely alter our states of consciousness through conventional means such as alcohol, tobacco, caffeine, and prescription drugs. Fifty-one percent of Americans use alcohol regularly and nearly 35% have tried marijuana at some time in their lives.[23] Even in the context of school, today's teenagers have witnessed the Ritalinization of difficult-to-manage students.[24] In today's society, teenage drug use seems to mirror American proclivities.[25] In this context, some psychologists argue, experimentation with mind-altering substances, legal or illegal, might instead be defined as normal, given the nature of our culture.[26]

Another flaw in drug education is its assumption that drug *use* is the same as drug *abuse*. Some programs use the terms interchangeably; others utilize an exaggerated definition of use that in effect defines anything other than one-time experimentation and any use of illegal drugs as abuse. But teenagers know the difference. Most have observed their parents and other adults who use alcohol, itself a drug, without abusing it. Virtually all studies have found that the vast majority of students who try drugs do *not* become abusers.[27] Programs that blur the distinctions between use and abuse are ineffective because students' own experiences tell them the information presented to them is not believable.[28]

The "gateway" theory, a mainstay in drug education, argues that the use of marijuana leads to the use of "harder" drugs such as cocaine and heroin.[29] There is no evidence, however, that the use of one drug causes the use of another. For example, several researchers, as well as the federal government, have found that the vast majority of marijuana smokers do not progress to the use of more dangerous drugs.[30] Based on the National Institute on Drug Abuse Household Survey, Professor Lynn Zimmer and Dr. John P. Morgan calculated that for every 100 people who have tried marijuana, only one is a current user of cocaine.[31] Teenagers know from their own experience and observation that marijuana use does not inevitably, or even usually, lead to the use of harder drugs. In fact, the majority of teens who try marijuana do not even use marijuana itself on a regular basis.[32] Therefore, when such information is given, students discount both the message and the messenger.

A common belief among many educators, policymakers, and parents is that if teenagers simply understood the *dangers* of drug experimentation they would abstain.[33] In an effort to encourage abstinence, "risk" and "danger" messages are grossly exaggerated, and sometimes even completely false. Although the *Reefer Madness* messages have been replaced by assertions that we now have "scientific evidence" of the dangers of drugs, when studies are critically evaluated, few of the most common assertions (especially about marijuana) hold up.

Marijuana, the drug second only to alcohol in popularity among teens, has been routinely demonized in drug education today. Many "drug education" websites, including that of the Office of National Drug Control Policy "Project kNOw," include misinformation about marijuana's potency, its relationship to cancer, memory, the immune system, personality alteration, addiction, and sexual dysfunction.[34] In their 1997 book, *Marijuana Myths, Marijuana Facts: A Review of the Scientific Evidence,* Professors Zimmer and Morgan examined the scientific evidence relevant to each of these alleged dangers. They found, in essentially every case, that the *claims of marijuana's dangerousness did not hold up.*[35] Over the years, the same conclusions have been reached by numerous official commissions, including the La Guardia Commission in 1944, the National Commission on Marijuana and Drug Abuse in 1972, the National Academy of Sciences in 1982, and, in 1999, the Institute of Medicine.

The consistent mischaracterization of marijuana may be the Achilles' heel of conventional approaches to drug education because these false messages are inconsistent with students' *actual* observations and experience. As a result, teenagers lose confidence in what we, as parents and teachers, tell

them. They are thus less likely to turn to us as credible sources of information. As one 17-year-old girl, an 11th-grader in Fort Worth, Texas, put it, "They told my little sister that you'd get addicted to marijuana the first time, and it's not like that. You hear that, and then you do it, and you say, 'Ah, they lied to me.' "[36]

Ultimately the problem with delivering unbelievable messages, particularly about marijuana, is that students define the entire drug education exercise as a joke. But their dismissal of warnings should not be taken lightly. A frightening ramification of imparting misinformation to them is that teenagers, like the heroin addict I interviewed over two decades ago, will ignore our warnings completely and put themselves in real danger. She did not find the negative claims about marijuana credible, discounted the entire message, and tried heroin. Today's increased purity and availability of "hard drugs," coupled with teenagers' refusal to heed warnings they don't trust, have resulted in *increased* risk of fatal overdose such as those we've witnessed among the children of celebrities and in affluent communities like Plano, Texas.[37]

> **The consistent mischaracterization of marijuana may be the Achilles' heel of conventional approaches to drug education because these false messages are inconsistent with students' *actual* observations and experience.**

Another problem with government-funded drug education programs is that they are mandated simply to *prevent* drug use. After admonitions and instructions to abstain, the lessons end. There is no information on how to reduce risks, avoid problems, or prevent abuse. Abstinence is seen as the sole measure of success and the only acceptable teaching option.

While the abstinence-only mandate is well-meaning, it is misguided. According to the government's own General Accounting Office, the expectation that teenagers, at a time in their lives when they are most amenable to risk-taking, will be inoculated from experimentation with consciousness alteration is unrealistic at best.[38, 39] In fact, more than *half* of all American teenagers have tried marijuana by the time they graduate from high school, and four out of five have used alcohol.[40] The insistence on complete abstinence has meant the inevitable failure of programs that make this their primary goal.[41]

The abstinence-only mandate leaves teachers and parents with *nothing* to say to the 50% of students who say "maybe" or "sometimes" or "yes," the very teens we most need to reach. As seasoned drug education researchers Gilbert Botvin and Ken Resnicow note:

> As mandated by federal guidelines, most current substance-use prevention programs emphasize "zero tolerance" and abstinence. Although controversial, programs that include messages of responsible use, however, may be more credible, and ultimately more effective. . . . The primary goal of substance abuse prevention programs should, it could be argued, be the reduction of heavy use and abuse rather than limiting experimentation among individuals unlikely to become frequent users.[42]

Increasing numbers of educators are becoming frustrated by the abstinence-only mandate of federally funded drug education. While attending a local summit on teens and drugs, a county-funded drug educator pulled me aside and whispered that he would like to give his students (whom he knew smoked marijuana) information that might help them minimize its dangers (e.g., not to smoke and drive). But for him to admit that they might use it at all would violate the abstinence-only school policy dictated by federal funding regulations. He believed his hands were tied, and he could not really educate his students at all. This man was only one of dozens who have expressed such frustrations to me.

Safety First: A Reality-Based Alternative

A *safety-first* strategy for drug education requires *reality-based* assumptions about drug use and drug education. Whether we like it or not, many teenagers will experiment with drugs. Some will use drugs more regularly. At the same time we stress abstinence, we should also provide a fallback strategy for risk reduction, providing students with information and resources so they do the least possible harm to themselves and those around them.

We must approach alcohol and other drugs as we approach other potentially dangerous substances and activities. For instance, instead of banning automobiles, which kill far more teenagers than drugs do, we enforce traffic laws, prohibit driving while intoxicated, and insist that drivers wear seat belts. Reality-based alcohol education provides a model, with Students Against Drunk Driving (SADD), "Alive at 25," as well as many "designated driver" programs adopting a risk-reduction approach. Such "responsible use" messages are being introduced in alcohol education as an alternative to zero-tolerance.[43]

The first assumption of *safety-first* drug education is that *teenagers can make responsible decisions* if given honest, science-based drug education. Few young people are interested in destroying their lives or their health. Many already know the pitfalls, having experimented with drugs before, during, and after receiving drug education, and/or having seen [the] consequences [of drug use] in their own families and communities.

The majority of teenagers do make wise decisions about drug use. According to the 1998 Household Survey, 90% of 12–17-year-olds *refrained* from regular use.[44] In fact, studies conducted to discover the reasons why students quit using marijuana found they were motivated by health reasons and negative drug effects, *which they themselves experienced.* Thus, any form of drug education should respect and build upon teenagers abilities to reason and to learn from their own experiences.[45]

A second assumption of a *safety-first* drug education program is that *total abstinence may not be a realistic alternative for all teenagers.* Drugs have always been, and are likely to remain, a part of American culture. To proclaim a "drug-free America by the year 2008" or some other arbitrary date is pure wishful thinking. Teenagers know this, and most parents and teachers know that they know it.

Instead, a realistic perspective emphasizes safety and a reduction in drug problems rather than abstinence as the key measure of success of any program.

> **At the same time we stress abstinence, we should also provide a fallback strategy for risk reduction.**

A third assumption of *safety-first* drug education is that the *use of mind-altering substances does not necessarily constitute abuse.* The majority of drug use (with the possible exception of nicotine, which is the most addictive of all substances) does not lead to addiction or abuse. Instead, 80–90 percent of users *control* their use of psychoactive substances.[46] According to Professor Erich Goode, author of the best-selling text *Drugs in American Society:* "The truth is, as measured by harm to the user, most illicit drug users, like most drinkers of alcohol, use their drug or drugs of choice wisely non-abusively in moderation; with most, use does not escalate to abuse or compulsive use."[47]

Students who, despite our strong admonitions to abstain, use marijuana, need to understand that there is a huge difference between use and abuse, between occasional and daily use. If they persist, students need to know that they can and *must* control their use by using moderation and limiting use. It is *never* appropriate to use marijuana at school, at work, while participating in sports, or while driving. As the late Harvard psychiatrist Dr. Norman Zinberg stressed, users must recognize the complex interaction between the drug they are ingesting, their own mind-set, and the setting in which they use substances, which combine to form the context of drug use.[48] As with sexual activity and alcohol use, teenagers need to understand the importance of context in order to make wise decisions, control their use, and stay safe and healthy.

Some 'How To's' of Safety-First Drug Education

Communication is key in *safety-first* drug education. We must keep the channels of communication open, find ways to keep the conversation going, and listen, listen, listen. If we become indignant and punitive, teenagers will stop talking to us. It's that simple.

Safety-first drug education should be *age-specific* and begin in middle school, when teens are actually confronted with drugs. Courses should run continuously through high school, when most experimentation occurs, utilizing both student engagement and participation (which conventional drug education acknowledges as crucial) and reality- and science-based educational materials.

Almost any discussion of drugs captures the attention of students. Teenagers often know more than we (want to) think about drugs through experience, family and the media. We must include them, incorporating their observations and experience in any drug education curriculum if we want it to be credible.[49, 50] There must be *no negative repercussions* for their input and honesty.

Safety-first drug education affords us the opportunity to engage students in the broad study of how drugs affect the body and mind. Quality drug education may provide an introduction to physiology, including the psychopharmacology of drugs (how they work), as well as their health and psychological risks (and benefits). An exceptional text is Dr. Andrew Weil and Winifred Rosen's *From Chocolate to Morphine: Everything You Need to Know About Mind-Altering Drugs,*[51] which describes nearly every drug available to teenagers in a comprehensive but objective way. Finally, students should learn about the social context of drugs in America. Drug education courses provide an opportunity to teach history, sociology, anthropology, and political science.

Students must also understand the *legal* consequences of drug use in America. Because teens are underage, *all* drugs are illegal for them. With increasing methods of detection such as school drug testing and escalating "zero tolerance" efforts, drug education must acknowledge *illegality* as a risk factor in and of itself, extending well beyond the physical effects of drug use. There are real, lasting consequences of using drugs and being caught, including expulsion from school, denial of college loans, a criminal record, and lasting stigma.

The goals of realistic drug education, as noted, focus on safety. With such an education, students will more deeply understand the concrete risks inherent in the use of drugs. But if we are to capture and retain students' confidence, we must separate the real from the *imagined* dangers of substance use. Just as drugs can be dangerous, they can also provide users with psychological and medical benefits, which explains why use has persisted around the world since civilization began. Reality-based drug education will equip students with information they trust, the basis for making responsible decisions.

As the demand for reality-based drug education grows, programs are being developed in the United States and abroad. A listing of such programs can be found at the website of the Lindesmith Center: *www.lindesmith.org.*

Summary

Drug education has existed in America for over a century. It has utilized a variety of methods, from scare tactics to resistance techniques, in the effort to prevent young people from using drugs. Nonetheless, teenagers continue to experiment with a variety of substances. Despite the expansion of drug prevention programs, it is very difficult to know which, if any "work" better than others. The assumptions that shape conventional programs render them problematic: that drug experimentation constitutes deviance; that drug *use* is the same as drug *abuse;* that marijuana constitutes the "gateway" to "harder" substances; that exaggeration of risks will deter experimentation.

> **Reality-based drug education will equip students with information they trust, the basis for making responsible decisions.**

The main reasons many students fail to take programs seriously and continue to ex-

periment with drugs is that they have learned for themselves that America is hardly "drug-free"; there are vast differences between experimentation, abuse, and addiction; and the use of one drug does not inevitably lead to the use of others.

While youth *abstinence* is what we'd all prefer, this unrealistic goal means programs lack *risk-reduction* education for those 50% who do not "just say no." We need a fallback strategy of *safety first* in order to prevent drug *abuse* and drug *problems* among teenagers.

Educational efforts should acknowledge teens' ability to make reasoned decisions. Programs should differentiate between use and abuse, and stress the importance of moderation and context. Curricula should be age-specific, stress student participation and provide science-based, objective educational materials. In simple terms, it is our responsibility as parents and teachers to engage students and provide them with credible information so they can make responsible decisions, avoid drug abuse, and stay safe.

Notes

1. Bordin, R., *Women and Temperance: The Quest for Power and Liberty, 1873–1900,* Philadelphia: Temple University Press (1981).
2. Milgram, G. G., "A historical review of alcohol education: Research and comments," *Journal of Alcohol and Drug Education* 21:1–16 (1976).
3. Rathbone, J. L., *Tobacco, Alcohol and Narcotics,* New York: Oxford Guidance Life Pamphlets (1952).
4. Beck, J., "100 years of 'just say no' versus 'just say know': Reevaluating drug education goals for the coming century," *Evaluation Review,* 22(1):15–45 (1998).
5. Goode, E., *Drugs in American Society,* New York: McGraw-Hill (1993), p. 334. Goode also cites H. S. Resnick, *It Starts With People: Experiences in Drug Abuse Prevention,* Washington, D.C.: U.S. Department of Health, Education and Welfare (1978).
6. Baum, D., *Smoke and Mirrors: The War on Drugs and the Politics of Failure* (1981), Boston: Little Brown (1996).
7. U.S. Department of Education, *Drug Education Curricula: A Guide to Selection and Implementation,* Washington, D. C.: U.S. Government Printing Office (1981).
8. Perhaps the most thorough and informative drug education book available for high school students, *Chocolate to Morphine: Understanding Mind-Altering Drugs,* by Andrew Weil M.D. and Winifred Rosen (Boston: Houghton Mifflin), was hastily removed from drug education curricula shortly after its 1983 publication because it stressed non-abusive relationships with drugs rather than total abstinence.
9. Rosenbaum, M., *Kids, Drugs, and Drug Education: A Harm Reduction Approach,* San Francisco: National Council on Crime and Delinquency (1996).
10. For an exhaustive listing of the most popular programs, see *Making the Grade: A Guide to School Drug Prevention Programs,* Washington D.C.: Drug Strategies (1999).

11. *Making the Grade: A Guide to School Drug Prevention Programs*, Washington, D.C.: Drug Strategies (1999).

12. Dusenbury, L., Lake, A., and Falco, M., "A review of the evaluation of 47 drug abuse prevention curricula available nationally," *Journal of School Health* 67(4):127–132 (1997).

13. Skager, R., "Can science-based prevention deliver the goods in the real world?" *Prevention File* Winter: 11–14 (1998).

14. Gorman, D. M., "The irrelevance of evidence in the development of school-based drug prevention policy, 1986–1996," *Evaluation Review* 22(11):118–146 (1998).

15. Kreft, I. G. G., and Brown, J. H., eds., "Zero effects of drug prevention programs: Issues and solutions," *Evaluation Review* 22(1):3–14 (1998).

16. Wysong, S., Aniskiewicz, R., and Wright, D., "Truth and D.A.R.E.: Tracking drug education to graduation and as symbolic politics," *Social Problems* 41(3):448–472 (1994).

17. Ennett, S. T., Tobler, N. S., Ringwalt, C. L., and Flewelling, R., "How effective is drug abuse resistance education? A meta-analysis of project D.A.R.E. outcome evaluations," *American Journal of Public Health* 84(9):1394–1401 (1994).

18. Lynam, D. R., et al., "Project D.A.R.E.: No effects at 10-year follow-up," *Journal of Consulting and Clinical Psychology* 76(4):590–593 (1999).

19. Tobler, N. S., and Stratton, H. H., "Effectiveness of school-based drug prevention programs: A meta-analysis of the research," *The Journal of Primary Prevention* 18(1):71–128 (1997); Dukes, R. L., Ullman, J. B., and Stein, J. A., "A three-year follow-up of Drug Abuse Resistance Education (D.A.R.E.)," *Evaluation Review* 20:49–66 (1996); Clayton, R. R., Cattarello, A. M., and Johnstone, B. M., "The effectiveness of drug abuse resistance education (Project D.A.R.E): 5-year follow-up results," *Preventive Medicine* 25:307–318 (1996); Rosenbaum, D. P., and Hanson, G. S., *Assessing the Effects of School-Based Drug Education: A Six-Year Multi-Level Analysis of Project D.A.R.E.* Chicago, Department of Criminal Justice and Center for Research in Law and Justice, University of Illinois (1998).

20. Wysong, E., Aniskiewicz, R., and Wright, D., "Truth and D.A.R.E.: Tracking drug education to graduation and as symbolic politics," *Social Problems* 41(3):448–472 (1994).

21. Brown, J. H., D'Emidio-Caston, M., and Pollard, J., "Students and substances: Social power in drug education," *Educational Evaluation and Policy Analysis* 19:65–82 (1997).

22. Brown, J. H., "Listen to the kids," *American School Board Journal* 184:38–47 (1997).

23. SAMHSA, Office of Applied Studies, *National Household Survey on Drug Abuse: Main Findings 1998*, Washington, D.C.: National Clearinghouse for Alcohol and Drug Information (1999).

24. Knickerbocker, B., "Using drugs to rein in boys," *The Christian Science Monitor*, May 19 (1999).

25. For an excellent discussion of the role of drugs in American culture, see C. Reinarman and H. G. Levine, "The cultural contradictions of punitive prohibition," in Reinarman, C., and Levine, H. G., eds., *Crack in America: Demon Drugs and Social Justice*, Berkeley: University of California Press (1997).

26. Newcomb, M., and Bentler, P., *Consequences of Adolescent Drug Use: Impact on the Lives of Young Adults*, Newbury Park, CA: Sage (1988); Shedler, J., and Block, J., "Adolescent drug use and psychological health: A longitudinal inquiry," *American Psychologist* 45:612–630 (1990).

27. Brown, J. H., and Horowitz, J. E., "Deviance and deviants: Why adolescent substance use prevention programs do not work," *Evaluation Review* 17(5):529–555 (1993); Zimmer, L., and Morgan, J. P., *Exposing Marijuana Myths: A Review of the Scientific Evidence*, New York: Open Society Institute (1995).

28. Duncan, D. F., "Problems associated with three commonly used drugs: A survey of rural secondary school students," *Psychology of Addictive Behavior* 5(2):93–96 (1991); United States General Accounting Office, *Drug Use Among Youth:*

No Simple Answers to Guide Prevention, Washington, D.C.: U.S. General Accounting Office (1993).

29. Kandel, D., "Stages in adolescent involvement in drug use," *Science* 190:912–914 (1975); Gabany, S. G., and Plummer, P., "The marijuana perception inventory: The effects of substance abuse instruction," *Journal of Drug Education* 20(3):235–245 (1990).

30. Zimmer, L., and Morgan, J. P., *Marijuana Myths, Marijuana Facts: A Review of the Scientific Evidence*, New York: The Lindesmith Center (1997); Brown, J. H., and Horowitz, J. D., "Deviance and deviants: Why adolescent substance use prevention programs do not work," *Evaluation Review* 17(5):529–555 (1993); SAMHSA, Office of Applied Studies, *National Household Survey on Drug Abuse: Main Findings 1998*, Washington, D.C.: National Clearinghouse for Alcohol and Drug Information (1999).

31. Zimmer, L., and Morgan, J. P., *Marijuana Myths, Marijuana Facts: A Review of the Scientific Evidence*, New York: The Lindesmith Center (1997).

32. SAMHSA, Office of Applied Studies, *National Household Survey on Drug Abuse: Main Findings 1998*, Washington, D.C.: National Clearinghouse for Alcohol and Drug Information (1999).

33. Bachman, J. G., Johnston, L. D., and O'Malley, P. M., "Explaining the recent decline in cocaine use among young adults: Further evidence that perceived risks and disapproval lead to reduced drug use," *Journal of Health and Human Social Behavior* 31(2)1:173–184 (1990).

34. Office of National Drug Control Policy, http://www.projectknow.com (1999).

35. Zimmer, L., and Morgan, J. P., *Marijuana Myths, Marijuana Facts: A Review of the Scientific Evidence*, New York: The Lindesmith Center (1997).

36. Taylor, M., and Berard, Y., "Anti-drug programs face overhaul," *Ft. Worth Star Telegram*, November 1, 1998.

37. Gray, M., "Texas Heroin Massacre," *Rolling Stone*, May 27, 1999.

38. United States General Accounting Office, *Drug Use Among Youth: No Simple Answers to Guide Prevention*, Washington, D.C.: U.S. General Accounting Office (1993).

39. For an excellent discussion of teenagers and risk, see Ponton, L., *The Romance of Risk: Why Teenagers Do the Things They Do*, New York: Basic Books (1997).

40. SAMHSA, Office of Applied Studies, *National Household Survey on Drug Abuse: Main Findings 1998*, Washington, D.C.: National Clearinghouse for Alcohol and Drug Information (1999).

41. Ching, C. L., "The goal of abstinence: Implications for drug education," *Journal of Drug Education* 11(1):13–18 (1981).

42. Botvin, G., and Resnicow, K., "School-based substance use prevention programs: Why do effects decay?" *Preventive Medicine* 22(4):484–490 (1993).

43. Oldenberg, D., "Kids and alcohol: A controversial alternative to 'Just Say No,' " *Washington Post*, March 10, 1998; Milgram, G. G., "Responsible decision making regarding alcohol: A re-emerging prevention/education strategy for the 1990s," *Journal of Drug Education* 26(4):357–365 (1996).

44. SAMHSA, Office of Applied Studies, *National Household Survey on Drug Abuse: Main Findings 1998*, Washington, D.C.: National Clearinghouse for Alcohol and Drug Information (1999).

45. Martin, C. E., Duncan, D. F., and Zunich, E. M., "Students' motives for discontinuing illicit drug taking," *Health Values: Achieving High Level Wellness* 7(5):8–11 (1983); Skager, R., and Austin, G., *Sixth Biennial California Student Substance Use Survey*, Sacramento: Office of the Attorney General, State of California (1998).

46. Nicholson, T., "The primary prevention of illicit drug problems: An argument for decriminalization and legalization," *The Journal of Primary Prevention* 12(4):275–288 (1992); Winick, C., "Social Behavior, Public Policy and Nonharmful Drug Use," *The Milbank Quarterly* 69(3):437–457 (1991).

47. Goode, E., *Drugs in American Society*, New York: McGraw-Hill (1993), p. 335.

48. Zinberg, N., *Drug, Set, and Setting: The Basis for Controlled Intoxicant Use*, New Haven: Yale University Press (1984).

49. Martin, C. E., Duncan, D. F., and Zunich, E. M., "Students' motives for discontinuing illicit drug taking," *Health Values: Achieving High Level Wellness* 7(5):8–11 (1983).

50. For an excellent discussion of peer education see Cohen, J., "Achieving a reduction in drug-related harm through education," in Nick Heather, Alex Wodak, Ethan A. Nadelmann, and Pat O'Hare, eds., *Psychoactive Drugs and Harm Reduction: From Faith to Science*, London: Whurr (1993); and for confluent education see Brown, J. H., and Horowitz, J. E., "Deviance and deviants: Why adolescent substance use prevention programs do not work," *Evaluation Review* 17(5):529–555 (1993).

51. Weil, A., and Rosen, W., *From Chocolate to Morphine: Everything You Need to Know About Mind-Altering Drugs*, Boston: Houghton Mifflin (1993).

For Discussion

What type of role models, if any, might we utilize in a reality-based educational approach?

41

Commonsense Drug Policy

Ethan A. Nadelmann

Ethan Nadelmann argues that current drug policy is misguided. He criticizes supply reduction strategies and notes that consumption rates would likely continue even if we were able to reduce or eliminate the supply of drugs from other countries. Harm reduction strategies that have been implemented in various European countries are described, in contrast to strategies used in the United States. For example, methadone maintenance is available in the United States, but its use is more strictly controlled than in other countries. Nadelmann also describes the results from Swiss and other European studies that have examined the effects of prescribing heroin for addicted individuals. Those results and other harm reduction strategies implemented elsewhere show great promise and should be used to guide and modify U.S. drug policy.

First, Reduce Harm

In 1988 Congress passed a resolution proclaiming its goal of "a drug-free America by 1995." U.S. drug policy has failed persistently over the decades because it has preferred such rhetoric to reality and moralism to pragmatism. Politicians confess their youthful indiscretions, then call for tougher drug laws. Drug control officials make assertions with no basis in fact or science. Police officers, generals, politicians, and guardians of public morals qualify as drug czars—but not, to date, a single doctor or public health figure. Independent commissions are appointed to evaluate drug policies, only to see their recommendations ignored as politically risky. And drug policies are designed, implemented, and enforced with virtually no input from the millions of Americans they affect most: drug users. Drug abuse is a seri-ous problem, both for individual citizens and society at large, but the "war on drugs" has made matters worse, not better.

Drug warriors often point to the 1980s as a time in which the drug war really worked. Illicit drug use by teenagers peaked around 1980, then fell more than 50 percent over the next 12 years. During the 1996 presidential campaign, Republican challenger Bob Dole made much of the recent rise in teenagers' use of illicit drugs, contrasting it with the sharp drop during the Reagan and Bush administrations. President Clinton's response was tepid, in part because he accepted the notion that teen drug use is the principal measure of a drug policy's success or failure; at best, he could point out that the level was still barely half what it had been in 1980.

In 1980, however, no one had ever heard of the cheap, smokeable form of cocaine called crack, or drug-related HIV infection or AIDS. By the 1990s, both had reached epidemic proportions in American cities, largely driven by prohibitionist economics and morals indifferent to the human consequences of the drug war. In 1980, the federal budget for drug control was about $1 billion, and state and local budgets were perhaps two or three times that. By 1997, the federal drug control budget had ballooned to $16 billion, two-thirds of it for law enforcement agencies, and state and local funding to at least that. On any day in 1980, approximately 50,000 people were behind bars for violating a drug law. By 1997, the number had increased eightfold, to about 400,000. These are the results of a drug policy over reliant on criminal justice "solutions," ideologically wedded to abstinence-only treatment, and insulated from cost-benefit analysis.

Imagine instead a policy that starts by acknowledging that drugs are here to stay, and that we have no choice but to learn how to live with them so that they cause the least possible harm. Imagine a policy that focuses on reducing not illicit drug use per se but the crime and misery caused by both drug abuse and prohibitionist policies. And imagine a drug policy based not on the fear, prejudice, and ignorance that drive America's current approach but rather on common sense, science, public health concerns, and human rights. Such a policy is possible in the United

States, especially if Americans are willing to learn from the experiences of other countries where such policies are emerging.

Attitudes Abroad

Americans are not averse to looking abroad for solutions to the nation's drug problems. Unfortunately, they have been looking in the wrong places: Asia and Latin America, where much of the world's heroin and cocaine originates. Decades of U.S. efforts to keep drugs from being produced abroad and exported to American markets have failed. Illicit drug production is bigger business than ever before. The opium poppy, source of morphine and heroin, and *cannabis sativa*, from which marijuana and hashish are prepared, grow readily around the world; the coca plant, from whose leaves cocaine is extracted, can be cultivated far from its native environment in the Andes. Crop substitution programs designed to persuade Third World peasants to grow legal crops cannot compete with the profits that drug prohibition makes inevitable. Crop eradication campaigns occasionally reduce production in one country, but new suppliers pop up elsewhere. International law enforcement efforts can disrupt drug trafficking organizations and routes, but they rarely have much impact on U.S. drug markets.

> **Drug policy should reduce the damage to users and the society around them.**

Even if foreign supplies could be cut off, the drug abuse problem in the United States would scarcely abate. Most of America's drug-related problems are associated with domestically produced alcohol and tobacco. Much if not most of the marijuana, amphetamine, hallucinogens, and illicitly diverted pharmaceutical drugs consumed in the country are made in the United States. The same is true of the glue, gasoline, and other solvents used by kids too young or too poor to obtain other psychoactive substances. No doubt such drugs, as well as new products, would quickly substitute for imported heroin and cocaine if the flow from abroad dried up.

While looking to Latin America and Asia for supply-reduction solutions to America's drug problems is futile, the harm-reduction approaches spreading throughout Europe and Australia and even into corners of North America show promise. These approaches start by acknowledging that supply-reduction initiatives are inherently limited, that criminal justice responses can be costly and counterproductive, and that single-minded pursuit of a "drug-free society" is dangerously quixotic. Demand-reduction efforts to prevent drug abuse among children and adults are important, but so are harm-reduction efforts to lessen the damage to those unable or unwilling to stop using drugs immediately, and to those around them.

Most proponents of harm reduction do not favor legalization. They recognize that prohibition has failed to curtail drug abuse, that it is responsible for much of the crime, corruption, disease, and death associated with drugs, and that its costs mount every year. But they also see legalization as politically unwise and as risking increased drug use. The challenge is thus making drug prohibition work better, but with a focus on reducing the negative consequences of both drug use and prohibitionist policies.

Countries that have turned to harm-reduction strategies for help in alleviating their drug woes are not so different from the United States. Drugs, crime, and race problems, and other socioeconomic problems, are inextricably linked. As in America, criminal justice authorities still prosecute and imprison major drug traffickers as well as petty dealers who create public nuisances. Parents worry that their children might get involved with drugs. Politicians remain fond of drug war rhetoric. But by contrast with U.S. drug policy, public health goals have priority, and public health authorities have substantial influence. Doctors have far more latitude in treating addiction and associated problems. Police view the sale and use of illicit drugs as similar to prostitution—vice activities that cannot be stamped out but can be effectively regulated. Moralists focus less on any inherent evils of drugs than on the need to deal with drug use and addiction pragmatically and humanely. And more politicians dare to speak out in favor of alternatives to punitive prohibitionist policies.

Harm-reduction innovations include efforts to stem the spread of HIV by making sterile syringes readily available and collecting used syringes; allowing doctors to prescribe oral methadone for heroin addiction treatment, as well as heroin and other drugs for addicts who would otherwise buy them on the black market; establishing "safe injection rooms" so addicts do not congregate in public places or dangerous "shooting galleries"; employing drug analysis units at the large dance parties called raves to test the quality and potency of MDMA, known as Ecstasy, and other drugs that patrons buy and consume there; decriminalizing (but not legalizing) possession and retail sale of cannabis and, in some cases, possession of small amounts of "hard" drugs; and integrating harm-reduction policies and principles into community policing strategies. Some of these measures are under way or under consideration in parts of the United States, but rarely to the extent found in growing numbers of foreign countries.

Stopping HIV With Sterile Syringes

The spread of HIV, the virus that causes AIDS, among people who inject drugs illegally was what prompted governments in Europe and Australia to experiment with harm-reduction policies. During the early 1980s public health officials realized that infected users were spreading HIV by sharing needles. Having already experienced a hepatitis epidemic attributed to the same mode of transmission, the Dutch were the first to tell drug users about the risks of needle sharing and to make sterile syringes available and collect dirty needles through pharmacies, needle exchange and methadone programs, and public health services. Governments elsewhere in Europe and in Australia soon followed suit. The few countries in which a prescription was necessary to obtain a syringe dropped the requirement. Local authorities in Germany, Switzerland, and other European countries authorized needle exchange machines to ensure 24-hour access. In some European cities, addicts can exchange used syringes for clean ones at local police stations without fear of prosecution or harassment. Prisons are instituting similar policies to help discourage the spread of HIV among inmates, recognizing that illegal drug injecting cannot be eliminated even behind bars.

These initiatives were not adopted without controversy. Conservative politicians argued that needle-exchange programs condoned illicit and immoral behavior and that government policies should focus on punishing drug users or making them drug-free. But by the late 1980s, the consensus in most of Western Europe, Oceania, and Canada was that while drug abuse was a serious problem, AIDS was worse. Slowing the spread of a fatal disease for which no cure exists was the greater moral imperative. There was also a fiscal imperative. Needle-exchange programs' costs are minuscule compared with those of treating people who would otherwise become infected with HIV. Only in the United States has this logic not prevailed, even though AIDS was the leading killer of Americans ages 25 to 44 for most of the 1990s and is now Number Two. The Centers for Disease Control (CDC) estimates that half of new HIV infections in the country stem from injection drug use. Yet both the White House and Congress block allocation of AIDS or drug-abuse prevention funds for needle exchange, and virtually all state governments retain drug paraphernalia laws, pharmacy regulations, and other restrictions on access to sterile syringes. During the 1980s, AIDS activists engaging in civil disobedience set up more syringe exchange programs than state and local governments. There are now more than 100 such programs in 28 states, Washington, D.C., and Puerto Rico, but they reach only an estimated 10 percent of injection drug users.

> **Prejudice and political cowardice are poor excuses for allowing AIDS to spread.**

Governments at all levels in the United States refuse to fund needle exchange for political reasons, even though dozens of scientific studies, domestic and foreign, have found that needle exchange and other distribution programs reduce needle sharing, bring hard-to-reach drug users into contact with health care systems, and inform addicts about treatment programs, yet do not increase illegal drug use. In 1991 the National AIDS Commission appointed by President George Bush called the lack of federal support for such programs "bewildering and tragic." In 1993 a CDC-sponsored review of research on needle exchange recommended federal funding, but top officials in the Clinton administration suppressed a favorable evaluation of the report within the Department of Health and Human Services. In July 1996 President Clinton's Advisory Council on HIV/AIDS criticized the administration for its failure to heed the National Academy of Sciences' recommendation that it authorize the use of federal money to support needle-exchange programs. An independent panel convened by the National Institute of Health reached the same conclusion in February 1997. Last summer, the American Medical Association, the American Bar Association, and even the politicized U.S. Conference of Mayors endorsed the concept of needle exchange. In the fall, an endorsement followed from the World Bank.

To date, America's failure in this regard is conservatively estimated to have resulted in the infection of up to 10,000 people with HIV. Mounting scientific evidence and the stark reality of the continuing AIDS crisis have convinced the public, if not politicians, that needle exchange saves lives; polls consistently find that a majority of Americans support needle exchange, with approval highest among those most familiar with the notion. Prejudice and political cowardice are poor excuses for allowing more citizens to suffer from and die of AIDS, especially when effective interventions are cheap, safe, and easy.

Methadone and Other Alternatives

The United States pioneered the use of the synthetic opiate methadone to treat heroin addiction in the 1960s and 1970s, but now lags behind much of Europe and Australia in making methadone accessible and effective.

Methadone is the best available treatment in terms of reducing illicit heroin use and associated crime, disease, and death. In the early 1990s the National Academy of Sciences' Institute of Medicine stated that of all forms of drug treatment, "methadone maintenance has been the most rigorously studied modality and has yielded the most incontrovertibly positive results. . . . Consumption of all illicit drugs, especially heroin, declines. Crime is reduced, fewer individuals become HIV positive, and individual functioning is improved." However, the institute went on to declare, "Current policy . . . puts too much emphasis on protecting society from methadone, and not enough on protecting society from the epidemics of addiction, violence, and infectious diseases that methadone can help reduce."

Methadone is to street heroin what nicotine skin patches and chewing gum are to cigarettes—with the added benefit of legality. Taken orally, methadone has little of injected heroin's effect on mood or cognition. It can be consumed for decades with few if any negative health consequences, and its purity and concentration, unlike street heroin's, are assured. Like other opiates, it can create physical dependence if taken regularly, but the "addiction" is more like a diabetic's "addiction" to insulin than a heroin addict's to product bought on the street. Methadone patients can and do drive safely, hold good jobs, and care for their children. When prescribed adequate doses, they can be indistinguishable from people who have never used heroin or methadone.

Popular misconceptions and prejudice, however, have all but prevented any expansion of methadone treatment in the United States. The 115,000 Americans receiving methadone today represent only a small increase over the number 20 years ago. For every ten heroin addicts, there are only one or two methadone treatment slots. Methadone is the most tightly controlled drug in the pharmacopoeia, subject to unique federal and state restrictions. Doctors cannot prescribe it for addiction treatment outside designated programs. Regulations dictate not only security, documentation, and staffing requirements but maximum doses, admission criteria, time spent in the program, and a host of other specifics, none of which has much to do with quality of treatment. Moreover, the regulations do not prevent poor treatment; many clinics provide insufficient doses, prematurely detoxify clients, expel clients for offensive behavior, and engage in other practices that would be regarded as unethical in any other field of medicine. Attempts to open new clinics tend to be blocked by residents who don't want addicts in their neighborhood.

In much of Europe and Australia, methadone treatment was at first even more controversial than in the United States; some countries, including Germany, France, and Greece, prohibited it well into the 1980s and 1990s. But where methadone has been accepted, doctors have substantial latitude in deciding how and when to prescribe it so as to maximize its efficacy. There are methadone treatment programs for addicts looking for rehabilitation and programs for those simply trying to reduce their heroin consumption. Doctors in regular medical practice can prescribe the drug, and patients fill their prescriptions at local pharmacies. Thousands of general practitioners throughout Europe, Australia, New Zealand, and Canada (notably in Ontario and British Columbia) are now involved in methadone maintenance. In Belgium, Germany, and Australia this is the principal means of distribution. Integrating methadone with mainstream medicine makes treatment more accessible, improves its quality, and allocates ancillary services more efficiently. It also helps reduce the stigma of methadone programs and community resistance to them.

Many factors prevent American doctors from experimenting with the more flexible treatment programs of their European counterparts. The Drug Enforcement Administration contends that looser regulations would fuel the illicit market in diverted methadone. But the black market, in which virtually all buyers are heroin addicts who cannot or will not enroll in methadone programs, is primarily a product of the inadequate legal availability of methadone. Some conventional providers do not want to cede their near-monopoly over methadone treatment and are reluctant to take on addicts

who can't or won't commit to quitting heroin. And all efforts to make methadone more available in the United States run up against the many Americans who dismiss methadone treatment as substituting one addictive drug for another and are wary of any treatment that does not leave the patient "drug free."

Oral methadone works best for hundreds of thousands of heroin addicts, but some fare better with other opiate substitutes. In England, doctors prescribe injectable methadone for about 10 percent of recovering patients, who may like the modest "rush" upon injection or the ritual of injecting. Doctors in Austria, Switzerland, and Australia are experimenting with prescribing oral morphine to determine whether it works better than oral methadone for some users. Several treatment programs in the Netherlands have conducted trials with oral morphine and palfium. In Germany, where methadone treatment was initially shunned, thousands of addicts have been maintained on codeine, which many doctors and patients still prefer to methadone. The same is true of buprenorphine in France.

In England, doctors have broad discretion to prescribe whatever drugs help addicted patients manage their lives and stay away from illegal drugs and their dealers. Beginning in the 1920s, thousands of English addicts were maintained on legal prescriptions of heroin, morphine, amphetamine, cocaine, and other pharmaceutical drugs. This tradition flourished until the 1960s, and has reemerged in response to AIDS and to growing disappointment with the Americanization of British prescribing practices during the 1970s and 1980s, when illicit heroin use in Britain increased almost tenfold. Doctors in other European countries and Australia are also trying heroin prescription.

The Swiss government began a nationwide trial in 1994 to determine whether prescribing heroin, morphine, or injectable methadone could reduce crime, disease, and other drug-related ills. Some 1,000 volunteers—only heroin addicts with at least two unsuccessful experiences in methadone or other conventional treatment programs were considered—took part in the experiment. The trial quickly determined that virtually all participants preferred heroin, and doctors subsequently prescribed it for them. Last July the government reported the results so far: Criminal offenses and the number of criminal offenders dropped 60 percent, the percentage of income from illegal and semilegal activities fell from 69 to 10 percent, illegal heroin *and* cocaine use declined dramatically (although use of alcohol, cannabis, and tranquilizers like Valium remained fairly constant), stable employment increased from 14 to 32 percent, physical health improved enormously, and most participants greatly reduced their contact with the drug scene. There were no deaths from overdoses, and no prescribed drugs were diverted to the black market. More than half those who dropped out of the study switched to another form of drug treatment, including 83 who began abstinence therapy. A cost-benefit analysis of the program found a net economic benefit of $30 per patient per day, mostly because of reduced criminal justice and health care costs.

The Swiss study has undermined several myths about heroin and its habitual users. The results to date demonstrate that, given relatively unlimited availability, heroin users will voluntarily stabilize or reduce their dosage, and some will even choose abstinence; that long-addicted users can lead relatively normal, stable lives if provided legal access to their drug of choice; and that ordinary citizens will support such initiatives. In recent referendums in Zurich, Basel, and Zug, substantial majorities voted to continue funding local arms of the experiment. And last September, a nationwide referendum to end the government's heroin maintenance and other harm-reduction initiatives was rejected by 71 percent of Swiss voters, including majorities in all 26 cantons.

The Netherlands plans its own heroin prescription study in 1998, and similar trials are under consideration elsewhere in Europe, including Luxembourg and Spain, as well as Canada. In Germany, the federal government has opposed heroin prescription trials and other harm-reduction innovations, but the League of Cities has petitioned it for permission to undertake them; a survey early last year found that police chiefs in 10 of the country's 12 largest cities favored letting states implement controlled heroin distribution programs. In Australia last summer, a majority of state health ministers approved a heroin prescription trial, but Prime Minister John Howard blocked it. And in Denmark, a September 1996 poll found that 66 percent of voters supported an experiment that would provide registered addicts with free heroin to be consumed in centers set up for the purpose.

Switzerland, attempting to reduce overdoses, dangerous injecting practices, and shooting up in public places, has also taken the lead in establishing "safe injection rooms," where users can inject their drugs under secure, sanitary conditions. There are now about a dozen such rooms in the country, and initial evaluations are positive. In Germany, Frankfurt has set up three, and there are also officially sanctioned facilities in Hamburg and Saarbrücken. Cities elsewhere in Europe and in Australia are expected to open safe injection rooms soon.

Reefer Sanity

Cannabis, in the form of marijuana and hashish, is by far the most popular illicit drug in the United States. More than a quarter of Americans admit to having tried it. Marijuana's popularity peaked in 1980, dropped steadily until the early 1990s, and is now on the rise again. Although it is not entirely safe, especially when consumed by children, smoked heavily, or used when driving, it is clearly among the least dangerous psychoactive drugs in common use. In 1988 the administrative law judge for the Drug Enforcement Administration, Francis Young, reviewed the evidence and concluded that "marihuana, in its natural form, is one of the safest therapeutically active substances known to man."

As with needle exchange and methadone treatment, American politicians have ignored or spurned the findings of government commissions and scientific organizations concerning marijuana policy. In 1972 the National Commission on Marihuana and Drug Abuse—created by President Nixon and chaired by a former Republican governor, Raymond Shafer—recommended that possession of up to one ounce of marijuana be decriminalized. Nixon rejected the recommendation. In 1982 a panel appointed by the National Academy of Sciences reached the same conclusion as the Shafer Commission.

Between 1973 and 1978, with attitudes changing, 11 states approved decriminalization statutes that reclassified marijuana possession as a misdemeanor, petty offense, or civil violation punishable by no more than a $100 fine. Consumption trends in those states and in states that retained stricter sanctions were indistinguishable. A 1988 scholarly evaluation of the Moscone Act, California's 1976 decriminalization law, estimated that the state had saved half a billion dollars in arrest costs since the law's passage. Nonetheless, public opinion began to shift in 1978. No other states decriminalized marijuana, and some eventually recriminalized it.

Between 1973 and 1989, annual arrests on marijuana charges by state and local police ranged between 360,000 and 460,000. The annual total fell to 283,700 in 1991, but has since more than doubled. In 1996, 641,642 people were arrested for marijuana, 85 percent of them for possession, not sale, of the drug. Prompted by concern over rising marijuana use among adolescents and fears of being labeled soft on drugs, the Clinton administration launched its own anti-marijuana campaign in 1995. But the administration's claims to have identified new risks of marijuana consumption—including a purported link between marijuana and violent behavior—have not withstood scrutiny.[1] Neither Congress nor the White House seems likely to put the issue of marijuana policy before a truly independent advisory commission, given the consistency with which such commissions have reached politically unacceptable conclusions.

In contrast, governments in Europe and Australia, notably in the Netherlands, have reconsidered their cannabis policies. In 1976 the Baan Commission in the Netherlands recommended, and the Dutch government adopted, a policy of separating the "soft" and "hard" drug markets. Criminal penalties for and police efforts against heroin trafficking were increased, while those

against cannabis were relaxed. Marijuana and hashish can now be bought in hundreds of "coffee shops" throughout the country. Advertising, open displays, and sales to minors are prohibited. Police quickly close coffee shops caught selling hard drugs. Almost no one is arrested or even fined for cannabis possession, and the government collects taxes on the gray market sales.

In the Netherlands today, cannabis consumption for most age groups is similar to that in the United States. Young Dutch teenagers, however, are less likely to sample marijuana than their American peers; from 1992 to 1994, only 7.2 percent of Dutch youths between the ages of 12 and 15 reported having tried marijuana, compared to 13.5 percent of Americans in that age bracket. Far fewer Dutch youths, moreover, experiment with cocaine, buttressing officials' claims of success in separating the markets for hard and soft drugs. Most Dutch parents regard the "reefer madness" anti-marijuana campaigns of the United States as silly.

Dutch coffee shops have not been problem free. Many citizens have complained about the proliferation of coffee shops, as well as nuisances created by foreign youth flocking to party in Dutch border cities. Organized crime involvement in the growing domestic cannabis industry is of increasing concern. The Dutch government's efforts to address the problem by more openly and systematically regulating supplies to coffee shops, along with some of its other drug policy initiatives, have run up against pressure from abroad, notably from Paris, Stockholm, Bonn, and Washington. In late 1995 French President Jacques Chirac began publicly berating The Hague for its drug policies, even threatening to suspend implementation of the Schengen Agreement allowing the free movement of people across borders of European Union (EU) countries. Some of Chirac's political allies called the Netherlands a narco-state. Dutch officials responded with evidence of the relative success of their policies, while pointing out that most cannabis seized in France originates in Morocco (which Chirac has refrained from criticizing because of his government's close relations with King Hassan). The Hague, however, did announce reductions in the number of coffee shops and the amount of cannabis customers can buy there. But it still sanctions the coffee shops, and a few municipalities actually operate them.

Notwithstanding the attacks, in the 1990s the trend toward decriminalization of cannabis has accelerated in Europe. Across much of Western Europe, possession and even minor sales of the drug are effectively decriminalized. Spain decriminalized private use of cannabis in 1983. In Germany, the Federal Constitutional Court effectively sanctioned a cautious liberalization of cannabis policy in a widely publicized 1994 decision. German states vary considerably in their attitude; some, like Bavaria, persist in a highly punitive policy, but most now favor the Dutch approach. So far the Kohl administration has refused to approve state proposals to legalize and regulate cannabis sales, but it appears aware of the rising support in the country for Dutch and Swiss approaches to local drug problems.

In June 1996 Luxembourg's parliament voted to decriminalize cannabis and push for standardization of drug laws in the Benelux countries. The Belgian government is now considering a more modest decriminalization of cannabis combined with tougher measures against organized crime and heroin traffickers. In Australia, cannabis has been decriminalized in South Australia, the Australian Capital Territory (Canberra), and the Northern Territory, and other states are considering the step. Even in France, Chirac's outburst followed recommendations of cannabis decriminalization by three distinguished national commissions. Chirac must now contend with a new prime minister, Lionel Jospin, who declared himself in favor of decriminalization before his Socialist Party won the 1997 parliamentary elections. Public opinion is clearly shifting. A recent poll found that 51 percent of Canadians favor decriminalizing marijuana.

Will It Work?

Both at home and abroad, the U.S. government has attempted to block resolutions supporting harm reduction, suppress scientific studies that reached politically inconvenient conclusions, and silence critics of official drug policy. In May 1994 the State Department forced the last-minute cancellation of a World Bank conference on drug trafficking to which critics of U.S. drug policy had been invited. That December the U.S. delegation to an international meeting of the U.N. Drug Control Program refused to sign any statement incorporating the phrase "harm reduction." In early 1995 the State Department successfully pressured the World Health Organization to scuttle the release of a report it had commissioned from a panel that included many of the world's leading experts on cocaine because it included the scientifically incontrovertible observations that traditional use of coca leaf in the Andes causes little harm to users and that most consumers of cocaine use the drug in moderation with few detrimental effects. Hundreds of congressional hearings have addressed multitudinous aspects of the drug problem, but few have inquired into the European harm-reduction policies described above. When former Secretary of State George Shultz, then–Surgeon General M. Joycelyn Elders, and Baltimore Mayor Kurt Schmoke pointed to the failure of current policies and called for new approaches, they were mocked, fired, and ignored, respectively—and thereafter mischaracterized as advocating the outright legalization of drugs.

In Europe, in contrast, informed, public debate about drug policy is increasingly common in government, even at the EU level. In June 1995 the European Parliament issued a report acknowledging that "there will always be a demand for drugs in our societies . . . the policies followed so far have not been able to prevent the illegal drug trade from flourishing." The EU called for serious consideration of the Frankfurt Resolution, a statement of harm-reduction principles supported by a transnational coalition of 31 cities and regions. In October 1996 Emma Bonino, the European commissioner for consumer policy, advocated decriminalizing soft drugs and initiating a broad prescription program for hard drugs. Greece's minister for European affairs, George Papandreou, seconded her. Last February the monarch of Liechtenstein, Prince Hans Adam, spoke out in favor of controlled drug legalization. Even Raymond Kendall, secretary general of Interpol, was quoted in the August 20, 1994, *Guardian* as saying, "The prosecution of thousands of otherwise law-abiding citizens every year is both hypocritical and an affront to individual, civil and human rights. . . . Drug use should no longer be a criminal offense. I am totally against legalization, but in favor of decriminalization for the user."

One can, of course, exaggerate the differences between attitudes in the United States and those in Europe and Australia. Many European leaders still echo Chirac's U.S.-style antidrug pronouncements. Most capital cities endorse the Stockholm Resolution, a statement backing punitive prohibitionist policies that was drafted in response to the Frankfurt Resolution. And the Dutch have had to struggle against French and other efforts to standardize more punitive drug laws and policies within the EU.

Conversely, support for harm-reduction approaches is growing in the United States, notably and vocally among public health professionals but also, more discreetly, among urban politicians and police officials. Some of the world's most innovative needle exchange and other harm-reduction programs can be found in America. The 1996 victories at the polls for California's Proposition 215, which legalizes the medicinal use of marijuana, and Arizona's Proposition 200, which allows doctors to prescribe any drug they deem appropriate and mandates treatment rather than jail for those arrested for possession, suggest that Americans are more receptive to drug policy reform than politicians acknowledge.

But Europe and Australia are generally ahead of the United States in their willingness to discuss openly and experiment pragmatically with alternative policies that might reduce the harm to both addicts and society. Public health officials in many European cities work closely with police, politicians, private physicians, and others to coordinate efforts. Community policing treats drug dealers and users as elements of the community that need not be expelled but can be

made less troublesome. Such efforts, including crackdowns on open drug scenes in Zurich, Bern, and Frankfurt, are devised and implemented in tandem with initiatives to address health and housing problems. In the United States, in contrast, politicians presented with new approaches do not ask, "Will they work?" but only, "Are they tough enough?" Many legislators are reluctant to support drug treatment programs that are not punitive, coercive, and prison-based, and many criminal justice officials still view prison as a quick and easy solution for drug problems.

Lessons from Europe and Australia are compelling. Drug control policies should focus on reducing drug-related crime, disease, and death, not the number of casual drug users. Stopping the spread of HIV by and among drug users by making sterile syringes and methadone readily available must be the first priority. American politicians need to explore, not ignore or automatically condemn, promising policy options such as cannabis decriminalization, heroin prescription, and the integration of harm-reduction principles into community policing strategies. Central governments must back, or at least not hinder, the efforts of municipal officials and citizens to devise pragmatic approaches to local drug problems. Like citizens in Europe, the American public has supported such innovations when they are adequately explained and allowed to prove themselves. As the evidence comes in, what works is increasingly apparent. All that remains is mustering the political courage.

Note

1. Lynn Zimmer and John P. Morgan. (1997) *Marijuana Myths, Marijuana Facts: A Review of the Scientific Evidence.* New York: Lindesmith Center.

For Discussion

Why has the United States traditionally been so resistant to harm reduction strategies?

Reprinted from: Ethan A. Nadelmann, "Commonsense Drug Policy." In *Foreign Affairs* 77(1), pp. 111–126. Reprinted by permission of *Foreign Affairs*. Copyright © 1998 by the Council on Foreign Relations, Inc. ✦

42

Why Can't We Make Prohibition Work Better?

Some Consequences of Ignoring the Unattractive

Peter Reuter

In this chapter, Peter Reuter describes the huge costs and punitiveness of U.S. drug policies. Government initiatives to reduce the supply of drugs have failed to produce an increase in the price of drugs—in fact, Reuter observes that street prices for most drugs have declined since the most recent War on Drugs. Moreover, perceptions among young persons suggest that drugs are more available currently than in years past. Reuter discusses this paradox. He also notes that despite the enormous amount of funds designated for reducing the supply of drugs, evaluations into the impact of these expenditures are lacking.

Introduction

United States drug policies are punitive (in both rhetoric and reality), divisive (certainly by race, probably by age and perhaps by class), intrusive (in small ways for many and in large ways for some groups) and expensive ($30 billion annually). Even more distressingly, the nation has a drug problem more severe than that of any other rich Western society, whether measured in terms of the extent of drug use, dependence on expensive drugs, drug-related AIDS cases, or the level of violence and corruption associated with these drugs.

Many contend that the problems are a consequence of our policies. Either it is the harshness of those policies that has generated the disease and violent crime that sur-round drug use (the standard liberal critique)[1] or it is the lack of effective stringency that explains why drugs are so widely used and available (the hawks' critique).[2] Yet this may give too much credit to the role of policy, a common fallacy in modern American discussions, particularly in the nation's capital, whose business is precisely policy. Whether or not there is an epidemic of experimentation with a particular drug; what fraction of experimenters goes on to become dependent; and the severity of health and crime consequences of dependence may all be much more shaped by factors other than policy. Certainly, when comparing America's drug problems with those of other nations, most of the relevant differences appear to be rooted in broader features of societies; e.g., the United States is characterized by greater hedonism, weak informal social controls, a higher propensity for risk taking, inadequate provision of health care for the poor, unequal income distribution, and high level of criminal violence generally; it is also more intimately connected with cocaine and opium growing regions, such as Colombia and Mexico. All these factors promote use of illicit psychoactive drugs and/or worsen the problems associated with that use.

If policy is only moderately important in controlling drug use, then perhaps we can mitigate the harshness of our policies with little risk of seeing an expansion of drug use and related problems. Reducing our drug *policy* problem (i.e., the adverse consequences of the policies themselves) is worth a good deal, though it would obviously be even more desirable if we could also reduce our drug problem.

But it is hard to be highly prescriptive here, to say what good drug policy would look like, because one consequence of politicians' treating drug control as a moral crusade has been an absolute uninterest, bordering on gross negligence, in assessing the consequences, good or bad, of the emphasis on punishment. We cannot say, even approximately, whether locking up more drug dealers or seizing lots of assets has any substantial effect on prices or whether higher prices would have much effect on American drug usage or related violence. There is no credible basis for describing a policy that would reduce, in any important dimension, the extent of American drug problems by, say, one-third in the next five years.

What I will offer is a set of reasonable conjectures, but a central message of this paper is that without systematic evaluation of the consequences of drug enforcement and punishment, the current stagnation of drug policies will almost certainly continue.

Characterizing American Drug Policies and Problems

Policies

The most striking characteristics of the U.S. response to illicit drugs in the last decade have been its scale and its punitiveness. The federal government spends about $15 billion annually on drug control. State and local governments probably spend at least as much.[3] Thus drug control is a $30–35 billion government program in the mid-1990s, massively up from about $6–7 billion in 1985. By comparison, the figure for all public law enforcement expenditures was about $110 billion in 1996.

The intended punitiveness is reflected in budgets. About three-quarters of the national drug control budget is spent on apprehending and punishing drug dealers and users, with treatment getting about two-thirds of the remainder. State and local governments are even more enforcement-ori-ented than the federal government; budgetarily they exhibit a disdain for prevention, even though this is primarily a school-based activity which seems most naturally to flow from local governments.

The total punishment levied for drug control purposes has increased massively since 1981, when the concern with cocaine became prominent. The number of commitments to state and federal prison have risen approximately tenfold over the same period. By 1994, there were almost 400,000 people in prison or jail serving time for selling or using drugs; the comparable figure for 1980 was about 31,000 (see Table 42.1).

At the state level, one striking feature is the number of persons being imprisoned for drug *possession* felonies. This does not include possession with intent to distribute, which is classified as a distribution offense. In 1992 50,000 were sentenced to state prison for non-distribution offenses, mostly simple possession; some may be plea-bargained down from distribution charges.

Sentencing figures are of themselves insufficient to show that enforcement has become more stringent; that depends on the ratio of sentences (or years of prison time) to offenses. Imprisonment may hardly have kept up with the growth of drug markets. The number of offenses might have risen as rapidly as arrests/sentences/years of prison time between 1980 and 1985, when cocaine consumption was still expanding rapidly,

Table 42.1

Trends in Drug Enforcement, 1980–1994

	1980	1985	1990	1994
Drug Arrests	581,000	811,000	1,090,000	1,350,000
Heroin and cocaine only	70,000	240,000	590,000	635,000
	(12%)	(30%)	(54%)	(47%)
Distribution only	104,000	192,000	345,000	370,000
	(18%)	(30%)	(31%)	(27%)
Inmates [Total]	31,000	68,000	291,000	392,000
Local jails	7,000	19,000	111,000	137,000
State prisons	19,000	39,000	149,000	202,000
Federal prisons	4,900	9,500	30,500	51,800

Sources: Uniform Crime Reports, Correctional Population in the United States; jail figures are author's estimates.

but from 1985 to 1995 it is very likely that the number of offenses (transactions) and offenders (sales/sellers/users) was essentially flat; the risk of being imprisoned for a cocaine or heroin user or seller went up very sharply, perhaps nearly tenfold.

How risky is drug selling or drug possession? The aggregate data suggest that in 1994 a cocaine user had an 8 percent risk of being arrested; for a heroin user the figure may have been 10 percent. For drug selling, Robert MacCoun and I estimated in a study of the District of Columbia that, in 1988, street dealers of drugs faced about a 22 percent probability of imprisonment in the course of a year's selling and that, given expected time served, they spent about one-third of their selling career in prison.[4] These figures on sellers are somewhat higher than crude calculations at the national level for more recent years.

Does this make drug selling appropriately risky? One-third of a career in prison seems quite a lot. On the other hand, the risk per sale is very small indeed; in our Washington, D.C. study a seller who worked two days a week at this trade made about 1,000 transactions in the course of a year. His imprisonment risk per transaction was only about 1 in 4,500; by that metric, drug selling is a great deal less risky than, say, a burglary or robbery. Another way to assess the risk is to look at aggregate figures. It is estimated that American users consume 300 tons of cocaine per annum. If these are sold in 1 gram units, then this represents 300 million transactions, which result in fewer than 100,000 prison sentences; that generates a prison risk for a single cocaine sales transaction of about 1 in 3,000.

The punitiveness of American drug policy is not simply captured in numbers. It is also an element of rhetoric and other programs. The 1996 presidential candidates competed, albeit briefly and unconvincingly, in efforts to demonstrate their toughness; no other aspect of drug policy merited a mention. Senator Dole accused the administration of failing to make adequate use of the military, particularly in the interdiction campaign. President Clinton responded by proposing that teenagers be drug tested when they apply for a driver's license. More recently House Speaker Newt Gingrich, in what was billed as a major address on domestic policy initiatives, proposed life sentences for those trafficking across state boundaries, and death sentences for the second offense.

Even the new federal welfare reform package includes its very own antidrug clause; unless a state affirmatively opts out, it must deny federal benefits to any applicant who has been convicted of a post-1996 drug felony. As deterrence, it presumes a peculiar long-sightedness on the part of offenders. It can reasonably be called spiteful, though it is not as mean-spirited as Senator Gramm's original version, which imposed loss of a wide range of public benefits for any drug conviction. It certainly serves no welfare goal to cut off those convicted at age eighteen for simple possession of small amounts of crack, as in California, from a right to welfare at age thirty-five.

What Has Toughness Accomplished?

Toughness should raise prices, make drugs less accessible, and reinforce messages that drugs are disapproved of and harmful. This should lead to less drug use and, eventually, fewer drug-related problems. In fact illegal drugs are remarkably expensive, not universally accessible, and generally feared. Nevertheless, it is striking that, notwithstanding sharply increased stringency, prices are declining, many of the young see drugs as quite easy to get, and the fear of the most widely used drug (marijuana) is declining.[5]

Illicit drugs are very expensive by most measures. Marijuana is a cultivated weed like tobacco, but whereas a cigarette costs, even with excise taxes, hardly ten cents, an equivalent amount of marijuana costs $5 or more. Heroin, a processed agricultural good like sugar, is vastly more expensive than gold, costing about $5,000 per ounce (wholesale), compared to gold's $400.

All the same, cocaine and heroin prices have fallen steadily since 1981; by 1995, after adjusting for inflation, they were only about one-third of their 1981 levels. For marijuana, prices rose steadily and substantially from 1981 to 1992 and then fell in the next four years back to their 1981 level. Even more surprising is Jon Caulkins's finding that crack cocaine, singled out for tough sentencing, both at the national level and in some major states (e.g., California), is no more expensive at the retail level than powder cocaine in terms of price per pure milligram.

This failure of cocaine and heroin prices to rise with tougher enforcement is a major analytic and policy puzzle. Declining demand, reduced labor market opportunities for aging drug user/sellers, a decline in violence engendered by few new entrants and lower margins, and the locking up of criminal users are just some of the possible factors contributing to this. None has been subject to systematic examination.

If enforcement did not raise prices for the drugs, then it might still have been successful if it lowered availability. The only long-term data, from the annual survey of high school seniors, suggest otherwise. For example, 80 to 90 percent of the students report that they think marijuana is very available or available to them, a figure that has been stable for two decades. The percentage of seniors reporting that cocaine was available or readily available was 46 percent in 1995, compared to 30 percent in 1980, though down somewhat from its 1989 high of 55 percent. The finding that marijuana is perceived as more available to high school students than alcohol or cigarettes has been widely reported.

Drug use is estimated to be half as prevalent in 1995 as in the early 1980s, but it is now growing, albeit very slowly; in 1995 the percentage of those over twelve who reported using an illicit drug in the previous month was 6 percent, compared to 14 percent in 1981.[6] The numbers dependent on cocaine and heroin have been fairly stable over a long period of time, at about 2.5 million. It seems likely that the severity of the nation's drug problem as measured by the related violence and health costs has also been fairly stable over that period of time, though declining somewhat since about 1990.

In some cities it appears that local enforcement has driven open air markets indoors. Driving around with police in Washington, D.C., one certainly observes much more circumspect behavior than was true in the late 1980s. This may be a major accomplishment. Open air markets not only ease access for users moving from experimentation to regular consumption but also breed violence and disorder.[7]

In summary, increasing toughness has not accomplished its immediate objectives of raising price and reducing availability. Drug use has declined, but the most proximate cause, as reported in the high school senior survey, seems to be a shift in attitudes as to the risks and approval of use of specific drugs. Though enforcement might influence those perceptions, there is no correlation between crude measures of toughness and those perceptions.

But toughness has clearly had other consequences as well.

Divisiveness

It is hard to analyze drug enforcement in contemporary America without reference to race.[8] In 1992 blacks (12 percent of the general population) constituted two-thirds of admissions to state prison for drug offenses, compared to slightly less than one-half for all non-drug offenses. A similar disproportion existed for Hispanics; 10 percent of the population, they constituted 25 percent of all those sent to prison for drug offenses.

The origins of this disproportion are a matter of controversy. The standard critique is that the population of drug users is predominantly white; differences in prevalence rates for drugs (even crack) are far too modest to overcome the vastly larger white population. Ergo, drug sellers should be primarily white. This argument is at best incomplete. Sellers are a select group of users; they are likely to be poorer and more deviant than users generally since selling is risky and widely condemned. The urban poor are disproportionately minority.

Racism may play a role but a lot is driven by the police responsiveness to concerns about drug selling and the violence and disorder around inner-city markets. Focusing on those involved in the street selling of expensive drugs (essentially anything other than marijuana) is likely to generate disproportionate numbers of arrests among central city poor young males, who are tempted into this business both by the unattractiveness of their legitimate economic opportunities and the accessibility of these selling opportunities.[9] These populations are again disproportionately minorities.

Drug selling has indeed become a common activity among poor minority urban males. For Washington, D.C., my colleagues and I estimate that over one-quarter of African American males born in the 1960s were charged with drug selling between the ages of eighteen and twenty-four.[10] Most were charged with a drug felony and most will be convicted of that offense.

But it is what happens after arrest that generates much of the controversy. In particular, the disproportion in sentences for crack offenses, for which arrests are overwhelmingly of blacks and Hispanics, has been a major political issue. This, together with the difficulty of articulating any credible grounds for maintaining the current federal disparity, has increased suspicion in the black community that drug enforcement is an instrument of continuing white oppression. Tom and Mary Edsall report that focus groups in the early 1990s found that many blacks believed drug enforcement was part of an effort by the white community to oppress blacks.[11]

Nor is this the only division in society arising from tough drug policies. For the young the growing harshness of rhetoric and policy to marijuana, arrests for simple possession having doubled in the last five years, reduces the credibility of government generally. The claims about marijuana's dangers, both in public rhetoric and school prevention programs, seem grossly exaggerated and indeed lack much scientific basis. For HHS Secretary Shalala to say, as she did in a recent meeting, that marijuana is comparable to crack in its dangerousness, is to disparage science and reason.[12]

Marijuana is not good for health but represents less threat in that respect than do alcohol and cigarettes; no one dies of the acute effects of marijuana and even the long-term effects are surprisingly modest. The negative effects of marijuana use on adolescent development are clearer but still modest. These are not arguments for legalization (indeed, they argue rather more for prohibition of cigarettes and alcohol), but they create a tension when so much emphasis is placed on

the health effects of the only one of these substances that is not legally promoted, and is disproportionately consumed by the young.

Intrusiveness

A whole array of legal innovations have been justified by the need to end the "scourge of drugs," to use President Bush's memorable 1989 phrase. Drug dealer "profiling" by police has allowed police to undertake numerous searches with barely plausible cause; most of those searched are again either minority or young or both.[13] Drug testing of federal employees (such as those in the executive office of the president) for purely symbolic purposes has demeaned public service. Some states require that candidates for state office be drug tested for symbolic purposes; the Supreme Court in 1997 unanimously ruled against this requirement for Georgia. Preventive detention, a particularly chilling power, has been extended in the context of the Controlled Substances Act.

Drug policy is clearly getting harsher in this respect. Some jurisdictions are contemplating testing welfare recipients for drug use and disqualifying those who cannot remain drug-free. Abe Rosenthal of the *New York Times*, the most prominent of columnist drug hawks, quickly pounced on President Clinton's proposal that all teenaged applicants for driver's licenses be subject to a drug test, suggesting that this was not nearly enough, and that the logic and facts spoke to the need to do random tests of young adults as well, since they are the highest risk group.[14]

The Punitive Cycle

The response to emerging drug problems is invariably punitive: the first twitch is to raise the statutory penalty for some offense. This was true in 1996 when methamphetamine showed signs of moving out of its long-established western base in San Diego, Dallas, etc. It has not yet happened for marijuana at the federal level, somewhat surprisingly, but various states are moving in that direction. For example, the Virginia Senate recently passed an increase in maximum sentences for marijuana possession offenses; a second conviction can result in a four-year prison sentence.

This is truly a vicious cycle, since the argument for raising the sentence for offenses involving a particular drug are mostly that the current sentence is less than that for other drugs and hence encourages sellers to pick that drug. This systematically generates sentence inflation. Indeed, many in Congress responded to the claim of imbalance between crack and powder cocaine by suggesting dramatically increasing penalties for powder. In May 1997 the U.S. Sentencing Commission, defeated in its previous effort at reducing the crack-powder cocaine [disparity] by lowering the crack penalties, made recommendations that would indeed increase the powder penalties, while trying again to lower the discrepancy.

The intrusive and divisive elements of our policies are not inherent in prohibition. Even harsh punishment is not; consider how lightly we enforce laws against prostitution.[15] However, they arise remorselessly out of the logic of drug scares, under the assumption that tougher policies will make a difference. There is some understanding that racial disparity and loss of civil liberties are not trivial harms but this rubs up against the unquestioned assumption that another major goal is importantly served by these measures, namely reductions in drug problems.

Comparing the U.S. and Western Europe

Perhaps we suffer no more from illicit drugs and clumsy drug policies than other developed countries with more wealth than self-control. Robert MacCoun and I have been studying the experiences of ten Western European countries, all of which have had significant problems with heroin and marijuana; some have also experienced cocaine or amphetamine problems.[16]

European innovations in tolerant drug policy, such as the Dutch coffee shops and the Swiss heroin maintenance trials, attract a fair amount of attention in the United States. But most Western European drug policy is firmly in the prohibitionist legal framework and, with respect to drug selling, these countries are, by their standards, ag-

gressive both in enforcing the laws and in the length of sentences served by traffickers. They are, with Sweden and France as interesting exceptions, very much less aggressive toward drug users than is the U.S. They are, again with the exception of Sweden and France, strong supporters of needle exchange programs and other efforts to reduce HIV risk behaviors among intravenous drug users. As the British Advisory Council on the Misuse of Drugs said famously in 1987, "Drugs are an important problem. AIDS is a more important problem."[17]

None of these countries has a problem with illicit drugs comparable to that in the U.S., mostly because they have not experienced a major epidemic of cocaine use. The highest reported figure we have been able to find for lifetime marijuana use among high school seniors is 36 percent in Spain, compared to more than 50 percent in the U.S. in recent years; for most European countries the figure is closer to one-quarter. Heroin addiction in some countries, notably Italy, Spain, and Switzerland, approaches the U.S. rate of about 2–3 per 1,000 population. But if one adds in cocaine, the U.S. figures for the prevalence of addiction are at least twice that of any European country.

Even starker is the difference in violence, though this is all impressionistic. I interviewed a senior Zurich police official during the period when that the city allowed drug sellers and buyers to operate openly in a park, called the Platzspitz, near the train station. The official was complaining about how bad the crime situation had become because of the drug market. He showed me a list of the thirty-one major crime incidents in the park in 1990. The list included a fight with a policeman and precisely one homicide. This for a park in which many hundreds of drug dealers and buyers, using heroin and some cocaine, congregated every day! In other European cities the drug market generates theft and disorder but not high levels of violence.

AIDS related to intravenous drug use has been a significant problem in some European countries, with France, Italy, and Switzerland the most badly affected. But neither in terms of the fraction of [intravenous drug users] who are HIV-positive nor in the fraction of the population that is HIV positive as the result of drug use does any European country approach the U.S.

Should we attribute the smaller drug problems in Europe to their policies? MacCoun and I see little basis for this. Take the violence for example. The low level of violence in crime generally, perhaps itself the result of the small number of guns, is more plausible a factor than any policy action by police or the criminal justice system. The absence of a significant cocaine epidemic can hardly be attributed to enforcement; prices are now down near to U.S. levels despite increasing seizures. The greater strength of families in Southern Europe, the better safety net for those who are long-term unemployed, and the smaller fraction of young males growing up in poor female-headed households, are plausibly more important. It is hard to do any formal testing with the available data but this seems to us a reasonable interpretation.

Interestingly, the choice of drug policy by nations is more influenced by views about the role of government, as well as by views about what constitutes the drug problem. For example, the Swedish population accepts a paternalistic state and will tolerate highly intrusive rules, including compulsory drug treatment even without an arrest. In Spain there are no criminal penalties for the possession of small amounts of any psychoactive drug; this represents less a decision about drug policy than a response to the long experience with the authoritarian Franco regime, which has created a strong suspicion of any laws that allow the government to regulate private conduct. Europeans generally see illicit drugs as primarily a personal and health problem, a position consistent with the lower levels of drug-related violence. The U.S. public sees illegal drugs as a crime problem; almost all speeches and most newspaper articles refer to "drugs and crime." For a nation that sees crime as something to be solved by punishment, that is enough to sustain a set of laws and programs that make toughness their centerpiece.

A Role for Research

Clearly there are policy alternatives to our current regime, even if we stick with prohibition. For any proposal involving less harshness the central issue is assessing the consequences of a highly punitive approach. At a minimum it would be useful to say whether longer prison sentences, more drug seizures, or more intensive money-laundering investigations can increase prices or reduce availability, and what effect these changes would have on drug use by current and prospective users, and on drug-related problems. There is not a single empirical paper that attempts to answer that question. The closest one gets is a paper of twenty-five years ago, which found that higher prices for heroin increased property crimes in Detroit.[18] There has been a little progress lately in estimating the price elasticity of demand for various drugs and various populations[19] but that is just a baby first step.

Oddly enough, we can say a great deal more about the effects of treatment and prevention, which account for no more than 20 percent of this nation's public expenditures on drug control, than about the consequences of enforcement.[20] Even more oddly, that is the result of the dedication to punishment; any other program has to justify itself against the suspicion that it is kind to criminals (treatment) or too diffuse (prevention). Since punishment is what drug users and sellers deserve, there is little need (in the eyes of politicians and perhaps the public) for these programs to demonstrate their effectiveness. Thus the National Institute on Drug Abuse has a research budget of $450 million; research on drug enforcement has to fight for its share of the National Institute of Justice's paltry $30 million annual budget, albeit that money is tripled by various evaluations and earmarks. Twenty million dollars is certainly far too generous an estimate of the funding for research related to drug enforcement.

One can usefully adapt a complaint of the public health research world to explain this situation. Prevention researchers object that whereas surgical procedures only have to be shown to be safe and medicines safe and effective, prevention programs have to be demonstrated to be safe, effective, and cost-effective as well. The corollary for drug enforcement is that it doesn't even have to be shown to be safe, let alone effective or cost-effective. Drug enforcement has become a crusade, and crusaders scarcely need a map, let alone evaluation.

The federal enforcement agencies sponsor no research themselves, notwithstanding federal program expenditures of about $10 billion. The DEA and FBI may generously be called non-analytic; more accurately they are anti-analytic. Not only do they lack any internal policy analytic capacity, they seem to lack even the ability to contract with external research organizations. The DEA's inability to report price data in a meaningful way, despite gathering about five thousand observations each year, is just symptomatic of this. Surely no other federal agency in the 1990s would report as a range the very highest and lowest figures, without any measure of central tendency; to report that the price range for marijuana went from $25–$450 in 1993 to $40–$450 in 1994 is to simply inform the world that these data are irrelevant.

Clearly a large research and analysis program is needed that has the depth and durability to develop more credible measures of the intensity of treatment and the size of the drug problem in a particular community. We need to take account of the enormous variation in the intensity of enforcement and severity of sentencing that seems to exist across cities and states. For example, in Texas in 1992 the median prison sentence for those convicted of drug trafficking was ten years, compared to only two years for those in Washington State. It should be possible to build on the improvements in the drug data indicators being developed by various federal agencies.

Why is there so little research on drug enforcement? Surely part of the answer is simply that there is, as James Q. Wilson noted in a recent lecture,[21] shockingly little research on crime control generally. But another factor, I conjecture, is a curious confluence of liberal and conservative interests. Those who support tough drug enforcement see no gain in evaluation; Peter Rossi's oft-cited comment, "If you don't like a program, evaluate it," is highly relevant. Liberals find the whole effort distasteful enough that they simply want nothing to do with it; in particular, they do not want to evaluate it for the purposes of making it work better. They would much rather focus on the programs in which they have faith and in which they passionately believe, namely prevention and treatment.

Conclusion

But a society that deliberately averts its eyes from an honest assessment of a massive and frequently cruel intervention that sacrifices so many other goals for the one desideratum of drug abstinence can scarcely expect to find a well-grounded alternative. I am struck by the lack of any nuanced debate about drug policy, beyond the ungrounded and polarizing legalization shouting match and the banal and marginal discussion of how the federal drug budget should be spent. Welfare reform, public housing policies, and income support generally may do more to affect drug abuse and related problems than those programs that claim to explicitly target them, yet there is rarely any serious discussion of their role in drug policy.

In John Le Carré's *The Honorable Schoolboy*, George Smiley finds some evidence that a prominent Chinese businessman in Hong Kong may be a Communist spy. Launching an investigation in Hong Kong is both politically sensitive and expensive, so he has to convene a meeting of the Foreign Office, Treasury, and other agencies to get authorization and funds. The Foreign Office is aghast; if the investigation were to become public and the businessman were innocent, it would be a major political embarrassment. On the other hand, the governor in Hong Kong entertains and trusts this businessman, indeed may recommend him for a knighthood; it would be equally embarrassing if it turned out that he was a spy! They become increasingly panicked and press Smiley for a judgment; is he a spy? Smiley inscrutably says he cannot answer without doing the investigation. The end of the story is of course that they give him the money and the authority, because the answer must be found.

That is the situation we face with respect to drug policy. If you want to know the answer as to whether we can make prohibition less expensive, divisive, and intrusive and maybe reduce the American drug problem, then you can't expect anyone to give a persuasive answer, who is not provided the money and authority to find out what our tough enforcement actually accomplishes.

Doing less rarely attracts much support for dealing with a problem that still concerns large parts of the community. But this may be the only responsible recommendation that can be made now. Locking up drug offenders for shorter terms, worrying more about the racial disparities in sentencing policies, giving up fewer of our civil liberties for unlikely reductions in drug problems, may be the best one can do at the moment. That would mean less intrusive, divisive, and expensive policies and perhaps little increase in drug problems.

Researchers are always inclined to think that learning and understanding are important for policy. The failure of the repeated findings that drug treatment has a very high benefit–cost ratio to make a policy impact[22] is a sober reminder that the political decision making here is driven by other considerations. But we might actually see something approximating a reasonable discussion of the alternatives in front of the nation if there were a more credible base of empirical analysis available. In its absence we are doomed to rhetorical debate.

Notes

1. See, e.g., Skolnick, J., "Rethinking the Drug Problem," *Daedalus* 121.3 (1992): 133–60.

2. The most articulate statement of this position is contained in William Bennett's introduction to the first *National Drug Control Strategy* (Office of National Drug Control Policy, 1989).

3. Federal figures are published annually in the *National Drug Control Strategy* (Office of National Drug Control Policy). State and local figures are available only for 1990 and 1991; see *State and Local Spending on Drug Control Activities* (Office of National Drug Control Policy, 1993).

4. Reuter, MacCoun, and Murphy, *Money from Crime* (Santa Monica, Ca.: RAND, 1990).

5. The best data come from an annual survey of high school seniors conducted by the Institute of Social Research at the University of Michigan: Johnston, O'Malley and Bachman, *Monitoring the Future.*

6. Annual data on drug use in the general population are provided by the National Household Survey on Drug Abuse (Department of Health and Human Services).

7. On this and other enforcement effects see Kleiman, M., *Against Excess: Drug Policy for Results*, 1992, Chapter 6.

8. See Tonry, M., *Malign Neglect* (Oxford University Press, 1994).

9. The most compelling description of this world is provided in Bourgois, P., *In Search of Respect: Selling Crack in El Barrio* (University of California Press, 1996).

10. Saner, MacCoun, and Reuter, "On the Ubiquity of Drug Selling," *J. Quantitative Criminology* 11.4 (1995): 337–62.

11. Edsall, T. with M. Edsall, *Chain Reaction: The Impact of Race, Rights and Taxes on American Politics* (New York: W. W. Norton, 1991), 237.

12. This comment was reported by two participants in the meeting of the National Advisory Council of the Substance Abuse and Mental Health Administration in early 1997.

13. On these matters generally see Rudovsky, "The Impact of the War on Drugs on Procedural Fairness and Racial Equality," *Chicago Legal Forum* 23 (1994): 7–74.

14. Rosenthal, A., *New York Times*, September 1996.

15. On recent prostitution enforcement policies, showing that most arrestees receive very modest penalties, see Pearl, Julie, "The Highest Paying Customers: America's Cities and the Costs of Prostitution Control." *Hastings Law Journal* 38 (1987): 769–90.

16. On the problems of comparison here see MacCoun, Saiger, Kahan, and Reuter, "Drug Policies and Problems: The Promise and Pitfalls of Cross-National Comparison," in N. Heather, A. Wodak, E. Nadelmann and P. Ohare (eds.), *Psychoactive Drugs and Harm Reduction: From Faith to Science* (London: Whurr Publishers, 1993): 103–17.

17. Advisory Council on the Misuse of Drugs, *AIDS and Drug Misuse* (London, 1987).

18. Silverman, L. and N. Spruill, "Urban Crime and the Price of Heroin," *Journal of Urban Economics* 4 (1977): 80–103.

19. E.g., Saffer, Henry and Frank Chalcupka, "The Demand for Illicit Drugs," Working Paper No. 5238 (Cambridge, Mass.: National Bureau of Economic Research, 1995).

20. For a review see Anglin, M.D. and Y-I. Hser, "Treatment of Drug Abuse," in Tonry, M. and Wilson, J. Q. (eds.), *Drugs and Crime* (Chicago: University of Chicago Press, 1990).

21. Wilson, James Q., "What, if anything, can the federal government do to reduce crime?" *Perspectives on Crime and Justice*, National Institute of Justice, 1996.

22. The most important of these studies, which compares the costs of reducing cocaine consumption by one percent through treatment or enforcement, is Rydell, C.P. and S. Everingham, *Controlling Cocaine* (RAND, 1994).

For Discussion

What criteria should be used to evaluate the success or failure of the war on drugs?

43
Clinical and Societal Implications of Drug Legalization

Herbert D. Kleber
James A. Inciardi

In this chapter, Herbert Kleber and James Inciardi outline the arguments proposed by supporters of drug legalization. They then critically review evidence, which leads them to reject the arguments by legalization advocates. For example, supporters of legalization suggest that crime would decline if drugs were legally available. Kleber and Inciardi cite evidence to show that many individuals engage in crime before they initiate drug use. The authors examine the effects of legal drugs on individuals and society and examine the legalizaton debate cross-culturally.

The drug legalization debate is not particularly new. It did not begin during election year 2002 with the numerous proposals to modify state constitutions to remove the possession of marijuana from the criminal law. It did not begin with former Surgeon General Jocelyn Elders' off-the-cuff remark at the close of 1993 that "I do feel that we would markedly reduce our crime rate if drugs were legalized." Nor did it begin in 1988 when at a meeting of the U.S. Conference of Mayors, Baltimore Mayor Kurt L. Schmoke called for a national debate on American drug control strategies and the potential benefits of legalizing marijuana, heroin, cocaine, crack, and other illicit substances. Although it has received the most media attention since the late 1980s, the debate has been on-again, off-again for the better part of a century. Its most recent rendering reflects a potpourri of loosely conceptualized suggestions involving "legalization" and "decriminalization" at one end of the continuum, to "medicalization" and "harm reduction" at the other.

Briefly, the basic argument for legalizing drugs is that America's "War on Drugs" has been a miserable failure, emphasizing that the drug laws have created evils far worse than the drugs themselves (corruption, violence, street crime, and disrespect for the law), and the laws passed to control drugs have failed to reduce demand. By contrast, if marijuana, cocaine, heroin, and other drugs were legalized, some positive things would happen: (a) drug prices would fall; (b) users could obtain their drugs at low, government-regulated prices and would no longer be forced to engage in prostitution and street crime to support their habits; (c) levels of drug-related crime would significantly decline, resulting in less-crowded courts, jails, and prisons, [which would leave] law enforcement personnel free to focus their energies on the "real criminals" in society; (d) drug production, distribution, and sale would be removed from the criminal arena; no longer would it be within the province of organized crime, and thus, such criminal syndicates as the Colombian and Mexican cocaine cartels, the Jamaican posses, and the various "mafias" around the country and the world would be decapitalized, and the violence associated with drug-distribution rivalries would be eliminated; and (e) the often draconian measures undertaken by police to enforce the drug laws would be curtailed, thus restoring to the American public many of its hard-won civil liberties (1–3).

The counterargument from those opposed to legalizing drugs is that the drug prohibition has been extremely effective in limiting drug abuse. Furthermore, it is maintained that legalizing drugs would likely initiate a major public health problem characterized by increased abuse and addiction, drug-related health problems, and *more* crime, not less (4). Within the context of these opposing arguments, this chapter examines the evidence surrounding the anti-legalization points of view.

Historical Background

During the closing decades of the nineteenth century, opiates and cocaine were widely and legally available both in their pure form and as ingredients in patent medicines promoted as remedies for any variety of ailments ranging from hay fever, depression, and arthritis, to colds, consumption, teething, and even athlete's foot, cancer, and baldness (5). Heroin and cocaine, furthermore, were touted as nonaddictive painkillers and as cures for morphine and alcohol addiction. But as the twentieth century began with hundreds of thousands of individuals dependent on cocaine and opiates (6), concern rose about the abuse liability and addiction potential of these drugs. In fact, in 1910 President William H. Taft noted in a report to Congress that "the misuse of cocaine is undoubtedly an American habit, the most threatening of the drug habits that has appeared in this country . . ." (7).

This concern over the effects of the legal use of drugs led to federal and state actions, which by 1920 had led to sharp decreases in the use of opiates and cocaine in patent medicines and the requirement of a physician's prescription to obtain them. By the 1930s cocaine and opiate use had markedly declined, and legislation in 1937 led to the illegality of marijuana and its subsequent decreased use (5).

While the same drugs are illegal in all 50 states and many have adopted schedules similar to those of the federal government, state penalties for possession and distribution vary widely, particularly with respect to marijuana. In a few states, possession of small amounts of marijuana is a civil violation punishable by fine rather than a criminal offense, and more than half the states and the District of Columbia have legislation permitting the medicinal use of marijuana. At the same time, 19 states have mandatory minimum sentences for the possession and/or sale of marijuana, and 11 states have separate penalties for *crack-* versus *powder*-cocaine (8). Like the federal government, states set higher penalties for selling drugs to minors and outlaw possession of drug paraphernalia and operation of premises where drugs are sold and used (8).

Drug Policy Alternatives

The drug policy debate revolves around such alternatives as prohibition (and its critiques) versus legalization, which has been used to encompass a wide variety of options. Many different terms are commonly used, with much variation in each (9).

- *Prohibition* reflects current policy, with its supporters focusing on the necessity for prohibiting illegal drugs through severe penalties for their use, distribution, and sale.

- *Legalization* rests at the other end of the continuum from prohibition, and calls for the elimination of drug prohibitions and instituting some form of government regulation.

- *Decriminalization* refers to the removal of the criminal penalties associated with the possession of currently illegal drugs.

- *Medicalization* advocates giving physicians the responsibility for treating drug abusers, including the decision to maintain some users on the drug on which they have become dependent.

- *Harm reduction* is an approach that emphasizes a public health model for reducing the risks and consequences of drug abuse (10).

Before going further, however, two things must be emphasized. The first is that none of these approaches are mutually exclusive, for each contains elements of the others. Prohibition, for example, includes elements of harm reduction in the forms of substance abuse prevention and treatment. Furthermore, methadone-maintenance programs can exist under the prohibition, medicalization, and harm-reduction approaches. At the same time, legalization proposals often include aspects of both decriminalization and medicalization. The second point is that each of these five drug policy approaches means different things to different people, with the most confusion associated with harm reduction.

The problem is that harm reduction is a concept that is difficult to define with any degree of precision. Its essential feature, however, is the attempt to ameliorate the adverse health, social, legal, and/or economic consequences associated with the use of mood-altering drugs. As such, harm reduction is neither a policy nor a program, but rather, a principle that suggests that managing drug abuse is more appropriate than attempting to stop it altogether. Within this context, harm reduction can mean different things to different people, groups, cultures, and nations. Most broadly, it can refer to any variety or combination of policies and policy goals, including the following:

- *Advocacy for changes in drug policies*—legalization, decriminalization, ending the drug prohibition, reduction of criminal sanctions for drug-related crimes, changes in drug paraphernalia laws
- *Human immunodeficiency virus (HIV)/ acquired immunodeficiency syndrome (AIDS)-related interventions*—needle/ syringe exchange programs; HIV prevention/intervention programs; bleach and condom distribution programs; referrals for HIV and other sexually transmitted infections (STI) testing; referrals for HIV and other STI medical care and management; referrals for HIV/ AIDS-related psychological care and management
- *Broader drug treatment options*—methadone maintenance by primary care physicians, changes in methadone regulations, heroin substitution programs, new experimental treatments, treatment on demand
- *Drug-abuse management for those who wish to continue using drugs*—counseling and clinical case management programs that promote safer and more responsible drug use
- *Ancillary interventions*—housing and other entitlements, healing centers, support and advocacy groups (11)

Although harm reduction encompasses a wide range of alternatives, to some observers it is viewed as a more politically attractive cover for legalization (12). Or, as the former director of the Office of National Drug Control Policy General Barry McCaffrey noted in 1998, "Harm reduction is a hijacked concept that has become a euphemism for drug legalization. It's become a cover story for people who would lower the barriers to drug use" (13).

The Epidemiology of Drug Use

Most arguments for legalizing drugs begin with the contentions that the fight against the use of cocaine, heroin, and other illegal drugs has been lost, and that the array of criminal justice and social policies, which attempt to manage drug use and drug users, have been a total failure. Legalization advocates point to the more than 80 million Americans who have used drugs at some point during their lifetimes, arguing that the laws have been futile and a liberal democracy should not ban what so many people do (14, 15). In counterpoint, however, it should be pointed out that for the majority of these individuals, their drug use involved little more than brief experimentation with marijuana. The size of this number especially reflects the large number of young people who tried marijuana and hallucinogenic drugs during the late 1960s and the 1970s when drug use was so widely tolerated that the 1972 Shafer Commission, established during the Nixon administration, and, later, President Jimmy Carter called for decriminalization of marijuana (5, 16). It also reflects the period of the late 1970s when some physicians described cocaine as a relatively harmless drug, even as related problems were escalating rapidly (17).

Since then concerned public health and government leaders have mounted energetic efforts to denormalize drug use. As a result, current (past month) users of any illicit drugs, as measured by the National Household Survey on Drug Abuse, decreased from 24.8 million in 1979 to 15.9 million in 2001, a more than 35% drop. Over the same time period, current marijuana users dropped from 23 million to 12 million, and cocaine users from 4.4 million to 1.7 million (18). Given these data, combined with the fact that the national population increased by some 20% between 1979 and 2001, it is difficult to say that drug reduction efforts have failed. The declines in drug use occurred during a period of strict drug laws, societal disapproval, and increasing knowledge and awareness of the dangers and costs of illegal drug use.

Several factors, however, lead many to conclude that we have not made progress against drugs. This feeling of despair stems from the uneven nature of the success. While casual drug use and experimentation have declined substantially, certain neighborhoods and areas of the country remain infested with drugs and drug-related crime, and these continuing trouble spots draw media attention. At the same time, the number of drug addicts has not dropped significantly, and the spread of HIV among addicts has added a devastating dimension to the problem.

The number of chronic (more than 10 days per month) cocaine users (as estimated by the Office of National Drug Control Policy based on a number of surveys including the National Household Survey on Drug Abuse, the Arrestee Drug Abuse Monitoring program, and the Drug Abuse Warning Network), has remained steady at roughly 2.8 million since 1995 (19). The overall number of illicit drug addicts has hovered between 5 and 6 million, a situation that many experts attribute [to both] a lack of treatment facilities (20) and the large numbers of drug-using individuals already in the pipeline to addiction, even though overall casual use has dropped. Furthermore, after 13 years of sharp decline, teenage drug use increased somewhat from 1992 to 2001 (19).

While strict drug laws and criminal sanctions are not likely to deter hard-core addicts, increased resources can be dedicated to prevention and treatment without changing the legal status of drugs. It is difficult to carry out effective prevention campaigns when drugs are available on many street corners and in both urban and rural school corridors; witness the continued rise in teenage smoking in spite of major prevention efforts. The criminal justice system can be used to enhance treatment outcome by using such programs as an alternative to incarceration and by offering treatment in prisons. Though substantial problems remain, the significant progress in the struggle against drug abuse can be accelerated by improving the system rather than tearing it down.

Legalization and Public Health

Proponents of drug legalization claim that making drugs legally available would not significantly increase the number of drug dependent people. It is argued that "drugs are everywhere," in that they are already available to those who want them, and that a policy of legalization could be combined with education and prevention programs to discourage drug use (3, 15, 21). Some contend that legalization might even reduce the number of users, arguing that there would be no local dealers to lure new users, and drugs would lose the "forbidden fruit" allure of illegality (15, 21). Proponents of legalization also play down the consequences of drug use, saying that most drug users can function normally (22, 23). Some legalization advocates assert that a certain level of drug addiction is inevitable, so that even if legalization increased the number of users, it would have little effect on the numbers of users who become drug dependent (17).

The effects of legalization on the number of drug-involved people is an important question because the answer in large part determines whether legalization will reduce crime, improve public health, and lower the economic, social, and health care costs related to drug abuse, or will have the opposite effects. The claimed benefits of legal change evaporate if the number of users and addicts, particularly among children, increases significantly.

Does Availability Create Demand?

An examination of this question has three components: (a) access to drugs; (b) social acceptability and perceived consequences of drug use; and (c) the affordability of drugs.

Accessibility. It would appear that at present, drugs are not readily accessible to all. Although 88.5% of high school seniors reported in 2001 that they could obtain marijuana "fairly easily" or "very easily" only 45% and 32% believed that they could easily obtain cocaine and heroin, respectively (24). In the adult population age 26 years and older, 53% believed they could easily obtain marijuana, 30% believed they could easily obtain cocaine, and 19% believed they could easily obtain heroin. Thus, although marijuana is perceived as easily available by a large proportion of the youth and adult populations, other drugs are not as easily obtainable. After legalization, all drugs would be more widely and easily available.

Acceptability. In arguing that legalization would not result in increased use, proponents of legalization often cite public opinion polls, which indicate that the vast majority of Americans would not try drugs even if they were legally available (21, 25). They fail to take into account, however, that this strong public antagonism toward drugs was formed during a period of strict prohibition, when government and institutions at every level made clear the health and criminal justice consequences of drug use. Furthermore, even if only 15% of the population would use drugs after legalization, this would be more than double the current level of 7.1%.

Laws define what is acceptable conduct in a society and express the will of its citizens. Drug laws not only create a criminal sanction, they also serve as educational and normative statements that shape public attitudes (26). Criminal laws constitute a far stronger statement than civil laws, but even the latter can discourage individual consumption. Laws regulating smoking in public and workplaces, prohibiting certain types of tobacco advertising, and mandating warning labels are in part responsible for the decline in smoking prevalence among adults, which seems to be leveling off at the high rate of 48 million nicotine addicts.

The challenge of reducing drug abuse and addiction would be decidedly more difficult if society passed laws indicating that these substances are not sufficiently harmful to prohibit their use. Any move toward legalization would decrease the perception of risks and costs of drug use, which would lead to wider use (24). During the late 1960s and the 1970s, as social norms, laws, and police practices became more permissive about drug use, the number of individuals smoking marijuana and using heroin, hallucinogens, and other drugs rose sharply. During the 1980s, as attitudes became more restrictive and antidrug laws stricter and more vigorously enforced, the perceived harmfulness of marijuana and other illicit drugs increased and use decreased.

Some legalization advocates point to the campaign against smoking as proof that reducing use is possible while substances are legally available (14, 21, 27). But it has taken smoking more than 30 years to decline as much as illegal drug use did in 10 years (28, 29). Moreover, reducing use of legal drugs among the young has proven especially difficult. While use of illegal drugs by high school seniors has dropped significantly over the years, tobacco use remained virtually constant in the 1980s, rose sharply in the early 1990s, and only now has declined to where it was 20 years ago (24).

Affordability. Unless the general laws of economics are repealed, it is likely that reducing the price of drugs will increase consumption (26, 30, 31). Although interdiction and law enforcement have had limited success in reducing supply (28), the illegality of drugs has increased their price (32). Prices of illegal drugs are roughly six to ten times what they would cost to produce legally. Cocaine, for example, sells at $60 to $200 a gram (depending on purity, potency, and availability), but would cost less than $3 a gram to produce and distribute legally. That would set the price of a dose at about 15 to 20 cents, well within the reach of virtually every student in America. "Legalized cocaine would cost no more than about 3% of today's black market price and consumption would surely increase dramatically" (33).

Until the mid-1980s, cocaine was the drug of the middle and upper classes. Regular use was limited to those who had the money to purchase it or got the money through white collar crime or selling such assets as their car, house, or children's college funds. In the mid-1980s, the $5 crack cocaine vial made the drug inexpensive and more available to the poor and young. Use spread. Cocaine-exposed infants began to fill hospital neonatal wards, cocaine-related emergency room visits increased sharply, and cocaine-related crime and violence jumped (26). As such, history suggests that availability does indeed create demand.

Efforts to increase the price of legal drugs by taxing them heavily in order to discourage consumption would be accompanied by the black market, crime, violence, and corruption now associated with the illegal drug trade. Heroin addicts, who gradually build a tolerance to the drug, and cocaine addicts, who crave more of the drug as soon as its effects subside, would turn to a black market if an affordable and rising level of drugs were not made available to them legally.

Youth and Drugs

Drug use among youths is of particular concern because almost all individuals who use drugs begin doing so during their preteen or adolescent years. Because we have been unable to keep legal drugs, like tobacco, alcohol, and prescription stimulants and painkillers, out of the hands of youths, the legalization of illegal drugs could compound existing problems of drug use among youths.

Most advocates of legalization support a regulated system in which access to presently illicit drugs would be illegal for minors (21). Such regulations would retain for children the "forbidden fruit" and risk-taking allure that many argue legalization would eliminate. Furthermore, any such distinction between adults and minors could make drugs, like beer and cigarettes today, an attractive badge of adulthood.

The American experience with laws restricting access by children and adolescents to tobacco and alcohol makes it clear that keeping legal drugs away from minors would be a formidable, probably impossible, task. Currently, 61% of high school seniors have smoked, 30% in the past month (24). Some 29% of high school students are current cigarette smokers; 10 million underage Americans reported drinking alcohol in the past 30 days, and although alcohol use is illegal for every American under age 21 years, 73.3% of high school seniors report using alcohol in the past year, almost half in the past month (24). These rates of use persist despite school, community, and media activities that inform youths about the dangers of smoking and drinking and despite increasing public awareness of these risks. Moreover, in contrast to these high rates of alcohol and tobacco use, only 26% of seniors are current users of illicit drugs, which are illegal for the entire society (18). It is no acci-

dent that those substances, which are mostly easily obtainable—alcohol, cigarettes, and inhalants such as those found in household cleaning fluids—are those most widely used by the youngest students.

Hard-Core Addicts

A review of addiction in the past shows that the number of alcohol, heroin, and cocaine addicts, even when adjusted for changes in population, fluctuates widely over time, in response to changes in access, price, societal attitudes, and legal consequences. That alcohol and tobacco, the most accepted and available legal drugs, are the most widely abused, demonstrates that behavior is influenced by opportunity, stigma, and price. Many soldiers who were regular heroin users in Vietnam stopped once they returned to the United States where heroin was much more difficult and dangerous to get (5). Studies show that even among chronic alcoholics, alcohol taxes lower consumption (34). Similarly, as cigarette taxes increase, the number of smokers decreases.

Although not all new users become addicts, few individuals foresee their addiction when they start using. Most think they can control their consumption (35). Among the new users created by increased availability, many, including children, would find themselves unable to live without the drug, no longer able to work, attend school, or maintain personal relationships.

Drugs, Violence, and Criminal Justice

In an effort to begin unraveling the legalization/drugs–violence connection and the overall relationships between drugs and violence, it is important to understand Paul J. Goldstein's tripartite conceptual framework of psychopharmacological, economically compulsive, and systemic models of violence (36).

The *psychopharmacologic model of violence* suggests that some individuals, as the result of short-term or long-term ingestion of specific substances, may become excitable, irrational, and exhibit violent behavior. Research documents that chronic users of amphetamines, methamphetamine, and cocaine, in particular, tend to exhibit hostile and aggressive behaviors (37).

Psychopharmacologic violence can also be a product of a psychotic state induced by cocaine and other stimulants (38–41). As dose and duration of cocaine use increase, the likelihood of developing cocaine-related psychopathology also increases. Cocaine psychosis is generally preceded by a transitional period characterized by increased suspiciousness, compulsive behavior, fault finding, and eventually paranoia. When the psychotic state is reached, individuals may experience visual and/or auditory hallucinations, with persecutory voices commonly heard. Many believe that they are being followed by police or that family, friends, and others are plotting against them. Moreover, everyday events tend to be misinterpreted in a way that supports delusional beliefs. When coupled with the irritability and hyperactivity that the stimulant nature of cocaine tends to generate in almost all of its users, the cocaine-induced paranoia may lead to violent behavior as a means of "self-defense" against imagined persecutors. The violence associated with cocaine psychosis was a common feature in many crack houses across the United States during the late 1980s and early 1990s (42). Violence may also result from the irritability associated with the drug withdrawal syndromes. In addition, some users ingest drugs before committing crimes to both loosen inhibitions and bolster their resolve to break the law (43).

The economically compulsive model of violence holds that some drug users engage in economically oriented violent crime to support drug use. This model is illustrated in the many studies of drug use and criminal behavior which have demonstrated that while drug sales, property crimes, and prostitution are the primary economic offenses committed by users, armed robberies and muggings do indeed occur (37, 44, 45).

Analyzing the legalization/drugs–violence connection within this model is far more complex than with the psychopharmacologic pattern. The contention is that in a legalized market, the prices of "expensive drugs" would decline to more affordable levels, and, hence, predatory crimes would become unnecessary. But this argument is based on several premises. First, it assumes that addicts commit crimes because they are "enslaved" to drugs, that because of the high prices of heroin, cocaine, and other illicit chemicals on the drug black market, users are forced to commit crimes to support their drug habits. Interestingly, however, there is no solid empirical evidence to support this contention. Studies over the past three decades document that while drug use tends to intensify and perpetuate criminal behavior, it usually does not initiate criminal careers. In fact, the evidence suggests that among the majority of street drug users who are involved in crime, their criminal careers were well established prior to the onset of either narcotics or cocaine use. As such, it would appear that the "inference of causality"—that the high price of drugs on the black market *per se* causes crime—is simply not supported.

The second premise suggests that people addicted to drugs commit crimes only for the purpose of supporting their habits. However, a variety of studies document that drug use is not the only reason why addicts commit predatory crimes. They also do so to support their daily living expenses—food, clothing, and shelter. To cite but one example, researchers at the Center for Drug and Alcohol Studies at the University of Delaware studied crack users on the streets of Miami. Of the scores of active addicts interviewed, 85% of the men and 70% of the female interviewees paid for portions of their living expenses through street crime. In fact, half of the men and a fourth of the women paid for 90% or more of their living expenses through crime. And not surprisingly, 96% of the men and 99% of the women had not held a legal job in the 90-day period before being interviewed for the study (46).

The third premise holds that in a legalized market users could obtain as much of the drugs as they wanted, whenever they wanted. More than likely, however, there would be some sort of regulation, and, hence, drug black markets would persist for those whose addictions were beyond the medicalized or legalized allotments. In a decriminalized market, moreover, levels of drug-related violence would likely either remain unchanged, or increase (if drug use increased).

The final premise is that cheap drugs preclude the need to commit crimes to obtain them, but the evidence emphatically suggests that this is not at all the case. Consider crack-cocaine. Although crack "rocks" are available on the illegal market for as little as $2 in some locales, users are still involved in crime-driven endeavors to support their addictions (47). For example, researchers Miller and Gold surveyed 200 consecutive callers to the 1-800-COCAINE hotline who considered themselves to have a problem with crack (48). They found that despite the low cost of crack, 63% of daily users and 40% of nondaily users spent more than $200 per week on the drug. Similarly, interviews conducted by researchers in New York City with almost 400 drug users contacted in the streets, jails, and treatment programs, found that almost half spent more than $1,000 a month on crack (49). The study also documented that crack users—despite the low cost of their drug of choice—spent more money on drugs than did users of heroin, powder cocaine, marijuana, and alcohol. Other researchers have found this to be so in Miami, as well (46). Miller and Gold summarized the issue of crack and crime this way: "Once the severity of addictive use is established, the pattern of the cost of maintaining the addiction and its consequences is related to preoccupation with acquisition and compulsive use . . ." (48).

The systemic model of violence maintains that violent crime is intrinsic to the very involvement with illicit substances. As such, systemic violence refers to the traditionally aggressive patterns of interaction within systems of illegal drug trafficking and distribution. It is the systemic violence associated with trafficking in cocaine and crack in America's inner cities that has brought the most attention to drug-related violence in recent years. Moreover, it is concerns with this same violence that focused the current interest on the possibility of legalizing drugs. And it is certainly logical to assume that if heroin and cocaine were legal substances, systemic drug-related violence might indeed decline significantly. However, there are two very important questions in this regard. First, is drug-related violence more often psychopharmacologic than systemic? Second, is the great bulk of systemic violence related to the distribution of crack? Third, is crack-re-

lated violence still at the high levels of a decade ago? If most of the drug-related violence is psychopharmacologic in nature, and if systemic violence is typically related to crack, a drug generally excluded from consideration when legalization is argued, it might be logical to conclude that legalizing drugs would *not* reduce violent crime.

In retrospect, study after study documents that alcohol and other drugs have psychopharmacologic effects that result in violence. Cocaine in all of its forms is linked to aggressive behavior as a result of the irritability and paranoia it engenders. Also, alcohol and cocaine have been found to be present in both the perpetrators and victims of violence. Alcohol is legal and cocaine is not, suggesting that the legal status of a drug may be unrelated to the issue of psychopharmacologic violence. Hence, it is unlikely that such violence would decline if drugs were legalized. Studies of economically compulsive violence also suggest that in a legalized market, crime would not necessarily decline. Users who engage in predatory behaviors do so for a variety of reasons—not only to obtain drugs, but also to support themselves. And typically, as pointed out, a number of studies suggest drug-involved offenders were crime-involved before the onset of their careers in drugs. Too, even when a drug is inexpensive, it still may not be affordable if there is addiction and compulsive use. This is amply illustrated in the experience with crack.

As for systemic violence, much of it is unrelated to the use of drugs. When it *is* drug linked, the overwhelming majority seems to be associated with the use of alcohol or crack. Taking this point further, violence stems from many of the dysfunctional aspects of our society other than drug use. After studying the violence associated with crack distribution in Manhattan neighborhoods, Jeffrey Fagan and Ko-lin Chin concluded that crack has been integrated into behaviors that were evident before drug sellers' involvement with crack or its appearance on New York City streets (50). In other words, the crack users/dealers are often engaged in violent and crime-involved lifestyles, which would likely exist (and previously did) independent of their involvement with crack. Furthermore, although there is evidence that crack sellers are more violent than other drug sellers, this violence is not confined to the drug-selling context: violence potentials appear to precede involvement in selling (50).

It appears, then, that crack has been blamed for increasing violence in the marketplace, but perhaps this violence actually stems from the psychopharmacologic consequences of crack use. *Crack dealers* are generally *crack users*, and because crack is highly addictive yet comparatively inexpensive, there is a continuous demand for it. This leads to the competition that generates violence. Legalizing crack would likely reduce the competition but increase the demand. Researcher Ansley Hamid reasons that increases in crack-related violence are caused by the deterioration of informal and formal social controls throughout communities that have been destabilized by economic processes and political decisions (51). As such, does anyone really believe that we can improve on these complex social problems through the simple act of legalizing drugs?

Legalization advocates point to exploding prison populations and the failure of drug laws to lower crime rates (2, 3, 21). From 1980 to 2001, arrests for drug offenses doubled, with the result that the majority of state and federal inmates had histories of drug abuse, or had been arrested for drug law violations (52). Rising prison populations are generated in large part by stricter laws, tough enforcement, and mandatory minimum sentencing laws, policy choices of the public and Congress. But the growing number of prisoners is also a product of the high rate of recidivism, a phenomenon tied in good measure to the lack of treatment facilities, both in and out of prison. Eighty percent of state prisoners have prior convictions and 60% have served time in the past. Despite the fact that more than 60% of all state inmates have used illegal drugs regularly and 30% were under the influence of drugs at the time they committed the crime for which they were incarcerated, fewer than 20% of inmates with drug problems receive any treatment (53).

While strict laws and enforcement do not necessarily deter addicts from using drugs, the criminal justice system can actually play a harm-reduction role, by diverting drug-involved offenders into treatment. Because of the nature of addiction, most drug abusers do not seek treatment voluntarily, but many respond to outside pressures including the threat of incarceration. Where the criminal justice system is used to encourage treatment participation, addicts are more likely to complete treatment and stay off drugs (53).

Addiction and Casual Drug Use

To offset any increased use as a result of legalization, many proponents contend that money presently spent on criminal justice and law enforcement could be used for treatment of addicts and prevention (3). In 2002, the federal government spent $18.8 billion to fight drug abuse, nearly two thirds of that on law enforcement; state and local governments are spending at least another $16 billion on drug control efforts, largely on law enforcement (54). Legalization proponents argue that most of this money could be used to fund treatment on demand for all addicts who want it, and extensive public health campaigns to discourage new use.

While the number of new prisoners would initially decrease because many are currently there for drug law violations, as use increased, costs would quickly rise in health care, schools, and businesses and the wider use would lead to increased addiction. Increased criminal activity, as noted earlier, would occur, related to the psychological and physical effects of drug use, and criminal justice costs would rise again. The higher number of casual users and addicts would reduce worker productivity and students' ability and motivation to learn, cause more highway accidents and fatalities, and fill hospital beds with individuals suffering from ailments and injuries caused or aggravated by drug abuse. Law enforcement and treatment do not need to be conflicting activities. Community policing, for example, is both a supply and demand reduction activity. Well-run drug courts can improve the efficacy of treatment. Effective treatment can decrease crime. Rather than cut supply reduction activities, what is needed is an expansion and improvement of treatment, such as the $1.6 billion over 5 years proposed by President G.W. Bush (54). A recent study (55) suggests another danger of casual drug use, especially among adolescents. A review of 140 studies of addiction, adolescence, and brain structures noted that the adolescent's impulse toward novelty develops far more quickly than the mechanisms that inhibit urges and impulses. Teenagers are . . . more likely to experiment with drugs[,] and the experience produces more pronounced brain effects, which can be permanent.

Chambers and associates (55) found that "[g]reater motivational drives for novel experiences, coupled with an immature inhibitory control system, could predispose to performance of impulsive actions and risky behaviors, including experimentation with and abusive use of addictive drugs. . . . Direct pharmacological-motivational effects of addictive drugs on dopamine systems may be accelerated during these developmental epochs, enhancing the progression or permanency of neural changes underlying addiction."

The chronic relapsing nature of drug dependence and the difficulties in treating it are well documented (56). The mechanisms described by Chambers and associates (55) may increase our understanding of why this happens and emphasize that curing addiction may be even harder than preventing it initially. Casual drug use by adolescents and young adults, in short, may have long-lasting consequences for many of them. Those harm-reduction proponents who argue that because teens are going to do drugs anyway, it is best to focus efforts on giving them the knowledge on how to do it "safely" rather than not doing it at all, may not understand the possible long-term consequences of even "safe use."

Costs

It is doubtful whether legalization would produce any cost savings over time, even in the area of law enforcement. Indeed, the legal availability of alcohol has not eliminated law enforcement costs because of alcohol-related violence. A third of state prison inmates committed their crimes while under the influence of alcohol (57, 58). In 1998, there were approximately 16,000 alcohol-related traffic fatalities, approximately 40% of fatal motor vehicle crashes (59). Despite intense educational campaigns, there are about 1.5 million arrests annually for driving while intoxicated (57).

Like advocates of legalization today, opponents of alcohol prohibition claimed that taxes on the legal sale of alcohol would dramatically increase revenues and even help erase the federal deficit (60). The real-world result has been quite different. The more than $11 billion in 1995 state and federal revenues from alcohol taxes (61, 62) paid for less than half the $40 billion that alcohol abuse imposed in direct health care costs in 1995 (63), much less the costs laid on federal entitlement programs and the legal and criminal justice systems, to say nothing of lost economic productivity. The $13 billion in federal and state tobacco tax revenue (61, 62) was one-sixth of the $75 billion in direct health care costs attributable to tobacco (63). By the end of the decade, these ratios had remained approximately the same (64, 65). This discrepancy between excise tax revenue and alcohol- and tobacco-related costs does decrease if one takes into account the "savings" from such programs as Social Security and Medicare as a result of premature death. The idea that a tobacco policy resulting in more than 400,000 deaths a year provides any kind of model for dealing with illegal drugs is hard to imagine. Health care costs directly attributable to illegal drugs range from $14.9 billion to $30 billion (63), an amount that would increase significantly if use spread after legalization. Experience renders it unrealistic to expect that taxes could be imposed on newly legalized drugs sufficient to cover the costs of increased use and abuse. As noted later, the Dutch, in spite of effectively decriminalizing marijuana, have been unable to tax this $300 million a year business.

Public Health

Legalization proponents contend that prohibition has negative public health consequences such as the spread of HIV from addicts who share dirty needles, accidental poisoning, and overdoses from impure drugs of variable potency. Of those individuals who were living with AIDS in 1999, approximately one-third [were] drug users and their sexual partners (66).

Advocates of medicalization argue that while illicit drugs should not be freely available to all, doctors should be allowed to prescribe them (particularly heroin, but some also advocate cocaine) to addicts. They contend that giving addicts drugs assures purity and eliminates the need for addicts to steal to buy them.

Giving addicts drugs like heroin, however, poses many problems. Providing them by prescription raises the danger of diversion for sale on the black market as happened in England in the 1960s. The alternative—insisting that addicts take drugs on the prescribers' premises—entails at least two visits a day, thus interfering with the stated goal of many maintenance programs to enable addicts to hold jobs. The dropouts from the Swiss heroin-maintenance projects (approximately 40% in the Basel study, for example [67]) show that a substantial number of enrolled individuals are unwilling to make such ongoing visits and/or are unwilling to do without the heroin and cocaine combination they like, leading some of the organizers to propose take-out heroin and the ability to use cocaine as well. A variety of claims have been made as to success of the participants, such as improved health and social integration. However, the treatment effectiveness of the heroin maintenance *per se* has been deemed hard to judge because of the lack of randomized controls, pre- and postcomparisons were limited to treatment completers, and there was extensive mandatory psychosocial counseling (68). A more rigorous, recently completed, Dutch study may provide more useful scientific information.

Heroin addicts require two to four shots each day in increasing doses as they build tolerance to its euphoric effect. On the other hand, methadone can be given at a constant dose because euphoria is not the objective. Addicts maintained on methadone need only a single oral dose each day, eliminating the need for injection. Buprenorphine, a partial opioid agonist given sublingually, was ap-

proved for treatment of opioid dependence in 2002 by the FDA. It can last up to 3 days, is safer than methadone as far as overdose is concerned, and since the passage of the Drug Abuse Treatment Act of 2000, can be prescribed by qualified office-based physicians. The possible medical mainstreaming of opiate addiction treatment via buprenorphine makes heroin maintenance even less of a necessary or useful alternative (69). Its extensive use in France (70), for example, has markedly cut the heroin overdose death rate by more than half (71). Because cocaine produces an intense but short euphoria and an immediate desire for more (72), addicts would have to be given the drug even more often than heroin to satisfy their craving sufficiently to prevent them from seeking additional cocaine on the street. The binge nature of cocaine use renders it unlikely that cocaine could be given on a "medicalization" basis. Because powder cocaine can be readily converted into crack, any proposal to expand availability of the former will increase the number of crack users and addicts.

Other, less-radical, harm-reduction proposals also have serious flaws. As compared to comprehensive methadone maintenance, "low-threshold" methadone-maintenance programs, when objectively studied, show sharply increased rates of illicit drug use and drug-related problems, and a failure to reduce high-risk behaviors (73, 74). Distributing free needles does not ensure that addicts desperate for a high at inconvenient times would not continue to share them. But to the extent that needle exchange programs are effective in reducing the spread of the HIV virus, they can be adopted without legalizing drugs. Studies of whether needle exchange programs increase drug use, however, have generally focused on periods of no longer than 12 months. Although use does not seem to increase in this period, data are lacking on the long-term effects of such programs and whether they prompt attitude shifts that, in turn, lead to increased drug use (75). Furthermore, most states now permit over-the-counter pharmacy sales of syringes at prices usually less than 40 cents per syringe. Funds spent on needle exchange programs, which often seem to attract the older, more risk-aversive addicts, might be better spent on outreach programs that go into crack houses and shooting galleries to encourage hard-to-reach addicts to seek treatment.

Some individuals do die as a result of drug impurities. But while drug purity could be assured in a government-regulated system (although not for those drugs sold on the black market), careful use could not. An increase in the number of users would probably produce a rising number of overdose deaths, similar to those caused by acute alcohol overdose deaths today. The deaths and costs as a result of unregulated drug quality pale in comparison to the negative impact that legalization would have on drug users, their families, and society. Casual drug use is dangerous, not simply because it can lead to addiction or accidental overdoses, but because it can be harmful *per se*, increasing worker accidents, highway fatalities, and children born with physical and psychological handicaps. Each year, roughly 500,000 newborns are exposed to illegal drugs *in utero;* many others are never born because of drug-induced spontaneous abortions (76, 77). Drug-exposed newborns are more likely to need intensive care and to suffer the numerous consequences of low birth weight and prematurity, including early death (76, 78). The additional costs just to raise drug-exposed infants would outweigh any potential savings of legalization in criminal justice expenditures (78).

Substance abuse both leads to and aggravates medical problems. Medicaid patients with a secondary diagnosis of substance abuse (including alcohol) remain in hospitals twice as long as patients with the same primary diagnosis but with no substance abuse problems. Girls and boys under age 15 years remain in the hospital three and four times as long, respectively, when they have a secondary diagnosis of substance abuse (79). One-third to one-half of individuals with psychiatric problems are also substance abusers (80). Young people who use drugs are at higher risk of mental health problems, including depression, suicide, and personality disorders, and are more likely to engage in risky behavior such as unprotected sex (81, 82). Such sexual behavior exposes these teens to increased risk of preg-nancy as well as to AIDS and other sexually transmitted diseases. The total economic cost of illegal drug use to society in 2000 was estimated at $160 billion, including health care costs of $14.9 billion, lost productivity of $110.5 billion, and crime and welfare of $35.2 billion (54).

In schools and families, drug abuse can be devastating. Students who use drugs not only limit their own ability to learn, they also disrupt classrooms. Drug-using parents are more likely to provide inadequate or no economic support and put their children at greater risk of becoming substance abusers themselves (76). With the advent of crack cocaine in the mid-1980s, foster care cases soared more than 50% nationwide in 5 years; more than 70% of these cases involved families in which at least one parent abused drugs (83).

Decreased coordination and impaired motor skills that result from drug use are dangerous not just to the individual but also to society at large. A study in Tennessee found that 59% of reckless drivers, having been stopped by the police and tested negative for alcohol, test positive for marijuana and/or cocaine (84). The extent of driving while high on marijuana and other illegal drugs is still not well known because usually the police do not have the same capability for roadside drug testing as they do for alcohol testing. However, data from the 2001 National Household Survey found that more than 8 million persons reported driving under the influence of illegal drugs during the past year (18).

The Workplace

Approximately 75% of illegal drug users are employed full- or part-time (65); in one survey, 60% of respondents knew people who went to work under the influence of alcohol or drugs (65). These workers impose costs on their employers, and eventually society, through their decreased productivity, health care needs, workplace accidents, and absenteeism. They drive buses and trucks, operate nuclear power plants, run the air traffic control system, perform surgery, deliver mail, and teach children.

Workers who use cocaine and marijuana are twice as likely to be absent from work and to be injured, and 15 times more likely to be involved in an accident (76). Overall, workers who use drugs are three times likelier to be late for work, ten times likelier to miss work, and three to six times likelier to injure themselves or others. Drug-using workers are responsible for 40% of industrial fatalities and experience more than 300% higher medical and benefits costs (85). Between 1992 and 2000, it is estimated that lost productivity as a consequence of illegal drugs totaled $110.5 billion (86, 87).

The Lessons of Prohibition

Legalization advocates often cite the era of national alcohol prohibition from 1920 to 1934 to support their case. As ratified in the 18th Amendment, Prohibition banned the "manufacture, sale, or transportation of intoxicating liquors within, the importation thereof into, or the exportation thereof from the United States. . . ." Proponents of legalization contend that the failure of the 18th Amendment supports their argument that prohibitions of this kind of individual behavior are not effective (25).

The alcohol prohibition–drug control law analogy is a false one. There are two important distinctions between Prohibition and current drug laws. First, Prohibition was in fact decriminalization because possession for personal consumption was not illegal. Second, alcohol, unlike illegal drugs, has a long history of widespread social acceptance and use in Western culture dating at least as far back as the Old Testament and Ancient Greece. Most Americans who drink do not get into trouble with alcohol. Thus, the public and political consensus favoring Prohibition was short-lived. By the early 1930s, most Americans no longer supported it. Today, however, the public overwhelmingly favors keeping illegal drugs illegal.

Despite these differences, which made alcohol prohibition more difficult to enforce than current drug laws, Prohibition reduced the amount of alcohol consumed, as well as the incidence of alcohol-related medical problems and violence. It is important not to confuse federal Prohibition with state laws restricting alcohol. Advocates of legalization point to the decline in consumption and cir-

rhosis pre-1919 to argue that consumption declined more before the 18th Amendment than after. Given that by 1919, 36 of the 48 states had established some form of prohibition, this argument is true but disingenuous. At the beginning of the twentieth century, Americans consumed 2.6 gallons of alcohol per person [per year]. By 1919, this amount dropped to 1.96 gallons per person [per year]. In 1934, the first full year after repeal of national Prohibition, alcohol use stood at 0.97 gallons per person. From then on, consumption rose steadily to roughly three times as high as that immediately after Prohibition (88).

Death rates from cirrhosis of the liver corroborate available consumption statistics. Cirrhosis death rates fell from 12 per 100,000 in 1916 to 5 per 100,000 in 1920, and remained at that level throughout Prohibition before beginning to rise steadily again after repeal (89). Among men such rates declined even more sharply, from 29.5 per 100,000 in 1911 to 10.7 per 100,000 in 1929 (60).

The decrease in consumption had other positive health consequences. Admissions to mental health institutions for alcoholic psychosis dropped by more than 60% from 1919 to 1922. Arrests for drunkenness and disorderly conduct dropped 50% between 1916 and 1922, and welfare agencies reported dramatic declines in the number of cases as a consequence of alcohol-related family problems (60).

Nor is Hollywood's guns and gangsters depiction of Prohibition accurate. Homicide experienced a higher rate of increase between 1900 and 1910 than during Prohibition, and organized crime was well established in cities before 1920 (60).

Legalization proponents also argue that during Prohibition, an increased number of drinkers died from the consumption of dangerous wood and denatured alcohol, which were used as substitutes for commercial alcohol, just as today addicts die from impure drugs. The data do not bear this out. Through 1927, the rate of death from these substitutes remained nearly constant at its 1920 level (60).

The public may agree that the freedom to drink is worth the public health consequences. Worried by the high rate of alcohol-related disease and crime, the residents of Barrow, Alaska, the northernmost city in the United States voted in 1994 to ban alcohol completely. Despite the 70% drop in crime and the immediate and persistent decline in alcohol-related emergency room visits from 118 in the month before the ban to 23 in the following month, residents voted to repeal the ban in 1995. In the 2 weeks after the ban was lifted, the detoxification center began to fill with patients and alcohol-related murders were on the rise (90).

These facts are presented to set the record straight and to dispel the exaggerated or false consequences often attributed to Prohibition. They are not an argument for the resumption of alcohol prohibition, which we oppose, but they do offer some lessons on the relevance of illegality to reducing drug use.

The Lessons of Legal Drugs

Legalization proponents point out that alcohol and tobacco cost society much more in lost productivity, increased health care, and criminal justice expenditures, and lead to more deaths than all illegal drugs combined (14, 27, 91). From that they conclude that we spend too much time and energy fighting illegal drugs, as compared to legal drugs. Alcohol and tobacco are, indeed, responsible for far more deaths and costs to society than illegal drugs, but this is a combination of their potential toxicity and legal status, which makes them widely available, used, and abused.

Illegal drug-related deaths are estimated at 20,000 annually. Tobacco is responsible for more than 400,000 deaths and alcohol for more than 100,000 deaths every year (92). Approximately 40% of fatal motor vehicle crashes involve alcohol. Fetal alcohol syndrome is the leading known cause of mental retardation (93). Smoking by pregnant women kills up to 7,000 newborns annually and leads to as many as 141,000 miscarriages (94). Cigarettes are as addictive as heroin and spawn health problems ranging from lung cancer to emphysema and heart disease (95). Of the $66 billion that substance abuse cost federal health and disability entitlement programs in 1995, $56 billion

were attributable to alcohol and tobacco (96). Of the $29 billion in Medicare costs attributable to substance abuse, 80% was related to smoking. Seventy percent of the $21 billion that Medicaid spent because of substance abuse was because of cigarettes and alcohol (63).

The high costs attributed to legal drugs do not indicate that we are concentrating prohibition on the wrong drugs, but rather that when drugs are legal, and therefore widely acceptable and available, they adversely affect more individuals and require more attention and resources. Indeed, the nation's experience with tobacco and alcohol send[s] a warning about the dangers of making illegal drugs readily available. As drug policy expert Mark Kleiman has noted, "Until success is achieved in imposing reasonable controls on the currently licit killers, alcohol and nicotine, the case for adding a third or fourth recreational drug . . . will remain hopelessly speculative" (97).

Another argument made by legalization proponents is that the general decrease in consumption rates of both legal and illegal drugs in the past 20 years has nothing to do with law enforcement policy, but rather with education and increased societal concern with personal health (91). Yet despite widespread awareness of the risks of smoking and heavy media attention to tobacco-related problems, roughly 25% of Americans continue to smoke, and smoking by adolescents is substantially higher than their marijuana use and close to where it was in 1979. On the other hand, as noted earlier, the number of illegal drug users has dropped from 24.8 million in 1979 to 15.9 million in 2001, while the national population increased by 20% in the same period (18). Arguing that we should treat illicit drugs as we do tobacco, using education instead of prohibition, also implies a false dichotomy between education and prohibitive laws. In curbing illegal drug use, when law enforcement and education complement and reinforce each other, they are most effective.

There are more than 48 million nicotine addicts, 12 to 18 million alcoholics and alcohol abusers, and 5 to 6 million illegal drug addicts. Making illegal drugs more available would drive the number of marijuana, heroin, and cocaine users closer to the number of alcohol and tobacco users.

Marijuana

Marijuana is the most commonly used illegal drug in the United States and its use is particularly high among adolescents. Because relatively little street-level violence attends the marijuana trade, the legalization and decriminalization debate here centers on how harmful the drug is to the user, whether marijuana use leads to the use of harder drugs, whether marijuana use would increase, and whether any increase would translate into a decrease in alcohol use (25, 98).

While clearly not as dangerous as snorting cocaine or shooting heroin, smoking marijuana is detrimental both physically and mentally, especially to adolescents. The effects of one marijuana joint on the lungs are equivalent to four cigarettes, placing the user at increased risk of bronchitis, emphysema, and bronchial asthma. The active ingredient in marijuana, tetrahydrocannabinol (THC), is fat-soluble and remains in the brain, lungs, and reproductive organs for weeks. Marijuana weakens the immune system, and regular use can disrupt the menstrual cycle and suppress ovarian function (99, 100). Regardless of socioeconomic status, prenatal use of marijuana by the mother appears to reduce significantly the IQs of babies (101). Marijuana impairs short-term memory and the ability to concentrate (102) at a time when the main task of its young users is education. And marijuana use diminishes motor control functions, distorts perception, and impairs judgment, leading, among other things, to increased car accidents and vandalism. Marijuana toxicity, especially anxiety and panic attacks, is a frequently cited cause of emergency room visits, and treatment of marijuana dependence has become a common reason for seeking substance abuse treatment, treatment which is usually psychologic rather than pharmacologic. As Millman and Beeder note, stopping chronic cannabis use often results in "a marked and rapid improvement in mental clarity and energy levels" (103).

The link between the use of marijuana and the subsequent use of harder drugs has been the subject of much debate (104), with supporters of marijuana decriminalization and legalization arguing that many individuals who smoke marijuana never use hard drugs. While the latter is true, the statistical association between the teenage use of marijuana and the later use of other drugs such as cocaine is powerful. Even though the biomedical or other causal relationship for this has not yet been adequately explained, 12- to 17-year-olds who smoke marijuana are 85 times more likely to use cocaine than those who do not. Adults who as adolescents smoked marijuana are 17 times likelier to use cocaine regularly. According to data of the National Household Survey, 60% of adolescents who use marijuana before age 15 years will later use cocaine, compared to only 16% who began marijuana use after age 21 years (105). These correlations are many times higher than the initial relationships found between smoking and lung cancer in the 1964 Surgeon General's report (nine to ten times). Individuals who used cannabis by age 17 years had odds of other drug use, alcohol dependence, and drug abuse/dependence 2.1 to 5.2 times higher than their twin who did not use cannabis before age 17 years (106, 107). Marijuana use is associated with many high-risk behaviors among young people. According to the U.S. Centers for Disease Control and Prevention, adolescents who smoke marijuana are twice as likely to attempt suicide and to carry a weapon as those who do not. Adolescent marijuana smokers are three times as likely to have sex and far more likely to do so without a condom, putting themselves at much greater risk of teen pregnancy and sexually transmitted diseases (108).

Past experiences with marijuana decriminalization illustrate the consequences of more tolerant policies. During the 1970s, 11 states decriminalized personal possession of marijuana by making the offense a civil violation punishable by a fine. In 1975, the Alaska State Supreme Court decriminalized at-home personal use of small amounts of marijuana for individuals older than age 19 years. By 1988, 12- to 17-year-olds in Alaska were smoking joints at more than twice the national average. Marijuana use became part of the lifestyle of many teenagers and the age of initiation declined (109, 110). Because of this, in a 1990 referendum, Alaskans voted to recriminalize personal possession.

Proponents of legalization cite several surveys and studies, which report that when Oregon, Maine, and California decriminalized marijuana, rates of use among teenagers did not increase significantly (111). These surveys, however, have severe shortcomings. They lack controls for other historical and demographic factors, such as sex, income, and education, and employ vaguely defined measurement criteria to estimate the prevalence of marijuana use (112, 113). They do not reflect the impact of legalization on long-term usage rates because they were conducted only 1 to 3 years after decriminalization laws were passed. Although reported marijuana use increased only slightly following decriminalization, the time period surveyed was not long enough to allow the educational and attitude-forming aspects of the previous strict drug laws to dissipate.

Measurement problems also exist in trying to compare usage rates in states that decriminalized marijuana use versus states that did not. The comparison is problematic because many states that did not decriminalize marijuana use did reduce penalties for marijuana use, and others chose not to enforce laws prohibiting personal use of marijuana. During the 1970s, many states and the federal government adopted more tolerant attitudes toward the drug. Nationwide, use rose significantly during this time, reaching almost 40% of high school seniors before beginning its long decline in 1979 (24).

Teenagers are not likely to stop using alcohol when they begin smoking marijuana. While on individual occasions teens may choose to get high on either marijuana or alcohol, these drugs are often used together. From 1975 to 1978, as the percentage of teens using marijuana increased from 27% to 37%, the percentage of teens that drank increased from 68% to 72%. Marijuana use then dropped to 12% of teens by 1992; alcohol use dropped to 51%. The rise in teenage marijuana use in the 1990s was accompanied by a rise, albeit smaller, in the percentage of students who drink, and especially in binge drinking (24).

Proponents of legalization argue that while smoking pot has detrimental health and social effects, so does use of our two legal drugs, alcohol and tobacco, and to be consistent, we should legalize marijuana. But legalizing marijuana would add a third drug that combines some of the most serious risks of the other two. Marijuana offers both the intoxicating effects of alcohol and the long-term lung damage of tobacco. It would be irresponsible to legalize or decriminalize marijuana and create a third legal drug, especially when we are still learning about its physical and psychological health effects, as well as its relationship to other drugs and a variety of dangerous behaviors. One of the most serious drawbacks of marijuana legalization, Kleiman notes, is its "virtual irreversibility if it goes badly wrong" (113). He also noted regarding marijuana legalization: "Low tax, high potency marijuana could lead to severe social costs within user populations of the greatest concern; high tax, low potency marijuana could sustain black markets and their associated costs while increasing consumption more modestly" (114).

The European Experiences

Many legalization advocates point to the policies of European countries as models for approaches to the American drug problem. They claim that some countries, notably the Netherlands and Great Britain, are more innovative because their aim is to minimize the harmful impact of drug use on the user and society, even if this requires legal change.

While the Netherlands' laws regarding illegal drugs remain unchanged, Dutch enforcement policy since 1976 has distinguished between "drugs presenting an unacceptable risk" (commonly termed "hard drugs," such as cocaine and heroin) and "cannabis products" (89). Special "coffee shops" were established where anyone age 18 years or older can purchase marijuana. Legalization proponents claim that this policy has not increased drug use among young people or the population in general (22, 115, 116).

The reality is more nuanced. Although marijuana use did not explode immediately following decriminalization, it did increase significantly following "commercialization" via the coffee shops (117), suggesting that the effects of decriminalization are related to a variety of factors and may only be fully realized in the longer term. Between 1984 and 1992, Dutch adolescent marijuana use increased nearly 200% (118); over the same period, marijuana use among American adolescents plummeted 66%. From 1988 to 1995, the Dutch had a 22% increase in the total number of registered addicts, and a 30% increase, from 1991 to 1993, in the number of registered cannabis addicts (119). From 1990 to 1995, the proportion of users who had smoked cannabis for the previous 5 years increased from 2% to 9%, suggesting that increased availability would be associated with longer-term use (120). The same study found that between 1990 and 1995, the percentage of 11- to 18-year-olds who had ever used marijuana more than doubled, from 7% to 17% (120). A number of marijuana "coffee shops" in Amsterdam have been shut down for illegally selling hard drugs or breaking other rules. Responding to pressure from other European countries and its own citizens, the Dutch Parliament passed restrictions in 1996 pledging to cut the number of coffee houses in half and reducing the amount of marijuana an individual can buy from 30 g to 5 g (121). It appears that only the reduction in quantity to be purchased has actually happened. By 1998 there had been only approximately a 10% reduction in the number of coffee shops because of legal tactics used by their owners (122), illustrating again how hard it becomes to change these policies once in place. Ironically, even though the marijuana trade may now be worth more than $300 million per year, the government, because of legal rulings, has been unable to tax it.

Another country that legalization advocates cite favorably is Great Britain for its policy of allowing specially licensed doctors to prescribe drugs to addicts. Prescribing heroin to addicts, it is claimed, has lowered the rate of addiction and reduced crime (123); neither of these claims has been verified.

Nationwide, British doctors maintain 17,000 heroin addicts on methadone and less than 400 on heroin. Given the 150,000 heroin addicts in England, claims that maintaining a few hundred of them on heroin have driven drug dealers and drug-related crimes from the streets are unfounded. There has been no movement among doctors in England to adopt heroin maintenance on a large scale (124).

In general, much confusion surrounds British policies. Until 1968, the government allowed all doctors to prescribe drugs to addicts in the context of their medical treatment, but this policy, while initially successful, in the 1960s failed to contain the problem of addiction. Some doctors carelessly or willfully abused their privilege and unlawfully supplied drugs to many individuals. Addicts diverted legally obtained drugs to the general population. In response to increasing rates of addiction, Britain mandated in 1968 that only doctors specially licensed by the Home Office could prescribe illegal drugs and that doctors must register all addicts with the Home Office (125). More than 100 doctors are licensed, of whom fewer than 20 prescribed such drugs for most of the 1990s.

The rate of increase in heroin addiction in England subsequently slowed until the late 1970s, when a large influx of black market heroin from southwest Asia fueled a sudden increase in new addicts that continued through the 1980s (126). This increase was not, as some legalization proponents claim, a result of the fact that the British, following the American lead, adopted harsher drug laws. While on the national level, the government responded to this increase in addiction by emphasizing supply reduction, prevention, and criminal justice deterrents, at the local level officials emphasized harm reduction and loosely enforced antidrug laws. These conflicting national and local approaches persisted until the late 1980s, when concern over the spread of AIDS by injection drug users prompted national policy makers to shift toward harm-reduction programs such as needle exchanges and condom distribution (127).

In short, the increasing number of addicts in Britain was not a result of strict national laws and "zero tolerance" policies. Rather, these policies were a response to the increased addiction. Moreover, strict national antidrug laws mean little if local enforcement is lax.

One celebrated experiment in harm reduction and drug tolerance is less often mentioned now that it has been terminated. Beginning in 1987, Switzerland allowed all addicts and users to congregate in a park—the "Platzspitz," or "Needle Park," as it became known—in the center of downtown Zurich, where they could buy and use drugs freely. Strict enforcement of antidrug laws continued in the rest of the city and country. Like many proponents of harm reduction, Swiss policy makers believed that if drug dealing and use was going to happen anyway, it might as well occur in the open where the police and health officials could monitor it. In Needle Park, public health officials gave addicts free needles, condoms, medical care, counseling, and the opportunity for treatment (89).

This experiment in harm reduction had unintended consequences. The number of addicts in the park increased from a few hundred in 1987 to 20,000 in 1992. Twenty-five percent came from outside Switzerland, drawn to the park by its tolerant policies. Drug-related violence and crime rose rapidly in the area; 81 drug-related deaths were recorded in 1991, double the previous year. The city's chief medical officer reported that doctors were resuscitating an average of 12 people a day who had overdosed, and as many as 40 people on some days. Because of these high costs, the park was closed in 1992, but the fallout from this policy was damaging. The heroin-related death rate in Switzerland had become the highest in Europe and North America (128). Addicts wandered the city streets and open-air markets proliferated. Three years after the experiment ended, Swiss police tried to disperse the continuing drug bazaar that had moved to an unused railroad station. Ultimately, to deal with their burgeoning heroin problem, which may be the highest in Europe (122),

Swiss authorities began heroin maintenance trials, as noted earlier. As drug policy experts MacCoun and Reuter point out, however, "Heroin maintenance has a contradiction at its heart. Having chosen to prohibit the drug, society then makes an exception for those who cause sufficient damage, to themselves and to society. . . ." If society sets the bar high by requiring a lot of damage, it "is expensive . . . and inhumane. However, if it sets the barrier low, then access to heroin becomes too easy. . . ." "This raises a 'fundamental ethical concern. . . . [H]eroin maintenance itself is clearly social policy, not medicine—[S]ocial policy should not be dressed up as a therapeutic activity" (122).

Italy is infrequently mentioned by advocates of legalization despite its lenient drug laws. Personal possession of small amounts of drugs has not been a crime in Italy since 1975, other than for a brief period of "recriminalization" between 1990 and 1993 (though even then Italy permitted an individual to possess one daily dose of a drug). Under decriminalization, interpretation of the precise quantity allowed was left to individual judges, but generally, possession of two to three daily doses of drugs such as heroin was exempt from criminal sanction (129). Italy, in 1994, had 300,000 heroin addicts (130), one of the highest rates of heroin addiction in Europe (128). Seventy percent of all AIDS cases in Italy are attributable to drug use (130).

In contrast, Sweden offers an example of a successful restrictive drug policy. Sweden has tried a variety of approaches to drugs (although none have involved legalization) since its first experiment with the prescription of drugs, particularly amphetamines, to addicts in 1965. This experiment ended 2 years later because eligible addicts diverted prescribed drugs to friends and acquaintances and, contrary to the expectation that freely available drugs would decrease crime among addicts, crimes committed by legal users increased.

In 1972, Swedish policy shifted toward harm reduction; enforcement became more lax, concentrating primarily on drug kingpins. Arrests for drug offenses dropped by half and police allowed possession of up to a week's supply of a drug. During this time, drug use remained high and heroin use began on a large scale.

By 1980, increasing deaths from heroin use shifted public opinion and government policy toward a more restrictive approach to drugs. The aim of Swedish drug policy, like that of the United States, became a drug-free society. Possession of anything more than a single joint of marijuana was punished; drug arrests tripled in 3 years. In 1982, Sweden introduced mandatory treatment commitments. During the 1980s, drug use declined rapidly, particularly among the young. By 1988, the percentage of military conscripts using drugs fell by 75%; current use by ninth graders dropped 66%. The population of drug users aged considerably. In 1979, 37% of daily drug users were under age 25 years; in 1992, 10% were (131).

Thus, the claim that permissive drug policies in some European nations are a success and an example for the United States to emulate is both inaccurate and simplistic. Reality remains complex. If the numbers are correct, and that is a big "if" requiring a chapter in itself, the two countries in Europe with the lowest overall prevalence of drug addiction in the early 1990s were the two with the most diametrically opposed policies, Sweden and the Netherlands. This suggests both that factors other than stated policy may play a major role (122) and how difficult cross-national comparisons are.

Can We Improve the Present Situation?

For all of the above-mentioned reasons, particularly the increased numbers of users and addicts and the threat to our children, legalization would open a dangerous Pandora's box. The claimed panacea—change the legal status of drugs and the problems associated with them will disappear—is illusory. More questions and problems arise than are answered by proponents.

Legalization is a policy of despair, one that would write off millions of our citizens and lead to a terrible game of Russian roulette, particularly for children. It is not born of any new evidence regarding the nature of addiction or the pharmacologic, public health, or criminal effects of drug use. At the

beginning of the century, the visible results of widespread recreational opiate and cocaine use prompted the first antidrug laws. With so much more new knowledge about the devastating consequences of drug use, it would be foolhardy to turn back the clock.

To reject legal change, however, is not to accept all of current policy. We have not yet mounted an all-fronts assault on illegal drug use in America, a fact reflected in the increase in teenage drug use during the 1990s. We should provide equal protection in the enforcement of drug laws by ending the acceptance of open-air drug bazaars in poor communities, which would not be tolerated in more prosperous ones. Treatment needs to be both made more readily available and improved. We need to recognize that addiction can be a chronic relapsing disorder, which necessitates major changes in how treatment is delivered and financed. Given the high prevalence of psychiatric disorders in addicts, the staff of treatment programs needs to be upgraded as far as skills and training as well as compensation. Treatment in the criminal justice system needs to be expanded so that we have more treatment in prison, after prison, and instead of prison.

Research on abuse and addiction has been woefully underfunded but doubling of National Institute on Drug Abuse (NIDA)'s budget over 5 years has helped improve the balance with other National Institutes of Health (NIH) institutes. However, it is not clear that NIDA will continue its budget success in the era of large budget deficits. It is critical to have a steady, increasing approach without deep troughs that drive talented investigators from the field. The increased knowledge of possible long-term brain changes in experimenting adolescents (55) and the realization of the importance of such changes in perpetuating addiction (132) provide targets for enhanced research efforts in both treatment and prevention.

Prevention is the least-expensive way to reduce the burden of drugs on our society; a dollar spent on prevention can save up to $15 in health care, criminal justice, and other costs (133), but there is controversy about its effectiveness (134). An aggressive strategy of prevention should be aimed at the entire population, but with special attention to those currently at high risk of drug abuse. Prevention programs should target children and adolescents, because individuals who go from age 10 years to 20 years without trying illegal drugs are unlikely to use them. Community-wide organizations such as Community Partnership Programs and the Parents Corps should be supported and expanded. The motto of an Office of National Drug Control Policy (ONDCP)/Partnership for a Drug Free America campaign, "Parents—the Anti-Drug," stresses the essential role parents can play. Their task is an uphill one because a sizable percentage of music videos, movies, and television portray alcohol, tobacco, and drug use as behaviors people do naturally when they socialize without serious consequences, helping to normalize such behavior among viewers (135).

Treatment is both absolutely and relatively cost-effective. It pays for itself over time by saving $7 in criminal justice, health care, and welfare costs for every dollar invested (136). To reduce heavy cocaine use, an additional dollar spent on treatment is 7 times more cost-effective than an additional dollar spent on domestic enforcement and 20 times more cost-effective than attempting to control supply in source countries (137). Still, more research is needed to raise treatment success rates, as well as to discern which types of treatment are most effective for which individuals. We also need to adopt more innovative strategies to get addicts who are neither in treatment nor involved yet with the criminal justice system to seek treatment. Using a coupon for free treatment and rapid intake, Booth and associates (138) were able to get two-thirds of those who received the coupon to enter treatment.

Court-imposed treatment should be expanded and combined with programs that reintegrate the ex-offender into the community by providing continued substance abuse counseling and support groups, as well as education and job training. Treatment and aftercare can decrease recidivism by giving ex-offenders a new chance to become productive members of society. As many as 800,000 inmates have prior convictions. If treatment reduced recidivism by just 20%, there would be 160,000 fewer inmates; a 50% reduction would mean 400,000 fewer inmates.

Mandatory minimum sentencing laws need to be revisited so that we appropriately use and target the scarce commodity of prison cells. Alternatives to incarceration, especially those that coordinate the criminal justice and treatment systems, such as Drug Courts and Treatment Alternatives to Street Crime (TASC), should be expanded. Unfortunately in the past decade we went in the opposite direction. The number of prisoners in substance-abuse treatment programs decreased between 1991 and 1997, from 25% to 10% in state prisons, and from 16% to 9% in federal prisons (139). Unless there is real coordination and appropriate sanctions, however, referenda that simply mandate treatment in lieu of incarceration, for example, Proposition 136 in California, may end up disillusioning the public about treatment as addicts who lack any interest or incentive to stop use make treatment a revolving door. Mandated treatment needs a carefully thought out structure with believable rewards and sanctions actually carried out.

The objective of a drug-free America, derided by advocates of legalization, is a statement of hope that a generation of children can come of age less exposed to the life-destroying effects of illegal drugs. As James Q. Wilson so eloquently observed, ". . . (if) the legalizers prevail then we will have consigned millions of people, hundreds of thousands of infants, and hundreds of neighborhoods to a life of oblivion and disease. To the lives and families destroyed by alcohol we will have added countless more destroyed by cocaine, heroin, PCP [phencyclidine], and whatever else a basement scientist can invent (140)."

Our policies should aim to reduce drug use and addiction to a marginal phenomenon and to rehabilitate drug abusers. At its best, America strives to give all its citizens the chance to develop their talents. Cornering millions of individuals into drug addiction insults this fundamental value and demeans the dignity to which each is entitled.

Finally, we need to take the long view because, as the eminent historian of drug use epidemics, David Musto, has pointed out, "Demanding quick solutions to the drug problem inevitably leads to frustration because the decline rate is never as steep as promised—Promises of a quick fix may energize concerned citizens for a while, but the larger effect is to discourage them. Repeated, hyped, short-term drug campaigns to end drug abuse 'once and for all . . .' are reminiscent of cocaine use. Every time the same dose is taken, the impact lessens, the temptation to increase the dose escalates, and, finally, you have burnout" (141).

References

1. Inciardi JA. American drug policy: the continuing debate. In: Inciardi JA, ed. *The drug legalization debate*, 2nd ed. Thousand Oaks, CA: Sage Publications, 1999: 1–8.

2. Lock ED, Timberlake JM, Rasinski KA. Battle fatigue: is public support waning for "war"-centered drug control strategies? *Crime Delinquency* 2002; 48 (3): 380–398.

3. Gra M. *How we got into this mess and how we can get out.* New York: Routledge, 2000.

4. McBride DC, Terry YM, Inciardi JA. Alternative perspectives on the drug policy debate. In: Inciardi JA, ed. *The drug legalization debate*, 2nd ed. Thousand Oaks, CA: Sage Publications, 1999: 9–54.

5. Musto DF. *The American disease: origins of narcotic control*. New York: Oxford University Press, 1987.

6. Terry CE, Pellens M. *The opium problem*. Montclair, NJ: Patterson Smith, 1970.

7. Musto DF. Foreword. In: Erickson PG, Adlaf EM, Murray GF, et al. *The steel drug: cocaine in perspective*. Toronto: Lexington Books, 1987: XV–XVL.

8. Impacteen Illicit Drug Team. *Illicit drug policies: selected laws from the 50 states*. Berrien Springs, MI: Andrews University, 2002.

9. Inciardi J, ed. *Handbook of drug control in the United States*. New York: Greenwood Press, 1990.

10. Goode E. *Between politics and reason: the drug legalization debate*. New York: St. Martin Press, 1997.

11. Inciardi JA, Harrison LD. The concept of harm reduction. In: Inciardi JA, Harrison LD, eds. *Harm reduction: national and international perspectives*. Thousand Oaks, CA: Sage, 2000: viii.

12. DuPont R, Voth E. Drug legalization, harm reduction, and drug policy. *Ann Intern Med* 1995; 123 (6): 461–465.

13. *The New York Times* 1998 Jun 19: A29.

14. Smith M. The drug problem: is there an answer? In: Evans R, Berent I, eds. *Drug legalization: for and against*. LaSalle, IL: Open Court Press, 1992: 77–88.

15. Schmoke K. Decriminalizing drugs: it just might work—and nothing else does. In: Evans R, Berent I, eds. Drug legalization: for and against. La Salle, IL: Open Court Press, 1992: 215–220.

16. National Commission on Marijuana and Drug Abuse. *Marijuana: signal of misunderstanding*. Washington, DC: U.S. Government Printing Office, 1972.

17. Grinspoon L, Bakalar JB. Drug dependence: non-narcotic agents. In: Kaplan HI, Sadock BJ, eds. *Comprehensive textbook of psychiatry*, 3rd ed. Baltimore: Williams & Wilkins, 1980.

18. U.S. Department of Health and Human Services. *Results from the 2001 National Household Survey on Drug Abuse*. Rockville, MD: Office of Applied Studies, Substance Abuse and Mental Health Services Administration, 2002.

19. *Office of National Drug Control Policy, Drug use trends*. Rockville, MD: Drug Policy Information Clearinghouse, 2002.

20. Office of National Drug Control Policy. *Breaking the cycle of drug abuse*. Washington, DC: U.S. Government Printing Office, 1993.

21. Trebach A. For legalization of drugs. In: Trebach A, Inciardi J. *Legalize it? Debating American drug policy*. Washington, DC: American University Press, 1993: 7–138.

22. Nadelmann E. The case for legalization. In: Inciardi JA, ed. *The drug legalization debate*. Newbury Park, CA: Sage Publications, 1991: 17–44.

23. Gazzaniga M. The opium of the people: crack in perspective. In: Evans R, Berent I, eds. *Drug legalization: for and against*. La Salle, IL: Open Court Press, 1992: 231–246.

24. Johnston L, O'Malley P, Bachman J. *National survey results on drug use from the Monitoring the Future Study, 1975–2001*. Ann Arbor, MI: University of Michigan, 2002.

25. Grinspoon L, Bakalar J. The war on drugs—a peace proposal. *N Engl J Med* 1994; 330: 357–360.

26. Moore M. Drugs: getting a fix on the problem and the solution. In: Evans R, Berent I, eds. *Drug legalization: for and against*. La Salle, IL: Open Court Press, 1992: 123–156.

27. Brenner TA. The legalization of drugs: why prolong the inevitable? In: Evans R, Berent I, eds. *Drug legalization: for and against*, 1992: 157–180.

28. Office of National Drug Control Policy. *National drug control strategy: strengthening communities' response to drugs and crime*. Washington, DC: U.S. Government Printing Office, 1995.

29. U.S. Centers for Disease Control and Prevention. *MMWR Morbid Mortal Wkly Rep* 1994; 34: SS–3.

30. Moore M. Supply reduction and law enforcement. In: Tonry M, Wilson J, eds. *Drugs and crime*. Chicago: University of Chicago Press, 1990: 109–158.

31. Grossman M, Becker G, Murphy K. Rational addiction and the effect of price on consumption. In: Krauss M, Lazear E, eds. *Searching for alternatives, drug-control policy in the United States*. Stanford, CA: Hoover Institution Press, 1992: 77–86.

32. Farrell M, Strang J, Reuter P. The non-case for legalization. In: Stevenson RC, ed. *Winning the war on drugs: to legalize or not*. London: Institute of Economic Affairs, 1994: 83–90.

33. Caulkins, JP. *Do drug prohibition and enforcement work?* Lexington Institute, Lexington, MA 2000.

34. Cook P. The effect of liquor taxes on drinking, cirrhosis, and auto accidents. In: Moore M, Gerstein D, eds. *Alcohol and public policy: beyond the shadow of prohibition*. Washington, DC: National Academy Press, 1981: 255–285.

35. Kleber HD. Our current approach to drug abuse—progress, problems, proposals. *N Engl J Med* 1994; 330: 361–364.

36. Goldstein PJ. Drugs and violent behavior. *J Drug Issues* 1985; 15: 493–506.

37. Inciardi JA. *The War on Drugs III*. Boston: Allyn and Bacon, 2002.

38. Weiss RD, Mirin SM. *Cocaine*. Washington, DC: American Psychiatric Press, 1987.

39. Satel SI, Price LH, Palumbo JM, et al. Clinical phenomenology and neurobiology of cocaine abstinence: a prospective inpatient study. *Am J Psychiatry* 1991; 148: 1712—1716.

40. Brody SL. Violence associated with acute cocaine use in patients admitted to a medical emergency department. *NIDA Res Monogr* 1990; 103: 44–59.

41. Reiss AJ, Roth J. *Understanding and preventing violence. Vol. 3: societal influences*. Washington, DC: National Academy Press.

42. Inciardi JA, Lockwood D, Pottieger AE. *Women and crack-cocaine*. New York: Macmillan, 1993.

43. Tunnell KD. *Choosing crime: the criminal calculus of property offenders*. Chicago, IL: Nelson-Hall Publishers, 1992.

44. Fagan J, Chin K. Social processes of initiation into crack. *J Drug Issues* 1991; 21: 313–343.

45. Inciardi JA, Surratt HL. Drug use, street crime, and sex-trading among cocaine-dependent women: implications for public health and criminal justice policy. *J Psychoactive Drugs* 2001; 33 (4): 379–389.

46. Inciardi JA, Pottieger AE., Crack cocaine use and street crime. *J Drug Issues* 1994; 24 (2): 273–292.

47. Jacobs BA. *Dealing crack: the social world of streetcorner selling.* Boston: Northeastern University Press, 1999.

48. Miller N, Gold M. Criminal activity and crack addiction. *Int J Addict* 1994; 29 (8): 1069–1078.

49. Johnson BD, Natarajan M, Dunlap E, et al. Crack abusers and noncrack abusers: profiles of drug use, drug sales and nondrug criminality. *J Drug Issues* 1994; 24 (1): 117–141.

50. Fagan J, Chin K. Violence as regulation and social control in the distribution of crack. *NIDA Res Monogr* 1990; 103: 8–43.

51. Hamid A. The political economy of crack related violence. *Contemp Drug Probl* 1990; Spring: 31–78.

52. Leukefeld CG, Tims F, Farabee D, eds. *Treatment of drug offenders.* New York: Springer Publishing, 2002.

53. Inciardi JA. *Criminal justice*, 7th ed. Orlando, FL: Harcourt College Publishers, 2002.

54. Office of National Drug Control Policy. *National drug control strategy 2002.* Washington, DC: U.S. Government Printing Office, 2002.

55. Chambers RA, Taylor JR, Potenza MN. Developmental neurocircuitry of motivation in adolescence: a critical period of addiction vulnerability. *Am J Psychiatry* 2003; 160: 1041–1052.

56. McLellan AT, Lewis DC, O'Brien CP, et al. Drug dependence, a chronic medical illness. *JAMA* 2000; 284: 1689–1695.

57. Greenfield LR. *Alcohol & crime: an analysis of national data on the prevalence of alcohol involvement in crime.* Washington, DC: Bureau of Justice Statistics, 1998.

58. Bureau of Justice Statistics Prisoners in 1994. Washington, DC: U.S. Department of Justice, 1995.

59. U.S. Department of Transportation, National Highway Traffic Safety Administration, 1999.

60. Aaron P, Musto D. Temperance and prohibition in America: a historical overview. In: Moore M, Gerstein D, eds. *Alcohol and public policy: beyond the shadow of prohibition.* Washington, DC: National Academy Press, 1981: 127–181.

61. *Statistical release: alcohol, tobacco and firearms tax collections. Fiscal year 1995.* Washington, DC: Department of the Treasury, Bureau of Alcohol, Tobacco and Firearms, 1995.

62. State government tax collections: 1995. Available at *http://www.census.gov/govs/statetax/95tax001.txt*.

63. The National Center on Addiction and Substance Abuse at Columbia University. *The cost of substance abuse to America's health care system, final report.* New York: CASA, 1996.

64. State government tax collections 2000. Available at *http://www.census.gov/govs/statetax/0000usstax.html*.

65. Schneider Institute for Health Policy, Brandeis University. *Substance abuse: the nation's number one health problem.* Princeton, NJ: The Robert Wood Johnson Foundation, 2001.

66. U.S. Centers for Disease Control and Prevention. *HIV/AIDS Surveill Rep* 2000; 12 (2): 2001.

67. Sendi P, Hoffman M, Bucher HC, et al. Intravenous heroin maintenance in a cohort of injecting drug addicts. *Drug Alcohol Depend* 2003; 69: 183–188.

68. Rehm J, Gschwend P, Steffen T, et al. Feasibility, safety, and efficacy of injectable heroin prescription for refractory opioid addicts: a follow-up study. *Lancet* 2001; 358: 1417–1420.

69. Jaffe JH, O'Keeffe C. From morphine clinics to buprenorphine: regulating opioid agonist treatment of addiction in the United States. *Drug Alcohol Depend* 2003; 70 (S): S3–S11.

70. Thirion X, Lapierre V, Miscallef U, et al. Buprenorphine prescription by general practitioners in a French region. *Drug Alcohol Depend* 2002; 65: 197–204.

71. Ling W, Smith D. Buprenorphine: blending practice and research. *J Subst Abuse Treat* 2002; 23: 87–92.

72. Fischman MW, Haney M. Neurobiology of stimulants. In: Galanter M, Kleber HD, eds. *Textbook of substance abuse treatment*, 2nd ed. Washington, DC: American Psychiatric Press, 1999: 21–31.

73. McLellan AT, Arndt O, Metzger DS, et al. The effects of psychosocial services in substance abuse treatment. *JAMA* 1993; 269: 1953–1959.

74. Hartgers C, van den Hoek A, Krijnen P, et al. HIV prevalence and risk behavior among injection drug users who participate in "low threshold" methadone programs in Amsterdam. *Am J Public Health* 1992; 82: 547–551.

75. Normand J, Vlahov D, Moses LA, eds. *Panel on needle exchange and bleach distribution programs. Commission on Behavioral and Social Sciences and Education. National Research Council and Institute.* Washington, DC: National Academy Press, 1995.

76. US Department of Justice. *Drugs, crime and the criminal justice system: a national report.* Washington, DC: US Government Printing Office, 1992.

77. Taubman P. Externalities and decriminalization of drugs. In: Krauss M, Lazear E, eds. *Searching for alternatives: drug-control policy in the United States.* Stanford, CA: Hoover Institution Press, 1992: 90–111.

78. Hay J. The harm they do to others. In: Krauss M, Lazear E, eds. *Searching for alternatives: drug-control policy in the United States.* Stanford, CA: Hoover Institution Press, 1992: 200–225.

79. The National Center on Addiction and Substance Abuse at Columbia University. *The cost of substance abuse to America's health care system, report 1: Medicaid hospital costs.* New York: CASA, 1993.

80. Kessler R, et al. Lifetime and 12-month prevalence of DSM-III-R psychiatric disorders in the United States: results from the National Comorbidity Study. *Arch Gen Psychiatry* 1994; 51 (1): 8–19.

81. U.S. Centers for Disease Control and Prevention. *Youth Risk Behavior Survey, 1999.* Rockville, MD: U.S. Department of Health and Human Services, 1999.

82. Cooper ML, Pierce R, Huselid RF. Substance abuse and sexual risk taking among black adolescents and white adolescents. *Health Psychol* 1994; 13 (3): 251–262.

83. General Accounting Office. *Foster care: parental drug abuse has alarming impact on young children.* Washington, DC: U.S. Government Printing Office, 1994.

84. Brookoff B, et al. Testing reckless drivers for cocaine and marijuana. *N Engl J Med* 1994; 331 (8): 518–522.

85. Drug Strategies. *Keeping score.* Washington, DC: Author, 1995.

86. Office of National Drug Control Policy. *The economic costs of drug abuse in the United States, 1992–1998 (with projections for 1999–2000).* Washington, DC: US Government Printing Office, 2001.

87. Rice D. *The economic costs of alcohol and drug abuse and mental illness: 1995.* Washington, DC: US Department of Health and Human Services, 1999.

88. Lender ME, Martin JK. *Drinking in America: a history.* New York: Macmillan, 1982.

89. Goldstein A. *Addiction: from biology to public policy.* New York: WH Freeman, 1994.

90. McCoy C: Booze flows back into Barrow, Alaska after year-long ban. *Wall Street Journal* 1995 Nov 15: A1.

91. Wisotsky S. Statement before the Select Committee on Narcotics Abuse and Control. In: Evans R, Berent I, eds. *Drug legalization: for and against.* La Salle, IL: Open Court Press, 1992: 181–212.

92. McGinnis JM, Foege W. Actual causes of death in the United States. *JAMA* 1993; 270 (18): 2207–2212.

93. Pytkowicz A, et al. Fetal alcohol syndrome in adolescents and adults. *JAMA* 1991; 265 (15): 1961–1967.

94. DiFranza J, Lew R. Effect of maternal cigarette smoking on pregnancy complications and sudden infant death syndrome. *J Fam Pract* 1995; 40 (4): 385–394.

95. Office of the Surgeon General. *Nicotine addiction: the health consequences of smoking.* Washington, DC: U.S. Government Printing Office, 1988.

96. The National Center on Addiction and Substance Abuse at Columbia University. *Substance abuse and federal entitlement programs.* New York: CASA, 1995.

97. Kleiman M. Legalizing drugs [Letter]. *Economist* 1993 Jun 12–18: 8.

98. Grinspoon L. Marijuana in a time of psychopharmacological McCarthyism. In: Krauss M, Lazear E, eds. *Searching for alternatives: drug-control policy in the United States.* Stanford, CA: Hoover Institution Press, 1992: 379–389.

99. Hall W, Solowij N. Adverse effects of cannabis. *Lancet* 1998: 352: 1611–1616.

100. Gold MD, Frost-Pineda K, Jacobs WS. Marijuana. In: Galanter M, Kleber HD, eds. *Textbook of Substance Abuse Treatment* 2004. 3rd ed. Washington, DC: American Psychiatric Press (in press).

101. Day NL, Richardson GA, Gold Schmidt L, et al. Effect of prenatal marijuana exposure on the cognitive development of offspring at age three. *Neurotoxicol Teratol* 1994; 16 (2): 169–175.

102. Solowij N, Stephens RS, Roffman RA, et al. Cognitive functioning of long-term heavy cannabis users seeking treatment. *JAMA* 2002; 287: 1123–1131.

103. Millman R, Beeder AB. Cannabis. In: Galanter M, Kleber HD, eds. *Textbook of substance abuse treatment.* Washington, DC: American Psychiatric Press, 1994: 91–109.

104. Kandel DB, ed. *Stages & pathway of drug involvement: examining the gateway hypothesis.* Cambridge, U.K: Cambridge University Press, 2002.

105. Gfroerer JC, Wu LT, Penne MA *Initiation of marijuana use: trends: patterns and implications.* Office of Applied Studies, Washington, DC: SAMHSA, 2002.

106. Lynskey MT, Heath AC, Bucholz KK, et al. Escalation of drug use in early-onset cannabis users vs. co-twin controls. *JAMA* 2003; 289: 427–433.

107. Kandel DB. Does marijuana use cause the use of other drugs? *JAMA* 2003; 289: 482–483.

108. U.S. Centers for Disease Control and Prevention. *Youth Risk Behavior Survey, 1991.* Rockville, MD: U.S. Department of Health and Human Services, 1991.

109. Segal B, et al. *Patterns of drug use: school survey.* Anchorage: Center for Alcohol and Addiction Studies, University of Alaska, 1983.

110. Segal B. *Drug-taking behavior among Alaska youth—1988: a follow-up study.* Anchorage: Center for Alcohol and Addiction Studies, University of Alaska, with the State Office of Alcoholism and Drug Abuse, August 1989.

111. Maloff D. A review of the effects of the decriminalization of marijuana. *Contemp Drug Probl* 1981; Fall: 306–322.

112. Cuskey W, et al. The effects of marijuana decriminalization on drug use patterns: a literature review and research critique. *Contemp Drug Probl* 1978; Winter: 491–532.

113. Cuskey W. Critique of marijuana decriminalization research. *Contemp Drug Probl* 1981; Fall: 323–334.

114. Kleiman M. *Against excess: drug policy for results.* New York: Basic Books, 1992.

115. Karel R. A model legalization proposal. In: Inciardi J, ed. *The drug legalization debate.* Newbury Park, CA: Sage Publications, 1991: 80–102.

116. McVay D. Marijuana legalization: the time is now. In: Inciardi J, ed. *The drug legalization debate.* Newbury Park, CA: Sage Publications, 1991: 147–160.

117. MacCoun RJ, Reuter P. Interpreting Dutch cannabis policy: reasoning by analogy in the legalization debate. *Science* 1997; 278: 47–52.

118. de Zwart WM, Mensink C, Kuipers SBM. *Key data: smoking, drinking, drug use and gambling among pupils aged 10 years and older.* Utrecht, Netherlands: Institute for Alcohol and Drugs, 1994.

119. Gunning KF, president, Dutch National Commission on Drug Prevention. Rotterdam, Holland, February 20, 1995.

120. Spanjer M. Dutch schoolchildren's drug-taking doubles. *Lancet* 1996; 347 (9000): 534.

121. Kroon JR. Interview with Dutch Prime Minister Kim Wok. *International Herald Tribune* 1996 Apr 9: 5.

122. MacCoun RJ, Reuter P. *Drug war heresies: Learning from other vices, times, and places.* Cambridge, UK: Cambridge University Press, 2001.

123. Interview with Dr John Marks. *Psychiatric News* 1993 Dec 17: 8, 14.

124. Glaze J, British Home Office. Letter to Michael Snell, Esq., British Embassy in Washington, DC, December 30, 1992.

125. Spear B. The early years of the "British system" in practice. In: Strang J, Gossop M, eds. *Heroin addiction and drug policy: the British system.* New York: Oxford University Press, 1994: 3–28.

126. Power R. Drug trends since 1968. In: Strang J, Gossop M, eds. *Heroin addiction and drug policy: the British system.* New York: Oxford University Press, 1994: 29–41.

127. Turner D. Pragmatic incoherence: the changing face of British drug policy. In: Krauss M, Lazear E, eds. *Searching for alternatives: drug-control policy in the United States.* Stanford, CA: Hoover Institution Press, 1992: 175–190.

128. Reuter P, Falco M, MacCoun R. *Comparing Western European and North American drug policies: an international conference report.* Santa Monica, CA: RAND, 1993.

129. Di Gennaro G. Antidrug legislation in Italy: historical background and present status. *J Drug Issues* 1994; 24 (4): 673–678.

130. Mariani F, Guaiana R, Di Fiandra T, et al. An epidemiological overview of the situation of illicit drug abuse in Italy. *J Drug Issues* 1994; 24 (4): 579–595.

131. *A restrictive drug policy: the Swedish experience.* Stockholm: Swedish National Institute of Public Health, 1993.

132. Leshner AI. Addiction is a brain disease and it matters. *Science* 1997; 278: 45–47.

133. Kim S, et al. Benefit–cost analysis of drug abuse prevention programs: a macroscopic approach. *J Drug Educ* 1995; 25 (2): 111–128.

134. Caulkins JP, Rydell CP, Everingham SM, et al. *An ounce of prevention, a pound of uncertainty: the cost-effectiveness of school-based drug prevention programs.* Santa Monica, CA: RAND, 1999.

135. *Substance use in popular music videos.* Washington, DC: Office of National Drug Control Policy, 2002.

136. State of California, Department of Alcohol and Drug Programs. *Evaluating recovery services: the California drug and alcohol treatment assessment (CALDATA).* 1994.

137. Rydell CP, Everingham S. *Controlling cocaine: supply vs. demand programs.* Santa Monica, CA: RAND, 1994.

138. Booth RE, Corsi KF, Mikulich SK. Improving entry to methadone maintenance among out of treatment injection drug users. *J Subst Abuse Treat* 2003; 24: 305–311.

139. *Substance abuse and treatment—state and federal prisons, 1997.* Rockville, MD: US Department of Justice, Bureau of Justice Statistics, 1999.

140. Wilson JQ. Against the legalization of drugs. *Commentary* 1990 Feb: 21–28.

141. Musto DF. This 10-year war can be won. *Washington Post* 1998 Jun 14: C-7.

For Discussion

1. Some drugs are legal in the United States whereas others are not. If other

drugs were to be legalized, what criteria should be used to determine legality?

2. Would use of all drugs increase if all drugs were legalized? Why or why not?

Reprinted from: Herbert D. Kleber and James A. Inciardi, "Clinical and Societal Implications of Drug Legalization." In *Substance Abuse: A Comprehensive Textbook*, fourth edition, ed. Joyce H. Lowinson, pp. 1383–1400. Copyright © 2004. Reprinted with permission. ✦

44

Safer Injection Facilities in North America

Their Place in Public Policy and Health Initiatives

Robert S. Broadhead
Thomas H. Kerr
Jean-Paul C. Grund
Frederick L. Altice

Injecting drug users (IDUs) continue to be at risk for overdose, blood-borne viruses such as HIV and Hepatitis C virus, and other health problems. The illegal status of drugs as well as the nature of drug dependence contribute to risk and ill health among IDUs. Safer injection facilities are authorized by governments in various countries and allow IDUs to inject drugs more safely in semipublic spaces. In this next chapter, Robert Broadhead and his colleagues draw on their observations of safer injection facilities located primarily in Europe. The authors describe how these facilities operate, the "house rules," and referral mechanisms to other services. The authors suggest that safer injection facilities can reduce risk for IDUs as well as the communities in which they reside or inject.

Introduction

Injection drug use continues to be associated with an array of significant health and social consequences throughout North America. These consequences are tied directly to the consumption of illicit drugs of unknown potency and composition, and the sharing of contaminated injection equipment; and indirectly, through unprotected sex with drug injectors, and through injectors' immersion in blackmarket pursuits that result frequently in violent exchanges with criminals and the police.

In the United States, injection drug use accounts for approximately 25% of all cumulative AIDS cases nationwide, but closer to 50% of all cases in several northeastern states (State of Connecticut Department of Health, 2000; State of New York Department of Public Health, 2000). The number of new HIV infections reported nationwide among injectors increased 300% in the 1990s, from 6,474 new infections in 1993, to 13,969 in 1995, 17,344 in 1998 and 18,882 in 1999 (Centers for Disease Control and Prevention, 2000). Injectors also suffer from very high rates of hepatitis C infection—90% of people who have injected for 5 years or more are infected—and from endocarditis, an acute infection of the heart valves that is not commonly seen among young adults (Centre for Disease Control, 1998; Gershon, 1998). Fatal and nonfatal drug overdose (OD) is also a prevalent medical problem among injectors, and hospital emergency rooms throughout the country attend to ODs virtually every day (Greenblatt, 1997; Sporer, Firestone, & Isaacs, 1996). Emergency room (ER) visits involving heroin alone doubled from 33,900 in 1990 to 70,500 in 1996, and some medical experts have recently declared that the United States is in the midst of another heroin epidemic (Sporer, 1999). On the other hand, injectors are known to use primary care services erratically and only after they are very sick, which drives up health care costs (Cherubin & Sapira, 1993; Mor, Fleishman, Dresser, & Piette, 1992). Injectors' pattern of avoiding primary care services, and over-relying on emergency rooms and acute care hospitalizations, has been well documented since the 1960s (Jouria, Hensle, & Rose, 1967; Sapira, 1968). Similarly, the vast majority of users are not interested in drug treatment; only 10–15% are enrolled at any given time, and drop-out rates are high (Bux, Iguchi, Lidz, Baxter, & Platt, 1993; Haverkos, 1991).

In Canada, the National Task Force on HIV, AIDS and Injection Drug Use declared that "Canada is in the midst of a public health crisis concerning HIV, AIDS, and injection drug use. . . . The number of new HIV infections among injectors is increasing rapidly, with Vancouver now having the highest reported rate in North America" (Canadian National Task Force on HIV, AIDS and Injection Drug Use [CNTF], 1997, pp. 2–3). As recently as 1997, the HIV prevalence rate among injectors in Vancouver [was] between 23–28% with 18.6 new infections for every 100 person-years, compared to a 20% prevalence rate in Montreal with 8.2 new infections for every 100 person-years (CNTF, 1997; Strathdee et al., 1997). The proportion of new HIV infections due to drug injection has also increased. Injectors accounted for 24% of new HIV infections between 1987 and 1990, but this increased to 46% by 1996 (Canadian Centre for Infectious Disease Prevention and Control, 2000). Like the United States, hepatitis C infection among injectors in Canada is also extremely high: 85% in Vancouver and 70% in Montreal with annual incidence rates of 26% and 27% respectively (Laboratory Centre for Disease Control, 1999). As the CNTF emphasized, "Despite clear indications of an escalating problem since the mid-1980s and the use of a variety of approaches to address it, the spread of HIV among injectors is increasing, as is the incidence of hepatitis and tuberculosis" (CNTF, 1997, p. 4).

In light of the continuing threat posed by HIV, HCV, and other drug injection-related health problems in both the United States and Canada, there is a clear need for further development of innovative interventions for injectors for disease prevention, reduction of drug-related deaths, and for increasing the number of injectors enrolled in drug treatment and other health care programs.

Governmentally sanctioned "safer injection facilities" (SIFs) are a health service that several countries around the world have been adding to the array of public health programs they offer. These countries include:

- Canada where the federal government, in collaboration with the Federal, Territorial and Provincial Advisory Committee on Population Health, has created a task force to examine the feasibility of a national research-based trial of SIFs

(Kerr & Palepu, 2001); Vancouver, B.C. where SIFs are included in the Mayor's "Four Pillar Drug Strategy," and a formal proposal to implement 2 SIFs has been put forward (Kerr, 2000; MacPherson, 2001)

- Germany with 13 SIFs operating in 4 cities
- The Netherlands with 16 SIFs operating in 9 cities
- Switzerland with 17 SIFs operating in 12 cities
- Spain with 1 SIF operating in Madrid
- Australia where an SIF began operations in May, 2001 in Sydney, and legislation has been approved to operate an SIF in Canberra and is pending in Melbourne (New York Times, 2001; Dolan [et al.], 2000).

Public health efforts for injectors in all of these cities, as well as in many major cities throughout the United States and Canada, typically include a range of street-based outreach services, needle exchange programs, HIV-test counseling centers, drug treatment/ drug-substitution programs, and broad-based, multi-targeted educational initiatives (Kerr, 2000; Normand, Vlahov, & Moses, 1995). As such, SIFs are clearly additions to, but still only parts of, much larger comprehensive public health approaches to reduce drug-related harm.

To date, there have been no systematic evaluations conducted on the operation and effectiveness of SIFs. However, a significant body of program evaluations, government and conference reports, and research articles has accumulated. Two comprehensive and frequently updated compilations where some of these materials can be found are the Lindesmith Center-Drug Policy Foundation website (*www.lindesmith.org/cites_sources/cites.html*) and the Australian Drug Foundation website (*www.adf. org.au/injectingrooms/index.htm*).

The discussion below draws on these materials, and from field observations and interviews made by the authors who, as a team, divided-up and visited 18 SIFs in Germany, Switzerland and the Netherlands over a ten day period in November, 2000. The first author also visited the SIF in Sydney, Australia in the following year. Below, we examine whether SIFs offer a significant, public health option that more communities in North America may wish to consider adding to their array of public health services for injectors. Specifically, we address the following policy questions:

- What specific problems do SIFs address over other services in responding to drug-related harms?
- What agreements need to be considered and negotiated in order to implement an SIF within a municipality?
- What rules of operation do SIFs generally follow?

First, however, we provide an overview of how SIFs are described and defined in various countries, including their staffing requirements and services offered.

An Overview of SIFs

In Hannover, Germany in November, 1999 the Addiction and Drug Research faculty of Carl von Ossietsky University, under the auspices of the German Federal Commissioner for Drugs (1999), sponsored the symposium entitled *Consumption Rooms as a Professional Service in Addictions-Health: International Conference for the Development of Guidelines*. The SIF Conference was attended by over 180 social workers, psychologists, nurses, doctors, public prosecutors, lawyers, and police officers from Germany, the Netherlands, Switzerland, Austria, France, and Australia. In the Conference *Guidelines* drafted by the conference participants, and in other documents, SIFs are referred to by several different names around the world, including "Gassenzimmer," "health-rooms," "safer injection rooms," "laneroom," "fix-rooms," "Fixerstubli," "drug consumption rooms," "consumption rooms," "medically supervised injecting centres," "supervised injecting places," "supervised consumption rooms," and "off-street injecting facilities" (Schneider & Stöver, 1999, p. 19). Despite the difference in names, the conference participants found common agreement on a simple definition: "[SIFs] are legal facilities that enable the consumption of pre-obtained drugs in an anxiety and stress-free atmosphere, under hygienic and low risk conditions" (Schneider & Stöver, 1999, p. 19). SIFs, therefore, stand in sharp contrast to what are generally referred to as "shooting galleries," which are private rooms or spaces in abandoned buildings, outdoor areas, and so on, that "operate informally and illegally . . . are unsterile, do not provide clean syringes or needles or the means of safe disposal, are unsupervised and do not provide medical assistance. These should not be confused with [SIFs] under discussion here" (Australian Drug Foundation, 1998, p. 2).

A distinction has been made between "pure" versus "comprehensive" SIFs, referring to the range of services that different projects offer (Schneider & Stöver, 1999). At one end of a continuum are "pure" SIFs that offer a safe and hygienic environment in which injectors can consume their pre-obtained drugs using sterile equipment provided on-site, overseen by a staff trained in basic first aid and cardiopulmonary resuscitation. At the other end are "comprehensive" SIFs that, in addition to the above, offer a much larger array of health and social services for injectors administered by professionals.

In actuality, all of the SIFs we observed in Western Europe, as well as those discussed in the existing literature, are comprehensive programs. For example, Dolan and Wodak (1996) described the SIFs they observed in 1996 in Bern, Zurich and Basel, Switzerland as "housed within Centres that also contain a cafe, a counseling room and a clinic for primary medical care. The injecting rooms are discrete rooms within the Centres" (p. 3). (While some SIFs offer spaces for smoking drugs and "chasing the dragon," these facilities—which are more broadly referred to as "consumption rooms"—are not reported on in this analysis.) Similarly, the 19 SIFs we visited in Germany, Switzerland, the Netherlands and Australia offered [a] comprehensive range of services on-site (see Table 44.1).

Finally, all of the SIF planning documents in Australia and Vancouver, B.C. make a point of emphasizing the comprehensive nature of the programs being proposed, especially the services or referral capabilities to be offered on-site for linking injectors di-

Table 44.1

SIFs in Germany, Switzerland, the Netherlands, and Australia

Name of SIF	Injection Spaces	Injection Equip.	Medical Care	Methadone	Counseling	Café	Beds	Laundry/ Shower	Job Training	Needle Exchange
Frankfurt										
Niddastrasse	12	Yes	Yes	No	Yes	No	No	No	No	Yes
Elbestrasse	8	Yes	Yes	Yes	Yes	Yes	17	L+S	No	Yes
La Strada	6	Yes	No	No	Yes	Yes	22	L+S	No	Yes
Eastside	8	Yes	Yes	Yes	Yes	Yes	80	L+S	Yes	Yes
Hamburg										
Drop-In	7	Yes	Yes	No	Yes	Yes	No	L+S	No	Yes
Fix Stern	7	Yes	Yes	No	Yes	Yes	No	No	No	Yes
Zurich										
Neufrankengasse	6	Yes	Yes	No	Yes	Yes	No	L+S	Yes	Yes
Selnaustrausse	10	Yes	Yes	No	Yes	Yes	No	L+S	Yes	Yes
Seilergraben	5	Yes	Yes	No	Yes	Yes	No	L+S	Yes	Yes
Allmendstrasse	6	Yes	Yes	No	Yes	Yes	No	L+S	Yes	Yes
Wallisellenstrasse	5	Yes	Yes	No	Yes	Yes	No	L+S	Yes	Yes
Bern										
Anlaufstelle Naegeligasse	10	Yes	Yes	No	Yes	Yes	No	L+S	No	Yes
Rotterdam										
St. Paul's Church	20	Yes	Yes	No	Yes	Yes	80	L	Yes	Yes
Community Center	6	Yes	Yes	No	Yes	No	No	L+S	No	Yes
Keetje Tippel	8	Yes	No	No	Yes	Yes	No	L+S	No	Yes
Amsterdam										
HVO	1	Yes	Yes	No	Yes	Yes	No	L+S	No	Yes
AMOC	5	Yes	Yes	No	Yes	Yes	No	L+S	No	Yes
Arnhem										
IT	5	Yes	Yes	Yes	Yes	Yes	No	No	No	Yes
Sydney										
MSIC	8	Yes	Yes	No	Yes	Yes	No	No	No	Yes

rectly to drug treatment, primary care, counseling, and other social supports (Australian Drug Foundation, 1998; Kerr, 2000).

Because SIFs tend to offer many of the same services in general, what is most significant to note in comparing them is the amount of resources that different SIFs are able to invest in any given service. In this re-spect, SIFs can be found to vary widely. For instance, virtually all SIFs offer "counseling" to injectors, but the type and level of counseling offered by different programs can vary significantly. For example, during the site visit to an SIF in Hamburg, a professional social worker commented that, "We'd like to think of ourselves as a counseling and referral agency that also offers a consumption room. But frequently we feel like we offer a consumption room and offer counseling on the side." This comment is interesting in light of the fact that the SIF in question enjoys a large staff of 11 full-time social workers and nurses, in addition to a front-line staff to oversee everyday operations. Being highly trained, the professional staff place a great deal of emphasis not just on counseling clients, but on "quality" counseling; ie., working in-depth with clients over time in helping them deal with the many difficult problems injectors commonly struggle with: eviction, homelessness, legal entanglements, loss of custody, mental illness, debt, deportation and, of course, drug addiction, a problem that many clients regard as less urgent than other problems. The social worker's comment above, therefore, must be understood in context: she works in an SIF that invests considerable resources in counseling as a service, and the staff of professionals embrace high standards of what "real" counseling involves. But because of such high standards and investment of resources, in the face of very high client-need, the professionals feel they are falling short professionally.

In comparison, during a site visit to an SIF in Frankfurt, a staff member commented, "Most of the time I feel like we are basically referees." This comment is interesting because the SIF in question also lists "counseling" as a service that it offers. However, the resources of this SIF are very different, and invested very differently, than those of the SIF in Hamburg. The Frankfurt SIF is administered by a large, part-time staff of university students, supervised by two professional social workers. The students are trained in basic first aid and cardio-pulmonary resuscitation, as well as in how to work with clients in a nonjudgmental manner. The staff feel like "referees" because the main focus of their work is on monitoring clients, enforcing the house rules, reacting to problems as they arise, and moving clients along at a reasonable pace to minimize congestion in the SIF. The SIF provides "counseling," but this primarily means orienting injectors on how to behave in the SIF, responding to clients' questions, engaging clients in mundane interactions and information-sharing, and referring clients who request help to on- or off-site services.

Similarly, virtually all SIFs offer medical care, yet what this means in terms of the nature and availability of actual services on-site, and the types of medical practitioners available, is highly variable. Some SIFs have medical practitioners on-site at most times providing basic primary care services, as well as training and assistance to clients experiencing problems in the injection room. Other SIFs provide medical care, but only with limited hours of operation by visiting practitioners, who offer a more limited range of medical services. To date, primary care facilities, themselves, have not incorporated SIFs into their own comprehensive planning and prevention programs, and the majority of SIFs rely on referral to outside facilities for many primary care services.

Given that SIFs, in general, offer similar services, and differ only in the resources they invest in them, SIFs tend to share similar logistical arrangements.

To begin with, SIFs have a main entrance for clients that staff monitor and control in order to prevent over-crowding inside, to receive and direct visitors to different services, and to block clients who have been temporarily or permanently expelled from the SIF for disciplinary reasons. (In Zurich, a police official checks clients' documents to ensure that they have legal residency in the city before allowing them to enter.) In general, the entrance leads to a waiting room from which all other services and amenities emanate. SIF staff emphasize that the larger the waiting room is, the better. They also prefer that a cafe be part of the waiting room in order for the staff to interact and monitor clients with ease. A large waiting room minimizes the need for injectors to loiter outside a project before gaining entrance, which helps protect an SIF's public image and relationships with neighbors. It also reduces the risk that injectors will be identified as SIF-clients. (An exception to the above is the Sydney SIF. The waiting area is large enough to accommodate 8–10 clients, but usually much fewer are waiting because the staff attempt to usher clients into the injection room quickly. As they leave the injection room, clients enter into a large lounge area where they are encouraged to remain, have some coffee or tea, relax for awhile, and to stabilize under the staff's supervision.)

Access to an SIF site may be limited by a number of factors. First, local police activity may limit potential clients from entering. For example, to reduce individuals from outlying Cantons or counties from using public services, police in Zurich monitor the SIFs to allow only Zurich citizens to frequent them. To be a citizen, individuals must reside in the city for two or more years in order to obtain an identification card that allows access to services. In general, however, SIF staff in other cities report that routine policing poses no obstacle for their clients. For instance, in Frankfurt, police on foot patrol are seen frequently around downtown SIFs, but they work to prevent serious offenses and maintain public order. The many SIF-clients we spoke to, both within SIFs and on the street, reported that they are seldom if ever hassled by the police.

Once inside the SIF waiting room, the staff requires clients to sign-up for admission to the injection room on a first-come, first-serve basis. SIF-staff allow clients to enter the injection room after their name or some other identifier has been called. As clients enter the room, a staff member may ask clients to display a registration card, to register at that time, to sign a liability release form, or to provide some other information. Clients are then given the sterile injection equipment they need, which typically includes a preferred type of syringe, water, dissolving agent, cooker, cotton filter, tourniquet, alcohol wipes, bandages, and paper towels for cleaning-up after themselves.

Injection rooms generally provide 7 to 12 injection spaces, and clients are allowed 30–45 minutes to inject. The SIF Conference *Guidelines* state that, "experience indicates that the capacity of a room should not exceed 10–12 places and that there should be enough space for safe consumption, movement, and for the management of drug consumption related emergencies" (Schneider & Stöver, 1999). At least one staff member is present in the injection room at all times to monitor clients and respond to problems. Clients sit at either stainless steel tables or

along counters bolted to the wall. Injection rooms also contain a large sink with a soap and paper-towel dispenser for clients to use before and after injecting. There is a cabinet containing additional injection materials for clients from which the staff can draw, as well as basic medical equipment such as mechanical respiration devices (resuscitation mask, air bag), biting wedges, a blood pressure apparatus, oxygen, stretcher, blanket, first-aid kit, dressing materials and ointment. The injection room is also equipped with a buzzer that allows the staff to signal for help, and a telephone to call for outside emergency assistance.

Finally, the total client-load that any single SIF can hope to accommodate is far less than the number of active injectors in most large cities. That is why cities that sponsor SIFs, or propose to, typically have more than one SIF (Dolan et al., 2000; Kerr, 2000). In addition, the optimum operating schedule of SIFs in many cities may be 7 days a week, 24 hours a day, as the SIF Conference *Guidelines* recommend (Schneider & Stöver, 1999). However, due to the practical politics of funding, SIFs typically have far shorter schedules (Dolan et al., 2000; Schneider & Stöver, 1999). Thus, for planning purposes, conservative estimates would suggest that a 10-space SIF open 12 hours a day, allowing clients 30 minutes per visit in the injection room, can accommodate approximately 200–250 client-episodes a day, approximately 800–1,000 a week, or around 3,500–4,000 client-episodes a month. Assuming this involves approximately 1,000–1,500 separate individuals per month, managing such a client-load is challenging, especially for an SIF of several fulltime social workers, medical practitioners and frontline staff whose mandate is to get to know all clients, individually, and move as many of them as possible into drug treatment, primary care, or some form of counseling/rehabilitation service.

Problems Addressed by SIFs

A point emphasized in the SIF Conference *Guidelines* is that a "prerequisite in setting up of consumption rooms is . . . to *point out service delivery gaps* and to do so in close cooperation with drug assistance agencies, the police, the public prosecutor's office and public health authorities, etc." (Schneider & Stöver, 1999, p. 19). This point was highlighted because gaining community support for SIFs is frequently dependent on SIFs coming to be seen as overcoming important deficiencies in a municipality's array of public health efforts for injectors, and/or if the number of HIV-infections and other health problems among injectors continue to increase despite the operation of conventional services in place. As already noted, many cities in North America already typically provide street-based outreach services, needle exchange programs, HIV-test counseling centers, drug treatment facilities, and broad-based, multi-targeted educational initiatives.

The available literature indicates that SIFs target three significant problems largely neglected by conventional public health efforts for injectors.

I. Reducing Rates and Risks of Drug Injection in Public Spaces. SIFs are seen as targeting the significant health risks that injectors run when they inject in public spaces. Needle exchange and street-based outreach services work with injectors in providing harm reduction materials and education, but there is no evidence that such services lead to a reduction in injectors' use of public spaces for injection. But to prevent or ameliorate the onset of withdrawal symptoms, or to get high as fast as possible, injectors commonly consume drugs close to where they are purchased (McCoy & Inciardi, 1995). Doing so results in injectors frequently injecting drugs in public and quasi-public spaces, such as restaurant and public restrooms, abandoned buildings, cars, stairwells, parks, and alleys. Injection in public spaces is not limited to injectors situated in large urban areas. A study by the first author in Windham, Connecticut, a rural town of 22,000 residents, found that injectors regularly injected in four outdoor areas: two in the woods surrounding a 600-unit public housing project (where many of the injectors live), and two other sites located on the banks of a river running through downtown (Broadhead, van Hulst, & Heckathorn, 1999).

Injectors' use of public spaces to inject drugs creates a number of risks to their health and well-being. It increases their risk of being assaulted and robbed by street-predators, or confronted by the police. In reaction, injectors are prone to rush when injecting in public spaces, which leads to mistakes and carelessness: in the preparation of injection sites, in the injection procedure, and in following important risk reduction measures throughout the process (Canadian HIV/AIDS Legal Network, 1999). When people inject in haste, mistakes are more likely to spiral into crises, such as when users have trouble hitting a vein and begin digging and jabbing themselves in a panic. Cutting-corners in order to save time increases risks, especially when drugs are injected quickly (eg., not tested for strength) and when injection equipment is re-used but not properly cleaned (increasing the likelihood of bacterial and viral infections). Carrying out risk reduction measures takes time and resources. For example, cleaning a used syringe with bleach requires that it first be flushed several times with clean water, then filled entirely with bleach at least 3 times, and leaving the bleach in the syringe for at least 30 seconds. After removing the bleach, the syringe then needs to be flushed several more times with clean water. All other used injection equipment, such as spoons or cookers, must also be cleaned with bleach and rinsed with clean water (Normand, Vlahov, & Moses, 1995). The pressures and anxieties of injecting in public spaces work against users' ability to adhere calmly and carefully to these risk-reduction procedures.

In addition, when injecting outdoors, injectors are more likely to lack the supplies needed for safer injection. For example, injectors are often reluctant to carry injection equipment when they are out and about town, usually from fear of the police (Grund, Broadhead, Heckathorn, & Anthony, 1995). After copping, they may then not be able to obtain new syringes because local pharmacies and needle exchange services may be closed or far away. Not being able to obtain sterile injection equipment increases injectors' risks of using contaminated equipment, either by borrowing someone else's syringe or using one that has been discarded. Injectors may be good at keeping a supply of new injection equipment at home, but that does not help them when they are away from home and run into unexpected opportunities to get high. Finally, temporary and long-term homelessness is common among injectors. Many do not have a living space in which to store new injection supplies.

The public spaces in which injectors inject are also unhygienic. Typically there is no source of clean water or clean injection equipment on-site, and used paraphernalia is frequently scattered about, including syringes. When injecting outside, injectors typically must proceed without cleaning either their hands or their injection sites, or cleaning and dressing their wound sites afterwards.

Finally, just as the risk of fatal drug-overdose increases when drug users inject by themselves, research indicates it also increases when they inject in public spaces. There are frequently no telephones on-site to call for help; many spaces, such as alleys, abandoned buildings and parked cars have no real address to guide emergency workers to; some spaces are difficult to reach with emergency equipment; and competent bystanders are less likely to be available in many spaces, such as alleys, abandoned buildings, and highway and railroad underpasses, to help or seek assistance (McGregor, Darke, Ali, & Christie, 1998; Sporer, 1999).

Thus, SIFs are seen as overcoming a significant service gap in existing public health programs. They provide an alternative "public" space for injectors to use that offers a hygienic and relaxed environment, clean injection materials, and trained personnel to respond to emergencies, and to enroll injectors in drug treatment, primary care and other support services. Some observers find it ironic that many municipalities offer needle exchange services but not SIFs, as an Australian observer pointed out:

A central anomaly in the current policy regarding needle-exchange services is that, while federal and state governments support programs where sterile needles and syringes are given out to injecting injectors, those same users are often forced into unhygienic environments (. . . toilet blocks, alleyways or behind business pre-

mises) in order to inject (Micallef, 1998, p. 5).

II. Creating Opportunities to Work with Injectors. SIFs are seen as providing a far greater opportunity for health workers to connect meaningfully with injectors than conventional public health services and programs. First, needle exchange and street-outreach workers make frequent contact with injectors, but it normally happens when injectors are out and about town, intent on "taking care of business" (ie. when they are working to cop drugs or get the money needed to buy them). The great majority of these interactions, therefore, tend to be cursory and on-the-run (Broadhead & Fox, 1993; Murphy, Sales, Choe, McKearin, & Murphy, 2000). As the Drugs and Crime Prevention Committee (1999) of the Victoria Parliament found, "[I]n contrast to needle exchange outlets where clients generally visit briefly, [SIFs] allow for a more prolonged interaction between health-care staff and client" (p. 16). This is because SIFs place trained staff in direct proximity with injectors while they are waiting to consume their drugs, as well as after they have done so and have returned to the waiting room to relax. SIFs that offer a cafe and other services give clients even more reason to remain on-site and interact with staff, during which time the clients become further stabilized.

Moreover, compared to needle exchange and street-outreach, SIFs provide greater opportunity for health workers to engage clients because they offer many needed services on-site: needle exchange, counseling, primary medical care, and frequently drug treatment, shower and laundry, temporary sleeping accommodations, and still other services depending on resources. There is substantial research that indicates that injectors will avail themselves of drug treatment and other services at much higher rates if they are offered on-site rather than referring them to such services elsewhere (Altice & Friedland, 1993; Umbricht-Schneiter, Ginn, Pabst, & Bigelow, 1994). In addition, when services are offered in a comprehensive package, as SIFs do, then staff members have frequent contact with clients which creates a *social support mechanism* that facilitates injectors' abilities to follow through and adhere to appointments, regimens, and schedules (Broadhead et al., in press).

As noted above, once inside an SIF waiting room, clients must sign-up to gain admission for the injection room and then wait their turn. While they are waiting, clients and staff have the opportunity to connect with one another, discuss problems, or make arrangements to see a counselor or a health provider. If nothing else, clients have the opportunity to relax and reflect in a non-threatening environment. When clients finish in the injection room, they are encouraged to return or go to a waiting room and stay for a half-hour or so until they have stabilized. This gives staff a further opportunity to monitor clients' condition and connect with them at a time when they are not agitated, stressed-out or dope-sick. Because many people inject drugs simply to "get straight" and feel "normal," one of the best times for staff to interact with clients can be when they return to the waiting room after using the injection room (Rosenbaum, 1981; Siegel, 1989; Waldorf, 1973). In general, an SIF's waiting room is the most opportune space for staff to engage clients, either as a group in terms of presentations, videos, and announcements; or as individuals, in terms of getting to know them as persons, enrolling them in counseling or medical and drug treatment, or consulting with them about any number of things. If an SIF runs a cafe, this makes the waiting area even more inviting for clients to spend time in, which further increases the staffs' opportunity to work with them.

Within the waiting area, clients gain access to all other services and/or amenities an SIF may make available: medical, drug treatment and counseling services; private consultations; safe sex and injection education; needle exchange; restrooms, showers and laundry; overnight beds; and other possible activities such as playing pool, ping pong, cards, chess, bingo, watching television or videos, reading newspapers and magazines, and checking bulletin and message boards. These combined opportunities and experiences create the potential for far greater and more meaningful contact between health workers and IDU-clients than any other type

of risk reduction service. Still, this optimum situation should not be over-drawn; connecting meaningfully with active drug injectors is still a challenge. While waiting to shoot-up in an SIF, some IDUs are anxious or dope sick, and not in the mood to communicate. After shooting-up, they may go on the nod for a half hour or so before stabilizing. Yet, despite these obstacles, SIFs appear to provide much better opportunities to interact with active IDUs than do street outreach or needle-exchange programs, in order to help injectors deal with, and take responsibility for, any number of problem they may be facing. This includes outpatient methadone programs as well, since they typically discourage "patients" from hanging out after they have received their dose.

III. Reducing the Burden of Illicit Drug Use on the Community. SIFs are described in the available literature as reducing the nuisance, costs, and risks to the larger community caused by drug injection in public spaces. Injecting in public spaces results in large amounts of litter that is unsightly and costly to collect. Such litter, particularly discarded syringes, pose[s] a health risk of accidental needle sticks and the transmission of blood-borne pathogens, especially to municipal workers and custodians who collect such litter, and trash haulers and sorters who separate and process it. Needle exchange programs endeavor to collect as many needles and syringes as they dispense. But some programs are more successful than others and, to our knowledge, no program in operation works to collect any drug-related litter other than syringes (Broadhead, van Hulst, & Heckathorn, 1999). For example, in the four outdoor injection areas in Windham, Connecticut mentioned above, the scheduled surveys that were carried out of drug-related litter found syringes, plastic syringe wrappers and caps, paper and plastic dope bags, bottle caps (cookers), one-ounce plastic bottles for bleach or water, filters, condoms and wrappers, match books, and assorted cans and bottles. In terms of dope bags alone that had been discarded in only one of the outdoor areas, 776 and 534 dope bags were collected in the summer and fall of 1997, respectively, and 643 bags in the summer of 1998 (Broadhead, van Hulst, & Heckathorn, 1999).

But in addition to the problem of drug-related litter, congregations of injectors are widely regarded by the public-at-large as a nuisance and a threat. Moreover, some inner-city areas have been *de facto* expropriated by injectors, including whole sections of municipal parks, street corners, vacant lots, sidewalks, and alleys. SIFs are seen as offering an innovative way to reduce significantly the expropriation of such public spaces, as well as the nuisance and fear that public drug use creates, by giving injectors a sanctioned, alternative space that accommodates the needs and sensibilities of both injectors and the larger community. As the State of Victoria Drug Policy Expert Committee (2000) reported, "Overseas experience suggests that communities find a well run [SIF] more acceptable in their neighborhood than the intense street-using situations that preceded them" (p. 17).

Conversely, there is no evidence in the available literature that indicates that the establishment of an SIF results in an increase in improperly discarded injection equipment, an increase in drug users congregating in public spaces and becoming a greater nuisance, or an increase in drug dealing and other forms of drug-related crime within a community.

Negotiating SIFs' Place in the Community

In seeing SIFs as a public health option that municipalities throughout North America may wish to pursue to overcome deficiencies in their existing efforts, the active involvement and support of four different components of the community is essential: law enforcement, city officials, drug assistance agencies, and injectors themselves.

Law Enforcement

Law enforcement agencies in the United States and Canada vigorously pursue illicit injectors, dealers, traffickers and producers. However in many municipalities throughout North America, law enforcement agencies have also entered into a "hands-off" rela-

tionship, working in collaboration with public health programs for injectors. They have agreed, sometimes under court pressure, to curb their surveillance and arrest efforts of injectors utilizing health services such as needle exchange, and to not interfere with outreach workers attempting to access injectors for the purpose of disseminating health education and risk reduction materials (American Civil Liberties Union, 2001). In municipalities that may wish to implement SIFs, a similar collaborative agreement with the police is necessary. As the Australian Drug Foundation (1998) advised in its *Position on the Provision of Injecting Facilities*, "the legal issue must be addressed to protect both the injectors and those working and running the facilities" (p. 3). Legally, what SIFs need is the same working agreement that the police already honor for the clients and staff of needle exchange programs, street-based outreach services, HIV test counseling centers, drug treatment facilities, and other public health programs. Honoring such an agreement, as Malkin (2001) observed, ". . . does not ever require going one step further than what has already taken place with the establishment of syringe and needle exchange" (p. 17). For example, during our site visits in Western Europe, we found that police enter SIFs only if called, or if there is a pressing need to find someone. In Bern, the police station is directly across the street from the SIF, but the police pay little attention to it as long as the "public nuisance" outside the SIF is minimized. Such a policy allows the police to focus their energy on reducing upper-level forms of drug trafficking and organized crime. As an alternative to these types of working agreements, some countries have opted to create new legislation specific to the operation of SIFs in order to ensure the full legal protection of injectors and staff (Malkin, 2001).

Lastly, it is important to note that, like most countries, both the United States and Canada are signatories to various international covenants pertaining to illicit drugs. The most notable covenants are the 1961 Single Convention on Narcotic Drugs, the 1971 Convention on Psychotropic Substances, and the relevant portions of the 1998 United Nations Convention against

Illicit Traffic in Narcotic Drugs and Psychotropic Substances (cited in Gilmour, 1995). While it is commonly assumed that these conventions require signatories to adopt a criminal-prohibitionist approach to dealing with illicit injectors, each contain provisions allowing for public health approaches. For example, two recent international reviews found that all three conventions advocate for the "treatment, education, aftercare, rehabilitation and social reintegration" of injectors, and require signatories to "take all practical measures" for reducing disease and addiction (Swiss Institute of Comparative Law, 2000, p. 1; Gilmour, 1995). While the conventions do not specify what these measures should be, many countries, including the United States and Canada, already offer needle exchange, street-based outreach, drug treatment, and other services for injectors. As Australia and several western European countries have demonstrated, there are no treaty-based legal obstacles to adding SIFs to this list of public health measures for drug injectors.

Local Government

Community implementation of an SIF requires the knowledge and endorsement of local governmental officials, especially from the offices of the major, city council, city attorney, zoning and planning, health department, and relevant task forces. Officials need to be informed sufficiently about the public health implications of a proposed SIF in order to explain it to others, and to defend its goals and operations. Ideally, officials should be integrated into the development and implementation of an SIF, including deciding where it will be located, the range of services it will offer, its operational procedures, and the composition of its staff.

In addition, it will be incumbent on officials to work out the legal framework within which an SIF can operate. This legal framework will articulate the rights and obligations of an SIF's sponsoring agency and staff, and circumscribe its potential liabilities. By rights, we mean the program staff's authority to specify and enforce the SIF's rules of operation and code of conduct for clients and staff. Obligations include the staff's "duty to care" for eligible clients, and the

protocols staff members will be expected to follow in conducting business, and in responding to problems and emergencies. Finally, an SIF's liabilities can be limited through the use of a legally binding release-form signed by all clients. In the release form, clients will acknowledge, and accept full responsibility for, the risks they will take as free adults in using an SIF to inject illicit drugs. The release-form will explicitly state that an SIF is free of responsibility for morbid outcomes that any given client may experience in the injection room, despite the staff's good faith efforts to prevent such outcomes (Drug Policy Expert Committee, 2000). Naturally, in the event of gross negligence or recklessness on the part of a staff member, an SIF would be liable, but in the same way that conventional health-care facilities are already legally vulnerable, including needle exchange programs and HIV counseling centers. An SIF would need to take steps to indemnify itself, but such steps do not appear to involve anything out of the ordinary.

Finally, agencies that receive government funding, at least in the United States, are required to certify that they provide a "drug-free" workplace for their employees. For example, they are required to notify "employees that the unlawful manufacture, distribution, dispensation, possession, or use of a controlled substance is prohibited in the workplace and specifying the actions that will be taken against employees for violation of such prohibition" (U.S. Government, 1988, p. 1). These legal requirements apply to agency employees rather than clients. For example, needle exchange and street-outreach workers, drug treatment providers, and medical practitioners interact with clients who are commonly in the possession of controlled substances. Many personnel also work in the immediate vicinity of persons [who are] consuming drugs, or are high. The agencies of such personnel, however, are still able to certify that their employees work in a drug-free workplace. The sponsoring agency of an SIF would be able to do so as well.

Drug Assistance Services

The SIF Conference *Guidelines* uses the term "drug assistance services" to refer to the full range of programs to help injectors and the community in reducing drug-related problems, including access to drug treatment, risk reduction, medical care, and social-welfare programs (Schneider & Stöver, 1999, p. 20). Because SIFs can provide many services on-site, and refer clients to still others in the community, local drug assistance agencies have essential contributions to make in the development and ongoing operation of an SIF. As the SIF Conference *Guidelines* emphasize, "[t]he primary goal is . . . a consumption room model embedded in the existing service delivery system" (Schneider & Stöver, 1999, p. 20). To this end, in implementing an SIF, memoranda of understanding will need to be developed on how SIF staff can call upon the many different drug assistance agencies that make up most [cities'] health and social service system[s] to help SIF clients.

But, in addition to establishing referral arrangements for services elsewhere, it is important to recall that SIFs are by design meant to offer a comprehensive array of services on-site. Thus, the optimum is for drug assistance services within a municipality to set-up ancillary operations within safer injection facilities themselves, and SIFs are ideal venues for maximizing the delivery of such services. For example, it is well established that active drug users use primary medical care services erratically and only after they are very sick. As a result, they also over-use emergency rooms. This pattern significantly drives up health care costs (Cherubin & Sapira, 199[3]). It is also well documented that if drug users are offered medical care services on-site, as part of other services which they may be receiving, their utilization of, and adherence to, care increases substantially while minimizing its cost (Umbricht-Schneiter et al., 1994). SIFs create the opportunity to offer primary care services to injectors in a very cost-effective manner, and the need for such care is enormous. The spectrum of diseases that drug injectors suffer from, especially if HIV and HCV infected, puts them in a class all their own (O'Connor, Selwyn, & Schottenfeld, 1994). Injectors have much higher rates of bacterial infections, including pneumonia, endocarditis, sepsis, and sexually transmit-

ted diseases, all of which can be treated on-site in an SIF. Injection drug use was identified as a risk factor for tuberculosis even before the AIDS epidemic (Reichman, Felton, & Edsall, 1979), which can also be tested for and treated within an SIF. Injectors also suffer from very high rates of dermatological problems such as staphylococcus infections, abscesses and skin ulcers, which are highly responsive to lo-tech primary care if treated. Finally, comprehensive SIFs are ideal locations for the provision of gynecological and prenatal health care for women injectors.

In general, the potential cost-savings and effectiveness of offering primary care and social services to drug injectors within SIFs should not be underestimated. Whether those services include a full range of drug treatment interventions, medical care, and multi-faceted counseling and testing services, is a decision that officials must decide as they consider the role that safer injection facilities can play in reducing the drug-related public health problems that exist in their own communities.

Active Injectors

Successful implementation of an SIF requires support and advice from active members of the drug-using community. Their expertise in representing the needs and concerns of injectors is critical in identifying the best location to establish an SIF, and how to maximize the SIF's relevance and appeal to injectors. In turn, injectors' ability to vouch for an SIF, to spread the word about its services—including its concern for protecting clients' confidentiality—is invaluable for successful implementation and ongoing operations. As such, injectors who are indigenous leaders within the drug-using community need to sit on an SIF's board of directors, and play an active, advisory role along with representatives from drug assistant agencies, local government, and law enforcement (Latkin, 1998).

SIF 'House Rules'

Examination of the research literature, plus our own site visits, revealed a number of house rules that are commonly applied to

SIF-clients and staff. These are listed below with minimal discussion.

Rules Governing SIF Clients

SIFs post some of the rules below, as well as distribute printed copies of house rules to clients:

- Clients are prohibited from dealing drugs on-site, or from injecting anywhere except in specifically designated rooms.
- Some SIFs allow clients to divide-up the drugs they bring into a SIF together, and assist one another in injecting.
- Some SIFs require clients to be registered and show an I.D. before admission to the injection room, and/or to demonstrate that they are injectors, city residents, and of minimum age (typically 18 years).
- SIFs limit the amount of time clients can use the injection room (30–45 minutes), but clients are allowed to return to the room several times throughout the day or evening.
- Clients are prohibited from threatening or intimidating staff members and other clients, and from using loud or offensive language.
- Clients are required to clean up after their use of an injection space and to dispose of all used materials in garbage containers before leaving.
- Clients are encouraged to assist in keeping the SIF clean, and to collect drug-related debris in the SIF's vicinity.

Rules Governing Facilities

- Staff members are generally prohibited from assisting clients in preparing or injecting their drugs, although some SIFs allow medical professionals to provide clients with safer injection training.
- Staff members are expected to be "acceptance-oriented" toward clients; that is, nonjudgmental about clients' behavior that does not affect others, including whether or not to follow the staff's advice or referral to other services.

- SIFs need to be physically located in or near neighborhoods with large number of injectors.
- SIF-staffing and operating hours should be determined based on need, which may require some facilities to never close.
- Staff members are trained to follow written protocols on how to manage the facility, to discipline clients who violate house rules, and to respond to emergencies.
- Many SIFs have direct phone lines to police and ambulance services.
- At least one staff member is in the injection room at all times.
- Staff members rotate their time in the injection room at appropriate intervals.
- The atmosphere in an injection room is to be peaceful and unhurried.
- All necessary injection equipment and supplies are provided for each client in an injection room, as well as the means for disposal.
- The floors and walls of an SIF are regularly cleaned and disinfected.
- SIFs employ a queuing system that requires clients to wait their turn before entering the injection room.

Our observations of the 19 SIFs we visited found that these rules are enforced, and that SIF staffs are able to work in an environment that is as orderly, safe and routinized as is found in methadone clinics, drop-in shelters, needle exchanges and primary care centers that provide care to large populations of impoverished inner-city residents. The same problems of stress and burnout that are found in those settings are also found in SIFs, but the latter are not qualitatively different work environments in terms of occupational risks (Broadhead & Fox, 1993).

Concluding Discussion

Our review suggests that SIF target several public health problems that municipalities in North America may wish to consider, problems largely unaddressed by needle exchange, street-outreach, education campaigns, HIV counseling, and other conventional services. SIF target injectors' use of public spaces to inject drugs in order to reduce the many risks associated with the practice. Compared to conventional services, SIFs provide greater opportunities for health workers to connect with injectors, and to move them into primary care, drug treatment, and other rehabilitation services. Finally, SIFs target the "nuisance factor" of drug scenes—the hazardous litter and intimidating presence of injectors congregating in city parks, public playgrounds and on street corners—by offering them an alternative, supervised "public" space. Our review also suggests that, for municipalities considering SIFs in order to address these problems, their implementation would not necessarily require any significant or fundamental changes in public policy or law: SIFs require the *same* working agreements with social service providers and the police that needle exchange, street-outreach, drug treatment and similar health programs for injectors already receive. As Malkin observed, SIFs "could sit comfortably alongside what already exists . . ." (Malkin, 200[1], p. 18).

Still, systematic evaluations of the effectiveness of SIFs have yet to be conducted. What evidence is available, while considerable, consists primarily of descriptive reports of SIFs operating in Western Europe. But this evidence bears on very important matters. For example, in Frankfurt, where SIFs were first implemented in the early 1990s, the number of fatal drug overdoses fell from 147 in 1991 to 22 in 1997, and none of those fatalities occurred in an SIF (Kerr, 2000). In addition, individuals overdosing in SIFs are 10 times less likely to receive hospitalization than those who overdose on the street (Böllinger, Stöver, & Fietzek, 199[8]). Finally, "so far, there has not been a single death in a [SIF] in Europe, although an overdose occurs approximately once every 500 visits" (Wodak, 2000, p. 2). This remarkable result follows thousands upon thousands of injections within safer injection facilities, some of which have been in operation for over 10 years.

With respect to "the nuisance factor," there are several reports of public drug use declining since the implementation of SIFs in several western European cities (Nickolai, 1997; Kemesies, 1999; Ronco, Spuhler, Coda, & Schopfer, 1996), as well as reports of fewer discarded syringes found in all Swiss cities that have implemented SIFs (Haemmig, 1996). While the nuisance factor is less of an issue in most North American cities, namely because the drug scene has been driven underground, the most compelling reasons to consider implementation of an SIF are public health and medical.

Finally, SIFs have been described as effective gateways to other systems of care and treatment. For example, data collected at an SIF in Frankfurt in 1997 revealed that 194 clients asked for referral to detoxification services and 64 were successful in completing the detoxification process, while an additional 93 clients were referred to treatment, resulting in 34 admissions to treatment programs (MacPherson, 1999). Projects have also reported that SIF-clients' contact with other health and social services on-site or via referral improved their general health, stability and level of functioning (MacPherson, 1999).

Given the resistance to needle exchange programs in North America, many may argue that the likelihood of SIFs being implemented is remote, regardless of the specific public health problems they address over existing services, and the evidence regarding their effectiveness. However, it must be remembered that 15 years ago, many communities actively resisted projects that proposed distributing small bottles of bleach to active injectors for use in disinfect[ing] their used syringes, but now "bleach kits" are standard prevention materials given out to IDUs by health departments and service agencies throughout the United States and Canada (Broadhead, 1991; Normand, Vlahov, & Moses, 1995). Approximately 10 years ago, needle exchange services in North America were virtually nonexistent, but now, according to the North American Syringe Exchange Network, there are 164 needle exchange programs operating throughout North America, most of which are legal and part of larger health and social service networks within local communities (Coffin, 2001). So it is fair to predict that, in light of the evidence reviewed above, it is likely that municipalities in North America will being considering the implementation of SIFs in order to increase significantly the effectiveness of their public health efforts at combating HIV, HCV, over-dose, and other problems related to drug injection. In light of the evidence, certainly the time has come for government support within North America of research initiatives, in terms of controlled field trials and community demonstration projects, for studying the impact and effectiveness of safer injection facilities to better protect the public's health. . . .

References

Altice, F. L., & Friedland, G. H. 1998. The era of adherence to antiretroviral therapy. *Annals of Internal Medicine*, 129, 503–506.

American Civil Liberties Union. 2001. CT court is first in the nation to protect needle exchange from police harassment. Retrieved on November 13, 2001 from *http://www.aclu.org/news/2001/n011901a.html*.

Australian Drug Foundation. 1998. ADF position on the provision of injecting facilities. Retrieved on November 13, 2001 from *http://www.adf.org.au/inside/position/injec.htm*.

Böllinger, L., Stöver, H., & Fietzek, L. 1998. Injection rooms: Places where intravenous drug use is tolerated. In L. Böllinger, H. Stöver, & L. Fietzek (Eds.), *Drogenpraxis, Drogenrecht, Drogenpolitik (Frankfurt: Fachlochschulverlag 1995), Integrative Drogenhilfe: Annual report 1997*. Unpublished paper. Integrative Drogenhilfe an der Fachhochschule Frankfurt am Main e.

Broadhead, R. S. 1991. Social construction of bleach in combating AIDS among injection drug users. *Journal of Drug Issues*, 21 (4), 713–737.

Broadhead, R. S., & Fox, K. J. 1993. The occupational risks of harm reduction work. In G. L. Albrecht & R. Zimmerman (Eds.), *Advances in medical sociology, Vol. III: The social and behavioral aspects of AIDS* (pp. 123–142). Greenwich, Connecticut: JAI Press.

Broadhead, R. S., Heckathorn, D. D., & Altice, F. L. (in press). *Increasing drug injectors' adherence to HIV therapeutics. Social Science and Medicine*.

Broadhead, R. S., van Hulst, Y., & Heckathorn, D. D. 1999. Termination of an established needle exchange: A study of claims and their impact. *Social Problems*, 46 (1), 48–66.

Bux, D. A., Iguchi, M. Y., Lidz, V., Baxter, R. C., & Platt, J. J. 1993. Participation in an outreach-based coupon distribution program for free methadone detoxification. *Hospital and Community Pharmacy*, 44 (11), 1066–72.

Canadian Centre for Infectious Disease Prevention and Control. 2000. Bureau of HIV/AIDS, STD and TB update series: HIV/AIDS epidemiological Update—April, 2000. Retrieved on November 13, 2001 from *http://www.hc-sc.gc.ca/hpb/lcdc/bah/epi/ahcan-e.html*.

Canadian HIV/AIDS Legal Network. 1999. *Injection drug use and HIV/AIDS: Legal and ethical issues*. Montreal: Canadian HIV/AIDS Legal Network.

Canadian National Task Force on HIV, AIDS and Injection Drug Use. 1997. *HIV/AIDS and injection drug use: A national action plan*. Retrieved on November 13, 2001 from *http://www.cfdp.ca/hivaids.html*.

Centre for Disease Control. 1998. *Morbidity and mortality weekly report: Recommendations for prevention and control of hepatitis C virus (HCV) infection and HCV-related chronic disease. Vol. 47, no. RR-19*.

Centers for Disease Control and Prevention. 2000. *HIV/AIDS surveillance report, December 6, 2000*. Available from Centers for Disease Control and Prevention. Retrieved on November 13, 2001 from *http://www.cdc.gov/*.

Cherubin, C. E., & Sapira, J. D. 1993. The medical complications of drug addiction and the medical assessment of the IV drug user: Twenty-five years later. *Annals of Internal Medicine*, 119, 1017–1028.

Coffin, P. 2001. *Research brief. Syringe access*. Retrieved on November 13, 2001 from *http://www.lindesmith.org/cites_sources/brief5.html*.

Dolan, K., Kimber, J., Fray, C., Fitzgerald, J., McDonald D., & Trautmann, F. 2000. Drug consumption facilities in Europe and the establishment of supervised injecting centres in Australia. *Drug and Alcohol Review*, 19, 337–46.

Dolan, K., & Wodak, A. 1996. Final report on injecting rooms in Switzerland. Unpublished manuscript. Retrieved on November 13, 2001 from *www.lindesmith.org/library/dolan2.html*.

Drugs and Crime Prevention Committee. 1999. *Safe injecting facilities: Their justification and viability in the Victorian setting*. Available from Drugs and Crime Prevention, Parliament of Victoria. Retrieved on November 13, 2001 from *http://www.parliament.vic.gov.au/dcpc*.

Drug Policy Expert Committee. 2000. *Heroin: Facing the issues*. Retrieved on November 13, 2001 from *http://www.dhs.vic.gov.au/phd/dpec/index.htm*.

Farfien, R. S., Vlahov, D., Galai, N., Doherty, M. C., & Nelson, K. E. 1996. Viral infections in short-term injectors: The prevalence of the hepatitis C, hepatitis B, human immunodeficiency, and human T-lymphotrophic viruses. *American Journal of Public Health*, 86 (5), 655–61.

Gershon, R. R. 1998. Infection control basis for recommending one-time use of sterile syringes and aseptic procedures for injection drug users. *Journal of Acquired Immune Deficiency Syndrome & Human Retrovirology*, 18 (Suppl. 1), S20-4.

Gilmour, G. 1995. *The international covenants prohibiting drug activities*. Paper submitted to Canada's Senate Standing Committee on Legal and Constitutional Affairs. Retrieved on November 13, 2001 from *http://www.cfdp.ca/gilmour.html*.

Greenblatt, J. 1997. *Year-end preliminary estimates from 1996*. Drug Abuse Warning Network. Rockville, MD: Office of Applied Statistics, U.S. Department of Human Services.

Grund, J. P. C., Broadhead, R. S., Heckathorn, D. D., & Anthony, D. L. 1995. In eastern Connecticut injectors purchase syringes from pharmacies but don't carry syringes. *Journal of Acquired Immune Deficiency Syndrome and Human Retrovirology*, 10 (1), 104–5.

Haemmig, R. B. 1996. *Swiss experiences with heroin dispension, fixer rooms and harm reduction in prison*. Paper presented at Conference Overlast en Verlichting. Utrecht, the Netherlands.

Haverkos, H. W. 1991. Infectious diseases and drug abuse: Prevention and treatment in the drug abuse treatment system. *Journal of Substance Abuse Treatment*, 8, 269–275.

Jouria, D. B., Hensle, R., & Rose, J. 1967. The major medical complications of narcotic addiction. *Annals of Internal Medicine*, 67, 1–31.

Kemesies, U. E., 1999. *The open drug scene and the safe injection room offers in Frankfurt am Main 1995: Final report*. Stadt Frankfurt/Dezernat Frauen and Gesundheit, Drogenreferat. Retrieved on November 13, 2001 from *http://home.muenster.net/-indro/injection_room.htm*.

Kerr, T. 2000. *Safe injection facilities: A proposal for a Vancouver pilot project*. Harm Reduction Action Society. Retrieved on November 13, 2001 from *http://www.cfdp.ca/safei.pdf*.

Kerr, T., & Palepu, A. 2001. Safe injection facilities: Is it time? *Canadian Medical Association Journal*, 165 (4), 436–437.

Laboratory Centre for Disease Control. 1999. Hepatitis C—prevention and control: A public health consensus, vol. 2552. *Health Canada*. Retrieved on November 13, 2001 from *http://www.hcsc.gc.ca/hpb/lcdc/publicat/ccdr/99vo125/25s2/index.html*.

Latkin, C. A. 1998. Outreach in natural settings: The use of peer leaders for HIV prevention among injecting drug users' networks. *Public Health Reports*, 113 (Suppl. 1), 151–64.

Malkin, I. 2001. *Establishing supervise injecting facilities: A morally and legally responsible way to help minimize harm.* Unpublished manuscript. University of Melbourne, Australia.

MacPherson, D. 1999. *Comprehensive systems of care for drug users in Switzerland and Frankfurt, Germany: A report from the 10th international conference on the reduction of drug related harm and a tour of harm reduction services in Frankfurt, Germany.* Vancouver: City of Vancouver, Social Planning Department.

——. 2001. *A framework for action: A four-pillar approach to drug problems in Vancouver.* Vancouver, BC: City of Vancouver.

McCoy, C. B., & Inciardi, J. A. 1995. *Sex, drugs, and the continuing spread of AIDS.* Los Angeles: Roxbury Publishing.

McGregor, C., Darke, S., Ali, R., & Christie, P. 1998. Experience of non-fatal overdose among heroin users in Adelaide, Australia: Circumstances and risk perceptions. *Addiction*, 93 (5), 701–711.

Micallef, E. 1998. *Safer injection facilities: Should Victoria have an SIF pilot-trial?* Unpublished paper. Retrieved on November 13, 2001 from *http://lindesmith.org/library/micallef.html.*

Mor, V., Fleishman, J. A., Dresser, M., & Piette, J. 1992. Variations in health service use among HIV-infected patients. *Medical Care*, 30, 17–29.

Murphy, P., Sales, P., Choe, J., McKearin, G., & Murphy, S. 2000. *The dynamics of needle exchange and other service provision.* Paper presented at the meeting of the American Society of Criminology, San Francisco, CA.

New York Times. 2001. Australia allows addicts' center to be opened in Sydney. (2001, May 10). *The New York Times*, p. 3.

Nejedly, M. M., & Bürki, C. 1996. *Monitoring HIV risk behaviors in a street agency with injection room in Switzerland.* Medizinischen Fakultät: University of Bern.

Nickolai, M. 1997. Evolution of Frankfurt's approach to the drug problem. *Euromet021hwork*, 12, 3–4.

Normand, J., Vlahov, D., & Moses, L. E. 1995. *Preventing HIV transmission: The role of sterile needles and bleach.* Washington, DC: National Academy Press.

O'Connor, P. A., Selwyn, P. A., & Schottenfeld, R. S. 1994. Medical care for injection drug users with human immunodeficiency virus infection. *New England Journal of Medicine*, 331, 450–59.

Reichman, L. B., Felton, C. P., & Edsall, J. R. 1979. Drug dependence: A possible new risk factor for tuberculosis disease. *Archives of Internal Medicine*, 139 (3), 337–39.

Ronco, C., Spuhler, G., Coda, P., & Schopfer, R. 1996. Evaluation for alley-rooms I, II, and III in Basel. *Social and Preventive Medicine*, 41, S58-68.

Rosenbaum, M. 1981. *Women on heroin.* New Jersey: Rutgers University Press.

Sapira, J. D. 1968. The narcotic addict as a medical patient. *American Journal of Medicine*, 45, 555–588.

Schneider, W., & Stöver, H. (Eds.). 1998. Guidelines for the operation and use of consumption rooms. Proceedings of the conference: Consumption rooms as a professional service in addictions—health (J. Kimber, Trans.). Munster: akzept

Bundeserband. Retrieved on November 13, 2001 from *http://www.uni-oldenburg.de/fb3/politik2/saus/en/index.html?2.*

Siegel, R. K. 1989. *Intoxication: Life in pursuit of artificial paradise.* New York: Dutton/Plume.

Sporer, K. A. 1999. Acute heroin overdose. *Annals of Internal Medicine*, 130 (7), 584–590.

Sporer, K. A., Firestone, J., & Isaacs, S. M. 1996. Out-of-hospital treatment of opioid overdoses in an urban setting. *Academic Emergency Medicine*, 3, 660–67.

State of Connecticut Department of Public Health. (n.d.). AIDS/HIV case data through June 30, 2000—Table I. Retrieved on November 13, 2001 from *http://www.state.ct.us/dph/Publications/publications.htm.*

State of New York Department of Health. 2000. AIDS in New York State: 1998–1999 edition. Retrieved on November 13, 2001 from *http://www.health.state.ny.us/nysdoh/aids/98/main.htm.*

Strathdee, S. A., Patrick, D. M., Currie, S., Cornelisse, P. G. A., Rekart, M. L., Montaner, J. S. G., Schechter, M. T., & O'Shaughnessy, M. 1997. Needle exchange is not enough: Lessons from the Vancouver injection drug use study. *AIDS*, 11 (8), F59-65.

Swiss Institute of Comparative Law. 2000. Use of narcotic drugs in public injection rooms under public international law. Retrieved on November 13, 2001 from *http://www.drugtext.org/articles/useroomavis.*

Umbricht-Schneiter, A., Ginn, D. H., Pabst, K. M., & Bigelow, G. E. 1994. Providing medical care to methadone clinic patients: Referral vs. on-site care. *American Journal of Public Health*, 84, 207–210.

U.S. Government. 1988. *The Drug-free Workplace Act of 1988 (Public Law 100-690, Title V, Subtitle D).* Washington, DC: U.S. Government Printing Office.

Waldorf, D. 1973. *Careers in dope.* New Jersey: Prentice-Hall.

Wodak, A. 2000. Guest editorial: Responding to the epidemic of drug overdose death. *Current Therapeutics.* Retrieved on November 13, 2001 from *http://www.ctonline.com.au/geditor.asp.*

For Discussion

Safer injection facilities represent a harm-reduction approach to drug use. Compare safer injection facilities with other harm-reduction strategies, such as, "chill-out" rooms, tablet testing, and free accessible water in clubs that cater to Ecstasy users. Are some harm-reduction strategies more acceptable than others?

Robert S. Broadhead, Thomas H. Kerr, Jean-Paul C. Grund, Frederick L. Altice, "Safer Injection Facilities in North America: Their Place in Public Policy and Health Intiatives." In the *Journal of Drug Issues* (Winter), pp. 329–356. Copyright © 2002 by the Journal of Drug Issues. Reprinted with permission. ✦

Websites for The American Drug Scene, 5th Edition

Data and Information About Drugs

Media Awareness Project *(www. mapinc.org/drugnews/index.htm)*

This website features an excellent drug news archive, with a searchable database that provides the newspaper source of the news article, the website of newspaper, and the date of the news report. Search by topic and the results include an abstract or the first few lines or paragraph of a news report. A search can specify a range of dates for news reports. The home page of this site (*www.mapinc.org/index.htm*) provides additional links and information.

Substance Abuse and Mental Health Services Administration, Office of Applied Statistics *(www.oas.samhsa.gov)*

This website provides survey and other data, as well as statistics and reports about drug use in the United States. Several reports are based on data collected through the National Survey on Drug Use and Health (formerly the National Household Survey on Drug Abuse). Other data and reports draw from drug treatment agencies and organizations. This website also features data and reports associated with the Drug Abuse Warning Network (DAWN). The database includes information collected by hospital emergency departments and medical examiners, reflecting information on visits to emergency rooms for drug reactions, overdose, etc., and data on fatal overdoses.

Monitoring the Future *(www. monitoringthefuture.org)*

The Monitoring the Future studies focus on self-reported drug information collected from high school and college students and other young adults. Some longitudinal data are collected. This website provides general information, tables, figures, and several publications. Most of the monographs from the year 2000 to the present are available in full-text version, and online through this website. There are journal articles available as well, although only the abstracts are available for some articles.

Online Articles and Searchable Databases

Drugtext *(www.drugtext.org)*

This website provides several full-text articles on drug use and drug policy in various countries.

Lindesmith Library *(Library.soros.org/ lindesmith.html)*

A searchable database of documents pertaining largely to drug use, drug policy, and drug history. Bibliographic information is provided for each document, and some documents are full-text.

Multidisciplinary Association for Psychedelic Studies *(www.maps.org)*

This organization advocates research into medical marijuana and psychedelic drugs. Searchable database and extensive bibliography.

Vaults of Erowid *(www.erowid.org)*

This website provides extensive information, including academic research, on various drugs. Searchable database; some articles are full-text.

Drug Policy and Alternatives

Office of National Drug Control Policy *(www.whitehousedrugpolicy.gov)*

This website describes the National Drug Control Strategy, national "priorities," expenditures, and news. Publications can be accessed here from various U.S. government agencies that have an interest in drug use and drug policy.

International Harm Reduction Association *(www.ihra.net)*

The Association advocates a harm reduction philosophy in relation to drug prevention, intervention, treatment, and policy.

With an international perspective, the website provides documents, papers, news, discussions, and debates. The Association sponsors *International Journal of Drug Policy.*

Drug Policy Alliance: Alternatives to Marijuana Prohibition and the Drug War *(www.lindesmith.org/homepage.cfm)*

The Alliance advocates a human rights perspective in its effort to end the U.S. War on Drugs. The website features publications, newsletters, projects, and suggestions for activists.

Common Sense for Drug Policy *(www. csdp.org)*

An organization that opposes the current U.S. War on Drugs, and offers information on medical marijuana and harm reduction strategies and projects.

Government-Sponsored Websites ('Facts,' Statistics, and Research Findings)

United Nations Office on Drugs and Crime *(unodc.org/unodc/world_drug_report.html)*

This website presents information and resources on drug production and seizures as well as patterns of use in several countries. It features legal information, policies, treaties, and up-to-date news reports. Through the "publication" link, one can access various editions of the *World Drug Report.* For a historical review, consult the articles featured in the *Bulletin on Narcotics,* with online access issues from the late 1940s.

National Institute on Drug Abuse *(www.nida.nih.gov)*

A U.S. government organization that claims to be one of the largest research funding agencies in the world. The website presents material on patterns and trends, prevention, treatment, and other interventions. Much of the information derives from research. Extensive publication directory, with full texts available for several articles.

National Institute of Justice *(www.ojp. usdoj.gov/nij)*

Government agency that presents research findings on drugs and crime, for example, drug use among persons in jail and prison, drug courts, and forfeiture. Access online publications through the "publications" link.

Drug Outreach

DanceSafe *(www.dancesafe.org)*

An organization that advocates harm reduction and provides nonjudgemental information about drugs, particularly those that have been associated with club settings. Various local chapters provide outreach in club and dance venues. At one time the organization disseminated information on tablets sold as Ecstasy; however, funding for the testing project was not available in 2005–2006.

Injecting Drug Use and Bloodborne Viruses

Centers for Disease Control *(www.cdc. gov)*

This website offers HIV/AIDS surveillance reports, information about Hepatitis C virus, testing, prevention, and syringe exchange programs in the United States.

Prescription Drugs

U.S. Food and Drug Administration, Center for Drug Evaluation and Research *(www.fda.gov/cder)*

This website provides information on prescription drugs (brand and generic) that are available in the United States. Information is also available on over-the-counter medicines. The site provides good search facilities and an excellent A–Z index of topics. Here you will find topics such as the Federal guidelines on marijuana for medical use, historical information on drug regulations, and a host of other issues.

Drug Enforcement Administration, Office of Diversion Control *(www. deadiversion.usdoj.gov)*

This website features information on the diversion of drugs, controlled substances and scheduling of drugs (e.g., Schedule I), selected drugs and chemicals with associated "street names," and a host of related information with good links. There are several online publications available. ◆